C++

Primer Plus

Fifth Edition

Stephen Prata

SAMS

800 East 96th St., Indianapolis, Indiana, 46240 USA

C++ Primer Plus

International Standard Book Number: 0-672-32697-3

Library of Congress Catalog Card Number: 2004095067

Printed in the United States of America

First Printing: November, 2004

10   12 13

Trademarks

All terms mentioned in this book that are known to be trademarks or service marks have been appropriately capitalized. Sams Publishing cannot attest to the accuracy of this information. Use of a term in this book should not be regarded as affecting the validity of any trademark or service mark.

Warning and Disclaimer

Every effort has been made to make this book as complete and as accurate as possible, but no warranty or fitness is implied. The information provided is on an "as is" basis.

Bulk Sales

Sams Publishing offers excellent discounts on this book when ordered in quantity for bulk purchases or special sales. For more information, please contact

U.S. Corporate and Government Sales

1-800-382-3419

corpsales@pearsontechgroup.com

For sales outside of the U.S., please contact

International Sales

international@pearsoned.com

ASSOCIATE PUBLISHER
Paul Boger

ACQUISITIONS EDITOR
Loretta Yates

DEVELOPMENT EDITOR
Songlin Qiu

MANAGING EDITOR
Charlotte Clapp

PROJECT EDITOR
George E. Nedeff

COPY EDITOR
Kitty Jarrett

INDEXER
Erika Millen

PROOFREADER
Suzanne Thomas

TECHNICAL EDITOR
David Horvath

PUBLISHING COORDINATOR
Cindy Teeters

MULTIMEDIA DEVELOPER
Dan Scherf

BOOK DESIGNER
Gary Adair

CONTENTS AT A GLANCE

TABLE OF CONTENTS

ABOUT THE AUTHOR

Stephen Prata teaches astronomy, physics, and computer science at the College of Marin in Kentfield, California. He received his B.S. from the California Institute of Technology and his Ph.D. from the University of California, Berkeley. Stephen has authored or coauthored more than a dozen books for The Waite Group. He wrote The Waite Group's *New C Primer Plus*, which received the Computer Press Association's 1990 Best How-to Computer Book Award, and The Waite Group's *C++ Primer Plus*, nominated for the Computer Press Association's Best How-to Computer Book Award in 1991.

DEDICATION

To my colleagues and students at the College of Marin, with whom it is a pleasure to work.

—Stephen Prata

ACKNOWLEDGMENTS

Acknowledgments for the Fifth Edition

I'd like to thank Loretta Yates and Songlin Qiu of Sams Publishing for guiding and managing this project. Thanks to my colleague Fred Schmitt for several useful suggestions. Once again, I'd like to thank Ron Liechty of Metrowerks for his helpfulness.

Acknowledgments for the Fourth Edition

Several editors from Pearson and from Sams helped originate and maintain this project; thanks to Linda Sharp, Karen Wachs, and Laurie McGuire. Thanks, too, to Michael Maddox, Bill Craun, Chris Maunder, and Phillipe Bruno for providing technical review and editing. And thanks again to Michael Maddox and Bill Craun for supplying the material for the Real World Notes. Finally, I'd like to thank Ron Liechty of Metrowerks and Greg Comeau of Comeau Computing for their aid with C++ compilers.

Acknowledgments for the Third Edition

I'd like to thank the editors from Macmillan and The Waite Group for the roles they played in putting this book together: Tracy Dunkelberger, Susan Walton, and Andrea Rosenberg. Thanks, too, to Russ Jacobs for his content and technical editing. From Metrowerks, I'd like to thank Dave Mark, Alex Harper, and especially Ron Liechty, for their help and cooperation.

Acknowledgments for the Second Edition

I'd like to thank Mitchell Waite and Scott Calamar for supporting a second edition and Joel Fugazzotto and Joanne Miller for guiding the project to completion. Thanks to Michael Marcotty of Metrowerks for dealing with my questions about their beta version CodeWarrior compiler. I'd also like to thank the following instructors for taking the time to give us feedback on the first edition: Jeff Buckwalter, Earl Brynner, Mike Holland, Andy Yao, Larry Sanders,

Shahin Momtazi, and Don Stephens. Finally, I wish to thank Heidi Brumbaugh for her helpful content editing of new and revised material.

Acknowledgments for the First Edition

Many people have contributed to this book. In particular, I wish to thank Mitch Waite for his work in developing, shaping, and reshaping this book, and for reviewing the manuscript. I appreciate Harry Henderson's work in reviewing the last few chapters and in testing programs with the Zortech C++ compiler. Thanks to David Gerrold for reviewing the entire manuscript and for championing the needs of less-experienced readers. Also thanks to Hank Shiffman for testing programs using Sun C++ and to Kent Williams for testing programs with AT&T cfront and with G++. Thanks to Nan Borreson of Borland International for her responsive and cheerful assistance with Turbo C++ and Borland C++. Thank you, Ruth Myers and Christine Bush, for handling the relentless paper flow involved with this kind of project. Finally, thanks to Scott Calamar for keeping everything on track.

WE WANT TO HEAR FROM YOU!

As the reader of this book, *you* are our most important critic and commentator. We value your opinion and want to know what we're doing right, what we could do better, what areas you'd like to see us publish in, and any other words of wisdom you're willing to pass our way.

As the publisher for Sams Publishing, I welcome your comments. You can email or write me directly to let me know what you did or didn't like about this book—as well as what we can do to make our books better.

Please note that I cannot help you with technical problems related to the topic of this book. We do have a User Services group, however, where I will forward specific technical questions related to the book.

When you write, please be sure to include this book's title and author as well as your name, email address, and phone number. I will carefully review your comments and share them with the author and editors who worked on the book.

Email: feedback@samspublishing.com

Mail: Paul Boger
          Publisher
          Sams Publishing
          800 East 96th Street
          Indianapolis, IN 46240 USA

For more information about this book or another Sams Publishing title, visit our web site at `www.samspublishing.com`. Type the ISBN (0672326973) or the title of a book in the Search field to find the page you're looking for.

INTRODUCTION

Preface to the Fifth Edition

Learning C++ is an adventure of discovery, particularly because the language accommodates several programming paradigms, including object-oriented programming, generic programming, and the traditional procedural programming. C++ was a moving target as the language added new features, but now, with the ISO/ANSI C++ Standard, Second Edition (2003), in place, the language has stabilized. Contemporary compilers support most or all of the features mandated by the standard, and programmers have had time to get used to applying these features. The fifth edition of this book, *C++ Primer Plus,* reflects the ISO/ANSI standard and describes this matured version of C++.

C++ Primer Plus discusses the basic C language and presents C++ features, making this book self-contained. It presents C++ fundamentals and illustrates them with short, to-the-point programs that are easy to copy and experiment with. You'll learn about input/output (I/O), how to make programs perform repetitive tasks and make choices, the many ways to handle data, and how to use functions. You'll learn about the many features C++ has added to C, including the following:

- Classes and objects

- Inheritance

- Polymorphism, virtual functions, and runtime type identification (RTTI)

- Function overloading

- Reference variables

- Generic, or type-independent, programming, as provided by templates and the Standard Template Library (STL)

- The exception mechanism for handling error conditions

- Namespaces for managing names of functions, classes, and variables

The Primer Approach

C++ Primer Plus brings several virtues to the task of presenting all this material. It builds on the primer tradition begun by *C Primer Plus* nearly two decades ago and embraces its successful philosophy:

- A primer should be an easy-to-use, friendly guide.

- A primer doesn't assume that you are already familiar with all relevant programming concepts.

- A primer emphasizes hands-on learning with brief, easily typed examples that develop your understanding, a concept or two at a time.

- A primer clarifies concepts with illustrations.

- A primer provides questions and exercises to let you test your understanding, making the book suitable for self-learning or for the classroom.

Following these principles, the book helps you understand this rich language and how to use it. For example:

- It provides conceptual guidance about when to use particular features, such as using public inheritance to model what are known as *is-a* relationships.

- It illustrates common C++ programming idioms and techniques.

- It provides a variety of sidebars, including tips, cautions, things to remember, compatibility notes, and real-world notes.

The author and editors of this book do our best to keep the presentation to-the-point, simple, and fun. Our goal is that by the end of the book, you'll be able to write solid, effective programs and enjoy yourself doing so.

Sample Code Used in This Book

This book provides an abundance of sample code, most of it in the form of complete programs. Like the previous editions, this book practices generic C++ so that it is not tied to any particular kind of computer, operating system, or compiler. Thus, the examples were tested on a Windows XP system, a Macintosh OS X system, and a Linux system. Only a few programs were affected by compiler non-conformance issues. Compiler compliance with the C++ standard has improved since the previous edition of this book first appeared.

The sample code for the complete programs described in this book is available on the Sams website, at www.samspublishing.com. Enter this book's ISBN (without the hyphens) in the Search box and click Search. When the book's title is displayed, click the title to go to a page where you can download the code. You also can find solutions to selected programming exercises at this site.

How This Book Is Organized

This book is divided into 17 chapters and 10 appendixes, summarized here.

Chapter 1: Getting Started

Chapter 1 relates how Bjarne Stroustrup created the C++ programming language by adding object-oriented programming support to the C language. You'll learn the distinctions between procedural languages, such as C, and object-oriented languages, such as C++. You'll read about the joint ANSI/ISO work to develop a C++ standard. This chapter discusses the mechanics of creating a C++ program, outlining the approach for several current C++ compilers. Finally, it describes the conventions used in this book.

Chapter 2: Setting Out to C++

Chapter 2 guides you through the process of creating simple C++ programs. You'll learn about the role of the `main()` function and about some of the kinds of statements that C++ programs use. You'll use the predefined `cout` and `cin` objects for program output and input, and you'll learn about creating and using variables. Finally, you'll be introduced to functions, C++'s programming modules.

Chapter 3: Dealing with Data

C++ provides built-in types for storing two kinds of data: integers (numbers with no fractional parts) and floating-point numbers (numbers with fractional parts). To meet the diverse requirements of programmers, C++ offers several types in each category. Chapter 3 discusses those types, including creating variables and writing constants of various types. You'll also learn how C++ handles implicit and explicit conversions from one type to another.

Chapter 4: Compound Types

C++ lets you construct more elaborate types from the basic built-in types. The most advanced form is the class, discussed in Chapters 9 through 13. Chapter 4 discusses other forms, including arrays, which hold several values of a single type; structures, which hold several values of unlike types; and pointers, which identify locations in memory. You'll also learn how to create and store text strings and to handle text I/O by using C-style character arrays and the C++ `string` class. Finally, you'll learn some of the ways C++ handles memory allocation, including using the `new` and `delete` operators for managing memory explicitly.

Chapter 5: Loops and Relational Expressions

Programs often must perform repetitive actions, and C++ provides three looping structures for that purpose: the `for` loop, the `while` loop, and the `do while` loop. Such loops must know when they should terminate, and the C++ relational operators enable you to create tests to guide such loops. In Chapter 5 you learn how to create loops that read and process input character-by-character. Finally, you'll learn how to create two-dimensional arrays and how to use nested loops to process them.

Chapter 6: Branching Statements and Logical Operators

Programs can behave intelligently if they can tailor their behavior to circumstances. In Chapter 6 you'll learn how to control program flow by using the `if`, `if else`, and `switch` statements and the conditional operator. You'll learn how to use logical operators to help express decision-making tests. Also, you'll meet the `cctype` library of functions for evaluating character relations, such as testing whether a character is a digit or a nonprinting character. Finally, you'll get an introductory view of file I/O.

Chapter 7: Functions: C++'s Programming Modules

Functions are the basic building blocks of C++ programming. Chapter 7 concentrates on features that C++ functions share with C functions. In particular, you'll review the general format of a function definition and examine how function prototypes increase the reliability of programs. Also, you'll investigate how to write functions to process arrays, character strings, and structures. Next, you'll learn about recursion, which is when a function calls itself, and see how it can be used to implement a divide-and-conquer strategy. Finally, you'll meet pointers to functions, which enable you to use a function argument to tell one function to use a second function.

Chapter 8: Adventures in Functions

Chapter 8 explores the new features C++ adds to functions. You'll learn about inline functions, which can speed program execution at the cost of additional program size. You'll work with reference variables, which provide an alternative way to pass information to functions. Default arguments let a function automatically supply values for function arguments that you omit from a function call. Function overloading lets you create functions having the same name but taking different argument lists. All these features have frequent use in class design. Also, you'll learn about function templates, which allow you to specify the design of a family of related functions.

Chapter 9: Memory Models and Namespaces

Chapter 9 discusses putting together multifile programs. It examines the choices in allocating memory, looking at different methods of managing memory and at scope, linkage, and namespaces, which determine what parts of a program know about a variable.

Chapter 10: Objects and Classes

A class is a user-defined type, and an object (such as a variable) is an instance of a class. Chapter 10 introduces you to object-oriented programming and to class design. A class declaration describes the information stored in a class object and also the operations (class methods) allowed for class objects. Some parts of an object are visible to the outside world (the public portion), and some are hidden (the private portion). Special class methods (constructors and destructors) come into play when objects are created and destroyed. You will learn about all this and other class details in this chapter, and you'll see how classes can be used to implement ADTs, such as a stack.

Chapter 11: Working with Classes

In Chapter 11 you'll further your understanding of classes. First, you'll learn about operator overloading, which lets you define how operators such as + will work with class objects. You'll learn about friend functions, which can access class data that's inaccessible to the world at large. You'll see how certain constructors and overloaded operator member functions can be used to manage conversion to and from class types.

Chapter 12: Classes and Dynamic Memory Allocation

Often it's useful to have a class member point to dynamically allocated memory. If you use new in a class constructor to allocate dynamic memory, you incur the responsibilities of providing an appropriate destructor, of defining an explicit copy constructor, and of defining an explicit assignment operator. Chapter 12 shows you how and discusses the behavior of the member functions generated implicitly if you fail to provide explicit definitions. You'll also expand your experience with classes by using pointers to objects and studying a queue simulation problem.

Chapter 13: Class Inheritance

One of the most powerful features of object-oriented programming is inheritance, by which a derived class inherits the features of a base class, enabling you to reuse the base class code. Chapter 13 discusses public inheritance, which models *is-a* relationships, meaning that a derived object is a special case of a base object. For example, a physicist is a special case of a scientist. Some inheritance relationships are polymorphic, meaning you can write code using a mixture of related classes for which the same method name may invoke behavior that depends on the object type. Implementing this kind of behavior necessitates using a new kind of member function called a virtual function. Sometimes using abstract base classes is the best approach to inheritance relationships. This chapter discusses these matters, pointing out when public inheritance is appropriate and when it is not.

Chapter 14: Reusing Code in C++

Public inheritance is just one way to reuse code. Chapter 14 looks at several other ways. Containment is when one class contains members that are objects of another class. It can be used to model *has-a* relationships, in which one class has components of another class. For example, an automobile has a motor. You also can use private and protected inheritance to model such relationships. This chapter shows you how and points out the differences among the different approaches. Also, you'll learn about class templates, which let you define a class in terms of some unspecified generic type, and then use the template to create specific classes in terms of specific types. For example, a stack template enables you to create a stack of integers or a stack of strings. Finally, you'll learn about multiple public inheritance, whereby a class can derive from more than one class.

Chapter 15: Friends, Exceptions, and More

Chapter 15 extends the discussion of friends to include friend classes and friend member functions. Then it presents several new developments in C++, beginning with exceptions, which provide a mechanism for dealing with unusual program occurrences, such an inappropriate function argument values and running out of memory. Then you'll learn about RTTI, a mechanism for identifying object types. Finally, you'll learn about the safer alternatives to unrestricted typecasting.

Chapter 16: The `string` Class and the Standard Template Library

Chapter 16 discusses some useful class libraries recently added to the language. The `string` class is a convenient and powerful alternative to traditional C-style strings. The `auto_ptr` class helps manage dynamically allocated memory. The STL provides several generic containers, including template representations of arrays, queues, lists, sets, and maps. It also provides an efficient library of generic algorithms that can be used with STL containers and also with ordinary arrays. The `valarray` template class provides support for numeric arrays.

Chapter 17: Input, Output, and Files

Chapter 17 reviews C++ I/O and discusses how to format output. You'll learn how to use class methods to determine the state of an input or output stream and to see, for example, whether there has been a type mismatch on input or whether the end-of-file has been detected. C++ uses inheritance to derive classes for managing file input and output. You'll learn how to open files for input and output, how to append data to a file, how to use binary files, and how to get random access to a file. Finally, you'll learn how to apply standard I/O methods to read from and write to strings.

Appendix A: Number Bases

Appendix A discusses octal, hexadecimal, and binary numbers.

Appendix B: C++ Reserved Words

Appendix B lists C++ keywords.

Appendix C: The ASCII Character Set

Appendix C lists the ASCII character set, along with decimal, octal, hexadecimal, and binary representations.

Appendix D: Operator Precedence

Appendix D lists the C++ operators in order of decreasing precedence.

Appendix E: Other Operators

Appendix E summarizes the C++ operators, such as the bitwise operators, not covered in the main body of the text.

Appendix F: The `string` Template Class

Appendix F summarizes `string` class methods and functions.

Appendix G: The STL Methods and Functions

Appendix G summarizes the STL container methods and the general STL algorithm functions.

Appendix H: Selected Readings and Internet Resources

Appendix H lists some books that can further your understanding of C++.

Appendix I: Converting to ANSI/ISO Standard C++

Appendix I provides guidelines for moving from C and older C++ implementations to ANSI/ISO C++.

Appendix J: Answers to Review Questions

Appendix J contains the answers to the review questions posed at the end of each chapter.

Note to Instructors

One of the goals of this edition of *C++ Primer Plus* is to provide a book that can be used as either a teach-yourself book or as a textbook. Here are some of the features that support using *C++ Primer Plus,* Fifth Edition, as a textbook:

- This book describes generic C++, so it isn't dependent on a particular implementation.

- The contents track the ISO/ANSI C++ standards committee's work and include discussions of templates, the STL, the `string` class, exceptions, RTTI, and namespaces.

- It doesn't assume prior knowledge of C, so it can be used without a C prerequisite. (Some programming background is desirable, however.)

- Topics are arranged so that the early chapters can be covered rapidly as review chapters for courses that do have a C prerequisite.

- Chapters include review questions and programming exercises. Appendix J provides the answers to the review questions. Solutions to selected programming exercises can be found at the Sams website (www.samspublishing.com).

- The book introduces several topics that are appropriate for computer science courses, including abstract data types (ADTs), stacks, queues, simple lists, simulations, generic programming, and using recursion to implement a divide-and-conquer strategy.

- Most chapters are short enough to cover in a week or less.

- The book discusses *when* to use certain features as well as *how* to use them. For example, it links public inheritance to *is-a* relationships and composition and private inheritance to *has-a* relationships, and it discusses when to use virtual functions and when not to.

Conventions Used in This Book

This book uses several typographic conventions to distinguish among various kinds of text:

- Code lines, commands, statements, variables, filenames, and program output appear in a `computer typeface`:

```
#include <iostream>
int main()
{
    using namespace std;
    cout << "What's up, Doc!\n";
    return 0;
}
```

- Program input that you should type appears in **bold computer typeface**:

```
Please enter your name:
Plato
```

- Placeholders in syntax descriptions appear in an *italic computer typeface*. You should replace a placeholder with the actual filename, parameter, or whatever element it represents.

- *Italic type* is used for new terms.

This book includes several elements intended to illuminate specific points:

Compatibility Note

Most compilers are not yet 100% compliant with the ISO/ANSI Standard, and these notes warn you of discrepancies you may encounter.

Remember

These notes highlight points that are important to remember.

Real-World Note

Several professional programmers offer observations based on their experiences.

Sidebar

A sidebar provides a deeper discussion or additional background to help illuminate a topic.

Tip

Tips present short, helpful guides to particular programming situations.

Caution

A caution alerts you to potential pitfalls.

Note

The notes provide a catch-all category for comments that don't fall into one of the other categories.

Systems Used to Develop This Book's Programming Examples

For the record, the examples in this book were developed using Microsoft Visual C++ 7.1 (the version that comes with Microsoft Visual Studio .NET 2003) and Metrowerks CodeWarrior Development Studio 9 on a Pentium PC with a hard disk and running under Windows XP Professional. Most programs were checked using the Borland C++ 5.5 command-line compiler and GNU `gpp` 3.3.3 on the same system, using Comeau 4.3.3 and GNU g++ 3.3.1 on an IBM-compatible Pentium running SuSE 9.0 Linux, and using Metrowerks Development Studio 9 on a Macintosh G4 under OS 10.3. This book reports discrepancies stemming from lagging behind the standard generically, as in "older implementations use `ios::fixed` instead of `ios_base::fixed`." This book reports some bugs and idiosyncrasies in older compilers that would prove troublesome or confusing; most of these have been fixed in current releases.

C++ offers a lot to the programmer; learn and enjoy!

CHAPTER 1

GETTING STARTED

> **In this chapter you'll learn about the following:**
>
> - The history and philosophy of C and of C++
> - Procedural versus object-oriented programming
> - How C++ adds object-oriented concepts to the C language
> - How C++ adds generic programming concepts to the C language
> - Programming language standards
> - The mechanics of creating a program

Welcome to C++! This exciting language, which blends the C language with support for object-oriented programming, became one of the most important programming languages of the 1990s and continues strongly into the 2000s. Its C ancestry brings to C++ the tradition of an efficient, compact, fast, and portable language. Its object-oriented heritage brings C++ a fresh programming methodology, designed to cope with the escalating complexity of modern programming tasks. Its template features bring yet another new programming methodology: generic programming. This triple heritage is both a blessing and a bane. It makes the language very powerful, but it also means there's a lot to learn.

This chapter explores C++'s background further and then goes over some of the ground rules for creating C++ programs. The rest of the book teaches you to use the C++ language, going from the modest basics of the language to the glory of object-oriented programming (OOP) and its supporting cast of new jargon—objects, classes, encapsulation, data hiding, polymorphism, and inheritance—and then on to its support of generic programming. (Of course, as you learn C++, these terms will be transformed from buzzwords to the necessary vocabulary of cultivated discourse.)

Learning C++: What Lies Before You

C++ joins three separate programming traditions: the procedural language tradition, represented by C; the object-oriented language tradition, represented by the class enhancements C++ adds to C; and generic programming, supported by C++ templates. This chapter looks into those traditions. But first, let's consider what this heritage implies about learning C++. One reason to use C++ is to avail yourself of its object-oriented features. To do so, you need a sound background in standard C, for that language provides the basic types, operators, control structures, and syntax rules. So if you already know C, you're poised to learn C++. But it's not just a matter of learning a few more keywords and constructs. Going from C to C++ involves about as much work as learning C in the first place. Also, if you know C, you must unlearn some programming habits as you make the transition to C++. If you don't know C, you have to master the C components, the OOP components, and the generic components to learn C++, but at least you may not have to unlearn programming habits. If you are beginning to think that learning C++ may involve some mind-stretching effort on your part, you're right. This book will guide you through the process in a clear, helpful manner, one step at a time, so the mind-stretching will be sufficiently gentle to leave your brain resilient.

C++ Primer Plus approaches C++ by teaching both its C basis and its new components, so it assumes that you have no prior knowledge of C. You'll start by learning the features C++ shares with C. Even if you know C, you may find this part of the book a good review. Also, it points out concepts that will become important later, and it indicates where C++ differs from C. After you have a good grounding in the basics of C, you'll learn about the C++ superstructure. At that point, you'll learn about objects and classes and how C++ implements them. And you will learn about templates.

This book is not intended to be a complete C++ reference; it doesn't explore every nook and cranny of the language. But you will learn all the major features of the language, including some, such as templates, exceptions, and namespaces, that are more recent additions.

Now let's take a brief look at some of C++'s background.

The Origins of C++: A Little History

Computer technology has evolved at an amazing rate over the past few decades. Today a notebook computer can compute faster and store more information than the mainframe computers of the 1960s. (Quite a few programmers can recall bearing offerings of decks of punched cards to be submitted to a mighty, room-filling computer system with a majestic 100KB of memory—not enough memory to run a good personal computer game today.) Computer languages have evolved, too. The changes may not be as dramatic, but they are important. Bigger, more powerful computers spawn bigger, more complex programs, which, in turn, raise new problems in program management and maintenance.

In the 1970s, languages such as C and Pascal helped usher in an era of structured programming, a philosophy that brought some order and discipline to a field badly in need of these qualities. Besides providing the tools for structured programming, C also produced compact, fast-running programs, along with the ability to address hardware matters, such as managing communication ports and disk drives. These gifts helped make C the dominant programming language in the 1980s. Meanwhile, the 1980s witnessed the growth of a new programming paradigm: object-oriented programming, or OOP, as embodied in languages such as SmallTalk and C++. Let's examine these C and OOP a bit more closely.

The C Language

In the early 1970s, Dennis Ritchie of Bell Laboratories was working on a project to develop the Unix operating system. (An *operating system* is a set of programs that manages a computer's resources and handles its interactions with users. For example, it's the operating system that puts the system prompt onscreen and that runs programs for you.) For this work Ritchie needed a language that was concise, that produced compact, fast programs, and that could control hardware efficiently. Traditionally, programmers met these needs by using assembly language, which is closely tied to a computer's internal machine language. However, assembly language is a *low-level* language—that is, it is specific to a particular computer processor. So if you want to move an assembly program to a different kind of computer, you may have to completely rewrite the program, using a different assembly language. It was a bit as if each time you bought a new car, you found that the designers decided to change where the controls went and what they did, forcing you to relearn how to drive. But Unix was intended to work on a variety of computer types (or platforms). That suggested using a high-level language. A *high-level* language is oriented toward problem solving instead of toward specific hardware. Special programs called *compilers* translate a high-level language to the internal language of a particular computer. Thus, you can use the same high-level language program on different platforms by using a separate compiler for each platform. Ritchie wanted a language that combined low-level efficiency and hardware access with high-level generality and portability. So, building from older languages, he created C.

C Programming Philosophy

Because C++ grafts a new programming philosophy onto C, we should first take a look at the older philosophy that C follows. In general, computer languages deal with two concepts—data and algorithms. The *data* constitutes the information a program uses and processes. The *algorithms* are the methods the program uses (see Figure 1.1). Like most mainstream languages when C was created, C is a *procedural* language. That means it emphasizes the algorithm side of programming. Conceptually, procedural programming consists of figuring out the actions a computer should take and then using the programming language to implement those actions. A program prescribes a set of procedures for the computer to follow to produce a particular outcome, much as a recipe prescribes a set of procedures for a cook to follow to produce a cake.

Earlier procedural languages, such as FORTRAN and BASIC, ran into organizational problems as programs grew larger. For example, programs often use branching statements, which route execution to one or another set of instructions, depending on the result of some sort of test. Many older programs had such tangled routing (called "spaghetti programming") that it was virtually impossible to understand a program by reading it, and modifying such a program was an invitation to disaster. In response, computer scientists developed a more disciplined style of programming called *structured programming*. C includes features to facilitate this approach. For example, structured programming limits branching (choosing which instruction to do next) to a small set of well-behaved constructions. C incorporates these constructions (the `for` loop, the `while` loop, the `do while` loop, and the `if else` statement) into its vocabulary.

FIGURE 1.1
Data + algorithms = program.

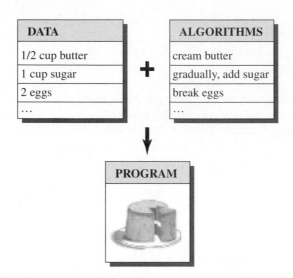

Top-down design was another of the new principles. With C, the idea is to break a large program into smaller, more manageable tasks. If one of these tasks is still too broad, you divide it into yet smaller tasks. You continue with this process until the program is compartmentalized into small, easily programmed modules. (Organize your study. Aargh! Well, organize your desk, your table top, your filing cabinet, and your bookshelves. Aargh! Well, start with the desk and organize each drawer, starting with the middle one. Hmmm, perhaps I can manage that task.) C's design facilitates this approach, encouraging you to develop program units called *functions* to represent individual task modules. As you may have noticed, the structured programming techniques reflect a procedural mind-set, thinking of a program in terms of the actions it performs.

The C++ Shift: Object-Oriented Programming

Although the principles of structured programming improved the clarity, reliability, and ease of maintenance of programs, large-scale programming still remains a challenge. OOP brings a new approach to that challenge. Unlike procedural programming, which emphasizes algorithms, OOP emphasizes the data. Rather than try to fit a problem to the procedural approach of a language, OOP attempts to fit the language to the problem. The idea is to design data forms that correspond to the essential features of a problem.

In C++, a *class* is a specification describing such a new data form, and an *object* is a particular data structure constructed according to that plan. For example, a class could describe the general properties of a corporation executive (name, title, salary, unusual abilities, for example), while an object would represent a specific executive (Guilford Sheepblat, vice president, $325,000, knows how to restore the Windows registry). In general, a class defines what data is used to represent an object *and* the operations that can be performed on that data. For example, suppose you were developing a computer drawing program capable of drawing a rectangle. You could define a class to describe a rectangle. The data part of the specification could include such things as the location of the corners, the height and width, the color and style of the boundary line, and the color and pattern used to fill the rectangle. The operations part of the specification could include methods for moving the rectangle, resizing it, rotating it, changing colors and patterns, and copying the rectangle to another location. If you then used your program to draw a rectangle, it would create an object according to the class specification. That object would hold all the data values describing the rectangle, and you could use the class methods to modify that rectangle. If you drew two rectangles, the program would create two objects, one for each rectangle.

The OOP approach to program design is to first design classes that accurately represent those things with which the program deals. For example, a drawing program might define classes to represent rectangles, lines, circles, brushes, pens, and the like. The class definitions, recall, include a description of permissible operations for each class, such as moving a circle or rotating a line. Then you would proceed to design a program, using objects of those classes. The process of going from a lower level of organization, such as classes, to a higher level, such as program design, is called *bottom-up* programming.

There's more to OOP than the binding of data and methods into a class definition. For example, OOP facilitates creating reusable code, and that can eventually save a lot of work. Information hiding safeguards data from improper access. Polymorphism lets you create multiple definitions for operators and functions, with the programming context determining which definition is used. Inheritance lets you derive new classes from old ones. As you can see, OOP introduces many new ideas and involves a different approach to programming than does procedural programming. Instead of concentrating on tasks, you concentrate on representing concepts. Instead of taking a top-down programming approach, you sometimes take a bottom-up approach. This book will guide you through all these points, with plenty of easily grasped examples.

Designing a useful, reliable class can be a difficult task. Fortunately, OOP languages make it simple to incorporate existing classes into your own programming. Vendors provide a variety of useful class libraries, including libraries of classes designed to simplify creating programs for environments such as Windows or the Macintosh. One of the real benefits of C++ is that it lets you easily reuse and adapt existing, well-tested code.

C++ and Generic Programming

Generic programming is yet another programming paradigm supported by C++. It shares with OOP the aim of making it simpler to reuse code and the technique of abstracting general concepts. But whereas OOP emphasizes the data aspect of programming, generic programming emphasizes the algorithmic aspect. And its focus is different. OOP is a tool for managing large projects, whereas generic programming provides tools for performing common tasks, such as sorting data or merging lists. The term *generic* refers to create code that is type independent. C++ data representations come in many types—integers, numbers with fractional parts, characters, strings of characters, and user-defined compound structures of several types. If, for example, you wanted to sort data of these various types, you would normally have to create a separate sorting function for each type. Generic programming involves extending the language so that you can write a function for a generic (that is, not specified) type once and use it for a variety of actual types. C++ templates provide a mechanism for doing that.

The Genesis of C++

Like C, C++ began its life at Bell Labs, where Bjarne Stroustrup developed the language in the early 1980s. In Stroustrup's own words, "C++ was designed primarily so that my friends and I would not have to program in assembler, C, or various modern high-level languages. Its main purpose was to make writing good programs easier and more pleasant for the individual programmer" (Bjarne Stroustrup, *The C++ Programming Language*, Third Edition. Reading, MA: Addison-Wesley, 1997).

Real-World Note: Bjarne Stroustrup's Home Page

Bjarne Stroustrup designed and implemented the C++ programming language and is the author of the definitive reference manuals *The C++ Programming Language* and *The Design and Evolution of C++*. His personal website at AT&T Labs Research should be the first C++ bookmark, or favorite, you create:

`www.research.att.com/~bs`

This site includes an interesting historical perspective of the hows and whys of the C++ language, Stroustrup's biographical material, and C++ FAQs. Surprisingly, Stroustrup's most frequently asked question is how to pronounce *Bjarne Stroustrup*. Download the `.WAV` file to hear for yourself!

Stroustrup was more concerned with making C++ useful than with enforcing particular programming philosophies or styles. Real programming needs are more important than theoretical purity in determining C++ language features. Stroustrup based C++ on C because of C's brevity, its suitability to system programming, its widespread availability, and its close ties to the Unix operating system. C++'s OOP aspect was inspired by a computer simulation language called Simula67. Stroustrup added OOP features and generic programming support to C without significantly changing the C component. Thus C++ is a superset of C, meaning that any valid C program is a valid C++ program, too. There are some minor discrepancies, but nothing crucial. C++ programs can use existing C software libraries. *Libraries* are collections of programming modules that you can call up from a program. They provide proven solutions to many common programming problems, thus saving you much time and effort. This has helped the spread of C++.

The name *C++* comes from the C increment operator ++, which adds one to the value of a variable. Therefore, the name C++ correctly suggests an augmented version of C.

A computer program translates a real-life problem into a series of actions to be taken by a computer. While the OOP aspect of C++ gives the language the ability to relate to concepts involved in the problem, the C part of C++ gives the language the ability to get close to the hardware (see Figure 1.2). This combination of abilities has enabled the spread of C++. It may also involve a mental shift of gears as you turn from one aspect of a program to another. (Indeed, some OOP purists regard adding OOP features to C as being akin to adding wings to a pig, albeit a lean, efficient pig.) Also, because C++ grafts OOP onto C, you can ignore C++'s object-oriented features. But you'll miss a lot if that's all you do.

FIGURE 1.2
C++ duality.

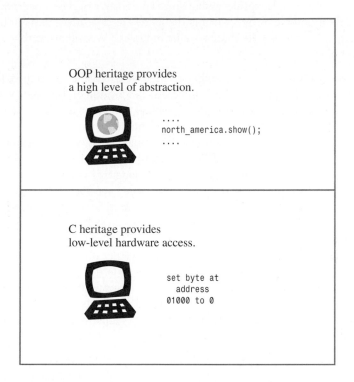

Only after C++ achieved some success did Stroustrup add templates, enabling generic programming. And only after the template feature had been used and enhanced did it become apparent that templates were perhaps as significant an addition as OOP—or even more significant, some would argue. The fact that C++ incorporates both OOP and generic programming, as well as the more traditional procedural approach, demonstrates that C++ emphasizes the utilitarian over the ideological approach, and that is one of the reasons for the language's success.

Portability and Standards

Say you've written a handy C++ program for the elderly Pentium PC computer at work, but management decides to replace the machine with a Macintosh G5—a computer using a different processor and a different operating system. Can you run your program on the new platform? Of course, you'll have to recompile the program, using a C++ compiler designed for the new platform. But will you have to make any changes to the code you wrote? If you can recompile the program without making changes and it runs without a hitch, we say the program is *portable*.

There are a couple obstacles to portability, the first of which is hardware. A program that is hardware specific is not likely to be portable. One that takes direct control of an IBM PC video board, for example, speaks gibberish as far as, say, a Sun is concerned. (You can minimize portability problems by localizing the hardware-dependent parts in function modules; then you just have to rewrite those specific modules.) We will avoid that sort of programming in this book.

The second obstacle to portability is language divergence. Certainly, that can be a problem with spoken languages. A Yorkshireman's description of the day's events may not be portable to Brooklyn, even though English is spoken in both areas. Computer languages, too, can develop dialects. Is the Windows XP C++ implementation the same as the Red Hat Linux implementation or the Macintosh OS X implementation? Although most implementers would like to make their versions of C++ compatible with others, it's difficult to do so without a published standard describing exactly how the language works. Therefore, the American National Standards Institute (ANSI) created a committee in 1990(ANSI X3J16) to develop a standard for C++. (ANSI had already developed a standard for C.) The International Organization for Standardization (ISO) soon joined the process with its own committee (ISO-WG-21), creating a joint ANSI/ISO effort to develop the a standard for C++. These committees met jointly three times a year, and we'll simply lump them together notationally as the ANSI/ISO committee. ANSI/ISO committee's decision to create a standard emphasizes that C++ has become an important and widespread language. It also indicates that C++ has reached a certain level of maturity, for it's not productive to introduce standards while a language is developing rapidly. Nonetheless, C++ has undergone significant changes since the ANSI/ISO committee began its work.

Work on the ANSI/ISO C++ Standard began in 1990. The committee issued some interim working papers in the following years. In April 1995 it released a Committee Draft (CD) for public comment. In December 1996 it released a second version (CD2) for further public review. These documents not only refined the description of existing C++ features but also extended the language with exceptions, runtime type identification (RTTI), templates, and the Standard Template Library (STL). The final International Standard (ISO/IEC 14882:1998) was adopted in 1998 by the ISO, International Electrotechnical Commission (IEC), and ANSI. 2003 brought the publication of the second edition of the C++ standard (IOS/IEC 14882:2003); the new edition is a technical revision, meaning that it tidies up the first edition—fixing typos, reducing ambiguities, and the like—but doesn't change the language features. This book is based on that standard.

The ANSI/ISO C++ Standard additionally draws on the ANSI C Standard because C++ is supposed to be, as far as possible, a superset of C. That means that any valid C program ideally should also be a valid C++ program. There are a few differences between ANSI C and the corresponding rules for C++, but they are minor. Indeed, ANSI C incorporates some features first introduced in C++, such as function prototyping and the `const` type qualifier.

Prior to the emergence of ANSI C, the C community followed a de facto standard based on the book *The C Programming Language*, by Kernighan and Ritchie (Addison-Wesley Publishing

Company, Reading, MA, 1978). This standard was often termed K&R C; with the emergence of ANSI C, the simpler K&R C is now sometimes called *classic C*.

The ANSI C Standard not only defines the C language, it also defines a standard C library that ANSI C implementations must support. C++ also uses that library; this book refers to it as the *standard C library* or the *standard library*. In addition, the ANSI/ISO C++ standard provides a standard library of C++ classes.

More recently, the C Standard has been revised; the new standard, often called C99, was adopted by the ISO in 1999 and ANSI in 2000. This standard adds some features to C, such as a new integer type, that some C++ compilers support. Although not part of the current C++ Standard, these features may become part of the next C++ Standard.

Before the ANSI/ISO C++ committee began its work, many people accepted the most recent Bell Labs version of C++ as a standard. For example, a compiler might describe itself as being compatible with Release 2.0 or Release 3.0 of C++.

C++ continues to evolve, and work has already begun on producing the next version of the standard. The new version is informally labeled C++0X because the expected completion date is near the end of this decade, around 2009.

This book describes the ISO/ANSI C++ Standard, second edition (ISO/IEC 14882:2003), so the examples should work with any C++ implementation that is compatible with that standard. (At least, this is the vision and hope of portability.) However, the C++ Standard is still new, and you may find a few discrepancies. For example, if your compiler is not a recent version, it may lack namespaces or the newest template features. Support for the STL, described in Chapter 16, "The `string` Class and the Standard Template Library," is spotty for older compilers. Some older Unix systems use a front-end translator that passes the translated code to a C compiler that is not fully ANSI compatible, resulting in some language features being left unimplemented and in some standard ANSI library functions and header files not being supported. Even if a compiler does conform to the Standard, some things, such as the number of bytes used to hold an integer, are implementation dependent.

Before getting to the C++ language proper, let's cover some of the groundwork related to creating programs.

The Mechanics of Creating a Program

Suppose you've written a C++ program. How do you get it running? The exact steps depend on your computer environment and the particular C++ compiler you use, but they should resemble the following steps (see Figure 1.3):

1. Use a text editor of some sort to write the program and save it in a file. This file constitutes the *source code* for your program.

2. Compile the source code. This means running a program that translates the source code to the internal language, called *machine language,* used by the host computer. The file containing the translated program is the *object code* for your program.

3. Link the object code with additional code. For example, C++ programs normally use *libraries.* A C++ library contains object code for a collection of computer routines, called *functions,* to perform tasks such as displaying information onscreen or calculating the square root of a number. Linking combines your object code with object code for the functions you use and with some standard startup code to produce a runtime version of your program. The file containing this final product is called the *executable code.*

You will encounter the term *source code* throughout this book, so be sure to file it away in your personal random-access memory.

FIGURE 1.3
Programming steps.

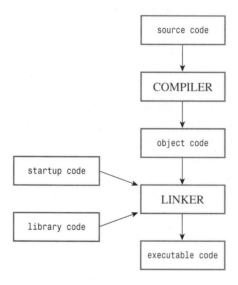

The programs in this book are generic and should run in any system that supports modern C++. (However, you may need one of the latest versions to get support for namespaces and the newest template features.) The steps for putting together a program may vary. Let's look a little further at these steps.

Creating the Source Code File

The rest of the book deals with what goes into a source file; this section discusses the mechanics of creating one. Some C++ implementations, such as Microsoft Visual C++, Borland C++ (various versions), Watcom C++, Digital Mars C++, and Metrowerks CodeWarrior, provide *Integrated Development Environments* (*IDEs*) that let you manage all steps of program development, including editing, from one master program. Other implementations, such as AT&T C++ or GNU C++ on Unix and Linux, and the free versions of the Borland and Digital Mars compilers, just handle the compilation and linking stages and expect you to type commands on the system command line. In such cases, you can use any available text editor to create and modify source code. On a Unix system, for example, you can use `vi` or `ed` or `ex` or `emacs`. On a DOS system, you can use `edlin` or `edit` or any of several available program editors. You can even use a word processor, provided that you save the file as a standard DOS ASCII text file instead of in a special word processor format.

In naming a source file, you must use the proper suffix to identify the file as a C++ file. This not only tells you that the file is C++ source code, it tells the compiler that, too. (If a Unix compiler complains to you about a "bad magic number," that's just its endearingly obscure way of saying that you used the wrong suffix.) The suffix consists of a period followed by a character or group of characters called the *extension* (see Figure 1.4).

FIGURE 1.4

The parts of a source code filename.

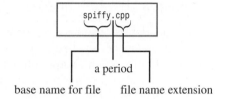

The extension you use depends on the C++ implementation. Table 1.1 shows some common choices. For example, `spiffy.C` is a valid Unix C++ source code filename. Note that Unix is case sensitive, meaning you should use an uppercase C character. Actually, a lowercase `c` extension also works, but standard C uses that extension. So, to avoid confusion on Unix systems, you should use `c` with C programs and `C` with C++ programs. If you don't mind typing an extra character or two, you can also use the `cc` and `cxx` extensions with some Unix systems. DOS, being a bit simple-minded compared to Unix, doesn't distinguish between uppercase and lowercase, so DOS implementations use additional letters, as shown in Table 1.1, to distinguish between C and C++ programs.

TABLE 1.1   Source Code Extensions

C++ Implementation	Source Code Extension(s)
Unix	C, cc, cxx, c
GNU C++	C, cc, cxx, cpp, c++
Digital Mars	cpp, cxx
Borland C++	cpp
Watcom	cpp
Microsoft Visual C++	cpp, cxx, cc
Metrowerks CodeWarrior	cpp, cp, cc, cxx, c++

Compilation and Linking

Originally, Stroustrup implemented C++ with a C++-to-C compiler program instead of developing a direct C++-to-object code compiler. This program, called `cfront` (for *C front end*), translated C++ source code to C source code, which could then be compiled by a standard C compiler. This approach simplified introducing C++ to the C community. Other implementations have used this approach to bring C++ to other platforms. As C++ has developed and grown in popularity, more and more implementers have turned to creating C++ compilers that generate object code directly from C++ source code. This direct approach speeds up the compilation process and emphasizes that C++ is a separate, if similar, language.

Often the distinction between a `cfront` translator and a compiler is nearly invisible to the user. For example, on a Unix system the `CC` command may first pass your program to the `cfront` translator and then automatically pass the translator's output on to the C compiler, which is called `cc`. Henceforth, we'll use the term *compiler* to include translate-and-compile combinations. The mechanics of compiling depend on the implementation, and the following sections outline a few common forms. These sections outline the basic steps, but they are no substitute for consulting the documentation for your system.

If you have access to the `cfront` translator and know C, you may want to inspect the C translations of your C++ programs to get an inside look at how some C++ features are implemented.

Unix Compiling and Linking

The traditional C++ Unix system compiler is invoked with the `CC` command. However, these days a Unix computer instead might have no compiler, a proprietary compiler, or a third-party compiler, perhaps commercial, perhaps freeware, such as the GNU `g++` compiler. In many of these other cases (but not in the no-compiler case!), the `CC` command still works, with the actual compiler being invoked differing from system to system. For simplicity, you should assume that `CC` is available, but realize that you might have to substitute a different command for `CC` in the following discussion.

You use the `CC` command to compile your program. The name is in uppercase letters to distinguish it from the standard Unix C compiler `cc`. The `CC` compiler is a command-line compiler, meaning you type compilation commands on the Unix command line.

For example, to compile the C++ source code file `spiffy.C`, you would type this command at the Unix prompt:

```
CC spiffy.C
```

If, through skill, dedication, or luck, your program has no errors, the compiler generates an object code file with an `o` extension. In this case, the compiler produces a file named `spiffy.o`.

Next, the compiler automatically passes the object code file to the system linker, a program that combines your code with library code to produce the executable file. By default, the executable file is called `a.out`. If you used just one source file, the linker also deletes the `spiffy.o` file because it's no longer needed. To run the program, you just type the name of the executable file:

a.out

Note that if you compile a new program, the new **a.out** executable file replaces the previous **a.out**. (That's because executable files take a lot of space, so overwriting old executable files helps reduce storage demands.) But if you develop an executable program you want to keep, you just use the Unix `mv` command to change the name of the executable file.

In C++, as in C, you can spread a program over more than one file. (Many of the programs in this book in Chapters 8, "Adventures in Functions," through 16 do this.) In such a case, you can compile a program by listing all the files on the command line, like this:

`CC my.C precious.C`

If there are multiple source code files, the compiler does not delete the object code files. That way, if you just change the `my.C` file, you can recompile the program with this command:

`CC my.C precious.o`

This recompiles the `my.C` file and links it with the previously compiled **precious.o** file.

You might have to identify some libraries explicitly. For example, to access functions defined in the math library, you may have to add the `-lm` flag to the command line:

`CC usingmath.C -lm`

Linux Compiling and Linking

Linux systems most commonly use `g++`, the GNU C++ compiler from the Free Software Foundation. The compiler is included in most Linux distributions, but it may not always be installed. The `g++` compiler works much like the standard Unix compiler. For example,

`g++ spiffy.cxx`

produces an executable file call **a.out**.

Some versions might require that you link in the C++ library:

`g++ spiffy.cxx -lg++`

To compile multiple source files, you just list them all in the command line:

`g++ my.cxx precious.cxx`

This produces an executable file called **a.out** and two object code files, **my.o** and **precious.o**. If you subsequently modify just one of the source code files, say **my.cxx**, you can recompile by using **my.cxx** and the **precious.o**:

`g++ my.cxx precious.o`

The Comeau C++ compiler (see www.comeaucomputing.com) is another possibility; it requires the presence of the GNU compiler. However, the Comeau compiler provides the most complete and rigorous implementation of the C++ standard.

The GNU compiler is available for many platforms, including the command-line mode for Windows-based PCs as well as for Unix systems on a variety of platforms.

Command-Line Compilers for Windows Command-Line Mode

The most inexpensive route for compiling C++ programs on a Windows PC is to download a free command-line compiler that runs in a Windows MS-DOS window. The MS-DOS version of the GNU C++ compiler is called **gpp**, and it is available at www.delorie.com/djgpp. Borland provides a free command-line compiler at www.borland.com/bcppbuilder/freecompiler. A slightly newer version of this compiler comes with the relatively inexpensive personal version of Borland C++BuilderX. Digital Mars has a free command-line compiler at www.digitalmars.com. The C++BuilderX installation is pretty automatic. For the rest, you need to read the installation directions carefully because parts of the installation processes are not automatic.

To use the **gpp** compiler, you first open an MS-DOS window. To compile a source code file named **great.cpp**, you type the following command at the prompt:

```
gpp great.cpp
```

If the program compiles successfully, the resulting executable file is named **a.exe**.

To use the Borland online compiler, you first open an MS-DOS window. To compile a source code file named **great.cpp**, you type the following command at the prompt:

```
bcc32 great.cpp
```

If the program compiles successfully, the resulting executable file is named **great.exe**.

Windows Compilers

Windows products are too abundant and too often revised to make it reasonable to describe them all individually. Popular ones include Microsoft, Borland, Metrowerks, and Digital Mars. Despite different designs and goals, they share some common features.

Typically, you must create a project for a program and add to the project the file or files constituting the program. Each vendor supplies an IDE with menu options and, possibly, automated assistance, in creating a project. One very important matter you have to establish is the kind of program you're creating. Typically, the compiler offers many choices, such as a Windows application, an MFC Windows application, a dynamic link library, an ActiveX control, a DOS or character-mode executable, a static library, or a console application. Some of these may be available in both 16-bit and 32-bit versions.

Because the programs in this book are generic, you should avoid choices that require platform-specific code, such as Windows applications. Instead, you want to run in a character-based mode. The choice depends on the compiler. For Microsoft Visual C++, you use the Win32 Console Application option. (If you are using Visual Studio .NET, you can also check the Empty Project option I Application Settings.) Metrowerks compilers offer a Win32 Console C++ App option and a Win32 WinSIOUX C++ App option, both of which work. (The former runs the compiled program in a DOS window; the latter runs it in a standard Windows window.) Some Borland versions feature an EasyWin choice that emulates a DOS session; other versions offer a Console option. In general, you should look to see if there is an option labeled Console, character-mode, or DOS executable, and try that.

After you have the project set up, you have to compile and link your program. The IDE typically gives you several choices, such as Compile, Build, Make, Build All, Link, Execute, and Run (but not necessarily all these choices in the same IDE!):

- *Compile* typically means compile the code in the file that is currently open.

- *Build* or *Make* typically means compile the code for all the source code files in the project. This is often an incremental process. That is, if the project has three files, and you change just one, then just that one is recompiled.

- *Build All* typically means compile all the source code files from scratch.

- As described earlier, *Link* means combine the compiled source code with the necessary library code.

- *Run* or *Execute* means run the program. Typically, if you have not yet done the earlier steps, Run does them before trying to run a program.

A compiler generates an error message when you violate a language rule and identifies the line that has the problem. Unfortunately, when you are new to a language, you may find it difficult to understand the message. Sometimes the actual error may occur before the identified line, and sometimes a single error generates a chain of error messages.

Tip

When fixing errors, fix the first error first. If you can't find it on the line identified as the line with the error, check the preceding line.

Be aware that the fact that a particular compiler accepts a program doesn't necessarily mean that the program is valid C++. And the fact that a particular compiler rejects a program doesn't necessarily mean that the program is invalid C++. Current compilers are more compliant with the Standard than their predecessors of two or three years ago. At this time, the Comeau compiler (and other users of the Edison Design Group front end) comes closest an exact image of the standard.

Tip

Occasionally, compilers get confused after incompletely building a program and respond by giving meaningless error messages that cannot be fixed. In such cases, you can clear things up by selecting Build All to restart the process from scratch. Unfortunately, it is difficult to distinguish this situation from the more common one in which the error messages merely seem to be meaningless.

Usually, the IDE lets you run the program in an auxiliary window. Some IDEs close the window as soon as the program finishes execution, and some leave it open. If your compiler closes the window, you'll have a hard time seeing the output, unless you have quick eyes and a photographic memory. To see the output, you must place some additional code at the end of the program:

```
cin.get();  // add this statement
cin.get();  // and maybe this, too
return 0;
}
```

The `cin.get()` statement reads the next keystroke, so this statement causes the program to wait until you press the Enter key. (No keystrokes get sent to a program until you press Enter, so there's no point in pressing another key.) The second statement is needed if the program otherwise leaves an unprocessed keystroke after its regular input. For example, if you enter a number, you type the number and then press Enter. The program reads the number but leaves the Enter keystroke unprocessed, and it is then read by the first `cin.get()`.

The Borland C++Builder compiler departs a bit from more traditional designs. Its primary aim is Windows programming. To use older versions for generic programs, you select File, New. Then you select Console App. A window opens that includes a skeleton version of `main()`. You should retain the following two nonstandard lines if they appear in the skeleton:

```
#include <vcl\condefs.h>
#pragma hdrstop
```

For C++BuilderX, select File, New, New Console. You don't get a skeleton `main()`. Instead, you need to select File, New File and add a new `.cpp` file to the project.

C++ on the Macintosh

The primary Macintosh C++ compiler is Metrowerks CodeWarrior. It provides project-based IDEs that are similar, in basic concepts, to what you would find in a Windows compiler. You start by selecting File, New Project. You are then given a choice of project types. For CodeWarrior, choose MacOS:C/C++:ANSI C++ Console in older versions, or MacOS:C/C++:Standard Console:Std C++ Console in mid-vintage versions, or MacOS C++ Stationery:Mac OS Carbon:Standard Console:C++ Console Carbon. (You can make other valid choices; for example, you might opt for Classic instead of Carbon or C++ Console Carbon Altivec instead of plain C++ Console Carbon.)

CodeWarrior supplies a small source code file as part of the initial project. You can try compiling and running that program to see if you have your system set up properly. However, after you provide your own code, you should delete this file from the project. You do so by highlighting the file in the project window and then selecting Project, Remove.

Next, you must add your source code to the project. You can use File, New to create a new file or File, Open to open an existing file. You should use a proper suffix, such as `.cp` or `.cpp`. You use the Project menu to add this file to the project list. Some programs in this book require that you add more than one source code file. When you are ready, you select Project, Run.

Tip

To save time, you can use just one project for all the sample programs. You should delete the previous sample source code file from the project list and add the current source code. This saves disk space.

The compiler includes a debugger to help you locate the causes of runtime problems.

Summary

As computers have grown more powerful, computer programs have become larger and more complex. In response to these conditions, computer languages have evolved so that it's easier to manage the programming process. The C language incorporated features such as control structures and functions to better control the flow of a program and to enable a more structured, modular approach. To these tools C++ adds support for object-oriented programming and generic programming. This enables even more modularity and facilitates the creation of reusable code, which saves time and increases program reliability.

The popularity of C++ has resulted in a large number of implementations for many computing platform; the ISO/ANSI C++ Standard provides a basis for keeping these many implementations mutually compatible. The Standard establishes the features the language should have, the behavior the language should display, and a standard library of functions, classes, and templates. The Standard supports the goal of a portable language across different computing platforms and different implementations of the language.

To create a C++ program, you create one or more source files containing the program as expressed in the C++ language. These are text files that must be compiled and linked to produce the machine-language files that constitute executable programs. These tasks are often accomplished in an IDE that provides a text editor for creating the source files, a compiler and a linker for producing executable files, and other resources, such as project management and debugging capabilities. But the same tasks can also be performed in a command-line environment by invoking the appropriate tools individually.

CHAPTER 2

SETTING OUT TO C++

In this chapter you'll learn about the following:

- How to create a C++ program

- The general format for a C++ program

- The #include directive

- The main() function

- How to use the cout object for output

- How to place comments in a C++ program

- How and when to use endl

- How to declare and use variables

- How to use the cin object for input

- How to define and use simple functions

When you construct a simple home, you begin with the foundation and the framework. If you don't have a solid structure from the beginning, you'll have trouble later filling in the details, such as windows, door frames, observatory domes, and parquet ballrooms. Similarly, when you learn a computer language, you should begin by learning the basic structure for a program. Only then can you move on to the details, such as loops and objects. This chapter gives you an overview of the essential structure of a C++ program and previews some topics—notably functions and classes—covered in much greater detail in later chapters. (The idea is to introduce at least some of the basic concepts gradually en route to the great awakenings that come later.)

C++ Initiation

Let's begin with a simple C++ program that displays a message. Listing 2.1 uses the C++ cout (pronounced "see-out") facility to produce character output. The source code includes several comments to the reader; these lines begin with //, and the compiler ignores them. C++ is *case sensitive*; that is, it discriminates between uppercase characters and lowercase characters. This means you must be careful to use the same case as in the examples. For example, this program uses cout, and if you substitute Cout or COUT, the compiler rejects your offering and accuses you of using unknown identifiers. (The compiler is also spelling sensitive, so don't try **kout** or **coot**, either.) The **cpp** filename extension is a common way to indicate a C++ program; you might need to use a different extension, as described in Chapter 1, "Getting Started."

LISTING 2.1 myfirst.cpp

```
// myfirst.cpp--displays a message

#include <iostream>                         // a PREPROCESSOR directive
int main()                                  // function header
{                                           // start of function body
    using namespace std;                    // make definitions visible
    cout << "Come up and C++ me some time."; // message
    cout << endl;                           // start a new line
    cout << "You won't regret it!" << endl; // more output
    return 0;                               // terminate main()
}                                           // end of function body
```

Compatibility Note

If you're using an older compiler, you might need to use `#include <iostream.h>` instead of `#include <iostream>`; in that case, you also would omit the `using namespace std;` line. That is, you'd replace

```
#include <iostream>     // the way of the future
```

with

```
#include <iostream.h>  // in case the future has not yet arrived
```

and you'd omit the following completely:

```
using namespace std;     // also the way of the future
```

(Some very old compilers use `#include <stream.h>` instead of `#include <iostream.h>`; if you have a compiler that old, you should get either a newer compiler or an older book.) The switch from `iostream.h` to `iostream` is relatively recent, and you may run across compilers that haven't implemented it yet.

Some windowing environments run the program in a separate window and then automatically close the window when the program finishes. As discussed in Chapter 1, you can make the window stay open until you strike a key by adding the following line of code before the return statement:

```
cin.get();
```

For some programs you must add two of these lines. This code causes the program to wait for a keystroke. You'll learn more about this code in Chapter 4, "Compound Types."

Program Adjustments

You might find that you must alter the examples in this book to run on your system. The two most common changes are those the first Compatibility Note in this chapter mentions. One is a matter of language standards; if your compiler is not up to date, you must include `iostream.h` instead of iostream and omit the `namespace` line. The second is a matter of the programming environment; you might need to add one or two `cin.get()` statements to keep the program output visible onscreen. Because these adjustments apply equally to every example in this book, the Compatibility Note is the only alert to them you get. Don't forget them! Future Compatibility Notes alert you to other possible alterations you might have to make.

After you use your editor of choice to copy this program (or else use the source code files from the Sams Publishing website, at www.samspublishing.com), you can use your C++ compiler to create the executable code, as Chapter 1 outlines. Here is the output from running the compiled program in Listing 2.1:

```
Come up and C++ me some time.
You won't regret it!
```

C Input and Output

If you're used to programming in C, seeing `cout` instead of the `printf()` function might come as a minor shock. C++ can, in fact, use `printf()`, `scanf()`, and all the other standard C input and output functions, provided that you include the usual C `stdio.h` file. But this is a C++ book, so it uses C++'s input facilities, which improve in many ways upon the C versions.

You construct C++ programs from building blocks called *functions*. Typically, you organize a program into major tasks and then design separate functions to handle those tasks. The example shown in Listing 2.1 is simple enough to consist of a single function named `main()`. The `myfirst.cpp` example has the following elements:

- Comments, indicated by the `//` prefix
- A preprocessor `#include` directive
- A function header: `int main()`
- A `using namespace` directive
- A function body, delimited by `{` and `}`
- Statements that uses the C++ `cout` facility to display a message
- A return statement to terminate the `main()` function

Let's look at these various elements in greater detail. The `main()` function is a good place to start because some of the features that precede `main()`, such as the preprocessor directive, are simpler to understand after you see what `main()` does.

The `main()` Function

Stripped of the trimmings, the sample program shown in Listing 2.1 has the following fundamental structure:

```
int main()
{
    statements
    return 0;
}
```

These lines state that there is a function called `main()`, and they describe how the function behaves. Together they constitute a *function definition*. This definition has two parts: the first line, `int main()`, which is called the *function header*, and the portion enclosed in braces (`{` and `}`), which is the *function body*. Figure 2.1 shows the `main()` function. The function header is a capsule summary of the function's interface with the rest of the program, and the function body represents instructions to the computer about what the function should do. In C++ each complete instruction is called a *statement*. You must terminate each statement with a semicolon, so don't omit the semicolons when you type the examples.

FIGURE 2.1

The `main()` function.

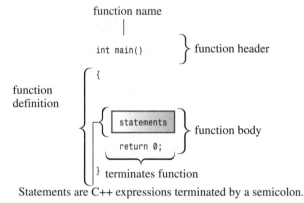

Statements are C++ expressions terminated by a semicolon.

The final statement in `main()`, called a *return statement*, terminates the function. You'll learn more about the return statement as you read through this chapter.

Statements and Semicolons

A statement represents a complete instruction to a computer. To understand your source code, a compiler needs to know when one statement ends and another begins. Some languages use a statement separator. FORTRAN, for example, uses the end of the line to separate one statement from the next. Pascal uses a semicolon to separate one statement from the next. In Pascal you can omit the semicolon in certain cases, such as after a statement just before an END, when you aren't actually separating two statements. (Pragmatists and minimalists will disagree about whether *can* implies *should*.) But C++, like C, uses a semicolon as a *terminator* rather than as a separator. The difference is that a semicolon acting as a terminator is *part* of the statement rather than a marker *between* statements. The practical upshot is that in C++ you should never omit the semicolon.

The Function Header as an Interface

Right now the main point to remember is that C++ syntax requires you to begin the definition of the main() function with this header: int main(). This chapter discusses the function header syntax in more detail later, in the section "Functions," but, for those who can't put their curiosity on hold, here's a preview.

In general, a C++ function is activated, or *called*, by another function, and the function header describes the interface between a function and the function that calls it. The part preceding the function name is called the *function return type*; it describes information flow from a function back to the function that calls it. The part within the parentheses following the function name is called the *argument list* or *parameter list*; it describes information flow from the calling function to the called function. This general format is a bit confusing when you apply it to main() because you normally don't call main() from other parts of your program. Typically, however, main() is called by startup code that the compiler adds to your program to mediate between the program and the operating system (Unix, Windows XP, or whatever). In effect, the function header describes the interface between main() and the operating system.

Consider the interface for main(), beginning with the int part. A C++ function called by another function can return a value to the activating (calling) function. That value is called a *return value*. In this case, main() can return an integer value, as indicated by the keyword int. Next, note the empty parentheses. In general, a C++ function can pass information to another function when it calls that function. The portion of the function header enclosed in parentheses describes that information. In this case, the empty parentheses mean that the main() function takes no information, or, in the usual terminology, main() takes no arguments. (To say that main() takes no arguments doesn't mean that main() is an unreasonable, authoritarian function. Instead, *argument* is the term computer buffs use to refer to information passed from one function to another.)

In short, the header

```
int main()
```

states that the main() function returns an integer value to the function that calls it and that main() takes no information from the function that calls it.

Many existing programs use the classic C header instead:

```
main()      // original C style
```

Under classic C, omitting the return type is the same as saying that the function is type int. However, C++ has phased out that usage.

You can also use this variant:

```
int main(void)      // very explicit style
```

Using the keyword void in the parentheses is an explicit way of saying that the function takes no arguments. Under C++ (but not C), leaving the parentheses empty is the same as using `void` in the parentheses. (In C, leaving the parentheses empty means you are remaining silent about whether there are arguments.)

Some programmers use this header and omit the return statement:

```
void main()
```

This is logically consistent because a `void` return type means the function doesn't return a value. However, although this variant works on some systems, it's not part of the C++ Standard. Thus, on other systems it fails. So you should avoid this form and use the C++ Standard form; it doesn't require that much more effort to do it right.

Finally, the ANSI/ISO C++ Standard makes a concession to those who complain about the tiresome necessity of having to place a return statement at the end of `main()`. If the compiler reaches the end of `main()` without encountering a return statement, the effect will be the same as if you ended `main()` with this statement:

```
return 0;
```

This implicit return is provided only for `main()` and not for any other function.

Why `main()` by Any Other Name Is Not the Same

There's an extremely compelling reason to name the function in the `myfirst.cpp` program `main()`: You must do so. Ordinarily, a C++ program requires a function called `main()`. (And not, by the way, `Main()` or `MAIN()` or `mane()`. Remember, case and spelling count.) Because the `myfirst.cpp` program has only one function, that function must bear the responsibility of being `main()`. When you run a C++ program, execution always begins at the beginning of the `main()` function. Therefore, if you don't have `main()`, you don't have a complete program, and the compiler points out that you haven't defined a `main()` function.

There are exceptions. For example, in Windows programming you can write a dynamic link library (DLL) module. This is code that other Windows programs can use. Because a DLL module is not a standalone program, it doesn't need a `main()`. Programs for specialized environments, such as for a controller chip in a robot, might not need a `main()`. But your ordinary standalone program does need a `main()`; this books discusses that sort of program.

C++ Comments

The double slash (`//`) introduces a C++ comment. A *comment* is a remark from the programmer to the reader that usually identifies a section of a program or explains some aspect of the code. The compiler ignores comments. After all, it knows C++ at least as well as you do, and, in any case, it's incapable of understanding comments. As far as the compiler is concerned, Listing 2.1 looks as if it were written without comments, like this:

```
#include <iostream>
int main()
{
    using namespace std;
    cout << "Come up and C++ me some time.";
    cout << endl;
```

```
    cout << "You won't regret it!" << endl;
    return 0;
}
```

C++ comments run from the // to the end of the line. A comment can be on its own line or it can be on the same line as code. Incidentally, note the first line in Listing 2.1:

```
// myfirst.cpp -- displays a message
```

In this book all programs begin with a comment that gives the filename for the source code and a brief program summary. As mentioned in Chapter 1, the filename extension for source code depends on your C++ system. Other systems might use `myfirst.C` or `myfirst.cxx` for names.

Tip
You should use comments to document your programs. The more complex the program, the more valuable comments are. Not only do they help others to understand what you have done, but also they help you understand what you've done, especially if you haven't looked at the program for a while.

C-Style Comments
C++ also recognizes C comments, which are enclosed between /* and */ symbols:

```
#include <iostream> /* a C-style comment */
```

Because the C-style comment is terminated by */ rather than by the end of a line, you can spread it over more than one line. You can use either or both styles in your programs. However, try sticking to the C++ style. Because it doesn't involve remembering to correctly pair an end symbol with a begin symbol, it's less likely to cause problems. Indeed, C99 has added the // comment to the C language.

The C++ Preprocessor and the `iostream` File

Here's the short version of what you need to know. If your program is to use the usual C++ input or output facilities, you provide these two lines:

```
#include <iostream>
using namespace std;
```

If your compiler doesn't like these lines (for example, if it complains that it can't find the file `iostream`), you should try the following single line instead:

```
#include <iostream.h >    // compatible with older compilers
```

That's all you really must know to make your programs work, but now let's take a more in-depth look.

C++, like C, uses a *preprocessor*. This is a program that processes a source file before the main compilation takes place. (Some C++ implementations, as you might recall from Chapter 1, use a translator program to convert a C++ program to C. Although the translator is also a form of preprocessor, we're not discussing that preprocessor; instead, we're discussing the one that handles directives whose names begin with #.) You don't have to do anything special to invoke this preprocessor. It automatically operates when you compile the program.

Listing 2.1 uses the `#include` directive:

```
#include <iostream>    // a PREPROCESSOR directive
```

This directive causes the preprocessor to add the contents of the `iostream` file to your program. This is a typical preprocessor action: adding or replacing text in the source code before it's compiled.

This raises the question of why you should add the contents of the `iostream` file to the program. The answer concerns communication between the program and the outside world. The `io` in `iostream` refers to *input*, which is information brought into the program, and to *output*, which is information sent out from the program. C++'s input/output scheme involves several definitions found in the `iostream` file. Your first program needs these definitions to use the `cout` facility to display a message. The `#include` directive causes the contents of the `iostream` file to be sent along with the contents of your file to the compiler. In essence, the contents of the `iostream` file replace the `#include <iostream>` line in the program. Your original file is not altered, but a composite file formed from your file and `iostream` goes on to the next stage of compilation.

Remember

Programs that use `cin` and `cout` for input and output must include the `iostream` file (or, on some systems, `iostream.h`).

Header Filenames

Files such as `iostream` are called *include files* (because they are included in other files) or *header files* (because they are included at the beginning of a file). C++ compilers come with many header files, each supporting a particular family of facilities. The C tradition has been to use the `h` extension with header files as a simple way to identify the type of file by its name. For example, the C `math.h` header file supports various C math functions. Initially, C++ did the same. For example, the header file supporting input and output was named `iostream.h`. More recently, however, C++ usage has changed. Now the `h` extension is reserved for the old C header files (which C++ programs can still use), whereas C++ header files have no extension. There are also C header files that have been converted to C++ header files. These files have been renamed by dropping the `h` extension (making it a C++-style name) and prefixing the filename with a `c` (indicating that it comes from C). For example, the C++ version of `math.h` is the `cmath` header file. Sometimes the C and C++ versions of C header files are identical, whereas in other cases the new version might have a few changes. For purely C++ header files such as `iostream`, dropping the `h` is more than a cosmetic change, for the `h`-free header files also incorporate namespaces, the next topic in this chapter. Table 2.1 summarizes the naming conventions for header files.

TABLE 2.1   Header File Naming Conventions

Kind of Header	Convention	Example	Comments
C++ old style	Ends in .h	iostream.h	Usable by C++ programs
C old style	Ends in .h	math.h	Usable by C and C++ programs
C++ new style	No extension	iostream	Usable by C++ programs, uses `namespace std`
Converted C	c prefix, no extension	cmath	Usable by C++ programs, might use non-C features, such as `namespace std`

In view of the C tradition of using different filename extensions to indicate different file types, it appears reasonable to have some special extension, such as `.hx` or `.hxx`, to indicate C++ header files. The ANSI/ISO committee felt so, too. The problem was agreeing on which extension to use, so eventually they agreed on nothing.

Namespaces

If you use `iostream` instead of `iostream.h`, you should use the following namespace directive to make the definitions in `iostream` available to your program:

```
using namespace std;
```

This is called a `using` *directive*. The simplest thing to do is to accept this for now and worry about it later (for example, in Chapter 9, "Memory Models and Namespaces"). But so that you won't be left completely in the dark, here's an overview of what's happening.

Namespace support is a fairly new C++ feature designed to simplify the writing of programs that combine preexisting code from several vendors. One potential problem is that you might use two prepackaged products that both have, say, a function called `wanda()`. If you then use the `wanda()` function, the compiler won't know which version you mean. The namespace facility lets a vendor package its wares in a unit called a *namespace* so that you can use the name of a namespace to indicate which vendor's product you want. So Microflop Industries could place its definitions in a namespace called `Microflop`. Then `Microflop::wanda()` would become the full name for its `wanda()` function. Similarly, `Piscine::wanda()` could denote Piscine Corporation's version of `wanda()`. Thus, your program could now use the namespaces to discriminate between various versions:

```
Microflop::wanda("go dancing?");        // use Microflop namespace version
Piscine::wanda("a fish named Desire");  // use Piscine namespace version
```

In this spirit, the classes, functions, and variables that are a standard component of C++ compilers are now placed in a namespace called `std`. This takes place in the h-free header files. This means, for example, that the `cout` variable used for output and defined in `iostream` is really called `std::cout` and that `endl` is really `std::endl`. Thus, you can omit the `using` directive and code in the following style:

```
std::cout << "Come up and C++ me some time.";
std::cout << std::endl;
```

However, most users don't feel like converting pre-namespace code, which uses `iostream.h` and `cout`, to namespace code, which uses `iostream` and `std::cout`, unless they can do so without a lot of hassle. This is where the `using` directive comes in. The following line means you can use names defined in the `std` namespace without using the `std::` prefix:

```
using namespace std;
```

This `using` directive makes all the names in the `std` namespace available. Modern practice regards this as a bit lazy. The preferred approach is to make available just those names you need, with something called a `using` declaration:

```
using std::cout;   // make cout available
using std::endl;   // make endl available
using std::cin;    // make cin available
```

If you use these directives instead of this:

```
using namespace std;   // lazy approach, all names available
```

you can use `cin` and `cout` without attaching `std::` to them. But if you need to use other names from `iostream`, you have to add them to the `using` list individually. This book initially uses the lazy approach for a couple reasons. First, for simple programs, it's not really a big issue which namespace management technique you use. Second, I'd rather emphasize the more basic aspects about learning C++. Later, the book uses the other namespace techniques.

C++ Output with `cout`

Now let's look at how to display a message. The `myfirst.cpp` program uses the following C++ statement:

```
cout << "Come up and C++ me some time.";
```

The part enclosed within the double quotation marks is the message to print. In C++, any series of characters enclosed in double quotation marks is called a *character string*, presumably because it consists of several characters strung together into a larger unit. The `<<` notation indicates that the statement is sending the string to `cout`; the symbols point the way the information flows. And what is `cout`? It's a predefined object that knows how to display a variety of things, including strings, numbers, and individual characters. (An *object*, as you might remember from Chapter 1, is a particular instance of a class, and a *class* defines how data is stored and used.)

Well, using objects so soon is a bit awkward because you won't learn about objects for several more chapters. Actually, this reveals one of the strengths of objects. You don't have to know the innards of an object in order to use it. All you must know is its interface—that is, how to use it. The `cout` object has a simple interface. If `string` represents a string, you can do the following to display it:

```
cout << string;
```

This is all you must know to display a string, but now take a look at how the C++ conceptual view represents the process. In this view, the output is a stream—that is, a series of characters flowing from the program. The `cout` object, whose properties are defined in the `iostream` file, represents that stream. The object properties for `cout` include an insertion operator (`<<`) that inserts the information on its right into the stream. Consider the following statement (note the terminating semicolon):

```
cout << "Come up and C++ me some time.";
```

It inserts the string "Come up and C++ me some time." into the output stream. Thus, rather than say that your program displays a message, you can say that it inserts a string into the output stream. Somehow, that sounds more impressive. (See Figure 2.2.)

FIGURE 2.2

Displaying a string by using `cout`.

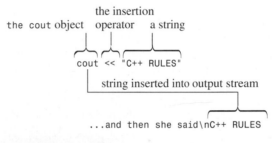

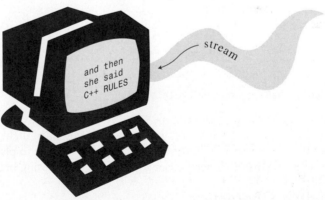

A First Look at Operator Overloading

If you're coming to C++ from C, you probably noticed that the insertion operator (`<<`) looks just like the bitwise left-shift operator (`<<`). This is an example of *operator overloading*, by which the same operator symbol can have different meanings. The compiler uses the context to figure out which meaning is intended. C itself has some operator overloading. For example, the `&` symbol represents both the address operator and the bitwise AND operator. The * symbol represents both multiplication and dereferencing a pointer. The important point here is not the exact function of these operators but that the same symbol can have more than one meaning, with the compiler determining the proper meaning from the context. (You do much the same when you determine the meaning of "sound" in "sound card" versus "sound financial basis.") C++ extends the operator overloading concept by letting you redefine operator meanings for the user-defined types called classes.

The Manipulator `endl`

Now let's examine an odd-looking notation that appears in the second output statement in Listing 2.1:

```
cout << endl;
```

`endl` is a special C++ notation that represents the important concept of beginning a new line. Inserting `endl` into the output stream causes the screen cursor to move to the beginning of the next line. Special notations like `endl` that have particular meanings to `cout` are dubbed *manipulators*. Like `cout`, `endl` is defined in the `iostream` header file and is part of the `std` namespace.

Note that the `cout` facility does not move automatically to the next line when it prints a string, so the first `cout` statement in Listing 2.1 leaves the cursor positioned just after the period at the end of the output string. The output for each `cout` statement begins where the last output ended, so omitting `endl` would result in this output for Listing 2.1:

```
Come up and C++ me some time.You won't regret it!
```

Note that the Y immediately follows the period. Let's look at another example. Suppose you try this code:

```
cout << "The Good, the";
cout << "Bad, ";
cout << "and the Ukulele";
cout << endl;
```

It produces the following output:

```
The Good, theBad, and the Ukulele
```

Again, note that the beginning of one string comes immediately after the end of the preceding string. If you want a space where two strings join, you must include it in one of the strings. (Remember that to try out these output examples, you have to place them in a complete program, with a `main()` function header and opening and closing braces.)

The Newline Character

C++ has another, more ancient, way to indicate a new line in output—the C notation \n:

```
cout << "What's next?\n";     // \n means start a new line
```

The \n combination is considered to be a single character called the *newline* character.

If you are displaying a string, you need less typing to include the newline as part of the string than to tag an `endl` onto the end:

```
cout << "Jupiter is a large planet.\n";        // displays sentence, goes to next
line
cout << "Jupiter is a large planet." << endl;  // displays sentence, goes to next
line
```

On the other hand, if you want to generate a newline by itself, both approaches take the same amount of typing, but most people find the keystrokes for `endl` to be more comfortable:

```
cout << "\n";   // start a new line
cout << endl;   // start a new line
```

Typically, this book uses an embedded newline character (`\n`) when displaying quoted strings and the `endl` manipulator otherwise.

The newline character is one example of special keystroke combinations termed "escape sequences"; they are further discussed in Chapter 3, "Dealing with Data."

C++ Source Code Formatting

Some languages, such as FORTRAN, are line oriented, with one statement to a line. For these languages, the carriage return serves to separate statements. In C++, however, the semicolon marks the end of each statement. This leaves C++ free to treat the carriage return in the same way as a space or a tab. That is, in C++ you normally can use a space where you would use a carriage return and vice versa. This means you can spread a single statement over several lines or place several statements on one line. For example, you could reformat `myfirst.cpp` as follows:

```
#include <iostream>
     int
main
() {   using
    namespace
        std; cout
          <<
"Come up and C++ me some time."
;    cout <<
endl; cout <<
"You won't regret it!" <<
endl;return 0; }
```

This is visually ugly, but valid, code. You do have to observe some rules. In particular, in C and C++ you can't put a space, tab, or carriage return in the middle of an element such as a name, nor can you place a carriage return in the middle of a string. Here are examples of what you can't do:

```
int ma  in()     // INVALID -- space in name
re
turn 0; // INVALID -- carriage return in word
cout << "Behold the Beans
 of Beauty!"; // INVALID -- carriage return in string
```

Tokens and White Space

The indivisible elements in a line of code are called *tokens*. (See Figure 2.3.) Generally, you must separate one token from the next with a space, tab, or carriage return, which collectively are termed *white space*. Some single characters, such as parentheses and commas, are tokens that need not be set off by white space. Here are some examples that illustrate when white space can be used and when it can be omitted:

```
return0;            // INVALID, must be return 0;
return(0);          // VALID, white space omitted
return (0);         // VALID, white space used
intmain();          // INVALID, white space omitted
int main()          // VALID, white space omitted in ()
int main ( )        // ALSO VALID, white space used in ( )
```

FIGURE 2.3
Tokens and white space.

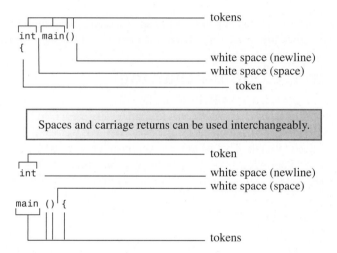

C++ Source Code Style

Although C++ gives you much formatting freedom, your programs will be easier to read if you follow a sensible style. Having valid but ugly code should leave you unsatisfied. Most programmers use the style of Listing 2.1, which observes these rules:

- One statement per line

- An opening brace and a closing brace for a function, each of which is on its own line

- Statements in a function indented from the braces

- No whitespace around the parentheses associated with a function name

The first three rules have the simple intent of keeping the code clean and readable. The fourth helps to differentiate functions from some built-in C++ structures, such as loops, that also use parentheses. This book alerts you to other guidelines as they come up.

C++ Statements

A C++ program is a collection of functions, and each function is a collection of statements. C++ has several kinds of statements, so let's look at some of the possibilities. Listing 2.2 provides two new kinds of statements. First, a *declaration statement* creates a variable. Second, an *assignment statement* provides a value for that variable. Also, the program shows a new capability for cout.

LISTING 2.2   `carrots.cpp`

```cpp
// carrots.cpp -- food processing program
// uses and displays a variable

#include <iostream>

int main()
{
    using namespace std;

    int carrots;            // declare an integer variable

    carrots = 25;             // assign a value to the variable
    cout << "I have ";
    cout << carrots;        // display the value of the variable
    cout << " carrots.";
    cout << endl;
    carrots = carrots - 1;  // modify the variable
    cout << "Crunch, crunch. Now I have " << carrots << " carrots." << endl;
    return 0;
}
```

A blank line separates the declaration from the rest of the program. This practice is the usual C convention, but it's somewhat less common in C++. Here is the program output for Listing 2.2:

```
I have 25 carrots.
Crunch, crunch. Now I have 24 carrots.
```

The next few pages examine this program.

Declaration Statements and Variables

Computers are precise, orderly machines. To store an item of information in a computer, you must identify both the storage location and how much memory storage space the information requires. One relatively painless way to do this in C++ is to use a *declaration statement* to indicate the type of storage and to provide a label for the location. For example, the program in Listing 2.2 has this declaration statement (note the semicolon):

```cpp
int carrots;
```

This statement declares that the program uses enough storage to hold an integer, for which C++ used the label `int`. The compiler takes care of the details of allocating and labeling memory for that task. C++ can handle several kinds, or types, of data, and the `int` is the most basic data type. It corresponds to an integer, a number with no fractional part. The C++ `int` type can be positive or negative, but the size range depends on the implementation. Chapter 3 provides the details on `int` and the other basic types.

Besides giving the type, the declaration statement declares that henceforth the program will use the name `carrots` to identify the value stored at that location. `Carrots` is called a *variable* because you can change its value. In C++ you must declare all variables. If you were to omit the declaration in `carrots.cpp`, the compiler would report an error when the program attempts to use `carrots` further on. (In fact, you might want to try omitting the declaration just to see how your compiler responds. Then, if you see that response in the future, you'll know to check for omitted declarations.)

Why Must Variables Be Declared?

Some languages, notably BASIC, create a new variable whenever you use a new name, without the aid of explicit declarations. That might seem friendlier to the user, and it is—in the short term. The problem is that if you misspell the name of a variable, you inadvertently can create a new variable without realizing it. That is, in BASIC, you can do something like the following:

```
CastleDark = 34
...
CastleDank = CastleDark + MoreGhosts
...
PRINT CastleDark
```

Because `CastleDank` is misspelled (the *r* was typed as an *n*), the changes you make to it leave `CastleDark` unchanged. This kind of error can be hard to trace because it breaks no rules in BASIC. However, in C++, `CastleDark` would be declared while the misspelled `CastleDank` would not be declared. Therefore, the equivalent C++ code breaks the rule about the need to declare a variable for you to use it, so the compiler catches the error and stomps the potential bug.

In general, then, a declaration indicates the type of data to be stored and the name the program will use for the data that's stored there. In this particular case, the program creates a variable called `carrots` in which it can store an integer. (See Figure 2.4.)

FIGURE 2.4
A variable declaration.

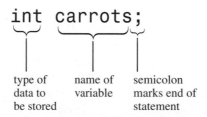

type of data to be stored   name of variable   semicolon marks end of statement

The declaration statement in the program is called a *defining declaration* statement, or *definition*, for short. This means that its presence causes the compiler to allocate memory space for the variable. In more complex situations, you can also have *reference declarations*. These tell the computer to use a variable that has already been defined elsewhere. In general, a declaration need not be a definition, but in this example it is.

If you're familiar with C or Pascal, you're already familiar with variable declarations. You also might have a modest surprise in store for you. In C and Pascal, all variable declarations normally come at the very beginning of a function or procedure. But C++ has no such restriction. Indeed, the usual C++ style is to declare a variable just before it is first used. That way, you don't have to rummage back through a program to see what the type is. You'll see an example of this later in this chapter. This style does have the disadvantage of not gathering all your variable names in one place; thus, you can't tell at a glance what variables a function uses. (Incidentally, C99 now makes the rules for C declarations much the same as for C++.)

Tip

The C++ style for declaring variables is to declare a variable as close to its first use as possible.

Assignment Statements

An assignment statement assigns a value to a storage location. For example, the statement

```
carrots = 25;
```

assigns the integer 25 to the location represented by the variable **carrots**. The = symbol is called the *assignment operator*. One unusual feature of C++ (and C) is that you can use the assignment operator serially. For example, the following is valid code:

```
int steinway;
int baldwin;
int yamaha;
yamaha = baldwin = steinway = 88;
```

The assignment works from right to left. First, **88** is assigned to **steinway**; then the value of **steinway**, which is now 88, is assigned to **baldwin**; then **baldwin**'s value of 88 is assigned to **yamaha**. (C++ follows C's penchant for allowing weird-appearing code.)

The second assignment statement in Listing 2.2 demonstrates that you can change the value of a variable:

```
carrots = carrots - 1;   // modify the variable
```

The expression to the right of the assignment operator (**carrots - 1**) is an example of arithmetic. The computer will subtract 1 from 25, the value of **carrots**, obtaining 24. The assignment operator then stores this new value in the **carrots** location.

A New Trick for cout

Up until now, the examples in this chapter have given `cout` strings to print. Listing 2.2 also gives `cout` a variable whose value is an integer:

```
cout << carrots;
```

The program doesn't print the word `carrots`; instead, it prints the integer value stored in `carrots`, which is 25. Actually, this is two tricks in one. First, `cout` replaces `carrots` with its current numeric value of 25. Second, it translates the value to the proper output characters.

As you can see, `cout` works with both strings and integers. This might not seem particularly remarkable to you, but keep in mind that the integer `25` is something quite different from the string `"25"`. The string holds the characters with which you write the number (that is, a 2 character and a 5 character). The program internally stores the code for the 2 character and the 5 character. To print the string, `cout` simply prints each character in the string. But the integer `25` is stored as a numeric value. Rather than store each digit separately, the computer stores 25 as a binary number. (Appendix A, "Number Bases," discusses this representation.) The main point here is that `cout` must translate a number in integer form into character form before it can print it. Furthermore, `cout` is smart enough to recognize that `carrots` is an integer that requires conversion.

Perhaps the contrast with old C will indicate how clever `cout` is. To print the string `"25"` and the integer `25` in C, you could use C's multipurpose output function `printf()`:

```
printf("Printing a string: %s\n", "25");
printf("Printing an integer: %d\n", 25);
```

Without going into the intricacies of `printf()`, note that you must use special codes (`%s` and `%d`) to indicate whether you are going to print a string or an integer. And if you tell `printf()` to print a string but give it an integer by mistake, `printf()` is too unsophisticated to notice your mistake. It just goes ahead and displays garbage.

The intelligent way in which `cout` behaves stems from C++'s object-oriented features. In essence, the C++ insertion operator (`<<`) adjusts its behavior to fit the type of data that follows it. This is an example of operator overloading. In later chapters, when you take up function overloading and operator overloading, you'll learn how to implement such smart designs yourself.

---

cout and printf()

If you are used to C and `printf()`, you might think `cout` looks odd. You might even prefer to cling to your hard-won mastery of `printf()`. But `cout` actually is no stranger in appearance than `printf()`, with all its conversion specifications. More importantly, `cout` has significant advantages. Its capability to recognize types reflects a more intelligent and foolproof design. Also, it is *extensible*. That is, you can redefine the `<<` operator so that `cout` can recognize and display new data types you develop. And if you relish the fine control `printf()` provides, you can accomplish the same effects with more advanced uses of `cout` (see Chapter 17, "Input, Output, and Files").

More C++ Statements

Let's look at a couple more examples of statements. The program in Listing 2.3 expands on the preceding example by allowing you to enter a value while the program is running. To do so, it uses cin (pronounced "see-in"), the input counterpart to cout. Also, the program shows yet another way to use that master of versatility, the cout object.

LISTING 2.3 getinfo.cpp

```cpp
// getinfo.cpp -- input and output
#include <iostream>

int main()
{
    using namespace std;

    int carrots;

    cout << "How many carrots do you have?" << endl;
    cin >> carrots;                 // C++ input
    cout << "Here are two more. ";
    carrots = carrots + 2;
// the next line concatenates output
    cout << "Now you have " << carrots << " carrots." << endl;
    return 0;
}
```

Here is an example of output from the program in Listing 2.3:

```
How many carrots do you have?
12
Here are two more. Now you have 14 carrots.
```

The program has two new features: using cin to read keyboard input and combining four output statements into one. Let's take a look.

Using cin

As the output from Listing 2.3 demonstrates, the value typed from the keyboard (12) is eventually assigned to the variable carrots. The following statement performs that wonder:

```cpp
cin >> carrots;
```

Looking at this statement, you can practically see information flowing from cin into carrots. Naturally, there is a slightly more formal description of this process. Just as C++ considers output to be stream of characters flowing out of the program, it considers input to be stream of characters flowing into the program. The iostream file defines cin as an object that represents this stream. For output, the << operator inserts characters into the output stream. For input, cin uses the >> operator to extract characters from the input stream. Typically, you provide a variable to the right of the operator to receive the extracted information. (The symbols << and >> were chosen to visually suggest the direction in which information flows.)

Like `cout`, `cin` is a smart object. It converts input, which is just a series of characters typed from the keyboard, into a form acceptable to the variable receiving the information. In this case, the program declares `carrots` to be an integer variable, so the input is converted to the numeric form the computer uses to store integers.

Concatenating with `cout`

The second new feature of `getinfo.cpp` is combining four output statements into one. The `iostream` file defines the `<<` operator so that you can combine (that is, concatenate) output as follows:

```
cout << "Now you have " << carrots << " carrots." << endl;
```

This allows you to combine string output and integer output in a single statement. The resulting output is the same as what the following code produces:

```
cout << "Now you have ";
cout << carrots;
cout << " carrots";
cout << endl;
```

While you're still in the mood for `cout` advice, you can also rewrite the concatenated version this way, spreading the single statement over four lines:

```
cout << "Now you have "
     << carrots
     << " carrots."
     << endl;
```

That's because C++'s free format rules treat newlines and spaces between tokens interchangeably. This last technique is convenient when the line width cramps your style.

Another point to note is that

```
Now you have 14 carrots.
```

appears on the same line as

```
Here are two more.
```

That's because, as noted before, the output of one `cout` statement immediately follows the output of the preceding `cout` statement. This is true even if there are other statements in between.

`cin` and `cout`: A Touch of Class

You've seen enough of `cin` and `cout` to justify your exposure to a little object lore. In particular, in this section you'll learn more about the notion of classes. As Chapter 1 outlined briefly, classes are one of the core concepts for object-oriented programming (OOP) in C++.

A *class* is a data type the user defines. To define a class, you describe what sort of information it can represent and what sort of actions you can perform with that data. A class bears the same relationship to an object that a type does to a variable. That is, a class definition describes a data form and how it can be used, whereas an object is an entity created according to the data form specification. Or, in noncomputer terms, if a class is analogous to a category such as famous actors, then an object is analogous to a particular example of that category, such as Kermit the Frog. To extend the analogy, a class representation of actors would include definitions of possible actions relating to the class, such as Reading for a Part, Expressing Sorrow, Projecting Menace, Accepting an Award, and the like. If you've been exposed to different OOP terminology, it might help to know that the C++ class corresponds to what some languages term an *object type*, and the C++ object corresponds to an object instance or instance variable.

Now let's get a little more specific. Recall the following declaration of a variable:

```
int carrots;
```

This creates a particular variable (`carrots`) that has the properties of the `int` type. That is, `carrots` can store an integer and can be used in particular ways—for addition and subtraction, for example. Now consider `cout`. It is an object created to have the properties of the `ostream` class. The ostream class definition (another inhabitant of the `iostream` file) describes the sort of data an `ostream` object represents and the operations you can perform with and to it, such as inserting a number or string into an output stream. Similarly, `cin` is an object created with the properties of the `istream` class, also defined in `iostream`.

Remember

The class describes all the properties of a data type, and an object is an entity created according to that description.

You have learned that classes are user-defined types, but as a user, you certainly didn't design the `ostream` and `istream` classes. Just as functions can come in function libraries, classes can come in class libraries. That's the case for the `ostream` and `istream` classes. Technically, they are not built in to the C++ language; instead, they are examples of classes that happen to come with the language. The class definitions are laid out in the `iostream` file and are not built into the compiler. You can even modify these class definitions if you like, although that's not a good idea. (More precisely, it is a truly dreadful idea.) The `iostream` family of classes and the related `fstream` (or file I/O) family are the only sets of class definitions that came with all early implementations of C++. However, the ANSI/ISO C++ committee added a few more class libraries to the Standard. Also, most implementations provide additional class definitions as part of the package. Indeed, much of the current appeal of C++ is the existence of extensive and useful class libraries that support Unix, Macintosh, and Windows programming.

The class description specifies all the operations that can be performed on objects of that class. To perform such an allowed action on a particular object, you send a message to the object. For example, if you want the `cout` object to display a string, you send it a message that says, in effect, "Object! Display this!" C++ provides a couple ways to send messages. One way, using a class method, is essentially a function call like the ones you'll see soon. The other way, which is the one used with `cin` and `cout`, is to redefine an operator. Thus the statement

```
cout << "I am not a crook."
```

uses the redefined << operator to send the "display message" to cout. In this case, the message comes with an argument, which is the string to be displayed. (See Figure 2.5.)

FIGURE 2.5
Sending a message to an object.

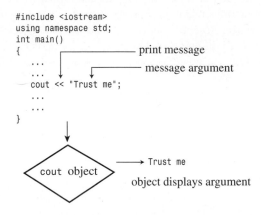

```
#include <iostream>
using namespace std;
int main()
{
    ...
    ...
    cout << "Trust me";
    ...
    ...
}
```

print message

message argument

cout object → Trust me

object displays argument

Functions

Because functions are the modules from which C++ programs are built and because they are essential to C++ OOP definitions, you should become thoroughly familiar with them. Some aspects of functions are advanced topics, so the main discussion of functions comes later, in Chapters 7, "Functions: C++'s Programming Modules," and 8, "Adventures in Functions." However, if we deal now with some basic characteristics of functions, you'll be more at ease and more practiced with functions later. The rest of this chapter introduces you to these function basics.

C++ functions come in two varieties: those with return values and those without them. You can find examples of each kind in the standard C++ library of functions, and you can create your own functions of each type. Let's look at a library function that has a return value and then examine how you can write your own simple functions.

Using a Function That Has a Return Value

A function that has a return value produces a value that you can assign to a variable. For example, the standard C/C++ library includes a function called sqrt() that returns the square root of a number. Suppose you want to calculate the square root of 6.25 and assign it to the variable x. You can use the following statement in your program:

```
x = sqrt(6.25); // returns the value 2.5 and assigns it to x
```

The expression sqrt(6.25) invokes, or *calls*, the sqrt() function. The expression sqrt(6.25) is termed a *function call*, the invoked function is termed the *called function*, and the function containing the function call is termed the *calling function*. (See Figure 2.6.)

FIGURE 2.6
Calling a function.

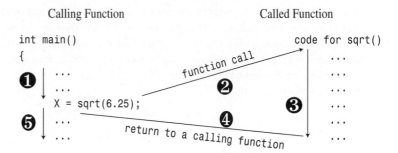

The value in the parentheses (6.25, in this example) is information that is sent to the function; it is said to be *passed* to the function. A value that is sent to a function this way is called an *argument* or *parameter*. (See Figure 2.7.) The `sqrt()` function calculates the answer to be 2.5 and sends that value back to the calling function; the value sent back is called the *return value* of the function. Think of the return value as what is substituted for the function call in the statement after the function finishes its job. Thus, this example assigns the return value to the variable `x`. In short, an argument is information sent to the function, and the return value is a value sent back from the function.

FIGURE 2.7
Function call syntax.

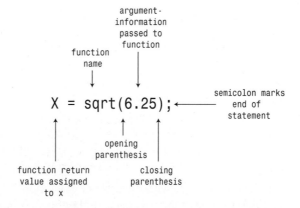

That's practically all there is to it, except that before the C++ compiler uses a function, it must know what kind of arguments the function uses and what kind of return value it has. That is, does the function return an integer? a character? a number with a decimal fraction? a guilty verdict? or something else? If it lacks this information, the compiler won't know how to interpret the return value. The C++ way to convey this information is to use a function prototype statement.

Remember

A C++ program should provide a prototype for each function used in the program.

A function prototype does for functions what a variable declaration does for variables: It tells what types are involved. For example, the C++ library defines the `sqrt()` function to take a number with (potentially) a fractional part (like 6.25) as an argument and to return a number of the same type. Some languages refer to such numbers as *real numbers*, but the name C++ uses for this type is `double`. (You'll see more of `double` in Chapter 3.) The function prototype for `sqrt()` looks like this:

```
double sqrt(double);    // function prototype
```

The initial `double` means `sqrt()` returns a type `double` value. The `double` in the parentheses means `sqrt()` requires a `double` argument. So this prototype describes `sqrt()` exactly as used in the following code:

```
double x;        // declare x as a type double variable
x = sqrt(6.25);
```

The terminating semicolon in the prototype identifies it as a statement and thus makes it a prototype instead of a function header. If you omit the semicolon, the compiler interprets the line as a function header and expects you to follow it with a function body that defines the function.

When you use `sqrt()` in a program, you must also provide the prototype. You can do this in either one of two ways:

- You can type the function prototype into your source code file yourself.

- You can include the `cmath` (`math.h` on older systems) header file, which has the prototype in it.

The second way is better because the header file is even more likely than you to get the prototype right. Every function in the C++ library has a prototype in one or more header files. Just check the function description in your manual or with online help, if you have it, and the description tells you which header file to use. For example, the description of the `sqrt()` function should tell you to use the `cmath` header file. (Again, you might have to use the older `math.h` header file, which works for both C and C++ programs.)

Don't confuse the function prototype with the function definition. The prototype, as you've seen, only describes the function interface. That is, it describes the information sent to the function and the information sent back. The definition, however, includes the code for the function's workings—for example, the code for calculating the square root of a number. C and C++ divide these two features—prototype and definition—for library functions. The library files contain the compiled code for the functions, whereas the header files contain the prototypes.

You should place a function prototype ahead of where you first use the function. The usual practice is to place prototypes just before the definition of the `main()` function. Listing 2.4 demonstrates the use of the library function `sqrt()`; it provides a prototype by including the `cmath` file.

LISTING 2.4   `sqrt.cpp`

```cpp
// sqrt.cpp -- using the sqrt() function

#include <iostream>
#include <cmath>     // or math.h

int main()
{
    using namespace std;

    double area;
    cout << "Enter the floor area, in square feet, of your home: ";
    cin >> area;
    double side;
    side = sqrt(area);
    cout << "That's the equivalent of a square " << side
        << " feet to the side." << endl;
    cout << "How fascinating!" << endl;
    return 0;
}
```

Compatibility Note

If you're using an older compiler, you might have to use `#include <math.h>` instead of `#include <cmath>` in Listing 2.4.

Using Library Functions

C++ library functions are stored in library files. When the compiler compiles a program, it must search the library files for the functions you've used. Compilers differ on which library files they search automatically. If you try to run Listing 2.4 and get a message that `_sqrt` is an undefined external (sounds like a condition to avoid!), chances are that your compiler doesn't automatically search the math library. (Compilers like to add an underscore prefix to function names—another subtle reminder that they have the last say about your program.) If you get such a message, check your compiler documentation to see how to have the compiler search the correct library. The usual Unix implementations, for example, require that you use the `-lm` option (for *l*ibrary *m*ath) at the end of the command line:

`CC sqrt.C -lm`

Using the Gnu compiler under Linux is similar:

`g++ sqrt.C -lm`

Merely including the `cmath` header file provides the prototype but does not necessarily cause the compiler to search the correct library file.

Here's a sample run of the program in Listing 2.4:

```
Enter the floor area, in square feet, of your home: 1536
That's the equivalent of a square 39.1918 feet to the side.
How fascinating!
```

Because `sqrt()` works with type `double` values, the example makes the variables that type. Note that you declare a type `double` variable by using the same form, or syntax, as when you declare a type `int` variable:

```
type-name variable-name;
```

Type `double` allows the variables `area` and `side` to hold values with decimal fractions, such as `536.0` and `39.1918`. An apparent integer, such as `536`, is stored as a real value with a decimal fraction part of `.0` when stored in a type `double` variable. As you'll see in Chapter 3, type `double` encompasses a much greater range of values than type `int`.

C++ allows you to declare new variables anywhere in a program, so `sqrt.cpp` didn't declare `side` until just before using it. C++ also allows you to assign a value to a variable when you create it, so you could also have done this:

```
double side = sqrt(area);
```

You'll learn more about this process, called *initialization*, in Chapter 3.

Note that `cin` knows how to convert information from the input stream to type `double`, and `cout` knows how to insert type `double` into the output stream. As noted earlier, these objects are smart.

Function Variations

Some functions require more than one item of information. These functions use multiple arguments separated by commas. For example, the math function `pow()` takes two arguments and returns a value equal to the first argument raised to the power given by the second argument. It has this prototype:

```
double pow(double, double);  // prototype of a function with two arguments
```

If, say, you wanted to find 5^8 (5 to eighth power), you would use the function like this:

```
answer = pow(5.0, 8.0);       // function call with a list of arguments
```

Other functions take no arguments. For example, one of the C libraries (the one associated with the `cstdlib` or the `stdlib.h` header file) has a `rand()` function that has no arguments and that returns a random integer. Its prototype looks like this:

```
int rand(void);        // prototype of a function that takes no arguments
```

The keyword `void` explicitly indicates that the function takes no arguments. If you omit `void` and leave the parentheses empty, C++ interprets this as an implicit declaration that there are no arguments. You could use the function this way:

```
myGuess = rand();      // function call with no arguments
```

Note that, unlike some computer languages, in C++ you must use the parentheses in the function call even if there are no arguments.

There also are functions that have no return value. For example, suppose you wrote a function that displayed a number in dollars-and-cents format. You could send to it an argument of, say, 23.5, and it would display $23.50 onscreen. Because this function sends a value to the screen instead of to the calling program, it doesn't return a value. You indicate this in the prototype by using the keyword `void` for the return type:

```
void bucks(double);  // prototype for function with no return value
```

Because `bucks()` doesn't return a value, you can't use this function as part of an assignment statement or of some other expression. Instead, you have a pure function call statement:

```
bucks(1234.56);      // function call, no return value
```

Some languages reserve the term *function* for functions with return values and use the terms *procedure* or *subroutine* for those without return values, but C++, like C, uses the term *function* for both variations.

User-Defined Functions

The standard C library provides more than 140 predefined functions. If one fits your needs, by all means use it. But often you have to write your own, particularly when you design classes. Anyway, it's fun to design your own functions, so now let's examine that process. You've already used several user-defined functions, and they have all been named `main()`. Every C++ program must have a `main()` function, which the user must define. Suppose you want to add a second user-defined function. Just as with a library function, you can call a user-defined function by using its name. And, as with a library function, you must provide a function prototype before using the function, which you typically do by placing the prototype above the `main()` definition. The new element is that you also must provide the source code for the new function. The simplest way is to place the code in the same file, after the code for `main()`. Listing 2.5 illustrates these elements.

LISTING 2.5   ourfunc.cpp

```cpp
// ourfunc.cpp -- defining your own function
#include <iostream>
void simon(int);    // function prototype for simon()

int main()
{
    using namespace std;
    simon(3);        // call the simon() function
    cout << "Pick an integer: ";
    int count;
    cin >> count;
    simon(count);    // call it again
    cout << "Done!" << endl;
```

LISTING 2.5   Continued

```
    return 0;
}

void simon(int n)    // define the simon() function
{
    using namespace std;
    cout << "Simon says touch your toes " << n << " times." << endl;
}                    // void functions don't need return statements
```

The `main()` function calls the `simon()` function twice, once with an argument of 3 and once with a variable argument `count`. In between, the user enters an integer that's used to set the value of `count`. The example doesn't use a newline character in the `cout` prompting message. This results in the user input appearing on the same line as the prompt. Here is a sample run of the program in Listing 2.5:

```
Simon says touch your toes 3 times.
Pick an integer: 512
Simon says touch your toes 512 times.
Done!
```

Function Form

The definition for the `simon()` function in Listing 2.5 follows the same general form as the definition for `main()`. First, there is a function header. Then, enclosed in braces, comes the function body. You can generalize the form for a function definition as follows:

```
type functionname(argumentlist)
{
    statements
}
```

Note that the source code that defines `simon()` follows the closing brace of `main()`. Like C, and unlike Pascal, C++ does not allow you to embed one function definition inside another. Each function definition stands separately from all others; all functions are created equal. (See Figure 2.8.)

Function Headers

The `simon()` function in Listing 2.5 has this header:

```
void simon(int n)
```

The initial `void` means that `simon()` has no return value. So calling `simon()` doesn't produce a number that you can assign to a variable in `main()`. Thus, the first function call looks like this:

```
simon(3);             // ok for void functions
```

Because poor `simon()` lacks a return value, you can't use it this way:

```
simple = simon(3);    // not allowed for void functions
```

FIGURE 2.8

Function definitions occur sequentially in a file.

```
#include <iostream>
using namespace std;
```

function prototypes
```
void simon(int);
double taxes(double);
```

function #1
```
int main()
{
    ...
    return 0;
}
```

function #2
```
void simon(int n)
{
    ...
}
```

function #3
```
double taxes(double t)
{
    ...
    return 2 * t;
}
```

The `int n` within the parentheses means that you are expected to use `simon()` with a single argument of type `int`. The `n` is a new variable assigned the value passed during a function call. Thus, the function call

```
simon(3);
```

assigns the value 3 to the `n` variable defined in the `simon()` header. When the `cout` statement in the function body uses `n`, it uses the value passed in the function call. That's why `simon(3)` displays a `3` in its output. The call to `simon(count)` in the sample run causes the function to display `512` because that's the value given to `count`. In short, the header for `simon()` tells you that this function takes a single type `int` argument and that it doesn't have a return value.

Let's review `main()`'s function header:

```
int main()
```

The initial `int` means that `main()` returns an integer value. The empty parentheses (which, optionally, could contain `void`) means that `main()` has no arguments. Functions that have return values should use the keyword `return` to provide the return value and to terminate the function. That's why you've been using the following statement at the end of `main()`:

```
return 0;
```

This is logically consistent: `main()` is supposed to return a type `int` value, and you have it return the integer 0. But, you might wonder, to what are you returning a value? After all, nowhere in any of your programs have you seen anything calling `main()`:

```
squeeze = main();    // absent from our programs
```

The answer is that you can think of your computer's operating system (Unix, say, or DOS) as calling your program. So `main()`'s return value is returned not to another part of the program but to the operating system. Many operating systems can use the program's return value. For example, Unix shell scripts and DOS batch files can be designed to run programs and test their return values, usually called *exit values*. The normal convention is that an exit value of zero means the program ran successfully, whereas a nonzero value means there was a problem. Thus, you can design a C++ program to return a nonzero value if, say, it fails to open a file. You can then design a shell script or batch file to run that program and to take some alternative action if the program signals failure.

Keywords

Keywords are the vocabulary of a computer language. This chapter has used four C++ keywords: `int`, `void`, `return`, and `double`. Because these keywords are special to C++, you can't use them for other purposes. That is, you can't use `return` as the name for a variable or `double` as the name of a function. But you can use them as part of a name, as in `painter` (with its hidden `int`) or `return_aces`. Appendix B, "C++ Reserved Words," provides a complete list of C++ keywords. Incidentally, `main` is not a keyword because it's not part of the language. Instead, it is the name of a required function. You can use `main` as a variable name. (That can cause a problem in circumstances too esoteric to describe here, and because it is confusing in any case, you'd best not.) Similarly, other function names and object names are not keywords. However, using the same name, say `cout`, for both an object and a variable in a program confuses the compiler. That is, you can use `cout` as a variable name in a function that doesn't use the `cout` object for output, but you can't use `cout` both ways in the same function.

Using a User-Defined Function That Has a Return Value

Let's go one step further and write a function that uses the return statement. The `main()` function already illustrates the plan for a function with a return value: Give the return type in the function header and use `return` at the end of the function body. You can use this form to solve a weighty problem for those visiting the United Kingdom. In the United Kingdom, many bathroom scales are calibrated in *stone* instead of in U.S. pounds or international kilograms. The word *stone* is both singular and plural in this context. (The English language does lack the internal consistency of, say, C++.) One stone is 14 pounds, and the program in Listing 2.6 uses a function to make this conversion.

LISTING 2.6   `convert.cpp`

```cpp
// convert.cpp -- converts stone to pounds
#include <iostream>
int stonetolb(int);      // function prototype
int main()
{
    using namespace std;
    int stone;
    cout << "Enter the weight in stone: ";
    cin >> stone;
    int pounds = stonetolb(stone);
    cout << stone << " stone = ";
```

LISTING 2.6   *Continued*

```
        cout << pounds << " pounds." << endl;
        return 0;
}

int stonetolb(int sts)
{
        return 14 * sts;
}
```

Here's a sample run of the program in Listing 2.6:

```
Enter the weight in stone: 14
14 stone = 196 pounds.
```

In `main()`, the program uses `cin` to provide a value for the integer variable `stone`. This value is passed to the `stonetolb()` function as an argument and is assigned to the variable `sts` in that function. `stonetolb()` then uses the `return` keyword to return the value of `14 * sts` to `main()`. This illustrates that you aren't limited to following `return` with a simple number. Here, by using a more complex expression, you avoid the bother of having to create a new variable to which to assign the value before returning it. The program calculates the value of that expression (196 in this example) and returns the resulting value. If returning the value of an expression bothers you, you can take the longer route:

```
int stonetolb(int sts)
{
        int pounds = 14 * sts;
        return pounds;
}
```

Both versions produce the same result, but the second version takes slightly longer to do so.

In general, you can use a function with a return value wherever you would use a simple constant of the same type. For example, `stonetolb()` returns a type `int` value. This means you can use the function in the following ways:

```
int aunt = stonetolb(20);
int aunts = aunt + stonetolb(10);
cout << "Ferdie weighs " << stonetolb(16) << " pounds." << endl;
```

In each case, the program calculates the return value and then uses that number in these statements.

As these examples show, the function prototype describes the function interface—that is, how the function interacts with the rest of the program. The argument list shows what sort of information goes into the function, and the function type shows the type of value returned. Programmers sometimes describe functions as *black boxes* (a term from electronics) specified by the flow of information into and out of them. The function prototype perfectly portrays that point of view. (See Figure 2.9.)

FIGURE 2.9
The function prototype
and the function as a
black box.

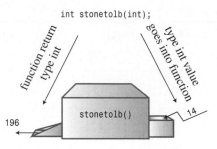

The `stonetolb()` function is short and simple, yet it embodies a full range of functional features:

- It has a header and a body.

- It accepts an argument.

- It returns a value.

- It requires a prototype.

Consider `stonetolb()` as a standard form for function design. You'll further explore functions in Chapters 7 and 8. In the meantime, the material in this chapter should give you a good feel for how functions work and how they fit into C++.

Placing the `using` Directive in Multifunction Programs

Notice that Listing 2.5 places a `using` directive in each of the two functions:

```
using namespace std;
```

This is because each function uses **cout** and thus needs access to the **cout** definition from the **std** namespace.

There's another way to make the **std** namespace available to both functions in Listing 2.5, and that's to place the directive outside and above both functions:

```
// ourfunc1.cpp - repositioning the using directive
#include <iostream>
using namespace std; // affects all function definitions in this file
void simon(int);

int main()
{
    simon(3);
    cout << "Pick an integer: ";
    int count;
    cin >> count;
    simon(count);
```

```
    cout << "Done!" << endl;
    return 0;
}

void simon(int n)
{
    cout << "Simon says touch your toes " << n << " times." << endl;
}
```

The current prevalent philosophy is that it's preferable to be more discriminating and limit access to the `std` namespace to only those functions that need access. For example, in Listing 2.6, only `main()` uses `cout`, so there is no need to make the `std` namespace available to the `stonetolb()` function. Thus, the `using` directive is placed inside the `main()` function only, limiting `std` namespace access to just that function.

In summary, you have several choices for making `std` namespace elements available to a program. Here are some:

- You can place

  ```
  using std namespace;
  ```

  above the function definitions in a file, making all the contents of the `std` namespace available to every function in the file.

- You can place

  ```
  using std namespace;
  ```

  in a specific function definition, making all the contents of the `std` namespace available to that specific function.

- Instead of using

  ```
  using std namespace;
  ```

  you can place directives like

  ```
  using std::cout;
  ```

  in a specific function definition and make a particular element, such as `cout`, available to that function.

- You can omit the `using` directives entirely and use the `std::` prefix whenever you use elements from the `std` namespace:

  ```
  std::cout << "I'm using cout and endl from the std namespace" << std::endl;
  ```

Real-World Note: Naming Conventions

C++ programmers are blessed (or cursed) with myriad options when naming functions, classes, and variables. Programmers have strong and varied opinions about style, and these often surface as holy wars in public forums. Starting with the same basic idea for a function name, a programmer might select any of the following:

```
MyFunction( )
myfunction( )
myFunction( )
my_function( )
my_funct( )
```

The choice will depend on the development team, the idiosyncrasies of the technologies or libraries used, and the tastes and preferences of the individual programmer. Rest assured that all legal styles are correct, as far as the C++ language is concerned, and can be used based on your own judgment.

Language allowances aside, it is worth noting that a personal naming style—one that aids you through consistency and precision—is well worth pursuing. A precise, recognizable personal naming convention is a hallmark of good software engineering, and it will aid you throughout your programming career.

Summary

A C++ program consists of one or more modules called functions. Programs begin executing at the beginning of the function called `main()` (all lowercase), so you should always have a function by this name. A function, in turn, consists of a header and a body. The function header tells you what kind of return value, if any, the function produces and what sort of information it expects arguments to pass to it. The function body consists of a series of C++ statements enclosed in paired braces (`{}`).

C++ statement types include the following:

- **Declaration statement**—A declaration statement announces the name and the type of a variable used in a function.

- **Assignment statement**—An assignment statement uses the assignment operator (=) to assign a value to a variable.

- **Message statement**—A message statement sends a message to an object, initiating some sort of action.

- **Function call**—A function call activates a function. When the called function terminates, the program returns to the statement in the calling function immediately following the function call.

- **Function prototype**—A function prototype declares the return type for a function, along with the number and type of arguments the function expects.

- **Return statement**—A return statement sends a value from a called function back to the calling function.

A class is a user-defined specification for a data type. This specification details how information is to be represented and also the operations that can be performed with the data. An object is an entity created according to a class prescription, just as a simple variable is an entity created according to a data type description.

C++ provides two predefined objects (`cin` and `cout`) for handling input and output. They are examples of the `istream` and `ostream` classes, which are defined in the `iostream` file. These classes view input and output as streams of characters. The insertion operator (`<<`), which is defined for the `ostream` class, lets you insert data into the output stream, and the extraction operator (`>>`), which is defined for the `istream` class, lets you extract information from the input stream. Both `cin` and `cout` are smart objects, capable of automatically converting information from one form to another according to the program context.

C++ can use the extensive set of C library functions. To use a library function, you should include the header file that provides the prototype for the function.

Now that you have an overall view of simple C++ programs, you can go on in the next chapters to fill in details and expand horizons.

Review Questions

You can find the answers to the review questions at the end of each chapter in Appendix J, "Answers to Review Questions."

1. What are the modules of C++ programs called?

2. What does the following preprocessor directive do?

   ```
   #include <iostream>
   ```

3. What does the following statement do?

   ```
   using namespace std;
   ```

4. What statement would you use to print the phrase "Hello, world" and then start a new line?

5. What statement would you use to create an integer variable with the name `cheeses`?

6. What statement would you use to assign the value 32 to the variable `cheeses`?

7. What statement would you use to read a value from keyboard input into the variable `cheeses`?

8. What statement would you use to print "We have X varieties of cheese," where the current value of the `cheeses` variable replaces X?

9. What do the following function prototypes tell you about the functions?

   ```
   int froop(double t);
   void rattle(int n);
   int prune(void);
   ```

10. When do you not have to use the keyword `return` when you define a function?

Programming Exercises

1. Write a C++ program that displays your name and address.

2. Write a C++ program that asks for a distance in furlongs and converts it to yards. (One furlong is 220 yards.)

3. Write a C++ program that uses three user-defined functions (counting `main()` as one) and produces the following output:

   ```
   Three blind mice
   Three blind mice
   See how they run
   See how they run
   ```

   One function, called two times, should produce the first two lines, and the remaining function, also called twice, should produce the remaining output.

4. Write a program that has `main()` call a user-defined function that takes a Celsius temperature value as an argument and then returns the equivalent Fahrenheit value. The program should request the Celsius value as input from the user and display the result, as shown in the following code:

   ```
   Please enter a Celsius value: 20
   20 degrees Celsius is 68 degrees Fahrenheit.
   ```

   For reference, here is the formula for making the conversion:

   Fahrenheit = 1.8 × degrees Celsius + 32.0

5. Write a program that has `main()` call a user-defined function that takes a distance in light years as an argument and then returns the distance in astronomical units. The program should request the light year value as input from the user and display the result, as shown in the following code:

   ```
   Enter the number of light years: 4.2
   4.2 light years = 265608 astronomical units.
   ```

   An astronomical unit is the average distance from the earth to the sun (about 150,000,000 km or 93,000,000 miles), and a light year is the distance light travels in a year (about 10 trillion kilometers or 6 trillion miles). (The nearest star after the sun is about 4.2 light years away.) Use type `double` (as in Listing 2.4) and this conversion factor:

   1 light year = 63,240 astronomical units

6. Write a program that asks the user to enter an hour value and a minute value. The `main()` function should then pass these two values to a type `void` function that displays the two values in the format shown in the following sample run:

   ```
   Enter the number of hours: 9
   Enter the number of minutes: 28
   Time: 9:28
   ```

CHAPTER 3

DEALING WITH DATA

In this chapter you'll learn about the following:

- Rules for naming C++ variables

- C++'s built-in integer types:
  `unsigned long`, `long`, `unsigned int`, `int`, `unsigned short`, `short`, `char`, `unsigned char`, `signed char`, and `bool`

- The `climits` file, which represents system limits for various integer types

- Numeric constants of various integer types

- Using the `const` qualifier to create symbolic constants

- C++'s built-in floating-point types: `float`, `double`, and `long double`

- The `cfloat` file, which represents system limits for various floating-point types

- Numeric constants of various floating-point types

- C++'s arithmetic operators

- Automatic type conversions

- Forced type conversions (type casts)

The essence of object-oriented programming (OOP) is designing and extending your own data types. Designing your own data types represents an effort to make a type match the data. If you do this properly, you'll find it much simpler to work with the data later. But before you can create your own types, you must know and understand the types that are built in to C++ because those types will be your building blocks.

The built-in C++ types come in two groups: fundamental types and compound types. In this chapter you'll meet the fundamental types, which represent integers and floating-point numbers. That might sound like just two types; however, C++ recognizes that no one integer type and no one floating-point type match all programming requirements, so it offers several variants on these two data themes. Chapter 4, "Compound Types," follows up by covering several types that are built on the basic types; these additional compound types include arrays, strings, pointers, and structures.

Of course, a program also needs a means to identify stored data. In this chapter you'll examine one method for doing so—using variables. Then, you'll look at how to do arithmetic in C++. Finally, you'll see how C++ converts values from one type to another.

Simple Variables

Programs typically need to store information—perhaps the current price of IBM stock, the average humidity in New York City in August, the most common letter in the U.S. Constitution and its relative frequency, or the number of available Elvis impersonators. To store an item of information in a computer, the program must keep track of three fundamental properties:

- Where the information is stored

- What value is kept there

- What kind of information is stored

The strategy the examples in this book have used so far is to declare a variable. The type used in the declaration describes the kind of information, and the variable name represents the value symbolically. For example, suppose Chief Lab Assistant Igor uses the following statements:

```
int braincount;
braincount = 5;
```

These statements tell the program that it is storing an integer and that the name `braincount` represents the integer's value, 5 in this case. In essence, the program locates a chunk of memory large enough to hold an integer, notes the location, assigns the label `braincount` to the location, and copies the value 5 into the location. These statements don't tell you (or Igor) where in memory the value is stored, but the program does keep track of that information, too. Indeed, you can use the `&` operator to retrieve `braincount`'s address in memory. You'll learn about that operator in the next chapter, when you investigate a second strategy for identifying data—using pointers.

Names for Variables

C++ encourages you to use meaningful names for variables. If a variable represents the cost of a trip, you should call it `cost_of_trip` or `costOfTrip`, not just `x` or `cot`. You do have to follow a few simple C++ naming rules:

- The only characters you can use in names are alphabetic characters, numeric digits, and the underscore (_) character.

- The first character in a name cannot be a numeric digit.

- Uppercase characters are considered distinct from lowercase characters.

- You can't use a C++ keyword for a name.

- Names beginning with two underscore characters or with an underscore character followed by an uppercase letter are reserved for use by the implementation—that is, the compiler and the resources it uses. Names beginning with a single underscore character are reserved for use as global identifiers by the implementation.

- C++ places no limits on the length of a name, and all characters in a name are significant.

The next-to-last point is a bit different from the preceding points because using a name such as `__time_stop` or `_Donut` doesn't produce a compiler error; instead, it leads to undefined behavior. In other words, there's no telling what the result will be. The reason there is no compiler error is that the names are not illegal but rather are reserved for the implementation to use. The bit about global names refers to where the names are declared; Chapter 4 touches on that topic.

The final point differentiates C++ from ANSI C (C99), which guarantees only that the first 63 characters in a name are significant. (In ANSI C, two names that have the same first 63 characters are considered identical, even if the 64th characters differ.)

Here are some valid and invalid C++ names:

```
int poodle;      // valid
int Poodle;      // valid and distinct from poodle
int POODLE;      // valid and even more distinct
Int terrier;     // invalid -- has to be int, not Int
int my_stars3    // valid
int _Mystars3;   // valid but reserved -- starts with underscore
int 4ever;       // invalid because starts with a digit
int double;      // invalid -- double is a C++ keyword
int begin;       // valid -- begin is a Pascal keyword
int __fools;     // valid but reserved - starts with two underscores
int the_very_best_variable_i_can_be_version_112;  // valid
int honky-tonk;         // invalid -- no hyphens allowed
```

If you want to form a name from two or more words, the usual practice is to separate the words with an underscore character, as in `my_onions`, or to capitalize the initial character of each word after the first, as in `myEyeTooth`. (C veterans tend to use the underscore method in the C tradition, whereas Pascalians prefer the capitalization approach.) Either form makes it easier to see the individual words and to distinguish between, say, `carDrip` and `cardRip`, or `boat_sport` and `boats_port`.

Real-World Note: Variable Names

Schemes for naming variables, like schemes for naming functions, provide fertile ground for fervid discussion. Indeed, this topic produces some of the most strident disagreements in programming. Again, as with function names, the C++ compiler doesn't care about your variable names as long as they are within legal limits, but a consistent, precise personal naming convention will serve you well.

As in function naming, capitalization is a key issue in variable naming (see the sidebar "Naming Conventions" in Chapter 2, "Setting Out to C++"), but many programmers may insert an additional level of information in a variable name—a prefix that describes the variable's type or contents. For instance, the integer `myWeight` might be named `nMyWeight`; here, the n prefix is used to represent an integer value, which is useful when you are reading code and the definition of the variable isn't immediately at hand. Alternatively, this variable might be named `intMyWeight`, which is more precise and legible, although it does include a couple extra letters (anathema to many programmers). Other prefixes are commonly used in like fashion: `str` or `sz` might be used to represent a null-terminated string of characters, `b` might represent a Boolean value, `p` a pointer, `c` a single character.

As you progress into the world of C++, you will find many examples of the prefix naming style (including the handsome `m_lpctstr` prefix—a class member value that contains a long pointer to a constant, null-terminated string of characters), as well as other, more bizarre and possibly counterintuitive styles that you may or may not adopt as your own. As in all the stylistic, subjective parts of C++, consistency and precision are best. You should use variable names to fit your own needs, preferences, and personal style. (Or, if required, choose names that fit the needs, preferences, and personal style of your employer.)

Integer Types

`Integers` are numbers with no fractional part, such as 2, 98, −5286, and 0. There are lots of integers, assuming that you consider an infinite number to be a lot, so no finite amount of computer memory can represent all possible integers. Thus, a language can represent only a subset of all integers. Some languages, such as standard Pascal, offer just one integer type (one type fits all!), but C++ provides several choices. This gives you the option of choosing the integer type that best meets a program's particular requirements. This concern with matching type to data presages the designed data types of OOP.

The various C++ integer types differ in the amount of memory they use to hold an integer. A larger block of memory can represent a larger range in integer values. Also, some types (signed types) can represent both positive and negative values, whereas others (unsigned types) can't represent negative values. The usual term for describing the amount of memory used for an integer is `width`. The more memory a value uses, the wider it is. C++'s basic integer types, in order of increasing width, are `char`, `short`, `int`, and `long`. Each comes in both signed and unsigned versions. That gives you a choice of eight different integer types! Let's look at these integer types in more detail. Because the `char` type has some special properties (it's most often used to represent characters instead of numbers), this chapter covers the other types first.

The `short`, `int`, and `long` Integer Types

Computer memory consists of units called `bits`. (See the "Bits and Bytes" sidebar, later in this chapter.) By using different numbers of bits to store values, the C++ types `short`, `int`, and `long` can represent up to three different integer widths. It would be convenient if each type were always some particular width for all systems—for example, if `short` were always 16 bits, `int` were always 32 bits, and so on. But life is not that simple. However, no one choice is suitable for all computer designs. C++ offers a flexible standard with some guaranteed minimum sizes, which it takes from C. Here's what you get:

- A `short` integer is at least 16 bits wide.

- An `int` integer is at least as big as `short`.

- A `long` integer is at least 32 bits wide and at least as big as `int`.

Bits and Bytes

The fundamental unit of computer memory is the `bit`. Think of a bit as an electronic switch that you can set to either off or on. Off represents the value 0, and on represents the value 1. An 8-bit chunk of memory can be set to 256 different combinations. The number 256 comes from the fact that each bit has two possible settings, making the total number of combinations for 8 bits $2 \times 2 \times 2 \times 2 \times 2 \times 2 \times 2 \times 2$, or 256. Thus, an 8-bit unit can represent, say, the values 0 through 255 or the values –128 through 127. Each additional bit doubles the number of combinations. This means you can set a 16-bit unit to 65,536 different values and a 32-bit unit to 4,294,672,296 different values.

A `byte` usually means an 8-bit unit of memory. `Byte` in this sense is the unit of measurement that describes the amount of memory in a computer, with a kilobyte equal to 1,024 bytes and a megabyte equal to 1,024 kilobytes. However, C++ defines `byte` differently. The C++ `byte` consists of at least enough adjacent bits to accommodate the basic character set for the implementation. That is, the number of possible values must equal or exceed the number of distinct characters. In the United States, the basic character sets are usually the ASCII and EBCDIC sets, each of which can be accommodated by 8 bits, so the C++ byte is typically 8 bits on systems using those character sets. However, international programming can require much larger character sets, such as Unicode, so some implementations may use a 16-bit byte or even a 32-bit byte.

Many systems currently use the minimum guarantee, making `short` 16 bits and `long` 32 bits. This still leaves several choices open for `int`. It could be 16, 24, or 32 bits in width and meet the standard. Typically, `int` is 16 bits (the same as `short`) for older IBM PC implementations and 32 bits (the same as `long`) for Windows 98, Windows NT, Windows XP, Macintosh OS X, VAX, and many other minicomputer implementations. Some implementations give you a choice of how to handle `int`. (What does your implementation use? The next example shows you how to determine the limits for your system without your having to open a manual.) The differences between implementations for type widths can cause problems when you move a C++ program from one environment to another. But a little care, as discussed later in this chapter, can minimize those problems.

You use these type names to declare variables just as you would use `int`:

```
short score;        // creates a type short integer variable
int temperature;    // creates a type int integer variable
long position;      // creates a type long integer variable
```

Actually, `short` is short for `short int` and `long` is short for `long int`, but hardly anyone uses the longer forms.

The three types, `int`, `short`, and `long`, are signed types, meaning each splits its range approximately equally between positive and negative values. For example, a 16-bit `int` might run from –32,768 to +32,767.

If you want to know how your system's integers size up, you can use C++ tools to investigate type sizes with a program. First, the `sizeof` operator returns the size, in bytes, of a type or a variable. (An `operator` is a built-in language element that operates on one or more items to produce a value. For example, the addition operator, represented by +, adds two values.) Note that the meaning of `byte` is implementation dependent, so a 2-byte `int` could be 16 bits on one system and 32 bits on another. Second, the `climits` header file (or, for older implementations, the `limits.h` header file) contains information about integer type limits. In particular, it defines symbolic names to represent different limits. For example, it defines `INT_MAX` as the largest possible `int` value and `CHAR_BIT` as the number of bits in a byte. Listing 3.1 demonstrates how to use these facilities. The program also illustrates `initialization`, which is the use of a declaration statement to assign a value to a variable.

LISTING 3.1   `limits.cpp`

```
// limits.cpp -- some integer limits
#include <iostream>
#include <climits>               // use limits.h for older systems
int main()
{
    using namespace std;
    int n_int = INT_MAX;         // initialize n_int to max int value
    short n_short = SHRT_MAX;     // symbols defined in limits.h file
    long n_long = LONG_MAX;

    // sizeof operator yields size of type or of variable
    cout << "int is " << sizeof (int) << " bytes." << endl;
    cout << "short is " << sizeof n_short << " bytes." << endl;
    cout << "long is " << sizeof n_long << " bytes." << endl << endl;

    cout << "Maximum values:" << endl;
    cout << "int: " << n_int << endl;
    cout << "short: " << n_short << endl;
    cout << "long: " << n_long << endl << endl;

    cout << "Minimum int value = " << INT_MIN << endl;
    cout << "Bits per byte = " << CHAR_BIT << endl;
    return 0;
}
```

Compatibility Note

The `climits` header file is the C++ version of the ANSI C `limits.h` header file. Some earlier C++ platforms have neither header file available. If you're using such a system, you must limit yourself to experiencing this example in spirit only.

Here is the output from the program in Listing 3.1, using Microsoft Visual C++ 7.1:

```
int is 4 bytes.
short is 2 bytes.
long is 4 bytes.

Maximum values:
int: 2147483647
short: 32767
long: 2147483647

Minimum int value = -2147483648
Bits per byte = 8
```

Here is the output for a second system, running Borland C++ 3.1 for DOS:

```
int is 2 bytes.
short is 2 bytes.
long is 4 bytes.

Maximum values:
int: 32767
short: 32767
long: 2147483647

Minimum int value = -32768
Bits per byte = 8
```

Program Notes

The following sections look at the chief programming features for this program.

The sizeof *Operator and the* climits *Header File*

The `sizeof` operator reports that `int` is 4 bytes on the base system, which uses an 8-bit byte. You can apply the `sizeof` operator to a type name or to a variable name. When you use the `sizeof` operator with a type name, such as `int`, you enclose the name in parentheses. But when you use the operator with the name of the variable, such as `n_short`, parentheses are optional:

```
cout << "int is " << sizeof (int) << " bytes.\n";
cout << "short is " << sizeof n_short << " bytes.\n";
```

The `climits` header file defines symbolic constants (see the sidebar "Symbolic Constants the Preprocessor Way," later in this chapter) to represent type limits. As mentioned previously, `INT_MAX` represents the largest value type `int` can hold; this turned out to be 32,767 for our DOS system. The compiler manufacturer provides a `climits` file that reflects the values appropriate to that compiler. For example, the `climits` file for Windows XP, which uses a 32-bit `int`, defines `INT_MAX` to represent 2,147,483,647. Table 3.1 summarizes the symbolic constants defined in the `climits` file; some pertain to types you have not yet learned.

TABLE 3.1   Symbolic Constants from `climits`

Symbolic Constant	Represents
CHAR_BIT	Number of bits in a `char`
CHAR_MAX	Maximum `char` value
CHAR_MIN	Minimum `char` value
SCHAR_MAX	Maximum `signed char` value
SCHAR_MIN	Minimum `signed char` value
UCHAR_MAX	Maximum `unsigned char` value

TABLE 3.1   Continued

Symbolic Constant	Represents
SHRT_MAX	Maximum short value
SHRT_MIN	Minimum short value
USHRT_MAX	Maximum unsigned short value
INT_MAX	Maximum int value
INT_MIN	Minimum int value
UINT_MAX	Maximum unsigned int value
LONG_MAX	Maximum long value
LONG_MIN	Minimum long value
ULONG_MAX	Maximum unsigned long value

Initialization

Initialization combines assignment with declaration. For example, the statement

```
int n_int = INT_MAX;
```

declares the n_int variable and sets it to the largest possible type int value. You can also use regular constants to initialize values. You can initialize a variable to another variable, provided that the other variable has been defined first. You can even initialize a variable to an expression, provided that all the values in the expression are known when program execution reaches the declaration:

```
int uncles = 5;               // initialize uncles to 5
int aunts = uncles;           // initialize aunts to 5
int chairs = aunts + uncles + 4;   // initialize chairs to 14
```

Moving the uncles declaration to the end of this list of statements would invalidate the other two initializations because then the value of uncles wouldn't be known at the time the program tries to initialize the other variables.

The initialization syntax shown previously comes from C; C++ has a second initialization syntax that is not shared with C:

```
int owls = 101;  // traditional C initialization
int wrens(432);  // alternative C++ syntax, set wrens to 432
```

Remember

If you don't initialize a variable that is defined inside a function, the variable's value is undefined. That means the value is whatever happened to be sitting at that memory location prior to the creation of the variable.

If you know what the initial value of a variable should be, initialize it. True, separating the declaring of a variable from assigning it a value can create momentary suspense:

```
short year;       // what could it be?
year = 1492;      // oh
```

But initializing the variable when you declare it protects you from forgetting to assign the value later.

Symbolic Constants the Preprocessor Way

The `climits` file contains lines similar to the following:

```
#define INT_MAX 32767
```

Recall that the C++ compilation process first passes the source code through a preprocessor. Here `#define`, like `#include`, is a preprocessor directive. What this particular directive tells the preprocessor is this: Look through the program for instances of `INT_MAX` and replace each occurrence with `32767`. So the `#define` directive works like a global search-and-replace command in a text editor or word processor. The altered program is compiled after these replacements occur. The preprocessor looks for independent tokens (separate words) and skips embedded words. That is, the preprocessor doesn't replace `PINT_MAXIM` with `P32767IM`. You can use `#define` to define your own symbolic constants, too. (See Listing 3.2.) However, the `#define` directive is a C relic. C++ has a better way of creating symbolic constants (using the `const` keyword, discussed in a later section), so you won't be using `#define` much. But some header files, particularly those designed to be used with both C and C++, do use it.

Unsigned Types

Each of the three integer types you just learned about comes in an unsigned variety that can't hold negative values. This has the advantage of increasing the largest value the variable can hold. For example, if `short` represents the range –32,768 to +32,767, the unsigned version can represent the range 0 to 65,535. Of course, you should use unsigned types only for quantities that are never negative, such as populations, bean counts, and happy face manifestations. To create unsigned versions of the basic integer types, you just use the keyword `unsigned` to modify the declarations:

```
unsigned short change;       // unsigned short type
unsigned int rovert;         // unsigned int type
unsigned quarterback;        // also unsigned int
unsigned long gone;          // unsigned long type
```

Note that `unsigned` by itself is short for `unsigned int`.

Listing 3.2 illustrates the use of unsigned types. It also shows what might happen if your program tries to go beyond the limits for integer types. Finally, it gives you one last look at the preprocessor `#define` statement.

LISTING 3.2   exceed.cpp

```cpp
// exceed.cpp -- exceeding some integer limits
#include <iostream>
#define ZERO 0        // makes ZERO symbol for 0 value
#include <climits>   // defines INT_MAX as largest int value
int main()
{
    using namespace std;
    short sam = SHRT_MAX;        // initialize a variable to max value
    unsigned short sue = sam;// okay if variable sam already defined

    cout << "Sam has " << sam << " dollars and Sue has " << sue;
    cout << " dollars deposited." << endl
         << "Add $1 to each account." << endl << "Now ";
    sam = sam + 1;
    sue = sue + 1;
    cout << "Sam has " << sam << " dollars and Sue has " << sue;
    cout << " dollars deposited.\nPoor Sam!" << endl;
    sam = ZERO;
    sue = ZERO;
    cout << "Sam has " << sam << " dollars and Sue has " << sue;
    cout << " dollars deposited." << endl;
    cout << "Take $1 from each account." << endl << "Now ";
    sam = sam - 1;
    sue = sue - 1;
    cout << "Sam has " << sam << " dollars and Sue has " << sue;
    cout << " dollars deposited." << endl << "Lucky Sue!" << endl;
    return 0;
}
```

Compatibility Note

Listing 3.2, like Listing 3.1, uses the `climits` file; older compilers might need to use `limits.h`, and some very old compilers might not have either file available.

Here's the output from the program in Listing 3.2:

```
Sam has 32767 dollars and Sue has 32767 dollars deposited.
Add $1 to each account.
Now Sam has -32768 dollars and Sue has 32768 dollars deposited.
Poor Sam!
Sam has 0 dollars and Sue has 0 dollars deposited.
Take $1 from each account.
Now Sam has -1 dollars and Sue has 65535 dollars deposited.
Lucky Sue!
```

The program sets a **short** variable (**sam**) and an **unsigned short** variable (**sue**) to the largest **short** value, which is 32,767 on our system. Then, it adds 1 to each value. This causes no problems for **sue** because the new value is still much less than the maximum value for an unsigned integer. But **sam** goes from 32,767 to −32,768! Similarly, subtracting 1 from 0 creates no problems for **sam**, but it makes the unsigned variable **sue** go from 0 to 65,535. As you can see, these integers behave much like an odometer. If you go past the limit, the values just start over at the other end of the range. (See Figure 3.1.) C++ guarantees that unsigned types behave in this fashion. However, C++ doesn't guarantee that signed integer types can exceed their limits (overflow and underflow) without complaint, but that is the most common behavior on current implementations.

FIGURE 3.1

Typical overflow behavior for integers.

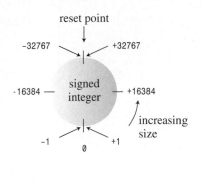

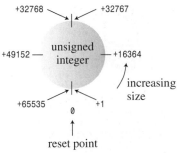

Beyond long

C99 has added a couple new types that most likely will be part of the next edition of the C++ Standard. Indeed, many C++ compilers already support them. The types are `long long` and `unsigned long long`. Both are guaranteed to be at least 64 bits and to be at least as wide as the `long` and `unsigned long` types.

Choosing an Integer Type

With the richness of C++ integer types, which should you use? Generally, `int` is set to the most "natural" integer size for the target computer. `Natural size` refers to the integer form that the computer handles most efficiently. If there is no compelling reason to choose another type, you should use `int`.

Now look at reasons why you might use another type. If a variable represents something that is never negative, such as the number of words in a document, you can use an unsigned type; that way the variable can represent higher values.

If you know that the variable might have to represent integer values too great for a 16-bit integer, you should use `long`. This is true even if `int` is 32 bits on your system. That way, if you transfer your program to a system with a 16-bit `int`, your program won't embarrass you by suddenly failing to work properly. (See Figure 3.2.)

FIGURE 3.2
For portability, use `long` for big integers.

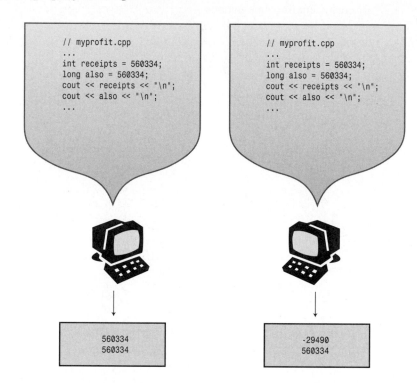

```
// myprofit.cpp
...
int receipts = 560334;
long also = 560334;
cout << receipts << "\n";
cout << also << "\n";
...
```

```
// myprofit.cpp
...
int receipts = 560334;
long also = 560334;
cout << receipts << "\n";
cout << also << "\n";
...
```

```
560334
560334
```

```
-29490
560334
```

Type `int` worked on this computer.   Type `int` failed on this computer.

Using `short` can conserve memory if `short` is smaller than `int`. Most typically, this is important only if you have a large array of integers. (An `array` is a data structure that stores several values of the same type sequentially in memory.) If it is important to conserve space, you should use `short` instead of `int`, even if the two are the same size. Suppose, for example, that you move your program from a 16-bit `int` DOS PC system to a 32-bit `int` Windows XP system. That doubles the amount of memory needed to hold an `int` array, but it doesn't affect the requirements for a `short` array. Remember, a bit saved is a bit earned.

If you need only a single byte, you can use `char`. We'll examine that possibility soon.

Integer Constants

An integer constant is one you write out explicitly, such as 212 or 1776. C++, like C, lets you write integers in three different number bases: base 10 (the public favorite), base 8 (the old Unix favorite), and base 16 (the hardware hacker's favorite). Appendix A, "Number Bases," describes these bases; here we'll look at the C++ representations. C++ uses the first digit or two to identify the base of a number constant. If the first digit is in the range 1–9, the number is base 10 (decimal); thus 93 is base 10. If the first digit is 0 and the second digit is in the range 1–7, the number is base 8 (octal); thus 042 is octal and equal to 34 decimal. If the first two characters are 0x or 0X, the number is base 16 (hexadecimal); thus 0x42 is hex and equal to 66 decimal. For hexadecimal values, the characters a–f and A–F represent the hexadecimal digits corresponding to the values 10–15. 0xF is 15 and 0xA5 is 165 (10 sixteens plus 5 ones). Listing 3.3 is tailor-made to show the three bases.

LISTING 3.3   hexoct1.cpp

```
// hexoct1.cpp -- shows hex and octal constants
#include <iostream>
int main()
{
    using namespace std;
    int chest = 42;      // decimal integer constant
    int waist = 0x42;    // hexadecimal integer constant
    int inseam = 042;    // octal integer constant

    cout << "Monsieur cuts a striking figure!\n";
    cout << "chest = " << chest << "\n";
    cout << "waist = " << waist << "\n";
    cout << "inseam = " << inseam << "\n";
    return 0;
}
```

By default, cout displays integers in decimal form, regardless of how they are written in a program, as the following output shows:

```
Monsieur cuts a striking figure!
chest = 42 (42 in decimal)
waist = 66 (0x42 in hex)
inseam = 34 (042 in octal)
```

Keep in mind that these notations are merely notational conveniences. For example, if you read that the CGA video memory segment is B000 in hexadecimal, you don't have to convert the value to base 10 45,056 before using it in your program. Instead, you can simply use 0xB000. But whether you write the value ten as 10, 012, or 0xA, it's stored the same way in the computer—as a binary (base 2) value.

By the way, if you want to display a value in hexadecimal or octal form, you can use some special features of cout. Recall that the iostream header file provides the endl manipulator to give cout the message to start a new line. Similarly, it provides the dec, hex, and oct manipulators to give cout the messages to display integers in decimal, hexadecimal, and octal formats, respectively. Listing 3.4 uses hex and oct to display the decimal value 42 in three formats. (Decimal is the default format, and each format stays in effect until you change it.)

LISTING 3.4   hexoct2.cpp

```cpp
// hexoct2.cpp -- display values in hex and octal
#include <iostream>
using namespace std;
int main()
{
    using namespace std;
    int chest = 42;
    int waist = 42;
    int inseam = 42;

    cout << "Monsieur cuts a striking figure!"  << endl;
    cout << "chest = " << chest << " (decimal)" << endl;
    cout << hex;        // manipulator for changing number base
    cout << "waist = " << waist << " hexadecimal" << endl;
    cout << oct;        // manipulator for changing number base
    cout << "inseam = " << inseam << " (octal)" << endl;
    return 0;
}
```

Here's the program output for Listing 3.4:

```
Monsieur cuts a striking figure!
chest = 42 (decimal)
waist = 2a hexadecimal
inseam = 52 (octal)
```

Note that code like

```
cout << hex;
```

doesn't display anything onscreen. Instead, it changes the way cout displays integers. Thus, the manipulator hex is really a message to cout that tells it how to behave. Also note that because the identifier hex is part of the std namespace and the program uses that namespace, this program can't use hex as the name of a variable. However, if you omitted the using directive and instead used std::cout, std::endl, std::hex, and std::oct, you could still use plain hex as the name for a variable.

How C++ Decides What Type a Constant Is

A program's declarations tell the C++ compiler the type of a particular integer variable. But what about constants? That is, suppose you represent a number with a constant in a program:

```
cout << "Year = " << 1492 << "\n";
```

Does the program store 1492 as an int, a long, or some other integer type? The answer is that C++ stores integer constants as type int unless there is a reason to do otherwise. Two such reasons are if you use a special suffix to indicate a particular type or if a value is too large to be an int.

First, look at the suffixes. These are letters placed at the end of a numeric constant to indicate the type. An l or L suffix on an integer means the integer is a type long constant, a u or U suffix indicates an unsigned int constant, and ul (in any combination of orders and uppercase and lowercase) indicates a type unsigned long constant. (Because a lowercase l can look much like the digit 1, you should use the uppercase L for suffixes.) For example, on a system using a 16-bit int and a 32-bit long, the number 22022 is stored in 16 bits as an int, and the number 22022L is stored in 32 bits as a long. Similarly, 22022LU and 22022UL are unsigned long.

Next, look at size. C++ has slightly different rules for decimal integers than it has for hexadecimal and octal integers. (Here decimal means base 10, just as hexadecimal means base 16; the term decimal does not necessarily imply a decimal point.) A decimal integer without a suffix is represented by the smallest of the following types that can hold it: int, long, or unsigned long. On a computer system using a 16-bit int and a 32-bit long, 20000 is represented as type int, 40000 is represented as long, and 3000000000 is represented as unsigned long. A hexadecimal or octal integer without a suffix is represented by the smallest of the following types that can hold it: int, unsigned int, long, or unsigned long. The same computer system that represents 40000 as long represents the hexadecimal equivalent 0x9C40 as an unsigned int. That's because hexadecimal is frequently used to express memory addresses, which intrinsically are unsigned. So unsigned int is more appropriate than long for a 16-bit address.

The char Type: Characters and Small Integers

It's time to turn to the final integer type: char. As you probably suspect from its name, the char type is designed to store characters, such as letters and numeric digits. Now, whereas storing numbers is no big deal for computers, storing letters is another matter. Programming languages take the easy way out by using number codes for letters. Thus, the char type is another integer type. It's guaranteed to be large enough to represent the entire range of basic symbols—all the letters, digits, punctuation, and the like—for the target computer system. In practice, most systems support fewer than 256 kinds of characters, so a single byte can represent the whole range. Therefore, although char is most often used to handle characters, you can also use it as an integer type that is typically smaller than short.

The most common symbol set in the United States is the ASCII character set, described in Appendix C, "The ASCII Character Set." A numeric code (the ASCII code) represents each character in the set. For example, 65 is the code for the character A, and 77 is the code for the character M. For convenience, this book assumes ASCII code in its examples. However, a C++ implementation uses whatever code is native to its host system—for example, EBCDIC (pronounced "eb-se-dik") on an IBM mainframe. Neither ASCII nor EBCDIC serve international needs that well, and C++ supports a wide-character type that can hold a larger range of values, such as are used by the international Unicode character set. You'll learn about this wchar_t type later in this chapter.

Try the char type in Listing 3.5.

LISTING 3.5   `chartype.cpp`

```cpp
// chartype.cpp -- the char type
#include <iostream>
int main( )
{
    using namespace std;
    char ch;          // declare a char variable

    cout << "Enter a character: " << endl;
    cin >> ch;
    cout << "Holla! ";
    cout << "Thank you for the " << ch << " character." << endl;
    return 0;
}
```

Here's the output from the program in Listing 3.5:

```
Enter a character:
M
Holla! Thank you for the M character.
```

The interesting thing is that you type an M, not the corresponding character code, 77. Also, the program prints an M, not 77. Yet if you peer into memory, you find that 77 is the value stored in the ch variable. The magic, such as it is, lies not in the char type but in cin and cout. These worthy facilities make conversions on your behalf. On input, cin converts the keystroke input M to the value 77. On output, cout converts the value 77 to the displayed character M; cin and cout are guided by the type of variable. If you place the same value 77 into an int variable, cout displays it as 77. (That is, cout displays two 7 characters.) Listing 3.6 illustrates this point. It also shows how to write a character constant in C++: Enclose the character within two single quotation marks, as in 'M'. (Note that the example doesn't use double quotation marks. C++ uses single quotation marks for a character and double quotation marks for a string. The cout object can handle either, but, as Chapter 4 discusses, the two are quite different from one another.) Finally, the program introduces a cout feature, the cout.put() function, which displays a single character.

LISTING 3.6   `morechar.cpp`

```cpp
// morechar.cpp -- the char type and int type contrasted
#include <iostream>
int main()
{
    using namespace std;
    char ch = 'M';       // assign ASCII code for M to ch
    int i = ch;          // store same code in an int
    cout << "The ASCII code for " << ch << " is " << i << endl;

    cout << "Add one to the character code:" << endl;
    ch = ch + 1;         // change character code in c
    i = ch;              // save new character code in i
    cout << "The ASCII code for " << ch << " is " << i << endl;
```

LISTING 3.6 *Continued*

```cpp
    // using the cout.put() member function to display a char
    cout << "Displaying char ch using cout.put(ch): ";
    cout.put(ch);

    // using cout.put() to display a char constant
    cout.put('!');

    cout << endl << "Done" << endl;
    return 0;
}
```

Here is the output from the program in Listing 3.6:

```
The ASCII code for M is 77
Add one to the character code:
The ASCII code for N is 78
Displaying char ch using cout.put(ch): N!
Done
```

Program Notes

In the program in Listing 3.6, the notation `'M'` represents the numeric code for the M character, so initializing the `char` variable `ch` to `'M'` sets `ch` to the value `77`. The program then assigns the identical value to the `int` variable `i`, so both `ch` and `i` have the value `77`. Next, `cout` displays `ch` as M and `i` as `77`. As previously stated, a value's type guides `cout` as it chooses how to display that value—just another example of smart objects.

Because `ch` is really an integer, you can apply integer operations to it, such as adding 1. This changes the value of `ch` to 78. The program then resets `i` to the new value. (Equivalently, you can simply add 1 to `i`.) Again, `cout` displays the `char` version of that value as a character and the `int` version as a number.

The fact that C++ represents characters as integers is a genuine convenience that makes it easy to manipulate character values. You don't have to use awkward conversion functions to convert characters to ASCII and back.

Finally, the program uses the `cout.put()` function to display both `ch` and a character constant.

A Member Function: `cout.put()`

Just what is `cout.put()`, and why does it have a period in its name? The `cout.put()` function is your first example of an important C++ OOP concept, the `member function`. Remember that a class defines how to represent data and how to manipulate it. A member function belongs to a class and describes a method for manipulating class data. The `ostream` class, for example, has a `put()` member function that is designed to output characters. You can use a member function only with a particular object of that class, such as the `cout` object, in this case. To use a class member function with an object such as `cout`, you use a period to combine the object name (`cout`) with the function name (`put()`). The period is called the `membership operator`. The notation `cout.put()` means to use the class member function `put()` with the class object `cout`. You'll learn about this in greater detail when you reach classes in Chapter 10, "Objects and Classes." Now, the only classes you have are the `istream` and `ostream` classes, and you can experiment with their member functions to get more comfortable with the concept.

The `cout.put()` member function provides an alternative to using the `<<` operator to display a character. At this point you might wonder why there is any need for `cout.put()`. Much of the answer is historical. Before Release 2.0 of C++, `cout` would display character `variables` as characters but display character `constants`, such as `'M'` and `'N'`, as numbers. The problem was that earlier versions of C++, like C, stored character constants as type `int`. That is, the code `77` for `'M'` would be stored in a 16-bit or 32-bit unit. Meanwhile, `char` variables typically occupied 8 bits. A statement like

```
char c = 'M';
```

copied 8 bits (the important 8 bits) from the constant `'M'` to the variable `c`. Unfortunately, this meant that, to `cout`, `'M'` and `c` looked quite different from one another, even though both held the same value. So a statement like

```
cout << '$';
```

would print the ASCII code for the `$` character rather than simply display `$`. But

```
cout.put('$');
```

would print the character, as desired. Now, after Release 2.0, C++ stores single-character constants as type `char`, not type `int`. Therefore, `cout` now correctly handles character constants.

The `cin` object has a couple different ways of reading characters from input. You can explore these by using a program that uses a loop to read several characters, so we'll return to this topic when we cover loops in Chapter 5, "Loops and Relational Expressions."

char Constants

You have several options for writing character constants in C++. The simplest choice for ordinary characters, such as letters, punctuation, and digits, is to enclose the character in single quotation marks. This notation stands for the numeric code for the character. For example, an ASCII system has the following correspondences:

`'A'` is **65**, the ASCII code for A
`'a'` is **97**, the ASCII code for a
`'5'` is **53**, the ASCII code for the digit 5
`' '` is **32**, the ASCII code for the space character
`'!'` is **33**, the ASCII code for the exclamation point

Using this notation is better than using the numeric codes explicitly. It's clearer, and it doesn't assume a particular code. If a system uses EBCDIC, then **65** is not the code for A, but `'A'` still represents the character.

There are some characters that you can't enter into a program directly from the keyboard. For example, you can't make the newline character part of a string by pressing the Enter key; instead, the program editor interprets that keystroke as a request for it to start a new line in your source code file. Other characters have difficulties because the C++ language imbues them with special significance. For example, the double quotation mark character delimits strings, so you can't just stick one in the middle of a string. C++ has special notations, called *escape sequences*, for several of these characters, as shown in Table 3.2. For example, \a represents the alert character, which beeps your terminal's speaker or rings its bell. The escape sequence \n represents a newline. And \" represents the double quotation mark as an ordinary character instead of a string delimiter. You can use these notations in strings or in character constants, as in the following examples:

```
char alarm = '\a';
cout << alarm << "Don't do that again!\a\n";
cout << "Ben \"Buggsie\" Hacker\nwas here!\n";
```

TABLE 3.2   C++ Escape Sequence Codes

Character Name	ASCII Symbol	C++ Code	ASCII Decimal Code	ASCII Hex Code
Newline	NL (LF)	\n	10	0xA
Horizontal tab	HT	\t	9	0x9
Vertical tab	VT	\v	11	0xB
Backspace	BS	\b	8	0x8
Carriage return	CR	\r	13	0xD
Alert	BEL	\a	7	0x7
Backslash	\	\\	92	0x5C
Question mark	?	\?	63	0x3F
Single quote	'	\'	39	0x27
Double quote	"	\"	34	0x22

The last line produces the following output:

```
Ben "Buggsie" Hacker
was here!
```

Note that you treat an escape sequence, such as \n, just as a regular character, such as Q. That is, you enclose it in single quotes to create a character constant and don't use single quotes when including it as part of a string.

The newline character provides an alternative to `endl` for inserting new lines into output. You can use the newline character in character constant notation (`'\n'`) or as character in a string (`"\n"`). All three of the following move the screen cursor to the beginning of the next line:

```
cout << endl;     // using the endl manipulator
cout << '\n';     // using a character constant
cout << "\n";     // using a string
```

You can embed the newline character in a longer string; this is often more convenient than using `endl`. For example, the following two `cout` statements produce the same output:

```
cout << endl << endl << "What next?" << endl << "Enter a number:" << endl;
cout << "\n\nWhat next?\nEnter a number:\n";
```

When you're displaying a number, `endl` is a bit easier to type than `"\n"` or `'\n'`, but, when you're displaying a string, ending the string with a newline character requires less typing:

```
cout << x << endl;     // easier than cout << x << "\n";
cout << "Dr. X.\n";    // easier than cout << "Dr. X."  << endl;
```

Finally, you can use escape sequences based on the octal or hexadecimal codes for a character. For example, Ctrl+Z has an ASCII code of 26, which is 032 in octal and 0x1a in hexadecimal. You can represent this character with either of the following escape sequences: `\032` or `\x1a`. You can make character constants out of these by enclosing them in single quotes, as in `'\032'`, and you can use them as parts of a string, as in `"hi\x1a there"`.

Tip

When you have a choice between using a numeric escape sequence or a symbolic escape sequence, as in `\0x8` versus `\b`, use the symbolic code. The numeric representation is tied to a particular code, such as ASCII, but the symbolic representation works with all codes and is more readable.

Listing 3.7 demonstrates a few escape sequences. It uses the alert character to get your attention, the newline character to advance the cursor (one small step for a cursor, one giant step for cursorkind), and the backspace character to back the cursor one space to the left. (Houdini once painted a picture of the Hudson River using only escape sequences; he was, of course, a great escape artist.)

LISTING 3.7   `bondini.cpp`

```cpp
// bondini.cpp -- using escape sequences
#include <iostream>
int main()
{
    using namespace std;
    cout << "\aOperation \"HyperHype\" is now activated!\n";
    cout << "Enter your agent code:_____\b\b\b\b\b\b\b";
    long code;
    cin >> code;
```

LISTING 3.7 Continued

```
        cout << "\aYou entered " << code << "...\n";
        cout << "\aCode verified! Proceed with Plan Z3!\n";
        return 0;
}
```

Compatibility Note

Some C++ systems based on pre-ANSI C compilers don't recognize \a. You can substitute \007 for \a on systems that use the ASCII character code. Some systems might behave differently, displaying the \b as a small rectangle rather than backspacing, for example, or perhaps erasing while backspacing, perhaps ignoring \a.

When you start the program in Listing 3.7, it puts the following text onscreen:

```
Operation "HyperHype" is now activated!
Enter your agent code:_____
```

After printing the underscore characters, the program uses the backspace character to back up the cursor to the first underscore. You can then enter your secret code and continue. Here's a complete run:

```
Operation "HyperHype" is now activated!
Enter your agent code:42007007
You entered 42007007...
Code verified! Proceed with Plan Z3!
```

Universal Character Names

C++ implementations support a basic source character set—that is, the set of characters you can use to write source code. It consists of the letters (uppercase and lowercase) and digits found on a standard U.S. keyboard, the symbols, such as { and =, used in the C language, and a scattering of other characters, such as newline and space characters. Then there is a basic execution character set (that is, characters that can be produced by the execution of a program), which adds a few more characters, such as backspace and alert. The C++ Standard also allows an implementation to offer extended source character sets and extended execution character sets. Furthermore, those additional characters that qualify as letters can be used as part of the name of an identifier. Thus, a German implementation might allow you to use umlauted vowels and a French implementation might allow accented vowels. C++ has a mechanism for representing such international characters that is independent of any particular keyboard: the use of *universal character names*.

Using universal character names is similar to using escape sequences. A universal character name begins either with \u or \U. The \u form is followed by 8 hexadecimal digits, and the \U form by 16 hexadecimal digits. These digits represent the ISO 10646 code for the character. (ISO 10646 is an international standard under development that provides numeric codes for a wide range of characters. See "Unicode and ISO 10646," later in this chapter.)

If your implementation supports extended characters, you can use universal character names in identifiers, as character constants, and in strings. For example, consider the following code:

```
int k\u00F6rper;
cout << "Let them eat g\u00E2teau.\n";
```

The ISO 10646 code for ö is 00F6, and the code for â is 00E2. Thus, this C++ code would set the variable name to `körper` and display the following output:

```
Let them eat gâteau.
```

If your system doesn't support ISO 10646, it might display some other character for â or perhaps simply display the word `gu00E2teau`.

Unicode and ISO 10646

Unicode provides a solution to the representation of various character sets by providing standard numeric codes for a great number of characters and symbols, grouping them by type. For example, the ASCII code is incorporated as a subset of Unicode, so U.S. Latin characters such as A and Z have the same representation under both systems. But Unicode also incorporates other Latin characters, such as those used in European languages; characters from other alphabets, including Greek, Cyrillic, Hebrew, Arabic, Thai, and Bengali; and ideographs, such as those used for Chinese and Japanese. So far Unicode represents more than 96,000 symbols and 49 scripts, and it is still under development. If you want to know more, you can check the Unicode Consortium's website, at `www.unicode.org`.

The International Organization for Standardization (ISO) established a working group to develop ISO 10646, also a standard for coding multilingual text. The ISO 10646 group and the Unicode group have worked together since 1991 to keep their standards synchronized with one another.

---

signed char and unsigned char

Unlike `int`, `char` is not signed by default. Nor is it unsigned by default. The choice is left to the C++ implementation in order to allow the compiler developer to best fit the type to the hardware properties. If it is vital to you that `char` has a particular behavior, you can use `signed char` or `unsigned char` explicitly as types:

```
char fodo;              // may be signed, may be unsigned
unsigned char bar;      // definitely unsigned
signed char snark;      // definitely signed
```

These distinctions are particularly important if you use `char` as a numeric type. The `unsigned char` type typically represents the range 0 to 255, and `signed char` typically represents the range −128 to 127. For example, suppose you want to use a `char` variable to hold values as large as 200. That works on some systems but fails on others. You can, however, successfully use `unsigned char` for that purpose on any system. On the other hand, if you use a `char` variable to hold a standard ASCII character, it doesn't really matter whether `char` is signed or unsigned, so you can simply use `char`.

For When You Need More: wchar_t

Programs might have to handle character sets that don't fit within the confines of a single 8-bit byte (for example, the Japanese kanji system). C++ handles this in a couple ways. First, if a large set of characters is the basic character set for an implementation, a compiler vender can define `char` as a 16-bit byte or larger. Second, an implementation can support both a small basic character set and a larger extended character set. The usual 8-bit `char` can represent the basic character set, and another type, called `wchar_t` (for wide `character type`), can represent the extended character set. The `wchar_t` type is an integer type with sufficient space to represent the largest extended character set used on the system. This type has the same size and sign properties as one of the other integer types, which is called the `underlying` type. The choice of underlying type depends on the implementation, so it could be `unsigned short` on one system and `int` on another.

The `cin` and `cout` family consider input and output as consisting of streams of `chars`, so they are not suitable for handling the `wchar_t` type. The latest version of the `iostream` header file provides parallel facilities in the form of `wcin` and `wcout` for handling `wchar_t` streams. Also, you can indicate a wide-character constant or string by preceding it with an `L`. The following code stores a `wchar_t` version of the letter `P` in the variable `bob` and displays a `whar_t` version of the word `tall`:

```
wchar_t bob = L'P';        // a wide-character constant
wcout << L"tall" << endl;  // outputting a wide-character string
```

On a system with a 2-byte `wchar_t`, this code stores each character in a 2-byte unit of memory. This book doesn't use the wide-character type, but you should be aware of it, particularly if you become involved in international programming or in using Unicode or ISO 10646.

The `bool` Type

The ANSI/ISO C++ Standard has added a new type (new to C++, that is), called `bool`. It's named in honor of the English mathematician George Boole, who developed a mathematical representation of the laws of logic. In computing, a `Boolean variable` is one whose value can be either `true` or `false`. In the past, C++, like C, has not had a Boolean type. Instead, as you'll see in greater detail in Chapters 5 and 6, "Branching Statements and Logical Operators," C++ interprets nonzero values as true and zero values as false. Now, however, you can use the `bool` type to represent true and false, and the predefined literals `true` and `false` represent those values. That is, you can make statements like the following:

```
bool isready = true;
```

The literals `true` and `false` can be converted to type `int` by promotion, with `true` converting to 1 and `false` to 0:

```
int ans = true;          // ans assigned 1
int promise = false;     // promise assigned 0
```

Also, any numeric or pointer value can be converted implicitly (that is, without an explicit type cast) to a `bool` value. Any nonzero value converts to `true`, whereas a zero value converts to `false`:

```
bool start = -100;       // start assigned true
bool stop = 0;           // stop assigned false
```

After the book introduces `if` statements (in Chapter 6), the `bool` type will become a common feature in the examples.

The `const` Qualifier

Now let's return to the topic of symbolic names for constants. A symbolic name can suggest what the constant represents. Also, if the program uses the constant in several places and you need to change the value, you can just change the single symbol definition. The note about `#define` statements earlier in this chapter (see the sidebar "Symbolic Constants the Preprocessor Way") promises that C++ has a better way to handle symbolic constants. That way is to use the `const` keyword to modify a variable declaration and initialization. Suppose, for example, that you want a symbolic constant for the number of months in a year. You enter this line in a program:

```
const int MONTHS = 12;   // Months is symbolic constant for 12
```

Now you can use `MONTHS` in a program instead of `12`. (A bare `12` in a program might represent the number of inches in a foot or the number of donuts in a dozen, but the name `MONTHS` tells you what the value `12` represents.) After you initialize a constant such as `MONTHS`, its value is set. The compiler does not let you subsequently change the value `MONTHS`. If you try to, for example, Borland C++ gives an error message stating that an `lvalue` is required. This is the same message you get if you try, say, to assign the value `4` to `3`. (An `lvalue` is a value, such as a variable, that appears on the left side of the assignment operator.) The keyword `const` is termed a `qualifier` because it qualifies the meaning of a declaration.

A common practice is to use all uppercase for the name to help remind yourself that `MONTHS` is a constant. This is by no means a universal convention, but it helps separate the constants from the variables when you read a program. Another convention is to capitalize just the first character in the name. Yet another convention is to begin constant names with the letter k, as in `kmonths`. And there are yet other conventions. Many organizations have particular coding conventions they expect their programmers to follow.

The general form for creating a constant is this:

```
const type name = value;
```

Note that you initialize a `const` in the declaration. The following sequence is no good:

```
const int toes;      // value of toes undefined at this point
toes = 10;           // too late!
```

If you don't provide a value when you declare the constant, it ends up with an unspecified value that you cannot modify.

If your background is in C, you might feel that the `#define` statement, which is discussed earlier, already does the job adequately. But `const` is better. For one thing, it lets you specify the type explicitly. Second, you can use C++'s scoping rules to limit the definition to particular functions or files. (Scoping rules describe how widely known a name is to different modules; you'll learn about this in more detail in Chapter 9, "Memory Models and Namespaces.") Third, you can use `const` with more elaborate types, such as arrays and structures, as discussed in Chapter 4.

Tip

If you are coming to C++ from C and you are about to use `#define` to define a symbolic constant, use `const` instead.

ANSI C also uses the `const` qualifier, which it borrows from C++. If you're familiar with the ANSI C version, you should be aware that the C++ version is slightly different. One difference relates to the scope rules, and Chapter 9 covers that point. The other main difference is that in C++ (but not in C), you can use a `const` value to declare the size of an array. You'll see examples in Chapter 4.

Floating-Point Numbers

Now that you have seen the complete line of C++ integer types, let's look at the floating-point types, which compose the second major group of fundamental C++ types. These numbers let you represent numbers with fractional parts, such as the gas mileage of an M1 tank (0.56 MPG). They also provide a much greater range in values. If a number is too large to be represented as type `long`—for example, the number of stars in our galaxy (an estimated 400,000,000,000)—you can use one of the floating-point types.

With floating-point types, you can represent numbers such as 2.5 and 3.14159 and 122442.32—that is, numbers with fractional parts. A computer stores such values in two parts. One part represents a value, and the other part scales that value up or down. Here's an analogy. Consider the two numbers 34.1245 and 34124.5. They're identical except for scale. You can represent the first one as 0.341245 (the base value) and 100 (the scaling factor). You can represent the second as 0.341245 (the same base value) and 100,000 (a bigger scaling factor). The scaling factor serves to move the decimal point, hence the term `floating-point`. C++ uses a similar method to represent floating-point numbers internally, except it's based on binary numbers, so the scaling is by factors of 2 instead of by factors of 10. Fortunately, you don't have to know much about the internal representation. The main points are that floating-point numbers let you represent fractional, very large, and very small values, and they have internal representations much different from those of integers.

Writing Floating-Point Numbers

C++ has two ways of writing floating-point numbers. The first is to use the standard decimal-point notation you've been using much of your life:

```
12.34         // floating-point
939001.32     // floating-point
0.00023       // floating-point
8.0           // still floating-point
```

Even if the fractional part is 0, as in 8.0, the decimal point ensures that the number is represented in floating-point format and not as an integer. (The C++ Standard does allow for implementations to represent different locales—for example, providing a mechanism for using the European method of using a comma instead of a period for the decimal point. However, these choices govern how the numbers can appear in input and output, not in code.)

The second method for representing floating-point values is called E notation, and it looks like this: `3.45E6`. This means that the value 3.45 is multiplied by 1,000,000; the E6 means 10 to the 6th power, which is 1 followed by 6 zeros. Thus `3.45E6` means 3,450,000. The 6 is called an `exponent`, and the 3.45 is termed the `mantissa`. Here are more examples:

```
2.52e+8          // can use E or e, + is optional
8.33E-4          // exponent can be negative
7E5              // same as 7.0E+05
-18.32e13        // can have + or - sign in front
7.123e12         // U.S. public debt, early 2004
5.98E24          // mass of earth in kilograms
9.11e-31         // mass of an electron in kilograms
```

As you might have noticed, E notation is most useful for very large and very small numbers.

E notation guarantees that a number is stored in floating-point format, even if no decimal point is used. Note that you can use either `E` or `e`, and the exponent can have a positive or negative sign. (See Figure 3.3.) However, you can't have spaces in the number, so, for example, `7.2 E6` is invalid.

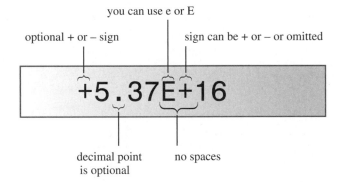

FIGURE 3.3
E notation.

To use a negative exponent means to divide by a power of 10 instead of to multiply by a power of 10. So 8.33E-4 means 8.33 / 10⁴, or 0.000833. Similarly, the electron mass 9.11e-31 kg means 0.000000000000000000000000000000911 kg. Take your choice. (Incidentally, note that 911 is the usual emergency telephone number in the United States and that telephone messages are carried by electrons. Coincidence or scientific conspiracy? You be the judge.) Note that –8.33E4 means –83300. A sign in front applies to the number value, and a sign in the exponent applies to the scaling.

Floating-Point Types

Like ANSI C, C++ has three floating-point types: `float`, `double`, and `long double`. These types are described in terms of the number of significant figures they can represent and the minimum allowable range of exponents. **Significant figures** are the meaningful digits in a number. For example, writing the height of Mt. Shasta in California as 14,162 feet uses five significant figures, for it specifies the height to the nearest foot. But writing the height of Mt. Shasta as about 14,000 feet tall uses two significant figures, for the result is rounded to the nearest thousand feet; in this case, the remaining three digits are just placeholders. The number of significant figures doesn't depend on the location of the decimal point. For example, you can write the height as 14.162 thousand feet. Again, this uses five significant digits because the value is accurate to the fifth digit.

In effect, the C and C++ requirements for significant digits amount to `float` being at least 32 bits, `double` being at least 48 bits and certainly no smaller than `float`, and `long double` being at least as big as `double`. All three can be the same size. Typically, however, `float` is 32 bits, `double` is 64 bits, and `long double` is 80, 96, or 128 bits. Also, the range in exponents for all three types is at least –37 to +37. You can look in the `cfloat` or `float.h` header files to find the limits for your system. (`cfloat` is the C++ version of the C `float.h` file.) Here, for example, are some annotated entries from the `float.h` file for Borland C++ Builder:

```
// the following are the minimum number of significant digits
#define DBL_DIG 15        // double
#define FLT_DIG 6         // float
#define LDBL_DIG 18       // long double

// the following are the number of bits used to represent the mantissa
#define DBL_MANT_DIG    53
#define FLT_MANT_DIG    24
#define LDBL_MANT_DIG   64

// the following are the maximum and minimum exponent values
#define DBL_MAX_10_EXP    +308
#define FLT_MAX_10_EXP    +38
#define LDBL_MAX_10_EXP   +4932

#define DBL_MIN_10_EXP    -307
#define FLT_MIN_10_EXP    -37
#define LDBL_MIN_10_EXP   -4931
```

Listing 3.8 examines types `float` and `double` and how they can differ in the precision to which they represent numbers (that's the significant figure aspect). The program previews an `ostream` method called `setf()` from Chapter 17, "Input, Output, and Files." This particular call forces output to stay in fixed-point notation so that you can better see the precision. It prevents the program from switching to E notation for large values and causes the program to display six digits to the right of the decimal. The arguments `ios_base::fixed` and `ios_base::floatfield` are constants provided by including `iostream`.

LISTING 3.8   `floatnum.cpp`

```cpp
// floatnum.cpp -- floating-point types
#include <iostream>
int main()
{
    using namespace std;
    cout.setf(ios_base::fixed, ios_base::floatfield); // fixed-point
    float tub = 10.0 / 3.0;     // good to about 6 places
    double mint = 10.0 / 3.0;   // good to about 15 places
    const float million = 1.0e6;

    cout << "tub = " << tub;
    cout << ", a million tubs = " << million * tub;
    cout << ",\nand ten million tubs = ";
    cout << 10 * million * tub << endl;

    cout << "mint = " << mint << " and a million mints = ";
    cout << million * mint << endl;
    return 0;
}
```

Here is the output from the program in Listing 3.8:

```
tub = 3.333333, a million tubs = 3333333.250000,
and ten million tubs = 33333332.000000
mint = 3.333333 and a million mints = 3333333.333333
```

Compatibility Note

The C++ Standard has replaced `ios::fixed` with `ios_base::fixed` and `ios::floatfield` with `ios_base::floatfield`. If your compiler does not accept the `ios_base` forms, try using `ios` instead; that is, substitute `ios::fixed` for `ios_base::fixed`, etc. By default, older versions of C++, when they display floating-point values, display six digits to the right of the decimal, as in 2345.831541. Standard C++, by default, displays a total of six digits (2345.83), switching to E notation when values reach a million or greater (2.34583E+06). However, the nondefault display modes, such as `fixed` in the preceding example, display six digits to the right of the decimal in both old and new versions.

The default setting also suppresses trailing zeros, displaying 23.4500 as 23.45. Implementations differ in how they respond to using the `setf()` statement to override the default settings. Older versions, such as Borland C++ 3.1 for DOS, suppress trailing zeros in this mode as well. Versions conforming to the standard, such as Microsoft Visual C++ 7.0, Metrowerks CodeWarrior 9, Gnu GCC 3.3, and Borland C++ 5.5, display the zeros, as shown in Listing 3.8.

Program Notes

Normally `cout` drops trailing zeros. For example, it would display 3333333.250000 as 3333333.25. The call to `cout.setf()` overrides that behavior, at least in new implementations. The main thing to note in Listing 3.8 is how `float` has less precision than `double`. Both `tub` and `mint` are initialized to 10.0 / 3.0. That should evaluate to 3.33333333333333333...(etc.). Because `cout` prints six figures to the right of the decimal, you can see that both `tub` and `mint` are accurate that far. But after the program multiplies each number by a million, you see that `tub` diverges from the proper value after the 7th three. `tub` is good to 7 significant figures. (This system guarantees 6 significant figures for `float`, but that's the worst-case scenario.) The type `double` variable, however, shows 13 threes, so it's good to at least 13 significant figures. Because the system guarantees 15, this shouldn't surprise you. Also, note that multiplying a million `tub`s by 10 doesn't quite result in the correct answer; this again points out the limitations of `float` precision.

The `ostream` class to which `cout` belongs has class member functions that give you precise control over how the output is formatted—field widths, places to the right of the decimal point, decimal form or E form, and so on. Chapter 17 outlines those choices. This book's examples keep it simple and usually just use the `<<` operator. Occasionally, this practice displays more digits than necessary, but that causes only esthetic harm. If you do mind, you can skim Chapter 17 to see how to use the formatting methods. Don't, however, expect to fully follow the explanations at this point.

Real-World Note: Reading Include Files

The include directives found at the top of C++ source files often take on the air of a magical incantation; novice C++ programmers learn, through reading and experience, which header files add particular functionalities, and they include them solely to make their programs work. Don't rely on the include files only as a source of mystic and arcane knowledge; feel free to open them up and read them. They are text files, so you can read them easily. All the files you include in your programs exist on your computer, or in a place where your computer can use them. Find the includes you use and see what they contain. You'll quickly see that the source and header files that you use are an excellent source of knowledge and information—in some cases, the best documentation available. Later, as you progress into more complex inclusions and begin to use other, nonstandard libraries in your applications, this habit will serve you well.

Floating-Point Constants

When you write a floating-point constant in a program, in which floating-point type does the program store it? By default, floating-point constants such as 8.24 and 2.4E8 are type `double`. If you want a constant to be type `float`, you use an `f` or `F` suffix. For type `long double`, you use an `l` or `L` suffix. (Because the lowercase `l` looks a lot like the digit `1`, the uppercase `L` is a better choice.) Here are some samples:

```
1.234f        // a float constant
2.45E20F      // a float constant
2.345324E28   // a double constant
2.2L          // a long double constant
```

Advantages and Disadvantages of Floating-Point Numbers

Floating-point numbers have two advantages over integers. First, they can represent values between integers. Second, because of the scaling factor, they can represent a much greater range of values. On the other hand, floating-point operations are slower than integer operations, at least on computers without math coprocessors, and you can lose precision. Listing 3.9 illustrates the last point.

LISTING 3.9   `fltadd.cpp`

```cpp
// fltadd.cpp -- precision problems with float
#include <iostream>
int main()
{
    using namespace std;
    float a = 2.34E+22f;
    float b = a + 1.0f;

    cout << "a = " << a << endl;
    cout << "b - a = " << b - a << endl;
    return 0;
}
```

Compatibility Note

Some ancient C++ implementations based on pre-ANSI C compilers don't support the `f` suffix for indicating type `float` constants. If you find yourself facing this problem, you can replace `2.34E+22f` with `2.34E+22` and replace `1.0f` with `(float) 1.0`.

The program in Listing 3.9 takes a number, adds 1, and then subtracts the original number. That should result in a value of 1. Does it? Here is the output from the program in Listing 3.9 for one system:

```
a = 2.34e+022
b - a = 0
```

The problem is that 2.34E+22 represents a number with 23 digits to the left of the decimal. By adding 1, you are attempting to add 1 to the 23rd digit in that number. But type `float` can represent only the first 6 or 7 digits in a number, so trying to change the 23rd digit has no effect on the value .

Classifying Data Types

C++ brings some order to its basic types by classifying them into families. Types `signed char`, `short`, `int`, and `long` are termed `signed integer` types. The unsigned versions are termed `unsigned integer` types. The `bool`, `char`, `wchar_t`, signed integer, and unsigned integer types together are termed `integral` types or `integer` types. The `float`, `double`, and `long double` types are termed `floating-point` types. Integer and floating-point types are collectively termed `arithmetic` types.

C++ Arithmetic Operators

Perhaps you have warm memories of doing arithmetic drills in grade school. You can give that same pleasure to your computer. C++ uses operators to do arithmetic. It provides operators for five basic arithmetic calculations: addition, subtraction, multiplication, division, and taking the modulus. Each of these operators uses two values (called `operands`) to calculate a final answer. Together, the operator and its operands constitute an `expression`. For example, consider the following statement:

```
int wheels = 4 + 2;
```

The values 4 and 2 are operands, the + symbol is the addition operator, and 4 + 2 is an expression whose value is 6.

Here are C++'s five basic arithmetic operators:

- The + operator adds its operands. For example, 4 + 20 evaluates to 24.

- The - operator subtracts the second operand from the first. For example, 12 - 3 evaluates to 9.

- The * operator multiplies its operands. For example, 28 * 4 evaluates to 112.

- The / operator divides its first operand by the second. For example, 1000 / 5 evaluates to 200. If both operands are integers, the result is the integer portion of the quotient. For example, 17 / 3 is 5, with the fractional part discarded.

- The % operator finds the modulus of its first operand with respect to the second. That is, it produces the remainder of dividing the first by the second. For example, 19 % 6 is 1 because 6 goes into 19 three times, with a remainder of 1. Both operands must be integer types; using the % operator with floating-point values causes a compile-time error. If one of the operands is negative, the sign of the result depends on the implementation.

Of course, you can use variables as well as constants for operands. Listing 3.10 does just that. Because the % operator works only with integers, we'll leave it for a later example.

LISTING 3.10   arith.cpp

```cpp
// arith.cpp -- some C++ arithmetic
#include <iostream>
int main()
{
    using namespace std;
    float hats, heads;
```

LISTING 3.10   Continued

```
cout.setf(ios_base::fixed, ios_base::floatfield); // fixed-point
cout << "Enter a number: ";
cin >> hats;
cout << "Enter another number: ";
cin >> heads;

cout << "hats = " << hats << "; heads = " << heads << endl;
cout << "hats + heads = " << hats + heads << endl;
cout << "hats - heads = " << hats - heads << endl;
cout << "hats * heads = " << hats * heads << endl;
cout << "hats / heads = " << hats / heads << endl;
return 0;
}
```

Compatibility Note

If your compiler does not accept the `ios_base` forms in `setf()`, try using the older `ios` forms instead; that is, substitute `ios::fixed` for `ios_base::fixed`, etc.

As you can see in the following sample output from the program in Listing 3.10, you can trust C++ to do simple arithmetic:

```
Enter a number: 50.25
Enter another number: 11.17
hats = 50.250000; heads = 11.170000
hats + heads = 61.419998
hats - heads = 39.080002
hats * heads = 561.292480
hats / heads = 4.498657
```

Well, maybe you can't trust it completely. Adding 11.17 to 50.25 should yield 61.42, but the output reports 61.419998. This is not an arithmetic problem; it's a problem with the limited capacity of type `float` to represent significant figures. Remember, C++ guarantees just six significant figures for `float`. If you round 61.419998 to six figures, you get 61.4200, which is the correct value to the guaranteed precision. The moral is that if you need greater accuracy, you should use `double` or `long double`.

Order of Operation: Operator Precedence and Associativity

Can you trust C++ to do complicated arithmetic? Yes, but you must know the rules C++ uses. For example, many expressions involve more than one operator. That can raise questions about which operator gets applied first. For example, consider this statement:

```
int flyingpigs = 3 + 4 * 5;   // 35 or 23?
```

The 4 appears to be an operand for both the + and * operators. When more than one operator can be applied to the same operand, C++ uses **precedence** rules to decide which operator is used first. The arithmetic operators follow the usual algebraic precedence, with multiplication, division, and the taking of the modulus done before addition and subtraction. Thus `3 + 4 * 5` means `3 + (4 * 5)`, not `(3 + 4) * 5`. So the answer is `23`, not `35`. Of course, you can use parentheses to enforce your own priorities. Appendix D, "Operator Precedence," shows precedence for all the C++ operators. Note that `*`, `/`, and `%` are all in the same row in Appendix D. That means they have equal precedence. Similarly, addition and subtraction share a lower precedence.

Sometimes the precedence list is not enough. Consider the following statement:

```
float logs = 120 / 4 * 5;     // 150 or 6?
```

Once again, 4 is an operand for two operators. But the `/` and `*` operators have the same precedence, so precedence alone doesn't tell the program whether to first divide 120 by 4 or multiply 4 by 5. Because the first choice leads to a result of 150 and the second to a result of 6, the choice is an important one. When two operators have the same precedence, C++ looks at whether the operators have a left-to-right `associativity` or a right-to-left associativity. Left-to-right associativity means that if two operators acting on the same operand have the same precedence, you apply the left-hand operator first. For right-to-left associativity, you apply the right-hand operator first. The associativity information, too, is in Appendix D. Appendix D shows that multiplication and division associate left-to-right. That means you use 4 with the leftmost operator first. That is, you divide 120 by 4, get 30 as a result, and then multiply the result by 5 to get 150.

Note that the precedence and associativity rules come into play only when two operators share the same operand. Consider the following expression:

```
int dues = 20 * 5 + 24 * 6;
```

Operator precedence tells you two things: The program must evaluate `20 * 5` before doing addition, and the program must evaluate `24 * 6` before doing addition. But neither precedence nor associativity says which multiplication takes place first. You might think that associativity says to do the leftmost multiplication first, but in this case, the two `*` operators do not share a common operand, so the rules don't apply. In fact, C++ leaves it to the implementation to decide which order works best on a system. For this example, either order gives the same result, but there are circumstances in which the order can make a difference. You'll see one in Chapter 5, which discusses the increment operator.

Division Diversions

You have yet to see the rest of the story about the division operator (`/`). The behavior of this operator depends on the type of the operands. If both operands are integers, C++ performs integer division. That means any fractional part of the answer is discarded, making the result an integer. If one or both operands are floating-point values, the fractional part is kept, making the result floating-point. Listing 3.11 illustrates how C++ division works with different types of values. As in Listing 3.10, Listing 3.11 invokes the `setf()` member function to modify how the results are displayed.

LISTING 3.11   `divide.cpp`

```cpp
// divide.cpp -- integer and floating-point division
#include <iostream>
int main()
{
    using namespace std;
    cout.setf(ios_base::fixed, ios_base::floatfield);
    cout << "Integer division: 9/5 = " << 9 / 5  << endl;
    cout << "Floating-point division: 9.0/5.0 = ";
    cout << 9.0 / 5.0 << endl;
    cout << "Mixed division: 9.0/5 = " << 9.0 / 5  << endl;
    cout << "double constants: 1e7/9.0 = ";
    cout << 1.e7 / 9.0 <<  endl;
    cout << "float constants: 1e7f/9.0f = ";
    cout << 1.e7f / 9.0f <<  endl;
    return 0;
}
```

Compatibility Note

If your compiler does not accept the `ios_base` forms in `setf()`, try using the older `ios` forms instead.

Some C++ implementations based on pre-ANSI C compilers don't support the `f` suffix for floating-point constants. If you find yourself facing this problem, you can replace `1.e7f / 9.0f` with `(float) 1.e7 /(float) 9.0`.

Some implementations suppress trailing zeros.

Here is the output from the program in Listing 3.11 for one implementation:

```
Integer division: 9/5 = 1
Floating-point division: 9.0/5.0 = 1.800000
Mixed division: 9.0/5 = 1.800000
double constants: 1e7/9.0 = 1111111.111111
float constants: 1e7f/9.0f = 1111111.125000
```

The first output line shows that dividing the integer 9 by the integer 5 yields the integer 1. The fractional part of 4 / 5 (or 0.8) is discarded. (You'll see a practical use for this kind of division when you learn about the modulus operator, later in this chapter.) The next two lines show that when at least one of the operands is floating-point, you get a floating-point answer of 1.8. Actually, when you try to combine mixed types, C++ converts all the concerned types to the same type. You'll learn about these automatic conversions later in this chapter. The relative precisions of the last two lines show that the result is type **double** if both operands are **double** and that it is **float** if both operands are **float**. Remember, floating-point constants are type **double** by default.

A Glimpse at Operator Overloading

In Listing 3.11, the division operator represents three distinct operations: `int` division, `float` division, and `double` division. C++ uses the context—in this case the type of operands—to determine which operator is meant. The process of using the same symbol for more than one operation is called `operator overloading`. C++ has a few examples of overloading built in to the language. C++ also lets you extend operator overloading to user-defined classes, so what you see here is a precursor of an important OOP property. (See Figure 3.4.)

FIGURE 3.4
Different divisions.

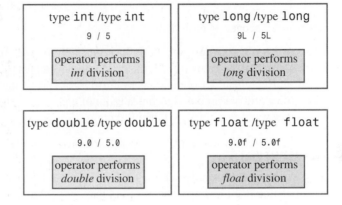

The Modulus Operator

Most people are more familiar with addition, subtraction, multiplication, and division than with the modulus operation, so let's take a moment to look at the modulus operator in action. The modulus operator returns the remainder of an integer division. In combination with integer division, the modulus operation is particularly useful in problems that require dividing a quantity into different integral units, such as converting inches to feet and inches or converting dollars to quarters, dimes, nickels, and pennies. In Chapter 2, Listing 2.6 converts weight in British stone to pounds. Listing 3.12 reverses the process, converting weight in pounds to stone. A stone, you remember, is 14 pounds, and most British bathroom scales are calibrated in this unit. The program uses integer division to find the largest number of whole stone in the weight, and it uses the modulus operator to find the number of pounds left over.

LISTING 3.12   modulus.cpp

```cpp
// modulus.cpp -- uses % operator to convert lbs to stone
#include <iostream>
int main()
{
    using namespace std;
    const int Lbs_per_stn = 14;
    int lbs;

    cout << "Enter your weight in pounds: ";
    cin >> lbs;
```

LISTING 3.12   Continued

```
    int stone = lbs / Lbs_per_stn;     // whole stone
    int pounds = lbs % Lbs_per_stn;    // remainder in pounds
    cout << lbs << " pounds are " << stone
         << " stone, " << pounds << " pound(s).\n";
    return 0;
}
```

Here is a sample run of the program in Listing 3.12:

```
Enter your weight in pounds: 177
184 pounds are 12 stone, 9 pound(s).
```

In the expression `lbs / Lbs_per_stn`, both operands are type `int`, so the computer performs integer division. With a `lbs` value of 177, the expression evaluates to 12. The product of 12 and 14 is 168, so the remainder of dividing 14 into 177 is 9, and that's the value of `lbs % Lbs_per_stn`. Now you are prepared technically, if not emotionally, to respond to questions about your weight when you travel in Great Britain.

Type Conversions

C++'s profusion of types lets you match the type to the need. It also complicates life for the computer. For example, adding two `short` values may involve different hardware instructions than adding two `long` values. With 11 integral types and 3 floating-point types, the computer can have a lot of different cases to handle, especially if you start mixing types. To help deal with this potential mishmash, C++ makes many type conversions automatically:

- C++ converts values when you assign a value of one arithmetic type to a variable of another arithmetic type.
- C++ converts values when you combine mixed types in expressions.
- C++ converts values when you pass arguments to functions.

If you don't understand what happens in these automatic conversions, you might find some program results baffling, so let's take a more detailed look at the rules.

Conversion on Assignment

C++ is fairly liberal in allowing you to assign a numeric value of one type to a variable of another type. Whenever you do so, the value is converted to the type of the receiving variable. For example, suppose `so_long` is type `long`, `thirty` is type `short`, and you have the following statement in a program:

```
so_long = thirty;            // assigning a short to a long
```

The program takes the value of `thirty` (typically a 16-bit value) and expands it to a `long` value (typically a 32-bit value) upon making the assignment. Note that the expansion creates a new value to place into `so_long`; the contents of `thirty` are unaltered.

Assigning a value to a type with a greater range usually poses no problem. For example, assigning a `short` value to a `long` variable doesn't change the value; it just gives the value a few more bytes in which to laze about. However, assigning a large `long` value such as 2111222333 to a `float` variable results in the loss of some precision. Because `float` can have just six significant figures, the value can be rounded to 2.11122E9. So, while some conversions are safe, some may pose difficulties. Table 3.3 points out some possible conversion problems.

TABLE 3.3 Potential Numeric Conversion Problems

Conversion Type	Potential Problems
Bigger floating-point type to smaller floating-point type, such as `double` to `float`	Loss of precision (significant figures); value might be out of range for target type, in which case result is undefined
Floating-point type to integer type	Loss of fractional part; original value might be out of range for target type, in which case result is undefined
Bigger integer type to smaller integer type, such as `long` to `short`	Original value might be out of range for target type; typically just the low-order bytes are copied

A zero value assigned to a `bool` variable is converted to `false`, and a nonzero value is converted to `true`.

Assigning floating-point values to integer types poses a couple problems. First, converting floating-point to integer results in truncating the number (discarding the fractional part). Second, a `float` value might be too big to fit in a cramped `int` variable. In that case, C++ doesn't define what the result should be; that means different implementations can respond differently. Listing 3.13 shows a few conversions by assignment.

LISTING 3.13 `assign.cpp`

```
// assign.cpp -- type changes on assignment
#include <iostream>
int main()
{
    using namespace std;
    cout.setf(ios_base::fixed, ios_base::floatfield);
    float tree = 3;     // int converted to float
    int guess = 3.9832; // float converted to int
    int debt = 7.2E12;  // result not defined in C++
    cout << "tree = " << tree << endl;
    cout << "guess = " << guess << endl;
    cout << "debt = " << debt << endl;
    return 0;
}
```

Here is the output from the program in Listing 3.13 for one system:

```
tree = 3.000000
guess = 3
debt = 1634811904
```

In this case, `tree` is assigned the floating-point value 3.0. Assigning 3.9832 to the `int` variable `guess` causes the value to be truncated to 3; C++ uses truncation (discarding the fractional part) and not rounding (finding the closest integer value) when converting floating-point types to integer types. Finally, note that the `int` variable `debt` is unable to hold the value 7.2E12. This creates a situation in which C++ doesn't define the result. On this system, `debt` ends up with the value 1634811904, or about 1.6E09. Well, that's a novel way to reduce massive indebtedness!

Some compilers warn you of possible data loss for those statements that initialize integer variables to floating-point values. Also, the value displayed for `debt` varies from compiler to compiler. For example, running the same program from Listing 3.13 on a second system produced a value of 2147483647.

Conversions in Expressions

Consider what happens when you combine two different arithmetic types in one expression. C++ makes two kinds of automatic conversions in that case. First, some types are automatically converted whenever they occur. Second, some types are converted when they are combined with other types in an expression.

First, let's examine the automatic conversions. When it evaluates expressions, C++ converts `bool`, `char`, `unsigned char`, `signed char`, and `short` values to `int`. In particular, `true` is promoted to 1 and `false` to 0. These conversions are termed *integral promotions*. For example, consider the following fowl statements:

```
short chickens = 20;        // line 1
short ducks = 35;           // line 2
short fowl = chickens + ducks; // line 3
```

To execute the statement on line 3, a C++ program takes the values of `chickens` and `ducks` and converts both to `int`. Then, the program converts the result back to type `short` because the answer is assigned to a type `short` variable. You might find this a bit roundabout, but it does make sense. The `int` type is generally chosen to be the computer's most natural type, which means the computer probably does calculations fastest for that type.

There's some more integral promotion: The `unsigned short` type is converted to `int` if `short` is smaller than `int`. If the two types are the same size, `unsigned short` is converted to `unsigned int`. This rule ensures that there's no data loss in promoting `unsigned short`. Similarly, `wchar_t` is promoted to the first of the following types that is wide enough to accommodate its range: `int`, `unsigned int`, `long`, or `unsigned long`.

Then there are the conversions that take place when you arithmetically combine different types, such as adding an `int` to a `float`. When an operation involves two types, the smaller is converted to the larger. For example, the program in Listing 3.11 divides 9.0 by 5. Because 9.0

is type `double`, the program converts 5 to type `double` before it does the division. More generally, the compiler goes through a checklist to determine which conversions to make in an arithmetic expression. Here's the list, which the compiler goes through in order:

1. If either operand is type `long double`, the other operand is converted to `long double`.

2. Otherwise, if either operand is `double`, the other operand is converted to `double`.

3. Otherwise, if either operand is `float`, the other operand is converted to `float`.

4. Otherwise, the operands are integer types and the integral promotions are made.

5. In that case, if either operand is `unsigned long`, the other operand is converted to `unsigned long`.

6. Otherwise, if one operand is `long int` and the other is `unsigned int`, the conversion depends on the relative sizes of the two types. If `long` can represent possible `unsigned int` values, `unsigned int` is converted to `long`.

7. Otherwise, both operands are converted to `unsigned long`.

8. Otherwise, if either operand is `long`, the other is converted to `long`.

9. Otherwise, if either operand is `unsigned int`, the other is converted to `unsigned int`.

10. If the compiler reaches this point in the list, both operands should be `int`.

ANSI C follows the same rules as C++, but classic K&R C has slightly different rules. For example, classic C always promotes `float` to `double`, even if both operands are `float`.

Conversions in Passing Arguments

Normally, C++ function prototyping controls type conversions for the passing of arguments, as you'll learn in Chapter 7, "Functions: C++'s Programming Modules." However, it is possible, although usually unwise, to waive prototype control for argument passing. In that case, C++ applies the integral promotions to the `char` and `short` types (`signed` and `unsigned`). Also, to preserve compatibility with huge amounts of code in classic C, C++ promotes `float` arguments to `double` when passing them to a function that waives prototyping.

Type Casts

C++ empowers you to force type conversions explicitly via the type cast mechanism. (C++ recognizes the need for type rules, and it also recognizes the need to occasionally override those rules.) The type cast comes in two forms. For example, to convert an `int` value stored in a variable called `thorn` to type `long`, you can use either of the following expressions:

```
(long) thorn     // returns a type long conversion of thorn
long (thorn)     // returns a type long conversion of thorn
```

The type cast doesn't alter the `thorn` variable itself; instead, it creates a new value of the indicated type, which you can then use in an expression, as in the following:

```
cout << int('Q');  // displays the integer code for 'Q'
```

More generally, you can do the following:

```
(typeName) value    // converts value to typeName type
typeName (value)    // converts value to typeName type
```

The first form is straight C. The second form is pure C++. The idea behind the new form is to make a type cast look like a function call. This makes type casts for the built-in types look like the type conversions you can design for user-defined classes.

C++ also introduces four type cast operators that are more restrictive in how they can be used. Chapter 15, "Friends, Exceptions, and More," covers them. Of the four, the `static_cast<>` operator, can be used for converting values from one numeric type to another. For example, using it to convert `thorn` to a type `long` value looks like this:

```
static_cast<long> (thorn)      // returns a type long conversion of thorn
```

More generally, you can do the following:

```
static_cast<typeName> (value)    // converts value to typeName type
```

As Chapter 15 discusses further, Stroustrup felt that the traditional C-style type cast is dangerously unlimited in its possibilities.

Listing 3.14 briefly illustrates both forms. Imagine that the first section of this listing is part of a powerful ecological modeling program that does floating-point calculations that are converted to integral numbers of birds and animals. The results you get depend on when you convert. The calculation for `auks` first adds the floating-point values and then converts the sum to `int` upon assignment. But the calculations for `bats` and `coots` first use type casts to convert the floating-point values to `int` and then sum the values. The final part of the program shows how you can use a type cast to display the ASCII code for a type `char` value.

LISTING 3.14 typecast.cpp

```
// typecast.cpp -- forcing type changes
#include <iostream>
int main()
{
    using namespace std;
    int auks, bats, coots;

    // the following statement adds the values as double,
    // then converts the result to int
    auks = 19.99 + 11.99;

    // these statements add values as int
    bats = (int) 19.99 + (int) 11.99;    // old C syntax
    coots = int (19.99) + int (11.99);   // new C++ syntax
    cout << "auks = " << auks << ", bats = " << bats;
    cout << ", coots = " << coots << endl;
```

LISTING 3.14   Continued

```
    char ch = 'Z';
    cout << "The code for " << ch << " is ";    // print as char
    cout << int(ch) << endl;                     // print as int
    return 0;
}
```

Here is the result of the program in Listing 3.14:

```
auks = 31, bats = 30, coots = 30
The code for Z is 90
```

First, adding 19.99 to 11.99 yields 31.98. When this value is assigned to the `int` variable `auks`, it's truncated to 31. But using type casts truncates the same two values to 19 and 11 before addition, making 30 the result for both `bats` and `coots`. The final `cout` statement uses a type cast to convert a type `char` value to `int` before it displays the result. This causes `cout` to print the value as an integer rather than as a character.

This program illustrates two reasons to use type casting. First, you might have values that are stored as type `double` but are used to calculate a type `int` value. For example, you might be fitting a position to a grid or modeling integer values, such as populations, with floating-point numbers. You might want the calculations to treat the values as `int`. Type casting enables you to do so directly. Notice that you get a different result, at least for these values, when you convert to `int` and add than you do when you add first and then convert to `int`.

The second part of the program shows the most common reason to use a type cast: the capability to compel data in one form to meet a different expectation. In Listing 3.14, for example, the `char` variable ch holds the code for the letter Z. Using `cout` with ch displays the character Z because `cout` zeros in on the fact that ch is type `char`. But by type casting ch to type `int`, you get `cout` to shift to `int` mode and print the ASCII code stored in ch.

Summary

C++'s basic types fall into two groups. One group consists of values that are stored as integers. The second group consists of values that are stored in floating-point format. The integer types differ from each other in the amount of memory used to store values and in whether they are signed or unsigned. From smallest to largest, the integer types are `bool`, `char`, `signed char`, `unsigned char`, `short`, `unsigned short`, `int`, `unsigned int`, `long`, and `unsigned long`. There is also a `wchar_t` type whose placement in this sequence of size depends on the implementation. C++ guarantees that `char` is large enough to hold any member of the system's basic character set, `wchar_t` can hold any member of the system's extended character set, `short` is at least 16 bits, `int` is at least as big as `short`, and `long` is at least 32 bits and at least as large as `int`. The exact sizes depend on the implementation.

Characters are represented by their numeric codes. The I/O system determines whether a code is interpreted as a character or as a number.

The floating-point types can represent fractional values and values much larger than integers can represent. The three floating-point types are `float`, `double`, and `long double`. C++ guarantees that `float` is no larger than `double` and that `double` is no larger than `long double`. Typically, `float` uses 32 bits of memory, `double` uses 64 bits, and `long double` uses 80 to 128 bits.

By providing a variety of types in different sizes and in both signed and unsigned varieties, C++ lets you match the type to particular data requirements.

C++ uses operators to provide the usual arithmetical support for numeric types: addition, subtraction, multiplication, division, and taking the modulus. When two operators seek to operate on the same value, C++'s precedence and associativity rules determine which operation takes place first.

C++ converts values from one type to another when you assign values to a variable, mix types in arithmetic, and use type casts to force type conversions. Many type conversions are "safe," meaning you can make them with no loss or alteration of data. For example, you can convert an `int` value to a `long` value with no problems. Others, such as conversions of floating-point types to integer types, require more care.

At first, you might find the large number of basic C++ types a little excessive, particularly when you take into account the various conversion rules. But most likely you will eventually find occasions when one of the types is just what you need at the time, and you'll thank C++ for having it.

Review Questions

1. Why does C++ have more than one integer type?

2. Declare variables matching the following descriptions:

    a. A `short` integer with the value 80

    b. An `unsigned int` integer with the value 42,110

    c. An integer with the value 3,000,000,000

3. What safeguards does C++ provide to keep you from exceeding the limits of an integer type?

4. What is the distinction between 33L and 33?

5. Consider the two C++ statements that follow:

```
char grade = 65;
char grade = 'A';
```

    Are they equivalent?

6. How could you use C++ to find out which character the code 88 represents? Come up with at least two ways.

7. Assigning a `long` value to a `float` can result in a rounding error. What about assigning `long` to `double`?

8. Evaluate the following expressions as C++ would:

    a. 8 * 9 + 2

    b. 6 * 3 / 4

    c. 3 / 4 * 6

    d. 6.0 * 3 / 4

    e. 15 % 4

9. Suppose `x1` and `x2` are two type `double` variables that you want to add as integers and assign to an integer variable. Construct a C++ statement for doing so.

Programming Exercises

1. Write a short program that asks for your height in integer inches and then converts your height to feet and inches. Have the program use the underscore character to indicate where to type the response. Also, use a `const` symbolic constant to represent the conversion factor.

2. Write a short program that asks for your height in feet and inches and your weight in pounds. (Use three variables to store the information.) Have the program report your body mass index (BMI). To calculate the BMI, first convert your height in feet and inches to your height in inches (1 foot = 12 inches). Then, convert your height in inches to your height in meters by multiplying by 0.0254. Then, convert your weight in pounds into your mass in kilograms by dividing by 2.2. Finally, compute your BMI by dividing your mass in kilograms by the square of your height in meters. Use symbolic constants to represent the various conversion factors.

3. Write a program that asks the user to enter a latitude in degrees, minutes, and seconds and that then displays the latitude in decimal format. There are 60 seconds of arc to a minute and 60 minutes of arc to a degree; represent these values with symbolic constants. You should use a separate variable for each input value. A sample run should look like this:

```
Enter a latitude in degrees, minutes, and seconds:
First, enter the degrees: 37
Next, enter the minutes of arc: 51
Finally, enter the seconds of arc: 19
37 degrees, 51 minutes, 19 seconds = 37.8553 degrees
```

4. Write a program that asks the user to enter the number of seconds as an integer value (use type `long`) and that then displays the equivalent time in days, hours, minutes, and seconds. Use symbolic constants to represent the number of hours in the day, the num-

ber of minutes in an hour, and the number of seconds in a minute. The output should look like this:

```
Enter the number of seconds: 31600000
31600000 seconds = 365 days, 46 minutes, 40 seconds
```

5. Write a program that asks how many miles you have driven and how many gallons of gasoline you have used and then reports the miles per gallon your car has gotten. Or, if you prefer, the program can request distance in kilometers and petrol in liters and then report the result European style, in liters per 100 kilometers.

6. Write a program that asks you to enter an automobile gasoline consumption figure in the European style (liters per 100 kilometers) and converts to the U.S. style of miles per gallon. Note that in addition to using different units of measurement, the U.S approach (distance / fuel) is the inverse of the European approach (fuel / distance). Note that 100 kilometers is 62.14 miles, and 1 gallon is 3.875 liters. Thus, 19 mpg is about 12.4 l/100 km, and 27 mpg is about 8.7 l/100 km.

CHAPTER 4

COMPOUND TYPES

In this chapter you'll learn about the following:

- How to create and use arrays

- How to create and use C-style strings

- How to create and use string-class strings

- How to use the getline() and get() methods for reading strings

- How to mix string and numeric input

- How to create and use structures

- How to create and use unions

- How to create and use enumerations

- How to create and use pointers

- How to manage dynamic memory with new and delete

- How to create dynamic arrays

- How to create dynamic structures

- Automatic, static, and dynamic storage

Say you've developed a computer game called User-Hostile in which players match wits with a cryptic and abusive computer interface. Now you must write a program that keeps track of your monthly game sales for a five-year period. Or you want to inventory your accumulation of hacker-hero trading cards. You soon conclude that you need something more than C++'s simple basic types to meet these data requirements, and C++ offers something more—compound types. These are types built from the basic integer and floating-point types. The most far-reaching compound type is the class, that bastion of OOP toward which we are progressing. But C++ also supports several more modest compound types taken from C. The array, for example, can hold several values of the same type. A particular kind of array can hold a string, which is a series of characters. Structures can hold several values of differing types. Then there are pointers, which are variables that tell a computer where data is placed. You'll examine all these compound forms (except classes) in this chapter, take a first look at new and delete and how you can use them to manage data, and take an introductory look at the C++ string class, which gives you an alternative way to work with strings.

Introducing Arrays

An *array* is a data form that can hold several values, all of one type. For example, an array can hold 60 type `int` values that represent five years of game sales data, 12 `short` values that represent the number of days in each month, or 365 `float` values that indicate your food expenses for each day of the year. Each value is stored in a separate array element, and the computer stores all the elements of an array consecutively in memory.

To create an array, you use a declaration statement. An array declaration should indicate three things:

- The type of value to be stored in each element
- The name of the array
- The number of elements in the array

You accomplish this in C++ by modifying the declaration for a simple variable and adding brackets that contain the number of elements. For example, the declaration

```
short months[12];    // creates array of 12 short
```

creates an array named `months` that has 12 elements, each of which can hold a type `short` value. Each element, in essence, is a variable that you can treat as a simple variable.

This is the general form for declaring an array:

```
typeName arrayName[arraySize];
```

The expression *arraySize*, which is the number of elements, must be an integer constant, such as 10 or a `const` value, or a constant expression, such as `8 * sizeof (int)`, for which all values are known at the time compilation takes place. In particular, *arraySize* cannot be a variable whose value is set while the program is running. However, later in this chapter you'll learn how to use the `new` operator to get around that restriction.

The Array as Compound Type

An array is called a *compound type* because it is built from some other type. (C uses the term *derived type,* but, because C++ uses the term *derived* for class relationships, it had to come up with a new term.) You can't simply declare that something is an array; it always has to be an array of some particular type. There is no generalized array type. Instead, there are many specific array types, such as array of `char` or array of `long`. For example, consider this declaration:

```
float loans[20];
```

The type for `loans` is not "array"; rather, it is "array of `float`." This emphasizes that the `loans` array is built from the `float` type.

Much of the usefulness of the array comes from the fact that you can access array elements individually. The way to do this is to use a *subscript*, or an *index*, to number the elements. C++ array numbering starts with zero. (This is nonnegotiable; you have to start at zero. Pascal and

BASIC users will have to adjust.) C++ uses a bracket notation with the index to specify an array element. For example, `months[0]` is the first element of the `months` array, and `months[11]` is the last element. Note that the index of the last element is one less than the size of the array. (See Figure 4.1.) Thus, an array declaration enables you to create a lot of variables with a single declaration, and you can then use an index to identify and access individual elements.

FIGURE 4.1

Creating an array.

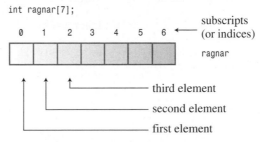

`ragnar` is an array holding seven values, each of which is a type `int` variable

---

The Importance of Valid Subscript Values

The compiler does not check to see if you use a valid subscript. For instance, the compiler won't complain if you assign a value to the nonexistent element `months[101]`. But that assignment could cause problems when the program runs, possibly corrupting data or code, possibly causing the program to abort. So it is your responsibility to make sure that your program uses only valid subscript values.

The yam analysis program in Listing 4.1 demonstrates a few properties of arrays, including declaring an array, assigning values to array elements, and initializing an array.

LISTING 4.1   `arrayone.cpp`

```cpp
// arrayone.cpp -- small arrays of integers
#include <iostream>
int main()
{
    using namespace std;
    int yams[3];     // creates array with three elements
    yams[0] = 7;     // assign value to first element
    yams[1] = 8;
    yams[2] = 6;

    int yamcosts[3] = {20, 30, 5}; // create, initialize array
// NOTE: If your C++ compiler or translator can't initialize
// this array, use static int yamcosts[3] instead of
// int yamcosts[3]
```

LISTING 4.1   Continued

```
        cout << "Total yams = ";
        cout << yams[0] + yams[1] + yams[2] << endl;
        cout << "The package with " << yams[1] << " yams costs ";
        cout << yamcosts[1] << " cents per yam.\n";
        int total = yams[0] * yamcosts[0] + yams[1] * yamcosts[1];
        total = total + yams[2] * yamcosts[2];
        cout << "The total yam expense is " << total << " cents.\n";

        cout << "\nSize of yams array = " << sizeof yams;
        cout << " bytes.\n";
        cout << "Size of one element = " << sizeof yams[0];
        cout << " bytes.\n";
        return 0;
}
```

Compatibility Note

Current versions of C++, as well as ANSI C, allow you to initialize ordinary arrays defined in a function. However, in some older implementations that use a C++ translator instead of a true compiler, the C++ translator creates C code for a C compiler that is not fully ANSI C compliant. In such a case, you can get an error message like the following example from a Sun C++ 2.0 system:

```
"arrayone.cc", line 10: sorry, not implemented: initialization of
yamcosts (automatic aggregate) Compilation failed
```

The fix is to use the keyword `static` in the array declaration:

```
// pre-ANSI initialization
static int yamcosts[3] = {20, 30, 5};
```

The keyword `static` causes the compiler to use a different memory scheme for storing the array, one that allows initialization even under pre-ANSI C. Chapter 9, "Memory Models and Namespaces," discusses this use of `static`.

Here is the output from the program in Listing 4.1:

```
Total yams = 21
The package with 8 yams costs 30 cents per yam.
The total yam expense is 410 cents.
Size of yams array = 12 bytes.
Size of one element = 4 bytes.
```

Program Notes

First, the program in Listing 4.1 creates a three-element array called **yams**. Because **yams** has three elements, the elements are numbered from **0** through **2**, and **arrayone.cpp** uses index values of **0** through **2** to assign values to the three individual elements. Each individual **yam** element is an **int** with all the rights and privileges of an **int** type, so **arrayone.cpp** can, and does, assign values to elements, add elements, multiply elements, and display elements.

The program uses the long way to assign values to the `yam` elements. C++ also lets you initialize array elements within the declaration statement. Listing 4.1 uses this shortcut to assign values to the `yamcosts` array:

```
int yamcosts[3] = {20, 30, 5};
```

It simply provides a comma-separated list of values (the *initialization list*) enclosed in braces. The spaces in the list are optional. If you don't initialize an array that's defined inside a function, the element values remain undefined. That means the element takes on whatever value previously resided at that location in memory.

Next, the program uses the array values in a few calculations. This part of the program looks cluttered with all the subscripts and brackets. The `for` loop, coming up in Chapter 5, "Loops and Relational Expressions," provides a powerful way to deal with arrays and eliminates the need to write each index explicitly. For the time being, we'll stick to small arrays.

As you should recall, the `sizeof` operator returns the size, in bytes, of a type or data object. Note that if you use the `sizeof` operator with an array name, you get the number of bytes in the whole array. But if you use `sizeof` with an array element, you get the size, in bytes, of the element. This illustrates that `yams` is an array, but `yams[1]` is just an `int`.

Initialization Rules for Arrays

C++ has several rules about initializing arrays. They restrict when you can do it, and they determine what happens if the number of array elements doesn't match the number of values in the initializer. Let's examine these rules.

You can use the initialization form *only* when defining the array. You cannot use it later, and you cannot assign one array wholesale to another:

```
int cards[4] = {3, 6, 8, 10};        // okay
int hand[4];                         // okay
hand[4] = {5, 6, 7, 9};              // not allowed
hand = cards;                        // not allowed
```

However, you can use subscripts and assign values to the elements of an array individually.

When initializing an array, you can provide fewer values than array elements. For example, the following statement initializes only the first two elements of `hotelTips`:

```
float hotelTips[5] = {5.0, 2.5};
```

If you partially initialize an array, the compiler sets the remaining elements to zero. Thus, it's easy to initialize all the elements of an array to zero—just explicitly initialize the first element to zero and then let the compiler initialize the remaining elements to zero:

```
long totals[500] = {0};
```

Note that if you initialize to `{1}` instead of to `{0}`, just the first element is set to `1`; the rest get set to `0`.

If you leave the square brackets (`[]`) empty when you initialize an array, the C++ compiler counts the elements for you. Suppose, for example, that you make this declaration:

```
short things[] = {1, 5, 3, 8};
```

The compiler makes `things` an array of four elements.

Letting the Compiler Do It

Normally, letting the compiler count the number of elements is poor practice, for its count can be different from what you think it is. However, this approach can be a safe one for initializing a character array to a string, as you'll soon see. And if your main concern is that the program, not you, knows how large an array is, you can do something like this:

```
short things[] = {1, 5, 3, 8};
int num_elements = sizeof things / sizeof (short);
```

Whether this is useful or lazy depends on the circumstances.

The C++ Standard Template Library (STL) provides an alternative to arrays called the *vector template class*. This alternative is more sophisticated and flexible than the built-in array composite type. Chapter 16, "The `string` Class and the Standard Template Library," discusses the STL and the `vector` template class.

Strings

A *string* is a series of characters stored in consecutive bytes of memory. C++ has two ways of dealing with strings. The first, taken from C and often called a *C-style string*, is the first one this chapter examines. Later, this chapter discusses an alternative method based on a `string` class library.

The idea of a series of characters stored in consecutive bytes implies that you can store a string in an array of `char`, with each character kept in its own array element. Strings provide a convenient way to store text information, such as messages to the user (*"Please tell me your secret Swiss bank account number"*) or responses from the user (*"You must be joking"*). C-style strings have a special feature: The last character of every string is the *null character*. This character, written \0, is the character with ASCII code 0, and it serves to mark the string's end. For example, consider the following two declarations:

```
char dog [5] = { 'b', 'e', 'a', 'u', 'x'};     // not a string!
char cat[5] = {'f', 'a', 't', 's', '\0'};     // a string!
```

Both of these arrays are arrays of `char`, but only the second is a string. The null character plays a fundamental role in C-style strings. For example, C++ has many functions that handle strings, including those used by `cout`. They all work by processing a string character-by-character until they reach the null character. If you ask `cout` to display a nice string like `cat` in the preceding example, it displays the first four characters, detects the null character, and stops. But if you are ungracious enough to tell `cout` to display the `dog` array from the preceding example, which is not a string, `cout` prints the five letters in the array and then keeps marching through memory byte-by-byte, interpreting each byte as a character to print, until it reached a null character. Because null characters, which really are bytes set to zero, tend to be common in memory, the damage is usually contained quickly; nonetheless, you should not treat nonstring character arrays as strings.

The `cat` array example makes initializing an array to a string look tedious—all those single quotes and then having to remember the null character. Don't worry. There is a better way to initialize a character array to a string. Just use a quoted string, called a *string constant* or *string literal*, as in the following:

```
char bird[10] = "Mr. Cheeps";    // the \0 is understood
char fish[] = "Bubbles";         // let the compiler count
```

Quoted strings always include the terminating null character implicitly, so you don't have to spell it out. (See Figure 4.2.) Also, the various C++ input facilities for reading a string from keyboard input into a `char` array automatically add the terminating null character for you. (If, when you run the program in Listing 4.1, you discover that you have to use the keyword `static` to initialize an array, you have to use it with these `char` arrays, too.)

FIGURE 4.2

Initializing an array to a string.

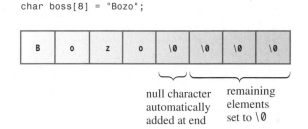

```
char boss[8] = "Bozo";
```

null character automatically added at end

remaining elements set to \0

Of course, you should make sure the array is large enough to hold all the characters of the string, including the null character. Initializing a character array with a string constant is one case where it may be safer to let the compiler count the number of elements for you. There is no harm, other than wasted space, in making an array larger than the string. That's because functions that work with strings are guided by the location of the null character, not by the size of the array. C++ imposes no limits on the length of a string.

Remember

When determining the minimum array size necessary to hold a string, remember to include the terminating null character in your count.

Note that a string constant (with double quotes) is not interchangeable with a character constant (with single quotes). A character constant, such as `'S'`, is a shorthand notation for the code for a character. On an ASCII system, `'S'` is just another way of writing 83. Thus, the statement

```
char shirt_size = 'S';          // this is fine
```

assigns the value 83 to `shirt_size`. But `"S"` represents the string consisting of two characters, the `S` and the `\0` characters. Even worse, `"S"` actually represents the memory address at which the string is stored. So a statement like

```
char shirt_size = "S";          // illegal type mismatch
```

attempts to assign a memory address to `shirt_size`! Because an address is a separate type in C++, a C++ compiler won't allow this sort of nonsense. (We'll return to this point later in this chapter, after we've discussed pointers.)

Concatenating String Constants

Sometimes a string may be too long to conveniently fit on one line of code. C++ enables you to concatenate string constants—that is, to combine two quoted strings into one. Indeed, any two string constants separated only by whitespace (spaces, tabs, and newlines) are automatically joined into one. Thus, all the following output statements are equivalent to each other:

```
cout << "I'd give my right arm to be" " a great violinist.\n";
cout << "I'd give my right arm to be a great violinist.\n";
cout << "I'd give my right ar"
"m to be a great violinist.\n";
```

Note that the join doesn't add any spaces to the joined strings. The first character of the second string immediately follows the last character, not counting `\0`, of the first string. The `\0` character from the first string is replaced by the first character of the second string.

Using Strings in an Array

The two most common ways of getting a string into an array are to initialize an array to a string constant and to read keyboard or file input into an array. Listing 4.2 demonstrates these approaches by initializing one array to a quoted string and using `cin` to place an input string in a second array. The program also uses the standard library function `strlen()` to get the length of a string. The standard `cstring` header file (or `string.h` for older implementations) provides declarations for this and many other string-related functions.

LISTING 4.2   `strings.cpp`

```
// strings.cpp -- storing strings in an array
#include <iostream>
#include <cstring>  // for the strlen() function
int main()
{
    using namespace std;
    const int Size = 15;
    char name1[Size];                 // empty array
```

LISTING 4.2   Continued

```
char name2[Size] = "C++owboy";  // initialized array
// NOTE: some implementations may require the static keyword
// to initialize the array name2

cout << "Howdy! I'm " << name2;
cout << "! What's your name?\n";
cin >> name1;
cout << "Well, " << name1 << ", your name has ";
cout << strlen(name1) << " letters and is stored\n";
cout << "in an array of " << sizeof(name1) << " bytes.\n";
cout << "Your initial is " << name1[0] << ".\n";
name2[3] = '\0';                 // null character
cout << "Here are the first 3 characters of my name: ";
cout << name2 << endl;
return 0;
}
```

Compatibility Note

If your system doesn't provide the `cstring` header file, try the older `string.h` version.

Here is a sample run of the program in Listing 4.2:

```
Howdy! I'm C++owboy! What's your name?
Basicman
Well, Basicman, your name has 8 letters and is stored
in an array of 15 bytes.
Your initial is B.
Here are the first 3 characters of my name: C++
```

Program Notes

What can you learn from Listing 4.2? First, note that the `sizeof` operator gives the size of the entire array, 15 bytes, but the `strlen()` function returns the size of the string stored in the array and not the size of the array itself. Also, `strlen()` counts just the visible characters and not the null character. Thus, it returns a value of **8**, not **9**, for the length of `Basicman`. If `cosmic` is a string, the minimum array size for holding that string is `strlen(cosmic) + 1`.

Because `name1` and `name2` are arrays, you can use an index to access individual characters in the array. For example, the program uses `name1[0]` to find the first character in that array. Also, the program sets `name2[3]` to the null character. That makes the string end after three characters, even though more characters remain in the array. (See Figure 4.3.)

Note that the program in Listing 4.2 uses a symbolic constant for the array size. Often, the size of an array appears in several statements in a program. Using a symbolic constant to represent the size of an array simplifies revising the program to use a different array size; you just have to change the value once, where the symbolic constant is defined.

FIGURE 4.3
Shortening a string
with \0.

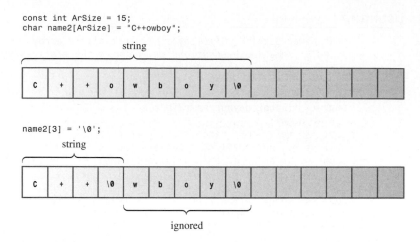

```
const int ArSize = 15;
char name2[ArSize] = "C++owboy";
```

Adventures in String Input

The `strings.cpp` program has a blemish that is concealed through the often useful technique of carefully selected sample input. Listing 4.3 removes the veils and shows that string input can be tricky.

LISTING 4.3   instr1.cpp

```cpp
// instr1.cpp -- reading more than one string
#include <iostream>
int main()
{
    using namespace std;
    const int ArSize = 20;
    char name[ArSize];
    char dessert[ArSize];

    cout << "Enter your name:\n";
    cin >> name;
    cout << "Enter your favorite dessert:\n";
    cin >> dessert;
    cout << "I have some delicious " << dessert;
    cout << " for you, " << name << ".\n";
    return 0;
}
```

The intent of the program in Listing 4.3 is simple: Read a user's name and favorite dessert from the keyboard and then display the information. Here is a sample run:

```
Enter your name:
Alistair Dreeb
Enter your favorite dessert:
I have some delicious Dreeb for you, Alistair.
```

We didn't even get a chance to respond to the dessert prompt! The program showed it and then immediately moved on to display the final line.

The problem lies with how `cin` determines when you've finished entering a string. You can't enter the null character from the keyboard, so `cin` needs some other means for locating the end of a string. The `cin` technique is to use whitespace—spaces, tabs, and newlines—to delineate a string. This means `cin` reads just one word when it gets input for a character array. After it reads this word, `cin` automatically adds the terminating null character when it places the string into the array.

The practical result in this example is that `cin` reads `Alistair` as the entire first string and puts it into the `name` array. This leaves poor `Dreeb` still sitting in the input queue. When `cin` searches the input queue for the response to the favorite dessert question, it finds `Dreeb` still there. Then `cin` gobbles up `Dreeb` and puts it into the `dessert` array. (See Figure 4.4.)

FIGURE 4.4
The `cin` view of string input.

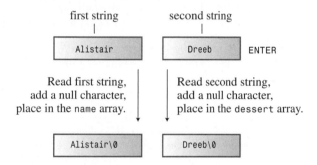

Another problem, which didn't surface in the sample run, is that the input string might turn out to be longer than the destination array. Using `cin` as this example did offers no protection against placing a 30-character string in a 20-character array.

Many programs depend on string input, so it's worthwhile to explore this topic further. We'll have to draw on some of the more advanced features of `cin`, which are described in Chapter 17, "Input, Output, and Files."

Reading String Input a Line at a Time

Reading string input a word at a time is often not the most desirable choice. For instance, suppose a program asks the user to enter a city, and the user responds with **New York** or **Sao Paulo**. You would want the program to read and store the full names, not just `New` and `Sao`. To be able to enter whole phrases instead of single words as a string, you need a different approach to string input. Specifically, you need a line-oriented method instead of a word-oriented method. You are in luck, for the `istream` class, of which `cin` is an example, has some line-oriented class member functions: `getline()` and `get()`. Both read an entire input line—that is, up until a newline character. However, `getline()` then discards the newline character, whereas `get()` leaves it in the input queue. Let's look at the details, beginning with `getline()`.

Line-Oriented Input with `getline()`

The getline() function reads a whole line, using the newline character transmitted by the Enter key to mark the end of input. You invoke this method by using `cin.getline()` as a function call. The function takes two arguments. The first argument is the name of the array destined to hold the line of input, and the second argument is a limit on the number of characters to be read. If this limit is, say, 20, the function reads no more than 19 characters, leaving room to automatically add the null character at the end. The `getline()` member function stops reading input when it reaches this numeric limit or when it reads a newline character, whichever comes first.

For example, suppose you want to use `getline()` to read a name into the 20-element name array. You would use this call:

```
cin.getline(name,20);
```

This reads the entire line into the `name` array, provided that the line consists of 19 or fewer characters. (The `getline()` member function also has an optional third argument, which Chapter 17 discusses.)

Listing 4.4 modifies Listing 4.3 to use `cin.getline()` instead of a simple `cin`. Otherwise, the program is unchanged.

LISTING 4.4   `instr2.cpp`

```cpp
// instr2.cpp -- reading more than one word with getline
#include <iostream>
int main()
{
    using namespace std;
    const int ArSize = 20;
    char name[ArSize];
    char dessert[ArSize];

    cout << "Enter your name:\n";
    cin.getline(name, ArSize);  // reads through newline
    cout << "Enter your favorite dessert:\n";
    cin.getline(dessert, ArSize);
    cout << "I have some delicious " << dessert;
    cout << " for you, " << name << ".\n";
    return 0;
}
```

Compatibility Note

Some early C++ versions don't fully implement all facets of the current C++ I/O package. In particular, the `getline()` member function isn't always available. If this affects you, just read about this example and go on to the next one, which uses a member function that predates `getline()`. Early releases of Turbo C++ implement `getline()` slightly differently so that it does store the newline character in the string. Microsoft Visual C++ 5.0 and 6.0 have a bug in `getline()` as implemented in the `iostream` header file but not in the `ostream.h` version; Service Pack 5 for Microsoft Visual C++ 6.0, available at the `msdn.microsoft.com/vstdio` website, fixes that bug.

Here is some sample output for Listing 4.4:

```
Enter your name:
Dirk Hammernose
Enter your favorite dessert:
Radish Torte
I have some delicious Radish Torte for you, Dirk Hammernose.
```

The program now reads complete names and delivers the user her just desserts! The `getline()` function conveniently gets a line at a time. It reads input through the newline character marking the end of the line, but it doesn't save the newline character. Instead, it replaces it with a null character when storing the string. (See Figure 4.5.)

FIGURE 4.5

`getline()` reads and replaces the newline character.

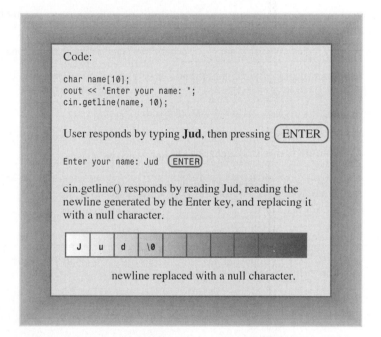

Code:

```
char name[10];
cout << "Enter your name: ";
cin.getline(name, 10);
```

User responds by typing **Jud**, then pressing (ENTER)

Enter your name: Jud (ENTER)

cin.getline() responds by reading Jud, reading the newline generated by the Enter key, and replacing it with a null character.

| J | u | d | \0 | | | | |

newline replaced with a null character.

Line-Oriented Input with `get()`

Let's try another approach. The `istream` class has another member function, `get()`, which comes in several variations. One variant works much like `getline()`. It takes the same arguments, interprets them the same way, and reads to the end of a line. But rather than read and discard the newline character, `get()` leaves that character in the input queue. Suppose you use two calls to `get()` in a row:

```
cin.get(name, ArSize);
cin.get(dessert, Arsize);   // a problem
```

Because the first call leaves the newline character in the input queue, that newline character is the first character the second call sees. Thus, `get()` concludes that it's reached the end of line without having found anything to read. Without help, `get()` just can't get past that newline character.

Fortunately, there is help in the form of a variation of `get()`. The call `cin.get()` (with no arguments) reads the single next character, even if it is a newline, so you can use it to dispose of the newline character and prepare for the next line of input. That is, this sequence works:

```
cin.get(name, ArSize);      // read first line
cin.get();                  // read newline
cin.get(dessert, Arsize);   // read second line
```

Another way to use `get()` is to *concatenate*, or join, the two class member functions, as follows:

```
cin.get(name, ArSize).get(); // concatenate member functions
```

What makes this possible is that `cin.get(name, ArSize)` returns the `cin` object, which is then used as the object that invokes the `get()` function. Similarly, the statement

```
cin.getline(name1, ArSize).getline(name2, ArSize);
```

reads two consecutive input lines into the arrays `name1` and `name2`; it's equivalent to making two separate calls to `cin.getline()`.

Listing 4.5 uses concatenation. In Chapter 11, "Working with Classes," you'll learn how to incorporate this feature into your class definitions.

LISTING 4.5   instr3.cpp

```cpp
// instr3.cpp -- reading more than one word with get() & get()
#include <iostream>
int main()
{
    using namespace std;
    const int ArSize = 20;
    char name[ArSize];
    char dessert[ArSize];

    cout << "Enter your name:\n";
    cin.get(name, ArSize).get();    // read string, newline
    cout << "Enter your favorite dessert:\n";
    cin.get(dessert, ArSize).get();
    cout << "I have some delicious " << dessert;
    cout << " for you, " << name << ".\n";
    return 0;
}
```

Compatibility Note

Some older C++ versions don't implement the `get()` variant that has no arguments. They do, however, implement yet another `get()` variant, one that takes a single `char` argument. To use it instead of the argument-free `get()`, you need to declare a `char` variable first:

```
char ch;
cin.get(name, ArSize).get(ch);
```

You can use this code instead of what is found in Listing 4.5. Chapters 5, 6, "Branching Statements and Logical Operators," and 17 further discuss the `get()` variants.

Here is a sample run of the program in Listing 4.5:

```
Enter your name:
Mai Parfait
Enter your favorite dessert:
Chocolate Mousse
I have some delicious Chocolate Mousse for you, Mai Parfait.
```

One thing to note is how C++ allows multiple versions of functions, provided that they have different argument lists. If you use, say, `cin.get(name, ArSize)`, the compiler notices you're using the form that puts a string into an array and sets up the appropriate member function. If, instead, you use `cin.get()`, the compiler realizes you want the form that reads one character. Chapter 8, "Adventures in Functions," explores this feature, which is called *function overloading*.

Why use `get()` instead of `getline()` at all? First, older implementations may not have `getline()`. Second, `get()` lets you be a bit more careful. Suppose, for example, you used `get()` to read a line into an array. How can you tell if it read the whole line rather than stopped because the array was filled? Look at the next input character. If it is a newline character, then the whole line was read. If it is not a newline character, then there is still more input on that line. Chapter 17 investigates this technique. In short, `getline()` is a little simpler to use, but `get()` makes error checking simpler. You can use either one to read a line of input; just keep the slightly different behaviors in mind.

Empty Lines and Other Problems

What happens after `getline()` or `get()` reads an empty line? The original practice was that the next input statement picked up where the last `getline()` or `get()` left off. However, the current practice is that after `get()` (but not `getline()`) reads an empty line, it sets something called the *failbit*. The implications of this act are that further input is blocked but you can restore input with the following command:

```
cin.clear();
```

Another potential problem is that the input string could be longer than the allocated space. If the input line is longer than the number of characters specified, both `getline()` and `get()` leave the remaining characters in the input queue. However, `getline()` additionally sets the failbit and turns off further input.

Chapters 5, 6, and 17 investigate these properties and how to program around them.

Mixing String and Numeric Input

Mixing numeric input with line-oriented string input can cause problems. Consider the simple program in Listing 4.6.

LISTING 4.6   `numstr.cpp`

```
// numstr.cpp -- following number input with line input
#include <iostream>
int main()
{
    using namespace std;
    cout << "What year was your house built?\n";
    int year;
    cin >> year;
    cout << "What is its street address?\n";
    char address[80];
    cin.getline(address, 80);
    cout << "Year built: " << year << endl;
    cout << "Address: " << address << endl;
    cout << "Done!\n";
    return 0;
}
```

Running the program in Listing 4.6 would look something like this:

```
What year was your house built?
1966
What is its street address?
Year built: 1966
Address
Done!
```

You never get the opportunity to enter the address. The problem is that when `cin` reads the year, it leaves the newline generated by the Enter key in the input queue. Then, `cin.getline()` reads the newline as an empty line and assigns a null string to the `address` array. The fix is to read and discard the newline before reading the address. This can be done several ways, including by using `get()` with no argument or with a `char` argument, as described in the preceding example. You can make this call separately:

```
cin >> year;
cin.get();   // or cin.get(ch);
```

Or you can concatenate the call, making use of the fact that the expression `cin >> year` returns the `cin` object:

```
(cin >> year).get();   // or (cin >> year).get(ch);
```

If you make one of these changes to Listing 4.6, it works properly:

```
What year was your house built?
1966
What is its street address?
43821 Unsigned Short Street
```

```
Year built: 1966
Address: 43821 Unsigned Short Street
Done!
```

C++ programs frequently use pointers instead of arrays to handle strings. We'll take up that aspect of strings after talking a bit about pointers. Meanwhile, let's take a look at a more recent way to handle strings: the C++ `string` class.

Introducing the `string` Class

The ISO/ANSI C++ Standard expanded the C++ library by adding a `string` class. So now, instead of using a character array to hold a string, you can use a type `string` variable (or object, to use C++ terminology). As you'll see, the `string` class is simpler to use than the array and also provides a truer representation of a string as a type.

To use the `string` class, a program has to include the `string` header file. The `string` class is part of the `std` namespace, so you have to provide a `using` directive or else refer to the class as `std::string`. The class definition hides the array nature of a string and lets you treat a string much like an ordinary variable. Listing 4.7 illustrates some of the similarities and differences between `string` objects and character arrays.

LISTING 4.7   `strtype1.cpp`

```cpp
// strtype1.cpp -- using the C++ string class
#include <iostream>
#include <string>                // make string class available
int main()
{
    using namespace std;
    char charr1[20];             // create an empty array
    char charr2[20] = "jaguar"; // create an initialized array
    string str1;                 // create an empty string object
    string str2 = "panther";     // create an initialized string

    cout << "Enter a kind of feline: ";
    cin >> charr1;
    cout << "Enter another kind of feline: ";
    cin >> str1;                 // use cin for input
    cout << "Here are some felines:\n";
    cout << charr1 << " " << charr2 << " "
        << str1 << " " << str2 // use cout for output
        << endl;
    cout << "The third letter in " << charr2 << " is "
        << charr2[2] << endl;
    cout << "The third letter in " << str2 << " is "
        << str2[2] << endl;    // use array notation

    return 0;
}
```

Here is a sample run of the program in Listing 4.7:

```
Enter a kind of feline: ocelot
Enter another kind of feline: tiger
Here are some felines:
ocelot jaguar tiger panther
The third letter in jaguar is g
The third letter in panther is n
```

You should learn from this example that in many ways, you can use a string object in the same manner as a character array:

- You can initialize a `string` object to a C-style string.

- You can use `cin` to store keyboard input in a `string` object.

- You can use `cout` to display a `string` object.

- You can use array notation to access individual characters stored in a `string` object.

The main difference between `string` objects and character arrays shown in Listing 4.7 is that you declare a `string` object as a simple variable, not as an array:

```
string str1;               // create an empty string object
string str2 = "panther";   // create an initialized string
```

The class design allows the program to handle the sizing automatically. For instance, the declaration for `str1` creates a `string` object of length zero, but the program automatically resizes `str1` when it reads input into `str1`:

```
cin >> str1;               // str1 resized to fit input
```

This makes using a `string` object both more convenient and safer than using an array. Conceptually, one thinks of an array of `char` as a collection of `char` storage units used to store a string but of a `string` class variable as a single entity representing the string.

Assignment, Concatenation, and Appending

The `string` class makes some operations simpler than is the case for arrays. For example, you can't simply assign one array to another. But you can assign one string object to another:

```
char charr1[20];               // create an empty array
char charr2[20] = "jaguar"; // create an initialized array
string str1;                   // create an empty string object
string str2 = "panther";       // create an initialized string
charr1 = charr2;               // INVALID, no array assignment
str1 = str2;                   // VALID, object assignment ok
```

The `string` class simplifies combining strings. You can use the + operator to add two `string` objects together and the += operator to tack on a string to the end of an existing `string` object. Continuing with the preceding code, we have the following possibilities:

```
string str3;
str3 = str1 + str2;        // assign str3 the joined strings
str1 += str2;              // add str2 to the end of str1
```

Listing 4.8 illustrates these usages. Note that you can add and append C-style strings as well as `string` objects to a `string` object.

LISTING 4.8   strtype2.cpp

```cpp
// strtype2.cpp -- assigning, adding, and appending
#include <iostream>
#include <string>                  // make string class available
int main()
{
    using namespace std;
    string s1 = "penguin";
    string s2, s3;

    cout << "You can assign one string object to another: s2 = s1\n";
    s2 = s1;
    cout << "s1: " << s1 << ", s2: " << s2 << endl;
    cout << "You can assign a C-style string to a string object.\n";
    cout << "s2 = \"buzzard\"\n";
    s2 = "buzzard";
    cout << "s2: " << s2 << endl;
    cout << "You can concatenate strings: s3 = s1 + s2\n";
    s3 = s1 + s2;
    cout << "s3: " << s3 << endl;
    cout << "You can append strings.\n";
    s1 += s2;
    cout <<"s1 += s2 yields s1 = " << s1 << endl;
    s2 += " for a day";
    cout <<"s2 += \" for a day\" yields s2 = " << s2 << endl;

    return 0;
}
```

Recall that the escape sequence \" represents a double quotation mark that is used as a literal character rather than as marking the limits of a string. Here is the output from the program in Listing 4.8:

```
You can assign one string object to another: s2 = s1
s1: penguin, s2: penguin
You can assign a C-style string to a string object.
s2 = "buzzard"
s2: buzzard
You can concatenate strings: s3 = s1 + s2
s3: penguinbuzzard
You can append strings.
s1 += s2 yields s1 = penguinbuzzard
s2 += " for a day" yields s2 = buzzard for a day
```

More `string` Class Operations

Even before the string class was added to C++, programmers needed to do things like assign strings. For C-style strings, they used functions from the C library for these tasks. The `cstring` header file (formerly `string.h`) supports these functions. For example, you can use the `strcpy()` function to copy a string to a character array, and you can use the `strcat()` function to append a string to a character array:

```
strcpy(charr1, charr2);  // copy charr2 to charr1
strcat(charr1, charr2);  // append contents of charr2 to char1
```

Listing 4.9 compares techniques used with `string` objects with techniques used with character arrays.

LISTING 4.9   `strtype3.cpp`

```
// strtype3.cpp -- more string class features
#include <iostream>
#include <string>              // make string class available
#include <cstring>             // C-style string library
int main()
{
    using namespace std;
    char charr1[20];
    char charr2[20] = "jaguar";
    string str1;
    string str2 = "panther";

    // assignment for string objects and character arrays
    str1 = str2;               // copy str2 to str2
    strcpy(charr1, charr2);    // copy charr2 to charr1

    // appending for string objects and character arrays
    str1 += " paste";          // add paste to end of str1
    strcat(charr1, " juice");  // add juice to end of charr1

    // finding the length of a string object and a C-style string
    int len1 = str1.size();    // obtain length of str1
    int len2 = strlen(charr1); // obtain length of charr1

    cout << "The string " << str1 << " contains "
        << len1 << " characters.\n";
    cout << "The string " << charr1 << " contains "
        << len2 << " characters.\n";

    return 0;
}
```

Here is the output from the program in Listing 4.9:

```
The string panther paste contains 13 characters.
The string jaguar juice contains 12 characters.
```

Working with string objects tends to be simpler than using the C string functions. This is especially true for more complex operations. For example, the library equivalent of

```
str3 = str1 + str2;
```

is this:

```
strcpy(charr3, charr1);
strcat(charr3, charr2);
```

Furthermore, with arrays, there is always the danger of the destination array being too small to hold the information, as in this example:

```
char site[10] = "house";
strcat(site, " of pancakes");  // memory problem
```

The `strcat()` function would attempt to copy all 12 characters into the `site` array, thus over-running adjacent memory. This might cause the program to abort, or the program might continue running, but with corrupted data. The `string` class, with its automatic resizing as necessary, avoids this sort of problem. The C library does provide cousins to `strcat()` and `strcpy()`, called `strncat()` and `strncpy()`, that work more safely by taking a third argument to indicate the maximum allowed size of the target array, but using them adds another layer of complexity in writing programs.

Notice the different syntax used to obtain the number of characters in a string:

```
int len1 = str1.size();      // obtain length of str1
int len2 = strlen(charr1);   // obtain length of charr1
```

The `strlen()` function is a regular function that takes a C-style string as its argument and that returns the number of characters in the string. The `size()` function basically does the same thing, but the syntax for it is different. Instead of appearing as a function argument, `str1` precedes the function name and is connected to it with a dot. As you saw with the `put()` method in Chapter 3, "Dealing with Data," this syntax indicates that `str1` is an object and that `size()` is a class method. A method is a function that can be invoked only by an object belonging to the same class as the method. In this particular case, `str1` is a `string` object, and `size()` is a `string` method. In short, the C functions use a function argument to identify which string to use, and the C++ `string` class objects use the object name and the dot operator to indicate which string to use.

More on `string` Class I/O

As you've seen, you can use `cin` with the `>>` operator to read a `string` object and `cout` with the `>>` operator to display a `string` object using the same syntax you use with a C-style string. But reading a line at a time instead of a word at time uses a different syntax. Listing 4.10 shows this difference.

LISTING 4.10 `strtype4.cpp`

```
// strtype4.cpp -- line input
#include <iostream>
#include <string>                 // make string class available
#include <cstring>                // C-style string library
int main()
{
    using namespace std;
```

LISTING 4.10   Continued

```
    char charr[20];
    string str;

    cout << "Length of string in charr before input: "
        << strlen(charr) << endl;
    cout << "Length of string in str before input: "
        << str.size() << endl;
    cout << "Enter a line of text:\n";
    cin.getline(charr, 20);     // indicate maximum length
    cout << "You entered: " << charr << endl;
    cout << "Enter another line of text:\n";
    getline(cin, str);          // cin now an argument; no length specifier
    cout << "You entered: " << str << endl;
    cout << "Length of string in charr after input: "
        << strlen(charr) << endl;
    cout << "Length of string in str after input: "
        << str.size() << endl;

    return 0;
}
```

Here's a sample run of the program in Listing 4.10:

```
Length of string in charr before input: 27
Length of string in str before input: 0
Enter a line of text:
peanut butter
You entered: peanut butter
Enter another line of text:
blueberry jam
You entered: blueberry jam
Length of string in charr after input: 13
Length of string in str after input: 13
```

Note that the program says the length of the string in the array `charr` before input is 27, which is larger than the size of the array! Two things are going on here. The first is that the contents of an uninitialized array are undefined. The second is that the `strlen()` function works by starting at the first element of the array and counting bytes until it reaches a null character. In this case, the first null character doesn't appear until several bytes *after* the end of the array. Where the first null character appears in uninitialized data is essentially random, so you very well could get a different numeric result using this program.

Also note that the length of the string in `str` before input is 0. That's because an uninitialized `string` object is automatically set to zero size.

This is the code for reading a line into an array:

```
cin.getline(charr, 20);
```

The dot notation indicates that the `getline()` function is a class method for the `istream` class. (Recall that `cin` is an `istream` object.) As mentioned earlier, the first argument indicates the destination array, and the second argument is the array size, which `getline()` used to avoid overrunning the array.

This is the code for reading a line into a `string` object:

```
getline(cin,str);
```

There is no dot notation, which indicates that *this* `getline()` is *not* a class method. So it takes `cin` as an argument that tells it where to find the input. Also, there isn't an argument for the size of the string because the `string` object automatically resizes to fit the string.

So why is one `getline()` an `istream` class method and the other `getline()` not? The `istream` class was part of C++ long before the `string` class was added. So the `istream` design recognizes basic C++ types such as `double` and `int`, but it is ignorant of the `string` type. Therefore, there are `istream` class methods for processing `double`, `int`, and the other basic types, but there are no `istream` class methods for processing `string` objects.

Because there are no `istream` class methods for processing string objects, you might wonder why code like this works:

```
cin >> str;  // read a word into the str string object
```

It turns out that code like this:

```
cin >> x;  // read a value into a basic C++ type
```

does (in disguised notation) use a member function of the `istream` class. But the `string` class equivalent uses a friend function (also in disguised notation) of the `string` class. You'll have to wait until Chapter 11 to see what a friend function is and how this technique works. In the meantime, you can use `cin` and `cout` with `string` objects and not worry about the inner workings.

Now let's go on to another compound type, the structure.

Introducing Structures

Suppose you want to store information about a basketball player. You might want to store his or her name, salary, height, weight, scoring average, free-throw percentage, assists, and so on. You'd like some sort of data form that could hold all this information in one unit. An array won't do. Although an array can hold several items, each item has to be the same type. That is, one array can hold 20 `int`s and another can hold 10 `float`s, but a single array can't store `int`s in some elements and `float`s in other elements.

The answer to your desire (the one about storing information about a basketball player) is the C++ structure. A *structure* is a more versatile data form than an array because a single structure can hold items of more than one data type. This enables you to unify your data representation by storing all the related basketball information in a single structure variable. If you want to keep track of a whole team, you can use an array of structures. The structure type is also a stepping stone to that bulwark of C++ OOP, the class. Learning a little about structures now takes you that much closer to the OOP heart of C++.

A structure is a user-definable type, with a structure declaration serving to define the type's data properties. After you define the type, you can create variables of that type. Thus, creating a structure is a two-part process. First, you define a structure description that describes and labels the different types of data that can be stored in a structure. Then, you can create structure variables, or, more generally, structure data objects, that follow the description's plan.

For example, suppose that Bloataire, Inc., wants to create a type to describe members of its product line of designer inflatables. In particular, the type should hold the name of the item, its volume in cubic feet, and its selling price. Here is a structure description that meets those needs:

```
struct inflatable    // structure declaration
{
    char name[20];
    float volume;
    double price;
};
```

The keyword `struct` indicates that the code defines the layout for a structure. The identifier `inflatable` is the name, or *tag*, for this form; this makes `inflatable` the name for the new type. Thus, you can now create variables of type `inflatable` just as you create variables of type `char` or `int`. Next, between braces are the list of data types to be held in the structure. Each list item is a declaration statement. You can use any of the C++ types here, including arrays and other structures. This example uses an array of `char`, which is suitable for storing a string, a `float`, and a `double`. Each individual item in the list is called a structure *member*, so the inflatable structure has three members. (See Figure 4.6.)

FIGURE 4.6

Parts of a structure description.

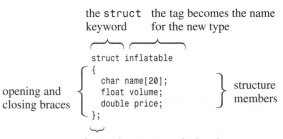

After you have the template, you can create variables of that type:

```
inflatable hat;              // hat is a structure variable of type inflatable
inflatable woopie_cushion;   // type inflatable variable
inflatable mainframe;        // type inflatable variable
```

If you're familiar with C structures, you'll notice (probably with pleasure) that C++ allows you to drop the keyword `struct` when you declare structure variables:

```
struct inflatable goose;     // keyword struct required in C
inflatable vincent;          // keyword struct not required in C++
```

In C++, the structure tag is used just like a fundamental type name. This change emphasizes that a structure declaration defines a new type. It also removes omitting `struct` from the list of curse-inducing errors.

Given that **hat** is type **inflatable**, you use the membership operator (.) to access individual members. For example, **hat.volume** refers to the **volume** member of the structure, and **hat.price** refers to the **price** member. Similarly, **vincent.price** is the **price** member of the **vincent** variable. In short, the member names enable you to access members of a structure much as indices enable you to access elements of an array. Because the **price** member is declared as type **double**, **hat.price** and **vincent.price** are both equivalent to type **double** variables and can be used in any manner an ordinary type **double** variable can be used. In short, **hat** is a structure, but **hat.price** is a **double**. By the way, the method used to access class member functions such as **cin.getline( )** has its origins in the method used to access structure member variables such as **vincent.price**.

Using a Structure in a Program

Now that we've covered some of the main features of structures, it's time to put the ideas together in a structure-using program. Listing 4.11 illustrates these points about a structure. Also, it shows how to initialize one.

LISTING 4.11   structur.cpp

```cpp
// structur.cpp -- a simple structure
#include <iostream>
struct inflatable    // structure declaration
{
    char name[20];
    float volume;
    double price;
};

int main()
{
    using namespace std;
    inflatable guest =
    {
        "Glorious Gloria",  // name value
        1.88,               // volume value
        29.99               // price value
    };  // guest is a structure variable of type inflatable
// It's initialized to the indicated values
    inflatable pal =
    {
        "Audacious Arthur",
        3.12,
        32.99
    };  // pal is a second variable of type inflatable
// NOTE: some implementations require using
// static inflatable guest =

    cout << "Expand your guest list with " << guest.name;
    cout << " and " << pal.name << "!\n";
// pal.name is the name member of the pal variable
    cout << "You can have both for $";
```

LISTING 4.11   Continued

```
        cout << guest.price + pal.price << "!\n";
        return 0;
}
```

Compatibility Note

Just as some older versions of C++ do not yet implement the capability to initialize an ordinary array defined in a function, they also do not implement the capability to initialize an ordinary structure defined in a function. Again, the solution is to use the keyword `static` in the declaration.

Here is the output from the program in Listing 4.11:

```
Expand your guest list with Glorious Gloria and Audacious Arthur!
You can have both for $62.98!
```

Program Notes

One important matter related to the program in Listing 4.11 is where to place the structure declaration. There are two choices for `structur.cpp`. You could place the declaration inside the `main()` function, just after the opening brace. The second choice, and the one made here, is to place it outside and preceding `main()`. When a declaration occurs outside any function, it's called an *external declaration*. For this program, there is no practical difference between the two choices. But for programs consisting of two or more functions, the difference can be crucial. The external declaration can be used by all the functions following it, whereas the internal declaration can be used only by the function in which the declaration is found. Most often, you want an external structure declaration so that all the functions can use structures of that type. (See Figure 4.7.)

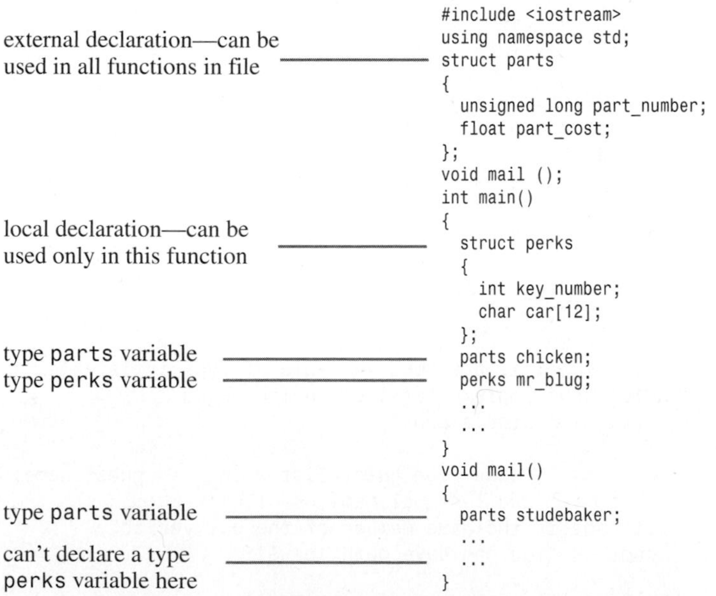

FIGURE 4.7

Local and external structure declarations.

external declaration—can be used in all functions in file

local declaration—can be used only in this function

type `parts` variable
type `perks` variable

type `parts` variable

can't declare a type `perks` variable here

```
#include <iostream>
using namespace std;
struct parts
{
    unsigned long part_number;
    float part_cost;
};
void mail ();
int main()
{
    struct perks
    {
        int key_number;
        char car[12];
    };
    parts chicken;
    perks mr_blug;
    ...
    ...
}
void mail()
{
    parts studebaker;
    ...
    ...
}
```

Variables, too, can be defined internally or externally, with external variables shared among functions. (Chapter 9 looks further into that topic.) C++ practices discourage the use of external variables but encourage the use of external structure declarations. Also, it often makes sense to declare symbolic constants externally.

Next, notice the initialization procedure:

```
inflatable guest =
{
    "Glorious Gloria",  // name value
    1.88,               // volume value
    29.99               // price value
};
```

As with arrays, you use a comma-separated list of values enclosed in a pair of braces. The program places one value per line, but you can place them all on the same line. Just remember to separate items with commas:

```
inflatable duck = {"Daphne", 0.12, 9.98};
```

You can initialize each member of the structure to the appropriate kind of data. For example, the `name` member is a character array, so you can initialize it to a string.

Each structure member is treated as a variable of that type. Thus, `pal.price` is a `double` variable and `pal.name` is an array of `char`. And when the program uses `cout` to display `pal.name`, it displays the member as a string. By the way, because `pal.name` is a character array, we can use subscripts to access individual characters in the array. For example, `pal.name[0]` is the character `A`. But `pal[0]` is meaningless because `pal` is a structure, not an array.

Can a Structure Use a `string` Class Member?

Can you use a `string` class object instead of a character array for the `name` member? That is, can you declare a structure like this:

```
#include <string>
struct inflatable    // structure template
{
    std::string name;
    float volume;
    double price;
};
```

In principle, the answer is yes. In practice, the answer depends on which compiler you use because some (including Borland C++ 5.5 and Microsoft Visual C++ prior to version 7.1) do not support initialization of structures with `string` class members.

If your compiler does support this usage, make sure that the structure definition has access to the `std` namespace. You can do this by moving the `using` directive so that it is above the structure definition. Alternatively, as shown previously, you can declare `name` as having type `std::string`.

Other Structure Properties

C++ makes user-defined types as similar as possible to built-in types. For example, you can pass structures as arguments to a function, and you can have a function use a structure as a return value. Also, you can use the assignment operator (=) to assign one structure to another of the same type. Doing so causes each member of one structure to be set to the value of the corresponding member in the other structure, even if the member is an array. This kind of assignment is called *memberwise assignment*. We'll defer passing and returning structures until we discuss functions in Chapter 7, "Functions: C++'s Programming Modules," but we can take a quick look at structure assignment now. Listing 4.12 provides an example.

LISTING 4.12   assgn_st.cpp

```cpp
// assgn_st.cpp -- assigning structures
#include <iostream>
struct inflatable
{
    char name[20];
    float volume;
    double price;
};
int main()
{
    using namespace std;
    inflatable bouquet =
    {
        "sunflowers",
        0.20,
        12.49
    };
    inflatable choice;
    cout << "bouquet: " << bouquet.name << " for $";
    cout << bouquet.price << endl;

    choice = bouquet;  // assign one structure to another
    cout << "choice: " << choice.name << " for $";
    cout << choice.price << endl;
    return 0;
}
```

Here's the output from the program in Listing 4.12:

```
bouquet: sunflowers for $12.49
choice: sunflowers for $12.49
```

As you can see, memberwise assignment is at work, for the members of the **choice** structure are assigned the same values stored in the **bouquet** structure.

You can combine the definition of a structure form with the creation of structure variables. To do so, you follow the closing brace with the variable name or names:

```
struct perks
{
    int key_number;
    char car[12];
} mr_smith, ms_jones;    // two perks variables
```

You even can initialize a variable you create in this fashion:

```
struct perks
{
    int key_number;
    char car[12];
} mr_glitz =
{
    7,              // value for mr_glitz.key_number member
    "Packard"       // value for mr_glitz.car member
};
```

However, keeping the structure definition separate from the variable declarations usually makes a program easier to read and follow.

Another thing you can do with structures is create a structure with no type name. You do this by omitting a tag name while simultaneously defining a structure form and a variable:

```
struct          // no tag
{
    int x;      // 2 members
    int y;
} position;     // a structure variable
```

This creates one structure variable called **position**. You can access its members with the membership operator, as in **position.x**, but there is no general name for the type. You can't subsequently create other variables of the same type. This book doesn't use that limited form of structure.

Aside from the fact that a C++ program can use the structure tag as a type name, C structures have all the features discussed so far for C++ structures. But C++ structures go further. Unlike C structures, for example, C++ structures can have member functions in addition to member variables. But these more advanced features most typically are used with classes rather than structures, so we'll discuss them when we cover classes, beginning with Chapter 10, "Objects and Classes."

Arrays of Structures

The **inflatable** structure contains an array (the **name** array). It's also possible to create arrays whose elements are structures. The technique is exactly the same as for creating arrays of the fundamental types. For example, to create an array of 100 **inflatable** structures, you could do the following:

```
inflatable gifts[100];  // array of 100 inflatable structures
```

This makes `gifts` an array of `inflatable`s. Hence each element of the array, such as `gifts[0]` or `gifts[99]`, is an `inflatable` object and can be used with the membership operator:

```
cin >> gifts[0].volume;          // use volume member of first struct
cout << gifts[99].price << endl; // display price member of last struct
```

Keep in mind that `gifts` itself is an array, not a structure, so constructions such as `gifts.price` are not valid.

To initialize an array of structures, you combine the rule for initializing arrays (a brace-enclosed, comma-separated list of values for each element) with the rule for structures (a brace-enclosed, comma-separated list of values for each member). Because each element of the array is a structure, its value is represented by a structure initialization. Thus, you wind up with a brace-enclosed, comma-separated list of values, each of which itself is a brace-enclosed, comma-separated list of values:

```
inflatable guests[2] =              // initializing an array of structs
    {
        {"Bambi", 0.5, 21.99},      // first structure in array
        {"Godzilla", 2000, 565.99}  // next structure in array
    };
```

As usual, you can format this the way you like. For example, both initializations can be on the same line, or each separate structure member initialization can get a line of its own.

Listing 4.13 shows a short example that uses an array of structures. Note that because `guests` is an array of `inflatable`, `guest[0]` is type `inflatable`, so you can use it with the dot operator to access a member of the `inflatable` structure.

LISTING 4.13 `arrstruc.cpp`

```
// arrstruc.cpp -- an array of structures
#include <iostream>
struct inflatable
{
    char name[20];
    float volume;
    double price;
};
int main()
{
    using namespace std;
    inflatable guests[2] =              // initializing an array of structs
    {
        {"Bambi", 0.5, 21.99},      // first structure in array
        {"Godzilla", 2000, 565.99}  // next structure in array
    };

    cout << "The guests " << guests[0].name << " and " << guests[1].name
         << "\nhave a combined volume of "
         << guests[0].volume + guests[1].volume << " cubic feet.\n";
    return 0;
}
```

Here is the output of the program in Listing 4.13:

```
The guests Bambi and Godzilla
have a combined volume of 2000.5 cubic feet.
```

Bit Fields in Structures

C++, like C, enables you to specify structure members that occupy a particular number of bits. This can be handy for creating a data structure that corresponds, say, to a register on some hardware device. The field type should be an integral or enumeration type (enumerations are discussed later in this chapter), and a colon followed by a number indicates the actual number of bits to be used. You can use unnamed fields to provide spacing. Each member is termed a *bit field*. Here's an example:

```
struct torgle_register
{
    unsigned int SN : 4;    // 4 bits for SN value
    unsigned int : 4;       // 4 bits unused
    bool goodIn : 1;        // valid input (1 bit)
    bool goodTorgle : 1;    // successful torgling
};
```

You can initialize the fields in the usual manner, and you use standard structure notation to access bit fields:

```
torgle_register tr = { 14, true, false };
...
if (tr.goodIn)    // if statement covered in Chapter 6
...
```

Bit fields are typically used in low-level programming. Often, using an integral type and the bitwise operators listed in Appendix E, "Other Operators," provides an alternative approach.

Unions

A *union* is a data format that can hold different data types but only one type at a time. That is, whereas a structure can hold, say, an **int** *and* a **long** *and* a **double**, a union can hold an **int** *or* a **long** *or* a **double**. The syntax is like that for a structure, but the meaning is different. For example, consider the following declaration:

```
union one4all
{
    int int_val;
    long long_val;
    double double_val;
};
```

You can use a **one4all** variable to hold an **int**, a **long**, or a **double**, just as long as you do so at different times:

```
one4all pail;
pail.int_val = 15;        // store an int
cout << pail.int_val;
pail.double_val = 1.38;   // store a double, int value is lost
cout << pail.double_val;
```

Thus, `pail` can serve as an `int` variable on one occasion and as a `double` variable at another time. The member name identifies the capacity in which the variable is acting. Because a union holds only one value at a time, it has to have space enough to hold its largest member. Hence, the size of the union is the size of its largest member.

One use for a union is to save space when a data item can use two or more formats but never simultaneously. For example, suppose you manage a mixed inventory of widgets, some of which have an integer ID, and some of which have a string ID. In that case, you could use the following:

```
struct widget
{
char brand[20];
int type;
union id                 // format depends on widget type
{
    long id_num;         // type 1 widgets
    char id_char[20];    // other widgets
} id_val;
};
...
widget prize;
...
if (prize.type == 1)                 // if-else statement (Chapter 6)
    cin >> prize.id_val.id_num;      // use member name to indicate mode
else
    cin >> prize.id_val.id_char;
```

An *anonymous union* has no name; in essence, its members become variables that share the same address. Naturally, only one member can be current at a time:

```
struct widget
{
    char brand[20];
    int type;
    union                    // anonymous union
    {
        long id_num;         // type 1 widgets
        char id_char[20];    // other widgets
    };
};
...
widget prize;
...
if (prize.type == 1)
    cin >> prize.id_num;
else
    cin >> prize.id_char;
```

Because the union is anonymous, `id_num` and `id_char` are treated as two members of `prize` that share the same address. The need for an intermediate identifier *id_val* is eliminated. It is up to the programmer to keep track of which choice is active.

Enumerations

The C++ `enum` facility provides an alternative to `const` for creating symbolic constants. It also lets you define new types but in a fairly restricted fashion. The syntax for `enum` resembles structure syntax. For example, consider the following statement:

```
enum spectrum {red, orange, yellow, green, blue, violet, indigo, ultraviolet};
```

This statement does two things:

- It makes `spectrum` the name of a new type; `spectrum` is termed an *enumeration*, much as a `struct` variable is called a structure.

- It establishes `red`, `orange`, `yellow`, and so on, as symbolic constants for the integer values 0–7. These constants are called *enumerators*.

By default, enumerators are assigned integer values starting with 0 for the first enumerator, 1 for the second enumerator, and so forth. You can override the default by explicitly assigning integer values. You'll see how later in this chapter.

You can use an enumeration name to declare a variable of the enumeration type:

```
spectrum band;  // band a variable of type spectrum
```

An enumeration variable has some special properties, which we'll examine now.

The only valid values that you can assign to an enumeration variable without a type cast are the enumerator values used in defining the type. Thus, we have the following:

```
band = blue;       // valid, blue is an enumerator
band = 2000;       // invalid, 2000 not an enumerator
```

Thus, a `spectrum` variable is limited to just eight possible values. Some compilers issue a compiler error if you attempt to assign an invalid value, whereas others issue a warning. For maximum portability, you should regard assigning a non-`enum` value to an `enum` variable as an error.

Only the assignment operator is defined for enumerations. In particular, arithmetic operations are not defined:

```
band = orange;          // valid
++band;                 // not valid, ++ discussed in Chapter 5
band = orange + red;    // not valid, but a little tricky
...
```

However, some implementations do not honor this restriction. That can make it possible to violate the type limits. For example, if `band` has the value `ultraviolet`, or 7, then `++band`, if valid, increments `band` to `8`, which is not a valid value for a `spectrum` type. Again, for maximum portability, you should adopt the stricter limitations.

Enumerators are of integer type and can be promoted to type `int`, but `int` types are not converted automatically to the enumeration type:

```
int color = blue;         // valid, spectrum type promoted to int
band = 3;                 // invalid, int not converted to spectrum
color = 3 + red;          // valid, red converted to int
...
```

Note that in this example, even though `3` corresponds to the enumerator `green`, assigning `3` to `band` is a type error. But assigning `green` to `band` is fine because they are both type `spectrum`. Again, some implementations do not enforce this restriction. In the expression `3 + red`, addition isn't defined for enumerators. However, `red` is converted to type `int`, and the result is type `int`. Because of the conversion from enumeration to `int` in this situation, you can use enumerations in arithmetic expressions to combine them with ordinary integers, even though arithmetic isn't defined for enumerations themselves.

The earlier example

```
band = orange + red;      // not valid, but a little tricky
```

fails for a somewhat involved reason. It is true that the `+` operator is not defined for enumerators. But it is also true that enumerators are converted to integers when used in arithmetic expressions, so the expression `orange + red` gets converted to `1 + 0`, which is a valid expression. But it is of type `int` and hence cannot be assigned to the type `spectrum` variable `band`.

You can assign an `int` value to an `enum`, provided that the value is valid and that you use an explicit type cast:

```
band = spectrum(3);            // typecast 3 to type spectrum
```

What if you try to type cast an inappropriate value? The result is undefined, meaning that the attempt won't be flagged as an error but that you can't rely on the value of the result:

```
band = spectrum(40003);    // undefined
```

(See the section "Value Ranges for Enumerations," later in this chapter, for a discussion of what values are and are not appropriate.)

As you can see, the rules governing enumerations are fairly restrictive. In practice, enumerations are used more often as a way of defining related symbolic constants than as a means of defining new types. For example, you might use an enumeration to define symbolic constants for a `switch` statement. (See Chapter 6 for an example.) If you plan to use just the constants and not create variables of the enumeration type, you can omit an enumeration type name, as in this example:

```
enum {red, orange, yellow, green, blue, violet, indigo, ultraviolet};
```

Setting Enumerator Values

You can set enumerator values explicitly by using the assignment operator:

```
enum bits{one = 1, two = 2, four = 4, eight = 8};
```

The assigned values must be integers. You also can define just some of the enumerators explicitly:

```
enum bigstep{first, second = 100, third};
```

In this case, `first` is `0` by default. Subsequent uninitialized enumerators are larger by one than their predecessors. So, `third` would have the value `101`.

Finally, you can create more than one enumerator with the same value:

```
enum {zero, null = 0, one, numero_uno = 1};
```

Here, both `zero` and `null` are `0`, and both `one` and `numero_uno` are `1`. In earlier versions of C++, you could assign only `int` values (or values that promote to `int`) to enumerators, but that restriction has been removed so that you can use type `long` values.

Value Ranges for Enumerations

Originally, the only valid values for an enumeration were those named in the declaration. However, C++ has expanded the list of valid values that can be assigned to an enumeration variable through the use of a type cast. Each enumeration has a *range*, and you can assign any integer value in the range, even if it's not an enumerator value, by using a type cast to an enumeration variable. For example, suppose that `bits` and `myflag` are defined this way:

```
enum bits{one = 1, two = 2, four = 4, eight = 8};
bits myflag;
```

In this case, the following is valid:

```
myflag = bits(6);    // valid, because 6 is in bits range
```

Here `6` is not one of the enumerations, but it lies in the range the enumerations define.

The range is defined as follows. First, to find the upper limit, you take the largest enumerator value. Then you find the smallest power of two greater than this largest value and subtract one; the result is the upper end of the range. (For example, the largest `bigstep` value, as previously defined, is 101. The smallest power of two greater than this is 128, so the upper end of the range is 127.) Next, to find the lower limit, you find the smallest enumerator value. If it is 0 or greater, the lower limit for the range is 0. If the smallest enumerator is negative, you use the same approach as for finding the upper limit but toss in a minus sign. (For example, if the smallest enumerator is -6, the next power of two [times a minus sign] is -8, and the lower limit is -7.)

The idea is that the compiler can choose how much space to use to hold an enumeration. It might use 1 byte or less for an enumeration with a small range and 4 bytes for an enumeration with type `long` values.

Pointers and the Free Store

The beginning of Chapter 3 mentions three fundamental properties of which a computer program must keep track when it stores data. To save the book the wear and tear of your thumbing back to that chapter, here are those properties again:

- Where the information is stored

- What value is kept there

- What kind of information is stored

You've used one strategy for accomplishing these ends: defining a simple variable. The declaration statement provides the type and a symbolic name for the value. It also causes the program to allocate memory for the value and to keep track of the location internally.

Let's look at a second strategy now, one that becomes particularly important in developing C++ classes. This strategy is based on pointers, which are variables that store addresses of values rather than the values themselves. But before discussing pointers, let's talk about how to explicitly find addresses for ordinary variables. You just apply the address operator, represented by **&**, to a variable to get its location; for example, if **home** is a variable, **&home** is its address. Listing 4.14 demonstrates this operator.

LISTING 4.14 `address.cpp`

```cpp
// address.cpp -- using the & operator to find addresses
#include <iostream>
int main()
{
    using namespace std;
    int donuts = 6;
    double cups = 4.5;

    cout << "donuts value = " << donuts;
    cout << " and donuts address = " << &donuts << endl;
// NOTE: you may need to use unsigned (&donuts)
// and unsigned (&cups)
    cout << "cups value = " << cups;
    cout << " and cups address = " << &cups << endl;
    return 0;
}
```

Compatibility Note

cout is a smart object, but some versions are smarter than others. Thus, some implementations might not be up to the requirement of the C++ Standard and fail to recognize pointer types. In that case, you have to type cast the address to a recognizable type, such as unsigned int. The appropriate type cast depends on the memory model. The default DOS memory model uses a 2-byte address, hence unsigned int is the proper cast. Some DOS memory models, however, use a 4-byte address, which requires a cast to unsigned long.

Here is the output from the program in Listing 4.14 on one system:

```
donuts value = 6 and donuts address = 0x0065fd40
cups value = 4.5 and cups address = 0x0065fd44
```

The particular implementation of `cout` shown here uses hexadecimal notation when display-ing address values because that is the usual notation used to specify a memory address. (Some implementations use base 10 notation instead.) Our implementation stores `donuts` at a lower memory location than `cups`. The difference between the two addresses is 0x0065fd44 – 0x0065fd40, or 4. This makes sense because `donuts` is type `int`, which uses 4 bytes. Different systems, of course, will give different values for the address. Also, some may store `cups` first, then `donuts`, giving a difference of 8 bytes because `cups` is `double`. And some may not even use adjacent locations.

Using ordinary variables, then, treats the value as a named quantity and the location as a derived quantity. Now let's look at the pointer strategy, one that is essential to the C++ pro-gramming philosophy of memory management. (See the following sidebar, "Pointers and the C++ Philosophy.")

Pointers and the C++ Philosophy

Object-oriented programming differs from traditional procedural programming in that OOP empha-sizes making decisions during runtime instead of during compile time. *Runtime* means while a pro-gram is running, and *compile time* means when the compiler is putting a program together. A runtime decision is like, when on vacation, choosing what sights to see depending on the weather and your mood at the moment, whereas a compile-time decision is more like adhering to a preset schedule, regardless of the conditions.

Runtime decisions provide the flexibility to adjust to current circumstances. For example, consider allocating memory for an array. The traditional way is to declare an array. To declare an array in C++, you have to commit yourself to a particular array size. Thus, the array size is set when the program is compiled; it is a compile-time decision. Perhaps you think an array of 20 elements is sufficient 80% of the time but that occasionally the program will need to handle 200 elements. To be safe, you use an array with 200 elements. This results in your program wasting memory most of the time it's used. OOP tries to make a program more flexible by delaying such decisions until runtime. That way, after the program is running, you can tell it you need only 20 elements one time or that you need 205 elements another time.

In short, with OOP you would like to make the array size a runtime decision. To make this approach possible, the language has to allow you to create an array—or the equivalent—while the program runs. The C++ method, as you soon see, involves using the keyword `new` to request the correct amount of memory and using pointers to keep track of where the newly allocated memory is found.

The new strategy for handling stored data switches things around by treating the location as the named quantity and the value as a derived quantity. A special type of variable—the *pointer*—holds the address of a value. Thus, the name of the pointer represents the location. Applying the `*` operator, called the *indirect value* or the *dereferencing* operator, yields the value at the location. (Yes, this is the same `*` symbol used for multiplication; C++ uses the context to determine whether you mean multiplication or dereferencing.) Suppose, for example, that `manly` is a pointer. In that case, `manly` represents an address, and `*manly` represents the value at that address. The combination `*manly` becomes equivalent to an ordinary type `int` variable. Listing 4.15 demonstrates these ideas. It also shows how to declare a pointer.

LISTING 4.15   `pointer.cpp`

```
// pointer.cpp -- our first pointer variable
#include <iostream>
int main()
{
    using namespace std;
    int updates = 6;        // declare a variable
    int * p_updates;        // declare pointer to an int

    p_updates = &updates;   // assign address of int to pointer

// express values two ways
    cout << "Values: updates = " << updates;
    cout << ", *p_updates = " << *p_updates << endl;

// express address two ways
    cout << "Addresses: &updates = " << &updates;
    cout << ", p_updates = " << p_updates << endl;

// use pointer to change value
    *p_updates = *p_updates + 1;
    cout << "Now updates = " << updates << endl;
    return 0;
}
```

Here is the output from the program in Listing 4.15:

```
Values: updates = 6, *p_updates = 6
Addresses: &updates = 0x0065fd48, p_updates = 0x0065fd48
Now updates = 7
```

As you can see, the `int` variable `updates` and the pointer variable `p_updates` are just two sides of the same coin. The `updates` variable represents the value as primary and uses the `&` operator to get the address, whereas the `p_updates` variable represents the address as primary and uses the `*` operator to get the value. (See Figure 4.8.) Because `p_updates` points to `updates`, `*p_updates` and `updates` are completely equivalent. You can use `*p_updates` exactly as you would use a type `int` variable. As the program in Listing 4.15 shows, you can even assign values to `*p_updates`. Doing so changes the value of the pointed-to value, `updates`.

FIGURE 4.8

Two sides of a coin.

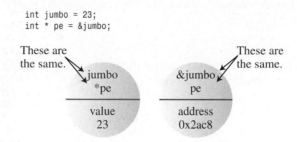

Declaring and Initializing Pointers

Let's examine the process of declaring pointers. A computer needs to keep track of the type of value to which a pointer refers. For example, the address of a `char` typically looks the same as the address of a `double`, but `char` and `double` use different numbers of bytes and different internal formats for storing values. Therefore, a pointer declaration must specify what type of data to which the pointer points.

For example, the preceding example has this declaration:

```
int * p_updates;
```

This states that the combination `* p_updates` is type `int`. Because you use the `*` operator by applying it to a pointer, the `p_updates` variable itself must *be* a pointer. We say that `p_updates` points to type `int`. We also say that the type for `p_updates` is pointer-to-`int` or, more concisely, `int *`. To repeat: `p_updates` is a pointer (an address), and `*p_updates` is an `int` and not a pointer. (See Figure 4.9.)

FIGURE 4.9

Pointers store addresses.

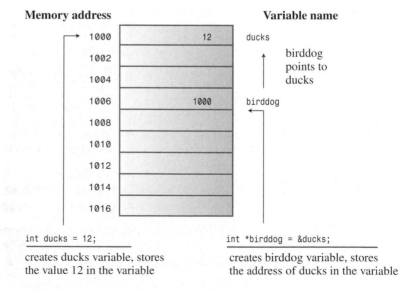

Incidentally, the use of spaces around the * operator are optional. Traditionally, C programmers have used this form:

```
int *ptr;
```

This accentuates the idea that the combination *ptr is a type int value. Many C++ programmers, on the other hand, use this form:

```
int* ptr;
```

This emphasizes the idea that int* is a type, pointer-to-int. Where you put the spaces makes no difference to the compiler. Be aware, however, that this declaration:

```
int* p1, p2;
```

creates one pointer (p1) and one ordinary int (p2). You need an * for each pointer variable name.

Remember

In C++, the combination int * is a compound type, pointer-to-int.

You use the same syntax to declare pointers to other types:

```
double * tax_ptr; // tax_ptr points to type double
char * str;       // str points to type char
```

Because you declare tax_ptr as a pointer-to-double, the compiler knows that *tax_ptr is a type double value. That is, it knows that *tax_ptr represents a number stored in floating-point format that occupies (on most systems) 8 bytes. A pointer variable is never simply a pointer. It is always a pointer to a specific type. tax_ptr is type pointer-to-double (or type double *) and str is type pointer-to-char (or char *). Although both are pointers, they are pointers of two different types. Like arrays, pointers are based on other types.

Note that whereas tax_ptr and str point to data types of two different sizes, the two variables tax_ptr and str themselves are typically the same size. That is, the address of a char is the same size as the address of a double, much as 1016 might be the street address for a department store, whereas 1024 could be the street address of a small cottage. The size or value of an address doesn't really tell you anything about the size or kind of variable or building you find at that address. Usually, addresses require 2 or 4 bytes, depending on the computer system. (Some systems might have larger addresses, and a system can use different address sizes for different types.)

You can use a declaration statement to initialize a pointer. In that case, the pointer, not the pointed-to value, is initialized. That is, the statements

```
int higgens = 5;
int * pt = &higgens;
```

set pt and not *pt to the value &higgens.

Listing 4.16 demonstrates how to initialize a pointer to an address.

LISTING 4.16   `init_ptr.cpp`

```cpp
// init_ptr.cpp -- initialize a pointer
#include <iostream>
int main()
{
    using namespace std;
    int higgens = 5;
    int * pt = &higgens;

    cout << "Value of higgens = " << higgens
         << "; Address of higgens = " << &higgens << endl;
    cout << "Value of *pt = " << *pt
         << "; Value of pt = " << pt << endl;
    return 0;
}
```

Here is the output from the program in Listing 4.16:

```
Value of higgens = 5; Address of higgens = 0012FED4
Value of *pt = 5; Value of pt = 0012FED4
```

You can see that the program initializes `pt`, not `*pt`, to the address of `higgens`.

Pointer Danger

Danger awaits those who incautiously use pointers. One extremely important point is that when you create a pointer in C++, the computer allocates memory to hold an address, but it does not allocate memory to hold the data to which the address points. Creating space for the data involves a separate step. Omitting that step, as in the following, is an invitation to disaster:

```cpp
long * fellow;        // create a pointer-to-long
*fellow = 223323;     // place a value in never-never land
```

Sure, `fellow` is a pointer. But where does it point? The code failed to assign an address to `fellow`. So where is the value `223323` placed? We can't say. Because `fellow` wasn't initialized, it could have any value. Whatever that value is, the program interprets it as the address at which to store `223323`. If `fellow` happens to have the value `1200`, then the computer attempts to place the data at address `1200`, even if that happens to be an address in the middle of your program code. Chances are that wherever `fellow` points, that is not where you want to put the number `223323`. This kind of error can produce some of the most insidious and hard-to-trace bugs.

Caution

Pointer Golden Rule: *Always* initialize a pointer to a definite and appropriate address before you apply the dereferencing operator (*) to it.

Pointers and Numbers

Pointers are not integer types, even though computers typically handle addresses as integers. Conceptually, pointers are distinct types from integers. Integers are numbers you can add, subtract, divide, and so on. But a pointer describes a location, and it doesn't make sense, for example, to multiply two locations by each other. In terms of the operations you can perform with them, pointers and integers are different from each other. Consequently, you can't simply assign an integer to a pointer:

```
int * pt;
pt = 0xB8000000;   // type mismatch
```

Here, the left side is a pointer to `int`, so you can assign it an address, but the right side is just an integer. You might know that 0xB8000000 is the combined segment-offset address of video memory on your system, but nothing in the statement tells the program that this number is an address. C prior to C99 lets you make assignments like this. But C++ more stringently enforces type agreement, and the compiler will give you an error message saying you have a type mismatch. If you want to use a numeric value as an address, you should use a type cast to convert the number to the appropriate address type:

```
int * pt;
pt = (int *) 0xB8000000; // types now match
```

Now both sides of the assignment statement represent addresses of integers, so the assignment is valid. Note that just because it is the address of a type `int` value doesn't mean that `pi` itself is type `int`. For example, in the large memory model on an IBM PC using DOS, type `int` is a 2-byte value, whereas the addresses are 4-byte values.

Pointers have some other interesting properties that we'll discuss as they become relevant. Meanwhile, let's look at how pointers can be used to manage runtime allocation of memory space.

Allocating Memory with `new`

Now that you have a feel for how pointers work, let's see how they can implement that important OOP technique of allocating memory as a program runs. So far, you've initialized pointers to the addresses of variables; the variables are *named* memory allocated during compile time, and each pointers merely provides an alias for memory you could access directly by name anyway. The true worth of pointers comes into play when you allocate *unnamed* memory during runtime to hold values. In this case, pointers become the only access to that memory. In C, you can allocate memory with the library function `malloc()`. You can still do so in C++, but C++ also has a better way: the `new` operator.

Let's try out this new technique by creating unnamed runtime storage for a type `int` value and accessing the value with a pointer. The key is the C++ `new` operator. You tell `new` for what data type you want memory; `new` finds a block of the correct size and returns the address of the block. You assign this address to a pointer, and you're in business. Here's an example of the technique:

```
int * pn = new int;
```

The `new int` part tells the program you want some `new` storage suitable for holding an `int`. The `new` operator uses the type to figure out how many bytes are needed. Then it finds the memory and returns the address. Next, you assign the address to `pn`, which is declared to be of type pointer-to-`int`. Now `pn` is the address and `*pn` is the value stored there. Compare this with assigning the address of a variable to a pointer:

```
int higgens;
int * pt = &higgens;
```

In both cases (`pn` and `pt`), you assign the address of an `int` to a pointer. In the second case, you can also access the `int` by name: `higgens`. In the first case, your only access is via the pointer. That raises a question: Because the memory to which `pn` points lacks a name, what do you call it? We say that `pn` points to a *data object*. This is not "object" in the sense of "object-oriented programming"; it's just "object" in the sense of "thing." The term "data object" is more general than the term "variable" because it means any block of memory allocated for a data item. Thus, a variable is also a data object, but the memory to which `pn` points is not a variable. The pointer method for handling data objects may seem more awkward at first, but it offers greater control over how your program manages memory.

The general form for obtaining and assigning memory for a single data object, which can be a structure as well as a fundamental type, is this:

```
typeName pointer_name = new typeName;
```

You use the data type twice: once to specify the kind of memory requested and once to declare a suitable pointer. Of course, if you've already declared a pointer of the correct type, you can use it rather than declare a new one. Listing 4.17 illustrates using `new` with two different types.

LISTING 4.17   `use_new.cpp`

```cpp
// use_new.cpp -- using the new operator
#include <iostream>
int main()
{
    using namespace std;
    int * pt = new int;         // allocate space for an int
    *pt = 1001;                 // store a value there

    cout << "int ";
    cout << "value = " << *pt << ": location = " << pt << endl;

    double * pd = new double;   // allocate space for a double
    *pd = 10000001.0;           // store a double there

    cout << "double ";
    cout << "value = " << *pd << ": location = " << pd << endl;
    cout << "size of pt = " << sizeof(pt);
    cout << ": size of *pt = " << sizeof(*pt) << endl;
    cout << "size of pd = " << sizeof pd;
    cout << ": size of *pd = " << sizeof(*pd) << endl;
    return 0;
}
```

Here is the output from the program in Listing 4.17:

```
int value = 1001: location = 0x004301a8
double value = 1e+07: location = 0x004301d8
size of pt = 4: size of *pt = 4
size of pd = 4: size of *pd = 8
```

Of course, the exact values for the memory locations differ from system to system.

Program Notes

The program in Listing 4.17 uses `new` to allocate memory for the type `int` and type `double` data objects. This occurs while the program is running. The pointers `pt` and `pd` point to these two data objects. Without them, you cannot access those memory locations. With them, you can use `*pt` and `*pd` just as you would use variables. You assign values to `*pt` and `*pd` to assign values to the new data objects. Similarly, you print `*pt` and `*pd` to display those values.

The program in Listing 4.17 also demonstrates one of the reasons you have to declare the type a pointer points to. An address in itself reveals only the beginning address of the object stored, not its type or the number of bytes used. Look at the addresses of the two values. They are just numbers with no type or size information. Also, note that the size of a pointer-to-`int` is the same as the size of a pointer-to-`double`. Both are just addresses. But because `use_new.cpp` declares the pointer types, the program knows that `*pd` is a `double` value of 8 bytes, whereas `*pt` is an `int` value of 4 bytes. When `use_new.cpp` prints the value of `*pd`, `cout` can tell how many bytes to read and how to interpret them.

Out of Memory?

It's possible that a computer might not have sufficient memory available to satisfy a `new` request. When that is the case, `new` returns the value `0`. In C++, a pointer with the value `0` is called the *null pointer*. C++ guarantees that the null pointer never points to valid data, so it is often used to indicate failure for operators or functions that otherwise return usable pointers. After you learn about `if` statements in Chapter 6, you can check to see if `new` returns the null pointer and thus protects your program from attempting to exceed its bounds. In addition to returning the null pointer upon failure to allocate memory, `new` might throw a `bad_alloc` exception. Chapter 15, "Friends, Exceptions, and More," discusses the exception mechanism.

Freeing Memory with `delete`

Using `new` to request memory when you need it is just the more glamorous half of the C++ memory-management package. The other half is the `delete` operator, which enables you to return memory to the memory pool when you are finished with it. That is an important step toward making the most effective use of memory. Memory that you return, or *free*, can then be reused by other parts of the program. You use `delete` by following it with a pointer to a block of memory originally allocated with `new`:

```
int * ps = new int; // allocate memory with new
   . . .              // use the memory
delete ps;           // free memory with delete when done
```

This removes the memory to which ps points; it doesn't remove the pointer ps itself. You can reuse ps, for example, to point to another new allocation. You should always balance a use of new with a use of delete; otherwise, you can wind up with a *memory leak*—that is, memory that has been allocated but can no longer be used. If a memory leak grows too large, it can bring a program seeking more memory to a halt.

You should not attempt to free a block of memory that you have previously freed. The C++ Standard says the result of such an attempt is undefined, meaning that the consequences could be anything. Also, you cannot use delete to free memory created by declaring ordinary variables:

```
int * ps = new int;     // ok
delete ps;              // ok
delete ps;              // not ok now
int jugs = 5;           // ok
int * pi = &jugs;       // ok
delete pi;              // not allowed, memory not allocated by new
```

Caution
You should use delete only to free memory allocated with new. However, it is safe to apply delete to a null pointer.

Note that the critical requirement for using delete is to use it with memory allocated by new. This doesn't mean you have to use the same pointer you used with new; instead, you have to use the same address:

```
int * ps = new int;     // allocate memory
int * pq = ps;          // set second pointer to same block
delete pq;              // delete with second pointer
```

Ordinarily, you won't create two pointers to the same block of memory because that raises the possibility that you will mistakenly try to delete the same block twice. But, as you'll soon see, using a second pointer does make sense when you work with a function that returns a pointer.

Using new to Create Dynamic Arrays

If all a program needs is a single value, you might as well declare a simple variable, for that is simpler, if less impressive, than using new and a pointer to manage a single small data object. More typically, you use new with larger chunks of data, such as arrays, strings, and structures. This is where new is useful. Suppose, for example, you're writing a program that might or might not need an array, depending on information given to the program while it is running. If you create an array by declaring it, the space is allocated when the program is compiled. Whether or not the program finally uses the array, the array is there, using up memory. Allocating the array during compile time is called *static binding*, meaning that the array is built in to the program at compile time. But with new, you can create an array during runtime if you need it and skip creating the array if you don't need it. Or you can select an array size after the program is running. This is called *dynamic binding*, meaning that the array is created while the program is running. Such an array is called a *dynamic array*. With static binding, you must specify the array size when you write the program. With dynamic binding, the program can decide on an array size while the program runs.

For now, we'll look at two basic matters concerning dynamic arrays: how to use C++'s `new` operator to create an array and how to use a pointer to access array elements.

Creating a Dynamic Array with `new`

It's easy to create a dynamic array in C++; you tell `new` the type of array element and number of elements you want. The syntax requires that you follow the type name with the number of elements, in brackets. For example, if you need an array of 10 `int`s, you use this:

```
int * psome = new int [10]; // get a block of 10 ints
```

The `new` operator returns the address of the first element of the block. In this example, that value is assigned to the pointer `psome`. You should balance the call to `new` with a call to `delete` when the program finishes using that block of memory.

When you use `new` to create an array, you should use an alternative form of `delete` which indicates that you are freeing an array:

```
delete [] psome;                // free a dynamic array
```

The presence of the brackets tells the program that it should free the whole array, not just the element pointed to by the pointer. Note that the brackets are between `delete` and the pointer. If you use `new` without brackets, you should use `delete` without brackets. If you use `new` with brackets, you should use `delete` with brackets. Earlier versions of C++ might not recognize the bracket notation. For the ANSI/ISO Standard, however, the effect of mismatching `new` and `delete` forms is undefined, meaning that you can't rely on some particular behavior. Here's an example:

```
int * pt = new int;
short * ps = new short [500];
delete [] pt;  // effect is undefined, don't do it
delete ps;     // effect is undefined, don't do it
```

In short, you should observe these rules when you use `new` and `delete`:

- Don't use `delete` to free memory that `new` didn't allocate.
- Don't use `delete` to free the same block of memory twice in succession.
- Use `delete []` if you used `new []` to allocate an array.
- Use `delete` (no brackets) if you used `new` to allocate a single entity.
- It's safe to apply `delete` to the null pointer (nothing happens).

Now let's return to the dynamic array. Note that `psome` is a pointer to a single `int`, the first element of the block. It's your responsibility to keep track of how many elements are in the block. That is, because the compiler doesn't keep track of the fact that `psome` points to the first of 10 integers, you have to write your program so that it keeps track of the number of elements.

Actually, the program does keep track of the amount of memory allocated so that it can be correctly freed at a later time when you use the `delete [ ]` operator. But that information isn't publicly available; you can't use the `sizeof` operator, for example, to find the number of bytes in a dynamically allocated array.

The general form for allocating and assigning memory for an array is this:

```
type_name pointer_name = new type_name [num_elements];
```

Invoking the `new` operator secures a block of memory large enough to hold *num_elements* elements of type *type_name*, with *pointer_name* pointing to the first element. As you're about to see, you can use *pointer_name* in many of the same ways you can use an array name.

Using a Dynamic Array

After you create a dynamic array, how do you use it? First, think about the problem conceptually. The statement

```
int * psome = new int [10]; // get a block of 10 ints
```

creates a pointer `psome` that points to the first element of a block of 10 `int` values. Think of it as a finger pointing to that element. Suppose an `int` occupies 4 bytes. Then, by moving your finger 4 bytes in the correct direction, you can point to the second element. Altogether, there are 10 elements, which is the range over which you can move your finger. Thus, the `new` statement supplies you with all the information you need to identify every element in the block.

Now think about the problem practically. How do you access one of these elements? The first element is no problem. Because `psome` points to the first element of the array, `*psome` is the value of the first element. That leaves 9 more elements to access. The simplest way to access the elements may surprise you if you haven't worked with C: Just use the pointer as if it were an array name. That is, you can use `psome[0]` instead of `*psome` for the first element, `psome[1]` for the second element, and so on. It turns out to be very simple to use a pointer to access a dynamic array, even if it may not immediately be obvious why the method works. The reason you can do this is that C and C++ handle arrays internally by using pointers anyway. This near equivalence of arrays and pointers is one of the beauties of C and C++. You'll learn more about this equivalence in a moment. First, Listing 4.18 shows how you can use `new` to create a dynamic array and then use array notation to access the elements. It also points out a fundamental difference between a pointer and a true array name.

LISTING 4.18   `arraynew.cpp`.

```
// arraynew.cpp -- using the new operator for arrays
#include <iostream>
int main()
{
    using namespace std;
    double * p3 = new double [3]; // space for 3 doubles
    p3[0] = 0.2;                   // treat p3 like an array name
    p3[1] = 0.5;
    p3[2] = 0.8;
```

LISTING 4.18   Continued

```
    cout << "p3[1] is " << p3[1] << ".\n";
    p3 = p3 + 1;                    // increment the pointer
    cout << "Now p3[0] is " << p3[0] << " and ";
    cout << "p3[1] is " << p3[1] << ".\n";
    p3 = p3 - 1;                    // point back to beginning
    delete [] p3;                   // free the memory
    return 0;
}
```

Here is the output from the program in Listing 4.18:

```
p3[1] is 0.5.
Now p3[0] is 0.5 and p3[1] is 0.8.
```

As you can see, `arraynew.cpp` uses the pointer `p3` as if it were the name of an array, with `p3[0]` as the first element, and so on. The fundamental difference between an array name and a pointer appears in the following line:

```
p3 = p3 + 1; // okay for pointers, wrong for array names
```

You can't change the value of an array name. But a pointer is a variable, hence you can change its value. Note the effect of adding 1 to `p3`. The expression `p3[0]` now refers to the former second element of the array. Thus, adding 1 to `p3` causes it to point to the second element instead of the first. Subtracting one takes the pointer back to its original value so that the program can provide `delete []` with the correct address.

The actual addresses of consecutive `int`s typically differ by 2 or 4 bytes, so the fact that adding 1 to `p3` gives the address of the next element suggests that there is something special about pointer arithmetic. There is.

Pointers, Arrays, and Pointer Arithmetic

The near equivalence of pointers and array names stems from *pointer arithmetic* and how C++ handles arrays internally. First, let's check out the arithmetic. Adding one to an integer variable increases its value by one, but adding one to a pointer variable increases its value by the number of bytes of the type to which it points. Adding one to a pointer to `double` adds 8 to the numeric value on systems with 8-byte `double`, whereas adding one to a pointer-to-`short` adds two to the pointer value if `short` is 2 bytes. Listing 4.19 demonstrates this amazing point. It also shows a second important point: C++ interprets the array name as an address.

LISTING 4.19   `addpntrs.cpp`

```
// addpntrs.cpp -- pointer addition
#include <iostream>
int main()
{
```

LISTING 4.19 Continued

```
    using namespace std;
    double wages[3] = {10000.0, 20000.0, 30000.0};
    short stacks[3] = {3, 2, 1};

// Here are two ways to get the address of an array
    double * pw = wages;      // name of an array = address
    short * ps = &stacks[0]; // or use address operator
// with array element
    cout << "pw = " << pw << ", *pw = " << *pw << endl;
    pw = pw + 1;
    cout << "add 1 to the pw pointer:\n";
    cout << "pw = " << pw << ", *pw = " << *pw << "\n\n";

    cout << "ps = " << ps << ", *ps = " << *ps << endl;
    ps = ps + 1;
    cout << "add 1 to the ps pointer:\n";
    cout << "ps = " << ps << ", *ps = " << *ps << "\n\n";

    cout << "access two elements with array notation\n";
    cout << "stacks[0] = " << stacks[0]
        << ", stacks[1] = " << stacks[1] << endl;
    cout << "access two elements with pointer notation\n";
    cout << "*stacks = " << *stacks
        << ", *(stacks + 1) =  " << *(stacks + 1) << endl;

    cout << sizeof(wages) << " = size of wages array\n";
    cout << sizeof(pw) << " = size of pw pointer\n";
    return 0;
}
```

Here is the output from the program in Listing 4.19:

```
pw = 0012FEBC, *pw = 10000
add 1 to the pw pointer:
pw = 0012FEC4, *pw = 20000

ps = 0012FEAC, *ps = 3
add 1 to the ps pointer:
ps = 0012FEAE, *ps = 2

access two elements with array notation
stacks[0] = 3, stacks[1] = 2
access two elements with pointer notation
*stacks = 3, *(stacks + 1) =  2
24 = size of wages array
4 = size of pw pointer
```

Program Notes

In most contexts, C++ interprets the name of an array as the address of its first element. Thus, the statement

```
double * pw = wages;
```

makes pw a pointer to type **double** and then initializes pw to **wages**, which is the address of the first element of the **wages** array. For **wages**, as with any array, we have the following equality:

```
wages = &wages[0] = address of first element of array
```

Just to show that this is no jive, the program explicitly uses the address operator in the expression **&stacks[0]** to initialize the **ps** pointer to the first element of the stacks array.

Next, the program inspects the values of pw and *pw. The first is an address and the second is the value at that address. Because pw points to the first element, the value displayed for *pw is that of the first element, **10000**. Then, the program adds one to pw. As promised, this adds eight (fd24 + 8 = fd2c in hexadecimal) to the numeric address value because **double** on this system is 8 bytes. This makes pw equal to the address of the second element. Thus, *pw is now **20000**, the value of the second element. (See Figure 4.10.) (The address values in the figure are adjusted to make the figure clearer.)

FIGURE 4.10
Pointer addition.

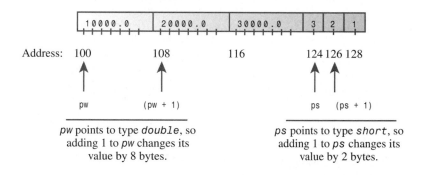

```
double wages[3] = {10000.0, 20000.0, 30000.0};
short stacks[3] = {3, 2, 1};
double * pw = wages;
short * ps = &stacks[0];
```

pw points to type *double*, so adding 1 to *pw* changes its value by 8 bytes.

ps points to type *short*, so adding 1 to *ps* changes its value by 2 bytes.

After this, the program goes through similar steps for **ps**. This time, because **ps** points to type **short** and because **short** is 2 bytes, adding one to the pointer increases its value by two. Again, the result is to make the pointer point to the next element of the array.

Remember

Adding one to a pointer variable increases its value by the number of bytes of the type to which it points.

Now consider the array expression **stacks[1]**. The C++ compiler treats this expression exactly as if you wrote it as ***(stacks + 1)**. The second expression means calculate the address of the second element of the array and then find the value stored there. The end result is precisely what **stacks[1]** means. (Operator precedence requires that you use the parentheses. Without them, one would be added to ***stacks** instead of to **stacks**.)

The program output demonstrates that `*(stacks + 1)` and `stacks[1]` are the same. Similarly, `*(stacks + 2)` is the same as `stacks[2]`. In general, wherever you use array notation, C++ makes the following conversion:

```
arrayname[i] becomes *(arrayname + i)
```

And if you use a pointer instead of an array name, C++ makes the same conversion:

```
pointername[i] becomes *(pointername + i)
```

Thus, in many respects you can use pointer names and array names in the same way. You can use the array brackets notation with either. You can apply the dereferencing operator (`*`) to either. In most expressions, each represents an address. One difference is that you can change the value of a pointer, whereas an array name is a constant:

```
pointername = pointername + 1; // valid
arrayname = arrayname + 1;     // not allowed
```

The second difference is that applying the `sizeof` operator to an array name yields the size of the array, but applying `sizeof` to a pointer yields the size of the pointer, even if the pointer points to the array. For example, in Listing 4.19, both `pw` and `wages` refer to the same array. But applying the `sizeof` operator to them produces the following results:

```
24 = size of wages array ← displaying sizeof wages
4 = size of pw pointer ← displaying sizeof pw
```

This is one case in which C++ doesn't interpret the array name as an address.

In short, using `new` to create an array and using a pointer to access the different elements is a simple matter. You just treat the pointer as an array name. Understanding why this works, however, is an interesting challenge. If you actually want to understand arrays and pointers, you should review their mutual relationships carefully.

Summarizing Pointer Points

You've been exposed to quite a bit of pointer knowledge lately, so let's summarize what's been revealed about pointers and arrays to date.

Declaring Pointers

To declare a pointer to a particular type, use this form:

```
typeName * pointerName;
```

Here are some examples:

```
double * pn;       // pn can point to a double value
char * pc;         // pc can point to a char value
```

Here `pn` and `pc` are pointers and `double *` and `char *` are the C++ notations for the types pointer-to-`double` and pointer-to-`char`.

Assigning Values to Pointers

You should assign a memory address to a pointer. You can apply the **&** operator to a variable name to get an address of named memory, and the **new** operator returns the address of unnamed memory.

Here are some examples:

```
double * pn;           // pn can point to a double value
double * pa;           // so can pa
char * pc;             // pc can point to a char value
double bubble = 3.2;
pn = &bubble;          // assign address of bubble to pn
pc = new char;         // assign address of newly allocated char memory to pc
pa = new double[30];   // assign address of array of 30 double to pa
```

Dereferencing Pointers

Dereferencing a pointer means referring to the pointed-to value. You apply the dereferencing, or indirect value, operator (*****) to a pointer to dereference it. Thus, if **pn** is a pointer to **bubble**, as in the preceding example, then ***pn** is the pointed-to value, or 3.2, in this case.

Here are some examples:

```
cout << *pn; // print the value of bubble
*pc = 'S';   // place 'S' into the memory location whose address is pc
```

Array notation is a second way to dereference a pointer; for instance, **pn[0]** is the same as ***pn**. You should never dereference a pointer that has not been initialized to a proper address.

Distinguishing Between a Pointer and the Pointed-to Value

Remember, if **pt** is a pointer-to-**int**, ***pt** is not a pointer-to-**int**; instead, ***pt** is the complete equivalent to a type **int** variable. It is **pt** that is the pointer.

Here are some examples:

```
int * pt = new int;    // assigns an address to the pointer pt
*pt = 5;               // stores the value 5 at that address
```

Array Names

In most contexts, C++ treats the name of an array as equivalent to the address of the first element of an array.

Here is an example:

```
int tacos[10];         // now tacos is the same as &tacos[0]
```

One exception is when you use the name of an array with the **sizeof** operator. In that case, **sizeof** returns the size of the entire array, in bytes.

Pointer Arithmetic

C++ allows you to add an integer to a pointer. The result of adding one equals the original address value plus a value equal to the number of bytes in the pointed-to object. You can also subtract an integer from a pointer to take the difference between two pointers. The last operation, which yields an integer, is meaningful only if the two pointers point into the same array (pointing to one position past the end is allowed, too); it then yields the separation between the two elements.

Here are some examples:

```
int tacos[10] = {5,2,8,4,1,2,2,4,6,8};
int * pt = tacos;       // suppose pf and tacos are the address 3000
pt = pt + 1;            // now pt is 3004 if a int is 4 bytes
int *pe = &tacos[9];    // pe is 3036 if an int is 4 bytes
pe = pe - 1;            // now pe is 3032, the address of tacos[8]
int diff = pe - pt;     // diff is 7, the separation between
                        // tacos[8] and tacos[1]
```

Dynamic Binding and Static Binding for Arrays

You can use an array declaration to create an array with static binding—that is, an array whose size is set

```
int tacos[10]; // static binding, size fixed at compile time
```

You use the `new []` operator to create an array with dynamic binding (a dynamic array)—that is, an array that is allocated and whose size can be set during runtime. You free the memory with `delete []` when you are done:

```
int size;
cin >> size;
int * pz = new int [size];   // dynamic binding, size set at run time
...
delete [] pz;                // free memory when finished
```

Array Notation and Pointer Notation

Using bracket array notation is equivalent to dereferencing a pointer:

```
tacos[0] means *tacos means the value at address tacos
tacos[3] means *(tacos + 3) means the value at address tacos + 3
```

This is true for both array names and pointer variables, so you can use either pointer notation or array notation with pointers and array names.

Here are some examples:

```
int * pt = new int [10];    // pt points to block of 10 ints
*pt = 5;                    // set element number 0 to 5
pt[0] = 6;                  // reset element number 0 to 6
pt[9] = 44;                 // set tenth element (element number 9) to 44
int coats[10];
*(coats + 4) = 12;          // set coats[4] to 12
```

Pointers and Strings

The special relationship between arrays and pointers extends to C-style strings. Consider the following code:

```
char flower[10] = "rose";
cout << flower << "s are red\n";
```

The name of an array is the address of its first element, so `flower` in the `cout` statement is the address of the `char` element containing the character `r`. The `cout` object assumes that the address of a `char` is the address of a string, so it prints the character at that address and then continues printing characters until it runs into the null character (`\0`). In short, if you give `cout` the address of a character, it prints everything from that character to the first null character that follows it.

The crucial element here is not that `flower` is an array name but that `flower` acts as the address of a `char`. This implies that you can use a pointer-to-`char` variable as an argument to `cout`, also, because it, too, is the address of a `char`. Of course, that pointer should point to the beginning of a string. We'll check that out in a moment.

But what about the final part of the preceding `cout` statement? If `flower` is actually the address of the first character of a string, what is the expression `"s are red\n"`? To be consistent with `cout`'s handling of string output, this quoted string should also be an address. And it is, for in C++ a quoted string, like an array name, serves as the address of its first element. The preceding code doesn't really send a whole string to `cout`; it just sends the string address. This means strings in an array, quoted string constants, and strings described by pointers are all handled equivalently. Each is really passed along as an address. That's certainly less work than passing each and every character in a string.

Remember

With `cout` and with most C++ expressions, the name of an array of `char`, a pointer-to-`char`, and a quoted string constant are all interpreted as the address of the first character of a string.

Listing 4.20 illustrates the use of the different forms of strings. It uses two functions from the string library. The `strlen()` function, which you've used before, returns the length of a string. The `strcpy()` function copies a string from one location to another. Both have function prototypes in the `cstring` header file (or `string.h`, on less up-to-date implementations). The program also uses comments to showcase some pointer misuses that you should try to avoid.

LISTING 4.20 ptrstr.cpp

```
// ptrstr.cpp -- using pointers to strings
#include <iostream>
#include <cstring>              // declare strlen(), strcpy()
int main()
{
```

LISTING 4.20   *Continued*

```
using namespace std;
char animal[20] = "bear";    // animal holds bear
const char * bird = "wren"; // bird holds address of string
char * ps;                   // uninitialized

cout << animal << " and ";  // display bear
cout << bird << "\n";        // display wren
// cout << ps << "\n";       //may display garbage, may cause a crash

cout << "Enter a kind of animal: ";
cin >> animal;               // ok if input < 20 chars
// cin >> ps; Too horrible a blunder to try; ps doesn't
//            point to allocated space

ps = animal;                 // set ps to point to string
cout << ps << "s!\n";        // ok, same as using animal
cout << "Before using strcpy():\n";
cout << animal << " at " << (int *) animal << endl;
cout << ps << " at " << (int *) ps << endl;

ps = new char[strlen(animal) + 1];  // get new storage
strcpy(ps, animal);          // copy string to new storage
cout << "After using strcpy():\n";
cout << animal << " at " << (int *) animal << endl;
cout << ps << " at " << (int *) ps << endl;
delete [] ps;
return 0;
}
```

Compatibility Note

If your system doesn't have the `cstring` header file, use the older `string.h` version.

Here is a sample run of the program in Listing 4.20:

```
bear and wren
Enter a kind of animal: fox
foxs!
Before using strcpy():
fox at 0x0065fd30
fox at 0x0065fd30
After using strcpy():
fox at 0x0065fd30
fox at 0x004301c8
```

Program Notes

The program in Listing 4.20 creates one `char` array (`animal`) and two pointers-to-`char` variables (`bird` and `ps`). The program begins by initializing the `animal` array to the `"bear"` string, just as you've initialized arrays before. Then, the program does something new. It initializes a pointer-to-`char` to a string:

```
const char * bird = "wren"; // bird holds address of string
```

Remember, `"wren"` actually represents the address of the string, so this statement assigns the address of `"wren"` to the `bird` pointer. (Typically, a compiler sets aside an area in memory to hold all the quoted strings used in the program source code, associating each stored string with its address.) This means you can use the pointer `bird` just as you would use the string `"wren"`, as in this example:

```
 cout << "A concerned " << bird << " speaks\n";
```

String literals are constants, which is why the code uses the `const` keyword in the declaration. Using `const` in this fashion means you can use `bird` to access the string but not to change it. Chapter 7 takes up the topic of `const` pointers in greater detail. Finally, the pointer `ps` remains uninitialized, so it doesn't point to any string. (As you know, that is usually a bad idea, and this example is no exception.)

Next, the program illustrates that you can use the array name `animal` and the pointer `bird` equivalently with `cout`. Both, after all, are the addresses of strings, and `cout` displays the two strings (`"bear"` and `"wren"`) stored at those addresses. If you activate the code that makes the error of attempting to display `ps`, you might get a blank line, you might get garbage displayed, and you might get a program crash. Creating an uninitialized pointer is a bit like distributing a blank signed check: You lack control over how it will be used.

For input, the situation is a bit different. It's safe to use the array `animal` for input as long as the input is short enough to fit into the array. It would not be proper to use `bird` for input, however:

- Some compilers treat string literals as read-only constants, leading to a runtime error if you try to write new data over them. That string literals be constants is the mandated behavior in C++, but not all compilers have made that change from older behavior yet.

- Some compilers use just one copy of a string literal to represent all occurrences of that literal in a program.

Let's amplify the second point. C++ doesn't guarantee that string literals are stored uniquely. That is, if you use a string literal `"wren"` several times in a program, the compiler might store several copies of the string or just one copy. If it does the latter, then setting `bird` to point to one `"wren"` makes it point to the only copy of that string. Reading a value into one string could affect what you thought was an independent string elsewhere. In any case, because the `bird` pointer is declared as `const`, the compiler prevents any attempt to change the contents of the location pointed to by `bird`.

Worse yet is trying to read information into the location to which `ps` points. Because `ps` is not initialized, you don't know where the information will wind up. It might even overwrite information that is already in memory. Fortunately, it's easy to avoid these problems: You just use a sufficiently large `char` array to receive input, and don't use string constants to receive input or uninitialized pointers to receive input. (Or you might sidestep all these issues and use `std::string` objects instead of arrays.)

Caution

When you read a string into a program, you should always use the address of previously allocated memory. This address can be in the form of an array name or of a pointer that has been initialized using `new`.

Next, notice what the following code accomplishes:

```
ps = animal;                // set ps to point to string
...
cout << animal << " at " << (int *) animal << endl;
cout << ps << " at " << (int *) ps << endl;
```

It produces the following output:

```
fox at 0x0065fd30
fox at 0x0065fd30
```

Normally, if you give `cout` a pointer, it prints an address. But if the pointer is type `char *`, `cout` displays the pointed-to string. If you want to see the address of the string, you have to type cast the pointer to another pointer type, such as `int *`, which this code does. So `ps` displays as the string `"fox"`, but `(int *) ps` displays as the address where the string is found. Note that assigning `animal` to `ps` does not copy the string; it copies the address. This results in two pointers (`animal` and `ps`) to the same memory location and string.

To get a copy of a string, you need to do more. First, you need to allocate memory to hold the string. You can do this by declaring a second array or by using `new`. The second approach enables you to custom fit the storage to the string:

```
ps = new char[strlen(animal) + 1]; // get new storage
```

The string `"fox"` doesn't completely fill the `animal` array, so this approach wastes space. This bit of code uses `strlen()` to find the length of the string; it adds one to get the length, including the null character. Then the program uses `new` to allocate just enough space to hold the string.

Next, you need a way to copy a string from the `animal` array to the newly allocated space. It doesn't work to assign `animal` to `ps` because that just changes the address stored in `ps` and thus loses the only way the program had to access the newly allocated memory. Instead, you need to use the `strcpy()` library function:

```
strcpy(ps, animal);                // copy string to new storage
```

The `strcpy()` function takes two arguments. The first is the destination address, and the second is the address of the string to be copied. It's up to you to make certain that the destination really is allocated and has sufficient space to hold the copy. That's accomplished here by using `strlen()` to find the correct size and using `new` to get free memory.

Note that by using `strcpy()` and `new`, you get two separate copies of `"fox"`:

```
fox at 0x0065fd30
fox at 0x004301c8
```

Also note that `new` located the new storage at a memory location quite distant from that of the array `animal`.

Often you encounter the need to place a string into an array. You use the = operator when you initialize an array; otherwise, you use `strcpy()` or `strncpy()`. You've seen the `strcpy()` function; it works like this:

```
char food[20] = "carrots"; // initialization
strcpy(food, "flan");      // otherwise
```

Note that something like this:

```
strcpy(food, "a picnic basket filled with many goodies");
```

can cause problems because the `food` array is smaller than the string. In this case, the function copies the rest of the string into the memory bytes immediately following the array, which can overwrite other memory the program is using. To avoid that problem, you should use `strncpy()` instead. It takes a third argument: the maximum number of characters to be copied. Be aware, however, that if this function runs out of space before it reaches the end of the string, it doesn't add the null character. Thus, you should use the function like this:

```
strncpy(food, "a picnic basket filled with many goodies", 19);
food[19] = '\0';
```

This copies up to 19 characters into the array and then sets the last element to the null character. If the string is shorter than 19 characters, `strncpy()` adds a null character earlier to mark the true end of the string.

Remember

Use `strcpy()` or `strncpy()`, not the assignment operator, to assign a string to an array.

Now that you've seen some aspects of using C-style strings and the `cstring` library, you can appreciate the comparative simplicity of using the C++ `string` type. You (normally) don't have to worry about a string overflowing an array, and you can use the assignment operator instead of `strcpy()` or `strncpy()`.

Using `new` to Create Dynamic Structures

You've seen how it can be advantageous to create arrays during runtime rather than at compile time. The same holds true for structures. You need to allocate space for only as many structures as a program needs during a particular run. Again, the `new` operator is the tool to use. With it, you can create dynamic structures. Again, *dynamic* means the memory is allocated during runtime, not at compile time. Incidentally, because classes are much like structures, you are able to use the techniques you'll learn in this section for structures with classes, too.

Using **new** with structures has two parts: creating the structure and accessing its members. To create a structure, you use the structure type with **new**. For example, to create an unnamed structure of the **inflatable** type and assign its address to a suitable pointer, you can use the following:

```
inflatable * ps = new inflatable;
```

This assigns to **ps** the address of a chunk of free memory large enough to hold a structure of the **inflatable** type. Note that the syntax is exactly the same as it is for C++'s built-in types.

The tricky part is accessing members. When you create a dynamic structure, you can't use the dot membership operator with the structure name because the structure has no name. All you have is its address. C++ provides an operator just for this situation: the arrow membership operator (`->`). This operator, formed by typing a hyphen and then a greater-than symbol, does for pointers to structures what the dot operator does for structure names. For example, if **ps** points to a type **inflatable** structure, then **ps->price** is the **price** member of the pointed-to structure. (See Figure 4.11.)

FIGURE 4.11

Identifying structure members.

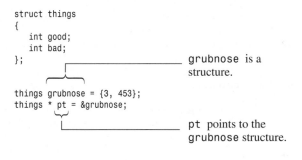

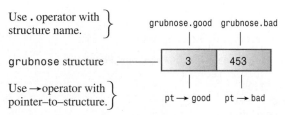

Remember

Sometimes new C++ users become confused about when to use the dot operator and when to use the arrow operator to specify a structure member. The rule is simple: If the structure identifier is the name of a structure, use the dot operator. If the identifier is a pointer to the structure, use the arrow operator.

A second, uglier approach to accessing structure members is to realize that if **ps** is a pointer to a structure, then ***ps** represents the pointed-to value—the structure itself. Then, because ***ps** is a structure, `(*ps).price` is the `price` member of the structure. C++'s operator precedence rules require that you use parentheses in this construction.

Listing 4.21 uses `new` to create an unnamed structure and demonstrates both pointer notations for accessing structure members.

LISTING 4.21 `newstrct.cpp`

```
// newstrct.cpp -- using new with a structure
#include <iostream>
struct inflatable   // structure template
{
    char name[20];
    float volume;
    double price;
};
int main()
{
    using namespace std;
    inflatable * ps = new inflatable; // allot memory for structure
    cout << "Enter name of inflatable item: ";
    cin.get(ps->name, 20);             // method 1 for member access
    cout << "Enter volume in cubic feet: ";
    cin >> (*ps).volume;               // method 2 for member access
    cout << "Enter price: $";
    cin >> ps->price;
    cout << "Name: " << (*ps).name << endl;         // method 2
    cout << "Volume: " << ps->volume << " cubic feet\n"; // method 1
    cout << "Price: $" << ps->price << endl;        // method 1
    delete ps;                         // free memory used by structure
    return 0;
}
```

Here is a sample run of the program in Listing 4.21:

```
Enter name of inflatable item: Fabulous Frodo
Enter volume in cubic feet: 1.4
Enter price: $27.99
Name: Fabulous Frodo
Volume: 1.4 cubic feet
Price: $27.99
```

An Example of Using `new` and `delete`

Let's look at an example that uses `new` and `delete` to manage storing string input from the keyboard. Listing 4.22 defines a function `getname()` that returns a pointer to an input string. This function reads the input into a large temporary array and then uses `new []` with an appropriate size to create a chunk of memory sized to fit to the input string. Then, the function returns the pointer to the block. This approach could conserve a lot of memory for programs that read in a large number of strings.

Suppose your program has to read 1,000 strings and that the largest string might be 79 characters long, but most of the strings are much shorter than that. If you used char arrays to hold the strings, you'd need 1,000 arrays of 80 characters each. That's 80,000 bytes, and much of that block of memory would wind up being unused. Alternatively, you could create an array of 1,000 pointers to char and then use new to allocate only the amount of memory needed for each string. That could save tens of thousands of bytes. Instead of having to use a large array for every string, you fit the memory to the input. Even better, you could also use new to find space to store only as many pointers as needed. Well, that's a little too ambitious for right now. Even using an array of 1,000 pointers is a little too ambitious for right now, but Listing 4.22 illustrates some of the technique. Also, just to illustrate how delete works, the program uses it to free memory for reuse.

LISTING 4.22   `delete.cpp`

```
// delete.cpp -- using the delete operator
#include <iostream>
#include <cstring>       // or string.h
using namespace std;
char * getname(void);    // function prototype
int main()
{
    char * name;         // create pointer but no storage

    name = getname();    // assign address of string to name
    cout << name << " at " << (int *) name << "\n";
    delete [] name;      // memory freed

    name = getname();    // reuse freed memory
    cout << name << " at " << (int *) name << "\n";
    delete [] name;      // memory freed again
    return 0;
}

char * getname()         // return pointer to new string
{
    char temp[80];       // temporary storage
    cout << "Enter last name: ";
    cin >> temp;
    char * pn = new char[strlen(temp) + 1];
    strcpy(pn, temp);    // copy string into smaller space

    return pn;           // temp lost when function ends
}
```

Here is a sample run of the program in Listing 4.22:

```
Enter last name: Fredeldumpkin
Fredeldumpkin at 0x004326b8
Enter last name: Pook
Pook at 0x004301c8
```

Program Notes

Consider the function `getname()` in the program in Listing 4.22. It uses `cin` to place an input word into the `temp` array. Next, it uses `new` to allocate new memory to hold the word. Including the null character, the program needs `strlen(temp) + 1` characters to store the string, so that's the value given to `new`. After the space becomes available, `getname()` uses the standard library function `strcpy()` to copy the string from `temp` to the new block. The function doesn't check to see whether the string fits, but `getname()` covers that by requesting the right number of bytes with `new`. Finally, the function returns `pn`, the address of the string copy.

In `main()`, the return value (the address) is assigned to the pointer `name`. This pointer is defined in `main()`, but it points to the block of memory allocated in the `getname()` function. The program then prints the string and the address of the string.

Next, after it frees the block pointed to by `name`, `main()` calls `getname()` a second time. C++ doesn't guarantee that newly freed memory is the first to be chosen the next time `new` is used, and in this sample run, it isn't.

Note in this example that `getname()` allocates memory and `main()` frees it. It's usually not a good idea to put `new` and `delete` in separate functions because that makes it easier to forget to use `delete`. But this example does separate `new` from `delete` just to show that it is possible.

To appreciate some of the more subtle aspects of this program, you should know a little more about how C++ handles memory. So let's preview some material that's covered more fully in Chapter 9.

Automatic Storage, Static Storage, and Dynamic Storage

C++ has three ways of managing memory for data, depending on the method used to allocate memory: automatic storage, static storage, and dynamic storage, sometimes called the *free store* or *heap*. Data objects allocated in these three ways differ from each other in how long they remain in existence. We'll take a quick look at each type.

Automatic Storage

Ordinary variables defined inside a function use *automatic storage* and are called *automatic variables*. These terms mean that the variables come into existence automatically when the function containing them is invoked, and they expire when the function terminates. For example, the `temp` array in Listing 4.22 exists only while the `getname()` function is active. When program control returns to `main()`, the memory used for `temp` is freed automatically. If `getname()`returned the address of `temp`, the `name` pointer in `main()` would be left pointing to a memory location that would soon be reused. That's one reason you have to use `new` in `getname()`.

Actually, automatic values are local to the block that contains them. A *block* is a section of code enclosed between braces. So far, all our blocks have been entire functions. But as you'll see in the next chapter, you can have blocks within a function. If you define a variable inside one of those blocks, it exists only while the program is executing statements inside the block.

Static Storage

Static storage is storage that exists throughout the execution of an entire program. There are two ways to make a variable static. One is to define it externally, outside a function. The other is to use the keyword `static` when declaring a variable:

```
static double fee = 56.50;
```

Under K&R C, you can initialize only static arrays and structures, whereas C++ Release 2.0 (and later) and ANSI C allow you to initialize automatic arrays and structures, too. However, as you may have discovered, some C++ implementations do not yet implement initialization for automatic arrays and structures.

Chapter 9 discusses static storage in more detail. The main point you should note now about automatic and static storage is that these methods rigidly define the lifetime of a variable. Either the variable exists for the entire duration of a program (a static variable) or it exists only while a particular function is being executed (an automatic variable).

Dynamic Storage

The `new` and `delete` operators provide a more flexible approach than automatic and static variables. They manage a pool of memory, which C++ refers to as the *free store*. This pool is separate from the memory used for static and automatic variables. As Listing 4.22 shows, `new` and `delete` enable you to allocate memory in one function and free it in another. Thus, the lifetime of the data is not tied arbitrarily to the life of the program or the life of a function. Using `new` and `delete` together gives you much more control over how a program uses memory than does using ordinary variables.

Real-World Note: Stacks, Heaps, and Memory Leaks

What happens if you *don't* call `delete` after creating a variable on the free store (or heap) with the `new` operator? The variable or construct dynamically allocated on the free store continues to persist if `delete` is not called, even though the memory that contains the pointer has been freed due to rules of scope and object lifetime. In essence, you have no way to access the construct on the free store because the pointer to the memory that contains it is gone. You have now created a *memory leak*. Memory that has been leaked remains unusable through the life of the program; it's been allocated but can't be de-allocated. In extreme (though not uncommon) cases, memory leaks can be so severe that they use up all the memory available to the application, causing it to crash with an out-of-memory error. In addition, these leaks may negatively affect some operating systems or other applications running in the same memory space, causing them, in turn, to fail.

Even the best programmers and software companies create memory leaks. To avoid them, it's best to get into the habit of joining your `new` and `delete` operators immediately, planning for and entering the deletion of your construct as soon as you dynamically allocate it on the free store.

Note

Pointers are among the most powerful of C++ tools. They are also the most dangerous because they permit computer-unfriendly actions, such as using an uninitialized pointer to access memory or attempting to free the same memory block twice. Furthermore, until you get used to pointer notation and pointer concepts through practice, pointers can be confusing. Because pointers are an important part of C++ programming, they weave in and out future discussions in this book. This book discusses pointers several more times. The hope is that each exposure will make you more comfortable with them.

Summary

Arrays, structures, and pointers are three C++ compound types. An array can hold several values, all of the same type, in a single data object. By using an index, or subscript, you can access the individual elements in an array.

A structure can hold several values of different types in a single data object, and you can use the membership operator (.) to access individual members. The first step in using structures is to create a structure template that defines what members the structure holds. The name, or tag, for this template then becomes a new type identifier. You can then declare structure variables of that type.

A union can hold a single value, but it can be of a variety of types, with the member name indicating which mode is being used.

Pointers are variables that are designed to hold addresses. We say a pointer points to the address it holds. The pointer declaration always states to what type of object a pointer points. Applying the dereferencing operator (*) to a pointer yields the value at the location to which the pointer points.

A string is a series of characters terminated by a null character. A string can be represented by a quoted string constant, in which case the null character is implicitly understood. You can store a string in an array of `char`, and you can represent a string with a pointer-to-`char` that is initialized to point to the string. The `strlen()` function returns the length of a string, not counting the null character. The `strcpy()` function copies a string from one location to another. When using these functions, you include the `cstring` or the `string.h` header file.

The C++ `string` class, supported by the `string` header file, offers an alternative, more user-friendly means to deal with strings. In particular, `string` objects are automatically resized to accommodate stored strings, and you can use the assignment operator to copy a string.

The `new` operator lets you request memory for a data object while a program is running. The operator returns the address of the memory it obtains, and you can assign that address to a pointer. The only means to access that memory is to use the pointer. If the data object is a simple variable, you can use the dereferencing operator (*) to indicate a value. If the data object is an array, you can use the pointer as if it were an array name to access the elements. If the data object is a structure, you can use the pointer dereferencing operator (`->`) to access structure members.

Pointers and arrays are closely connected. If `ar` is an array name, then the expression `ar[i]` is interpreted as `*(ar + i)`, with the array name interpreted as the address of the first element of the array. Thus, the array name plays the same role as a pointer. In turn, you can use a pointer name with array notation to access elements in an array allocated by `new`.

The `new` and `delete` operators let you explicitly control when data objects are allocated and when they are returned to the memory pool. Automatic variables, which are those declared within a function, and static variables, which are defined outside a function or with the keyword `static`, are less flexible. An automatic variable comes into being when the block containing it (typically a function definition) is entered, and it expires when the block is left. A static variable persists for the duration of a program.

Review Questions

1. How would you declare each of the following?

   a. `actors` is an array of 30 `char`.

   b. `betsie` is an array of 100 `short`.

   c. `chuck` is an array of 13 `float`.

   d. `dipsea` is an array of 64 `long double`.

2. Declare an array of five `int`s and initialize it to the first five odd positive integers.

3. Write a statement that assigns the sum of the first and last elements of the array in Question 2 to the variable `even`.

4. Write a statement that displays the value of the second element in the `float` array `ideas`.

5. Declare an array of `char` and initialize it to the string `"cheeseburger"`.

6. Devise a structure declaration that describes a fish. The structure should include the kind, the weight in whole ounces, and the length in fractional inches.

7. Declare a variable of the type defined in Question 6 and initialize it.

8. Use `enum` to define a type called `Response` with the possible values `Yes`, `No`, and `Maybe`. `Yes` should be `1`, `No` should be `0`, and `Maybe` should be `2`.

9. Suppose `ted` is a `double` variable. Declare a pointer that points to `ted` and use the pointer to display `ted`'s value.

10. Suppose `treacle` is an array of 10 `float`s. Declare a pointer that points to the first element of `treacle` and use the pointer to display the first and last elements of the array.

11. Write a code fragment that asks the user to enter a positive integer and then creates a dynamic array of that many `int`s.

12. Is the following valid code? If so, what does it print?

    ```
    cout << (int *) "Home of the jolly bytes";
    ```

13. Write a code fragment that dynamically allocates a structure of the type described in Question 6 and then reads a value for the kind member of the structure.

14. Listing 4.6 illustrates a problem created by following numeric input with line-oriented string input. How would replacing this:

    ```
    cin.getline(address,80);
    ```

    with this:

    ```
    cin >> address;
    ```

    affect the working of this program?

Programming Exercises

1. Write a C++ program that requests and displays information as shown in the following example of output:

   ```
   What is your first name? Betty Sue
   What is your last name? Yew
   What letter grade do you deserve? B
   What is your age? 22
   Name: Yew, Betty Sue
   Grade: C
   Age: 22
   ```

   Note that the program should be able to accept first names that comprise more than one word. Also note that the program adjusts the grade downward—that is, up one letter. Assume that the user requests an A, a B, or a C so that you don't have to worry about the gap between a D and an F.

2. Rewrite Listing 4.4, using the C++ `string` class instead of `char` arrays.

3. Write a program that asks the user to enter his or her first name and then last name, and that then constructs, stores, and displays a third string, consisting of the user's last name followed by a comma, a space, and first name. Use `char` arrays and functions from the `cstring` header file. A sample run could look like this:

   ```
   Enter your first name: Flip
   Enter your last name: Fleming
   Here's the information in a single string: Fleming, Flip
   ```

4. Write a program that asks the user to enter his or her first name and then last name, and that then constructs, stores, and displays a third string consisting of the user's last name

followed by a comma, a space, and first name. Use **string** objects and methods from the **string** header file. A sample run could look like this:

```
Enter your first name: Flip
Enter your last name: Fleming
Here's the information in a single string: Fleming, Flip
```

5. The **CandyBar** structure contains three members. The first member holds the brand name of a candy bar. The second member holds the weight (which may have a fractional part) of the candy bar, and the third member holds the number of calories (an integer value) in the candy bar. Write a program that declares such a structure and creates a **CandyBar** variable called **snack**, initializing its members to **"Mocha Munch"**, **2.3**, and **350**, respectively. The initialization should be part of the declaration for **snack**. Finally, the program should display the contents of the **snack** variable.

6. The **CandyBar** structure contains three members, as described in Programming Exercise 5. Write a program that creates an array of three **CandyBar** structures, initializes them to values of your choice, and then displays the contents of each structure.

7. William Wingate runs a pizza-analysis service. For each pizza, he needs to record the following information:

   • The name of the pizza company, which can consist of more than one word

   • The diameter of the pizza

   • The weight of the pizza

   Devise a structure that can hold this information and write a program that uses a structure variable of that type. The program should ask the user to enter each of the preceding items of information, and then the program should display that information. Use **cin** (or its methods) and **cout**.

8. Do Programming Exercise 7, but use **new** to allocate a structure instead of declaring a structure variable. Also, have the program request the pizza diameter before it requests the pizza company name.

9. Do Programming Exercise 6, but, instead of declaring an array of three **CandyBar** structures, use **new** to allocate the array dynamically.

CHAPTER 5

LOOPS AND RELATIONAL EXPRESSIONS

In this chapter you'll learn about the following:

- The `for` loop
- Expressions and statements
- The increment and decrement operators: ++ and - -
- Combination assignment operators
- Compound statements (blocks)
- The comma operator

- Relational operators: >, >=, ==, <=, <, and !=
- The `while` loop
- The `typedef` facility
- The `do while` loop
- The `get()` character input method
- The end-of-file condition
- Nested loops and two-dimensional arrays

C omputers do more than store data. They analyze, consolidate, rearrange, extract, modify, extrapolate, synthesize, and otherwise manipulate data. Sometimes they even distort and trash data, but we'll try to steer clear of that kind of behavior. To perform their manipulative miracles, programs need tools for performing repetitive actions and for making decisions. Of course, C++ provides such tools. Indeed, it uses the same `for` loops, `while` loops, `do while` loops, `if` statements, and `switch` statements that regular C employs, so if you know C, you can zip through chapter and Chapter 6, "Branching Statements and Logical Operators." (But don't zip too fast—you don't want to miss how `cin` handles character input!) These various program control statements often use relational expressions and logical expressions to govern their behavior. This chapter discusses loops and relational expressions, and Chapter 6 follows up with branching statements and logical expressions.

Introducing `for` Loops

Circumstances often call on a program to perform repetitive tasks, such as adding together the elements of an array one by one or printing some paean to productivity 20 times. The C++ `for` loop makes such tasks easy to do. Let's look at a loop in Listing 5.1, see what it does, and then discuss how it works.

LISTING 5.1   `forloop.cpp`

```cpp
// forloop.cpp -- introducing the for loop
#include <iostream>
int main()
{
    using namespace std;
    int i;  // create a counter
//   initialize; test ; update
    for (i = 0; i < 5; i++)
        cout << "C++ knows loops.\n";
    cout << "C++ knows when to stop.\n";
    return 0;
}
```

Here is the output from the program in Listing 5.1:

```
C++ knows loops.
C++ knows loops.
C++ knows loops.
C++ knows loops.
C++ knows loops.
C++ knows when to stop.
```

This loop begins by setting the integer `i` to 0:

```
i = 0
```

This is the *loop initialization* part of the loop. Then, in the *loop test*, the program tests whether `i` is less than 5:

```
i < 5
```

If it is, the program executes the following statement, which is termed the *loop body*:

```
cout << "C++ knows loops.\n";
```

Then, the program uses the *loop update* part of the loop to increase `i` by 1:

```
i++
```

The *loop update* part of the loop uses the `++` operator, called the *increment operator*. It increments the value of its operand by 1. (The increment operator is not restricted to `for` loops. For example, you can use `i++;` instead of `i = i + 1;` as a statement in a program.) Incrementing `i` completes the first cycle of the loop.

Next, the loop begins a new cycle by comparing the new `i` value with 5. Because the new value (1) is also less than 5, the loop prints another line and then finishes by incrementing `i` again. That sets the stage for a fresh cycle of testing, executing a statement, and updating the value of `i`. The process continues until the loop updates `i` to 5. Then the next test fails, and the program moves on to the next statement after the loop.

`for` Loop Parts

A `for` loop provides a step-by-step recipe for performing repeated actions. Let's take a more detailed look at how it's set up. The usual parts of a `for` loop handle these steps:

1. Setting a value initially

2. Performing a test to see whether the loop should continue

3. Executing the loop actions

4. Updating value(s) used for the test

The C++ loop design positions these elements so that you can spot them at a glance. The initialization, test, and update actions constitute a three-part control section enclosed in parentheses. Each part is an expression, and semicolons separate the expressions from each other. The statement following the control section is called the *body* of the loop, and it is executed as long as the test expression remains true:

```
for (initialization; test-expression; update-expression)
    body
```

C++ syntax counts a complete `for` statement as a single statement, even though it can incorporate one or more statements in the body portion. (Having more than one statement requires using a compound statement, or block, as discussed later in this chapter.)

The loop performs initialization just once. Typically, programs use this expression to set a variable to a starting value and then use the variable to count loop cycles.

test-expression determines whether the loop body gets executed. Typically, this expression is a relational expression—that is, one that compares two values. Our example compares the value of `i` to 5, checking whether `i` is less than 5. If the comparison is true, the program executes the loop body. Actually, C++ doesn't limit *test-expression* to true/false comparisons. You can use any expression, and C++ will type cast it to type `bool`. Thus, an expression with a value of 0 is converted to the `bool` value `false`, and the loop terminates. If the expression evaluates to nonzero, it is type cast to the `bool` value `true`, and the loop continues. Listing 5.2 demonstrates this by using the expression `i` as the test condition. (In the update section, `i--` is similar to `i++` except that it decreases the value of `i` by 1 each time it's used.)

LISTING 5.2   num_test.cpp

```
// num_test.cpp -- use numeric test in for loop
#include <iostream>
int main()
{
    using namespace std;
    cout << "Enter the starting countdown value: ";
    int limit;
    cin >> limit;
    int i;
    for (i = limit; i; i--)      // quits when i is 0
        cout << "i = " << i << "\n";
    cout << "Done now that i = " << i << "\n";
    return 0;
}
```

Here is the output from the program in Listing 5.2:

```
Enter the starting countdown value: 4
i = 4
i = 3
i = 2
i = 1
Done now that i = 0
```

Note that the loop terminates when **i** reaches 0.

How do relational expressions, such as **i < 5**, fit into this framework of terminating a loop with a 0 value? Before the **bool** type was introduced, relational expressions evaluated to 1 if true and 0 if false. Thus, the value of the expression **3 < 5** was **1** and the value of **5 < 5** was **0**. Now that C++ has added the **bool** type, however, relational expressions evaluate to the **bool** literals **true** and **false** instead of 1 and 0. This change doesn't lead to incompatibilities, however, because a C++ program converts **true** and **false** to 1 and 0 where integer values are expected, and it converts **0** to **false** and nonzero to **true** where **bool** values are expected.

The **for** loop is an *entry-condition* loop. This means the test expression is evaluated *before* each loop cycle. The loop never executes the loop body when the test expression is false. For example, suppose you rerun the program in Listing 5.2 but give 0 as a starting value. Because the test condition fails the very first time it's evaluated, the loop body never gets executed:

```
Enter the starting countdown value: 0
Done now that i = 0
```

This look-before-you-loop attitude can help keep a program out of trouble.

update-expression is evaluated at the end of the loop, after the body has been executed. Typically, it's used to increase or decrease the value of the variable keeping track of the number of loop cycles. However, it can be any valid C++ expression, as can the other control expressions. This makes the **for** loop capable of much more than simply counting from 0 to 5, the way the first loop example does. You'll see some examples of this later.

The **for** loop body consists of a single statement, but you'll soon learn how to stretch that rule. Figure 5.1 summarizes the **for** loop design.

FIGURE 5.1

The design of `for` loops.

```
statement1
for (int_expr; test_expr; update_expr)
    statement2
statement3
```

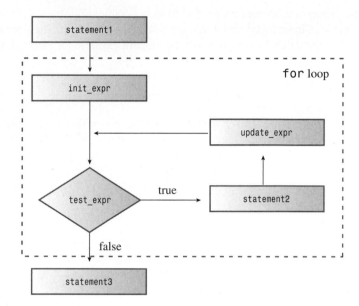

A `for` statement looks something like a function call because it uses a name followed by paired parentheses. However, `for`'s status as a C++ keyword prevents the compiler from thinking `for` is a function. It also prevents you from naming a function `for`.

Tip

Common C++ style is to place a space between `for` and the following parenthesis and to omit space between a function name and the following parenthesis:

```
for (i = 6; i < 10; i++)
    smart_function(i);
```

Other control statements, such as `if` and `while`, are treated similarly to `for`. This serves to visually reinforce the distinction between a control statement and a function call. Also, common practice is to indent the body of a `for` statement to make it stand out visually.

Expressions and Statements

A `for` control section uses three expressions. Within its self-imposed limits of syntax, C++ is a very expressive language. Any value or any valid combination of values and operators constitute an expression. For example, `10` is an expression with the value 10 (no surprise), and `28 * 20` is an expression with the value 560. In C++ every expression has a value. Often the value is obvious. For example, the expression

```
22 + 27
```

is formed from two values and the addition operator, and it has the value 49. Sometimes the value is less obvious. For example,

```
x = 20
```

is an expression because it's formed from two values and the assignment operator. C++ defines the value of an assignment expression to be the value of the member on the left, so the expression has the value 20. The fact that assignment expressions have values permits statements such as the following:

```
maids = (cooks = 4) + 3;
```

The expression `cooks = 4` has the value 4, so `maids` is assigned the value 7. However, just because C++ permits this behavior doesn't mean you should encourage it. But the same rule that makes this peculiar statement possible also makes the following useful statement possible:

```
x = y = z = 0;
```

This is a fast way to set several variables to the same value. The precedence table (see Appendix D, "Operator Precedence") reveals that assignment associates right-to-left, so first `0` is assigned to `z`, and then `z = 0` is assigned to `y`, and so on.

Finally, as mentioned previously, relational expressions such as `x < y` evaluate to the `bool` values `true` or `false`. The short program in Listing 5.3 illustrates some points about expression values. The `<<` operator has higher precedence than the operators used in the expressions, so the code uses parentheses to enforce the correct order.

LISTING 5.3   express.cpp

```cpp
// express.cpp -- values of expressions
#include <iostream>
int main()
{
    using namespace std;
    int x;

    cout << "The expression x = 100 has the value ";
    cout << (x = 100) << endl;
    cout << "Now x = " << x << endl;
    cout << "The expression x < 3 has the value ";
    cout << (x < 3) << endl;
    cout << "The expression x > 3 has the value ";
    cout << (x > 3) << endl;
    cout.setf(ios_base::boolalpha);    //a newer C++ feature
    cout << "The expression x < 3 has the value ";
    cout << (x < 3) << endl;
    cout << "The expression x > 3 has the value ";
    cout << (x > 3) << endl;
    return 0;
}
```

Compatibility Note

Older implementations of C++ may require using `ios::boolalpha` instead of `ios_base::boolal-pha` as the argument for `cout.setf()`. Even older implementations might not recognize either form.

Here is the output from the program in Listing 5.3:

```
The expression x = 100 has the value 100
Now x = 100
The expression x < 3 has the value 0
The expression x > 3 has the value 1
The expression x < 3 has the value false
The expression x > 3 has the value true
```

Normally, `cout` converts `bool` values to `int` before displaying them, but the `cout.setf(ios::boolalpha)` function call sets a flag that instructs `cout` to display the words `true` and `false` instead of `1` and `0`.

Remember

A C++ expression is a value or a combination of values and operators, and every C++ expression has a value.

To evaluate the expression `x = 100`, C++ must assign the value `100` to `x`. When the very act of evaluating an expression changes the value of data in memory, we say the evaluation has a *side effect*. Thus, evaluating an assignment expression has the side effect of changing the assignee's value. You might think of assignment as the intended effect, but from the standpoint of how C++ is constructed, evaluating the expression is the primary effect. Not all expressions have side effects. For example, evaluating `x + 15` calculates a new value, but it doesn't change the value of `x`. But evaluating `++x + 15` does have a side effect because it involves incrementing `x`.

From expression to statement is a short step; you just add a semicolon. Thus

```
age = 100
```

is an expression, whereas

```
age = 100;
```

is a statement. Any expression can become a statement if you add a semicolon, but the result might not make programming sense. For example, if `rodents` is a variable, then

```
rodents + 6;     // valid, but useless, statement
```

is a valid C++ statement. The compiler allows it, but the statement doesn't accomplish anything useful. The program merely calculates the sum, does nothing with it, and goes on to the next statement. (A smart compiler might even skip the statement.)

Nonexpressions and Statements

Some concepts, such as knowing the structure of a `for` loop, are crucial to understanding C++. But there are also relatively minor aspects of syntax that can suddenly bedevil you just when you think you understand the language. We'll look at a couple of them now.

Although it is true that adding a semicolon to any expression makes it a statement, the reverse is not true. That is, removing a semicolon from a statement does not necessarily convert it to an expression. Of the kinds of statements we've used so far, return statements, declaration statements, and `for` statements don't fit the *statement = expression + semicolon* mold. For example, this is a statement:

```
int toad;
```

But the fragment `int toad` is not an expression and does not have a value. This makes code such as the following invalid:

```
eggs = int toad * 1000;    // invalid, not an expression
cin >> int toad;           // can't combine declaration with cin
```

Similarly, you can't assign a `for` loop to a variable. In the following example, the `for` loop is not an expression, so it has no value and you can't assign it:

```
int fx = for (i = 0; i< 4; i++)
    cout >> i;   // not possible
```

Bending the Rules

C++ adds a feature to C loops that requires some artful adjustments to the `for` loop syntax. This was the original syntax:

```
for (expression; expression; expression)
    statement
```

In particular, the control section of a `for` structure consisted of three expressions, as defined earlier in this chapter, separated by semicolons. C++ loops allow you do to things like the following, however:

```
for (int i = 0; i < 5; i++)
```

That is, you can declare a variable in the initialization area of a `for` loop. This can be convenient, but it doesn't fit the original syntax because a declaration is not an expression. This once outlaw behavior was originally accommodated by defining a new kind of expression, the *declaration-statement expression*, which was a declaration stripped of the semicolon, and which could appear only in a `for` statement. That adjustment has been dropped, however. Instead, the syntax for the `for` statement has been modified to the following:

```
for (for-init-statement condition; expression)
    statement
```

At first glance, this looks odd because there is just one semicolon instead of two. But that's okay because *for-init-statement* is identified as a statement, and a statement has its own semicolon. As for *for-init-statement*, it's identified as either an expression-statement or a declaration. This syntax rule replaces an expression followed by a semicolon with a statement, which has its own semicolon. What this boils down to is that C++ programmers want to be able to declare and initialize a variable in a `for` loop initialization, and they'll do whatever is necessary to C++ syntax and to the English language to make it possible.

There's a practical aspect to declaring a variable in *for-init-statement* that you should know about. Such a variable exists only within the `for` statement. That is, after the program leaves the loop, the variable is eliminated:

```
for (int i = 0; i < 5; i++)
    cout << "C++ knows loops.\n";
cout << i << endl;  // oops! i no longer defined
```

Another thing you should know is that some C++ implementations follow an earlier rule and treat the preceding loop as if `i` were declared *before* the loop, thus making it available after the loop terminates. Use of this new option for declaring a variable in a `for` loop initialization results, at least at this time, in different behaviors on different systems.

Caution

At the time of writing, not all compilers have implemented the current rule that a variable declared in a `for` loop control section expires when the loop terminates. For example, Microsoft Visual C++ prior to 7.1 by default follows the old rule, mainly because much code in existing Microsoft libraries was written before the new rule was adopted. (Version 7.1, in a valiant, but nonstandard, attempt to live with both rules, accepts code written either way.)

Back to the `for` Loop

Let's be a bit more ambitious with loops. Listing 5.4 uses a loop to calculate and store the first 16 factorials. Factorials, which are handy for computing odds, are calculated the following way. Zero factorial, written as 0!, is defined to be 1. Then, 1! is 1 * 0!, or 1. Next, 2! is 2 * 1!, or 2. Then, 3! is 3 * 2!, or 6, and so on, with the factorial of each integer being the product of that integer with the preceding factorial. (One of the pianist Victor Borge's best-known monologues features phonetic punctuation, in which the exclamation mark is pronounced something like phffft pptz, with a moist accent. However, in this case, "!" is pronounced "factorial.") The program uses one loop to calculate the values of successive factorials, storing them in an array. Then it uses a second loop to display the results. Also, the program introduces the use of external declarations for values.

LISTING 5.4   `formore.cpp`

```
// formore.cpp -- more looping with for
#include <iostream>
using namespace std;
const int ArSize = 16;      // example of external declaration
int main()
{
```

LISTING 5.4   *Continued*

```
    double factorials[ArSize];
    factorials[1] = factorials[0] = 1.0;
 // int i;
    for (int i = 2; i < ArSize; i++)
        factorials[i] = i * factorials[i-1];
    for (i = 0; i < ArSize; i++)
        cout << i << "! = " << factorials[i] << endl;
    return 0;
}
```

Here is the output from the program in Listing 5.4:

```
0! = 1
1! = 1
2! = 2
3! = 6
4! = 24
5! = 120
6! = 720
7! = 5040
8! = 40320
9! = 362880
10! = 3.6288e+006
11! = 3.99168e+007
12! = 4.79002e+008
13! = 6.22702e+009
14! = 8.71783e+010
15! = 1.30767e+012
```

Factorials get big fast!

Program Notes

The program in Listing 5.4 creates an array to hold the factorial values. Element 0 is 0!, element 1 is 1!, and so on. Because the first two factorials equal 1, the program sets the first two elements of the `factorials` array to 1.0. (Remember, the first element of an array has an index value of 0.) After that, the program uses a loop to set each factorial to the product of the index with the previous factorial. The loop illustrates that you can use the loop counter as a variable in the body of the loop.

The program in Listing 5.4 demonstrates how the `for` loop works hand-in-hand with arrays by providing a convenient means to access each array member in turn. Also, `formore.cpp` uses `const` to create a symbolic representation (`ArSize`) for the array size. Then it uses `ArSize` wherever the array size comes into play, such as in the array definition and in the limits for the loops handling the array. Now, if you wish to extend the program to, say, 20 factorials, you just have to set `ArSize` to 20 in the program and recompile. By using a symbolic constant, you avoid having to change every occurrence of 16 to 20 individually.

Tip

It's usually a good idea to define a `const` value to represent the number of elements in an array. You can use the `const` value in the array declaration and in all other references to the array size, such as in a `for` loop.

The `limit i < ArSize` expression reflects the fact that subscripts for an array with `ArSize` elements run from `0` to `ArSize - 1`, so the array index should stop one short of `ArSize`. You could use the test `i <= ArSize - 1` instead, but it looks awkward in comparison.

Note that the program declares the `const int` variable `ArSize` outside the body of `main()`. As the end of Chapter 4, "Compound Types," mentions, this makes `ArSize` external data. The two consequences of declaring `ArSize` in this fashion are that `ArSize` exists for the duration of the program and that all functions in the program file can use it. In this particular case, the program has just one function, so declaring `ArSize` externally has little practical effect. But multi-function programs often benefit from sharing external constants, so we'll practice using them next.

Changing the Step Size

So far the loop examples in this chapter have increased or decreased the loop counter by one in each cycle. You can change that by changing the update expression. The program in Listing 5.5, for example, increases the loop counter by a user-selected step size. Rather than use `i++` as the update expression, it uses the expression `i = i + by`, where `by` is the user-selected step size.

LISTING 5.5 `bigstep.cpp`

```
// bigstep.cpp -- count as directed
#include <iostream>
int main()
{
    using namespace std;
    cout << "Enter an integer: ";
    int by;
    cin >> by;
    cout << "Counting by " << by << "s:\n";
    for (int i = 0; i < 100; i = i + by)
        cout << i << endl;
    return 0;
}
```

Here is a sample run of the program in Listing 5.5:

```
Enter an integer: 17
Counting by 17s:
0
17
34
```

```
51
68
85
```

When i reaches the value 102, the loop quits. The main point here is that the update expression can be any valid expression. For example, if you want to square i and add 10 in each cycle, you can use i = i * i + 10.

Inside Strings with the `for` Loop

The `for` loop provides a direct way to access each character in a string in turn. For example, Listing 5.6 enables you to enter a string and then displays the string character-by-character, in reverse order. You could use either a **string** class object or an array of **char** in this example because both allow you to use array notation to access individual characters in a string; Listing 5.6 uses a **string** class object. The **string** class `size()` method yields the number of characters in the string; the loop uses that value in its initializing expression to set i to the index of the last character in the string, not counting the null character. To count backward, the program uses the decrement operator (--) to decrease the array subscript by one in each loop. Also, Listing 5.6 uses the greater-than-or-equal-to relational operator (>=) to test whether the loop has reached the first element. We'll summarize all the relational operators soon.

LISTING 5.6   `forstr1.cpp`

```cpp
// forstr1.cpp -- using for with a string
#include <iostream>
#include <string>
int main()
{
    using namespace std;
    cout << "Enter a word: ";
    string word;
    cin >> word;

    // display letters in reverse order
    for (int i = word.size() - 1; i >= 0; i--)
        cout << word[i];
    cout << "\nBye.\n";
    return 0;
}
```

Here is a sample run of the program in Listing 5.6:

```
Enter a word: animal
lamina
Bye.
```

Yes, the program succeeds in printing **animal** backward; choosing **animal** as a test word more clearly illustrates the effect of this program than choosing, say, a palindrome such as **redder** or **stats**.

The Increment (++) and Decrement (--) Operators

C++ features several operators that are frequently used in loops; let's take a little time to examine them now. You've already seen two: the increment operator (++), which inspired the name C++, and the decrement operator (--). These operators perform two exceedingly common loop operations: increasing and decreasing a loop counter by one. However, there's more to their story than you've seen to this point. Each operator comes in two varieties. The *prefix* version comes before the operand, as in ++x. The *postfix* version comes after the operand, as in x++. The two versions have the same effect on the operand, but they differ in terms of when they take place. It's like getting paid for mowing the lawn in advance or afterward; both methods have the same final effect on your wallet, but they differ in when the money gets added. Listing 5.7 demonstrates this difference for the increment operator.

LISTING 5.7   plus_one.cpp

```cpp
// plus_one.cpp -- the increment operator
#include <iostream>
int main()
{
    using namespace std;
    int a = 20;
    int b = 20;

    cout << "a   = " << a << ":   b = " << b << "\n";
    cout << "a++ = " << a++ << ": ++b = " << ++b << "\n";
    cout << "a   = " << a << ":   b = " << b << "\n";
    return 0;
}
```

Here is the output from the program in Listing 5.7:

```
a     = 20:   b = 20
a++   = 20: ++b = 21
a     = 21:   b = 21
```

Roughly speaking, the notation a++ means "use the current value of a in evaluating an expression, and then increment the value of a." Similarly, the notation ++b means "first increment the value of b, and then use the new value in evaluating the expression." For example, we have the following relationships:

```cpp
int x = 5;
int y = ++x;        // change x, then assign to y
                    // y is 6, x is 6

int z = 5;
int y = z++;        // assign to y, then change z
                    // y is 5, z is 6
```

Using the increment and decrement operators is a concise, convenient way to handle the common task of increasing or decreasing values by one.

The increment and decrement operators are nifty little operators, but don't get carried away and increment or decrement the same value more than once in the same statement. The problem is that the use-then-change and change-then-use rules can become ambiguous. That is, a statement such as this

```
x = 2 * x++ * (3 - ++x);    // don't do it
```

can produce quite different results on different systems. C++ does not define correct behavior for this sort of statement.

Side Effects and Sequence Points

Let's take a closer look at what C++ does and doesn't say about when increment operators take effect. First, recall that a *side effect* is an effect that occurs when evaluating an expression modifies something, such as a value stored in a variable. A *sequence point* is a point in program execution at which all side effects are guaranteed to be evaluated before going on to the next step. In C++ the semicolon in a statement marks a sequence point. That means all changes made by assignment operators, increment operators, and decrement operators in a statement must take place before a program proceeds to the next statement. Some operators that we'll discuss in later chapters have sequence points. Also, the end of any full expression is a sequence point.

What's a full expression? It's an expression that's not a subexpression of a larger expression. Examples of full expressions include an expression portion of an expression statement and an expression that serves as a test condition for a `while` loop.

Sequence points help clarify when postfix incrementation takes place. Consider, for instance, the following code:

```
while (guests++ < 10)
    printf("%d \n", guests);
```

Sometimes C++ newcomers assume that "use the value, then increment it" means, in this context, to increment `guests` after it's used in the `printf()` statement. However, the `guests++ < 10` expression is a full expression because it is a `while` loop test condition, so the end of this expression is a sequence point. Therefore, C++ guarantees that the side effect (incrementing `guests`) takes place before the program moves on to `printf()`. Using the postfix form, however, guarantees that `guests` will be incremented after the comparison to `10` is made.

Now consider this statement:

```
y = (4 + x++) + (6 + x++);
```

The expression `4 + x++` is not a full expression, so C++ does not guarantee that `x` will be incremented immediately after the subexpression `4 + x++` is evaluated. Here the full expression is the entire assignment statement, and the semicolon marks the sequence point, so all that C++ guarantees is that `x` will have been incremented twice by the time the program moves to the following statement. C++ does not specify whether `x` is incremented after each subexpression is evaluated or only after all the expressions have been evaluated, which is why you should avoid statements of this kind.

Prefixing Versus Postfixing

Clearly, whether you use the prefix or postfix form makes a difference if the value is used for some purpose, such as a function argument or assigning to a variable. But what if the value of an increment or decrement expression isn't used? For example, are

```
x++;
```

and

```
++x;
```

different from one another? Or are

```
for (n = lim; n > 0; --n)
    ...;
```

and

```
for (n = lim; n > 0; n--)
    ...;
```

different from one another?

Logically, whether the prefix or postfix forms are used makes no difference in these two situations. The values of the expressions aren't used, so the only effects are the side effects. Here the expressions using the operators are full expressions, so the side effects of incrementing x and decrementing n are guaranteed to be performed by the time the program moves on to the next step; the prefix form and postfix form lead to the same final result.

However, although the choice between prefix and postfix forms has no effect on the program's behavior, it is possible for the choice to have a small effect on execution speed. For built-in types and modern compilers, this seems to be a non-issue. But C++ lets you define these operators for classes. In that case, the user defines a prefix function that works by incrementing a value and then returning it. But the postfix version works by first stashing a copy of the value, incrementing the value, and then returning the stashed copy. Thus, for classes, the prefix version is a bit more efficient than the postfix version.

In short, for built-in types, it mostly likely makes no difference which form you use. For user-defined types having user-defined increment and decrement operators, the prefix form is more efficient.

The Increment/Decrement Operators and Pointers

You can use increment operators with pointers as well as with basic variables. Recall that adding an increment operator to a pointer increases its value by the number of bytes in the type it points to. The same rule holds for incrementing and decrementing pointers:

```
double arr[5] = {21.1, 32.8, 23.4, 45.2, 37.4};
double *pt = arr;   // pt points to arr[0], i.e. to 21.1
++pt;               // pt points to arr[1], i.e. to 32.8
```

You can also use these operators to change the quantity a pointer points to by using them in conjunction with the * operator. Applying both * and ++ to a pointer raises the questions of what gets dereferenced and what gets incremented. Those actions are determined by the placement and precedence of the operators. The prefix increment, prefix decrement, and dereferencing operators all have the same precedence and associate from right to left. The postfix increment and decrement operators both have the same precedence, which is higher than the prefix precedence. These two operators associate from left to right.

The right-to-left association rule for prefix operators implies that `*++pt` means first apply `++` to `pt` (because the `++` is to the right of the `*`) and then apply `*` to the new value of `pt`:

```
*++pt;        // increment pointer, take the value; i.e., arr[2], or 23.4
```

On the other hand, `++*pt` means obtain the value that `pt` points to and then increment that value:

```
++*pt;        // increment the pointed to value; i.e., change 23.4 to 24.4
```

Here, `pt` remains pointing to `arr[2]`.

Next, consider this combination:

```
(*pt)++;      // increment pointed-to value
```

The parentheses indicate that first the pointer is dereferenced, yielding **24.4**. Then the `++` operator increments that value to **25.4**; `pt` remains pointing at `arr[2]`.

Finally, consider this combination:

```
*pt++;        // dereference original location, then increment pointer
```

The higher precedence of the postfix `++` operator means the `++` operator operates on `pt`, not on `*pt`, so the pointer is incremented. But the fact that the postfix operator is used means that the address that gets dereferenced is the original address, `&arr[2]`, not the new address. Thus, the value of `*pt++` is `arr[2]`, or **25.4**, but the value of `pt` after the statement completes is the address of `arr[3]`.

Remember

Incrementing and decrementing pointers follow pointer arithmetic rules. Thus, if `pt` points to the first member of an array, `++pt` changes `pt` so that it points to the second member.

Combination Assignment Operators

Listing 5.5 uses the following expression to update a loop counter:

```
i = i + by
```

C++ has a combined addition and assignment operator that accomplishes the same result more concisely:

```
i += by
```

The += operator adds the values of its two operands and assigns the result to the operand on the left. This implies that the left operand must be something to which you can assign a value, such as a variable, an array element, a structure member, or data you identify by dereferencing a pointer:

```
int k = 5;
k += 3;                    // ok, k set to 8
int *pa = new int[10];     // pa points to pa[0]
pa[4] = 12;
pa[4] += 6;                // ok, pa[4] set to 18
*(pa + 4) += 7;            // ok, pa[4] set to 25
pa += 2;                   // ok, pa points to the former pa[2]
34 += 10;                  // quite wrong
```

Each arithmetic operator has a corresponding assignment operator, as summarized in Table 5.1. Each operator works analogously to +=. Thus, for example, the statement

```
k *= 10;
```

replaces the current value of k with a value 10 times greater.

TABLE 5.1   Combined Assignment Operators

Operator	Effect (L=left operand, R=right operand)
+=	Assigns L + R to L
-=	Assigns L – R to L
*=	Assigns L * R to L
/=	Assigns L / R to L
%=	Assigns L % R to L

Compound Statements, or Blocks

The format, or syntax, for writing a C++ **for** statement might seem restrictive to you because the body of the loop must be a single statement. That's awkward if you want the loop body to contain several statements. Fortunately, C++ provides a syntax loophole through which you may stuff as many statements as you like into a loop body. The trick is to use paired braces to construct a *compound statement*, or *block*. The block consists of paired braces and the statements they enclose and, for the purposes of syntax, counts as a single statement. For example, the program in Listing 5.8 uses braces to combine three separate statements into a single block. This enables the body of the loop to prompt the user, read input, and do a calculation. The program calculates the running sum of the numbers you enter, and this provides a natural occasion for using the += operator.

LISTING 5.8   block.cpp

```cpp
// block.cpp -- use a block statement
#include <iostream>
int main()
{
    using namespace std;
    cout << "The Amazing Accounto will sum and average ";
    cout << "five numbers for you.\n";
    cout << "Please enter five values:\n";
    double number;
    double sum = 0.0;
    for (int i = 1; i <= 5; i++)
    {                                       // block starts here
        cout << "Value " << i << ": ";
        cin >> number;
        sum += number;
    }                                       // block ends here
    cout << "Five exquisite choices indeed! ";
    cout << "They sum to " << sum << endl;
    cout << "and average to " << sum / 5 << ".\n";
    cout << "The Amazing Accounto bids you adieu!\n";
    return 0;
}
```

Here is a sample run of the program in Listing 5.8:

```
The Amazing Accounto will sum and average five numbers for you.
Please enter five values:
Value 1: 1942
Value 2: 1948
Value 3: 1957
Value 4: 1974
Value 5: 1980
Five exquisite choices indeed! They sum to 9801
and average to 1960.2.
The Amazing Accounto bids you adieu!
```

Suppose you leave in the indentation but omit the braces:

```cpp
for (int i = 1; i <= 5; i++)
        cout << "Value " << i << ": ";      // loop ends here
        cin >> number;                      // after the loop
        sum += number;
cout << "Five exquisite choices indeed! ";
```

The compiler ignores indentation, so only the first statement would be in the loop. Thus, the loop would print the five prompts and do nothing more. After the loop completes, the program moves to the following lines, reading and summing just one number.

Compound statements have another interesting property. If you define a new variable inside a block, the variable persists only as long as the program is executing statements within the block. When execution leaves the block, the variable is deallocated. That means the variable is known only within the block:

```
#include  <iostream>
using namespace std;
int main()
{
    int x = 20;
    {                           // block starts
        int y = 100;
        cout << x << endl;      // ok
        cout << y << endl;      // ok
    }                           // block ends
     cout << x << endl;  // ok
     cout << y << endl;         // invalid, won't compile
     return 0;
}
```

Note that a variable defined in an outer block is still defined in the inner block.

What happens if you declare a variable in a block that has the same name as one outside the block? The new variable hides the old one from its point of appearance until the end of the block. Then, the old one becomes visible again, as in this example:

```
int main()
{
    int x = 20;             // original x
    {                       // block starts
       cout << x << endl;   // use original x
       int x = 100;         // new x
       cout << x << endl;   // use new x
    }                       // block ends
    cout << x << endl;      // use original x
    return 0;
}
```

The Comma Operator (or More Syntax Tricks)

As you have seen, a block enables you to sneak two or more statements into a place where C++ syntax allows just one statement. The comma operator does the same for expressions, enabling you to sneak two expressions into a place where C++ syntax allows only one expression. For example, suppose you have a loop in which one variable increases by one each cycle and a second variable decreases by one each cycle. Doing both in the update part of a `for` loop control section would be convenient, but the loop syntax allows just one expression there. The solution is to use the comma operator to combine the two expressions into one:

```
++j, --i   // two expressions count as one for syntax purposes
```

The comma is not always a comma operator. For example, the comma in this declaration serves to separate adjacent names in a list of variables:

```
int i, j;  // comma is a separator here, not an operator
```

Listing 5.9 uses the comma operator twice in a program that reverses the contents of a `string` class object. (You could also write the program by using an array of `char`, but the length of the word would be limited by your choice of array size.) Note that Listing 5.6 displays the contents of an array in reverse order, but Listing 5.9 actually moves characters around in the array. The program in Listing 5.9 also uses a block to group several statements into one.

LISTING 5.9   forstr2.cpp

```
// forstr2.cpp -- reversing an array
#include <iostream>
#include <string>
int main()
{
    using namespace std;
    cout << "Enter a word: ";
    string word;
    cin >> word;

    // physically modify string object
    char temp;
    int i, j;
    for (j = 0, i = word.size() - 1; j < i; --i, ++j)
    {                           // start block
        temp = word[i];
        word[i] = word[j];
        word[j] = temp;
    }                           // end block
    cout << word << "\nDone\n";
    return 0;
}
```

Here is a sample run of the program in Listing 5.9:

```
Enter a word: parts
strap
Done
```

By the way, the `string` class offers more concise ways to reverse a string, but we'll leave those for Chapter 16, "The `string` Class and the Standard Template Library."

Program Notes

Look at the `for` control section of the program in Listing 5.9.

First, it uses the comma operator to squeeze two initializations into one expression for the first part of the control section. Then it uses the comma operator again to combine two updates into a single expression for the last part of the control section.

Next, look at the body. The program uses braces to combine several statements into a single unit. In the body, the program reverses the word by switching the first element of the array with the last element. Then it increments `j` and decrements `i` so that they now refer to the next-to-the-first element and the next-to-the-last element. After this is done, the program swaps those elements. Note that the test condition `j<i` makes the loop stop when it reaches the center of the array. If it were to continue past that point, it would begin swapping the switched elements back to their original positions. (See Figure 5.2.)

FIGURE 5.2

Reversing a string.

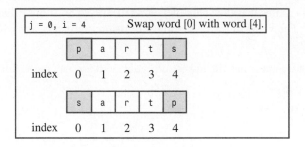

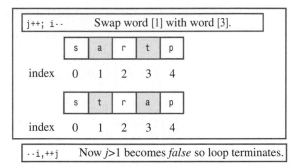

Another thing to note is the location for declaring the variables `temp`, `i`, and `j`. The code declares `i` and `j` before the loop because you can't combine two declarations with a comma operator. That's because declarations already use the comma for another purpose—separating items in a list. You can use a single declaration-statement expression to create and initialize two variables, but it's a bit confusing visually:

```
int j = 0, i = word.size() - 1;
```

In this case the comma is just a list separator, not the comma operator, so the expression declares and initializes both `j` and `i`. However, it looks as if it declares only `j`.

Incidentally, you can declare `temp` inside the `for` loop:

```
int temp = word[i];
```

This may result in `temp` being allocated and deallocated in each loop cycle. This might be a bit slower than declaring `temp` once before the loop. On the other hand, after the loop is finished, `temp` is discarded if it's declared inside the loop.

Comma Operator Tidbits

By far the most common use for the comma operator is to fit two or more expressions into a single `for` loop expression. But C++ does provide the operator with two additional properties. First, it guarantees that the first expression is evaluated before the second expression. (In other words, the comma operator is a sequence point.) Expressions such as the following are safe:

```
i = 20, j = 2 * i       // i set to 20, j set to 40
```

Second, C++ states that the value of a comma expression is the value of the second part of the expression. The value of the preceding expression, for example, is 40, because that is the value of `j = 2 * i`.

The comma operator has the lowest precedence of any operator. For example, this statement:

```
cats = 17,240;
```

gets read as this:

```
(cats = 17), 240;
```

That is, `cats` is set to `17`, and `240` does nothing. But, because parentheses have high precedence, this:

```
cats = (17,240);
```

results in `cats` being set to `240`, the value of the expression on the right of the comma.

Relational Expressions

Computers are more than relentless number crunchers. They have the capability to compare values, and this capability is the foundation of computer decision making. In C++ relational operators embody this ability. C++ provides six relational operators to compare numbers. Because characters are represented by their ASCII codes, you can use these operators with characters, too. They don't work with C-style strings, but they do work with `string` class objects. Each relational expression reduces to the `bool` value `true` if the comparison is true and to the `bool` value `false` if the comparison is false, so these operators are well suited for use in a loop test expression. (Older implementations evaluate true relational expressions to 1 and false relational expressions to 0.) Table 5.2 summarizes these operators.

TABLE 5.2 Relational Operators

Operator	Meaning
<	Is less than
<=	Is less than or equal to
==	Is equal to
>	Is greater than
>=	Is greater than or equal to
!=	Is not equal to

The six relational operators exhaust the comparisons C++ enables you to make for numbers. If you want to compare two values to see which is the more beautiful or the luckier, you must look elsewhere.

Here are some sample tests:

```
for (x = 20; x > 5; x--) // continue while x is greater than 5
for (x = 1; y != x; ++x) // continue while y is not equal to x
for (cin >> x; x == 0; cin >> x))    // continue while x is 0
```

The relational operators have a lower precedence than the arithmetic operators. That means this expression:

```
x + 3 > y - 2              // Expression 1
```

corresponds to this:

```
(x + 3) > (y - 2)          // Expression 2
```

and not to the following:

```
x + (3 > y) - 2            // Expression 3
```

Because the expression (`3 > y`) is either `1` or `0` after the `bool` value is promoted to `int`, Expressions 2 and 3 are both valid. But most of us would want Expression 1 to mean Expression 2, and that is what C++ does.

A Mistake You'll Probably Make

Don't confuse testing the is-equal-to operator (`==`) with the assignment operator (`=`). This expression:

```
musicians == 4    // comparison
```

asks the musical question Is `musicians` equal to 4? The expression has the value `true` or `false`. This expression:

```
musicians = 4     // assignment
```

assigns the value `4` to `musicians`. The whole expression, in this case, has the value `4` because that's the value of the left side.

The flexible design of the `for` loop creates an interesting opportunity for error. If you accidentally drop an equals sign (`=`) from the `==` operator and use an assignment expression instead of a relational expression for the test part of a `for` loop, you still produce valid code. That's because you can use any valid C++ expression for a `for` loop test condition. Remember that nonzero values test as `true` and zero tests as `false`. An expression that assigns 4 to `musicians` has the value `4` and is treated as `true`. If you come from a language, such as Pascal or BASIC, that uses `=` to test for equality, you might be particularly prone to this slip.

Listing 5.10 shows a situation in which you can make this sort of error. The program attempts to examine an array of quiz scores and stops when it reaches the first score that's not 20. It shows a loop that correctly uses comparison and then one that mistakenly uses assignment in the test condition. The program also has another egregious design error that you'll see how to fix later. (You learn from your mistakes, and Listing 5.10 is happy to help in that respect.)

LISTING 5.10   `equal.cpp`

```cpp
// equal.cpp -- equality vs assignment
#include <iostream>
int main()
{
    using namespace std;
    int quizscores[10] =
        { 20, 20, 20, 20, 20, 19, 20, 18, 20, 20};

    cout << "Doing it right:\n";
    int i;
    for (i = 0; quizscores[i] == 20; i++)
        cout << "quiz " << i << " is a 20\n";

    cout << "Doing it dangerously wrong:\n";
    for (i = 0; quizscores[i] = 20; i++)
        cout << "quiz " << i << " is a 20\n";

    return 0;
}
```

Because the program in Listing 5.10 has a serious problem, you might prefer reading about it to actually running it. Here is some sample output from the program:

```
Doing it right:
quiz 0 is a 20
quiz 1 is a 20
quiz 2 is a 20
quiz 3 is a 20
quiz 4 is a 20
Doing it dangerously wrong:
quiz 0 is a 20
quiz 1 is a 20
quiz 2 is a 20
quiz 3 is a 20
quiz 4 is a 20
quiz 5 is a 20
quiz 6 is a 20
quiz 7 is a 20
quiz 8 is a 20
quiz 9 is a 20
quiz 10 is a 20
quiz 11 is a 20
quiz 12 is a 20
quiz 13 is a 20
...
```

The first loop correctly halts after displaying the first five quiz scores. But the second starts by displaying the whole array. Worse than that, it says every value is 20. And worse still, it doesn't stop at the end of the array!

Where things go wrong, of course, is with the following test expression:

```
quizscores[i] = 20
```

First, simply because it assigns a nonzero value to the array element, the expression is always nonzero, hence always true. Second, because the expression assigns values to the array elements, it actually changes the data. Third, because the test expression remains true, the program continues changing data beyond the end of the array. It just keeps putting more and more 20s into memory! This is not good.

The difficulty with this kind of error is that the code is syntactically correct, so the compiler won't tag it as an error. (However, years and years of C and C++ programmers making this error has eventually led many compilers to issue a warning, asking if that's what you really meant to do.)

Caution

Don't use = to compare for equality; use ==.

Like C, C++ grants you more freedom than most programming languages. This comes at the cost of requiring greater responsibility on your part. Nothing but your own good planning prevents a program from going beyond the bounds of a standard C++ array. However, with C++ classes, you can design a protected array type that prevents this sort of nonsense. Chapter 13, "Class Inheritance," provides an example. For now, you should build the protection into your programs when you need it. For example, the loop in Listing 5.10 should include a test that keeps it from going past the last member. That's true even for the "good" loop. If all the scores were 20s, the "good" loop, too, would exceed the array bounds. In short, the loop needs to test the values of the array and the array index. Chapter 6 shows how to use logical operators to combine two such tests into a single condition.

Comparing C-Style Strings

Suppose you want to see if a string in a character array is the word `mate`. If `word` is the array name, the following test might not do what you think it should do:

```
word == "mate"
```

Remember that the name of an array is a synonym for its address. Similarly, a quoted string constant is a synonym for its address. Thus, the preceding relational expression doesn't test whether the strings are the same; it checks whether they are stored at the same address. The answer to that is no, even if the two strings have the same characters.

Because C++ handles C-style strings as addresses, you get little satisfaction if you try to use the relational operators to compare strings. Instead, you can go to the C-style string library and use the `strcmp()` function to compare strings. This function takes two string addresses as arguments. That means the arguments can be pointers, string constants, or character array names. If the two strings are identical, the function returns the value `0`. If the first string precedes the second alphabetically, `strcmp()` returns a negative value, and if the first string follows the second alphabetically, `strcmp()` returns a positive value. Actually, "in the system collating sequence" is more accurate than "alphabetically." This means that characters are compared according to the system code for characters. For example, in ASCII code, uppercase letters have smaller codes than the lowercase letters, so uppercase precedes lowercase in the collating sequence. Therefore, the string "Zoo" precedes the string "aviary". The fact that comparisons are based on code values also means that uppercase and lowercase letters differ, so the string "FOO" is different from the string "foo".

In some languages, such as BASIC and standard Pascal, strings stored in differently sized arrays are necessarily unequal to each other. But C-style strings are defined by the terminating null character, not by the size of the containing array. This means that two strings can be identical even if they are contained in differently sized arrays:

```
char big[80] = "Daffy";          // 5 letters plus \0
char little[6] = "Daffy";        // 5 letters plus \0
```

By the way, although you can't use relational operators to compare strings, you can use them to compare characters because characters are actually integer types. So this:

```
for (ch = 'a'; ch <= 'z'; ch++)
    cout << ch;
```

is valid code, at least for the ASCII character set, for displaying the characters of the alphabet.

The program in Listing 5.11 uses strcmp() in the test condition of a for loop. The program displays a word, changes its first letter, displays the word again, and keeps going until strcmp() determines that word is the same as the string "mate". Note that the listing includes the cstring file because it provides a function prototype for strcmp().

LISTING 5.11   compstr1.cpp

```
// compstr1.cpp -- comparing strings using arrays
#include <iostream>
#include <cstring>       // prototype for strcmp()
int main()
{
    using namespace std;
    char word[5] = "?ate";

    for (char ch = 'a'; strcmp(word, "mate"); ch++)
    {
        cout << word << endl;
        word[0] = ch;
    }
    cout << "After loop ends, word is " << word << endl;
    return 0;
}
```

Compatibility Note

You might have to use string.h instead of cstring. Also, the code in Listing 5.11 assumes that the system uses the ASCII character code set. In that set, the codes for the letters a through z are consecutive, and the code for the ? character immediately precedes the code for a.

Here is the output for the program in Listing 5.11:

```
?ate
aate
bate
cate
date
eate
fate
gate
hate
iate
jate
kate
late
After loop ends, word is mate
```

Program Notes

The program in Listing 5.11 has some interesting points. One, of course, is the test. You want the loop to continue as long as `word` is not `mate`. That is, you want the test to continue as long as `strcmp()` says the two strings are not the same. The most obvious test for that is this:

```
strcmp(word, "mate") != 0     // strings are not the same
```

This statement has the value `1` (`true`) if the strings are unequal and the value `0` (`false`) if they are equal. But what about `strcmp(word, "mate")` by itself? It has a nonzero value (`true`) if the strings are unequal and the value `0` (`false`) if the strings are equal. In essence, the function returns `true` if the strings are different and `false` if they are the same. You can use just the function instead of the whole relational expression. This produces the same behavior and involves less typing. Also, it's the way C and C++ programmers have traditionally used `strcmp()`.

Remember

You can use `strcmp()` to test C-style strings for equality or order. The expression

```
strcmp(str1,str2) == 0
```

is true if `str1` and `str2` are identical; the expressions

```
strcmp(str1, str2) != 0
```

and

```
strcmp(str1, str2)
```

are true if `str1` and `str2` are not identical; the expression

```
strcmp(str1,str2) < 0
```

is true if `str1` precedes `str2`; and the expression

```
strcmp(str1, str2) > 0
```

is true if `str1` follows `str2`. Thus, the `strcmp()` function can play the role of the `==`, `!=`, `<`, and `>` operators, depending on how you set up a test condition.

Next, compstr1.cpp uses the increment operator to march the variable `ch` through the alphabet:

```
ch++
```

You can use the increment and decrement operators with character variables because type `char` really is an integer type, so the operation actually changes the integer code stored in the variable. Also, note that using an array index makes it simple to change individual characters in a string:

```
word[0] = ch;
```

Comparing `string` Class Strings

Life is a bit simpler if you use `string` class strings instead of C-style strings because the class design allows you to use relational operators to make the comparisons. This is possible because you define class functions that "overload", or redefine, operators. Chapter 12, "Classes and Dynamic Memory Allocation," discusses how to incorporate this feature into class designs, but, from a practical standpoint, all you need to know now is that you can use the relational operators with `string` class objects. Listing 5.12 revises Listing 5.11 to use a `string` object instead of an array of `char`.

LISTING 5.12   compstr2.cpp

```cpp
// compstr2.cpp -- comparing strings using arrays
#include <iostream>
#include <string>      // string class
int main()
{
    using namespace std;
    string word = "?ate";

    for (char ch = 'a'; word != "mate"; ch++)
    {
        cout << word << endl;
        word[0] = ch;
    }
    cout << "After loop ends, word is " << word << endl;
    return 0;
}
```

The output from the program in Listing 5.12 is the same as that for the program in Listing 5.11.

Program Notes

In Listing 5.12, the test condition

```
word != "mate"
```

uses a relational operator with a `string` object on the left and a C-style string on the right. The way the `string` class overloads the `!=` operator allows you to use it as long as at least one of the operands is a `string` object; the remaining operand can be either a `string` object or a C-style string.

The `string` class design allows you to use a `string` object as a single entity, as in the relational test expression, or as an aggregate object for which you can use array notation to extract individual characters.

Finally, unlike most of the `for` loops you have seen to this point, the last two loops aren't counting loops. That is, they don't execute a block of statements a specified number of times. Instead, each of these loops watches for a particular circumstance (`word` being `"mate"`) to signal that it's time to stop. More typically, C++ programs use `while` loops for this second kind of test, so let's examine that form next.

The `while` Loop

The `while` loop is a `for` loop stripped of the initialization and update parts; it has just a test condition and a body:

```
while (test-condition)
        body
```

First, a program evaluates the parenthesized *test-condition* expression. If the expression evaluates to `true`, the program executes the statement(s) in the body. As with a `for` loop, the body consists of a single statement or a block defined by paired braces. After it finishes with the body, the program returns to the test condition and reevaluates it. If the condition is nonzero, the program executes the body again. This cycle of testing and execution continues until the test condition evaluates to `false`. (See Figure 5.3.) Clearly, if you want the loop to terminate eventually, something within the loop body must do something to affect the *test-condition* expression. For example, the loop can increment a variable used in the test condition or read a new value from keyboard input. Like the `for` loop, the `while` loop is an entry-condition loop. Thus, if *test-condition* evaluates to `false` at the beginning, the program never executes the body of the loop.

Listing 5.13 puts a `while` loop to work. The loop cycles through each character in a string and displays the character and its ASCII code. The loop quits when it reaches the null character. This technique of stepping through a string character-by-character until reaching the null character is a standard C++ method for processing strings. Because a string contains its own termination marker, programs often don't need explicit information about how long a string is.

FIGURE 5.3
The structure of `while` loops.

statement1
while (test_expr)
   statement2
statement3

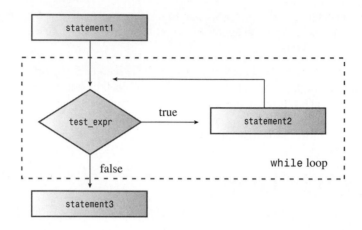

LISTING 5.13 `while.cpp`

```cpp
// while.cpp -- introducing the while loop
#include <iostream>
const int ArSize = 20;
int main()
{
    using namespace std;
    char name[ArSize];

    cout << "Your first name, please: ";
    cin >> name;
    cout << "Here is your name, verticalized and ASCIIized:\n";
    int i = 0;                   // start at beginning of string
    while (name[i] != '\0')      // process to end of string
    {
        cout << name[i] << ": " << int(name[i]) << endl;
        i++;                     // don't forget this step
    }
    return 0;
}
```

Here is a sample run of the program in Listing 5.13:

```
Your first name, please: Muffy
Here is your name, verticalized and ASCIIized:
M: 77
u: 117
f: 102
f: 102
y: 121
```

(No, verticalized and ASCIIized are not real words or even good would-be words. But they do add an endearing technoid tone to the output.)

Program Notes

The `while` condition in Listing 5.13 looks like this:

```
while (name[i] != '\0')
```

It tests whether a particular character in the array is the null character. For this test to eventually succeed, the loop body needs to change the value of `i`. It does so by incrementing `i` at the end of the loop body. Omitting this step keeps the loop stuck on the same array element, printing the character and its code until you manage to kill the program. Getting such an infinite loop is one of the most common problems with loops. Often you can cause it when you forget to update some value within the loop body.

You can rewrite the `while` line this way:

```
while (name[i])
```

With this change, the program works just as it did before. That's because when `name[i]` is an ordinary character, its value is the character code, which is nonzero, or `true`. But when `name[i]` is the null character, its character-code value is `0`, or `false`. This notation is more concise (and more commonly used) but less clear than what Listing 5.13 uses. Dumb compilers might produce faster code for the second version, but smart compilers produce the same code for both.

To print the ASCII code for a character, the program uses a type cast to convert `name[i]` to an integer type. Then `cout` prints the value as an integer rather than interpret it as a character code.

Unlike a C-style string, a `string` class object doesn't use a null character to identify the end of a string, so you can't convert Listing 5.13 to a `string` class version merely by replacing the array of `char` with a `string` object. Chapter 16 discusses techniques you can use with a `string` object to identify the last character.

for Versus while

In C++ the `for` and `while` loops are essentially equivalent. For example, this `for` loop:

```
for (init-expression; test-expression; update-expression)
{
    statement(s)
}
```

could be rewritten this way:

```
init-expression;
while (test-expression)
{
    statement(s)
    update-expression;
}
```

Similarly, this `while` loop:

```
while (test-expression)
    body
```

could be rewritten this way:

```
for ( ;test-expression;)
    body
```

This `for` loop requires three expressions (or, more technically, one statement followed by two expressions), but they can be empty expressions (or statements). Only the two semicolons are mandatory. Incidentally, a missing test expression in a `for` loop is construed as true, so this loop runs forever:

```
for ( ; ; )
    body
```

Because `for` loops and `while` loops are nearly equivalent, the one you use is a matter of style. (There is a slight difference if the body includes a `continue` statement, which is discussed in Chapter 6.) Typically, programmers use `for` loops for counting loops because the `for` loop format enables you to place all the relevant information—initial value, terminating value, and method of updating the counter—in one place. Programmers most often use `while` loops when they don't know in advance precisely how many times a loop will execute.

Tip

Keep in mind the following guidelines when you design a loop:

- Identify the condition that terminates loop execution.
- Initialize that condition before the first test.
- Update the condition in each loop cycle, before the condition is tested again.

One nice thing about `for` loops is that their structure provides a place to implement these three guidelines, thus helping you to remember to do so.

Bad Punctuation

Both `for` loops and `while` loops have bodies that consist of a single statement following the parenthesized expressions. As you've seen, that single statement can be a block, which can contain several statements. Keep in mind that braces, not indentation, define a block. Consider the following loop, for example:

```
i = 0;
while (name[i] != '\0')
        cout << name[i] << endl;
        i++;
cout << "Done\n";
```

The indentation tells you that the program author intended the `i++;` statement to be part of the loop body. The absence of braces, however, tells the compiler that the body consists solely of the first `cout` statement. Thus, the loop keeps printing the first character of the array indefinitely. The program never reaches the `i++;` statement because it is outside the loop.

The following example shows another potential pitfall:

```cpp
i = 0;
while (name[i] != '\0');     // problem semicolon
{
      cout << name[i] << endl;
      i++;
}
cout << "Done\n";
```

This time the code gets the braces right, but it also inserts an extra semicolon. Remember, a semicolon terminates a statement, so this semicolon terminates the `while` loop. In other words, the body of the loop is a *null statement*—that is, nothing followed by a semicolon. All the material in braces now comes *after* the loop and is never reached. Instead, the loop cycles, doing nothing forever. Beware the straggling semicolon.

Just a Moment—Building a Time-Delay Loop

Sometimes it's useful to build a time delay into a program. For example, you might have encountered programs that flash a message onscreen and then go on to something else before you can read the message. You end up being afraid that you've missed irretrievable information of vital importance. It would be much nicer if the program paused 5 seconds before moving on. The `while` loop is handy for producing this effect. A technique from the early days of personal computers was to make the computer count for a while to use up time:

```cpp
long wait = 0;
while (wait < 10000)
    wait++;               // counting silently
```

The problem with this approach is that you have to change the counting limit when you change computer processor speed. Several games written for the original IBM PC, for example, became unmanageably fast when run on its faster successors. A better approach is to let the system clock do the timing for you.

The ANSI C and the C++ libraries have a function to help you do this. The function is called `clock()`, and it returns the system time elapsed since a program started execution. There are a couple complications, though. First, `clock()` doesn't necessarily return the time in seconds. Second, the function's return type might be `long` on some systems, `unsigned long` on others, and perhaps some other type on others.

But the `ctime` header file (`time.h` on less current implementations) provides solutions to these problems. First, it defines a symbolic constant, `CLOCKS_PER_SEC`, that equals the number of system time units per second. So dividing the system time by this value yields seconds. Or you can multiply seconds by `CLOCKS_PER_SEC` to get time in the system units. Second, `ctime` establishes `clock_t` as an alias for the `clock()` return type. (See the sidebar "Type Aliases," later in this chapter.) This means you can declare a variable as type `clock_t`, and the compiler converts it to `long` or `unsigned int` or whatever is the proper type for your system.

Compatibility Note

Systems that haven't added the `ctime` header file can use `time.h` instead. Some C++ implementations might have problems with `waiting.cpp` if the implementation's library component is not fully ANSI C compliant. That's because the `clock()` function is an ANSI addition to the traditional C library. Also, some premature implementations of ANSI C use `CLK_TCK` or `TCK_CLK` instead of the longer `CLOCKS_PER_SEC`. Some older versions of C++ don't recognize any of these defined constants. Some environments have problems with the alarm character `\a` and coordinating the display with the time delay.

Listing 5.14 shows how to use `clock()` and the `ctime` header to create a time-delay loop.

LISTING 5.14   `waiting.cpp`

```
// waiting.cpp -- using clock() in a time-delay loop
#include <iostream>
#include <ctime> // describes clock() function, clock_t type
int main()
{
    using namespace std;
    cout << "Enter the delay time, in seconds: ";
    float secs;
    cin >> secs;
    clock_t delay = secs * CLOCKS_PER_SEC;   // convert to clock ticks
    cout << "starting\a\n";
    clock_t start = clock();
    while (clock() - start < delay )          // wait until time elapses
        ;                                     // note the semicolon
    cout << "done \a\n";
    return 0;
}
```

By calculating the delay time in system units instead of in seconds, the program in Listing 5.14 avoids having to convert system time to seconds in each loop cycle.

Type Aliases

C++ has two ways to establish a new name as an alias for a type. One is to use the preprocessor:

`#define BYTE char // preprocessor replaces BYTE with char`

The preprocessor then replaces all occurrences of `BYTE` with `char` when you compile a program, thus making `BYTE` an alias for `char`.

The second method is to use the C++ (and C) keyword `typedef` to create an alias. For example, to make `byte` an alias for `char`, you use this:

`typedef char byte;    // makes byte an alias for char`

Here's the general form:

```
typedef typeName aliasName;
```

In other words, if you want `aliasName` to be an alias for a particular type, you declare `aliasName` as if it were a variable of that type and then prefix the declaration with the `typedef` keyword. For example, to make `byte_pointer` an alias for pointer-to-char, you could declare `byte_pointer` as a pointer-to-char and then stick `typedef` in front:

```
typedef char * byte_pointer; // pointer to char type
```

You could try something similar with `#define`, but that wouldn't work if you declared a list of variables. For example, consider the following:

```
#define FLOAT_POINTER float *
FLOAT_POINTER pa, pb;
```

Preprocessor substitution converts the declaration to this:

```
float * pa, pb;  // pa a pointer to float, pb just a float
```

The `typedef` approach doesn't have that problem. Its ability to handle more complex type aliases makes using `typedef` a better choice than `#define`—and sometimes it is the only choice.

Notice that `typedef` doesn't create a new type. It just creates a new name for an old type. If you make `word` an alias for `int`, `cout` treats a type `word` value as the `int` it really is.

The `do while` Loop

You've now seen the `for` loop and the `while` loop. The third C++ loop is the `do while`. It's different from the other two because it's an *exit-condition* loop. That means this devil-may-care loop first executes the body of the loop and only then evaluates the test expression to see whether it should continue looping. If the condition evaluates to **false**, the loop terminates; otherwise, a new cycle of execution and testing begins. Such a loop always executes at least once because its program flow must pass through the body of the loop before reaching the test. Here's the syntax for the `do while` loop:

```
do
      body
while (test-expression);
```

The *body* portion can be a single statement or a brace-delimited statement block. Figure 5.4 summarizes the program flow for `do while` loops.

Usually, an entry-condition loop is a better choice than an exit-condition loop because the entry-condition loop checks before looping. For example, suppose Listing 5.13 used `do while` instead of `while`. In that case, the loop would print the null character and its code before finding that it had already reached the end of the string. But sometimes a `do while` test does make sense. For example, if you're requesting user input, the program has to obtain the input before testing it. Listing 5.15 shows how to use `do while` in such a situation.

FIGURE 5.4
The structure of do
while loops.

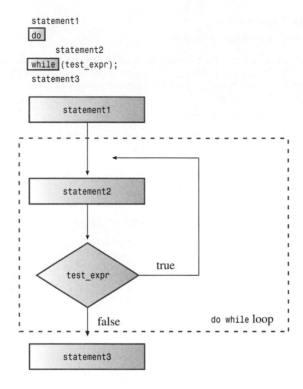

```
statement1
do
  statement2
while (test_expr);
statement3
```

LISTING 5.15 dowhile.cpp

```cpp
// dowhile.cpp -- exit-condition loop
#include <iostream>
int main()
{
    using namespace std;
    int n;

    cout << "Enter numbers in the range 1-10 to find ";
    cout << "my favorite number\n";
    do
    {
        cin >> n;       // execute body
    } while (n != 7);   // then test
    cout << "Yes, 7 is my favorite.\n" ;
    return 0;
}
```

Here's a sample run of the program in Listing 5.15:

```
Enter numbers in the range 1-10 to find my favorite number
9
4
7
Yes, 7 is my favorite.
```

Real-World Note: Strange for loops

It's not terribly common, but you may occasionally see code that resembles the following:

```
for(;;)   // sometimes called a "forever loop"
{
    I++;
    // do something ...
    if (30 >= I) break;     // if statement and break (Chapter 6)
}
```

or another variation:

```
for(;;I++)
{
    if (30 >= I) break;
        // do something ...
 }
```

The code relies on the fact that an empty test condition in a `for` loop is treated as being true. Neither of these examples is easy to read, and neither should be used as a general model of writing a loop. The functionality of the first example can be more clearly expressed in a `do while` loop:

```
do {
    I++;
    // do something;
while (30 < I);
```

Similarly, the second example can be expressed more clearly as a `while` loop:

```
while (I < 30)
{
    // do something
    I++;
}
```

In general, writing clear, easily understood code is a more useful goal than demonstrating the ability to exploit obscure features of the language.

Loops and Text Input

Now that you've seen how loops work, let's look at one of the most common and important tasks assigned to loops: reading text character-by-character from a file or from the keyboard. For example, you might want to write a program that counts the number of characters, lines, and words in the input. Traditionally, C++, like C, uses the `while` loop for this sort of task. We'll next investigate how that is done. If you already know C, don't skim through the following sections too fast. Although the C++ `while` loop is the same as C's, C++'s I/O facilities are different. This can give the C++ loop a somewhat different look from the C loop. In fact, the `cin` object supports three distinct modes of single-character input, each with a different user interface. Let's look at how to use these choices with `while` loops.

Using Unadorned `cin` for Input

If a program is going to use a loop to read text input from the keyboard, it has to have some way of knowing when to stop. How can it know when to stop? One way is to choose some special character, sometimes called a *sentinel character*, to act as a stop sign. For example, Listing 5.16 stops reading input when the program encounters a # character. The program counts the number of characters it reads and the echoes them. That is, it redisplays the characters that have been read. (Pressing a keyboard key doesn't automatically place a character onscreen; programs have to do that drudge work by echoing the input character. Typically, the operating system handles that task. In this case, both the operating system and the test program echo the input.) When it is finished, the program reports the total number of characters processed. Listing 5.16 shows the program.

LISTING 5.16 `textin1.cpp`

```cpp
// textin1.cpp -- reading chars with a while loop
#include <iostream>
int main()
{
    using namespace std;
    char ch;
    int count = 0;         // use basic input
    cout << "Enter characters; enter # to quit:\n";
    cin >> ch;             // get a character
    while (ch != '#')      // test the character
    {
        cout << ch;        // echo the character
        ++count;           // count the character
        cin >> ch;         // get the next character
    }
    cout << endl << count << " characters read\n";
    return 0;
}
```

Here's a sample run of the program in Listing 5.16:

```
Enter characters; enter # to quit:
see ken run#really fast
seekenrun
9 characters read
```

Apparently, Ken runs so fast that he obliterates space itself—or at least the space characters in the input.

Program Notes

Note the structure of the program in Listing 5.16. The program reads the first input character before it reaches the loop. That way, the first character can be tested when the program reaches the loop statement. This is important because the first character might be #. Because `textin1.cpp` uses an entry-condition loop, the program correctly skips the entire loop in that case. And because the variable `count` was previously set to `0`, `count` has the correct value.

Suppose the first character read is not a #. In that case, the program enters the loop, displays the character, increments the count, and reads the next character. This last step is vital. Without it, the loop repeatedly processes the first input character forever. With the last step, the program advances to the next character.

Note that the loop design follows the guidelines mentioned earlier. The condition that terminates the loop is if the last character read is #. That condition is initialized by reading a character before the loop starts. The condition is updated by reading a new character at the end of the loop.

This all sounds reasonable. So why does the program omit the spaces on output? Blame `cin`. When reading type `char` values, just as when reading other basic types, `cin` skips over spaces and newline characters. The spaces in the input are not echoed, so they are not counted.

To further complicate things, the input to `cin` is buffered. That means the characters you type don't get sent to the program until you press Enter. This is why you are able to type characters after the # when running the program in Listing 5.16. After you press Enter, the whole sequence of characters is sent to the program, but the program quits processing the input after it reaches the # character.

cin.get(char) **to the Rescue**

Usually, programs that read input character-by-character need to examine every character, including spaces, tabs, and newlines. The `istream` class (defined in `iostream`), to which `cin` belongs, includes member functions that meet this need. In particular, the member function `cin.get(ch)` reads the next character, even if it is a space, from the input and assigns it to the variable `ch`. By replacing `cin>>ch` with this function call, you can fix Listing 5.16. Listing 5.17 shows the result.

LISTING 5.17   `textin2.cpp`

```
// textin2.cpp -- using cin.get(char)
#include <iostream>
int main()
{
    using namespace std;
    char ch;
    int count = 0;

    cout << "Enter characters; enter # to quit:\n";
    cin.get(ch);        // use the cin.get(ch) function
    while (ch != '#')
    {
        cout << ch;
        ++count;
        cin.get(ch);    // use it again
    }
    cout << endl << count << " characters read\n";
    return 0;
}
```

Here is a sample run of the program in Listing 5.17:

Did you use a #2 pencil?
Did you use a
14 characters read

Now the program echoes and counts every character, including the spaces. Input is still buffered, so it is still possible to type more input than what eventually reaches the program.

If you are familiar with C, this program may strike you as terribly wrong. The `cin.get(ch)` call places a value in the `ch` variable, which means it alters the value of the variable. In C you must pass the address of a variable to a function if you want to change the value of that variable. But the call to `cin.get()` in Listing 5.17 passes `ch`, not `&ch`. In C, code like this won't work. In C++ it can work, provided that the function declares the argument as a *reference*. This is a feature type that is new to C++. The `iostream` header file declares the argument to `cin.get(ch)` as a reference type, so this function can alter the value of its argument. You'll learn the details in Chapter 8, "Adventures in Functions." Meanwhile, the C mavens among you can relax; ordinarily, argument passing in C++ works just as it does in C. For `cin.get(ch)`, however, it doesn't.

Which `cin.get()`?

Listing 4.5 in Chapter 4 uses this code:

```
char name[ArSize];
...
cout << "Enter your name:\n";
cin.get(name, ArSize).get();
```

The last line is equivalent to two consecutive function calls:

```
cin.get(name, ArSize);
cin.get();
```

One version of `cin.get()` takes two arguments: the array name, which is the address of the string (technically, type `char*`), and `ArSize`, which is an integer of type `int`. (Recall that the name of an array is the address of its first element, so the name of a character array is type `char*`.) Then, the program uses `cin.get()` with no arguments. And, most recently, we've used `cin.get()` this way:

```
char ch;
cin.get(ch);
```

This time `cin.get()` has one argument, and it is type `char`.

Once again it is time for those of you familiar with C to get excited or confused. In C if a function takes a pointer-to-`char` and an `int` as arguments, you can't successfully use the same function with a single argument of a different type. But you can do so in C++ because the language supports an OOP feature called *function overloading*. Function overloading allows you to create different functions that have the same name, provided that they have different argument lists. If, for example, you use `cin.get(name, ArSize)` in C++, the compiler finds the version of `cin.get()` that uses a `char*` and an `int` as arguments. But if you use `cin.get(ch)`, the compiler fetches the version that uses a single type `char` argument. And if the code provides no arguments, the compiler uses the version of `cin.get()` that takes no arguments. Function overloading enables you to use the same name for related functions that perform the same basic task in different ways or for different types. This is another topic awaiting you in Chapter 8. Meanwhile, you can get accustomed to function overloading by using the `get()` examples that come with the `istream` class. To distinguish between the different function versions, we'll include the argument list when referring to them. Thus, `cin.get()` means the version that takes no arguments, and `cin.get(char)` means the version that takes one argument.

The End-of-File Condition

As Listing 5.17 shows, using a symbol such as `#` to signal the end of input is not always satisfactory because such a symbol might be part of legitimate input. The same is true of other arbitrarily chosen symbols, such as `@` and `%`. If the input comes from a file, you can employ a much more powerful technique—detecting the end-of-file (EOF). C++ input facilities cooperate with the operating system to detect when input reaches the end of a file and report that information back to a program.

At first glance, reading information from files seems to have little to do with `cin` and keyboard input, but there are two connections. First, many operating systems, including Unix and MS-DOS, support *redirection*, which enables you to substitute a file for keyboard input. For example, suppose that in MS-DOS you have an executable program called `gofish.exe` and a text file called `fishtale`. In that case, you can give this command line at the DOS prompt:

```
gofish <fishtale
```

This causes the program to take input from the `fishtale` file instead of from the keyboard. The `<` symbol is the redirection operator for both Unix and DOS.

Second, many operating systems allow you to simulate the EOF condition from the keyboard. In Unix you do so by pressing Ctrl+D at the beginning of a line. In DOS, you press Ctrl+Z and then press Enter anywhere on the line. Some implementations of C++ support similar behavior even though the underlying operating system doesn't. The EOF concept for keyboard entry is actually a legacy of command-line environments. However, Symantec C++ for the Mac imitates Unix and recognizes Ctrl+D as a simulated EOF. Metrowerks Codewarrior recognizes Ctrl+Z in the Macintosh and Windows environments. Microsoft Visual C++ 7.0, Borland C++ 5.5, and GNU C++ for the PC recognize Ctrl+Z when it's the first character on a line, but they require a subsequent Enter. In short, many PC programming environment recognize Ctrl+Z as a simulated EOF, but the exact details (anywhere on a line versus first character on a line, Enter key required or not required) vary.

If your programming environment can test for the EOF, you can use a program similar to Listing 5.17 with redirected files and you can use it for keyboard input in which you simulate the EOF. That sounds useful, so let's see how it's done.

When `cin` detects the EOF, it sets two bits (the *eofbit* and the *failbit*) to `1`. You can use a member function named `eof()` to see whether the eofbit has been set; the call `cin.eof()` returns the `bool` value `true` if the EOF has been detected and `false` otherwise. Similarly, the `fail()`

member function returns `true` if either the eofbit or the failbit has been set to 1 and `false` otherwise. Note that the `eof()` and `fail()` methods report the result of the most recent attempt to read; that is, they report on the past rather than look ahead. So a `cin.eof()` or `cin.fail()` test should always follow an attempt to read. The design of Listing 5.18 reflects this fact. It uses `fail()` instead of `eof()` because the former method appears to work with a broader range of implementations.

Compatibility Note

Some systems do not support simulated EOF from the keyboard. Other systems support it imperfectly. If you have been using `cin.get()` to freeze the screen until you can read it, that won't work here because detecting the EOF turns off further attempts to read input. However, you can use a timing loop like that in Listing 5.14 to keep the screen visible for a while.

LISTING 5.18   `textin3.cpp`

```
// textin3.cpp -- reading chars to end of file
#include <iostream>
int main()
{
    using namespace std;
    char ch;
    int count = 0;
    cin.get(ch);          // attempt to read a char
    while (cin.fail() == false)  // test for EOF
    {
        cout << ch;       // echo character
        ++count;
        cin.get(ch);      // attempt to read another char
    }
    cout << endl << count << " characters read\n";
    return 0;
}
```

Here is sample output from the program in Listing 5.18:

```
The green bird sings in the winter.<ENTER>
The green bird sings in the winter.
Yes, but the crow flies in the dawn.<ENTER>
Yes, but the crow flies in the dawn.
<CTRL><Z>
73 characters read
```

Because I ran the program on a Windows XP system, I pressed Ctrl+Z and then Enter to simulate the EOF condition. Unix and Linux users would press Ctrl+D instead.

By using redirection, you can use the program in Listing 5.18 to display a text file and report how many characters it has. This time, we have a program read, echo, and count a two-line file on a Unix system (the $ is a Unix prompt):

```
$ textin3 < stuff
I am a Unix file. I am proud
to be a Unix file.
49 characters read
$
```

EOF Ends Input

Remember that when a `cin` method detects the EOF, it sets a flag in the `cin` object, indicating the EOF condition. When this flag is set, `cin` does not read anymore input, and further calls to `cin` have no effect. For file input, this makes sense because you shouldn't read past the end of a file. For keyboard input, however, you might use a simulated EOF to terminate a loop but then want to read more input later. The `cin.clear()` method clears the EOF flag and lets input proceed again. Chapter 17, "Input, Output, and Files," discusses this further. Keep in mind, however, that in some systems, typing Ctrl+Z effectively terminates both input and output beyond the powers of `cin.clear()` to restore them.

Common Idioms for Character Input

The following is the essential design of a loop intended to read text a character at a time until EOF:

```
cin.get(ch);         // attempt to read a char
while (cin.fail() == false)  // test for EOF
{
    ...              // do stuff
    cin.get(ch);     // attempt to read another char
}
```

There are some shortcuts you can take with this code. Chapter 6 introduces the `!` operator, which toggles `true` to `false` and vice versa. You can use it to rewrite the `while` test to look like this:

```
while (!cin.fail())    // while input has not failed
```

The return value for the `cin.get(char)` method is `cin`, an object. However, the `istream` class provides a function that can convert an `istream` object such as `cin` to a `bool` value; this conversion function is called when `cin` occurs in a location where a `bool` is expected, such as in the test condition of a `while` loop. Furthermore, the `bool` value for the conversion is `true` if the last attempted read was successful and `false` otherwise. This means you can rewrite the `while` test to look like this:

```
while (cin)    // while input is successful
```

This is a bit more general than using `!cin.fail()` or `!cin.eof()` because it detects other possible causes of failure, such as disk failure.

Finally, because the return value of `cin.get(char)` is `cin`, you can condense the loop to this format:

```
while (cin.get(ch))  // while input is successful
{
    ...                // do stuff
}
```

Here, `cin.get(char)` is called once in the test condition instead of twice—once before the loop and once at the end of the loop. To evaluate the loop test, the program first has to execute the call to `cin.get(ch)`, which, if successful, places a value into `ch`. Then the program obtains the return value from the function call, which is `cin`. Then it applies the `bool` conversion to `cin`, which yields `true` if input worked and `false` otherwise. The three guidelines (identifying the termination condition, initializing the condition, and updating the condition) are all compressed into one loop test condition.

Yet Another Version of `cin.get()`

Nostalgic C users might yearn for C's character I/O functions, `getchar()` and `putchar()`. They are available in C++ if you want them. You just use the `stdio.h` header file as you would in C (or use the more current `cstdio`). Or you can use member functions from the `istream` and `ostream` classes that work in much the same way. Let's look at that approach next.

Compatibility Note

Some older C++ implementations don't support the `cin.get()` member function (no arguments) discussed here.

The `cin.get()` member function with no arguments returns the next character from the input. That is, you use it in this way:

```
ch = cin.get();
```

(Recall that `cin.get(ch)` returns an object, not the character read.) This function works much the same as C's `getchar()`, returning the character code as a type `int` value. Similarly, you can use the `cout.put()` function (see Chapter 3, "Dealing with Data") to display the character:

```
cout.put(ch);
```

It works much like C's `putchar()`, except that its argument should be type `char` instead of type `int`.

Compatibility Note

Originally, the `put()` member had the single prototype `put(char)`. You could pass to it an `int` argument, which would then be type cast to `char`. The Standard also calls for a single prototype. However, many current C++ implementations provide three prototypes: `put(char)`, `put(signed char)`, and `put(unsigned char)`. Using `put()` with an `int` argument in these implementations generates an error message because there is more than one choice for converting the `int`. An explicit type cast, such as `cin.put(char(ch))`, works for `int` types.

To use `cin.get()` successfully, you need to know how it handles the EOF condition. When the function reaches the EOF, there are no more characters to be returned. Instead, `cin.get()` returns a special value, represented by the symbolic constant `EOF`. This constant is defined in the `iostream` header file. The `EOF` value must be different from any valid character value so that the program won't confuse EOF with a regular character. Typically, EOF is defined as the value -1 because no character has an ASCII code of -1, but you don't need to know the actual value. You can just use EOF in a program. For example, the heart of Listing 5.18 looks like this:

```
char ch;
cin.get(ch);
while (cin.fail() == false)  // test for EOF
{
    cout << ch;
    ++count;
    cin.get(ch);
}
```

You can use int ch, replace cin.get(char) with cin.get(), replace cout with cout.put(), and replace the cin.fail() test with a test for EOF:

```
int ch;       /// for compatibility with EOF value
ch = cin.get();
while (ch != EOF)
{
    cout.put(ch);   // cout.put(char(ch)) for some implementations
    ++count;
    ch = cin.get();
}
```

If ch is a character, the loop displays it. If ch is EOF, the loop terminates.

Tip

You should realize that EOF does not represent a character in the input. Instead, it's a signal that there are no more characters.

There's a subtle but important point about using cin.get() beyond the changes made so far. Because EOF represents a value outside the valid character codes, it's possible that it might not be compatible with the char type. For example, on some systems type char is unsigned, so a char variable could never have the usual EOF value of -1. For this reason, if you use cin.get() (with no argument) and test for EOF, you must assign the return value to type int instead of to type char. Also, if you make ch type int instead of type char, you might have to do a type cast to char when displaying ch.

Listing 5.19 incorporates the cin.get() approach into a new version of Listing 5.18. It also condenses the code by combining character input with the while loop test.

LISTING 5.19   textin4.cpp

```
// textin4.cpp -- reading chars with cin.get()
#include <iostream>
int main(void)
{
```

LISTING 5.19   Continued

```
using namespace std;
int ch;                           // should be int, not char
int count = 0;

while ((ch = cin.get()) != EOF) // test for end-of-file
{
    cout.put(char(ch));
    ++count;
}
cout << endl << count << " characters read\n";
return 0;
}
```

Compatibility Note

Some systems either do not support simulated EOF from the keyboard or support it imperfectly, and that may prevent the example in Listing 5.19 from running as described. If you have been using `cin.get()` to freeze the screen until you can read it, that won't work here because detecting the EOF turns off further attempts to read input. However, you can use a timing loop like that in Listing 5.14 to keep the screen visible for a while.

Here's a sample run of the program in Listing 5.19:

```
The sullen mackerel sulks in the shadowy shallows.<ENTER>
The sullen mackerel sulks in the shadowy shallows.
Yes, but the blue bird of happiness harbors secrets.<ENTER>
Yes, but the blue bird of happiness harbors secrets.
^Z
104 characters read
```

Let's analyze the loop condition:

```
while ((ch = cin.get()) != EOF)
```

The parentheses that enclose the subexpression `ch = cin.get()` cause the program to evaluate that expression first. To do the evaluation, the program first has to call the `cin.get()` function. Next, it assigns the function return value to `ch`. Because the value of an assignment statement is the value of the left operand, the whole subexpression reduces to the value of `ch`. If this value is `EOF`, the loop terminates; otherwise, it continues. The test condition needs all the parentheses. Suppose you leave some parentheses out:

```
while (ch = cin.get() != EOF)
```

The `!=` operator has higher precedence than `=`, so first the program compares `cin.get()`'s return value to `EOF`. A comparison produces a `false` or `true` result; that `bool` value is converted to `0` or `1`, and that's the value that gets assigned to `ch`.

Using `cin.get(ch)` (with an argument) for input, on the other hand, doesn't create any type problems. Remember that the `cin.get(char)` function doesn't assign a special value to `ch` at the EOF. In fact, it doesn't assign anything to `ch` in that case. `ch` is never called on to hold a non-`char` value. Table 5.3 summarizes the differences between `cin.get(char)` and `cin.get()`.

TABLE 5.3 `cin.get(ch)` Versus `cin.get()`

Property	cin.get(ch)	ch=cin.get()
Method for conveying input character	Assign to argument `ch`	Use function return value to assign to `ch`
Function return value for character input	A class `istream` object (`true` after `bool` conversion)	Code for character as type `int` value
Function return value at EOF	A class `istream` object (`false` after `bool` conversion)	EOF

So which should you use, `cin.get()` or `cin.get(char)`? The form with the character argument is integrated more fully into the object approach because its return value is an `istream` object. This means, for example, that you can chain uses. For example, the following code means read the next input character into `ch1` and the following input character into `ch2`:

```
cin.get(ch1).get(ch2);
```

This works because the function call `cin.get(ch1)` returns the `cin` object, which then acts as the object to which `get(ch2)` is attached.

Probably the main use for the `get()` form is to let you make quick-and-dirty conversions from the `getchar()` and `putchar()` functions of `stdio.h` to the `cin.get()` and `cout.put()` methods of `iostream`. You just replace one header file with the other and globally replace `getchar()` and `putchar()` with their act-alike method equivalents. (If the old code uses a type `int` variable for input, you have to make further adjustments if your implementation has multiple prototypes for `put()`.)

Nested Loops and Two-Dimensional Arrays

Earlier in this chapter you saw that the `for` loop is a natural tool for processing arrays. Now let's go a step further and look at how a `for` loop within a `for` loop (nested loops) serves to handle two-dimensional arrays.

First, let's examine what a two-dimensional array is. The arrays used so far in this chapter are termed *one-dimensional arrays* because you can visualize each array as a single row of data. You can visualize a two-dimensional array as being more like a table, having both rows and columns of data. You can use a two-dimensional array, for example, to represent quarterly sales figures for six separate districts, with one row of data for each district. Or you can use a two-dimensional array to represent the position of RoboDork on a computerized game board.

C++ doesn't provide a special two-dimensional array type. Instead, you create an array for which each element is itself an array. For example, suppose you want to store maximum temperature data for five cities over a 4-year period. In that case, you can declare an array as follows:

```
int maxtemps[4][5];
```

This declaration means that `maxtemps` is an array with four elements. Each of these elements is an array of five integers. (See Figure 5.5.) You can think of the `maxtemps` array as representing four rows of five temperature values each.

FIGURE 5.5
An array of arrays.

maxtemps is an array of 4 elements

```
int maxtemps[4][5];
```

Each element is an array of 5 ints.

The maxtemps array

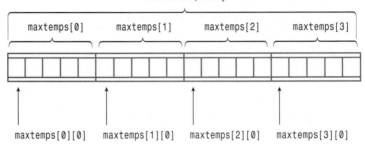

The expression `maxtemps[0]` is the first element of the `maxtemps` array; hence `maxtemps[0]` is itself an array of five `int`s. The first element of the `maxtemps[0]` array is `maxtemps[0][0]`, and this element is a single `int`. Thus, you need to use two subscripts to access the `int` elements. You can think of the first subscript as representing the row and the second subscript as representing the column. (See Figure 5.6.)

FIGURE 5.6
Accessing array elements with subscripts.

```
int maxtemps[4][5];
```

The `maxtemps` array viewed as a table:

		0	1	2	3	4
maxtemps[0]	0	maxtemps[0][0]	maxtemps[0][1]	maxtemps[0][2]	maxtemps[0][3]	maxtemps[0][4]
maxtemps[1]	1	maxtemps[1][0]	maxtemps[1][1]	maxtemps[1][2]	maxtemps[1][3]	maxtemps[1][4]
maxtemps[2]	2	maxtemps[2][0]	maxtemps[2][1]	maxtemps[2][2]	maxtemps[2][3]	maxtemps[2][4]
maxtemps[3]	3	maxtemps[3][0]	maxtemps[3][1]	maxtemps[3][2]	maxtemps[3][3]	maxtemps[3][4]

Suppose you want to print all the array contents. In that case, you can use one `for` loop to change rows and a second, nested, `for` loop to change columns:

```
for (int row = 0; row < 4; row++)
{
    for (int col = 0; col < 5; ++col)
        cout << maxtemps[row][col] << "\t";
    cout << endl;
}
```

For each value of `row`, the inner `for` loop cycles through all the `col` values. This example prints a tab character (`\t` in C++ escape character notation) after each value and a newline character after each complete row.

Initializing a Two-Dimensional Array

When you create a two-dimensional array, you have the option of initializing each element. The technique is based on that for initializing a one-dimensional array. Remember that you do this by providing a comma-separated list of values enclosed in braces:

```
// initializing a one-dimensional array
int btus[5] = { 23, 26, 24, 31, 28};
```

For a two-dimensional array, each element is itself an array, so you can initialize each element by using a form like that in the previous code example. Thus, the initialization consists of a comma-separated series of one-dimensional initializations, all enclosed in a set of braces:

```
int maxtemps[4][5] =                // 2-D array
{
    {94, 98, 87, 103, 101},        // values for maxtemps[0]
    {98, 99, 91, 107, 105},        // values for maxtemps[1]
    {93, 91, 90, 101, 104},        // values for maxtemps[2]
    {95, 100, 88, 105, 103}        // values for maxtemps[3]
};
```

The term `{94, 98, 87, 103, 101}` initializes the first row, represented by `maxtemps[0]`. As a matter of style, placing each row of data on its own line, if possible, makes the data easier to read.

Listing 5.20 incorporates an initialized two-dimensional array and a nested loop into a program. This time the program reverses the order of the loops, placing the column loop (city index) on the outside and the row loop (year index) on the inside. Also, it uses a common C++ practice of initializing an array of pointers to a set of string constants. That is, `cities` is declared as an array of pointers-to-`char`. That makes each element, such as `cities[0]`, a pointer-to-`char` that can be initialized to the address of a string. The program initializes `cities[0]` to the address of the `"Gribble City"` string, and so on. Thus, this array of pointers behaves like an array of strings.

LISTING 5.20   nested.cpp

```cpp
// nested.cpp -- nested loops and 2-D array
#include <iostream>
const int Cities = 5;
const int Years = 4;
int main()
{
    using namespace std;
    const char * cities[Cities] =   // array of pointers
    {                               // to 5 strings
        "Gribble City",
        "Gribbletown",
        "New Gribble",
        "San Gribble",
        "Gribble Vista"
    };

    int maxtemps[Years][Cities] =   // 2-D array
    {
        {95, 99, 86, 100, 104},   // values for maxtemps[0]
        {95, 97, 90, 106, 102},   // values for maxtemps[1]
        {96, 100, 940, 107, 105}, // values for maxtemps[2]
        {97, 102, 89, 108, 104}   // values for maxtemps[3]
    };

    cout << "Maximum temperatures for 2002 - 2005\n\n";
    for (int city = 0; city < Cities; ++city)
    {
        cout << cities[city] << ":\t";
        for (int year = 0; year < Years; ++year)
            cout << maxtemps[year][city] << "\t";
        cout << endl;
    }

    return 0;
}
```

Here is the output for the program in Listing 5.20:

```
Maximum temperatures for 1999 - 2002

Gribble City:    95  95  96  97
Gribbletown:     99  97  100 102
New Gribble:     86  90  940 89
San Gribble:     100 106 107 108
Gribble Vista:   104 102 105 104
```

Using tabs in the output spaces the data more regularly than using spaces would. However, different tab settings can cause the output to vary in appearance from one system to another. Chapter 17 presents more precise, but more complex, methods for formatting output.

More awkwardly, you could use an array of arrays of **char** instead of an array of pointers for the string data. The declaration would look like this:

```
char cities[25][Cities] =    // array of 5 arrays of 25 char
{
    "Gribble City",
    "Gribbletown",
    "New Gribble",
    "San Gribble",
    "Gribble Vista"
};
```

This approach limits each of the five strings to a maximum of 24 characters. The array of pointers stores the addresses of the five string literals, but the array of `char` arrays copies each of the five string literals to the corresponding five arrays of 25 `char`. Thus, the array of pointers is much more economical in terms of space. However, if you intended to modify any of the strings, the two-dimensional array would be a better choice. Oddly enough, both choices use the same initialization list and the same `for` loop code to display the strings.

Also, you could use an array of `string` class objects instead of an array of pointers for the string data. The declaration would look like this:

```
const string cities[Cities] =    // array of 5 strings
{
    "Gribble City",
    "Gribbletown",
    "New Gribble",
    "San Gribble",
    "Gribble Vista"
};
```

If you intended for the strings to be modifiable, you would omit the `const` qualifier. This form uses the same initializer list and the same `for` loop display code as the other two forms. If you want modifiable strings, the automatic sizing feature of the `string` class makes this approach more convenient to use than the two-dimensional array approach.

Summary

C++ offers three varieties of loops: `for` loops, `while` loops, and `do while` loops. A loop cycles through the same set of instructions repetitively, as long as the loop test condition evaluates to `true` or nonzero, and the loop terminates execution when the test condition evaluates to `false` or zero. The `for` loop and the `while` loop are entry-condition loops, meaning that they examine the test condition before executing the statements in the body of the loop. The `do while` loop is an exit-condition loop, meaning that it examines the test condition after executing the statements in the body of the loop.

The syntax for each loop calls for the loop body to consist of a single statement. However, that statement can be a compound statement, or block, formed by enclosing several statements within paired curly braces.

Relational expressions, which compare two values, are often used as loop test conditions. Relational expressions are formed by using one of the six relational operators: <, <=, ==, >=, >, or !=. Relational expressions evaluate to the type `bool` values `true` and `false`.

Many programs read text input or text files character-by-character. The `istream` class provides several ways to do this. If `ch` is a type `char` variable, the statement

```
cin >> ch;
```

reads the next input character into `ch`. However, it skips over spaces, newlines, and tabs. The member function call

```
cin.get(ch);
```

reads the next input character, regardless of its value, and places it in `ch`. The member function call `cin.get()` returns the next input character, including spaces, newlines, and tabs, so it can be used as follows:

```
ch = cin.get();
```

The `cin.get(char)` member function call reports encountering the EOF condition by returning a value with the `bool` conversion of `false`, whereas the `cin.get()` member function call reports the EOF by returning the value `EOF`, which is defined in the `iostream` file.

A nested loop is a loop within a loop. Nested loops provide a natural way to process two-dimensional arrays.

Review Questions

1. What's the difference between an entry-condition loop and an exit-condition loop? Which kind is each of the C++ loops?

2. What would the following code fragment print if it were part of a valid program?

```
int i;
for (i = 0; i < 5; i++)
      cout << i;
      cout << endl;
```

3. What would the following code fragment print if it were part of a valid program?

```
int j;
for (j = 0; j < 11; j += 3)
      cout << j;
cout << endl << j << endl;
```

4. What would the following code fragment print if it were part of a valid program?

```
int j = 5;
while ( ++j < 9)
      cout << j++ << endl;
```

5. What would the following code fragment print if it were part of a valid program?

```
int k = 8;
do
      cout <<" k = " << k << endl;
while (k++ < 5);
```

6. Write a `for` loop that prints the values 1 2 4 8 16 32 64 by increasing the value of a counting variable by a factor of two in each cycle.

7. How do you make a loop body include more than one statement?

8. Is the following statement valid? If not, why not? If so, what does it do?

```
int x = (1,024);
```

What about the following?

```
int y;
y = 1,024;
```

9. How does `cin>>ch` differ from `cin.get(ch)` and `ch=cin.get()` in how it views input?

Programming Exercises

1. Write a program that requests the user to enter two integers. The program should then calculate and report the sum of all the integers between and including the two integers. At this point, assume that the smaller integer is entered first. For example, if the user enters **2** and **9**, the program should report that the sum of all the integers from 2 through 9 is 44.

2. Write a program that asks the user to type in numbers. After each entry, the program should report the cumulative sum of the entries to date. The program should terminate when the user enters **0**.

3. Daphne invests $100 at 10% simple interest. That is, every year, the investment earns 10% of the original investment, or $10 each and every year:

interest = 0.10 × original balance

At the same time, Cleo invests $100 at 5% compound interest. That is, interest is 5% of the current balance, including previous additions of interest:

interest = 0.05 × current balance

Cleo earns 5% of $100 the first year, giving her $105. The next year she earns 5% of $105, or $5.25, and so on. Write a program that finds how many years it takes for the value of Cleo's investment to exceed the value of Daphne's investment and then displays the value of both investments at that time.

4. You sell the book *C++ for Fools*. Write a program that has you enter a year's worth of monthly sales (in terms of number of books, not of money). The program should use a loop to prompt you by month, using an array of `char *` (or an array of `string` objects, if you prefer) initialized to the month strings and storing the input data in an array of `int`. Then, the program should find the sum of the array contents and report the total sales for the year.

5. Do Programming Exercise 4, but use a two-dimensional array to store input for 3 years of monthly sales. Report the total sales for each individual year and for the combined years.

6. Design a structure called `car` that holds the following information about an automobile: its make, as a string in a character array or in a `string` object, and the year it was built, as an integer. Write a program that asks the user how many cars to catalog. The program should then use `new` to create a dynamic array of that many `car` structures. Next, it should prompt the user to input the make (which might consist of more than one word) and year information for each structure. Note that this requires some care because it alternates reading strings with numeric data (see Chapter 4). Finally, it should display the contents of each structure. A sample run should look something like the following:

```
How many cars do you wish to catalog? 2
Car #1:
Please enter the make: Hudson Hornet
Please enter the year made: 1952
Car #2:
Please enter the make: Kaiser
Please enter the year made: 1951
Here is your collection:
1952 Hudson Hornet
1951 Kaiser
```

7. Write a program that uses an array of `char` and a loop to read one word at a time until the word `done` is entered. The program should then report the number of words entered (not counting `done`). A sample run could look like this:

```
Enter words (to stop, type the word done):
anteater birthday category dumpster
envy finagle geometry done for sure
You entered a total of 7 words.
```

You should include the `cstring` header file and use the `strcmp()` function to make the comparison test.

8. Write a program that matches the description of the program in Programming Exercise 7, but use a `string` class object instead of an array. Include the `string` header file and use a relational operator to make the comparison test.

9. Write a program using nested loops that asks the user to enter a value for the number of rows to display. It should then display that many rows of asterisks, with one asterisk in the first row, two in the second row, and so on. For each row, the asterisks are preceded by the number of periods needed to make all the rows display a total number of characters equal to the number of rows. A sample run would look like this:

```
Enter number of rows: 5
....*
...**
..***
.****
*****
```

CHAPTER 6

BRANCHING STATEMENTS AND LOGICAL OPERATORS

In this chapter you'll learn about the following:

- The `if` statement
- The `if else` statement
- Logical operators: &&, ||, and !
- The `cctype` library of character functions
- The conditional operator: ?:
- The `switch` statement
- The `continue` and `break` statements
- Number-reading loops
- Basic File input/output

One of the keys to designing intelligent programs is to give them the ability to make decisions. Chapter 5, "Loops and Relational Expressions," shows one kind of decision making—looping—in which a program decides whether to continue looping. This investigates how C++ lets you use branching statements to decide among alternative actions. Which vampire-protection scheme (garlic or cross) should the program use? What menu choice has the user selected? Did the user enter a zero? C++ provides the `if` and `switch` statements to implement decisions, and they are this chapter's main topics. This chapter also looks at the conditional operator, which provides another way to make a choice, and the logical operators, which let you combine two tests into one. Finally, the chapter takes a first look at file input/output.

The `if` Statement

When a C++ program must choose whether to take a particular action, you usually implement the choice with an `if` statement. The `if` comes in two forms: `if` and `if else`. Let's investigate the simple `if` first. It's modeled after ordinary English, as in "If you have a Captain Cookie card, you get a free cookie." The `if` statement directs a program to execute a statement or statement block if a test condition is true and to skip that statement or block if the condition is false. Thus, an `if` statement lets a program decide whether a particular statement should be executed.

The syntax for the `if` statement is similar to the that of the `while` syntax:

```
if (test-condition)
    statement
```

A true *test-condition* causes the program to execute *statement*, which can be a single statement or a block. A false *test-condition* causes the program to skip *statement*. (See Figure 6.1.) As with loop test conditions, an `if` test condition is type cast to a `bool` value, so zero becomes `false` and nonzero becomes `true`. The entire `if` construction counts as a single statement.

FIGURE 6.1

The structure of `if` statements.

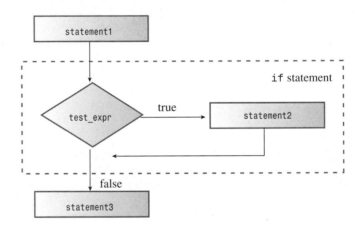

Most often, *test-condition* is a relational expression such as those used to control loops. Suppose, for example, that you want a program that counts the spaces in the input as well as the total number of characters. You can use `cin.get(char)` in a `while` loop to read the characters and then use an `if` statement to identify and count the space characters. Listing 6.1 does just that, using the period (.) to recognize the end of a sentence.

LISTING 6.1   `if.cpp`

```
// if.cpp -- using the if statement
#include <iostream>
int main()
{
    using namespace std;
    char ch;
```

LISTING 6.1   Continued

```
        int spaces = 0;
        int total = 0;
        cin.get(ch);
        while (ch != '.')    // quit at end of sentence
        {
            if (ch == ' ')   // check if ch is a space
                ++spaces;
            ++total;          // done every time
            cin.get(ch);
        }
        cout << spaces << " spaces, " << total;
        cout << " characters total in sentence\n";
        return 0;
}
```

Here's some sample output from the program in Listing 6.1:

The balloonist was an airhead
with lofty goals.
6 spaces, 46 characters total in sentence

As the comments in Listing 6.1 indicate, the `++spaces;` statement is executed only when `ch` is a space. Because it is outside the `if` statement, the `++total;` statement is executed in every loop cycle. Note that the total count includes the newline character that is generated by pressing Enter.

The `if else` Statement

Whereas an `if` statement lets a program decide whether a *particular* statement or block is executed, an `if else` statement lets a program decide which of *two* statements or blocks is executed. It's an invaluable statement for creating alternative courses of action. The C++ `if else` statement is modeled after simple English, as in "If you have a Captain Cookie card, you get a Cookie Plus Plus, else you just get a Cookie d'Ordinaire." The `if else` statement has this general form:

```
if (test-condition)
    statement1
else
    statement2
```

If *test-condition* is `true`, or nonzero, the program executes *statement1* and skips over *statement2*. Otherwise, when *test-condition* is `false`, or zero, the program skips *statement1* and executes *statement2* instead. So this code fragment:

```
if (answer == 1492)
    cout << "That's right!\n";
else
    cout << "You'd better review Chapter 1 again.\n";
```

prints the first message if `answer` is `1492` and prints the second message otherwise. Each statement can be either a single statement or a statement block delimited by braces. (See Figure 6.2.) The entire `if else` construct counts syntactically as a single statement.

FIGURE 6.2

The structure of `if else` statements.

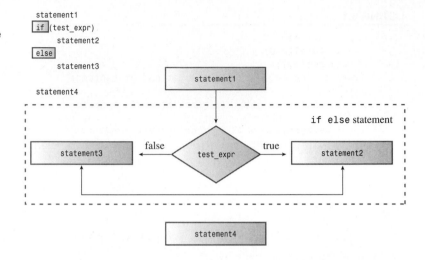

For example, suppose you want to alter incoming text by scrambling the letters while keeping the newline character intact. In that case, each line of input is converted to an output line of equal length. This means you want the program to take one course of action for newline characters and a different course of action for all other characters. As Listing 6.2 shows, `if else` makes this task easy.

LISTING 6.2   ifelse.cpp

```cpp
// ifelse.cpp -- using the if else statement
#include <iostream>
int main()
{
    using namespace std;
    char ch;

    cout << "Type, and I shall repeat.\n";
    cin.get(ch);
    while (ch != '.')
    {
        if (ch == '\n')
            cout << ch;       // done if newline
        else
            cout << ++ch;     // done otherwise
        cin.get(ch);
    }
// try ch + 1 instead of ++ch for interesting effect
    cout << "\nPlease excuse the slight confusion.\n";
    return 0;
}
```

Here's some sample output from the program in Listing 6.2:

```
Type, and I shall repeat.
I am extraordinarily pleased
J!bn!fyusbpsejobsjmz!qmfbtfe
to use such a powerful computer.
up!vtf!tvdi!b!qpxfsgvm!dpnqvufs
Please excuse the slight confusion.
```

Note that one of the comments in Listing 6.2 suggests that changing ++ch to ch+1 has an interesting effect. Can you deduce what it will be? If not, try it out and then see if you can explain what's happening. (Hint: Think about how cout handles different types.)

Formatting if else Statements

Keep in mind that the two alternatives in an if else statement must be single statements. If you need more than one statement, you must use braces to collect them into a single block statement. Unlike some languages, such as BASIC and FORTRAN, C++ does not automatically consider everything between if and else a block, so you have to use braces to make the statements a block. The following code, for example, produces a compiler error:

```
if (ch == 'Z')
    zorro++;        // if ends here
    cout << "Another Zorro candidate\n";
else                // wrong
    dull++;
    cout << "Not a Zorro candidate\n";
```

The compiler sees it as a simple if statement that ends with the zorro++; statement. Then there is a cout statement. So far, so good. But then there is what the compiler perceives as an unattached else, and that is flagged as a syntax error.

You add braces to convert the code to what you want:

```
if (ch == 'Z')
{                           // if true block
    zorro++;
    cout << "Another Zorro candidate\n";
}
else
{                           // if false block
    dull++;
    cout << "Not a Zorro candidate\n";
}
```

Because C++ is a free-form language, you can arrange the braces as you like, as long as they enclose the statements. The preceding code shows one popular format. Here's another:

```
if (ch == 'Z') {
    zorro++;
    cout << "Another Zorro candidate\n";
    }
```

```
else {
    dull++;
    cout << "Not a Zorro candidate\n";
    }
```

The first form emphasizes the block structure for the statements, whereas the second form more closely ties the blocks to the keywords `if` and `else`. Either style is clear and consistent and should serve you well; however, you may encounter an instructor or employer with strong and specific views on the matter.

The `if else if else` Construction

Computer programs, like life, might present you with a choice of more than two selections. You can extend the C++ `if else` statement to meet such a need. As you've seen, the `else` should be followed by a single statement, which can be a block. Because an `if else` statement itself is a single statement, it can follow an `else`:

```
if (ch == 'A')
    a_grade++;                // alternative # 1
else
    if (ch == 'B')            // alternative # 2
        b_grade++;            // subalternative # 2a
    else
        soso++;               // subalternative # 2b
```

If `ch` is not `'A'`, the program goes to the `else`. There, a second `if else` subdivides that alternative into two more choices. C++'s free formatting enables you to arrange these elements into an easier-to-read format:

```
if (ch == 'A')
    a_grade++;                // alternative # 1
else if (ch == 'B')
    b_grade++;                // alternative # 2
else
    soso++;                   // alternative # 3
```

This looks like a new control structure—an `if else if else` structure. But actually it is one `if else` contained within a second. This revised format looks much cleaner, and it enables you to skim through the code to pick out the different alternatives. This entire construction still counts as one statement.

Listing 6.3 uses this preferred formatting to construct a modest quiz program.

LISTING 6.3   `ifelseif.cpp`

```
// ifelseif.cpp -- using if else if else
#include <iostream>
const int Fave = 27;
int main()
{
```

LISTING 6.3   Continued

```
using namespace std;
int n;

cout << "Enter a number in the range 1-100 to find ";
cout << "my favorite number: ";
do
{
    cin >> n;
    if (n < Fave)
        cout << "Too low -- guess again: ";
    else if (n > Fave)
        cout << "Too high -- guess again: ";
    else
        cout << Fave << " is right!\n";
} while (n != Fave);
return 0;
}
```

Here's some sample output from the program in Listing 6.3:

```
Enter a number in the range 1-100 to find my favorite number: 50
Too high -- guess again: 25
Too low -- guess again: 37
Too high -- guess again: 31
Too high -- guess again: 28
Too high -- guess again: 27
27 is right!
```

Real-World Note: Conditional Operators and Bug Prevention

Many programmers reverse the more intuitive expression *variable* == *value* to *value* == *variable* in order to catch errors where the equality is mistyped as an assignment operator. For example, entering the conditional as

```
if (3 == myNumber)
```

is valid and will work properly. However, if you happen to mistype

```
if (3 = myNumber)
```

the compiler will generate an error message, as it believes you are attempting to assign a value to a literal (3 always equals 3 and can't be assigned another value). Suppose you made a similar mistake made, using the former notation:

```
if (myNumber = 3)
```

The compiler would simply assign the value 3 to myNumber, and the block within the if would run— a very common error, and a difficult error to find. As a general rule, writing code that allows the compiler to find errors is much easier than repairing the causes of mysterious faulty results.

Logical Expressions

Often you must test for more than one condition. For example, for a character to be a lower-case letter, its value must be greater than or equal to `'a'` and less than or equal to `'z'`. Or, if you ask a user to respond with a **y** or an **n**, you want to accept uppercase (**Y** and **N**) as well as lowercase. To meet this kind of need, C++ provides three logical operators to combine or modify existing expressions. The operators are logical OR, written `||`; logical AND, written `&&`; and logical NOT, written `!`. Let's examine them now.

The Logical OR Operator: ||

In English, the word *or* can indicate when one or both of two conditions satisfy a requirement. For example, you can go to the MegaMicro company picnic if you *or* your spouse work for MegaMicro, Inc. The C++ equivalent is the logical OR operator, written `||`. This operator combines two expressions into one. If either or both of the original expressions is `true`, or nonzero, the resulting expression has the value `true`. Otherwise, the expression has the value `false`. Here are some examples:

```
5 ==5 || 5 == 9     // true because first expression is true
5 > 3 || 5 > 10     // true because first expression is true
5 > 8 || 5 < 10     // true because second expression is true
5 < 8 || 5 > 2      // true because both expressions are true
5 > 8 || 5 < 2      // false because both expressions are false
```

Because the `||` has a lower precedence than the relational operators, you don't need to use parentheses in these expressions. Table 6.1 summarizes how the `||` operator works.

TABLE 6.1   The `||` Operator

	The Value of expr1 `||` expr2	
	expr1 == true	expr1 == false
expr2 == true	true	true
expr2 == false	true	false

C++ provides that the `||` operator is a *sequence point*. That is, any value changes indicated on the left side take place before the right side is evaluated. For example, consider the following expression:

```
i++ < 6 || i == j
```

Suppose **i** originally has the value **10**. By the time the comparison with **j** takes place, **i** has the value **11**. Also, C++ won't bother evaluating the expression on the right if the expression on the left is true, for it only takes one true expression to make the whole logical expression true. (The semicolon and the comma operator, recall, are also sequence points.)

Listing 6.4 uses the || operator in an if statement to check for both uppercase and lowercase versions of a character. Also, it uses C++'s string concatenation feature (see Chapter 4, "Compound Types") to spread a single string over three lines.

LISTING 6.4   or.cpp

```
// or.cpp -- using the logical OR operator
#include <iostream>
int main()
{
    using namespace std;
    cout << "This program may reformat your hard disk\n"
            "and destroy all your data.\n"
            "Do you wish to continue? <y/n> ";
    char ch;
    cin >> ch;
    if (ch == 'y' || ch == 'Y')            // y or Y
        cout << "You were warned!\a\a\n";
    else if (ch == 'n' || ch == 'N')       // n or N
        cout << "A wise choice ... bye\n";
    else
        cout << "That wasn't a y or an n, so I guess I'll "
                "trash your disk anyway.\a\a\a\n";
    return 0;
}
```

Here is a sample run of the program in Listing 6.4:

```
This program may reformat your hard disk
and destroy all your data.
Do you wish to continue? <y/n> N
A wise choice ... bye
```

The program reads just one character, so only the first character in the response matters. That means the user could have input **NO!** instead of **N**. The program would just read the **N**. But if the program tried to read more input later, it would start at the **O**.

The Logical AND Operator: &&

The logical AND operator, written &&, also combines two expressions into one. The resulting expression has the value true only if both of the original expressions are true. Here are some examples:

```
5 == 5 && 4 == 4   // true because both expressions are true
5 == 3 && 4 == 4   // false because first expression is false
5 > 3 && 5 > 10    // false because second expression is false
5 > 8 && 5 < 10    // false because first expression is false
5 < 8 && 5 > 2     // true because both expressions are true
5 > 8 && 5 < 2     // false because both expressions are false
```

Because the && has a lower precedence than the relational operators, you don't need to use parentheses in these expressions. Like the || operator, the && operator acts as a sequence point, so the left side is evaluated, and any side effects are carried out before the right side is evaluated. If the left side is false, the whole logical expression must be false, so C++ doesn't bother evaluating the right side in that case. Table 6.2 summarizes how the **&&** operator works.

TABLE 6.2   The **&&** Operator

| | The Value of *expr1* **&&** *expr2* | |
	expr1 == true	expr1 == false
expr2 == true	true	false
expr2 == false	false	false

Listing 6.5 shows how to use **&&** to cope with a common situation, terminating a `while` loop, for two different reasons. In the listing, a `while` loop reads values into an array. One test (`i < ArSize`) terminates the loop when the array is full. The second test (`temp >= 0`) gives the user the option of quitting early by entering a negative number. The program uses the **&&** operator to combine the two tests into a single condition. The program also uses two `if` statements, an `if else` statement, and a `for` loop, so it demonstrates several topics from this chapter and Chapter 5.

LISTING 6.5   and.cpp

```cpp
// and.cpp -- using the logical AND operator
#include <iostream>
const int ArSize = 6;
int main()
{
    using namespace std;
    float naaq[ArSize];
    cout << "Enter the NAAQs (New Age Awareness Quotients) "
         << "of\nyour neighbors. Program terminates "
         << "when you make\n" << ArSize << " entries "
         << "or enter a negative value.\n";

    int i = 0;
    float temp;
    cout << "First value: ";
    cin >> temp;
    while (i < ArSize && temp >= 0) // 2 quitting criteria
    {
        naaq[i] = temp;
        ++i;
        if (i < ArSize)             // room left in the array,
        {
            cout << "Next value: ";
            cin >> temp;            // so get next value
        }
    }
```

LISTING 6.5   Continued

```
            if (i == 0)
                cout << "No data--bye\n";
            else
            {
                cout << "Enter your NAAQ: ";
                float you;
                cin >> you;
                int count = 0;
                for (int j = 0; j < i; j++)
                    if (naaq[j] > you)
                        ++count;
                cout << count;
                cout << " of your neighbors have greater awareness of\n"
                        << "the New Age than you do.\n";
            }
            return 0;
}
```

Note that the program in Listing 6.5 places input into the temporary variable `temp`. Only after it verifies that the input is valid does the program assign the value to the array.

Here are a couple of sample runs of the program. One terminates after six entries:

```
Enter the NAAQs (New Age Awareness Quotients) of
your neighbors. Program terminates when you make
6 entries or enter a negative value.
First value: 28
Next value: 72
Next value: 15
Next value: 6
Next value: 130
Next value: 145
Enter your NAAQ: 50
3 of your neighbors have greater awareness of
the New Age than you do.
```

The second run terminates after a negative value is entered:

```
Enter the NAAQs (New Age Awareness Quotients) of
your neighbors. Program terminates when you make
6 entries or enter a negative value.
First value: 123
Next value: 119
Next value: 4
Next value: 89
Next value: -1
Enter your NAAQ: 123.031
0 of your neighbors have greater awareness of
the New Age than you do.
```

Program Notes

The following is the input part of the program in Listing 6.5:

```
cin >> temp;
while (i < ArSize && temp >= 0)   // 2 quitting criteria
{
    naaq[i] = temp;
    ++i;
    if (i < ArSize)               // room left in the array,
    {
        cout << "Next value: ";
        cin >> temp;              // so get next value
    }
}
```

The program begins by reading the first input value into a temporary variable called `temp`. Then the `while` test condition checks whether there is still room left in the array (`i < ArSize`) and whether the input value is nonnegative (`temp >= 0`). If it is, the program copies the `temp` value to the array and increases the array index by one. At that point, because array numbering starts at zero, `i` equals the total number of entries to date. That is, if `i` starts out at `0`, the first cycle through the loop assigns a value to `naaq[0]` and then sets `i` to `1`.

The loop terminates when the array is filled or when the user enters a negative number. Note that the loop reads another value into `temp` only if `i` is less than `ArSize`—that is, only if there is still room left in the array.

After it gets data, the program uses an `if else` statement to comment if no data was entered (that is, if the first entry was a negative number) and to process the data if any is present.

Setting Up Ranges with &&

The `&&` operator also lets you set up a series of `if else if else` statements, with each choice corresponding to a particular range of values. Listing 6.6 illustrates the approach. It also shows a useful technique for handling a series of messages. Just as a pointer-to-`char` variable can identify a single string by pointing to its beginning, an array of pointers-to-`char` can identify a series of strings. You simply assign the address of each string to a different array element. Listing 6.6 uses the `qualify` array to hold the addresses of four strings. For example, `qualify[1]` holds the address of the string `"mud tug-of-war\n"`. The program can then use `qualify[1]` as it would any other pointer to a string—for example, with `cout` or with `strlen()` or `strcmp()`. Using the `const` qualifier protects these strings from accidental alterations.

LISTING 6.6   more_and.cpp

```
// more_and.cpp -- using the logical AND operator
#include <iostream>
const char * qualify[4] =        // an array of pointers
{                                // to strings
    "10,000-meter race.\n",
    "mud tug-of-war.\n",
    "masters canoe jousting.\n",
```

LISTING 6.6 Continued

```
        "pie-throwing festival.\n"
};
int main()
{
    using namespace std;
    int age;
    cout << "Enter your age in years: ";
    cin >> age;
    int index;

    if (age > 17 && age < 35)
        index = 0;
    else if (age >= 35 && age < 50)
        index = 1;
    else if (age >= 50 && age < 65)
        index = 2;
    else
        index = 3;

    cout << "You qualify for the " << qualify[index];
    return 0;
}
```

Compatibility Note

You might recall that some C++ implementations require that you use the keyword `static` in an array declaration in order to make it possible to initialize that array. That restriction, as discussed in Chapter 9, "Memory Models and Namespaces," applies to arrays declared inside a function body. When an array is declared outside a function body, as is `qualify` in Listing 6.6, it's termed an *external* array and can be initialized even in pre-ANSI C implementations.

Here is a sample run of the program in Listing 6.6:

```
Enter your age in years: 87
You qualify for the pie-throwing festival.
```

The entered age doesn't match any of the test ranges, so the program sets `index` to `3` and then prints the corresponding string.

Program Notes

In Listing 6.6, the expression `age > 17 && age < 35` tests for ages between the two values—that is, ages in the range 18–34. The expression `age >= 35 && age < 50` uses the `<=` operator to include 35 in its range, which is 35–49. If the program used `age > 35 && age < 50`, the value 35 would be missed by all the tests. When you use range tests, you should check that the ranges don't have holes between them and that they don't overlap. Also, you need to be sure to set up each range correctly; see the sidebar "Range Tests," later in this section.

The `if else` statement serves to select an array index, which, in turn, identifies a particular string.

Range Tests

Note that each part of a range test should use the AND operator to join two complete relational expressions:

```
if (age > 17 && age < 35)    // OK
```

Don't borrow from mathematics and use the following notation:

```
if (17 < age < 35)           // Don't do this!
```

If you make this mistake, the compiler won't catch it as an error because it is still valid C++ syntax. The < operator associates from left to right, so the previous expression means the following:

```
if ( (17 < age) < 35)
```

But 17 < age is either true, or 1, or else false, or 0. In either case, the expression 17 < age is less than 35, so the entire test is always true!

The Logical NOT Operator: !

The ! operator negates, or reverses the truth value of, the expression that follows it. That is, if expression is true, then !expression is false—and vice versa. More precisely, if expression is true, or nonzero, then !expression is false. Incidentally, many people call the exclamation point *bang*, making !x "bang-ex" and !!x "bang-bang-ex."

Usually you can more clearly express a relationship without using the ! operator:

```
if (!(x > 5))                 // if (x <= 5) is clearer
```

But the ! operator can be useful with functions that return true/false values or values that can be interpreted that way. For example, strcmp(s1,s2) returns a nonzero (true) value if the two C-style strings s1 and s2 are different from each other and a zero value if they are the same. This implies that !strcmp(s1,s2) is true if the two strings are equal.

Listing 6.7 uses the technique of applying the ! operator to a function return value to screen numeric input for suitability to be assigned to type int. The user-defined function is_int(), which we'll discuss further in a moment, returns true if its argument is within the range of values that can be assigned to type int. The program then uses the test while(!is_int(num)) to reject values that don't fit in the range.

LISTING 6.7   not.cpp

```
// not.cpp -- using the not operator
#include <iostream>
#include <climits>
bool is_int(double);
int main()
{
    using namespace std;
    double num;

    cout << "Yo, dude! Enter an integer value: ";
    cin >> num;
```

LISTING 6.7   *Continued*

```
    while (!is_int(num))      // continue while num is not int-able
    {
        cout << "Out of range -- please try again: ";
        cin >> num;
    }
    int val = int (num);      // type cast
    cout << "You've entered the integer " << val << "\nBye\n";
    return 0;
}

bool is_int(double x)
{
    if (x <= INT_MAX && x >= INT_MIN)    // use climits values
        return true;
    else
        return false;
}
```

Compatibility Note

If your system doesn't provide `climits`, use `limits.h`.

Here is a sample run of the program in Listing 6.7 on a system with a 32-bit `int`:

```
Yo, dude! Enter an integer value: 6234128679
Out of range -- please try again: -8000222333
Out of range -- please try again: 99999
You've entered the integer 99999
Bye
```

Program Notes

If you enter a too-large value to a program reading a type `int`, many C++ implementations simply truncate the value to fit, without informing you that data was lost. The program in Listing 6.7 avoids that by first reading the potential `int` as a `double`. The `double` type has more than enough precision to hold a typical `int` value, and its range is much greater.

The Boolean function `is_int()` uses the two symbolic constants (`INT_MAX` and `INT_MIN`), defined in the `climits` file (discussed in Chapter 3, "Dealing with Data"), to determine whether its argument is within the proper limits. If so, the program returns a value of `true`; otherwise, it returns `false`.

The `main()` program uses a `while` loop to reject invalid input until the user gets it right. You could make the program friendlier by displaying the `int` limits when the input is out of range. After the input has been validated, the program assigns it to an `int` variable.

Logical Operator Facts

As mentioned earlier in this chapter, the C++ logical OR and logical AND operators have a lower precedence than relational operators. This means that an expression such as this

```
x > 5 && x < 10
```

is read this way:

```
(x > 5) && (x < 10)
```

The ! operator, on the other hand, has a higher precedence than any of the relational or arithmetic operators. Therefore, to negate an expression, you should enclose the expression in parentheses, like this:

```
!(x > 5)     // is it false that x is greater than 5
!x > 5       // is !x greater than 5
```

Incidentally, the second expression here is always `false` because `!x` can have only the values `true` or `false`, which get converted to `1` or `0`.

The logical AND operator has a higher precedence than the logical OR operator. Thus this expression:

```
age > 30 && age < 45 || weight > 300
```

means the following:

```
(age > 30 && age < 45) || weight > 300
```

That is, one condition is that `age` be in the range 31–44, and the second condition is that `weight` be greater than 300. The entire expression is `true` if one or the other or both of these conditions are `true`.

You can, of course, use parentheses to tell the program the interpretation you want. For example, suppose you want to use `&&` to combine the condition that `age` be greater than 50 or `weight` be greater than 300 with the condition that `donation` be greater than 1,000. You have to enclose the OR part within parentheses:

```
(age > 50 || weight > 300) && donation > 1000
```

Otherwise, the compiler combines the `weight` condition with the `donation` condition instead of with the `age` condition.

Although the C++ operator precedence rules often make it possible to write compound comparisons without using parentheses, the simplest course of action is to use parentheses to group the tests, whether or not the parentheses are needed. It makes the code easier to read, it doesn't force someone else to look up some of the less commonly used precedence rules, and it reduces the chance of making errors because you don't quite remember the exact rule that applies.

C++ guarantees that when a program evaluates a logical expression, it evaluates it from left to right and stops evaluation as soon as it knows what the answer is. Suppose, for example, that you have this condition:

```
x != 0  && 1.0 / x > 100.0
```

If the first condition is `false`, then the whole expression must be `false`. That's because for this expression to be `true`, each individual condition must be `true`. Knowing the first condition is `false`, the program doesn't bother evaluating the second condition. That's fortunate in this example because evaluating the second condition would result in dividing by zero, which is not in a computer's repertoire of possible actions.

Alternative Representations

Not all keyboards provide all the symbols used for the logical operators, so the C++ Standard provides alternative representations, as shown in Table 6.3. The identifiers `and`, `or`, and `not` are C++ reserved words, meaning that you can't use them as names for variables and so on. They are not considered keywords because they are alternative representations of existing language features. Incidentally, these are not reserved words in C, but a C program can use them as operators, provided that the program includes the `iso646.h` header file. C++ does not require using a header file.

TABLE 6.3   Logical Operators: Alternative Representations

Operator	Alternative Representation
&&	and
||	or
!	not

The `cctype` Library of Character Functions

C++ has inherited from C a handy package of character-related functions, prototyped in the `cctype` header file (`ctype.h`, in the older style), that simplify such tasks as determining whether a character is an uppercase letter or a digit or punctuation. For example, the `isalpha(ch)` function returns a nonzero value if `ch` is a letter and a zero value otherwise. Similarly, the `ispunct(ch)` function returns a `true` value only if `ch` is a punctuation character, such as a comma or period. (These functions have return type `int` rather than `bool`, but the usual `bool` conversions allow you to treat them as type `bool`.)

Using these functions is more convenient than using the AND and OR operators. For example, here's how you might use AND and OR to test whether a character `ch` is an alphabetic character:

```
if ((ch >= 'a' && ch <= 'z') || (ch >= 'A' && ch <= 'Z'))
```

Compare that to using `isalpha()`:

```
if (isalpha(ch))
```

Not only is `isalpha()` easier to use, it is more general. The AND/OR form assumes that character codes for A through Z are in sequence, with no other characters having codes in that range. This assumption is true for ASCII codes, but it isn't always true in general.

Listing 6.8 demonstrates some functions from the `cctype` family. In particular, it uses `isalpha()`, which tests for alphabetic characters; `isdigits()`, which tests for digit characters, such as 3; `isspace()`, which tests for whitespace characters, such as newlines, spaces, and tabs; and `ispunct()`, which tests for punctuation characters. The program also reviews the `if else if` structure and using a `while` loop with `cin.get(char)`.

LISTING 6.8   `cctypes.cpp`

```cpp
// cctypes.cpp -- using the ctype.h library
#include <iostream>
#include <cctype>               // prototypes for character functions
int main()
{
    using namespace std;
    cout << "Enter text for analysis, and type @"
            " to terminate input.\n";
    char ch;
    int whitespace = 0;
    int digits = 0;
    int chars = 0;
    int punct = 0;
    int others = 0;

    cin.get(ch);                // get first character
    while(ch != '@')            // test for sentinel
    {
        if(isalpha(ch))         // is it an alphabetic character?
            chars++;
        else if(isspace(ch))    // is it a whitespace character?
            whitespace++;
        else if(isdigit(ch))    // is it a digit?
            digits++;
        else if(ispunct(ch))    // is it punctuation?
            punct++;
        else
            others++;
        cin.get(ch);            // get next character
    }
    cout << chars << " letters, "
         << whitespace << " whitespace, "
         << digits << " digits, "
         << punct << " punctuations, "
         << others << " others.\n";
    return 0;
}
```

Here is a sample run of the program in Listing 6.8 (note that the whitespace count includes newlines):

```
Enter text for analysis, and type @ to terminate input.
Jody "Java-Java" Joystone, noted restaurant critic,
celebrated her 39th birthday with a carafe of 1982
Chateau Panda.@
89 letters, 16 whitespace, 6 digits, 6 punctuations, 0 others.
```

Table 6.4 summarizes the functions available in the `cctype` package. Some systems may lack some of these functions or have additional ones.

TABLE 6.4   The `cctype` Character Functions

Function Name	Return Value
`isalnum()`	This function returns `true` if the argument is alphanumeric (that is, a letter or a digit).
`isalpha()`	This function returns `true` if the argument is alphabetic.
`isblank()`	This function returns `true` if the argument is a space or a horizontal tab.
`iscntrl()`	This function returns `true` if the argument is a control character.
`isdigit()`	This function returns `true` if the argument is a decimal digit (0–9).
`isgraph()`	This function returns `true` if the argument is any printing character other than a space.
`islower()`	This function returns `true` if the argument is a lowercase letter.
`isprint()`	This function returns `true` if the argument is any printing character, including a space.
`ispunct()`	This function returns `true` if the argument is a punctuation character.
`isspace()`	This function returns `true` if the argument is a standard whitespace character (that is, a space, formfeed, newline, carriage return, horizontal tab, vertical tab).
`isupper()`	This function returns `true` if the argument is an uppercase letter.
`isxdigit()`	This function returns `true` if the argument is a hexadecimal digit character (that is, 0–9, a–f, or A–F).
`tolower()`	If the argument is an uppercase character, `tolower()` returns the lowercase version of that character; otherwise, it returns the argument unaltered.
`toupper()`	If the argument is a lowercase character, `toupper()` returns the uppercase version of that character; otherwise, it returns the argument unaltered.

The ?: Operator

C++ has an operator that can often be used instead of the `if else` statement. This operator is called the *conditional operator*, written `?:`, and, for you trivia buffs, it is the only C++ operator that requires three operands. The general form looks like this:

expression1 ? *expression2* : *expression3*

If *expression1* is `true`, then the value of the whole conditional expression is the value of *expression2*. Otherwise, the value of the whole expression is the value of *expression3*. Here are two examples that show how the operator works:

```
5 > 3 ? 10 : 12  // 5 > 3 is true, so expression value is 10
3 == 9? 25 : 18  // 3 == 9 is false, so expression value is 18
```

We can paraphrase the first example this way: If 5 is greater than 3, the expression evaluates to 10; otherwise, it evaluates to 12. In real programming situations, of course, the expressions would involve variables.

Listing 6.9 uses the conditional operator to determine the larger of two values.

LISTING 6.9   `condit.cpp`

```cpp
// condit.cpp -- using the conditional operator
#include <iostream>
int main()
{
    using namespace std;
    int a, b;
    cout << "Enter two integers: ";
    cin >> a >> b;
    cout << "The larger of " << a << " and " << b;
    int c = a > b ? a : b;   // c = a if a > b, else c = b
    cout << " is " << c << endl;
    return 0;
}
```

Here is a sample run of the program in Listing 6.9:

```
Enter two numbers: 25 28
The larger of 25 and 28 is 28
```

The key part of the program is this statement:

```
int c = a > b ? a : b;
```

It produces the same result as the following statements:

```
int c;
if (a > b)
    c = a;
else
    c = b;
```

Compared to the `if else` sequence, the conditional operator is more concise but, at first, less obvious. One difference between the two approaches is that the conditional operator produces an expression and hence a single value that can be assigned or be incorporated into a larger expression, as the program in Listing 6.9 does when it assigns the value of the conditional expression to the variable `c`. The conditional operator's concise form, unusual syntax, and overall weird appearance make it a great favorite among programmers who appreciate those qualities. One favorite trick for the reprehensible goal of concealing the purpose of code is to nest conditional expressions within one another, as the following mild example shows:

```
const char x[2] [20] = {"Jason ","at your service\n"};
const char * y = "Quillstone ";

for (int i = 0; i < 3; i++)
    cout << ((i < 2)? !i ? x [i] : y : x[1]);
```

This is merely an obscure (but, by no means maximally obscure) way to print the three strings in the following order:

```
Jason Quillstone at your service
```

In terms of readability, the conditional operator is best suited for simple relationships and simple expression values:

```
x = (x > y) ? x : y;
```

If the code becomes more involved, it can probably be expressed more clearly as an `if else` statement.

The `switch` Statement

Suppose you create a screen menu that asks the user to select one of five choices—for example, Cheap, Moderate, Expensive, Extravagant, and Excessive. You can extend an `if else if else` sequence to handle five alternatives, but the C++ `switch` statement more easily handles selecting a choice from an extended list. Here's the general form for a `switch` statement:

```
switch (integer-expression)
{
    case label1 : statement(s)
    case label2 : statement(s)
    ...
    default     : statement(s)
}
```

A C++ `switch` statement acts as a routing device that tells the computer which line of code to execute next. On reaching a `switch` statement, a program jumps to the line labeled with the value corresponding to the value of *integer-expression*. For example, if *integer-expression* has the value 4, the program goes to the line that has a `case 4:` label. The value *integer-expression*, as the name suggests, must be an expression that reduces to an integer value. Also, each label must be an integer constant expression. Most often, labels are simple `int` or `char` constants, such as 1 or `'q'`, or enumerators. If *integer-expression* doesn't match any of the labels, the program jumps to the line labeled `default`. The `default` label is optional. If you omit it and there is no match, the program jumps to the next statement following the `switch`. (See Figure 6.3.)

FIGURE 6.3
The structure of `switch` statements.

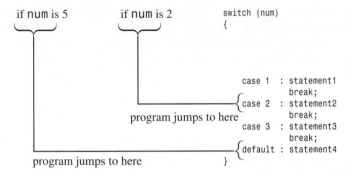

The `switch` statement is different from similar statements in languages such as Pascal in a very important way. Each C++ case label functions only as a line label, not as a boundary between choices. That is, after a program jumps to a particular line in a `switch`, it then sequentially executes all the statements following that line in the switch unless you explicitly direct it otherwise. Execution does *not* automatically stop at the next case. To make execution stop at the end of a particular group of statements, you must use the `break` statement. This causes execution to jump to the statement following the `switch`.

Listing 6.10 shows how to use `switch` and `break` together to implement a simple menu for executives. The program uses a `showmenu()` function to display a set of choices. A `switch` statement then selects an action based on the user's response.

Compatibility Note

Some C++ implementations treat the `\a` escape sequence (used in `case 1` in Listing 6.10) as silent.

LISTING 6.10   `switch.cpp`

```
// switch.cpp -- using the switch statement
#include <iostream>
using namespace std;
void showmenu();    // function prototypes
void report();
void comfort();
int main()
{
    showmenu();
    int choice;
    cin >> choice;
```

LISTING 6.10 Continued

```
    while (choice != 5)
    {
        switch(choice)
        {
            case 1 :    cout << "\a\n";
                        break;
            case 2 :    report();
                        break;
            case 3 :    cout << "The boss was in all day.\n";
                        break;
            case 4 :    comfort();
                        break;
            default :   cout << "That's not a choice.\n";
        }
        showmenu();
        cin >> choice;
    }
    cout << "Bye!\n";
    return 0;
}

void showmenu()
{
    cout << "Please enter 1, 2, 3, 4, or 5:\n"
            "1) alarm           2) report\n"
            "3) alibi           4) comfort\n"
            "5) quit\n";
}
void report()
{
    cout << "It's been an excellent week for business.\n"
        "Sales are up 120%. Expenses are down 35%.\n";
}
void comfort()
{
    cout << "Your employees think you are the finest CEO\n"
        "in the industry. The board of directors think\n"
        "you are the finest CEO in the industry.\n";
}
```

Here is a sample run of the executive menu program in Listing 6.10:

```
Please enter 1, 2, 3, 4, or 5:
1) alarm           2) report
3) alibi           4) comfort
5) quit
4
Your employees think you are the finest CEO
in the industry. The board of directors think
you are the finest CEO in the industry.
```

```
Please enter 1, 2, 3, 4, or 5:
1) alarm              2) report
3) alibi              4) comfort
5) quit
2
It's been an excellent week for business.
Sales are up 120%. Expenses are down 35%.
Please enter 1, 2, 3, 4, or 5:
1) alarm              2) report
3) alibi              4) comfort
5) quit
6
That's not a choice.
Please enter 1, 2, 3, 4, or 5:
1) alarm              2) report
3) alibi              4) comfort
5) quit
5
Bye!
```

The `while` loop terminates when the user enters **5**. Entering **1** through **4** activates the corresponding choice from the `switch` list, and entering **6** triggers the default statements.

As noted earlier, this program needs the `break` statements to confine execution to a particular portion of a `switch` statement. To see that this is so, you can remove the `break` statements from Listing 6.10 and see how it works afterward. You'll find, for example, that entering **2** causes the program to execute *all* the statements associated with case labels 2, 3, 4, and the default. C++ works this way because that sort of behavior can be useful. For one thing, it makes it simple to use multiple labels. For example, suppose you rewrote Listing 6.10 using characters instead of integers as menu choices and switch labels. In that case, you could use both an uppercase and a lowercase label for the same statements:

```
char choice;
cin >> choice;
while (choice != 'Q' && choice != 'q')
{
    switch(choice)
    {
        case 'a':
        case 'A': cout << "\a\n";
                  break;
        case 'r':
        case 'R': report();
                  break;
        case 'l':
        case 'L': cout << "The boss was in all day.\n";
                  break;
        case 'c':
        case 'C': comfort();
                  break;
        default : cout << "That's not a choice.\n";
    }
```

```
    showmenu();
    cin >> choice;
}
```

Because there is no `break` immediately following `case 'a'`, program execution passes on to the next line, which is the statement following `case 'A'`.

Using Enumerators as Labels

Listing 6.11 illustrates using `enum` to define a set of related constants and then using the constants in a `switch` statement. In general, `cin` doesn't recognize enumerated types (it can't know how you will define them), so the program reads the choice as an `int`. When the `switch` statement compares the `int` value to an enumerator case label, it promotes the enumerator to `int`. Also, the enumerators are promoted to type `int` in the `while` loop test condition.

LISTING 6.11 `enum.cpp`

```cpp
// enum.cpp -- using enum
#include <iostream>
// create named constants for 0 - 6
enum {red, orange, yellow, green, blue, violet, indigo};

int main()
{
    using namespace std;
    cout << "Enter color code (0-6): ";
    int code;
    cin >> code;
    while (code >= red && code <= indigo)
    {
        switch (code)
        {
            case red     : cout << "Her lips were red.\n"; break;
            case orange  : cout << "Her hair was orange.\n"; break;
            case yellow  : cout << "Her shoes were yellow.\n"; break;
            case green   : cout << "Her nails were green.\n"; break;
            case blue    : cout << "Her sweatsuit was blue.\n"; break;
            case violet  : cout << "Her eyes were violet.\n"; break;
            case indigo  : cout << "Her mood was indigo.\n"; break;
        }
        cout << "Enter color code (0-6): ";
        cin >> code;
    }
    cout << "Bye\n";
    return 0;
}
```

Here's sample output from the program in Listing 6.11:

```
Enter color code (0-6): 3
Her nails were green.
Enter color code (0-6): 5
```

```
Her eyes were violet.
Enter color code (0-6): 2
Her shoes were yellow.
Enter color code (0-6): 8
Bye
```

switch and if else

Both the `switch` statement and the `if else` statement let a program select from a list of alternatives. The `if else` is the more versatile of the two. For example, it can handle ranges, as in the following:

```
if (age > 17 && age < 35)
    index = 0;
else if (age >= 35 && age < 50)
    index = 1;
else if (age >= 50 && age < 65)
    index = 2;
else
    index = 3;
```

The `switch` statement, on the other hand, isn't designed to handle ranges. Each `switch` case label must be a single value. Also, that value must be an integer (which includes `char`), so a `switch` statement can't handle floating-point tests. And the case label value must be a constant. If your alternatives involve ranges or floating-point tests or comparing two variables, you should use `if else`.

If, however, all the alternatives can be identified with integer constants, you can use a `switch` or an `if else` statement. Because that's precisely the situation that the `switch` statement is designed to process, the `switch` statement is usually the more efficient choice in terms of code size and execution speed, unless there are only a couple alternatives from which to choose.

Tip

If you can use either an `if else if` sequence or a `switch` statement, the usual rule is to use `switch` if you have three or more alternatives.

The break and continue Statements

The `break` and `continue` statements enable a program to skip over parts of the code. You can use the `break` statement in a `switch` statement and in any of the loops. It causes program execution to pass to the next statement following the `switch` or the loop. The `continue` statement is used in loops and causes a program to skip the rest of the body of the loop and then start a new loop cycle. (See Figure 6.4.)

FIGURE 6.4

The structure of `continue` and `break` statements.

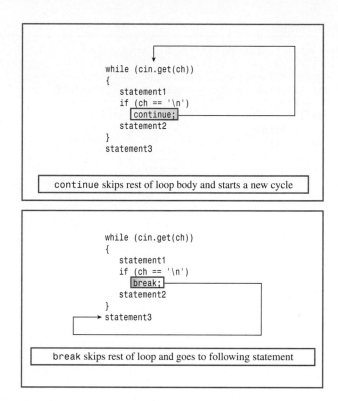

Listing 6.12 shows how the two statements work. The program lets you enter a line of text. The loop echoes each character and uses **break** to terminate the loop if the character is a period. This shows how you can use **break** to terminate a loop from within when some condition becomes **true**. Next the program counts spaces but not other characters. The loop uses **continue** to skip over the counting part of the loop when the character isn't a space.

LISTING 6.12   jump.cpp

```cpp
// jump.cpp -- using continue and break
#include <iostream>
const int ArSize = 80;
int main()
{
    using namespace std;
    char line[ArSize];
    int spaces = 0;

    cout << "Enter a line of text:\n";
    cin.get(line, ArSize);
    cout << "Complete line:\n" << line << endl;
    cout << "Line through first period:\n";
```

LISTING 6.12   Continued

```cpp
    for (int i = 0; line[i] != '\0'; i++)
    {
        cout << line[i];     // display character
        if (line[i] == '.') // quit if it's a period
            break;
        if (line[i] != ' ') // skip rest of loop
            continue;
        spaces++;
    }
    cout << "\n" << spaces << " spaces\n";
    cout << "Done.\n";
    return 0;
}
```

Here's a sample run of the program in Listing 6.12:

```
Enter a line of text:
Let's do lunch today. You can pay!
Complete line:
Let's do lunch today. You can pay!
Line through first period:
Let's do lunch today.
3 spaces
Done.
```

Program Notes

Note that whereas the `continue` statement causes the program in Listing 6.12 to skip the rest of the loop body, it doesn't skip the loop update expression. In a `for` loop, the `continue` statement makes the program skip directly to the update expression and then to the test expression. For a `while` loop, however, `continue` makes the program go directly to the test expression. So any update expression in a `while` loop body following the `continue` would be skipped. In some cases, that could be a problem.

This program doesn't have to use `continue`. Instead, it could use this code:

```cpp
if (line[i] == ' ')
    spaces++;
```

However, the `continue` statement can make the program more readable when several statements follow the `continue`. That way, you don't need to make all those statements part of an `if` statement.

C++, like C, also has a `goto` statement. A statement like this:

```cpp
goto paris;
```

means to jump to the location that has the label `paris:`. That is, you can have code like this:

```cpp
char ch;
cin >> ch;
if (ch == 'P')
```

```
        goto paris;
cout << ...
...
paris: cout << "You've just arrived at Paris.\n";
```

In most circumstances (some would say in all circumstances), using `goto` is a bad hack, and you should use structured controls, such as `if else`, `switch`, `continue`, and the like, to control program flow.

Number-Reading Loops

Say you're preparing a program to read a series of numbers into an array. You want to give the user the option to terminate input before filling the array. One way to do this is utilize how `cin` behaves. Consider the following code:

```
int n;
cin >> n;
```

What happens if the user responds by entering a word instead of a number? Four things occur in such a mismatch:

- The value of `n` is left unchanged.

- The mismatched input is left in the input queue.

- An error flag is set in the `cin` object.

- The call to the `cin` method, if converted to type `bool`, returns `false`.

The fact that the method returns `false` means that you can use non-numeric input to terminate a number-reading loop. The fact that non-numeric input sets an error flag means that you have to reset the flag before the program can read more input. The `clear()` method, which also resets the end-of-file (EOF) condition (see Chapter 5), resets the bad input flag. (Either bad input or the EOF can cause `cin` to return `false`. Chapter 17, "Input, Output, and Files," discusses how to distinguish between the two cases.) Let's look at a couple examples that illustrate these techniques.

Say you want to write a program that calculates the average weight of your day's catch of fish. There's a five-fish limit, so a five-element array can hold all the data, but it's possible that you could catch fewer fish. Listing 6.13 uses a loop that terminates if the array is full or if you enter non-numeric input.

LISTING 6.13 `cinfish.cpp`
_____

```
// cinfish.cpp -- non-numeric input terminates loop
#include <iostream>
const int Max = 5;
int main()
{
    using namespace std;
```

LISTING 6.13   Continued

```
// get data
    double fish[Max];
    cout << "Please enter the weights of your fish.\n";
    cout << "You may enter up to " << Max
            << " fish <q to terminate>.\n";
    cout << "fish #1: ";
    int i = 0;
    while (i < Max && cin >> fish[i]) {
        if (++i < Max)
            cout << "fish #" << i+1 << ": ";
    }
// calculate average
    double total = 0.0;
    for (int j = 0; j < i; j++)
        total += fish[j];
// report results
    if (i == 0)
        cout << "No fish\n";
    else
        cout << total / i << " = average weight of "
            << i << " fish\n";
    cout << "Done.\n";
    return 0;
}
```

Compatibility Note

Some older Borland compilers give a warning about this:

```
cout << "fish #" << i+1 << ": ";
```

that says that ambiguous operators need parentheses. Don't worry. Such a compiler is just warning about a possible grouping error if << is used in its original meaning as a left-shift operator.

The expression `cin >> fish[i]` in Listing 6.13 is really a `cin` method function call, and the function returns `cin`. If `cin` is part of a test condition, it's converted to type **bool**. The conversion value is **true** if input succeeds and **false** otherwise. A **false** value for the expression terminates the loop. By the way, here's a sample run of the program:

```
Please enter the weights of your fish.
You may enter up to 5 fish <q to terminate>.
fish #1: 30
fish #2: 35
fish #3: 25
fish #4: 40
fish #5: q
32.5 = average weight of 4 fish
Done.
```

Note the following line of code:

```
while (i < Max && cin >> fish[i]) {
```

Recall that C++ doesn't evaluate the right side of a logical AND expression if the left side is `false`. In such a case, evaluating the right side means using `cin` to place input into the array. If `i` does equal `Max`, the loop terminates without trying to read a value into a location past the end of the array.

The preceding example doesn't attempt to read any input after non-numeric input. Let's look at a case that does. Suppose you are required to submit exactly five golf scores to a C++ program to establish your average. If a user enters non-numeric input, the program should object, insisting on numeric input. As you've seen, you can use the value of a `cin` input expression to test for non-numeric input. Suppose the program finds that the user enters the wrong stuff. It needs to take three steps:

1. Reset `cin` to accept new input.

2. Get rid of the bad input.

3. Prompt the user to try again.

Note that the program has to reset `cin` before getting rid of the bad input. Listing 6.14 shows how these tasks can be accomplished.

LISTING 6.14 `cingolf.cpp`

```cpp
// cingolf.cpp -- non-numeric input skipped
#include <iostream>
const int Max = 5;
int main()
{
    using namespace std;
// get data
    int golf[Max];
    cout << "Please enter your golf scores.\n";
    cout << "You must enter " << Max << " rounds.\n";
    int i;
    for (i = 0; i < Max; i++)
    {
        cout << "round #" << i+1 << ": ";
        while (!(cin >> golf[i])) {
            cin.clear();      // reset input
            while (cin.get() != '\n')
                continue;     // get rid of bad input
            cout << "Please enter a number: ";
        }
    }
// calculate average
    double total = 0.0;
    for (i = 0; i < Max; i++)
        total += golf[i];
// report results
    cout << total / Max << " = average score "
         << Max << " rounds\n";
    return 0;
}
```

Compatibility Note

Some older Borland compilers give a warning about this:

```
cout << "round #" << i+1 << ": ";
```

that says that ambiguous operators need parentheses. Don't worry. Such compilers are just warning about a possible grouping error if << is used in its original meaning as a left-shift operator.

Here is a sample run of the program in Listing 6.14:

```
Please enter your golf scores.
You must enter 5 rounds.
round #1: 88
round #2: 87
round #3: must i?
Please enter a number: 103
round #4: 94
round #5: 86
91.6 = average score 5 rounds
```

Program Notes

The heart of the error-handling code in Listing 6.14 is the following:

```
while (!(cin >> golf[i])) {
    cin.clear();     // reset input
    while (cin.get() != '\n')
        continue; // get rid of bad input
    cout << "Please enter a number: ";
}
```

If the user enters **88**, the `cin` expression is **true**, a value is placed in the array, the expression `!(cin >> golf[i])` is **false**, and this inner loop terminates. But if the user enters **must i?**, the `cin` expression is **false**, nothing is placed into the array, the expression `!(cin >> golf[i])` is **true**, and the program enters the inner `while` loop. The first statement in the loop uses the `clear()` method to reset input. If you omit this statement, the program refuses to read any more input. Next, the program uses `cin.get()` in a `while` loop to read the remaining input through the end of the line. This gets rid of the bad input, along with anything else on the line. Another approach is to read to the next whitespace, which gets rid of bad input one word at a time instead of one line at a time. Finally, the program tells the user to enter a number.

Simple File Input/Output

Sometimes keyboard input is not the best choice. For example, suppose you've written a program to analyze stocks, and you've downloaded a file of 1,000 stock prices. It would be far more convenient to have the program read the file directly than to hand-enter all the values. Similarly, it can be convenient to have a program write output to a file so that you have a permanent record of the results.

Fortunately, C++ makes it simple to transfer the skills you've acquired for keyboard input and display output (collectively termed *console I/O*) to file input and output (*file I/O*). Chapter 17 explores these topics more extensively, but we'll look at simple text file I/O now.

Text I/O and Text Files

Let's reexamine the concept of text *I/O*. When you use `cin` for input, the program views input as a series of bytes, with each byte being interpreted as a character code. No matter what the destination data type, the input begins as character data—that is, text data. The `cin` object then has the responsibility of translating text to other types. To see how this works, let's examine how different code handles the same line of input.

Suppose you have the following sample line of input:

38.5 19.2

Let's see how this line of input is handled by `cin` when used with different data types. First, let's try type `char`:

```
char ch;
cin >> ch;
```

The first character in the input line is assigned to `ch`. In this case, the first character is the digit **3**, and the character code (in binary) for this digit is stored in `ch`. The input and the destination are both characters, so no translation is needed. (Note that it's not the numeric value **3** that is stored; rather, it is the character code for the digit 3.) After the input statement, the digit character **8** is the next character in the input queue and will be the next character examined by the next input operation.

Next, let's try the `int` type:

```
int n;
cin >> n;
```

In this case, `cin` reads up to the first non-digit character. That is, it reads the **3** digit and the **8** digit, leaving the period as the next character in the input queue. Then `cin` computes that these two characters correspond to the numeric value **38**, and the binary code for **38** is copied to `n`.

Next, let's try the `double` type:

```
double x;
cin >> x;
```

In this case, `cin` reads up to the first character that's not part of a floating-point number. That is, it reads the **3** digit, the **8** digit, the period character, and the **5** digit, leaving the space as the next character in the input queue. Then `cin` computes that these four characters correspond to the numeric value **38.5**, and the binary code (floating-point format) for 38.5 is copied to `x`.

Next, let's try the `char` array type:

```
char word[50];
cin >> word;
```

In this case, `cin` reads up to the whitespace character. That is, it reads the **3** digit, the **8** digit, the period character, and the **5** digit, leaving the space as the next character in the input queue. Then `cin` stores the character code for these four characters in the array `word` and adds a terminating null character. No translation is needed.

Finally, let's try an input variant for the `char` array type:

```
char word[50];
cin.geline(word,50);
```

In this case, `cin` reads up through the newline character. All the characters through the final **2** digit are stored in the array `word`, and a null character is added. The newline character is discarded, and the next character in the input queue will be the first character on the next line. No translation is needed.

On output, the opposite translations take place. That is, integers are converted to sequences of digit characters, and floating-point numbers are converted to sequences of digits and other characters (for example, 284.53 or -1.587E+06). Character data requires no translation.

The main point to this is that all the input starts out as text. Therefore, the file equivalent to console input is a text file—that is, a file in which each byte stores a character code. Not all files are text files. For example, databases and spreadsheets store numeric data in numeric forms—that is, in binary integer or binary floating-point form. Also, word processing files may contain text information, but they also contain non-text data to describe formatting, fonts, printers, and the like.

The file I/O discussed in this chapter parallels console I/O and thus should be used with text files. To create a text file for input, you use a text editor, such as EDIT for DOS, Notepad for Windows, or vi or emacs for Unix/Linux. You can use a word processor, as long as you save the file in text format. The code editors that are part of IDEs also produce text files; indeed, the source code files are examples of text files. Similarly, you can use text editors to look at files created with text output.

Writing to a Text File

For file output, C++ uses analogs to `cout`. So, to prepare for file output, let's review some basic facts about using `cout for console output`:

- You must include the `iostream` header file.

- The `iostream` header file defines an `ostream` class for handling output.

- The `iostream` header file declares an `ostream` variable, or object, called `cout`.

- You must account for the `std` namespace; for example, you can use the `using` directive or the `std::` prefix for elements such as `cout` and `endl`.

- You can use `cout` with the `>>` operator to read a variety of data types.

File output parallels this very closely:

- You must include the `fstream` header file.

- The `fstream` header file defines an `ofstream` class for handling output.

- You need to declare one or more `ofstream` variables, or objects, which you can name as you please, as long as you respect the usual naming conventions.

- You must account for the `std` namespace; for example, you can use the `using` directive or the `std::` prefix for elements such as `ofstream`.

- You need to associate a specific `ofstream` object with a specific file; one way to do so is to use the `open()` method.

- When you're finished with a file, you should use the `close()` method to close the file.

- You can use an `ofstream` object with the `>>` operator to output a variety of data types.

Note that although the `iostream` header file provides a predefined `ostream` object called `cout`, you have to declare your own `ofstream` object, choosing a name for it and associating it with a file. Here's how you declare such objects:

```
ofstream outFile;        // outFile an ofstream object
ofstream fout;           // fout an ofstream object
```

Here's how you can associate the objects with particular files:

```
outFile.open("fish.txt");   // outFile used to write to the fish.txt file
char filename[50];
cin >> filename;            // user specifies a name
fout.open(filename);        // fout used to read specified file
```

Note that the `open()` method requires a C-style string as its argument. This can be a literal string or a string stored in an array.

Here's how you can use these objects:

```
double wt = 125.8;
outFile << wt;          // write a number to fish.txt
char line[81] = "Objects are closer than they appear.";
fin << line << endl;    // write a line of text
```

The important point is that after you've declared an `ofstream` object and associated it with a file, you use it exactly as you would use `cout`. All the operations and methods available to `cout`, such as `<<`, `endl`, and `setf()`, are also available to `ofstream` objects, such as `outFile` and `fout` in the preceding examples.

In short, these are the main steps for using file output:

1. Include the `fstream` header file.

2. Create an `ofstream` object.

3. Associate the `ofstream` object with a file.

4. Use the `ofstream` object in the same manner you would use `cout`.

The program in Listing 6.15 demonstrates this approach. It solicits information from the user, sends output to the display, and then sends the same output to a file. You can use a text editor to examine the output file.

LISTING 6.15   `outfile.cpp`

```
// outfile.cpp -- writing to a file
#include <iostream>
#include <fstream>                       // for file I/O

int main()
{
    using namespace std;

    char automobile[50];
    int year;
    double a_price;
    double d_price;

    ofstream outFile;                    // create object for output
    outFile.open("carinfo.txt");         // associate with a file

    cout << "Enter the make and model of automobile: ";
    cin.getline(automobile, 50);
    cout << "Enter the model year: ";
    cin >> year;
    cout << "Enter the original asking price: ";
    cin >> a_price;
    d_price = 0.913 * a_price;

// display information on screen with cout

    cout << fixed;
    cout.precision(2);
    cout.setf(ios_base::showpoint);
    cout << "Make and model: " << automobile << endl;
    cout << "Year: " << year << endl;
    cout << "Was asking $" << a_price << endl;
    cout << "Now asking $" << d_price << endl;

// now do exact same things using outFile instead of cout

    outFile << fixed;
    outFile.precision(2);
    outFile.setf(ios_base::showpoint);
    outFile << "Make and model: " << automobile << endl;
    outFile << "Year: " << year << endl;
    outFile << "Was asking $" << a_price << endl;
    outFile << "Now asking $" << d_price << endl;

    outFile.close();                     // done with file
    return 0;
}
```

Note that the final section of the program in Listing 6.15 duplicates the `cout` section, with `cout` replaced by `outFile`. Here is a sample run of this program:

```
Enter the make and model of automobile: Flitz Pinata
Enter the model year: 2001
Enter the original asking price: 28576
Make and model: Flitz Pinata
Year: 2001
Was asking $28576.00
Now asking $26089.89
```

The screen output comes from using `cout`. If you check the directory or folder that contains the executable program, you should find a new file called `carinfo.txt`. It contains the output generated by using `outFile`. If you open it with a text editor, you should find the following contents:

```
Make and model: Flitz Pinata
Year: 2001
Was asking $28576.00
Now asking $26089.89
```

As you can see, `outFile` sends precisely the same sequence of characters to the `carinfo.txt` file that `cout` sends to the display.

Program Notes

After the program in Listing 6.15 declares an `ofstream` object, you can use the `open()` method to associate the object with a particular file:

```
ofstream outFile;               // create object for output
outFile.open("carinfo.txt");    // associate with a file
```

When the program is done using a file, it should close the connection:

```
outFile.close();
```

Notice that the `close()` method doesn't require a filename. That's because `outFile` has already been associated with a particular file. If you forget to close a file, the program will close it automatically if the program terminates normally.

Notice that `outFile` can use the same methods that `cout` does. Not only can it use the `<<` operator, but it can use the various formatting methods, such as `setf()` and `precision()`. These methods affect only the object that invokes the method. For example, you can provide different values for different objects:

```
cout.precision(2);       // use a precision of 2 for the display
outFile.precision(4);    // use a precision of 4 for file output
```

The main point you should remember is that after you set up an `ofstream` object such as `outFile`, you use it in precisely the same matter as you use `cout`.

Let's go back to the `open()` method:

```
outFile.open("carinfo.txt");
```

In this case, the file `carinfo.txt` does not exist before the program runs. In this circumstance, the `open()` method creates a brand new file by that name. When the file `carinfo.txt` exists, what happens if you run the program again? By default, `open()` first truncates the file; that is, it trims `carinfo.txt` to zero length, discarding the current contents. The contents are then replaced with the new output. Chapter 17 reveals how to override this default behavior.

Caution

When you open an existing file for output, by default it is truncated to a length of zero bytes, so the contents are lost.

It is possible that an attempt to open a file for output might fail. For example, a file having the requested name might already exist and have restricted access. Therefore, a careful programmer would check to see if the attempt succeeded. You'll learn the technique for this in the next example.

Reading from a Text File

Next, let's examine text file input. It's based on console input, which has many elements. So let's begin with a summary those elements.

- You must include the `iostream` header file.

- The `iostream` header file defines an `istream` class for handling input.

- The `iostream` header file declares an `istream` variable, or object, called `cin`.

- You must account for the `std` namespace; for example, you can use the `using` directive or the `std::` prefix for elements such as `cin`.

- You can use `cin` with the `<<` operator to read a variety of data types.

- You can use `cin` with the `get()` method to read individual characters and with the `getline()` method to read a line of characters at a time.

- You can use `cin` with methods such as `eof()` and `fail()` to monitor the success of an input attempt.

- The object `cin` itself, when used as a test condition, is converted to the Boolean value `true` if the last read attempt succeeded and to `false` otherwise.

File input parallels this very closely:

- You must include the `fstream` header file.

- The `fstream` header file defines an `ifstream` class for handling input.

- You need to declare one or more `ifstream` variables, or objects, which you can name as you please, as long as you respect the usual naming conventions.

- You must account for the `std` namespace; for example, you can use the `using` directive or the `std::` prefix for elements such as `ifstream`.

- You need to associate a specific `ifstream` object with a specific file; one way to do so is to use the `open()` method.

- When you're finished with a file, you should use the `close()` method to close the file.

- You can use an `ifstream` object with the `<<` operator to read a variety of data types.

- You can use an `ifstream` object with the `get()` method to read individual characters and with the `getline()` method to read a line of characters at a time.

- You can use an `ifstream` object with methods such as `eof()` and `fail()` to monitor the success of an input attempt.

- An `ifstream` object itself, when used as a test condition, is converted to the Boolean value `true` if the last read attempt succeeded and to `false` otherwise.

Note that although the `iostream` header file provides a predefined `istream` object called `cin`, you have to declare your own `ifstream` object, choosing a name for it and associating it with a file. Here's how you declare such objects:

```
ifstream inFile;          // inFile an ifstream object
ifstream fin;             // fin an ifstream object
```

Here's how you can associate them with particular files:

```
inFile.open("bowling.txt");  // inFile used to read bowling.txt file
char filename[50];
cin >> filename;             // user specifies a name
fin.open(filename);          // fin used to read specified file
```

Note that the `open()` method requires a C-style string as its argument. This can be a literal string or a string stored in an array.

Here's how you can use these objects:

```
double wt;
inFile >> wt;          // read a number from bowling.txt
char line[81];
fin.getline(line, 81); // read a line of text
```

The important point is that after you've declared an `ifstream` object and associated it with a file, you can use it exactly as you would use `cin`. All the operations and methods available to `cin` are also available to `ifstream` objects, such as `inFile` and `fin` in the preceding examples.

What happens if you attempt to open a non-existent file for input? This error causes subsequent attempts to use the `ifstream` object for input to fail. The preferred way to check whether a file was opened successfully is to use the `is_open()` method. You can use code like this:

```
inFile.open("bowling.txt");
if (!inFile.is_open())
{
    exit(EXIT_FAILURE);
}
```

The `is_open()` method returns `true` if the file was opened successfully, so the expression `!inFile.is_open()` is `true` if the attempt fails. The `exit()` function is prototyped in the `cstdlib` header file, which also defines `EXIT_FAILURE` as an argument value used to communicate with the operating system. The `exit()` function terminates the program.

The `is_open()` method is relatively new to C++. If your compiler doesn't support it, you can use the older `good()` method instead. As Chapter 17 discusses, `good()` doesn't check quite as extensively as `is_open()` for possible problems.

The program in Listing 6.16 opens a file specified by the user, reads numbers from the file, and reports the number of values, their sum, and their average. It's important that you design the input loop correctly, and the following "Program Notes" section discusses this in more detail. Notice that this program makes good use of `if` statements.

LISTING 6.16   sumafile.cpp

```cpp
// sumafile.cpp -- functions with an array argument
#include <iostream>
#include <fstream>              // file I/O support
#include <cstdlib>              // support for exit()
const int SIZE = 60;
int main()
{
    using namespace std;
    char filename[SIZE];
    ifstream inFile;           // object for handling file input

    cout << "Enter name of data file: ";
    cin.getline(filename, SIZE);
    inFile.open(filename);  // associate inFile with a file
    if (!inFile.is_open())  // failed to open file
    {
        cout << "Could not open the file " << filename << endl;
        cout << "Program terminating.\n";
        exit(EXIT_FAILURE);
    }
    double value;
    double sum = 0.0;
    int count = 0;             // number of items read

    inFile >> value;           // get first value
    while (inFile.good())      // while input good and not at EOF
    {
        ++count;               // one more item read
        sum += value;          // calculate running total
        inFile >> value;       // get next value
    }
    if (inFile.eof())
        cout << "End of file reached.\n";
    else if (inFile.fail())
        cout << "Input terminated by data mismatch.\n";
```

LISTING 6.16   Continued

```
else
    cout << "Input terminated for unknown reason.\n";
if (count == 0)
    cout << "No data processed.\n";
else
{
    cout << "Items read: " << count << endl;
    cout << "Sum: " << sum << endl;
    cout << "Average: " << sum / count << endl;
}
inFile.close();            // finished with the file
return 0;
}
```

Compatibility Note

Some older compilers don't recognize the `is_open()` method. For them, you can replace this:

```
if (!inFile.is_open())
```

with the following:

```
if (!inFile.good())
```

This provides a slightly less rigorous test for whether the program succeeded in opening the file.

To use the program in Listing 6.16, you first have to create a text file that contains numbers. You can use a text editor, such as the text editor you use to write source code, to create this file. Let's assume that the file is called `scores.txt` and has the following contents:

```
18 19 18.5 13.5 14
16 19.5 20 18 12 18.5
17.5
```

Caution

The proper format for a DOS/Windows text file requires a newline character at the end of each line. Some text editors, such as the Metrowerks CodeWarrior IDE editor, don't automatically add a newline character to the final line. Therefore, if you use such an editor, you need to press the Enter key after typing the final text and before exiting the file.

Here's a sample run of the program in Listing 6.16:

```
Enter name of data file: scores.txt
End of file reached.
Items read: 12
Sum: 204.5
Average: 17.0417
```

Program Notes

Instead of hard-coding a filename, the program in Listing 6.16 stores a user-supplied name in the character array `filename`. Then the array is used as an argument to `open()`:

```
inFile.open(filename);
```

As discussed earlier in this chapter, it's vital to test whether the attempt to open the file succeeded. Here are a few of the things that might go wrong: The file might not exist, the file might be located in another directory or file folder, access might be denied, and the user might mistype the name or omit a file extension. Many a beginner has spent a long time trying to figure what's wrong with a file-reading loop when the real problem was that the program didn't open the file. Testing for file-opening failure can save you such misspent effort.

You need to pay close attention to the proper design of a file-reading loop. There are several things to test for when reading from a file. First, the program should not try to read past the EOF. The `eof()` method returns `true` if the most recent attempt to read data ran into the EOF. Second, the program might encounter a type mismatch. For instance, Listing 6.16 expects a file containing only numbers. The `fail()` method returns `true` if the most recent read attempt encountered a type mismatch. (This method also returns `true` if the EOF is encountered.) Finally, something unexpected may go wrong—for example, a corrupted file or a hardware failure. The `bad()` method returns `true` if the most recent read attempt encountered such a problem. Rather than test for these conditions individually, it's simpler to use the `good()` method, which returns `true` if nothing went wrong:

```
while (inFile.good())    // while input good and not at EOF
{
    ...
}
```

Then, if you like, you can use the other methods to determine exactly why the loop terminated:

```
if (inFile.eof())
    cout << "End of file reached.\n";
else if (inFile.fail())
    cout << "Input terminated by data mismatch.\n";
else
    cout << "Input terminated for unknown reason.\n";
```

This code comes immediately after the loop so that it investigates why the loop terminated. Because `eof()` tests just for the EOF and `fail()` tests for both the EOF and type mismatch, this code tests for the EOF first. That way, if execution reaches the `else if` test, the EOF has already been excluded, so a `true` value for `fail()` unambiguously identifies type mismatch as the cause of loop termination.

It's particularly important that you understand that `good()` reports on the most recent attempt to read input. That means there should be an attempt to read input *immediately* before applying the test. A standard way of doing that is to have one input statement immediately before the loop, just before the first execution of the loop test, and a second input statement at the end of the loop, just before subsequent executions of the loop test:

```
// standard file-reading loop design
inFile >> value;          // get first value
while (inFile.good())    // while input good and not at EOF
{
    // loop body goes here
    inFile >> value;      // get next value
}
```

You can condense this somewhat by using the fact that the expression

```
inFile >> value
```

evaluates to `inFile` and that `inFile`, when placed in a context in which a `bool` value is expected, evaluates to `inFile.good()`—that is, to `true` or `false`. Thus, you can replace the two input statements with a single input statement used as a loop test. That is, you can replace the preceding loop structure with this:

```
// abbreviated file-reading loop design
// omit pre-loop input
while (inFile >> value)    // read and test for success
{
    // loop body goes here
    // omit end-of-loop input
}
```

This design still follows the precept of attempting to read before testing because to evaluate the expression `inFile >> value`, the program first has to attempt to read a number into `value`.

Now you know the rudiments of file I/O.

Summary

Programs and programming become more interesting when you introduce statements that guide the program through alternative actions. (Whether this also makes the programmer more interesting is a point I've not fully researched.) C++ provides the `if` statement, the `if else` statement, and the `switch` statement as means for managing choices. The C++ `if` statement lets a program execute a statement or statement block conditionally. That is, the program executes the statement or block if a particular condition is met. The C++ `if else` statement lets a program select from two choices which statement or statement block to execute. You can append additional `if else` statements to such a statement to present a series of choices. The C++ `switch` statement directs the program to a particular case in a list of choices.

C++ also provides operators to help in decision making. Chapter 5 discusses the relational expressions, which compare two values. The `if` and `if else` statements typically use relational expressions as test conditions. By using C++'s logical operators (`&&`, `||`, and `!`), you can combine or modify relational expressions to construct more elaborate tests. The conditional operator (`?:`) provides a compact way to choose from two values.

The `cctype` library of character functions provides a convenient and powerful set of tools for analyzing character input.

Loops and selection statements are useful tools for file I/O, which closely parallels console I/O. After you declare `ifstream` and `ofstream` objects and associate them with files, you can use these objects in the same manner you use `cin` and `cout`.

With C++'s loops and decision-making statements, you have the tools for writing interesting, intelligent, and powerful programs. But we've only begun to investigate the real powers of C++. Next, we'll look at functions.

Review Questions

1. Consider the following two code fragments for counting spaces and newlines:

```
// Version 1
while (cin.get(ch))     // quit on eof
{
     if (ch == ' ')
           spaces++;
     if (ch == '\n')
          newlines++;
}
```

```
// Version 2
while (cin.get(ch))     // quit on eof
{
     if (ch == ' ')
           spaces++;
     else if (ch == '\n')
          newlines++;
}
```

What advantages, if any, does the second form have over the first?

2. In Listing 6.2, what is the effect of replacing `++ch` with `ch+1`?

3. Carefully consider the following program:

```
#include <iostream>
using namespace std;
int main()
{
    char ch;
    int ct1, ct2;

    ct1 = ct2 = 0;
    while ((ch = cin.get()) != '$')
    {
        cout << ch;
        ct1++;
        if (ch = '$')
            ct2++;
        cout << ch;
    }
```

```
    cout <<"ct1 = " << ct1 << ", ct2 = " << ct2 << "\n";
    return 0;
}
```

Suppose you provide the following input, where ➡ represents pressing Enter:

Hi!➡
Send $10 or $20 now! ➡

What is the output? (Recall that input is buffered.)

4. Construct logical expressions to represent the following conditions:

   a. `weight` is greater than or equal to 115 but less than 125.

   b. `ch` is `q` or `Q`.

   c. `x` is even but is not `26`.

   d. `x` is even but is not a multiple of `26`.

   e. `donation` is in the range 1,000–2,000 or `guest` is `1`.

   f. `ch` is a lowercase letter or an uppercase letter. (Assume that lowercase letters are coded sequentially and that uppercase letters are coded sequentially but that there is a gap in the code between uppercase and lowercase.)

5. In English, the statement "I will not not speak" means the same as "I will speak." In C++, is `!!x` the same as `x`?

6. Construct a conditional expression that is equal to the absolute value of a variable. That is, if a variable `x` is positive, the value of the expression is just `x`, but if `x` is negative, the value of the expression is `-x`, which is positive.

7. Rewrite the following fragment using `switch`:

```
if (ch == 'A')
    a_grade++;
else if (ch == 'B')
    b_grade++;
else if (ch == 'C')
    c_grade++;
else if (ch == 'D')
    d_grade++;
else
    f_grade++;
```

8. In Listing 6.10, what advantage would there be in using character labels, such as `a` and `c`, instead of numbers for the menu choices and switch cases? (Hint: Think about what happens if the user types `q` in either case and what happens if the user types `5` in either case.)

9. Consider the following code fragment:

```
int line = 0;
char ch;
```

```cpp
while (cin.get(ch))
{
    if (ch == 'Q')
            break;
    if (ch != '\n')
            continue;
    line++;
}
```

Rewrite this code without using `break` or `continue`.

Programming Exercises

1. Write a program that reads keyboard input to the @ symbol and that echoes the input except for digits, converting each uppercase character to lowercase, and vice versa. (Don't forget the `cctype` family.)

2. Write a program that reads up to 10 donation values into an array of `double`. The program should terminate input on non-numeric input. It should report the average of the numbers and also report how many numbers in the array are larger than the average.

3. Write a precursor to a menu-driven program. The program should display a menu offering four choices, each labeled with a letter. If the user responds with a letter other than one of the four valid choices, the program should prompt the user to enter a valid response until the user complies. Then the program should use a switch to select a simple action based on the user's selection. A program run could look something like this:

```
Please enter one of the following choices:
c) carnivore          p) pianist
t) tree               g) game
f
Please enter a c, p, t, or g: q
Please enter a c, p, t, or g: t
A maple is a tree.
```

4. When you join the Benevolent Order of Programmers, you can be known at BOP meetings by your real name, your job title, or your secret BOP name. Write a program that can list members by real name, by job title, by secret name, or by a member's preference. Base the program on the following structure:

```cpp
// Benevolent Order of Programmers name structure
struct bop {
    char fullname[strsize];  // real name
    char title[strsize];     // job title
    char bopname[strsize];   // secret BOP name
    int preference;          // 0 = fullname, 1 = title, 2 = bopname
};
```

In the program, create a small array of such structures and initialize it to suitable values. Have the program run a loop that lets the user select from different alternatives:

```
a. display by name      b. display by title
c. display by bopname   d. display by preference
q. quit
```

Note that "display by preference" does not mean display the preference member; it means display the member corresponding to the preference number. For instance, if preference is 1, choice **d** would display the programmer's job title. A sample run may look something like the following:

```
Benevolent Order of Programmers Report
a. display by name      b. display by title
c. display by bopname   d. display by preference
q. quit
Enter your choice: a
Wimp Macho
Raki Rhodes
Celia Laiter
Hoppy Hipman
Pat Hand
Next choice: d
Wimp Macho
Junior Programmer
MIPS
Analyst Trainee
LOOPY
Next choice: q
Bye!
```

5. The Kingdom of Neutronia, where the unit of currency is the tvarp, has the following income tax code:

first 5,000 tvarps: 0% tax

next 10,000 tvarps: 10% tax

next 20,000 tvarps: 15% tax

tvarps after 35,000: 20% tax

For example, someone earning 38,000 tvarps would owe $5,000 \times 0.00 + 10,000 \times 0.10 + 20,000 \times 0.15 + 3,000 \times 0.20$, or 4,600 tvarps. Write a program that uses a loop to solicit incomes and to report tax owed. The loop should terminate when the user enters a negative number or nonnumeric input.

6. Put together a program that keeps track of monetary contributions to the Society for the Preservation of Rightful Influence. It should ask the user to enter the number of contributors and then solicit the user to enter the name and contribution of each contributor. The information should be stored in a dynamically allocated array of structures. Each structure should have two members: a character array (or else a **string** object) to store the name and a **double** member to hold the amount of the contribution. After reading all the data, the program should display the names and amounts donated for all donors who contributed $10,000 or more. This list should be headed by the label Grand Patrons. After that, the program should list the remaining donors. That list should be

headed Patrons. If there are no donors in one of the categories, the program should print the word "none." Aside from displaying two categories, the program need do no sorting.

7. Write a program that reads input a word at a time until a lone **q** is entered. The program should then report the number of words that began with vowels, the number that began with consonants, and the number that fit neither of those categories. One approach is to use `isalpha()` to discriminate between words beginning with letters and those that don't and then use an `if` or `switch` statement to further identify those passing the `isalpha()` test that begin with vowels. A sample run might look like this:

```
Enter words (q to quit):
The 12 awesome oxen ambled
quietly across 15 meters of lawn. q
5 words beginning with vowels
4 words beginning with consonants
2 others
```

8. Write a program that opens a text file, reads it character-by-character to the end of the file, and reports the number of characters in the file.

9. Do Programming Exercise 6, but modify it to get information from a file. The first item in the file should be the number of contributors, and the rest of the file should consist of pairs of lines, with the first line of each pair being a contributor's name and the second line being a contribution. That is, the file should look like this:

```
4
Sam Stone
2000
Freida Flass
100500
Tammy Tubbs
5000
Rich Raptor
55000
```

CHAPTER 7

FUNCTIONS: C++'S PROGRAMMING MODULES

In this chapter you'll learn about the following:

- Function basics
- Function prototypes
- How to pass function arguments by value
- How to design functions to process arrays
- How to use const pointer parameters

- How to design functions to process text strings
- How to design functions to process structures
- How to design functions to objects of the string class
- Functions that call themselves (recursion)
- Pointers to functions

Fun is where you find it. Look closely, and you can find it in functions. C++ comes with a large library of useful functions (the standard ANSI C library plus several C++ classes), but real programming pleasure comes with writing your own functions. This chapter and Chapter 8, "Adventures in Functions," examine how to define functions, convey information to them, and retrieve information from them. After reviewing how functions work, this chapter concentrates on how to use functions in conjunction with arrays, strings, and structures. Finally, it touches on recursion and pointers to functions. If you've paid your C dues, you'll find much of this chapter familiar. But don't be lulled into a false sense of expertise. C++ has made several additions to what C functions can do, and Chapter 8 deals primarily with those. Meanwhile, let's attend to the fundamentals.

Function Review

Let's review what you've already seen about functions. To use a C++ function, you must do the following:

- Provide a function definition.
- Provide a function prototype.
- Call the function.

If you're using a library function, the function has already been defined and compiled for you. Also, you can use a standard library header file to provide the prototype. All that's left to do is call the function properly. The examples so far in this book have done that several times. For example, the standard C library includes the `strlen()` function for finding the length of the string. The associated standard header file `cstring` contains the function prototype for `strlen()` and several other string-related functions. This advance work allows you to use the `strlen()` function in programs without further worries.

But when you create your own functions, you have to handle all three aspects—defining, prototyping, and calling—yourself. Listing 7.1 shows these steps in a short example.

LISTING 7.1   `calling.cpp`

```cpp
// calling.cpp -- defining, prototyping, and calling a function
#include <iostream>

void simple();    // function prototype

int main()
{
    using namespace std;
    cout << "main() will call the simple() function:\n";
    simple();      // function call
    return 0;
}

// function definition
void simple()
{
    using namespace std;
    cout << "I'm but a simple function.\n";
}
```

Here's the output of the program in Listing 7.1:

```
main() will call the simple() function:
I'm but a simple function.
```

This example places a `using` directive inside each function definition because each function uses `cout`. Alternatively, the program could place a single `using` directive above the function definitions.

Let's take a more detailed look at these steps now.

Defining a Function

You can group functions into two categories: those that don't have return values and those that do. Functions without return values are termed type `void` functions and have the following general form:

```
void functionName(parameterList)
{
    statement(s)
    return;          // optional
}
```

Here *parameterList* specifies the types and number of arguments (parameters) passed to the function. This chapter more fully investigates this list later. The optional return statement marks the end of the function. Otherwise, the function terminates at the closing brace. Type `void` functions correspond to Pascal procedures, FORTRAN subroutines, and modern BASIC subprogram procedures. Typically, you use a `void` function to perform some sort of action. For example, a function to print *Cheers!* a given number (n) of times could look like this:

```
void cheers(int n)          // no return value
{
    using namespace std;
    for (int i = 0; i < n; i++)
        cout << "Cheers! ";
    cout << endl;
}
```

The `int n` parameter list means that `cheers()` expects to have an `int` value passed to it as an argument when you call this function.

A function with a return value produces a value that it returns to the function that called it. In other words, if the function returns the square root of 9.0 (`sqrt(9.0)`), the function call has the value `3.0`. Such a function is declared as having the same type as the value it returns. Here is the general form:

```
typeName functionName(parameterList)
{
    statements
    return value;    // value is type cast to type typeName
}
```

Functions with return values require that you use a return statement so that the value is returned to the calling function. The value itself can be a constant, a variable, or a more general expression. The only requirement is that the expression reduce to a value that has, or is convertible to, the *typeName* type. (If the declared return type is, say, `double`, and the function returns an `int` expression, the `int` value is type cast to type `double`.) The function then returns the final value to the function that called it. C++ does place a restriction on what types you can use for a return value: The return value cannot be an array. Everything else is possible—integers, floating-point numbers, pointers, and even structures and objects! (Interestingly, even though a C++ function can't return an array directly, it can return an array that's part of a structure or object.)

As a programmer, you don't need to know how a function returns a value, but knowing the method might clarify the concept for you. (Also, it gives you something to talk about with your friends and family.) Typically, a function returns a value by copying the return value to a specified CPU register or memory location. Then, the calling program examines that location. Both the returning function and the calling function have to agree on the type of data at that location. The function prototype tells the calling program what to expect, and the function definition tells the called program what to return (see Figure 7.1). Providing the same information in the prototype as in the definition might seem like extra work, but it makes good sense. Certainly, if you want a courier to pick up something from your desk at the office, you enhance the odds of the task being done right if you provide a description of what you want both to the courier and to someone at the office.

FIGURE 7.1
A typical return value mechanism.

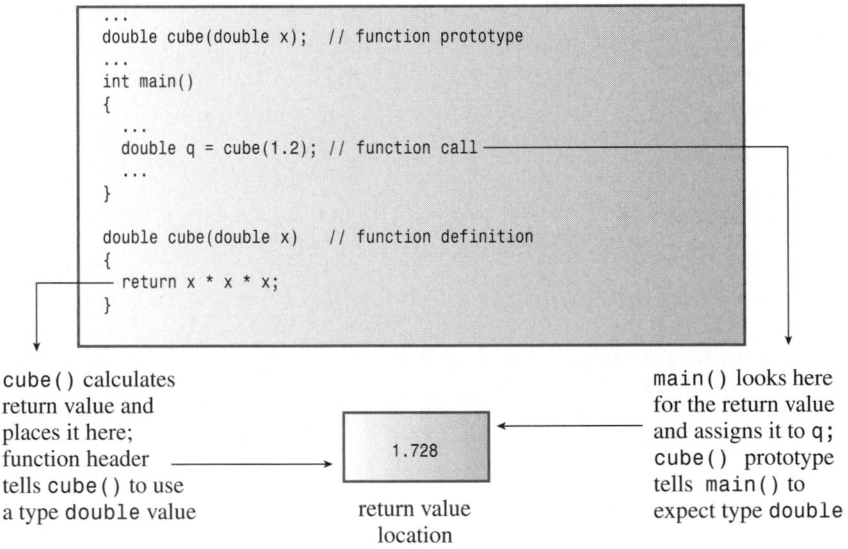

```
...
double cube(double x);   // function prototype
...
int main()
{
    ...
    double q = cube(1.2); // function call
    ...
}

double cube(double x)    // function definition
{
    return x * x * x;
}
```

cube() calculates return value and places it here; function header tells cube() to use a type double value

1.728

return value location

main() looks here for the return value and assigns it to q; cube() prototype tells main() to expect type double

A function terminates after executing a return statement. If a function has more than one return statement—for example, as alternatives to different if else selections—the function terminates after it executes the first return statement it reaches. For example, in the following example, the else isn't needed, but it does help the casual reader understand the intent:

```
int bigger(int a, int b)
{
    if (a > b )
        return a;  // if a > b, function terminates here
```

```
        else
            return b;  // otherwise, function terminates here
}
```

Functions with return values are much like functions in Pascal, FORTRAN, and BASIC. They return a value to the calling program, which can then assign that value to a variable, display the value, or otherwise use it. Here's a simple example that returns the cube of a type `double` value:

```
double cube(double x)    // x times x times x
{
    return x * x * x; // a type double value
}
```

For example, the function call `cube(1.2)` returns the value `1.728`. Note that this return statement uses an expression. The function computes the value of the expression (`1.728`, in this case) and returns the value.

Prototyping and Calling a Function

By now you are familiar with making function calls, but you may be less comfortable with function prototyping because that's often been hidden in the `include` files. Listing 7.2 shows the `cheers()` and `cube()` functions used in a program; notice the function prototypes.

LISTING 7.2   protos.cpp

```cpp
// protos.cpp -- using prototypes and function calls
#include <iostream>
void cheers(int);        // prototype: no return value
double cube(double x);   // prototype: returns a double
int main(void)
{
    using namespace std;
    cheers(5);              // function call
    cout << "Give me a number: ";
    double side;
    cin >> side;
    double volume = cube(side);     // function call
    cout << "A " << side <<"-foot cube has a volume of ";
    cout << volume << " cubic feet.\n";
    cheers(cube(2));    // prototype protection at work
    return 0;
}

void cheers(int n)
{
    using namespace std;
    for (int i = 0; i < n; i++)
        cout << "Cheers! ";
    cout << endl;
}
```

LISTING 7.2 Continued

```
double cube(double x)
{
    return x * x * x;
}
```

The program in Listing 7.2 places a `using` directive in only those functions that use the members of the `std` namespace. Here's a sample run:

```
Cheers! Cheers! Cheers! Cheers! Cheers!
Give me a number: 5
A 5-foot cube has a volume of 125 cubic feet.
Cheers! Cheers! Cheers! Cheers! Cheers! Cheers! Cheers! Cheers!
```

Note that `main()` calls the type `void` function `cheers()` by using the function name and arguments followed by a semicolon: `cheers(5);`. This is an example of a function call statement. But because `cube()` has a return value, `main()` can use it as part of an assignment statement:

```
double volume = cube(side);
```

But I said earlier that you should concentrate on the prototypes. What should you know about prototypes? First, you should understand why C++ requires prototypes. Then, because C++ requires prototypes, you should know the proper syntax. Finally, you should appreciate what the prototype does for you. Let's look at these points in turn, using Listing 7.2 as a basis for discussion.

Why Prototypes?

A prototype describes the function interface to the compiler. That is, it tells the compiler what type of return value, if any, the function has, and it tells the compiler the number and type of function arguments. Consider, for example, how a prototype affects this function call from Listing 7.2:

```
double volume = cube(side);
```

First, the prototype tells the compiler that `cube()` should have one type `double` argument. If the program fails to provide the argument, prototyping allows the compiler to catch the error. Second, when the `cube()` function finishes its calculation, it places its return value at some specified location—perhaps in a CPU register, perhaps in memory. Then, the calling function, `main()` in this case, retrieves the value from that location. Because the prototype states that `cube()` is type `double`, the compiler knows how many bytes to retrieve and how to interpret them. Without that information, the compiler could only guess, and that is something compilers won't do.

Still, you might wonder, why does the compiler need a prototype? Can't it just look further in the file and see how the functions are defined? One problem with that approach is that it is not very efficient. The compiler would have to put compiling `main()` on hold while searching the rest of the file. An even more serious problem is the fact that the function might not even be in the file. C++ allows you to spread a program over several files, which you can compile independently and then combine later. In such a case, the compiler might not have access to the function code when it's compiling `main()`. The same is true if the function is part of a library. The only way to avoid using a function prototype is to place the function definition before its first use. That is not always possible. Also, the C++ programming style is to put `main()` first because it generally provides the structure for the whole program.

Prototype Syntax

A function prototype is a statement, so it must have a terminating semicolon. The simplest way to get a prototype is to copy the function header from the function definition and add a semicolon. That's what the program in Listing 7.2 does for `cube()`:

```
double cube(double x); // add ; to header to get prototype
```

However, the function prototype does not require that you provide names for the variables; a list of types is enough. The program in Listing 7.2 prototypes `cheers()` by using only the argument type:

```
void cheers(int); // okay to drop variable names in prototype
```

In general, you can either include or exclude variable names in the argument lists for prototypes. The variable names in the prototype just act as placeholders, so if you do use names, they don't have to match the names in the function definition.

C++ Versus ANSI C Prototyping

ANSI C borrowed prototyping from C++, but the two languages do have some differences. The most important is that ANSI C, to preserve compatibility with classic C, made prototyping optional, whereas C++ makes prototyping mandatory. For example, consider the following function declaration:

```
void say_hi();
```

In C++, leaving the parentheses empty is the same as using the keyword `void` within the parentheses. It means the function has no arguments. In ANSI C, leaving the parentheses empty means that you are declining to state what the arguments are. That is, it means you're forgoing prototyping the argument list. The C++ equivalent for not identifying the argument list is to use an ellipsis:

```
void say_bye(...);    // C++ abdication of responsibility
```

Normally this use of an ellipsis is needed only for interfacing with C functions having a variable number of arguments, such as `printf()`.

What Prototypes Do for You

You've seen that prototypes help the compiler. But what do they do for you? They greatly reduce the chances of program errors. In particular, prototypes ensure the following:

- The compiler correctly handles the function return value.

- The compiler checks that you use the correct number of function arguments.

- The compiler checks that you use the correct type of arguments. If you don't, it converts the arguments to the correct type, if possible.

We've already discussed how to correctly handle the return value. Let's look now at what happens when you use the wrong number of arguments. For example, suppose you make the following call:

```
double z = cube();
```

Without function prototyping, the compiler lets this go by. When the function is called, it looks where the call to `cube()` should have placed a number and uses whatever value happens to be there. This is how C worked before ANSI C borrowed prototyping from C++. Because prototyping is optional for ANSI C, this is how some C programs still work. But in C++ prototyping is not optional, so you are guaranteed protection from that sort of error.

Next, suppose you provide an argument but it is the wrong type. In C, this could create weird errors. For example, if a function expects a type `int` value (assume that's 16 bits) and you pass a `double` (assume that's 64 bits), the function looks at just the first 16 bits of the 64 and tries to interpret them as an `int` value. However, C++ automatically converts the value you pass to the type specified in the prototype, provided that both are arithmetic types. For example, Listing 7.2 manages to get two type mismatches in one statement:

```
cheers(cube(2));
```

First, the program passes the `int` value of `2` to `cube()`, which expects type `double`. The compiler, noting that the `cube()` prototype specifies a type `double` argument, converts `2` to `2.0`, a type `double` value. Then, `cube()` returns a type `double` value (`8.0`) to be used as an argument to `cheers()`. Again, the compiler checks the prototypes and notes that `cheers()` requires an `int`. It converts the return value to the integer `8`. In general, prototyping produces automatic type casts to the expected types. (Function overloading, discussed in Chapter 8, can create ambiguous situations, however, that prevent some automatic type casts.)

Automatic type conversion doesn't head off all possible errors. For example, if you pass a value of `8.33E27` to a function that expects an `int`, such a large value cannot be converted correctly to a mere `int`. Some compilers warn you of possible data loss when there is an automatic conversion from a larger type to a smaller.

Also, prototyping results in type conversion only when it makes sense. It won't, for example, convert an integer to a structure or pointer.

Prototyping takes place during compile time and is termed *static type checking*. Static type checking, as you've just seen, catches many errors that are much more difficult to catch during runtime.

Function Arguments and Passing by Value

It's time to take a closer look at function arguments. C++ normally passes arguments *by value*. That means the numeric value of the argument is passed to the function, where it is assigned to a new variable. For example, Listing 7.2 has this function call:

```
double volume = cube(side);
```

Here `side` is a variable that, in the sample run, had the value **5**. The function header for `cube()`, recall, was this:

```
double cube(double x)
```

When this function is called, it creates a new type **double** variable called **x** and assigns the value **5** to it. This insulates data in `main()` from actions that take place in `cube()` because `cube()` works with a copy of `side` rather than with the original data. You'll see an example of this protection soon. A variable that's used to receive passed values is called a *formal argument* or *formal parameter*. The value passed to the function is called the *actual argument* or *actual parameter*. To simplify matters a bit, the C++ Standard uses the word *argument* by itself to denote an actual argument or parameter and the word *parameter* by itself to denote a formal argument or parameter. Using this terminology, argument passing assigns the argument to the parameter. (See Figure 7.2.)

FIGURE 7.2

Passing by value.

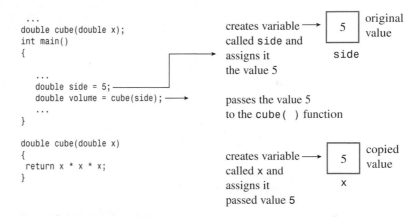

Variables, including parameters, declared within a function are private to the function. When a function is called, the computer allocates the memory needed for these variables. When the function terminates, the computer frees the memory that was used for those variables. (Some C++ literature refers to this allocating and freeing of memory as *creating and destroying variables*. That does make it sound much more exciting.) Such variables are called *local variables* because they are localized to the function. As mentioned previously, this helps preserve data integrity. It also means that if you declare a variable called **x** in `main()` and another variable called **x** in some other function, these are two distinct, unrelated variables, much as the Albany in California is distinct from the Albany in New York. (See Figure 7.3.) Such variables are also termed *automatic variables* because they are allocated and deallocated automatically during program execution.

FIGURE 7.3
Local variables.

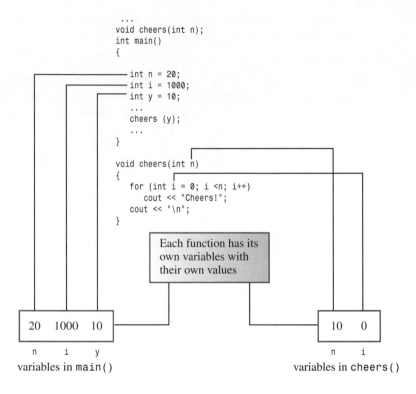

Multiple Arguments

A function can have more than one argument. In the function call, you just separate the arguments with commas:

```
n_chars('R', 25);
```

This passes two arguments to the function `n_chars()`, which will be defined shortly.

Similarly, when you define the function, you use a comma-separated list of parameter declarations in the function header:

```
void n_chars(char c, int n)   // two arguments
```

This function header states that the function `n_chars()` takes one type `char` argument and one type `int` argument. The parameters `c` and `n` are assigned the values passed to the function. If a function has two parameters of the same type, you have to give the type of each parameter separately. You can't combine declarations the way you can when you declare regular variables:

```
void fifi(float a, float b)   // declare each variable separately
void fufu(float a, b)         // NOT acceptable
```

As with other functions, you just add a semicolon to get a prototype:

```
void n_chars(char c, int n); // prototype, style 1
```

As with single arguments, you don't have to use the same variable names in the prototype as in the definition, and you can omit the variable names in the prototype:

```
void n_chars(char, int);      // prototype, style 2
```

However, providing variable names can make the prototype more understandable, particularly if two parameters are the same type. Then, the names can remind you which argument is which:

```
double melon_density(double weight, double volume);
```

Listing 7.3 shows an example of a function with two arguments. It also illustrates how changing the value of a formal parameter in a function has no effect on the data in the calling program.

LISTING 7.3   twoarg.cpp

```
// twoarg.cpp -- a function with 2 arguments
#include <iostream>
using namespace std;
void n_chars(char, int);
int main()
{
    int times;
    char ch;

    cout << "Enter a character: ";
    cin >> ch;
    while (ch != 'q')        // q to quit
    {
        cout << "Enter an integer: ";
        cin >> times;
        n_chars(ch, times); // function with two arguments
        cout << "\nEnter another character or press the"
                " q-key to quit: ";
            cin >> ch;
    }
    cout << "The value of times is " << times << ".\n";
    cout << "Bye\n";
    return 0;
}

void n_chars(char c, int n) // displays c n times
{
    while (n-- < 0)          // continue until n reaches 0
        cout << c;
}
```

The program in Listing 7.3 illustrates placing a `using` directive above the function definitions rather than within the functions. Here is a sample run:

```
Enter a character: W
Enter an integer: 50
WWWWWWWWWWWWWWWWWWWWWWWWWWWWWWWWWWWWWWWWWWWWWWWWWWWW
```

```
Enter another character or press the q-key to quit: a
Enter an integer: 20
aaaaaaaaaaaaaaaaaaaa
Enter another character or press the q-key to quit: q
The value of times is 20.
Bye
```

Program Notes

The `main()` function in Listing 7.3 uses a `while` loop to provide repeated input (and to keep your loop skills fresh). Note that it uses `cin >> ch` rather than `cin.get(ch)` or `ch = cin.get()` to read a character. There's a good reason for this. Recall that the two `cin.get()` functions read all input characters, including spaces and newlines, whereas `cin >>` skips spaces and newlines. When you respond to the program prompt, you have to press Enter at the end of each line, thus generating a newline character. The `cin >> ch` approach conveniently skips over these newlines, but the `cin.get()` siblings read the newline following each number entered as the next character to display. You can program around this nuisance, but it's simpler to use `cin` as the program in Listing 7.3 does.

The `n_chars()` function takes two arguments: a character `c` and an integer `n`. It then uses a loop to display the character the number of times the integer specifies:

```
while (n-- > 0)           // continue until n reaches 0
    cout << c;
```

Notice that the program keeps count by decrementing the `n` variable, where `n` is the formal parameter from the argument list. This variable is assigned the value of the `times` variable in `main()`. The `while` loop then decreases `n` to `0`, but, as the sample run demonstrates, changing the value of `n` has no effect on `times`.

Another Two-Argument Function

Let's create a more ambitious function—one that performs a nontrivial calculation. Also, the function will illustrate the use of local variables other than the function's formal arguments.

Many states in the United States now sponsor a lottery with some form of Lotto game. Lotto lets you pick a certain number of choices from a card. For example, you might get to pick 6 numbers from a card having 51 numbers. Then, the Lotto managers pick 6 numbers at random. If your choice exactly matches theirs, you win a few million dollars or so. Our function will calculate the probability that you have a winning pick. (Yes, a function that successfully predicts the winning picks themselves would be more useful, but C++, although powerful, has yet to implement psychic faculties.)

First, you need a formula. If you have to pick 6 values out of 51, mathematics says that you have 1 chance in `R` of winning, where the following formula gives `R`:

$$R = \frac{51 \times 50 \times 49 \times 48 \times 47 \times 46}{6 \times 5 \times 4 \times 3 \times 2 \times 1}$$

For 6 choices, the denominator is the product of the first 6 integers, or 6 factorial. The numerator is also the product of 6 consecutive numbers, this time starting with 51 and going down. More generally, if you pick picks values out of numbers numbers, the denominator is picks factorial and the numerator is the product of picks integers, starting with the value numbers and working down. You can use a for loop to make that calculation:

```
long double result = 1.0;
for (n = numbers, p = picks; p > 0; n--, p--)
    result = result * n / p ;
```

Rather than multiply all the numerator terms first, the loop begins by multiplying 1.0 by the first numerator term and then dividing by the first denominator term. Then, in the next cycle, the loop multiplies and divides by the second numerator and denominator terms. This keeps the running product smaller than if you did all the multiplication first. For example, compare

```
(10 * 9) / (2 * 1)
```

with

```
(10 / 2) * (9 / 1)
```

The first evaluates to 90 / 2 and then to 45, whereas the second evaluates to 5 × 9 and then to 45. Both give the same answer, but the first method produces a larger intermediate value (90) than does the second. The more factors you have, the bigger the difference gets. For large numbers, this strategy of alternating multiplication with division can keep the calculation from overflowing the maximum possible floating-point value.

Listing 7.4 incorporates this formula into a probability() function. Because the number of picks and the total number of choices should be positive values, the program uses the unsigned int type (unsigned, for short) for those quantities. Multiplying several integers can produce pretty large results, so lotto.cpp uses the long double type for the function's return value. Also, terms such as 49 / 6 produce a truncation error for integer types.

Compatibility Note

Some C++ implementations don't support type long double. If your implementation falls into that category, try ordinary double instead.

LISTING 7.4   lotto.cpp

```
// lotto.cpp -- probability of winning
#include <iostream>
// Note: some implementations require double instead of long double
long double probability(unsigned numbers, unsigned picks);
int main()
{
    using namespace std;
    double total, choices;
    cout << "Enter the total number of choices on the game card and\n"
            "the number of picks allowed:\n";
```

LISTING 7.4   Continued

```
    while ((cin >> total >> choices) && choices <= total)
    {
        cout << "You have one chance in ";
        cout << probability(total, choices);      // compute the odds
        cout << " of winning.\n";
        cout << "Next two numbers (q to quit): ";
    }
    cout << "bye\n";
    return 0;
}

// the following function calculates the probability of picking picks
// numbers correctly from numbers choices
long double probability(unsigned numbers, unsigned picks)
{
    long double result = 1.0;  // here come some local variables
    long double n;
    unsigned p;

    for (n = numbers, p = picks; p > 0; n--, p--)
        result = result * n / p ;
    return result;
}
```

Here's a sample run of the program in Listing 7.4:

```
Enter the total number of choices on the game card and
the number of picks allowed:
49 6
You have one chance in 1.39838e+007 of winning.
Next two numbers (q to quit): 51 6
You have one chance in 1.80095e+007 of winning.
Next two numbers (q to quit): 38 6
You have one chance in 2.76068e+006 of winning.
Next two numbers (q to quit): q
bye
```

Notice that increasing the number of choices on the game card greatly increases the odds against winning.

Program Notes

The `probability()` function in Listing 7.4 illustrates two kinds of local variables you can have in a function. First, there are the formal parameters (`numbers` and `picks`), which are declared in the function header before the opening brace. Then come the other local variables (`result`, `n`, and `p`). They are declared in between the braces bounding the function definition. The main difference between the formal parameters and the other local variables is that the formal parameters get their values from the function that calls `probability()`, whereas the other variables get values from within the function.

Functions and Arrays

So far the sample functions in this book have been simple, using only the basic types for arguments and return values. But functions can be the key to handling more involved types, such as arrays and structures. Let's take a look now at how arrays and functions get along with each other.

Suppose you use an array to keep track of how many cookies each person has eaten at a family picnic. (Each array index corresponds to a person, and the value of the element corresponds to the number of cookies that person has eaten.) Now you want the total. That's easy to find; you just use a loop to add all the array elements. But adding array elements is such a common task that it makes sense to design a function to do the job. Then, you won't have to write a new loop every time you have to sum an array.

Let's consider what the function interface involves. Because the function calculates a sum, it should return the answer. If you keep your cookies intact, you can use a function with a type `int` return value. So that the function knows what array to sum, you want to pass the array name as an argument. And to make the function general so that it is not restricted to an array of a particular size, you pass the size of the array. The only new ingredient here is that you have to declare that one of the formal arguments is an array name. Let's see what that and the rest of the function header look like:

```
int sum_arr(int arr[], int n) // arr = array name, n = size
```

This looks plausible. The brackets seem to indicate that `arr` is an array, and the fact that the brackets are empty seems to indicate that you can use the function with an array of any size. But things are not always as they seem: `arr` is not really an array; it's a pointer! The good news is that you can write the rest of the function just as if `arr` were an array. First, let's ensure that this approach works, and then let's look into why it works.

Listing 7.5 illustrates using a pointer as if it were an array name. The program initializes the array to some values and uses the `sum_arr()` function to calculate the sum. Note that the `sum_arr()` function uses `arr` as if it were an array name.

LISTING 7.5   `arrfun1.cpp`

```cpp
// arrfun1.cpp -- functions with an array argument
#include <iostream>
const int ArSize = 8;
int sum_arr(int arr[], int n);          // prototype
int main()
{
    using namespace std;
    int cookies[ArSize] = {1,2,4,8,16,32,64,128};
// some systems require preceding int with static to
// enable array initialization

    int sum = sum_arr(cookies, ArSize);
    cout << "Total cookies eaten: " << sum <<  "\n";
```

LISTING 7.5 Continued

```
    return 0;
}

// return the sum of an integer array
int sum_arr(int arr[], int n)
{
    int total = 0;

    for (int i = 0; i < n; i++)
        total = total + arr[i];
    return total;
}
```

Here is the output of the program in Listing 7.5:

```
Total cookies eaten: 255
```

As you can see, the program works. Now let's look at why it works.

How Pointers Enable Array-Processing Functions

The key to the program in Listing 7.5 is that C++, like C, in most contexts treats the name of an array as if it were a pointer. Recall from Chapter 4, "Compound Types," that C++ interprets an array name as the address of its first element:

```
cookies == &cookies[0]  // array name is address of first element
```

(There are two exceptions to this rule. First, the array declaration uses the array name to label the storage. Second, applying `sizeof` to an array name yields the size of the whole array, in bytes.)

Listing 7.5 makes the following function call:

```
int sum = sum_arr(cookies, ArSize);
```

Here `cookies` is the name of an array, hence by C++ rules `cookies` is the address of the array's first element. The function passes an address. Because the array has type `int` elements, `cookies` must be type pointer-to-`int`, or `int *`. This suggests that the correct function header should be this:

```
int sum_arr(int * arr, int n) // arr = array name, n = size
```

Here `int *arr` has replaced `int arr[]`. It turns out that both headers are correct because in C++ the notations `int *arr` and `int arr[]` have the identical meaning when (and *only* when) used in a function header or function prototype. Both mean that `arr` is a pointer-to-`int`. However, the array notation version (`int arr[]`) symbolically reminds you that `arr` not only points to an `int`, it points to the first `int` in an array of `int`s. This book uses the array notation when the pointer is to the first element of an array, and it uses the pointer notation when the pointer is to an isolated value. Remember that the notations `int *arr` and `int arr[]` are not synonymous in any other context. For example, you can't use the notation `int tip[]` to declare a pointer in the body of a function.

Given that the variable `arr` actually is a pointer, the rest of the function makes sense. As you might recall from the discussion of dynamic arrays in Chapter 4, you can use the bracket array notation equally well with array names or with pointers to access elements of an array. Whether `arr` is a pointer or an array name, the expression `arr[3]` means the fourth element of the array. And it probably will do no harm at this point to remind you of the following two identities:

```
arr[i] == *(ar + i)     // values in two notations
&arr[i] == ar + i       // addresses in two notations
```

Remember that adding one to a pointer, including an array name, actually adds a value equal to the size, in bytes, of the type to which the pointer points. Pointer addition and array subscription are two equivalent ways of counting elements from the beginning of an array.

The Implications of Using Arrays as Arguments

Let's look at the implications of Listing 7.5. The function call `sum_arr(cookies, ArSize)` passes the address of the first element of the `cookies` array and the number of elements of the array to the `sum_arr()` function. The `sum_arr()` function assigns the `cookies` address to the pointer variable `arr` and assigns `ArSize` to the `int` variable n. This means Listing 7.5 doesn't really pass the array contents to the function. Instead, it tells the function where the array is (the address), what kind of elements it has (the type), and how many elements it has (the n variable). (See Figure 7.4.) Armed with this information, the function then uses the original array. If you pass an ordinary variable, the function works with a copy. But if you pass an array, the function works with the original. Actually, this difference doesn't violate C++'s pass-by-value approach. The `sum_arr()` function still passes a value that's assigned to a new variable. But that value is a single address, not the contents of an array.

FIGURE 7.4
Telling a function about an array.

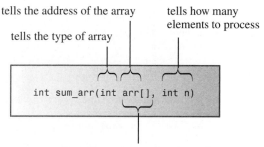

Is the correspondence between array names and pointers a good thing? Indeed, it is. The design decision to use array addresses as arguments saves the time and memory needed to copy an entire array. The overhead for using copies can be prohibitive if you're working with large arrays. With copies, not only does a program need more computer memory, but it has to spend time copying large blocks of data. On the other hand, working with the original data raises the possibility of inadvertent data corruption. That's a real problem in classic C, but ANSI C and C++'s `const` modifier provides a remedy. You'll soon see an example. But first, let's alter Listing 7.5 to illustrate some points about how array functions operate. Listing 7.6 demonstrates that `cookies` and `arr` have the same value. It also shows how the pointer concept makes the `sum_arr` function more versatile than it may have appeared at first. To provide a bit of variety and to show you what it looks like, the program uses the `std::` qualifier instead of the `using` directive to provide access to `cout` and `endl`.

LISTING 7.6   `arrfun2.cpp`

```cpp
// arrfun2.cpp -- functions with an array argument
#include <iostream>
const int ArSize = 8;
int sum_arr(int arr[], int n);
// use std:: instead of using directive
int main()
{
    int cookies[ArSize] = {1,2,4,8,16,32,64,128};
//  some systems require preceding int with static to
//  enable array initialization

    std::cout << cookies << " = array address, ";
//  some systems require a type cast: unsigned (cookies)

    std::cout << sizeof cookies << " = sizeof cookies\n";
    int sum = sum_arr(cookies, ArSize);
    std::cout << "Total cookies eaten: " << sum <<  std::endl;
    sum = sum_arr(cookies, 3);         // a lie
    std::cout << "First three eaters ate " << sum << " cookies.\n";
    sum = sum_arr(cookies + 4, 4);     // another lie
    std::cout << "Last four eaters ate " << sum << " cookies.\n";
    return 0;
}

// return the sum of an integer array
int sum_arr(int arr[], int n)
{
    int total = 0;
    std::cout << arr << " = arr, ";
// some systems require a type cast: unsigned (arr)

    std::cout << sizeof arr << " = sizeof arr\n";
    for (int i = 0; i < n; i++)
        total = total + arr[i];
    return total;
}
```

Here's the output of the program in Listing 7.6:

```
0x0065fd24 = array address, 32 = sizeof cookies
0x0065fd24 = arr, 4 = sizeof arr
Total cookies eaten: 255
0x0065fd24 = arr, 4 = sizeof arr
First three eaters ate 7 cookies.
0x0065fd34 = arr, 4 = sizeof arr
Last four eaters ate 240 cookies.
```

Note that the address values and the array and integer sizes will vary from system to system. Also, some implementations will display the addresses in base 10 notation instead of in hexadecimal.

Program Notes

Listing 7.6 illustrates some very interesting points about array functions. First, note that `cookies` and `arr` both evaluate to the same address, exactly as claimed. But `sizeof cookies` is `16`, whereas `sizeof arr` is only `4`. That's because `sizeof cookies` is the size of the whole array, whereas `sizeof arr` is the size of the pointer variable. (This program execution takes place on a system that uses 4-byte addresses.) By the way, this is why you have to explicitly pass the size of the array rather than use `sizeof arr` in `sum_arr()`.

Because the only way `sum_arr()` knows the number of elements in the array is through what you tell it with the second argument, you can lie to the function. For example, the second time the program uses the function, it makes this call:

```
sum = sum_arr(cookies, 3);
```

By telling the function that `cookies` has just three elements, you get the function to calculate the sum of the first three elements.

Why stop there? You can also lie about where the array starts:

```
sum = sum_arr(cookies + 4, 4);
```

Because `cookies` acts as the address of the first element, `cookies + 4` acts as the address of the fifth element. This statement sums the fifth, sixth, seventh, and eighth elements of the array. Note in the output how the third call to the function assigns a different address to `arr` than the first two calls did. And yes, you can use `&cookies[4]` instead of `cookies + 4` as the argument; they both mean the same thing.

Remember

To indicate the kind of array and the number of elements to an array-processing function, you pass the information as two separate arguments:

```
void fillArray(int arr[], int size);    // prototype
```

Don't try to pass the array size by using brackets notation:

```
void fillArray(int arr[size]);           // NO -- bad prototype
```

More Array Function Examples

When you choose to use an array to represent data, you are making a design decision. But design decisions should go beyond how data is stored; they should also involve how the data is used. Often, you'll find it profitable to write specific functions to handle specific data operations. (The profits here include increased program reliability, ease of modification, and ease of debugging.) Also, when you begin integrating storage properties with operations when you think about a program, you are taking an important step toward the OOP mind-set; that, too, might prove profitable in the future.

Let's examine a simple case. Suppose you want to use an array to keep track of the dollar values of your real estate. (If necessary, suppose you have real estate.) You have to decide what type to use. Certainly, `double` is less restrictive in its range than `int` or `long`, and it provides enough significant digits to represent the values precisely. Next, you have to decide on the number of array elements. (With dynamic arrays created with `new`, you can put off that decision, but let's keep things simple.) Let's say that you have no more than five properties, so you can use an array of five `doubles`.

Now consider the possible operations you might want to execute with the real estate array. Two very basic ones are reading values into the array and displaying the array contents. Let's add one more operation to the list: reassessing the value of the properties. For simplicity, assume that all your properties increase or decrease in value at the same rate. (Remember, this is a book on C++, not on real estate management.) Next, fit a function to each operation and then write the code accordingly. We'll go through the steps of creating these pieces of a program next. Afterward, we'll fit them into a complete example.

Filling the Array

Because a function with an array name argument accesses the original array, not a copy, you can use a function call to assign values to array elements. One argument to the function will be the name of the array to be filled. In general, a program might manage more than one person's investments, hence more than one array, so you don't want to build the array size into the function. Instead, you pass the array size as a second argument, as in the previous example. Also, it's possible that you might want to quit reading data before filling the array, so you want to build that feature in to the function. Because you might enter fewer than the maximum number of elements, it makes sense to have the function return the actual number of values entered. These considerations suggest the following function prototype:

```
int fill_array(double ar[], int limit);
```

The function takes an array name argument and an argument specifying the maximum number of items to be read, and the function returns the actual number of items read. For example, if you use this function with an array of five elements, you pass 5 as the second argument. If you then enter only three values, the function returns 3.

You can use a loop to read successive values into the array, but how can you terminate the loop early? One way is to use a special value to indicate the end of input. Because no property should have a negative value, you can use a negative number to indicate the end of input. Also, the function should do something about bad input, such as terminating further input. Given this, you can code the function as follows:

```
int fill_array(double ar[], int limit)
{
    using namespace std;
    double temp;
    int i;
    for (i = 0; i < limit; i++)
    {
        cout << "Enter value #" << (i + 1) << ": ";
        cin >> temp;
```

```
        if (!cin)    // bad input
        {
            cin.clear();
            while (cin.get() != '\n')
                continue;
            cout << "Bad input; input process terminated.\n";
            break;
        }
        else if (temp < 0)     // signal to terminate
            break;
        ar[i] = temp;
    }
    return i;
}
```

Note that this code includes a prompt to the user. If the user enters a non-negative value, the value is assigned to the array. Otherwise, the loop terminates. If the user enters only valid values, the loop terminates after it reads `limit` values. The last thing the loop does is increment `i`, so after the loop terminates, `i` is one greater than the last array index, hence it's equal to the number of filled elements. The function then returns that value.

Showing the Array and Protecting It with `const`

Building a function to display the array contents is simple. You pass the name of the array and the number of filled elements to the function, which then uses a loop to display each element. But there is another consideration—guaranteeing that the display function doesn't alter the original array. Unless the purpose of a function is to alter data passed to it, you should safeguard it from doing so. That protection comes automatically with ordinary arguments because C++ passes them by value, and the function works with a copy. But functions that use an array work with the original. After all, that's why the `fill_array()` function is able to do its job. To keep a function from accidentally altering the contents of an array argument, you can use the keyword `const` (discussed in Chapter 3, "Dealing with Data") when you declare the formal argument:

```
void show_array(const double ar[], int n);
```

The declaration states that the pointer `ar` points to constant data. This means that you can't use `ar` to change the data. That is, you can use a value such as `ar[0]`, but you can't change that value. Note that this doesn't mean that the original array needs be constant; it just means that you can't use `ar` in the `show_array()` function to change the data. Thus, `show_array()` treats the array as read-only data. Suppose you accidentally violate this restriction by doing something like the following in the `show_array()` function:

```
ar[0] += 10;
```

In this case, the compiler will put a stop to your wrongful ways. Borland C++, for example, gives an error message like this (edited slightly):

```
Cannot modify a const object in function
    show_array(const double *,int)
```

Other compilers may choose to express their displeasure in different words.

The message reminds you that C++ interprets the declaration `const double ar[]` to mean `const double *ar`. Thus, the declaration really says that `ar` points to a constant value. We'll discuss this in detail when we finish with the current example. Meanwhile, here is the code for the `show_array()` function:

```cpp
void show_array(const double ar[], int n)
{
    using namespace std;
    for (int i = 0; i < n; i++)
    {
        cout << "Property #" << (i + 1) << ": $";
        cout << ar[i] << endl;
    }
}
```

Modifying the Array

The third operation for the array in this example is multiplying each element by the same revaluation factor. You need to pass three arguments to the function: the factor, the array, and the number of elements. No return value is needed, so the function can look like this:

```cpp
void revalue(double r, double ar[], int n)
{
    for (int i = 0; i < n; i++)
        ar[i] *= r;
}
```

Because this function is supposed to alter the array values, you don't use `const` when you declare `ar`.

Putting the Pieces Together

Now that you've defined a data type in terms of how it's stored (an array) and how it's used (three functions), you can put together a program that uses the design. Because you've already built all the array-handling tools, you've greatly simplified programming `main()`. Most of the remaining programming work consists of having `main()` call the functions you've just developed. Listing 7.7 shows the result. It places a `using` directive in just those functions that use the `iostream` facilities.

LISTING 7.7   `arrfun3.cpp`

```cpp
// arrfun3.cpp -- array functions and const
#include <iostream>
const int Max = 5;

// function prototypes
int fill_array(double ar[], int limit);
void show_array(const double ar[], int n);  // don't change data
void revalue(double r, double ar[], int n);

int main()
{
```

LISTING 7.7   *Continued*

```
    using namespace std;
    double properties[Max];

    int size = fill_array(properties, Max);
    show_array(properties, size);
    cout << "Enter revaluation factor: ";
    double factor;
    cin >> factor;
    revalue(factor, properties, size);
    show_array(properties, size);
    cout << "Done.\n";
    return 0;
}

int fill_array(double ar[], int limit)
{
    using namespace std;
    double temp;
    int i;
    for (i = 0; i < limit; i++)
    {
        cout << "Enter value #" << (i + 1) << ": ";
        cin >> temp;
        if (!cin)      // bad input
        {
            cin.clear();
            while (cin.get() != '\n')
                continue;
            cout << "Bad input; input process terminated.\n";
            break;
        }
        else if (temp < 0)      // signal to terminate
            break;
        ar[i] = temp;
    }
    return i;
}

// the following function can use, but not alter,
// the array whose address is ar
void show_array(const double ar[], int n)
{
    using namespace std;
    for (int i = 0; i < n; i++)
    {
        cout << "Property #" << (i + 1) << ": $";
        cout << ar[i] << endl;
    }
}
```

LISTING 7.7   Continued

```
// multiplies each element of ar[] by r
void revalue(double r, double ar[], int n)
{
    for (int i = 0; i < n; i++)
        ar[i] *= r;
}
```

Here are two sample runs of the program in Listing 7.7:

```
Enter value #1: 100000
Enter value #2: 80000
Enter value #3: 222000
Enter value #4: 240000
Enter value #5: 118000
Property #1: $100000
Property #2: $80000
Property #3: $222000
Property #4: $240000
Property #5: $118000
Enter reassessment rate: 1.10
Property #1: $110000
Property #2: $88000
Property #3: $244200
Property #4: $264000
Property #5: $129800
Done.

Enter value #1: 200000
Enter value #2: 84000
Enter value #3: 160000
Enter value #4: -2
Property #1: $200000
Property #2: $84000
Property #3: $160000
Enter reassessment rate: 1.20
Property #1: $240000
Property #2: $100800
Property #3: $192000
Done.
```

Recall that `fill_array()` prescribes that input should quit when the user enters five properties or enters a negative number, whichever comes first. The first output example illustrates reaching the five-property limit, and the second output example illustrates that entering a negative value terminates the input phase.

Program Notes

We've already discussed the important programming details related to the real estate example, so let's reflect on the process. You began by thinking about the data type and designed appropriate functions to handle the data. Then, you assembled these functions into a program. This is sometimes called *bottom-up programming* because the design process moves from the component parts to the whole. This approach is well suited to OOP, which concentrates on data representation and manipulation first. Traditional procedural programming, on the other hand, leans toward *top-down programming*, in which you develop a modular grand design first and then turn your attention to the details. Both methods are useful, and both lead to modular programs.

Functions Using Array Ranges

As you've seen, C++ functions that process arrays need to be informed about the kind of data in the array, the location of the beginning of the array, and the number of elements in the array. The traditional C/C++ approach to functions that process arrays is to pass a pointer to the start of the array as one argument and to pass the size of the array as a second argument. (The pointer tells the function both where to find the array and the kind of data in it.) That gives the function the information it needs to find all the data.

There is another approach to giving a function the information it needs: to specify a *range* of elements. This can be done by passing two pointers—one identifying the start of the array and one identifying the end of the array. The C++ Standard Template Library (STL; presented in Chapter 16, "The `string` Class and the Standard Template Library"), for example, generalizes the range approach. The STL approach uses the concept of "one past the end" to indicate an extent. That is, in the case of an array, the argument identifying the end of the array would be a pointer to the location just after the last element. For example, suppose you have this declaration:

```
double elbuod[20];
```

Then the two pointers `elboud` and `elboud + 20` define the range. First, `elboub`, being the name of the array, points to the first element. The expression `elboud + 19` points to the last element (that is, `elboud[19]`), so `elboud + 20` points to one past the end of the array. Passing a range to a function tells it which elements to process. Listing 7.8 modifies Listing 7.6 to use two pointers to specify a range.

LISTING 7.8 `arrfun4.cpp`

```cpp
// arrfun4.cpp -- functions with an array range
#include <iostream>
const int ArSize = 8;
int sum_arr(const int * begin, const int * end);
int main()
{
    using namespace std;
    int cookies[ArSize] = {1,2,4,8,16,32,64,128};
//  some systems require preceding int with static to
//  enable array initialization

    int sum = sum_arr(cookies, cookies + ArSize);
    cout << "Total cookies eaten: " << sum <<  endl;
    sum = sum_arr(cookies, cookies + 3);        // first 3 elements
    cout << "First three eaters ate " << sum << " cookies.\n";
    sum = sum_arr(cookies + 4, cookies + 8);    // last 4 elements
```

LISTING 7.8   *Continued*

```
        cout << "Last four eaters ate " << sum << " cookies.\n";
        return 0;
}

// return the sum of an integer array
int sum_arr(const int * begin, const int * end)
{
    const int * pt;
    int total = 0;

    for (pt = begin; pt != end; pt++)
        total = total + *pt;
    return total;
}
```

Here's the output of the program in Listing 7.8:

```
Total cookies eaten: 255
First three eaters ate 7 cookies.
Last four eaters ate 240 cookies.
```

Program Notes

In Listing 7.8, notice the `for` loop in the `sum_array()` function:

```
for (pt = begin; pt != end; pt++)
    total = total + *pt;
```

It sets `pt` to point to the first element to be processed (the one pointed to by `begin`) and adds `*pt` (the value of the element) to `total`. Then the loop updates `pt` by incrementing it, causing it to point to the next element. The process continues as long as `pt != end`. When `pt` finally equals `end`, it's pointing to the location following the last element of the range, so the loop halts.

Second, notice how the different function calls specify different ranges within the array:

```
int sum = sum_arr(cookies, cookies + ArSize);
...
sum = sum_arr(cookies, cookies + 3);        // first 3 elements
...
sum = sum_arr(cookies + 4, cookies + 8);    // last 4 elements
```

The pointer value `cookies + ArSize` points to the location following the last element. (The array has `ArSize` elements, so `cookies[ArSize - 1]` is the last element, and its address is `cookies + ArSize - 1`.) So the range `cookies, cookies + ArSize` specifies the entire array. Similarly, `cookies, cookies + 3` specifies the first three elements, and so on.

Note, by the way, that the rules for pointer subtraction imply that, in `sum_arr()`, the expression `end - begin` is an integer value equal to the number of elements in the range.

Pointers and `const`

Using `const` with pointers has some subtle aspects (pointers always seem to have subtle aspects), so let's take a closer look. You can use the `const` keyword two different ways with pointers. The first way is to make a pointer point to a constant object, and that prevents you from using the pointer to change the pointed-to value. The second way is to make the pointer itself constant, and that prevents you from changing where the pointer points. Now for the details.

First, let's declare a pointer `pt` that points to a constant:

```
int age = 39;
const int * pt = &age;
```

This declaration states that `pt` points to a `const int` (`39`, in this case). Therefore, you can't use `pt` to change that value. In other words, the value `*pt` is `const` and cannot be modified:

```
*pt += 1;          // INVALID because pt points to a const int
cin >> *pt;        // INVALID for the same reason
```

Now for a subtle point. This declaration for `pt` doesn't necessarily mean that the value it points to is really a constant; it just means the value is a constant insofar as `pt` is concerned. For example, `pt` points to `age`, and `age` is not `const`. You can change the value of `age` directly by using the `age` variable, but you can't change the value indirectly via the `pt` pointer:

```
*pt = 20;          // INVALID because pt points to a const int
age = 20;          // VALID because age is not declared to be const
```

In the past, you've assigned the address of a regular variable to a regular pointer. Now you've assigned the address of a regular variable to a pointer-to-`const`. That leaves two other possibilities: assigning the address of a `const` variable to a pointer-to-`const` and assigning the address of a `const` to a regular pointer. Are they both possible? The first is, and the second isn't:

```
const float g_earth = 9.80;
const float * pe = &g_earth;     // VALID

const float g_moon = 1.63;
float * pm = &g_moon;            // INVALID
```

For the first case, you can use neither `g_earth` nor `pe` to change the value `9.80`. C++ doesn't allow the second case for a simple reason: If you can assign the address of `g_moon` to `pm`, then you can cheat and use `pm` to alter the value of `g_moon`. That makes a mockery of `g_moon`'s `const` status, so C++ prohibits you from assigning the address of a `const` to a non-`const` pointer. (If you are really desperate, you can use a type cast to override the restriction; see Chapter 15 for a discussion of the `const_cast` operator.)

The situation becomes a bit more complex if you have pointers to pointers. As you saw earlier, assigning a non-`const` pointer to a `const` pointer is okay, provided that you're dealing with just one level of indirection:

```
int age = 39;          // age++ is a valid operation
int * pd = &age;       // *pd = 41 is a valid operation
const int * pt = pd;   // *pt = 42 is an invalid operation
```

But pointer assignments that mix **const** and non-**const** in this manner are no longer safe when you go to two levels of indirection. If mixing **const** and non-**const** were allowed, you could do something like this:

```
const int **pp2;
int *p1;
const int n = 13;
pp2 = &p1; // not allowed, but suppose it were
*pp2 = &n; // valid, both const, but sets p1 to point at n
*p1 = 10;  // valid, but changes const n
```

Here the code assigns a non-**const** address (**&p1**) to a **const** pointer (**pp2**), and that allows **p1** to be used to alter **const** data. So the rule that you can assign a non-**const** address or pointer to a **const** pointer works only if there is just one level of indirection—for example, if the pointer points to a fundamental data type.

Remember

You can assign the address of either **const** data or non-**const** data to a pointer-to-**const**, provided that the data type is not itself a pointer, but you can assign the address of non-**const** data only to a non-**const** pointer.

Suppose you have an array of **const** data:

```
const int months[12] = {31,28,31,30,31,30, 31, 31,30,31,30,31};
```

The prohibition against assigning the address of a constant array means that you cannot pass the array name as an argument to a function by using a non-constant formal argument:

```
int sum(int arr[], int n);  // should have been const int arr[]
...
int j = sum(months, 12);    // not allowed
```

This function call attempts to assign a **const** pointer (**months**) to a non-**const** pointer (**arr**), and the compiler disallows the function call.

Using const When You Can

There are two strong reasons to declare pointer arguments as pointers to constant data:

- It protects you against programming errors that inadvertently alter data.
- Using **const** allows a function to process both **const** and non-**const** actual arguments, whereas a function that omits **const** in the prototype can accept only non-**const** data.

You should declare formal pointer arguments as pointers to **const** whenever it's appropriate to do so.

For yet another subtle point, consider the following declarations:

```
int age = 39;
const int * pt = &age;
```

The const in the second declaration only prevents you from changing the value to which pt points, which is 39. It doesn't prevent you from changing the value of pt itself. That is, you can assign a new address to pt:

```
int sage = 80;
pt = &sage; // okay to point to another location
```

But you still can't use pt to change the value to which it points (now 80).

The second way to use const makes it impossible to change the value of the pointer itself:

```
int sloth = 3;
const int * ps = &sloth;        // a pointer to const int
int * const finger = &sloth;    // a const pointer to int
```

Note that the last declaration has repositioned the keyword const. This form of declaration constrains finger to point only to sloth. However, it allows you to use finger to alter the value of sloth. The middle declaration does not allow you to use ps to alter the value of sloth, but it permits you to have ps point to another location. In short, finger and *ps are both const, and *finger and ps are not const. (See Figure 7.5.)

FIGURE 7.5

Pointers-to-const and const pointers.

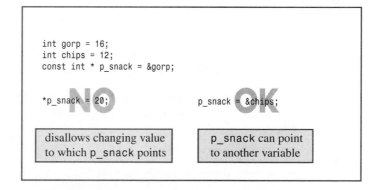

If you like, you can declare a const pointer to a const object:

```
double trouble = 2.0E30;
const double * const stick = &trouble;
```

Here `stick` can point only to `trouble`, and `stick` cannot be used to change the value of `trouble`. In short, both `stick` and `*stick` are `const`.

Typically you use the pointer-to-`const` form to protect data when you pass pointers as function arguments. For example, recall the `show_array()` prototype from Listing 7.5:

```
void show_array(const double ar[], int n);
```

Using `const` in this declaration means that `show_array()` cannot alter the values in any array that is passed to it. This technique works as long as there is just one level of indirection. Here, for example, the array elements are a fundamental type. But if they were pointers or pointers-to-pointers, you wouldn't use `const`.

Functions and Two-Dimensional Arrays

To write a function that has a two-dimensional array as an argument, you need to remember that the name of an array is treated as its address, so the corresponding formal parameter is a pointer, just as for one-dimensional arrays. The tricky part is declaring the pointer correctly. Suppose, for example, that you start with this code:

```
int data[3][4] = {{1,2,3,4}, {9,8,7,6}, {2,4,6,8}};
int total = sum(data, 3);
```

What should the prototype for `sum()` look like? And why does the function pass the number of rows (**3**) as an argument and not also the number of columns (**4**)?

Well, `data` is the name of an array with three elements. The first element is, itself, an array of four `int` values. Thus, the type of `data` is pointer-to-array-of-four-`int`, so an appropriate prototype would be this:

```
int sum(int (*ar2)[4], int size);
```

The parentheses are needed because the declaration

```
int *ar2[4]
```

would declare an array of four pointers-to-`int` instead of a single pointer-to-array-of-four-`int`, and a function parameter cannot be an array. There's an alternative format that means exactly the same thing as this first prototype, but, perhaps, is easier to read:

```
int sum(int ar2[][4], int size);
```

Either prototype states that `ar2` is a pointer, not an array. Also note that the pointer type specifically says it points to an array of four `int`s. Thus, the pointer type specifies the number of columns, which is why the number of columns is not passed as a separate function argument.

Because the pointer type specifies the number of columns, the `sum()` function only works with arrays with four columns. But the number of rows is specified by the variable size, so `sum()` can work with a varying number of rows:

```
int a[100][4];
int b[6][4];
...
int total1 = sum(a, 100);    // sum all of a
int total2 = sum(b, 6);      // sum all of b
int total3 = sum(a, 10);     // sum first 10 rows of a
int total4 = sum(a+10, 20);  // sum next 20 rows of a
```

Given that the parameter `ar2` is a pointer to an array, how do you use it in the function definition? The simplest way is to use `ar2` as if it were the name of a two-dimensional array. Here's a
possible function definition:

```
int sum(int ar2[][4], int size)
{
    int total = 0;
    for (int r = 0; r < size; r++)
        for (int c = 0; c < 4; c++)
            total += ar2[r][c];
    return total;
}
```

Again, note that the number of rows is whatever is passed to the `size` parameter, but the number of columns is fixed at four, both in the parameter declaration for `ar2` and in the inner `for`
loop.

Here's why you can use array notation. Because `ar2` points to the first element (element 0) of
an array whose elements are array-of-four-`int`, the expression `ar2 + r` points to element number `r`. Therefore `ar2[r]` is element number `r`. That element is itself an array-of-four-`int`, so
`ar2[r]` is the name of that array-of-four-`int`. Applying a subscript to an array name gives an
array element, so `ar2[r][c]` is an element of the array-of-four-`int`, hence is a single `int` value.
The pointer `ar2` has to be dereferenced twice to get to the data. The simplest way is to use
brackets twice, as in `ar2[r][c]`. But it is possible, if ungainly, to use the `*` operator twice:

```
ar2[r][c] == *(*(ar2 + r) + c)   // same thing
```

To understand this, you can work out the meaning of the subexpressions from the inside out:

```
ar2            // pointer to first row of an array of 4 int
ar2 + r        // pointer to row r (an array of 4 int)
*(ar2 + r)     // row r (an array of 4 int, hence the name of an array,
               // thus a pointer to the first int in the row, i.e., ar2[r]

*(ar2 +r) + c     // pointer int number c in row r, i.e., ar2[r] + c
*(*(ar2 + r) + c  // value of int number c in row r, i.e. ar2[r][c]
```

Incidentally, the code for `sum()` doesn't use `const` in declaring the parameter `ar2` because that
technique is for pointers to fundamental types, and `ar2` is a pointer to a pointer.

Functions and C-Style Strings

Recall that a C-style string consists of a series of characters terminated by the null character.
Much of what you've learned about designing array functions applies to string functions, too.

For example, passing a string as an argument means passing an address, and you can use const to protect a string argument from being altered. But there are a few special twists to strings that we'll unravel now.

Functions with C-Style String Arguments

Suppose you want to pass a string as an argument to a function. You have three choices for representing a string:

- An array of char

- A quoted string constant (also called a *string literal*)

- A pointer-to-char set to the address of a string

All three choices, however, are type pointer-to-char (more concisely, type char *), so you can use all three as arguments to string-processing functions:

```
char ghost[15] = "galloping";
char * str = "galumphing";
int n1 = strlen(ghost);        // ghost is &ghost[0]
int n2 = strlen(str);          // pointer to char
int n3 = strlen("gamboling");  // address of string
```

Informally, you can say that you're passing a string as an argument, but you're really passing the address of the first character in the string. This implies that a string function prototype should use type char * as the type for the formal parameter representing a string.

One important difference between a C-style string and a regular array is that the string has a built-in terminating character. (Recall that a char array containing characters but no null character is just an array and not a string.) That means you don't have to pass the size of the string as an argument. Instead, the function can use a loop to examine each character in the string in turn until the loop reaches the terminating null character. Listing 7.9 illustrates that approach with a function that counts the number of times a given character appears in a string.

LISTING 7.9   strgfun.cpp

```
// strgfun.cpp -- functions with a string argument
#include <iostream>
int c_in_str(const char * str, char ch);
int main()
{
    using namespace std;
    char mmm[15] = "minimum";    // string in an array
// some systems require preceding char with static to
// enable array initialization

    char *wail = "ululate";    // wail points to string

    int ms = c_in_str(mmm, 'm');
    int us = c_in_str(wail, 'u');
```

LISTING 7.9   *Continued*

```
        cout << ms << " m characters in " << mmm << endl;
        cout << us << " u characters in " << wail << endl;
        return 0;
}

// this function counts the number of ch characters
// in the string str
int c_in_str(const char * str, char ch)
{
    int count = 0;

    while (*str)            // quit when *str is '\0'
    {
        if (*str == ch)
            count++;
        str++;          // move pointer to next char
    }
    return count;
}
```

Here's the output of the program in Listing 7.9:

```
3 m characters in minimum
2 u characters in ululate
```

Program Notes

Because the `c_int_str()` function in Listing 7.9 shouldn't alter the original string, it uses the `const` modifier when it declares the formal parameter `str`. Then, if you mistakenly let the function alter part of the string, the compiler catches your error. Of course, you can use array notation instead to declare `str` in the function header:

```
int c_in_str(const char str[], char ch) // also okay
```

However, using pointer notation reminds you that the argument doesn't have to be the name of an array but can be some other form of pointer.

The function itself demonstrates a standard way to process the characters in a string:

```
while (*str)
{
    statements
    str++;
}
```

Initially, `str` points to the first character in the string, so `*str` represents the first character itself. For example, immediately after the first function call, `*str` has the value m, the first character in `minimum`. As long as the character is not the null character (`\0`), `*str` is nonzero, so the loop continues. At the end of each loop, the expression `str++` increments the pointer by 1 byte so that it points to the next character in the string. Eventually, `str` points to the terminating null character, making `*str` equal to `0`, which is the numeric code for the null character. That condition terminates the loop. (Why are string-processing functions ruthless? Because they stop at nothing.)

Functions That Return C-Style Strings

Now suppose you want to write a function that returns a string. Well, a function can't do that. But it can return the address of a string, and that's more efficient. Listing 7.10, for example, defines a function called `buildstr()` that returns a pointer. This function takes two arguments: a character and a number. Using `new`, the function creates a string whose length equals the number, and then it initializes each element to the character. Then, it returns a pointer to the new string.

LISTING 7.10   `strgback.cpp`

```cpp
// strgback.cpp -- a function that returns a pointer to char
#include <iostream>
char * buildstr(char c, int n);      // prototype
int main()
{
    using namespace std;
    int times;
    char ch;

    cout << "Enter a character: ";
    cin >> ch;
    cout << "Enter an integer: ";
    cin >> times;
    char *ps = buildstr(ch, times);
    cout << ps << endl;
    delete [] ps;                    // free memory
    ps = buildstr('+', 20);          // reuse pointer
    cout << ps << "-DONE-" << ps << endl;
    delete [] ps;                    // free memory
    return 0;
}

// builds string made of n c characters
char * buildstr(char c, int n)
{
    char * pstr = new char[n + 1];
    pstr[n] = '\0';            // terminate string
    while (n-- > 0)
        pstr[n] = c;           // fill rest of string
    return pstr;
}
```

Here's a sample run of the program in Listing 7.10:

```
Enter a character: V
Enter an integer: 46
VVVVVVVVVVVVVVVVVVVVVVVVVVVVVVVVVVVVVVVVVVVVVVVV
++++++++++++++++++++-DONE-++++++++++++++++++++
```

Program Notes

To create a string of n visible characters, you need storage for n + 1 characters in order to have space for the null character. So the function in Listing 7.10 asks for n + 1 bytes to hold the string. Next, it sets the final byte to the null character. Then, it fills in the rest of the array from back to front. In Listing 7.10, the loop

```
while (n-- > 0)
    pstr[n] = c;
```

cycles n times as n decreases to 0, filling n elements. At the start of the final cycle, n has the value 1. Because n-- means use the value and then decrement it, the `while` loop test condition compares 1 to 0, finds the test to be `true`, and continues. But after making the test, the function decrements n to 0, so pstr[0] is the last element set to c. The reason for filling the string from back to front instead of front to back is to avoid using an additional variable. Using the other order would involve something like this:

```
int i = 0;
while (i < n)
    pstr[i++] = c;
```

Note that the variable `pstr` is local to the `buildstr` function, so when that function terminates, the memory used for `pstr` (but not for the string) is freed. But because the function returns the value of `pstr`, the program is able to access the new string through the `ps` pointer in `main()`.

The program in Listing 7.10 uses `delete` to free memory used for the string after the string is no longer needed. Then it reuses `ps` to point to the new block of memory obtained for the next string and frees that memory. The disadvantage to this kind of design (having a function return a pointer to memory allocated by `new`) is that it makes it the programmer's responsibility to remember to use `delete`. In Chapter 12, "Classes and Dynamic Memory Allocation," you'll see how C++ classes, by using constructors and destructors, can take care of these details for you.

Functions and Structures

Let's move from arrays to structures. It's easier to write functions for structures than for arrays. Although structure variables resemble arrays in that both can hold several data items, structure variables behave like basic, single-valued variables when it comes to functions. That is, unlike an array, a structure ties its data in to a single entity that will be treated as a unit. Recall that you can assign one structure to another. Similarly, you can pass structures by value, just as you do with ordinary variables. In that case, the function works with a copy of the original structure. Also, a function can return a structure. There's no funny business like the name of an array being the address of its first element. The name of a structure is simply the name of the structure, and if you want its address, you have to use the & address operator. (C++ and C both use the & symbol to denote the address operator. C++ additionally uses this operator to identify reference variables, to be discussed in Chapter 8.)

The most direct way to program by using structures is to treat them as you would treat the basic types—that is, pass them as arguments and use them, if necessary, as return values. However, there is one disadvantage to passing structures by value. If the structure is large, the space and effort involved in making a copy of a structure can increase memory requirements and slow down the system. For those reasons (and because, at first, C didn't allow the passing of structures by value), many C programmers prefer passing the address of a structure and then using a pointer to access the structure contents. C++ provides a third alternative, called *passing by reference*, that is discussed in Chapter 8. Let's examine the other two choices now, beginning with passing and returning entire structures.

Passing and Returning Structures

Passing structures by value makes the most sense when the structure is relatively compact, so let's look at a couple examples along those lines. The first example deals with travel time (not to be confused with time travel). Some maps will tell you that it is 3 hours, 50 minutes, from Thunder Falls to Bingo City and 1 hour, 25 minutes, from Bingo City to Grotesquo. You can use a structure to represent such times, using one member for the hour value and a second member for the minute value. Adding two times is a little tricky because you might have to transfer some of the minutes to the hours part. For example, the two preceding times sum to 4 hours, 75 minutes, which should be converted to 5 hours, 15 minutes. Let's develop a structure to represent a time value and then a function that takes two such structures as arguments and returns a structure that represents their sum.

Defining the structure is simple:

```
struct travel_time
{
    int hours;
    int mins;
};
```

Next, consider the prototype for a `sum()` function that returns the sum of two such structures. The return value should be type `travel_time`, and so should the two arguments. Thus, the prototype should look like this:

```
travel_time sum(travel_time t1, travel_time t2);
```

To add two times, you first add the minute members. Integer division by 60 yields the number of hours to carry over, and the modulus operation (`%`) yields the number of minutes left. Listing 7.11 incorporates this approach into the `sum()` function and adds a `show_time()` function to display the contents of a `travel_time` structure.

LISTING 7.11   `travel.cpp`

```
// travel.cpp -- using structures with functions
#include <iostream>
struct travel_time
{
    int hours;
    int mins;
```

LISTING 7.11   Continued

```
    };
    const int Mins_per_hr = 60;

    travel_time sum(travel_time t1, travel_time t2);
    void show_time(travel_time t);

    int main()
    {
        using namespace std;
        travel_time day1 = {5, 45};      // 5 hrs, 45 min
        travel_time day2 = {4, 55};      // 4 hrs, 55 min

        travel_time trip = sum(day1, day2);
        cout << "Two-day total: ";
        show_time(trip);

        travel_time day3= {4, 32};
        cout << "Three-day total: ";
        show_time(sum(trip, day3));

        return 0;
    }

    travel_time sum(travel_time t1, travel_time t2)
    {
        travel_time total;

        total.mins = (t1.mins + t2.mins) % Mins_per_hr;
        total.hours = t1.hours + t2.hours +
                    (t1.mins + t2.mins) / Mins_per_hr;
        return total;
    }

    void show_time(travel_time t)
    {
        using namespace std;
        cout << t.hours << " hours, "
            << t.mins << " minutes\n";
    }
```

Here `travel_time` acts just like a standard type name; you can use it to declare variables, function return types, and function argument types. Because variables such as `total` and `t1` are `travel_time` structures, you can apply the dot membership operator to them. Note that because the `sum()` function returns a `travel_time` structure, you can use it as an argument for the `show_time()` function. Because C++ functions, by default, pass arguments by value, the `show_time(sum(trip, day3))` function call first evaluates the `sum(trip, day3)` function call in order to find its return value. The `show_time()` call then passes `sum()`'s return value, not the function itself, to `show_time()`. Here's the output of the program in Listing 7.11:

```
Two-day total: 10 hours, 40 minutes
Three-day total: 15 hours, 12 minutes
```

Another Example of Using Functions with Structures

Much of what you learn about functions and C++ structures carries over to C++ classes, so it's worth looking at a second example. This time let's deal with space instead of time. In particular, this example defines two structures representing two different ways of describing positions and then develops functions to convert one form to the other and show the result. This example is a bit more mathematical than the last, but you don't have to follow the mathematics to follow the C++.

Suppose you want to describe the position of a point on the screen or a location on a map relative to some origin. One way is to state the horizontal offset and the vertical offset of the point from the origin. Traditionally, mathematicians use the symbol x to represent the horizontal offset and y to represent the vertical offset. (See Figure 7.6.) Together, x and y constitute *rectangular coordinates*. You can define a structure consisting of two coordinates to represent a position:

```
struct rect
{
    double x;        // horizontal distance from origin
    double y;        // vertical distance from origin
};
```

FIGURE 7.6

Rectangular coordinates.

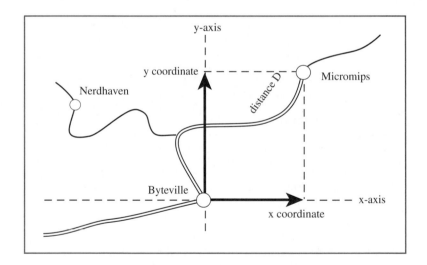

rectangular coordinates of Micromips relative to Byteville

A second way to describe the position of a point is to state how far it is from the origin and in what direction it is (for example, 40 degrees north of east). Traditionally, mathematicians have measured the angle counterclockwise from the positive horizontal axis. (See Figure 7.7.) The distance and angle together constitute *polar coordinates*. You can define a second structure to represent this view of a position:

```
struct polar
{
        double distance;    // distance from origin
        double angle;       // direction from origin
};
```

FIGURE 7.7

Polar coordinates.

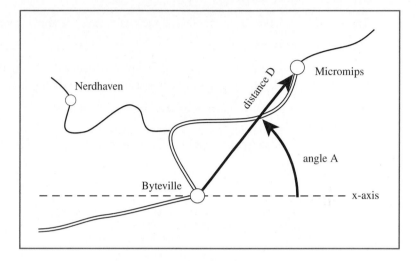

polar coordinates of Micromips relative to Byteville

Let's construct a function that displays the contents of a type **polar** structure. The math functions in the C++ library assume that angles are in radians, so you need to measure angles in that unit. But for display purposes, you can convert radian measure to degrees. This means multiplying by $180/\pi$, which is approximately 57.29577951. Here's the function:

```
// show polar coordinates, converting angle to degrees
void show_polar (polar dapos)
{
    using namespace std;
    const double Rad_to_deg = 57.29577951;

    cout << "distance = " << dapos.distance;
    cout << ", angle = " << dapos.angle * Rad_to_deg;
    cout << " degrees\n";
}
```

Notice that the formal variable is type **polar**. When you pass a **polar** structure to this function, the structure contents are copied into the **dapos** structure, and the function then uses that copy in its work. Because **dapos** is a structure, the function uses the membership (dot) operator (see Chapter 4) to identify structure members.

Next, let's try something more ambitious and write a function that converts rectangular coordinates to polar coordinates. You should have the function accept a **rect** structure as its argument and return a **polar** structure to the calling function. This involves using functions from the math library, so the program has to include the `math.h` header file. Also, on some systems you have to tell the compiler to load the math library (see Chapter 1, "Getting Started"). You can use the Pythagorean theorem to get the distance from the horizontal and vertical components:

```
distance = sqrt( x * x + y * y)
```

The `atan2()` function from the math library calculates the angle from the **x** and **y** values:

```
angle = atan2(y, x)
```

(There's also an `atan()` function, but it doesn't distinguish between angles 180 degrees apart. That uncertainty is no more desirable in a math function than it is in a wilderness guide.)

Given these formulas, you can write the function as follows:

```
// convert rectangular to polar coordinates
polar rect_to_polar(rect xypos)    // type polar
{
    polar answer;

    answer.distance =
        sqrt( xypos.x * xypos.x + xypos.y * xypos.y);
    answer.angle = atan2(xypos.y, xypos.x);
    return answer;      // returns a polar structure
}
```

Now that the functions are ready, writing the rest of the program is straightforward. Listing 7.12 presents the result.

LISTING 7.12 `strctfun.cpp`

```
// strctfun.cpp -- functions with a structure argument
#include <iostream>
#include <cmath>

// structure declarations
struct polar
{
    double distance;        // distance from origin
    double angle;           // direction from origin
};
struct rect
{
    double x;               // horizontal distance from origin
    double y;               // vertical distance from origin
};

// prototypes
polar rect_to_polar(rect xypos);
void show_polar(polar dapos);

int main()
{
```

LISTING 7.12   Continued

```
    using namespace std;
    rect rplace;
    polar pplace;

    cout << "Enter the x and y values: ";
    while (cin >> rplace.x >> rplace.y)  // slick use of cin
    {
        pplace = rect_to_polar(rplace);
        show_polar(pplace);
        cout << "Next two numbers (q to quit): ";
    }
    cout << "Done.\n";
    return 0;
}

// convert rectangular to polar coordinates
polar rect_to_polar(rect xypos)
{
    using namespace std;
    polar answer;

    answer.distance =
        sqrt( xypos.x * xypos.x + xypos.y * xypos.y);
    answer.angle = atan2(xypos.y, xypos.x);
    return answer;       // returns a polar structure
}

// show polar coordinates, converting angle to degrees
void show_polar (polar dapos)
{
    using namespace std;
    const double Rad_to_deg = 57.29577951;

    cout << "distance = " << dapos.distance;
    cout << ", angle = " << dapos.angle * Rad_to_deg;
    cout << " degrees\n";
}
```

	Compatibility Note

Some C++ implementations still use `math.h` instead of the newer `cmath` header file. Some compilers require explicit instructions to search the math library. For example, older versions of g++ uses this command line:

```
g++ structfun.C -lm
```

Here is a sample run of the program in Listing 7.12:

```
Enter the x and y values: 30 40
distance = 50, angle = 53.1301 degrees
Next two numbers (q to quit): -100 100
distance = 141.421, angle = 135 degrees
Next two numbers (q to quit): q
```

Program Notes

We've already discussed the two functions in Listing 7.12, so let's review how the program uses `cin` to control a `while` loop:

```
while (cin >> rplace.x >> rplace.y)
```

Recall that `cin` is an object of the `istream` class. The extraction operator (`>>`) is designed in such a way that `cin >> rplace.x` also is an object of that type. As you'll see in Chapter 11, "Working with Classes," class operators are implemented with functions. What really happens when you use `cin >> rplace.x` is that the program calls a function that returns a type `istream` value. If you apply the extraction operator to the `cin >> rplace.x` object (as in `cin >> rplace.x >> rplace.y`), you again get an object of the `istream` class. Thus, the entire `while` loop test expression eventually evaluates to `cin`, which, as you may recall, when used in the context of a test expression, is converted to a `bool` value of `true` or `false`, depending on whether input succeeded. In the loop in Listing 7.12, for example, `cin` expects the user to enter two numbers. If, instead, the user enters q, as shown in the sample output, `cin >>` recognizes that q is not a number. It leaves the q in the input queue and returns a value that's converted to `false`, terminating the loop.

Compare that approach for reading numbers to this simpler one:

```
for (int i = 0; i < limit; i++)
    {
        cout << "Enter value #" << (i + 1) << ": ";
        cin >> temp;
        if (temp < 0)
            break;
        ar[i] = temp;
    }
```

To terminate this loop early, you enter a negative number. This restricts input to non-negative values. This restriction fits the needs of some programs, but more typically you would want a means of terminating a loop that doesn't exclude certain numeric values. Using `cin >>` as the test condition eliminates such restrictions because it accepts all valid numeric input. You should keep this trick in mind when you need an input loop for numbers. Also, you should keep in mind that non-numeric input sets an error condition that prevents the reading of any more input. If a program needs input subsequent to the input loop, you must use `cin.clear()` to reset input, and you might then need to get rid of the offending input by reading it. Listing 7.7 illustrates those techniques.

Passing Structure Addresses

Suppose you want to save time and space by passing the address of a structure instead of passing the entire structure. This requires rewriting the functions so that they use pointers to structures. First, let's look at how you rewrite the `show_polar()` function. You need to make three changes:

- When calling the function, pass it the address of the structure (`&pplace`) rather than the structure itself (`pplace`).

- Declare the formal parameter to be a pointer-to-`polar`—that is, type `polar *`. Because the function shouldn't modify the structure, use the `const` modifier.

- Because the formal parameter is a pointer instead of a structure, use the indirect membership operator (`->`) rather than the membership operator (dot).

After these changes are made, the function looks like this:

```
// show polar coordinates, converting angle to degrees
void show_polar (const polar * pda)
{
    using namespace std;
    const double Rad_to_deg = 57.29577951;

    cout << "distance = " << pda->distance;
    cout << ", angle = " << pda->angle * Rad_to_deg;
    cout << " degrees\n";
}
```

Next, let's alter `rect_to_polar`. This is more involved because the original `rect_to_polar` function returns a structure. To take full advantage of pointer efficiency, you should use a pointer instead of a return value. The way to do this is to pass two pointers to the function. The first points to the structure to be converted, and the second points to the structure that's to hold the conversion. Instead of *returning* a new structure, the function *modifies* an existing structure in the calling function. Hence, although the first argument is `const` pointer, the second is not `const`. Otherwise, you apply the same principles used to convert `show_polar()` to pointer arguments. Listing 7.13 shows the reworked program.

LISTING 7.13 `strctptr.cpp`

```
// strctptr.cpp -- functions with pointer to structure arguments
#include <iostream>
#include <cmath>

// structure templates
struct polar
{
    double distance;      // distance from origin
    double angle;         // direction from origin
};
struct rect
{
    double x;             // horizontal distance from origin
    double y;             // vertical distance from origin
};

// prototypes
void rect_to_polar(const rect * pxy, polar * pda);
void show_polar (const polar * pda);

int main()
{
```

LISTING 7.13   Continued

```cpp
    using namespace std;
    rect rplace;
    polar pplace;

    cout << "Enter the x and y values: ";
    while (cin >> rplace.x >> rplace.y)
    {
        rect_to_polar(&rplace, &pplace);    // pass addresses
        show_polar(&pplace);         // pass address
        cout << "Next two numbers (q to quit): ";
    }
    cout << "Done.\n";
    return 0;
}

// show polar coordinates, converting angle to degrees
void show_polar (const polar * pda)
{
    using namespace std;
    const double Rad_to_deg = 57.29577951;

    cout << "distance = " << pda->distance;
    cout << ", angle = " << pda->angle * Rad_to_deg;
    cout << " degrees\n";
}

// convert rectangular to polar coordinates
void rect_to_polar(const rect * pxy, polar * pda)
{
    using namespace std;
    pda->distance =
        sqrt(pxy->x * pxy->x + pxy->y * pxy->y);
    pda->angle = atan2(pxy->y, pxy->x);
}
```

Compatibility Note

Some C++ implementations still use `math.h` instead of the newer `cmath` header file. Some compilers require explicit instructions to search the math library.

From the user's standpoint, the program in Listing 7.13 behaves like that in Listing 7.12. The hidden difference is that Listing 7.12 works with copies of structures, whereas Listing 7.13 uses pointers to the original structures.

Functions and `string` Class Objects

Although C-style strings and `string` class objects serve much the same purpose, a `string` class object is more closely related to a structure than to an array. For example, you can assign a structure to another structure and an object to another object. You can pass a structure as a complete entity to a function, and you can pass an object as a complete entity. If you need several strings, you can declare a one-dimensional array of **string** objects instead of a two-dimensional array of **char**.

Listing 7.14 provides a short example that declares an array of string objects and passes the array to a function that displays the contents.

LISTING 7.14 `topfive.cpp`

```cpp
// topfive.cpp -- handling an array of string objects
#include <iostream>
#include <string>
using namespace std;
const int SIZE = 5;
void display(const string sa[], int n);
int main()
{
    string list[SIZE];     // an array holding 5 string object
    cout << "Enter your " << SIZE << " favorite astronomical sights:\n";
    for (int i = 0; i < SIZE; i++)
    {
        cout << i + 1 << ": ";
        getline(cin,list[i]);
    }

    cout << "Your list:\n";
    display(list, SIZE);

    return 0;
}

void display(const string sa[], int n)
{
    for (int i = 0; i < n; i++)
        cout << i + 1 << ": " << sa[i] << endl;
}
```

Compatibility Notes

Some older versions of Visual C++ have a bug that throws off the synchronization of the input and output statements. With one of these versions, you may have to type a response before the computer displays the prompt for that response.

Here's a sample run of the program in Listing 7.14:

```
Enter your 5 favorite astronomical sights:
1: Orion Nebula
2: M13
3: Saturn
```

```
4: Jupiter
5: Moon
Your list:
1: Orion Nebula
2: M13
3: Saturn
4: Jupiter
5: Moon
```

The main point to note in this example is that, aside from the `getline()` function, this program treats `string` just as it would treat any of the built-in types, such as `int`. If you want an array of `string`, you just use the usual array-declaration format:

```
string list[SIZE];     // an array holding 5 string object
```

Each element of the `list` array, then, is a `string` object and can be used as such:

```
getline(cin,list[i]);
```

Similarly, the formal argument `sa` is a pointer to a `string` object, so `sa[i]` is a `string` object and can be used accordingly:

```
cout << i + 1 << ": " << sa[i] << endl;
```

Recursion

And now for something completely different. A C++ function has the interesting characteristic that it can call itself. (Unlike C, however, C++ does not let `main()` call itself.) This ability is termed *recursion*. Recursion is an important tool in certain types of programming, such as artificial intelligence, but we'll just take a superficial look (artificial shallowness) at how it works.

Recursion with a Single Recursive Call

If a recursive function calls itself, then the newly called function calls itself, and so on, ad infinitum unless the code includes something to terminate the chain of calls. The usual method is to make the recursive call part of an `if` statement. For example, a type `void` recursive function called `recurs()` can have a form like this:

```
void recurs(argumentlist)
{
    statements1
    if (test)
            recurs(arguments)
    statements2
}
```

With luck or foresight, *test* eventually becomes `false`, and the chain of calls is broken.

Recursive calls produce an intriguing chain of events. As long as the `if` statement remains `true`, each call to `recurs()` executes *statements1* and then invokes a new incarnation of `recurs()` without reaching *statements2*. When the `if` statement becomes `false`, the current call then proceeds to *statements2*. Then, when the current call terminates, program control returns to the previous version of `recurs()` that called it. Then, that version of `recurs()` completes executing its *statements2* section and terminates, returning control to the prior call, and so on. Thus, if `recurs()` undergoes five recursive calls, first the *statements1* section is executed five times in the order in which the functions were called, and then the *statements2* section is executed five times in the opposite order from the order in which the functions were called. After going into five levels of recursion, the program then has to back out through the same five levels. Listing 7.15 illustrates this behavior.

LISTING 7.15   `recur.cpp`

```cpp
// recur.cpp -- using recursion
#include <iostream>
void countdown(int n);

int main()
{
    countdown(4);           // call the recursive function
    return 0;
}

void countdown(int n)
{
    using namespace std;
    cout << "Counting down ... " << n << endl;
    if (n > 0)
        countdown(n-1);     // function calls itself
    cout << n << ": Kaboom!\n";
}
```

Here's the annotated output of the program in Listing 7.15:

```
Counting down ... 4     ←level 1; adding levels of recursion
Counting down ... 3     ←level 2
Counting down ... 2     ←level 3
Counting down ... 1     ←level 4
Counting down ... 0     ←level 5; final recursive call
0: Kaboom!              ←level 5; beginning to back out
1: Kaboom!              ←level 4
2: Kaboom!              ←level 3
3: Kaboom!              ←level 2
4: Kaboom!              ←level 1
```

Note that each recursive call creates its own set of variables, so by the time the program reaches the fifth call, it has five separate variables called n, each with a different value. You can verify this for yourself by modifying Listing 7.15 so that it displays the address of n as well as its value:

```cpp
cout << "Counting down ... " << n << " (n at " << &n << ")" << endl;
...
cout << n << ": Kaboom!"; << "        (n at " << &n << ")" << endl;
```

Doing so produces output like the following:

```
Counting down ... 4 (n at 0012FE0C)
Counting down ... 3 (n at 0012FD34)
Counting down ... 2 (n at 0012FC5C)
Counting down ... 1 (n at 0012FB84)
Counting down ... 0 (n at 0012FAAC)
0: Kaboom!        (n at 0012FAAC)
1: Kaboom!        (n at 0012FB84)
2: Kaboom!        (n at 0012FC5C)
3: Kaboom!        (n at 0012FD34)
4: Kaboom!        (n at 0012FE0C)
```

Note how the n having the value 4 is stored at one location (memory address 0012FE0C in this example), the n having the value 3 is stored at a second location (memory address 0012FD34), and so on.

Recursion with Multiple Recursive Calls

Recursion is particularly useful for situations that call for repeatedly subdividing a task into two smaller, similar tasks. For example, consider this approach to drawing a ruler. Mark the two ends, locate the midpoint, and mark it. Then, apply this same procedure to the left half of the ruler and then to the right half. If you want more subdivisions, apply the same procedure to each of the current subdivisions. This recursive approach is sometimes called the *divide-and-conquer strategy*. Listing 7.16 illustrates this approach, with the recursive function `subdivide()`. It uses a string initially filled with spaces except for a | character at each end. The main program uses a loop to call the `subdivide()` function six times, each time increasing the number of recursion levels and printing the resulting string. Thus, each line of output represents an additional level of recursion. To remind you that it's an option, the program uses the `std::` qualifier instead of a `using` directive.

LISTING 7.16   `ruler.cpp`
```cpp
// ruler.cpp -- using recursion to subdivide a ruler
#include <iostream>
const int Len = 66;
const int Divs = 6;
void subdivide(char ar[], int low, int high, int level);
int main()
{
    char ruler[Len];
    int i;
    for (i = 1; i < Len - 2; i++)
        ruler[i] = ' ';
    ruler[Len - 1] = '\0';
    int max = Len - 2;
    int min = 0;
    ruler[min] = ruler[max] = '|';
    std::cout << ruler << std::endl;
    for (i = 1; i <= Divs; i++)
    {
```

LISTING 7.16   Continued

```
        subdivide(ruler,min,max, i);
        std::cout << ruler << std::endl;
        for (int j = 1; j < Len - 2; j++)
            ruler[j] = ' ';  // reset to blank ruler
    }

    return 0;
}

void subdivide(char ar[], int low, int high, int level)
{
    if (level == 0)
        return;
    int mid = (high + low) / 2;
    ar[mid] = '|';
    subdivide(ar, low, mid, level - 1);
    subdivide(ar, mid, high, level - 1);
}
```

Here is the output of the program in Listing 7.16:

```
|                                                               |
|                              |                                |
|              |               |               |                |
|      |       |       |       |       |       |       |        |
|   |   |   |   |   |   |   |   |   |   |   |   |   |   |   |    |
| | | | | | | | | | | | | | | | | | | | | | | | | | | | | | | | |
|||||||||||||||||||||||||||||||||||||||||||||||||||||||||||||||||
```

Program Notes

The `subdivide()` function in Listing 7.16 uses the variable `level` to control the recursion level. When the function calls itself, it reduces `level` by one, and the function with a `level` of 0 terminates. Note that `subdivide()` calls itself twice, once for the left subdivision and once for the right subdivision. The original midpoint becomes the right end for one call and the left end for the other call. Notice that the number of calls grows geometrically. That is, one call generates two, which generate four calls, which generate eight, and so on. That's why the level 6 call is able to fill in 64 elements ($2^6 = 64$). This continued doubling of the number of function calls (and hence of the number of variables stored) make this form of recursion a poor choice if many levels of recursion are required. But it is an elegant and simple choice if the necessary levels of recursion are few.

Pointers to Functions

No discussion of C or C++ functions would be complete without mention of pointers to functions. We'll take a quick look at this topic and leave the full exposition of the possibilities to more advanced texts.

Functions, like data items, have addresses. A function's address is the memory address at which the stored machine language code for the function begins. Normally, it's neither important nor useful for you or the user to know that address, but it can be useful to a program. For example, it's possible to write a function that takes the address of another function as an argument. That enables the first function to find the second function and run it. This approach is more awkward than simply having the first function call the second one directly, but it leaves open the possibility of passing different function addresses at different times. That means the first function can use different functions at different times.

Function Pointer Basics

Let's clarify this process with an example. Suppose you want to design an `estimate()` function that estimates the amount of time necessary to write a given number of lines of code, and you want different programmers to use the function. Part of the code for `estimate()` will be the same for all users, but the function will allow each programmer to provide his or her own algorithm for estimating time. The mechanism for that will be to pass to `estimate()` the address of the particular algorithm function the programmer wants to use. To implement this plan, you need to be able to do the following:

- Obtain the address of a function.

- Declare a pointer to a function.

- Use a pointer to a function to invoke the function.

Obtaining the Address of a Function

Obtaining the address of a function is simple: You just use the function name without trailing parentheses. That is, if `think()` is a function, then `think` is the address of the function. To pass a function as an argument, you pass the function name. Be sure you distinguish between passing the *address* of a function and passing the *return value* of a function:

```
process(think);     // passes address of think() to process()
thought(think());   // passes return value of think() to thought()
```

The `process()` call enables the `process()` function to invoke the `think()` function from within `process()`. The `thought()` call first invokes the `think()` function and then passes the return value of `think()` to the `thought()` function.

Declaring a Pointer to a Function

To declare pointers to a data type, the declaration has had to specify exactly to what type the pointer points. Similarly, a pointer to a function has to specify to what type of function the pointer points. This means the declaration should identify the function's return type and the function's signature (its argument list). That is, the declaration should provide the same information about a function that a function prototype does. For example, suppose Pam LeCoder has written a time-estimating function with the following prototype:

```
double pam(int);   // prototype
```

Here's what a declaration of an appropriate pointer type looks like:

```
double (*pf)(int);    // pf points to a function that takes
                      // one int argument and that
                      // returns type double
```

Note that this looks just like the `pam()` declaration, with `(*pf)` playing the part of `pam`. Because `pam` is a function, so is `(*pf)`. And if `(*pf)` is a function, then `pf` is a pointer to a function.

Tip
In general, to declare a pointer to a particular kind of function, you can first write a prototype for a regular function of the desired kind and then replace the function name with an expression in the form `(*pf)`. In this case, `pf` is a pointer to a function of that type.

The declaration requires the parentheses around `*pf` to provide the proper operator precedence. Parentheses have a higher precedence than the `*` operator, so `*pf(int)` means `pf()` is a function that returns a pointer, whereas `(*pf)(int)` means `pf` is a pointer to a function:

```
double (*pf)(int); // pf points to a function that returns double
double *pf(int);   // pf() a function that returns a pointer-to-double
```

After you declare `pf` properly, you can assign to it the address of a matching function:

```
double pam(int);
double (*pf)(int);
pf = pam;            // pf now points to the pam() function
```

Note that `pam()` has to match `pf` in both signature and return type. The compiler rejects non-matching assignments:

```
double ned(double);
int ted(int);
double (*pf)(int);
pf = ned;          // invalid -- mismatched signature
pf = ted;          // invalid -- mismatched return types
```

Let's return to the `estimate()` function mentioned earlier. Suppose you want to pass to it the number of lines of code to be written and the address of an estimating algorithm, such as the `pam()` function. It could have the following prototype:

```
void estimate(int lines, double (*pf)(int));
```

This declaration says the second argument is a pointer to a function that has an `int` argument and a `double` return value. To have `estimate()` use the `pam()` function, you pass `pam()`'s address to it:

```
estimate(50, pam); // function call telling estimate() to use pam()
```

Clearly, the tricky part about using pointers to functions is writing the prototypes, whereas passing the address is very simple.

Using a Pointer to Invoke a Function

Now we get to the final part of the technique, which is using a pointer to call the pointed-to function. The clue comes in the pointer declaration. There, recall, `(*pf)` plays the same role as a function name. Thus, all you have to do is use `(*pf)` as if it were a function name:

```cpp
double pam(int);
double (*pf)(int);
pf = pam;                // pf now points to the pam() function
double x = pam(4);   // call pam() using the function name
double y = (*pf)(5); // call pam() using the pointer pf
```

Actually, C++ also allows you to use `pf` as if it were a function name:

```cpp
double y = pf(5);    // also call pam() using the pointer pf
```

Using the first form is uglier, but it provides a strong visual reminder that the code is using a function pointer.

History Versus Logic

Holy syntax! How can `pf` and `(*pf)` be equivalent? One school of thought maintains that because `pf` is a pointer to a function, `*pf` is a function; hence, you should use `(*pf)()` as a function call. A second school maintains that because the name of a function is a pointer to that function, a pointer to that function should act like the name of a function; hence you should use `pf()` as a function call. C++ takes the compromise view that both forms are correct, or at least can be allowed, even though they are logically inconsistent with each other. Before you judge that compromise too harshly, reflect that the ability to hold views that are not logically self-consistent is a hallmark of the human mental process.

A Function Pointer Example

Listing 7.17 demonstrates using function pointers in a program. It calls the `estimate()` function twice, once passing the `betsy()` function address and once passing the `pam()` function address. In the first case, `estimate()` uses `betsy()` to calculate the number of hours necessary, and in the second case, `estimate()` uses `pam()` for the calculation. This design facilitates future program development. When Ralph develops his own algorithm for estimating time, he doesn't have to rewrite `estimate()`. Instead, he merely needs to supply his own `ralph()` function, making sure it has the correct signature and return type. Of course, rewriting `estimate()` isn't a difficult task, but the same principle applies to more complex code. Also, the function pointer method allows Ralph to modify the behavior of `estimate()`, even if he doesn't have access to the source code for `estimate()`.

LISTING 7.17   fun_ptr.cpp

```cpp
// fun_ptr.cpp -- pointers to functions
#include <iostream>
double betsy(int);
double pam(int);
```

LISTING 7.17   Continued

```
// second argument is pointer to a type double function that
// takes a type int argument
void estimate(int lines, double (*pf)(int));

int main()
{
    using namespace std;
    int code;

    cout << "How many lines of code do you need? ";
    cin >> code;
    cout << "Here's Betsy's estimate:\n";
    estimate(code, betsy);
    cout << "Here's Pam's estimate:\n";
    estimate(code, pam);
    return 0;
}

double betsy(int lns)
{
    return 0.05 * lns;
}

double pam(int lns)
{
    return 0.03 * lns + 0.0004 * lns * lns;
}

void estimate(int lines, double (*pf)(int))
{
    using namespace std;
    cout << lines << " lines will take ";
    cout << (*pf)(lines) << " hour(s)\n";
}
```

Here is a sample run of the program in Listing 7.17:

```
How many lines of code do you need? 30
Here's Betsy's estimate:
30 lines will take 1.5 hour(s)
Here's Pam's estimate:
30 lines will take 1.26 hour(s)
```

Here is a second sample run of the program:

```
How many lines of code do you need? 100
Here's Betsy's estimate:
100 lines will take 5 hour(s)
Here's Pam's estimate:
100 lines will take 7 hour(s)
```

Summary

Functions are the C++ programming modules. To use a function, you need to provide a definition and a prototype, and you have to use a function call. The function definition is the code that implements what the function does. The function prototype describes the function interface: how many and what kinds of values to pass to the function and what sort of return type, if any, to get from it. The function call causes the program to pass the function arguments to the function and to transfer program execution to the function code.

By default, C++ functions pass arguments by value. This means that the formal parameters in the function definition are new variables that are initialized to the values provided by the function call. Thus, C++ functions protect the integrity of the original data by working with copies.

C++ treats an array name argument as the address of the first element of the array. Technically, this is still passing by value because the pointer is a copy of the original address, but the function uses the pointer to access the contents of the original array. When you declare formal parameters for a function (and only then), the following two declarations are equivalent:

```
typeName arr[]
typeName * arr
```

Both of these mean that `arr` is a pointer to *typeName*. When you write the function code, however, you can use `arr` as if it were an array name in order to access elements: `arr[i]`. Even when passing pointers, you can preserve the integrity of the original data by declaring the formal argument to be a pointer to a `const` type. Because passing the address of an array conveys no information about the size of the array, you normally pass the array size as a separate argument.

C++ provides three ways to represent C-style strings: by using a character array, a string constant, or a pointer to a string. All are type `char*` (pointer-to-`char`), so they are passed to a function as a type `char*` argument. C++ uses the null character (`\0`) to terminate strings, and string functions test for the null character to determine the end of any string they are processing.

C++ also provides the `string` class to represent strings. A function can accept `string` objects as arguments and use a `string` object as a return value. The `string` class `size()` method can be used to determine the length of a stored string.

C++ treats structures the same as basic types, meaning that you can pass them by value and use them as function return types. However, if a structure is large, it might be more efficient to pass a pointer to the structure and let the function work with the original data.

A C++ function can be recursive; that is, the code for a particular function can include a call of itself.

The name of a C++ function acts as the address of the function. By using a function argument that is a pointer to a function, you can pass to a function the name of a second function that you want the first function to evoke.

Review Questions

1. What are the three steps in using a function?

2. Construct function prototypes that match the following descriptions:

    a. `igor()` takes no arguments and has no return value.

    b. `tofu()` takes an `int` argument and returns a `float`.

    c. `mpg()` takes two type `double` arguments and returns a `double`.

    d. `summation()` takes the name of a `long` array and an array size as values and returns a `long` value.

    e. `doctor()` takes a string argument (the string is not to be modified) and returns a `double` value.

    f. `ofcourse()` takes a `boss` structure as an argument and returns nothing.

    g. `plot()` takes a pointer to a `map` structure as an argument and returns a string.

3. Write a function that takes three arguments: the name of an `int` array, the array size, and an `int` value. Have the function set each element of the array to the `int` value.

4. Write a function that takes three arguments: a pointer to the first element of a range in an array, a pointer to the element following the end of a range in an array, and an `int` value. Have the function set each element of the array to the `int` value.

5. Write a function that takes a `double` array name and an array size as arguments and returns the largest value in that array. Note that this function shouldn't alter the contents of the array.

6. Why don't you use the `const` qualifier for function arguments that are one of the fundamental types?

7. What are the three forms a C-style string can take in a C++ program?

8. Write a function that has this prototype:

```
int replace(char * str, char c1, char c2);
```

Have the function replace every occurrence of `c1` in the string `str` with `c2`, and have the function return the number of replacements it makes.

9. What does the expression `*"pizza"` mean? What about `"taco"[2]`?

10. C++ enables you to pass a structure by value, and it lets you pass the address of a structure. If `glitz` is a structure variable, how would you pass it by value? How would you pass its address? What are the trade-offs of the two approaches?

11. The function `judge()` has a type `int` return value. As an argument, it takes the address of a function. The function whose address is passed, in turn, takes a pointer to a `const` `char` as an argument and returns an `int`. Write the function prototype.

Programming Exercises

1. Write a program that repeatedly asks the user to enter pairs of numbers until at least one of the pair is **0**. For each pair, the program should use a function to calculate the harmonic mean of the numbers. The function should return the answer to `main()`, which should report the result. The harmonic mean of the numbers is the inverse of the average of the inverses and can be calculated as follows:

   harmonic mean = 2.0 × x × y / (x + y)

2. Write a program that asks the user to enter up to 10 golf scores, which are to be stored in an array. You should provide a means for the user to terminate input prior to entering 10 scores. The program should display all the scores on one line and report the average score. Handle input, display, and the average calculation with three separate array-processing functions.

3. Here is a structure declaration:

   ```
   struct box
   {
        char maker[40];
        float height;
        float width;
        float length;
        float volume;
   };
   ```

   a. Write a function that passes a **box** structure by value and that displays the value of each member.

   b. Write a function that passes the address of a **box** structure and that sets the **volume** member to the product of the other three dimensions.

   c. Write a simple program that uses these two functions.

4. Many state lotteries use a variation of the simple lottery portrayed by Listing 7.4. In these variations you choose several numbers from one set and call them the field numbers. For example, you might select 5 numbers from the field of 1–47). You also pick a single number (called a mega number or a power ball, etc.) from a second range, such as 1–27. To win the grand prize, you have to guess all the picks correctly. The chance of winning is the product of the probability of picking all the field numbers times the probability of picking the mega number. For instance, the probability of winning the example described here is the product of the probability of picking 5 out of 47 correctly times the probability of picking 1 out of 27 correctly. Modify Listing 7.4 to calculate the probability of winning this kind of lottery.

5. Define a recursive function that takes an integer argument and returns the factorial of that argument. Recall that 3 factorial, written 3!, equals 3 × 2!, and so on, with 0! defined as 1. In general, if n is greater than zero, n! = n * (n − 1)!. Test your function in a program that uses a loop to allow the user to enter various values for which the program reports the factorial.

6. Write a program that uses the following functions:

   Fill_array() takes as arguments the name of an array of **double** values and an array size. It prompts the user to enter **double** values to be entered in the array. It ceases taking input when the array is full or when the user enters non-numeric input, and it returns the actual number of entries.

   Show_array() takes as arguments the name of an array of **double** values and an array size and displays the contents of the array.

   Reverse_array() takes as arguments the name of an array of **double** values and an array size and reverses the order of the values stored in the array.

   The program should use these functions to fill an array, show the array, reverse the array, show the array, reverse all but the first and last elements of the array, and then show the array.

7. Redo Listing 7.7, modifying the three array-handling functions to each use two pointer parameters to represent a range. The **fill_array()** function, instead of returning the actual number of items read, should return a pointer to the location after the last location filled; the other functions can use this pointer as the second argument to identify the end of the data.

8. This exercise provides practice in writing functions dealing with arrays and structures. The following is a program skeleton. Complete it by providing the described functions:

```
#include <iostream>
using namespace std;

const int SLEN = 30;
struct student {
    char fullname[SLEN];
    char hobby[SLEN];
    int ooplevel;
};
// getinfo() has two arguments: a pointer to the first element of
// an array of student structures and an int representing the
// number of elements of the array. The function solicits and
// stores data about students. It terminates input upon filling
// the array or upon encountering a blank line for the student
// name. The function returns the actual number of array elements
// filled.
int getinfo(student pa[], int n);

// display1() takes a student structure as an argument
// and displays its contents
void display1(student st);

// display2() takes the address of student structure as an
// argument and displays the structure's contents
void display2(const student * ps);
```

```
// display3() takes the address of the first element of an array
// of student structures and the number of array elements as
// arguments and displays the contents of the structures
void display3(const student pa[], int n);

int main()
{
    cout << "Enter class size: ";
    int class_size;
    cin >> class_size;
    while (cin.get() != '\n')
        continue;

    student * ptr_stu = new student[class_size];
    int entered = getinfo(ptr_stu, class_size);
    for (int i = 0; i < entered; i++)
    {
        display1(ptr_stu[i]);
        display2(&ptr_stu[i]);
    }
    display3(ptr_stu, entered);
    delete [] ptr_stu;
    cout << "Done\n";
    return 0;
}
```

9. Design a function `calculate()` that takes two type `double` values and a pointer to a function that takes two `double` arguments and returns a `double`. The `calculate()` function should also be type `double`, and it should return the value that the pointed-to function calculates, using the double arguments to `calculate()`. For example, suppose you have this definition for the `add()` function:

```
double add(double x, double y)
{
    return x + y;
}
```

Then, the function call in

```
double q = calculate(2.5, 10.4, add);
```

would cause `calculate()` to pass the values `2.5` and `10.4` to the `add()` function and then return the `add()` return value (`12.9`).

Use these functions and at least one additional function in the `add()` mold in a program. The program should use a loop that allows the user to enter pairs of numbers. For each pair, use `calculate()` to invoke `add()` and at least one other function. If you are feeling adventurous, try creating an array of pointers to `add()`-style functions and use a loop to successively apply `calculate()` to a series of functions by using these pointers. Hint: Here's how to declare such an array of three pointers:

```
double (*pf[3])(double, double);
```

You can initialize such an array by using the usual array initialization syntax and function names as addresses.

CHAPTER 8

ADVENTURES IN FUNCTIONS

In this chapter you'll learn about the following:

- Inline functions

- Reference variables

- How to pass function arguments by reference

- Default arguments

- Function overloading

- Function templates

- Function template specializations

With Chapter 7, "Functions: C++'s Programming Modules," under your belt, you now know a lot about C++ functions, but there's much more to come. C++ provides many new function features that separate C++ from its C heritage. The new features include inline functions, by-reference variable passing, default argument values, function overloading (polymorphism), and template functions. This chapter, more than any other you've read so far, explores features found in C++ but not C, so it marks your first major foray into plus-plussedness.

C++ Inline Functions

Inline functions are a C++ enhancement designed to speed up programs. The primary distinction between normal functions and inline functions is not in how you code them but in how the C++ compiler incorporates them into a program. To understand the distinction between inline functions and normal functions, you need to peer more deeply into a program's innards than we have so far. Let's do that now.

The final product of the compilation process is an executable program, which consists of a set of machine language instructions. When you start a program, the operating system loads these instructions into the computer's memory so that each instruction has a particular memory address. The computer then goes through these instructions step-by-step. Sometimes, as when you have a loop or a branching statement, program execution skips over instructions, jumping backward or forward to a particular address. Normal function calls also involve having a program jump to another address (the function's address) and then jump back when the function terminates. Let's look at a typical implementation of that process in a little more detail. When a program reaches the function call instruction, the program stores the memory address of the instruction immediately following the function call, copies function arguments to the stack (a block of memory reserved for that purpose), jumps to the memory location that marks the beginning of the function, executes the function code (perhaps placing a return value in a register), and then jumps back to the instruction whose address it saved.[1] Jumping back and forth and keeping track of where to jump means that there is an overhead in elapsed time to using functions.

C++ inline functions provide an alternative. In an inline function, the compiled code is "in line" with the other code in the program. That is, the compiler replaces the function call with the corresponding function code. With inline code, the program doesn't have to jump to another location to execute the code and then jump back. Inline functions thus run a little faster than regular functions, but they come with a memory penalty. If a program calls an inline function at 10 separate locations, then the program winds up with 10 copies of the function inserted into the code. (See Figure 8.1.)

FIGURE 8.1

Inline functions versus regular functions.

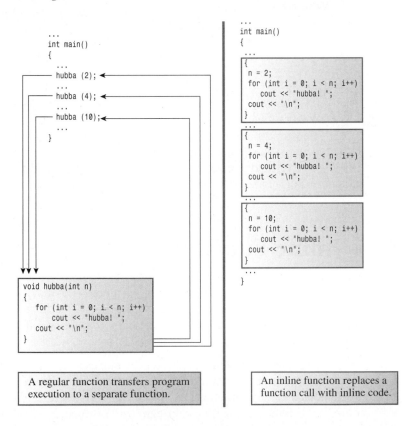

A regular function transfers program execution to a separate function.

An inline function replaces a function call with inline code.

---

[1] It's a bit like having to leave off reading some text to find out what a footnote says and then, upon finishing the footnote, returning to where you were reading in the text.

You should be selective about using inline functions. If the time needed to execute the function code is long compared to the time needed to handle the function call mechanism, then the time saved is a relatively small portion of the entire process. If the code execution time is short, then an inline call can save a large portion of the time used by the non-inline call. On the other hand, you are now saving a large portion of a relatively quick process, so the absolute time savings may not be that great unless the function is called frequently.

To use this feature, you must take at least one of two actions:

- Preface the function declaration with the keyword `inline`.

- Preface the function definition with the keyword `inline`.

A common practice is to omit the prototype and to place the entire definition (meaning the function header and all the function code) where the prototype would normally go.

The compiler does not have to honor your request to make a function inline. It might decide the function is too large or notice that it calls itself (recursion is not allowed or indeed possible for inline functions), or the feature might not be turned on or implemented for your particular compiler.

Listing 8.1 illustrates the inline technique with an inline `square()` function that squares its argument. Note that placed the entire definition is on one line. That's not required, but if the definition doesn't fit on one line, the function is probably a poor candidate for an inline function.

LISTING 8.1   `inline.cpp`

```cpp
// inline.cpp -- using an inline function
#include <iostream>

// an inline function definition
inline double square(double x) { return x * x; }

int main()
{
    using namespace std;
    double a, b;
    double c = 13.0;

    a = square(5.0);
    b = square(4.5 + 7.5);    // can pass expressions
    cout << "a = " << a << ", b = " << b << "\n";
    cout << "c = " << c;
    cout << ", c squared = " << square(c++) << "\n";
    cout << "Now c = " << c << "\n";
    return 0;
}
```

Here's the output of the program in Listing 8.1:

```
a = 25, b = 144
c = 13, c squared = 169
Now c = 14
```

This output illustrates that inline functions pass arguments by value just like regular functions do. If the argument is an expression, such as **4.5 + 7.5**, the function passes the value of the expression—**12** in this case. This makes C++'s inline facility far superior to C's macro definitions. See the "Inline Versus Macros" sidebar.

Even though the program doesn't provide a separate prototype, C++'s prototyping features are still in play. That's because the entire definition, which comes before the function's first use, serves as a prototype. This means you can use **square()** with an **int** argument or a **long** argument, and the program automatically type casts the value to type **double** before passing it to the function.

Inline Versus Macros

The **inline** facility is an addition to C++. C uses the preprocessor **#define** statement to provide *macros*, which are crude implementations of inline code. For example, here's a macro for squaring a number:

```
#define SQUARE(X) X*X
```

This works not by passing arguments but through text substitution, with the X acting as a symbolic label for the "argument":

```
a = SQUARE(5.0); is replaced by a = 5.0*5.0;
b = SQUARE(4.5 + 7.5); is replaced by b = 4.5 + 7.5 * 4.5 + 7.5;
d = SQUARE(c++); is replaced by d = c++*c++;
```

Only the first example here works properly. You can improve matters with a liberal application of parentheses:

```
#define SQUARE(X) ((X)*(X))
```

Still, the problem remains that macros don't pass by value. Even with this new definition, **SQUARE(c++)** increments c twice, but the inline **square()** function in Listing 8.1 evaluates c, passes that value to be squared, and then increments c once.

The intent here is not to show you how to write C macros. Rather, it is to suggest that if you have been using C macros to perform function-like services, you should consider converting them to C++ inline functions.

Reference Variables

C++ adds a new compound type to the language—the reference variable. A *reference* is a name that acts as an alias, or an alternative name, for a previously defined variable. For example, if you make **twain** a reference to the **clemens** variable, you can use **twain** and **clemens** interchangeably to represent that variable. Of what use is such an alias? Is it to help people who are embarrassed by their choice of variable names? Maybe, but the main use for a reference variable is as a formal argument to a function. If you use a reference as an argument, the function works with the original data instead of with a copy. References provide a convenient alternative to pointers for processing large structures with a function, and they are essential for designing classes. Before you see how to use references with functions, however, let's examine the basics of defining and using a reference. Keep in mind that the purpose of the following discussion is to illustrate how references work, not how they are typically used.

Creating a Reference Variable

You might recall that C and C++ use the & symbol to indicate the address of a variable. C++ assigns an additional meaning to the & symbol and presses it into service for declaring references. For example, to make `rodents` an alternative name for the variable `rats`, you could do the following:

```
int rats;
int & rodents = rats;    // makes rodents an alias for rats
```

In this context, & is not the address operator. Instead, it serves as part of the type identifier. Just as `char *` in a declaration means pointer-to-`char`, `int &` means reference-to-`int`. The reference declaration allows you to use `rats` and `rodents` interchangeably; both refer to the same value and the same memory location. Listing 8.2 illustrates the truth of this claim.

LISTING 8.2 `firstref.cpp`

```cpp
// firstref.cpp -- defining and using a reference
#include <iostream>
int main()
{
    using namespace std;
    int rats = 101;
    int & rodents = rats;    // rodents is a reference

    cout << "rats = " << rats;
    cout << ", rodents = " << rodents << endl;
    rodents++;
    cout << "rats = " << rats;
    cout << ", rodents = " << rodents << endl;

// some implementations require type casting the following
// addresses to type unsigned
    cout << "rats address = " << &rats;
    cout << ", rodents address = " << &rodents << endl;
    return 0;
}
```

Note that the & operator in the statement

```
int & rodents = rats;
```

is not the address operator but declares that `rodents` is of type `int &`—that is, it is a reference to an `int` variable. But the `&` operator in the statement

```
cout <<", rodents address = " << &rodents << endl;
```

is the address operator, with `&rodents` representing the address of the variable to which `rodents` refers. Here is the output of the program in Listing 8.2:

```
rats = 101, rodents = 101
rats = 102, rodents = 102
rats address = 0x0065fd48, rodents address = 0x0065fd48
```

As you can see, both `rats` and `rodents` have the same value and the same address. (The address values and display format vary from system to system.) Incrementing `rodents` by one affects both variables. More precisely, the `rodents++` operation increments a single variable for which there are two names. (Again, keep in mind that although this example shows you how a reference works, it doesn't represent the typical use for a reference, which is as a function parameter, particularly for structure and object arguments. We'll look into these uses pretty soon.)

References tend to be a bit confusing at first to C veterans coming to C++ because they are tantalizingly reminiscent of pointers, yet somehow different. For example, you can create both a reference and a pointer to refer to `rats`:

```
int rats = 101;
int & rodents = rats;   // rodents a reference
int * prats = &rats;    // prats a pointer
```

Then, you could use the expressions `rodents` and `*prats` interchangeably with `rats` and use the expressions `&rodents` and `prats` interchangeably with `&rats`. From this standpoint, a reference looks a lot like a pointer in disguised notation in which the `*` dereferencing operator is understood implicitly. And, in fact, that's more or less what a reference is. But there are differences besides those of notation. For one, it is necessary to initialize the reference when you declare it; you can't declare the reference and then assign it a value later the way you can with a pointer:

```
int rat;
int & rodent;
rodent = rat;   // No, you can't do this.
```

Remember

You should initialize a reference variable when you declare it.

A reference is rather like a `const` pointer; you have to initialize it when you create it, and once a reference pledges its allegiance to a particular variable, it sticks to its pledge. That is,

```
int & rodents = rats;
```

is, in essence, a disguised notation for something like this:

```
int * const pr = &rats;
```

Here, the reference `rodents` plays the same role as the expression `*pr`.

Listing 8.3 shows what happens if you try to make a reference change allegiance from a `rats` variable to a `bunnies` variable.

LISTING 8.3 `secref.cpp`

```
// secref.cpp -- defining and using a reference
#include <iostream>
int main()
{
    using namespace std;
    int rats = 101;
    int & rodents = rats;    // rodents is a reference

    cout << "rats = " << rats;
    cout << ", rodents = " << rodents << endl;

    cout << "rats address = " << &rats;
    cout << ", rodents address = " << &rodents << endl;

    int bunnies = 50;
    rodents = bunnies;       // can we change the reference?
    cout << "bunnies = " << bunnies;
    cout << ", rats = " << rats;
    cout << ", rodents = " << rodents << endl;

    cout << "bunnies address = " << &bunnies;
    cout << ", rodents address = " << &rodents << endl;
    return 0;
}
```

Here's the output of the program in Listing 8.3:

```
rats = 101, rodents = 101
rats address = 0x0065fd44, rodents address = 0x0065fd44
bunnies = 50, rats = 50, rodents = 50
bunnies address = 0x0065fd48, rodents address = 0x0065fd4
```

Initially, `rodents` refers to `rats`, but then the program apparently attempts to make `rodents` a reference to `bunnies`:

```
rodents = bunnies;
```

For a moment, it looks as if this attempt has succeeded because the value of `rodents` changes from `101` to `50`. But closer inspection reveals that `rats` also has changed to `50` and that `rats` and `rodents` still share the same address, which differs from the `bunnies` address. Because `rodents` is an alias for `rats`, the assignment statement really means the same as the following:

```
rats = bunnies;
```

That is, it means "Assign the value of the `bunnies` variable to the `rat` variable." In short, you can set a reference by an initializing declaration, not by assignment.

Suppose you tried the following:

```
int rats = 101;
int * pt = &rats;
int & rodents = *pt;
int bunnies = 50;
pt = &bunnies;
```

Initializing `rodents` to `*pt` makes `rodents` refer to `rats`. Subsequently altering `pt` to point to `bunnies` does not alter the fact that `rodents` refers to `rats`.

References as Function Parameters

Most often, references are used as function parameters, making a variable name in a function an alias for a variable in the calling program. This method of passing arguments is called *passing by reference*. Passing by reference allows a called function to access variables in the calling function. C++'s addition of the feature is a break from C, which only passes by value. Passing by value, recall, results in the called function working with copies of values from the calling program. (See Figure 8.2.) Of course, C lets you get around the passing by value limitation by using pointers.

FIGURE 8.2

Passing by value and passing by reference.

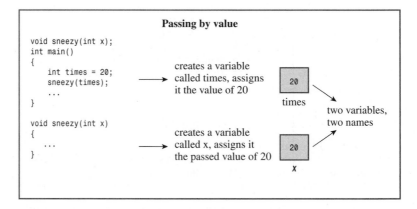

Let's compare using references and using pointers in a common computer problem: swapping the values of two variables. A swapping function has to be able to alter values of variables in the calling program. That means the usual approach of passing variables by value won't work because the function will end up swapping the contents of copies of the original variables instead of the variables themselves. If you pass references, however, the function can work with the original data. Alternatively, you can pass pointers in order to access the original data. Listing 8.4 shows all three methods, including the one that doesn't work, so that you can compare them.

LISTING 8.4   swaps.cpp

```cpp
// swaps.cpp -- swapping with references and with pointers
#include <iostream>
void swapr(int & a, int & b);    // a, b are aliases for ints
void swapp(int * p, int * q);    // p, q are addresses of ints
void swapv(int a, int b);        // a, b are new variables
int main()
{
    using namespace std;
    int wallet1 = 300;
    int wallet2 = 350;

    cout << "wallet1 = $" << wallet1;
    cout << " wallet2 = $" << wallet2 << endl;

    cout << "Using references to swap contents:\n";
    swapr(wallet1, wallet2);    // pass variables
    cout << "wallet1 = $" << wallet1;
    cout << " wallet2 = $" << wallet2 << endl;

    cout << "Using pointers to swap contents again:\n";
    swapp(&wallet1, &wallet2); // pass addresses of variables
    cout << "wallet1 = $" << wallet1;
    cout << " wallet2 = $" << wallet2 << endl;

    cout << "Trying to use passing by value:\n";
    swapv(wallet1, wallet2);    // pass values of variables
    cout << "wallet1 = $" << wallet1;
    cout << " wallet2 = $" << wallet2 << endl;
    return 0;
}

void swapr(int & a, int & b)     // use references
{
    int temp;

    temp = a;        // use a, b for values of variables
    a = b;
    b = temp;
}
```

LISTING 8.4   Continued

```
void swapp(int * p, int * q)     // use pointers
{
    int temp;

    temp = *p;      // use *p, *q for values of variables
    *p = *q;
    *q = temp;
}

void swapv(int a, int b)         // try using values
{
    int temp;

    temp = a;       // use a, b for values of variables
    a = b;
    b = temp;
}
```

Here's the output of the program in Listing 8.4:

```
wallet1 = $300 wallet2 = $350             ← original values
Using references to swap contents:
wallet1 = $350 wallet2 = $300             ← values swapped
Using pointers to swap contents again:
wallet1 = $300 wallet2 = $350             ← values swapped again
Trying to use passing by value:
wallet1 = $300 wallet2 = $350             ← swap failed
```

As you'd expect, the reference and pointer methods both successfully swap the contents of the two wallets, whereas the passing by value method fails.

Program Notes

First, note how each function in Listing 8.4 is called:

```
swapr(wallet1, wallet2);        // pass variables
swapp(&wallet1, &wallet2);      // pass addresses of variables
swapv(wallet1, wallet2);        // pass values of variables
```

Passing by reference (`swapr(wallet1, wallet2)`) and passing by value (`swapv(wallet1, wallet2)`) look identical. The only way you can tell that `swapr()` passes by reference is by looking at the prototype or the function definition. However, the presence of the address operator (`&`) makes it obvious when a function passes by address (`(swapp(&wallet1, &wallet2)`). (Recall that the type declaration `int *p` means that `p` is a pointer to an `int` and therefore the argument corresponding to `p` should be an address, such as `&wallet1`.)

Next, compare the code for the functions `swapr()` (passing by reference) and `swapv()` (passing by value). The only outward difference between the two is how the function parameters are declared:

```
void swapr(int & a, int & b)
void swapv(int a, int b)
```

The internal difference, of course, is that in `swapr()` the variables a and b serve as aliases for `wallet1` and `wallet2`, so swapping a and b swaps `wallet1` and `wallet2`. But in `swapv()`, the variables a and b are new variables that copy the values of `wallet1` and `wallet2`, so swapping a and b has no effect on `wallet1` and `wallet2`.

Finally, compare the functions `swapr()` (passing a reference) and `swapp()` (passing a pointer). The first difference is in how the function parameters are declared:

```
void swapr(int & a, int & b)
void swapp(int * p, int * q)
```

The second difference is that the pointer version requires using the * dereferencing operator throughout when the function uses p and q.

Earlier, I said you should initialize a reference variable when you define it. You can consider reference function arguments as being initialized to the argument passed by the function call. That is, the function call

```
swapr(wallet1, wallet2);
```

initializes the formal parameter a to `wallet1` and the formal parameter b to `wallet2`.

Reference Properties and Oddities

Using reference arguments has several twists you need to know about. First, consider Listing 8.5. It uses two functions to cube an argument. One takes a type `double` argument, and the other takes a reference to `double`. The actual code for cubing is purposefully a bit odd to illustrate a point.

LISTING 8.5 `cubes.cpp`

```cpp
// cubes.cpp -- regular and reference arguments
#include <iostream>
double cube(double a);
double refcube(double &ra);
int main ()
{
    using namespace std;
    double x = 3.0;

    cout << cube(x);
    cout << " = cube of " << x << endl;
    cout << refcube(x);
    cout << " = cube of " << x << endl;
    return 0;
}

double cube(double a)
{
    a *= a * a;
    return a;
}
```

LISTING 8.5   *Continued*

```
double refcube(double &ra)
{
    ra *= ra * ra;
    return ra;
}
```

Here is the output of the program in Listing 8.5:

```
27 = cube of 3
27 = cube of 27
```

Note that the `refcube()` function modifies the value of x in `main()` and `cube()` doesn't, which reminds you why passing by value is the norm. The variable a is local to `cube()`. It is initialized to the value of x, but changing a has no effect on x. But because `refcube()` uses a reference argument, the changes it makes to `ra` are actually made to x. If your intent is that a function use the information passed to it without modifying the information, and if you're using a reference, you should use a constant reference. Here, for example, you should use `const` in the function prototype and function header:

```
double refcube(const double &ra);
```

If you do this, the compiler generates an error message when it finds code altering the value of `ra`.

Incidentally, if you need to write a function along the lines of this example, you should use passing by value rather than the more exotic passing by reference. Reference arguments become useful with larger data units, such as structures and classes, as you'll soon see.

Functions that pass by value, such as the `cube()` function in Listing 8.5, can use many kinds of actual arguments. For example, all the following calls are valid:

```
double z = cube(x + 2.0);    // evaluate x + 2.0, pass value
z = cube(8.0);               // pass the value 8.0
int k = 10;
z = cube(k);                 // convert value of k to double, pass value
double yo[3] = { 2.2, 3.3, 4.4};
z = cube (yo[2]);            // pass the value 4.4
```

Suppose you try similar arguments for a function with a reference parameter. It would seem that passing a reference should be more restrictive. After all, if `ra` is the alternative name for a variable, then the actual argument should be that variable. Something like

```
double z = refcube(x + 3.0);  // may not compile
```

doesn't appear to make sense because the expression x + 3.0 is not a variable. For example, you can't assign a value to such an expression:

```
x + 3.0 = 5.0;   // nonsensical
```

What happens if you try a function call like `refcube(x + 3.0)`? In contemporary C++, that's an error, and some compilers will tell you so. Others give you a warning along the following lines:

```
Warning: Temporary used for parameter 'ra' in call to refcube(double &)
```

The reason for this milder response is that C++, in its early years, did allow you to pass expressions to a reference variable. In some cases, it still does. What happens is that because x + 3.0 is not a type double variable, the program creates a temporary, nameless variable, initializing it to the value of the expression x + 3.0. Then, ra becomes a reference to that temporary variable. Let's take a closer look at temporary variables and see when they are and are not created.

Temporary Variables, Reference Arguments, and const

C++ can generate a temporary variable if the actual argument doesn't match a reference argument. Currently, C++ permits this only if the argument is a const reference, but this is a new restriction. Let's look at the cases in which C++ does generate temporary variables and see why the restriction to a const reference makes sense.

First, when is a temporary variable created? Provided that the reference parameter is a const, the compiler generates a temporary variable in two kinds of situations:

- When the actual argument is the correct type but isn't an lvalue

- When the actual argument is of the wrong type, but it's of a type that can be converted to the correct type

An argument that's an *lvalue* is a data object that can be referenced. For example, a variable, an array element, a structure member, a reference, and a dereferenced pointer are lvalues. Non-lvalues include literal constants and expressions with multiple terms. For example, suppose you redefine refcube() so that it has a constant reference argument:

```
double refcube(const double &ra)
{
    return ra * ra * ra;
}
```

Now consider the following code:

```
double side = 3.0;
double * pd = &side;
double & rd = side;
long edge = 5L;
double lens[4] = { 2.0, 5.0, 10.0, 12.0};
double c1 = refcube(side);        // ra is side
double c2 = refcube(lens[2]);     // ra is lens[2]
double c3 = refcube(rd);          // ra is rd is side
double c4 = refcube(*pd);         // ra is *pd is side
double c5 = refcube(edge);        // ra is temporary variable
double c6 = refcube(7.0);         // ra is temporary variable
double c7 = refcube(side + 10.0); // ra is temporary variable
```

The arguments side, lens[2], rd, and *pd are type double data objects with names, so it is possible to generate a reference for them, and no temporary variables are needed. (Recall that an element of an array behaves like a variable of the same type as the element.) But although edge is a variable, it is of the wrong type. A reference to a double can't refer to a long. The arguments 7.0 and side + 10.0, on the other hand, are the right type, but they are not named data objects. In each of these cases, the compiler generates a temporary, anonymous variable and makes `ra` refer to it. These temporary variables last for the duration of the function call, but then the compiler is free to dump them.

So why is this behavior okay for constant references but not otherwise? Recall the `swapr()` function from Listing 8.4:

```
void swapr(int & a, int & b)   // use references
{
    int temp;

    temp = a;      // use a, b for values of variables
    a = b;
    b = temp;
}
```

What would happen if you did the following under the freer rules of early C++?

```
long a = 3, b = 5;
swapr(a, b);
```

Here there is a type mismatch, so the compiler would create two temporary `int` variables, initialize them to 3 and 5, and then swap the contents of the temporary variables, leaving `a` and `b` unaltered.

In short, if the intent of a function with reference arguments is to modify variables passed as arguments, situations that create temporary variables thwart that purpose. The solution is to prohibit creating temporary variables in these situations, and that is what the C++ Standard now does. (However, some compilers still, by default, issue warnings instead of error messages, so if you see a warning about temporary variables, don't ignore it.)

Now think about the `refcube()` function. Its intent is merely to use passed values, not to modify them, so temporary variables cause no harm and make the function more general in the sorts of arguments it can handle. Therefore, if the declaration states that a reference is `const`, C++ generates temporary variables when necessary. In essence, a C++ function with a `const` reference formal argument and a nonmatching actual argument mimics the traditional passing by value behavior, guaranteeing that the original data is unaltered and using a temporary variable to hold the value.

Remember

If a function call argument isn't an `lvalue` or does not match the type of the corresponding `const` reference parameter, C++ creates an anonymous variable of the correct type, assigns the value of the function call argument to the anonymous variable, and has the parameter refer to that variable.

Use const When You Can

There are three strong reasons to declare reference arguments as references to constant data:

- Using const protects you against programming errors that inadvertently alter data.
- Using const allows a function to process both const and non-const actual arguments, whereas a function that omits const in the prototype only can accept non-const data.
- Using a const reference allows the function to generate and use a temporary variable appropriately.

You should declare formal reference arguments as const whenever it's appropriate to do so.

Using References with a Structure

References work wonderfully with structures and classes, C++'s user-defined types. Indeed, references were introduced primarily for use with these types, not for use with the basic built-in types.

The method for using a reference to a structure is the same as the method for using a reference to a basic variable: You just use the & reference operator when declaring a structure parameter. The program in Listing 8.6 does exactly that. It also adds an interesting twist by having a function return a reference to the structure. This works a bit differently from returning a structure. There are some cautions to note, and often it is best to make the returned reference a const. I'll explain these points during the next few examples. The program has a use() function that displays two members of a structure and increments a third member. Thus, the third member can keep track of how many times a particular structure has been handled by the use() function.

LISTING 8.6   strtref.cpp

```cpp
// strtref.cpp -- using structure references
#include <iostream>
using namespace std;
struct sysop
{
    char name[26];
    char quote[64];
    int used;
};

const sysop & use(sysop & sysopref);  // function with a reference return type

int main()
{
// NOTE: some implementations require using the keyword static
// in the two structure declarations to enable initialization
    sysop looper =
    {
        "Rick \"Fortran\" Looper",
        "I'm a goto kind of guy.",
```

LISTING 8.6   Continued

```
        0
    };

    use(looper);            // looper is type sysop
    cout << "Looper: " << looper.used << " use(s)\n";
    sysop copycat;
    copycat = use(looper);
    cout << "Looper: " << looper.used << " use(s)\n";
    cout << "Copycat: " << copycat.used << " use(s)\n";
    cout << "use(looper): " << use(looper).used << " use(s)\n";
    return 0;
}

// use() returns the reference passed to it
const sysop & use(sysop & sysopref)
{
    cout << sysopref.name << " says:\n";
    cout << sysopref.quote << endl;
    sysopref.used++;
    return sysopref;
}
```

Here's the output of the program in Listing 8.6:

```
Rick "Fortran" Looper says:
I'm a goto kind of guy.
Looper: 1 use(s)
Rick "Fortran" Looper says:
I'm a goto kind of guy.
Looper: 2 use(s)
Copycat: 2 use(s)
Rick "Fortran" Looper says:
I'm a goto kind of guy.
use(looper): 3 use(s)
```

Program Notes

The program in Listing 8.6 ventures into three new areas. The first is using a reference to a structure, illustrated by the first function call:

```
use(looper);
```

It passes the structure `looper` by reference to the `use()` function, making `sysopref` a synonym for `looper`. When the `use()` function displays the `name` and `quote` members of `sysopref`, it really displays the members of `looper`. Also, when the function increments `sysopref.used` to 1, it really increments `looper.used`, as the program output shows:

```
Rick "Fortran" Looper says:
I'm a goto kind of guy.
1 use(s)
```

The second new area is using a reference as a return value. Normally, the return mechanism copies the returned value to a temporary storage area, which the calling program then accesses. Returning a reference, however, means that the calling program accesses the return value directly, without there being a copy. Typically, the reference refers to a reference passed to the function in the first place, so the calling function actually winds up directly accessing one of its own variables. Here, for example, `sysopref` is a reference to `looper`, so the return value is the original `looper` variable in `main()`. Consider this line of code:

```
copycat = use(looper);
```

If the `use()` function simply returned a structure, the contents of `sysopref` would be copied to a temporary return location, and then the contents of the temporary return location would be copied to `copycat`. But because `use()` returns a reference to `looper`, in this case the contents of `looper` are copied directly to `copycat`. This illustrates one of the main benefits of returning a reference to a structure instead of returning a structure: efficiency.

Remember

A function that returns a reference is actually an alias for the referred-to variable.

The third new area is that the program uses the function call to access a structure member:

```
cout << "use(looper): " << use(looper).used << " use(s)\n";
```

Because `use()` returns a reference to `looper`, this line has the same effect as the following two:

```
use(looper);
cout << "use(looper): " << looper.used << " use(s)\n";
```

The notation `use(looper).used` accesses the `used` member of `looper`. If the function returned a structure instead of a reference to a structure, the code would access the `used` member of the temporary return copy of `looper`.

Being Careful About What a Return Reference Refers To

The single most important point to remember when returning a reference is avoid returning a reference to a memory location that ceases to exist when the function terminates. What you want to avoid is code along these lines:

```
const sysop & clone2(sysop & sysopref)
{
     sysop newguy;          // first step to big error
     newguy = sysopref;     // copy info
     return newguy;         // return reference to copy
}
```

This has the unfortunate effect of returning a reference to a temporary variable (`newguy`) that passes from existence as soon as the function terminates. (Chapter 9, "Memory Models and Namespaces," discusses the persistence of various kinds of variables.) Similarly, you should avoid returning pointers to such temporary variables.

The simplest way to avoid this problem is to return a reference that was passed as an argument to the function. A reference parameter will refer to data used by the calling function, hence the returned reference will refer to that same data.

A second method is to use new to create new storage. You've already seen examples in which new creates space for a string and the function returns a pointer to that space. Here's how you could do something similar with a reference:

```
const sysop & clone(sysop & sysopref)
{
    sysop * psysop = new sysop;
    *psysop = sysopref;   // copy info
    return *psysop;       // return reference to copy
}
```

The first statement creates a nameless **sysop** structure. The pointer **psysop** points to the structure, so *psysop is the structure. The code appears to return the structure, but the function declaration indicates that the function really returns a reference to this structure. You could then use the function this way:

```
sysop & jolly = clone(looper);
```

This makes **jolly** a reference to the new structure. There is a problem with this approach: You should use **delete** to free memory allocated by **new** when the memory is no longer needed. A call to **clone()** hides the call to **new**, making it simpler to forget to use **delete** later. The **auto_ptr** template discussed in Chapter 16, "The **string** Class and the Standard Template Library," can help automate the deletion process.

Why Use const with a Reference Return?

The **use()** function return type in the preceding example is **const sysop &**. You may be wondering about the purpose of **const** in this usage. It doesn't mean that the **sysop** structure itself is **const**; it just means that you can't use the return value directly to modify the structure. For instance, if you omitted **const**, you could use code like this:

```
use(looper).used = 10;
```

Because **use()** returns a reference to **looper**, this code would have the same effect as the following:

```
use(looper);          // display structure, increment used member
looper.used = 10;     // reset used member to 10
```

Or you could use this:

```
sysop newgal = {"Polly Morf", "Polly's not a hacker.", 0};
use(looper) = newgal;
```

This would have the same effect as the following:

```
sysop newgal = {"Polly Morf", "Polly's not a hacker.", 0};
use(looper);          // display structure, increment used member
looper = newgal;      // replace looper contents with newgal contents
```

In short, by omitting **const**, you can write shorter but more obscure-looking code.

Usually, you're better off avoiding the addition of obscure features to a design because obscure features often expand the opportunities to make obscure errors. Making the return type a `const` reference thus protects you from the temptation of obfuscation. Occasionally, omitting `const` does make sense. The overloaded `<<` operator discussed in Chapter 11, "Working with Classes," is an example.

Using References with a Class Object

The usual C++ practice for passing class objects to a function is to use references. For instance, you would use reference parameters for functions taking objects of the `string`, `ostream`, `istream`, `ofstream`, and `ifstream` classes as arguments.

Let's look at an example that uses the `string` class and illustrates some different design choices, some of them bad. The general idea is to create a function that adds a given string to each end of another string. Listing 8.7 provides three functions that are intended to do this. However, one of the designs is so flawed that it may cause the program to crash or even not compile.

LISTING 8.7   `strquote.cpp`

```cpp
// strquote.cpp  -- different designs
#include <iostream>
#include <string>
using namespace std;
string version1(const string & s1, const string & s2);
const string & version2(string & s1, const string & s2);  // has side effect
const string & version3(string & s1, const string & s2);  // bad design

int main()
{
    string input;
    string copy;
    string result;

    cout << "Enter a string: ";
    getline(cin, input);
    copy = input;
    cout << "Your string as entered: " << input << endl;
    result = version1(input, "***");
    cout << "Your string enhanced: " << result << endl;
    cout << "Your original string: " << input << endl;

    result = version2(input, "###");
    cout << "Your string enhanced: " << result << endl;
    cout << "Your original string: " << input << endl;

    cout << "Resetting original string.\n";
    input = copy;
    result = version3(input, "@@@");
    cout << "Your string enhanced: " << result << endl;
    cout << "Your original string: " << input << endl;
```

LISTING 8.7   Continued

```
    return 0;
}

string version1(const string & s1, const string & s2)
{
    string temp;

    temp = s2 + s1 + s2;;
    return temp;
}

const string & version2(string & s1, const string & s2)    // has side effect
{
    s1 = s2 + s1 + s2;
// safe to return reference passed to function
    return s1;
}

const string & version3(string & s1, const string & s2)    // bad design
{
    string temp;

    temp = s2 + s1 + s2;
// unsafe to return reference to local variable
    return temp;
}
```

Here is a sample run of the program in Listing 8.7:

```
Enter a string: It's not my fault.
Your string as entered: It's not my fault.
Your string enhanced: ***It's not my fault.***
Your original string: It's not my fault.
Your string enhanced: ###It's not my fault.###
Your original string: ###It's not my fault.###
Resetting original string.
```

At this point the program crashes.

Program Notes

Version 1 of the function in Listing 8.7 is the most straightforward of the three:

```
string version1(const string & s1, const string & s2)
{
    string temp;

    temp = s2 + s1 + s2;;
    return temp;
}
```

It takes two **string** arguments and uses **string** class addition to create a new string that has the desired properties. Note that the two function arguments are **const** references. The function would produce the same end result if it just passed **string** objects:

```
string version4(string s1, string & s2)  // would work the same
```

In this case, **s1** and **s2** would be brand-new **string** objects. Thus, using references is more efficient because the function doesn't have to create new objects and copy data from the old objects to the new. The use of the **const** qualifier indicates that this function will use, but not modify, the original strings.

The **temp** object is a new object, local to the **version1()** function, and it ceases to exist when the function terminates. Thus, returning **temp** as a reference won't work, so the function type is **string**. This means the contents of **temp** will be copied to a temporary return location. Then, in **main()**, the contents of the return location are copied to the string named **result**:

```
result = version1(input, "***");
```

Passing a C-Style String Argument to a `string` Object Reference Parameter

You may have noticed a rather interesting fact about the version1() function: Both formal parameters (s1 and s2) are type const string &, but the actual arguments (input and "***") are type string and const char *, respectively. Because input is type string, there is no problem having s1 refer to it. But how is it that the program accepts passing a pointer-to-char argument to a string reference?

Two things are going on here. One is that the string class defines a char *-to-string conversion, which makes it possible to initialize a string object to a C-style string. The second is a property of const reference formal parameters that is discussed earlier in this chapter. Suppose the actual argument type doesn't match the reference parameter type but can be converted to the reference type. Then the program creates a temporary variable of the correct type, initializes it to the converted value, and passes a reference to the temporary variable. Earlier this chapter you saw, for instance, that a const double & parameter can handle an int argument in this fashion. Similarly, a const string & parameter can handle a char * or const char * argument in this fashion.

The convenient outcome of this is that if the formal parameter is type const string &, the actual argument used in the function call can be a string object or a C-style string, such as a quoted string literal, a null-terminated array of char, or a pointer variable that points to a char. Hence the following works fine:

```
result = version1(input, "***");
```

The **version2()** function doesn't create a temporary string. Instead, it directly alters the original string:

```
const string & version2(string & s1, const string & s2)   // has side effect
{
    s1 = s2 + s1 + s2;
// safe to return reference passed to function
    return s1;
}
```

This function is allowed to alter **s1** because **s1**, unlike **s2**, is not declared using **const**.

Because `s1` is a reference to an object (`input`) in `main()`, it's safe to return `s1` as a reference. Because `s1` is a reference to `input`, the line

```
result = version2(input, "###");
```

essentially becomes equivalent to the following:

```
version2(input, "###");      // input altered directly by version2()
result = input;              // reference to s1 is reference to input
```

However, because `s1` is a reference to `input`, calling this function has the side effect of altering `input` also:

```
Your original string: It's not my fault.
Your string enhanced: ###It's not my fault.###
Your original string: ###It's not my fault.###
```

Thus, if you want to keep the original string unaltered, this is the wrong design.

The third version in Listing 8.7 is a reminder of what not to do:

```
const string & version3(string & s1, const string & s2)    // bad design
{
    string temp;

    temp = s2 + s1 + s2;
// unsafe to return reference to local variable
    return temp;
}
```

It has the fatal flaw of returning a reference to a variable declared locally inside `version3()`. This function compiles (with a warning), but the program crashes when attempting to execute the function. Specifically, the assignment aspect of

```
result = version3(input, "@@@");
```

causes the problem. The program attempts to refer to memory that is no longer in use.

Another Object Lesson: Objects, Inheritance, and References

The `ostream` and `ofstream` classes bring an interesting property of references to the fore. As you may recall from Chapter 6, "Branching Statements and Logical Operators," objects of the `ofstream` type can use `ostream` methods, allowing file input/output to use the same forms as console input/output. The language feature that makes it possible to pass features from one class to another is called *inheritance*, and Chapter 13, "Class Inheritance," discusses this feature in detail. In brief, `ostream` is termed a base class (because the `ofstream` class is based on it) and `ofstream` is termed a *derived class* (because it is derived from `ostream`). A derived class inherits the base class methods, which means that an `ofstream` object can use base class features such as the `precision()` and `setf()` formatting methods.

Another aspect of inheritance is that a base class reference can refer to a derived class object without requiring a type cast. The practical upshot of this is that you can define a function having a base class reference parameter, and that function can be used with base class objects and also with derived objects. For example, a function with a type `ostream &` parameter can accept an `ostream` object, such as `cout`, or an `ofstream` object, such as you might declare, equally well.

Listing 8.8 demonstrates this point by using the same function to write data to a file and to display the data onscreen; only the function call argument is changed. This program solicits the focal length of a telescope objective (its main mirror or lens) and of some eyepieces. Then it calculates and displays the magnification each eyepiece would produce in that telescope. The magnification equals the focal length of the telescope divided by the focal length of the eyepiece used, so the calculation is simple. The program also uses some formatting methods, which, as promised, work equally well with `cout` and with `ofstream` objects (`fout`, in this example).

LISTING 8.8 `filefunc.cpp`

```cpp
//filefunc.cpp -- function with ostream & parameter
#include <iostream>
#include <fstream>
#include <cstdlib>
using namespace std;

void file_it(ostream & os, double fo, const double fe[],int n);
const int LIMIT = 5;
int main(void)
{
    ofstream fout;
    const char * fn = "ep-data.txt";
    fout.open(fn);
    if (!fout.is_open())
    {
        cout << "Can't open " << fn << ". Bye.\n";
        exit(EXIT_FAILURE);
    }
    double objective;
    cout << "Enter the focal length of your "
            "telescope objective in mm: ";
    cin >> objective;
    double eps[LIMIT];
    cout << "Enter the focal lengths, in mm, of " << LIMIT << " eyepieces:\n";
    for (int i = 0; i < LIMIT; i++)
    {
        cout << "Eyepiece #" << i + 1 << ": ";
        cin >> eps[i];
    }
    file_it(fout, objective, eps, LIMIT);
    file_it(cout, objective, eps, LIMIT);
    cout << "Done\n";
    return 0;
}
```

LISTING 8.8   *Continued*

```
void file_it(ostream & os, double fo, const double fe[],int n)
{
    ios_base::fmtflags initial;
    initial = os.setf(ios_base::fixed); // save initial formatting state
    os.precision(0);
    os << "Focal length of objective: " << fo << " mm\n";
    os.setf(ios::showpoint);
    os.precision(1);
    os.width(12);
    os << "f eyepiece";
    os.width(15);
    os << "magnification" << endl;
    for (int i = 0; i < n; i++)
    {
        os.width(12);
        os << fe[i];
        os.width(15);
        os << int (fo/fe[i] + 0.5) << endl;
    }
    os.setf(initial);    // restore initial formatting state
}
```

Here is a sample run of the program in Listing 8.8:

```
Enter the focal length of your telescope objective in mm: 1800
Enter the focal lengths, in mm, of 5 eyepieces:
Eyepiece #1: 30
Eyepiece #2: 19
Eyepiece #3: 14
Eyepiece #4: 8.8
Eyepiece #5: 7.5
Focal length of objective: 1800 mm
  f eyepiece   magnification
        30.0             60
        19.0             95
        14.0            129
         8.8            205
         7.5            240
Done
```

The line

```
file_it(fout, objective, eps, LIMIT);
```

writes the eyepiece data to the file **ep-data.txt**, and the line

```
file_it(cout, objective, eps, LIMIT);
```

writes the identical information in the identical format to the screen.

Program Notes

The main point of Listing 8.8 is that the **os** parameter, which is type **ostream &**, can refer to an **ostream** object such as **cout** and to an **ofstream** object such as **fout**. But the program also illustrates how `ostream` formatting methods can be used for both types. Let's review, or, in some cases, examine for the first time, some of these methods. (Chapter 17, "Input, Output, and Files," provides a fuller discussion.)

The `setf()` method allows you to set various formatting states. For example, the method call `setf(ios_base::fixed)` places an object in the mode of using fixed decimal-point notation. The call `setf(ios_base:showpoint)` places an object in the mode of showing a trailing decimal point, even if the following digits are zeros. The `precision()` method indicates the number of figures to be shown to the right of the decimal (provided that the object is in `fixed` mode). All these settings stay in place unless they're reset by another method call. The `width()` call sets the field width to be used for the next output action. This setting holds for displaying one value only, and then it reverts to the default. (The default is a field width of zero, which is then expanded to just fit the actual quantity being displayed.)

The `file_it()` function uses an interesting pair of method calls:

```
ios_base::fmtflags initial;
initial = os.setf(ios_base::fixed); // save initial formatting state
...
os.setf(initial);   // restore initial formatting state
```

The `setf()` method returns a copy of all the formatting settings in effect before the call was made. `ios_base::fmtflags` is a fancy name for the type needed to store this information. So the assignment to `initial` stores the settings that were in place before the `file_it()` function was called. The `initial` variable can then be used as an argument to `setf()` to reset all the formatting settings to this original value. Thus, the function restores the object to the state it had before being passed to `file_it()`.

Knowing more about classes will help you understand better how these methods work and, why, for example, `ios_base` keeps popping up. But you don't have to wait until Chapter 17 to use these methods.

One final point: Each object stores its own formatting settings. So when the program passes `cout` to `file_it()`, `cout`'s settings are altered and then restored. When the program passes `fout` to `file_it()`, `fout`'s settings are altered and then restored.

When to Use Reference Arguments

There are two main reasons for using reference arguments:

- To allow you to alter a data object in the calling function

- To speed up a program by passing a reference instead of an entire data object

The second reason is most important for larger data objects, such as structures and class objects. These two reasons are the same reasons you might have for using a pointer argument. This makes sense because reference arguments are really just a different interface for pointer-based code. So when should you use a reference? use a pointer? pass by value? The following are some guidelines.

A function uses passed data without modifying it:

- If the data object is small, such as a built-in data type or a small structure, pass it by value.

- If the data object is an array, use a pointer because that's your only choice. Make the pointer a pointer to `const`.

- If the data object is a good-sized structure, use a `const` pointer or a `const` reference to increase program efficiency. You save the time and space needed to copy a structure or a class design. Make the pointer or reference `const`.

- If the data object is a class object, use a `const` reference. The semantics of class design often require using a reference, which is the main reason C++ added this feature. Thus, the standard way to pass class object arguments is by reference.

A function modifies data in the calling function:

- If the data object is a built-in data type, use a pointer. If you spot code like `fixit(&x)`, where x is an `int`, it's pretty clear that this function intends to modify x.

- If the data object is an array, use your only choice: a pointer.

- If the data object is a structure, use a reference or a pointer.

- If the data object is a class object, use a reference.

Of course, these are just guidelines, and there might be reasons for making different choices. For example, `cin` uses references for basic types so that you can use `cin >> n` instead of `cin >> &n`.

Default Arguments

Let's look at another topic from C++'s bag of new tricks: the default argument. A *default argument* is a value that's used automatically if you omit the corresponding actual argument from a function call. For example, if you set up `void wow(int n)` so that n has a default value of `1`, the function call `wow()` is the same as `wow(1)`. This gives you flexibility in how you use a function. Suppose you have a function called `left()` that returns the first n characters of a string, with the string and n as arguments. More precisely, the function returns a pointer to a new string consisting of the selected portion of the original string. For example, the call `left("theory", 3)` constructs a new string `"the"` and returns a pointer to it. Now suppose you establish a default value of `1` for the second argument. The call `left("theory", 3)` would work as before, with your choice of `3` overriding the default. But the call `left("theory")`, instead of being an error, would assume a second argument of `1` and return a pointer to the string `"t"`. This kind of default is helpful if your program often needs to extract a one-character string but occasionally needs to extract longer strings.

How do you establish a default value? You must use the function prototype. Because the compiler looks at the prototype to see how many arguments a function uses, the function prototype also has to alert the program to the possibility of default arguments. The method is to assign a value to the argument in the prototype. For example, here's the prototype fitting this description of left():

```
char * left(const char * str, int n = 1);
```

You want the function to return a new string, so its type is char*, or pointer-to-char. You want to leave the original string unaltered, so you use the const qualifier for the first argument. You want n to have a default value of 1, so you assign that value to n. A default argument value is an initialization value. Thus, the preceding prototype initializes n to the value 1. If you leave n alone, it has the value 1, but if you pass an argument, the new value overwrites the 1.

When you use a function with an argument list, you must add defaults from right to left. That is, you can't provide a default value for a particular argument unless you also provide defaults for all the arguments to its right:

```
int harpo(int n, int m = 4, int j = 5);        // VALID
int chico(int n, int m = 6, int j);            // INVALID
int groucho(int k = 1, int m = 2, int n = 3);  // VALID
```

For example, the harpo() prototype permits calls with one, two, or three arguments:

```
beeps = harpo(2);       // same as harpo(2,4,5)
beeps = harpo(1,8);     // same as harpo(1,8,5)
beeps = harpo (8,7,6);  // no default arguments used
```

The actual arguments are assigned to the corresponding formal arguments from left to right; you can't skip over arguments. Thus, the following isn't allowed:

```
beeps = harpo(3, ,8);    // invalid, doesn't set m to 4
```

Default arguments aren't a major programming breakthrough; rather, they are a convenience. When you begin working with class design, you'll find that they can reduce the number of constructors, methods, and method overloads you have to define.

Listing 8.9 puts default arguments to use. Note that only the prototype indicates the default. The function definition is the same as it would be without default arguments.

LISTING 8.9   left.cpp

```
// left.cpp -- string function with a default argument
#include <iostream>
const int ArSize = 80;
char * left(const char * str, int n = 1);
int main()
{
    using namespace std;
    char sample[ArSize];
    cout << "Enter a string:\n";
    cin.get(sample,ArSize);
    char *ps = left(sample, 4);
    cout << ps << endl;
```

LISTING 8.9   *Continued*

```
    delete [] ps;        // free old string
    ps = left(sample);
    cout << ps << endl;
    delete [] ps;        // free new string
    return 0;
}

// This function returns a pointer to a new string
// consisting of the first n characters in the str string.
char * left(const char * str, int n)
{
    if(n < 0)
        n = 0;
    char * p = new char[n+1];
    int i;
    for (i = 0; i < n && str[i]; i++)
        p[i] = str[i];   // copy characters
    while (i <= n)
        p[i++] = '\0';   // set rest of string to '\0'
    return p;
}
```

Here's a sample run of the program in Listing 8.9:

```
Enter a string:
forthcoming
fort
f
```

Program Notes

The program in Listing 8.9 uses **new** to create a new string for holding the selected characters. One awkward possibility is that an uncooperative user may request a negative number of characters. In that case, the function sets the character count to **0** and eventually returns the null string. Another awkward possibility is that an irresponsible user may request more characters than the string contains. The function protects against this by using a combined test:

```
i < n && str[i]
```

The `i < n` test stops the loop after **n** characters have been copied. The second part of the test, the expression `str[i]`, is the code for the character about to be copied. If the loop reaches the null character, the code is **0**, and the loop terminates. The final **while** loop terminates the string with the null character and then sets the rest of the allocated space, if any, to null characters.

Another approach for setting the size of the new string is to set **n** to the smaller of the passed value and the string length:

```
int len = strlen(str);
n = (n < len) ? n : len;    // the lesser of n and len
char * p = new char[n+1];
```

This ensures that `new` doesn't allocate more space than what's needed to hold the string. That can be useful if you make a call such as `left("Hi!", 32767)`. The first approach copies the `"Hi!"` into an array of 32767 characters, setting all but the first 3 characters to the null character. The second approach copies `"Hi!"` into an array of 4 characters. But, by adding another function call (`strlen()`), it increases the program size, slows the process, and requires that you remember to include the `cstring` (or `string.h`) header file. C programmers have tended to opt for faster running, more compact code and leave a greater burden on the programmer to use functions correctly. However, the C++ tradition places greater weight on reliability. After all, a slower program that works correctly is better than a fast program that works incorrectly. If the time taken to call `strlen()` turns out to be a problem, you can let `left()` determine the lesser of n and the string length directly. For example, the following loop quits when m reaches n or the end of the string, whichever comes first:

```
int m = 0;
while ( m <= n && str[m] != '\0')
      m++;
char * p = new char[m+1]:
// use m instead of n in rest of code
```

Function Overloading

Function polymorphism is a neat C++ addition to C's capabilities. Whereas default arguments let you call the same function by using varying numbers of arguments, *function polymorphism*, also called *function overloading*, lets you use multiple functions sharing the same name. The word *polymorphism* means having many forms, so *function polymorphism* lets a function have many forms. Similarly, the expression *function overloading* means you can attach more than one function to the same name, thus overloading the name. Both expressions boil down to the same thing, but we'll usually use the expression *function overloading*—it sounds harder working. You can use function overloading to design a family of functions that do essentially the same thing, but using different argument lists.

Overloaded functions are analogous to verbs having more than one meaning. For example, Miss Piggy can root at the ball park for the home team, and she can root in soil for truffles. The context (one hopes) tells you which meaning of *root* is intended in each case. Similarly, C++ uses the context to decide which version of an overloaded function is intended.

The key to function overloading is a function's argument list, also called the *function signature*. If two functions use the same number and types of arguments in the same order, they have the same signature; the variable names don't matter. C++ enables you to define two functions by the same name, provided that the functions have different signatures. The signature can differ in the number of arguments or in the type of arguments, or both. For example, you can define a set of `print()` functions with the following prototypes:

```
void print(const char * str, int width);   // #1
void print(double d, int width);           // #2
void print(long l, int width);             // #3
void print(int i, int width);              // #4
void print(const char *str);               // #5
```

When you then use a `print()` function, the compiler matches your use to the prototype that has the same signature:

```
print("Pancakes", 15);          // use #1
print("Syrup");                 // use #5
print(1999.0, 10);              // use #2
print(1999, 12);                // use #4
print(1999L, 15);               // use #3
```

For example, `print("Pancakes", 15)` uses a string and an integer as arguments, and it matches Prototype #1.

When you use overloaded functions, you need to be sure you use the proper argument types in the function call. For example, consider the following statements:

```
unsigned int year = 3210;
print(year, 6);                 // ambiguous call
```

Which prototype does the `print()` call match here? It doesn't match any of them! A lack of a matching prototype doesn't automatically rule out using one of the functions because C++ will try to use standard type conversions to force a match. If, say, the *only* `print()` prototype were #2, the function call `print(year, 6)` would convert the `year` value to type `double`. But in the earlier code there are three prototypes that take a number as the first argument, providing three different choices for converting `year`. Faced with this ambiguous situation, C++ rejects the function call as an error.

Some signatures that appear to be different from each other nonetheless can't coexist. For example, consider these two prototypes:

```
double cube(double x);
double cube(double & x);
```

You might think this is a place you could use function overloading because the function signatures appear to be different. But consider things from the compiler's standpoint. Suppose you have code like this:

```
cout << cube(x);
```

The `x` argument matches both the `double x` prototype and the `double &x` prototype. The compiler has no way of knowing which function to use. Therefore, to avoid such confusion, when it checks function signatures, the compiler considers a reference to a type and the type itself to be the same signature.

The function-matching process does discriminate between `const` and non-`const` variables. Consider the following prototypes:

```
void dribble(char * bits);          // overloaded
void dribble (const char *cbits);   // overloaded
void dabble(char * bits);           // not overloaded
void drivel(const char * bits);     // not overloaded
```

Here's what various function calls would match:

```
const char p1[20] = "How's the weather?";
char p2[20] = "How's business?";
dribble(p1);        // dribble(const char *);
dribble(p2);        // dribble(char *);
dabble(p1);         // no match
dabble(p2);         // dabble(char *);
drivel(p1);         // drivel(const char *);
drivel(p2);         // drivel(const char *);
```

The `dribble()` function has two prototypes—one for `const` pointers and one for regular pointers—and the compiler selects one or the other, depending on whether the actual argument is `const`. The `dabble()` function only matches a call with a non-`const` argument, but the `drivel()` function matches calls with either `const` or non-`const` arguments. The reason for this difference in behavior between `drivel()` and `dabble()` is that it's valid to assign a non-`const` value to a `const` variable, but not vice versa.

Keep in mind that the signature, not the function type, enables function overloading. For example, the following two declarations are incompatible:

```
long gronk(int n, float m);        // same signatures,
double gronk(int n, float m);      // hence not allowed
```

Therefore, C++ doesn't permit you to overload `gronk()` in this fashion. You can have different return types, but only if the signatures are also different:

```
long gronk(int n, float m);        // different signatures,
double gronk(float n, float m);    // hence allowed
```

After we discuss templates later in this chapter, we'll further discuss function matching.

An Overloading Example

In this chapter you've already developed a `left()` function that returns a pointer to the first n characters in a string. Let's add a second `left()` function, one that returns the first n digits in an integer. You can use it, for example, to examine the first three digits of a U.S. postal zip code stored as an integer, which is useful if you want to sort for urban areas.

The integer function is a bit more difficult to program than the string version because you don't have the benefit of each digit being stored in its own array element. One approach is to first compute the number of digits in the number. Dividing a number by 10 lops off one digit, so you can use division to count digits. More precisely, you can do so with a loop, like this:

```
unsigned digits = 1;
while (n /= 10)
    digits++;
```

This loop counts how many times you can remove a digit from n until none are left. Recall that n /= 10 is short for n = n / 10. If n is 8, for example, the test condition assigns to n the value 8 / 10, or 0, because it's integer division. That terminates the loop, and `digits` remains at 1. But if n is 238, the first loop test sets n to 238 / 10, or 23. That's nonzero, so the loop increases `digits` to 2. The next cycle sets n to 23 / 10, or 2. Again, that's nonzero, so `digits` grows to 3. The next cycle sets n to 2 / 10, or 0, and the loop quits, leaving `digits` set to the correct value, 3.

Now suppose you know that the number has five digits, and you want to return the first three digits. You can get that value by dividing the number by 10 and then dividing the answer by 10 again. Each division by 10 lops one more digit off the right end. To calculate the number of digits to lop, you just subtract the number of digits to be shown from the total number of digits. For example, to show four digits of a nine-digit number, you lop off the last five digits. You can code this approach as follows:

```
ct = digits - ct;
while (ct--)
    num /= 10;
return num;
```

Listing 8.10 incorporates this code into a new `left()` function. The function includes some additional code to handle special cases, such as asking for zero digits or asking for more digits than the number possesses. Because the signature of the new `left()` differs from that of the old `left()`, you can use both functions in the same program.

LISTING 8.10 `leftover.cpp`

```cpp
// leftover.cpp -- overloading the left() function
#include <iostream>
unsigned long left(unsigned long num, unsigned ct);
char * left(const char * str, int n = 1);

int main()
{
    using namespace std;
    char * trip = "Hawaii!!";   // test value
    unsigned long n = 12345678; // test value
    int i;
    char * temp;

    for (i = 1; i < 10; i++)
    {
        cout << left(n, i) << endl;
        temp = left(trip,i);
        cout << temp << endl;
        delete [] temp; // point to temporary storage
    }
    return 0;

}

// This function returns the first ct digits of the number num.
unsigned long left(unsigned long num, unsigned ct)
{
    unsigned digits = 1;
    unsigned long n = num;
```

LISTING 8.10   *Continued*

```
    if (ct == 0 || num == 0)
        return 0;        // return 0 if no digits
    while (n /= 10)
        digits++;
    if (digits > ct)
    {
    ct = digits - ct;
    while (ct--)
        num /= 10;
    return num;          // return left ct digits
    }
    else                 // if ct >= number of digits
        return num;      // return the whole number
}

// This function returns a pointer to a new string
// consisting of the first n characters in the str string.
char * left(const char * str, int n)
{
    if(n < 0)
        n = 0;
    char * p = new char[n+1];
    int i;
    for (i = 0; i < n && str[i]; i++)
        p[i] = str[i];   // copy characters
    while (i <= n)
        p[i++] = '\0';   // set rest of string to '\0'
    return p;
}
```

Here's the output of the program in Listing 8.10:

```
1
H
12
Ha
123
Haw
1234
Hawa
12345
Hawai
123456
Hawaii
1234567
Hawaii!
12345678
Hawaii!!
12345678
Hawaii!!
```

When to Use Function Overloading

You might find function overloading fascinating, but you shouldn't overuse it. You should reserve function overloading for functions that perform basically the same task but with different forms of data. Also, you might want to check whether you can accomplish the same end by using default arguments. For example, you could replace the single, string-oriented `left()` function with two overloaded functions:

```
char * left(const char * str, unsigned n);    // two arguments
char * left(const char * str);                // one argument
```

But using the single function with a default argument is simpler. There's just one function to write, instead of two, and the program requires memory for just one function, instead of two. If you decide to modify the function, you have to edit only one. However, if you require different types of arguments, default arguments are of no avail, so in that case, you should use function overloading.

Real-World Note: What Is Name Decoration?

How does C++ keep track of which overloaded function is which? It assigns a secret identity to each of these functions. When you use the editor of your C++ development tool to write and compile programs, your C++ compiler performs a bit of magic on your behalf—known as *name decoration* or *name mangling*—through which each function name is encrypted, based on the formal parameter types specified in the function's prototype. Consider the following undecorated function prototype:

```
long MyFunctionFoo(int, float);
```

This format is fine for us humans; we know that the function accepts two arguments of type `int` and `float`, and it returns a value of type `long`. For its own use, the compiler documents this interface by transforming the name into an internal representation with a more unsightly appearance, perhaps something like this:

```
?MyFunctionFoo@@YAXH@Z
```

The apparent gibberish decorating the original name (or mangling it, depending on your attitude) encodes the number and types of parameters. A different function signature would result in a different set of symbols being added, and different compilers would use different conventions for their efforts at decorating.

Function Templates

Contemporary C++ compilers implement one of the newer C++ additions: function templates. A *function template* is a generic function description; that is, it defines a function in terms of a generic type for which a specific type, such as `int` or `double`, can be substituted. By passing a type as a parameter to a template, you cause the compiler to generate a function for that particular type. Because templates let you program in terms of a generic type instead of a specific type, the process is sometimes termed *generic programming*. Because types are represented by parameters, the template feature is sometimes referred to as *parameterized types*. Let's see why such a feature is useful and how it works.

Earlier you defined a function that swapped two `int` values. Suppose you want to swap two `double` values instead. One approach is to duplicate the original code but replace each `int` with `double`. If you need to swap two `char` values, you can use the same technique again. Still, it's wasteful of your valuable time to have to make these petty changes, and there's always the possibility of making an error. If you make the changes by hand, you might overlook an `int`. If you do a global search-and-replace to substitute, say, `double` for `int`, you might do something such as converting

```
int x;
short interval;
```

to the following:

```
double x;              // intended change of type
short doubleerval;    // unintended change of variable name
```

C++'s function template capability automates the process, saving you time and providing greater reliability.

Function templates enable you to define a function in terms of some arbitrary type. For example, you can set up a swapping template like this:

```
template <class Any>
void Swap(Any &a, Any &b)
{
    Any temp;
    temp = a;
    a = b;
    b = temp;
}
```

The first line specifies that you are setting up a template and that you're naming the arbitrary type `Any`. The keywords `template` and `class` are obligatory, except that you can use the keyword `typename` instead of `class`. Also, you must use the angle brackets. The type name (`Any`, in this example) is your choice, as long as you follow the usual C++ naming rules; many programmers use simple names such as `T`. The rest of the code describes the algorithm for swapping two values of type `Any`. The template does not create any functions. Instead, it provides the compiler with directions about how to define a function. If you want a function to swap `int`s, then the compiler creates a function following the template pattern, substituting `int` for `Any`. Similarly, if you need a function to swap `double`s, the compiler follows the template, substituting the `double` type for `Any`.

The keyword `typename` is a recent addition to C++. You can use it instead of the keyword `class` in this particular context. That is, you can write the template definition this way:

```
template <typename Any>
void Swap(Any &a, Any &b)
{
    Any temp;
    temp = a;
    a = b;
    b = temp;
}
```

The `typename` keyword makes it a bit more obvious that the parameter `Any` represents a type; however, large libraries of code have already been developed by using the older keyword `class`. The C++ Standard treats the two keywords identically when they are used in this context.

Tip

You should use templates if you need functions that apply the same algorithm to a variety of types. If you aren't concerned with backward compatibility and can put up with the effort of typing a longer word, you should use the keyword `typename` rather than `class` when you declare type parameters.

To let the compiler know that you need a particular form of swap function, you just use a function called `Swap()` in your program. The compiler checks the argument types you use and then generates the corresponding function. Listing 8.11 shows how this works. The program layout follows the usual pattern for ordinary functions, with a template function prototype near the top of the file and the template function definition following `main()`.

Compatibility Note

Noncurrent versions of C++ compilers might not support templates. New versions accept the keyword `typename` as an alternative to `class`. Older versions of g++ require that both the template prototype and the template definition appear before the template is used, but this has been fixed in newer releases.

LISTING 8.11   `funtemp.cpp`

```
// funtemp.cpp -- using a function template
#include <iostream>
// function template prototype
template <class Any>   // or typename Any
void Swap(Any &a, Any &b);

int main()
{
    using namespace std;
    int i = 10;
    int j = 20;
    cout << "i, j = " << i << ", " << j << ".\n";
    cout << "Using compiler-generated int swapper:\n";
    Swap(i,j);  // generates void Swap(int &, int &)
    cout << "Now i, j = " << i << ", " << j << ".\n";

    double x = 24.5;
    double y = 81.7;
    cout << "x, y = " << x << ", " << y << ".\n";
    cout << "Using compiler-generated double swapper:\n";
```

LISTING 8.11   Continued

```
    Swap(x,y);  // generates void Swap(double &, double &)
    cout << "Now x, y = " << x << ", " << y << ".\n";

    return 0;
}

// function template definition
template <class Any>  // or typename Any
void Swap(Any &a, Any &b)
{
    Any temp;    // temp a variable of type Any
    temp = a;
    a = b;
    b = temp;
}
```

The first `Swap()` function in Listing 8.11 has two `int` arguments, so the compiler generates an `int` version of the function. That is, it replaces each use of `Any` with `int`, producing a definition that looks like this:

```
void Swap(int &a, int &b)
{
    int temp;
    temp = a;
    a = b;
    b = temp;
}
```

You don't see this code, but the compiler generates and then uses it in the program. The second `Swap()` function has two `double` arguments, so the compiler generates a `double` version. That is, it replaces `Any` with `double`, generating this code:

```
void Swap(double &a, double &b)
{
    double temp;
    temp = a;
    a = b;
    b = temp;
}
```

Here's the output of the program in Listing 8.11, which shows that the process has worked:

```
i, j = 10, 20.
Using compiler-generated int swapper:
Now i, j = 20, 10.
x, y = 24.5, 81.7.
Using compiler-generated double swapper:
Now x, y = 81.7, 24.5.
```

Note that function templates don't make executable programs any shorter. In Listing 8.11, you still wind up with two separate function definitions, just as you would if you defined each function manually. And the final code doesn't contain any templates; it just contains the actual functions generated for the program. The benefits of templates are that they make generating multiple function definitions simpler and more reliable.

Overloaded Templates

You use templates when you need functions that apply the same algorithm to a variety of types, as in Listing 8.11. It might be, however, that not all types would use the same algorithm. To handle this possibility, you can overload template definitions, just as you overload regular function definitions. As with ordinary overloading, overloaded templates need distinct function signatures. For example, Listing 8.12 adds a new swapping template—one for swapping elements of two arrays. The original template has the signature (`Any &, Any &`), whereas the new template has the signature (`Any [], Any [], int`). Note that the final parameter in this case happens to be a specific type (`int`) rather than a generic type. Not all template arguments have to be template parameter types.

When, in `twotemps.cpp`, the compiler encounters the first use of `Swap()`, it notices that it has two `int` arguments and matches `Swap()` to the original template. The second use, however, has two `int` arrays and an `int` value as arguments, and this matches the new template.

LISTING 8.12   `twotemps.cpp`

```
// twotemps.cpp -- using overloaded template functions
#include <iostream>
template <class Any>     // original template
void Swap(Any &a, Any &b);

template <class Any>     // new template
void Swap(Any *a, Any *b, int n);

void Show(int a[]);
const int Lim = 8;
int main()
{
    using namespace std;
    int i = 10, j = 20;
    cout << "i, j = " << i << ", " << j << ".\n";
    cout << "Using compiler-generated int swapper:\n";
    Swap(i,j);               // matches original template
    cout << "Now i, j = " << i << ", " << j << ".\n";

    int d1[Lim] = {0,7,0,4,1,7,7,6};
    int d2[Lim] = {0,6,2,0,1,9,6,9};
    cout << "Original arrays:\n";
    Show(d1);
    Show(d2);
    Swap(d1,d2,Lim);         // matches new template
    cout << "Swapped arrays:\n";
    Show(d1);
    Show(d2);
```

LISTING 8.12   Continued

```
    return 0;
}

template <class Any>
void Swap(Any &a, Any &b)
{
    Any temp;
    temp = a;
    a = b;
    b = temp;
}

template <class Any>
void Swap(Any a[], Any b[], int n)
{
    Any temp;
    for (int i = 0; i < n; i++)
    {
        temp = a[i];
        a[i] = b[i];
        b[i] = temp;
    }
}

void Show(int a[])
{
    using namespace std;
    cout << a[0] << a[1] << "/";
    cout << a[2] << a[3] << "/";
    for (int i = 4; i < Lim; i++)
        cout << a[i];
    cout << endl;
}
```

Compatibility Note

Noncurrent versions of C++ compilers might not support templates. New versions might accept the keyword `typename` as an alternative to `class`. Older versions of C++ are more picky about type matching and require the following code to make the `const int Lim` match the template requirement for an ordinary `int`:

```
Swap(d1,d2, int (Lim));          // typecast Lim to non-const int
```

Older versions of g++ require that the template definitions be placed ahead of `main()`.

Here is the output of the program in Listing 8.12:

```
i, j = 10, 20.
Using compiler-generated int swapper:
Now i, j = 20, 10.
Original arrays:
07/04/1776
```

```
07/20/1969
Swapped arrays:
07/20/1969
07/04/1776
```

Explicit Specializations

Suppose you define a structure like the following:

```
struct job
{
    char name[40];
    double salary;
    int floor;
};
```

Also, suppose you want to be able to swap the contents of two such structures. The original template uses the following code to effect a swap:

```
temp = a;
a = b;
b = temp;
```

Because C++ allows you to assign one structure to another, this works fine, even if type Any is a job structure. But suppose you only want to swap the salary and floor members, keeping the name members unchanged. This requires different code, but the arguments to Swap() would be the same as for the first case (references to two job structures), so you can't use template overloading to supply the alternative code.

However, you can supply a specialized function definition, called an *explicit specialization*, with the required code. If the compiler finds a specialized definition that exactly matches a function call, it uses that definition without looking for templates.

The specialization mechanism has changed with the evolution of C++. We'll look at the current form as mandated by the C++ Standard and then look at two older forms supported by older compilers.

Third-Generation Specialization (ISO/ANSI C++ Standard)

After C++ experimented with the specialization approaches described later in this chapter, the C++ Standard settled on this approach:

- For a given function name, you can have a non-template function, a template function, and an explicit specialization template function, along with overloaded versions of all of these.

- The prototype and definition for an explicit specialization should be preceded by template <> and should mention the specialized type by name.

- A specialization overrides the regular template, and a non-template function overrides both.

Here's how prototypes for swapping type `job` structures would look for these three forms:

```
// non-template function prototype
void Swap(job &, job &);

// template prototype
template <class Any>
void Swap(Any &, Any &);

// explicit specialization for the job type
template <> void Swap<job>(job &, job &);
```

As mentioned previously, if more than one of these prototypes is present, the compiler chooses the non-template version over explicit specializations and template versions, and it chooses an explicit specialization over a version generated from a template. For example, in the following code, the first call to `Swap()` uses the general template, and the second call uses the explicit specialization, based on the `job` type:

```
...
template <class Any>          // template
void Swap(Any &, Any &);

// explicit specialization for the job type
template <> void Swap<job>(job &, job &);
int main()
{
    double u, v;
    ...
    Swap(u,v);  // use template
    job a, b;
    ...
    Swap(a,b);  // use void Swap<job>(job &, job &)
}
```

The `<job>` in `Swap<job>` is optional because the function argument types indicate that this is a specialization for `job`. Thus, the prototype can also be written this way:

```
template <> void Swap(job &, job &);   // simpler form
```

In case you have to work with an older compiler, we'll come back to pre-C++ Standard usage soon, but first, let's see how explicit specializations are supposed to work.

An Example of Explicit Specialization

Listing 8.13 illustrates how explicit specialization works. It's set up to follow the C++ Standard.

LISTING 8.13 `twoswap.cpp`

```
// twoswap.cpp -- specialization overrides a template
#include <iostream>
template <class Any>
void Swap(Any &a, Any &b);
```

LISTING 8.13   Continued

```cpp
struct job
{
    char name[40];
    double salary;
    int floor;
};

// explicit specialization
template <> void Swap<job>(job &j1, job &j2);
void Show(job &j);

int main()
{
    using namespace std;
    cout.precision(2);
    cout.setf(ios::fixed, ios::floatfield);
    int i = 10, j = 20;
    cout << "i, j = " << i << ", " << j << ".\n";
    cout << "Using compiler-generated int swapper:\n";
    Swap(i,j);    // generates void Swap(int &, int &)
    cout << "Now i, j = " << i << ", " << j << ".\n";

    job sue = {"Susan Yaffee", 73000.60, 7};
    job sidney = {"Sidney Taffee", 78060.72, 9};
    cout << "Before job swapping:\n";
    Show(sue);
    Show(sidney);
    Swap(sue, sidney); // uses void Swap(job &, job &)
    cout << "After job swapping:\n";
    Show(sue);
    Show(sidney);

    return 0;
}

template <class Any>
void Swap(Any &a, Any &b)      // general version
{
    Any temp;
    temp = a;
    a = b;
    b = temp;
}

// swaps just the salary and floor fields of a job structure

template <> void Swap<job>(job &j1, job &j2)   // specialization
{
    double t1;
    int t2;
    t1 = j1.salary;
    j1.salary = j2.salary;
```

LISTING 8.13   Continued

```
    j2.salary = t1;
    t2 = j1.floor;
    j1.floor = j2.floor;
    j2.floor = t2;
}

void Show(job &j)
{
    using namespace std;
    cout << j.name << ": $" << j.salary
        << " on floor " << j.floor << endl;
}
```

Compatibility Note

The version of the program in Listing 8.13 requires ISO/ANSI C++ support.

Here's the output of the program in Listing 8.13:

```
i, j = 10, 20.
Using compiler-generated int swapper:
Now i, j = 20, 10.
Before job swapping:
Susan Yaffee: $73000.60 on floor 7
Sidney Taffee: $78060.72 on floor 9
After job swapping:
Susan Yaffee: $78060.72 on floor 9
Sidney Taffee: $73000.60 on floor 7
```

Earlier Approaches to Specialization

If Listing 8.13 doesn't work with your compiler, you might have to revert to earlier usage. The simplest way is to provide an ordinary function, defined for the particular type you want to process. That is, in Listing 8.13, you would replace

```
template <> void Swap<job>(job &j1, job &j2);
```

with

```
void Swap(int & n, int & m);    // regular prototype
```

and replace

```
template <> void Swap<job>(job &j1, job &j2)  // specialization
{
...
}
```

with

```
void Swap(job &j1, job &j2)    // regular function
{
...// code unchanged
}
```

When the compiler reaches the `Swap(sue, sidney)` function call, it has the choice of generating a function definition using the template or of using the non-template `Swap(job &, job &)` function. The original template facility (as well as the current standard) has the compiler use the non-template version.

If this approach doesn't work for you, you might be using a compiler that installed a non-official predraft version of templates in which templates were chosen *ahead* of ordinary functions. With that predraft version of the rule in effect, the compiler would use the template `Swap()` instead of the `job` version. So to get the desired effect, you'd have to use an explicit specialization that didn't quite have the modern form. That is, instead of using

```
template <> void Swap<job>(job &j1, job &j2);   // ISO/ANSI C++
```

you would use the following form:

```
void Swap<job>(job &, job &);    // earlier form of specialization
```

Notice that this is missing the `template <>` preface. You'd make the same adjustment in the function header. That is,

```
template <> void Swap<job>(job &j1, job &j2)   // specialization
{
...
}
```

becomes

```
void Swap<job>(job &j1, job &j2)   // old form  of specialization
{
...// code unchanged
}
```

If you're using a contemporary C++ compiler (and I hope you are), you won't have to deal with these adjustments.

Instantiations and Specializations

To extend your understanding of templates, let's investigate the terms *instantiation* and *specialization*. Keep in mind that including a function template in your code does not in itself generate a function definition. It's merely a plan for generating a function definition. When the compiler uses the template to generate a function definition for a particular type, the result is termed an *instantiation* of the template. For example, in Listing 8.13, the function call `Swap(i,j)` causes the compiler to generate an instantiation of `Swap()`, using `int` as the type. The template *is not* a function definition, but the specific instantiation using `int` *is* a function definition. This type of instantiation is termed *implicit instantiation* because the compiler deduces the necessity for making the definition by noting that the program uses a `Swap()` function with `int` parameters.

Originally, using implicit instantiation was the only way the compiler generated function definitions from templates, but now C++ allows for *explicit instantiation*. That means you can instruct the compiler to create a particular instantiation—for example, `Swap<int>()`—directly.

The syntax is to declare the particular variety you want, using the <> notation to indicate the type and prefixing the declaration with the keyword `template`:

```
template void Swap<int>(int, int);  // explicit instantiation
```

A compiler that implements this feature will, upon seeing this declaration, use the `Swap()` template to generate an instantiation, using the `int` type. That is, this declaration means "Use the `Swap()` template to generate a function definition for the `int` type."

Contrast the explicit instantiation with the explicit specialization, which uses one or the other of these equivalent declarations:

```
template <> void Swap<int>(int &, int &);  // explicit specialization
template <> void Swap(int &, int &);       // explicit specialization
```

The difference is that these declarations mean "Don't use the `Swap()` template to generate a function definition. Instead, use a separate, specialized function definition explicitly defined for the `int` type." These prototypes have to be coupled with their own function definitions. The explicit specialization declaration has <> after the keyword template, whereas the explicit instantiation omits the <>.

	Caution

It is an error to try to use both an explicit instantiation and an explicit specialization for the same type(s) in the same programming unit.

Implicit instantiations, explicit instantiations, and explicit specializations collectively are termed *specializations*. What they all have in common is that they represent a function definition that uses specific types rather than one that is a generic description.

The addition of the explicit instantiation led to the new syntax of using `template` and `template <>` prefixes in declarations to distinguish between the explicit instantiation and the explicit specialization. As in many other cases, the cost of doing more is more syntax rules. The following fragment summarizes these concepts:

```
...
template <class Any>
void Swap (Any &, Any &);  // template prototype

template <> void Swap<job>(job &, job &);   // explicit specialization for job
int main(void)
{
  template void Swap<char>(char &, char &); // explicit instantiation for char
  short a, b;
  ...
  Swap(a,b);    // implicit template instantiation for short
  job n, m;
  ...
  Swap(n, m);   // use explicit specialization for job
  char g, h;
  ...
```

```
    Swap(g, h);  // use explicit template instantiation for char
    ...
}
```

When the compiler reaches the explicit instantiation for `char`, it uses the template definition to generate a `char` version of `Swap()`. For the remaining uses of `Swap()`, the compiler matches a template to the actual arguments used in the function call. For example, when the compiler reaches the function call `Swap(a,b)`, it generates a `short` version of `Swap()` because the two arguments are type `short`. When the compiler reaches `Swap(n,m)`, it uses the separate definition (the explicit specialization) provided for the `job` type. When the compiler reaches `Swap(g,h)`, it uses the template specialization it already generated when it processed the explicit instantiation.

Which Function Version Does the Compiler Pick?

What with function overloading, function templates, and function template overloading, C++ needs, and has, a well-defined strategy for deciding which function definition to use for a function call, particularly when there are multiple arguments. The process is called *overload resolution*. Detailing the complete strategy would take a small chapter, so let's take just a broad look at how the process works:

- **Phase 1**—Assemble a list of candidate functions. These are functions and template functions that have the same names as the called functions.

- **Phase 2**—From the candidate functions, assemble a list of viable functions. These are functions with the correct number of arguments and for which there is an implicit conversion sequence, which includes the case of an exact match for each type of actual argument to the type of the corresponding formal argument. For example, a function call with a type `float` argument could have that value converted to a `double` to match a type `double` formal parameter, and a template could generate an instantiation for `float`.

- **Phase 3**—Determine whether there is a best viable function. If so, you use that function. Otherwise, the function call is an error.

Consider a case with just one function argument—for example, the following call:

```
may('B');    // actual argument is type char
```

First, the compiler rounds up the suspects, which are functions and function templates that have the name `may()`. Then, it finds those that can be called with one argument. For example, the following pass muster because they have the same name:

```
void may(int);                          // #1
float may(float, float = 3);            // #2
void may(char);                         // #3
char * may(const char *);               // #4
char may(const char &);                 // #5
template<class T> void may(const T &);  // #6
template<class T> void may(T *);        // #7
```

Note that just the signatures and not the return types are considered. Two of these candidates (#4 and #7), however, are not viable because an integral type cannot be converted implicitly (that is, without an explicit type cast) to a pointer type. The remaining template is used to generate a specialization, with T taken as type `char`. That leaves five viable functions, each of which could be used if it were the only function declared.

Next, the compiler has to determine which of the viable functions is best. It looks at the conversion required to make the function call argument match the viable candidate's argument. In general, the ranking from best to worst is this:

1. Exact match, with regular functions outranking templates.

2. Conversion by promotion (for example, the automatic conversions of `char` and `short` to `int` and of `float` to `double`)

3. Conversion by standard conversion (for example, converting `int` to `char` or `long` to `double`)

4. User-defined conversions, such as those defined in class declarations

For example, Function #1 is better than Function #2 because `char`-to-`int` is a promotion (refer to Chapter 3, "Dealing with Data"), whereas `char`-to-`float` is a standard conversion (refer to Chapter 3). Functions #3, #5, and #6 are better than either #1 or #2 because they are exact matches. Both #3 and #5 are better than #6 because #6 is a template. This analysis raises a couple questions. What is an exact match? And what happens if you get two of them? Usually, as is the case with this example, two exact matches are an error; but a couple special cases are exceptions to this rule. Clearly, we need to investigate the matter further!

Exact Matches and Best Matches

C++ allows some "trivial conversions" when making an exact match. Table 8.1 lists them, with *Type* standing for some arbitrary type. For example, an `int` actual argument is an exact match to an `int &` formal parameter. Note that *Type* can be something like `char &`, so these rules include converting `char &` to `const char &`. The *Type (argument-list)* entry means that a function name as an actual argument matches a function pointer as a formal parameter, as long as both have the same return type and argument list. (Remember function pointers from Chapter 7. Also recall that you can pass the name of a function as an argument to a function that expects a pointer to a function.) We'll discuss the `volatile` keyword later in this chapter.

TABLE 8.1 Trivial Conversions Allowed for an Exact Match

From an Actual Argument	To a Formal Argument
Type	*Type* &
Type &	*Type*
Type []	* *Type*

TABLE 8.1 Continued

From an Actual Argument	To a Formal Argument
Type (argument-list)	Type (*)(argument-list)
Type	const Type
Type	volatile Type
Type *	const Type *
Type *	volatile Type *

Suppose you have the following function code:

```
struct blot {int a; char b[10];};
blot ink = {25, "spots"};
...
recycle(ink);
```

In that case, all the following prototypes would be exact matches:

```
void recycle(blot);         // #1  blot-to-blot
void recycle(const blot);   // #2  blot-to-(const blot)
void recycle(blot &);       // #3  blot-to-(blot &)
void recycle(const blot &); // #4  blot-to-(const blot &)
```

As you might expect, the result of having several matching prototypes is that the compiler cannot complete the overload resolution process. There is no best viable function, and the compiler generates an error message, probably using words such as *ambiguous*.

However, sometimes there can be overload resolution even if two functions are an exact match. First, pointers and references to non-**const** data are preferentially matched to non-**const** pointer and reference parameters. That is, if only Functions #3 and #4 were available in the `recycle()` example, #3 would be chosen because `ink` wasn't declared as **const**. However, this discrimination between **const** and non-**const** applies just to data referred to by pointers and references. That is, if only #1 and #2 were available, you would get an ambiguity error.

Another case in which one exact match is better than another is when one function is a non-template function and the other isn't. In that case, the non-template is considered better than a template, including explicit specializations.

If you wind up with two exact matches that both happen to be template functions, the template function that is the more specialized, if either, is the better function. That means, for example, that an explicit specialization is chosen over one generated implicitly from the template pattern:

```
struct blot {int a; char b[10];};
template <class Type> void recycle (Type t); // template
template <> void recycle<blot> (blot & t);   // specialization for blot
...
```

```
blot ink = {25, "spots"};
...
recycle(ink);  // use specialization
```

The term *most specialized* doesn't necessarily imply an explicit specialization; more generally, it indicates that fewer conversions take place when the compiler deduces what type to use. For example, consider the following two templates:

```
template <class Type> void recycle (Type t);    // #1
template <class Type> void recycle (Type * t);  // #2
```

Suppose the program that contains those templates also contains the following code:

```
struct blot {int a; char b[10];};
blot ink = {25, "spots"};
...
recycle(&ink);  // address of a structure
```

The recycle(&ink) call matches Template #1, with Type interpreted as blot *. The recycle(&ink) function call also matches Template #2, this time with Type being ink. This combination sends two implicit instantiations, recycle<blot *>(blot *) and recycle<blot>(blot *), to the viable function pool.

Of these two template functions, recycle<blot *>(blot *) is considered the more specialized because it underwent fewer conversions in being generated. That is, Template #2 already explicitly said that the function argument was pointer-to-*Type*, so *Type* could be directly identified with blot. However, Template #1 had *Type* as the function argument, so *Type* had to be interpreted as pointer-to-blot. That is, in Template #2, *Type* was already specialized as a pointer, hence it is "more specialized."

The rules for finding the most specialized template are called the *partial ordering rules* for function templates. Like explicit instantiations, they are new additions to the C++ language.

A Partial Ordering Rules Example

Let's examine a complete program that uses the partial ordering rules for identifying which template definition to use. Listing 8.14 has two template definitions for displaying the contents of an array. The first definition (Template A) assumes that the array that is passed as an argument contains the data to be displayed. The second definition (Template B) assumes that the array argument contains pointers to the data to be displayed.

LISTING 8.14   tempover.cpp

```
// tempover.cpp --- template overloading
#include <iostream>

template <typename T>          // template A
void ShowArray(T arr[], int n);

template <typename T>          // template B
void ShowArray(T * arr[], int n);
```

LISTING 8.14   *Continued*

```cpp
struct debts
{
    char name[50];
    double amount;
};

int main(void)
{
    using namespace std;
    int things[6] = {13, 31, 103, 301, 310, 130};
    struct debts mr_E[3] =
    {
        {"Ima Wolfe", 2400.0},
        {"Ura Foxe ", 1300.0},
        {"Iby Stout", 1800.0}
    };
    double * pd[3];

// set pointers to the amount members of the structures in the arr mr_E
    for (int i = 0; i < 3; i++)
        pd[i] = &mr_E[i].amount;

    cout << "Listing Mr. E's counts of things:\n";
// things is an array of int
    ShowArray(things, 6);   // uses template A
    cout << "Listing Mr. E's debts:\n";
// pd is an array of pointers to double
    ShowArray(pd, 3);       // uses template B (more specialized)
    return 0;
}

template <typename T>
void ShowArray(T arr[], int n)
{
    using namespace std;
    cout << "template A\n";
    for (int i = 0; i < n; i++)
        cout << arr[i] << ' ';
    cout << endl;
}

template <typename T>
void ShowArray(T * arr[], int n)
{
    using namespace std;
    cout << "template B\n";
    for (int i = 0; i < n; i++)
        cout << *arr[i] << ' ';
    cout << endl;
}
```

Consider this function call:

```
ShowArray(things, 6);
```

The identifier **things** is the name of an array of **int**, so it matches the template

```
template <typename T>             // template A
void ShowArray(T arr[], int n);
```

with **T** taken to be type **int**.

Next, consider this function call:

```
ShowArray(pd, 3);
```

Here, **pd** is the name of an array of **double ***. This could be matched by Template A:

```
template <typename T>             // template A
void ShowArray(T arr[], int n);
```

Here, **T** would be taken to be type **double ***. In this case, the template function would display the contents of the **pd** array: three addresses. The function call could also be matched by Template B:

```
template <typename T>             // template B
void ShowArray(T * arr[], int n);
```

In this case, **T** is type **double**, and the function displays the dereferenced elements ***arr[i]**— that is, the **double** values pointed to by the array contents. Of the two templates, Template B is the more specialized because it makes the specific assumption that the array contents are pointers, so it is the template that gets used.

Here's the output of the program in Listing 8.14:

```
Listing Mr. E's counts of things:
template A
13 31 103 301 310 130
Listing Mr. E's debts:
template B
2400 1300 1800
```

If you remove Template B from the program, the compiler then uses Template A for listing the contents of **pd**, so it lists the addresses instead of the values.

In short, the overload resolution process looks for a function that's the best match. If there's just one, that function is chosen. If more than one are otherwise tied, but only one is a non-template function, that non-template function is chosen. If more than one candidates are otherwise tied and all are template functions, but one template is more specialized than the rest, that one is chosen. If there are two or more equally good non-template functions, or if there are two or more equally good template functions, none of which is more specialized than the rest, the function call is ambiguous and an error. If there are no matching calls, of course, that is also an error.

Functions with Multiple Arguments

Where matters really get involved is when a function call with multiple arguments is matched to prototypes with multiple arguments. The compiler must look at matches for all the arguments. If it can find a function that is better than all the other viable functions, it is chosen. For one function to be better than another function, it has to provide at least as good a match for all arguments and a better match for at least one argument.

This book does not intend to challenge the matching process with complex examples. The rules are there so that there is a well-defined result for any possible set of function prototypes and templates.

Summary

C++ has expanded C function capabilities. By using an inline keyword with a function definition and by placing that definition ahead of the first call to that function, you suggest to the C++ compiler that it make the function inline. That is, instead of having the program jump to a separate section of code to execute the function, the compiler replaces the function call with the corresponding code inline. An inline facility should be used only when the function is short.

A reference variable is a kind of disguised pointer that lets you create an alias (that is, a second name) for a variable. Reference variables are primarily used as arguments to functions that process structures and class objects. Normally, an identifier declared as a reference to a particular type can refer only to data of that type. However, when one class is derived from another, such as `ofstream` from `ostream`, a reference to the base type may also refer to the derived type.

C++ prototypes enable you to define default values for arguments. If a function call omits the corresponding argument, the program uses the default value. If the function includes an argument value, the program uses that value instead of the default. Default arguments can be provided only from right to left in the argument list. Thus, if you provide a default value for a particular argument, you must also provide default values for all arguments to the right of that argument.

A function's signature is its argument list. You can define two functions having the same name, provided that they have different signatures. This is called *function polymorphism*, or *function overloading*. Typically, you overload functions to provide essentially the same service to different data types.

Function templates automate the process of overloading functions. You define a function by using a generic type and a particular algorithm, and the compiler generates appropriate function definitions for the particular argument types you use in a program.

Review Questions

1. What kinds of functions are good candidates for inline status?

2. Suppose the `song()` function has this prototype:

   ```
   void song(char * name, int times);
   ```

   a. How would you modify the prototype so that the default value for `times` is `1`?

   b. What changes would you make in the function definition?

   c. Can you provide a default value of `"O, My Papa"` for `name`?

3. Write overloaded versions of `iquote()`, a function that displays its argument enclosed in double quotation marks. Write three versions: one for an `int` argument, one for a `double` argument, and one for a `string` argument.

4. The following is a structure template:

   ```
   struct box
   {
       char maker[40];
       float height;
       float width;
       float length;
       float volume;
   };
   ```

   a. Write a function that has a reference to a `box` structure as its formal argument and displays the value of each member.

   b. Write a function that has a reference to a `box` structure as its formal argument and sets the `volume` member to the product of the other three dimensions.

5. The following are some desired effects. Indicate whether each can be accomplished with default arguments, function overloading, both, or neither. Provide appropriate prototypes.

   a. `mass(density, volume)` returns the mass of an object having a density of `density` and a volume of `volume`, whereas `mass(density)` returns the mass having a density of `density` and a volume of 1.0 cubic meters. All quantities are type `double`.

   b. `repeat(10, "I'm OK")` displays the indicated string 10 times, and `repeat("But you're kind of stupid")` displays the indicated string 5 times.

   c. `average(3,6)` returns the `int` average of two `int` arguments, and `average(3.0, 6.0)` returns the `double` average of two `double` values.

   d. `mangle("I'm glad to meet you")` returns the character `I` or a pointer to the string `"I'm mad to gleet you"`, depending on whether you assign the return value to a `char` variable or to a `char*` variable.

6. Write a function template that returns the larger of its two arguments.

7. Given the template of Review Question 6 and the **box** structure of Review Question 4, provide a template specialization that takes two **box** arguments and returns the one with the larger volume.

Programming Exercises

1. Write a function that normally takes one argument, the address of a string, and prints that string once. However, if a second, type **int**, argument is provided and is nonzero, the function should print the string a number of times equal to the number of times that function has been called at that point. (Note that the number of times the string is printed is not equal to the value of the second argument; it is equal to the number of times the function has been called.) Yes, this is a silly function, but it makes you use some of the techniques discussed in this chapter. Use the function in a simple program that demonstrates how the function works.

2. The **CandyBar** structure contains three members. The first member holds the brand name of a candy bar. The second member holds the weight (which may have a fractional part) of the candy bar, and the third member holds the number of calories (an integer value) in the candy bar. Write a program that uses a function that takes as arguments a reference to **CandyBar**, a pointer-to-**char**, a **double**, and an **int** and uses the last three values to set the corresponding members of the structure. The last three arguments should have default values of "Millennium Munch," 2.85, and 350. Also, the program should use a function that takes a reference to a **CandyBar** as an argument and displays the contents of the structure. Use **const** where appropriate.

3. Write a function that takes a reference to a **string** object as its parameter and that converts the contents of the **string** to uppercase. Use the **toupper()** function described in Table 6.4. Write a program that uses a loop which allows you to test the function with different input. A sample run might look like this:

```
Enter a string (q to quit): go away
GO AWAY
Next string (q to quit): good grief!
GOOD GRIEF!
Next string (q to quit): q
Bye.
```

4. The following is a program skeleton:

```cpp
#include <iostream>
using namespace std;
#include <cstring>        // for strlen(), strcpy()
struct stringy {
    char * str;           // points to a string
    int ct;               // length of string (not counting '\0')
    };
```

```
// prototypes for set(), show(), and show() go here
int main()
{
    stringy beany;
    char testing[] = "Reality isn't what it used to be.";

    set(beany, testing);    // first argument is a reference,
                // allocates space to hold copy of testing,
                // sets str member of beany to point to the
                // new block, copies testing to new block,
                // and sets ct member of beany
    show(beany);        // prints member string once
    show(beany, 2);     // prints member string twice
    testing[0] = 'D';
    testing[1] = 'u';
    show(testing);      // prints testing string once
    show(testing, 3);   // prints testing string thrice
    show("Done!");
    return 0;
}
```

Complete this skeleton by providing the described functions and prototypes. Note that there should be two `show()` functions, each using default arguments. Use `const` arguments when appropriate. Note that `set()` should use `new` to allocate sufficient space to hold the designated string. The techniques used here are similar to those used in designing and implementing classes. (You might have to alter the header filenames and delete the `using` directive, depending on your compiler.)

5. Write a template function `max5()` that takes as its argument an array of five items of type `T` and returns the largest item in the array. (Because the size is fixed, it can be hard-coded into the loop instead of being passed as an argument.) Test it in a program that uses the function with an array of five `int` value and an array of five `double` values.

6. Write a template function `maxn()` that takes as its arguments an array of items of type `T` and an integer representing the number of elements in the array and that returns the largest item in the array. Test it in a program that uses the function template with an array of six `int` value and an array of four `double` values. The program should also include a specialization that takes an array of pointers-to-`char` as an argument and the number of pointers as a second argument and that returns the address of the longest string. If multiple strings are tied for having the longest length, the function should return the address of the first one tied for longest. Test the specialization with an array of five string pointers.

7. Modify Listing 8.14 so that the template functions return the sum of the array contents instead of displaying the contents. The program now should report the total number of things and the sum of all the debts.

CHAPTER 9

MEMORY MODELS AND NAMESPACES

In this chapter you'll learn about the following:

- Separate compilation of programs
- Storage duration, scope, and linkage
- Placement new
- Namespaces

C++ offers many choices for storing data in memory. You have choices for how long data remains in memory (storage duration) and choices for which parts of a program have access to data (scope and linkage). You can allocate memory dynamically by using new, and placement new offers a variation on that technique. The C++ namespace facility provides additional control over access. Larger programs typically consist of several source code files that may share some data in common. Such programs involve the separate compilation of the program files, and this chapter begins with that topic.

Separate Compilation

C++, like C, allows and even encourages you to locate the component functions of a program in separate files. As Chapter 1, "Getting Started," describes, you can compile the files separately and then link them into the final executable program. (A C++ compiler typically compiles programs and also manages the linker program.) If you modify just one file, you can recompile just that one file and then link it to the previously compiled versions of the other files. This facility makes it easier to manage large programs. Furthermore, most C++ environments provide additional facilities to help with the management. Unix and Linux systems, for example, have make programs, which keep track of which files a program depends on and when they were last modified. If you run make, and it detects that you've changed one or more source files since the last compilation, make remembers the proper steps needed to reconstitute the program. The Borland C++, Microsoft Visual C++, and Metrowerks CodeWarrior Integrated Development Environments (IDEs) provide similar facilities with their Project menus.

Let's look at a simple example. Instead of looking at compilation details, which depend on the implementation, let's concentrate on more general aspects, such as design.

Suppose, for example, that you decide to break up the program in Listing 7.12 by placing the two supporting functions in a separate file. Recall that Listing 7.12 converts rectangular coordinates to polar coordinates and then displays the result. You can't simply cut the original file on a dotted line after the end of `main()`. The problem is that `main()` and the other two functions use the same structure declarations, so you need to put the declarations in both files. Simply typing them in is an invitation to error. Even if you copy the structure declarations correctly, you have to remember to modify both sets of declarations if you make changes later. In short, spreading a program over multiple files creates new problems.

Who wants more problems? The developers of C and C++ didn't, so they've provided the `#include` facility to deal with this situation. Instead of placing the structure declarations in each file, you can place them in a header file and then include that header file in each source code file. That way, if you modify the structure declaration, you can do so just once, in the header file. Also, you can place the function prototypes in the header file. Thus, you can divide the original program into three parts:

- A header file that contains the structure declarations and prototypes for functions that use those structures
- A source code file that contains the code for the structure-related functions
- A source code file that contains the code that calls the structure-related functions

This is a useful strategy for organizing a program. If, for example, you write another program that uses those same functions, you can just include the header file and add the functions file to the project or `make` list. Also, this organization reflects the OOP approach. One file, the header file, contains the definition of the user-defined types. A second file contains the function code for manipulating the user-defined types. Together, they form a package you can use for a variety of programs.

You shouldn't put function definitions or variable declarations into a header file. That might work for a simple setup, but usually it leads to trouble. For example, if you had a function definition in a header file and then included the header file in two other files that are part of a single program, you'd wind up with two definitions of the same function in a single program, which is an error, unless the function is inline. Here are some things commonly found in header files:

- Function prototypes
- Symbolic constants defined using `#define` or `const`
- Structure declarations
- Class declarations
- Template declarations
- Inline functions

It's okay to put structure declarations in a header file because they don't create variables; they just tell the compiler how to create a structure variable when you declare one in a source code file. Similarly, template declarations aren't code to be compiled; they are instructions to the compiler on how to generate function definitions to match function calls found in the source code. Data declared `const` and inline functions have special linkage properties (described shortly) that allow them to be placed in header files without causing problems.

Listings 9.1, 9.2, and 9.3 show the result of dividing Listing 7.12 into separate parts. Note that you use `"coordin.h"` instead of `<coordin.h>` when including the header file. If the filename is enclosed in angle brackets, the C++ compiler looks at the part of the host system's file system that holds the standard header files. But if the filename is enclosed in double quotation marks, the compiler first looks at the current working directory or at the source code directory (or some such choice, depending on the compiler). If it doesn't find the header file there, it then looks in the standard location. So you should use quotation marks, not angle brackets, when including your own header files.

Figure 9.1 outlines the steps for putting this program together on a Unix system. Note that you just give the `CC` compile command, and the other steps follow automatically. The g++ and gpp command-line compilers and the Borland C++ command-line compiler (`bcc32.exe`) also behave that way. Borland C++, Turbo C++, Metrowerks CodeWarrior, and Microsoft Visual C++ go through essentially the same steps, but, as outlined in Chapter 1, you initiate the process differently, using menus that let you create a project and associate source code files with it. Note that you only add source code files, not header files, to projects. That's because the `#include` directive manages the header files. Also, you shouldn't use `#include` to include source code files because that can lead to multiple declarations.

Caution

In IDEs, don't add header files to the project list, and don't use `#include` to include source code files in other source code files.

LISTING 9.1   `coordin.h`

```
// coordin.h -- structure templates and function prototypes
// structure templates
#ifndef COORDIN_H_
#define COORDIN_H_

struct polar
{
    double distance;    // distance from origin
    double angle;        // direction from origin
};
struct rect
{
```

LISTING 9.1   Continued

```
    double x;        // horizontal distance from origin
    double y;        // vertical distance from origin
};

// prototypes
polar rect_to_polar(rect xypos);
void show_polar(polar dapos);

#endif
```

Header File Management

You should include a header file just once in a file. That might seem to be an easy thing to remember, but it's possible to include a header file several times without knowing you did so. For example, you might use a header file that includes another header file. There's a standard C/C++ technique for avoiding multiple inclusions of header files. It's based on the preprocessor `#ifndef` (for *if n*ot *defi*ned) directive. A code segment like

```
#ifndef COORDIN_H_
...
#endif
```

means process the statements between the `#ifndef` and `#endif` only if the name `COORDIN_H_` has not been defined previously by the preprocessor `#define` directive.

Normally, you use the `#define` statement to create symbolic constants, as in the following:

```
#define MAXIMUM 4096
```

But simply using `#define` with a name is enough to establish that a name is defined, as in the following:

```
#define COORDIN_H_
```

The technique that Listing 9.1 uses is to wrap the file contents in an `#ifndef`:

```
#ifndef COORDIN_H_
#define COORDIN_H_
// place include file contents here
#endif
```

The first time the compiler encounters the file, the name `COORDIN_H_` should be undefined. (I chose a name based on the `include` filename, with a few underscore characters tossed in to create a name that is unlikely to be defined elsewhere.) That being the case, the compiler looks at the material between the `#ifndef` and the `#endif`, which is what you want. In the process of looking at the material, the compiler reads the line defining `COORDIN_H_`. If it then encounters a second inclusion of `coordin.h` in the same file, the compiler notes that `COORDIN_H_` is defined and skips to the line following the `#endif`. Note that this method doesn't keep the compiler from including a file twice. Instead, it makes the compiler ignore the contents of all but the first inclusion. Most of the standard C and C++ header files use this guarding scheme.

LISTING 9.2 `file1.cpp`

```
// file1.cpp -- example of a three-file program
#include <iostream>
#include "coordin.h" // structure templates, function prototypes
using namespace std;
int main()
{
    rect rplace;
    polar pplace;

    cout << "Enter the x and y values: ";
    while (cin >> rplace.x >> rplace.y)  // slick use of cin
    {
        pplace = rect_to_polar(rplace);
        show_polar(pplace);
        cout << "Next two numbers (q to quit): ";
    }
    cout << "Bye!\n";
    return 0;
}
```

LISTING 9.3 `file2.cpp`

```
// file2.cpp -- contains functions called in file1.cpp
#include <iostream>
#include <cmath>
#include "coordin.h" // structure templates, function prototypes

// convert rectangular to polar coordinates
polar rect_to_polar(rect xypos)
{
    using namespace std;
    polar answer;

    answer.distance =
        sqrt( xypos.x * xypos.x + xypos.y * xypos.y);
    answer.angle = atan2(xypos.y, xypos.x);
    return answer;        // returns a polar structure
}

// show polar coordinates, converting angle to degrees
void show_polar (polar dapos)
{
    using namespace std;
    const double Rad_to_deg = 57.29577951;

    cout << "distance = " << dapos.distance;
    cout << ", angle = " << dapos.angle * Rad_to_deg;
    cout << " degrees\n";
}
```

Compiling and linking these two source code files along with the new header file produces an executable program. Here is a sample run:

```
Enter the x and y values: 120 80
distance = 144.222, angle = 33.6901 degrees
Next two numbers (q to quit): 120 50
distance = 130, angle = 22.6199 degrees
Next two numbers (q to quit): q
```

FIGURE 9.1

Compiling a multifile C++ program on a Unix system.

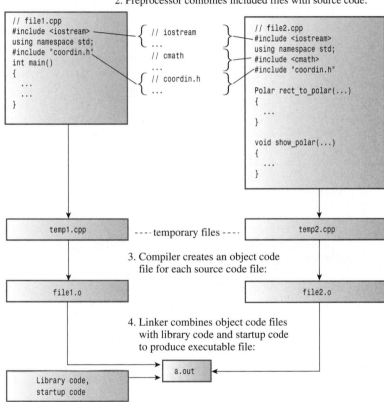

1. Give UNIX compile command for two source files:
   `CC file1.cpp file2.ccp`

2. Preprocessor combines included files with source code:

3. Compiler creates an object code file for each source code file:

4. Linker combines object code files with library code and startup code to produce executable file:

By the way, although we've discussed separate compilation in terms of files, the C++ Standard uses the term *translation unit* instead of *file* in order to preserve greater generality; the file metaphor is not the only possible way to organize information for a computer.

Real-World Note: Multiple Library Linking

The C++ Standard allows each compiler designer the latitude to implement name decoration or mangling (see the Real-World Note "Real-World Note: What Is Name Decoration?" in Chapter 8,

"Adventures in Functions") as it sees fit, so you should be aware that binary modules (object-code files) created with different compilers will, most likely, not link properly. That is, the two compilers will generate different decorated names for the same function. This name difference will prevent the linker from matching the function call generated by one compiler with the function definition generated by a second compiler. When attempting to link compiled modules, you should make sure that each object file or library was generated with the same compiler. If you are provided with the source code, you can usually resolve link errors by recompiling the source with your compiler.

Storage Duration, Scope, and Linkage

Now that you've seen a multifile program, it's a good time to extend the discussion of memory schemes in Chapter 4, "Compound Types," because storage categories affect how information can be shared across files. It might have been a while since you last read Chapter 4, so let's review what it says about memory. C++ uses three separate schemes for storing data, and the schemes differ in how long they preserve data in memory:

- **Automatic storage duration**—Variables declared inside a function definition—including function parameters—have automatic storage duration. They are created when program execution enters the function or block in which they are defined, and the memory used for them is freed when execution leaves the function or block. C++ has two kinds of automatic storage duration variables.

- **Static storage duration**—Variables defined outside a function definition or else by using the keyword `static` have static storage duration. They persist for the entire time a program is running. C++ has three kinds of static storage duration variables.

- **Dynamic storage duration**—Memory allocated by the `new` operator persists until it is freed with the `delete` operator or until the program ends, whichever comes first. This memory has dynamic storage duration and sometimes is termed the *free store*.

You'll get the rest of the story now, including fascinating details about when variables of different types are in scope, or visible (that is, usable by the program), and about linkage, which determines what information is shared across files.

Scope and Linkage

Scope describes how widely visible a name is in a file (translation unit). For example, a variable defined in a function can be used in that function, but not in another, whereas a variable defined in a file above the function definitions can be used in all the functions. *Linkage* describes how a name can be shared in different units. A name with *external linkage* can be shared across files, and a name with *internal linkage* can be shared by functions within a single file. Names of automatic variables have no linkage because they are not shared.

A C++ variable can have one of several scopes. A variable that has *local scope* (also termed *block scope*) is known only within the block in which it is defined. Recall that a block is a series of statements enclosed in braces. A function body, for example, is a block, but you can have other blocks nested within the function body. A variable that has *global scope* (also termed *file scope*) is known throughout the file after the point where it is defined. Automatic variables have local scope, and a static variable can have either scope, depending on how it is defined. Names used in a *function prototype scope* are known just within the parentheses enclosing the argument list. (That's why it doesn't really matter what they are or if they are even present.) Members declared in a class have *class scope* (see Chapter 10, "Objects and Classes"). Variables declared in a namespace have *namespace scope*. (Now that namespaces have been added to the C++ language, the global scope has become a special case of namespace scope.)

C++ functions can have class scope or namespace scope, including global scope, but they can't have local scope. (Because a function can't be defined inside a block, if a function were to have local scope, it could only be known to itself, and hence couldn't be called by another function. Such a function couldn't function.)

The various C++ storage choices are characterized by their storage duration, their scope, and their linkage. Let's look at C++'s storage classes in terms of these properties. We'll begin by examining the situation before namespaces were added to the mix and then see how namespaces modify the picture.

Automatic Storage Duration

Function parameters and variables declared inside a function have, by default, automatic storage duration. They also have local scope and no linkage. That is, if you declare a variable called `texas` in `main()` and you declare another variable with the same name in a function called `oil()`, you've created two independent variables, each known only in the function in which it's defined. Anything you do to the `texas` in `oil()` has no effect on the `texas` in `main()`, and vice versa. Also, each variable is allocated when program execution enters the innermost block containing the definition, and each fades from existence when its function terminates. (Note that the variable is allocated when execution enters the block, but the scope begins only after the point of declaration.)

If you define a variable inside a block, the variable's persistence and scope are confined to that block. Suppose, for example, that you define a variable called `teledeli` at the beginning of `main()`. Now suppose you start a new block within `main()` and define a new variable, called `websight`, in the block. Then, `teledeli` is visible in both the outer and inner blocks, whereas `websight` exists only in the inner block and is in scope only from its point of definition until program execution passes the end of the block:

```
int main()
{
    int teledeli = 5;
    {                               // websight allocated
        cout << "Hello\n";
        int websight = -2;    // websight scope begins
        cout << websight << ' ' << teledeli << endl;
    }                               // websight expires
    cout << teledeli << endl;
    ...
}
```

But what if you name the variable in the inner block `teledeli` instead of `websight` so that you have two variables of the same name, with one in the outer block and one in the inner block? In this case, the program interprets the `teledeli` name to mean the local block variable while the program executes statements within the block. We say the new definition *hides* the prior definition. The new definition is in scope, and the old definition is temporarily out of scope. When the program leaves the block, the original definition comes back into scope. (See Figure 9.2.)

FIGURE 9.2

Blocks and scope.

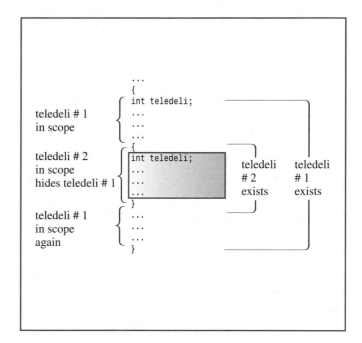

Listing 9.4 illustrates how automatic variables are localized to the functions or blocks that contain them.

LISTING 9.4   `auto.cpp`

```cpp
// auto.cpp -- illustrating scope of automatic variables
#include <iostream>
void oil(int x);
int main()
{
    using namespace std;

    int texas = 31;
    int year = 1999;
    cout << "In main(), texas = " << texas << ", &texas = ";
    cout << &texas << endl;
    cout << "In main(), year = " << year << ", &year = ";
```

LISTING 9.4 Continued

```cpp
    cout << &year << endl;
    oil(texas);
    cout << "In main(), texas = " << texas << ", &texas = ";
    cout << &texas << endl;
    cout << "In main(), year = " << year << ", &year = ";
    cout << &year << endl;
    return 0;
}

void oil(int x)
{
    using namespace std;
    int texas = 5;

    cout << "In oil(), texas = " << texas << ", &texas = ";
    cout << &texas << endl;
    cout << "In oil(), x = " << x << ", &x = ";
    cout << &x << endl;
    {                                // start a block
        int texas = 113;
        cout << "In block, texas = " << texas;
        cout << ", &texas = " << &texas << endl;
                cout << "In block, x = " << x << ", &x = ";
        cout << &x << endl;
    }                                // end a block
    cout << "Post-block texas = " << texas;
    cout << ", &texas = " << &texas << endl;
}
```

Here is the output from the program in Listing 9.4:

```
In main(), texas = 31, &texas = 0012FED4
In main(), year = 1999, &year = 0012FEC8
In oil(), texas = 5, &texas = 0012FDE4
In oil(), x = 31, &x = 0012FDF4
In block, texas = 113, &texas = 0012FDD8
In block, x = 31, &x = 0012FDF4
Post-block texas = 5, &texas = 0012FDE4
In main(), texas = 31, &texas = 0012FED4
In main(), year = 1999, &year = 0012FEC8
```

Notice that each of the three **texas** variables in Listing 9.4 has its own distinct address and that the program uses only the particular variable in scope at the moment, so assigning the value 113 to the **texas** in the inner block in **oil()** has no effect on the other variables of the same name. (As usual, the actual address values and address format will differ from system to system.)

Let's summarize the sequence of events. When **main()** starts, the program allocates space for **texas** and **year**, and these variables come into scope. When the program calls **oil()**, these variables remain in memory but pass out of scope. Two new variables, **x** and **texas**, are allocated and come into scope. When program execution reaches the inner block in **oil()**, the new `texas` passes out of scope because it is superseded by an even newer definition. The variable `x`, however, stays in scope because the block doesn't define a new `x`. When execution exits the block, the memory for the newest `texas` is freed, and `texas` #2 comes back into scope. When the `oil()` function terminates, that `texas` and `x` expire, and the original `texas` and `year` come back into scope.

Incidentally, you can use the C++ (and C) keyword `auto` to indicate the storage class explicitly:

```
int froob(int n)
{
    auto float ford;
    ...
}
```

Because you can use the `auto` keyword only with variables that are already automatic by default, programmers rarely bother using it. Occasionally, the `auto` keyword is used to clarify code to the reader. For example, you can use it to indicate that you are purposely creating an automatic variable that overrides a global definition, such as those that are discussed a little later in this chapter, in the section "Static Duration, External Linkage."

Initialization of Automatic Variables

You can initialize an automatic variable with any expression whose value will be known when the declaration is reached. The following example shows the variables `x`, `y`, and `z` being initialized:

```
int w;          // value of w is indeterminate
int x = 5;      // initialized with a constant expression
int y = 2 * x;  // use previously determined value of x
cin >> w;
int z = 3 * w;  // use new value of w
```

Automatic Variables and the Stack

You might gain a better understanding of automatic variables if you look at how a typical C++ compiler implements them. Because the number of automatic variables grows and shrinks as functions start and terminate, the program has to manage automatic variables as it runs. The usual means is to set aside a section of memory and treat it as a stack for managing the flow and ebb of variables. It's called a *stack* because new data is figuratively stacked atop old data (that is, at an adjacent location, not at the same location) and then removed from the stack when a program is finished with it. The default size of the stack depends on the implementation, but a compiler generally provides the option of changing the size. The program keeps track of the stack by using two pointers. One points to the base of the stack, where the memory set aside for the stack begins, and one points to the top of the stack, which is the next free memory location. When a function is called, its automatic variables are added to the stack, and the pointer to the top points to the next available free space following the variables. When the function terminates, the top pointer is reset to the value it had before the function was called, effectively freeing the memory that had been used for the new variables.

A stack is a LIFO (last-in, first-out) design, meaning the last variables added to the stack are the first to go. The design simplifies argument passing. The function call places the values of its arguments on top of the stack and resets the top pointer. The called function uses the description of its formal parameters to determine the addresses of each argument. For example, Figure 9.3 shows a `fib()` function that, when called, passes a 2-byte `int` and a 4-byte `long`. These values go on the stack. When `fib()` begins execution, it associates the names `real` and `tell` with the two values. When `fib()` terminates, the top-of-stack pointer is relocated to its former position. The new values aren't erased, but they are no longer labeled, and the space they occupy will be used by the next process that places values on the stack. (Figure 9.3 is somewhat simplified because function calls may pass additional information, such as a return address.)

FIGURE 9.3

Passing arguments by using a stack.

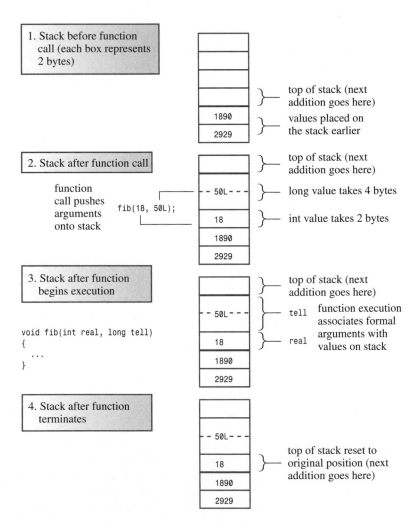

Register Variables

C++, like C, supports the `register` keyword for declaring local variables. A register variable is another form of automatic variable, so it has automatic storage duration, local scope, and no linkage. The `register` keyword is a hint to the compiler that you want it to provide fast access to the variable, perhaps by using a CPU register instead of the stack to handle a particular variable. The idea is that the CPU can access a value in one of its registers more rapidly than it can access memory in the stack. To declare a register variable, you preface the type with the keyword `register`:

```
register int count_fast;  // request for a register variable
```

You've probably noticed the qualifying words *hint* and *request*. The compiler doesn't have to honor the request. For example, the registers may already be occupied, or you might request a type that doesn't fit in a register. Many programmers feel that modern compilers are often smart enough not to need the hint. If you write a `for` loop, for example, the compiler might take it upon itself to use a register for the loop index.

If a variable is stored in a register, it doesn't have a memory address; therefore, you can't apply the address operator to a register variable. Thus, in the following code, it's okay to take the address of the variable `x` but not of the register variable `y`:

```
void gromb(int *);     // function that expects an address
int main()
{
    int x;
    register int y;
    gromb(&x);         // ok
    gromb(&y);         // not allowed
    ...
```

Using `register` in the declaration is enough to invoke this restriction, even if the compiler doesn't actually use a register for the variable.

In short, an ordinary local variable, a local variable declared using `auto`, and a local variable declared using `register` all have automatic storage duration, local scope, and no linkage. The following code illustrates these three cases:

```
int main()
{
    short waffles;          // auto variable by default
    auto short pancakes;    // explicitly auto
    register int muffins;   // register variable
```

Declaring a local variable without a specifier is the same as declaring it with `auto`, and such a variable is typically handled by being placed on a memory stack. Using the `register` specifier is a hint that the variable will be heavily used, and the compiler may choose to use something other than the memory stack (for example, a CPU register) to hold it.

Static Duration Variables

C++, like C, provides static storage duration variables with three kinds of linkage: external linkage, internal linkage, and no linkage. All three last for the duration of the program; they are less ephemeral than automatic variables. Because the number of static variables doesn't change as the program runs, the program doesn't need a special device such as a stack to manage them. Instead, the compiler allocates a fixed block of memory to hold all the static variables, and those variables stay present as long as the program executes. Also, if you don't explicitly initialize a static variable, the compiler sets it to **0**. Static arrays and structures have all the bits of each element or member set to **0** by default.

Compatibility Note

Classic K&R C does not allow you to initialize automatic arrays and structures, but it does allow you to initialize static arrays and structures. ANSI C and C++ allow you to initialize both kinds. But some older C++ translators use C compilers that are not fully ANSI C compliant. If you are using such an implementation, you might need to use one of the three varieties of static storage classes for initializing arrays and structures.

Let's look at how to create the three different kinds of static duration variables; then we can go on to examine their properties. To create a static duration variable with external linkage, you declare it outside any block. To create a static duration variable with internal linkage, you declare it outside any block and use the **static** storage class modifier. To create a static duration variable with no linkage, you declare it inside a block, using the **static** modifier. The following code fragment shows these three variations:

```
...
int global = 1000;          // static duration, external linkage
static int one_file = 50;    // static duration, internal linkage
int main()
{
...
}
void funct1(int n)
{
    static int count = 0;   // static duration, no linkage
    int llama = 0;
...
}
void funct2(int q)
{
...
}
```

As stated previously, all the static duration variables (**global**, **one_file**, and **count**, in this example) persist from the time the program begins execution until it terminates. The variable **count**, which is declared inside **funct1()**, has local scope and no linkage, which means it can be used only inside the **funct1()** function, just like the automatic variable **llama**. But, unlike `llama`, `count` remains in memory even when the `funct1()` function is not being executed. Both `global` and `one_file` have file scope, meaning they can be used from the point of declaration until the end of the file. In particular, both can be used in `main()`, `funct1()`, and `funct2()`. Because `one_file` has internal linkage, it can be used only in the file containing this code. Because `global` has external linkage, it also can be used in other files that are part of the program.

All static duration variables share the following two initialization features:

• An uninitialized static variable has all its bits set to `0`.

• A static variable can be initialized only with a constant expression.

A constant expression can use literal constants, `const` and `enum` constants, and the `sizeof` operator. The following code fragment illustrates these points:

```
int x;                      // x set to 0
int y = 49;                 // 49 is a constant expression
int z = 2 * sizeof(int) + 1; // also a constant expression
int m = 2 * z;              // invalid, z not a constant
int main() {...}
```

Table 9.1 summarizes the storage class features as used in the pre-namespace era. Next, we'll examine the static duration varieties in more detail.

TABLE 9.1   The Five Kinds of Variable Storage

Storage Description	Duration	Scope	Linkage	How Declared
Automatic	Automatic	Block	None	In a block (optionally with the keyword `auto`)
Register	Automatic	Block	None	In a block with the keyword `register`
Static with no linkage	Static	Block	None	In a block with the keyword `static`
Static with external linkage	Static	File	External	Outside all functions
Static with internal linkage	Static	File	Internal	Outside all functions with the keyword `static`

Static Duration, External Linkage

Variables with external linkage are often simply called *external variables*. They necessarily have static storage duration and file scope. External variables are defined outside, and hence external to, any function. For example, they could be declared above the `main()` function. You can use an external variable in any function that follows the external variable's definition in the file. Thus, external variables are also termed *global variables*, in contrast to automatic variables, which are local variables. However, if you define an automatic variable that has the same name as an external variable, the automatic variable is the one that is in scope when the program executes that particular function. Listing 9.5 illustrates these points. It also shows how you can use the keyword `extern` to redeclare an external variable defined earlier and how you can use C++'s scope-resolution operator to access an otherwise hidden external variable. Because this example is a one-file program, it doesn't illustrate the external linkage property; an example later in this chapter does that.

LISTING 9.5 `external.cpp`

```cpp
// external.cpp -- external variables
#include <iostream>
using namespace std;
// external variable
double warming = 0.3;

// function prototypes
void update(double dt);
void local();

int main()                 // uses global variable
{
    cout << "Global warming is " << warming << " degrees.\n";
    update(0.1);           // call function to change warming
    cout << "Global warming is " << warming << " degrees.\n";
    local();               // call function with local warming
    cout << "Global warming is " << warming << " degrees.\n";
    return 0;
}

void update(double dt)     // modifies global variable
{
    extern double warming; // optional redeclaration
    warming += dt;
    cout << "Updating global warming to " << warming;
    cout << " degrees.\n";
}

void local()               // uses local variable
{
    double warming = 0.8;  // new variable hides external one

    cout << "Local warming = " << warming << " degrees.\n";
        // Access global variable with the
```

LISTING 9.5   Continued

```
        // scope resolution operator
    cout << "But global warming = " << ::warming;
    cout << " degrees.\n";
}
```

Here is the output from the program in Listing 9.5:

```
Global warming is 0.3 degrees.
Updating global warming to 0.4 degrees.
Global warming is 0.4 degrees.
Local warming = 0.8 degrees.
But global warming = 0.4 degrees.
Global warming is 0.4 degrees.
```

Program Notes

The output of the program in Listing 9.5 illustrates that both `main()` and `update()` can access the external variable `warming`. Note that the change that `update()` makes to `warming` shows up in subsequent uses of the variable.

The `update()` function redeclares the `warming` variable by using the keyword `extern`. This keyword means "Use the variable by this name previously defined externally." Because that is what `update()` would do anyway if you omitted the entire declaration, this declaration is optional. It serves to document that the function is designed to use the external variable. The original declaration

```
double warming = 0.3;
```

is called a *defining declaration* or, simply, a *definition*. It causes storage for the variable to be allocated. The redeclaration

```
extern double warming;
```

is called a *referencing declaration* or, simply, a *declaration*. It does not cause storage to be allocated because it refers to an existing variable. You can use the `extern` keyword only in declarations referring to variables defined elsewhere (or functions—as you'll learn later). In essence, this declaration says "Use the `warming` variable defined externally elsewhere." A referencing declaration should specify the same type as the defining declaration. Also, you cannot initialize a variable in a referencing declaration:

```
extern double warming = 0.5;   // INVALID
```

You can initialize a variable in a declaration only if the declaration allocates the variable—that is, only in a defining declaration. After all, the term *initialization* refers to the assigning of a value to a memory location when that location is allocated.

The `local()` function demonstrates that when you define a local variable that has the same name as a global variable, the local version hides the global version. The `local()` function, for example, uses the local definition of `warming` when it displays the value of `warming`.

C++ goes a step beyond C by offering the *scope-resolution operator* (`::`). When it is prefixed to the name of a variable, this operator means to use the global version of that variable. Thus, `local()` displays `warming` as `0.8`, but it displays `::warming` as `0.4`. You'll encounter this operator again in namespaces and classes.

Global Versus Local Variables

Now that you have a choice of using global or local variables, which should you use? At first, global variables have a seductive appeal—because all functions have access to a global variable, you don't have to bother passing arguments. But this easy access has a heavy price: unreliable programs. Computing experience has shown that the better job your program does of isolating data from unnecessary access, the better job the program does in preserving the integrity of the data. Most often, you should use local variables and pass data to functions on a need-to-know basis rather than make data available indiscriminately by using global variables. As you will see, OOP takes this data isolation a step further.

Global variables do have their uses, however. For example, you might have a block of data that's to be used by several functions, such as an array of month names or the atomic weights of the elements. The external storage class is particularly suited to representing constant data because you can use the keyword `const` to protect the data from change:

```cpp
const char * const months[12] =
{
    "January", "February", "March", "April", "May",
    "June", "July", "August", "September", "October",
    "November", "December"
};
```

In this example, the first `const` protects the strings from change, and the second `const` makes sure that each pointer in the array remains pointing to the same string to which it pointed initially.

Static Duration, Internal Linkage

Applying the `static` modifier to a file-scope variable gives it internal linkage. The difference between internal linkage and external linkage becomes meaningful in multifile programs. In that context, a variable with internal linkage is local to the file that contains it. But a regular external variable has external linkage, meaning that it can be used in different files. For external linkage, one and only one file can contain the external definition for the variable. Other files that want to use that variable must use the keyword `extern` in a reference declaration. (See Figure 9.4.)

If a file doesn't provide the `extern` declaration of a variable, it can't use an external variable defined in a different file:

```cpp
// file1
int errors = 20;      // global declaration
...
-------------------------------------------
// file 2
...                     // missing an extern int errors declaration
void froobish()
{
    cout << errors;  // doomed attempt to use errors
..
```

FIGURE 9.4

Defining declaration and referencing declaration.

```
// file1.cpp
#include <iostream>
using namespace std;

// function prototypes
#include "mystuff.h"

// defining an external variable
int process_status = 0;

void promise ();
int main()
{
    ...
}

void promise ()
{
    ...
}
```

```
// file2.cpp
#include <iostream>
using namespace std;

// function prototypes
#include "mystuff.h"

// referencing an external variable
extern int process_status;

int manipulate(int n)
{
    ...
}

char * remark(char * str)
{
    ...
}
```

This file defines the variable process_status, causing the compiler to allocate space for it.

This file uses extern to instruct the program to use the variable process_status that was defined in another file.

If a file attempts to define a second external variable by the same name, that's an error:

```
// file1
int errors = 20;           // external declaration
...
-------------------------------------------------
// file 2
int errors;                // invalid declaration
void froobish()
{
    cout << errors;        // doomed attempt to use errors
...
```

The correct approach is to use the keyword **extern** in the second file:

```
// file1
int errors = 20;           // external declaration
...
-------------------------------------------------
// file 2
extern int errors;         // refers to errors from file1
void froobish()
{
    cout << errors;        // uses errors defined in file1
```

But if a file declares a static external variable that has the same name as an ordinary external variable declared in another file, the static version is the one in scope for that file:

```
// file1
int errors = 20;           // external declaration
...
-------------------------------------------------
// file2
```

```
static int errors = 5;   // known to file2 only
void froobish()
{
    cout << errors;   // uses errors defined in file2
    ...
```

You should use an external variable to share data among different parts of a multifile program. You should use a static variable with internal linkage to share data among functions found in just one file. (Namespaces offer an alternative method for this, and the C++ Standard indicates that using **static** to create internal linkage will be phased out in the future.) Also, if you make a file-scope variable static, you needn't worry about its name conflicting with file-scope variables found in other files.

Listings 9.6 and 9.7 show how C++ handles variables with external and internal linkage. Listing 9.6 (**twofile1.cpp**) defines the external variables **tom** and **dick** and the static external variable **harry**. The **main()** function in that file displays the addresses of the three variables and then calls the **remote_access()** function, which is defined in a second file. Listing 9.7 (**twofile2.cpp**) shows that file. In addition to defining **remote_access()**, the file uses the **extern** keyword to share **tom** with the first file. Next, the file defines a static variable called **dick**. The **static** modifier makes this variable local to the file and overrides the global definition. Then, the file defines an external variable called **harry**. It can do so without conflicting with the **harry** of the first file because the first **harry** has internal linkage only. Then, the **remote_access()** function displays the addresses of these three variables so that you can compare them with the addresses of the corresponding variables in the first file. Remember that you need to compile both files and link them to get the complete program.

LISTING 9.6   twofile1.cpp

```
// twofile1.cpp -- variables with external and internal linkage
#include <iostream>       // to be compiled with two file2.cpp
int tom = 3;              // external variable definition
int dick = 30;            // external variable definition
static int harry = 300;   // static, internal linkage

// function prototype
void remote_access();

int main()
{
    using namespace std;
    cout << "main() reports the following addresses:\n";
    cout << &tom << " = &tom, " << &dick << " = &dick, ";
```

LISTING 9.6   Continued

```
        cout << &harry << " = &harry\n";
        remote_access();
        return 0;
    }
```

LISTING 9.7   twofile2.cpp

```
// twofile2.cpp -- variables with internal and external linkage
#include <iostream>
extern int tom;          // tom defined elsewhere
static int dick = 10;    // overrides external dick
int harry = 200;         // external variable definition,
                         // no conflict with twofile1 harry

void remote_access()
{
    using namespace std;
    cout << "remote_access() reports the following addresses:\n";
    cout << &tom << " = &tom, " << &dick << " = &dick, ";
    cout << &harry << " = &harry\n";
}
```

Here is the output from the program produced by compiling Listings 9.6 and 9.7 together:

```
main() reports the following addresses:
0x0041a020 = &tom, 0x0041a024 = &dick, 0x0041a028 = &harry
remote_access() reports the following addresses:
0x0041a020 = &tom, 0x0041a450 = &dick, 0x0041a454 = &harry
```

As you can see from the addresses, both files use the same `tom` variable but different `dick` and `harry` variables. (The particular address values and formatting may be different on your system, but the `tom` addresses will match each other and the `dick` and `harry` addresses won't.)

Static Storage Duration, No Linkage

So far, we've looked at a file-scope variable with external linkage and a file-scope variable with internal linkage. Now let's look at the third member of the static duration family: local variables with no linkage. You create such a variable by applying the `static` modifier to a variable defined inside a block. When you use it inside a block, `static` causes a local variable to have static storage duration. This means that even though the variable is known within that block, it exists even while the block is inactive. Thus, a static local variable can preserve its value between function calls. (Static variables would be useful for reincarnation—you could use them to pass secret account numbers for a Swiss bank to your next appearance.) Also, if you initialize a static local variable, the program initializes the variable once, when the program starts up. Subsequent calls to the function don't reinitialize the variable the way they do for automatic variables. Listing 9.8 illustrates these points.

LISTING 9.8   `static.cpp`

```cpp
// static.cpp -- using a static local variable
#include <iostream>
// constants
const int ArSize = 10;

// function prototype
void strcount(const char * str);

int main()
{
    using namespace std;
    char input[ArSize];
    char next;

    cout << "Enter a line:\n";
    cin.get(input, ArSize);
    while (cin)
    {
        cin.get(next);
        while (next != '\n')     // string didn't fit!
            cin.get(next);
        strcount(input);
        cout << "Enter next line (empty line to quit):\n";
        cin.get(input, ArSize);
    }
    cout << "Bye\n";
    return 0;
}

void strcount(const char * str)
{
    using namespace std;
    static int total = 0;       // static local variable
    int count = 0;              // automatic local variable

    cout << "\"" << str <<"\" contains ";
    while (*str++)              // go to end of string
        count++;
    total += count;
    cout << count << " characters\n";
    cout << total << " characters total\n";
}
```

Incidentally, the program in Listing 9.8 shows one way to deal with line input that may exceed the size of the destination array. Recall that the `cin.get(input,ArSize)` input method reads up to the end of the line or up to `ArSize` - `1` characters, whichever comes first. It leaves the newline character in the input queue. This program uses `cin.get(next)` to read the character that follows the line input. If `next` is a newline character, then the preceding call to `cin.get(input, ArSize)` read the whole line. If `next` isn't a newline character, there are more characters left on the line. This program then uses a loop to reject the rest of the line, but you can modify the code to use the rest of the line for the next input cycle. The program also uses the fact that attempting to read an empty line with `get(char *, int)` causes `cin` to test as `false`.

Compatibility Note

Some older compilers don't implement the requirement that when `cin.get(char *,int)` reads an empty line, it sets the failbit error flag, causing `cin` to test as `false`. In that case, you can replace the test

```
while (cin)
```

with this:

```
while (input[0])
```

Or, for a test that works for both old and new implementations, you can use this:

```
while (cin && input[0])
```

Here is the output of the program in Listing 9.8:

```
Enter a line:
nice pants
"nice pant" contains 9 characters
9 characters total
Enter next line (empty line to quit):
thanks
"thanks" contains 6 characters
15 characters total
Enter next line (empty line to quit):
parting is such sweet sorrow
"parting i" contains 9 characters
24 characters total
Enter next line (empty line to quit):
ok
"ok" contains 2 characters
26 characters total
Enter next line (empty line to quit):

Bye
```

Note that because the array size is `10`, the program does not read more than nine characters per line. Also note that the automatic variable `count` is reset to `0` each time the function is called. However, the static variable `total` is set to `0` once, at the beginning. After that, `total` retains its value between function calls, so it's able to maintain a running total.

Specifiers and Qualifiers

Certain C++ keywords, called *storage class specifiers* and *cv-qualifiers*, provide additional information about storage. Here's a list of the storage class specifiers:

```
auto
register
static
extern
mutable
```

You've already seen most of these, and you can use no more than one of them in a single declaration. To review, the keyword `auto` can be used in a declaration to document that the variable is an automatic variable. The keyword `register` is used in a declaration to indicate the register storage class. The keyword `static`, when used with a file-scope declaration, indicates internal linkage. When used with a local declaration, it indicates static storage duration for a local variable. The keyword `extern` indicates a reference declaration—that is, that the declaration refers to a variable defined elsewhere. The keyword `mutable` is explained in terms of `const`, so let's look at the cv-qualifiers first before returning to `mutable`.

Here are the cv-qualifiers:

```
const
volatile
```

(As you may have guessed, *cv* stands for `const` and `volatile`.) The most commonly used cv-qualifier is `const`, and you've already seen its purpose: It indicates that memory, once initialized, should not be altered by a program. We'll come back to `const` in a moment.

The `volatile` keyword indicates that the value in a memory location can be altered even though nothing in the program code modifies the contents. This is less mysterious than it sounds. For example, you could have a pointer to a hardware location that contains the time or information from a serial port. In this case, the hardware, not the program, changes the contents. Or two programs may interact, sharing data. The intent of this keyword is to improve the optimization abilities of compilers. For example, suppose the compiler notices that a program uses the value of a particular variable twice within a few statements. Rather than have the program look up the value twice, the compiler might cache the value in a register. This optimization assumes that the value of the variable doesn't change between the two uses. If you don't declare a variable as `volatile`, then the compiler can feel free to make this optimization. If you do declare a variable as `volatile`, you're telling the compiler not to make that sort of optimization.

Now let's return to `mutable`. You can use it to indicate that a particular member of a structure (or class) can be altered even if a particular structure (or class) variable is a `const`. For example, consider the following code:

```
struct data
{
    char name[30];
    mutable int accesses;
    ...
};
const data veep = {"Claybourne Clodde", 0, ... };
strcpy(veep.name, "Joye Joux");   // not allowed
veep.accesses++;                  // allowed
```

The `const` qualifier to `veep` prevents a program from changing `veep`'s members, but the `muta-ble` specifier to the `accesses` member shields `accesses` from that restriction.

This book doesn't use `volatile` or `mutable`, but there is more to learn about `const`.

More About `const`

In C++ (but not C), the `const` modifier alters the default storage classes slightly. Whereas a global variable has external linkage by default, a `const` global variable has internal linkage by default. That is, C++ treats a global `const` definition, such as in the following code fragment, as if the `static` specifier had been used:

```
const int fingers = 10;    // same as static const int fingers;
int main(void)
{
    ...
```

C++ has altered the rules for constant types to make life easier for you. Suppose, for example, that you have a set of constants that you'd like to place in a header file and that you use this header file in several files in the same program. After the preprocessor includes the header file contents in each source file, each source file will contain definitions like this:

```
const int fingers = 10;
const char * warning = "Wak!";
```

If global `const` declarations had external linkage as regular variables do, this would be an error because you can define a global variable in one file only. That is, only one file can contain the preceding declaration, and the other files have to provide reference declarations using the `extern` keyword. Moreover, only the declarations without the `extern` keyword can initialize values:

```
// extern would be required if const had external linkage
extern const int fingers;      // can't be initialized
extern const char * warning;
```

So, you would need one set of definitions for one file and a different set of declarations for the other files. Instead, because externally defined `const` data has internal linkage, you can use the same declarations in all files.

Internal linkage also means that each file gets its own set of constants rather than sharing them. Each definition is private to the file that contains it. This is why it's a good idea to put constant definitions in a header file. That way, as long as you include the same header file in two source code files, they receive the same set of constants.

If, for some reason, you want to make a constant have external linkage, you can use the `extern` keyword to override the default internal linkage:

```
extern const int states = 50;    // external linkage
```

You must use the `extern` keyword to declare the constant in all files that use the constant. This differs from regular external variables, in which you don't use the keyword `extern` when you define a variable, but you use `extern` in other files using that variable. Also, unlike regular variables, you can initialize an `extern const` value. Indeed, you have to because `const` data requires initialization.

When you declare a `const` within a function or block, it has block scope, which means the constant is usable only when the program is executing code within the block. This means that you can create constants within a function or block and not have to worry about the names conflicting with constants defined elsewhere.

Functions and Linkage

Like variables, functions have linkage properties, although the selection is more limited than for variables. C++, like C, does not allow you to define one function inside another, so all functions automatically have static storage duration, meaning they are all present as long as the program is running. By default, functions have external linkage, meaning they can be shared across files. You can, in fact, use the keyword `extern` in a function prototype to indicate that the function is defined in another file, but that is optional. (For the program to find the function in another file, that file must be one of the files being compiled as part of the program or a library file searched by the linker.) You can also use the keyword `static` to give a function internal linkage, confining its use to a single file. You would apply this keyword to the prototype and to the function definition:

```
static int private(double x);
...
static int private(double x)
{
    ...
}
```

This means the function is known only in that file. It also means you can use the same name for another function in a different file. As with variables, a static function overrides an external definition for the file containing the static declaration, so a file containing a static function definition will use that version of the function even if there is an external definition of a function that has the same name.

C++ has a "one definition rule" which states that every program shall contain exactly one definition of every non-inline function. For functions with external linkage, this means that only one file of a multifile program can contain the function definition. However, each file that uses the function should have the function prototype.

Inline functions are excepted from this rule to allow you to place inline function definitions in a header file. Thus, each file that includes the header file ends up having the inline function definition. However, C++ does require that all the inline definitions for a particular function be identical.

Where C++ Finds Functions

Suppose you call a function in a particular file in a program. Where does C++ look for the function definition? If the function prototype in that file indicates that the function is static, the compiler looks only in that file for the function. Otherwise, the compiler (and the linker, too) looks in all the program files. If it finds two definitions, the compiler sends you an error message because you can have only one definition for an external function. If it fails to find any definition in the files, the function then searches the libraries. This implies that if you define a function that has the same name as a library function, the compiler uses your version rather than the library version. (However, C++ reserves the names of the standard library functions, so you shouldn't reuse them.) Some compiler-linkers need explicit instructions to identify which libraries to search.

Language Linking

Another form of linking, called *language linking*, affects functions. First, a little background. A linker needs a different symbolic name for each distinct function. In C, this is simple to implement because there can be only one C function with a given name. So, for internal purposes, a C compiler might translate a C function name such as `spiff` to `_spiff`. The C approach is termed *C language linkage*. However, C++ can have several functions with the same C++ name that have to be translated to separate symbolic names. Thus, the C++ compiler indulges in the process of name mangling or name decoration (as discussed in Chapter 8) to generate different symbolic names for overloaded functions. For example, it could convert `spiff(int)` to, say, `_spiff_i`, and `spiff(double, double)` to `_spiff_d_d`. The C++ approach is *C++ language linkage*.

When the linker looks for a function to match a C++ function call, it uses a different look-up method than it does to match a C function call. But suppose you want to use a precompiled function from a C library in a C++ program? For example, suppose you have this code:

```
spiff(22); // want spiff(int) from a C library
```

Its symbolic name in the C library file is `_spiff`, but, for our hypothetical linker, the C++ look-up convention is to look for the symbolic name `_spiff_i`. To get around this problem, you can use the function prototype to indicate which protocol to use:

```
extern "C" void spiff(int);    // use C protocol for name look-up
extern void spoff(int);        // use C++ protocol for name look-up
extern "C++" void spaff(int);  // use C++ protocol for name look-up
```

The first example here uses C language linkage. The second and third examples use C++ language linkage; the second does so by default, and the third does so explicitly.

Storage Schemes and Dynamic Allocation

You've seen the five schemes C++ uses to allocate memory for variables (including arrays and structures). They don't apply to memory allocated by using the C++ `new` operator (or by using the older C `malloc()` function). We call that kind of memory *dynamic memory*. As you saw in Chapter 4, dynamic memory is controlled by the `new` and `delete` operators, not by scope and linkage rules. Thus, dynamic memory can be allocated from one function and freed from another function. Unlike automatic memory, dynamic memory is not LIFO; the order of allocation and freeing depends on when and how `new` and `delete` are used. Typically, the compiler uses three separate memory chunks: one for static variables (this chunk might be subdivided), one for automatic variables, and one for dynamic storage.

Although the storage scheme concepts don't apply to dynamic memory, they do apply to automatic and static pointer variables used to keep track of dynamic memory. For example, suppose you have the following statement inside a function:

```
float * p_fees = new float [20];
```

The 80 bytes (assuming that a `float` is 4 bytes) of memory allocated by `new` remains in memory until the `delete` operator frees it. But the `p_fees` pointer passes from existence when the function containing this declaration terminates. If you want to have the 80 bytes of allocated memory available to another function, you need to pass or return its address to that function. On the other hand, if you declare `p_fees` with external linkage, the `p_fees` pointer will be available to all the functions following that declaration in the file. And by using

```
extern float * p_fees;
```

in a second file, you make that same pointer available in the second file. Note, however, that a statement that uses `new` to set `p_fees` has to be in a function, as in the following sample code, because static storage variables can only be initialized with constant expressions:

```
float * p_fees;    // ok to create a static storage pointer
// float * p2 = new float[20];  // initialization with non-const not allowed here
int main()
{
    p_fees = new float [20];
...
```

Compatibility Note

Memory allocated by `new` is typically freed when the program terminates. However, this is not always true. Under some less robust operating systems, for example, in some circumstances a request for a large block of memory can result in a block that is not deleted automatically when the program terminates. The best practice is to use `delete` to free memory allocated by `new`.

The Placement new Operator

Normally, the `new` operator has the responsibility of finding in the heap a block of memory that is large enough to handle the amount of memory you request. The `new` operator has a variation, called *placement* new, that allows you to specify the location to be used. A programmer might use this feature to set up his or her own memory-management procedures or to deal with hardware that is accessed via a particular address.

To use the placement `new` feature, you first include the `new` header file, which provides a prototype for this version of `new`. Then you use `new` with an argument that provides the intended address. Aside from this argument, the syntax is the same as for regular `new`. In particular, you can use placement `new` either without or with brackets. The following code fragment shows the syntax for using these four forms of `new`:

```
#include <new>
struct chaff
{
    char dross[20];
    int slag;
};
char buffer1[50];
char buffer2[500];
int main()
{
    chaff *p1, *p2;
    int *p3, *p4;
// first, the regular forms of new
    p1 = new chaff;                 // place structure in heap
    p3 = new int[20];               // place int array in heap
// now, the two forms of placement new
    p2 = new (buffer1) chaff;       // place structure in buffer1
    p4 = new (buffer2) int[20];     // place int array in buffer2
...
```

For simplicity, this example uses two static arrays to provide memory space for placement new. So this code allocates space for a chaff structure in buffer1 and space for an array of 20 ints in buffer2.

Now that you've made your acquaintance with placement new, let's look at a sample program. Listing 9.9 uses both new and placement new to create dynamically allocated arrays. This program illustrates some important differences between new and placement new that we'll discuss after seeing the output.

LISTING 9.9   newplace.cpp

```
// newplace.cpp -- using placement new
#include <iostream>
#include <new>              // for placement new
const int BUF = 512;
const int N = 5;
char buffer[BUF];          // chunk of memory
int main()
{
    using namespace std;

    double *pd1, *pd2;
    int i;
    cout << "Calling new and placement new:\n";
    pd1 = new double[N];            // use heap
    pd2 = new (buffer) double[N];   // use buffer array
    for (i = 0; i < N; i++)
        pd2[i] = pd1[i] = 1000 + 20.0 * i;
    cout << "Buffer addresses:\n" << "  heap: " << pd1
        << "  static: " << (void *) buffer  <<endl;
    cout << "Buffer contents:\n";
    for (i = 0; i < N; i++)
```

LISTING 9.9   Continued

```
    {
        cout << pd1[i] << " at " << &pd1[i] << "; ";
        cout << pd2[i] << " at " << &pd2[i] << endl;
    }

    cout << "\nCalling new and placement new a second time:\n";
    double *pd3, *pd4;
    pd3= new double[N];
    pd4 = new (buffer) double[N];
    for (i = 0; i < N; i++)
        pd4[i] = pd3[i] = 1000 + 20.0 * i;
    cout << "Buffer contents:\n";
    for (i = 0; i < N; i++)
    {
        cout << pd3[i] << " at " << &pd3[i] << "; ";
        cout << pd4[i] << " at " << &pd4[i] << endl;
    }

    cout << "\nCalling new and placement new a third time:\n";
    delete [] pd1;
    pd1= new double[N];
    pd2 = new (buffer + N * sizeof(double)) double[N];
    for (i = 0; i < N; i++)
        pd2[i] = pd1[i] = 1000 + 20.0 * i;
    cout << "Buffer contents:\n";
    for (i = 0; i < N; i++)
    {
        cout << pd1[i] << " at " << &pd1[i] << "; ";
        cout << pd2[i] << " at " << &pd2[i] << endl;
    }
    delete [] pd1;
    delete [] pd3;

    return 0;
}
```

Here is an example of output from the program in Listing 9.9 on one system:

```
Calling new and placement new:
Buffer addresses:
  heap: 0xc9d34  static: 0x42e10
Buffer contents:
1000 at 0xc9d34; 1000 at 0x42e10
1020 at 0xc9d3c; 1020 at 0x42e18
1040 at 0xc9d44; 1040 at 0x42e20
1060 at 0xc9d4c; 1060 at 0x42e28
1080 at 0xc9d54; 1080 at 0x42e30

Calling new and placement new a second time:
Buffer contents:
1000 at 0xc9d64; 1000 at 0x42e10
1020 at 0xc9d6c; 1020 at 0x42e18
```

```
1040 at 0xc9d74; 1040 at 0x42e20
1060 at 0xc9d7c; 1060 at 0x42e28
1080 at 0xc9d84; 1080 at 0x42e30

Calling new and placement new a third time:
Buffer contents:
1000 at 0xc9d34; 1000 at 0x42e38
1020 at 0xc9d3c; 1020 at 0x42e40
1040 at 0xc9d44; 1040 at 0x42e48
1060 at 0xc9d4c; 1060 at 0x42e50
1080 at 0xc9d54; 1080 at 0x42e58
```

Program Notes

The first thing to note about Listing 9.9 is that placement new does, indeed, place the p2 array in the buffer array; both p2 and buffer have the value 0x42e10. Meanwhile, regular new locates the p1 array rather far away in memory, at location 0xc9d34, which is part of the dynamically managed heap.

The second point to note is that the second call to regular new results in new finding a new block of memory—one beginning at 0xc9d64. But the second call to placement new results in the same block of memory being used as before—that is, the block beginning at 0x42e10. The important fact here is that placement new simply uses the address that is passed to it; it doesn't keep track of whether that location has already been used, and it doesn't search the block for unused memory. This shifts some of the burden of memory management to the programmer. For example, the third call to placement new provides an offset into the buffer array so that new memory is used:

```
pd2 = new (buffer + N * sizeof(double)) double[N]; // offset of 40 bytes
```

The third point has to do with the use and non-use of delete. For regular new, the statement

```
delete [] pd1;
```

frees up the block of memory beginning at 0xc9d34, and, as a result, the next call to new is able to reuse that block. In contrast, the program in Listing 9.9 does not use delete to free the memory used by placement new. In fact, in this case, it can't. The memory specified by buffer is static memory, and delete can be used only with a pointer to heap memory allocated by regular new. That is, the buffer array is outside the jurisdiction of delete, and the statement

```
delete [] pd2;    // won't work
```

will produce a runtime error. On the other hand, if you use regular new to create a buffer in the first place, you use regular delete to free that entire block.

The situation becomes more involved when you use placement new with class objects. Chapter 12, "Classes and Dynamic Memory Allocation," continues this story.

Namespaces

Names in C++ can refer to variables, functions, structures, enumerations, classes, and class and structure members. When programming projects grow large, the potential for name conflicts increases. When you use class libraries from more than one source, you can get name conflicts. For example, two libraries might both define classes named `List`, `Tree`, and `Node`, but in incompatible ways. You might want the `List` class from one library and the `Tree` from the other, and each might expect its own version of `Node`. Such conflicts are termed *namespace problems*.

The C++ Standard provides namespace facilities to provide greater control over the scope of names. It has taken a while for compilers to incorporate namespaces, but, by now, support has become common.

Traditional C++ Namespaces

Before looking at the new namespace facilities in C++, let's review the namespace properties that already exist in C++ and introduce some terminology. This can help make the idea of namespaces seem more familiar.

One term you need to be aware of is *declarative region*. A declarative region is a region in which declarations can be made. For example, you can declare a global variable outside any function. The declarative region for that variable is the file in which it is declared. If you declare a variable inside a function, its declarative region is the innermost block in which it is declared.

A second term you need to be aware of is *potential scope*. The potential scope for a variable begins at its point of declaration and extends to the end of its declarative region. So the potential scope is more limited than the declarative region because you can't use a variable above the point where it is first defined.

However, a variable might not be visible everywhere in its potential scope. For example, it might be hidden by another variable of the same name declared in a nested declarative region. For example, a local variable declared in a function (for this variable, the declarative region is the function) hides a global variable declared in the same file (for this variable, the declarative region is the file). The portion of the program that can actually see the variable is termed the *scope*, which is the way we've been using the term all along. Figures 9.5 and 9.6 illustrate the terms *declarative region*, *potential scope*, and *scope*.

C++'s rules about global and local variables define a kind of namespace hierarchy. Each declarative region can declare names that are independent of names declared in other declarative regions. A local variable declared in one function doesn't conflict with a local variable declared in a second function.

FIGURE 9.5
Declarative regions.

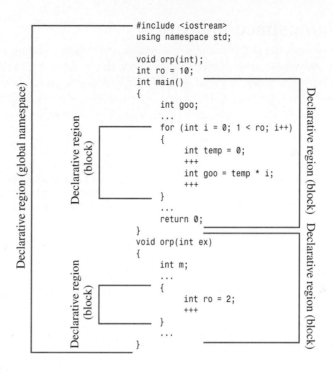

FIGURE 9.6
Potential scope and scope.

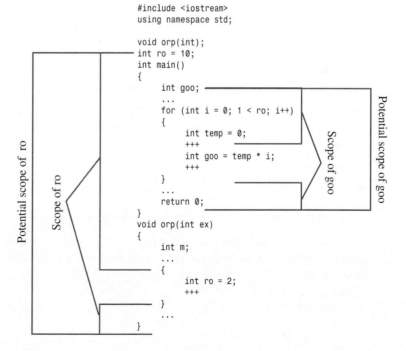

New Namespace Features

C++ now adds the ability to create named namespaces by defining a new kind of declarative region, one whose main purpose is to provide an area in which to declare names. The names in one namespace don't conflict with the same names declared in other namespaces, and there are mechanisms for letting other parts of a program use items declared in a namespace. The following code, for example, uses the new keyword `namespace` to create two namespaces, `Jack` and `Jill`:

```
namespace Jack {
    double pail;                       // variable declaration
    void fetch();                      // function prototype
    int pal;                           // variable declaration
    struct Well { ... };               // structure declaration
}
namespace Jill {
    double bucket(double n) { ... }    // function definition
    double fetch;                      // variable declaration
    int pal;                           // variable declaration
    struct Hill { ... };               // structure declaration
}
```

Namespaces can be located at the global level or inside other namespaces, but they cannot be placed in a block. Thus, a name declared in a namespace has external linkage by default (unless it refers to a constant).

In addition to user-defined namespaces, there is one more namespace, the *global namespace*. This corresponds to the file-level declarative region, so what used to be termed *global variables* are now described as being part of the global namespace.

The names in any one namespace don't conflict with names in another namespace. Thus, the `fetch` in `Jack` can coexist with the `fetch` in `Jill`, and the `Hill` in `Jill` can coexist with an external `Hill`. The rules governing declarations and definitions in a namespace are the same as the rules for global declarations and definitions.

Namespaces are *open*, meaning that you can add names to existing namespaces. For example, the statement

```
namespace Jill {
    char * goose(const char *);
}
```

adds the name `goose` to the existing list of names in `Jill`.

Similarly, the original `Jack` namespace provides a prototype for a `fetch()` function. You can provide the code for the function later in the file (or in another file) by using the `Jack` namespace again:

```
namespace Jack {
    void fetch()
    {
        ...
    }
}
```

Of course, you need a way to access names in a given namespace. The simplest way is to use `::`, the scope-resolution operator, to *qualify* a name with its namespace:

```
Jack::pail = 12.34;   // use a variable
Jill::Hill mole;      // create a type Hill structure
Jack::fetch();        // use a function
```

An unadorned name, such as `pail`, is termed the *unqualified name*, whereas a name with the namespace, as in `Jack::pail`, is termed a *qualified name*.

using Declarations and using Directives

Having to qualify names every time they are used is not an appealing prospect, so C++ provides two mechanisms—the `using` *declaration* and the `using` *directive*—to simplify using namespace names. The `using` declaration lets you make particular identifiers available, and the `using` directive makes the entire namespace accessible.

The `using` declaration involves preceding a qualified name with the keyword `using`:

```
using Jill::fetch;    // a using declaration
```

A `using` declaration adds a particular name to the declarative region in which it occurs. For example, the `using` declaration of `Jill::fetch` in `main()` adds `fetch` to the declarative region defined by `main()`. After making this declaration, you can use the name `fetch` instead of `Jill::fetch`. The following code fragment illustrates these points:

```
namespace Jill {
    double bucket(double n) { ... }
    double fetch;
    struct Hill { ... };
}
char fetch;
int main()
{
    using Jill::fetch;   // put fetch into local namespace
    double fetch;        // Error! Already have a local fetch
    cin >> fetch;        // read a value into Jill::fetch
    cin >> ::fetch;      // read a value into global fetch
    ...
}
```

Because a `using` declaration adds the name to the local declarative region, this example precludes creating another local variable by the name of `fetch`. Also, like any other local variable, `fetch` would override a global variable by the same name.

Placing a `using` declaration at the external level adds the name to the global namespace:

```
void other();
namespace Jill {
    double bucket(double n) { ... }
    double fetch;
    struct Hill { ... };
}
```

```
using Jill::fetch;    // put fetch into global namespace
int main()
{
    cin >> fetch;     // read a value into Jill::fetch
    other()
...
}

void other()
{
    cout << fetch;    // display Jill::fetch
...
}
```

A `using` declaration, then, makes a single name available. In contrast, the `using` directive makes all the names available. A `using` directive involves preceding a namespace name with the keywords `using namespace`, and it makes *all* the names in the namespace available, without the use of the scope-resolution operator:

```
using namespace Jack;  // make all the names in Jack available
```

Placing a `using` directive at the global level makes the namespace names available globally. You've seen this in action a few times in this book in the following form:

```
#include <iostream>    // places names in namespace std
using namespace std;   // make names available globally
```

Placing a `using` directive in a particular function makes the names available just in that function. Here's an example:

```
int main()
{
    using namespace jack; // make names available in vorn()
...
}
```

You've seen this form often in this book with the `std` namespace.

One thing to keep in mind about `using` directives and `using` declarations is that they increase the possibility of name conflicts. That is, if you have both namespace `jack` and namespace `jill` available, and you use the scope-resolution operator, there is no ambiguity:

```
jack::pal = 3;
jill::pal =10;
```

The variables `jack::pal` and `jill::pal` are distinct identifiers for distinct memory locations. However, if you employ `using` declarations, the situation changes:

```
using jack::pal;
using jill::pal;
pal = 4;              // which one? now have a conflict
```

In fact, the compiler won't let you use both of these `using` declarations because of the ambiguity that would be created.

using Directives Versus using Declarations

Using a using directive to import all the names from a namespace wholesale is *not* the same as using multiple using declarations. It's more like the mass application of a scope-resolution operator. When you use a using declaration, it is as if the name is declared at the location of the using declaration. If a particular name is already declared in a function, you can't import the same name with a using declaration. When you use a using directive, however, name resolution takes place as if you declared the names in the smallest declarative region containing both the using declaration and the namespace itself. For the following example, that would be the global namespace. If you use a using directive to import a name that is already declared in a function, the local name will hide the namespace name, just as it would hide a global variable of the same name. However, you can still use the scope-resolution operator, as in the following example:

```
namespace Jill {
    double bucket(double n) { ... }
    double fetch;
    struct Hill { ... };
}
char fetch;                 // global namespace
int main()
{
    using namespace Jill;      // import all namespace names
    Hill Thrill;               // create a type Jill::Hill structure
    double water = bucket(2);  // use Jill::bucket();
    double fetch;              // not an error; hides Jill::fetch
    cin >> fetch;              // read a value into the local fetch
    cin >> ::fetch;            // read a value into global fetch
    cin >> Jill::fetch;        // read a value into Jill::fetch
    ...
}

int foom()
{
    Hill top;                  // ERROR
    Jill::Hill crest;          // valid
}
```

Here, in main(), the name Jill::fetch is placed in the local namespace. It doesn't have local scope, so it doesn't override the global fetch. But the locally declared fetch hides both Jill::fetch and the global fetch. However, both of the last two fetch variables are available if you use the scope-resolution operator. You might want to compare this example to the preceding one, which uses a using declaration.

One other point of note is that although a using directive in a function treats the namespace names as being declared outside the function, it doesn't make those names available to other functions in the file. Hence in the preceding example, the foom() function can't use the unqualified Hill identifier.

Generally speaking, the `using` declaration is safer to use than a `using` directive because it shows exactly what names you are making available. And if the name conflicts with a local name, the compiler lets you know. The `using` directive adds all names, even ones you might not need. If a local name conflicts, it overrides the namespace version, and you aren't warned. Also, the open nature of namespaces means that the complete list of names in a namespace might be spread over several locations, making it difficult to know exactly which names you are adding.

This is the approach used for most of this book's examples:

```
#include <iostream>int main()
{
    using namespace std;
```

First, the `iostream` header file puts everything in the `std` namespace. Then, the `using` directive makes the names available within `main()`. Some examples do this instead:

```
#include <iostream>
using namespace std;
int main()
{
```

This exports everything from the `std` namespace into the global namespace. The main rationale for this approach is expediency. It's easy to do, and if your system doesn't have namespaces, you can replace the first two of the preceding code lines with the original form:

```
#include <iostream.h>
```

However, namespace proponents hope that you will be more selective and use either the scope-resolution operator or the `using` declaration. That is, you shouldn't use the following:

```
using namespace std;  // avoid as too indiscriminate
```

Instead, you should use this:

```
int x;
std::cin >> x;
std::cout << x << std::endl;
```

Or you could use this:

```
using std::cin;
using std::cout;
using std::endl;
int x;
cin >> x;
cout << x << endl;
```

You can use nested namespaces, as described in the following section, to create a namespace that holds the `using` declarations you commonly use.

More Namespace Features

You can nest namespace declarations, like this:

```
namespace elements
{
    namespace fire
    {
        int flame;
        ...
    }
    float water;
}
```

In this case, you refer to the `flame` variable as `elements::fire::flame`. Similarly, you can make the inner names available with this `using` directive:

```
using namespace elements::fire;
```

Also, you can use `using` directives and `using` declarations inside namespaces, like this:

```
namespace myth
{
    using Jill::fetch;
    using namespace elements;
    using std::cout;
    using std::cin;
}
```

Suppose you want to access `Jill::fetch`. Because `Jill::fetch` is now part of the `myth` namespace, where it can be called `fetch`, you can access it this way:

```
std::cin >> myth::fetch;
```

Of course, because it is also part of the `Jill` namespace, you still can call it `Jill::fetch`:

```
std::cout << Jill::fetch;  // display value read into myth::fetch
```

Or you can do this, provided that no local variables conflict:

```
using namespace myth;
cin >> fetch;       // really std::cin and Jill::fetch
```

Now consider applying a `using` directive to the *myth* namespace. The `using` directive is *transitive*. We say that an operation *op* is transitive if A *op* B and B *op* C implies A *op* C. For example, the `>` operator is transitive. (That is, A bigger than B and B bigger than C implies A bigger than C.) In this context, the upshot is that the statement

```
using namespace myth;
```

results in the `elements` namespace being added via a `using` directive also, so it is the same as the following:

```
using namespace myth;
using namespace elements;
```

You can create an alias for a namespace. For example, suppose you have a namespace defined as follows:

```
namespace my_very_favorite_things { ... };
```

You can make `mvft` an alias for `my_very_favorite_things` by using the following statement:

```
namespace mvft = my_very_favorite_things;
```

You can use this technique to simplify using nested namespaces:

```
namespace MEF = myth::elements::fire;
using MEF::flame;
```

Unnamed Namespaces

You can create an *unnamed namespace* by omitting the namespace name:

```
namespace           // unnamed namespace
{
    int ice;
    int bandycoot;
}
```

This code behaves as if it were followed by a `using` directive; that is, the names declared in this namespace are in potential scope until the end of the declarative region that contains the unnamed namespace. In this respect, names in an unnamed namespace are like global variables. However, if a namespace has no name, you can't explicitly use a `using` directive or `using` declaration to make the names available elsewhere. In particular, you can't use names from an unnamed namespace in a file other than the one that contains the namespace declaration. This provides an alternative to using static variables with internal linkage. Indeed, the C++ Standard deprecates the use of the keyword `static` in namespaces and global scope. (*Deprecate* is a term that the C++ Standard uses to indicate practices that are currently valid but most likely will be rendered invalid by future revisions of the Standard.) Suppose, for example, you have this code:

```
static int counts;    // static storage, internal linkage
int other();
int main()
{
...
}

int other()
{
...
 }
```

The intent of the C++ Standard is that you should do this instead:

```
namespace
{
    int counts;    // static storage, internal linkage
}
```

```
int other();
int main()
{
    ...
}

int other()
{
    ...
}
```

A Namespace Example

Let's take a look at a multifile example that demonstrates some of the features of namespaces. The first file in this example (see Listing 9.10) is a header file that contains some items normally found in header files—constants, structure definitions, and function prototypes. In this case, the items are placed in two namespaces. The first namespace, pers, contains a definition of a Person structure, plus prototypes for a function that fills a structure with a person's name and a function that displays the structure's contents. The second namespace, debts, defines a structure for storing the name of a person and the amount of money owed to that person. This structure uses the Person structure, so the debts namespace has a using directive to make the names in the pers namespace available in the debts namespace. The debts namespace also contains some prototypes.

LISTING 9.10   `namesp.h`

```
// namesp.h
// create the pers and debts namespaces
namespace pers
{
    const int LEN = 40;
    struct Person
    {
        char fname[LEN];
        char lname[LEN];
    };
    void getPerson(Person &);
    void showPerson(const Person &);
}

namespace debts
{
    using namespace pers;
    struct Debt
    {
        Person name;
        double amount;
    };
```

LISTING 9.10 Continued

```
        void getDebt(Debt &);
        void showDebt(const Debt &);
        double sumDebts(const Debt ar[], int n);
}
```

The second file in this example (see Listing 9.11) follows the usual pattern of having a source code file provide definitions for functions prototyped in a header file. The function names, which are declared in a namespace, have namespace scope, so the definitions need to be in the same namespace as the declarations. This is where the open nature of namespaces comes in handy. The original namespaces are brought in by including `namesp.h` (refer to Listing 9.10). The file then adds the function definitions to the two namespaces, as shown in Listing 9.11. Also, the `namesp.cpp` file illustrates bringing in elements of the `std` namespace with the `using` declaration and the scope-resolution operator.

LISTING 9.11 `namesp.cpp`

```
// namesp.cpp -- namespaces
#include <iostream>
#include "namesp.h"

namespace pers
{
    using std::cout;
    using std::cin;
    void getPerson(Person & rp)
    {
        cout << "Enter first name: ";
        cin >> rp.fname;
        cout << "Enter last name: ";
        cin >> rp.lname;
    }

    void showPerson(const Person & rp)
    {
        std::cout << rp.lname << ", " << rp.fname;
    }
}

namespace debts
{
    void getDebt(Debt & rd)
    {
        getPerson(rd.name);
        std::cout << "Enter debt: ";
        std::cin >> rd.amount;
    }

    void showDebt(const Debt & rd)
    {
        showPerson(rd.name);
```

LISTING 9.11   Continued

```
            std::cout <<": $" << rd.amount << std::endl;
    }

    double sumDebts(const Debt ar[], int n)
    {
        double total = 0;
        for (int i = 0; i < n; i++)
            total += ar[i].amount;
        return total;
    }
}
```

Finally, the third file of this program (see Listing 9.12) is a source code file that uses the structures and functions declared and defined in the namespaces. Listing 9.12 shows several methods of making the namespace identifiers available.

LISTING 9.12   `usenmsp.cpp`

```
// usenmsp.cpp -- using namespaces
#include <iostream>
#include "namesp.h"

void other(void);
void another(void);
int main(void)
{
    using debts::Debt;
    using debts::showDebt;
    Debt golf = { {"Benny", "Goatsniff"}, 120.0 };
    showDebt(golf);
    other();
    another();

    return 0;
}

void other(void)
{
    using std::cout;
    using std::endl;
    using namespace debts;
    Person dg = {"Doodles", "Glister"};
    showPerson(dg);
    cout << endl;
    Debt zippy[3];
    int i;

    for (i = 0; i < 3; i++)
        getDebt(zippy[i]);
```

LISTING 9.12 *Continued*

```
    for (i = 0; i < 3; i++)
        showDebt(zippy[i]);
    cout << "Total debt: $" << sumDebts(zippy, 3) << endl;.cpp;.cpp;.cpp;

    return;
}

void another(void)
{
    using pers::Person;;

    Person collector = { "Milo", "Rightshift" };
    pers::showPerson(collector);
    std::cout << std::endl;
}
```

In Listing 9.12, `main()` begins by using two `using` declarations:

```
using debts::Debt;        // makes the Debt structure definition available
using debts::showDebt;    // makes the showDebt function available
```

Note that `using` declarations just use the name; for example, the second example here doesn't describe the return type or function signature for `showDebt`; it just gives the name. (Thus, if a function were overloaded, a single `using` declaration would import all the versions.) Also, although both `Debt` and `showDebt()` use the `Person` type, it isn't necessary to import any of the `Person` names because the `debt` namespace already has a `using` directive that includes the `pers` namespace.

Next, the `other()` function takes the less desirable approach of importing the entire namespace with a `using` directive:

```
using namespace debts;    // make all debts and pers names available to other()
```

Because the `using` directive in `debts` imports the `pers` namespace, the `other()` function can use the `Person` type and the `showPerson()` function.

Finally, the `another()` function uses a `using` declaration and the scope-resolution operator to access specific names:

```
using pers::Person;;
pers::showPerson(collector);
```

Here is a sample run of the program built from Listings 9.10, 9.11, and 9.12:

```
Goatsniff, Benny: $120
Glister, Doodles
Enter first name: Arabella
Enter last name: Binx
Enter debt: 100
Enter first name: Cleve
Enter last name: Delaproux
Enter debt: 120
Enter first name: Eddie
```

```
Enter last name: Fiotox
Enter debt: 200
Binx, Arabella: $100
Delaproux, Cleve: $120
Fiotox, Eddie: $200
Total debt: $420
Rightshift, Milo
```

Namespaces and the Future

As programmers become more familiar with namespaces, common programming idioms will emerge. Here are some current guidelines:

- Use variables in a named namespace instead of using external global variables.

- Use variables in an unnamed namespace instead of using static global variables.

- If you develop a library of functions or classes, place them in a namespace. Indeed, C++ currently already calls for placing standard library functions in a namespace called `std`. This extends to functions brought in from C. For example, the `math.c` header file, which is C compatible, doesn't use namespaces, but the C++ `cmath` header file should place the various math library functions in the `std` namespace. (In practice, not all compiler have made this transition yet.)

- Use the `using` directive only as a temporary means of converting old code to namespace usage.

- Don't use `using` directives in header files; for one thing, doing so conceals which names are being made available. Also, the ordering of header files may affect behavior. If you use a `using` directive, place it after all the preprocessor `#include` directives.

- Preferentially import names by using the scope-resolution operator or a `using` declaration.

- Preferentially use local scope instead of global scope for `using` declarations.

Bear in mind that the main motivation for using namespaces is to simplify management of large programming projects. For simple, one-file programs, using a `using` directive is no great sin.

As mentioned earlier, changes in the header filenames reflect namespace changes. The older-style header files, such as `iostream.h`, do not use namespaces, but the newer `iostream` header file should use the `std` namespace.

Summary

C++ encourages the use of multiple files in developing programs. An effective organizational strategy is to use a header file to define user types and provide function prototypes for functions to manipulate the user types. You should use a separate source code file for the function definitions. Together, the header file and the source file define and implement the user-defined type and how it can be used. Then, `main()` and other functions using those functions can go into a third file.

C++'s storage schemes determine how long variables remain in memory (storage duration) and what parts of a program have access to them (scope and linkage). Automatic variables are variables that are defined within a block, such as a function body or a block within the body. They exist and are known only while the program executes statements in the block that contains the definition. Automatic variables may be declared by using the storage class specifiers `auto` and `register` or with no specifier at all, which is the same as using `auto`. The `register` specifier is a hint to the compiler that the variable is heavily used.

Static variables exist for the duration of a program. A variable defined outside any function is known to all functions in the file following its definition (file scope) and is made available to other files in the program (external linkage). For another file to use such a variable, that file must declare it by using the `extern` keyword. A variable that is shared across files should have a defining declaration in one file (`extern` is not used) and reference declarations in the other files (`extern` is used). A variable defined outside any function but qualified with the keyword `static` has file scope but is not made available to other files (internal linkage). A variable defined inside a block but qualified with the keyword `static` is local to that block (local scope, no linkage) but retains its value for the duration of the program.

By default, C++ functions have external linkage, so they can be shared across files. But functions qualified with the keyword `static` have internal linkage and are confined to the defining file.

Namespaces let you define named regions in which you can declare identifiers. The intent is to reduce name conflicts, particularly in large programs that use code from several vendors. You can make available identifiers in a namespace by using the scope-resolution operator, by using a `using` declaration, or by using a `using` directive.

Review Questions

1. What storage scheme would you use for the following situations?

    a. `homer` is a formal argument (parameter) to a function.

    b. The `secret` variable is to be shared by two files.

    c. The `topsecret` variable is to be shared by the functions in one file but hidden from other files.

    d. `beencalled` keeps track of how many times the function containing it has been called.

2. Describe the differences between a `using` declaration and a `using` directive.

3. Rewrite the following so that it doesn't use **using** declarations or **using** directives:

```
#include <iostream>
using namespace std;
int main()
{
    double x;
    cout << "Enter value: ";
    while (! (cin >> x) )
    {
        cout << "Bad input. Please enter a number: ";
        cin.clear();
        while (cin.get() != '\n')
            continue;
    }
    cout << "Value = " << x << endl;
    return 0;
}
```

4. Rewrite the following so that it uses **using** declarations instead of the **using** directive:

```
#include <iostream>
using namespace std;
int main()
{
    double x;
    cout << "Enter value: ";
    while (! (cin >> x) )
    {
        cout << "Bad input. Please enter a number: ";
        cin.clear();
        while (cin.get() != '\n')
            continue;
    }
    cout << "Value = " << x << endl;
    return 0;
}
```

5. Say that the **average(3,6)** function returns an **int** average of the two **int** arguments when it is called in one file, and it returns a **double** average of the two **int** arguments when it is called in a second file in the same program. How could you set this up?

6. What will the following two-file program display?

```
// file1.cpp
#include <iostream>
using namespace std;
void other();
void another();
int x = 10;
int y;

int main()
{
```

```cpp
    cout << x << endl;
    {
        int x = 4;
        cout << x << endl;
        cout << y << endl;
    }
    other();
    another();
    return 0;
}

void other()
{
    int y = 1;
    cout << "Other: " << x << ", " << y << endl;
}

// file 2.cpp
#include <iostream>
using namespace std;
extern int x;
namespace
{
    int y = -4;
}

void another()
{
    cout << "another(): " << x << ", " << y << endl;
}
```

7. What will the following program display?

```cpp
#include <iostream>
using namespace std;
void other();
namespace n1
{
    int x = 1;
}

namespace n2
{
    int x = 2;
}


int main()
{
    using namespace n1;
    cout << x << endl;
    {
        int x = 4;
```

```
        cout << x << ", " << n1::x << ", " << n2::x << endl;
    }
    using n2::x;
    cout << x << endl;

    other();
    return 0;
}

void other()
{
    using namespace n2;
    cout << x << endl;
    {
        int x = 4;
        cout << x << ", " << n1::x << ", " << n2::x << endl;
    }
    using n2::x;
    cout << x << endl;
}
```

Programming Exercises

1. Here is a header file:

```
// golf.h -- for pe9-1.cpp

const int Len = 40;
struct golf
{
    char fullname[Len];
    int handicap;
};

// non-interactive version:
//   function sets golf structure to provided name, handicap
//   using values passed as arguments to the function
void setgolf(golf & g, const char * name, int hc);

// interactive version:
//   function solicits name and handicap from user
//   and sets the members of g to the values entered
//   returns 1 if name is entered, 0 if name is empty string
int setgolf(golf & g);

// function resets handicap to new value
void handicap(golf & g, int hc);

// function displays contents of golf structure
void showgolf(const golf & g);
```

Note that `setgolf()` is overloaded. Using the first version of `setgolf()` would look like this:

```
golf ann;
setgolf(ann, "Ann Birdfree", 24);
```

The function call provides the information that's stored in the `ann` structure. Using the second version of `setgolf()` would look like this:

```
golf andy;
setgolf(andy);
```

The function would prompt the user to enter the name and handicap and store them in the `andy` structure. This function could (but doesn't need to) use the first version internally.

Put together a multifile program based on this header. One file, named `golf.cpp`, should provide suitable function definitions to match the prototypes in the header file. A second file should contain `main()` and demonstrate all the features of the prototyped functions. For example, a loop should solicit input for an array of golf structures and terminate when the array is full or the user enters an empty string for the golfer's name. The `main()` function should use only the prototyped functions to access the golf structures.

2. Redo Listing 9.8, replacing the character array with a `string` object. The program should no longer have to check whether the input string fits, and it can compare the input string to `""` to check for an empty line.

3. Begin with the following structure declaration:

```
struct chaff
{
    char dross[20];
    int slag;
};
```

Write a program that uses placement `new` to place an array of two such structures in a buffer. Then assign values to the structure members (remembering to use `strcpy()` for the `char` array) and use a loop to display the contents. Option 1 is to use a static array, like that in Listing 9.9, for the buffer. Option 2 is to use regular `new` to allocate the buffer.

4. Write a three-file program based on the following namespace:

```
namespace SALES
{
    const int QUARTERS = 4;
    struct Sales
    {
        double sales[QUARTERS];
        double average;
        double max;
        double min;
    };
```

```
    // copies the lesser of 4 or n items from the array ar
    // to the sales member of s and computes and stores the
    // average, maximum, and minimum values of the entered items;
    // remaining elements of sales, if any, set to 0
    void setSales(Sales & s, const double ar[], int n);

    // gathers sales for 4 quarters interactively, stores them
    // in the sales member of s and computes and stores the
    // average, maximum, and minumum values
    void setSales(Sales & s);

    // display all information in structure s
    void showSales(const Sales & s);
}
```

The first file should be a header file that contains the namespace. The second file should be a source code file that extends the namespace to provide definitions for the three prototyped functions. The third file should declare two **Sales** objects. It should use the interactive version of **setSales()** to provide values for one structure and the non-interactive version of **setSales()** to provide values for the second structure. It should display the contents of both structures by using **showSales()**.

CHAPTER 10

OBJECTS AND CLASSES

In this chapter you'll learn about the following:

- Procedural and object-oriented programming
- The concept of classes
- How to define and implement a class
- Public and private class access
- Class data members
- Class methods (also called class function members)
- Creating and using class objects
- Class constructors and destructors
- `const` member functions
- The `this` pointer
- Creating arrays of objects
- Class scope
- Abstract data types

bject-oriented programming (OOP) is a particular conceptual approach to designing programs, and C++ has enhanced C with features that ease the way to applying that approach. The following are the most important OOP features:

- Abstraction

- Encapsulation and data hiding

- Polymorphism

- Inheritance

- Reusability of code

The class is the single most important C++ enhancement for implementing these features and tying them together. This chapter begins an examination of classes. It explains abstraction, encapsulation, and data hiding, and shows how classes implement these features. It discusses how to define a class, provide a class with public and private sections, and create member functions that work with the class data. Also, this chapter acquaints you with constructors and destructors, which are special member functions for creating and disposing of objects that belong to a class. Finally, you'll meet the `this` pointer, an important component of some class programming. The following chapters extend this discussion to operator overloading (another variety of polymorphism) and inheritance, the basis for reusing code.

Procedural and Object-Oriented Programming

Although in this book we have occasionally explored the OOP perspective on programming, we've usually stuck pretty close to the standard procedural approach of languages such as C, Pascal, and BASIC. Let's look at an example that clarifies how the OOP outlook differs from that of procedural programming.

As the newest member of the Genre Giants softball team, you've been asked to keep the team statistics. Naturally, you turn to your computer for help. If you were a procedural programmer, you might think along these lines:

> Let's see, I want to enter the name, times at bat, number of hits, batting averages (for those who don't follow baseball or softball, the batting average is the number of hits divided by the player's official number of times at bat; an at bat terminates when a player gets on base or makes an out, but certain events, such as getting a walk, don't count as official times at bat), and all those other great basic statistics for each player. Wait, the computer is supposed to make life easier for me, so I want to have it figure out some of that stuff, such as the batting average. Also, I want the program to report the results. How should I organize this? I guess I should do things right and use functions. Yeah, I'll make `main()` call a function to get the input, call another function to make the calculations, and then call a third function to report the results. Hmmm, what happens when I get data from the next game? I don't want to start from scratch again. Okay, I can add a function to update the statistics. Golly, maybe I'll need a menu in `main()` to select between entering, calculating, updating, and showing the data. Hmmm...how am I going to represent the data? I could use an array of strings to hold the players' names, another array to hold the at bats for each player, yet another array to hold the hits, and so on. No, that's dumb. I can design a structure to hold all the information for a single player and then use an array of those structures to represent the whole team.

In short, with a procedural approach, you first concentrate on the procedures you will follow and then think about how to represent the data. (Note: So that you don't have to keep the program running the whole season, you probably also want to be able to save data to a file and read data from a file.)

Now let's see how your perspective changes when you don your OOP hat (in an attractive polymorphic design). You begin by thinking about the data. Furthermore, you think about the data not only in terms of how to represent it but in terms of how it's to be used:

Let's see, what am I keeping track of? A ball player, of course. So, I want an object that represents the whole player, not just her batting average or times at bat. Yeah, that'll be my fundamental data unit, an object representing the name and statistics for a player. I'll need some methods to handle this object. Hmmm, I guess I need a method to get basic information into this unit. The computer should calculate some of the stuff, like the batting averages—I can add methods to do calculations. And the program should do those calculations automatically, without the user having to remember to ask to have them done. Also, I'll need methods for updating and displaying the information. So the user gets three ways to interact with the data: initialization, updating, and reporting. That's the user interface.

In short, with an OOP approach, you concentrate on the object as the user perceives it, thinking about the data you need to describe the object and the operations that will describe the user's interaction with the data. After you develop a description of that interface, you move on to decide how to implement the interface and data storage. Finally, you put together a program to use your new design.

Abstraction and Classes

Life is full of complexities, and one way we cope with complexity is to frame simplifying abstractions. You are a collection of more than an octillion atoms. Some students of the mind would say that your mind is a collection of semiautonomous agents. But it's much simpler to think of yourself as a single entity. In computing, abstraction is the crucial step of representing information in terms of its interface with the user. That is, you abstract the essential operational features of a problem and express a solution in those terms. In the softball statistics example, the interface describes how the user initializes, updates, and displays the data. From abstraction, it is a short step to the user-defined type, which in C++ is a class design that implements the abstract interface.

What Is a Type?

Let's think a little more about what constitutes a type. For example, what is a nerd? If you subscribe to the popular stereotype, you might think of a nerd in visual terms—thick, black-rimmed glasses, pocket protector full of pens, and so on. After a little reflection, you might conclude that a nerd is better defined operationally—for example, in terms of how he or she responds to an awkward social situation. You have a similar situation, if you don't mind stretched analogies, with a procedural language such as C. At first, you tend to think of a data type in terms of its appearance—how it is stored in memory. A `char`, for example, is 1 byte of memory, and a `double` is often 8 bytes of memory. But a little reflection leads you to conclude that a data type is also defined in terms of the operations that can be performed on it. For example, the `int` type can use all the arithmetic operations. You can add, subtract, multiply, and divide integers. You can also use the modulus operator (%) with them.

On the other hand, consider pointers. A pointer might very well require the same amount of memory as an `int`. It might even be represented internally as an integer. But a pointer doesn't allow the same operations that an integer does. You can't, for example, multiply two pointers by each other. The concept makes no sense, so C++ doesn't implement it. Thus, when you declare a variable as an `int` or as a pointer-to-`float`, you're not just allocating memory—you are also establishing which operations can be performed with the variable. In short, specifying a basic type does three things:

- It determines how much memory is needed for a data object.

- It determines how the bits in memory are interpreted. (A `long` and a `float` might use the same number of bits in memory, but they are translated into numeric values differently.)

- It determines what operations, or methods, can be performed using the data object.

For built-in types, the information about operations is built in to the compiler. But when you define a user-defined type in C++, you have to provide the same kind of information yourself. In exchange for this extra work, you gain the power and flexibility to custom fit new data types to match real-world requirements.

Classes in C++

A *class* is a C++ vehicle for translating an abstraction to a user-defined type. It combines data representation and methods for manipulating that data into one neat package. Let's look at a class that represents stocks.

First, you have to think a bit about how to represent stocks. You could take one share of stock as the basic unit and define a class to represent a share. However, that implies that you would need 100 objects to represent 100 shares, and that's not practical. Instead, you can represent a person's current holdings in a particular stock as a basic unit. The number of shares owned would be part of the data representation. A realistic approach would have to maintain records of such things as initial purchase price and date of purchase, for tax purposes. Also, it would have to manage events such as stock splits. That seems a bit ambitious for your first effort at defining a class, so you can instead take an idealized, simplified view of matters. In particular, you should limit the operations you can perform to the following:

- Acquire stock in a company.

- Buy more shares of the same stock.

- Sell stock.

- Update the per-share value of a stock.

- Display information about the holdings.

You can use this list to define the public interface for the stock class. (And you can add additional features later if you're interested.) To support this interface, you need to store some information. Again, you can use a simplified approach. For example, you shouldn't worry about the U.S. practice of evaluating stocks in multiples of eighths of a dollar. (Apparently the New York Stock Exchange must have seen this simplification in a previous edition of the book because it has decided to change over to the system used here.) You should store the following information:

- Name of company

- Number of stocks owned

- Value of each share

- Total value of all shares

Next, you can define the class. Generally, a class specification has two parts:

- A *class declaration*, which describes the data component, in terms of data members, and the public interface, in terms of member functions, termed *methods*

- The *class method definitions*, which describe how certain class member functions are implemented

Roughly speaking, the class declaration provides a class overview, whereas the method definitions supply the details.

What Is an Interface?

An *interface* is a shared framework for interactions between two systems—for instance, between a computer and a printer or between a user and a computer program. For example, the user might be you and the program might be a word processor. When you use the word processor, you don't transfer words directly from your mind to the computer memory. Instead, you interact with the interface provided by the program. You press a key, and the computer shows you a character on the screen. You move the mouse, and the computer moves a cursor on the screen. You click the mouse accidentally, and something weird happens to the paragraph you were typing. The program interface manages the conversion of your intentions to specific information stored in the computer.

For classes, we speak of the public interface. In this case, the public is the program using the class, the interacting system consists of the class objects, and the interface consists of the methods provided by whoever wrote the class. The interface enables you, the programmer, to write code that interacts with class objects, and thus it enables the program to use the class objects. For example, to find the number of characters in a `string` object, you don't open up the object to what is inside; you just use the `size()` method provided by the class creators. It turns out that the class design denies direct access to the public user. But the public is allowed to use the `size()` method. The `size()` method, then, is part of the public interface between the user and a `string` class object. Similarly, the `getline()` method is part of the `istream` class public interface; a program using `cin` doesn't tinker directly with the innards of a `cin` object to read a line of input; instead, `getline()` does the work.

If you want a more personal relationship, instead of thinking of the program using a class as the public user, you can think of the person writing the program using the class as the public user. But in any case, to use a class, you need to know its public interface; to write a class, you need to create its public interface.

Developing a class and a program using it requires several steps. Rather than take them all at once, let's break up the development into smaller stages; later the code for these stages is merged together into Listing 10.3. Listing 10.1 presents the first stage, a tentative class declaration for a class called `Stock`. (To help identify classes, this book follows a common, but not universal, convention of capitalizing class names.) You'll notice that Listing 10.1 looks like a structure declaration with a few additional wrinkles, such as member functions and public and private sections. You'll improve on this declaration shortly (so don't use it as a model), but first let's see how this definition works.

LISTING 10.1   The First Part of `stocks.cpp`

```
// beginning of stocks.cpp file
#include <iostream>
#include <cstring>

class Stock   // class declaration
{
private:
    char company[30];
    int shares;
    double share_val;
    double total_val;
    void set_tot() { total_val = shares * share_val; }
public:
    void acquire(const char * co, int n, double pr);
    void buy(int num, double price);
    void sell(int num, double price);
    void update(double price);
    void show();
};    // note semicolon at the end
```

You'll get a closer look at the class details later, but first let's examine the more general features. To begin, the C++ keyword `class` identifies the code in Listing 10.1 as defining the design of a class. The syntax identifies `Stock` as the type name for this new class. This declaration enables you to declare variables, called *objects*, or *instances*, of the `Stock` type. Each individual object represents a single holding. For example, the declarations

```
Stock sally;
Stock solly;
```

create two `Stock` objects called `sally` and `solly`. The `sally` object, for example, could represent Sally's stock holdings in a particular company.

Next, notice that the information you decided to store appears in the form of class data members, such as `company` and `shares`. The `company` member of `sally`, for example, holds the name of the company, the `share` member holds the number of shares Sally owns, the `share_val` member holds the value of each share, and the `total_val` member holds the total value of all the shares. Similarly, the operations you want appear as class function members (or methods), such as `sell()` and `update()`. A member function can be defined in place—for example, `set_tot()`—or it can be represented by a prototype, like the other member functions in this class. The full definitions for the other member functions come later, but the prototypes suffice to describe the function interfaces. The binding of data and methods into a single unit is the most striking feature of the class. Because of this design, creating a `Stock` object automatically establishes the rules governing how that object can be used.

You've already seen how the `istream` and `ostream` classes have member functions, such as `get()` and `getline()`. The function prototypes in the `Stock` class declaration demonstrate how member functions are established. The `iostream` header file, for example, has a `getline()` prototype in the `istream` class declaration.

Also new are the keywords `private` and `public`. These labels describe *access control* for class members. Any program that uses an object of a particular class can access the public portions directly. A program can access the private members of an object *only* by using the public member functions (or, as you'll see in Chapter 11, "Working with Classes," via a friend function). For example, the only way to alter the `shares` member of the `Stock` class is to use one of the `Stock` member functions. Thus, the public member functions act as go-betweens between a program and an object's private members; they provide the interface between object and program. This insulation of data from direct access by a program is called *data hiding*. (C++ provides a third access-control keyword, `protected`, which we'll discuss when we cover class inheritance in Chapter 13, "Class Inheritance.") (See Figure 10.1.) Whereas data hiding may be an unscrupulous act in, say, a stock fund prospectus, it's a good practice in computing because it preserves the integrity of the data.

FIGURE 10.1

The `Stock` class.

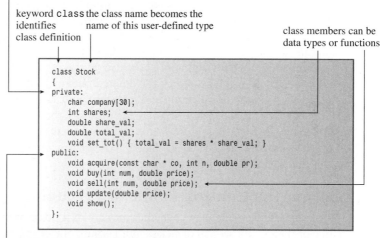

keyword `private` identifies class members that can be accessed only through the public member functions (data hiding)

keyword `class` the class name becomes the
identifies   name of this user-defined type
class definition

class members can be
data types or functions

```
class Stock
{
private:
    char company[30];
    int shares;
    double share_val;
    double total_val;
    void set_tot() { total_val = shares * share_val; }
public:
    void acquire(const char * co, int n, double pr);
    void buy(int num, double price);
    void sell(int num, double price);
    void update(double price);
    void show();
};
```

keyword `public` identifies class members that constitute the public interface for the class (abstraction)

A class design attempts to separate the public interface from the specifics of the implementation. The public interface represents the abstraction component of the design. Gathering the implementation details together and separating them from the abstraction is called *encapsulation*. *Data hiding* (putting data into the private section of a class) is an instance of encapsulation, and so is hiding functional details of an implementation in the private section, as the

`Stock` class does with `set_tot()`. Another example of encapsulation is the usual practice of placing class function definitions in a separate file from the class declaration.

OOP and C++

OOP is a programming style that you can use to some degree with any language. Certainly, you can incorporate many OOP ideas into ordinary C programs. For example, Chapter 9, "Memory Models and Namespaces," provides an example (see Listings 9.1, 9.2, 9.3) in which a header file contains a structure prototype along with the prototypes for functions to manipulate that structure. The `main()` function simply defines variables of that structure type and uses the associated functions to handle those variables; `main()` does not directly access structure members. In essence, that example defines an abstract type that places the storage format and the function prototypes in a header file, hiding the actual data representation from `main()`. C++ includes features specifically intended to implement the OOP approach, so it enables you to take the process a few steps further than you can with C. First, placing the data representation and the function prototypes into a single class declaration instead of keeping them separate unifies the description by placing everything in one class declaration. Second, making the data representation private enforces the stricture that data is accessed only by authorized functions. If, in the C example, `main()` directly accesses a structure member, it violates the spirit of OOP, but it doesn't break any C language rules. However, trying to directly access, say, the `shares` member of a `Stock` object does break a C++ language rule, and the compiler will catch it.

Note that data hiding not only prevents you from accessing data directly, but it also absolves you (in the roll as a user of the class) from needing to know how the data is represented. For example, the `show()` member displays, among other things, the total value of a holding. This value can be stored as part of an object, as the code in Listing 10.1 does, or it can be calculated when needed. From the standpoint of the user, it makes no difference which approach is used. What you do need to know is what the different member functions accomplish; that is, you need to know what kinds of arguments a member function takes and what kind of return value it has. The principle is to separate the details of the implementation from the design of the interface. If you later find a better way to implement the data representation or the details of the member functions, you can change those details without changing the program interface, and that makes programs much easier to maintain.

Member Access Control: Public or Private?

You can declare class members, whether they are data items or member functions, either in the public or the private section of a class. But because one of the main precepts of OOP is to hide the data, data items normally go into the private section. The member functions that constitute the class interface go into the public section; otherwise, you can't call those functions from a program. As the `Stock` declaration shows, you can also put member functions in the private section. You can't call such functions directly from a program, but the public methods can use them. Typically, you use private member functions to handle implementation details that don't form part of the public interface.

You don't have to use the keyword `private` in class declarations because that is the default access control for class objects:

```
class World
{
    float mass;         // private by default
    char name[20];      // private by default
public:
    void tellall(void);
    ...
};
```

However, this book explicitly uses the `private` label in order to emphasize the concept of data hiding.

Classes and Structures
Class descriptions look much like structure declarations with the addition of member functions and the `public` and `private` visibility labels. In fact, C++ extends to structures the same features classes have. The only difference is that the default access type for a structure is `public`, whereas the default type for a class is `private`. C++ programmers commonly use classes to implement class descriptions while restricting structures to representing pure data objects or, occasionally, classes with no private components.

Implementing Class Member Functions

You still have to create the second part of the class specification: providing code for those member functions represented by a prototype in the class declaration. Member function definitions are much like regular function definitions. Each has a function header and a function body. Member function definitions can have return types and arguments. But they also have two special characteristics:

- When you define a member function, you use the scope-resolution operator (`::`) to identify the class to which the function belongs.

- Class methods can access the `private` components of the class.

Let's look at these points now.

First, the function header for a member function uses the scope-resolution operator (`::`) to indicate to which class the function belongs. For example, the header for the `update()` member function looks like this:

```
void Stock::update(double price)
```

This notation means you are defining the `update()` function that is a member of the `Stock` class. Not only does this identify `update()` as a member function, it means you can use the same name for a member function for a different class. For example, an `update()` function for a `Buffoon` class would have this function header:

```
void Buffoon::update()
```

Thus, the scope-resolution operator resolves the identity of the class to which a method definition applies. We say that the identifier `update()` has *class scope*. Other member functions of the `Stock` class can, if necessary, use the `update()` method without using the scope-resolution operator. That's because they belong to the same class, making `update()` in scope. Using `update()` outside the class declaration and method definitions, however, requires special measures, which we'll get to soon.

One way of looking at method names is that the complete name of a class method includes the class name. `Stock::update()` is called the *qualified name* of the function. A simple `update()`, on the other hand, is an abbreviation (the *unqualified name*) for the full name—one that can be used just in class scope.

The second special characteristic of methods is that a method can access the private members of a class. For example, the `show()` method can use code like this:

```
cout << "Company: " << company
     << "  Shares: " << shares << endl
     << "  Share Price: $" << share_val
     << "  Total Worth: $" << total_val << endl;
```

Here `company`, `shares`, and so on are private data members of the `Stock` class. If you try to use a nonmember function to access these data members, the compiler stops you cold in your tracks. (However, friend functions, which Chapter 11 discusses, provide an exception.)

With these two points in mind, you can implement the class methods as shown in Listing 10.2. These method definitions can go in a separate file or in the same file with the class declaration. Because you are beginning simply, you can assume that these definitions follow the class declaration in the same file. This is the easiest, although not the best, way to make the class declaration available to the method definitions. (The best way, which you'll apply later in this chapter, is to use a header file for the class declaration and a separate source code file for the class member function definitions.) To provide more namespace experience, the code uses the `std::` qualifier in some methods and `using` declarations in others.

LISTING 10.2   `stocks.cpp` Continued

```cpp
//more stocks.cpp -- implementing the class member functions
void Stock::acquire(const char * co, int n, double pr)
{
    std::strncpy(company, co, 29);   // truncate co to fit company
    company[29] = '\0';
    if (n < 0)
    {
        std::cerr << "Number of shares can't be negative; "
                  << company << " shares set to 0.\n";
        shares = 0;
    }
    else
        shares = n;
    share_val = pr;
    set_tot();
}
```

LISTING 10.2 Continued

```cpp
void Stock::buy(int num, double price)
{
     if (num < 0)
     {
        std::cerr << "Number of shares purchased can't be negative. "
                  << "Transaction is aborted.\n";
     }
     else
     {
        shares += num;
        share_val = price;
        set_tot();
     }
}

void Stock::sell(int num, double price)
{
    using std::cerr;
    if (num < 0)
    {
        cerr << "Number of shares sold can't be negative. "
             << "Transaction is aborted.\n";
    }
    else if (num > shares)
    {
        cerr << "You can't sell more than you have! "
             << "Transaction is aborted.\n";
    }
    else
    {
        shares -= num;
        share_val = price;
        set_tot();
    }
}

void Stock::update(double price)
{
    share_val = price;
    set_tot();
}

void Stock::show()
{
    using std::cout;
    using std::endl;
    cout << "Company: " << company
         << "  Shares: " << shares << endl
         << "  Share Price: $" << share_val
         << "  Total Worth: $" << total_val << endl;
}
```

Member Function Notes

The `acquire()` function manages the first acquisition of stock for a given company, whereas `buy()` and `sell()` manage adding to or subtracting from an existing holding. The `buy()` and `sell()` methods make sure that the number of shares bought or sold is not a negative number. Also, if the user attempts to sell more shares than he or she has, the `sell()` function terminates the transaction. The technique of making the data private and limiting access to public functions gives you control over how the data can be used; in this case, it allows you to insert these safeguards against faulty transactions.

Four of the member functions set or reset the `total_val` member value. Rather than write this calculation four times, the class has each function call the `set_tot()` function. Because this function is merely the means of implementing the code and not part of the public interface, the class makes `set_tot()` a private member function. (That is, `set_tot()` is a member function used by the person writing the class but not used by someone writing code that uses the class.) If the calculation were lengthy, this could save some typing and code space. Here, however, the main value is that by using a function call instead of retyping the calculation each time, you ensure that exactly the same calculation gets done. Also, if you have to revise the calculation (which is not likely in this particular case), you have to revise it in just one location.

The `acquire()` method uses `strncpy()` to copy the string. In case you've forgotten, the call `strncpy(s2, s1, n)` copies `s1` to `s2` or else up to `n` characters from `s1` to `s2`, whichever comes first. If `s1` contains fewer characters than `n`, the `strncpy()` function pads `s2` with null characters. That is, `strncpy(firstname,"Tim", 6)` copies the characters `T`, `i`, and `m` to `firstname` and then adds three null characters to bring the total to six characters. But if `s1` is longer than `n`, no null characters are appended. That is, `strncpy(firstname, "Priscilla", 4)` just copies the characters `P`, `r`, `i`, and `s` to `firstname`, making it a character array but, because it lacks a terminating null character, not a string. Therefore, `acquire()` places a null character at the end of the array to guarantee that it is a string.

The `cerr` Object

The `cerr` object, like `cout`, is an `ostream` object. The difference is that operating system redirection affects `cout` but not `cerr`. The `cerr` object is used for error messages. Thus, if you redirect program output to a file and there is an error, you still get the error message onscreen. (In Unix, you can redirect `cout` and `cerr` independently of one another. The > command-line operator redirects `cout`, and the 2> operator redirects `cerr`.)

Inline Methods

Any function with a definition in the class declaration automatically becomes an inline function. Thus, `Stock::set_tot()` is an inline function. Class declarations often use inline functions for short member functions, and `set_tot()` qualifies on that account.

You can, if you like, define a member function outside the class declaration and still make it inline. To do so, you just use the `inline` qualifier when you define the function in the class implementation section:

```
class Stock
{
private:
    ...
    void set_tot();  // definition kept separate
public:
    ...
};

inline void Stock::set_tot()  // use inline in definition
{
    total_val = shares * share_val;
}
```

The special rules for inline functions require that they be defined in each file in which they are used. The easiest way to make sure that inline definitions are available to all files in a multifile program is to include the inline definition in the same header file in which the corresponding class is defined. (Some development systems may have smart linkers that allow the inline definitions to go into a separate implementation file.)

Incidentally, according to the *rewrite rule*, defining a method in a class declaration is equivalent to replacing the method definition with a prototype and then rewriting the definition as an inline function immediately after the class declaration. That is, the original inline definition of set_tot() in Listing 10.2 is equivalent to the one just shown, with the definition following the class declaration.

Which Object Does a Method Use?

Now we come to one of the most important aspects of using objects: how you apply a class method to an object. Code such as

```
shares += num;
```

uses the shares member of an object. But which object? That's an excellent question! To answer it, first consider how you create an object. The simplest way is to declare class variables:

```
Stock kate, joe;
```

This creates two objects of the Stock class, one named kate and one named joe.

Next, consider how to use a member function with one of these objects. The answer, as with structures and structure members, is to use the membership operator:

```
kate.show();    // the kate object calls the member function
joe.show();     // the joe object calls the member function
```

The first call here invokes show() as a member of the kate object. This means the method interprets shares as kate.shares and share_val as kate.share_val. Similarly, the call joe.show() makes the show() method interpret shares and share_val as joe.shares and joe.share_val, respectively.

> ### Remember
>
> When you call a member function, it uses the data members of the particular object used to invoke the member function.

Similarly, the function call `kate.sell()` invokes the `set_tot()` function as if it were `kate.set_tot()`, causing that function to get its data from the `kate` object.

Each new object you create contains storage for its own internal variables, the class members. But all objects of the same class share the same set of class methods, with just one copy of each method. Suppose, for example, that `kate` and `joe` are `Stock` objects. In that case, `kate.shares` occupies one chunk of memory and `joe.shares` occupies a second chunk of memory. But `kate.show()` and `joe.show()` both invoke the same method—that is, both execute the same block of code. They just apply the code to different data. Calling a member function is what some OOP languages term *sending a message*. Thus, sending the same message to two different objects invokes the same method but applies it to two different objects. (See Figure 10.2.)

FIGURE 10.2
Objects, data, and member functions.

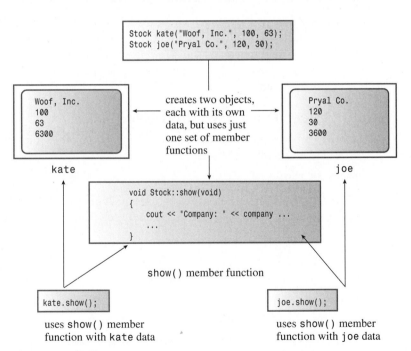

Using Classes

In this chapter you've seen how to define a class and its class methods. The next step is to produce a program that creates and uses objects of a class. The C++ goal is to make using classes as similar as possible to using the basic, built-in types, such as `int` and `char`. You can create a class object by declaring a class variable or using `new` to allocate an object of a class type. You can pass objects as arguments, return them as function return values, and assign one object to another. C++ provides facilities for initializing objects, teaching `cin` and `cout` to recognize objects, and even providing automatic type conversions between objects of similar classes. It will be a while before you can do all those things, but let's start now with the simpler properties. Indeed, you've already seen how to declare a class object and call a member function. Listing 10.3 combines those techniques with the class declaration and the member function definitions to form a complete program. It creates a `Stock` object named `stock1`. The program is simple, but it tests the features you have built in to the class.

LISTING 10.3   The Full `stocks.cpp` Program

```cpp
// stocks.cpp -- the whole program
#include <iostream>
#include <cstring>

class Stock  // class declaration
{
private:
    char company[30];
    int shares;
    double share_val;
    double total_val;
    void set_tot() { total_val = shares * share_val; }
public:
    void acquire(const char * co, int n, double pr);
    void buy(int num, double price);
    void sell(int num, double price);
    void update(double price);
    void show();
};    // note semicolon at the end

void Stock::acquire(const char * co, int n, double pr)
{
    std::strncpy(company, co, 29);  // truncate co to fit company
    company[29] = '\0';
    if (n < 0)
    {
        std::cerr << "Number of shares can't be negative; "
                  << company << " shares set to 0.\n";
        shares = 0;
    }
    else
        shares = n;
    share_val = pr;
    set_tot();
}

void Stock::buy(int num, double price)
{
     if (num < 0)
     {
```

LISTING 10.3 Continued

```cpp
        std::cerr << "Number of shares purchased can't be negative. "
            << "Transaction is aborted.\n";
    }
    else
    {
        shares += num;
        share_val = price;
        set_tot();
    }
}

void Stock::sell(int num, double price)
{
    using std::cerr;
    if (num < 0)
    {
        cerr << "Number of shares sold can't be negative. "
            << "Transaction is aborted.\n";
    }
    else if (num > shares)
    {
        cerr << "You can't sell more than you have! "
            << "Transaction is aborted.\n";
    }
    else
    {
        shares -= num;
        share_val = price;
        set_tot();
    }
}

void Stock::update(double price)
{
    share_val = price;
    set_tot();
}

void Stock::show()
{
    using std::cout;
    using std::endl;
    cout << "Company: " << company
        << "  Shares: " << shares << endl
        << "  Share Price: $" << share_val
        << "  Total Worth: $" << total_val << endl;
}

int main()
{
    using std::cout;
    using std::ios_base;
```

LISTING 10.3   Continued

```
        Stock stock1;
        stock1.acquire("NanoSmart", 20, 12.50);
        cout.setf(ios_base::fixed);      // #.## format
        cout.precision(2);               // #.## format
        cout.setf(ios_base::showpoint);  // #.## format
        stock1.show();
        stock1.buy(15, 18.25);
        stock1.show();
        stock1.sell(400, 20.00);
        stock1.show();
        return 0;
}
```

The program in Listing 10.3 uses three formatting commands:

```
cout.setf(ios_base::fixed);      // use fixed decimal point format
cout.precision(2);               // two places to right of decimal
cout.setf(ios_base::showpoint);  // show trailing zeros
```

It also has this `using` declaration:

```
using std::ios_base;
```

This is a case of nested namespaces. The `fixed` and `showpoint` identifiers are part of the `ios_base` namespace, and the `ios_base` namespace is part of the `std` namespace. The net effect of the formatting statements is to display two digits to the right of the decimal, including trailing zeros. Actually, only the first two are needed, according to current practices, and older C++ implementations just need the first and third. Using all three produces the same output for both newer and older implementations. See Chapter 17, "Input, Output, and Files," for the details. Meanwhile, here is the output of the program in Listing 10.3:

```
Company: NanoSmart  Shares: 20
  Share Price: $12.50  Total Worth: $250.00
Company: NanoSmart  Shares: 35
  Share Price: $18.25  Total Worth: $638.75
You can't sell more than you have! Transaction is aborted.
Company: NanoSmart  Shares: 35
  Share Price: $18.25  Total Worth: $638.75
```

Note that `main()` is just a vehicle for testing the design of the `Stock` class. When the `Stock` class works as you want it to, you can use it as a user-defined type in other programs. The critical point in using the new type is to understand what the member functions do; you shouldn't have to think about the implementation details. See the following sidebar, "The Client/Server Model."

The Client/Server Model

OOP programmers often discuss program design in terms of a client/server model. In this conceptualization, the *client* is a program that uses the class. The class declaration, including the class methods, constitute the *server*, which is a resource that is available to the programs that need it. The client uses the server through the publicly defined interface only. This means that the client's only responsibility, and, by extension, the client's programmer's only responsibility, is to know that interface. The server's responsibility, and, by extension, the server's designer's responsibility, is to see that the server reliably and accurately performs according to that interface. Any changes the server designer makes to the class design should be to details of implementation, not to the interface. This allows programmers to improve the client and the server independently of each other, without changes in the server having unforeseen repercussions on the client's behavior.

Reviewing Our Story to Date

The first step in specifying a class design is to provide a class declaration. The class declaration is modeled after a structure declaration and can include data members and function members. The declaration has a private section, and members declared in that section can be accessed only through the member functions. The declaration also has a public section, and members declared there can be accessed directly by a program using class objects. Typically, data members go into the private section and member functions go into the public section, so a typical class declaration has this form:

```
class className
{
private:
    data member declarations
public:
    member function prototypes
};
```

The contents of the public section constitute the abstract part of the design, the public interface. Encapsulating data in the private section protects the integrity of the data and is called *data hiding*. Thus, using a class is the C++ way of making it easy to implement the OOP features abstraction, data hiding, and encapsulation.

The second step in specifying a class design is to implement the class member functions. You can use a complete function definition instead of a function prototype in the class declaration, but the usual practice, except with very brief functions, is to provide the function definitions separately. In that case, you need to use the scope-resolution operator to indicate to which class a member function belongs. For example, suppose the `Bozo` class has a member function called `Retort()` that returns a pointer to a `char`. The function header would look like this:

```
char * Bozo::Retort()
```

In other words, `Retort()` is not just a type `char *` function; it is a type `char *` function that belongs to the `Bozo` class. The full, or qualified, name of the function is `Bozo::Retort()`. The name `Retort()`, on the other hand, is an abbreviation of the qualified name, and it can be used only in certain circumstances, such as in the code for the class methods.

Another way of describing this situation is to say that the name `Retort` has class scope, so the scope-resolution operator is needed to qualify the name when it is used outside the class declaration and a class method.

To create an object, which is a particular example of a class, you use the class name as if it were a type name:

```
Bozo bozetta;
```

This works because a class *is* a user-defined type.

You invoke a class member function, or method, by using a class object. You do so by using the dot membership operator:

```
cout << Bozetta.Retort();
```

This invokes the `Retort()` member function, and whenever the code for that function refers to a particular data member, the function uses the value that member has in the `bozetta` object.

Class Constructors and Destructors

At this point, you need to do more with the `Stock` class. There are certain standard functions, called *constructors* and *destructors*, that you should normally provide for a class. Let's talk about why they are needed and how to write them.

One of C++'s aims is to make using class objects similar to using standard types. However, the code provided so far in this chapter doesn't let you initialize a `Stock` object the way you can an ordinary `int` or `struct`. That is, the usual initialization syntax doesn't carry over for the `Stock` type:

```
int year = 2001;                              // valid initialization
struct thing
{
    char * pn;
    int m;
};
thing amabob = {"wodget", -23};               // valid initialization
Stock hot = {"Sukie's Autos, Inc.", 200, 50.25};   // NO! compile error
```

The reason you can't initialize a `Stock` object this way is because the data parts have private access status, which means a program cannot access the data members directly. As you've seen, the only way a program can access the data members is through a member function. Therefore, you need to devise an appropriate member function if you're to succeed in initializing an object. (You could initialize a class object as just shown if you made the data members public instead of private, but making the data public goes against one of the main justifications for using classes: data hiding.)

In general, it's best that all objects be initialized when they are created. For example, consider the following code:

```
Stock gift;
gift.buy(10, 24.75);
```

With the current implementation of the `Stock` class, the `gift` object has no value for the `company` member. The class design assumes that the user calls `acquire()` before calling any other member functions, but there is no way to enforce that assumption. One way around this difficulty is to have objects initialized automatically when they are created. To accomplish this, C++ provides for special member functions, called *class constructors*, especially for constructing new objects and assigning values to their data members. More precisely, C++ provides a name for these member functions and a syntax for using them, and you provide the method definition. The name is the same as the class name. For example, a possible constructor for the `Stock` class is a member function called `Stock()`. The constructor prototype and header have an interesting property: Although the constructor has no return value, it's not declared type `void`. In fact, a constructor has no declared type.

Declaring and Defining Constructors

Now you need to build a `Stock` constructor. Because a `Stock` object has three values to be provided from the outside world, you should give the constructor three arguments. (The fourth value, the `total_val` member, is calculated from `shares` and `share_val`, so you don't have to provide it to the constructor.) Possibly, you may want to provide just the `company` member value and set the other values to zero; you can do this by using default arguments (see Chapter 8, "Adventures in Functions"). Thus, the prototype would look like this:

```
// constructor prototype with some default arguments
Stock(const char * co, int n = 0, double pr = 0.0);
```

The first argument is a pointer to the string that is used to initialize the `company` character array member. The `n` and `pr` arguments provide values for the `shares` and `share_val` members. Note that there is no return type. The prototype goes in the public section of the class declaration.

Next, here's one possible definition for the constructor:

```
// constructor definition
Stock::Stock(const char * co, int n, double pr)
{
    std::strncpy(company, co, 29);
    company[29] = '\0';

    if (n < 0)
    {
        std::cerr << "Number of shares can't be negative; "
                  << company << " shares set to 0.\n";
        shares = 0;
    }
    else
        shares = n;
    share_val = pr;
    set_tot();
}
```

This is the same code that you used for the **acquire()** function earlier in this chapter. The difference is that in this case, a program automatically invokes the constructor when it declares an object.

Caution

Often those new to constructors try to use the class member names as arguments to the constructor, as in this example:

```
// NO!
Stock::Stock(const char * company, int shares, double share_val)
{
...
}
```

This is wrong. The constructor arguments don't represent the class members; they represent values that are assigned to the class members. Thus, they must have distinct names, or you end up with confusing code like this:

```
shares = shares;
```

One common coding practice to help avoid such confusion is to use an m_ prefix to identify data member names:

```
class Stock
{
private:
    string m_company;
    int m_shares;
    ....
```

Using Constructors

C++ provides two ways to initialize an object by using a constructor. The first is to call the constructor explicitly:

```
Stock food = Stock("World Cabbage", 250, 1.25);
```

This sets the **company** member of the **food** object to the string **"World Cabbage"**, the **shares** member to **250**, and so on.

The second way is to call the constructor implicitly:

```
Stock garment("Furry Mason", 50, 2.5);
```

This more compact form is equivalent to the following explicit call:

```
Stock garment = Stock("Furry Mason", 50, 2.5));
```

C++ uses a class constructor whenever you create an object of that class, even when you use **new** for dynamic memory allocation. Here's how to use the constructor with **new**:

```
Stock *pstock = new Stock("Electroshock Games", 18, 19.0);
```

This statement creates a `Stock` object, initializes it to the values provided by the arguments, and assigns the address of the object to the `pstock` pointer. In this case, the object doesn't have a name, but you can use the pointer to manage the object. We'll discuss pointers to objects further in Chapter 11.

Constructors are used differently from the other class methods. Normally, you use an object to invoke a method:

```
stock1.show();  // stock1 object invokes show() method
```

However, you can't use an object to invoke a constructor because until the constructor finishes its work of making the object, there is no object. Rather than being invoked by an object, the constructor is used to create the object.

Default Constructors

A *default constructor* is a constructor that is used to create an object when you don't provide explicit initialization values. That is, it's a constructor that is used for declarations like this:

```
Stock stock1;  // uses the default constructor
```

Hey, Listing 10.3 already did that! The reason this statement works is that if you fail to provide any constructors, C++ automatically supplies a default constructor. It's an implicit version of a default constructor, and it does nothing. For the `Stock` class, the default constructor would look like this:

```
Stock::Stock() { }
```

The net result is that the `stock1` object is created with its members uninitialized, just as

```
int x;
```

creates x without providing a value for x. The fact that the default constructor has no arguments reflects the fact that no values appear in the declaration.

A curious fact about default constructors is that the compiler provides one only if you don't define any constructors. After you define any constructor for a class, the responsibility for providing a default constructor for that class passes from the compiler to you. If you provide a nondefault constructor, such as `Stock(const char * co, int n, double pr)`, and don't provide your own version of a default constructor, then a declaration like

```
Stock stock1;  // not possible with current constructor
```

becomes an error. The reason for this behavior is that you might want to make it impossible to create uninitialized objects. If, however, you wish to create objects without explicit initialization, you must define your own default constructor. This is a constructor that takes no arguments. You can define a default constructor two ways. One is to provide default values for all the arguments to the existing constructor:

```
Stock(const char * co = "Error", int n = 0, double pr = 0.0);
```

The second is to use function overloading to define a second constructor, one that has no arguments:

```
Stock();
```

You can have only one default constructor, so be sure that you don't do both. (With early versions of C++, you could use only the second method for creating a default constructor.)

Actually, you should usually initialize objects in order to ensure that all members begin with known, reasonable values. Thus, a default constructor typically provides implicit initialization for all member values. For example, this is how you might define one for the `Stock` class:

```
Stock::Stock()          // default constructor
{
    std::strcpy(company, "no name");
    shares = 0;
    share_val = 0.0;
    total_val = 0.0;
}
```

Tip

When you design a class, you should usually provide a default constructor that implicitly initializes all class members.

After you've used either method (no arguments or default values for all arguments) to create the default constructor, you can declare object variables without initializing them explicitly:

```
Stock first;             // calls default constructor implicitly
Stock first = Stock();   // calls it explicitly
Stock *prelief = new Stock; // calls it implicitly
```

However, you shouldn't be misled by the implicit form of the nondefault constructor:

```
Stock first("Concrete Conglomerate");    // calls constructor
Stock second();                          // declares a function
Stock third;                             // calls default constructor
```

The first declaration here calls the nondefault constructor—that is, the one that takes arguments. The second declaration states that `second()` is a function that returns a `Stock` object. When you implicitly call the default constructor, you don't use parentheses.

Destructors

When you use a constructor to create an object, the program undertakes the responsibility of tracking that object until it expires. At that time, the program automatically calls a special member function bearing the formidable title *destructor*. The destructor should clean up any debris, so it actually serves a useful purpose. For example, if your constructor uses `new` to allocate memory, the destructor should use `delete` to free that memory. The `Stock` constructor doesn't do anything fancy like using `new`, so the `Stock` class destructor doesn't really have any tasks to perform. In such a case, you can simply let the compiler generate an implicit, do-nothing destructor, which is exactly what the first version of the `Stock` class does. On the other hand, it's certainly worth looking into how to declare and define destructors, so let's provide one for the `Stock` class.

Like a constructor, a destructor has a special name: It is formed from the class name preceded by a tilde (~). Thus, the destructor for the `Stock` class is called `~Stock()`. Also, like a constructor, a destructor can have no return value and has no declared type. Unlike a constructor, a destructor must have no arguments. Thus, the prototype for a `Stock` destructor must be this:

```
~Stock();
```

Because a `Stock` destructor has no vital duties, you can code it as a do-nothing function:

```
Stock::~Stock()
{
}
```

However, just so that you can see when the destructor is called, you can code it this way:

```
Stock::~Stock()    // class destructor
{
    cout << "Bye, " << company << "!\n";
}
```

When should a destructor be called? The compiler handles this decision; normally your code shouldn't explicitly call a destructor. (See the section "Looking Again at Placement `new`" in Chapter 12 for an exception.) If you create a static storage class object, its destructor is called automatically when the program terminates. If you create an automatic storage class object, as the examples have been doing, its destructor is called automatically when the program exits the block of code in which the object is defined. If the object is created by using `new`, it resides in heap memory, or the free store, and its destructor is called automatically when you use `delete` to free the memory. Finally, a program can create temporary objects to carry out certain operations; in that case, the program automatically calls the destructor for the object when it has finished using it.

Because a destructor is called automatically when a class object expires, there ought to be a destructor. If you don't provide one, the compiler implicitly declares a default constructor and, if it detects code that leads to the destruction of an object, it provides a definition for the destructor.

Improving the `Stock` Class

At this point you need to incorporate the constructors and the destructor into the class and method definitions. This time you should follow the usual C++ practice and organize the program into separate files. You can place the class declaration in a header file called `stock1.h`. (This name suggests the possibility of further revisions.) The class methods go into a file called `stock1.cpp`. In general, the header file containing the class declaration and the source code file containing the methods definitions should have the same base name so that you can keep track of which files belong together. Using separate files for the class declaration and the member functions separates the abstract definition of the interface (the class declaration) from the details of implementation (the member function definitions). You could, for example, distribute the class declaration as a text header file but distribute the function definitions as compiled code. Finally, you place the program using these resources in a third file, which you can call `usestok1.cpp`.

The Header File

Listing 10.4 shows the header file for the stock program. It adds prototypes for the constructor and destructor functions to the original class declaration. Also, it dispenses with the `acquire()` function, which is no longer necessary now that the class has constructors. The file also uses the `#ifndef` technique described in Chapter 9 to protect against multiple inclusion of this file.

LISTING 10.4   `stock1.h`

```
// stock1.h -- Stock class declaration with constructors, destructor added
#ifndef STOCK1_H_
#define STOCK1_H_

class Stock
{
private:
    char company[30];
    int shares;
    double share_val;
    double total_val;
    void set_tot() { total_val = shares * share_val; }
public:
    Stock();          // default constructor
    Stock(const char * co, int n = 0, double pr = 0.0);
    ~Stock();         // noisy destructor
    void buy(int num, double price);
    void sell(int num, double price);
    void update(double price);
    void show();
};

#endif
```

The Implementation File

Listing 10.5 provides the method definitions for the stock program. It includes the `stock1.h` file in order to provide the class declaration. (Recall that enclosing the filename in double quotation marks instead of in brackets causes the compiler to search for it at the same location where your source files are located.) Also, Listing 10.5 includes the `iostream` header file to provide I/O support and the `cstring` header file to support `strcpy()` and `strncpy()`. The listing also provides using declarations and qualified names (such as `std::string`) to provide access to various declarations in the header files. This file adds the constructor and destructor method definitions to the prior methods. To help you see when these methods are called, they each display a message. This is not a usual feature of constructors and destructors, but it can help you better visualize how classes use them.

LISTING 10.5   `stock1.cpp`

```cpp
// stock1.cpp -- Stock class implementation with constructors, destructor added
#include <iostream>
#include "stock1.h"

// constructors (verbose versions)
Stock::Stock()          // default constructor
{
    std::cout << "Default constructor called\n";
    std::strcpy(company, "no name");
    shares = 0;
    share_val = 0.0;
    total_val = 0.0;
}

Stock::Stock(const char * co, int n, double pr)
{
    std::cout << "Constructor using " << co << " called\n";
    std::strncpy(company, co, 29);
    company[29] = '\0';

    if (n < 0)
    {
        std::cerr << "Number of shares can't be negative; "
                  << company << " shares set to 0.\n";
        shares = 0;
    }
    else
        shares = n;
    share_val = pr;
    set_tot();
}
// class destructor
Stock::~Stock()          // verbose class destructor
{
    std::cout << "Bye, " << company << "!\n";
}

// other methods
void Stock::buy(int num, double price)
{
     if (num < 0)
    {
        std::cerr << "Number of shares purchased can't be negative. "
            << "Transaction is aborted.\n";
    }
    else
    {
        shares += num;
        share_val = price;
        set_tot();
    }
}
```

LISTING 10.5 Continued

```cpp
void Stock::sell(int num, double price)
{
    using std::cerr;
    if (num < 0)
    {
        cerr << "Number of shares sold can't be negative. "
            << "Transaction is aborted.\n";
    }
    else if (num > shares)
    {
        cerr << "You can't sell more than you have! "
            << "Transaction is aborted.\n";
    }
    else
    {
        shares -= num;
        share_val = price;
        set_tot();
    }
}

void Stock::update(double price)
{
    share_val = price;
    set_tot();
}

void Stock::show()
{
    using std::cout;
    using std::endl;
    cout << "Company: " << company
        << "  Shares: " << shares << endl
        << "  Share Price: $" << share_val
        << "  Total Worth: $" << total_val << endl;
}
```

A Client File

Listing 10.6 provides a short program for testing the new methods in the stock program. Because it simply uses the `Stock` class, this listing is a client of the `Stock` class. Like `stock1.cpp`, it includes the `stock1.h` file to provide the class declaration. The program demonstrates constructors and destructors. It also uses the same formatting commands invoked by Listing 10.3. To compile the complete program, you use the techniques for multi-file programs described in Chapters 1, "Getting Started," and 8.

LISTING 10.6   usestok1.cpp

```cpp
// usestok1.cpp -- using the Stock class
#include <iostream>
#include "stock1.h"

int main()
{
    using std::cout;
    using std::ios_base;
    cout.precision(2);                          // #.## format
    cout.setf(ios_base::fixed, ios_base::floatfield);// #.## format
    cout.setf(ios_base::showpoint);             // #.## format

    cout << "Using constructors to create new objects\n";
    Stock stock1("NanoSmart", 12, 20.0);        // syntax 1
    stock1.show();
    Stock stock2 = Stock ("Boffo Objects", 2, 2.0); // syntax 2
    stock2.show();

    cout << "Assigning stock1 to stock2:\n";
    stock2 = stock1;
    cout << "Listing stock1 and stock2:\n";
    stock1.show();
    stock2.show();

    cout << "Using a constructor to reset an object\n";
    stock1 = Stock("Nifty Foods", 10, 50.0);    // temp object
    cout << "Revised stock1:\n";
    stock1.show();
    cout << "Done\n";
    return 0;
}
```

Compatibility Note

You might have to use the older `ios::` instead of `ios_base::`.

Compiling the program represented by Listings 10.4, 10.5, and 10.6 produces an executable program. Here's one compiler's output from the executable program:

```
Using constructors to create new objects
Constructor using NanoSmart called
Company: NanoSmart  Shares: 12
  Share Price: $20.00  Total Worth: $240.00
Constructor using Boffo Objects called
Company: Boffo Objects  Shares: 2
  Share Price: $2.00  Total Worth: $4.00
Assigning stock1 to stock2:
Listing stock1 and stock2:
Company: NanoSmart  Shares: 12
  Share Price: $20.00  Total Worth: $240.00
```

```
Company: NanoSmart  Shares: 12
  Share Price: $20.00  Total Worth: $240.00
Using a constructor to reset an object
Constructor using Nifty Foods called
Bye, Nifty Foods!
Revised stock1:
Company: Nifty Foods  Shares: 10
  Share Price: $50.00  Total Worth: $500.00
Done
Bye, NanoSmart!
Bye, Nifty Foods!
```

Some compilers may produce a program with the following initial output, which has one additional line:

```
Using constructors to create new objects
Constructor using NanoSmart called
Company: NanoSmart  Shares: 12
  Share Price: $20.00  Total Worth: $240.00
Constructor using Boffo Objects called
Bye, Boffo Objects!                          ←additional line
Company: Boffo Objects  Shares: 2
  Share Price: $2.00  Total Worth: $4.00
...
```

The "Program Notes" section explain the `"Bye, Boffo Objects!"` line of this output.

Program Notes

In Listing 10.6, the statement

```
Stock stock1("NanoSmart", 12, 20.0);
```

creates a `Stock` object called `stock1` and initializes its data members to the indicated values:

```
Constructor using NanoSmart called
Company: NanoSmart  Shares: 12
```

The statement

```
Stock stock2 = Stock ("Boffo Objects", 2, 2.0);
```

uses another syntax to create and initialize an object called `stock2`. The C++ Standard gives a compiler a couple ways to execute this second syntax. One is to make it behave exactly like the first syntax:

```
Constructor using Boffo Objects called
Company: Boffo Objects  Shares: 2
```

The second way is to allow the call to the constructor to create a temporary object that is then copied to `stock2`. Then the temporary object is discarded. If the compiler uses this option, the destructor is called for the temporary object, producing this output instead:

```
Constructor using Boffo Objects called
Bye, Boffo Objects!
Company: Boffo Objects  Shares: 2
```

The compiler that produced this output disposed of the temporary object immediately, but it's possible that a compiler might wait longer, in which case the destructor message would be displayed later.

The statement

```
stock2 = stock1;     // object assignment
```

illustrates that you can assign one object to another of the same type. As with structure assignment, class object assignment, by default, copies the members of one object to the other. In this case, the original contents of stock2 are overwritten.

Remember

When you assign one object to another of the same class, by default C++ copies the contents of each data member of the source object to the corresponding data member of the target object.

You can use the constructor for more than initializing a new object. For example, the program has this statement in main():

```
stock1 = Stock("Nifty Foods", 10, 50.0);
```

The stock1 object already exists. Therefore, instead of initializing stock1, this statement assigns new values to the object. It does so by having the constructor create a new, temporary object and then copying the contents of the new object to stock1. Then the program disposes of the temporary object, invoking the destructor as it does so, as illustrated by the following annotated output:

```
Using a constructor to reset an object
Constructor using Nifty Foods called ←temporary object created
Bye, Nifty Foods!                     ←temporary object destroyed
Revised stock1:
Company: Nifty Foods   Shares: 10     ←data now copied to stock1
  Share Price: $50.00   Total Worth: $500.00
```

Some compilers might dispose of the temporary object later, delaying the destructor call.

Finally, at the end, the program displays this:

```
Done
Bye, NanoSmart!
Bye, Nifty Foods!
```

When the main() function terminates, its local variables (stock1 and stock2) pass from your plane of existence. Because such automatic variables go on the stack, the last object created is the first deleted, and the first created is the last deleted. (Recall that "NanoSmart" was originally in stock1 but was later transferred to stock2, and stock1 was reset to "Nifty Foods".)

The output points out that there is a fundamental difference between the following two statements:

```
Stock stock2 = Stock ("Boffo Objects", 2, 2.0);
stock1 = Stock("Nifty Foods", 10, 50.0); // temporary object
```

The first of these statements invokes initialization; it creates an object with the indicated value, and it may or may not create a temporary object. The second statement invokes assignment. Using a constructor in an assignment statement in this fashion always causes the creation of a temporary object before assignment occurs.

Tip

If you can set object values either through initialization or by assignment, choose initialization. It is usually more efficient.

`const` Member Functions

Consider the following code snippet:

```
const Stock land = Stock("Kludgehorn Properties");
land.show();
```

With current C++, the compiler should object to the second line. Why? Because the code for `show()` fails to guarantee that it won't modify the invoking object, which, because it is `const`, should not be altered. You've solved this kind of problem before by declaring a function's argument to be a `const` reference or a pointer to `const`. But here you have a syntax problem: The `show()` method doesn't have any arguments. Instead, the object it uses is provided implicitly by the method invocation. What you need is a new syntax, one that says a function promises not to modify the invoking object. The C++ solution is to place the `const` keyword after the function parentheses. That is, the `show()` declaration should look like this:

```
void show() const;        // promises not to change invoking object
```

Similarly, the beginning of the function definition should look like this:

```
void stock::show() const   // promises not to change invoking object
```

Class functions declared and defined this way are called `const` member functions. Just as you should use `const` references and pointers as formal function arguments whenever appropriate, you should make class methods `const` whenever they don't modify the invoking object. We'll follow this rule from here on out.

Constructors and Destructors in Review

Now that we've gone through a few examples of constructors and destructors, you might want to pause and assimilate what has passed. To help you, here is a summary of these methods.

A constructor is a special class member function that's called whenever an object of that class is created. A class constructor has the same name as its class, but, through the miracle of function overloading, you can have more than one constructor with the same name, provided that each has its own signature, or argument list. Also, a constructor has no declared type. Usually, a constructor is used to initialize members of a class object. Your initialization should match the constructor's argument list. For example, suppose the `Bozo` class has the following proto-type for a class constructor:

```
Bozo(const char * fname, const char * lname);   // constructor prototype
```

In this case, you would use it to initialize new objects as follows:

```
Bozo bozetta = bozo("Bozetta", "Biggens");   // primary form
Bozo fufu("Fufu", "O'Dweeb");                // short form
Bozo *pc = new Bozo("Popo", "Le Peu");       // dynamic object
```

If a constructor has just one argument, that constructor is invoked if you initialize an object to a value that has the same type as the constructor argument. For example, suppose you have this constructor prototype:

```
Bozo(int age);
```

Then you can use any of the following forms to initialize an object:

```
Bozo dribble = bozo(44);   // primary form
Bozo roon(66);             // secondary form
Bozo tubby = 32;           // special form for one-argument constructors
```

Actually, the third example is a new point, not a review point, but it seemed like a nice time to tell you about it. Chapter 11 mentions a way to turn off this feature.

Remember

A constructor that you can use with a single argument allows you to use assignment syntax to initial-ize an object to a value:

```
Classname object = value;
```

A default constructor has no arguments, and it is used if you create an object without explicitly initializing it. If you fail to provide any constructors, the compiler defines a default constructor for you. Otherwise, you have to supply your own default constructor. It can have no argu-ments or else it must have default values for all arguments:

```
Bozo();                               // default constructor prototype
Bistro(const char * s = "Chez Zero"); // default for Bistro class
```

The program uses the default constructor for uninitialized objects:

```
Bozo bubi;             // use default
Bozo *pb = new Bozo;   // use default
```

Just as a program invokes a constructor when an object is created, it invokes a destructor when an object is destroyed. You can have only one destructor per class. It has no return type (not even **void**), it has no arguments, and its name is the class name preceded by a tilde. For example, the `Bozo` class destructor has the following prototype:

```
~Bozo();   // class destructor
```

Class destructors that use **delete** become necessary when class constructors use **new**.

Knowing Your Objects: The `this` Pointer

You can do still more with the `Stock` class. So far each class member function has dealt with but a single object: the object that invokes it. Sometimes, however, a method might need to deal with two objects, and doing so may involve a curious C++ pointer called `this`. Let's look at how the need for `this` can unfold.

Although the `Stock` class declaration displays data, it's deficient in analytic power. For example, by looking at the `show()` output, you can tell which of your holdings has the greatest value, but the program can't tell because it can't access `total_val` directly. The most direct way of letting a program know about stored data is to provide methods to return values. Typically, you use inline code for this, as in the following example:

```
class Stock
{
private:
    ...
    double total_val;
    ...
public:
    double total() const { return total_val; }
    ...
};
```

This definition, in effect, makes `total_val` read-only memory as far as a direct program access is concerned. That is, you can use the `total_val()` method to obtain the value, but the class doesn't provide a method for specifically resetting the value of `total_val`. (Other methods, such as `buy()`, `sell()`, and `update()`, do modify `total_val` as a by-product of resetting the `shares` and `share_val` members.)

By adding this function to the class declaration, you can let a program investigate a series of stocks to find the one with the greatest value. However, you can take a different approach, one that helps you learn about the `this` pointer. The approach is to define a member function that looks at two `Stock` objects and returns a reference to the larger of the two. Attempting to implement this approach raises some interesting questions, which we'll look into now.

First, how do you provide the member function with two objects to compare? Suppose, for example, that you decide to name the method `topval()`. Then, the function call `stock1.topval()` accesses the data of the `stock1` object, whereas the message `stock2.top-val()` accesses the data of the `stock2` object. If you want the method to compare two objects, you have to pass the second object as an argument. For efficiency, you can pass the argument by reference. That is, you can have the `topval()` method use a type `const Stock &` argument.

Second, how do you communicate the method's answer back to the calling program? The most direct way is to have the method return a reference to the object that has the larger total value. Thus, the comparison method should have the following prototype:

```
const Stock & topval(const Stock & s) const;
```

This function accesses one object implicitly and one object explicitly, and it returns a reference to one of those two objects. The `const` in parentheses states that the function won't modify the explicitly accessed object, and the `const` that follows the parentheses states that the function won't modify the implicitly accessed object. Because the function returns a reference to one of the two `const` objects, the return type also has to be a `const` reference.

Suppose, then, that you want to compare the `Stock` objects `stock1` and `stock2` and assign the one with the greater total value to the object `top`. You can use either of the following statements to do so:

```
top = stock1.topval(stock2);
top = stock2.topval(stock1);
```

The first form accesses `stock1` implicitly and `stock2` explicitly, whereas the second accesses `stock1` explicitly and `stock2` implicitly. (See Figure 10.3.) Either way, the method compares the two objects and returns a reference to the one with the higher total value.

FIGURE 10.3
Accessing two objects by using a member function.

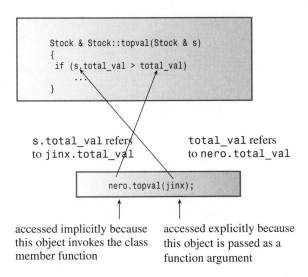

Actually, this notation is a bit confusing. It would be clearer if you could somehow use the relational operator `>` to compare the two objects. You can do so with operator overloading, which Chapter 11 discusses.

Meanwhile, there's still the implementation of `topval()` to attend to. It raises a slight problem. Here's a partial implementation that highlights the problem:

```
const Stock & Stock::topval(const Stock & s) const
{
    if (s.total_val > total_val)
        return s;                // argument object
    else
        return ?????;            // invoking object
}
```

Here `s.total_val` is the total value for the object passed as an argument, and `total_val` is the total value for the object to which the message is sent. If `s.total_val` is greater than `total_val`, the function returns `s`. Otherwise, it returns the object used to evoke the method. (In OOP talk, that is the object to which the `topval` message is sent.) Here's the problem: What do you call that object? If you make the call `stock1.topval(stock2)`, then `s` is a reference for `stock2` (that is, an alias for `stock2`), but there is no alias for `stock1`.

The C++ solution to this problem is to use a special pointer called `this`. The `this` pointer points to the object used to invoke a member function. (Basically, `this` is passed as a hidden argument to the method.) Thus, the function call `stock1.topval(stock2)` sets `this` to the address of the `stock1` object and makes that pointer available to the `topval()` method. Similarly, the function call `stock2.topval(stock1)` sets `this` to the address of the `stock2` object. In general, all class methods have a `this` pointer set to the address of the object that invokes the method. Indeed, `total_val` in `topval()` is just shorthand notation for `this->total_val`. (Recall from Chapter 4, "Compound Types," that you use the `->` operator to access structure members via a pointer. The same is true for class members.) (See Figure 10.4.)

FIGURE 10.4

`this` points to the invoking object.

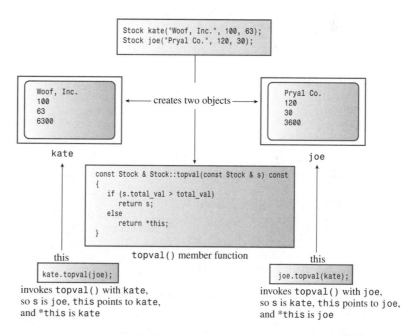

The `this` Pointer

Each member function, including constructors and destructors, has a `this` pointer. The special property of the `this` pointer is that it points to the invoking object. If a method needs to refer to the invoking object as a whole, it can use the expression `*this`. Using the `const` qualifier after the function argument parentheses qualifies `this` as being `const`; in that case, you can't use `this` to change the object's value.

What you want to return, however, is not `this` because `this` is the address of the object. You want to return the object itself, and that is symbolized by `*this`. (Recall that applying the dereferencing operator `*` to a pointer yields the value to which the pointer points.) Now you can complete the method definition by using `*this` as an alias for the invoking object:

```
const Stock & Stock::topval(const Stock & s) const
{
    if (s.total_val > total_val)
        return s;              // argument object
    else
        return *this;          // invoking object
}
```

The fact that the return type is a reference means that the returned object is the invoking object itself rather than a copy passed by the return mechanism. Listing 10.7 shows the new header file.

LISTING 10.7   stock2.h

```
// stock2.h -- augmented version
#ifndef STOCK2_H_
#define STOCK2_H_

class Stock
{
private:
    char company[30];
    int shares;
    double share_val;
    double total_val;
    void set_tot() { total_val = shares * share_val; }
public:
    Stock();           // default constructor
    Stock(const char * co, int n = 0, double pr = 0.0);
    ~Stock();          // do-nothing destructor
    void buy(int num, double price);
    void sell(int num, double price);
    void update(double price);
    void show()const;
    const Stock & topval(const Stock & s) const;
};

#endif
```

Listing 10.8 presents the revised class methods file. It includes the new `topval()` method. Also, now that you've seen how the constructors and destructor work, Listing 10.8 replaces them with silent versions.

LISTING 10.8   stock2.cpp

```cpp
// stock2.cpp -- improved version
#include <iostream>
#include "stock2.h"

// constructors
Stock::Stock()          // default constructor
{
    std::strcpy(company, "no name");
    shares = 0;
    share_val = 0.0;
    total_val = 0.0;
}

Stock::Stock(const char * co, int n, double pr)
{
    std::strncpy(company, co, 29);
    company[29] = '\0';

    if (n < 0)
    {
        std::cerr << "Number of shares can't be negative; "
                  << company << " shares set to 0.\n";
        shares = 0;
    }
    else
        shares = n;
    share_val = pr;
    set_tot();
}

// class destructor
Stock::~Stock()         // quiet class destructor
{
}

// other methods
void Stock::buy(int num, double price)
{
    if (num < 0)
    {
        std::cerr << "Number of shares purchased can't be negative. "
            << "Transaction is aborted.\n";
    }
    else
    {
        shares += num;
        share_val = price;
        set_tot();
    }
}
```

LISTING 10.8 *Continued*

```cpp
void Stock::sell(int num, double price)
{
    using std::cerr;
    if (num < 0)
    {
        cerr << "Number of shares sold can't be negative. "
            << "Transaction is aborted.\n";
    }
    else if (num > shares)
    {
        cerr << "You can't sell more than you have! "
            << "Transaction is aborted.\n";
    }
    else
    {
        shares -= num;
        share_val = price;
        set_tot();
    }
}

void Stock::update(double price)
{
    share_val = price;
    set_tot();
}

void Stock::show() const
{
    using std::cout;
    using std::endl;
    cout << "Company: " << company
        << "  Shares: " << shares << endl
        << "  Share Price: $" << share_val
        << "  Total Worth: $" << total_val << endl;
}

const Stock & Stock::topval(const Stock & s) const
{
    if (s.total_val > total_val)
        return s;
    else
        return *this;
}
```

Of course, you want to see if the **this** pointer works, and a natural place to use the new method is in a program with an array of objects, which leads us to the next topic.

An Array of Objects

Often, as with the `Stock` examples, you want to create several objects of the same class. You can create separate object variables, as the examples have done so far in this chapter, but it might make more sense to create an array of objects. That might sound like a major leap into the unknown, but, in fact, you declare an array of objects the same way you declare an array of any of the standard types:

```
Stock mystuff[4]; // creates an array of 4 Stock objects
```

Recall that a program always calls the default class constructor when it creates class objects that aren't explicitly initialized. This declaration requires either that the class explicitly define no constructors at all, in which case the implicit do-nothing default constructor is used, or, as in this case, that an explicit default constructor be defined. Each element—`mystuff[0]`, `mystuff[1]`, and so on—is a `Stock` object and thus can be used with the `Stock` methods:

```
mystuff[0].update();      // apply update() to 1st element
mystuff[3].show();        // apply show() to 4th element
Stock tops = mystuff[2].topval(mystuff[1]);
                          // compare 3rd and 2nd elements
```

You can use a constructor to initialize the array elements. In that case, you have to call the constructor for each individual element:

```
const int STKS = 4;
Stock stocks[STKS] = {
    Stock("NanoSmart", 12.5, 20),
    Stock("Boffo Objects", 200, 2.0),
    Stock("Monolithic Obelisks", 130, 3.25),
    Stock("Fleep Enterprises", 60, 6.5)
};
```

Here the code uses the standard form for initializing an array: a comma-separated list of values enclosed in braces. In this case, a call to the constructor method represents each value. If the class has more than one constructor, you can use different constructors for different elements:

```
const int STKS = 10;
Stock stocks[STKS] = {
    Stock("NanoSmart", 12.5, 20),
    Stock(),
    Stock("Monolithic Obelisks", 130, 3.25),
};
```

This initializes `stocks[0]` and `stocks[2]` using the `Stock(const char * co, int n, double pr)` constructor and `stocks[1]` using the `Stock()` constructor. Because this declaration only partially initializes the array, the remaining seven members are initialized using the default constructor.

The scheme for initializing an array of objects still initially uses the default constructor to create the array elements. Then, the constructors in the braces create temporary objects whose contents are copied to the vector. Thus, a class must have a default constructor if you want to create arrays of class objects.

Caution

If you want to create an array of class objects, the class must have a default constructor.

Listing 10.9 applies these principles to a short program that initializes four array elements, displays their contents, and tests the elements to find the one with the highest total value. Because `topval()` examines just two objects at a time, the program uses a `for` loop to examine the whole array. This listing uses the Listing 10.7 header file and the Listing 10.8 methods file.

LISTING 10.9   `usestok2.cpp`

```
// usestok2.cpp -- using the Stock class
// compile with stock2.cpp
#include <iostream>
#include "stock2.h"

const int STKS = 4;
int main()
{
    using std::cout;
    using std::ios_base;

// create an array of initialized objects
    Stock stocks[STKS] = {
        Stock("NanoSmart", 12, 20.0),
        Stock("Boffo Objects", 200, 2.0),
        Stock("Monolithic Obelisks", 130, 3.25),
        Stock("Fleep Enterprises", 60, 6.5)
        };

    cout.precision(2);                              // #.## format
    cout.setf(ios_base::fixed, ios_base::floatfield);// #.## format
    cout.setf(ios_base::showpoint);                 // #.## format

    cout << "Stock holdings:\n";
    int st;
    for (st = 0; st < STKS; st++)
        stocks[st].show();

    Stock top = stocks[0];
    for (st = 1; st < STKS; st++)
        top = top.topval(stocks[st]);
    cout << "\nMost valuable holding:\n";
    top.show();

    return 0;
}
```

Here is the output from the program in Listing 10.9:

```
Stock holdings:
Company: NanoSmart  Shares: 12
  Share Price: $20.00  Total Worth: $240.00
Company: Boffo Objects  Shares: 200
  Share Price: $2.00  Total Worth: $400.00
Company: Monolithic Obelisks  Shares: 130
  Share Price: $3.25  Total Worth: $422.50
Company: Fleep Enterprises  Shares: 60
  Share Price: $6.50  Total Worth: $390.00

Most valuable holding:
Company: Monolithic Obelisks  Shares: 130
  Share Price: $3.25  Total Worth: $422.50
```

One thing to note about Listing 10.9 is that most of the work goes into designing the class. When that's done, writing the program itself is rather simple.

Incidentally, knowing about the **this** pointer makes it easier to see how C++ works under the skin. For example, the C++ front-end **cfront** converts C++ programs to C programs. To handle method definitions, all it has to do is convert a C++ method definition like

```
void Stock::show() const
{
    cout << "Company: " << company
        << "  Shares: " << shares << '\n'
        << "  Share Price: $" << share_val
        << "  Total Worth: $" << total_val << '\n';
}
```

to the following C-style definition:

```
void show(const Stock * this)
{
    cout << "Company: " << this->company
        << "  Shares: " << this->shares << '\n'
        << "  Share Price: $" << this->share_val
        << "  Total Worth: $" << this->total_val << '\n';
}
```

That is, it converts a **Stock::** qualifier to a function argument that is a pointer to **Stock** and then uses the pointer to access class members.

Similarly, the front end converts function calls like

```
top.show();
```

to this:

```
show(&top);
```

In this fashion, the `this` pointer is assigned the address of the invoking object. (The actual details might be more involved.)

The Interface and Implementation Revisited

By using a character array with 30 elements, the `Stock` class limits the length of a name that it can store to 29 characters. For example, the statement

```
Stock firm ("Dunkelmeister, Dostoyevsky, and Delderfield Construction", 8, 2.5);
```

results in the truncated string `"Dunkelmeister, Dostoyevsky, a"` being stored in the `firm` object.

You can remove the length restriction by changing the class implementation. One approach is to increase the array size, but that leads to space often being wasted. Another approach is to use a `string` object instead of an array, relying on the automatic sizing of `string` objects. This entails three changes.

The first change is to add `string` class support by including the `string` header file in `stock2.h`. Because `stock2.cpp` includes `stock2.h`, the `string` class gets supported in `stock2.cpp`, also.

The second change is to modify the private section of the class definition in `stock2.h`. You change

```
class Stock
{
private:
    char company[30];
...
```

to the following:

```
class Stock
{
private:
    std::string company;
...
```

The third change is to modify the constructor definition in `stock2.cpp`. You change

```
Stock::Stock(const char * co, int n, double pr)
{
    std::strncpy(company, co, 29);
    company[29] = '\0';
    ...
```

to this:

```
Stock::Stock(const char * co, int n, double pr)
{
    company = co;    // assign C-style string to string object
    ...
```

These changes are examples of changing the implementation. You've made changes in the private section of the class declaration, and you've made changes in the implementation file. However, you haven't changed the public section of the class. Someone using the class still has the same list of methods from which to choose. Thus, the class interface is unchanged. True, a `Stock` object can store all of `"Dunkelmeister, Dostoyevsky, and Delderfield Construction"`, but the code remains unchanged:

```
Stock firm ("Dunkelmeister, Dostoyevsky, and Delderfield Construction", 8, 2.5);
```

You could also add a new constructor:

```
Stock(const std::string & co, int n, double pr);
```

This would be an interface change. The list of available methods would be changed, and a programmer using the class would have new options. For example, a program could use this:

```
string business;
getline(cout, business);
Stock mine(business, 10, 120.5);   // use new constructor
```

In short, changes in the private section of a class and in the implementation file are implementation changes; changes in the public section of a class are interface changes. Implementation changes alter the internal workings of a class, and interface changes alter the coding choices available to someone using the class.

Perhaps you're wondering about using a class object as a member of another class. It's okay to use objects as class members; after all, one of the goals of classes is to make these user-defined types as similar as possible to built-in types. A class constructor automatically sees to it that the constructors for any object members get called. There is a language feature called the *member initialization list* that can improve the efficiency of constructor design; Chapter 14, "Reusing Code in C++," pursues that topic further.

Class Scope

Chapter 9 discusses global (or file) scope and local (or block) scope. Recall that you can use a variable with global scope anywhere in the file that contains its definition, whereas a variable with local scope is local to the block that contains its definition. Function names, too, can have global scope, but they never have local scope. C++ classes introduce a new kind of scope: class scope.

Class scope applies to names defined in a class, such as the names of class data members and class member functions. Items that have class scope are known within the class but not outside the class. Thus, you can use the same class member names in different classes without conflict. For example, the `shares` member of the `Stock` class is distinct from the `shares` member of a `JobRide` class. Also, class scope means you can't directly access members of a class from the outside world. This is true even for public function members. That is, to invoke a public member function, you have to use an object:

```
Stock sleeper("Exclusive Ore", 100, 0.25);  // create object
sleeper.show();      // use object to invoke a member function
show();              // invalid -- can't call method directly
```

Similarly, you have to use the scope-resolution operator when you define member functions:

```
void Stock::update(double price)
{
    ...
}
```

In short, within a class declaration or a member function definition you can use an unadorned member name (the unqualified name), as when `sell()` calls the `set_tot()` member function. A constructor name is recognized when it is called because its name is the same as the class name. Otherwise, you must use the direct membership operator (.), the indirect membership operator (->), or the scope-resolution operator (::), depending on the context, when you use a class member name. The following code fragment illustrates how identifiers with class scope can be accessed:

```
class Ik
{
private:
    int fuss;         // fuss has class scope
public:
    Ik(int f  = 9) {fuss = f; }  // fuss is in scope
    void ViewIk() const;         // ViewIk has class scope
};

void Ik::ViewIk() const    //Ik:: places ViewIk into scope
{
    cout << fuss << endl;   // fuss in scope within class methods
}
...
int main()
{
    Ik * pik = new Ik;
    Ik ee = Ik(8); // constructor in scope because has class name
    ee.ViewIk();   // class object brings ViewIk into scope
    pik->ViewIk(); // pointer-to-Ik brings ViewIk into scope
...
```

Class Scope Constants

Sometimes it would be nice to have symbolic constants with class scope. For example, the `Stock` class declaration uses the literal `30` to specify the array size for `company`. Also, because the constant is the same for all objects, it would be nice to create a single constant shared by all objects. You might think the following would be a solution:

```
class Stock
{
private:
    const int Len = 30;    // declare a constant? FAILS
    char company[Len];
    ...
```

But this won't work because declaring a class describes what an object looks like but doesn't create an object. Hence, until you create an object, there's no place to store a value. There are, however, a couple ways to achieve essentially the same desired effect.

First, you can declare an enumeration within a class. An enumeration given in a class declaration has class scope, so you can use enumerations to provide class scope symbolic names for integer constants. That is, you can start off the `Stock` declaration this way:

```
class Stock
{
private:
    enum {Len = 30};  // class-specific constant
    char company[Len];
    ...
```

Note that declaring an enumeration in this fashion does not create a class data member. That is, each individual object does not carry an enumeration in it. Rather, `Len` is just a symbolic name that the compiler replaces with `30` when it encounters it in code in class scope.

Because this uses the enumeration merely to create a symbolic constant, with no intent of creating variables of the enumeration type, you needn't provide an enumeration tag. Incidentally, for many implementations, the `ios_base` class does something similar in its public section; that's the source of identifiers such as `ios_base::fixed`. Here `fixed` is typically an enumerator defined in the `ios_base` class.

More recently, C++ has introduced a second way of defining a constant within a class—using the keyword `static`:

```
class Stock
{
private:
    static const int Len = 30;    // declare a constant! WORKS
    char company[Len];
    ...
```

This creates a single constant called `Len` that is stored with other static variables rather than in an object. Thus, there is only one `Len` constant shared by all `Stock` objects. Chapter 12, "Classes and Dynamic Memory Allocation," looks further into static class members. You can use this technique only for declaring static constants with integral and enumeration values. You can't store a `double` constant this way.

Abstract Data Types

The `Stock` class is pretty specific. Often, however, programmers define classes to represent more general concepts. For example, using classes is a good way to implement what computer scientists describe as abstract data types (ADTs). As the name suggests, an *ADT* describes a data type in a general fashion, without bringing in language or implementation details. Consider, for example, the stack. By using the stack, you can store data so that data is always added to or deleted from the top of the stack. For example, C++ programs use a stack to manage automatic variables. As new automatic variables are generated, they are added to the top of the stack. When they expire, they are removed from the stack.

Let's look at the properties of a stack in a general, abstract way. First, a stack holds several items. (That property makes it a *container*, an even more general abstraction.) Next, a stack is characterized by the operations you can perform on it:

- You can create an empty stack.

- You can add an item to the top of a stack (that is, you can *push* an item).

- You can remove an item from the top (that is, you can *pop* an item).

- You can check whether the stack is full.

- You can check whether the stack is empty.

You can match this description with a class declaration in which the public member functions provide an interface that represents the stack operations. The private data members take care of storing the stack data. The class concept is a nice match to the ADT approach.

The private section has to commit itself to how to hold the data. For example, you can use an ordinary array, a dynamically allocated array, or some more advanced data structure, such as a linked list. However, the public interface should hide the exact representation. Instead, it should be expressed in general terms, such as creating a stack, pushing an item, and so on. Listing 10.10 shows one approach. It assumes that the `bool` type has been implemented. If it hasn't been implemented on your system, you can use `int`, `0`, and `1` rather than `bool`, `false`, and `true`.

LISTING 10.10   `stack.h`

```
// stack.h -- class definition for the stack ADT
#ifndef STACK_H_
#define STACK_H_

typedef unsigned long Item;

class Stack
{
private:
    enum {MAX = 10};    // constant specific to class
    Item items[MAX];    // holds stack items
    int top;            // index for top stack item
public:
    Stack();
    bool isempty() const;
    bool isfull() const;
    // push() returns false if stack already is full, true otherwise
    bool push(const Item & item);    // add item to stack
    // pop() returns false if stack already is empty, true otherwise
    bool pop(Item & item);           // pop top into item
};
#endif
```

In the example in Listing 10.10, the private section shows that the stack is implemented by using an array, but the public section doesn't reveal that fact. Thus, you can replace the array with, say, a dynamic array without changing the class interface. This means changing the stack implementation doesn't require that you recode programs that use the stack. You just recompile the stack code and link it with existing program code.

The interface is redundant in that `pop()` and `push()` return information about the stack status (full or empty) instead of being type `void`. This provides the programmer with a couple options as to how to handle exceeding the stack limit or emptying the stack. He or she can use `isempty()` and `isfull()` to check before attempting to modify the stack, or else use the return value of `push()` and `pop()` to determine whether the operation is successful.

Rather than define the stack in terms of some particular type, the class describes it in terms of a general `Item` type. In this case, the header file uses `typedef` to make `Item` the same as `unsigned long`. If you want, say, a stack of `double`s or of a structure type, you can change the `typedef` and leave the class declaration and method definitions unaltered. Class templates (see Chapter 14) provide a more powerful method for isolating from the class design the type of data stored.

Next, you need to implement the class methods. Listing 10.11 shows one possibility.

LISTING 10.11   stack.cpp

```cpp
// stack.cpp -- Stack member functions
#include "stack.h"
Stack::Stack()    // create an empty stack
{
    top = 0;
}

bool Stack::isempty() const
{
    return top == 0;
}

bool Stack::isfull() const
{
    return top == MAX;
}

bool Stack::push(const Item & item)
{
    if (top < MAX)
```

LISTING 10.11   Continued

```cpp
    {
        items[top++] = item;
        return true;
    }
    else
        return false;
}

bool Stack::pop(Item & item)
{
    if (top > 0)
    {
        item = items[--top];
        return true;
    }
    else
        return false;
}
```

The default constructor guarantees that all stacks are created empty. The code for **pop()** and **push()** guarantees that the top of the stack is managed properly. Guarantees like this are one of the things that make OOP reliable. Suppose that, instead, you create a separate array to represent the stack and an independent variable to represent the index of the top. In that case, it is your responsibility to get the code right each time you create a new stack. Without the protection that private data offers, there's always the possibility of making some program blunder that alters data unintentionally.

Let's test this stack. Listing 10.12 models the life of a clerk who processes purchase orders from the top of his in-basket, using the LIFO (last-in, first-out) approach of a stack.

LISTING 10.12   `stacker.cpp`

```cpp
// stacker.cpp -- testing the Stack class
#include <iostream>
#include <cctype>   // or ctype.h
#include "stack.h"
int main()
{
    using namespace std;
    Stack st; // create an empty stack
    char ch;
    unsigned long po;
    cout << "Please enter A to add a purchase order,\n"
        << "P to process a PO, or Q to quit.\n";
    while (cin >> ch && toupper(ch) != 'Q')
    {
        while (cin.get() != '\n')
            continue;
        if (!isalpha(ch))
        {
```

LISTING 10.12 Continued

```
                    cout << '\a';
                    continue;
                }
                switch(ch)
                {
                    case 'A':
                    case 'a': cout << "Enter a PO number to add: ";
                              cin >> po;
                              if (st.isfull())
                                  cout << "stack already full\n";
                              else
                                  st.push(po);
                              break;
                    case 'P':
                    case 'p': if (st.isempty())
                                  cout << "stack already empty\n";
                              else {
                                  st.pop(po);
                                  cout << "PO #" << po << " popped\n";
                              }
                              break;
                }
                cout << "Please enter A to add a purchase order,\n"
                     << "P to process a PO, or Q to quit.\n";
            }
            cout << "Bye\n";
            return 0;
        }
```

The little `while` loop in Listing 10.12 that gets rid of the rest of the line isn't absolutely necessary at this point, but it will come in handy in a modification of this program in Chapter 14.
Here's a sample run:

```
Please enter A to add a purchase order,
P to process a PO, or Q to quit.
A
Enter a PO number to add: 17885
Please enter A to add a purchase order,
P to process a PO, or Q to quit.
P
PO #17885 popped
Please enter A to add a purchase order,
P to process a PO, or Q to quit.
A
Enter a PO number to add: 17965
Please enter A to add a purchase order,
P to process a PO, or Q to quit.
A
Enter a PO number to add: 18002
Please enter A to add a purchase order,
P to process a PO, or Q to quit.
```

```
P
PO #18002 popped
Please enter A to add a purchase order,
P to process a PO, or Q to quit.
P
PO #17965 popped
Please enter A to add a purchase order,
P to process a PO, or Q to quit.
P
stack already empty
Please enter A to add a purchase order,
P to process a PO, or Q to quit.
Q
Bye
```

Real-World Note: Minimizing Class Size with Selective Data Typing

When designing classes, you need to give careful thought to the data types you use for class members. Imprudent use of nonstandard or platform-dependent data types inflates the size of your classes, thereby increasing the memory footprint, or working set, of your programs. This is both inefficient and considered bad form.

A classic example that demonstrates this point involves using a nonstandard BOOL typedef instead of the standard bool data type. Consider these simple classes:

```cpp
typedef int BOOL;
class BadClassDesign
{
  BOOL m_b1;
  BOOL m_b2;
  BOOL m_b3;
  BOOL m_b4;
  BOOL m_b5;
  BOOL m_b6;
};

class GoodClassDesign
{
  bool m_b1;
  bool m_b2;
  bool m_b3;
  bool m_b4;
  bool m_b5;
  bool m_b6;
};
```

Unlike bool, which usually occupies only 1 byte on most platforms, each BOOL typically occupies 4 bytes. If the intent for the class members is to manage a true Boolean value of true or false, only 1 byte is actually required. For the typical Intel platform machine, the class BadClassDesign occupies 24 bytes, and the class ClassGoodDesign uses only 6 bytes. That's a 400% savings!

You should always strive to use appropriate data types that minimize the amount of memory your program requires.

Summary

OOP emphasizes how a program represents data. The first step toward solving a programming problem by using the OOP approach is to describe the data in terms of its interface with the program, specifying how the data is used. Next, you need to design a class that implements the interface. Typically, private data members store the information, whereas public member functions, also called methods, provide the only access to the data. The class combines data and methods into one unit, and the private aspect accomplishes data hiding.

Usually, you separate a class declaration into two parts, typically kept in separate files. The class declaration proper goes into a header file, with the methods represented by function prototypes. The source code that defines the member functions goes into a methods file. This approach separates the description of the interface from the details of the implementation. In principle, you need to know only the public class interface to use the class. Of course, you can look at the implementation (unless it's been supplied to you in compiled form only), but your program shouldn't rely on details of the implementation, such as knowing that a particular value is stored as an `int`. As long as a program and a class communicate only through methods defining the interface, you are free to improve either part separately without worrying about unforeseen interactions.

A class is a user-defined type, and an object is an instance of a class. This means an object is a variable of that type or the equivalent of a variable, such as memory allocated by `new` according to the class specification. C++ tries to make user-defined types as similar as possible to standard types, so you can declare objects, pointers to objects, and arrays of objects. You can pass objects as arguments, return them as function return values, and assign one object to another of the same type. If you provide a constructor method, you can initialize objects when they are created. If you provide a destructor method, the program executes that method when the object expires.

Each object holds its own copies of the data portion of a class declaration, but they share the class methods. If `mr_object` is the name of a particular object and `try_me()` is a member function, you invoke the member function by using the dot membership operator: `mr_object.try_me()`. OOP terminology describes this function call as sending a `try_me` message to the `mr_object` object. Any reference to class data members in the `try_me()` method then applies to the data members of the `mr_object` object. Similarly, the function call `i_object.try_me()` accesses the data members of the `i_object` object.

If you want a member function to act on more than one object, you can pass additional objects to the method as arguments. If a method needs to refer explicitly to the object that evoked it, it can use the `this` pointer. The `this` pointer is set to the address of the evoking object, so `*this` is an alias for the object itself.

Classes are well matched to describing ADTs. The public member function interface provides the services described by an ADT, and the class's private section and the code for the class methods provide an implementation that is hidden from clients of the class.

Review Questions

1. What is a class?

2. How does a class accomplish abstraction, encapsulation, and data hiding?

3. What is the relationship between an object and a class?

4. In what way, aside from being functions, are class function members different from class data members?

5. Define a class to represent a bank account. Data members should include the depositor's name, the account number (use a string), and the balance. Member functions should allow the following:

   - Creating an object and initializing it.

   - Displaying the depositor's name, account number, and balance

   - Depositing an amount of money given by an argument

   - Withdrawing an amount of money given by an argument

   Just show the class declaration, not the method implementations. (Programming Exercise 1 provides you with an opportunity to write the implementation.)

6. When are class constructors called? When are class destructors called?

7. Provide code for a constructor for the bank account class from Review Question 5.

8. What is a default constructor? What is the advantage of having one?

9. Modify the `Stock` class (the version in `stock2.h`) so that it has member functions that return the values of the individual data members. Note: A member that returns the company name should not provide a weapon for altering the array. That is, it can't simply return a `char *`. It could return a `const` pointer, or it could return a pointer to a copy of the array, manufactured by using `new`.

10. What are `this` and `*this`?

Programming Exercises

1. Provide method definitions for the class described in Review Question 5 and write a short program that illustrates all the features.

2. Here is a rather simple class definition:

```
class Person {
private:
    static const LIMIT = 25;
    string lname;       // Person's last name
    char fname[LIMIT];  // Person's first name
public:
```

```
    Person() {lname = ""; fname[0] = '\0';  } // #1
    Person(const string & ln, const char * fn = "Heyyou");   // #2
// the following methods display lname and fname
    void Show() const;        // firstname lastname format
    void FormalShow() const;  // lastname, firstname format
};
```

Write a program that completes the implementation by providing code for the undefined methods. The program in which you use the class should also use the three possible constructor calls (no arguments, one argument, and two arguments) and the two display methods. Here's an example that uses the constructors and methods:

```
Person one;                          // use default constructor
Person two("Smythecraft");           // use #2 with one default argument
Person three("Dimwiddy", "Sam");     // use #2, no defaults
one.Show();
cout << endl;
one.FormalShow();
// etc. for two and three
```

3. Do Programming Exercise 1 from Chapter 9, but replace the code shown there with an appropriate golf class declaration. Replace setgolf(golf &, const char *, int) with a constructor with the appropriate argument for providing initial values. Retain the interactive version of setgolf(), but implement it by using the constructor. (For example, for the code for setgolf(), obtain the data, pass the data to the constructor to create a temporary object, and assign the temporary object to the invoking object, which is *this.)

4. Do Programming Exercise 4 from Chapter 9, but convert the Sales structure and its associated functions to a class and its methods. Replace the setSales(Sales &, double [], int) function with a constructor. Implement the interactive setSales(Sales &) method by using the constructor. Keep the class within the namespace SALES.

5. Consider the following structure declaration:

```
struct customer {
    char fullname[35];
    double payment;
};
```

Write a program that adds and removes customer structures from a stack, represented by a Stack class declaration. Each time a customer is removed, his or her payment should be added to a running total, and the running total should be reported. Note: You should be able to use the Stack class unaltered; just change the typedef declaration so that Item is type customer instead of unsigned long.

6. Here's a class declaration:

```
class Move
{
private:
    double x;
    double y;
```

```
public:
    Move(double a = 0, double b = 0);   // sets x, y to a, b
    showmove() const;                   // shows current x, y values
    Move add(const Move & m) const;
// this function adds x of m to x of invoking object to get new x,
// adds y of m to y of invoking object to get new y, creates a new
// move object initialized to new x, y values and returns it
    reset(double a = 0, double b = 0);  // resets x,y to a, b
};
```

Create member function definitions and a program that exercises the class.

7. A Betelgeusean plorg has these properties:

Data

A plorg has a name with no more than 19 letters.

A plorg has a contentment index (CI), which is an integer.

Operations

A new plorg starts out with a name and a CI of 50.

A plorg's CI can change.

A plorg can report its name and CI.

The default plorg has the name `"Plorga"`.

Write a `Plorg` class declaration (including data members and member function prototypes) that represents a plorg. Write the function definitions for the member functions. Write a short program that demonstrates all the features of the `Plorg` class.

8. You can describe a simple list as follows:

- The simple list can hold zero or more items of some particular type.

- You can create an empty list.

- You can add items to the list.

- You can determine whether the list is empty.

- You can determine whether the list is full.

- You can visit each item in the list and perform some action on it.

As you can see, this list really is simple; it doesn't allow insertion or deletion, for example.

Design a `List` class to represent this abstract type. You should provide a `list.h` header file with the class declaration and a `list.cpp` file with the class method implementations. You should also create a short program that utilizes your design.

The main reason for keeping the list specification simple is to simplify this programming exercise. You can implement the list as an array or, if you're familiar with the data type, as a linked list. But the public interface should not depend on your choice. That is, the public interface should not have array indices, pointers to nodes, and so on. It should be expressed in the general concepts of creating a list, adding an item to the list, and so on. The usual way to handle visiting each item and performing an action is to use a function that takes a function pointer as an argument:

```
void visit(void (*pf)(Item &));
```

Here `pf` points to a function (not a member function) that takes a reference to `Item` argument, where `Item` is the type for items in the list. The `visit()` function applies this function to each item in the list. You can use the `Stack` class as a general guide.

CHAPTER 11

WORKING WITH CLASSES

In this chapter you'll learn about the following:

- Operator overloading

- Friend functions

- Overloading the << operator for output

- State members

- Using rand() to generate random values

- Automatic conversions and type casts for classes

- Class conversion functions

C++ classes are feature-rich, complex, and powerful. In Chapter 9, "Memory Models and Namespaces," you began a journey toward object-oriented programming by learning to define and use a simple class. You saw how a class defines a data type by defining the type of data to be used to represent an object and by also defining, through member functions, the operations that can be performed with that data. And you learned about two special member functions, the constructor and the destructor, that manage creating and discarding objects made to a class specification. This chapter takes you a few steps further in the exploration of class properties, concentrating on class design techniques rather than on general principles. You'll probably find some of the features covered here straightforward and some a bit more subtle. To best understand these new features, you should try the examples and experiment with them: What happens if you use a regular argument instead of a reference argument for this function? What happens if you leave something out of a destructor? Don't be afraid to make mistakes; usually you can learn more from unraveling an error than by doing something correctly but by rote. (However, don't assume that a maelstrom of mistakes inevitably leads to incredible insight.) In the end, you'll be rewarded with a fuller understanding of how C++ works and of what C++ can do for you.

This chapter starts with operator overloading, which lets you use standard C++ operators such as = and + with class objects. Then it examines friends, the C++ mechanism for letting non-member functions access private data. Finally, it looks at how you can instruct C++ to perform automatic type conversions with classes. As you go through this chapter and Chapter 12, "Classes and Dynamic Memory Allocation," you'll gain a greater appreciation of the roles class constructors and class destructors play. Also, you'll see some of the stages you may go through as you develop and improve a class design.

One difficulty with learning C++, at least by the time you've gotten this far into the subject, is that there is an awful lot to remember. And it's unreasonable to expect to remember it all until you've logged enough experience on which to hang your memories. Learning C++, in this respect, is like learning a feature-laden word processor or spreadsheet program. No one feature is that daunting, but, in practice, most people really know well only those features they use regularly, such as searching for text or italicizing. You may recall having read somewhere how to generate alternative characters or create a table of contents, but those skills probably won't be part of your daily repertoire until you face a situation in which you need them frequently. Probably the best approach to absorbing the wealth of material in this chapter is to begin incorporating just some of these new features into your own C++ programming. As your experiences enhance your understanding and appreciation of these features, you can begin adding other C++ features. As Bjarne Stroustrup, the creator of C++, suggested at a C++ conference for professional programmers: "Ease yourself into the language. Don't feel you have to use all of the features, and don't try to use them all on the first day."

Operator Overloading

Let's look at a technique for giving object operations a prettier look. *Operator overloading* is an example of C++ polymorphism. In Chapter 8, "Adventures in Functions," you saw how C++ enables you to define several functions that have the same name, provided that they have different signatures (argument lists). That is called *function overloading*, or *functional polymorphism*. Its purpose is to let you use the same function name for the same basic operation, even though you apply the operation to different data types. (Imagine how awkward English would be if you had to use a different verb form for each different type of object—for example, lift_lft your left foot, but lift_sp your spoon.) Operator overloading extends the overloading concept to operators, letting you assign multiple meanings to C++ operators. Actually, many C++ (and C) operators already are overloaded. For example, the * operator, when applied to an address, yields the value stored at that address. But applying * to two numbers yields the product of the values. C++ uses the number and type of operands to decide which action to take.

C++ lets you extend operator overloading to user-defined types, permitting you, say, to use the + symbol to add two objects. Again, the compiler uses the number and type of operands to determine which definition of addition to use. Overloaded operators can often make code look more natural. For example, a common computing task is adding two arrays. Usually, this winds up looking like the following `for` loop:

```
for (int i = 0; i < 20; i++)
        evening[i] = sam[i] + janet[i];   // add element by element
```

But in C++, you can define a class that represents arrays and that overloads the + operator so that you can do this:

```
evening = sam + janet;                 // add two array objects
```

This simple addition notation conceals the mechanics and emphasizes what is essential, and that is another goal of OOP.

To overload an operator, you use a special function form called an *operator function*. An operator function has the form

```
operatorop(argument-list)
```

where *op* is the symbol for the operator being overloaded. For example, `operator+()` overloads the + operator and `operator*()` overloads the * operator. The *op* has to be a valid C++ operator; you can't just make up a new symbol. For example, you can't have an `operator@()` function because C++ has no @ operator. But the `operator[]()` function would overload the [] operator because [] is the array-indexing operator. Suppose, for example, that you have a `Salesperson` class for which you define an `operator+()` member function to overload the + operator so that it adds sales figures of one salesperson object to another. Then, if `district2`, `sid`, and `sara` are all objects of the `Salesperson` class, you can write this equation:

```
district2 = sid + sara;
```

The compiler, recognizing the operands as belonging to the `Salesperson` class, replaces the operator with the corresponding operator function:

```
district2 = sid.operator+(sara);
```

The function then uses the `sid` object implicitly (because it invoked the method) and the `sara` object explicitly (because it's passed as an argument) to calculate the sum, which it then returns. Of course, the nice part is that you can use the nifty + operator notation instead of the clunky function notation.

C++ imposes some restrictions on operator overloading, but they're easiest to understand after you've seen how overloading works. So let's develop a few examples to clarify the process and then discuss the limitations.

Time on Our Hands: Developing an Operator Overloading Example

If you worked on the Priggs account for 2 hours 35 minutes in the morning and 2 hours 40 minutes in the afternoon, how long did you work altogether on the account? Here's an example where the concept of addition makes sense, but the units that you are adding (a mixture of hours and minutes) don't match a built-in type. Chapter 7, "Functions: C++'s Programming Modules," handles a similar case by defining a `travel_time` structure and a `sum()` function for adding such structures. Now let's generalize that to a `Time` class, using a method to handle addition. Let's begin with an ordinary method, called `Sum()`, and then see how to convert it to an overloaded operator. Listing 11.1 shows the class declaration.

LISTING 11.1   `mytime0.h`

```
// mytime0.h -- Time class before operator overloading
#ifndef MYTIME0_H_
#define MYTIME0_H_
```

LISTING 11.1   Continued

```
class Time
{
private:
    int hours;
    int minutes;
public:
    Time();
    Time(int h, int m = 0);
    void AddMin(int m);
    void AddHr(int h);
    void Reset(int h = 0, int m = 0);
    Time Sum(const Time & t) const;
    void Show() const;
};
#endif
```

The `Time` class provides methods for adjusting and resetting times, for displaying time values, and for adding two times. Listing 11.2 shows the methods definitions; note how the `AddMin()` and `Sum()` methods use integer division and the modulus operator to adjust the `minutes` and `hours` values when the total number of minutes exceeds 59. Also, because the only `iostream` feature used is `cout`, and because it is used only once, it seems economical to use `std::cout` rather than use the whole `std` namespace.

LISTING 11.2   mytime0.cpp

```
// mytime0.cpp  -- implementing Time methods
#include <iostream>
#include "mytime0.h"

Time::Time()
{
    hours = minutes = 0;
}

Time::Time(int h, int m )
{
    hours = h;
    minutes = m;
}

void Time::AddMin(int m)
{
    minutes += m;
    hours += minutes / 60;
    minutes %= 60;
}
void Time::AddHr(int h)
{
    hours += h;
}
```

LISTING 11.2   Continued

```cpp
void Time::Reset(int h, int m)
{
    hours = h;
    minutes = m;
}

Time Time::Sum(const Time & t) const
{
    Time sum;
    sum.minutes = minutes + t.minutes;
    sum.hours = hours + t.hours + sum.minutes / 60;
    sum.minutes %= 60;
    return sum;
}

void Time::Show() const
{
    std::cout << hours << " hours, " << minutes << " minutes";
}
```

Consider the code for the `Sum()` function. Note that the argument is a reference but that the return type is not a reference. The reason for making the argument a reference is efficiency. The code would produce the same results if the `Time` object were passed by value, but it's usually faster and more memory-efficient to just pass a reference.

However, the return value cannot be a reference. The reason is that the function creates a new `Time` object (`sum`) that represents the sum of the other two `Time` objects. Returning the object, as this code does, creates a copy of the object that the calling function can use. If the return type were `Time &`, however, the reference would be to the `sum` object. But the `sum` object is a local variable and is destroyed when the function terminates, so the reference would be a reference to a nonexistent object. Using a `Time` return type, however, means the program constructs a *copy* of `sum` before destroying it, and the calling function gets the copy.

Caution

Don't return a reference to a local variable or another temporary object. When the function terminates and the local variable or temporary object disappears, the reference becomes a reference to non-existent data.

Finally, Listing 11.3 tests the time summation part of the `Time` class.

LISTING 11.3   usetime0.cpp

```cpp
// usetime0.cpp -- using the first draft of the Time class
// compile usetime0.cpp and mytime0.cpp together
#include <iostream>
#include "mytime0.h"
```

LISTING 11.3 Continued

```
int main()
{
    using std::cout;
    using std::endl;
    Time planning;
    Time coding(2, 40);
    Time fixing(5, 55);
    Time total;

    cout << "planning time = ";
    planning.Show();
    cout << endl;

    cout << "coding time = ";
    coding.Show();
    cout << endl;

    cout << "fixing time = ";
    fixing.Show();
    cout << endl;

    total = coding.Sum(fixing);
    cout << "coding.Sum(fixing) = ";
    total.Show();
    cout << endl;

    return 0;
}
```

Here is the output of the program in Listings 11.1, 11.2, and 11.3:

```
planning time = 0 hours, 0 minutes
coding time = 2 hours, 40 minutes
fixing time = 5 hours, 55 minutes
coding.Sum(fixing) = 8 hours, 35 minutes
```

Adding an Addition Operator

It's a simple matter to convert the `Time` class to using an overloaded addition operator. You just change the name of `Sum()` to the odder-looking name `operator+()`. That's right: You just append the operator symbol (+, in this case) to the end of `operator` and use the result as a method name. This is one place where you can use a character other than a letter, a digit, or an underscore in an identifier name. Listings 11.4 and 11.5 reflect this small change.

LISTING 11.4 mytime1.h

```
// mytime1.h -- Time class before operator overloading
#ifndef MYTIME1_H_
#define MYTIME1_H_
```

LISTING 11.4   Continued

```cpp
class Time
{
private:
    int hours;
    int minutes;
public:
    Time();
    Time(int h, int m = 0);
    void AddMin(int m);
    void AddHr(int h);
    void Reset(int h = 0, int m = 0);
    Time operator+(const Time & t) const;
    void Show() const;
};
#endif
```

LISTING 11.5   mytime1.cpp

```cpp
// mytime1.cpp  -- implementing Time methods
#include <iostream>
#include "mytime1.h"

Time::Time()
{
    hours = minutes = 0;
}

Time::Time(int h, int m )
{
    hours = h;
    minutes = m;
}

void Time::AddMin(int m)
{
    minutes += m;
    hours += minutes / 60;
    minutes %= 60;
}
void Time::AddHr(int h)
{
    hours += h;
}

void Time::Reset(int h, int m)
{
    hours = h;
    minutes = m;
}
```

LISTING 11.5   Continued

```
Time Time::operator+(const Time & t) const
{
    Time sum;
    sum.minutes = minutes + t.minutes;
    sum.hours = hours + t.hours + sum.minutes / 60;
    sum.minutes %= 60;
    return sum;
}

void Time::Show() const
{
    std::cout << hours << " hours, " << minutes << " minutes";
}
```

Like Sum(), operator+() is invoked by a Time object, takes a second Time object as an argument, and returns a Time object. Thus, you can invoke the operator+() method by using the same syntax that Sum() uses:

```
total = coding.operator+(fixing);    // function notation
```

But naming the method operator+() also lets you use operator notation:

```
total = coding + fixing;             // operator notation
```

Either notation invokes the operator+() method. Note that with the operator notation, the object to the left of the operator (coding, in this case) is the invoking object, and the object to the right (fixing, in this case) is the one passed as an argument. Listing 11.6 illustrates this point.

LISTING 11.6   usetime1.cpp

```
// usetime1.cpp -- using the second draft of the Time class
// compile usetime1.cpp and mytime1.cpp together
#include <iostream>
#include "mytime1.h"

int main()
{
    using std::cout;
    using std::endl;
    Time planning;
    Time coding(2, 40);
    Time fixing(5, 55);
    Time total;

    cout << "planning time = ";
    planning.Show();
    cout << endl;

    cout << "coding time = ";
    coding.Show();
    cout << endl;
```

LISTING 11.6   Continued

```
    cout << "fixing time = ";
    fixing.Show();
    cout << endl;

    total = coding + fixing;
    // operator notation
    cout << "coding + fixing = ";
    total.Show();
    cout << endl;

    Time morefixing(3, 28);
    cout << "more fixing time = ";
    morefixing.Show();
    cout << endl;
    total = morefixing.operator+(total);
    // function notation
    cout << "morefixing.operator+(total) = ";
    total.Show();
    cout << endl;

    return 0;
}
```

Here is the output of the program in Listings 11.4, 11.5, and 11.6:

```
planning time = 0 hours, 0 minutes
coding time = 2 hours, 40 minutes
fixing time = 5 hours, 55 minutes
coding + fixing = 8 hours, 35 minutes
more fixing time = 3 hours, 28 minutes
morefixing.operator+(total) = 12 hours, 3 minutes
```

In short, the name of the `operator+()` function allows it to be invoked by using either function notation or operator notation. The compiler uses the operand types to figure out what to do:

```
int a, b, c;
Time A, B, C;
c = a + b;       // use int addition
C = A + B;       // use addition as defined for Time objects
```

Can you add more than two objects? For example, if `t1`, `t2`, `t3`, and `t4` are all `Time` objects, can you do the following?

```
t4 = t1 + t2 + t3;                        // valid?
```

The way to answer this is to consider how the statement gets translated into functions calls. Because addition is a left-to-right operator, the statement is first translated to this:

```
t4 = t1.operator+(t2 + t3);               // valid?
```

Then the function argument is itself translated to a function call, giving the following:

```
t4 = t1.operator+(t2.operator+(t3));   // valid? YES
```

Is this valid? Yes, it is. The function call `t2.operator+(t3)` returns a `Time` object that represents the sum of `t2` and `t3`. This object then becomes the object of the `t1.operator+()` function call, and that call returns the sum of `t1` and the `Time` object that represents the sum of `t2` and `t3`. In short, the final return value is the sum of `t1`, `t2`, and `t3`, just as desired.

Overloading Restrictions

Most C++ operators (see Table 11.1) can be overloaded in the manner described in the preceding section. Overloaded operators (with some exceptions) don't necessarily have to be member functions. However, at least one of the operands has to be a user-defined type. Let's take a closer look at the limits C++ imposes on user-defined operator overloading:

- The overloaded operator must have at least one operand that is a user-defined type. This prevents you from overloading operators for the standard types. Thus, you can't redefine the minus operator (`-`) so that it yields the sum of two `double` values instead of their difference. This restriction preserves program sanity, although it may hinder creative accounting.

- You can't use an operator in a manner that violates the syntax rules for the original operator. For example, you can't overload the modulus operator (`%`) so that it can be used with a single operand:

```
int x;
Time shiva;
% x;        // invalid for modulus operator
% shiva;    // invalid for overloaded operator
```

Similarly, you can't alter operator precedence. So if you overload the addition operator to let you add two classes, the new operator has the same precedence as ordinary addition.

- You can't create new operator symbols. For example, you can't define an `operator**()` function to denote exponentiation.

- You cannot overload the following operators:

Operator	Description
sizeof	The `sizeof` operator
.	The membership operator
.*	The pointer-to-member operator
::	The scope-resolution operator
?:	The conditional operator
typeid	An RTTI operator
const_cast	A type cast operator

Operator	Description
dynamic_cast	A type cast operator
reinterpret_cast	A type cast operator
static_cast	A type cast operator

This still leaves all the operators in Table 11.1 available for overloading.

• Most of the operators in Table 11.1 can be overloaded by using either member or non-member functions. However, you can use *only* member functions to overload the following operators:

Operator	Description
=	Assignment operator
( )	Function call operator
[ ]	Subscripting operator
->	Class member access by pointer operator

Note
This chapter does not cover every operator mentioned in the list of restrictions or in Table 11.1. However, Appendix E, "Other Operators," summarizes the operators that are not covered in the main body of this text.

TABLE 11.1   Operators That Can Be Overloaded

+	-	*	/	%	^
&	|	~=	!	=	<
>	+=	-=	*=	/=	%=
^=	&=	|=	<<	>>	>>=
<<=	==	!=	<=	>=	&&
||	++	--	,	->*	->
( )	[ ]	new	delete	new [ ]	delete [ ]

In addition to these formal restrictions, you should use sensible restraint in overloading operators. For example, you shouldn't overload the * operator so that it swaps the data members of two `Time` objects. Nothing in the notation would suggest what the operator did, so it would be better to define a class method with an explanatory name such as `Swap()`.

More Overloaded Operators

Some other operations make sense for the `Time` class. For example, you might want to subtract one time from another or multiply a time by a factor. This suggests overloading the subtraction and multiplication operators. The technique is the same as for the addition operator: You create `operator-()` and `operator*()` methods. That is, you add the following prototypes to the class declaration:

```
Time operator-(const Time & t) const;
Time operator*(double n) const;
```

Listing 11.7 shows the new header file.

LISTING 11.7   mytime2.h

```
// mytime2.h -- Time class after operator overloading
#ifndef MYTIME2_H_
#define MYTIME2_H_

class Time
{
private:
    int hours;
    int minutes;
public:
    Time();
    Time(int h, int m = 0);
    void AddMin(int m);
    void AddHr(int h);
    void Reset(int h = 0, int m = 0);
    Time operator+(const Time & t) const;
    Time operator-(const Time & t) const;
    Time operator*(double n) const;
    void Show() const;
};
#endif
```

Then you add definitions for the new methods to the implementation file, as shown in Listing 11.8.

LISTING 11.8   mytime2.cpp

```
// mytime2.cpp  -- implementing Time methods
#include <iostream>
#include "mytime2.h"

Time::Time()
{
```

LISTING 11.8   Continued

```
        hours = minutes = 0;
    }

    Time::Time(int h, int m )
    {
        hours = h;
        minutes = m;
    }

    void Time::AddMin(int m)
    {
        minutes += m;
        hours += minutes / 60;
        minutes %= 60;
    }
    void Time::AddHr(int h)
    {
        hours += h;
    }

    void Time::Reset(int h, int m)
    {
        hours = h;
        minutes = m;
    }

    Time Time::operator+(const Time & t) const
    {
        Time sum;
        sum.minutes = minutes + t.minutes;
        sum.hours = hours + t.hours + sum.minutes / 60;
        sum.minutes %= 60;
        return sum;
    }

    Time Time::operator-(const Time & t) const
    {
        Time diff;
        int tot1, tot2;
        tot1 = t.minutes + 60 * t.hours;
        tot2 = minutes + 60 * hours;
        diff.minutes = (tot2 - tot1) % 60;
        diff.hours = (tot2 - tot1) / 60;
        return diff;
    }

    Time Time::operator*(double mult) const
    {
        Time result;
        long totalminutes = hours * mult * 60 + minutes * mult;
        result.hours = totalminutes / 60;
        result.minutes = totalminutes % 60;
```

LISTING 11.8   Continued

```
        return result;
}

void Time::Show() const
{
    std::cout << hours << " hours, " << minutes << " minutes";
}
```

With these changes made, you can test the new definitions with the code shown in Listing 11.9.

LISTING 11.9   usetime2.cpp

```
// usetime2.cpp -- using the third draft of the Time class
// compile usetime2.cpp and mytime2.cpp together
#include <iostream>
#include "mytime2.h"

int main()
{
    using std::cout;
    using std::endl;
    Time weeding(4, 35);
    Time waxing(2, 47);
    Time total;
    Time diff;
    Time adjusted;

    cout << "weeding time = ";
    weeding.Show();
    cout << endl;

    cout << "waxing time = ";
    waxing.Show();
    cout << endl;

    cout << "total work time = ";
    total = weeding + waxing;    // use operator+()
    total.Show();
    cout << endl;

    diff = weeding - waxing;     // use operator-()
    cout << "weeding time - waxing time = ";
    diff.Show();
    cout << endl;

    adjusted = total * 1.5;      // use operator+()
    cout << "adjusted work time = ";
    adjusted.Show();
    cout << endl;

    return 0;
}
```

Here is the output of the program in Listings 11.7, 11.8, and 11.9:

```
weeding time = 4 hours, 35 minutes
waxing time = 2 hours, 47 minutes
total work time = 7 hours, 22 minutes
weeding time - waxing time = 1 hours, 48 minutes
adjusted work time = 11 hours, 3 minutes
```

Introducing Friends

As you've seen, C++ controls access to the private portions of a class object. Usually, public class methods serve as the only access, but sometimes this restriction is too rigid to fit particular programming problems. In such cases, C++ provides another form of access: the *friend*. Friends come in three varieties:

- Friend functions

- Friend classes

- Friend member functions

By making a function a friend to a class, you allow the function the same access privileges that a member function of the class has. We'll look into friend functions now, leaving the other two varieties to Chapter 15, "Friends, Exceptions, and More."

Before seeing how to make friends, let's look into why they might be needed. Often, overloading a binary operator (that is, an operator with two arguments) for a class generates a need for friends. Multiplying a `Time` object by a real number provides just such a situation, so let's study that case.

In the `Time` class example, the overloaded multiplication operator is different from the other two overloaded operators in that it combines two different types. That is, the addition and subtraction operators each combine two `Time` values, but the multiplication operator combines a `Time` value with a `double` value. This restricts how the operator can be used. Remember, the left operand is the invoking object. That is,

```
A = B * 2.75;
```

translates to the following member function call:

```
A = B.operator*(2.75);
```

But what about the following statement?

```
A = 2.75 * B;     // cannot correspond to a member function
```

Conceptually, `2.75 * B` should be the same as `B * 2.75`, but the first expression cannot correspond to a member function because `2.75` is not a type `Time` object. Remember, the left operand is the invoking object, but `2.75` is not an object. So the compiler cannot replace the expression with a member function call.

One way around this difficulty is to tell everyone (and to remember yourself) that you can only write `B * 2.75` but never write `2.75 * B`. This is a server-friendly, client-beware solution, and that's not what OOP is about.

However, there is another possibility—using a nonmember function. (Remember, most operators can be overloaded using either member or nonmember functions.) A nonmember function is not invoked by an object; instead, any values it uses, including objects, are explicit arguments. Thus, the compiler could match the expression

```
A = 2.75 * B;     // cannot correspond to a member function
```

to the following nonmember function call:

```
A = operator*(2.75, B);
```

The function would have this prototype:

```
Time operator*(double m, const Time & t);
```

With the nonmember overloaded operator function, the left operand of an operator expression corresponds to the first argument of the operator function, and the right operand corresponds to the second argument. Meanwhile, the original member function handles operands in the opposite order—that is, a `Time` value multiplied by a `double` value.

Using a nonmember function solves the problem of getting the operands in the desired order (first `double` and then `Time`), but it raises a new problem: Nonmember functions can't directly access private data in a class. Well, at least ordinary nonmember functions lack access. But there is a special category of nonmember functions, called *friends*, that can access private members of a class.

Creating Friends

The first step toward creating a friend function is to place a prototype in the class declaration and prefix the declaration with the keyword `friend`:

```
friend Time operator*(double m, const Time & t);  // goes in class declaration
```

This prototype has two implications:

- Although the `operator*()` function is declared in the class declaration, it is not a member function. So it isn't invoked by using the membership operator.

- Although the `operator*()` function is not a member function, it has the same access rights as a member function.

The second step is to write the function definition. Because it is not a member function, you don't use the `Time::` qualifier. Also, you don't use the `friend` keyword in the definition. The definition should look like this:

```
Time operator*(double m, const Time & t)  // friend not used in definition
{
    Time result;
    long totalminutes = t.hours * mult * 60 +t. minutes * mult;
```

```
    result.hours = totalminutes / 60;
    result.minutes = totalminutes % 60;
    return result;
}
```

With this declaration and definition, the statement

```
A = 2.75 * B;
```

translates to

```
A = operator*(2.75, B);
```

and invokes the nonmember friend function you just defined.

In short, a friend function to a class is a nonmember function that has the same access rights as a member function.

Are Friends Unfaithful to OOP?

At first glance, it might seem that friends violate the OOP principle of data hiding because the friend mechanism allows nonmember functions to access private data. However, that's an overly narrow view. Instead, you should think of friend functions as part of an extended interface for a class. For example, from a conceptual point of view, multiplying a `double` by a `Time` value is pretty much the same as multiplying a `Time` value by a `double`. That the first requires a friend function whereas the second can be done with a member function is the result of C++ syntax, not of a deep conceptual difference. By using both a friend function and a class method, you can express either operation with the same user interface. Also, keep in mind that only a class declaration can decide which functions are friends, so the class declaration still controls which functions access private data. In short, class methods and friends are simply two different mechanisms for expressing a class interface.

Actually, you can write this particular friend function as a non-friend by altering the definition so that it switches which value comes first in the multiplication:

```
Time operator*(double m, const Time & t)
{
    return t * m;      // use t.operator*(m)
}
```

The original version accessed **t.minutes** and **t.hours** explicitly, so it had to be a friend. This version only uses the **Time** object **t** as a whole, letting a member function handle the private values, so this version doesn't have to be a friend. Nonetheless, it's still a good idea to make this version a friend, too. Most importantly, it ties the function in as part of the official class interface. Second, if you later find a need for the function to access private data directly, you only have to change the function definition and not the class prototype.

Tip

If you want to overload an operator for a class and you want to use the operator with a nonclass term as the first operand, you can use a friend function to reverse the operand order.

A Common Kind of Friend: Overloading the << Operator

One very useful features of classes is that you can overload the << operator so that you can use it with `cout` to display an object's contents. In some ways, this overloading is a bit trickier than the earlier examples, so we'll develop it in two steps instead of in one.

Suppose `trip` is a `Time` object. To display `Time` values, we've been using `Show()`. Wouldn't it be nice, however, if you could do the following?

```
cout << trip;  // make cout recognize Time class?
```

You can do this because << is one of the C++ operators that can be overloaded. In fact, it already is heavily overloaded. In its most basic incarnation, the << operator is one of C and C++'s bit manipulation operators; it shifts bits left in a value (see Appendix E). But the `ostream` class overloads the operator, converting it into an output tool. Recall that `cout` is an `ostream` object and that it is smart enough to recognize all the basic C++ types. That's because the `ostream` class declaration includes an overloaded `operator<<()` definition for each of the basic types. That is, one definition uses an `int` argument, one uses a `double` argument, and so on. So, one way to teach `cout` to recognize a `Time` object is to add a new function operator definition to the `ostream` class declaration. But it's a dangerous idea to alter the `iostream` file and mess around with a standard interface. It's better to use the `Time` class declaration to teach the `Time` class how to use `cout`.

The First Version of Overloading <<

To teach the `Time` class to use `cout`, you have to use a friend function. Why? Because a statement like

```
cout << trip;
```

uses two objects, with the `ostream` class object (`cout`) first. If you use a `Time` member function to overload <<, the `Time` object would come first, as it did when you overloaded the * operator with a member function. That means you would have to use the << operator this way:

```
trip << cout;   // if operator<<() were a Time member function
```

This would be confusing. But by using a friend function, you can overload the operator this way:

```
void operator<<(ostream & os, const Time & t)
{
    os << t.hours << " hours, " << t.minutes << " minutes";
}
```

This lets you use

```
cout << trip;
```

to print data in the following format:

```
4 hours, 23 minutes
```

Friend or No Friend?

The new `Time` class declaration makes the `operator<<()` function a friend function to the `Time` class. But this function, although not inimical to the `ostream` class, is not a friend to it. The `operator<<()` function takes an `ostream` argument and a `Time` argument, so it might seem that this function has to be a friend to both classes. If you look at the code for the function, however, you'll notice that the function accesses individual members of the `Time` object but only uses the `ostream` object as a whole. Because `operator<<()` accesses private `Time` object members directly, it has to be a friend to the `Time` class. But because it does not directly access private `ostream` object members, the function does not have to be a friend to the `ostream` class. That's nice because it means you don't have to tinker with the `ostream` definition.

Note that the new `operator<<()` definition uses the `ostream` reference `os` as its first argument. Normally, `os` refers to the `cout` object, as it does in the expression `cout << trip`. But you could use the operator with other `ostream` objects, in which case `os` would refer to those objects.

What? You Don't Know of Any Other `ostream` Objects?

Don't forget `cerr`, introduced in Chapter 10, "Objects and Classes." Also, recall that Chapter 6, "Branching Statements and Logical Operators," introduces `ofstream` objects, which can be used to send output to a file. Through the magic of inheritance (see Chapter 13, "Class Inheritance"), `ofstream` objects can use `ostream` methods. Thus you can use the `operator<<()` definition to write `Time` data to files as well as to the screen. You just pass a suitably initialized `ofstream` object instead of `cout` as the first argument.

The call `cout << trip` should use the `cout` object itself, not a copy, so the function passes the object as a reference instead of by value. Thus, the expression `cout << trip` causes `os` to be an alias for `cout`, and the expression `cerr << trip` causes `os` to be an alias for `cerr`. The `Time` object can be passed by value or by reference because either form makes the object values available to the function. Again, passing by reference uses less memory and time than passing by value.

The Second Version of Overloading <<

The implementation just presented has a problem. Statements such as

```
cout << trip;
```

work fine, but the implementation doesn't allow you to combine the redefined << operator with the ones `cout` normally uses:

```
cout << "Trip time: " << trip << " (Tuesday)\n"; // can't do
```

To understand why this doesn't work and what must be done to make it work, you first need to know a bit more about how `cout` operates. Consider the following statements:

```
int x = 5;
int y = 8;
cout << x << y;
```

C++ reads the output statement from left to right, meaning it is equivalent to the following:

```
(cout << x) << y;
```

The << operator, as defined in **iostream**, takes an **ostream** object to its left. Clearly, the expression **cout << x** satisfies that requirement because **cout** is an **ostream** object. But the output statement also requires that the whole expression (**cout << x**) be a type **ostream** object because that expression is to the left of << **y**. Therefore, the **ostream** class implements the **operator<<()** function so that it returns an **ostream** object. In particular, it returns the invoking object—**cout**, in this case. Thus, the expression (**cout << x**) is itself an **ostream** object, and it can be used to the left of the << operator.

You can take the same approach with the friend function. You just revise the **operator<<()** function so that it returns a reference to an **ostream** object:

```
ostream & operator<<(ostream & os, const Time & t)
{
    os << t.hours << " hours, " << t.minutes << " minutes";
    return os;
}
```

Note that the return type is **ostream &**. Recall that this means that the function returns a reference to an **ostream** object. Because a program passes an object reference to the function to begin with, the net effect is that the function's return value is just the object passed to it. That is, the statement

```
cout << trip;
```

becomes the following function call:

```
operator<<(cout, trip);
```

And that call returns the **cout** object. So now the following statement does work:

```
cout << "Trip time: " << trip << " (Tuesday)\n"; // can do
```

Let's break this into separate steps to see how it works. First,

```
cout << "Trip time: "
```

invokes the particular **ostream** definition of << that displays a string and returns the **cout** object, so the expression **cout << "Trip time: "** displays the string and then is replaced by its return value, **cout**. This reduces the original statement to the following one:

```
cout << trip << " (Tuesday)\n";
```

Next, the program uses the **Time** declaration of << to display the trip values and to return the **cout** object again. This reduces the statement to the following:

```
cout << " (Tuesday)\n";
```

The program now finishes up by using the **ostream** definition of << for strings to display the final string.

As a point of interest, this version of `operator<<()` can also be used for file output:

```
#include <fstream>
...
ofstream fout;
fout.open("savetime.txt");
Time trip(12, 40);
fout << trip;
```

The last statement becomes this:

```
operator<<(fout, trip);
```

And, as Chapter 8 points out, the properties of class inheritance allow an `ostream` reference to refer to `ostream` objects and to `ofstream` objects.

Tip

In general, to overload the << operator to display an object of class *c_name*, you use a friend function with a definition in this form:

```
ostream & operator<<(ostream & os, const c_name & obj)
{
    os << ... ;   // display object contents
    return os;
}
```

Listing 11.10 shows the class definition as modified to include the two friend functions `operator*()` and `operator<<()`. It implements the first of these as an inline function because the code is so short. (When the definition is also the prototype, as in this case, you use the `friend` prefix.)

Remember

You use the `friend` keyword only in the prototype found in the class declaration. You don't use it in the function definition, unless the definition is also the prototype.

LISTING 11.10   `mytime3.h`

```
// mytime3.h -- Time class with friends
#ifndef MYTIME3_H_
#define MYTIME3_H_
#include <iostream>

class Time
{
private:
    int hours;
    int minutes;
```

LISTING 11.10   Continued

```cpp
public:
    Time();
    Time(int h, int m = 0);
    void AddMin(int m);
    void AddHr(int h);
    void Reset(int h = 0, int m = 0);
    Time operator+(const Time & t) const;
    Time operator-(const Time & t) const;
    Time operator*(double n) const;
    friend Time operator*(double m, const Time & t)
        { return t * m; }   // inline definition
    friend std::ostream & operator<<(std::ostream & os, const Time & t);

};
#endif
```

Listing 11.11 shows the revised set of definitions. Note again that the methods use the `Time::` qualifier, whereas the friend function does not. Also note that because `mytime3.h` includes `iostream` and provides the `using` declaration `std::ostream`, including `mytime3.h` in `mytime3.cpp` provides support for using `ostream` in the implementation file.

LISTING 11.11   mytime3.cpp

```cpp
// mytime3.cpp  -- implementing Time methods
#include "mytime3.h"

Time::Time()
{
    hours = minutes = 0;
}

Time::Time(int h, int m )
{
    hours = h;
    minutes = m;
}

void Time::AddMin(int m)
{
    minutes += m;
    hours += minutes / 60;
    minutes %= 60;
}
void Time::AddHr(int h)
{
    hours += h;
}

void Time::Reset(int h, int m)
{
```

LISTING 11.11   Continued

```cpp
        hours = h;
        minutes = m;
    }

    Time Time::operator+(const Time & t) const
    {
        Time sum;
        sum.minutes = minutes + t.minutes;
        sum.hours = hours + t.hours + sum.minutes / 60;
        sum.minutes %= 60;
        return sum;
    }

    Time Time::operator-(const Time & t) const
    {
        Time diff;
        int tot1, tot2;
        tot1 = t.minutes + 60 * t.hours;
        tot2 = minutes + 60 * hours;
        diff.minutes = (tot2 - tot1) % 60;
        diff.hours = (tot2 - tot1) / 60;
        return diff;
    }

    Time Time::operator*(double mult) const
    {
        Time result;
        long totalminutes = hours * mult * 60 + minutes * mult;
        result.hours = totalminutes / 60;
        result.minutes = totalminutes % 60;
        return result;
    }

    std::ostream & operator<<(std::ostream & os, const Time & t)
    {
        os << t.hours << " hours, " << t.minutes << " minutes";
        return os;
    }
```

Listing 11.12 shows a sample program. Technically, `usetime3.cpp` doesn't have to include `iostream` because `mytime3.h` already includes that file. However, as a user of the `Time` class, you don't necessarily know which files are included in the class code, so you would take the responsibility of declaring those header files that you know your part of the code needs.

LISTING 11.12   usetime3.cpp

```cpp
//usetime3.cpp -- using the fourth draft of the Time class
// compile usetime3.cpp and mytime3.cpp together
#include <iostream>
#include "mytime3.h"
```

LISTING 11.12 Continued

```
int main()
{
    using std::cout;
    using std::endl;
    Time aida(3, 35);
    Time tosca(2, 48);
    Time temp;

    cout << "Aida and Tosca:\n";
    cout << aida<<"; " << tosca << endl;
    temp = aida + tosca;       // operator+()
    cout << "Aida + Tosca: " << temp << endl;
    temp = aida* 1.17;   // member operator*()
    cout << "Aida * 1.17: " << temp << endl;
    cout << "10 * Tosca: " << 10 * tosca << endl;

    return 0;
}
```

Here is the output of the program in Listings 11.10, 11.11, and 11.12:

```
Aida and Tosca:
3 hours, 35 minutes; 2 hours, 48 minutes
Aida + Tosca: 6 hours, 23 minutes
Aida * 1.17: 4 hours, 11 minutes
10 * Tosca: 28 hours, 0 minutes
```

Overloaded Operators: Member Versus Nonmember Functions

For many operators, you have a choice between using member functions or nonmember functions to implement operator overloading. Typically, the nonmember version is a friend function so that it can directly access the private data for a class. For example, consider the addition operator for the `Time` class. It has this prototype in the `Time` class declaration:

```
Time operator+(const Time & t) const;                          // member version
```

Instead, the class could use the following prototype:

```
friend Time operator+(const Time & t1, const Time & t2);   // nonmember version
```

The addition operator requires two operands. For the member function version, one is passed implicitly via the `this` pointer and the second is passed explicitly as a function argument. For the friend version, both are passed as arguments.

Remember
A nonmember version of an overloaded operator function requires as many formal parameters as the operator has operands. A member version of the same operator requires one fewer parameter because one operand is passed implicitly as the invoking object.

Either of these two prototypes matches the expression T2 + T3, where T2 and T3 are type Time objects. That is, the compiler can convert the statement

```
T1 = T2 + T3;
```

to either of the following:

```
T1 = T2.operator+(T3);    // member function
T1 = operator+(T2, T3);   // nonmember function
```

Keep in mind that you must choose one or the other form when defining a given operator, but not both. Because both forms match the same expression, defining both forms is an ambiguity error, leading to a compilation error.

Which form, then, is it best to use? For some operators, as mentioned earlier, the member function is the only valid choice. Otherwise, it often doesn't make much difference. Sometimes, depending on the class design, the nonmember version may have an advantage, particularly if you have defined type conversions for the class. The section "Conversions and Friends," near the end of this chapter, discusses this situation further.

More Overloading: A Vector Class

Let's look at another class design that uses operator overloading and friends—a class representing vectors. This class also illustrates further aspects of class design, such as incorporating two different ways of describing the same thing into an object. Even if you don't care for vectors, you can use many of the new techniques shown here in other contexts. A *vector*, as the term is used in engineering and physics, is a quantity that has both a magnitude (size) and a direction. For example, if you push something, the effect depends on how hard you push (the magnitude) and in what direction you push. A push in one direction can save a tottering vase, whereas a push in another direction can hasten its rush to doom. To fully describe the motion of your car, you should give both the speed (the magnitude) and the direction; arguing with the highway patrol that you were driving under the speed limit carries little weight if you were traveling in the wrong direction. (Immunologists and computer scientists may use the term *vector* differently; ignore them, at least until Chapter 16, "The string Class and the Standard Template Library," which looks at a computer science version, the vector template class.) The following sidebar tells you more about vectors, but understanding them completely isn't necessary for following the C++ aspects of the examples.

Vectors

Say you're a worker bee and have discovered a marvelous nectar cache. You rush back to the hive and announce that you've found nectar 120 yards away. "Not enough information," buzz the other bees. "You have to tell us the direction, too!" You answer, "It's 30 degrees north of the sun direction." Knowing both the distance (magnitude) and the direction, the other bees rush to the sweet site. Bees know vectors.

Many quantities involve both a magnitude and a direction. The effect of a push, for example, depends on both its strength and direction. Moving an object on a computer screen involves a distance and a direction. You can describe such things by using vectors. For example, you can describe moving (displacing) an object onscreen with a vector, which you can visualize as an arrow drawn from the starting position to the final position. The length of the vector is its magnitude, and that describes how far the point has been displaced. The orientation of the arrow describes the direction (see Figure 11.1). A vector representing such a change in position is called a *displacement vector*.

Now say you're Lhanappa, the great mammoth hunter. Scouts report a mammoth herd 14.1 kilometers to the northwest. But, because of a southeast wind, you don't want to approach from the southeast. So you go 10 kilometers west and then 10 kilometers north, approaching the herd from the south. You know these two displacement vectors bring you to the same location as the single 14.1-kilometer vector pointing northwest. Lhanappa, the great mammoth hunter, also knows how to add vectors.

Adding two vectors has a simple geometric interpretation. First, draw one vector. Then draw the second vector, starting from the arrow end of the first vector. Finally, draw a vector from the starting point of the first vector to the endpoint of the second vector. This third vector represents the sum of the first two (see Figure 11.2). Note that the length of the sum can be less than the sum of the individual lengths.

FIGURE 11.1
Describing a displacement with a vector.

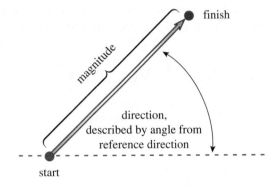

FIGURE 11.2
Adding two vectors.

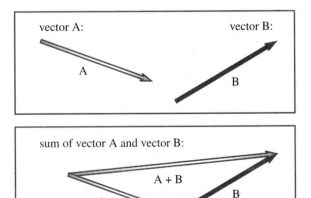

Vectors are a natural choice for operator overloading. First, you can't represent a vector with a single number, so it makes sense to create a class to represent vectors. Second, vectors have analogs to ordinary arithmetic operations such as addition and subtraction. This parallel suggests overloading the corresponding operators so you can use them with vectors.

To keep things simple, in this section you'll implement a two-dimensional vector, such as a screen displacement, instead of a three-dimensional vector, such as might represent movement of a helicopter or a gymnast. You need just two numbers to describe a two-dimensional vector, but you have a choice of what set of two numbers:

- You can describe a vector by its magnitude (length) and direction (an angle).

- You can represent a vector by its x and y components.

The components are a horizontal vector (the x component) and a vertical vector (the y component), which add up to the final vector. For example, you can describe a motion as moving a point 30 units to the right and 40 units up (see Figure 11.3). That motion puts the point at the same spot as moving 50 units at an angle of 53.1° from the horizontal. Therefore, a vector with a magnitude of 50 and an angle of 53.1° is equivalent to a vector having a horizontal component of 30 and a vertical component of 40. What counts with displacement vectors is where you start and where you end up, not the exact route taken to get there. This choice of representation is basically the same thing covered with the Chapter 7 program that converts between rectangular and polar coordinates.

FIGURE 11.3

x and y components of a vector.

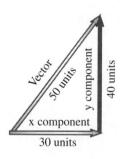

Two ways of describing the same vector:

vector: 50 units at 53.1 degrees

or

vector: x = 30, y = 40

Sometimes one form is more convenient, sometimes the other, so you'll incorporate both representations into the class description. (See the sidebar "Multiple Representations and Classes," later in this chapter.) Also, you'll design the class so that if you alter one representation of a vector, the object automatically updates the other representation. The ability to build such intelligence into an object is another C++ class virtue. Listing 11.13 presents a class declaration. To refresh your memory about namespaces, the listing places the class declaration inside the VECTOR namespace.

Compatibility Note

If your system does not support namespaces, you can remove the following lines:

```
namespace VECTOR
{
```

and

```
}    // end namespace VECTOR
```

LISTING 11.13 vect.h

```
// vect.h -- Vector class with <<, mode state
#ifndef VECTOR_H_
#define VECTOR_H_
#include <iostream>
namespace VECTOR
{
    class Vector
    {
    private:
        double x;          // horizontal value
        double y;          // vertical value
        double mag;        // length of vector
        double ang;        // direction of vector
        char mode;         // 'r' = rectangular, 'p' = polar
    // private methods for setting values
        void set_mag();
        void set_ang();
        void set_x();
        void set_y();
    public:
        Vector();
        Vector(double n1, double n2, char form = 'r');
        void set(double n1, double n2, char form = 'r');
        ~Vector();
        double xval() const {return x;}      // report x value
        double yval() const {return y;}      // report y value
        double magval() const {return mag;}  // report magnitude
        double angval() const {return ang;}  // report angle
        void polar_mode();                   // set mode to 'p'
        void rect_mode();                    // set mode to 'r'
    // operator overloading
        Vector operator+(const Vector & b) const;
        Vector operator-(const Vector & b) const;
        Vector operator-() const;
        Vector operator*(double n) const;
    // friends
        friend Vector operator*(double n, const Vector & a);
```

LISTING 11.13   Continued

```
        friend std::ostream & operator<<(std::ostream & os, const Vector & v);
    };

}   // end namespace VECTOR
#endif
```

Notice that the four functions in Listing 11.13 that report component values are defined in the class declaration. This automatically makes them inline functions. The fact that these functions are so short makes them excellent candidates for inlining. None of them should alter object data, so they are declared using the `const` modifier. As you may recall from Chapter 10, this is the syntax for declaring a function that doesn't modify the object it implicitly accesses.

Listing 11.14 shows all the methods and friend functions declared in Listing 11.13. The listing uses the open nature of namespaces to add the method definitions to the `VECTOR` namespace. Note how the constructor functions and the `set()` function each set both the rectangular and the polar representations of the vector. Thus, either set of values is available immediately, without further calculation, should you need them. Also, as mentioned in Chapters 4, "Compound Types," and 7, C++'s built-in math functions use angles in radians, so the functions build conversion to and from degrees into the methods. The `Vector` class implementation hides such things as converting from polar coordinates to rectangular coordinates or converting radians to degrees from the user. All the user needs to know is that the class uses angles in degrees and that it makes a vector available in two equivalent representations.

LISTING 11.14   `vect.cpp`

```
// vect.cpp -- methods for the Vector class
#include <cmath>
#include "vect.h"    // includes <iostream>
using std::sin;
using std::cos;
using std::atan2;
using std::cout;

namespace VECTOR
{

    const double Rad_to_deg = 57.2957795130823;

    // private methods
    // calculates magnitude from x and y
    void Vector::set_mag()
    {
        mag = sqrt(x * x + y * y);
    }

    void Vector::set_ang()
    {
        if (x == 0.0 && y == 0.0)
            ang = 0.0;
```

LISTING 11.14   Continued

```cpp
    else
        ang = atan2(y, x);
}
// set x from polar coordinate
void Vector::set_x()
{
    x = mag * cos(ang);
}

// set y from polar coordinate
void Vector::set_y()
{
    y = mag * sin(ang);
}

// public methods
Vector::Vector()                // default constructor
{
    x = y = mag = ang = 0.0;
    mode = 'r';
}

// construct vector from rectangular coordinates if form is r
// (the default) or else from polar coordinates if form is p
Vector::Vector(double n1, double n2, char form)
{
    mode = form;
    if (form == 'r')
     {
        x = n1;
        y = n2;
        set_mag();
        set_ang();
    }
    else if (form == 'p')
    {
        mag = n1;
        ang = n2 / Rad_to_deg;
        set_x();
        set_y();
    }
    else
    {
        cout << "Incorrect 3rd argument to Vector() -- ";
        cout << "vector set to 0\n";
        x = y = mag = ang = 0.0;
        mode = 'r';
    }
}

// set vector from rectangular coordinates if form is r (the
// default) or else from polar coordinates if form is p
```

LISTING 11.14   Continued

```cpp
void Vector:: set(double n1, double n2, char form)
{
    mode = form;
    if (form == 'r')
     {
         x = n1;
         y = n2;
         set_mag();
         set_ang();
    }
    else if (form == 'p')
    {
         mag = n1;
         ang = n2 / Rad_to_deg;
         set_x();
         set_y();
    }
    else
    {
         cout << "Incorrect 3rd argument to Vector() -- ";
         cout << "vector set to 0\n";
         x = y = mag = ang = 0.0;
         mode = 'r';
    }
}

Vector::~Vector()     // destructor
{
}

void Vector::polar_mode()     // set to polar mode
{
    mode = 'p';
}

void Vector::rect_mode()      // set to rectangular mode
{
    mode = 'r';
}

// operator overloading
// add two Vectors
Vector Vector::operator+(const Vector & b) const
{
    return Vector(x + b.x, y + b.y);
}

// subtract Vector b from a
Vector Vector::operator-(const Vector & b) const
{
    return Vector(x - b.x, y - b.y);
}
```

LISTING 11.14 Continued

```cpp
// reverse sign of Vector
Vector Vector::operator-() const
{
    return Vector(-x, -y);
}

// multiple vector by n
Vector Vector::operator*(double n) const
{
    return Vector(n * x, n * y);
}

// friend methods
// multiply n by Vector a
Vector operator*(double n, const Vector & a)
{
    return a * n;
}

// display rectangular coordinates if mode is r,
// else display polar coordinates if mode is p
std::ostream & operator<<(std::ostream & os, const Vector & v)
{
    if (v.mode == 'r')
        os << "(x,y) = (" << v.x << ", " << v.y << ")";
    else if (v.mode == 'p')
    {
        os << "(m,a) = (" << v.mag << ", "
            << v.ang * Rad_to_deg << ")";
    }
    else
        os << "Vector object mode is invalid";
    return os;
}

}  // end namespace VECTOR
```

You could design the class differently. For example, the object could store the rectangular coordinates and not the polar coordinates. In that case, the computation of polar coordinates could be moved to the `magval()` and `angval()` methods. For applications in which conversions are seldom used, this could be a more efficient design. Also, the `set()` method isn't really needed. Suppose `shove` is a `Vector` object and that you have the following code:

```cpp
shove.set(100,300);
```

You can get the same result by using a constructor instead:

```cpp
shove = Vector(100,300);    // create and assign a temporary object
```

However, the `set()` method alters the contents of `shove` directly, whereas using the constructor adds the extra steps of creating a temporary object and assigning it to `shove`.

These design decisions follow the OOP tradition of having the class interface concentrate on the essentials (the abstract model) while hiding the details. Thus, when you use the `Vector` class, you can think about a vector's general features, such as that they can represent displacements and that you can add two vectors. Whether you express a vector in component notation or in magnitude, direction notation becomes secondary because you can set a vector's values and display them in whichever format is most convenient at the time.

We'll look at some of the features the `Vector` class in more detail next.

Compatibility Note

Some systems may still use `math.h` instead of `cmath`. Also, some C++ systems don't automatically search the math library. For example, some Unix systems require that you do the following:

```
$ CC source_file(s) -lm
```

The `-lm` option instructs the linker to search the math library. So, when you eventually compile programs that use the `Vector` class, if you get a message about undefined externals, you should try the `-lm` option or check whether your system requires something similar.

As with the header file, if your system does not support namespaces, you can remove the following lines:

```
namespace VECTOR
{
```

and

```
}   // end namespace VECTOR
```

Using a State Member

The Vector class stores both the rectangular coordinates and the polar coordinates for a vector. It uses a member called `mode` to control which form the constructor, the `set()` method, and the overloaded `operator<<()` function use, with `'r'` representing the rectangular mode (the default) and `'p'` the polar mode. Such a member is termed a *state member* because it describes the state an object is in. To see what this means, look at the code for the constructor:

```
Vector::Vector(double n1, double n2, char form)
{
    mode = form;
    if (form == 'r')
     {
         x = n1;
         y = n2;
         set_mag();
         set_ang();
    }
    else if (form == 'p')
    {
         mag = n1;
         ang = n2 / Rad_to_deg;
         set_x();
         set_y();
    }
```

```
        else
        {
            cout << "Incorrect 3rd argument to Vector() -- ";
            cout << "vector set to 0\n";
            x = y = mag = ang = 0.0;
            mode = 'r';
        }
    }
```

If the third argument is `'r'` or if it is omitted (the prototype assigns a default value of `'r'`), the inputs are interpreted as rectangular coordinates, whereas a value of `'p'` causes them to be interpreted as polar coordinates:

```
Vector folly(3.0, 4.0);          // set x = 3, y = 4
Vector foolery(20.0, 30.0, 'p'); // set mag = 20, ang = 30
```

Note that the constructor uses the private methods **set_mag()** and **set_ang()** to set the magnitude and angle values if you provide x and y values, and it uses the private **set_x()** and **set_y()** methods to set x and y values if you provide magnitude and angle values. Also note that the constructor delivers a warning message and sets the state to `'r'` if something other than `'r'` or `'p'` is specified.

Similarly, **the operator<<()** function uses the mode to determine how values are displayed:

```
// display rectangular coordinates if mode is r,
// else display polar coordinates if mode is p
ostream & operator<<(ostream & os, const Vector & v)
{
    if (v.mode == 'r')
        os << "(x,y) = (" << v.x << ", " << v.y << ")";
    else if (v.mode == 'p')
    {
        os << "(m,a) = (" << v.mag << ", "
            << v.ang * Rad_to_deg << ")";
    }
    else
        os << "Vector object mode is invalid";
    return os;
}
```

The various methods that can set the mode are careful to accept only `'r'` and `'p'` as valid values, so the final **else** in this function should never be reached. Still, it's often a good idea to check; such a check can help catch an otherwise obscure programming error.

Multiple Representations and Classes

Quantities that have different, but equivalent, representations are common. For example, you can measure gasoline consumption in miles per gallon, as done in the United States, or in liters per 100 kilometers, as done in Europe. You can represent a number in string form or numeric form, and you can represent intelligence as an IQ or in kiloturkeys. Classes lend themselves nicely to encompassing different aspects and representations of an entity in a single object. First, you can store multiple representations in one object. Second, you can write the class functions so that assigning values for one representation automatically assigns values for the other representation(s). For example, the set_by_polar() method for the Vector class sets the mag and ang members to the function arguments, but it also sets the x and y members. By handling conversions internally, a class can help you think of a quantity in terms of its essential nature rather than in terms of its representation.

Overloading Arithmetic Operators for the Vector Class

Adding two vectors is very simple when you use x,y coordinates. You just add the two x components to get the x component of the answer and add the two y components to get the y component of the answer. From this description, you might be tempted to use this code:

```
Vector Vector::operator+(const Vector & b) const
{
    Vector sum;
    sum.x = x + b.x;
    sum.y = y + b.y;
    return sum;           // incomplete version
}
```

And this would be fine if the object stored only the x and y components. Unfortunately, this version of the code fails to set the polar values. You could fix this problem by adding more code:

```
Vector Vector::operator+(const Vector & b) const
{
    Vector sum;
    sum.x = x + b.x;
    sum.y = y + b.y;
    sum.set_ang(sum.x, sum.y);
    sum.set_mag(sum.x, sum.y);
    return sum;            // version duplicates needlessly
}
```

But it is much simpler and more reliable to let a constructor do the work:

```
Vector Vector::operator+(const Vector & b) const
{
    return Vector(x + b.x, y + b.y);        // return the constructed Vector
}
```

Here, the code hands the **Vector** constructor the two new values for the x and y components. The constructor then creates a nameless new object, using these values, and the function returns a copy of that object. This way, you guarantee that the new **Vector** object is created according to the standard rules you lay down in the constructor.

Tip

If a method needs to compute a new class object, you should see if you can use a class constructor to do the work. Not only does that save you trouble, it ensures that the new object is constructed in the proper fashion.

Multiplication

In visual terms, multiplying a vector by a number makes the vector longer or shorter by that factor. So multiplying a vector by 3 produces a vector with three times the length, but still pointed in the same direction. It's easy to translate that image into how the Vector class represents a vector. In polar terms, you multiply the magnitude and leave the angle alone. In rectangular terms, you multiply a vector by a number by multiplying its x and y components separately by the number. That is, if a vector has components of 5 and 12, multiplying by 3 makes the components 15 and 36. And that is what the overloaded multiplication operator does:

```
Vector Vector::operator*(double n) const
{
    return Vector(n * x, n * y);
}
```

As with overloaded addition, the code lets a constructor create the correct Vector object from the new x and y components. This handles multiplying a Vector value by a double value. Just as in the Time example, you can use an inline friend function to handle double times Vector:

```
Vector operator*(double n, const Vector & a)  // friend function
{
    return a * n;   // convert double times Vector to Vector times double
}
```

More Refinement: Overloading an Overloaded Operator

In ordinary C++, the - operator already has two meanings. First, when used with two operands, it's the subtraction operator. The subtraction operator is termed a *binary operator* because it has exactly two operands. Second, when used with one operand, as in -x, it's a minus sign operator. This form is termed a *unary operator*, meaning it has exactly one operand. Both operations—subtraction and sign reversal—make sense for vectors, too, so the Vector class has both.

To subtract Vector B from Vector A, you simply subtract components, so the definition for overloading subtraction is quite similar to the one for addition:

```
Vector operator-(const Vector & b) const;          // prototype
Vector Vector::operator-(const Vector & b) const    // definition
{
    return Vector(x - b.x, y - b.y);  // return the constructed Vector
}
```

Here, it's important to get the correct order. Consider the following statement:

```
diff = v1 - v2;
```

It's converted to a member function call:

```
diff = v1.operator-(v2);
```

This means the vector that is passed as the explicit argument is subtracted from the implicit vector argument, so you should use `x - b.x` and not `b.x - x`.

Next, consider the unary minus operator, which takes just one operand. Applying this operator to a regular number, as in -x, changes the sign of the value. Thus, applying this operator to a vector reverses the sign of each component. More precisely, the function should return a new vector that is the reverse of the original. (In polar terms, negation leaves the magnitude unchanged but reverses the direction. Many politicians with little or no mathematical training, nonetheless, have an intuitive mastery of this operation.) Here are the prototype and definition for overloading negation:

```
Vector operator-() const;
Vector Vector::operator-() const
{
    return Vector (-x, -y);
}
```

Note that now there are two separate definitions for `operator-()`. That's fine because the two definitions have different signatures. You can define both binary and unary versions of the - operator because C++ provides both binary and unary versions of that operator to begin with. An operator that has only a binary form, such as division (/), can only be overloaded as a binary operator.

Remember
Because operator overloading is implemented with functions, you can overload the same operator many times, as long as each operator function has a distinct signature and as long as each operator function has the same number of operands as the corresponding built-in C++ operator.

An Implementation Comment

The implementation described in the preceding sections stores both rectangular and polar coordinates for a vector in the `Vector` object. However, the public interface doesn't depend on this fact. All the interface calls for is that both representations can be displayed and that individual values can be returned. The internal implementation could be quite different. As mentioned earlier, the object could store just the x and y components. Then, say, the `magval()` method, which returns the value of the magnitude of the vector, could calculate the magnitude from the x and y values instead of just looking up the value as stored in the object. Such an approach changes the implementation but leaves the user interface unchanged. This separation of interface from implementation is one of the goals of OOP. It lets you fine-tune an implementation without changing the code in programs that use the class.

Both of these implementations have advantages and disadvantages. Storing the data means that the object occupies more memory and that code has to be careful to update both rectangular and polar representations each time a `Vector` object is changed. But data look-up is faster. If an application often needs to access both representations of a vector, the implementation used in this example would be preferable; if polar data were needed only infrequently, the other implementation would be better. You could choose to use one implementation in one program and the second implementation in another, yet retain the same user interface for both.

Taking the `Vector` Class on a Random Walk

Listing 11.15 provides a short program that uses the revised `Vector` class. It simulates the famous Drunkard's Walk problem. Actually, now that drunks are recognized as people with a serious health problem rather than as a source of amusement, it's usually called the Random Walk problem. The idea is that you place someone at a lamppost. The person begins walking, but the direction of each step varies randomly from the direction of the preceding step. One way of phrasing the problem is How many steps does it take the random walker to travel, say, 50 feet away from the post? In terms of vectors, this amounts to adding a bunch of randomly oriented vectors until the sum exceeds 50 feet.

Listing 11.15 lets you select the target distance to be traveled and the length of the wanderer's step. It maintains a running total that represents the position after each step (represented as a vector), and reports the number of steps needed to reach the target distance, along with the walker's location (in both formats). As you'll see, the walker's progress is quite inefficient. A journey of 1,000 steps, each 2 feet long, may carry the walker only 50 feet from the starting point. The program divides the net distance traveled (50 feet, in this case) by the number of steps to provide a measure of the walker's inefficiency. All the random direction changes make this average much smaller than the length of a single step. To select directions randomly, the program uses the standard library functions `rand()`, `srand()`, and `time()`, described in the following "Program Notes" section. Be sure to compile Listing 11.14 along with Listing 11.15.

LISTING 11.15   `randwalk.cpp`

```cpp
// randwalk.cpp -- using the Vector class
// compile with the vect.cpp file
#include <iostream>
#include <cstdlib>      // rand(), srand() prototypes
#include <ctime>        // time() prototype
#include "vect.h"
int main()
{
    using namespace std;
    using VECTOR::Vector;
    srand(time(0));     // seed random-number generator
    double direction;
    Vector step;
    Vector result(0.0, 0.0);
    unsigned long steps = 0;
    double target;
    double dstep;
    cout << "Enter target distance (q to quit): ";
    while (cin >> target)
    {
        cout << "Enter step length: ";
        if (!(cin >> dstep))
            break;

        while (result.magval() < target)
        {
```

LISTING 11.15   Continued

```
            direction = rand() % 360;
            step.set(dstep, direction, 'p');
            result = result + step;
            steps++;
        }
        cout << "After " << steps << " steps, the subject "
            "has the following location:\n";
        cout << result << endl;
        result.polar_mode();
        cout << " or\n" << result << endl;
        cout << "Average outward distance per step = "
            << result.magval()/steps << endl;
        steps = 0;
        result.set(0.0, 0.0);
        cout << "Enter target distance (q to quit): ";
    }
    cout << "Bye!\n";

    return 0;
}
```

Compatibility Note

You might have to use `stdlib.h` instead of `cstdlib` and `time.h` instead of `ctime`. If your system doesn't support namespaces, omit the following line:

`using VECTOR::Vector;`

Here is a sample run of the program in Listings 11.13, 11.14, and 11.15:

```
Enter target distance (q to quit): 50
Enter step length: 2
After 253 steps, the subject has the following location:
(x,y) = (46.1512, 20.4902)
 or
(m,a) = (50.495, 23.9402)
Average outward distance per step = 0.199587
Enter target distance (q to quit): 50
Enter step length: 2
After 951 steps, the subject has the following location:
(x,y) = (-21.9577, 45.3019)
 or
(m,a) = (50.3429, 115.8593)
Average outward distance per step = 0.0529362
Enter target distance (q to quit): 50
Enter step length: 1
After 1716 steps, the subject has the following location:
(x,y) = (40.0164, 31.1244)
 or
(m,a) = (50.6956, 37.8755)
```

```
Average outward distance per step = 0.0295429
Enter target distance (q to quit): q
Bye!
```

The random nature of the process produces considerable variation from trial to trial, even if the initial conditions are the same. On average, however, halving the step size quadruples the number of steps needed to cover a given distance. Probability theory suggests that, on average, the number of steps (N) of length s needed to reach a net distance of D is given by the following equation:

$$N = (D/s)^2$$

This is just an average, but there will be considerable variations from trial to trial. For example, 1,000 trials of attempting to travel 50 feet in 2-foot steps yielded an average of 636 steps (close to the theoretical value of 625) to travel that far, but the range was from 91 to 3,951. Similarly, 1,000 trials of traveling 50 feet in 1-foot steps averaged 2,557 steps (close to the theoretical value of 2,500), with a range of 345 to 10,882. So if you find yourself walking randomly, be confident and take long steps. You still won't have any control over the direction you wind up going, but at least you'll get farther.

Program Notes

First, let's note how painless it was to use the **VECTOR** namespace in Listing 11.15. The **using** declaration

```
using VECTOR::Vector;
```

places the name of the **Vector** class in scope. Because all the **Vector** class methods have class scope, importing the class name also makes the **Vector** methods available, without the need for any further **using** declarations.

Next, let's talk about random numbers. The standard ANSI C library, which also comes with C++, includes a **rand()** function that returns a random integer in the range from 0 to some implementation-dependent value. Your random walk program uses the modulus operator to get an angle value in the range 0 to 359. The **rand()** function works by applying an algorithm to an initial seed value to get a random value. That value is used as the seed for the next function call, and so on. The numbers are really *pseudorandom* because 10 consecutive calls normally produce the same set of 10 random numbers. (The exact values depend on the implementation.) However, the **srand()** function lets you override the default seed value and initiate a different sequence of random numbers. This program uses the return value of **time(0)** to set the seed. The **time(0)** function returns the current calendar time, often implemented as the number of seconds since some specific date. (More generally, **time()** takes the address of a type **time_t** variable and puts the time into that variable and also returns it. Using **0** for the address argument obviates the need for an otherwise unneeded **time_t** variable.) Thus, the statement

```
srand(time(0));
```

sets a different seed each time you run the program, making the random output appear even more random. The `cstdlib` header file (formerly `stdlib.h`) contains the prototypes for `srand()` and `rand()`, whereas `ctime` (formerly `time.h`) contains the `time()` prototype.

The program uses the `result` vector to keep track of the walker's progress. On each cycle of the inner loop, the program sets the `step` vector to a new direction and adds it to the current `result` vector. When the magnitude of `result` exceeds the target distance, the loop terminates.

By setting the vector mode, the program displays the final position in rectangular terms and in polar terms.

Incidentally, the statement

```
result = result + step;
```

has the effect of placing `result` in the `'r'` mode, regardless of the initial modes of `result` and `step`. Here's why. First, the addition operator function creates and returns a new vector that holds the sum of the two arguments. The function creates that vector by using the default constructor, which creates vectors in the `'r'` mode. Thus, the vector being assigned to `result` is in the `'r'` mode. By default, assignment assigns each member variable individually, so `'r'` is assigned to `result.mode`. If you would prefer some other behavior, such as `result` retaining its original mode, you can override default assignment by defining an assignment operator for the class. Chapter 12 shows examples of this.

By the way, it's a simple matter to save successive positions in a file. First, you include `<fstream>`, declare an `ofstream` object, and associate the object with a file:

```
#include <fstream>
...
ofstream fout;
fout.open("thewalk.txt");
```

Then, in the loop that calculates the result, you insert something like this:

```
fout << result << endl;
```

This invokes the friend function call `operator<<(fout, result)`, causing the `os` reference parameter to refer to `fout`, thus sending output to the file. You could also use `fout` to write other information to the file, such as the summary information currently displayed by `cout`.

Automatic Conversions and Type Casts for Classes

The next topic on the class menu is type conversion. We'll look into how C++ handles conversions to and from user-defined types. To set the stage, let's first review how C++ handles conversions for its built-in types. When you make a statement that assigns a value of one standard type to a variable of another standard type, C++ automatically converts the value to the same type as the receiving variable, provided that the two types are compatible. For example, the following statements all generate numeric type conversions:

```
long count = 8;      // int value 8 converted to type long
double time = 11;    // int value 11 converted to type double
int side = 3.33;     // double value 3.33 converted to type int 3
```

These assignments work because C++ recognizes that the diverse numeric types all represent the same basic thing—a number—and because C++ incorporates built-in rules for making the conversions. Recall from Chapter 3, "Dealing with Data," however, that you can lose some precision in these conversions. For example, assigning 3.33 to the int variable side results in side getting the value 3, losing the 0.33 part.

The C++ language does not automatically convert types that are not compatible. For example, the statement

```
int * p = 10;  // type clash
```

fails because the left side is a pointer type, whereas the right side is a number. And even though a computer may represent an address internally with an integer, integers and pointers are conceptually quite different. For example, you wouldn't square a pointer. However, when automatic conversions fail, you may use a type cast:

```
int * p = (int *) 10;   // ok, p and (int *) 10 both pointers
```

This sets a pointer to the address 10 by type casting 10 to type pointer-to-int (that is, type int *).

You may define a class sufficiently related to a basic type or to another class that it makes sense to convert from one form to another. In such a case, you can tell C++ how to make such conversions automatically or, perhaps, via a type cast. To see how that works, you can recast the pounds-to-stone program from Chapter 3 into class form. First, you need to design an appropriate type. Fundamentally, you're representing one thing (a weight) two ways (pounds and stone). A class provides an excellent way to incorporate two representations of one concept into a single entity. Therefore, it makes sense to place both representations of weight into the same class and then provide class methods for expressing the weight in different forms. Listing 11.16 provides the class header.

LISTING 11.16   stonewt.h

```
// stonewt.h -- definition for the Stonewt class
#ifndef STONEWT_H_
#define STONEWT_H_
class Stonewt
{
private:
    enum {Lbs_per_stn = 14};    // pounds per stone
    int stone;                  // whole stones
    double pds_left;            // fractional pounds
    double pounds;              // entire weight in pounds
public:
```

LISTING 11.16   Continued

```
    Stonewt(double lbs);       // constructor for double pounds
    Stonewt(int stn, double lbs); // constructor for stone, lbs
    Stonewt();                 // default constructor
    ~Stonewt();
    void show_lbs() const;     // show weight in pounds format
    void show_stn() const;     // show weight in stone format
};
#endif
```

As mentioned in Chapter 10, enum provides a convenient way to define class-specific constants, provided that they are integers. New compilers allow the following alternative:

```
static const int Lbs_per_stn = 14;
```

Note that the Stonewt class has three constructors. They allow you to initialize a Stonewt
object to a floating-point number of pounds or to a combination of stone and pounds. Or you
can create a Stonewt object without initializing it:

```
Stonewt blossem(132);      // weight = 132 pounds
Stonewt buttercup(10, 2);  // weight = 10 stone, 2 pounds
Stonewt bubbles;           // weight = default value
```

Also, the Stonewt class provides two display functions. One displays the weight in pounds,
and the other displays the weight in stone and pounds. Listing 11.17 shows the class methods
implementation. Note that each constructor assigns values to all three private members. Thus,
creating a Stonewt object automatically sets both representations of weight.

LISTING 11.17   stonewt.cpp

```
// stonewt.cpp -- Stonewt methods
#include <iostream>
using std::cout;
#include "stonewt.h"

// construct Stonewt object from double value
Stonewt::Stonewt(double lbs)
{
    stone = int (lbs) / Lbs_per_stn;   // integer division
    pds_left = int (lbs) % Lbs_per_stn + lbs - int(lbs);
    pounds = lbs;
}

// construct Stonewt object from stone, double values
Stonewt::Stonewt(int stn, double lbs)
{
    stone = stn;
    pds_left = lbs;
    pounds =  stn * Lbs_per_stn +lbs;
}

Stonewt::Stonewt()            // default constructor, wt = 0
{
```

LISTING 11.17   Continued

```
        stone = pounds = pds_left = 0;
}

Stonewt::~Stonewt()          // destructor
{
}

// show weight in stones
void Stonewt::show_stn() const
{
    cout << stone << " stone, " << pds_left << " pounds\n";
}

// show weight in pounds
void Stonewt::show_lbs() const
{
    cout << pounds << " pounds\n";
}
```

Because a `Stonewt` object represents a single weight, it makes sense to provide ways to convert an integer or a floating-point value to a `Stonewt` object. And you have already done so! In C++, any constructor that takes a single argument acts as a blueprint for converting a value of that argument type to the class type. Thus the constructor

```
Stonewt(double lbs);  // template for double-to-Stonewt conversion
```

serves as instructions for converting a type `double` value to a type `Stonewt` value. That is, you can write code like the following:

```
Stonewt myCat;        // create a Stonewt object
myCat = 19.6;         // use Stonewt(double) to convert 19.6 to Stonewt
```

The program uses the `Stonewt(double)` constructor to construct a temporary `Stonewt` object, using `19.6` as the initialization value. Then memberwise assignment copies the contents of the temporary object into `myCat`. This process is termed an *implicit conversion* because it happens automatically, without the need of an explicit type cast.

Only a constructor that can be used with just one argument works as a conversion function. The constructor

```
Stonewt(int stn, double lbs);
```

has two arguments, so it cannot be used to convert types.

Having a constructor work as an automatic type-conversion function seems like a nice feature. As programmers acquired more experience working with C++, however, they found that the automatic aspect isn't always desirable because it can lead to unexpected conversions. So recent C++ implementations have a new keyword, `explicit`, to turn off the automatic aspect. That is, you can declare the constructor this way:

```
explicit Stonewt(double lbs);   // no implicit conversions allowed
```

This turns off implicit conversions such as the preceding example but still allows explicit conversions—that is, conversions using explicit type casts:

```
Stonewt myCat;           // create a Stonewt object
myCat = 19.6;            // not valid if Stonewt(double) is declared as explicit
mycat = Stonewt(19.6);   // ok, an explicit conversion
mycat = (Stonewt) 19.6;  // ok, old form for explicit typecast
```

Remember

A C++ constructor that contains one argument defines a type conversion from the argument type to the class type. If the constructor is qualified with the keyword `explicit`, the constructor is used for explicit conversions only; otherwise, it is also used for implicit conversions.

When does the compiler use the `Stonewt(double)` function? If the keyword `explicit` is used in the declaration, `Stonewt(double)` is used only for an explicit type cast; otherwise, it is also used for the following implicit conversions:

- When you initialize a `Stonewt` object to a type `double` value
- When you assign a type `double` value to a `Stonewt` object
- When you pass a type `double` value to a function that expects a `Stonewt` argument
- When a function that's declared to return a `Stonewt` value tries to return a `double` value
- When any of the preceding situations uses a built-in type that can unambiguously be converted to type `double`

Let's look at the last point in more detail. The argument-matching process provided by function prototyping lets the `Stonewt(double)` constructor act as conversions for other numerical types. That is, both of the following statements work by first converting `int` to `double` and then using the `Stonewt(double)` constructor:

```
Stonewt Jumbo(7000);     // uses Stonewt(double), converting int to double
Jumbo = 7300;            // uses Stonewt(double), converting int to double
```

However, this two-step conversion process works only if there is an unambiguous choice. That is, if the class also defined a `Stonewt(long)` constructor, the compiler would reject these statements, probably pointing out that an `int` can be converted to either a `long` or a `double`, so the call is ambiguous.

Listing 11.18 uses the class constructors to initialize some `Stonewt` objects and to handle type conversions. Be sure to compile Listing 11.17 along with Listing 11.18.

LISTING 11.18   stone.cpp

```
// stone.cpp -- user-defined conversions
// compile with stonewt.cpp
#include <iostream>
using std::cout;
```

LISTING 11.18 Continued

```
#include "stonewt.h"
void display(const Stonewt & st, int n);
int main()
{
    Stonewt pavarotti = 260; // uses constructor to initialize
    Stonewt wolfe(285.7);    // same as Stonewt wolfe = 285.7;
    Stonewt taft(21, 8);

    cout << "The tenor weighed ";
    pavarotti.show_stn();
    cout << "The detective weighed ";
    wolfe.show_stn();
    cout << "The President weighed ";
    taft.show_lbs();
    pavarotti = 265.8;       // uses constructor for conversion
    taft = 325;              // same as taft = Stonewt(325);
    cout << "After dinner, the tenor weighed ";
    pavarotti.show_stn();
    cout << "After dinner, the President weighed ";
    taft.show_lbs();
    display(taft, 2);
    cout << "The wrestler weighed even more.\n";
    display(422, 2);
    cout << "No stone left unearned\n";
    return 0;
}

void display(const Stonewt & st, int n)
{
    for (int i = 0; i < n; i++)
    {
        cout << "Wow! ";
        st.show_stn();
    }
}
```

Here is the output of the program in Listing 11.18:

```
The tenor weighed 18 stone, 8 pounds
The detective weighed 20 stone, 5.7 pounds
The President weighed 302 pounds
After dinner, the tenor weighed 18 stone, 13.8 pounds
After dinner, the President weighed 325 pounds
Wow! 23 stone, 3 pounds
Wow! 23 stone, 3 pounds
The wrestler weighed even more.
Wow! 30 stone, 2 pounds
Wow! 30 stone, 2 pounds
No stone left unearned
```

Program Notes

Note that when a constructor has a single argument, you can use the following form when initializing a class object:

```
// a syntax for initializing a class object when
// using a constructor with one argument
Stonewt pavarotti = 260;
```

This is equivalent to the other two forms you've used:

```
// standard syntax forms for initializing class objects
Stonewt pavarotti(260);
Stonewt pavarotti = Stonewt(260);
```

However, the last two forms can also be used with constructors that have multiple arguments.

Next, note the following two assignments from Listing 11.18:

```
pavarotti = 265.8;
taft = 325;
```

The first of these assignments uses the constructor with a type `double` argument to convert `265.8` to a type `Stonewt` value. This sets the `pounds` member of `pavarotti` to `265.8`. Because it uses the constructor, this assignment also sets the `stone` and `pds_left` members of the class. Similarly, the second assignment converts a type `int` value to type `double` and then uses `Stonewt(double)` to set all three member values in the process.

Finally, note the following function call:

```
display(422, 2);    // convert 422 to double, then to Stonewt
```

The prototype for `display()` indicates that its first argument should be the `Stonewt` object. (Either a `Stonewt` or a `Stonewt &` formal parameter matches a `Stonewt` argument.) Confronted with an `int` argument, the compiler looks for a `Stonewt(int)` constructor to convert the `int` to the desired `Stonewt` type. Failing to find that constructor, the compiler looks for a constructor with some other built-in type to which an `int` can be converted. The `Stonewt(double)` constructor fits the bill. So the compiler converts `int` to `double` and then uses `Stonewt (double)` to convert the result to a `Stonewt` object.

Conversion Functions

Listing 11.18 converts a number to a `Stonewt` object. Can you do the reverse? That is, can you convert a `Stonewt` object to a `double` value, as in the following?

```
Stonewt wolfe(285.7);
double host = wolfe;  // ?? possible ??
```

The answer is that you can do this—but not by using constructors. Constructors only provide for converting another type *to* the class type. To do the reverse, you have to use a special form of a C++ operator function called a *conversion function*.

Conversion functions are user-defined type casts, and you can use them the way you would use a type cast. For example, if you define a `Stonewt`-to-`double` conversion function, you can use the following conversions:

```
Stonewt wolfe(285.7);
double host = double (wolfe);     // syntax #1
double thinker = (double) wolfe;  // syntax #2
```

Or you can let the compiler figure out what to do:

```
Stonewt wells(20, 3);
double star = wells;    // implicit use of conversion function
```

The compiler, noting that the right side is type `Stonewt` and the left side is type `double`, looks to see if you've defined a conversion function that matches this description. (If it can't find such a definition, the compiler generates an error message to the effect that it can't assign a `Stonewt` to a `double`.)

So how do you create a conversion function? To convert to type *typeName*, you use a conversion function in this form:

```
operator typeName();
```

Note the following points:

- The conversion function must be a class method.
- The conversion function must not specify a return type.
- The conversion function must have no arguments.

For example, a function to convert to type `double` would have this prototype:

```
operator double();
```

The *typeName* part (in this case *typeName* is `double`) tells the conversion the type to which to convert, so no return type is needed. The fact that the function is a class method means it has to be invoked by a particular class object, and that tells the function which value to convert. Thus, the function doesn't need arguments.

To add functions that convert `stone_wt` objects to type `int` and to type `double`, then, requires adding the following prototypes to the class declaration:

```
operator int();
operator double();
```

Listing 11.19 shows the modified class declaration.

LISTING 11.19   stonewt1.h

```
// stonewt1.h -- revised definition for the Stonewt class
#ifndef STONEWT1_H_
#define STONEWT1_H_
class Stonewt
{
```

LISTING 11.19   Continued

```
private:
    enum {Lbs_per_stn = 14};      // pounds per stone
    int stone;                    // whole stones
    double pds_left;              // fractional pounds
    double pounds;                // entire weight in pounds
public:
    Stonewt(double lbs);          // construct from double pounds
    Stonewt(int stn, double lbs); // construct from stone, lbs
    Stonewt();                    // default constructor
    ~Stonewt();
    void show_lbs() const;        // show weight in pounds format
    void show_stn() const;        // show weight in stone format
// conversion functions
    operator int() const;
    operator double() const;
};            ;
#endif
```

Listing 11.20 shows Listing 11.18 modified to include the definitions for these two conversion functions. Note that each function returns the desired value, even though there is no declared return type. Also note that the `int` conversion definition rounds to the nearest integer rather than truncating. For example, if `pounds` is `114.4`, then `pounds + 0.5` is `114.9`, and `int (114.9)` is `114`. But if `pounds` is `114.6`, `pounds + 0.5` is `115.1`, and `int (115.1)` is `115`.

LISTING 11.20   stonewt1.cpp

```cpp
// stonewt1.cpp -- Stonewt class methods + conversion functions
#include <iostream>
using std::cout;
#include "stonewt1.h"

// construct Stonewt object from double value
Stonewt::Stonewt(double lbs)
{
    stone = int (lbs) / Lbs_per_stn;    // integer division
    pds_left = int (lbs) % Lbs_per_stn + lbs - int(lbs);
    pounds = lbs;
}

// construct Stonewt object from stone, double values
Stonewt::Stonewt(int stn, double lbs)
{
    stone = stn;
    pds_left = lbs;
    pounds =  stn * Lbs_per_stn +lbs;
}

Stonewt::Stonewt()              // default constructor, wt = 0
{
    stone = pounds = pds_left = 0;
}
```

LISTING 11.20   Continued

```cpp
Stonewt::~Stonewt()          // destructor
{
}

// show weight in stones
void Stonewt::show_stn() const
{
    cout << stone << " stone, " << pds_left << " pounds\n";
}

// show weight in pounds
void Stonewt::show_lbs() const
{
    cout << pounds << " pounds\n";
}


// conversion functions
Stonewt::operator int() const
{

    return int (pounds + 0.5);

}

Stonewt::operator double()const
{
    return pounds;
}
```

Listing 11.21 tests the new conversion functions. The assignment statement in the program uses an implicit conversion, whereas the final **cout** statement uses an explicit type cast. Be sure to compile Listing 11.20 along with Listing 11.21.

LISTING 11.21   stone1.cpp

```cpp
// stone1.cpp -- user-defined conversion functions
// compile with stonewt1.cpp
#include <iostream>
#include "stonewt1.h"

int main()
{
    using std::cout;
    Stonewt poppins(9,2.8);      // 9 stone, 2.8 pounds
    double p_wt = poppins;       // implicit conversion
    cout << "Convert to double => ";
    cout << "Poppins: " << p_wt << " pounds.\n";
    cout << "Convert to int => ";
    cout << "Poppins: " << int (poppins) << " pounds.\n";
    return 0;
}
```

Here's the output from the program in Listings 11.19, 11.20, and 11.21, which shows the result of converting the type `Stonewt` object to type `double` and to type `int`:

```
Convert to double => Poppins: 128.8 pounds.
Convert to int => Poppins: 129 pounds.
```

Applying Type Conversions Automatically

Listing 11.21 uses `int (poppins)` with `cout`. Suppose that, instead, it omitted the explicit type cast:

```
cout << "Poppins: " << poppins << " pounds.\n";
```

Would the program use an implicit conversion, as in the following statement?

```
double p_wt = poppins;
```

The answer is no. In the `p_wt` example, the context indicates that `poppins` should be converted to type `double`. But in the `cout` example, nothing indicates whether the conversion should be to `int` or to `double`. Facing this lack of information, the compiler would complain that you were using an ambiguous conversion. Nothing in the statement indicates what type to use.

Interestingly, if the class defined only the `double` conversion function, the compiler would accept the statement. That's because with only one conversion possible, there is no ambiguity.

You can have a similar situation with assignment. With the current class declarations, the compiler rejects the following statement as being ambiguous:

```
long gone = poppins;    // ambiguous
```

In C++, you can assign both `int` and `double` values to a `long` variable, so the compiler legitimately can use either conversion function. The compiler doesn't want the responsibility of choosing which. But if you eliminate one of the two conversion functions, the compiler accepts the statement. For example, suppose you omit the `double` definition. Then the compiler will use the `int` conversion to convert `poppins` to a type `int` value. Then it converts the `int` value to type `long` when assigning it to `gone`.

When the class defines two or more conversions, you can still use an explicit type cast to indicate which conversion function to use. You can use either of these type cast notations:

```
long gone = (double) poppins;   // use double conversion
long gone = int (poppins);      // use int conversion
```

The first of these statements converts `poppins` weight to a `double` value, and then assignment converts the `double` value to type `long`. Similarly, the second statement converts `poppins` first to type `int` and then to `long`.

Like conversion constructors, conversion functions can be a mixed blessing. The problem with providing functions that make automatic, implicit conversions is that they may make conversions when you don't expect them. Suppose, for example, that you happen to write the following code when you're sleep deprived:

```
int ar[20];
...
Stonewt temp(14, 4);
...
int Temp = 1;
...
cout << ar[temp] << "!\n";   // used temp instead of Temp
```

Normally, you'd expect the compiler to catch a blunder such as using an object instead of an integer as an array index. But the `Stonewt` class defines an `operator int()`, so the `Stonewt` object `temp` is converted to the `int 200` and be used as an array index. The moral is that often it's best to use explicit conversions and exclude the possibility of implicit conversions. The keyword `explicit` doesn't work with conversion functions, but all you have to do is replace a conversion function with a nonconversion function that does the same task—but only if called explicitly. That is, you can replace

```
Stonewt::operator int() { return int (pounds + 0.5); }
```

with

```
int Stonewt::Stone_to_Int() { return int (pounds + 0.5); }
```

This disallows

```
int plb = poppins;
```

but, if you really need a conversion, it allows the following:

```
int plb = poppins.Stone_to_Int();
```

Caution

You should use implicit conversion functions with care. Often, a function that can only be invoked explicitly is the best choice.

In summary, then, C++ provides the following type conversions for classes:

- A class constructor that has but a single argument serves as an instruction for converting a value of the argument type to the class type. For example, the `Stonewt` class constructor with a type `int` argument is invoked automatically when you assign a type `int` value to a `Stonewt` object. However, using `explicit` in the constructor declaration eliminates implicit conversions and allows only explicit conversions.

- A special class member operator function called a *conversion function* serves as an instruction for converting a class object to some other type. The conversion function is a class member, has no declared return type, has no arguments, and is called `operator` *typeName*`()`, where *typeName* is the type to which the object is to be converted. This conversion function is invoked automatically when you assign a class object to a variable of that type or use the type cast operator to that type.

Conversions and Friends

Let's bring addition to the `Stonewt` class. As mentioned in the discussion of the `Time` class, you can use either a member function or a friend function to overload addition. (To simplify matters, assume that no conversion functions of the `operator double()` form are defined.) You can implement addition with the following member function:

```
Stonewt Stonewt::operator+(const Stonewt & st) const
{
    double pds = pounds + st.pounds;
    Stonewt sum(pds);
    return sum;
}
```

Or you can implement addition as a friend function this way:

```
Stonewt operator+(const Stonewt & st1, const Stonewt & st2)
{
    double pds = st1.pounds + st2.pounds;
    Stonewt sum(pds);
    return sum;
}
```

Remember, you can provide the method definition or the friend definition, but not both. Either form lets you do the following:

```
Stonewt jennySt(9, 12);
Stonewt bennySt(12, 8);
Stonewt total;
total = jennySt + bennySt;
```

Also, given the `Stonewt(double)` constructor, each form lets you do the following:

```
Stonewt jennySt(9, 12);
double kennyD = 176.0;
Stonewt total;
total = jennySt + kennyD;
```

But only the friend function lets you do this:

```
Stonewt jennySt(9, 12);
double pennyD = 146.0;
Stonewt total;
total = pennyD + jennySt;
```

To see why, you can translate each addition into the corresponding function calls. First,

```
total = jennySt + bennySt;
```

becomes

```
total = jennySt.operator+(bennySt);   // member function
```

or else

```
total = operator+(jennySt, bennySt);  // friend function
```

In either case, the actual argument types match the formal arguments. Also, the member function is invoked, as required, by a `Stonewt` object.

Next,

```
total = jennySt + kennyD;
```

becomes

```
total = jennySt.operator+(kennyD);   // member function
```

or else

```
total = operator+(jennySt, kennyD);  // friend function
```

Again, the member function is invoked, as required, by a `Stonewt` object. This time, in each case, one argument (`kennyD`) is type `double`, which invokes the `Stonewt(double)` constructor to convert the argument to a `Stonewt` object.

By the way, having an `operator double()` member function defined would create confusion at this point because that would create another option for interpretation. Instead of converting `kennyD` to `double` and performing `Stonewt` addition, the compiler could convert `jennySt` to `double` and perform `double` addition. Having too many conversion functions creates ambiguities.

Finally,

```
total = pennyD + jennySt;
```

becomes

```
total = operator+(pennyD, jennySt);  // friend function
```

Here, both arguments are type `double`, which invokes the `Stonewt(double)` constructor to convert them to `Stonewt` objects. The member function cannot be invoked, however.

```
total = pennyD.operator+(jennySt);   // not meaningful
```

The reason is that only a class object can invoke a member function. C++ does not attempt to convert `pennyD` to a `Stonewt` object. Conversion takes place for member function arguments, not for member function invokers.

The lesson here is that defining addition as a friend makes it easier for a program to accommodate automatic type conversions. The reason is that both operands become function arguments, so function prototyping comes into play for both operands.

Choices in Implementing Addition

Given that you want to add `double` quantities to `Stonewt` quantities, you have a couple choices. The first, as you just saw, is to define

```
operator+(const Stonewt &, const Stonewt &)
```

as a friend function and have the `Stonewt(double)` constructor handle conversions of type `double` arguments to type `Stonewt` arguments.

The second choice is to further overload the addition operator with functions that explicitly use one type **double** argument:

```
Stonewt operator+(double x);  // member function
friend Stonewt operator+(double x, Stonewt & s);
```

That way, the statement

```
total = jennySt + kennyD; // Stonewt + double
```

exactly matches the **operator+(double x)** member function, and the statement

```
total = pennyD + jennySt; // double + Stonewt
```

exactly matches the **operator+(double x, Stonewt & s)** friend function. Earlier, you did something similar for **Vector** multiplication.

Each choice has advantages. The first choice (relying on implicit conversions) results in a shorter program because you define fewer functions. That also implies less work for you and fewer chances to mess up. The disadvantage is the added overhead in time and memory needed to invoke the conversion constructor whenever a conversion is needed. The second choice (additional functions explicitly matching the types), however, is the mirror image. It makes for a longer program and more work on your part, but it runs a bit faster.

If your program makes intensive use of adding **double** values to **Stonewt** objects, it may pay to overload addition to handle such cases directly. If the program uses such addition only occasionally, it's simpler to rely on automatic conversions, or, if you want to be more careful, on explicit conversions.

Real-World Note: Calling Bootstrap Functions Before main()

Although the first function called in any executable is always its main() entry point, there are a few tricks you can perform to alter this behavior. For example, consider a scheduling program that coordinates the production of golf clubs. Normally, when the program is started, information from a variety of sources is required to accurately schedule the daily production run of golf clubs. So you might want some "bootstrap" functions to be called first to prepare the ground for main().

A *global object* (that is, an object with file scope) is precisely what you're looking for because global objects are guaranteed to be constructed before a program's main() function is called. What you can do is create a class with a default constructor that invokes all your bootstrap functions. These could, for example, initialize various data components of the object. Then you can create a global object. The following code illustrates this technique:

```
class CompileRequirements
{
  private:
    // essential information
  public:
    CompileRequirements()    // default constructor
    {
      GetDataFromSales();          // various
      GetDataFromManufacturing();  // bootstrap
```

```
            GetDataFromFinance();           // functions
        }
};

//Instance of Req class has global scope
CompileRequirements Req;      // uses default constructor

int main(void)
{
  // Read Req and build schedule
  BuildScheduleFromReq();

  //
  // rest of program code
  //
}
```

Summary

This chapter covers many important aspects of defining and using classes. Some of the material in this chapter may seem vague to you until your own experiences enrich your understanding.

Normally, the only way you can access private class members is by using a class method. C++ alleviates that restriction with friend functions. To make a function a friend function, you declare the function in the class declaration and preface the declaration with the keyword `friend`.

C++ extends overloading to operators by letting you define special operator functions that describe how particular operators relate to a particular class. An operator function can be a class member function or a friend function. (A few operators can only be class member functions.) C++ lets you invoke an operator function either by calling the function or by using the overloaded operator with its usual syntax. An operator function for the operator *op* has this form:

operator*op*(*argument-list*)

argument-list represents operands for the operator. If the operator function is a class member function, then the first operand is the invoking object and isn't part of *argument-list*. For example, in this chapter you overloaded addition by defining an **operator+()** member function for the **Vector** class. If **up**, **right**, and **result** are three vectors, you can use either of the following statements to invoke vector addition:

```
result = up.operator+(right);
result = up + right;
```

For the second version, the fact that the operands **up** and **right** are type **Vector** tells C++ to use the **Vector** definition of addition.

When an operator function is a member function, the first operand is the object invoking the function. In the preceding statements, for example, the **up** object is the invoking object. If you want to define an operator function so that the first operand is not a class object, you must use a friend function. Then you can pass the operands to the function definition in whichever order you want.

One of the most common tasks for operator overloading is defining the **<<** operator so that it can be used in conjunction with the **cout** object to display an object's contents. To allow an **ostream** object to be the first operand, you define the operator function as a friend. To allow the redefined operator to be concatenated with itself, you make the return type **ostream &**. Here's a general form that satisfies those requirements:

```
ostream & operator<<(ostream & os, const c_name & obj)
{
    os << ... ;   // display object contents
    return os;
}
```

If, however, the class has methods that return values for the data members you want to display, you can use those methods instead of direct access in **operator<<()**. In that case, the function needn't (and shouldn't) be a friend.

C++ lets you establish conversions to and from class types. First, any class constructor that takes a single argument acts as a conversion function, converting values of the argument type to the class type. C++ invokes the constructor automatically if you assign a value of the argument type to an object. For example, suppose you have a **String** class with a constructor that takes a **char *** value as its sole argument. Then, if **bean** is a **String** object, you can use the following statement:

```
bean = "pinto";   // converts type char * to type String
```

If, however, you precede the constructor declaration with the keyword **explicit**, the constructor can be used only for explicit conversions:

```
bean = String("pinto");   // converts type char * to type String explicitly
```

To convert from a class to another type, you must define a conversion function and provide instruction about how to make the conversion. A conversion function must be a member function. If it is to convert to type *typeName*, it should have the following prototype:

```
operator typeName();
```

Note that it must have no declared return type, must have no arguments, and must (despite having no declared return type) return the converted value. For example, a function to convert type **Vector** to type **double** would have this function form:

```
Vector::operator double()
{
    ...
    return a_double_value;
}
```

Experience has shown that often it is better not to rely on such implicit conversion functions.

As you might have noticed, classes require much more care and attention to detail than do simple C-style structures. In return, they do much more for you.

Review Questions

1. Use a member function to overload the multiplication operator for the `Stonewt` class; have the operator multiply the data members by a type `double` value. Note that this will require carryover for the stone–pound representation. That is, twice 10 stone 8 pounds is 21 stone 2 pounds.

2. What are the differences between a friend function and a member function?

3. Does a nonmember function have to be a friend to access a class's members?

4. Use a friend function to overload the multiplication operator for the `Stonewt` class; have the operator multiply the `double` value by the `Stone` value.

5. Which operators cannot be overloaded?

6. What restriction applies to overloading the following operators? `=`, `()`, `[]`, and `->`

7. Define a conversion function for the `Vector` class that converts a `Vector` object to a type `double` value that represents the vector's magnitude.

Programming Exercises

1. Modify Listing 11.15 so that it writes the successive locations of the random walker in a file. Label each position with the step number. Also have the program write the initial conditions (target distance and step size) and the summarized results to the file. The file contents might look like this:

```
Target Distance: 100, Step Size: 20
0: (x,y) = (0, 0)
1: (x,y) = (-11.4715, 16.383)
2: (x,y) = (-8.68807, -3.42232)
...
26: (x,y) = (42.2919, -78.2594)
27: (x,y) = (58.6749, -89.7309)
After 27 steps, the subject has the following location:
(x,y) = (58.6749, -89.7309)
 or
(m,a) = (107.212, -56.8194)
Average outward distance per step = 3.97081
```

2. Modify the `Vector` class header and implementation files (Listings 11.13 and 11.14) so that the magnitude and angle are no longer stored as data components. Instead, they should be calculated on demand when the `magval()` and `angval()` methods are called.

You should leave the public interface unchanged (the same public methods with the same arguments), but alter the private section, including some of the private method, and the method implementations. Test the modified version with Listing 11.15, which should be left unchanged because the public interface of the **Vector** class is unchanged.

3. Modify Listing 11.15 so that instead of reporting the results of a single trial for a particular target/step combination, it reports the highest, lowest, and average number of steps for N trials, where N is an integer entered by the user.

4. Rewrite the final **Time** class example (Listings 11.10, 11.11, and 11.12) so that all the overloaded operators are implemented using friend functions.

5. Rewrite the **Stonewt** class (Listings 11.16 and 11.17) so that it has a state member that governs whether the object is interpreted in stone form, integer pounds form, or floating-point pounds form. Overload the **<<** operator to replace the **show_stn()** and **show_lbs()** methods. Overload the addition, subtraction, and multiplication operators so that one can add, subtract, and multiply **Stonewt** values. Test your class with a short program that uses all the class methods and friends.

6. Rewrite the **Stonewt** class (Listings 11.16 and 11.17) so that it overloads all six relational operators. The operators should compare the **pounds** members and return a type **bool** value. Write a program that declares an array of six **Stonewt** objects and initializes the first three objects in the array declaration. Then it should use a loop to read in values used to set the remaining three array elements. Then it should report the smallest element, the largest element, and how many elements are greater or equal to 11 stone. (The simplest approach is to create a **Stonewt** object initialized to 11 stone and to compare the other objects with that object.)

7. A complex number has two parts: a real part and an imaginary part. One way to write an imaginary number is this: (3.0, 4.0). Here 3.0 is the real part and 4.0 is the imaginary part. Suppose a = (A,Bi) and c = (C,Di). Here are some complex operations:

   - Addition: $a + c = (A + C, (B + D)i)$

   - Subtraction: $a - c = (A - C, (B - D)i)$

   - Multiplication: $a \times c = (A \times C - B \times D, (A \times D + B \times C)i)$

   - Multiplication: (x a real number): $x \times c = (x \times C, x \times Di)$

   - Conjugation: $\sim a = (A, -Bi)$

Define a complex class so that the following program can use it with correct results:

```
#include <iostream>
using namespace std;
#include "complex0.h"  // to avoid confusion with complex.h
int main()
{
    complex a(3.0, 4.0);   // initialize to (3,4i)
    complex c;
    cout << "Enter a complex number (q to quit):\n";
```

```
    while (cin >> c)
    {
        cout << "c is " << c << '\n';
        cout << "complex conjugate is " << ~c << '\n';
        cout << "a is " << a << '\n';
        cout << "a + c is " << a + c << '\n';
        cout << "a - c is " << a - c << '\n';
        cout << "a * c is " << a * c << '\n';
        cout << "2 * c is " << 2 * c << '\n';
        cout << "Enter a complex number (q to quit):\n";
    }
    cout << "Done!\n";
    return 0;
}
```

Note that you have to overload the << and >> operators. Many systems already have complex support in a `complex.h` header file, so use `complex0.h` to avoid conflicts. Use `const` whenever warranted.

Here is a sample run of the program:

```
Enter a complex number (q to quit):
real: 10
imaginary: 12
c is (10,12i)
complex conjugate is (10,-12i)
a is (3,4i)
a + c is (13,16i)
a - c is (-7,-8i)
a * c is (-18,76i)
2 * c is (20,24i)
Enter a complex number (q to quit):
real: q
Done!
```

Note that `cin >> c`, through overloading, now prompts for real and imaginary parts.

CHAPTER 12

CLASSES AND DYNAMIC MEMORY ALLOCATION

In this chapter you'll learn about the following:

- Using dynamic memory allocation for class members

- Implicit and explicit copy constructors

- Implicit and explicit overloaded assignment operators

- What you must do if you use new in a constructor

- Using static class members

- Using placement new with objects

- Using pointers to objects

- Implementing a queue abstract data type (ADT)

This chapter looks at how to use new and delete with classes and how to deal with some of the subtle problems that using dynamic memory can cause. This may sound like a short list of topics, but these topics affect constructor design, destructor design, and operator overloading.

Let's look at a specific example of how C++ can add to your memory load. Suppose you want to create a class with a member that represents someone's last name. The simplest way is to use a character array member to hold the name. But this has some drawbacks. You might use a 14-character array and then run into Bartholomew Smeadsbury-Crafthovingham. Or, to be safer, you might use a 40-character array. But, if you then create an array of 2,000 such objects, you'll waste a lot of memory with character arrays that are only partly filled. (At that point, you're adding to the computer's memory load.) There is an alternative.

Often it is much better to decide many matters, such as how much storage to use, when a program runs rather than when it's compiled. The usual C++ approach to storing a name in an object is to use the new operator in a class constructor to allocate the correct amount of memory while the program is running. But introducing new to a class constructor raises several new problems unless you remember to take a series of additional steps, such as expanding the class destructor, bringing all constructors into harmony with the new destructor, and writing additional class methods to facilitate correct initialization and assignment. (This chapter, of course, explains all these steps.) If you're just learning C++, you might be better off initially sticking to the simple, if inferior, character array approach. Then, when a class design works well, you can return to your OOP workbench and enhance the class declaration by using new. In short, you might want to gradually grow into C++.

Dynamic Memory and Classes

What would you like for breakfast, lunch, and dinner for the next month? How many ounces of milk for dinner on the 3rd day? How many raisins in your cereal for breakfast on the 15th day? If you're like most people, you'd rather postpone some of those decisions until the actual mealtimes. Part of the strategy in C++ is to take the same attitude toward memory allocation, letting the program decide about memory during runtime rather than during compile time. That way, memory use can depend on the needs of a program instead of on a rigid set of storage-class rules. Remember that to gain dynamic control of memory, C++ utilizes the new and delete operators. Unhappily, using these operators with classes can pose some new programming problems. As you'll see, destructors can become necessary instead of merely ornamental. And sometimes, you have to overload an assignment operator to get a program to behave properly. We'll look into these matters now.

A Review Example and Static Class Members

We haven't used new and delete for a while, so let's review them with a short program. While we're at it, let's look at a new storage class: the static class member. The vehicle will be a StringBad class, later to be superseded by the slightly more able String class. (You've already seen the standard C++ string class, and you'll learn more about it in Chapter 16, "The string Class and the Standard Template Library." Meanwhile, the humble StringBad and String classes in this chapter provide some insight into what underlies such a class. A lot of programming techniques go into providing such a friendly interface.)

StringBad and String class objects will hold a pointer to a string and a value representing the string length. You'll use the StringBad and String classes primarily to give an inside look at how new, delete, and static class members operate. For that reason, the constructors and destructors will display messages when called so that you can follow the action. Also, you'll omit several useful member and friend functions, such as overloaded ++ and >> operators and a conversion function, in order to simplify the class interface. (But rejoice! The review questions for this chapter give you the opportunity to add those useful support functions.) Listing 12.1 shows the class declaration.

LISTING 12.1   strngbad.h

```
// strngbad.h -- flawed string class definition
#include <iostream>
#ifndef STRNGBAD_H_
#define STRNGBAD_H_
class StringBad
{
private:
    char * str;                 // pointer to string
    int len;                    // length of string
    static int num_strings;     // number of objects
public:
    StringBad(const char * s); // constructor
    StringBad();                // default constructor
    ~StringBad();               // destructor
// friend function
    friend std::ostream & operator<<(std::ostream & os,
                        const StringBad & st);
};
#endif
```

Why call the class StringBad? This is to remind you that StringBad is an example under development. It's the first stage of developing a class by using dynamic memory allocation, and it does the obvious things correctly; for example, it uses new and delete correctly in the constructors and destructor. It doesn't really do bad things, but the design omits doing some additional good things that are necessary but not at all obvious. Seeing the problems the class has should help you understand and remember the non-obvious changes you will make later, when you convert it to the more functional String class.

You should note two points about this declaration. First, it uses a pointer-to-char instead of a char array to represent a name. This means that the class declaration does not allocate storage space for the string itself. Instead, it uses new in the constructors to allocate space for the string. This arrangement avoids straitjacketing the class declaration with a predefined limit to the string size.

Second, the definition declares the num_strings member as belonging to the static storage class. A *static class member* has a special property: A program creates only one copy of a static class variable, regardless of the number of objects created. That is, a static member is shared among all objects of that class, much as a phone number might be shared among all members of a family. If, say, you create 10 StringBad objects, there would be 10 str members and 10 len members, but just 1 shared num_strings member (see Figure 12.1). This is convenient for data that should be private to a class but that should have the same value for all class objects. The num_strings member, for example, is intended to keep track of the number of objects created.

FIGURE 12.1

A static data member.

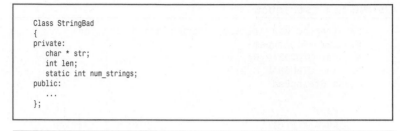

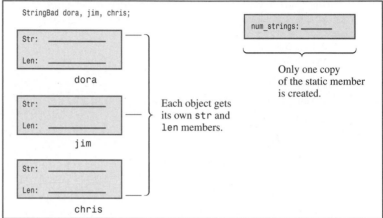

Each object gets its own str and len members.

Only one copy of the static member is created.

By the way, Listing 12.1 uses the `num_strings` member as a convenient means of illustrating static data members and as a device to point out potential programming problems. In general, a string class doesn't need such a member.

Take a look at the implementation of the class methods in Listing 12.2. Notice how it handles using a pointer and using a static member.

LISTING 12.2 strngbad.cpp

```cpp
// strngbad.cpp -- StringBad class methods
#include <cstring>                    // string.h for some
#include "strngbad.h"
using std::cout;

// initializing static class member
int StringBad::num_strings = 0;

// class methods

// construct StringBad from C string
StringBad::StringBad(const char * s)
{
    len = std::strlen(s);                    // set size
    str = new char[len + 1];          // allot storage
```

LISTING 12.2   Continued

```
    std::strcpy(str, s);                     // initialize pointer
    num_strings++;                    // set object count
    cout << num_strings << ": \"" << str
        << "\" object created\n";    // For Your Information
}

StringBad::StringBad()                // default constructor
{
    len = 4;
    str = new char[4];
    std::strcpy(str, "C++");                 // default string
    num_strings++;
    cout << num_strings << ": \"" << str
        << "\" default object created\n";  // FYI
}

StringBad::~StringBad()               // necessary destructor
{
    cout << "\"" << str << "\" object deleted, ";    // FYI
    --num_strings;                           // required
    cout << num_strings << " left\n"; // FYI
    delete [] str;                           // required
}

std::ostream & operator<<(std::ostream & os, const StringBad & st)
{
    os << st.str;
    return os;
}
```

First, notice the following statement from Listing 12.2:

```
int StringBad::num_strings = 0;
```

This statement initializes the static `num_strings` member to `0`. Note that you cannot initialize a static member variable inside the class declaration. That's because the declaration is a description of how memory is to be allocated, but it doesn't allocate memory. You allocate and initialize memory by creating an object using that format. In the case of a static class member, you initialize the static member independently, with a separate statement outside the class declaration. That's because the static class member is stored separately rather than as part of an object. Note that the initialization statement gives the type and uses the scope operator.

This initialization goes in the methods file, not in the class declaration file. That's because the class declaration is in a header file, and a program may include a header file in several other files. That would result in multiple copies of the initialization statement, which is an error.

The exception to the noninitialization of a static data member inside the class declaration (see Chapter 10, "Objects and Classes") is if the static data member is a `const` of integral or enumeration type.

Remember

A static data member is declared in the class declaration and is initialized in the file containing the class methods. The scope operator is used in the initialization to indicate to which class the static member belongs. However, if the static member is a `const` integral type or an enumeration type, it can be initialized in the class declaration itself.

Next, notice that each constructor contains the expression `num_strings++`. This ensures that each time a program creates a new object, the shared variable `num_strings` increases by one, keeping track of the total number of `String` objects. Also, the destructor contains the expression `--num_strings`. Thus, the `String` class also keeps track of deleted objects, keeping the value of the `num_strings` member current.

Now look at the first constructor in Listing 12.2, which initializes a `String` object with a regular C string:

```
StringBad::StringBad(const char * s)
{
    len = std::strlen(s);       // set size
    str = new char[len + 1];    // allot storage
    std::strcpy(str, s);        // initialize pointer
    num_strings++;              // set object count
    cout << num_strings << ": \"" << str
        << "\" object created\n"; // For Your Information
}
```

Recall that the class `str` member is just a pointer, so the constructor has to provide the memory for holding a string. You can pass a string pointer to the constructor when you initialize an object:

```
String boston("Boston");
```

The constructor must then allocate enough memory to hold the string, and then it must copy the string to that location. Let's go through the process step-by-step.

First, the function initializes the `len` member, using the `strlen()` function to compute the length of the string. Next, it uses `new` to allocate sufficient space to hold the string, and then it assigns the address of the new memory to the `str` member. (Recall that `strlen()` returns the length of a string, not counting the terminating null character, so the constructor adds one to `len` to allow space for the string, including the null character.)

Next, the constructor uses `strcpy()` to copy the passed string into the new memory. Then it updates the object count. Finally, to help you monitor what's going on, the constructor displays the current number of objects and the string stored in the object. This feature will come in handy later, when you deliberately lead the `String` class into trouble.

To understand this approach, you should realize that the string is not stored in the object. The string is stored separately, in heap memory, and the object merely stores information that tells where to find the string.

Note that you do not use this:

```
str = s;  // not the way to go
```

This merely stores the address without making a copy of the string.

The default constructor behaves similarly, except that it provides a default string of `"C++"`.

The destructor contains the example's most important addition to the handling of classes:

```
StringBad::~StringBad()               // necessary destructor
{
    cout << "\"" << str << "\" object deleted, ";    // FYI
    --num_strings;                    // required
    cout << num_strings << " left\n"; // FYI
    delete [] str;                    // required
}
```

The destructor begins by announcing when the destructor gets called. This part is informative but not essential. However, the `delete` statement is vital. Recall that the `str` member points to memory allocated with `new`. When a `StringBad` object expires, the `str` pointer expires. But the memory `str` pointed to remains allocated unless you use `delete` to free it. Deleting an object frees the memory occupied by the object itself, but it does not automatically free memory pointed to by pointers that were object members. For that, you must use the destructor. By placing the `delete` statement in the destructor, you ensure that the memory that a constructor allocates with `new` is freed when the object expires.

Remember

Whenever you use `new` in a constructor to allocate memory, you should use `delete` in the corresponding destructor to free that memory. If you use `new [ ]` (with brackets), then you should use `delete [ ]` (with brackets).

Listing 12.3, which is taken from a program under development at *The Daily Vegetable*, illustrates when and how the `StringBad` constructors and destructors work. Be sure to compile Listing 12.2 along with Listing 12.3.

LISTING 12.3   vegnews.cpp

```
// vegnews.cpp -- using new and delete with classes
// compile with strngbad.cpp
#include <iostream>
using std::cout;
#include "strngbad.h"

void callme1(StringBad &);  // pass by reference
void callme2(StringBad);    // pass by value

int main()
{
```

LISTING 12.3   *Continued*

```
    using std::endl;
    StringBad headline1("Celery Stalks at Midnight");
    StringBad headline2("Lettuce Prey");
    StringBad sports("Spinach Leaves Bowl for Dollars");
    cout << "headline1: " << headline1 << endl;
    cout << "headline2: " << headline2 << endl;
    cout << "sports: " << sports << endl;
    callme1(headline1);
    cout << "headline1: " << headline1 << endl;
    callme2(headline2);
    cout << "headline2: " << headline2 << endl;
    cout << "Initialize one object to another:\n";
    StringBad sailor = sports;
    cout << "sailor: " << sailor << endl;
    cout << "Assign one object to another:\n";
    StringBad knot;
    knot = headline1;
    cout << "knot: " << knot << endl;
    cout << "End of main()\n";

    return 0;
}

void callme1(StringBad & rsb)
{
    cout << "String passed by reference:\n";
    cout << "    \"" << rsb << "\"\n";
}

void callme2(StringBad sb)
{
    cout << "String passed by value:\n";
    cout << "    \"" << sb << "\"\n";
}
```

Compatibility Note

This first draft of a design for `StringBad` has some deliberate flaws that make the exact output undefined. Some compilers I used, for example, produced versions that aborted before completing. However, although the output details may differ, the basic problems and solutions (soon to be revealed!) are the same.

Here is the output produced after compiling the program in Listing 12.3 with the Borland C++ 5.5 command-line compiler:

```
1: "Celery Stalks at Midnight" object created
2: "Lettuce Prey" object created
3: "Spinach Leaves Bowl for Dollars" object created
headline1: Celery Stalks at Midnight
headline2: Lettuce Prey
```

```
sports: Spinach Leaves Bowl for Dollars
String passed by reference:
    "Celery Stalks at Midnight"
headline1: Celery Stalks at Midnight
String passed by value:
    "Lettuce Prey"
"Lettuce Prey" object deleted, 2 left
headline2: Dûº
Initialize one object to another:
sailor: Spinach Leaves Bowl for Dollars
Assign one object to another:
3: "C++" default object created
knot: Celery Stalks at Midnight
End of main()
"Celery Stalks at Midnight" object deleted, 2 left
"Spinach Leaves Bowl for Dollars" object deleted, 1 left
"Spinach Leaves Bowl for Doll8" object deleted, 0 left
"@g" object deleted, -1 left
"-|" object deleted, -2 left
```

The various nonstandard characters that appear in the output will vary from system to system; they are one of the signs that StringBad deserves to be called bad. Another sign is the negative object count. Newer compiler/operating system combinations typically abort the program just before displaying the line about having -1 objects left, and some of them report a General Protection Fault (GPF). A GPF indicates that a program tried to access a memory location forbidden to it; this is another bad sign.

Program Notes

The program in Listing 12.3 starts out fine, but it staggers to a strange and ultimately disastrous conclusion. Let's begin by looking at the good parts. The constructor announces that it has created three StringBad objects, it numbers them, and the program lists them, using the overloaded >> operator:

```
1: "Celery Stalks at Midnight" object created
2: "Lettuce Prey" object created
3: "Spinach Leaves Bowl for Dollars" object created
headline1: Celery Stalks at Midnight
headline2: Lettuce Prey
sports: Spinach Leaves Bowl for Dollars
```

Then the program passes headline1 to the callme1() function and redisplays headline1 after the call. Here's the code:

```
callme1(headline1);
cout << "headline1: " << headline1 << endl;
```

And here's the result:

```
String passed by reference:
    "Celery Stalks at Midnight"
headline1: Celery Stalks at Midnight
```

This section of code seems to work fine, too.

But then the program executes the following code:

```
callme2(headline2);
cout << "headline2: " << headline2 << endl;
```

Here, `callme2()` passes `headline2` by value instead of by reference, and the result indicates a serious problem:

```
String passed by value:
    "Lettuce Prey"
"Lettuce Prey" object deleted, 2 left
headline2: Dû°
```

First, passing `headline2` as a function argument somehow causes the destructor to be called. Second, although passing by value is supposed to protect the original argument from change, the function messes up the original string beyond recognition, and some nonstandard characters get displayed. (The exact display will depend on what happens to sitting in memory.)

Even worse, look at the end of the output, when the destructor gets called automatically for each of the objects created earlier:

```
End of main()
"Celery Stalks at Midnight" object deleted, 2 left
"Spinach Leaves Bowl for Dollars" object deleted, 1 left
"Spinach Leaves Bowl for Doll8" object deleted, 0 left
"@g" object deleted, -1 left
"-|" object deleted, -2 left
```

Because automatic storage objects are deleted in an order opposite to that in which they are created, the first three objects deleted are `knots`, `sailor`, and `sport`. The `knots` and `sailor` deletions look okay, but for `sport`, `Dollars` has become `Doll8`. The only thing the program does with `sport` is use it to initialize `sailor`, but that act appears to have altered `sport`. And the last two objects deleted, `headline2` and `headline1`, are unrecognizable. Something messes up these strings before they are deleted. Also, the counting is bizarre. How can there be -2 objects left?

Actually, the peculiar counting is a clue. Every object is constructed once and destroyed once, so the number of constructor calls should equal the number of destructor calls. Because the object count (`num_strings`) is decremented two times more than it is incremented, a constructor that doesn't increment `num_strings` must be creating two objects. The class definition declares and defines two constructors (both of which increment `num_strings`), but it turns out that the program uses three. For example, consider this line:

```
StringBad sailor = sports;
```

What constructor is used here? Not the default constructor, and not the constructor with a `const char *` parameter. Remember, initialization using this form is another syntax for the following:

```
StringBad sailor = StringBad(sports); //constructor using sports
```

Because `sports` is type `StringBad`, a matching constructor could have this prototype:

```
StringBad(const StringBad &);
```

And it turns out that the compiler automatically generates this constructor (called a *copy constructor* because it makes a copy of an object) if you initialize one object to another. The automatic version would not know about updating the `num_strings` static variable, so it would mess up the counting scheme. Indeed, all the problems exhibited by this example stem from member functions that the compiler generates automatically, so let's look at that topic now.

Implicit Member Functions

The problems with the `StringBad` class stem from implicit member functions that are defined automatically and whose behavior is inappropriate to this particular class design. In particular, C++ automatically provides the following member functions:

- A default constructor if you define no constructors
- A copy constructor if you don't define one
- An assignment operator if you don't define one
- A default destructor if you don't define one
- An address operator if you don't define one

More precisely, the compiler generates definitions for the last four items if a program uses objects in such a way as to require them. For example, if you assign one object to another, the program provides a definition for the assignment operator.

It turns out that the implicit copy constructor and the implicit assignment operator cause the `StringBad` class problems.

The implicit address operator returns the address of the invoking object (that is, the value of the `this` pointer). That's fine for our purposes, and we won't discuss this member function further. The default destructor does nothing, and we won't discuss it, either, other than to point out that the class has already provided a substitute for it. But the others do warrant more discussion.

Default Constructors

If you fail to provide any constructors at all, C++ provides you with a default constructor. For example, suppose you define a `Klunk` class and omit any constructors. In this case, the compiler supplies the following default:

```
Klunk::Klunk() { }  // implicit default constructor
```

That is, it supplies a constructor that takes no arguments and that does nothing. It's needed because creating an object always invokes a constructor:

```
Klunk lunk;  // invokes default constructor
```

The default constructor makes `lunk` like an ordinary automatic variable; that is, its value at initialization is unknown.

After you define any constructor, C++ doesn't bother to define a default constructor. If you want to create objects that aren't initialized explicitly, or if you want to create an array of objects, you then have to define a default constructor explicitly. It's a constructor with no arguments, but you can use it to set particular values:

```
Klunk::Klunk()  // explicit default constructor
{
    klunk_ct = 0;
    ...
}
```

A constructor with arguments still can be a default constructor if all its arguments have default values. For example, the `Klunk` class could have the following inline constructor:

```
Klunk(int n = 0) { klunk_ct = n; }
```

However, you can have only one default constructor. That is, you can't do this:

```
Klunk() { klunk_ct = 0 }              // constructor #1
Klunk(int n = 0) { klunk_ct = n; }   // ambiguous constructor #2
```

Why is this ambiguous? Consider the following two declarations:

```
Klunk kar(10);    // clearly matches Klunt(int n)
Klunk bus;        // could match either constructor
```

The second declaration matches constructor #1 (no argument), but it also matches constructor #2 (using the default argument `0`). This will cause the compiler to issue an error message.

Copy Constructors

A copy constructor is used to copy an object to a newly created object. That is, it's used during initialization, not during ordinary assignment. A copy constructor for a class normally has this prototype:

```
Class_name(const Class_name &);
```

Note that it takes a constant reference to a class object as its argument. For example, a copy constructor for the `String` class would have this prototype:

```
StringBad(const StringBad &);
```

You must know two things about a copy constructor: when it's used and what it does.

When a Copy Constructor Is Used

A copy constructor is invoked whenever a new object is created and initialized to an existing object of the same kind. This happens in several situations. The most obvious situation is when you explicitly initialize a new object to an existing object. For example, given that `motto` is a `StringBad` object, the following four defining declarations invoke a copy constructor:

```
StringBad ditto(motto);  // calls StringBad(const StringBad &)
StringBad metoo = motto; // calls StringBad(const StringBad &)
StringBad also = StringBad(motto);
```

```
                           // calls StringBad(const StringBad &)
StringBad * pStringBad = new StringBad(motto);
                           // calls StringBad(const StringBad &)
```

Depending on the implementation, the middle two declarations may use a copy constructor directly to create `metoo` and `also`, or they may use a copy constructor to generate temporary objects whose contents are then assigned to `metoo` and `also`. The last example initializes an anonymous object to `motto` and assigns the address of the new object to the `pstring` pointer.

Less obviously, a compiler uses a copy constructor whenever a program generates copies of an object. In particular, it's used when a function passes an object by value (as `callme2()` does in Listing 12.3) or when a function returns an object. Remember, passing by value means creating a copy of the original variable. A compiler also uses a copy constructor whenever it generates temporary objects. For example, a compiler might generate a temporary `Vector` object to hold an intermediate result when adding three `Vector` objects. Compilers vary as to when they generate temporary objects, but all invoke a copy constructor when passing objects by value and when returning them. In particular, this function call in Listing 12.3 invokes a copy constructor:

```
callme2(headline2);
```

The program uses a copy constructor to initialize `sb`, the formal `StringBad`-type parameter for the `callme2()` function.

By the way, the fact that passing an object by value involves invoking a copy constructor is a good reason for passing by reference instead. That saves the time of invoking the constructor and the space for storing the new object.

What the Copy Constructor Does

The default copy constructor performs a member-by-member copy of the nonstatic members (*memberwise copying*, also sometimes called *shallow copying*). Each member is copied by value. In Listing 12.3, the statement

```
StringBad sailor = sports;
```

amounts to the following (aside from the fact that it doesn't compile because access to private members is not allowed):

```
StringBad sailor;
sailor.str = sports.str;
sailor.len = sports.len;
```

If a member is itself a class object, the copy constructor for that class is used to copy one member object to another. Static members, such as `num_strings`, are unaffected because they belong to the class as a whole instead of to individual objects. Figure 12.2 illustrates the action of an implicit copy constructor.

FIGURE 12.2
An inside look at memberwise copying.

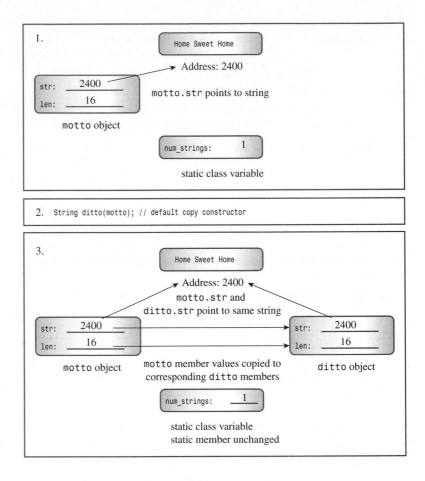

Where the Copy Constructor Goes Wrong

You are now in a position to understand the twofold weirdness of Listing 12.3. (Let's assume that the output is the one shown after the listing.) The first weirdness is that the program output indicates two more objects destroyed than constructed. The explanation is that the program does create two additional objects, using the default copy constructor. The copy constructor is used to initialize the formal parameter of `callme2()` when that function is called, and it is used to initialize the object `sailor` to `sports`. The default copy constructor doesn't vocalize its activities, so it doesn't announce its creations, and it doesn't increment the `num_strings` counter. However, the destructor does update the count, and it's invoked upon the demise of all objects, regardless of how they were constructed. This weirdness is a problem because it means the program doesn't keep an accurate object count. The solution is to provide an explicit copy constructor that does update the count:

```
String::String(const String & s)
{
    num_strings++;
    ...// important stuff to go here
}
```

Tip

If your class has a static data member whose value changes when new objects are created, you should provide an explicit copy constructor that handles the accounting.

The second weirdness is the more subtle and dangerous. One symptom is the garbled string contents:

```
headline2: Dû°
```

Another disturbing symptom is that many compiled versions of the program abort. Microsoft Visual C++ 7.1 (debug mode), for example, displays an error message window saying that a Debug Assertion failed, and gpp complains of a General Protection Fault. Other systems might provide different messages or even no message, but the same evil lurks within the programs.

The cause is that the implicit copy constructor copies by value. Consider Listing 12.3, for example. The effect, recall, is this:

```
sailor.str = sport.str;
```

This does not copy the string; it copies the pointer to a string. That is, after `sailor` is initialized to `sports`, you wind up with two pointers to the same string. That's not a problem when the `operator<<()` function uses the pointer to display the string. It *is* a problem when the destructor is called. Recall that the `StringBad` destructor frees the memory pointed to by the `str` pointer. The effect of destroying `sailor` is this:

```
delete [] sailor.str;     // delete the string that ditto.str points to
```

The `sailor.str` pointer points to `"Spinach Leaves Bowl for Dollars"` because it is assigned the value of `sports.str`, which points to that string. So the `delete` statement frees the memory occupied by the string `"Spinach Leaves Bowl for Dollars"`.

Next, the effect of destroying `sports` is this:

```
delete [] sports.str;   // effect is undefined
```

Here, `sports.str` points to the same memory location that has already been freed by the destructor for `sailor`, and this results in undefined, possibly harmful, behavior. In the case of Listing 12.3, the program produces mangled strings, which is usually a sign of memory mismanagement.

Fixing the Problem with an Explicit Copy Constructor

The cure for the problems in the class design is to make a *deep copy*. That is, rather than just copy the address of the string, the copy constructor should duplicate the string and assign the address of the duplicate to the `str` member. That way, each object gets its own string rather than referring to another object's string. And each call of the destructor frees a different string rather than making duplicate attempts at freeing the same string. Here's how you can code the `String` copy constructor:

```cpp
StringBad::StringBad(const StringBad & st)
{
    num_strings++;              // handle static member update
    len = st.len;               // same length
    str = new char [len + 1];   // allot space
    std:::strcpy(str, st.str);  // copy string to new location
    cout << num_strings << ": \"" << str
         << "\" object created\n"; // For Your Information
}
```

What makes defining the copy constructor necessary is the fact that some class members are `new`-initialized pointers to data rather than the data themselves. Figure 12.3 illustrates deep copying.

FIGURE 12.3

An inside look at deep copying.

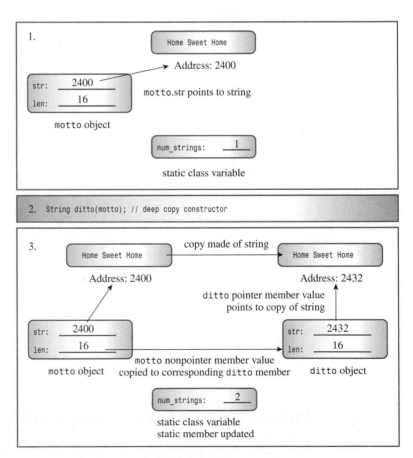

Caution
If a class contains members that are pointers initialized by new, you should define a copy constructor that copies the pointed-to data instead of copying the pointers themselves. This is termed *deep copying*. The alternative form of copying (*memberwise*, or *shallow*, *copying*) just copies pointer values. A shallow copy is just that—the shallow "scraping off" of pointer information for copying, rather than the deeper "mining" required to copy the constructs referred to by the pointers.

Assignment Operators

Not all the problems in Listing 12.3 can be blamed on the default copy constructor; you have to look at the default assignment operator, too. Just as ANSI C allows structure assignment, C++ allows class object assignment. It does so by automatically overloading an assignment operator for a class. This operator has the following prototype:

```
Class_name & Class_name::operator=(const Class_name &);
```

That is, it takes and returns a reference to an object of the class. For example, here's the prototype for the `StringBad` class:

```
StringBad & StringBad::operator=(const StringBad &);
```

When an Assignment Operator Is Used

An overloaded assignment operator is used when you assign one object to another existing object:

```
StringBad headline1("Celery Stalks at Midnight");
...
StringBad knot;
knot = headline1;    // assignment operator invoked
```

An assignment operator is not necessarily used when initializing an object:

```
StringBad metoo = knot; // use copy constructor, possibly assignment, too
```

Here `metoo` is a newly created object being initialized to `knot`'s values; hence, the copy constructor is used. However, as mentioned before, implementations have the option of handling this statement in two steps: using the copy constructor to create a temporary object and then using assignment to copy the values to the new object. That is, initialization always invokes a copy constructor, and forms using the = operator may also invoke an assignment operator.

What an Assignment Operator Does

Like a copy constructor, an implicit implementation of an assignment operator performs a member-to-member copy. If a member is itself an object of some class, the program uses the assignment operator defined for that class to do the copying for that particular member. Static data members are unaffected.

Where Assignment Goes Wrong

Listing 12.3 assigns `headline1` to `knot`:

```
knot = headline1;
```

When the destructor is called for `knot`, it displays this message:

```
"Celery Stalks at Midnight" object deleted, 2 left
```

When the destructor is called for `headline1`, it displays this message:

```
"-|" object deleted, -2 left
```

(Some implementations abort before getting this far.)

Here you see the same problem that the implicit copy constructor caused: corrupted data. Once again, the problem is memberwise copying, which causes both `headline1.str` and `knot.str` to point to the same address. Thus, when the destructor is called for `knot`, it deletes the string `"Celery Stalks at Midnight"`, and when it's called for `headline1`, it attempts to delete the previously deleted string. As mentioned earlier, the effect of attempting to delete previously deleted data is undefined, so it may change the memory contents, and it may cause a program to abort. As some like to point out, if the effect of a particular operation is undefined, your compiler can do anything it wants, including displaying the Declaration of Independence or freeing your hard disk of unsightly files.

Fixing Assignment

The solution for the problems created by an inappropriate default assignment operator is to provide your own assignment operator definition, one that makes a deep copy. The implementation is similar to that of the copy constructor, but there are some differences:

- Because the target object may already refer to previously allocated data, the function should use `delete []` to free former obligations.

- The function should protect against assigning an object to itself; otherwise, the freeing of memory described previously could erase the object's contents before they are reassigned.

- The function returns a reference to the invoking object.

By returning an object, the function can emulate the way ordinary assignment for built-in types can be chained. That is, if `S0`, `S1`, and `S2` are `StringBad` objects, you can write the following:

```
S0 = S1 = S2;
```

In function notation, this becomes the following:

```
S0.operator=(S1.operator=(S2));
```

Thus, the return value of `S1.operator=(S2)` becomes the argument of the `S0.operator=()` function. Because the return value is a reference to a `String` object, it is the correct argument type.

Here's how you could write an assignment operator for the `StringBad` class:

```
StringBad & StringBad::operator=(const StringBad & st)
{
    if (this == &st)              // object assigned to itself
        return *this;             // all done
    delete [] str;                // free old string
    len = st.len;
    str = new char [len + 1];     // get space for new string
    std::strcpy(str, st.str);     // copy the string
    return *this;                 // return reference to invoking object
}
```

First, the code checks for self-assignment. It does so by seeing if the address of the right-hand side of the assignment (`&s`) is the same as the address of the receiving object (`this`). If so, the program returns `*this` and terminates. You may recall from Chapter 10 that the assignment operator is one of the operators that can be overloaded only by a class member function.

Otherwise, the function proceeds to free the memory that `str` pointed to. The reason for this is that shortly thereafter `str` will be assigned the address of a new string. If you don't first apply the `delete` operator, the previous string will remain in memory. Because the program no longer has a pointer to the old string, that memory will be wasted.

Next, the program proceeds like a copy constructor, allocating enough space for the new string and then copying the string from the right-hand object to the new location.

When it is finished, the program returns `*this` and terminates.

Assignment does not create a new object, so you don't have to adjust the value of the static data member `num_strings`.

Adding the copy constructor and the assignment operator described previously to the `StringBad` class clears up all the problems. Here, for example, are the last few lines of output after these changes have been made:

```
End of main()
"Celery Stalks at Midnight" object deleted, 4 left
"Spinach Leaves Bowl for Dollars" object deleted, 3 left
"Spinach Leaves Bowl for Dollars" object deleted, 2 left
"Lettuce Prey" object deleted, 1 left
"Celery Stalks at Midnight" object deleted, 0 left
```

The object counting is correct now, and none of the strings have been mangled.

The New, Improved `String` Class

Now that you are a bit wiser, you can revise the `StringBad` class, renaming it `String`. First, you'll add the copy constructor and the assignment operator just discussed so that the class correctly manages the memory used by class objects. Next, now that you've seen when objects are constructed and destroyed, you can mute the class constructors and destructors so that they no longer announce each time they are used. Also, now that you're no longer watching the constructors at work, you can simplify the default constructor so that it constructs an empty string instead of `"C++"`.

Next, you can add a few capabilities to the class. A useful `String` class would incorporate all the functionality of the standard `cstring` library of string functions, but you'll add only enough to see what happens. (Keep in mind that this `String` class is an illustrative example and that the C++ standard `string` class is much more extensive.) In particular, you'll add the following methods:

```
int length () const { return len; }
friend bool operator<(const String &st, const String &st2);
friend bool operator>(const String &st1, const String &st2);
friend bool operator==(const String &st, const String &st2);
friend operator>>(istream & is, String & st);
char & operator[](int i);
const char & operator[](int i) const;
static int HowMany();
```

The first new method returns the length of the stored string. The next three friend functions allow you to compare strings. The `operator>>()` function provides simple input capabilities. The two `operator[]()` functions provide array-notation access to individual characters in a string. The static class method `HowMany()` complements the static class data member `num_strings`. Let's look at some details.

The Revised Default Constructor

The new default constructor merits notice. It look likes this:

```
String::String()
{
    len = 0;
    str = new char[1];
    str[0] = '\0';              // default string
}
```

You might wonder why the code uses

```
str = new char[1];
```

and not this:

```
str = new char;
```

Both forms allocate the same amount of memory. The difference is that the first form is compatible with the class destructor and the second is not. Recall that the destructor contains this code:

```
delete [] str;
```

Using `delete []` is compatible with pointers initialized by using `new []` and with the null pointer. So another possibility would be to replace

```
str = new char[1];
str[0] = '\0';              // default string
```

with this:

```
str = 0; // sets str to the null pointer
```

The effect of using `delete []` with any pointers initialized any other way is undefined:

```
char words[15] = "bad idea";
char * p1= words;
char * p2 = new char;
char * p3;
delete [] p1; // undefined, so don't do it
delete [] p2; // undefined, so don't do it
delete [] p3; // undefined, so don't do it
```

Comparison Members

Three of the methods in the `String` class perform comparisons. The `operator<()` function returns `true` if the first string comes before the second string alphabetically (or, more precisely, in the machine collating sequence). The simplest way to implement the string comparison functions is to use the standard `strcmp()` function, which returns a negative value if its first argument precedes the second alphabetically, `0` if the strings are the same, and a positive value if the first follows the second alphabetically. So, you can use `strcmp()` like this:

```
bool operator<(const String &st1, const String &st2)
{
    if (std::strcmp(st1.str, st2.str) > 0)
        return true;
    else
        return false;
}
```

Because the built-in > operator already returns a type `bool` value, you can simplify the code further to this:

```
bool operator<(const String &st1, const String &st2)
{
    return (std::strcmp(st1.str, st2.str) < 0);
}
```

Similarly, you can code the other two comparison functions like this:

```
bool operator>(const String &st1, const String &st2)
{
    return st2.str < st1.str;
}
bool operator==(const String &st1, const String &st2)
{
    return (std::strcmp(st1.str, st2.str) == 0);
}
```

The first definition expresses the > operator in terms of the < operator and would be a good choice for an inline function.

Making the comparison functions friends facilitates comparisons between `String` objects and regular C strings. For example, suppose `answer` is a `String` object and that you have the following code:

```
if ("love" == answer)
```

This gets translated to the following:

```
if (operator==("love", answer))
```

The compiler then uses one of the constructors to convert the code, in effect, to this:

```
if (operator==(String("love"), answer))
```

And this matches the prototype.

Accessing Characters by Using Bracket Notation

With a standard C-style string, you can use brackets to access individual characters:

```
char city[40] = "Amsterdam";
cout << city[0] << endl; // display the letter A
```

In C++ the two bracket symbols constitute a single operator, the bracket operator, and you can overload this operator by using a method called `operator[]()`. Typically, a binary C++ operator (one with two operands) puts the operator between the two operands, as in `2 + 5`. But the bracket operator places one operand in front of the first bracket and the other operand between the two brackets. Thus, in the expression `city[0]`, `city` is the first operand, `[]` is the operator, and `0` is the second operand.

Suppose that `opera` is a `String` object:

```
String opera("The Magic Flute");
```

If you use the expression `opera[4]`, C++ looks for a method with this name and signature:

```
operator[](int i)
```

If it finds a matching prototype, the compiler replaces the expression `opera[4]` with this function call:

```
opera.operator[](4)
```

The `opera` object invokes the method, and the array subscript `4` becomes the function argument.

Here's a simple implementation:

```
char & String::operator[](int i)
{
    return str[i];
}
```

With this definition, the statement

```
cout << opera[4];
```

becomes this:

```
cout << opera.operator[](4);
```

The return value is `opera.str[4]`, or the character `'M'`. So the public method gives access to private data.

Declaring the return type as type `char &` allows you to assign values to a particular element. For example, you can use the following:

```
String means("might");
means[0] = 'r';
```

The second statement is converted to an overloaded operator function call:

```
means.operator[][0] = 'r';
```

This assigns `'r'` to the method's return value. But the function returns a reference to `means.str[0]`, making the code equivalent to

```
means.str[0] = 'r';
```

This last line of code violates private access, but, because `operator[]()` is a class method, it is allowed to alter the array contents. The net effect of the code is that `"might"` becomes `"right"`.

Suppose you have a constant object:

```
const String answer("futile");
```

Then, if the only available definition for `operator[]()` is the one you've just seen, the following code is labeled an error:

```
cout << answer[1];  // compile-time error
```

The reason is that `answer` is `const`, and the method doesn't promise not to alter data. (In fact, sometimes the method's job is to alter data, so it can't promise not to.)

However, C++ distinguishes between `const` and non-`const` function signatures when overloading, so you can provide a second version of `operator[]()` that is used just by `const String` objects:

```
// for use with const String objects
const char & String::operator[](int i) const
{
    return str[i];
}
```

With the definitions, you have read/write access to regular `String` objects and read-only access to `const String` data:

```
String text("Once upon a time");
const String answer("futile");
cout << text[1];     // ok, uses non-const version of operator[]()
cout << answer[1];   // ok, uses const version of operator[]()
cin >> text[1];      // ok, uses non-const version of operator[]()
cin >> answer[1];    // compile-time error
```

Static Class Member Functions

It's possible to declare a member function as being static. (The keyword `static` should appear in the function declaration but not in the function definition, if the latter is separate.) This has two important consequences.

First, a static member function doesn't have to be invoked by an object; in fact, it doesn't even get a `this` pointer to play with. If the static member function is declared in the public section, it can be invoked using the class name and the scope-resolution operator. You can give the `String` class a static member function called `HowMany()` with the following prototype/definition in the class declaration:

```
static int HowMany() { return num_strings; }
```

It could be invoked like this:

```
int count = String::HowMany();  // invoking a static member function
```

The second consequence is that, because a static member function is not associated with a particular object, the only data members it can use are the static data members. For example, the `HowMany()` static method can access the `num_strings` static member, but not `str` or `len`.

Similarly, a static member function can be used to set a classwide flag that controls how some aspect of the class interface behaves. For example, it can control the formatting used by a method that displays class contents.

Further Assignment Operator Overloading

Before looking at the new listings for the `String` class example, let's consider another matter. Suppose you want to copy an ordinary string to a `String` object. For example, suppose you use `getline()` to read a string and you want to place it in a `String` object. The class methods already allow you to do the following:

```
String name;
char temp[40];
cin.getline(temp, 40);
name = temp;  // use constructor to convert type
```

However, this might not be a satisfactory solution if you have to do it often. To see why, let's review how the final statement works:

1. The program uses the `String(const char *)` constructor to construct a temporary `String` object containing a copy of the string stored in `temp`. Remember from Chapter 11, "Working with Classes," that a constructor with a single argument serves as a conversion function.

2. In Listing 12.6, later in this chapter, the program uses the `String & String::operator=(const String &)` function to copy information from the temporary object to the `name` object.

3. The program calls the `~String()` destructor to delete the temporary object.

The simplest way to make the process more efficient is to overload the assignment operator so that it works directly with ordinary strings. This removes the extra steps of creating and destroying a temporary object. Here's one possible implementation:

```
String & String::operator=(const char * s)
{
    delete [] str;
```

```
    len = std::strlen(s);
    str = new char[len + 1];
    std::strcpy(str, s);
    return *this;
}
```

As usual, you must deallocate memory formerly managed by str and allocate enough memory for the new string.

Listing 12.4 shows the revised class declaration. In addition to the changes already mentioned, it defines the constant CINLIM, which is used in implementing operator>>().

LISTING 12.4   string1.h

```
// string1.h -- fixed and augmented string class definition
#include <iostream>
using std::ostream;
using std::istream;

#ifndef STRING1_H_
#define STRING1_H_
class String
{
private:
    char * str;              // pointer to string
    int len;                 // length of string
    static int num_strings;  // number of objects
    static const int CINLIM = 80;  // cin input limit
public:
// constructors and other methods
    String(const char * s);  // constructor
    String();                // default constructor
    String(const String &);  // copy constructor
    ~String();               // destructor
    int length () const { return len; }
// overloaded operator methods
    String & operator=(const String &);
    String & operator=(const char *);
    char & operator[](int i);
    const char & operator[](int i) const;
// overloaded operator friends
    friend bool operator<(const String &st, const String &st2);
    friend bool operator>(const String &st1, const String &st2);
    friend bool operator==(const String &st, const String &st2);
    friend ostream & operator<<(ostream & os, const String & st);
    friend istream & operator>>(istream & is, String & st);
// static function
    static int HowMany();
};
#endif
```

Compatibility Note

You might have a compiler that has not implemented `bool`. In that case, you can use `int` instead of `bool`, `0` instead of `false`, and `1` instead of `true`. If your compiler doesn't support static class constants, you can define `CINLIM` with an enumeration:

```
enum {CINLIM = 90};
```

Listing 12.5 presents the revised method definitions.

LISTING 12.5   `string1.cpp`

```cpp
// string1.cpp -- String class methods
#include <cstring>                // string.h for some
#include "string1.h"              // includes <iostream>
using std::cin;
using std::cout;

// initializing static class member

int String::num_strings = 0;

// static method
int String::HowMany()
{
    return num_strings;
}

// class methods
String::String(const char * s)     // construct String from C string
{
    len = std::strlen(s);          // set size
    str = new char[len + 1];       // allot storage
    std::strcpy(str, s);           // initialize pointer
    num_strings++;                 // set object count
}

String::String()                   // default constructor
{
    len = 4;
    str = new char[1];
    str[0] = '\0';                 // default string
    num_strings++;
}

String::String(const String & st)
{
    num_strings++;                 // handle static member update
    len = st.len;                  // same length
    str = new char [len + 1];      // allot space
```

LISTING 12.5 Continued

```
    std::strcpy(str, st.str);  // copy string to new location
}

String::~String()                  // necessary destructor
{
    --num_strings;                 // required
    delete [] str;                 // required
}

// overloaded operator methods

    // assign a String to a String
String & String::operator=(const String & st)
{
    if (this == &st)
        return *this;
    delete [] str;
    len = st.len;
    str = new char[len + 1];
    std::strcpy(str, st.str);
    return *this;
}

    // assign a C string to a String
String & String::operator=(const char * s)
{
    delete [] str;
    len = std::strlen(s);
    str = new char[len + 1];
    std::strcpy(str, s);
    return *this;
}

    // read-write char access for non-const String
char & String::operator[](int i)
{
    return str[i];
}

    // read-only char access for const String
const char & String::operator[](int i) const
{
    return str[i];
}

// overloaded operator friends

bool operator<(const String &st1, const String &st2)
{
    return (std::strcmp(st1.str, st2.str) < 0);
}
```

LISTING 12.5   Continued

```
bool operator>(const String &st1, const String &st2)
{
    return st2.str < st1.str;
}

bool operator==(const String &st1, const String &st2)
{
    return (std::strcmp(st1.str, st2.str) == 0);
}

    // simple String output
ostream & operator<<(ostream & os, const String & st)
{
    os << st.str;
    return os;
}

    // quick and dirty String input
istream & operator>>(istream & is, String & st)
{
    char temp[String::CINLIM];
    is.get(temp, String::CINLIM);
    if (is)
        st = temp;
    while (is && is.get() != '\n')
        continue;
    return is;
}
```

The overloaded >> operator provides a simple way to read a line of keyboard input into a
`String` object. It assumes an input line of `String::CINLIM` or fewer characters and discards
any characters beyond that limit. Keep in mind that the value of an `istream` object in an `if`
condition evaluates to `false` if input fails for some reason, such as encountering an end-of-file
condition, or, in the case of `get(char *, int)`, reading an empty line.

Listing 12.6 exercises the String class with a short program that lets you enter a few strings.
The program has the user enter sayings, puts the strings into `String` objects, displays them,
and reports which string is the shortest and which comes first alphabetically.

LISTING 12.6   sayings1.cpp

```
// sayings1.cpp -- using expanded String class
// compile with string1.cpp
#include <iostream>
#include "string1.h"
const int ArSize = 10;
const int MaxLen =81;
```

LISTING 12.6   Continued

```
int main()
{
    using std::cout;
    using std::cin;
    using std::endl;
    String name;
    cout <<"Hi, what's your name?\n>> ";
    cin >> name;

    cout << name << ", please enter up to " << ArSize
         << " short sayings <empty line to quit>:\n";
    String sayings[ArSize];     // array of objects
    char temp[MaxLen];          // temporary string storage
    int i;
    for (i = 0; i < ArSize; i++)
    {
        cout << i+1 << ": ";
        cin.get(temp, MaxLen);
        while (cin && cin.get() != '\n')
            continue;
        if (!cin || temp[0] == '\0')    // empty line?
            break;                      // i not incremented
        else
            sayings[i] = temp;  // overloaded assignment
    }
    int total = i;              // total # of lines read

    cout << "Here are your sayings:\n";
    for (i = 0; i < total; i++)
        cout << sayings[i][0] << ": " << sayings[i] << endl;

    int shortest = 0;
    int first = 0;
    for (i = 1; i < total; i++)
    {
        if (sayings[i].length() < sayings[shortest].length())
            shortest = i;
        if (sayings[i] < sayings[first])
            first = i;
    }
    cout << "Shortest saying:\n" << sayings[shortest] << endl;;
    cout << "First alphabetically:\n" << sayings[first] << endl;
    cout << "This program used "<< String::HowMany()
         << " String objects. Bye.\n";

    return 0;
}
```

Compatibility Note

Older versions of `get(char *, int)` don't evaluate to `false` upon reading an empty line. For those versions, however, the first character in the string is a null character if an empty line is entered. This example uses the following code:

```
if (!cin || temp[0] == '\0')    // empty line?
    break;                       // i not incremented
```

If the implementation follows the current C++ Standard, the first test in the `if` statement detects an empty line, whereas the second test detects the empty line for older implementations.

The program in Listing 12.6 asks the user to enter up to 10 sayings. Each saying is read into a temporary character array and then copied to a `String` object. If the user enters a blank line, a `break` statement terminates the input loop. After echoing the input, the program uses the `length()` and `operator<()` member functions to locate the shortest string and the alphabetically earliest string. The program also uses the subscript operator (`[]`) to preface each saying with its initial character. Here's a sample run:

```
Hi, what's your name?
>> Misty Gutz
Misty Gutz, please enter up to 10 short sayings <empty line to quit>:
1: a fool and his money are soon parted
2: penny wise, pound foolish
3: the love of money is the root of much evil
4: out of sight, out of mind
5: absence makes the heart grow fonder
6: absinthe makes the hart grow fonder
7:
a: a fool and his money are soon parted
p: penny wise, pound foolish
t: the love of money is the root of much evil
o: out of sight, out of mind
a: absence makes the heart grow fonder
a: absinthe makes the hart grow fonder
Shortest saying:
penny wise, pound foolish
First alphabetically:
a fool and his money are soon parted
This program used 11 String objects. Bye.
```

Things to Remember When Using new in Constructors

By now you've noticed that you must take special care when using **new** to initialize pointer members of an object. In particular, you should do the following:

- If you use **new** to initialize a pointer member in a constructor, you should use **delete** in the destructor.

- The uses of **new** and **delete** should be compatible. You should pair **new** with **delete** and **new []** with **delete []**.

- If there are multiple constructors, all should use new the same way—either all with brackets or all without brackets. There's only one destructor, so all constructors have to be compatible to that destructor. However, it is permissible to initialize a pointer with new in one constructor and with the null pointer (NULL or 0) in another constructor because it's okay to apply the delete operation (with or without brackets) to the null pointer.

NULL or 0?

The null pointer can be represented by 0 or by NULL, a symbolic constant defined as 0 in several header files. C programmers often use NULL instead of 0 as a visual reminder that the value is a pointer value, just as they use '\0' instead of 0 for the null character as a visual reminder that this value is a character. The C++ tradition, however, seems to favor using a simple 0 instead of the equivalent NULL.

- You should define a copy constructor that initializes one object to another by doing deep copying. Typically, the constructor should emulate the following example:

```
String::String(const String & st)
{
    num_strings++;            // handle static member update if necessary
    len = st.len;             // same length
    str = new char [len + 1]; // allot space
    std::strcpy(str, st.str);   // copy string to new location
}
```

In particular, the copy constructor should allocate space to hold the copied data, and it should copy the data, not just the address of the data. Also, it should update any static class members whose value would be affected by the process.

- You should define an assignment operator that copies one object to another by doing deep copying. Typically, the class method should emulate the following example:

```
String & String::operator=(const String & st)
{
    if (this == &st)          // object assigned to itself
        return *this;         // all done
    delete [] str;            // free old string
    len = st.len;
    str = new char [len + 1]; // get space for new string
    std::strcpy(str, st.str);   // copy the string
    return *this;             // return reference to invoking object
}
```

In particular, the method should check for self-assignment; it should free memory formerly pointed to by the member pointer; it should copy the data, not just the address of the data; and it should return a reference to the invoking object.

The following excerpt contains two examples of what not to do and one example of a good constructor:

```cpp
String::String()
{
    str = "default string";    // oops, no new []
    len = std::strlen(str);
}

String::String(const char * s)
{
    len = std::strlen(s);
    str = new char;            // oops, no []
    std::strcpy(str, s);             // oops, no room
}

String::String(const String & st)
{
    len = st.len;
    str = new char[len + 1];       // good, allocate space
    std::strcpy(str, st.str);          // good, copy value
}
```

The first constructor fails to use **new** to initialize str. The destructor, when called for a default object, applies **delete** to str. The result of applying **delete** to a pointer not initialized by **new** is undefined, but it is probably bad. Any of the following would be okay:

```cpp
String::String()
{
    len = 0;
    str = new char[1];  // uses new with []
    str[0] = '\0';
}

String::String()
{
    len = 0;
    str = NULL;  // or the equivalent str = 0;
}

String::String()
{
    static const char * s = "C++";     // initialized just once
    len = std::strlen(s);
    str = new char[len + 1];           // uses new with []
    std::strcpy(str, s);
}
```

The second constructor in the original excerpt applies **new**, but it fails to request the correct amount of memory; hence, **new** returns a block containing space for just one character. Attempting to copy a longer string to that location is asking for memory problems. Also, the use of **new** without brackets is inconsistent with the correct form of the other constructors.

The third constructor is fine.

Finally, here's a destructor that *doesn't* work correctly with the previous constructors:

```
String::~String()
{
    delete str;        // oops, should be delete [] str;
}
```

The destructor uses `delete` incorrectly. Because the constructors request arrays of characters, the destructor should delete an array.

Observations About Returning Objects

When a member function or standalone function returns an object, you have choices. The function could return a reference to an object, a constant reference to an object, an object, or a constant object. By now, you've seen examples of all but the last, so it's a good time to review these options.

Returning a Reference to a `const` Object

The usual reason for using a `const` reference is efficiency, but there are restrictions on when this choice can be used. If a function returns an object that is passed to it, either by object invocation or as a method argument, you can increase the efficiency of the method by having it pass a reference. For example, suppose you wanted to write a function `Max()` that returned the larger of two `Vector` objects, where `Vector` is the class developed in Chapter 11. The function would be used in this manner:

```
Vector force1(50,60);
Vector force2(10,70);
Vector max;
max = Max(force1, force2);
```

Either of the following two implementations would work:

```
// version 1
Vector Max(const Vector & v1, const Vector & v2)
{
    if (v1.magval() > v2.magval())
        return v1;
    else
        return v2;
}

// version 2
const Vector & Max(const Vector & v1, const Vector & v2)
{
    if (v1.magval() > v2.magval())
        return v1;
    else
        return v2;
}
```

There are three important points here. First, recall that returning an object invokes the copy constructor, whereas returning a reference doesn't. Thus Version 2 does less work and is more efficient. Second, the reference should be to an object that exists when the calling function is executing. In this example, the reference is to either `force1` or `force2`, and both are objects defined in the calling function, so this requirement is met. Third, both `v1` and `v2` are declared as being `const` references, so the return type has to be `const` to match.

Returning a Reference to a Non-`const` Object

Two common examples of returning a non-`const` object are overloading the assignment operator and overloading the `<<` operator for use with `cout`. The first is done for reasons of efficiency, and the second for reasons of necessity.

The return value of `operator=()` is used for chained assignment:

```
String s1("Good stuff");
String s2, s3;
s3 = s2 = s1;
```

In this code, the return value of `s2.operator=(s1)` is assigned to `s3`. Returning either a `String` object or a reference to a `String` object would work, but, as with the `Vector` example, using a reference allows the function to avoid calling the `String` copy constructor to create a new `String` object. In this case, the return type is not `const` because the `operator=()` method returns a reference to `s2`, which it does modify.

The return value of `operator<<()` is used for chained output:

```
String s1("Good stuff");
cout << s1 << "is coming!";
```

Here, the return value of `operator<<(cout, s1)` becomes the object used to display the string `"is coming!"`. Here, the return type has to be `ostream &` and not just `ostream`. Using an `ostream` return type would require calling the `ostream` copy constructor, and, as it turns out, the `ostream` class does not have a public copy constructor. Fortunately, returning a reference to `cout` poses no problems because `cout` is already in scope in the calling function.

Returning an Object

If the object being returned is local to the called function, then it should not be returned by reference because the local object has its destructor called when the function terminates. Thus, when control returns to the calling function, there is no object left to which the reference can refer. In these circumstances, you should return an object, not a reference. Typically, overloaded arithmetic operators fall into this category. Consider this example, which uses the `Vector` class again:

```
Vector force1(50,60);
Vector force2(10,70);
Vector net;
net = force1 + force2;
```

The value being returned is not `force1`, which should be left unaltered by the process, nor `force2`, which should also be unaltered. Thus the return value can't be a reference to an object that is already present in the calling function. Instead, the sum is a new, temporary object computed in `Vector::operator+()`, and the function shouldn't return a reference to a temporary object, either. Instead, it should return an actual vector object, not a reference:

```
Vector Vector::operator+(const Vector & b) const
{
    return Vector(x + b.x, y + b.y);
}
```

There is the added expense of calling the copy constructor to create the returned object, but that is unavoidable.

One more observation: In the `Vector::operator+()` example, the constructor call `Vector(x + b.x, y + b.y)` creates an object that is accessible to the `operator+()` method; the implicit call to the copy constructor produced by the return statement, however, creates an object that is accessible to the calling program.

Returning a `const` Object

The preceding definition of `Vector::operator+()` has a bizarre property. The intended use is this:

```
net = force1 + force2;                          // 1: three Vector objects
```

However, the definition also allows you to use the following:

```
force1 + force2 = net;                          // 2: dyslectic programming
cout << (force1 + force2 = net).magval() << endl; // 3: demented programming
```

Three questions immediately arise. Why would anyone write such statements? Why are they possible? What do they do?

First, there is no sensible reason for writing such code, but not all code is written for sensible reasons. People, even programmers, make mistakes. For instance, if the comparison `operator==()` were defined for the `Vector` class, you might mistakenly type

```
if (force1 + force2 = net)
```

instead of this:

```
if (force1 + force2 == net)
```

Also, programmers tend to be ingenious, and this can lead to ingeniously adventurous mistakes.

Second, this code is possible because the copy constructor constructs a temporary object to represent the return value. So, in the preceding code, the expression `force1 + force2` stands for that temporary object. In Statement 1, the temporary object is assigned to `net`. In Statements 2 and 3, `net` is assigned to the temporary object.

Third, the temporary object is used and then discarded. For instance, in Statement 2, the program computes the sum of `force1` and `force2`, copies the answer into the temporary return object, overwrites the contents with the contents of `net`, and then discards the temporary object. The original vectors are all left unchanged. In Statement 3, the magnitude of the temporary object is displayed before the object is deleted.

If you are concerned about the potential for misuse and abuse created by this behavior, you have a simple recourse: Declare the return type as a `const` object. For instance, if `Vector::operator+()` is declared to have return type `const Vector`, then Statement 1 is still allowed but Statements 2 and 3 become invalid.

In summary, if a method or function returns a local object, it should return an object, not a reference. In this example, the program uses the copy constructor to generate the returned object. If a method or function returns an object of a class for which there is no public copy constructor, such as the `ostream` class, it must return a reference to an object. Finally, some methods and functions, such as the overloaded assignment operator, can return either an object or a reference to an object. In this example, the reference is preferred for reasons of efficiency.

Using Pointers to Objects

C++ programs often use pointers to objects, so let's get in a bit of practice. Listing 12.6 uses array index values to keep track of the shortest string and of the first string alphabetically. Another approach is to use pointers to point to the current leaders in these categories. Listing 12.7 implements this approach, using two pointers to `String`. Initially, the `shortest` pointer points to the first object in the array. Each time the program finds an object with a shorter string, it resets `shortest` to point to that object. Similarly, a `first` pointer tracks the alphabetically earliest string. Note that these two pointers do not create new objects; they merely point to existing objects. Hence they don't require using `new` to allocate additional memory.

For variety, the program in Listing 12.7 uses a pointer that does keep track of a new object:

```
String * favorite = new String(sayings[choice]);
```

Here the pointer `favorite` provides the only access to the nameless object created by `new`. This particular syntax means to initialize the new `String` object by using the object `sayings[choice]`. That invokes the copy constructor because the argument type for the copy constructor (`const String &`) matches the initialization value (`sayings[choice]`). The program uses `srand()`, `rand()`, and `time()` to select a value for choice at random.

LISTING 12.7   `sayings2.cpp`

```cpp
// sayings2.cpp -- using pointers to objects
// compile with string1.cpp
#include <iostream>
#include <cstdlib>        // (or stdlib.h) for rand(), srand()
#include <ctime>          // (or time.h) for time()
#include "string1.h"
const int ArSize = 10;
const int MaxLen = 81;
int main()
{
    using namespace std;
    String name;
```

LISTING 12.7   Continued

```cpp
    cout <<"Hi, what's your name?\n>> ";
    cin >> name;

    cout << name << ", please enter up to " << ArSize
         << " short sayings <empty line to quit>:\n";
    String sayings[ArSize];
    char temp[MaxLen];               // temporary string storage
    int i;
    for (i = 0; i < ArSize; i++)
    {
        cout << i+1 << ": ";
        cin.get(temp, MaxLen);
        while (cin && cin.get() != '\n')
            continue;
        if (!cin || temp[0] == '\0') // empty line?
            break;                   // i not incremented
        else
            sayings[i] = temp;       // overloaded assignment
    }
    int total = i;                   // total # of lines read

    if (total > 0)
    {
        cout << "Here are your sayings:\n";
        for (i = 0; i < total; i++)
            cout << sayings[i] << "\n";

// use pointers to keep track of shortest, first strings
        String * shortest = &sayings[0]; // initialize to first object
        String * first = &sayings[0];
        for (i = 1; i < total; i++)
        {
            if (sayings[i].length() < shortest->length())
                shortest = &sayings[i];
            if (sayings[i] < *first)     // compare values
                first = &sayings[i];     // assign address
        }
        cout << "Shortest saying:\n" << * shortest << endl;
        cout << "First alphabetically:\n" << * first << endl;

        srand(time(0));
        int choice = rand() % total;     // pick index at random
// use new to create, initialize new String object
        String * favorite = new String(sayings[choice]);
        cout << "My favorite saying:\n" << *favorite << endl;
        delete favorite;
    }
    else
        cout << "Not much to say, eh?\n";
    cout << "Bye.\n";
    return 0;
}
```

> ## Object Initialization with new
>
> In general, if *Class_name* is a class and if *value* is of type *Type_name*, the statement
>
> *Class_name* * pclass = new *Class_name*(*value*);
>
> invokes this constructor:
>
> *Class_name*(*Type_name*);
>
> There may be trivial conversions, such as to this:
>
> *Class_name*(const *Type_name* &);
>
> Also, the usual conversions invoked by prototype matching, such as from int to double, takes place as long as there is no ambiguity. An initialization in the form
>
> *Class_name* * ptr = new *Class_name*;
>
> invokes the default constructor.

> ## Compatibility Note
>
> Older C++ implementations might require including stdlib.h instead of cstdlib and time.h instead of ctime.

Here's a sample run of the program in Listing 12.7:

```
Hi, what's your name?
>> Kirt Rood
Kirt Rood, please enter up to 10 short sayings <empty line to quit>:
1: a friend in need is a friend indeed
2: neither a borrower nor a lender be
3: a stitch in time saves nine
4: a niche in time saves stine
5: it takes a crook to catch a crook
6: cold hands, warm heart
7:
Here are your sayings:
a friend in need is a friend indeed
neither a borrower nor a lender be
a stitch in time saves nine
a niche in time saves stine
it takes a crook to catch a crook
cold hands, warm heart
Shortest saying:
cold hands, warm heart
First alphabetically:
a friend in need is a friend indeed
My favorite saying:
a stitch in time saves nine
Bye
```

Because the program selects the favorite saying randomly, different samples runs will show different choices, even for identical input.

Looking Again at new and delete

Note that the program generated from Listings 12.4, 12.5, and 12.7 uses new and delete on two levels. First, it uses new to allocate storage space for the name strings for each object that is created. This happens in the constructor functions, so the destructor function uses delete to free that memory. Because each string is an array of characters, the destructor uses delete with brackets. Thus, memory used to store the string contents is freed automatically when an object is destroyed. Second, the code in Listing 12.7 uses new to allocate an entire object:

```
String * favorite = new String(sayings[choice]);
```

This allocates space not for the string to be stored but for the object—that is, for the str pointer that holds the address of the string and for the len member. (It does not allocate space for the num_strings member because it is a static member that is stored separately from the objects.) Creating the object, in turn, calls the constructor, which allocates space for storing the string and assigns the string's address to str. The program then uses delete to delete this object when it is finished with it. The object is a single object, so the program uses delete without brackets. Again, this frees only the space used to hold the str pointer and the len member. It doesn't free the memory used to hold the string str points to, but the destructor takes care of that final task. (See Figure 12.4.)

FIGURE 12.4

Calling destructors.

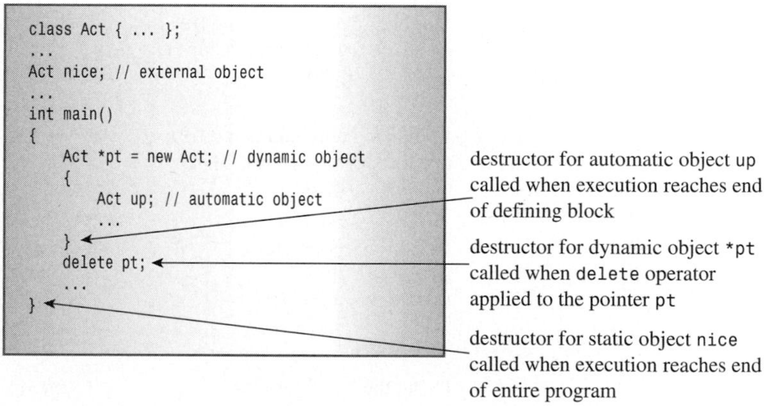

```
class Act { ... };
...
Act nice; // external object
...
int main()
{
    Act *pt = new Act; // dynamic object
    {
        Act up; // automatic object
        ...
    }
    delete pt;
    ...
}
```

destructor for automatic object up called when execution reaches end of defining block

destructor for dynamic object *pt called when delete operator applied to the pointer pt

destructor for static object nice called when execution reaches end of entire program

Again, destructors are called in the following situations (refer to Figure 12.4):

- If an object is an automatic variable, the object's destructor is called when the program exits the block in which the object is defined. Thus, in Listing 12.3 the destructor is called for headlines[0] and headlines[1] when the program exits main(), and the destructor for grub is called when the program exits callme1().

- If an object is a static variable (external, static, static external, or from a namespace), its destructor is called when the program terminates. This is what happened for the sports object in Listing 12.3.

- If an object is created by new, its destructor is called only when you explicitly use delete on the object.

Pointers and Objects Summary

You should note several points about using pointers to objects (refer to Figure 12.5 for a summary):

- You declare a pointer to an object by using the usual notation:

```
String * glamour;
```

- You can initialize a pointer to point to an existing object:

```
String * first = &sayings[0];
```

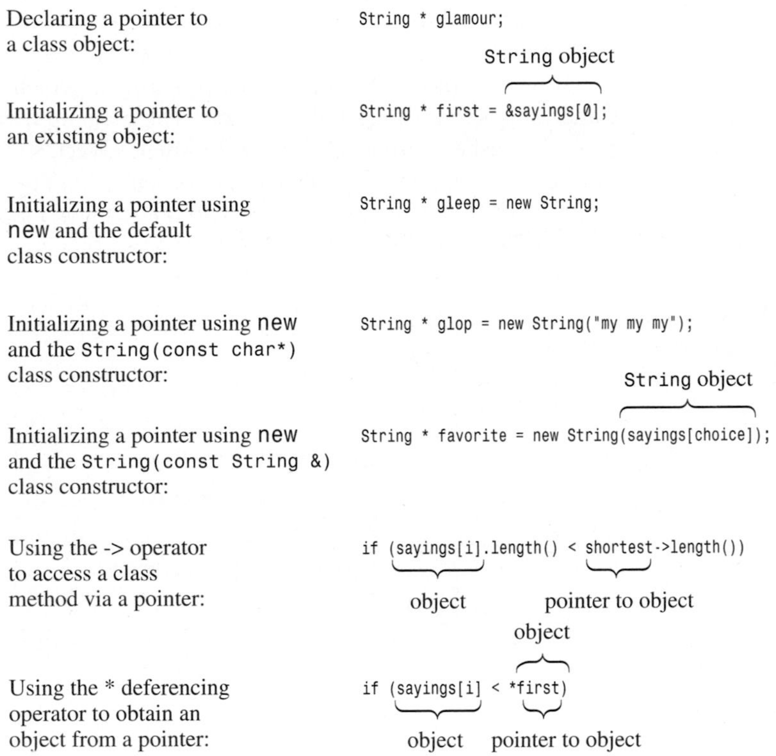

FIGURE 12.5
Pointers and objects.

Declaring a pointer to a class object:	`String * glamour;`
	String object
Initializing a pointer to an existing object:	`String * first = &sayings[0];`
Initializing a pointer using new and the default class constructor:	`String * gleep = new String;`
Initializing a pointer using new and the String(const char*) class constructor:	`String * glop = new String("my my my");`
	String object
Initializing a pointer using new and the String(const String &) class constructor:	`String * favorite = new String(sayings[choice]);`
Using the -> operator to access a class method via a pointer:	`if (sayings[i].length() < shortest->length())`
	object pointer to object
	object
Using the * dereferencing operator to obtain an object from a pointer:	`if (sayings[i] < *first)`
	object pointer to object

- You can initialize a pointer by using new; this creates a new object:

```
String * favorite = new String(sayings[choice]);
```

Also see Figure 12.6 for a more detailed look at an example of initializing a pointer with new.

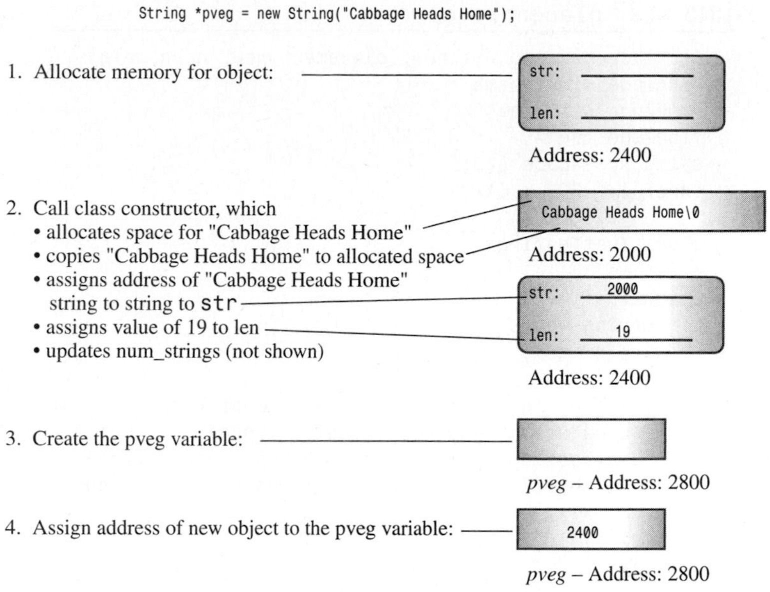

FIGURE 12.6

Creating an object with new.

`String *pveg = new String("Cabbage Heads Home");`

1. Allocate memory for object:

str: _____
len: _____

Address: 2400

2. Call class constructor, which
   • allocates space for "Cabbage Heads Home"
   • copies "Cabbage Heads Home" to allocated space
   • assigns address of "Cabbage Heads Home" string to string to str
   • assigns value of 19 to len
   • updates num_strings (not shown)

Cabbage Heads Home\0

Address: 2000

str: 2000
len: 19

Address: 2400

3. Create the pveg variable: _____

pveg – Address: 2800

4. Assign address of new object to the pveg variable: 2400

pveg – Address: 2800

- Using new with a class invokes the appropriate class constructor to initialize the newly created object:

```
// invokes default constructor
String * gleep = new String;

// invokes the String(const char *) constructor
String * glop = new String("my my my");

// invokes the String(const String &) constructor
String * favorite = new String(sayings[choice]);
```

- You use the `->` operator to access a class method via a pointer:

```
if (sayings[i].length() < shortest->length())
```

- You apply the dereferencing operator (`*`) to a pointer to an object to obtain an object:

```
if (sayings[i] < *first)    // compare object values
    first = &sayings[i];    // assign object address
```

Looking Again at Placement new

Recall that placement new allows you to specify the memory location used to allocate memory. Chapter 9, "Memory Models and Namespaces," discusses placement new in the context of built-in types. Using placement new with objects adds some new twists. Listing 12.8 uses placement new along with regular placement to allocate memory for objects. It defines a class with a chatty constructor and destructor so that you can follow the history of objects.

LISTING 12.8 placenew1.cpp

```cpp
// placenew1.cpp  -- new, placement new, no delete
#include <iostream>
#include <string>
#include <new>
using namespace std;
const int BUF = 512;

class JustTesting
{
private:
    string words;
    int number;
public:
    JustTesting(const string & s = "Just Testing", int n = 0)
    {words = s; number = n; cout << words << " constructed\n"; }
    ~JustTesting() { cout << words << " destroyed\n";}
    void Show() const { cout << words << ", " << number << endl;}
};
int main()
{
    char * buffer = new char[BUF];      // get a block of memory

    JustTesting *pc1, *pc2;

    pc1 = new (buffer) JustTesting;     // place object in buffer
    pc2 = new JustTesting("Heap1", 20); // place object on heap

    cout << "Memory block addresses:\n" << "buffer: "
        << (void *) buffer << "    heap: " << pc2 <<endl;
    cout << "Memory contents:\n";
    cout << pc1 << ": ";
    pc1->Show();
    cout << pc2 << ": ";
    pc2->Show();

    JustTesting *pc3, *pc4;
    pc3 = new (buffer) JustTesting("Bad Idea", 6);
    pc4 = new JustTesting("Heap2", 10);

    cout << "Memory contents:\n";
    cout << pc3 << ": ";
    pc3->Show();
    cout << pc4 << ": ";
    pc4->Show();

    delete pc2;                         // free Heap1
    delete pc4;                         // free Heap2
    delete [] buffer;                   // free buffer
    cout << "Done\n";
    return 0;
}
```

The program in Listing 12.8 uses new to create a memory buffer of 512 bytes. It then uses new to create two objects of type JustTesting on the heap and attempts to use placement new to create two objects of type JustTesting in the memory buffer. Finally, it uses delete to free the memory allocated by new. Here is the output:

```
Just Testing constructed
Heap1 constructed
Memory block addresses:
buffer: 00320AB0     heap: 00320CE0
Memory contents:
00320AB0: Just Testing, 0
00320CE0: Heap1, 20
Bad Idea constructed
Heap2 constructed
Memory contents:
00320AB0: Bad Idea, 6
00320EC8: Heap2, 10
Heap1 destroyed
Heap2 destroyed
Done
```

As usual, the formatting and exact values for the memory addresses will vary from system to system.

There are a couple problems with placement new in Listing 12.8. First, when creating a second object, placement new simply overwrites the same location used for the first object with a new object. Not only is this rude, it means that the destructor was never called for the first object. This, of course, would create real problems if, say, the class used dynamic memory allocation for its members.

Second, using delete with pc2 and pc4 automatically invokes the destructors for the two objects that pc2 and pc4 point to. But using delete [] with buffer does not invoke the destructors for the objects created with placement new.

One lesson to be learned here is the same lesson you learned in Chapter 9: It's up to you to manage the memory locations in a buffer that placement new populates. To use two different locations, you provide two different addresses within the buffer, making sure that the locations don't overlap. You can, for example, use this:

```
pc1 = new (buffer) JustTesting;
pc3 = new (buffer + sizeof (JustTesting)) JustTesting("Better Idea", 6);
```

Here the pointer pc3 is offset from pc1 by the size of a JustTesting object.

The second lesson to be learned here is that if you use placement new to store objects, you need to arrange for their destructors to be called. But how? For objects created on the heap, you can use this:

```
delete pc2;   // delete object pointed to by pc2
```

But you can't use this:

```
delete pc1;   // delete object pointed to by pc1? NO! Reason #1
delete pc3;   // delete object pointed to by pc2? NO! Reason #2
```

The reason is that `delete` works in conjunction with `new` but not with placement `new`. The pointer `pc3`, for example, does not receive an address returned by `new`, so `delete pc3` throws a runtime error. The pointer `pc1`, on the other hand, has the same numeric value as `buffer`, but `buffer` is initialized using `new []`, so it's freed using `delete []`, not `delete`. Even if `buffer` were initialized by `new` instead of `new []`, `delete pc1` would free `buffer`, not `pc1`. That's because the `new`/`delete` system knows about the 256-byte block that is allocated, but it doesn't know anything about what placement `new` does with the block.

Note that the program does free the buffer:

```
delete [] buffer;                // free buffer
```

As this comment suggests, `delete [] buffer;` deletes the entire block of memory allocated by `new`. But it doesn't call the destructors for any objects that placement `new` constructs in the block. You can tell this is so because this program uses chatty destructors, which report the demise of `"Heap1"` and `"Heap2"` but which remain silent about `"Just Testing"` and `"Bad Idea"`.

The solution to this quandary is that you must call the destructor explicitly for any object created by placement `new`. Normally, destructors are called automatically; this is one of the rare cases that require an explicit call. An explicit call to a destructor requires identifying the object to be destroyed. Because there are pointers to the objects, you can use these pointers:

```
pc3->~JustTesting();  // destroy object pointed to by pc3
pc1->~JustTesting();  // destroy object pointed to by pc1
```

Listing 12.9 fixes Listing 12.8 by managing memory locations used by placement `new` and by adding appropriate uses of `delete` and of explicit destructor calls. One important fact is the proper order of deletion. The objects constructed by placement `new` should be destroyed in order opposite that in which they were constructed. The reason is that, in principle, a later object might have dependencies on an earlier object. And the buffer used to hold the objects should be freed only after all the contained objects are destroyed.

LISTING 12.9   `placenew2.cpp`

```cpp
// placenew2.cpp  -- new, placement new, no delete
#include <iostream>
#include <string>
#include <new>
using namespace std;
const int BUF = 512;

class JustTesting
{
private:
    string words;
    int number;
public:
    JustTesting(const string & s = "Just Testing", int n = 0)
        {words = s; number = n; cout << words << " constructed\n"; }
```

LISTING 12.9 Continued

```
    ~JustTesting() { cout << words << " destroyed\n";}
    void Show() const { cout << words << ", " << number << endl;}
};
int main()
{
    char * buffer = new char[BUF];        // get a block of memory

    JustTesting *pc1, *pc2;

    pc1 = new (buffer) JustTesting;        // place object in buffer
    pc2 = new JustTesting("Heap1", 20);   // place object on heap

    cout << "Memory block addresses:\n" << "buffer: "
        << (void *) buffer << "     heap: " << pc2 <<endl;
    cout << "Memory contents:\n";
    cout << pc1 << ": ";
    pc1->Show();
    cout << pc2 << ": ";
    pc2->Show();

    JustTesting *pc3, *pc4;
// fix placement new location
    pc3 = new (buffer + sizeof (JustTesting))
                JustTesting("Better Idea", 6);
    pc4 = new JustTesting("Heap2", 10);

    cout << "Memory contents:\n";
    cout << pc3 << ": ";
    pc3->Show();
    cout << pc4 << ": ";
    pc4->Show();

    delete pc2;             // free Heap1
    delete pc4;             // free Heap2
// explicitly destroy placement new objects
    pc3->~JustTesting();   // destroy object pointed to by pc3
    pc1->~JustTesting();   // destroy object pointed to by pc1
    delete [] buffer;      // free buffer
    cout << "Done\n";
    return 0;
}
```

Here is the output of the program in Listing 12.9:

```
Just Testing constructed
Heap1 constructed
Memory block addresses:
buffer: 00320AB0    heap: 00320CE0
Memory contents:
00320AB0: Just Testing, 0
00320CE0: Heap1, 20
Better Idea constructed
Heap2 constructed
```

```
Memory contents:
00320AD0: Better Idea, 6
00320EC8: Heap2, 10
Heap1 destroyed
Heap2 destroyed
Better Idea destroyed
Just Testing destroyed
Done
```

The program in Listing 12.9 places the two placement new objects in adjacent location and calls the proper destructors.

Reviewing Techniques

By now, you've encountered several programming techniques for dealing with various class-related problems, and you may be having trouble keeping track of all of them. So the following sections summarize several techniques and when they are used.

Overloading the << Operator

To redefine the << operator so that you use it with cout to display an object's contents, you define a friend operator function that has the following form:

```
ostream & operator<<(ostream & os, const c_name & obj)
{
    os << ... ;  // display object contents
    return os;
}
```

Here *c_name* represents the name of the class. If the class provides public methods that return the required contents, you can use those methods in the operator function and dispense with the friend status.

Conversion Functions

To convert a single value to a class type, you create a class constructor that has the following prototype:

```
c_name(type_name value);
```

Here *c_name* represents the class name, and *type_name* represents the name of the type you want to convert.

To convert a class type to some other type, you create a class member function that has the following prototype:

```
operator type_name();
```

Although this function has no declared return type, it should return a value of the desired type.

Remember to use conversion functions with care. You can use the keyword explicit when declaring a constructor to prevent it from being used for implicit conversions.

Classes Whose Constructors Use new

You need to take several precautions when designing classes that use the new operator to allocate memory pointed to by a class member (yes, we summarized these precautions recently, but the rules are very important to remember, particularly because the compiler does not know them and, thus, won't catch your mistakes):

- Any class member that points to memory allocated by new should have the `delete` operator applied to it in the class destructor. This frees the allocated memory.

- If a destructor frees memory by applying `delete` to a pointer that is a class member, every constructor for that class should initialize that pointer, either by using new or by setting the pointer to the null pointer.

- Constructors should settle on using either new [ ] or new, but not a mixture of both. The destructor should use `delete` [ ] if the constructors use new [ ], and it should use `delete` if the constructors use new.

- You should define a copy constructor that allocates new memory rather than copying a pointer to existing memory. This enables a program to initialize one class object to another. The constructor should normally have the following prototype:

    ```
    className(const className &)
    ```

- You should define a class member function that overloads the assignment operator and that has a function definition with the following prototype (where c_pointer is a member of the *c_name* class and has the type pointer-to-*type_name*). The following example assumes that the constructors initialize the variable c_pointer by using new [ ]:

    ```
    c_name & c_name::operator=(const c_name & cn)
    {
        if (this == & cn_)
            return *this;       // done if self-assignment
        delete [] c_pointer;
        // set size number of type_name units to be copied
        c_pointer = new type_name[size];
        // then copy data pointed to by cn.c_pointer to
        // location pointed to by c_pointer
        ...
        return *this;
    }
    ```

A Queue Simulation

Let's apply your improved understanding of classes to a programming problem. The Bank of Heather wants to open an automatic teller machine (ATM) in the Food Heap supermarket. The Food Heap management is concerned about lines at the ATM interfering with traffic flow in the market and may want to impose a limit on the number of people allowed to line up at the ATM. The Bank of Heather people want estimates of how long customers will have to wait in line. Your task is to prepare a program that simulates the situation so that management can see what the effect of the ATM might be.

A rather natural way of representing the problem is to use a queue of customers. A queue is an abstract data type (ADT) that holds an ordered sequence of items. New items are added to the rear of the queue, and items can be removed from the front. A queue is a bit like a stack, except that a stack has additions and removals at the same end. This makes a stack a LIFO (last in, first out) structure, whereas the queue is a FIFO (first in, first out) structure. Conceptually, a queue is like a line at a checkout stand or an ATM, so it's ideally suited to the task. So, one part of the project is to define a **Queue** class. (In Chapter 16, you'll read about the Standard Template Library **queue** class, but you'll learn more by developing your own than by just reading about such a class.)

The items in the queue will be customers. A Bank of Heather representative tells you that, on average, a third of the customers will take one minute to be processed, a third will take two minutes, and a third will take three minutes. Furthermore, customers arrive at random intervals, but the average number of customers per hour is fairly constant. Two more parts of your project will be to design a class representing customers and to put together a program that simulates the interactions between customers and the queue (see Figure 12.7).

FIGURE 12.7
A queue.

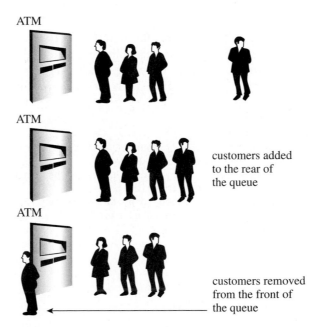

ATM

ATM

customers added
to the rear of
the queue

ATM

customers removed
from the front of
the queue

A Queue Class

The first order of business is to design a **Queue** class. First, you need to list the attributes of the kind of queue you'll need:

- A queue holds an ordered sequence of items.

- A queue has a limit on the number of items it can hold.

- You should be able to create an empty queue.

- You should be able to check whether a queue is empty.

- You should be able to check whether a queue is full.

- You should be able to add an item to the end of a queue.

- You should be able to remove an item from the front of a queue.

- You should be able to determine the number of items in the queue.

As usual when designing a class, you need to develop a public interface and a private implementation.

The Queue Class Interface

The queue attributes listed in the preceding section suggest the following public interface for a queue class:

```
class Queue
{
    enum {Q_SIZE = 10};
private:
// private representation to be developed later
public:
    Queue(int qs = Q_SIZE); // create queue with a qs limit
    ~Queue();
    bool isempty() const;
    bool isfull() const;
    int queuecount() const;
    bool enqueue(const Item &item); // add item to end
    bool dequeue(Item &item);       // remove item from front
};
```

The constructor creates an empty queue. By default, the queue can hold up to 10 items, but that can be overridden with an explicit initialization argument:

```
Queue line1;            // queue with 10-item limit
Queue line2(20);        // queue with 20-item limit
```

When using the queue, you can use a typedef to define Item. (In Chapter 14, "Reusing Code in C++," you'll learn how to use class templates instead.)

The Queue Class Implementation

After you determine the interface, you can implement it. First, you have to decide how to represent the queue data. One approach is to use new to dynamically allocate an array with the required number of elements. However, arrays aren't a good match to queue operations. For example, removing an item from the front of the array should be followed up by shifting every remaining element one unit closer to the front. Otherwise, you need to do something more elaborate, such as treat the array as circular. Using a linked list, however, is a reasonable fit to the requirements of a queue. A *linked list* consists of a sequence of nodes. Each *node* contains the information to be held in the list, plus a pointer to the next node in the list. For the queue in this example, each data part is a type `Item` value, and you can use a structure to represent a node:

```
struct Node
{
    Item item;              // data stored in the node
    struct Node * next;     // pointer to next node
};
```

Figure 12.8 illustrates a linked list.

FIGURE 12.8
A linked list.

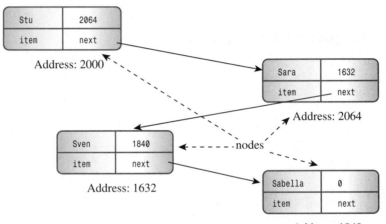

The example shown in Figure 12.8 is called a *singly linked list* because each node has a single link, or pointer, to another node. If you have the address of the first node, you can follow the pointers to each subsequent node in the list. Commonly, the pointer in the last node in the list is set to `NULL` (or, equivalently, to `0`) to indicate that there are no further nodes. To keep track of a linked list, you must know the address of the first node. You can use a data member of the `Queue` class to point to the beginning of the list. In principle, that's all the information you need because you can trace down the chain of nodes to find any other node. However, because a queue always adds a new item to the end of the queue, it is convenient to have a data member point to the last node, too (see Figure 12.9). In addition, you can use data members to keep track of the maximum number of items allowed in the queue and of the current number of items. Thus, the private part of the class declaration can look like this:

```
class Queue
{
private:
// class scope definitions
    // Node is a nested structure definition local to this class
```

```
    struct Node { Item item; struct Node * next;};
    enum {Q_SIZE = 10};
// private class members
    Node * front;        // pointer to front of Queue
    Node * rear;         // pointer to rear of Queue
    int items;           // current number of items in Queue
    const int qsize;     // maximum number of items in Queue
    ...
public:
//...
};
```

FIGURE 12.9

A `Queue` object.

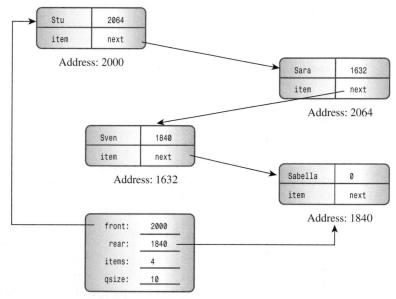

type `Queue` object

The declaration uses a new C++ feature: the ability to nest a structure or class declaration inside a class. By placing the `Node` declaration inside the `Queue` class, you give it class scope. That is, `Node` is a type that you can use to declare class members and as a type name in class methods, but the type is restricted to the class. That way, you don't have to worry about this declaration of `Node` conflicting with some global declaration or with a `Node` declared inside some other class. Not all compilers currently support nested structures and classes. If yours doesn't, then you have to define a `Node` structure globally, giving it file scope.

Nested Structures and Classes

A structure, a class, or an enumeration declared within a class declaration is said to be *nested* in the class. It has class scope. Such a declaration doesn't create a data object. Rather, it specifies a type that can be used internally within the class. If the declaration is made in the private section of the class, then the declared type can be used only within the class. If the declaration is made in the public section, then the declared type can also be used out of the class, through use of the scope-resolution operator. For example, if `Node` were declared in the public section of the `Queue` class, you could declare variables of type `Queue::Node` outside the `Queue` class.

After you settle on a data representation, the next step is to code the class methods.

The Class Methods

A class constructor should provide values for the class members. Because the queue in this example begins in an empty state, you should set the front and rear pointers to `NULL` (or `0`) and `items` to `0`. Also, you should set the maximum queue size `qsize` to the constructor argument `qs`. Here's an implementation that does not work:

```
Queue::Queue(int qs)
{
    front = rear = NULL;
    items = 0;
    qsize = qs;     // not acceptable!
}
```

The problem is that `qsize` is a `const`, so it can be *initialized to* a value, but it can't be *assigned* a value. Conceptually, calling a constructor creates an object before the code within the brackets is executed. Thus, calling the `Queue(int qs)` constructor causes the program to first allocate space for the four member variables. Then program flow enters the brackets and uses ordinary assignment to place values into the allocated space. Therefore, if you want to initialize a `const` data member, you have to do so when the object is created, before execution reaches the body of the constructor. C++ provides a special syntax for doing just that. It's called a *member initializer list*. The member initializer list consists of a comma-separated list of initializers preceded by a colon. It's placed after the closing parenthesis of the argument list and before the opening bracket of the function body. If a data member is named `mdata` and if it's to be initialized to the value `val`, the initializer has the form `mdata(val)`. Using this notation, you can write the `Queue` constructor like this:

```
Queue::Queue(int qs) : qsize(qs)    // initialize qsize to qs
{
    front = rear = NULL;
    items = 0;
}
```

In general, the initial value can involve constants and arguments from the constructor's argument list. The technique is not limited to initializing constants; you can also write the `Queue` constructor like this:

```
Queue::Queue(int qs) : qsize(qs), front(NULL), rear(NULL), items(0)
{
}
```

Only constructors can use this initializer-list syntax. As you've seen, you have to use this syntax for `const` class members. You also have to use it for class members that are declared as references:

```
class Agency {...};
class Agent
{
private:
    Agency & belong;     // must use initializer list to initialize
    ...
};
Agent::Agent(Agency & a) : belong(a) {...}
```

That's because references, like const data, can be initialized only when created. For simple data members, such as front and items, it doesn't make much difference whether you use a member initializer list or use assignment in the function body. As you'll see in Chapter 14, however, it's more efficient to use the member initializer list for members that are themselves class objects.

The Member Initializer List Syntax

If Classy is a class and if mem1, mem2, and mem3 are class data members, a class constructor can use the following syntax to initialize the data members:

```
Classy::Classy(int n, int m) :mem1(n), mem2(0), mem3(n*m + 2)
{
//...
}
```

This initializes mem1 to n, mem2 to 0, and mem3 to n*m + 2. Conceptually, these initializations take place when the object is created and before any code within the brackets is executed. Note the following:

- This form can be used only with constructors.
- You must use this form to initialize a nonstatic const data member.
- You must use this form to initialize a reference data member.

Data members are initialized in the order in which they appear in the class declaration, not in the order in which initializers are listed.

Caution

You can't use the member initializer list syntax with class methods other than constructors.

Incidentally, the parenthesized form used in the member initializer list can be used in ordinary initializations, too. That is, if you like, you can replace code like

```
int games = 162;
double talk = 2.71828;
```

with

```
int games(162);
double talk(2.71828);
```

This allows initializing built-in types to look like initializing class objects.

The code for `isempty()`, `isfull()`, and `queuecount()` is simple. If `items` is `0`, the queue is empty. If `items` is `qsize`, the queue is full. Returning the value of `items` answers the question of how many items are in the queue. You'll see the code later this chapter, in Listing 12.11.

Adding an item to the rear of the queue (enqueuing) is more involved. Here is one approach:

```cpp
bool Queue::enqueue(const Item & item)
{
    if (isfull())
        return false;
    Node * add = new Node;  // create node
    if (add == NULL)
        return false;       // quit if none available
    add->item = item;       // set node pointers
    add->next = NULL;
    items++;
    if (front == NULL)      // if queue is empty,
        front = add;        // place item at front
    else
        rear->next = add;   // else place at rear
    rear = add;             // have rear point to new node
    return true;
}
```

In brief, the method goes through the following phases (see Figure 12.10):

FIGURE 12.10

Enqueuing an item.

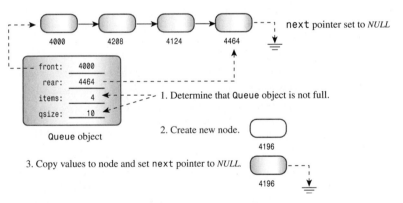

1. Determine that `Queue` object is not full.

2. Create new node.

3. Copy values to node and set `next` pointer to *NULL*.

4. and 5. Update `items` count, attach node to rear of queue, and reset `rear` pointer.

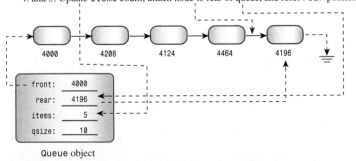

1. Terminate if the queue is already full. (For this implementation, the maximum size is selected by the user via the constructor.)

2. Create a new node, and terminate if it can't create a new node—for example, if the request for more memory fails.

3. Place proper values into the node. In this case, the code copies an `Item` value into the data part of the node and sets the node's next pointer to `NULL`. This prepares the node to be the last item in the queue.

4. Increase the item count (`items`) by one.

5. Attach the node to the rear of the queue. There are two parts to this process. The first is linking the node to the other nodes in the list. This is done by having the `next` pointer of the currently rear node point to the new rear node. The second part is to set the `Queue` member pointer `rear` to point to the new node so that the queue can access the last node directly. If the queue is empty, you must also set the `front` pointer to point to the new node. (If there's just one node, it's both the front and the rear node.)

Removing an item from the front of the queue (dequeuing) also has several steps. Here is one approach:

```
bool Queue::dequeue(Item & item)
{
    if (front == NULL)
        return false;
    item = front->item;      // set item to first item in queue
    items--;
    Node * temp = front;     // save location of first item
    front = front->next;     // reset front to next item
    delete temp;             // delete former first item
    if (items == 0)
        rear = NULL;
    return true;
}
```

In brief, the method goes through the following phases (see Figure 12.11):

1. Terminate if the queue is already empty.

2. Provide the first item in the queue to the calling function. This is accomplished by copying the data portion of the current `front` node into the reference variable passed to the method.

3. Decrease the item count (`items`) by one.

4. Save the location of the front node for later deletion.

5. Take the node off the queue. This is accomplished by setting the `Queue` member pointer `front` to point to the next node, whose address is provided by `front->next`.

6. To conserve memory, delete the former first node.

7. If the list is now empty, set `rear` to `NULL`. (The front pointer would already be `NULL` in this case, after setting `front->next`.)

Step 4 is necessary because step 5 erases the queue's memory of where the former first node is.

FIGURE 12.11
Dequeuing an item.

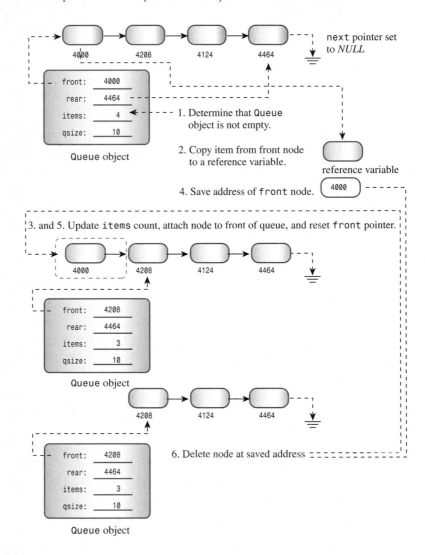

Other Class Methods?

Do you need any more methods? The class constructor doesn't use `new`, so, at first glance, it may appear that you don't have to worry about the special requirements of classes that do use `new` in the constructors. Of course, that first glance is misleading because adding objects to a queue does invoke **new** to create new nodes. It's true that the **dequeue()** method cleans up by deleting nodes, but there's no guarantee that a queue will be empty when it expires. Therefore, the class does require an explicit destructor—one that deletes all remaining nodes. Here's an implementation that starts at the front of the list and deletes each node in turn:

```
Queue::~Queue()
{
    Node * temp;
    while (front != NULL)    // while queue is not yet empty
    {
        temp = front;        // save address of front item
        front = front->next;// reset pointer to next item
        delete temp;         // delete former front
    }
}
```

Hmmm. You've seen that classes that use **new** usually require explicit copy constructors and assignment operators that do deep copying. Is that the case here? The first question to answer is Does the default memberwise copying do the right thing? The answer is no. Memberwise copying of a **Queue** object would produce a new object that points to the front and rear of the same linked list as the original. Thus, adding an item to the copy **Queue** object changes the shared linked list. That's bad enough. What's worse is that only the copy's rear pointer gets updated, essentially corrupting the list from the standpoint of the original object. Clearly, then, cloning or copying queues requires providing a copy constructor and an assignment constructor that do deep copying.

Of course, that raises the question of why you would want to copy a queue. Well, perhaps you would want to save snapshots of a queue during different stages of a simulation. Or you would like to provide identical input to two different strategies. Actually, it might be useful to have operations that split a queue, the way supermarkets sometimes do when opening an additional checkout stand. Similarly, you might want to combine two queues into one or truncate a queue.

But you don't want to do any of these things in this simulation. Can't you simply ignore those concerns and use the methods you already have? Of course you can. However, at some time in the future, you might need to use a queue again, but with copying. And you might forget that you failed to provide proper code for copying. In that case, your programs will compile and run, but they will generate puzzling results and crashes. So it would seem that it's best to provide a copy constructor and an assignment operator, even though you don't need them now.

Fortunately, there is a sneaky way to avoid doing this extra work while still protecting against future program crashes. The idea is to define the required methods as dummy private methods:

```
class Queue
{
private:
    Queue(const Queue & q) : qsize(0) { }   // preemptive definition
    Queue & operator=(const Queue & q) { return *this;}
//...
};
```

This has two effects. First, it overrides the default method definitions that otherwise would be generated automatically. Second, because these methods are private, they can't be used by the world at large. That is, if `nip` and `tuck` are `Queue` objects, the compiler won't allow the following:

```
Queue snick(nip);     // not allowed
tuck = nip;           // not allowed
```

Therefore, instead of being faced with mysterious runtime malfunctions in the future, you'll get an easier-to-trace compiler error, stating that these methods aren't accessible. Also, this trick is useful when you define a class whose objects should not be copied.

Are there any other effects to note? Yes. Recall that a copy constructor is invoked when objects are passed (or returned) by value. However, this is no problem if you follow the preferred practice of passing objects as references. Also, a copy constructor is used to create other temporary objects. But the `Queue` definition lacks operations that lead to temporary objects, such as overloading the addition operator.

The `Customer` Class

At this point, you need to design a customer class. In general, an ATM customer has many properties, such as a name, account numbers, and account balances. However, the only properties you need for the simulation are when a customer joins the queue and the time required for the customer's transaction. When the simulation produces a new customer, the program should create a new customer object, storing in it the customer's time of arrival and a randomly generated value for the transaction time. When the customer reaches the front of the queue, the program should note the time and subtract the queue-joining time to get the customer's waiting time. Here's how you can define and implement the `Customer` class:

```
class Customer
{
private:
    long arrive;        // arrival time for customer
    int processtime;    // processing time for customer
public:
    Customer() { arrive = processtime = 0; }
    void set(long when);
    long when() const { return arrive; }
    int ptime() const { return processtime; }
};
void Customer::set(long when)
{
    processtime = std::rand() % 3 + 1;
    arrive = when;
}
```

The default constructor creates a null customer. The `set()` member function sets the arrival time to its argument and randomly picks a value from 1 through 3 for the processing time.

Listing 12.10 gathers together the `Queue` and `Customer` class declarations, and Listing 12.11 provides the methods.

LISTING 12.10   queue.h

```
// queue.h -- interface for a queue
#ifndef QUEUE_H_
#define QUEUE_H_
// This queue will contain Customer items
class Customer
{
private:
    long arrive;        // arrival time for customer
    int processtime;    // processing time for customer
public:
    Customer() { arrive = processtime = 0; }
    void set(long when);
    long when() const { return arrive; }
    int ptime() const { return processtime; }
};

typedef Customer Item;

class Queue
{
private:
// class scope definitions
    // Node is a nested structure definition local to this class
    struct Node { Item item; struct Node * next;};
    enum {Q_SIZE = 10};
// private class members
    Node * front;       // pointer to front of Queue
    Node * rear;        // pointer to rear of Queue
    int items;          // current number of items in Queue
    const int qsize;    // maximum number of items in Queue
    // preemptive definitions to prevent public copying
    Queue(const Queue & q) : qsize(0) { }
    Queue & operator=(const Queue & q) { return *this;}
public:
    Queue(int qs = Q_SIZE); // create queue with a qs limit
    ~Queue();
    bool isempty() const;
    bool isfull() const;
    int queuecount() const;
    bool enqueue(const Item &item); // add item to end
    bool dequeue(Item &item);       // remove item from front
};
#endif
```

LISTING 12.11   queue.cpp

```
// queue.cpp -- Queue and Customer methods
#include "queue.h"
#include <cstdlib>              // (or stdlib.h) for rand()
```

LISTING 12.11   Continued

```
// Queue methods
Queue::Queue(int qs) : qsize(qs)
{
    front = rear = NULL;
    items = 0;
}

Queue::~Queue()
{
    Node * temp;
    while (front != NULL)    // while queue is not yet empty
    {
        temp = front;        // save address of front item
        front = front->next;// reset pointer to next item
        delete temp;         // delete former front
    }
}

bool Queue::isempty() const
{
    return items == 0;
}

bool Queue::isfull() const
{
    return items == qsize;
}

int Queue::queuecount() const
{
    return items;
}

// Add item to queue
bool Queue::enqueue(const Item & item)
{
    if (isfull())
        return false;
    Node * add = new Node;   // create node
    if (add == NULL)
        return false;        // quit if none available
    add->item = item;        // set node pointers
    add->next = NULL;
    items++;
    if (front == NULL)       // if queue is empty,
        front = add;         // place item at front
    else
        rear->next = add;    // else place at rear
    rear = add;              // have rear point to new node
    return true;
}
```

LISTING 12.11   Continued

```
// Place front item into item variable and remove from queue
bool Queue::dequeue(Item & item)
{
    if (front == NULL)
        return false;
    item = front->item;    // set item to first item in queue
    items--;
    Node * temp = front;   // save location of first item
    front = front->next;   // reset front to next item
    delete temp;           // delete former first item
    if (items == 0)
        rear = NULL;
    return true;
}


// customer method

// when is the time at which the customer arrives
// the arrival time is set to when and the processing
// time set to a random value in the range 1 - 3
void Customer::set(long when)
{
    processtime = std::rand() % 3 + 1;
    arrive = when;
}
```

Compatibility Note

You might have a compiler that has not implemented `bool`. In that case, you can use `int` instead of `bool`, `0` instead of `false`, and `1` instead of `true`. You might also have to use `stdlib.h` instead of the newer `cstdlib`.

The Simulation

You now have the tools needed for the ATM simulation. The program should allow the user to enter three quantities: the maximum queue size, the number of hours the program will simulate, and the average number of customers per hour. The program should use a loop in which each cycle represents one minute. During each minute cycle, the program should do the following:

1. Determine whether a new customer has arrived. If so, add the customer to the queue if there is room; otherwise, turn the customer away.

2. If no one is being processed, take the first person from the queue. Determine how long the person has been waiting and set a `wait_time` counter to the processing time that the new customer will need.

3. If a customer is being processed, decrement the `wait_time` counter by one minute.

4. Track various quantities, such as the number of customers served, the number of customers turned away, cumulative time spent waiting in line, and cumulative queue length.

When the simulation cycle is finished, the program should report various statistical findings.

An interesting matter is how the program determines whether a new customer has arrived. Suppose that on average, 10 customers arrive per hour. That amounts to a customer every 6 minutes. The program computes and stores that value in the variable `min_per_cust`. However, having a customer show up exactly every 6 minutes is unrealistic. What you really want (at least most of the time) is a more random process that averages to a customer every 6 minutes. The program uses this function to determine whether a customer shows up during a cycle:

```
bool newcustomer(double x)
{
    return (std::rand() * x / RAND_MAX < 1);
}
```

Here's how it works. The value `RAND_MAX` is defined in the `cstdlib` file (formerly `stdlib.h`) and represents the largest value the `rand()` function can return (`0` is the lowest value). Suppose that `x`, the average time between customers, is `6`. Then the value of `rand() * x / RAND_MAX` will be somewhere between `0` and `6`. In particular, it will be less than 1 one-sixth of the time, on average. However, it's possible that this function might yield two customers spaced 1 minute apart one time and two customers 20 minutes apart another time. This behavior leads to the clumpiness that often distinguishes real processes from the clocklike regularity of exactly one customer every 6 minutes. This particular method breaks down if the average time between arrivals drops below 1 minute, but the simulation is not intended to handle that scenario. If you did need to deal with such a case, you'd use a finer time resolution, perhaps letting each cycle represent 10 seconds.

Compatibility Note

Some compilers don't define `RAND_MAX`. If you face that situation, you can define a value for `RAND_MAX` yourself by using `#define` or else a `const int`. If you can't find the correct value documented, you can try using the largest possible `int` value, given by `INT_MAX` in the `climits` or the `limits.h` header file.

Listing 12.12 presents the details of the simulation. Running the simulation for a long time period provides insight into long-term averages, and running it for short times provides insight into short-term variations.

LISTING 12.12   `bank.cpp`

```
// bank.cpp -- using the Queue interface
// compile with queue.cpp
#include <iostream>
```

LISTING 12.12   Continued

```cpp
#include <cstdlib> // for rand() and srand()
#include <ctime>   // for time()
#include "queue.h"
const int MIN_PER_HR = 60;

bool newcustomer(double x); // is there a new customer?

int main()
{
    using std::cin;
    using std::cout;
    using std::endl;
    using std::ios_base;
// setting things up
    std::srand(std::time(0));    //  random initializing of rand()

    cout << "Case Study: Bank of Heather Automatic Teller\n";
    cout << "Enter maximum size of queue: ";
    int qs;
    cin >> qs;
    Queue line(qs);          // line queue holds up to qs people

    cout << "Enter the number of simulation hours: ";
    int hours;               //  hours of simulation
    cin >> hours;
    // simulation will run 1 cycle per minute
    long cyclelimit = MIN_PER_HR * hours; // # of cycles

    cout << "Enter the average number of customers per hour: ";
    double perhour;          //  average # of arrival per hour
    cin >> perhour;
    double min_per_cust;     //  average time between arrivals
    min_per_cust = MIN_PER_HR / perhour;

    Item temp;               //  new customer data
    long turnaways = 0;      //  turned away by full queue
    long customers = 0;      //  joined the queue
    long served = 0;         //  served during the simulation
    long sum_line = 0;       //  cumulative line length
    int wait_time = 0;       //  time until autoteller is free
    long line_wait = 0;      //  cumulative time in line


// running the simulation
    for (int cycle = 0; cycle < cyclelimit; cycle++)
    {
        if (newcustomer(min_per_cust))  // have newcomer
        {
            if (line.isfull())
                turnaways++;
            else
            {
```

LISTING 12.12   Continued

```cpp
                customers++;
                temp.set(cycle);     // cycle = time of arrival
                line.enqueue(temp); // add newcomer to line
            }
        }
        if (wait_time <= 0 && !line.isempty())
        {
            line.dequeue (temp);      // attend next customer
            wait_time = temp.ptime(); // for wait_time minutes
            line_wait += cycle - temp.when();
            served++;
        }
        if (wait_time > 0)
            wait_time--;
        sum_line += line.queuecount();
    }

// reporting results
    if (customers > 0)
    {
        cout << "customers accepted: " << customers << endl;
        cout << "  customers served: " << served << endl;
        cout << "         turnaways: " << turnaways << endl;
        cout << "average queue size: ";
        cout.precision(2);
        cout.setf(ios_base::fixed, ios_base::floatfield);
        cout.setf(ios_base::showpoint);
        cout << (double) sum_line / cyclelimit << endl;
        cout << " average wait time: "
             << (double) line_wait / served << " minutes\n";
    }
    else
        cout << "No customers!\n";
    cout << "Done!\n";

    return 0;
}

//  x = average time, in minutes, between customers
//  return value is true if customer shows up this minute
bool newcustomer(double x)
{
    return (std::rand() * x / RAND_MAX < 1);
}
```

Compatibility Note

You might have a compiler that has not implemented `bool`. In that case, you can use `int` instead of `bool`, `0` instead of `false`, and `1` instead of `true`. You might also have to use `stdlib.h` and `time.h` instead of the newer `cstdlib` and `ctime`. You might have to define `RAND_MAX` yourself.

Here are a few sample runs of the program built from Listings 12.10, 12.11, and 12.12 for a longer time period:

```
Case Study: Bank of Heather Automatic Teller
Enter maximum size of queue: 10
Enter the number of simulation hours: 100
Enter the average number of customers per hour: 15
customers accepted: 1485
  customers served: 1485
        turnaways: 0
average queue size: 0.15
 average wait time: 0.63 minutes

Case Study: Bank of Heather Automatic Teller
Enter maximum size of queue: 10
Enter the number of simulation hours: 100
Enter the average number of customers per hour: 30
customers accepted: 2896
  customers served: 2888
        turnaways: 101
average queue size: 4.64
 average wait time: 9.63 minutes

Case Study: Bank of Heather Automatic Teller
Enter maximum size of queue: 20
Enter the number of simulation hours: 100
Enter the average number of customers per hour: 30
customers accepted: 2943
  customers served: 2943
        turnaways: 93
average queue size: 13.06
 average wait time: 26.63 minutes
```

Note that going from 15 customers per hour to 30 customers per hour doesn't double the average wait time; it increases it by about a factor of 15. Allowing a longer queue just makes matters worse. However, the simulation doesn't allow for the fact that many customers, frustrated with a long wait, would simply leave the queue.

Here are a few more sample runs of the program in Listing 12.12; they illustrate the short-term variations you might see, even though the average number of customers per hour is kept constant:

```
Case Study: Bank of Heather Automatic Teller
Enter maximum size of queue: 10
Enter the number of simulation hours: 4
Enter the average number of customers per hour: 30
customers accepted: 114
  customers served: 110
        turnaways: 0
average queue size: 2.15
 average wait time: 4.52 minutes

Case Study: Bank of Heather Automatic Teller
Enter maximum size of queue: 10
```

```
Enter the number of simulation hours: 4
Enter the average number of customers per hour: 30
customers accepted: 121
  customers served: 116
        turnaways: 5
average queue size: 5.28
 average wait time: 10.72 minutes

Case Study: Bank of Heather Automatic Teller
Enter maximum size of queue: 10
Enter the number of simulation hours: 4
Enter the average number of customers per hour: 30
customers accepted: 112
  customers served: 109
        turnaways: 0
average queue size: 2.41
 average wait time: 5.16 minutes
```

Summary

This chapter covers many important aspects of defining and using classes. Several of these aspects are subtle—even difficult—concepts. If some of them seem obscure or unusually complex to you, don't feel bad; they affect most newcomers to C++ that way. Often, the way you come to really appreciate concepts such as copy constructors is through getting into trouble by ignoring them. So some of the material in this chapter may seem vague to you until your own experiences enrich your understanding.

You can use **new** in a class constructor to allocate memory for data and then assign the address of the memory to a class member. This enables a class, for example, to handle strings of various sizes without committing the class design in advance to a fixed array size. Using **new** in class constructors also raises potential problems when an object expires. If an object has member pointers pointing to memory allocated by **new**, freeing the memory used to hold the object does not automatically free the memory pointed to by the object member pointers. Therefore, if you use **new** in a class constructor to allocate memory, you should use **delete** in the class destructor to free that memory. That way, the demise of an object automatically triggers the deletion of pointed-to memory.

Objects that have members pointing to memory allocated by **new** also have problems with initializing one object to another or assigning one object to another. By default, C++ uses memberwise initialization and assignment, which means that the initialized or the assigned-to object winds up with exact copies of the original object's members. If an original member points to a block of data, the copy member points to the same block. When the program eventually deletes the two objects, the class destructor attempts to delete the same block of memory twice, which is an error. The solution is to define a special copy constructor that redefines initialization and to overload the assignment operator. In each case, the new definition should create duplicates of any pointed-to data and have the new object point to the copies. That way, both the old and the new objects refer to separate but identical data, with no overlap. The same reasoning applies to defining an assignment operator. In each case, the goal is to make a deep copy—that is, to copy the real data and not just pointers to the data.

When an object has automatic storage or external storage, the destructor for that object is called automatically when the object ceases to exist. If you allocate storage for an object by using new and assign its address to a pointer, the destructor for that object is called automatically when you apply `delete` to the pointer. However, if you allocate storage for class objects by using placement new instead of regular new, you also take on the responsibility of calling the destructor for that object explicitly by invoking the destructor method with a pointer to the object. C++ allows you to place structure, class, and enumeration definitions inside a class. Such nested types have class scope, meaning that they are local to the class and don't conflict with structures, classes, and enumerations of the same name that are defined elsewhere.

C++ provides a special syntax for class constructors that can be used to initialize data members. This syntax consists of a colon followed by a comma-separated list of initializers. This is placed after the closing parenthesis of the constructor arguments and before the opening brace of the function body. Each initializer consists of the name of the member being initialized followed by parentheses containing the initialization value. Conceptually, these initializations take place when the object is created and before any statements in the function body are executed. The syntax looks like this:

```
queue(int qs) : qsize(qs), items(0), front(NULL), rear(NULL) { }
```

This form is obligatory if the data member is a nonstatic `const` member or a reference.

As you might have noticed, classes require much more care and attention to detail than do simple C-style structures. In return, they do much more for you.

Review Questions

1. Suppose a `String` class has the following private members:

```
class String
{
private:
    char * str;     // points to string allocated by new
    int len;        // holds length of string
//...
};
```

   a. What's wrong with this default constructor?

```
String::String() {}
```

   b. What's wrong with this constructor?

```
String::String(const char * s)
{
    str = s;
    len = strlen(s);
}
```

c. What's wrong with this constructor?

```
String::String(const char * s)
{
    strcpy(str, s);
    len = strlen(s);
}
```

2. Name three problems that may arise if you define a class in which a pointer member is initialized by using **new**. Indicate how they can be remedied.

3. What class methods does the compiler generate automatically if you don't provide them explicitly? Describe how these implicitly generated functions behave.

4. Identify and correct the errors in the following class declaration:

```
class nifty
{
// data
    char personality[];
    int talents;
// methods
    nifty();
    nifty(char * s);
    ostream & operator<<(ostream & os, nifty & n);
}

nifty:nifty()
{
    personality = NULL;
    talents = 0;
}

nifty:nifty(char * s)
{
    personality = new char [strlen(s)];
    personality = s;
    talents = 0;
}

ostream & nifty:operator<<(ostream & os, nifty & n)
{
    os << n;
}
```

5. Consider the following class declaration:

```
class Golfer
{
private:
    char * fullname;     // points to string containing golfer's name
    int games;           // holds number of golf games played
    int * scores;        // points to first element of array of golf scores
public:
    Golfer();
```

```
    Golfer(const char * name, int g= 0);
     // creates empty dynamic array of g elements if g > 0
    Golfer(const Golfer & g);
    ~Golfer();
};
```

a. What class methods would be invoked by each of the following statements?

```
Golfer nancy;                          // #1
Golfer lulu("Little Lulu");            // #2
Golfer roy("Roy Hobbs", 12);           // #3
Golfer * par = new Golfer;             // #4
Golfer next = lulu;                    // #5
Golfer hazzard = "Weed Thwacker";      // #6
*par = nancy;                          // #7
nancy = "Nancy Putter";                // #8
```

b. Clearly, the class requires several more methods to make it useful. What additional method does it require to protect against data corruption?

Programming Exercises

1. Consider the following class declaration:

```
class Cow {
    char name[20];
    char * hobby;
    double weight;
public:
    Cow();
    Cow(const char * nm, const char * ho, double wt);
    Cow(const Cow c&);
    ~Cow();
    Cow & operator=(const Cow & c);
    void ShowCow() const;  // display all cow data
};
```

Provide the implementation for this class and write a short program that uses all the member functions.

2. Enhance the String class declaration (that is, upgrade string1.h to string2.h) by doing the following:

a. Overload the + operator to allow you to join two strings into one.

b. Provide a stringlow() member function that converts all alphabetic characters in a string to lowercase. (Don't forget the cctype family of character functions.)

c. Provide a stringup() member function that converts all alphabetic characters in a string to uppercase.

d. Provide a member function that takes a char argument and returns the number of times the character appears in the string.

Test your work in the following program:

```cpp
// pe12_2.cpp
#include <iostream>
using namespace std;
#include "string2.h"
int main()
{
    String s1(" and I am a C++ student.");
    String s2 = "Please enter your name: ";
    String s3;
    cout << s2;                 // overloaded << operator
    cin >> s3;                  // overloaded >> operator
    s2 = "My name is " + s3;    // overloaded =, + operators
    cout << s2 << ".\n";
    s2 = s2 + s1;
    s2.stringup();              // converts string to uppercase
    cout << "The string\n" << s2 << "\ncontains " << s2.has('A')
         << " 'A' characters in it.\n";
    s1 = "red";       // String(const char *),
                      // then String & operator=(const String&)
    String rgb[3] = { String(s1), String("green"), String("blue")};
    cout << "Enter the name of a primary color for mixing light: ";
    String ans;
    bool success = false;
    while (cin >> ans)
    {
        ans.stringlow();        // converts string to lowercase
        for (int i = 0; i < 3; i++)
        {
            if (ans == rgb[i])  // overloaded == operator
            {
                cout << "That's right!\n";
                success = true;
                break;
            }
        }
        if (success)
            break;
        else
            cout << "Try again!\n";
    }
    cout << "Bye\n";
    return 0;
}
```

Your output should look like this sample run:

```
Please enter your name: Fretta Farbo
My name is Fretta Farbo.
The string
MY NAME IS FRETTA FARBO AND I AM A C++ STUDENT.
contains 6 'A' characters in it.
```

```
Enter the name of a primary color for mixing light: yellow
Try again!
BLUE
That's right!
Bye
```

3. Rewrite the `Stock` class, as described in Listings 10.7 and 10.8 in Chapter 10, so that it uses dynamically allocated memory directly instead of using `string` class objects to hold the stock names. Also, replace the `show()` member function with an overloaded `operator<<()` definition. Test the new definition program in Listing 10.9.

4. Consider the following variation of the `Stack` class defined in Listing 10.10:

```
// stack.h -- class declaration for the stack ADT
typedef unsigned long Item;

class Stack
{
private:
    enum {MAX = 10};        // constant specific to class
    Item  * pitems;         // holds stack items
    int size;               // number of elements in stack
    int top;                // index for top stack item
public:
    Stack(int n = 10);      // creates stack with n elements
    Stack(const Stack & st);
    ~Stack();
    bool isempty() const;
    bool isfull() const;
    // push() returns false if stack already is full, true otherwise
    bool push(const Item & item); // add item to stack
    // pop() returns false if stack already is empty, true otherwise
    bool pop(Item & item);  // pop top into item
    Stack & operator=(const Stack & st);
};
```

As the private members suggest, this class uses a dynamically allocated array to hold the stack items. Rewrite the methods to fit this new representation and write a program that demonstrates all the methods, including the copy constructor and assignment operator.

5. The Bank of Heather has performed a study showing that ATM customers won't wait more than one minute in line. Using the simulation from Listing 12.10, find a value for number of customers per hour that leads to an average wait time of one minute. (Use at least a 100-hour trial period.)

6. The Bank of Heather would like to know what would happen if it added a second ATM. Modify the simulation in this chapter so that it has two queues. Assume that a customer will join the first queue if it has fewer people in it than the second queue and that the customer will join the second queue otherwise. Again, find a value for number of customers per hour that leads to an average wait time of one minute. (Note: This is a non-linear problem in that doubling the number of ATMs doesn't double the number of customers who can be handled per hour with a one-minute wait maximum.)

CHAPTER 13

CLASS INHERITANCE

In this chapter you'll learn about the following:

- Inheritance as an *is-a* relationship
- How to publicly derive one class from another
- Protected access
- Constructor member initializer lists
- Upcasting and downcasting
- Virtual member functions
- Early (static) binding and late (dynamic) binding
- Abstract base classes
- Pure virtual functions
- When and how to use public inheritance

One of the main goals of object-oriented programming is to provide reusable code. When you develop a new project, particularly if the project is large, it's nice to be able to reuse proven code rather than to reinvent it. Employing old code saves time and, because it has already been used and tested, can help suppress the introduction of bugs into a program. Also, the less you have to concern yourself with details, the better you can concentrate on overall program strategy.

Traditional C function libraries provide reusability through predefined, precompiled functions, such as `strlen()` and `rand()`, that you can use in your programs. Many vendors furnish specialized C libraries that provide functions beyond those of the standard C library. For example, you can purchase libraries of database management functions and of screen control functions. However, function libraries have a limitation: Unless the vendor supplies the source code for its library functions (and often it doesn't), you can't extend or modify the functions to meet your particular needs. Instead, you have to shape your program to meet the workings of the library. Even if the vendor does supply the source code, you run the risk of unintentionally modifying how part of a function works or of altering the relationships among library functions as you add your changes.

C++ classes bring a higher level of reusability. Many vendors now offer class libraries, which consist of class declarations and implementations. Because a class combines data representation with class methods, it provides a more integrated package than does a function library. A single class, for example, may provide all the resources for managing a dialog box. Often, class libraries are available in source code, which means you can modify them to meet your needs. But C++ has a better method than code modification for extending and modifying classes. This method, called *class inheritance*, lets you derive new classes from old ones, with the derived class inheriting the properties, including the methods, of the old class, called a *base class*. Just as inheriting a fortune is usually easier than earning one from scratch, deriving a class through inheritance is usually easier than designing a new one. Here are some things you can do with inheritance:

- You can add functionality to an existing class. For example, given a basic array class, you could add arithmetic operations.

- You can add to the data that a class represents. For example, given a basic string class, you could derive a class that adds a data member representing a color to be used when displaying the string.

- You can modify how a class method behaves. For example, given a `Passenger` class that represents the services provided to an airline passenger, you can derive a `FirstClassPassenger` class that provides a higher level of services.

Of course, you could accomplish the same aims by duplicating the original class code and modifying it, but the inheritance mechanism allows you to proceed by just providing the new features. You don't even need access to the source code to derive a class. Thus, if you purchase a class library that provides only the header files and the compiled code for class methods, you can still derive new classes based on the library classes. Conversely, you can distribute your own classes to others, keeping parts of your implementation secret, yet still giving your clients the option of adding features to your classes.

Inheritance is a splendid concept, and its basic implementation is quite simple. But managing inheritance so that it works properly in all situations requires some adjustments. This chapter looks at both the simple and the subtle aspects of inheritance.

Beginning with a Simple Base Class

When one class inherits from another, the original class is called a *base class* and the inheriting class is called a *derived class*. So, to illustrate inheritance, let's begin with a base class. The Webtown Social Club has decided to keep track of its members who play table tennis. As head programmer for the club, you have designed the simple `TableTennisPlayer` class defined in Listings 13.1 and 13.2.

LISTING 13.1 `tabtenn0.h`

```
// tabtenn0.h -- a table-tennis base class
#ifndef TABTENN0_H_
#define TABTENN0_H_
// simple base class
class TableTennisPlayer
{
```

LISTING 13.1   Continued

```
private:
    enum {LIM = 20};
    char firstname[LIM];
    char lastname[LIM];
    bool hasTable;
public:
    TableTennisPlayer (const char * fn = "none",
                        const char * ln = "none", bool ht = false);
    void Name() const;
    bool HasTable() const { return hasTable; };
    void ResetTable(bool v) { hasTable = v; };
};
#endif
```

LISTING 13.2   tabtenn0.cpp

```
//tabtenn0.cpp -- simple base-class methods
#include "tabtenn0.h"
#include <iostream>
#include <cstring>

TableTennisPlayer::TableTennisPlayer (const char * fn, const char * ln,
                bool ht)
{
    std::strncpy(firstname, fn, LIM - 1);
    firstname[LIM - 1] = '\0';
    std::strncpy(lastname, ln, LIM - 1);
    lastname[LIM - 1] = '\0';
    hasTable = ht;
}

void TableTennisPlayer::Name() const
{
    std::cout << lastname << ", " << firstname;
}
```

All the `TableTennisPlayer` class does is keep track of the players' names and whether they have tables. Listing 13.3 shows this modest class in action.

LISTING 13.3   usett0.cpp

```
// usett0.cpp -- using a base class
#include <iostream>
#include "tabtenn0.h"

int main ( void )
{
    using std::cout;
    TableTennisPlayer player1("Chuck", "Blizzard", true);
    TableTennisPlayer player2("Tara", "Boomdea", false);
```

LISTING 13.3   Continued

```
    player1.Name();
    if (player1.HasTable())
        cout << ": has a table.\n";
    else
        cout << ": hasn't a table.\n";
    player2.Name();
    if (player2.HasTable())
        cout << ": has a table";
    else
        cout << ": hasn't a table.\n";

    return 0;
}
```

And here's the output of the program in Listings 13.1, 13.2, and 13.3:

```
Blizzard, Chuck: has a table.
Boomdea, Tara: hasn't a table.
```

Deriving a Class

Some members of the Webtown Social Club have played in local table tennis tournaments, and they demand a class that includes the point ratings they've earned through their play. Rather than start from scratch, you can derive a class from the `TableTennisPlayer` class. The first step is to have the `RatedPlayer` class declaration show that it derives from the `TableTennisPlayer` class:

```
// RatedPlayer derives from the TableTennisPlayer base class
class RatedPlayer : public TableTennisPlayer
{
...
};
```

The colon indicates that the `RatedPlayer` class is based on the `TableTennisPlayer` class. This particular heading indicates that `TableTennisPlayer` is a public base class; this is termed *public derivation*. An object of a derived class incorporates a base class object. With public derivation, the public members of the base class become public members of the derived class. The private portions of a base class become part of the derived class, but they can be accessed only through public and protected methods of the base class. (We'll get to protected members in a bit.)

What does this accomplish? If you declare a `RatedPlayer` object, it has the following special properties:

- An object of the derived type has stored within it the data members of the base type. (The derived class inherits the base-class implementation.)

- An object of the derived type can use the methods of the base type. (The derived class inherits the base-class interface.)

Thus, a `RatedPlayer` object can store the first name and last name of each player and whether the player has a table. Also, a `RatedPlayer` object can use the `Name()`, `HasTable()`, and `ResetTable()` methods from the `TableTennisPlayer` class. (See Figure 13.1.)

FIGURE 13.1
Base-class and derived-class objects.

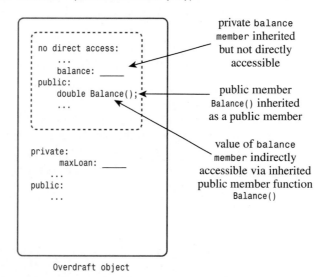

Overdraft object

What needs to be added to these inherited features?

- A derived class needs its own constructors.

- A derived class can add additional data members and member functions as needed.

In this particular case, the class needs one more data member to hold the `ratings` value. It should also have a method for retrieving the rating and a method for resetting the rating. So the class declaration could look like this:

```
// simple derived class
class RatedPlayer : public TableTennisPlayer
{
private:
    unsigned int rating;     // add a data member
```

```
public:
    RatedPlayer (unsigned int r = 0, const char * fn = "none",
                    const char * ln = "none", bool ht = false);
    RatedPlayer(unsigned int r, const TableTennisPlayer & tp);
    unsigned int Rating() { return rating; }       // add a method
    void ResetRating (unsigned int r) {rating = r;} // add a method
};
```

The constructors have to provide data for the new members, if any, and for the inherited members. The first `RatedPlayer` constructor uses a separate formal parameter for each member, and the second `RatedPlayer` constructor uses a `TableTennisPlayer` parameter, which bundles three items (`firstname`, `lastname`, and `hasTable`) into a single unit.

Constructors: Access Considerations

A derived class does not have direct access to the private members of the base class; it has to work through the base-class methods. For example, the `RatedPlayer` constructors cannot directly set the inherited members (`firstname`, `lastname`, and `hasTable`). Instead, they have to use public base-class methods to access private base-class members. In particular, the derived-class constructors have to use the base-class constructors.

When a program constructs a derived-class object, it first constructs the base-class object. Conceptually, that means the base-class object should be constructed before the program enters the body of the derived-class constructor. C++ uses the member initializer list syntax to accomplish this. Here, for instance, is the code for the first `RatedPlayer` constructor:

```
RatedPlayer::RatedPlayer(unsigned int r, const char * fn,
    const char * ln, bool ht) : TableTennisPlayer(fn, ln, ht)
{
    rating = r;
}
```

The

```
: TableTennisPlayer(fn, ln, ht)
```

part is the member initializer list. It's executable code, and it calls the `TableTennisPlayer` constructor. Suppose, for example, a program has the following declaration:

```
RatedPlayer rplayer1(1140, "Mallory", "Duck", true);
```

The `RatedPlayer` constructor assigns the actual arguments `"Mallory"`, `"Duck"`, and `true` to the formal parameters `fn`, `ln`, and `ht`. It then passes these parameters on as actual arguments to the `TableTennisPlayer` constructor. This constructor, in turn, creates the embedded `TableTennisPlayer` object and stores the data `"Mallory"`, `"Duck"`, and `true` in it. Then the program enters the body of the `RatedPlayer` constructor, completes the construction of the `RatedPlayer` object, and assigns the value of the parameter r (that is, `1140`) to the `rating` member. (See Figure 13.2.)

FIGURE 13.2

Passing arguments through to a base-class constructor.

derived-class constructor

passing arguments from the derived-class constructor to the base-class constructor

```
Overdraft::Overdraft(const char * s, long an, double bal,

        double ml, double r) : BandAccount(s, an, bal)
    {
        ...
    }
```

base-class constructor

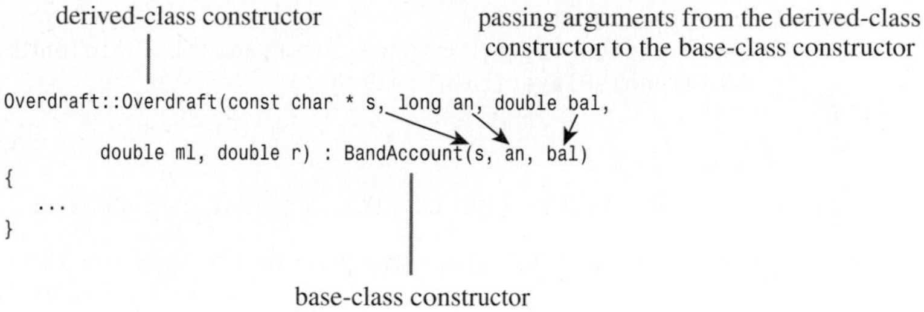

What if you omit the member initializer list?

```
RatedPlayer::RatedPlayer(unsigned int r, const char * fn,
    const char * ln, bool ht) // what if no initializer list?
{
    rating = r;
}
```

The base-class object must be created first, so if you omit calling a base-class constructor, the program uses the default base-class constructor. Therefore, the previous code is the same as the following:

```
RatedPlayer::RatedPlayer(unsigned int r, const char * fn,
    const char * ln, bool ht) // : TableTennisPlayer()
{
    rating = r;
}
```

Unless you want the default constructor to be used, you should explicitly provide the correct base-class constructor call.

Now let's look at code for the second constructor:

```
RatedPlayer::RatedPlayer(unsigned int r, const TableTennisPlayer & tp)
    : TableTennisPlayer(tp)
{
    rating = r;
}
```

Again, the `TableTennisPlayer` information is passed on to a `TableTennisPlayer` constructor:

```
TableTennisPlayer(tp)
```

Because `tp` is type `const TableTennisPlayer &`, this call invokes the base-class copy constructor. The base class doesn't define a copy constructor, but recall from Chapter 12, "Classes and Dynamic Memory Allocation," that the compiler automatically generates a copy constructor if one is needed and you haven't defined one already. In this case, the implicit copy constructor, which does memberwise copying, is fine because the class doesn't use dynamic memory allocation.

You may, if you like, also use member initializer list syntax for members of the derived class. In this case, you use the member name instead of the class name in the list. Thus, the second constructor can also be written in this manner:

```
// alternative version
RatedPlayer::RatedPlayer(unsigned int r, const TableTennisPlayer & tp)
    : TableTennisPlayer(tp), rating(r)
{
}
```

These are the key points about constructors for derived classes:

- The base-class object is constructed first.

- The derived-class constructor should pass base-class information to a base-class constructor via a member initializer list.

- The derived-class constructor should initialize the data members that were added to the derived class.

This example doesn't provide explicit destructors, so the implicit destructors are used. Destroying an object occurs in the opposite order used to construct an object. That is, the body of the derived-class destructor is executed first, and then the base-class destructor is called automatically.

Remember

When creating an object of a derived class, a program first calls the base-class constructor and then calls the derived-class constructor. The base-class constructor is responsible for initializing the inherited data members. The derived-class constructor is responsible for initializing any added data members. A derived-class constructor always calls a base-class constructor. You can use the initializer list syntax to indicate *which* base-class constructor to use. Otherwise, the default base-class constructor is used.

When an object of a derived class expires, the program first calls the derived-class destructor and then calls the base-class destructor.

Member Initializer Lists

A constructor for a derived class can use the initializer list mechanism to pass values along to a base-class constructor. Consider this example:

```
derived::derived(type1 x, type2 y) : base(x,y) // initializer list
{
    ...
}
```

Here, `derived` is the derived class, `base` is the base class, and x and y are variables used by the base-class constructor. If, say, the derived-class constructor receives the arguments 10 and 12, this mechanism then passes 10 and 12 on to the base-class constructor defined as taking arguments of these types. Except for the case of virtual base classes (see Chapter 14, "Reusing Code in C++"), a class can pass values back only to its immediate base class. However, that class can use the same mechanism to pass back information to its immediate base class, and so on. If you don't supply a base-class constructor in a member initializer list, the program uses the default base-class constructor. The member initializer list can be used *only* with constructors.

Using a Derived Class

To use a derived class, a program needs access to the base-class declarations. Listing 13.4 places both class declarations in the same header file. You could give each class its own header file, but because the two classes are related, it makes more organizational sense to keep the class declarations together.

LISTING 13.4   `tabtenn1.h`

```
// tabtenn1.h  -- simple inheritance
#ifndef TABTENN1_H_
#define TABTENN1_H_
// simple base class
class TableTennisPlayer
{
private:
    enum {LIM = 20};
    char firstname[LIM];
    char lastname[LIM];
    bool hasTable;
public:
    TableTennisPlayer (const char * fn = "none",
                       const char * ln = "none", bool ht = false);
    void Name() const;
    bool HasTable() const { return hasTable; } ;
    void ResetTable(bool v) { hasTable = v; };
};

// simple derived class
class RatedPlayer : public TableTennisPlayer
{
private:
    unsigned int rating;
public:
    RatedPlayer (unsigned int r = 0, const char * fn = "none",
                     const char * ln = "none", bool ht = false);
    RatedPlayer(unsigned int r, const TableTennisPlayer & tp);
    unsigned int Rating() { return rating; }
    void ResetRating (unsigned int r) {rating = r;}
};

#endif
```

Listing 13.5 provides the method definitions for both classes. Again, you could use separate files, but it's simpler to keep the definitions together.

LISTING 13.5   `tabtenn1.cpp`

```
// tabtenn1.cpp -- base-class methods and derived-class methods
#include "tabtenn1.h"
#include <iostream>
#include <cstring>
```

LISTING 13.5 Continued

```
// TableTennisPlayer methods
TableTennisPlayer::TableTennisPlayer (const char * fn, const char * ln,
            bool ht)
{
    std::strncpy(firstname, fn, LIM - 1);
    firstname[LIM - 1] = '\0';
    std::strncpy(lastname, ln, LIM - 1);
    lastname[LIM - 1] = '\0';
    hasTable = ht;
}

void TableTennisPlayer::Name() const
{
    std::cout << lastname << ", " << firstname;
}

// RatedPlayer methods
RatedPlayer::RatedPlayer(unsigned int r, const char * fn,
    const char * ln, bool ht) : TableTennisPlayer(fn, ln, ht)
{
    rating = r;
}

RatedPlayer::RatedPlayer(unsigned int r, const TableTennisPlayer & tp)
    : TableTennisPlayer(tp), rating(r)
{
}
```

Listing 13.6 creates objects of both the `TableTennisPlayer` class and the `RatedPlayer` class.
Notice that objects of both classes can use the `TableTennisPlayer` class `Name()` and
`HasTable()` methods.

LISTING 13.6 usett1.cpp

```
// usett1.cpp -- using base class and derived class
#include <iostream>
#include "tabtenn1.h"

int main ( void )
{
    using std::cout;
    using std::endl;
    TableTennisPlayer player1("Tara", "Boomdea", false);
    RatedPlayer rplayer1(1140, "Mallory", "Duck", true);
    rplayer1.Name();        // derived object uses base method
    if (rplayer1.HasTable())
        cout << ": has a table.\n";
    else
        cout << ": hasn't a table.\n";
    player1.Name();            // base object uses base method
```

LISTING 13.6   Continued

```
        if (player1.HasTable())
            cout << ": has a table";
        else
            cout << ": hasn't a table.\n";
        cout << "Name: ";
        rplayer1.Name();
        cout << "; Rating: " << rplayer1.Rating() << endl;
        RatedPlayer rplayer2(1212, player1);
        cout << "Name: ";
        rplayer2.Name();
        cout << "; Rating: " << rplayer2.Rating() << endl;

        return 0;
}
```

Here is the output of the program in Listings 13.4, 13.5, and 13.6:

```
Duck, Mallory: has a table.
Boomdea, Tara: hasn't a table.
Name: Duck, Mallory; Rating: 1140
Name: Boomdea, Tara; Rating: 1212
```

Special Relationships Between Derived and Base Classes

A derived class has some special relationships with the base class. One, which you've just seen, is that a derived-class object can use base-class methods, provided that the methods are not private:

```
RatedPlayer rplayer1(1140, "Mallory", "Duck", true);
rplayer1.Name();  // derived object uses base method
```

Two other important relationships are that a base-class pointer can point to a derived-class object without an explicit type cast and that a base-class reference can refer to a derived-class object without an explicit type cast:

```
RatedPlayer rplayer1(1140, "Mallory", "Duck", true);
TableTennisPlayer & rt = rplayer;
TableTennisPlayer * pt = &rplayer;
rt.Name();   // invoke Name() with reference
pt->Name();  // invoke Name() with pointer
```

However, a base-class pointer or reference can invoke just base-class methods, so you couldn't use rt or pt to invoke, say, the derived-class ResetRanking() method.

Ordinarily, C++ requires that references and pointer types match the assigned types, but this rule is relaxed for inheritance. However, the rule relaxation is just in one direction. You can't assign base-class objects and addresses to derived-class references and pointers:

```
TableTennisPlayer player("Betsy", "Bloop", true);
RatedPlayer & rr = player;      // NOT ALLOWED
RatedPlayer * pr = player;      // NOT ALLOWED
```

Both these sets of rules make sense. For example, consider the implications of having a base-class reference refer to a derived object. In this case, you can use the base-class reference to invoke base-class methods for the derived-class object. Because the derived class inherits the base-class methods and data members, this causes no problems. Now consider what would happen if you could assign a base-class object to a derived-class reference. The derived-class reference would be able to invoke derived-class methods for the base object, and that could cause problems. For example, applying the `RatedPlayer::Rating()` method to a `TableTennisPlayer` object makes no sense because the `TableTennisPlayer` object doesn't have a `rating` member.

The fact that base-class references and pointers can refer to derived-class objects has some interesting consequences. One is that functions defined with base-class reference or pointer arguments can be used with either base-class or derived-class objects. For instance, consider this function:

```
void Show(const TableTennisPlayer & rt)
{
    cout << "Name: ";
    rt.Name();
    cout << "\nTable: ";
    if (rt.HasTable())
        cout << "yes\n";
    else
        cout << "no\n";
}
```

The formal parameter `rt` is a reference to a base class, so it can refer to a base-class object or to a derived-class object. Thus, you can use `Show()` with either a `TableTennis` argument or a `RatedPlayer` argument:

```
TableTennisPlayer player1("Tara", "Boomdea", false);
RatedPlayer rplayer1(1140, "Mallory", "Duck", true);
Show(player1);   // works with TableTennisPlayer argument
Show(rplayer1);  // works with RatedPlayer argument
```

A similar relationship would hold for a function with a pointer-to-base-class formal parameter; it could be used with either the address of a base-class object or the address of a derived-class object as an actual argument:

```
void Wohs(const TableTennisPlayer * pt);  // function with pointer parameter
...
TableTennisPlayer player1("Tara", "Boomdea", false);
RatedPlayer rplayer1(1140, "Mallory", "Duck", true);
Wohs(&player1);   // works with TableTennisPlayer * argument
Wohs(&rplayer1);  // works with RatedPlayer * argument
```

The reference compatibility property also allows you to initialize a base-class object to a derived-class object, although somewhat indirectly. Suppose you have this code:

```
RatedPlayer olaf1(1840, "Olaf", "Loaf", true);
TableTennisPlayer olaf2(olaf1);
```

The exact match for initializing `olaf2` would be a constructor with this prototype:

```
TableTennisPlayer(const RatedPlayer &);          // doesn't exist
```

The class definitions don't include this constructor, but there is the implicit copy constructor:

```
// implicit copy constructor
TableTennisPlayer(const TableTennisPlayer &);
```

The formal parameter is a reference to the base type, so it can refer to a derived type. Thus, the attempt to initialize `olaf2` to `olaf1` uses this constructor, which copies the `firstname`, `lastname`, and `hasTable` members. In other words, it initializes `olaf2` to the `TableTennisPlayer` object embedded in the `RatedPlayer` object `olaf1`.

Similarly, you can assign a derived-class object to a base-class object:

```
RatedPlayer olaf1(1840, "Olaf", "Loaf", true);
TableTennisPlayer winner;
winner = olaf1; // assign derived to base object
```

In this case, the program uses the implicit overloaded assignment operator:

```
TableTennisPlayer & operator=(const TableTennisPlayer &) const;
```

Again, a base-class reference refers to a derived-class object, and just the base-class portion of `olaf1` is copied to `winner`.

Inheritance: An *Is-a* Relationship

The special relationship between a derived class and a base class is based on an underlying model for C++ inheritance. Actually, C++ has three varieties of inheritance: public, protected, and private. Public inheritance is the most common form, and it models an *is-a* relationship. This is shorthand for saying that an object of a derived class should also be an object of the base class. Anything you do with a base-class object, you should be able to do with a derived-class object. Suppose, for example, that you have a `Fruit` class. It could store, say, the weight and caloric content of a fruit. Because a banana is a particular kind of fruit, you could derive a `Banana` class from the `Fruit` class. The new class would inherit all the data members of the original class, so a `Banana` object would have members representing the weight and caloric content of a banana. The new `Banana` class also might add members that apply particularly to bananas and not to fruit in general, such as the Banana Institute Peel Index. Because the derived class can add features, it's probably more accurate to describe the relationship as an *is-a-kind-of* relationship, but *is-a* is the usual term.

To clarify *is-a* relationships, let's look at some examples that don't match that model. Public inheritance doesn't model a *has-a* relationship. A lunch, for example, might contain a fruit. But a lunch, in general, is not a fruit. Therefore, you should not derive a `Lunch` class from the `Fruit` class in an attempt to place fruit in a lunch. The correct way to handle putting fruit into a lunch is to consider the matter as a *has-a* relationship: A lunch has a fruit. As you'll see in Chapter 14, that's most easily modeled by including a `Fruit` object as a data member of a `Lunch` class (see Figure 13.3).

FIGURE 13.3

Is-a and *has-a* relationships.

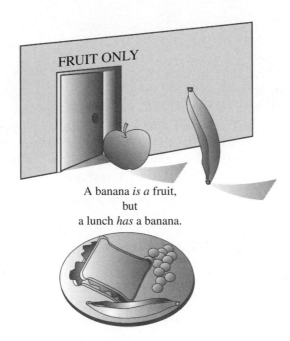

A banana *is a* fruit,
but
a lunch *has* a banana.

Public inheritance doesn't model an *is-like-a* relationship—that is, it doesn't do similes. It's often pointed out that lawyers are like sharks. But it is not literally true that a lawyer is a shark. For example, sharks can live underwater. Therefore, you shouldn't derive a `Lawyer` class from a `Shark` class. Inheritance can add properties to a base class; it doesn't remove properties from a base class. In some cases, shared characteristics can be handled by designing a class encompassing those characteristics and then using that class, either in an *is-a* or *has-a* relationship, to define the related classes.

Public inheritance doesn't model an *is-implemented-as-a* relationship. For example, you could implement a stack by using an array. However, it wouldn't be proper to derive a `Stack` class from an `Array` class. A stack is not an array. For example, array indexing is not a stack property. Also, a stack could be implemented in some other way, such as by using a linked list. A proper approach would be to hide the array implementation by giving the stack a private `Array` object member.

Public inheritance doesn't model a *uses-a* relationship. For example, a computer can use a laser printer, but it doesn't make sense to derive a `Printer` class from a `Computer` class, or vice versa. You might, however, devise friend functions or classes to handle communication between `Printer` objects and `Computer` objects.

Nothing in the C++ language prevents you from using public inheritance to model *has-a*, *is-implemented-as-a*, or *uses-a* relationships. However, doing so usually leads to programming problems. So let's stick to the *is-a* relationships.

Polymorphic Public Inheritance

The `RatedPlayer` example of inheritance is a simple one. Objects of the derived class use the base-class methods without change. But you can encounter situations in which you want a method to behave differently for the derived class than it does for the base class. That is, the way a particular method behaves may depend on the object that invokes it. This more sophisticated behavior is termed *polymorphic* ("having many forms") because you can have multiple behaviors for a method, depending on the context. There are two key mechanisms for implementing polymorphic public inheritance:

- Redefining base-class methods in a derived class

- Using virtual methods

It's time for another example. You have leveraged your experience with the Webtown Social Club to become head programmer for the Pontoon National Bank. The first thing the bank asks you to do is develop two classes. One class will represent its basic checking plan, the Brass Account, and the second class will represent the Brass Plus checking account, which adds an overdraft protection feature. That is, if a user writes a check larger (but not too much larger) than his or her balance, the bank will cover the check, charging the user for the excess payment and adding a surcharge. You can characterize the two accounts in terms of data to be stored and operations to be allowed.

First, here is the information for a Brass Account checking plan:

- Client name

- Account number

- Current balance

And here are the operations to be represented:

- Creating an account

- Depositing money into the account

- Withdrawing money from the account

- Displaying the account information

For the Brass Plus Account checking plan, the Pontoon National Bank wants all the features of the Brass Account as well as the following additional items of information:

- An upper limit to the overdraft protection

- An interest rate charged for overdraft loans

- The overdraft amount currently owed to the bank

No additional operations are needed, but two operations need to be implemented differently:

- The withdrawing money operation has to incorporate overdraft protection for the Brass Plus Account

- The display operation has to show the additional information required by the Brass Plus Account

Suppose you call one class `Brass` and the second class `BrassPlus`. Should you derive `BrassPlus` publicly from `Brass`? To answer this question, first answer another: Does the `BrassPlus` class meet the *is-a* test? Sure. Everything that is true of a `Brass` object will be true for a `BrassPlus` object. Both store a client name, an account number, and a balance. With both, you can make deposits and withdrawals and display account information. Note that the *is-a* relationship is not, in general, symmetric. A fruit, in general, is not a banana; similarly, a `Brass` object won't have all the capabilities of a `BrassPlus` object.

Developing the `Brass` and `BrassPlus` Classes

The Brass Account class information is pretty straightforward, but the bank hasn't told you enough details about how the overdraft system works. In response to your request for further information, the friendly Pontoon National Bank representative tells you the following:

- A Brass Plus Account limits how much money the bank will lend you to cover overdrafts. The default value is $500, but some customers may start with a different limit.

- The bank may change a customer's overdraft limit.

- A Brass Plus Account charges interest on the loan. The default value is 10%, but some customers may start with a different rate.

- The bank may change a customer's interest rate.

- The account keeps track of how much the customer owes the bank (overdraft loans plus interest). The user cannot pay off this amount through a regular deposit or through a transfer from another account. Instead, he or she must pay in cash to a special bank officer, who will, if necessary, seek out the customer. Once the debt is paid, the account can reset the amount owed to 0.

The last feature is an unusual way for a bank to do business, but it has the fortunate side effect of keeping the programming problem simpler.

This list suggests that the new class needs constructors that provide account information and that include a debt limit with a default value of $500 and an interest rate with a default value of 10%. Also, there should be methods for resetting the debt limit, interest rate, and current debt. These are all things to be added to the `Brass` class, and they will be declared in the `BrassPlus` class declaration.

The information about the two classes suggests class declarations like those in Listing 13.7.

LISTING 13.7 brass.h

```cpp
// brass.h  -- bank account classes
#ifndef BRASS_H_
#define BRASS_H_

// Brass Account Class
class Brass
{
private:
    enum {MAX = 35};
    char fullName[MAX];
    long acctNum;
    double balance;
public:
    Brass(const char *s = "Nullbody", long an = -1,
                double bal = 0.0);
    void Deposit(double amt);
    virtual void Withdraw(double amt);
    double Balance() const;
    virtual void ViewAcct() const;
    virtual ~Brass() {}
};

//Brass Plus Account Class
class BrassPlus : public Brass
{
private:
    double maxLoan;
    double rate;
    double owesBank;
public:
    BrassPlus(const char *s = "Nullbody", long an = -1,
            double bal = 0.0, double ml = 500,
            double r = 0.10);
    BrassPlus(const Brass & ba, double ml = 500, double r = 0.1);
    virtual void ViewAcct()const;
    virtual void Withdraw(double amt);
    void ResetMax(double m) { maxLoan = m; }
    void ResetRate(double r) { rate = r; };
    void ResetOwes() { owesBank = 0; }
};

#endif
```

There are several points to notice in Listing 13.7:

- The BrassPlus class adds three new private data members and three new public member functions to the Brass class.

- Both the Brass class and the BrassPlus class declare the ViewAcct() and Withdraw() methods; these are the methods that will behave differently for a BrassPlus object than they do with a Brass object.

- The **Brass** class uses the new keyword `virtual` in declaring `ViewAcct()` and `Withdraw()`. These methods are now termed *virtual methods*.

- The **Brass** class also declares a virtual destructor, even though the destructor does nothing.

The first point in the list is nothing new. The **RatedPlayer** class did something similar when it added a new data member and two new methods to the **TableTennisPlayer** class.

The second point in the list is how the declarations specify that methods are to behave differently for the derived class. The two `ViewAcct()` prototypes indicate that there will be two separate method definitions. The qualified name for the base-class version is `Brass::ViewAcct()`, and the qualified name for the derived-class version is `BrassPlus::ViewAcct()`. A program will use the object type to determine which version to use:

```
Brass dom("Dominic Banker", 11224, 4183.45);
BrassPlus dot("Dorothy Banker", 12118, 2592.00);
dom.ViewAcct();        // use Brass::ViewAcct()
dot.ViewAcct();        // use BrassPlus::ViewAcct()
```

Similarly, there will be two versions of `Withdraw()`: one that's used by **Brass** objects and one that's used by **BrassPlus** objects. Methods that behave the same for both classes, such as `Deposit()` and `Balance()`, are declared only in the base class.

The third point (the use of `virtual`) is more involved than the first two points. It determines which method is used if the method is invoked by a reference or a pointer instead of by an object. If you don't use the keyword `virtual`, the program chooses a method based on the reference type or pointer type. If you do use the keyword `virtual`, the program chooses a method based on the type of object the reference or pointer refers to. Here is how a program behaves if `ViewAcct()` is not virtual:

```
// behavior with non-virtual ViewAcct()
// method chosen according to reference type
Brass dom("Dominic Banker", 11224, 4183.45);
BrassPlus dot("Dorothy Banker", 12118, 2592.00);
Brass & b1_ref = dom;
Brass & b2_ref = dot;
b1_ref.ViewAcct();     // use Brass::ViewAcct()
b2_ref.ViewAcct();     // use Brass::ViewAcct()
```

The reference variables are type **Brass**, so `Brass::ViewAccount()` is chosen. Using pointers to **Brass** instead of references results in similar behavior.

In contrast, here is the behavior if `ViewAcct()` is virtual:

```
// behavior with virtual ViewAcct()
// method chosen according to object type
Brass dom("Dominic Banker", 11224, 4183.45);
BrassPlus dot("Dorothy Banker", 12118, 2592.00);
Brass & b1_ref = dom;
Brass & b2_ref = dot;
b1_ref.ViewAcct();     // use Brass::ViewAcct()
b2_ref.ViewAcct();     // use BrassPlus::ViewAcct()
```

In this case, both references are type `Brass`, but `b2_ref` refers to a `BrassPlus` object, so `BrassPlus::ViewAcct()` is used for it. Using pointers to `Brass` instead of references results in similar behavior.

It turns out, as you'll see in a bit, that this behavior of virtual functions is very handy. Therefore, it is the common practice to declare as virtual in the base class those methods that might be redefined in a derived class. When a method is declared virtual in a base class, it is automatically virtual in the derived class, but it is a good idea to document which functions are virtual by using the keyword `virtual` in the derived class declarations, too.

The fourth point is that the base class declares a virtual destructor. This is to make sure that the correct sequence of destructors is called when a derived object is destroyed. We'll discuss this point in more detail later in this chapter.

Remember

If you redefine a base-class method in a derived class, the usual practice is to declare the base-class method as virtual. This makes the program choose the method version based on object type instead of the type of a reference or pointer. It's also the usual practice to declare a virtual destructor for the base class.

Class Implementations

The next step is to prepare the class implementation. Part of this has been done already by the inline function definitions in the header file. Listing 13.8 provides the remaining method definitions. Note that the keyword `virtual` is used just in the method prototypes in the class declaration, not in the method definitions in Listing 13.8.

LISTING 13.8   `brass.cpp`

```
// brass.cpp -- bank account class methods
#include <iostream>
#include <cstring>
#include "brass.h"
using std::cout;
using std::ios_base;
using std::endl;
// Brass methods

Brass::Brass(const char *s, long an, double bal)
{
    std::strncpy(fullName, s, MAX - 1);
    fullName[MAX - 1] = '\0';
    acctNum = an;
    balance = bal;
}

void Brass::Deposit(double amt)
{
```

LISTING 13.8   *Continued*

```cpp
    if (amt < 0)
        cout << "Negative deposit not allowed; "
            << "deposit is cancelled.\n";
    else
        balance += amt;
}

void Brass::Withdraw(double amt)
{
    if (amt < 0)
        cout << "Withdrawal amount must be positive; "

            << "withdrawal canceled.\n";
    else if (amt <= balance)
        balance -= amt;
    else
        cout << "Withdrawal amount of $" << amt
            << " exceeds your balance.\n"
            << "Withdrawal canceled.\n";
}
double Brass::Balance() const
{
    return balance;
}

void Brass::ViewAcct() const
{
    // set up ###.## format
    ios_base::fmtflags initialState =
        cout.setf(ios_base::fixed, ios_base::floatfield);
    cout.setf(ios_base::showpoint);
    cout.precision(2);
    cout << "Client: " << fullName << endl;
    cout << "Account Number: " << acctNum << endl;
    cout << "Balance: $" << balance << endl;
    cout.setf(initialState); // restore original format
}

// BrassPlus Methods
BrassPlus::BrassPlus(const char *s, long an, double bal,
        double ml, double r) : Brass(s, an, bal)
{
    maxLoan = ml;
    owesBank = 0.0;
    rate = r;
}

BrassPlus::BrassPlus(const Brass & ba, double ml, double r)
        : Brass(ba)    // uses implicit copy constructor
{
    maxLoan = ml;
    owesBank = 0.0;
```

LISTING 13.8   Continued

```
        rate = r;
}

// redefine how ViewAcct() works
void BrassPlus::ViewAcct() const
{
    // set up ###.## format
    ios_base::fmtflags initialState =
        cout.setf(ios_base::fixed, ios_base::floatfield);
    cout.setf(ios_base::showpoint);
    cout.precision(2);

    Brass::ViewAcct();    // display base portion
    cout << "Maximum loan: $" << maxLoan << endl;
    cout << "Owed to bank: $" << owesBank << endl;
    cout << "Loan Rate: " << 100 * rate << "%\n";
    cout.setf(initialState);
}

// redefine how Withdraw() works
void BrassPlus::Withdraw(double amt)
{
    // set up ###.## format
    ios_base::fmtflags initialState =
        cout.setf(ios_base::fixed, ios_base::floatfield);
    cout.setf(ios_base::showpoint);
    cout.precision(2);

    double bal = Balance();
    if (amt <= bal)
        Brass::Withdraw(amt);
    else if ( amt <= bal + maxLoan - owesBank)
    {
        double advance = amt - bal;
        owesBank += advance * (1.0 + rate);
        cout << "Bank advance: $" << advance << endl;
        cout << "Finance charge: $" << advance * rate << endl;
        Deposit(advance);
        Brass::Withdraw(amt);
    }
    else
        cout << "Credit limit exceeded. Transaction cancelled.\n";
    cout.setf(initialState);
}
```

Before looking at details of Listing 13.8, such as handling of formatting in some of the methods, let's examine the aspects that relate directly to inheritance. Keep in mind that the derived class does not have direct access to private base-class data; the derived class has to use base-class public methods to access that data. The means of access depends on the method. Constructors use one technique, and other member functions use a different technique.

The technique that derived-class constructors use to initialize base-class private data is the member initializer list syntax. The `RatedPlayer` class constructors use that technique, and so do the `BrassPlus` constructors:

```
BrassPlus::BrassPlus(const char *s, long an, double bal,
            double ml, double r) : Brass(s, an, bal)
{
    maxLoan = ml;
    owesBank = 0.0;
    rate = r;
}

BrassPlus::BrassPlus(const Brass & ba, double ml, double r)
            : Brass(ba)    // uses implicit copy constructor
{
    maxLoan = ml;
    owesBank = 0.0;
    rate = r;
}
```

Each of these constructors uses the member initializer list syntax to pass base-class information to a base-class constructor and then uses the constructor body to initialize the new data items added by the `BrassPlus` class.

Non-constructors can't use the member initializer list syntax. But a derived-class method can call a public base-class method. For instance, ignoring the formatting aspect, the core of the `BrassPlus` version of `ViewAcct()` is this:

```
// redefine how ViewAcct() works
void BrassPlus::ViewAcct() const
{
...
    Brass::ViewAcct();    // display base portion
    cout << "Maximum loan: $" << maxLoan << endl;
    cout << "Owed to bank: $" << owesBank << endl;
    cout << "Loan Rate: " << 100 * rate << "%\n";
...
}
```

In other words, `BrassPlus::ViewAcct()` displays the added `BrassPlus` data members and calls on the base-class method `Brass::ViewAcct()` to display the base-class data members. Using the scope-resolution operator in a derived-class method to invoke a base-class method is a standard technique.

It's vital that the code use the scope-resolution operator. Suppose that, instead, you wrote the code this way:

```
// redefine how ViewAcct() works
void BrassPlus::ViewAcct() const
{
...
    ViewAcct();    // oops! recursive call
...
}
```

If the code doesn't use the scope-resolution operator, the compiler assumes that `ViewAcct()` is `BrassPlus::ViewAcct()`, and this creates a recursive function that has no termination—not a good thing.

Next, consider the `BrassPlus::Withdraw()` method. If the client withdraws an amount larger than the balance, the method should arrange for a loan. It can use `Brass::Withdraw()` to access the balance member, but `Brass::Withdraw()` issues an error message if the withdrawal amount exceeds the balance. This implementation avoids the message by using the `Deposit()` method to make the loan and then calling `Brass::Withdraw()` when sufficient funds are available:

```
// redefine how Withdraw() works
void BrassPlus::Withdraw(double amt)
{
...
    double bal = Balance();
    if (amt <= bal)
        Brass::Withdraw(amt);
    else if ( amt <= bal + maxLoan - owesBank)
    {
        double advance = amt - bal;
        owesBank += advance * (1.0 + rate);
        cout << "Bank advance: $" << advance << endl;
        cout << "Finance charge: $" << advance * rate << endl;
        Deposit(advance);
        Brass::Withdraw(amt);
    }
    else
        cout << "Credit limit exceeded. Transaction cancelled.\n";
...
}
```

Note that the method uses the base-class `Balance()` function to determine the original balance. The code doesn't have to use the scope-resolution operator for `Balance()` because this method has not been redefined in the derived class.

The `ViewAcct()` methods use formatting commands to set the output mode for floating-point values to fixed-point, two places to the right of the decimal. When these modes are set, output stays in that mode, so the polite thing for these methods to do is to reset the formatting mode to its state prior to calling the methods. Therefore, these methods capture the original format state with this code:

```
ios_base::fmtflags initialState =
    cout.setf(ios_base::fixed, ios_base::floatfield);
```

The `setf()` method returns a value representing the format state before the function was called. New C++ implementations define the `ios_base::fmtflags` type as the type for this value, and this statement saves the state in a variable (`initialState`) of that type. (Older versions of C++ might use `unsigned int` instead for the type.) When `ViewAcct()` finishes, it passes `initialState` to `setf()` as an argument:

```
cout.setf(initialState);
```

This restores the original format settings

Using the `Brass` and `BrassPlus` Classes

Listing 13.9 shows the class definitions with a `Brass` object and a `BrassPlus` object.

LISTING 13.9   usebrass1.cpp

```cpp
// usebrass1.cpp -- testing bank account classes
// compile with brass.cpp
#include <iostream>
#include "brass.h"

int main()
{
    using std::cout;
    using std::endl;

    Brass Piggy("Porcelot Pigg", 381299, 4000.00);
    BrassPlus Hoggy("Horatio Hogg", 382288, 3000.00);
    Piggy.ViewAcct();
    cout << endl;
    Hoggy.ViewAcct();
    cout << endl;
    cout << "Depositing $1000 into the Hogg Account:\n";
    Hoggy.Deposit(1000.00);
    cout << "New balance: $" << Hoggy.Balance() << endl;
    cout << "Withdrawing $4200 from the Pigg Account:\n";
    Piggy.Withdraw(4200.00);
    cout << "Pigg account balance: $" << Piggy.Balance() << endl;
    cout << "Withdrawing $4200 from the Hogg Account:\n";
    Hoggy.Withdraw(4200.00);
    Hoggy.ViewAcct();

    return 0;
}
```

In the following output of the program in Listing 13.9, note that Hogg gets overdraft protection and Pigg does not:

```
Client: Porcelot Pigg
Account Number: 381299
Balance: $4000.00

Client: Horatio Hogg
Account Number: 382288
Balance: $3000.00
Maximum loan: $500.00
```

```
Owed to bank: $0.00
Loan Rate: 10.00%

Depositing $1000 into the Hogg Account:
New balance: $4000.00
Withdrawing $4200 from the Pigg Account:
Withdrawal amount of $4200.00 exceeds your balance.
Withdrawal canceled.
Pigg account balance: $4000.00
Withdrawing $4200 from the Hogg Account:
Bank advance: $200.00
Finance charge: $20.00
Client: Horatio Hogg
Account Number: 382288
Balance: $0.00
Maximum loan: $500.00
Owed to bank: $220.00
Loan Rate: 10.00%
```

Showing Virtual Method Behavior

In Listing 13.9 the methods are invoked by objects, not pointers or references, so this program doesn't use the virtual method feature. Let's look at an example for which the virtual methods do come into play. Suppose you would like to manage a mixture of **Brass** and **BrassPlus** accounts. It would be nice if you could have a single array that holds a mixture of **Brass** and **BrassPlus** objects, but that's not possible. Every item in an array has to be of the same type, and **Brass** and **BrassPlus** are two separate types. However, you can create an array of pointers-to-**Brass**. In that case, every element is of the same type, but because of the public inheritance model, a pointer-to-**Brass** can point to either a **Brass** or a **BrassPlus** object. Thus, in effect, you have a way of representing a collection of more than one type of object with a single array. This is polymorphism, and Listing 13.10 shows a simple example.

LISTING 13.10   usebrass2.cpp

```cpp
// usebrass2.cpp -- polymorphic example
// compile with brass.cpp
#include <iostream>
#include "brass.h"
const int CLIENTS = 4;
const int LEN = 40;
int main()
{
    using std::cin;
    using std::cout;
    using std::endl;
    Brass * p_clients[CLIENTS];

    int i;
    for (i = 0; i < CLIENTS; i++)
    {
        char temp[LEN];
```

LISTING 13.10   *Continued*

```
            long tempnum;
            double tempbal;
            char kind;
            cout << "Enter client's name: ";
            cin.getline(temp, LEN);
            cout << "Enter client's account number: ";
            cin >> tempnum;
            cout << "Enter opening balance: $";
            cin >> tempbal;
            cout << "Enter 1 for Brass Account or "
                 << "2 for BrassPlus Account: ";
            while (cin >> kind && (kind != '1' && kind != '2'))
                cout <<"Enter either 1 or 2: ";
            if (kind == '1')
                p_clients[i] = new Brass(temp, tempnum, tempbal);
            else
            {
                double tmax, trate;
                cout << "Enter the overdraft limit: $";
                cin >> tmax;
                cout << "Enter the interest rate "
                     << "as a decimal fraction: ";
                cin >> trate;
                p_clients[i] = new BrassPlus(temp, tempnum, tempbal,
                                             tmax, trate);

            }
            while (cin.get() != '\n')
                continue;
    }
    cout << endl;
    for (i = 0; i < CLIENTS; i++)
    {
        p_clients[i]->ViewAcct();
        cout << endl;
    }

    for (i = 0; i < CLIENTS; i++)
    {
        delete p_clients[i];   // free memory
    }
    cout << "Done.\n";

    return 0;
}
```

The program in Listing 13.10 lets user input determine the type of account to be added and then uses **new** to create and initialize an object of the proper type.

Here is a sample run of the program in Listing 13.10:

```
Enter client's name: Harry Fishsong
Enter client's account number: 112233
Enter opening balance: $1500
```

```
Enter 1 for Brass Account or 2 for BrassPlus Account: 1
Enter client's name: Dinah Otternoe
Enter client's account number: 121213
Enter opening balance: $1800
Enter 1 for Brass Account or 2 for BrassPlus Account: 2
Enter the overdraft limit: $350
Enter the interest rate as a decimal fraction: 0.12
Enter client's name: Brenda Birdherd
Enter client's account number: 212118
Enter opening balance: $5200
Enter 1 for Brass Account or 2 for BrassPlus Account: 2
Enter the overdraft limit: $800
Enter the interest rate as a decimal fraction: 0.10
Enter client's name: Tim Turtletop
Enter client's account number: 233255
Enter opening balance: $688
Enter 1 for Brass Account or 2 for BrassPlus Account: 1

Client: Harry Fishsong
Account Number: 112233
Balance: $1500.00

Client: Dinah Otternoe
Account Number: 121213
Balance: $1800.00
Maximum loan: $350.00
Owed to bank: $0.00
Loan Rate: 12.00%

Client: Brenda Birdherd
Account Number: 212118
Balance: $5200.00
Maximum loan: $800.00
Owed to bank: $0.00
Loan Rate: 10.00%

Client: Tim Turtletop
Account Number: 233255
Balance: $688.00

Done.
```

The polymorphic aspect is provided by the following code:

```
for (i = 0; i < CLIENTS; i++)
{
    p_clients[i]->ViewAcct();
    cout << endl;
}
```

If the array member points to a `Brass` object, `Brass::ViewAcct()` is invoked; if the array member points to a `BrassPlus` object, `BrassPlus::ViewAcct()` is invoked. If `Brass::ViewAcct()` were been declared as virtual, `Brass:ViewAcct()` would be invoked in all cases.

The Need for Virtual Destructors

The code in Listing 13.10 that uses `delete` to free the objects allocated by `new` illustrates why the base class should have a virtual destructor, even if no destructor appears to be needed. If the destructors are not virtual, then just the destructor corresponding to the pointer type is called. In Listing 13.10, this means that only the `Brass` destructor would be called, even if the pointer pointed to a `BrassPlus` object. If the destructors are virtual, the destructor corresponding to the object type is called. So if a pointer points to a `BrassPlus` object, the `BrassPlus` destructor is called. And when a `BrassPlus` destructor finishes, it automatically calls the base-class constructor. Thus, using virtual destructors ensures that the correct sequence of destructors is called. In Listing 13.10, this correct behavior isn't essential because the destructors do nothing. But if, say, `BrassPlus` had a do-something destructor, it would be vital for `Brass` to have a virtual destructor, even if it did nothing.

Static and Dynamic Binding

Which block of executable code gets used when a program calls a function? The compiler has the responsibility of answering this question. Interpreting a function call in the source code as executing a particular block of function code is termed *binding* the function name. With C, the task is simple because each function name corresponds to a distinct function. With C++, the task is more complex because of function overloading. The compiler has to look at the function arguments as well as the function name to figure out which function to use. Nonetheless, this kind of binding is a task a C or C++ compiler could perform during the compiling process; binding that takes place during compilation is called *static binding* (or *early binding*). However, virtual functions make the job more difficult yet. As shown in Listing 13.10, the decision of which function to use can't be made at compile time because the compiler doesn't know which kind of object the user is going to choose to make. Therefore, the compiler has to generate code that allows the correct virtual method to be selected as the program runs; this is called *dynamic binding* (or *late binding*).

Now that you've seen virtual methods at work, let's look at this process in greater depth, beginning with how C++ handles pointer and reference type compatibility.

Pointer and Reference Type Compatibility

Dynamic binding in C++ is associated with methods invoked by pointers and references, and this is governed, in part, by the inheritance process. One way public inheritance models the *is-a* relationship is in how it handles pointers and references to objects. Normally, C++ does not allow you to assign an address of one type to a pointer of another type. Nor does it let a reference to one type refer to another type:

```
double x = 2.5;
int * pi = &x;    // invalid assignment, mismatched pointer types
long & rl = x;    // invalid assignment, mismatched reference type
```

However, as you've seen, a reference or a pointer to a base class can refer to a derived-class object without using an explicit type cast. For example, the following initializations are allowed:

```
BrassPlus dilly ("Annie Dill", 493222, 2000);
Brass * pb = &dilly;    // ok
Brass & rb = dilly;     // ok
```

Converting a derived-class reference or pointer to a base-class reference or pointer is called *upcasting*, and it is always allowed for public inheritance, without the need for an explicit type cast. This rule is part of expressing the *is-a* relationship. A `BrassPlus` object is a `Brass` object in that it inherits all the data members and member functions of a `Brass` object. Therefore, anything that you can do to a `Brass` object, you can do to a `BrassPlus` object. So a function designed to handle a `Brass` reference can, without fear of creating problems, perform the same acts on a `BrassPlus` object. The same idea applies if you pass a pointer to an object as a function argument. Upcasting is transitive. That is, if you derive a `BrassPlusPlus` class from `BrassPlus`, then a `Brass` pointer or reference can refer to a `Brass` object, a `BrassPlus` object, or a `BrassPlusPlus` object.

The opposite process, converting a base-class pointer or reference to a derived-class pointer or reference, is called *downcasting*, and it is not allowed without an explicit type cast. The reason for this restriction is that the *is-a* relationship is not, in general, symmetric. A derived class could add new data members, and the class member functions that used these data members wouldn't apply to the base class. For example, suppose you derive a `Singer` class from an `Employee` class, adding a data member representing a singer's vocal range and a member function, called `range()`, that reports the value for the vocal range. It wouldn't make sense to apply the `range()` method to an `Employee` object. But if implicit downcasting were allowed, you could accidentally set a pointer-to-`Singer` to the address of an `Employee` object and use the pointer to invoke the `range()` method (see Figure 13.4).

FIGURE 13.4

Upcasting and down-casting.

```
class Employee
{
private:
    char name[40];
    ...
public:
    void show_name();
    ...
};
class Singer : public Employee
{
    ...
public:
    void range();
    ...
};
...
Employee veep;
Singer trala;
...
Employee * pe = &trala;          ◄────── upcast—implicit type cast allowed
Singer * ps = (Singer *) &veep;  ◄────── downcast—explicit type cast required
...
pe->show_name();   ◄────── Upcasting leads to a safe operation because
ps->range();       ◄────── a Singer is an Employee (every Singer
                           inherits name).

                           Downcasting can lead to an unsafe operation
                           because an Employee isn't a Singer (an
                           Employee need not have a range() method).
```

Implicit upcasting makes it possible for a base-class pointer or reference to refer to either a base-class object or a derived-class object, and that produces the need for dynamic binding. Virtual member functions are the C++ answer to that need.

Virtual Member Functions and Dynamic Binding

Let's revisit the process of invoking a method with a reference or pointer. Consider the following code:

```
BrassPlus ophelia;     // derived-class object
Brass * bp;            // base-class pointer
bp = &ophelia;         // Brass pointer to BrassPlus object
bp->ViewAcct();        // which version?
```

As discussed before, if `ViewAcct()` is not declared as virtual in the base class, `bp->ViewAcct()` goes by the pointer type (`Brass *`) and invokes `Brass::ViewAcct()`. The pointer type is known at compile time, so the compiler can bind `ViewAcct()` to `Brass::ViewAcct()` at compile time. In short, the compiler uses static binding for nonvirtual methods.

But if `ViewAcct()` is declared as virtual in the base class, `bp->ViewAcct()` goes by the object type (`BrassPlus`) and invokes `BrassPlus::ViewAcct()`. In this example, you can see that the object type is `BrassPlus`, but, in general, (as in Listing 13.10) the object type might only be determined when the program is running. Therefore, the compiler generates code that binds `ViewAcct()` to `Brass::ViewAcct()` or `BrassPlus::ViewAcct()`, depending on the object type, while the program executes. In short, the compiler uses dynamic binding for virtual methods.

In most cases, dynamic binding is a good thing because it allows a program to choose the method designed for a particular type. Given this fact, you might be wondering about the following:

- Why have two kinds of binding?

- If dynamic binding is so good, why isn't it the default?

- How does it work?

We'll look at answers to these questions next.

Why Two Kinds of Binding and Why Static Is the Default

If dynamic binding allows you to redefine class methods but static binding makes a partial botch of it, why have static binding at all? There are two reasons: efficiency and a conceptual model.

First, let's consider efficiency. For a program to be able to make a runtime decision, it has to have some way to keep track of what sort of object a base-class pointer or reference refers to, and that entails some extra processing overhead. (You'll see one method of dynamic binding later.) If, for example, you design a class that won't be used as a base class for inheritance, you don't need dynamic binding. Similarly, if you have a derived class, such as the `RatedPlayer` example, that does not redefine any methods, you don't need dynamic binding. In these cases, it makes sense to use static binding and gain a little efficiency. The fact that static binding is more efficient is the reason it is the default choice for C++. Stroustrup says that one of the guiding principles of C++ is that you shouldn't have to pay (in memory usage or processing time) for features you don't use. You should therefore go to virtual functions only if the program design needs them.

Next, let's consider the conceptual model. When you design a class, you may have member functions that you don't want redefined in derived classes. For example, the `Brass::Balance()` function, which returns the account balance, seems like a function that shouldn't be redefined. By making this function nonvirtual, you accomplish two things. First, you make it more efficient. Second, you announce that it is your intention that this function not be redefined. That suggests reserving the virtual label just for methods you expect to be redefined.

Tip
If a method in a base class will be redefined in a derived class, you should make it virtual. If the method should not be redefined, you should make it nonvirtual.

Of course, when you design a class, it's not always obvious into which category a method falls. Like many aspects of real life, class design is not a linear process.

How Virtual Functions Work

C++ specifies how virtual functions should behave, but it leaves the implementation up to the compiler writer. You don't need to know the implementation method to use virtual functions, but seeing how it is done may help you understand the concepts better, so let's take a look.

The usual way compilers handle virtual functions is to add a hidden member to each object. The hidden member holds a pointer to an array of function addresses. Such an array is usually termed a *virtual function table* (*vtbl*). The vtbl holds the addresses of the virtual functions declared for objects of that class. For example, an object of a base class contains a pointer to a table of addresses of all the virtual functions for that class. An object of a derived class contains a pointer to a separate table of addresses. If the derived class provides a new definition of a virtual function, the vtbl holds the address of the new function. If the derived class doesn't redefine the virtual function, the vtbl holds the address of the original version of the function. If the derived class defines a new function and makes it virtual, its address is added to the vtbl (see Figure 13.5). Note that whether you define 1 or 10 virtual functions for a class, you add just one address member to an object; it's the table size that varies.

When you call a virtual function, the program looks at the vtbl address stored in an object and goes to the corresponding table of function addresses. If you use the first virtual function defined in the class declaration, the program uses the first function address in the array and executes the function that has that address. If you use the third virtual function in the class declaration, the program uses the function whose address is in the third element of the array.

FIGURE 13.5

A virtual function mechanism.

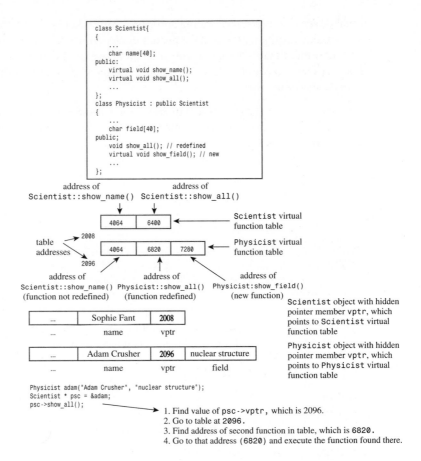

In short, using virtual functions has the following modest costs in memory and execution speed:

- Each object has its size increased by the amount needed to hold an address.

- For each class, the compiler creates a table (an array) of addresses of virtual functions.

- For each function call, there's an extra step of going to a table to look up an address.

Keep in mind that although nonvirtual functions are slightly more efficient than virtual functions, they don't provide dynamic binding.

Things to Know About Virtual Methods

We've already discussed the main points about virtual methods:

- Beginning a class method declaration with the keyword **virtual** in a base class makes the function virtual for the base class and all classes derived from the base class, including classes derived from the derived classes, and so on.

- If a virtual method is invoked by using a reference to an object or by using a pointer to an object, the program uses the method defined for the object type rather than the method defined for the reference or pointer type. This is called *dynamic*, or *late*, *binding*. This behavior is important because it's always valid for a base-class pointer or reference to refer to an object of a derived type.

- If you're defining a class that will be used as a base class for inheritance, you should declare as virtual functions the class methods that may have to be redefined in derived classes.

There are several other things you may need to know about virtual methods, some of which have been mentioned in passing already. Let's look at them next.

Constructors

Constructors can't be virtual. Creating a derived object invokes a derived-class constructor, not a base-class constructor. The derived-class constructor then uses a base-class constructor, but this sequence is distinct from the inheritance mechanism. Thus, a derived class doesn't inherit the base-class constructors, so usually there's not much point to making them virtual, anyway.

Destructors

Destructors should be virtual unless a class isn't to be used as a base class. For example, suppose `Employee` is a base class and `Singer` is a derived class that adds a `char *` member that points to memory allocated by `new`. Then, when a `Singer` object expires, it's vital that the `~Singer()` destructor be called to free that memory.

Now consider the following code:

```
Employee * pe = new Singer; // legal because Employee is base for Singer
...
delete pe;                   // ~Employee() or ~Singer()?
```

If the default static binding applies, the `delete` statement invokes the `~Employee()` destructor. This frees memory pointed to by the `Employee` components of the `Singer` object but not memory pointed to by the new class members. However, if the destructors are virtual, the same code invokes the `~Singer()` destructor, which frees memory pointed to by the `Singer` component, and then calls the `~Employee()` destructor to free memory pointed to by the `Employee` component.

Note that this implies that even if a base class doesn't require the services of an explicit destructor, you shouldn't rely on the default constructor. Instead, you should provide a virtual destructor, even if it has nothing to do:

```
virtual ~BaseClass() { }
```

By the way, it's not an error for a class to have a virtual destructor even if it is not intended to be a base class; it's just a matter of efficiency.

Tip

Normally, you should provide a base class with a virtual destructor, even if the class doesn't need a destructor.

Friends

Friends can't be virtual functions because friends are not class members, and only members can be virtual functions. If this poses a problem for a design, you might be able to sidestep it by having the friend function use virtual member functions internally.

No Redefinition

If a derived class fails to redefine a function (virtual or not), the class will use the base class version of the function. If a derived class is part of a long chain of derivations, it will use the most recently defined version of the function. The exception is if the base versions are hidden, as described next.

Redefinition Hides Methods

Suppose you create something like the following:

```
class Dwelling
{
public:
      virtual void showperks(int a) const;
...
};
class Hovel : public Dwelling
{
{
public:
      virtual void showperks() const;
...
};
```

This causes a problem. You might get a compiler warning similar to the following:

```
Warning: Hovel::showperks(void) hides Dwelling::showperks(int)
```

Or perhaps you won't get a warning. Either way, the code has the following implications:

```
Hovel trump;
trump.showperks();        // valid
trump.showperks(5);       // invalid
```

The new definition defines a `showperks()` function that takes no arguments. Rather than resulting in two overloaded versions of the function, this redefinition *hides* the base class version that takes an `int` argument. In short, redefining inherited methods is not a variation of overloading. If you redefine a function in a derived class, it doesn't just override the base class declaration with the same function signature. Instead, it hides *all* base-class methods of the same name, regardless of the argument signatures.

This fact of life leads to a couple rules of thumb. First, if you redefine an inherited method, you need to make sure you match the original prototype exactly. One relatively new exception to this rule is that a return type that is a reference or pointer to a base class can be replaced by a reference or pointer to the derived class. This feature is termed *covariance of return type* because the return type is allowed to vary in parallel with the class type:

```
class Dwelling
{
public:
// a base method
    virtual Dwelling & build(int n);
    ...
};
class Hovel : public Dwelling
{
public:
// a derived method with a covariant return type
    virtual Hovel & build(int n);  // same function signature
    ...
};
```

Note that this exception applies only to return values, not to arguments.

Second, if the base class declaration is overloaded, you need to redefine all the base-class versions in the derived class:

```
class Dwelling
{
public:
// three overloaded showperks()
    virtual void showperks(int a) const;
    virtual void showperks(double x) const;
    virtual void showperks() const;
    ...
};
class Hovel : public Dwelling
{
public:
// three redefined showperks()
    virtual void showperks(int a) const;
    virtual void showperks(double x) const;
    virtual void showperks() const;
    ...
};
```

If you redefine just one version, the other two become hidden and cannot be used by objects of the derived class. Note that if no change is needed, the redefinition can simply call the base-class version.

Access Control: `protected`

So far the class examples in this book have used the keywords `public` and `private` to control access to class members. There is one more access category, denoted with the keyword `protected`. The `protected` keyword is like `private` in that the outside world can access class members in a `protected` section only by using public class members. The difference between `private` and `protected` comes into play only within classes derived from the base class. Members of a derived class can access protected members of a base class directly, but they cannot directly access private members of the base class. So members in the protected category behave like private members as far as the outside world is concerned but behave like public members as far as derived classes are concerned.

For example, suppose the `Brass` class declared the `balance` member as protected:

```
class Brass
{
protected:
    double balance;
...
};
```

In this case, the `BrassPlus` class could access `balance` directly without using `Brass` methods. For example, the core of `BrassPlus::Withdraw()` could be written this way:

```
void BrassPlus::Withdraw(double amt)
{
    if (amt < 0)
        cout << "Withdrawal amount must be positive; "

             << "withdrawal canceled.\n";
    else if (amt <= balance)        // access balance directly
        balance -= amt;
    else if ( amt <= balance + maxLoan - owesBank)
    {
        double advance = amt - balance;
        owesBank += advance * (1.0 + rate);
        cout << "Bank advance: $" << advance << endl;
        cout << "Finance charge: $" << advance * rate << endl;
        Deposit(advance);
        balance -= amt;
    }
    else
        cout << "Credit limit exceeded. Transaction cancelled.\n";
}
```

Using protected data members may simplify writing the code, but it has a design defect. For example, continuing with the `BrassPlus` example, if `balance` were protected, you could write code like this:

```
void BrassPlus::Reset(double amt)
{
    balance = amt;
}
```

The `Brass` class was designed so that the `Deposit()` and `Withdraw()` interface provides the only means for altering `balance`. But the `Reset()` method essentially makes `balance` a public variable as far as `BrassPlus` objects are concerned, ignoring, for example, the safeguards found in `Withdraw()`.

Caution

You should prefer private to protected access control for class data members, and you should use base-class methods to provide derived classes access to base-class data.

However, protected access control can be quite useful for member functions, giving derived classes access to internal functions that are not available publicly.

Real-World Note: The Singleton Design Pattern

Often you can find a single general pattern that solves a variety of problems. This is true in human interactions; there's the recipe "take a deep breath and count to 10 before responding." In programming, too, common patterns emerge when you study software design problems. A design pattern is the software equivalent of a particular cooking style, in which the same approach can be applied to different selections of ingredients. You can apply a design pattern to create an elegant and consistent solution to your recurring problem domains. For example, you can use the singleton pattern when you want exactly one instance of a class to be returned to a caller. Here's how such a class might be declared:

```
class TheOnlyInstance
{
  public:
    static TheOnlyInstance* GetTheOnlyInstance();
    // other methods
  protected:
    TheOnlyInstance() {}
  private:
    // private data
};
```

By declaring the `TheOnlyInstance` constructor as `protected` and omitting any public constructor, you can ensure that no local instances can be created:

```
int main()
{
    TheOnlyInstance noCanDo;   // not allowed
```

The public static method `GetTheOnlyInstance` serves as the sole access point for the class during its lifetime. When called, it returns an instance of class `TheOnlyInstance`:

```
TheOnlyInstance* TheOnlyInstance::GetTheOnlyInstance()
{
    static TheOnlyInstance objTheOnlyInstance;
    return &objTheOnlyInstance;
}
```

The `GetTheOnlyInstance` method simply creates a static instance of class `TheOnlyInstance` the first time the static `GetTheOnlyInstance` method is called. A static object constructed in this manner remains valid until the program terminates, at which point it is automatically destroyed. To retrieve a pointer to the only instance of this class, a program can simply call the static method `GetTheOnlyInstance`, which returns the address of the singleton object:

```
TheOnlyInstance* pTheOnlyInstance = TheOnlyInstance::GetTheOnlyInstance();
```

Because a static variable remains in memory between function calls, subsequent calls of `GetTheOnlyInstance` return the address of the same static object.

Abstract Base Classes

So far you've seen simple inheritance and the more intricate polymorphic inheritance. The next step in increasing sophistication is the abstract base class (ABC). Let's look at some programming situations that provide the background for ABCs.

Sometimes applying the *is-a* rule is not as simple as it might appear. Suppose, for example, you are developing a graphics program that is supposed to represent, among other things, circles and ellipses. A circle is a special case of an ellipse: It's an ellipse whose long axis is the same as its short axis. Therefore, all circles are ellipses, and it is tempting to derive a `Circle` class from an `Ellipse` class. But when you get to the details, you may find problems.

To see this, first consider what you might include as part of an `Ellipse` class. Data members could include the coordinates of the center of the ellipse, the semimajor axis (half the long diameter), the semiminor axis (half the short diameter), and an orientation angle that gives the angle from the horizontal coordinate axis to the semimajor axis. Also, the class could include methods to move the ellipse, to return the area of the ellipse, to rotate the ellipse, and to scale the semimajor and semiminor axes:

```
class Ellipse
{
private:
    double x;      // x-coordinate of the ellipse's center
    double y;      // y-coordinate of the ellipse's center
    double a;      // semimajor axis
    double b;      // semiminor axis
    double angle;  // orientation angle in degrees
    ...
public:
    ...
    void Move(int nx, ny) { x = nx; y = ny; }
    virtual double Area() const { return 3.14159 * a * b; }
    virtual void Rotate(double nang) { angle += nang; }
    virtual void Scale(double sa, double sb)  { a *= sa; b *= sb; }
    ...
};
```

Now suppose you derive a `Circle` class from the `Ellipse` class:

```
class Circle : public Ellipse
{
    ...
};
```

Although a circle is an ellipse, this derivation is awkward. For example, a circle needs only a single value, its radius, to describe its size and shape instead of having a semimajor axis (**a**) and semiminor axis (**b**). The `Circle` constructors can take care of that by assigning the same value to both the **a** and **b** members, but then you have redundant representation of the same information. The `angle` parameter and the `Rotate()` method don't really make sense for a circle, and the `Scale()` method, as it stands, can change a circle to a non-circle by scaling the two axes differently. You can try fixing things with tricks, such as putting a redefined `Rotate()` method in the private section of the `Circle` class so that `Rotate()` can't be used publicly with a circle, but, on the whole, it seems simpler to define a `Circle` class without using inheritance:

```
class Circle        // no inheritance
{
private:
    double x;       // x-coordinate of the circle's center
    double y;       // y-coordinate of the circle's center
    double r;       // radius
    ...
public:
    ...
    void Move(int nx, ny) { x = nx; y = ny; }
    double Area() const { return 3.14159 * r * r; }
    void Scale(double sr)  { r *= sr; }
    ...
};
```

Now the class has only the members it needs. Yet this solution also seems weak. The `Circle` and `Ellipse` classes have a lot in common, but defining them separately ignores that fact.

There is another solution: You can abstract from the `Ellipse` and `Circle` classes what they have in common and place those features in an ABC. Next, you derive both the `Circle` and `Ellipse` classes from the ABC. Then, for example, you can use an array of base-class pointers to manage a mixture of `Ellipse` and `Circle` objects—that is, you can use a polymorphic approach. In this case, what the two classes have in common are the coordinates of the center of the shape; a `Move()` method, which is the same for both; and an `Area()` method, which works differently for the two classes. Indeed, the `Area()` method can't even be implemented for the ABC because it doesn't have the necessary data members. C++ has a way to provide an unimplemented function by using a *pure virtual function*. A pure virtual function has = **0** at the end of its declaration, as shown for the `Area()` method:

```
class BaseEllipse  // abstract base class
{
private:
    double x;    // x-coordinate of center
    double y;    // y-coordinate of center
    ...
public:
    BaseEllipse(double x0 = 0, double y0 = 0) : x(x0),y(y0) {}
    virtual ~BaseEllipse() {}
    void Move(int nx, ny) { x = nx; y = ny; }
    virtual double Area() const = 0; // a pure virtual function
    ...
}
```

When a class declaration contains a pure virtual function, you can't create an object of that class. The idea is that classes with pure virtual functions exist solely to serve as base classes. For a class to be a genuine ABC, it has to have at least one pure virtual function. It is the = 0 in the prototype that makes a virtual function a pure virtual function. In the case of the Area() method, the function has no definition, but C++ allows even a pure virtual function to have a definition. For example, perhaps all the base methods are like Move() in that they can be defined for the base class, but you still need to make the class abstract. You could then make the prototype virtual:

```
void Move(int nx, ny) = 0;
```

This makes the base class abstract. But then you could still provide a definition in the implementation file:

```
void BaseEllipse::Move(int nx, ny) { x = nx; y = ny; }
```

In short, the = 0 in the prototype indicates that the class is an abstract base class and that the class doesn't necessarily have to define the function.

Now you can derive the Ellipse class and Circle class from the BaseEllipse class, adding the members needed to complete each class. One point to note is that the Circle class always represents circles, whereas the Ellipse class represents ellipses that can also be circles. However, an Ellipse class circle can be rescaled to a non-circle, whereas a Circle class circle must remain a circle.

A program using these classes would be able to create Ellipse objects and Circle objects but no BaseEllipse objects. Because Circle and Ellipse objects have the same base class, a collection of such objects can be managed with an array of BaseEllipse pointers. Classes such as Circle and Ellipse are sometimes termed *concrete* classes to indicate that you can create objects of those types.

In short, an ABC describes an interface that uses a least one pure virtual function, and classes derived from an ABC use regular virtual functions to implement the interface in terms of the properties of the particular derived class.

Applying the ABC Concept

You'd probably like to see a complete example of an ABC, so let's apply the concept to representing the Brass and BrassPlus accounts, starting with an ABC called AcctABC. This class should contain all methods and data members that are common to both the Brass and the BrassPlus classes. The methods that are to work differently for the BrassPlus class than they do for the Brass class should be declared as virtual functions. At least one virtual function should be a pure virtual function in order to make the AcctABC class abstract.

Listing 13.11 is a header file that declares the AcctABC class (an ABC) and the Brass and BrassPlus classes (both concrete classes). To facilitate derived class access to base class data, AcctABC provides some protected methods. Recall that protected methods are methods that derived-class methods can call but that are not part of the public interface for derived-class objects. AcctABC also provides a protected member function to handle the formatting previously performed in several methods. Also, the AcctABC class has two pure virtual functions, so it is, indeed, an abstract class.

LISTING 13.11   `acctabc.h`

```
// acctabc.h  -- bank account classes
#ifndef ACCTABC_H_
#define ACCTABC_H_

// Abstract Base Class
class AcctABC
{
private:
    enum {MAX = 35};
    char fullName[MAX];
    long acctNum;
    double balance;
protected:
    const char * FullName() const {return fullName;}
    long AcctNum() const {return acctNum;}
    std::ios_base::fmtflags SetFormat() const;
public:
    AcctABC(const char *s = "Nullbody", long an = -1,
                double bal = 0.0);
    void Deposit(double amt) ;
    virtual void Withdraw(double amt) = 0; // pure virtual function
    double Balance() const {return balance;};
    virtual void ViewAcct() const = 0;     // pure virtual function
    virtual ~AcctABC() {}
};

// Brass Account Class
class Brass :public AcctABC
{
public:
    Brass(const char *s = "Nullbody", long an = -1,
            double bal = 0.0) : AcctABC(s, an, bal) { }
    virtual void Withdraw(double amt);
    virtual void ViewAcct() const;
    virtual ~Brass() {}
};

//Brass Plus Account Class
class BrassPlus : public AcctABC
{
private:
    double maxLoan;
    double rate;
    double owesBank;
public:
    BrassPlus(const char *s = "Nullbody", long an = -1,
            double bal = 0.0, double ml = 500,
```

LISTING 13.11   Continued

```
                    double r = 0.10);
        BrassPlus(const Brass & ba, double ml = 500, double r = 0.1);
        virtual void ViewAcct()const;
        virtual void Withdraw(double amt);
        void ResetMax(double m) { maxLoan = m; }
        void ResetRate(double r) { rate = r; };
        void ResetOwes() { owesBank = 0; }
};

#endif
```

The next step is to implement the methods that don't already have inline definitions. Listing 13.12 does that.

LISTING 13.12   `acctabc.cpp`

```
// acctabc.cpp -- bank account class methods
#include <iostream>
#include <cstring>
using std::cout;
using std::ios_base;
using std::endl;

#include "acctabc.h"

// Abstract Base Class
AcctABC::AcctABC(const char *s, long an, double bal)
{
    std::strncpy(fullName, s, MAX - 1);
    fullName[MAX - 1] = '\0';
    acctNum = an;
    balance = bal;
}

void AcctABC::Deposit(double amt)
{
    if (amt < 0)
        cout << "Negative deposit not allowed; "
             << "deposit is cancelled.\n";
    else
        balance += amt;
}

void AcctABC::Withdraw(double amt)
{
    balance -= amt;
}

// protected method
ios_base::fmtflags AcctABC::SetFormat() const
{
```

LISTING 13.12 Continued

```
    // set up ###.## format
      ios_base::fmtflags initialState =
          cout.setf(ios_base::fixed, ios_base::floatfield);
      cout.setf(ios_base::showpoint);
      cout.precision(2);
      return initialState;
}

// Brass methods
void Brass::Withdraw(double amt)
{
    if (amt < 0)
        cout << "Withdrawal amount must be positive; "
              << "withdrawal canceled.\n";
    else if (amt <= Balance())
        AcctABC::Withdraw(amt);
    else
        cout << "Withdrawal amount of $" << amt
              << " exceeds your balance.\n"
              << "Withdrawal canceled.\n";
}

void Brass::ViewAcct() const
{

    ios_base::fmtflags initialState = SetFormat();
    cout << "Brass Client: " << FullName() << endl;
    cout << "Account Number: " << AcctNum() << endl;
    cout << "Balance: $" << Balance() << endl;
    cout.setf(initialState);
}

// BrassPlus Methods
BrassPlus::BrassPlus(const char *s, long an, double bal,
          double ml, double r) : AcctABC(s, an, bal)
{
    maxLoan = ml;
    owesBank = 0.0;
    rate = r;
}

BrassPlus::BrassPlus(const Brass & ba, double ml, double r)
          : AcctABC(ba)    // uses implicit copy constructor
{
    maxLoan = ml;
    owesBank = 0.0;
    rate = r;
}

void BrassPlus::ViewAcct() const
{
    ios_base::fmtflags initialState = SetFormat();
```

LISTING 13.12 Continued

```cpp
    cout << "BrassPlus Client: " << FullName() << endl;
    cout << "Account Number: " << AcctNum() << endl;
    cout << "Balance: $" << Balance() << endl;
    cout << "Maximum loan: $" << maxLoan << endl;
    cout << "Owed to bank: $" << owesBank << endl;
    cout << "Loan Rate: " << 100 * rate << "%\n";
    cout.setf(initialState);
}

void BrassPlus::Withdraw(double amt)
{
    ios_base::fmtflags initialState = SetFormat();

    double bal = Balance();
    if (amt <= bal)
        AcctABC::Withdraw(amt);
    else if ( amt <= bal + maxLoan - owesBank)
    {
        double advance = amt - bal;
        owesBank += advance * (1.0 + rate);
        cout << "Bank advance: $" << advance << endl;
        cout << "Finance charge: $" << advance * rate << endl;
        Deposit(advance);
        AcctABC::Withdraw(amt);
    }
    else
        cout << "Credit limit exceeded. Transaction cancelled.\n";
    cout.setf(initialState);
}
```

The `FullName()` and `AcctNum()` protected methods provide read-only access to the `fullName` and `acctNum` data members and make it possible to customize `ViewAcct()` a little more individually for each derived class.

This new implementation of the `Brass` and `BrassPlus` accounts can be used in the same manner as the old one because the class methods have the same names and interfaces as before. For example, to convert Listing 13.10 to use the new implementation, you just need to take these steps to convert `usebrass2.cpp` to a `usebrass3.cpp` file:

- Link `usebrass2.cpp` with `acctabc.cpp` instead of with `brass.cpp`.

- Include `acctabc.h` instead of `brass.h`.

- Replace

  `Brass * p_clients[CLIENTS];`

  with

  `AcctABC * p_clients[CLIENTS];`

ABC Philosophy

The ABC methodology is a much more systematic, disciplined way to approach inheritance than the more ad hoc, spur-of-the-moment approach used by the **RatedPlayer** example. Before designing an ABC, you first have to develop a model of what classes are needed to represent a programming problem and how they relate to one another. One school of thought holds that if you design an inheritance hierarchy of classes, the only concrete classes should be those that never serve as a base class. This approach tends to produce cleaner designs with fewer complications.

Real-World Note: Enforcing Interface Rules with ABCs

One way of thinking about ABCs is to consider them an enforcement of interface. An ABC demands that its pure virtual functions be overridden in any concrete derived classes—forcing the derived class to obey the rules of interface the ABC has set. This model is common in component-based programming paradigms, in which the use of ABCs allows the component designer to create an "interface contract" where all components derived from the ABC are guaranteed to uphold *at least* the common functionality specified by the ABC.

Inheritance and Dynamic Memory Allocation

How does inheritance interact with dynamic memory allocation (the use of **new** and **delete**)? For example, if a base class uses dynamic memory allocation and redefines assignment and a copy constructor, how does that affect the implementation of the derived class? The answer depends on the nature of the derived class. If the derived class does not itself use dynamic memory allocation, you needn't take any special steps. If the derived class does also use dynamic memory allocation, then there are a couple new tricks to learn. Let's look at these two cases.

Case 1: Derived Class Doesn't Use new

Suppose you begin with the following base class that uses dynamic memory allocation:

```
// Base Class Using DMA
class baseDMA
{
private:
    char * label;
    int rating;

public:
    baseDMA(const char * l = "null", int r = 0);
    baseDMA(const baseDMA & rs);
    virtual ~baseDMA();
    baseDMA & operator=(const baseDMA & rs);
...
};
```

The declaration contains the special methods that are required when constructors use `new`: a destructor, a copy constructor, and an overloaded assignment operator.

Now suppose you derive a `lackDMA` class from `baseDMA` and that `lackDMA` does not use `new` or have other unusual design features that require special treatment:

```
// derived class without DMA
class lacksDMA :public baseDMA
{
private:
    char color[40];
public:
...
};
```

Do you now have to define an explicit destructor, copy constructor, and assignment operator for the `lackDMA` class? The answer is no.

First, consider the need for a destructor. If you don't define one, the compiler defines a default destructor that does nothing. Actually, the default destructor for a derived class always does something; it calls the base-class destructor after executing its own code. Because the `lackDMA` members, we assume, don't require any special action, the default destructor is fine.

Next, consider the copy constructor. As you saw in Chapter 12, the default copy constructor does memberwise copying, which is inappropriate for dynamic memory allocation. However, memberwise copying is fine for the new `lacksDMA` member. That leaves the matter of the inherited `baseDMA` object. What you need to know is that memberwise copying uses the form of copying that is defined for the data type in question. So copying a `long` to a `long` is done using ordinary assignment. But copying a class member or an inherited class component is done using the copy constructor for that class. Thus, the default copy constructor for the `lacksDMA` class uses the explicit `baseDMA` copy constructor to copy the `baseDMA` portion of a `lacksDMA` object. So the default copy constructor is fine for the new `lacksDMA` member, and it's also fine for the inherited `baseDMA` object.

Essentially the same situation holds for assignment. The default assignment operator for a class automatically uses the base-class assignment operator for the base-class component. So it, too, is fine.

These properties of inherited objects also hold true for class members that are themselves objects. For example, Chapter 10, "Objects and Classes," describes how you could implement the `Stock` class by using a `string` object instead of a `char` array to represent the company name. The standard `string` class, like our `String` example, uses dynamic memory allocation. Now you see why this wouldn't create problems. The default `Stock` copy constructor would use the `string` copy constructor to copy the `company` member of an object, the default `Stock` assignment operator would use the `string` assignment operator to assign the `company` member of an object, and the `Stock` destructor (default or otherwise) would automatically call the `string` destructor.

Case 2: Derived Class Does Use new

Suppose that the derived class uses new:

```
// derived class with DMA
class hasDMA :public baseDMA
{
private:
    char * style;  // use new in constructors
public:
...
};
```

In this case, of course, you do have to define an explicit destructor, copy constructor, and assignment operator for the derived class. Let's consider these methods in turn.

A derived class destructor automatically calls the base-class destructor, so its own responsibility is to clean up after what the derived-class constructors do. Thus, the hasDMA destructor has to free the memory managed by the style pointer and can rely on the baseDMA destructor to free the memory managed by the label pointer:

```
baseDMA::~baseDMA()  // takes care of baseDMA stuff
{
    delete [] label;
}

hasDMA::~hasDMA()       // takes care of hasDMA stuff
{
    delete [] style;
}
```

Next, consider copy constructors. The baseDMA copy constructor follows the usual pattern:

```
baseDMA::baseDMA(const baseDMA & rs)
{
    label = new char[std::strlen(rs.label) + 1];
    std::strcpy(label, rs.label);
    rating = rs.rating;
}
```

The hasDMA copy constructor only has access to hasDMA data, so it must invoke the baseDMA copy constructor to handle the baseDMA share of the data:

```
hasDMA::hasDMA(const hasDMA & hs)
        : baseDMA(hs)
{
    style = new char[std::strlen(hs.style) + 1];
    std::strcpy(style, hs.style);
}
```

The point to note is that the member initializer list passes a hasDMA reference to a baseDMA constructor. There is no baseDMA constructor with a type hasDMA reference parameter, but none is needed. That's because the baseDMA copy constructor has a baseDMA reference parameter, and a base class reference can refer to a derived type. Thus, the baseDMA copy constructor uses the `baseDMA` portion of the `hasDMA` argument to construct the `baseDMA` portion of the new object.

Next, consider assignment operators. The `baseDMA` assignment operator follows the usual pattern:

```
baseDMA & baseDMA::operator=(const baseDMA & rs)
{
    if (this == &rs)
        return *this;
    delete [] label;
    label = new char[std::strlen(rs.label) + 1];
    std::strcpy(label, rs.label);
    rating = rs.rating;
    return *this;
}
```

Because `hasDMA` also uses dynamic memory allocation, it, too, needs an explicit assignment operator. Being a `hasDMA` method, it only has direct access to `hasDMA` data. Nonetheless, an explicit assignment operator for a derived class also has to take care of assignment for the inherited base class `baseDMA` object. You can accomplish this by explicitly calling the base class assignment operator, as shown here:

```
hasDMA & hasDMA::operator=(const hasDMA & hs)
{
    if (this == &hs)
        return *this;
    baseDMA::operator=(hs);  // copy base portion
    style = new char[std::strlen(hs.style) + 1];
    std::strcpy(style, hs.style);
    return *this;
}
```

The statement

```
baseDMA::operator=(hs);  // copy base portion
```

may look a little odd. But using function notation instead of operator notation lets you use the scope-resolution operator. In effect, the statement means the following:

```
*this = hs;  // use baseDMA::operator=()
```

But, of course, the compiler ignores comments, so if you used the latter code, the compiler would use `hasDMA::operator=()` instead and create a recursive call. Using function notation gets the correct assignment operator called.

In summary, when both the base class and the derived class use dynamic memory allocation, the derived-class destructor, copy constructor, and assignment operator all must use their base-class counterparts to handle the base-class component. This common requirement is accomplished three different ways. For a destructor, it is done automatically. For a constructor, it is accomplished by invoking the base-class copy constructor in the member initialization list, or else the default constructor is invoked automatically. For the assignment operator, it is accomplished by using the scope-resolution operator in an explicit call of the base-class assignment operator.

An Inheritance Example with Dynamic Memory Allocation and Friends

To illustrate these ideas of inheritance and dynamic memory allocation, let's integrate the baseDMA, lacksDMA, and hasDMA classes just discussed into a single example. Listing 13.13 is a header file for these classes. To what we've already discussed, it adds a friend function that illustrates how derived classes can access friends to a base class.

LISTING 13.13 dma.h

```
// dma.h  -- inheritance and dynamic memory allocation
#ifndef DMA_H_
#define DMA_H_
#include <iostream>

//   Base Class Using DMA
class baseDMA
{
private:
    char * label;
    int rating;

public:
    baseDMA(const char * l = "null", int r = 0);
    baseDMA(const baseDMA & rs);
    virtual ~baseDMA();
    baseDMA & operator=(const baseDMA & rs);
    friend std::ostream & operator<<(std::ostream & os,
                                     const baseDMA & rs);
};

// derived class without DMA
// no destructor needed
// uses implicit copy constructor
// uses implicit assignment operator
class lacksDMA :public baseDMA
{
private:
    enum { COL_LEN = 40};
    char color[COL_LEN];
public:
    lacksDMA(const char * c = "blank", const char * l = "null",
             int r = 0);
    lacksDMA(const char * c, const baseDMA & rs);
    friend std::ostream & operator<<(std::ostream & os,
                                     const lacksDMA & rs);
};

// derived class with DMA
class hasDMA :public baseDMA
{
```

LISTING 13.13   Continued

```
private:
    char * style;
public:
    hasDMA(const char * s = "none", const char * l = "null",
               int r = 0);
    hasDMA(const char * s, const baseDMA & rs);
    hasDMA(const hasDMA & hs);
    ~hasDMA();
    hasDMA & operator=(const hasDMA & rs);
    friend std::ostream & operator<<(std::ostream & os,
                                     const hasDMA & rs);
};

#endif
```

Listing 13.14 provides the method definitions for the `baseDMA`, `lacksDMA`, and `hasDMA` classes.

LISTING 13.14   `dma.cpp`

```
// dma.cpp --dma class methods

#include "dma.h"
#include <cstring>

// baseDMA methods
baseDMA::baseDMA(const char * l, int r)
{
    label = new char[std::strlen(l) + 1];
    std::strcpy(label, l);
    rating = r;
}

baseDMA::baseDMA(const baseDMA & rs)
{
    label = new char[std::strlen(rs.label) + 1];
    std::strcpy(label, rs.label);
    rating = rs.rating;
}

baseDMA::~baseDMA()
{
    delete [] label;
}

baseDMA & baseDMA::operator=(const baseDMA & rs)
{
    if (this == &rs)
        return *this;
    delete [] label;
    label = new char[std::strlen(rs.label) + 1];
    std::strcpy(label, rs.label);
```

LISTING 13.14 Continued

```cpp
        rating = rs.rating;
        return *this;
    }

    std::ostream & operator<<(std::ostream & os, const baseDMA & rs)
    {
        os << "Label: " << rs.label << std::endl;
        os << "Rating: " << rs.rating << std::endl;
        return os;
    }

    // lacksDMA methods
    lacksDMA::lacksDMA(const char * c, const char * l, int r)
        : baseDMA(l, r)
    {
        std::strncpy(color, c, 39);
        color[39] = '\0';
    }

    lacksDMA::lacksDMA(const char * c, const baseDMA & rs)
        : baseDMA(rs)
    {
        std::strncpy(color, c, COL_LEN - 1);
        color[COL_LEN - 1] = '\0';
    }

    std::ostream & operator<<(std::ostream & os, const lacksDMA & ls)
    {
        os << (const baseDMA &) ls;
        os << "Color: " << ls.color << std::endl;
        return os;
    }

    // hasDMA methods
    hasDMA::hasDMA(const char * s, const char * l, int r)
            : baseDMA(l, r)
    {
        style = new char[std::strlen(s) + 1];
        std::strcpy(style, s);
    }

    hasDMA::hasDMA(const char * s, const baseDMA & rs)
            : baseDMA(rs)
    {
        style = new char[std::strlen(s) + 1];
        std::strcpy(style, s);
    }

    hasDMA::hasDMA(const hasDMA & hs)
            : baseDMA(hs)  // invoke base class copy constructor
    {
```

LISTING 13.14 Continued

```
    style = new char[std::strlen(hs.style) + 1];
    std::strcpy(style, hs.style);
}

hasDMA::~hasDMA()
{
    delete [] style;
}

hasDMA & hasDMA::operator=(const hasDMA & hs)
{
    if (this == &hs)
        return *this;
    baseDMA::operator=(hs);  // copy base portion
    style = new char[std::strlen(hs.style) + 1];
    std::strcpy(style, hs.style);
    return *this;
}

std::ostream & operator<<(std::ostream & os, const hasDMA & hs)
{
    os << (const baseDMA &) hs;
    os << "Style: " << hs.style << std::endl;
    return os;
}
```

The new feature to note in Listings 13.13 and 13.14 is how derived classes can make use of a friend to a base class. Consider, for example, the following friend to the `hasDMA` class:

```
friend std::ostream & operator<<(std::ostream & os,
                                 const hasDMA & rs);
```

Being a friend to the `hasDMA` class gives this function access to the `style` member. But there's a problem: This function is not a friend to the `baseDMA` class, so how can it access the `label` and `rating` members? The solution is to use the `operator<<()` function that is a friend to the `baseDMA` class. The next problem is that because friends are not member functions, you can't use the scope-resolution operator to indicate which function to use. The solution to this problem is to use a type cast so that prototype matching will select the correct function. Thus, the code type casts the type `const hasDMA &` parameter to a type `const baseDMA &` argument:

```
std::ostream & operator<<(std::ostream & os, const hasDMA & hs)
{
//  type cast to match operator<<(ostream & , const baseDMA &)
    os << (const baseDMA &) hs;
    os << "Style: " << hs.style << endl;
    return os;
}
```

Listing 13.15 tests the `baseDMA`, `lacksDMA`, and `hasDMA` classes in a short program.

LISTING 13.15   usedma.cpp

```
// usedma.cpp -- inheritance, friends, and DMA
// compile with dma.cpp
#include <iostream>
#include "dma.h"
int main()
{
    using std::cout;
    using std::endl;

    baseDMA shirt("Portabelly", 8);
    lacksDMA balloon("red", "Blimpo", 4);
    hasDMA map("Mercator", "Buffalo Keys", 5);
    cout << shirt << endl;
    cout << balloon << endl;
    cout << map << endl;
    lacksDMA balloon2(balloon);
    hasDMA map2;
    map2 = map;
    cout << balloon2 << endl;
    cout << map2 << endl;
    return 0;
}
```

Here's the output of the program in Listings 13.13, 13.14, and 13.15:

```
Label: Portabelly
Rating: 8

Label: Blimpo
Rating: 4
Color: red

Label: Buffalo Keys
Rating: 5
Style: Mercator

Label: Blimpo
Rating: 4
Color: red

Label: Buffalo Keys
Rating: 5
Style: Mercator
```

Class Design Review

C++ can be applied to a wide variety of programming problems, and you can't reduce class design to some paint-by-numbers routine. However, there are some guidelines that often apply, and this is as good a time as any to go over them, by reviewing and amplifying earlier discussions.

Member Functions That the Compiler Generates for You

As first discussed in Chapter 12, the compiler automatically generates certain public member functions. The fact that it does so suggests that these member functions are particularly important. Let's look again at some of them now.

Default Constructors

A default constructor is one that has no arguments, or else one for which all the arguments have default arguments. If you don't define any constructors, the compiler defines a default constructor for you. Its existence allows you to create objects. For example, suppose `Star` is a class. You need a default constructor to use the following:

```
Star rigel;        // create an object without explicit initialization
Star pleiades[6];  // create an array of objects
```

One more thing an automatic default constructor does is call the default constructors for any base classes and for any members that are objects of another class.

Also, if you write a derived-class constructor without explicitly invoking a base-class constructor in the member initializer list, the compiler uses the base class default constructor to construct the base class portion of the new object. If there is no base-class default constructor, you get a compile-time error in this situation.

If you define a constructor of any kind, the compiler does not define a default constructor for you. In that case, it's up to you to provide a default constructor if one is needed.

Note that one of the motivations for having constructors is to ensure that objects are always properly initialized. Also, if a class has any pointer members, they certainly should be initialized. Thus, it's a good idea to supply an explicit default constructor that initializes all class data members to reasonable values.

Copy Constructors

A copy constructor for a class is a constructor that takes an object of the class type as its argument. Typically, the declared parameter is a constant reference to the class type. For example, the copy constructor for a `Star` class would have this prototype:

```
Star(const Star &);
```

A class copy constructor is used in the following situations:

- When a new object is initialized to an object of the same class
- When an object is passed to a function by value
- When a function returns an object by value
- When the compiler generates a temporary object

If a program doesn't use a copy constructor (explicitly or implicitly), the compiler provides a prototype, but not a function definition. Otherwise, the program defines a copy constructor that performs memberwise initialization. That is, each member of the new object is initialized to the value of the corresponding member of the original object.

In some cases, memberwise initialization is undesirable. For example, member pointers initialized with new generally require that you institute deep copying, as with the baseDMA class example. Or a class may have a static variable that needs to be modified. In such cases, you need to define your own copy constructor.

Assignment Operators

A default assignment operator handles assigning one object to another object of the same class. Don't confuse assignment with initialization. If a statement creates a new object, it's using initialization, and if a statement alters the value of an existing object, it's assignment:

```
Star sirius;
Star alpha = sirius;     // initialization (one notation)
Star dogstar;
dogstar = sirius;        // assignment
```

If you need to define a copy constructor explicitly, you also need, for the same reasons, to define the assignment operator explicitly. The prototype for a Star class assignment operator is this:

```
Star & Star::operator=(const Star &);
```

Note that the assignment operator function returns a reference to a Star object. The baseDMA class shows a typical example of an explicit assignment operator function.

The compiler doesn't generate assignment operators for assigning one type to another. Suppose you want to be able to assign a string to a Star object. One approach is to define such an operator explicitly:

```
Star & Star::operator=(const char *) {...}
```

A second approach is to rely on a conversion function (see "Conversion Considerations" in the next section) to convert a string to a Star object and use the Star-to-Star assignment function. The first approach runs more quickly, but requires more code. The conversion function approach can lead to compiler-befuddling situations.

Other Class Method Considerations

There are several other points to keep in mind as you define a class. The following sections list some of them.

Constructor Considerations

Constructors are different from other class methods in that they create new objects, whereas other methods are invoked by existing objects. This is one reason constructors aren't inherited. Inheritance means a derived object can use a base-class method, but, in the case of constructors, the object doesn't exist until after the constructor has done its work.

Destructor Considerations

You need to remember to define an explicit destructor that deletes any memory allocated by new in the class constructors and takes care of any other special bookkeeping that destroying a class object requires. If the class is to be used as a base class, you should provide a virtual destructor even if the class doesn't require a destructor.

Conversion Considerations

Any constructor that can be invoked with exactly one argument defines conversion from the argument type to the class type. For example, consider the following constructor prototypes for a Star class:

```
Star(const char *);                         // converts char * to Star
Star(const Spectral &, int members = 1);    // converts Spectral to Star
```

Conversion constructors are used, for example, when a convertible type is passed to a function that is defined as taking a class argument. For example, suppose you have the following:

```
Star north;
north = "polaris";
```

The second statement would invoke the Star::operator=(const Star &) function, using Star::Star(const char *) to generate a Star object to be used as an argument for the assignment operator function. This assumes that you haven't defined a (char *)-to-Star assignment operator.

Using explicit in the prototype for a one-argument constructor disables implicit conversions but still allows explicit conversions:

```
class Star
{
...
public:
    explicit Star(const char *);
...
};
Star north;
north = "polaris";         // not allowed
north = Star("polaris");   // allowed
```

To convert from a class object to some other type, you define a conversion function (see Chapter 11, "Working with Classes"). A conversion function is a class member function with no arguments or declared return type that has the name of the type to be converted to. Despite having no declared return type, the function should return the desired conversion value. Here are some examples:

```
Star::Star double() {...}        // converts star to double
Star::Star const char * () {...}   // converts to const char
```

You should be judicious with such functions, only using them if they make good sense. Also, with some class designs, having conversion functions increases the likelihood of writing ambiguous code. For example, suppose you define a `double` conversion for the `vector` type of Chapter 11, and suppose you have the following code:

```
vector ius(6.0, 0.0);
vector lux = ius + 20.2;        // ambiguous
```

The compiler could convert `ius` to `double` and use `double` addition, or else it could convert `20.2` to `vector` (using one of the constructors) and use `vector` addition. Instead, it would do neither and inform you of an ambiguous construction.

Passing an Object by Value Versus Passing a Reference

In general, if you write a function using an object argument, you should pass the object by reference rather than by value. One reason for this is efficiency. Passing an object by value involves generating a temporary copy, which means calling the copy constructor and then later calling the destructor. Calling these functions takes time, and copying a large object can be quite a bit slower than passing a reference. If the function doesn't modify the object, you should declare the argument as a `const` reference.

Another reason for passing objects by reference is that, in the case of inheritance using virtual functions, a function defined as accepting a base-class reference argument can also be used successfully with derived classes, as you saw earlier in this chapter. (Also see the section "Virtual Methods," later in this chapter.)

Returning an Object Versus Returning a Reference

Some class methods return objects. You've probably noticed that some members return objects directly whereas others return references. Sometimes a method must return an object, but if it isn't necessary, you should use a reference instead. Let's look at this more closely.

First, the only coding difference between returning an object directly and returning a reference is in the function prototype and header:

```
Star nova1(const Star &);       // returns a Star object
Star & nova2(const Star &);     // returns a reference to a Star
```

Next, the reason you should return a reference rather than an object is that returning an object involves generating a temporary copy of the returned object. It's the copy that is made available to the calling program. Thus, returning an object involves the time cost of calling a copy constructor to generate the copy and the time cost of calling the destructor to get rid of the copy. Returning a reference saves time and memory use. Returning an object directly is analogous to passing an object by value: Both processes generate temporary copies. Similarly, returning a reference is analogous to passing an object by reference: Both the calling and the called function operate on the same object.

However, it's not always possible to return a reference. A function shouldn't return a reference to a temporary object created in the function because the reference becomes invalid when the function terminates and the object disappears. In this case, the code should return an object in order to generate a copy that will be available to the calling program.

As a rule of thumb, if a function returns a temporary object created in the function, you shouldn't use a reference. For example, the following method uses a constructor to create a new object, and it then returns a copy of that object:

```
Vector Vector::operator+(const Vector & b) const
{
    return Vector(x + b.x, y + b.y);
}
```

If a function returns an object that was passed to it via a reference or pointer, you should return the object by reference. For example, the following code returns, by reference, either the object that invokes the function or else the object passed as an argument:

```
const Stock & Stock::topval(const Stock & s) const
{
    if (s.total_val > total_val)
        return s;              // argument object
    else
        return *this;          // invoking object
}
```

Using const

You need to be alert to opportunities to use const. You can use it to guarantee that a method doesn't modify an argument:

```
Star::Star(const char * s) {...} // won't change the string to which s points
```

You can use const to guarantee that a method won't modify the object that invokes it:

```
void Star::show() const {...} // won't change invoking object
```

Here const means const Star * this, where this points to the invoking object.

Normally, a function that returns a reference can be on the left side of an assignment statement, which really means you can assign a value to the object referred to. But you can use const to ensure that a reference or pointer return value can't be used to modify data in an object:

```
const Stock & Stock::topval(const Stock & s) const
{
    if (s.total_val > total_val)
        return s;              // argument object
    else
        return *this;          // invoking object
}
```

Here the method returns a reference either to this or to s. Because this and s are both declared const, the function is not allowed to change them, which means the returned reference also must be declared const.

Note that if a function declares an argument as a reference or pointer to a const, it cannot pass along that argument to another function unless that function also guarantees not to change the argument.

Public Inheritance Considerations

Naturally, adding inheritance to a program brings up a number of considerations. Let's look at a few.

Is-a Relationships

You should be guided by the *is-a* relationship. If your proposed derived class is not a particular kind of the base class, you shouldn't use public derivation. For example, you shouldn't derive a `Programmer` class from a `Brain` class. If you want to represent the belief that a programmer has a brain, you should use a `Brain` class object as a member of the `Programmer` class.

In some cases the best approach may be to create an abstract data class with pure virtual functions and to derive other classes from it.

Remember that one expression of the *is-a* relationship is that a base class pointer can point to a derived-class object and that a base-class reference can refer to a derived-class object without an explicit type cast. Also remember that the reverse is not true; thus, you cannot have a derived-class pointer or reference refer to a base-class object without an explicit type cast. Depending on the class declarations, such an explicit type cast (a downcast) may or may not make sense. (You might want to review Figure 13.4.)

What's Not Inherited

Constructors are not inherited. That is, creating a derived object requires calling a derived-class constructor. However, derived-class constructors typically use the member-initializer list syntax to call on base-class constructors to construct the base class portion of a derived object. If the derived-class constructor doesn't explicitly call a base-class constructor by using the member-initializer list syntax, it uses the base class's default constructor. In an inheritance chain, each class can use a member initializer list to pass back information to its immediate base class.

Destructors are not inherited. However, when an object is destroyed, the program first calls the derived destructor and then the base destructor. If there is a default base class destructor, the compiler generates a default derived class destructor. Generally speaking, if a class serves as a base class, its destructor should be virtual.

Assignment Operators

Assignment operators are not inherited. The reason is simple. An inherited method has the same function signature in a derived class as it does in the base class. However, an assignment operator has a function signature that changes from class to class because it has a formal parameter that is the class type. Assignment operators do have some interesting properties, which we'll look at next.

If the compiler detects that a program assigns one object to another of the same class, it automatically supplies that class with an assignment operator. The default, or implicit, version of this operator uses memberwise assignment, with each member of the target object being assigned the value of the corresponding member of the source object. However, if the object belongs to a derived class, the compiler uses the base-class assignment operator to handle assignment for the base-class portion of the derived-class object. If you've explicitly provided an assignment operator for the base class, that operator is used. Similarly, if a class contains a member that is an object of another class, the assignment operator for that class is used for that member.

As you've seen several times, you need to provide an explicit assignment operator if class constructors use new to initialize pointers. Because C++ uses the base-class assignment operator for the base part of derived objects, you don't need to redefine the assignment operator for a derived class *unless* it adds data members that require special care. For example, the baseDMA class defines assignment explicitly, but the derived lacksDMA class uses the implicit assignment operator generated for that class.

Suppose, however, that a derived class does use new, and you have to provide an explicit assignment operator. The operator must provide for every member of the class, not just the new members. The hasDMA class illustrates how this can be done:

```
hasDMA & hasDMA::operator=(const hasDMA & hs)
{
    if (this == &hs)
        return *this;
    baseDMA::operator=(hs);   // copy base portion
    style = new char[std::strlen(hs.style) + 1];
    std::strcpy(style, hs.style);
    return *this;
}
```

What about assigning a derived-class object to a base-class object? (Note: This is not the same as initializing a base-class reference to a derived-class object.) Take a look at this example:

```
Brass blips;                                              // base class
BrassPlus snips("Rafe Plosh", 91191,3993.19, 600.0, 0.12); // derived class
blips = snips;                      // assign derived object to base object
```

Which assignment operator is used? Remember that the assignment statement is translated into a method that is invoked by the left-hand object:

```
blips.operator=(snips);
```

Here the left-hand object is a Brass object, so it invokes the Brass::operator=(const Brass &) function. The *is-a* relationship allows the Brass reference to refer to a derived-class object, such as snips. The assignment operator only deals with base-class members, so the maxLoan member and other BrassPlus members of snips are ignored in the assignment. In short, you can assign a derived object to a base object, and only the base-class members are involved.

What about the reverse? Can you assign a base-class object to a derived object? Take a look at this example:

```
Brass gp("Griff Hexbait", 21234, 1200);    // base class
BrassPlus temp;                             // derived class
temp = gp;   // possible?
```

Here the assignment statement would be translated as follows:

```
temp.operator=(gp);
```

The left-hand object is a `BrassPlus` object, so it invokes the `BrassPlus::operator=(const BrassPlus &)` function. However, a derived-class reference cannot automatically refer to a base-class object, so this code *won't* run unless there is *also* a conversion constructor:

```
BrassPlus(const Brass &);
```

It could be, as is the case for the `BrassPlus` class, that the conversion constructor is a constructor with a base-class argument plus additional arguments, provided that the additional arguments have default values:

```
BrassPlus(const Brass & ba, double ml = 500, double r = 0.1);
```

If there is a conversion constructor, the program uses this constructor to create a temporary `BrassPlus` object from `gp`, which is then used as an argument to the assignment operator.

Alternatively, you could define an assignment operator for assigning a base class to a derived class:

```
BrassPlus & BrassPlus ::operator=(const Brass &) {...}
```

Here the types match the assignment statement exactly, and no type conversions are needed.

In short, the answer to the question "Can you assign a base-class object to a derived object?" is "Maybe." You can if the derived class has a constructor that defines the conversion of a base-class object to a derived-class object. And you can if the derived class defines an assignment operator for assigning a base-class object to a derived object. If neither of these two conditions holds, then you can't make the assignment unless you use an explicit type cast.

Private Versus Protected Members

Remember that protected members act like public members as far as a derived class is concerned, but they act like private members for the world at large. A derived class can access protected members of a base class directly, but it can access private members only via base-class member functions. Thus, making base-class members private offers more security, whereas making them protected simplifies coding and speeds up access. Stroustrup, in his book *The Design and Evolution of C++*, indicates that it's better to use private data members than protected data members but that protected methods are useful.

Virtual Methods

When you design a base class, you have to decide whether to make class methods virtual. If you want a derived class to be able to redefine a method, you define the method as virtual in the base class. This enables late, or dynamic, binding. If you don't want the method to be redefined, you don't make it virtual. This doesn't prevent someone from redefining the method, but it should be interpreted as meaning that you don't want it redefined.

Note that inappropriate code can circumvent dynamic binding. Consider, for example, the following two functions:

```
void show(const Brass & rba)
{
    rba.ViewAcct();
    cout << endl;
}

void inadequate(Brass ba)
{
    ba.ViewAcct();
    cout << endl;
}
```

The first function passes an object by reference, and the second passes an object by value.

Now suppose you use each with a derived class argument:

```
BrassPlus buzz("Buzz Parsec", 00001111, 4300);
show(buzz);
inadequate(buzz);
```

The `show()` function call results in the `rba` argument being a reference to the `BrassPlus` object `buzz`, so `rba.ViewAcct()` is interpreted as the `BrassPlus` version, as it should be. But in the `inadequate()` function, which passes an object by value, `ba` is a `Brass` object constructed by the `Brass(const Brass &)` constructor. (Automatic upcasting allows the constructor argument to refer to a `BrassPlus` object.) Thus, in `inadequate()`, `ba.ViewAcct()` is the `Brass` version, so only the `Brass` component of `buzz` is displayed.

Destructors

As mentioned earlier, a base class destructor should be virtual. That way, when you delete a derived object via a base-class pointer or reference to the object, the program uses the derived-class destructor followed by the base-class destructor rather than using only the base-class destructor.

Friends

Because a friend function is not actually a class member, it's not inherited. However, you might still want a friend to a derived class to use a friend to the base class. The way to accomplish this is to type cast a derived-class reference or pointer to the base-class equivalent and to then use the type cast reference or pointer to invoke the base-class friend:

```
ostream & operator<<(ostream & os, const hasDMA & hs)
{
//  type cast to match operator<<(ostream & , const baseDMA &)
    os << (const baseDMA &) hs;
    os << "Style: " << hs.style << endl;
    return os;
}
```

You can also use the `dynamic_cast<>` operator, discussed in Chapter 15, "Friends, Exceptions, and More," for the type cast:

```
os << dynamic_cast<const baseDMA &> (hs);
```

For reasons discussed in Chapter 15, this would be the preferred form of type cast.

Observations on Using Base-Class Methods

Publicly derived objects can use base-class methods in many ways:

- A derived object automatically uses inherited base-class methods if the derived class hasn't redefined the method.

- A derived-class destructor automatically invokes the base-class constructor.

- A derived-class constructor automatically invokes the base-class default constructor if you don't specify another constructor in a member-initialization list.

- A derived-class constructor explicitly invokes the base-class constructor specified in a member-initialization list.

- Derived-class methods can use the scope-resolution operator to invoke public and protected base-class methods.

- Friends to a derived class can type cast a derived-class reference or pointer to a base-class reference or pointer and then use that reference or pointer to invoke a friend to the base class.

Class Function Summary

C++ class functions come in many variations. Some can be inherited, and some can't. Some operator functions can be either member functions or friends, and others can only be member functions. Table 13.1, based on a similar table from *The Annotated C++ Reference Manual*, summarizes these properties. In it, the notation *op*= stands for assignment operators of the form +=, *=, and so on. Note that the properties for the *op*= operators are no different from those of the "other operators" category. The reason for listing *op*= separately is to point out that these operators don't behave like the = operator.

TABLE 13.1 Member Function Properties

Function	Inherited	Member or Friend	Generated by Default	Can Be Virtual	Can Have a Return Type
Constructor	No	Member	Yes	No	No
Destructor	No	Member	Yes	Yes	No
=	No	Member	Yes	Yes	Yes
&	Yes	Either	Yes	Yes	Yes
Conversion	Yes	Member	No	Yes	No
( )	Yes	Member	No	Yes	Yes
[ ]	Yes	Member	No	Yes	Yes

TABLE 13.1 Continued

Function	Inherited	Member or Friend	Generated by Default	Can Be Virtual	Can Have a Return Type
->	Yes	Member	No	Yes	Yes
op=	Yes	Either	No	Yes	Yes
new	Yes	Static member	No	No	void *
delete	Yes	Static member	No	No	void
Other operators	Yes	Either	No	Yes	Yes
Other members	Yes	Member	No	Yes	Yes
Friends	No	Friend	No	No	Yes

Summary

Inheritance enables you to adapt programming code to your particular needs by defining a new class (a derived class) from an existing class (the base class). Public inheritance models an *is-a* relationship, meaning that a derived-class object should also be a kind of base-class object. As part of the *is-a* model, a derived class inherits the data members and most methods of the base class. However, a derived class doesn't inherit the base-class constructors, destructors, and assignment operators. A derived class can access the public and protected members of the base class directly and the private base-class members via the public and protected base-class methods. You can then add new data members and methods to the class, and you can use the derived class as a base class for further development. Each derived class requires its own constructors. When a program creates a derived-class object, it first calls a base-class constructor and then the derived-class constructor. When a program deletes an object, it first calls the derived-class destructor and then the base-class destructor.

If a class is meant to be a base class, you may choose to use protected members instead of private members so that derived classes can access those members directly. However, using private members, in general, reduces the scope for programming bugs. If you intend that a derived class can redefine a base-class method, you should make it a virtual function by declaring it with the keyword `virtual`. This enables objects accessed by pointers or references to be handled on the basis of the object type rather than on the basis of the reference type or pointer type. In particular, the destructor for a base class should normally be virtual.

You might want to define an ABC that defines an interface without getting into implementation matters. For example, you could define an abstract `Shape` class from which particular shape classes, such as `Circle` and `Square`, will be derived. An ABC must include at least one pure virtual method. You declare a pure virtual method by placing = 0 before the closing semicolon of the declaration:

```
virtual double area() const = 0;
```

You don't have to define pure virtual methods, and you can't create an object of a class that contains pure virtual members. Instead, pure virtual methods serve to define a common interface to be used by derived classes.

Review Questions

1. What does a derived class inherit from a base class?

2. What doesn't a derived class inherit from a base class?

3. Suppose the return type for the baseDMA::operator=() function were defined as void instead of baseDMA &. What effect, if any, would that have? What if the return type were baseDMA instead of baseDMA &?

4. In what order are class constructors and class destructors called when a derived-class object is created and deleted?

5. If a derived class doesn't add any data members to the base class, does the derived class require constructors?

6. Suppose a base class and a derived class both define a method with the same name and a derived-class object invokes the method. What method is called?

7. When should a derived class define an assignment operator?

8. Can you assign the address of an object of a derived class to a pointer to the base class? Can you assign the address of an object of a base class to a pointer to the derived class?

9. Can you assign an object of a derived class to an object of the base class? Can you assign an object of a base class to an object of the derived class?

10. Suppose you define a function that takes a reference to a base-class object as an argument. Why can this function also use a derived-class object as an argument?

11. Suppose you define a function that takes a base-class object as an argument (that is, the function passes a base-class object by value). Why can this function also use a derived-class object as an argument?

12. Why is it usually better to pass objects by reference than by value?

13. Suppose Corporation is a base class and PublicCorporation is a derived class. Also suppose that each class defines a head() member function, that ph is a pointer to the Corporation type, and that ph is assigned the address of a PublicCorporation object. How is ph->head() interpreted if the base class defines head() as a

    a. Regular nonvirtual method

    b. Virtual method

14. What's wrong, if anything, with the following code?

```
class Kitchen
{
private:
    double kit_sq_ft;
public:
    Kitchen() {kit_sq_ft = 0.0; }
    virtual double area() const { return kit_sq_ft * kit_sq_ft; }
};
class House : public Kitchen
{
private:
    double all_sq_ft;
public:
    House() {all_sq_ft += kit_sq_ft;}
    double area(const char *s) const { cout << s; return all_sq_ft; }
};
```

Programming Exercises

1. Start with the following class declaration:

```
// base class
class Cd {  // represents a CD disk
private:
    char performers[50];
    char label[20];
    int selections;   // number of selections
    double playtime;  // playing time in minutes
public:
    Cd(char * s1, char * s2, int n, double x);
    Cd(const Cd & d);
    Cd();
    ~Cd();
    void Report() const;  // reports all CD data
    Cd & operator=(const Cd & d);
};
```

Derive a **Classic** class that adds an array of **char** members that will hold a string identifying the primary work on the CD. If the base class requires that any functions be virtual, modify the base-class declaration to make it so. If a declared method is not needed, remove it from the definition. Test your product with the following program:

```
#include <iostream>
using namespace std;
#include "classic.h"      // which will contain #include cd.h
void Bravo(const Cd & disk);
int main()
{
    Cd c1("Beatles", "Capitol", 14, 35.5);
    Classic c2 = Classic("Piano Sonata in B flat, Fantasia in C",
```

```
                              "Alfred Brendel", "Philips", 2, 57.17);
        Cd *pcd = &c1;

        cout << "Using object directly:\n";
        c1.Report();    // use Cd method
        c2.Report();    // use Classic method

        cout << "Using type cd * pointer to objects:\n";
        pcd->Report();  // use Cd method for cd object
        pcd = &c2;
        pcd->Report();  // use Classic method for classic object

        cout << "Calling a function with a Cd reference argument:\n";
        Bravo(c1);
        Bravo(c2);

        cout << "Testing assignment: ";
        Classic copy;
        copy = c2;
        copy.Report()

        return 0;
}

void Bravo(const Cd & disk)
{
        disk.Report();
}
```

2. Do Programming Exercise 1, but use dynamic memory allocation instead of fixed-size arrays for the various strings tracked by the two classes.

3. Revise the baseDMA-lacksDMA-hasDMA class hierarchy so that all three classes are derived from an ABC. Test the result with a program similar to the one in Listing 13.10. That is, it should feature an array of pointers to the ABC and allow the user to make runtime decisions as to what types of objects are created. Add virtual View() methods to the class definitions to handle displaying the data.

4. The Benevolent Order of Programmers maintains a collection of bottled port. To describe it, the BOP Portmaster has devised a Port class, as declared here:

```
#include <iostream>
using namespace std;
class Port
{
private:
    char * brand;
    char style[20]; // i.e., tawny, ruby, vintage
    int bottles;
public:
    Port(const char * br = "none", const char * st = "none", int b = 0);
    Port(const Port & p);                    // copy constructor
    virtual ~Port() { delete [] brand; }
```

```
    Port & operator=(const Port & p);
    Port & operator+=(int b);              // adds b to bottles
    Port & operator-=(int b);              // subtracts b from bottles, if
available
    int BottleCount() const { return bottles; }
    virtual void Show() const;
    friend ostream & operator<<(ostream & os, const Port & p);
};
```

The `Show()` method presents information in the following format:

```
Brand: Gallo
Kind: tawny
Bottles: 20
```

The `operator<<()` function presents information in the following format (with no new-line character at the end):

```
Gallo, tawny, 20
```

The Portmaster completed the method definitions for the `Port` class and then derived the `VintagePort` class as follows before being relieved of his position for accidentally routing a bottle of '45 Cockburn to someone preparing an experimental barbecue sauce:

```
class VintagePort : public Port // style necessarily = "vintage"
{
private:
    char * nickname;           // i.e., "The Noble" or "Old Velvet", etc.
    int year;                  // vintage year
public:
    VintagePort();
    VintagePort(const char * br, int b, const char * nn, int y);
    VintagePort(const VintagePort & vp);
    ~VintagePort() { delete [] nickname; }
    VintagePort & operator=(const VintagePort & vp);
    void Show() const;
    friend ostream & operator<<(ostream & os, const VintagePort & vp);
};
```

You get the job of completing the `VintagePort` work.

a. Your first task is to re-create the `Port` method definitions because the former Portmaster immolated his upon being relieved.

b. Your second task is to explain why certain methods are redefined and others are not.

c. Your third task is to explain why `operator=()` and `operator<<()` are not virtual.

d. Your fourth task is to provide definitions for the `VintagePort` methods.

CHAPTER 14

REUSING CODE IN C++

In this chapter you'll learn about the following:

- *Has-a* relationships
- Classes with member objects (containment)
- The `valarray` template class
- Private and protected inheritance

- Multiple inheritance
- Virtual base classes
- Creating class templates
- Using class templates
- Template specializations

One of the main goals of C++ is to facilitate the reuse of code. Public inheritance is one mechanism for achieving this goal, but it's not the only one. This chapter investigates other choices. One technique is to use class members that are themselves objects of another class. This is referred to as *containment* or *composition* or *layering*. Another option is to use private or protected inheritance. Containment, private inheritance, and protected inheritance are typically used to implement *has-a* relationships—that is, relationships for which the new class has an object of another class. For example, a `HomeTheater` class might have a `DvdPlayer` object. Multiple inheritance lets you create classes that inherit from two or more base classes, combining their functionality.

Chapter 10, "Objects and Classes," introduces function templates. In this chapter we'll look at class templates, which provide another way of reusing code. A class template lets you define a class in generic terms. Then you can use the template to create specific classes defined for specific types. For example, you could define a general stack template and then use the template to create one class that represents a stack of `int` values and another class that represents a stack of `double` values. You could even generate a class that represents a stack of stacks.

Classes with Object Members

Let's begin with classes that include class objects as members. Some classes, such as the `string` class or the standard C++ class templates discussed in Chapter 16, "The `string` Class and the Standard Template Library," offer convenient ways of representing components of a more extensive class. Let's look at a particular example now.

What is a student? Someone enrolled in a school? Someone engaged in thoughtful investigation? A refugee from the harsh exigencies of the real world? Someone with an identifying name and a set of quiz scores? Clearly, the last definition is a totally inadequate characterization of a person, but it is well suited for a simple computer representation. So let's develop a `Student` class based on that definition.

Simplifying a student to a name and a set of quiz scores suggests using a class with two members: one to represent the name and one to represent the scores. For the name, you could use a character array, but that puts a size limitation on the name. Or you could use a `char` pointer and dynamic memory allocation. However, as Chapter 12, "Classes and Dynamic Memory Allocation," illustrates, that requires a lot of supporting code. Better yet, you could use an object of a class for which someone has already done all the work. For example, you could use an object of the `String` class (see Chapter 12) or of the standard C++ `string` class. The simpler choice is the `string` class because the C++ library already provides all the implementation code. (To use the `String` class, you'd have to make the `string1.cpp` implementation file part of your project.)

Representing the quiz scores presents similar choices. You could use a fixed-size array, which places a size limitation. You could use dynamic memory allocation and provide a large body of supporting code. You could use your own design of a class, using dynamic memory allocation to represent an array. You could look for a standard C++ library class that is capable of representing the data.

The problem with the third choice is that you haven't developed such a class. A simple version wouldn't be that difficult because an array of `double` shares many similarities with an array of `char`, so you could base the design of an array-of-`double` class on the `String` class design. And, in fact, that is what earlier editions of this book do.

But, of course, it is even easier if the library already provides a suitable class, and it does: the `valarray` class.

The `valarray` Class: A Quick Look

The `valarray` class is supported by the `valarray` header file. As its name suggests, the class is targeted to deal with numeric values (or with classes with similar properties), so it supports operations such as summing the contents and finding the largest and smallest values in an array. So that it can handle different data types, `valarray` is defined as a template class. Later, this chapter goes into how to define template classes, but all you need to know now is how to use one.

The template aspect means that you have to specify a specific type when declaring an object. To do so when declaring an object, you follow the identifier `valarray` with angle brackets that contain the desired type:

```
valarray<int> q_values;      // an array of int
valarray<double> weights;    // an array of double
```

This is the only new syntax you need to learn, and it's pretty easy.

The class aspect means that to use `valarray` objects, you need to know something about class constructors and other class methods. Here are several examples that use some of the constructors:

```
double gpa[5] = {3.1, 3.5, 3.8, 2.9, 3.3};
valarray<double> v1;        // an array of int, size 0
valarray<int> v2(8);        // an array of 8 int elements
valarray<int> v3(10,8);     // an array of 8 int elements,
                            // each set to 10
valarray<double> v4(gpa, 4); // an array of 4 elements
              // initialized to the first 4 elements of gpa
```

As you can see, you can create an empty array of zero size, an empty array of a given size, an array with all elements initialized to the same value, and an array initialized using the values from an ordinary array.

Next, here are a few of the methods:

- `operator[]()` provides access to individual elements.

- `size()` returns the number of elements.

- `sum()` returns the sum of the elements.

- `max()` returns the largest element.

- `min()` returns the smallest element.

There are many more methods, some of which are presented in Chapter 16, but you've already seen more than enough to proceed with this example.

The `Student` Class Design

At this point, the design plan for the `Student` class is to use a `string` object to represent the name and a `valarray<double>` object to represent the quiz scores. How should this be done? You might be tempted to publicly derive a `Student` class from these two classes. That would be an example of multiple public inheritance, which C++ allows, but it would be inappropriate here. The reason is that the relationship of a student to these classes doesn't fit the *is-a* model. A student is not a name. A student is not an array of quiz scores. What you have here is a *has-a* relationship. A student has a name, and a student has an array of quiz scores. The usual C++ technique for modeling *has-a* relationships is to use composition or containment—that is, to create a class composed of, or containing, members that are objects of another class. For example, you can begin a `Student` class declaration like this:

```
class Student
{
private:
    string name;              // use a string object for name
    valarray<double> scores;  // use a valarray<double> object for scores
    ...
};
```

As usual, the class makes the data members private. This implies that the `Student` class member functions can use the public interfaces of the `string` and `valarray<double>` classes to access and modify the `name` and `scores` objects, but the outside world cannot do so. The only access the outside world will have to `name` and `scores` is through the public interface defined for the `Student` class (see Figure 14.1). A common way of describing this is to say that the `Student` class acquires the implementation of its member objects but doesn't inherit the interface. For example, a `Student` object uses the `string` implementation rather than a `char * name` or a `char name[26]` implementation for holding the name. But a `Student` object does not innately have the ability to use the `string operator+=()` function for appending

FIGURE 14.1

Objects within objects: containment.

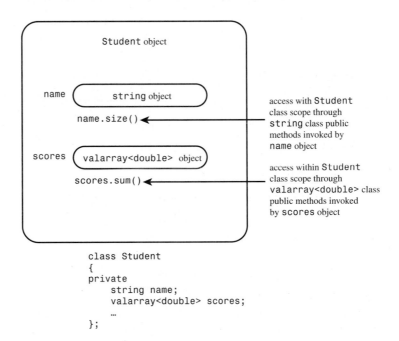

```
class Student
{
private
    string name;
    valarray<double> scores;
    ...
};
```

Interfaces and Implementations

With public inheritance, a class inherits an interface, and, perhaps, an implementation. (Pure virtual functions in a base class can provide an interface without an implementation.) Acquiring the interface is part of the *is-a* relationship. With composition, on the other hand, a class acquires the implementation without the interface. Not inheriting the interface is part of the *has-a* relationship.

The fact that a class object doesn't automatically acquire the interface of a contained object is a good thing for a *has-a* relationship. For example, `string` overloads the + operator to allow concatenating two strings, but, conceptually, it doesn't make sense to concatenate two `Student` objects. That's one reason not to use public inheritance in this case. On the other hand, parts of the interface for the contained class may make sense for the new class. For example, you might want to use the `operator<()` method from the `string` interface to sort `Student` objects by name. You can do so by defining a `Student::operator<()` member function that, internally, uses the `string::operator<()` function. Let's move on to some details.

The `Student` Class Example

At this point you need to provide the `Student` class declaration. It should, of course, include constructors and at least a few functions to provide an interface for the `Student` class. Listing 14.1 does this, defining all the constructors inline. It also supplies some friends for input and output.

LISTING 14.1   `studentc.h`

```
// studentc.h -- defining a Student class using containment
#ifndef STUDENTC_H_
#define STUDENTC_H_

#include <iostream>
#include <string>
#include <valarray>
class Student
{
private:
    typedef std::valarray<double> ArrayDb;
    std::string name;        // contained object
    ArrayDb scores;          // contained object
    // private method for scores output
    std::ostream & arr_out(std::ostream & os) const;
public:
    Student() : name("Null Student"), scores() {}
    Student(const std::string & s)
        : name(s), scores() {}
    explicit Student(int n) : name("Nully"), scores(n) {}
    Student(const std::string & s, int n)
        : name(s), scores(n) {}
    Student(const std::string & s, const ArrayDb & a)
        : name(s), scores(a) {}
    Student(const char * str, const double * pd, int n)
        : name(str), scores(pd, n) {}
    ~Student() {}
    double Average() const;
    const std::string & Name() const;
    double & operator[](int i);
    double operator[](int i) const;
// friends
    // input
    friend std::istream & operator>>(std::istream & is,
                                     Student & stu);  // 1 word
    friend std::istream & getline(std::istream & is,
                                  Student & stu);     // 1 line
    // output
```

LISTING 14.1   Continued

```
         friend std::ostream & operator<<(std::ostream & os,
                                          const Student & stu);
};

#endif
```

In order to simplify notation, the `Student` class contains this `typedef`:

```
typedef std::valarray<double> ArrayDb;
```

This enables the remaining code to use the more convenient notation `ArrayDb` instead of `std::valarray<double>`. Thus, methods and friends can refer to the `ArrayDb` type. Placing this `typedef` in the private portion of the class definition means that it can be used internally in the `Student` implementation but not by outside users of the `Student` class.

Note the use of the keyword `explicit`:

```
explicit Student(int n) : name("Nully"), scores(n) {}
```

Recall that a constructor that can be called with one argument serves as an implicit conversion function from the argument type to the class type. In this example, the first argument represents the number of elements in an array rather than a value for the array, so having the constructor serve as an `int`-to-`Student` conversion function does not make sense. Using `explicit` turns off implicit conversions. If this keyword were omitted, code like the following would be possible:

```
Student doh("Homer", 10);  // store "Homer", create array of 10 elements
doh = 5;   // reset name to "Nully", reset to empty array of 5 elments
```

Here, the inattentive programmer typed `doh` instead of `doh[0]`. If the constructor omitted `explicit`, 5 would be converted to a temporary `Student` object, using the constructor call `Student(5)`, with the value of `"Nully"` being used to set the `name` member. Then assignment would replace the original `doh` with the temporary object. With `explicit` in place, the compiler will catch the assignment operator as an error.

Real-World Note: C++ and Constraints

C++ is full of features that allow programmers to constrain programmatic constructs to certain limits—explicit to remove the implicit conversion of single-argument constructors, const to constrain the use of methods to modify data, and more. The underlying motive is simply this: Compile-time errors are better than runtime errors.

Initializing Contained Objects

Note that constructors all use the by-now-familiar member initializer list syntax to initialize the `name` and `scores` member objects. In some cases earlier in this book, such as the following, the constructors use it to initialize members that are built-in types:

```
Queue::Queue(int qs) : qsize(qs)  {...} // initialize qsize to qs
```

This code uses the name of the data member (`qsize`) in a member initializer list. Also, constructors from previous examples, such as the following, use a member initializer list to initialize the base-class portion of a derived object:

```
hasDMA::hasDMA(const hasDMA & hs) : baseDMA(hs) {...}
```

For *inherited* objects, constructors use the *class* name in the member initializer list to invoke a specific base class constructor. For *member* objects, constructors use the *member* name. For example, look at the last constructor in Listing 14.1:

```
Student(const char * str, const double * pd, int n)
        : name(str), scores(pd, n) {}
```

Because it initializes member objects, not inherited objects, this constructor uses the member names, not the class names, in the initialization list. Each item in this initialization list invokes the matching constructor. That is, `name(str)` invokes the `string(const char *)` constructor, and `scores(pd, n)` invokes the `ArrayDb(const double *, int)` constructor, which, because of the `typedef`, really is the `valarray<double>(const double *, int)` constructor.

What happens if you don't use the initialization list syntax? As with inherited components, C++ requires that all member objects be constructed before the rest of an object is constructed. So if you omit the initialization list, C++ uses the default constructors defined for the member objects' classes.

Initialization Order

When you have a member initializer list that initializes more than one item, the items are initialized in the order in which they were declared, not in the order in which they appear in the initializer list. For example, suppose you write a `Student` constructor this way:

```
Student(const char * str, const double * pd, int n)
        : scores(pd, n),  name(str) {}
```

The `name` member would still be initialized first because it is declared first in the class definition. The exact initialization order is not important for this example, but it would be important if the code used the value of one member as part of the initialization expression for a second member.

Using an Interface for a Contained Object

The interface for a contained object isn't public, but it can be used within the class methods. For example, here is how you can define a function that returns the average of a student's scores:

```
double Student::Average() const
{
    if (scores.size() > 0)
        return scores.sum()/scores.size();
    else
        return 0;
}
```

This defines a method that can be invoked by a `Student` object. Internally, it uses the valarray `size()` and `sum()` methods. That's because `scores` is a `valarray` object, so it can invoke the member functions of the `valarray` class. In short, the `Student` object invokes a `Student` method, and the `Student` method uses the contained `valarray` object to invoke `valarray` methods.

Similarly, you can define a friend function that uses the `string` version of the `<<` operator:

```
// use string version of operator<<()
ostream & operator<<(ostream & os, const Student & stu)
{
    os << "Scores for " << stu.name << ":\n";
    ...
}
```

Because `stu.name` is a `string` object, it invokes the `operator<<(ostream &, const string &)` function, which is provided as part of the `string` class package. Note that the `operator<<(ostream & os, const Student & stu)` function has to be a friend to the `Student` class so that it can access the `name` member. (Alternatively, the function could use the public `Name()` method instead of the private `name` data member.)

Similarly, the function could use the `valarray` implementation of `<<` for output; unfortunately, there is none. Therefore, the class defines a private helper method to handle this task:

```
// private method
ostream & Student::arr_out(ostream & os) const
{
    int i;
    int lim = scores.size();
    if (lim > 0)
    {
        for (i = 0; i < lim; i++)
        {
            os << scores[i] << " ";
            if (i % 5 == 4)
                os << endl;
        }
        if (i % 5 != 0)
            os << endl;
    }
    else
        os << " empty array ";
    return os;
}
```

Using a helper like this gathers the messy details together in one place and makes the coding of the friend function neater:

```
// use string version of operator<<()
ostream & operator<<(ostream & os, const Student & stu)
{
    os << "Scores for " << stu.name << ":\n";
    stu.arr_out(os);  // use private method for scores
    return os;
}
```

The helper function could also act as a building block for other user-level output functions, should you choose to provide them.

Listing 14.2 shows the class methods file for the **Student** class. It includes methods that allow you to use the **[ ]** operator to access individual scores in a **Student** object.

LISTING 14.2   studentc.cpp

```
// studentc.cpp -- Student class using containment
#include "studentc.h"
using std::ostream;
using std::endl;
using std::istream;
using std::string;

//public methods
double Student::Average() const
{
    if (scores.size() > 0)
        return scores.sum()/scores.size();
    else
        return 0;
}

const string & Student::Name() const
{
    return name;
}

double & Student::operator[](int i)
{
    return scores[i];         // use valarray<double>::operator[]()
}

double Student::operator[](int i) const
{
    return scores[i];
}

// private method
ostream & Student::arr_out(ostream & os) const
{
    int i;
    int lim = scores.size();
    if (lim > 0)
    {
        for (i = 0; i < lim; i++)
        {
            os << scores[i] << " ";
            if (i % 5 == 4)
                os << endl;
        }
    }
```

LISTING 14.2   Continued

```
            if (i % 5 != 0)
                os << endl;
        }
        else
            os << " empty array ";
        return os;
    }

    // friends

    // use string version of operator>>()
    istream & operator>>(istream & is, Student & stu)
    {
        is >> stu.name;
        return is;
    }

    // use string friend getline(ostream &, const string &)
    istream & getline(istream & is, Student & stu)
    {
        getline(is, stu.name);
        return is;
    }

    // use string version of operator<<()
    ostream & operator<<(ostream & os, const Student & stu)
    {
        os << "Scores for " << stu.name << ":\n";
        stu.arr_out(os);   // use private method for scores
        return os;
    }
```

Aside from the private helper method, Listing 14.2 doesn't require much new code. Using containment allows you to take advantage of the code you or someone else has already written.

Using the New Student Class

Let's put together a small program to test the new **Student** class. To keep things simple, it should use an array of just three **Student** objects, each holding five quiz scores. And it should use an unsophisticated input cycle that doesn't verify input and that doesn't let you cut the input process short. Listing 14.3 presents the test program. Be sure to compile it along with `studentc.cpp`.

LISTING 14.3   `use_stuc.cpp`

```
// use_stuc.cpp -- using a composite class
// compile with studentc.cpp
#include <iostream>
#include "studentc.h"
using std::cin;
```

LISTING 14.3 Continued

```
using std::cout;
using std::endl;

void set(Student & sa, int n);

const int pupils = 3;
const int quizzes = 5;

int main()
{
    Student ada[pupils] =
        {Student(quizzes), Student(quizzes), Student(quizzes)};

    int i;
    for (i = 0; i < pupils; ++i)
        set(ada[i], quizzes);
    cout << "\nStudent List:\n";
    for (i = 0; i < pupils; ++i)
        cout << ada[i].Name() << endl;
    cout << "\nResults:";
    for (i = 0; i < pupils; ++i)
    {
        cout << endl << ada[i];
        cout << "average: " << ada[i].Average() << endl;
    }
    cout << "Done.\n";
    return 0;
}

void set(Student & sa, int n)
{
    cout << "Please enter the student's name: ";
    getline(cin, sa);
    cout << "Please enter " << n << " quiz scores:\n";
    for (int i = 0; i < n; i++)
        cin >> sa[i];
    while (cin.get() != '\n')
        continue;
}
```

Compatibility Note

If your system doesn't correctly support the `string` friend `getline()` function, it won't run this program correctly. You could modify the program to use the `operator>>()` from Listing 14.2 instead. Because this friend function reads just one word, you would change the prompt to ask for just the last name.

Here is a sample run of the program in Listings 14.1, 14.2, and 14.3:

```
Please enter the student's name: Gil Bayts
Please enter 5 quiz scores:
92 94 96 93 95
Please enter the student's name: Pat Roone
Please enter 5 quiz scores:
83 89 72 78 95
Please enter the student's name: Fleur O'Day
Please enter 5 quiz scores:
92 89 96 74 64

Student List:
Gil Bayts
Pat Roone
Fleur O'Day

Results:
Scores for Gil Bayts:
92 94 96 93 95
average: 94

Scores for Pat Roone:
83 89 72 78 95
average: 83.4

Scores for Fleur O'Day:
92 89 96 74 64
average: 83
Done.
```

Private Inheritance

C++ has a second means of implementing the *has-a* relationship: private inheritance. With *private inheritance*, public and protected members of the base class become private members of the derived class. This means the methods of the base class do not become part of the public interface of the derived object. They can be used, however, inside the member functions of the derived class.

Let's look at the interface topic more closely. With public inheritance, the public methods of the base class become public methods of the derived class. In short, the derived class inherits the base-class interface. This is part of the *is-a* relationship. With private inheritance, the public methods of the base class become private methods of the derived class. In short, the derived class does not inherit the base-class interface. As you saw with contained objects, this lack of inheritance is part of the *has-a* relationship.

With private inheritance, a class does inherit the implementation. For example, if you base a `Student` class on a `string` class, the `Student` class winds up with an inherited `string` class component that can be used to store a string. Furthermore, the `Student` methods can use the `string` methods internally to access the `string` component.

Containment adds an object to a class as a named member object, whereas private inheritance adds an object to a class as an unnamed inherited object. This book uses the term *subobject* to denote an object added by inheritance or by containment.

Private inheritance, then, provides the same features as containment: Acquire the implementation, don't acquire the interface. Therefore it, too, can be used to implement a *has-a* relationship. In fact, you can produce a `Student` class that uses private inheritance and has the same public interface as the containment version. Thus the differences between the two approaches affect the implementation, not the interface. Let's see how you can use private inheritance to redesign the `Student` class.

The `Student` Class Example (New Version)

To get private inheritance, you use the keyword `private` instead of `public` when defining the class. (Actually, `private` is the default, so omitting an access qualifier also leads to private inheritance.) The `Student` class should inherit from two classes, so the declaration should list both:

```
class Student : private std::string, private std::valarray<double>
{
public:
    ...
};
```

Having more than one base class is called *multiple inheritance* (MI). In general, MI, particularly public MI, can lead to problems that have to be resolved with additional syntax rules. We'll talk about such matters later in this chapter. But in this particular case, MI causes no problems.

Note that the new class doesn't need private data. That's because the two inherited base classes already provide all the needed data members. The containment version of this example provides two explicitly named objects as members. Private inheritance, however, provides two nameless subobjects as inherited members. This is the first of the main differences in the two approaches.

Initializing Base-Class Components

Having implicitly inherited components instead of member objects affects the coding of this example because you can no longer use `name` and `scores` to describe the objects. Instead, you have to go back to the techniques you used for public inheritance. For example, consider constructors. Containment uses this constructor:

```
Student(const char * str, const double * pd, int n)
    : name(str), scores(pd, n) {}       // use object names for containment
```

The new version should use the member initializer list syntax for inherited classes, which uses the *class* name instead of a *member* name to identify a constructor:

```
Student(const char * str, const double * pd, int n)
    : std::string(str), ArrayDb(pd, n) {}  // use class names for inheritance
```

Here, as in the preceding example, `ArrayDb` is a `typedef` for `std::valarray<double>`. Be sure to note that the member initializer list uses terms such as `std::string(str)` instead of `name(str)`. This is the second main difference in the two approaches.

Listing 14.4 shows the new class declaration. The only changes are the omission of explicit object names and the use of class names instead of member names in the inline constructors.

LISTING 14.4   studenti.h

```
// studenti.h -- defining a Student class using private inheritance
#ifndef STUDENTC_H_
#define STUDENTC_H_

#include <iostream>
#include <valarray>
#include <string>
class Student : private std::string, private std::valarray<double>
{
private:
    typedef std::valarray<double> ArrayDb;
    // private method for scores output
    std::ostream & arr_out(std::ostream & os) const;
public:
    Student() : std::string("Null Student"), ArrayDb() {}
    Student(const std::string & s)
            : std::string(s), ArrayDb() {}
    Student(int n) : std::string("Nully"), ArrayDb(n) {}
    Student(const std::string & s, int n)
            : std::string(s), ArrayDb(n) {}
    Student(const std::string & s, const ArrayDb & a)
            : std::string(s), ArrayDb(a) {}
    Student(const char * str, const double * pd, int n)
            : std::string(str), ArrayDb(pd, n) {}
    ~Student() {}
    double Average() const;
    double & operator[](int i);
    double operator[](int i) const;
    const std::string & Name() const;
// friends
    // input
    friend std::istream & operator>>(std::istream & is,
                                     Student & stu);   // 1 word
    friend std::istream & getline(std::istream & is,
                                  Student & stu);      // 1 line
    // output
    friend std::ostream & operator<<(std::ostream & os,
                                     const Student & stu);
};

#endif
```

Accessing Base-Class Methods

Private inheritance limits the use of base-class methods to within derived-class methods. Sometimes, however, you might like to make a base-class facility available publicly. For example, the `Student` class declaration suggests the ability to use an `Average()` function. As with containment, the technique for doing this is to use the `valarray size()` and `sum()` methods within a public `Student::average()` function (see Figure 14.2). Containment invoked the methods with an object:

```
double Student::Average() const
{
    if (scores.size() > 0)
        return scores.sum()/scores.size();
    else
        return 0;
}
```

FIGURE 14.2

Objects within objects: private inheritance.

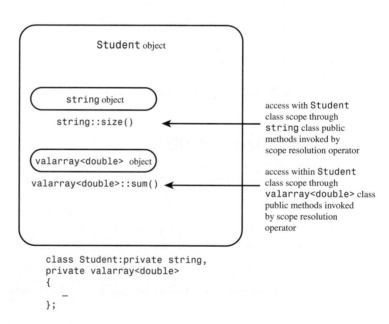

access with `Student` class scope through `string` class public methods invoked by scope resolution operator

access within `Student` class scope through `valarray<double>` class public methods invoked by scope resolution operator

```
class Student:private string,
private valarray<double>
{
    ...
};
```

Here, however, inheritance lets you use the class name and the scope-resolution operator to invoke base-class methods:

```
double Student::Average() const
{
    if (ArrayDb::size() > 0)
        return ArrayDb::sum()/ArrayDb::size();
    else
        return 0;
}
```

In short, the containment approach uses object names to invoke a method, whereas private inheritance uses the class name and the scope-resolution operator instead.

Accessing Base-Class Objects

The scope-resolution operator allows you access to a base-class method, but what if you need the base-class object itself? For example, the containment version of the `Student` class implements the `Name()` method by having the method return the `name` member `string` object. But with private inheritance, the `string` object has no name. How, then, can `Student` code access the inner `string` object?

The answer is to use a type cast. Because `Student` is derived from `string`, it's possible to type cast a `Student` object to a `string` object; the result is an inherited `string` object. Recall that the `this` pointer points to the invoking object, so `*this` is the invoking object—in this case, a type `Student` object. To avoid invoking constructors to create new objects, you use the type cast to create a reference:

```
const string & Student::Name() const
{
    return (const string &) *this;
}
```

This code returns a reference to the inherited `string` object residing in the invoking `Student` object.

Accessing Base-Class Friends

The technique of explicitly qualifying a function name with its class name doesn't work for friend functions because a friend function doesn't belong to a class. However, you can use an explicit type cast to the base class to invoke the correct functions. This is basically the same technique used to access a base-class object in a class method, but with friends you have a name for the `Student` object, so the code uses the name instead of `*this`. For example, consider the following friend function definition:

```
ostream & operator<<(ostream & os, const Student & stu)
{
    os << "Scores for " << (const string &) stu << ":\n";
...

}
```

If `plato` is a `Student` object, then the statement

```
cout << plato;
```

invokes that function, with `stu` being a reference to `plato` and `os` being a reference to `cout`. Within the code, the type cast in

```
os << "Scores for " << (const string &) stu << ":\n";
```

explicitly converts `stu` to a reference to a type `string` object and that matches the `operator<<(ostream &, const string &)` function.

The reference **stu** doesn't get converted automatically to a **string** reference. The fundamental reason is that with private inheritance, a reference or pointer to a base class cannot be assigned a reference or pointer to a derived class without an explicit type cast.

However, even if the example used public inheritance, it would have to use explicit type casts. One reason is that without a type cast, code like

```
os << stu;
```

matches the friend function prototype, leading to a recursive call. A second reason is that because the class uses MI, the compiler can't tell which base class to convert to if both base classes happen to provide an **operator<<()** function. Listing 14.5 shows all the **Student** class methods, other than those defined inline in the class declaration.

LISTING 14.5   studenti.cpp

```
// studenti.cpp -- Student class using private inheritance
#include "studenti.h"
using std::ostream;
using std::endl;
using std::istream;
using std::string;

// public methods
double Student::Average() const
{
    if (ArrayDb::size() > 0)
        return ArrayDb::sum()/ArrayDb::size();
    else
        return 0;
}

const string & Student::Name() const
{
    return (const string &) *this;
}

double & Student::operator[](int i)
{
    return ArrayDb::operator[](i);          // use ArrayDb::operator[]()
}

double Student::operator[](int i) const
{
    return ArrayDb::operator[](i);
}

// private method
ostream & Student::arr_out(ostream & os) const
{
    int i;
    int lim = ArrayDb::size();
```

LISTING 14.5   Continued

```
        if (lim > 0)
        {
            for (i = 0; i < lim; i++)
            {
                os << ArrayDb::operator[](i) << " ";
                if (i % 5 == 4)
                    os << endl;
            }
            if (i % 5 != 0)
                os << endl;
        }
        else
            os << " empty array ";
        return os;
    }

// friends
// use string version of operator>>()
istream & operator>>(istream & is, Student & stu)
{
    is >> (string &)stu;
    return is;
}

// use string friend getline(ostream &, const string &)
istream & getline(istream & is, Student & stu)
{
    getline(is, (string &)stu);
    return is;
}

// use string version of operator<<()
ostream & operator<<(ostream & os, const Student & stu)
{
    os << "Scores for " << (const string &) stu  << ":\n";
    stu.arr_out(os);  // use private method for scores
    return os;
}
```

Again, because the example reuses the `string` and `valarray` code, relatively little new code is needed, aside from the private helper method.

Using the Revised `Student` Class

Once again, it's time to test a new class. Note that the two versions of the `Student` class have exactly the same public interface, so you can test the two versions with exactly the same program. The only difference is that you have to include `studenti.h` instead of `studentc.h`, and you have to link the program with studenti.cpp instead of with studentc.cpp. Listing 14.6 shows the program. Be sure to compile it along with studenti.cpp.

LISTING 14.6   use_stui.cpp

```
// use_stui.cpp -- using a class with private inheritance
// compile with studenti.cpp
#include <iostream>
#include "studenti.h"
using std::cin;
using std::cout;
using std::endl;

void set(Student & sa, int n);

const int pupils = 3;
const int quizzes = 5;

int main()
{
    Student ada[pupils] =
        {Student(quizzes), Student(quizzes), Student(quizzes)};

    int i;
    for (i = 0; i < pupils; i++)
        set(ada[i], quizzes);
    cout << "\nStudent List:\n";
    for (i = 0; i < pupils; ++i)
        cout << ada[i].Name() << endl;
    cout << "\nResults:";
    for (i = 0; i < pupils; i++)
    {
        cout << endl << ada[i];
        cout << "average: " << ada[i].Average() << endl;
    }
    cout << "Done.\n";
    return 0;
}

void set(Student & sa, int n)
{
    cout << "Please enter the student's name: ";
    getline(cin, sa);
    cout << "Please enter " << n << " quiz scores:\n";
    for (int i = 0; i < n; i++)
        cin >> sa[i];
    while (cin.get() != '\n')
        continue;
}
```

Compatibility Note

If your system doesn't correctly support the `string` friend `getline()` function, it won't run this program correctly. You could modify the program to use `operator>>()` from Listing 14.5 instead. Because this friend function reads just one word, you could change the prompt to ask for just the last name.

Here is a sample run of the program in Listing 14.6:

```
Please enter the student's name: Gil Bayts
Please enter 5 quiz scores:
92 94 96 93 95
Please enter the student's name: Pat Roone
Please enter 5 quiz scores:
83 89 72 78 95
Please enter the student's name: Fleur O'Day
Please enter 5 quiz scores:
92 89 96 74 64

Student List:
Gil Bayts
Pat Roone
Fleur O'Day

Results:
Scores for Gil Bayts:
92 94 96 93 95
average: 94

Scores for Pat Roone:
83 89 72 78 95
average: 83.4

Scores for Fleur O'Day:
92 89 96 74 64
average: 83
Done.
```

The same input as before leads to the same output that the containment version produces.

Containment or Private Inheritance?

Given that you can model a *has-a* relationship either with containment or with private inheritance, which should you use? Most C++ programmers prefer containment. First, it's easier to follow. When you look at the class declaration, you see explicitly named objects representing the contained classes, and your code can refer to these objects by name. Using inheritance makes the relationship appear more abstract. Second, inheritance can raise problems, particularly if a class inherits from more than one base class. You may have to deal with issues such as separate base classes having methods with the same name or of separate base classes sharing a common ancestor. All in all, you're less likely to run into trouble using containment. Also, containment allows you to include more than one subobject of the same class. If a class needs three `string` objects, you can declare three separate `string` members by using the containment approach. But inheritance limits you to a single object. (It is difficult to tell objects apart when they are all nameless.)

However, private inheritance does offer features beyond those provided by containment. Suppose, for example, that a class has protected members, which could either be data members or member functions. Such members are available to derived classes but not to the world at large. If you include such a class in another class by using composition, the new class is part of the world at large, not a derived class. Hence it can't access protected members. But using inheritance makes the new class a derived class, so it can access protected members.

Another situation that calls for using private inheritance is if you want to redefine virtual functions. Again, this is a privilege accorded to a derived class but not to a containing class. With private inheritance, the redefined functions would be usable just within the class, not publicly.

Tip

In general, you should use containment to model a *has-a* relationship. You should use private inheritance if the new class needs to access protected members in the original class or if it needs to redefine virtual functions.

Protected Inheritance

Protected inheritance is a variation on private inheritance. It uses the keyword `protected` when listing a base class:

```
class Student : protected std::string,
                protected std::valarray<double>
{...};
```

With protected inheritance, public and protected members of a base class become protected members of the derived class. As with private inheritance, the interface for the base class is available to the derived class but not to the outside world. The main difference between private and protected inheritance occurs when you derive another class from the derived class. With private inheritance, this third-generation class doesn't get the internal use of the base class interface. That's because the public base-class methods become private in the derived class, and private members and methods can't be directly accessed by the next level of derivation. With protected inheritance, public base-class methods become protected in the second generation and so are available internally to the next level of derivation.

Table 14.1 summarizes public, private, and protected inheritance. The term *implicit upcasting* means that you can have a base class pointer or reference refer to a derived class object without using an explicit type cast.

TABLE 14.1 Varieties of Inheritance

Property	Public Inheritance	Protected Inheritance	Private Inheritance
Public members become	Public members of the derived class	Protected members of the derived class	Private members of the derived class
Protected members become	Protected members of the derived class	Protected members of the derived class	Private members of the derived class
Private members become	Accessible only through the base class interface	Accessible only through the base class interface	Accessible only through the base class interface
Implicit Upcasting	Yes	Yes (but only the derived class) within	No

Redefining Access with `using`

Public members of a base class become protected or private when you use protected or private derivation. Suppose you want to make a particular base-class method available publicly in the derived class. One option is to define a derived-class method that uses the base-class method. For example, suppose you want the `Student` class to be able to use the `valarray sum()` method. You can declare a `sum()` method in the class declaration and then define the method this way:

```
double Student::sum() const    // public Student method
{
    return std::valarray<double>::sum();    // use privately-inherited method
}
```

Then a `Student` object can invoke `Student::sum()`, which, in turn, applies the `valarray<double>::sum()` method to the embedded `valarray` object. (If the `ArrayDb` typedef is in scope, you can use `ArrayDb` instead of `std::valarray<double>`.)

There is an alternative to wrapping one function call in another: to use a `using` declaration (such as those used with namespaces) to announce that a particular base-class member can be used by the derived class, even though the derivation is private. For example, suppose you want to be able to use the `valarray min()` and `max()` methods with the `Student` class. In this case, in `studenti.h`, you can add `using` declarations to the public section:

```
class Student : private std::string, private std::valarray<double>
{
...
public:
    using std::valarray<double>::min;
    using std::valarray<double>::max;
    ...
};
```

The using declaration makes the valarray<double>::min() and valarray<double>::max() methods available as if they were public Student methods:

```
cout << "high score: " << ada[i].max() << endl;
```

Note that the using declaration just uses the member name—no parentheses, no function signatures, no return types. For example, to make the valarray operator[]() method available to the Student class, you'd place the following using declaration in the public section of the Student class declaration:

```
using std::valarray<double>::operator[];
```

This would make both versions (const and non-const) available. You could then remove the existing prototypes and definitions for Student::operator[](). The using declaration approach works only for inheritance and not for containment.

There is an older way to redeclare base-class methods in a privately derived class: You place the method name in the public section of the derived class. Here's how you would do that:

```
class Student : private std::string, private std::valarray<double>
{
public:
    std::valarray<double>::operator[];  // redeclare as public, just use name
    ...

};
```

This looks like a using declaration without the using keyword. This approach is *deprecated*, meaning that the intention is to phase it out. So if your compiler supports the using declaration, you can use it to make a method from a private base class available to the derived class.

Multiple Inheritance

MI describes a class that has more than one immediate base class. As with single inheritance, public MI should express an *is-a* relationship. For example, if you have a Waiter class and a Singer class, you could derive a SingingWaiter class from the two:

```
class SingingWaiter : public Waiter, public Singer {...};
```

Note that you must qualify each base class with the keyword public. That's because the compiler assumes private derivation unless instructed otherwise:

```
class SingingWaiter : public Waiter, Singer {...}; // Singer is a private base
```

As discussed earlier in this chapter, private and protected MI can express a *has-a* relationship; the studenti.h implementation of the Student class is an example. We'll concentrate on public inheritance now.

MI can introduce new problems for programmers. The two chief problems are inheriting different methods with the same name from two different base classes and inheriting multiple instances of a class via two or more related immediate base classes. Solving these problems involves introducing a few new rules and syntax variations. Thus, using MI can be more difficult and problem-prone than using single inheritance. For this reason, many in the C++ community object strongly to MI; some want it removed from the language. Others love MI and argue that it's very useful, even necessary, for particular projects. Still others suggest using MI cautiously and in moderation.

Let's explore a particular example and see what the problems and solutions are. You need several classes to create an MI situation. For this example, you need to define an abstract `Worker` base class and derive a `Waiter` class and a `Singer` class from it. Then you can use MI to derive a `SingingWaiter` class from the `Waiter` and `Singer` classes (see Figure 14.3). This is a case in which a base class (`Worker`) is inherited via two separate derivations, which is the circumstance that causes the most difficulties with MI. You can start with declarations for the `Worker`, `Waiter`, and `Singer` classes, as shown in Listing 14.7.

FIGURE 14.3
MI with a shared ancestor.

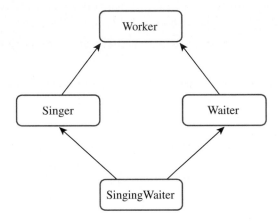

LISTING 14.7 `Worker0.h`

```cpp
// worker0.h  -- working classes
#ifndef WORKER0_H_
#define WORKER0_H_

#include <string>

class Worker    // an abstract base class
{
private:
    std::string fullname;
    long id;
public:
    Worker() : fullname("no one"), id(0L) {}
    Worker(const std::string & s, long n)
            : fullname(s), id(n) {}
    virtual ~Worker() = 0;    // pure virtual destructor
    virtual void Set();
```

LISTING 14.7   Continued

```cpp
    virtual void Show() const;
};

class Waiter : public Worker
{
private:
    int panache;
public:
    Waiter() : Worker(), panache(0) {}
    Waiter(const std::string & s, long n, int p = 0)
            : Worker(s, n), panache(p) {}
    Waiter(const Worker & wk, int p = 0)
            : Worker(wk), panache(p) {}
    void Set();
    void Show() const;
};

class Singer : public Worker
{
protected:
    enum {other, alto, contralto, soprano,
                    bass, baritone, tenor};
    enum {Vtypes = 7};
private:
    static char *pv[Vtypes];     // string equivs of voice types
    int voice;
public:
    Singer() : Worker(), voice(other) {}
    Singer(const std::string & s, long n, int v = other)
            : Worker(s, n), voice(v) {}
    Singer(const Worker & wk, int v = other)
            : Worker(wk), voice(v) {}
    void Set();
    void Show() const;
};

#endif
```

The class declarations in Listing 14.7 include some internal constants that represent voice types. An enumeration makes alto, contralto, and so on symbolic constants for voice types, and the static array pv holds pointers to the C-style string equivalents. The implementation file, shown in Listing 14.8, initializes this array and provides method definitions.

LISTING 14.8   worker0.cpp

```cpp
// worker0.cpp -- working class methods
#include "worker0.h"
#include <iostream>
using std::cout;
using std::cin;
```

LISTING 14.8   Continued

```cpp
using std::endl;
// Worker methods

// must implement virtual destructor, even if pure
Worker::~Worker() {}

void Worker::Set()
{
    cout << "Enter worker's name: ";
    getline(cin, fullname);
    cout << "Enter worker's ID: ";
    cin >> id;
    while (cin.get() != '\n')
        continue;
}

void Worker::Show() const
{
    cout << "Name: " << fullname << "\n";
    cout << "Employee ID: " << id << "\n";
}

// Waiter methods
void Waiter::Set()
{
    Worker::Set();
    cout << "Enter waiter's panache rating: ";
    cin >> panache;
    while (cin.get() != '\n')
        continue;
}

void Waiter::Show() const
{
    cout << "Category: waiter\n";
    Worker::Show();
    cout << "Panache rating: " << panache << "\n";
}

// Singer methods

char * Singer::pv[] = {"other", "alto", "contralto",
            "soprano", "bass", "baritone", "tenor"};

void Singer::Set()
{
    Worker::Set();
    cout << "Enter number for singer's vocal range:\n";
    int i;
    for (i = 0; i < Vtypes; i++)
    {
```

LISTING 14.8   Continued

```
            cout << i << ": " << pv[i] << "    ";
            if ( i % 4 == 3)
                cout << endl;
        }
        if (i % 4 != 0)
            cout << endl;
        cin >> voice;
        while (cin.get() != '\n')
            continue;
    }

void Singer::Show() const
{
    cout << "Category: singer\n";
    Worker::Show();
    cout << "Vocal range: " << pv[voice] << endl;
}
```

Listing 14.9 provides a brief test of the classes, using a polymorphic array of pointers.

LISTING 14.9   worktest.cpp

```
// worktest.cpp -- test worker class hierarchy
#include <iostream>
#include "worker0.h"
const int LIM = 4;
int main()
{
    Waiter bob("Bob Apple", 314L, 5);
    Singer bev("Beverly Hills", 522L, 3);
    Waiter w_temp;
    Singer s_temp;

    Worker * pw[LIM] = {&bob, &bev, &w_temp, &s_temp};

    int i;
    for (i = 2; i < LIM; i++)
        pw[i]->Set();
    for (i = 0; i < LIM; i++)
    {
        pw[i]->Show();
        std::cout << std::endl;
    }

    return 0;
}
```

Compatibility Note

If your system doesn't correctly support the `string` friend `getline()` function, it won't run this program correctly. You could modify the program to use `operator>>()` from Listing 14.8 instead. Because this friend function reads just one word, you could change the prompt to ask for just the last name.

Here is the output of the program in Listings 14.7, 14.8, and 14.9:

```
Enter waiter's name: Waldo Dropmaster
Enter worker's ID: 442
Enter waiter's panache rating: 3
Enter singer's name: Sylvie Sirenne
Enter worker's ID: 555
Enter number for singer's vocal range:
0: other   1: alto   2: contralto   3: soprano
4: bass   5: baritone   6: tenor
3
Category: waiter
Name: Bob Apple
Employee ID: 314
Panache rating: 5

Category: singer
Name: Beverly Hills
Employee ID: 522
Vocal range: soprano

Category: waiter
Name: Waldo Dropmaster
Employee ID: 442
Panache rating: 3

Category: singer
Name: Sylvie Sirenne
Employee ID: 555
Vocal range: soprano
```

The design seems to work, with pointers to `Waiter` invoking `Waiter::Show()` and `Waiter::Set()`, and pointers to `Singer` invoking `Singer::Show()` and `Singer::Set()`. However, it leads to some problems if you add a `SingingWaiter` class derived from both the `Singer` class and `Waiter` class. In particular, you'll need to face the following questions:

- How many workers?
- Which method?

How Many Workers?

Suppose you begin by publicly deriving `SingingWaiter` from `Singer` and `Waiter`:

```
class SingingWaiter: public Singer, public  Waiter {...};
```

Because both `Singer` and `Waiter` inherit a `Worker` component, `SingingWaiter` winds up with two `Worker` components (see Figure 14.4).

FIGURE 14.4
Inheriting two base-class objects.

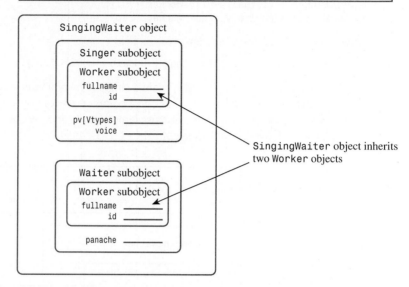

```
class Singer : public Worker { ...};
class Waiter : public Worker { ...};
class SingingWaiter : public Singer, public Waiter { ...};
```

As you might expect, this raises problems. For example, ordinarily you can assign the address of a derived-class object to a base-class pointer, but this becomes ambiguous now:

```
SingingWaiter ed;
Worker * pw = &ed;    // ambiguous
```

Normally, such an assignment sets a base-class pointer to the address of the base-class object within the derived object. But `ed` contains two `Worker` objects, so there are two addresses from which to choose. You could specify which object by using a type cast:

```
Worker * pw1 = (Waiter *) &ed;    // the Worker in Waiter
Worker * pw2 = (Singer *) &ed;    // the Worker in Singer
```

This certainly complicates the technique of using an array of base-class pointers to refer to a variety of objects (polymorphism).

Having two copies of a `Worker` object causes other problems, too. However, the real issue is why should you have two copies of a `Worker` object at all? A singing waiter, like any other worker, should have just one name and one ID. When C++ added MI to its bag of tricks, it added a virtual base classes to make this possible.

Virtual Base Classes

Virtual base classes allow an object derived from multiple bases that themselves share a common base to inherit just one object of that shared base class. For this example, you would make `Worker` a virtual base class to `Singer` and `Waiter` by using the keyword `virtual` in the class declarations (`virtual` and `public` can appear in either order):

```
class Singer : virtual public Worker {...};
class Waiter : public virtual Worker {...};
```

Then you would define `SingingWaiter` as before:

```
class SingingWaiter: public Singer, public  Waiter {...};
```

Now a `SingingWaiter` object will contain a single copy of a `Worker` object. In essence, the inherited `Singer` and `Waiter` objects share a common `Worker` object instead of each bringing in its own copy (see Figure 14.5). Because `SingingWaiter` now contains one `Worker` subobject, you can use polymorphism again.

FIGURE 14.5

Inheritance with a virtual base class.

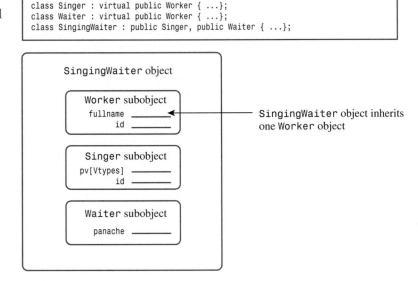

Let's look at some questions you might have:

- Why the term *virtual*?
- Why don't we dispense with declaring base classes virtual and make virtual behavior the norm for MI?
- Are there any catches?

First, why the term virtual? After all, there doesn't seem to be an obvious connection between the concepts of virtual functions and virtual base classes. It turns out that there is strong pressure from the C++ community to resist the introduction of new keywords. It would be awkward, for example, if a new keyword corresponded to the name of some important function or variable in a major program. So C++ merely recycled the keyword `virtual` for the new facility—a bit of keyword overloading.

Next, why don't we dispense with declaring base classes virtual and make virtual behavior the norm for MI? First, there are cases in which you might want multiple copies of a base. Second, making a base class virtual requires that a program do some additional accounting, and you shouldn't have to pay for that facility if you don't need it. Third, there are the disadvantages presented in the next paragraph.

Finally, are there catches? Yes. Making virtual base classes work requires adjustments to C++ rules, and you have to code some things differently. Also, using virtual base classes may involve changing existing code. For example, adding the `SingingWaiter` class to the `Worker` hierarchy requires that you go back and add the `virtual` keyword to the `Singer` and `Waiter` classes.

New Constructor Rules

Having virtual base classes requires a new approach to class constructors. With nonvirtual base classes, the *only* constructors that can appear in an initialization list are constructors for the immediate base classes. But these constructors can, in turn, pass information on to their bases. For example, you can have the following organization of constructors:

```cpp
class A
{
    int a;
public:
    A(int n = 0) { a = n; }
    ...
};
class B: public A
{
    int b;
public:
    B(int m = 0, int n = 0) : A(n)  { b = m; }
    ...
};
class C : public B
{
    int c;
public:
    C(int q = 0, int m = 0, int n = 0) : B(m, n) { c = q; }
    ...
};
```

A `C` constructor can invoke only constructors from the `B` class, and a `B` constructor can invoke only constructors from the `A` class. Here the `C` constructor uses the `q` value and passes the values of `m` and `n` back to the `B` constructor. The `B` constructor uses the value of `m` and passes the value of `n` back to the `A` constructor.

This automatic passing of information doesn't work if `Worker` is a virtual base class. For example, consider the following possible constructor for the MI example:

```
SingingWaiter(const Worker & wk, int p = 0, int v = Singer::other)
            : Waiter(wk,p), Singer(wk,v) {}  // flawed
```

The problem is that automatic passing of information would pass `wk` to the `Worker` object via two separate paths (`Waiter` and `Singer`). To avoid this potential conflict, C++ disables the automatic passing of information through an intermediate class to a base class *if* the base class is virtual. Thus, the previous constructor will initialize the `panache` and `voice` members, but the information in the `wk` argument *won't* get to the `Waiter` subobject. However, the compiler must construct a base object component before constructing derived objects; in this case, it will use the default `Worker` constructor.

If you want to use something other than the default constructor for a virtual base class, you need to invoke the appropriate base constructor explicitly. Thus, the constructor should look like this:

```
SingingWaiter(const Worker & wk, int p = 0, int v = Singer::other)
            : Worker(wk), Waiter(wk,p), Singer(wk,v) {}
```

Here the code explicitly invokes the `Worker(const Worker &)` constructor. Note that this usage is legal and often necessary for virtual base classes, and it is illegal for nonvirtual base classes.

Caution

If a class has an indirect virtual base class, a constructor for that class should explicitly invoke a constructor for the virtual base class unless all that is needed is the default constructor for the virtual base class.

Which Method?

In addition to introducing changes in class constructor rules, MI often requires other coding adjustments. Consider the problem of extending the `Show()` method to the `SingingWaiter` class. Because a `SingingWaiter` object has no new data members, you might think the class could just use the inherited methods. This brings up the first problem. Suppose you do omit a new version of `Show()` and try to use a `SingingWaiter` object to invoke an inherited `Show()` method:

```
SingingWaiter newhire("Elise Hawks", 2005, 6, soprano);
newhire.Show();  // ambiguous
```

With single inheritance, failing to redefine `Show()` results in using the most recent ancestral definition. In this case, each direct ancestor has a `Show()` function, which makes this call ambiguous.

You can use the scope-resolution operator to clarify what you mean:

```
SingingWaiter newhire("Elise Hawks", 2005, 6, soprano);
newhire.Singer::Show();  // use Singer version
```

However, a better approach is to redefine `Show()` for `SingingWaiter` and to have it specify which `Show()` to use. For example, if you want a `SingingWaiter` object to use the `Singer` version, you could use this:

```
void SingingWaiter::Show()
{
    Singer::Show();
}
```

This method of having the derived method call the base method works well enough for single inheritance. For example, suppose that the `HeadWaiter` class derives from the `Waiter` class. You could use a sequence of definitions like this, with each derived class adding to the information displayed by its base class:

```
void Worker::Show() const
{
    cout << "Name: " << fullname << "\n";
    cout << "Employee ID: " << id << "\n";
}

void Waiter::Show() const
{
    Worker::Show();
    cout << "Panache rating: " << panache << "\n";
}
void HeadWaiter::Show() const
{
    Waiter::Show();
    cout << "Presence rating: " << presence << "\n";
}
```

This incremental approach fails for the `SingingWaiter` case, however. The method

```
void SingingWaiter::Show()
{
    Singer::Show();
}
```

fails because it ignores the `Waiter` component. You can remedy that by called the `Waiter` version also:

```
void SingingWaiter::Show()
{
     Singer::Show();
     Waiter::Show();
}
```

This displays a person's name and ID twice because `Singer::Show()` and with `Waiter::Show()` both call `Worker::Show()`.

How can you fix this? One way is to use a modular approach instead of an incremental approach. That is, you an provide a method that displays only `Worker` components, another method that displays only `Waiter` components (instead of `Waiter` plus `Worker` components), and another that displays only `Singer` components. Then the `SingingWaiter::Show()` method can put those components together. For example, you could use this:

```
void Worker::Data() const
{
    cout << "Name: " << fullname << "\n";
    cout << "Employee ID: " << id << "\n";
}

void Waiter::Data() const
{
    cout << "Panache rating: " << panache << "\n";
}

void Singer::Data() const
{
    cout << "Vocal range: " << pv[voice] << "\n";
}

void SingingWaiter::Data() const
{
    Singer::Data();
    Waiter::Data();
}

void SingingWaiter::Show() const
{
    cout << "Category: singing waiter\n";
    Worker::Data();
    Data();
}
```

Similarly, the other `Show()` methods would be built from the appropriate `Data()` components.

With this approach, objects would still use the `Show()` method publicly. The `Data()` methods, on the other hand, should be internal to the classes; they should be helper methods used to facilitate the public interface. However, making the `Data()` methods private would prevent, say, `Waiter` code from using `Worker::Data()`. Here is just the kind of situation for which the protected access class is useful. If the `Data()` methods are protected, they can by used internally by all the classes in the hierarchy while being kept hidden from the outside world.

Another approach would be to make all the data components protected instead of private, but using protected methods instead of protected data puts tighter control on the allowable access to the data.

The Set() methods, which solicit data for setting object values, present a similar problem. For example, SingingWaiter::Set()should ask for Worker information once, not twice. The same solution used for Show() works. You can provide protected Get() methods that solicit information for just a single class, and then you can put together Set() methods that use the Get() methods as building blocks.

In short, introducing MI with a shared ancestor requires introducing virtual base classes, altering the rules for constructor initialization lists, and possibly recoding the classes if they were written with MI in mind. Listing 14.10 shows the modified class declarations with these changes institutes, and Listing 14.11 shows the implementation.

LISTING 14.10   workermi.h

```
// workermi.h  -- working classes with MI
#ifndef WORKERMI_H_
#define WORKERMI_H_

#include <string>

class Worker    // an abstract base class
{
private:
    std::string fullname;
    long id;
protected:
    virtual void Data() const;
    virtual void Get();
public:
    Worker() : fullname("no one"), id(0L) {}
    Worker(const std::string & s, long n)
            : fullname(s), id(n) {}
    virtual ~Worker() = 0; // pure virtual function
    virtual void Set() = 0;
    virtual void Show() const = 0;
};

class Waiter : virtual public Worker
{
private:
    int panache;
protected:
    void Data() const;
    void Get();
public:
    Waiter() : Worker(), panache(0) {}
    Waiter(const std::string & s, long n, int p = 0)
            : Worker(s, n), panache(p) {}
```

LISTING 14.10   Continued

```
            Waiter(const Worker & wk, int p = 0)
                    : Worker(wk), panache(p) {}
            void Set();
            void Show() const;
        };

        class Singer : virtual public Worker
        {
        protected:
        enum {other, alto, contralto, soprano,
                            bass, baritone, tenor};
            enum {Vtypes = 7};
            void Data() const;
            void Get();
        private:
            static char *pv[Vtypes];     // string equivs of voice types
            int voice;
        public:
            Singer() : Worker(), voice(other) {}
            Singer(const std::string & s, long n, int v = other)
                    : Worker(s, n), voice(v) {}
            Singer(const Worker & wk, int v = other)
                    : Worker(wk), voice(v) {}
            void Set();
            void Show() const;
        };

        // multiple inheritance
        class SingingWaiter : public Singer, public Waiter
        {
        protected:
            void Data() const;
            void Get();
        public:
            SingingWaiter()  {}
            SingingWaiter(const std::string & s, long n, int p = 0,
                                int v = other)
                    : Worker(s,n), Waiter(s, n, p), Singer(s, n, v) {}
            SingingWaiter(const Worker & wk, int p = 0, int v = other)
                    : Worker(wk), Waiter(wk,p), Singer(wk,v) {}
            SingingWaiter(const Waiter & wt, int v = other)
                     : Worker(wt),Waiter(wt), Singer(wt,v) {}
            SingingWaiter(const Singer & wt, int p = 0)
                    : Worker(wt),Waiter(wt,p), Singer(wt) {}
            void Set();
            void Show() const;
        };

        #endif
```

LISTING 14.11   `workermi.cpp`

```cpp
// workermi.cpp -- working class methods with MI
#include "workermi.h"
#include <iostream>
using std::cout;
using std::cin;
using std::endl;
// Worker methods
Worker::~Worker() { }

// protected methods
void Worker::Data() const
{
    cout << "Name: " << fullname << endl;
    cout << "Employee ID: " << id << endl;
}

void Worker::Get()
{
    getline(cin, fullname);
    cout << "Enter worker's ID: ";
    cin >> id;
    while (cin.get() != '\n')
        continue;
}

// Waiter methods
void Waiter::Set()
{
    cout << "Enter waiter's name: ";
    Worker::Get();
    Get();
}

void Waiter::Show() const
{
    cout << "Category: waiter\n";
    Worker::Data();
    Data();
}

// protected methods
void Waiter::Data() const
{
    cout << "Panache rating: " << panache << endl;
}

void Waiter::Get()
{
    cout << "Enter waiter's panache rating: ";
    cin >> panache;
    while (cin.get() != '\n')
```

LISTING 14.11   Continued

```cpp
            continue;
    }

    // Singer methods

    char * Singer::pv[Singer::Vtypes] = {"other", "alto", "contralto",
                "soprano", "bass", "baritone", "tenor"};

    void Singer::Set()
    {
        cout << "Enter singer's name: ";
        Worker::Get();
        Get();
    }

    void Singer::Show() const
    {
        cout << "Category: singer\n";
        Worker::Data();
        Data();
    }

    // protected methods
    void Singer::Data() const
    {
        cout << "Vocal range: " << pv[voice] << endl;
    }

    void Singer::Get()
    {
        cout << "Enter number for singer's vocal range:\n";
        int i;
        for (i = 0; i < Vtypes; i++)
        {
            cout << i << ": " << pv[i] << "    ";
            if ( i % 4 == 3)
                cout << endl;
        }
        if (i % 4 != 0)
            cout << '\n';
        cin >>  voice;
        while (cin.get() != '\n')
            continue;
    }

    // SingingWaiter methods
    void SingingWaiter::Data() const
    {
        Singer::Data();
        Waiter::Data();
    }
```

LISTING 14.11   Continued

```
void SingingWaiter::Get()
{
    Waiter::Get();
    Singer::Get();
}

void SingingWaiter::Set()
{
    cout << "Enter singing waiter's name: ";
    Worker::Get();
    Get();
}

void SingingWaiter::Show() const
{
    cout << "Category: singing waiter\n";
    Worker::Data();
    Data();
}
```

Of course, curiosity demands that you test these classes, and Listing 14.12 provides code to do so. Note that the program makes use of polymorphism by assigning the addresses of various kinds of classes to base-class pointers. Also, the program uses the C-style **string** library function **strchr()** in the following test:

```
while (strchr("wstq", choice) == NULL)
```

This function returns the address of the first occurrence of the **choice** character value in the string **"wstq"**; the function returns the **NULL** pointer if the character isn't found. This test is simpler to write than an **if** statement that compares **choice** to each letter individually.

Be sure to compile Listing 14.12 along with **workermi.cpp**.

LISTING 14.12   workmi.cpp

```
// workmi.cpp -- multiple inheritance
// compile with workermi.cpp
#include <iostream>
#include <cstring>
#include "workermi.h"
const int SIZE = 5;

int main()
{
    using std::cin;
    using std::cout;
    using std::endl;
    using std::strchr;

    Worker * lolas[SIZE];
```

LISTING 14.12   *Continued*

```cpp
    int ct;
    for (ct = 0; ct < SIZE; ct++)
    {
        char choice;
        cout << "Enter the employee category:\n"
            << "w: waiter  s: singer  "
            << "t: singing waiter  q: quit\n";
        cin >> choice;
        while (strchr("wstq", choice) == NULL)
        {
            cout << "Please enter a w, s, t, or q: ";
            cin >> choice;
        }
        if (choice == 'q')
            break;
        switch(choice)
        {
            case 'w':   lolas[ct] = new Waiter;
                        break;
            case 's':   lolas[ct] = new Singer;
                        break;
            case 't':   lolas[ct] = new SingingWaiter;
                        break;
        }
        cin.get();
        lolas[ct]->Set();
    }

    cout << "\nHere is your staff:\n";
    int i;
    for (i = 0; i < ct; i++)
    {
        cout << endl;
        lolas[i]->Show();
    }
    for (i = 0; i < ct; i++)
        delete lolas[i];
    cout << "Bye.\n";
    return 0;
}
```

Compatibility Note

If your system doesn't correctly support the `string` friend `getline()` function, it won't run this program correctly. You could modify the program to use `operator>>()` from Listing 14.11 instead. Because this friend function reads just one word, you could change the prompt to ask for just the last name.

Here is a sample run of the program in Listings 14.10, 14.11, and 14.12:

```
Enter the employee category:
w: waiter  s: singer  t: singing waiter  q: quit
w
Enter waiter's name: Wally Slipshod
Enter worker's ID: 1040
Enter waiter's panache rating: 4
Enter the employee category:
w: waiter  s: singer  t: singing waiter  q: quit
s
Enter singer's name: Sinclair Parma
Enter worker's ID: 1044
Enter number for singer's vocal range:
0: other   1: alto   2: contralto   3: soprano
4: bass   5: baritone   6: tenor
5
Enter the employee category:
w: waiter  s: singer  t: singing waiter  q: quit
t
Enter singing waiter's name: Natasha Gargalova
Enter worker's ID: 1021
Enter waiter's panache rating: 6
Enter number for singer's vocal range:
0: other   1: alto   2: contralto   3: soprano
4: bass   5: baritone   6: tenor
3
Enter the employee category:
w: waiter  s: singer  t: singing waiter  q: quit
q

Here is your staff:

Category: waiter
Name: Wally Slipshod
Employee ID: 1040
Panache rating: 4

Category: singer
Name: Sinclair Parma
Employee ID: 1044
Vocal range: baritone

Category: singing waiter
Name: Natasha Gargalova
Employee ID: 1021
Vocal range: soprano
Panache rating: 6
Bye.
```

Let's look at a few more matters concerning MI.

Mixed Virtual and Nonvirtual Bases

Let's consider again the case of a derived class that inherits a base class by more than one route. If the base class is virtual, the derived class contains one subobject of the base class. If the base class is not virtual, the derived class contains multiple subobjects. What if there is a mixture? Suppose, for example, that class B is a virtual base class to classes C and D and a nonvirtual base class to classes X and Y. Furthermore, suppose class M is derived from C, D, X, and Y. In this case, class M contains one class B subobject for all the virtually derived ancestors (that is, classes C and D) and a separate class B subobject for each nonvirtual ancestor (that is, classes X and Y). So, all told, it would contain three class B subobjects. When a class inherits a particular base class through several virtual paths and several nonvirtual paths, the class has one base-class subobject to represent all the virtual paths and a separate base-class subobject to represent each nonvirtual path.

Virtual Base Classes and Dominance

Using virtual base classes alters how C++ resolves ambiguities. With nonvirtual base classes, the rules are simple. If a class inherits two or more members (data or methods) with the same name from different classes, using that name without qualifying it with a class name is ambiguous. If virtual base classes are involved, however, such a use may or may not be ambiguous. In this case, if one name *dominates* all others, it can be used unambiguously without a qualifier.

So how does one member name dominate another? A name in a derived class dominates the same name in any ancestor class, whether direct or indirect. For example, consider the following definitions:

```
class B
{
public:
      short q();
      ...
};

class C : virtual public B
{
public:
      long q();
      int omb()
      ...
};

class D : public C
{
      ...
};

class E : virtual public B
{
private:
```

```
        int omb();
        ...
};

class F:  public D, public E
{
        ...
};
```

Here the definition of `q()` in class `C` dominates the definition in class `B` because `C` is derived from `B`. Thus, methods in `F` can use `q()` to denote `C::q()`. On the other hand, neither definition of `omb()` dominates the other because neither `C` nor `E` is a base class to the other. Therefore, an attempt by `F` to use an unqualified `omb()` would be ambiguous.

The virtual ambiguity rules pay no attention to access rules. That is, even though `E::omb()` is private and hence not directly accessible to class `F`, using `omb()` is ambiguous. Similarly, even if `C::q()` were private, it would dominate `D::q()`. In that case, you could call `B::q()` in class `F`, but an unqualified `q()` for that would refer to the inaccessible `C::q()`.

MI Synopsis

First, let's review MI without virtual base classes. This form of MI imposes no new rules. However, if a class inherits two members with the same name but from different classes, you need to use class qualifiers in the derived class to distinguish between the two members. That is, methods in the `BadDude` class, derived from `Gunslinger` and `PokerPlayer`, would use `Gunslinger::draw()` and `PokerPlayer::draw()` to distinguish between `draw()` methods inherited from the two classes. Otherwise, the compiler should complain about ambiguous usage.

If one class inherits from a nonvirtual base class by more than one route, then the class inherits one base class object for each nonvirtual instance of the base class. In some cases, this may be what you want, but more often, multiple instances of a base class are a problem.

Next, let's look at MI with virtual base classes. A class becomes a virtual base class when a derived class uses the keyword `virtual` when indicating derivation:

```
class marketing : public virtual reality { ... };
```

The main change, and the reason for virtual base classes, is that a class that inherits from one or more instances of a virtual base class inherits just one base class object. Implementing this feature entails other requirements:

- A derived class with an indirect virtual base class should have its constructors invoke the indirect base class constructors directly, which is illegal for indirect nonvirtual base classes.

- Name ambiguity is resolved via the dominance rule.

As you can see, MI can introduce programming complexities. However, most of these complexities arise when a derived class inherits from the same base class by more than one route. If you avoid that situation, about the only thing you need to watch for is qualifying inherited names when necessary.

Class Templates

Inheritance (public, private, or protected) and containment aren't always the solution when you want to reuse code. Consider, for example, the `Stack` class (see Chapter 10) and the `Queue` class (see Chapter 12). These are examples of *container classes*, which are classes designed to hold other objects or data types. The `Stack` class from Chapter 10, for example, stores `unsigned long` values. You could just as easily define a stack class for storing `double` values or `string` objects. The code would be identical except for the type of object stored. However, rather than write new class declarations, it would be nice if you could define a stack in a generic (that is, type-independent) fashion and then provide a specific type as a parameter to the class. Then you could use the same generic code to produce stacks of different kinds of values. In Chapter 10, the `Stack` example uses `typedef` as a first pass at dealing with this desire. However, that approach has a couple drawbacks. First, you have to edit the header file each time you change the type. Second, you can use the technique to generate just one kind of stack per program. That is, you can't have a `typedef` represent two different types simultaneously, so you can't use the method to define a stack of `int`s and a stack of `string`s in the same program.

C++'s class templates provide a better way to generate generic class declarations. (C++ originally did not support templates, and, since their introduction, templates have continued to evolve, so it is possible that your compiler may not support all the features presented here.) Templates provide *parameterized* types—that is, they are capable of passing a type name as an argument to a recipe for building a class or a function. By feeding the type name `int` to a `Queue` template, for example, you can get the compiler to construct a `Queue` class for queuing `int`s.

The C++ library provides several template classes. Earlier in this chapter, you worked with the `valarray` template class. C++'s Standard Template Library (STL), which Chapter 16 discusses in part, provides powerful and flexible template implementations of several container classes. This chapter explores designs of a more elementary nature.

Defining a Class Template

Let's use the `Stack` class from Chapter 10 as a model from which to build a template. Here's the original class declaration:

```
typedef unsigned long Item;

class Stack
{
private:
    enum {MAX = 10};        // constant specific to class
    Item items[MAX];        // holds stack items
    int top;                // index for top stack item
public:
    Stack();
```

```
      bool isempty() const;
      bool isfull() const;
      // push() returns false if stack already is full, true otherwise
      bool push(const Item & item);   // add item to stack
      // pop() returns false if stack already is empty, true otherwise
      bool pop(Item & item);          // pop top into item
};
```

The template approach will replace the `Stack` definition with a template definition and the `Stack` member functions with template member functions. As with template functions, you preface a template class with code that has the following form:

```
template <class Type>
```

The keyword `template` informs the compiler that you're about to define a template. The part in angle brackets is analogous to an argument list to a function. You can think of the keyword `class` as serving as a type name for a variable that accepts a type as a value, and of *Type* as representing a name for this variable.

Using `class` here doesn't mean that *Type* must be a class; it just means that *Type* serves as a generic type specifier for which a real type will be substituted when the template is used. Newer C++ implementations allow you to use the less confusing keyword `typename` instead of `class` in this context:

```
template <typename Type>  // newer choice
```

You can use your choice of generic type name in the *Type* position; the name rules are the same as those for any other identifier. Popular choices include `T` and `Type`; in this case, you should use the latter. When a template is invoked, *Type* will be replaced with a specific type value, such as `int` or `string`. Within the template definition, you can use the generic type name to identify the type to be stored in the stack. For the `Stack` case, that would mean using `Type` wherever the old declaration formerly used the `typedef` identifier `Item`. For example,

```
Item items[MAX];  // holds stack items
```

becomes the following:

```
Type items[MAX];  // holds stack items
```

Similarly, you can replace the class methods of the original class with template member functions. Each function heading will be prefaced with the same template announcement:

```
template <class Type>
```

Again, you should replace the `typedef` identifier `Item` with the generic type name `Type`. One more change is that you need to change the class qualifier from `Stack::` to `Stack<Type>::`. For example,

```
bool Stack::push(const Item & item)
{
...
}
```

becomes the following:

```
template <class Type>                        // or template <typename Type>
bool Stack<Type>::push(const Type & item)
{
...
}
```

If you define a method within the class declaration (an inline definition), you can omit the template preface and the class qualifier.

Listing 14.13 shows the combined class and member function templates. It's important to realize that these templates are not class and member function definitions. Rather, they are instructions to the C++ compiler about how to generate class and member function definitions. A particular actualization of a template, such as a stack class for handling `string` objects, is called an *instantiation* or a *specialization*. Unless you have a compiler that has implemented the new `export` keyword, placing the template member functions in a separate implementation file won't work. Because the templates aren't functions, they can't be compiled separately. Templates have to be used in conjunction with requests for particular instantiations of templates. The simplest way to make this work is to place all the template information in a header file and to include the header file in the file that will use the templates.

LISTING 14.13 `stacktp.h`

```
// stacktp.h -- a stack template
#ifndef STACKTP_H_
#define STACKTP_H_
template <class Type>
class Stack
{
private:
    enum {MAX = 10};    // constant specific to class
    Type items[MAX];    // holds stack items
    int top;            // index for top stack item
public:
    Stack();
    bool isempty();
    bool isfull();
    bool push(const Type & item); // add item to stack
    bool pop(Type & item);        // pop top into item
};

template <class Type>
Stack<Type>::Stack()
{
    top = 0;
}

template <class Type>
bool Stack<Type>::isempty()
{
    return top == 0;
}
```

LISTING 14.13   Continued

```
template <class Type>
bool Stack<Type>::isfull()
{
    return top == MAX;
}

template <class Type>
bool Stack<Type>::push(const Type & item)
{
    if (top < MAX)
    {
        items[top++] = item;
        return true;
    }
    else
        return false;
}

template <class Type>
bool Stack<Type>::pop(Type & item)
{
    if (top > 0)
    {
        item = items[--top];
        return true;
    }
    else
        return false;
}

#endif
```

If your compiler does implement the new `export` keyword, you can place the template method definitions in a separate file, provided that you preface each template declaration with `export`:

```
// stacktp.h -- a stack template
#ifndef STACKTP_H_
#define STACKTP_H_
export template <class Type>    // preface with export
class Stack
{
...
};
```

Then you could follow the same convention used for ordinary classes:

1. Place the template class declaration (with the keyword `export`) in a header file and use the `#include` directive to make the declaration available to a program.

2. Place the template class method definitions in a source code file, include the header file in that file, and use a project file or equivalent to make the definitions available to a program.

Using a Template Class

Merely including a template in a program doesn't generate a template class. You have to ask for an instantiation. To do this, you declare an object of the template class type, replacing the generic type name with the particular type you want. For example, here's how you would create two stacks, one for stacking `ints` and one for stacking `string` objects:

```
Stack<int> kernels;       // create a stack of ints
Stack<string> colonels;   // create a stack of string objects
```

Seeing these two declarations, the compiler will follow the `Stack<Type>` template to generate two separate class declarations and two separate sets of class methods. The `Stack<int>` class declaration will replace `Type` throughout with `int`, and the `Stack<string>` class declaration will replace `Type` throughout with `string`. Of course, the algorithms you use have to be consistent with the types. The `Stack` class, for example, assumes that you can assign one item to another. This assumption is true for basic types, structures, and classes (unless you make the assignment operator private) but not for arrays.

Generic type identifiers such as `Type` in the example are called *type parameters*, meaning that they act something like variables, but instead of assigning a numeric value to a type parameter, you assign a type to it. So in the `kernel` declaration, the type parameter `Type` has the value `int`.

Notice that you have to provide the desired type explicitly. This is different from ordinary function templates, for which the compiler can use the argument types to a function to figure out what kind of function to generate:

```
Template <class T>
void simple(T t) { cout << t << '\n';}
...
simple(2);        // generate void simple(int)
simple("two")     // generate void simple(char *)
```

Listing 14.14 modifies the original stack-testing program (Listing 10.12) to use string purchase order IDs instead of `unsigned long` values.

LISTING 14.14   `stacktem.cpp`

```
// stacktem.cpp -- testing the template stack class
#include <iostream>
#include <string>
#include <cctype>
#include "stacktp.h"
using std::cin;
using std::cout;

int main()
{
    Stack<std::string> st;   // create an empty stack
    char ch;
    std::string po;
```

LISTING 14.14 Continued

```
        cout << "Please enter A to add a purchase order,\n"
            << "P to process a PO, or Q to quit.\n";
    while (cin >> ch && std::toupper(ch) != 'Q')
    {
        while (cin.get() != '\n')
            continue;
        if (!std::isalpha(ch))
        {
            cout << '\a';
            continue;
        }
        switch(ch)
        {
            case 'A':
            case 'a': cout << "Enter a PO number to add: ";
                      cin >> po;
                      if (st.isfull())
                          cout << "stack already full\n";
                      else
                          st.push(po);
                      break;
            case 'P':
            case 'p': if (st.isempty())
                          cout << "stack already empty\n";
                      else {
                          st.pop(po);
                          cout << "PO #" << po << " popped\n";
                          break;
                      }
        }
        cout << "Please enter A to add a purchase order,\n"
            << "P to process a PO, or Q to quit.\n";
    }
    cout << "Bye\n";
    return 0;
}
```

Compatibility Note

You should use the older `ctype.h` header file if your C++ implementation doesn't provide `cctype`.

Here's a sample run of the program in Listing 14.14:

```
Please enter A to add a purchase order,
P to process a PO, or Q to quit.
A
Enter a PO number to add: red911porsche
Please enter A to add a purchase order,
P to process a PO, or Q to quit.
A
```

```
Enter a PO number to add: greenS8audi
Please enter A to add a purchase order,
P to process a PO, or Q to quit.
A
Enter a PO number to add: silver747boeing
Please enter A to add a purchase order,
P to process a PO, or Q to quit.
P
PO #silver747boeing popped
Please enter A to add a purchase order,
P to process a PO, or Q to quit.
P
PO #greenS8audi popped
Please enter A to add a purchase order,
P to process a PO, or Q to quit.
P
PO #red911porsche popped
Please enter A to add a purchase order,
P to process a PO, or Q to quit.
P
stack already empty
Please enter A to add a purchase order,
P to process a PO, or Q to quit.
Q
Bye
```

A Closer Look at the Template Class

You can use a built-in type or a class object as the type for the `Stack<Type>` class template. What about a pointer? For example, can you use a pointer to a `char` instead of a `string` object in Listing 14.14? After all, such pointers are the built-in way for handling C++ strings. The answer is that you can create a stack of pointers, but it won't work very well without major modifications in the program. The compiler can create the class, but it's your task to see that it's used sensibly. Let's see why such a stack of pointers doesn't work very well with Listing 14.14, and then let's look at an example where a stack of pointers is useful.

Using a Stack of Pointers Incorrectly

Let's quickly look at three simple, but flawed, attempts to adapt Listing 14.14 to use a stack of pointers. These attempts illustrate the lesson that you should keep the design of a template in mind and not just use it blindly. All three examples begin with this perfectly valid invocation of the `Stack<Type>` template:

```
Stack<char *> st; // create a stack for pointers-to-char
```

Version 1 then replaces

```
string po;
```

with

```
char * po;
```

The idea is to use a `char` pointer instead of a `string` object to receive the keyboard input. This approach fails immediately because merely creating a pointer doesn't create space to hold the input strings. (The program would compile, but it would quite possibly crash after `cin` tried to store input in some inappropriate location.)

Version 2 replaces

```
string po;
```

with

```
char po[40];
```

This allocates space for an input string. Furthermore, `po` is of type `char *`, so it can be placed on the stack. But an array is fundamentally at odds with the assumptions made for the `pop()` method:

```
template <class Type>
bool Stack<Type>::pop(Type & item)
{
    if (top > 0)
    {
        item = items[--top];
        return true;
    }
    else
        return false;
}
```

First, the reference variable `item` has to refer to an lvalue of some sort, not to an array name. Second, the code assumes that you can assign to `item`. Even if `item` could refer to an array, you can't assign to an array name. So this approach fails, too.

Version 3 replaces

```
string po;
```

with

```
char * po = new char[40];
```

This allocates space for an input string. Furthermore, `po` is a variable and hence compatible with the code for `pop()`. Here, however, you come up against the most fundamental problem: There is only one `po` variable, and it always points to the same memory location. True, the contents of the memory change each time a new string is read, but every push operation puts exactly the same address onto the stack. So when you pop the stack, you always get the same address back, and it always refers to the last string read into memory. In particular, the stack is not storing each new string separately as it comes in, and it serves no useful purpose.

Using a Stack of Pointers Correctly

One way to use a stack of pointers is to have the calling program provide an array of pointers, with each pointer pointing to a different string. Putting these pointers on a stack then makes sense because each pointer will refer to a different string. Note that it is the responsibility of the calling program, not the stack, to create the separate pointers. The stack's job is to manage the pointers, not create them.

For example, suppose you have to simulate the following situation. Someone has delivered a cart of folders to Plodson. If Plodson's in-basket is empty, he removes the top folder from the cart and places it in his in-basket. If his in-basket is full, Plodson removes the top file from the basket, processes it, and places it in his out-basket. If the in-basket is neither empty nor full, Plodson may process the top file in the in-basket, or he may take the next file from the cart and put it into his in-basket. In what he secretly regards as a bit of madcap self-expression, he flips a coin to decide which of these actions to take. You'd like to investigate the effects of his method on the original file order.

You can model this with an array of pointers to strings representing the files on the cart. Each string will contain the name of the person described by the file. You can use a stack to represent the in-basket, and you can use a second array of pointers to represent the out-basket. Adding a file to the in-basket is represented by pushing a pointer from the input array onto the stack, and processing a file is represented by popping an item from the stack and adding it to the out-basket.

Given the importance of examining all aspects of this problem, it would be useful to be able to try different stack sizes. Listing 14.15 redefines the Stack<Type> class slightly so that the Stack constructor accepts an optional size argument. This involves using a dynamic array internally, so the class now needs a destructor, a copy constructor, and an assignment operator. Also, the definition shortens the code by making several of the methods inline.

LISTING 14.15   stcktp1.h

```
// stcktp1.h -- modified Stack template
#ifndef STCKTP1_H_
#define STCKTP1_H_

template <class Type>
class Stack
{
private:
    enum {SIZE = 10};    // default size
    int stacksize;
    Type * items;        // holds stack items
    int top;             // index for top stack item
public:
    explicit Stack(int ss = SIZE);
    Stack(const Stack & st);
    ~Stack() { delete [] items; }
    bool isempty() { return top == 0; }
    bool isfull() { return top == stacksize; }
    bool push(const Type & item);   // add item to stack
    bool pop(Type & item);          // pop top into item
    Stack & operator=(const Stack & st);
};
```

LISTING 14.15   Continued

```cpp
template <class Type>
Stack<Type>::Stack(int ss) : stacksize(ss), top(0)
{
    items = new Type [stacksize];
}

template <class Type>
Stack<Type>::Stack(const Stack & st)
{
    stacksize = st.stacksize;
    top = st.top;
    items = new Type [stacksize];
    for (int i = 0; i < top; i++)
        items[i] = st.items[i];
}

template <class Type>
bool Stack<Type>::push(const Type & item)
{
    if (top < stacksize)
    {
        items[top++] = item;
        return true;
    }
    else
        return false;
}

template <class Type>
bool Stack<Type>::pop(Type & item)
{
    if (top > 0)
    {
        item = items[--top];
        return true;
    }
    else
        return false;
}

template <class Type>
Stack<Type> & Stack<Type>::operator=(const Stack<Type> & st)
{
    if (this == &st)
        return *this;
    delete [] items;
    stacksize = st.stacksize;
    top = st.top;
    items = new Type [stacksize];
    for (int i = 0; i < top; i++)
        items[i] = st.items[i];
```

LISTING 14.15   Continued

```
    return *this;
}

#endif
```

Compatibility Note

Some C++ implementations might not recognize `explicit`.

Notice that the prototype declares the return type for the assignment operator function to be a reference to `Stack`, and the actual template function definition identifies the type as `Stack<Type>`. The former is an abbreviation for the latter, but it can be used only within the class scope. That is, you can use `Stack` inside the template declaration and inside the template function definitions, but outside the class, as when identifying return types and when using the scope-resolution operator, you need to use the full `Stack<Type>` form.

The program in Listing 14.16 uses the new stack template to implement the Plodson simulation. It uses `rand()`, `srand()`, and `time()` in the same way previous simulations have used them to generate random numbers. In this case, randomly generating a 0 or a 1 simulates the coin toss.

LISTING 14.16   stkoptr1.cpp

```
// stkoptr1.cpp -- testing stack of pointers
#include <iostream>
#include <cstdlib>      // for rand(), srand()
#include <ctime>        // for time()
#include "stcktp1.h"
const int Num = 10;
int main()
{
    std::srand(std::time(0)); // randomize rand()
    std::cout << "Please enter stack size: ";
    int stacksize;
    std::cin >> stacksize;
// create an empty stack with stacksize slots
    Stack<const char *> st(stacksize);

// in basket
    const char * in[Num] = {
            " 1: Hank Gilgamesh", " 2: Kiki Ishtar",
            " 3: Betty Rocker", " 4: Ian Flagranti",
            " 5: Wolfgang Kibble", " 6: Portia Koop",
            " 7: Joy Almondo", " 8: Xaverie Paprika",
            " 9: Juan Moore", "10: Misha Mache"
            };
// out basket
    const char * out[Num];
```

LISTING 14.16 *Continued*

```
            int processed = 0;
            int nextin = 0;
            while (processed < Num)
            {
                if (st.isempty())
                    st.push(in[nextin++]);
                else if (st.isfull())
                    st.pop(out[processed++]);
                else if (std::rand() % 2  && nextin < Num)    // 50-50 chance
                    st.push(in[nextin++]);
                else
                    st.pop(out[processed++]);
            }
            for (int i = 0; i < Num; i++)
                std::cout << out[i] << std::endl;

            std::cout << "Bye\n";
            return 0;
        }
```

Compatibility Note

Some C++ implementations require `stdlib.h` instead of `cstdlib` and `time.h` instead of `ctime`.

Two sample runs of the program in Listing 14.16 follow (note that, thanks to the randomizing feature, the final file ordering can differ quite a bit from one trial to the next, even when the stack size is kept unaltered):

```
Please enter stack size: 5
 2: Kiki Ishtar
 1: Hank Gilgamesh
 3: Betty Rocker
 5: Wolfgang Kibble
 4: Ian Flagranti
 7: Joy Almondo
 9: Juan Moore
 8: Xaverie Paprika
 6: Portia Koop
10: Misha Mache
Bye

Please enter stack size: 5
 3: Betty Rocker
 5: Wolfgang Kibble
 6: Portia Koop
 4: Ian Flagranti
 8: Xaverie Paprika
 9: Juan Moore
10: Misha Mache
```

```
 7: Joy Almondo
 2: Kiki Ishtar
 1: Hank Gilgamesh
Bye
```

Program Notes

The strings in Listing 14.16 never move. Pushing a string onto the stack really creates a new pointer to an existing string. That is, it creates a pointer whose value is the address of an existing string. And popping a string off the stack copies that address value into the out array.

The program uses const char * as a type because the array of pointers is initialized to a set of string constants.

What effect does the stack destructor have on the strings? None. The class constructor uses new to create an array for holding pointers. The class destructor eliminates that array, not the strings to which the array elements pointed.

An Array Template Example and Non-Type Arguments

Templates are frequently used for container classes because the idea of type parameters matches well with the need to apply a common storage plan to a variety of types. Indeed, the desire to provide reusable code for container classes was the main motivation for introducing templates, so let's look at another example and explore a few more facets of template design and use. In particular, let's look at non-type, or expression, arguments and at using an array to handle an inheritance family.

Let's begin with a simple array template that lets you specify an array size. One technique, which the last version of the Stack template uses, is to use a dynamic array within the class and a constructor argument to provide the number of elements. Another approach is to use a template argument to provide the size for a regular array. Listing 14.17 shows how this can be done.

LISTING 14.17 arraytp.h

```
//arraytp.h  -- Array Template
#ifndef ARRAYTP_H_
#define ARRAYTP_H_

#include <iostream>
#include <cstdlib>

template <class T, int n>
class ArrayTP
{
private:
    T ar[n];
public:
    ArrayTP() {};
    explicit ArrayTP(const T & v);
```

LISTING 14.17   Continued

```cpp
    virtual T & operator[](int i);
    virtual T operator[](int i) const;
};

template <class T, int n>
ArrayTP<T,n>::ArrayTP(const T & v)
{
    for (int i = 0; i < n; i++)
        ar[i] = v;
}

template <class T, int n>
T & ArrayTP<T,n>::operator[](int i)
{
    if (i < 0 || i >= n)
    {
        std::cerr << "Error in array limits: " << i
            << " is out of range\n";
        std::exit(EXIT_FAILURE);
    }
    return ar[i];
}

template <class T, int n>
T ArrayTP<T,n>::operator[](int i) const
{
    if (i < 0 || i >= n)
    {
        std::cerr << "Error in array limits: " << i
            << " is out of range\n";
        std::exit(EXIT_FAILURE);
    }
    return ar[i];
}

#endif
```

Note the template heading in Listing 14.17:

```cpp
template <class T, int n>
```

The keyword `class` (or, equivalently in this context, `typename`) identifies `T` as a type parameter, or type argument. `int` identifies `n` as being an `int` type. This second kind of parameter, one that specifies a particular type instead of acting as a generic name for a type, is called a *non-type*, or *expression*, *argument*. Suppose you have the following declaration:

```cpp
ArrayTP<double, 12> eggweights;
```

This causes the compiler to define a class called `ArrayTP<double,12>` and to create an `eggweights` object of that class. When defining the class, the compiler replaces `T` with `double` and `n` with `12`.

Expression arguments have some restrictions. An expression argument can be an integral type, an enumeration type, a reference, or a pointer. Thus, `double m` is ruled out, but `double & rm` and `double * pm` are allowed. Also, the template code can't alter the value of the argument or take its address. Thus, in the `ArrayTP` template, expressions such as `n++` or `&n` would not be allowed. Also, when you instantiate a template, the value used for the expression argument should be a constant expression.

This approach for sizing an array has one advantage over the constructor approach used in `Stack`. The constructor approach uses heap memory managed by `new` and `delete`, whereas the expression argument approach uses the memory stack maintained for automatic variables. This provides faster execution time, particularly if you have a lot of small arrays.

The main drawback to the expression argument approach is that each array size generates its own template. That is, the declarations

```
ArrayTP<double, 12> eggweights;
ArrayTP(double, 13> donuts;
```

generate two separate class declarations. But the declarations

```
Stack<int> eggs(12);
Stack<int> dunkers(13);
```

generate just one class declaration, and the size information is passed to the constructor for that class.

Another difference is that the constructor approach is more versatile because the array size is stored as a class member rather than being hard-coded into the definition. This makes it possible, for example, to define assignment from an array of one size to an array of another size or to build a class that allows resizable arrays.

Template Versatility

You can apply the same techniques to template classes as you do to regular classes. Template classes can serve as base classes, and they can be component classes. They can themselves be type arguments to other templates. For example, you can implement a stack template by using an array template. Or you can have an array template that is used to construct an array whose elements are stacks based on a stack template. That is, you can have code along the following lines:

```
template <class T>
class Array
{
private:
    T entry;
    ...
};

template <class Type>
class GrowArray : public Array<Type> {...};  // inheritance
```

```
template <class Tp>
class Stack
{
     Array<Tp> ar;        // use an Array<> as a component
     ...
};
...
Array < Stack<int> > asi;  // an array of stacks of int
```

In the last statement, you must separate the two > symbols by at least one white-space character in order to avoid confusion with the >> operator.

Using a Template Recursively

Another example of template versatility is that you can use templates recursively. For example, given the earlier definition of an array template, you can use it as follows:

```
ArrayTP< ArrayTP<int,5>, 10> twodee;
```

This makes **twodee** an array of 10 elements, each of which is an array of five **int**s. The equivalent ordinary array would have this declaration:

```
int twodee[10][5];
```

Note that the syntax for templates presents the dimensions in the opposite order from that of the equivalent ordinary two-dimensional array. The program in Listing 14.18 tries this idea. It also uses the **ArrayTP** template to create one-dimensional arrays to hold the sum and average value of each of the 10 sets of five numbers. The method call **cout.width(2)** causes the next item to be displayed to use a field width of two characters, unless a larger width is needed to show the whole number.

LISTING 14.18   twod.cpp

```cpp
// twod.cpp -- making a 2-d array
#include <iostream>
#include "arraytp.h"
int main(void)
{
    using std::cout;
    using std::endl;
    ArrayTP<int, 10> sums;
    ArrayTP<double, 10> aves;
    ArrayTP< ArrayTP<int,5>, 10> twodee;

    int i, j;

    for (i = 0; i < 10; i++)
    {
        sums[i] = 0;
        for (j = 0; j < 5; j++)
        {
```

LISTING 14.18   Continued

```
            twodee[i][j] = (i + 1) * (j + 1);
            sums[i] += twodee[i][j];
        }
        aves[i] = (double) sums[i] / 10;
    }
    for (i = 0; i < 10; i++)
    {
        for (j = 0; j < 5; j++)
        {
            cout.width(2);
            cout << twodee[i][j] << ' ';
        }
        cout << ": sum = ";
        cout.width(3);
        cout  << sums[i] << ", average = " << aves[i] << endl;
    }

    cout << "Done.\n";

    return 0;
}
```

The output of the program in Listing 14.18 has one line for each of the 10 elements of twodee, each of which is a five-element array. Each line shows the values, sum, and average of an element of twodee:

```
 1  2  3  4  5 : sum =  15, average = 1.5
 2  4  6  8 10 : sum =  30, average = 3
 3  6  9 12 15 : sum =  45, average = 4.5
 4  8 12 16 20 : sum =  60, average = 6
 5 10 15 20 25 : sum =  75, average = 7.5
 6 12 18 24 30 : sum =  90, average = 9
 7 14 21 28 35 : sum = 105, average = 10.5
 8 16 24 32 40 : sum = 120, average = 12
 9 18 27 36 45 : sum = 135, average = 13.5
10 20 30 40 50 : sum = 150, average = 15
Done.
```

Using More Than One Type Parameter

You can have a template with more than one type parameter. For example, suppose you want a class that holds two kinds of values. You can create and use a Pair template class for holding two disparate values. (Incidentally, the STL provides a similar template called pair.) The short program in Listing 14.19 shows an example. In it, the first() const and second() const methods report the stored values, and the first() and second() methods, by virtue of returning references to the Pair data members, allow you to reset the stored values by using assignment.

LISTING 14.19   `pairs.cpp`

```cpp
// pairs.cpp -- defining and using a Pair template
#include <iostream>
#include <string>
template <class T1, class T2>
class Pair
{
private:
    T1 a;
    T2 b;
public:
    T1 & first();
    T2 & second();
    T1 first() const { return a; }
    T2 second() const { return b; }
    Pair(const T1 & aval, const T2 & bval) : a(aval), b(bval) { }
    Pair() {}
};

template<class T1, class T2>
T1 & Pair<T1,T2>::first()
{
    return a;
}
template<class T1, class T2>
T2 & Pair<T1,T2>::second()
{
    return b;
}

int main()
{
    using std::cout;
    using std::endl;
    using std::string;
    Pair<string, int> ratings[4] =
    {
        Pair<string, int>("The Purple Duke", 5),
        Pair<string, int>("Jake's Frisco Al Fresco", 4),
        Pair<string, int>("Mont Souffle", 5),
        Pair<string, int>("Gertie's Eats", 3)
    };

    int joints = sizeof(ratings) / sizeof (Pair<string, int>);
    cout << "Rating:\t Eatery\n";
    for (int i = 0; i < joints; i++)
        cout << ratings[i].second() << ":\t "
             << ratings[i].first() << endl;
    cout << "Oops! Revised rating:\n";
    ratings[3].first() = "Gertie's Fab Eats";
    ratings[3].second() = 6;
```

LISTING 14.19 Continued

```
    cout << ratings[3].second() << ":\t "
         << ratings[3].first() << endl;

    return 0;
}
```

One thing to note about Listing 14.19 is that in `main()`, you have to use `Pair<string,int>` to invoke the constructors and as an argument for `sizeof`. That's because `Pair<string,int>` and not `Pair` is the class name. Also, `Pair<char *,double>` would be the name of an entirely different class.

Here's the output of the program in Listing 14.19:

```
Rating:  Eatery
5:       The Purple Duke
4:       Jake's Frisco Al Fresco
5:       Mont Souffle
3:       Gertie's Eats
Oops! Revised rating:
6:       Gertie's Fab Eats
```

Default Type Template Parameters

Another new class template feature is that you can provide default values for type parameters:

```
template <class T1, class T2 = int> class Topo {...};
```

This causes the compiler to use `int` for the type `T2` if a value for `T2` is omitted:

```
Topo<double, double> m1; // T1 is double, T2 is double
Topo<double> m2;         // T1 is double, T2 is int
```

The STL (discussed in Chapter 16) often uses this feature, with the default type being a class.

Although you can provide default values for class template type parameters, you can't do so for function template parameters. However, you can provide default values for non-type parameters for both class and function templates.

Template Specializations

Class templates are like function templates in that you can have implicit instantiations, explicit instantiations, and explicit specializations, collectively known as *specializations*. That is, a template describes a class in terms of a general type, whereas a specialization is a class declaration generated by using a specific type.

Implicit Instantiations

The template examples you have seen so far in this chapter use *implicit instantiations*. That is, they declare one or more objects indicating the desired type, and the compiler generates a specialized class definition, using the recipe provided by the general template:

```
ArrayTP<int, 100> stuff; // implicit instantiation
```

The compiler doesn't generate an implicit instantiation of the class until it needs an object:

```
ArrayTP<double, 30> * pt;       // a pointer, no object needed yet
pt = new ArrayTP<double, 30>; // now an object is needed
```

The second statement causes the compiler to generate a class definition and also an object that is created according to that definition.

Explicit Instantiations

The compiler generates an *explicit instantiation* of a class declaration when you declare a class by using the keyword `template` and indicating the desired type or types. The declaration should be in the same namespace as the template definition. For example, the declaration

```
template class ArrayTP<string, 100>; // generate ArrayTP<string, 100> class
```

declares `ArrayTP<string, 100>` to be a class. In this case, the compiler generates the class definition, including method definitions, even though no object of the class has yet been created or mentioned. Just as with the implicit instantiation, the general template is used as a guide to generate the specialization.

Explicit Specializations

An *explicit specialization* is a definition for a particular type or types that is to be used instead of the general template. Sometimes you might need or want to modify a template to behave differently when instantiated for a particular type; in that case, you can create an explicit specialization. Suppose, for example, that you've defined a template for a class that represents a sorted array for which items are sorted as they are added to the array:

```
template <class T>
class SortedArray
{
    ...// details omitted
};
```

Also, suppose the template uses the `>` operator to compare values. This works well for numbers. It will work if `T` represents a class type, too, provided that you've defined a `T::operator>()` method. But it won't work if `T` is a string represented by type `char *`. Actually, the template will work, but the strings will wind up sorted by address rather than alphabetically. What is needed is a class definition that uses `strcmp()` instead of `>`. In such a case, you can provide an explicit template specialization. This takes the form of a template defined for one specific type instead of for a general type. When faced with the choice of a specialized template and a general template that both match an instantiation request, the compiler uses the specialized version.

A specialized class template definition has the following form:

```
template <> class Classname<specialized-type-name> { ... };
```

Older compilers may only recognize the older form, which dispenses with the template <>:

```
class Classname<specialized-type-name> { ... };
```

To provide a `SortedArray` template specialized for the `char *` type, using the new notation, you would use code like the following:

```
template <> class SortedArray<char *>
{
    ...// details omitted
};
```

Here the implementation code would use `strcmp()` instead of `>` to compare array values. Now, requests for a `SortedArray` template of `char *` will use this specialized definition instead of the more general template definition:

```
SortedArray<int> scores;    // use general definition
SortedArray<char *> dates;  // use specialized definition
```

Partial Specializations

C++ allows for *partial specializations*, which partially restrict the generality of a template. For example, a partial specialization can provide a specific type for one of the type parameters:

```
// general template
    template <class T1, class T2> class Pair {...};
// specialization with T2 set to int
    template <class T1> class Pair<T1, int> {...};
```

The `<>` following the keyword `template` declares the type parameters that are still unspecialized. So the second declaration specializes `T2` to `int` but leaves `T1` open. Note that specifying all the types leads to an empty bracket pair and a complete explicit specialization:

```
// specialization with T1 and T2 set to int
    template <> class Pair<int, int> {...};
```

The compiler uses the most specialized template if there is a choice:

```
Pair<double, double> p1; // use general Pair template
Pair<double, int> p2;    // use Pair<T1, int> partial specialization
Pair<int, int> p3;       // use Pair<int, int> explicit specialization
```

Or you can partially specialize an existing template by providing a special version for pointers:

```
template<class T>      // general version
class Feeb { ... };
template<class T*>     // pointer partial specialization
class Feeb { ... };    // modified code
```

If you provide a non-pointer type, the compiler uses the general version; if you provide a pointer, the compiler uses the pointer specialization:

```
Feeb<char> fb1;        // use general Feeb template, T is char
Feeb<char *> fb2;      // use Feeb T* specialization, T is char
```

Without the partial specialization, the second declaration would use the general template, interpreting `T` as type `char *`. With the partial specialization, it uses the specialized template, interpreting `T` as `char`.

The partial specialization feature allows for making a variety of restrictions. For example, you can use the following:

```
// general template
    template <class T1, class T2, class T3> class Trio{...};
// specialization with T3 set to T2
    template <class T1, class T2> class Trio<T1, T2, T2> {...};
// specialization with T3 and T2 set to T1*
    template <class T1> class Trio<T1, T1*, T1*> {...};
```

Given these declarations, the compiler would make the following choices:

```
Trio<int, short, char *> t1; // use general template
Trio<int, short> t2; // use Trio<T1, T2, T2>
Trio<char, char *, char *> t3; use Trio<T1, T1*, T1*>
```

Member Templates

Another of the more recent additions to C++ template support is that a template can be a member of a structure, class, or template class. The STL requires this feature to fully implement its design. Listing 14.20 provides a short example of a template class with a nested template class and a template function as members.

LISTING 14.20   `tempmemb.cpp`

```
// tempmemb.cpp -- template members
#include <iostream>
using std::cout;
using std::endl;

template <typename T>
class beta
{
private:
    template <typename V>  // nested template class member
    class hold
    {
    private:
        V val;
    public:
        hold(V v  = 0) : val(v) {}
        void show() const { cout << val << endl; }
        V Value() const { return val; }
    };
    hold<T> q;              // template object
    hold<int> n;            // template object
public:
    beta( T t, int i) : q(t), n(i) {}
    template<typename U>    // template method
    U blab(U u, T t) { return (n.Value() + q.Value()) * u / t; }
    void Show() const { q.show(); n.show();}
};
```

LISTING 14.20   Continued

```
int main()
{
    beta<double> guy(3.5, 3);

    guy.Show();
    cout << guy.blab(10, 2.3) << endl;
    cout << "Done\n";
    return 0;
}
```

The `hold` template is declared in the private section in Listing 14.20, so it is accessible only within the `beta` class scope. The `beta` class uses the `hold` template to declare two data members:

```
hold<T> q;              // template object
hold<int> n;            // template object
```

`n` is a `hold` object based on the `int` type, and the `q` member is a `hold` object based on the `T` type (the `beta` template parameter). In `main()`, the declaration

```
beta<double> guy(3.5, 3);
```

makes `T` represent `double`, making `q` type `hold<double>`.

The `blab()` method has one type (`U`) that is determined implicitly by the argument value when the method is called and one type (`T`) that is determined by the instantiation type of the object. In this example, the declaration for `guy` sets `T` to type `double`, and the first argument in the method call in

```
cout << guy.blab(10, 2.5) << endl;
```

sets `U` to type `int`, matching the value `10`. Thus, although the automatic type conversions brought about by mixed types cause the calculation in `blab()` to be done as type `double`, the return value, being type `U`, is an `int`, as the following program output shows:

```
3.5
3
28
Done
```

If you replace `10` with `10.0` in the call to `guy.blab()`, `U` is set to `double`, making the return type `double`, and you get this output instead:

```
3.5
3
28.2609
Done
```

As mentioned previously, the type of the second parameter is set to `double` by the declaration of the `guy` object. Unlike the first parameter, then, the type of the second parameter is not set by the function call. For instance, the statement

```
cout << guy.blab(10, 3) << endl;
```

would still implement `blah()` as `blah(int, double)`, and the 3 would be converted to type `double` by the usual function prototype rules.

You can declare the `hold` class and `blah` method in the `beta` template and define them outside the `beta` template. However, because implementing templates is still a new process, it may be more difficult to get the compiler to accept these forms. Some compilers may not accept template members at all, and others that accept them as shown in Listing 14.20 don't accept definitions outside the class. However, if your compiler is willing and able, here's how defining the template methods outside the `beta` template would look:

```cpp
template <typename T>
class beta
{
private:
    template <typename V>  // declaration
    class hold;
    hold<T> q;
    hold<int> n;
public:
    beta( T t, int i) : q(t), n(i) {}
    template<typename U>   // declaration
    U blab(U u, T t);
    void Show() const { q.show(); n.show();}
};

// member definition
template <typename T>
  template<typename V>
    class beta<T>::hold
    {
    private:
        V val;
    public:
        hold(V v  = 0) : val(v) {}
        void show() const { std::cout << val << std::endl; }
        V Value() const { return val; }
    };

// member definition
template <typename T>
  template <typename U>
    U beta<T>::blab(U u, T t)
    {
        return (n.Value() + q.Value()) * u / t;
    }
```

The definitions have to identify T, V, and U as template parameters. Because the templates are nested, you have to use the

```cpp
template <typename T>
  template <typename V>
```

syntax instead of the

```cpp
template<typename T, typename V>
```

syntax. The definitions also must indicate that `hold` and `blab` are members of the `beta<T>` class, and they use the scope-resolution operator to do so.

Templates as Parameters

You've seen that a template can have type parameters, such as `typename T`, and non-type parameters, such as `int n`. A template can also have a parameter that is itself a template. Such parameters are yet another recent template feature addition that is used to implement the STL.

Listing 14.21 shows an example for which the template parameter is `template <typename T> class Thing`. Here `template <typename T> class` is the type and `Thing` is the parameter. What does this imply? Suppose you have this declaration:

```
Crab<King> legs;
```

For this to be accepted, the template argument `King` has to be a template class whose declaration matches that of the template parameter `Thing`:

```
template <typename T>
class King {...};
```

The `Crab` declaration declares two objects:

```
Thing<int> s1;
Thing<double> s2;
```

The previous declaration for `legs` would then result in substituting `King<int>` for `Thing<int>` and `King<double>` for `Thing<double>`. However, Listing 14.21 has this declaration:

```
Crab<Stack> nebula;
```

Hence, in this case, `Thing<int>` is instantiated as `Stack<int>`, and `Thing<double>` is instantiated as `Stack<double>`. In short, the template parameter `Thing` is replaced by whatever template type is used as a template argument in declaring a `Crab` object.

The `Crab` class declaration makes three further assumptions about the template class represented by `Thing`. The class should have a `push()` method, the class should have a `pop()` method, and these methods should have a particular interface. The `Crab` class can use any template class that matches the `Thing` type declaration and that has the prerequisite `push()` and `pop()` methods. This chapter happens to have one such class, the `Stack` template defined in `stacktp.h`, so the example uses that class.

LISTING 14.21   `tempparm.cpp`

```
// tempparm.cpp -- templates as parameters
#include <iostream>
#include "stacktp.h"

template <template <typename T> class Thing>
class Crab
{
private:
```

LISTING 14.21 Continued

```cpp
        Thing<int> s1;
        Thing<double> s2;
public:
    Crab() {};
    // assumes the thing class has push() and pop() members
    bool push(int a, double x) { return s1.push(a) && s2.push(x); }
    bool pop(int & a, double & x){ return s1.pop(a) && s2.pop(x); }
};

int main()
{
    using std::cout;
    using std::cin;
    using std::endl;
    Crab<Stack> nebula;
// Stack must match template <typename T> class thing
    int ni;
    double nb;
    cout << "Enter int double pairs, such as 4 3.5 (0 0 to end):\n";
    while (cin>> ni >> nb && ni > 0 && nb > 0)
    {
        if (!nebula.push(ni, nb))
            break;
    }

    while (nebula.pop(ni, nb))
        cout << ni << ", " << nb << endl;
    cout << "Done.\n";

    return 0;
}
```

Here is a sample run of the program in Listing 14.21:

```
Enter int double pairs, such as 4 3.5 (0 0 to end):
50 22.48
25 33.87
60 19.12
0 0
60, 19.12
25, 33.87
50, 22.48
Done.
```

You can mix template parameters with regular parameters. For example, the **Crab** class declaration could start out like this:

```cpp
template <template <typename T> class Thing, typename U, typename V>
class Crab
{
private:
    Thing<U> s1;
    Thing<V> s2;
...
```

Now the types to be stored in the members s1 and s2 are generic types instead of hard-coded types. This would require the declaration of `nebula` in the program to be changed to this:

```
Crab<Stack, int, double> nebula; // T=Stack, U=int, V=double
```

The `template` parameter T represents a template type, and the type parameters U and V represent non-template types.

Template Classes and Friends

Template class declarations can have friends, too. You can classify friends of templates into three categories:

- Non-template friends

- Bound template friends, meaning the type of the friend is determined by the type of the class when a class is instantiated

- Unbound template friends, meaning that all specializations of the friend are friends to each specialization of the class

Let's look at examples of each.

Non-Template Friend Functions to Template Classes

Let's declare an ordinary function in a template class as a friend:

```
template <class T>
class HasFriend
{
    friend void counts();      // friend to all HasFriend instantiations
    ...
};
```

This declaration makes the `counts()` function a friend to all possible instantiations of the template. For example, it would be a friend to the `HasFriend<int>` class and the `HasFriend<string>` class.

The `counts()` function is not invoked by an object (it's a friend, not a member function) and it has no object parameters, so how does it access a `HasFriend` object? There are several possibilities. It could access a global object; it could access nonglobal objects by using a global pointer; it could create its own objects; and it could access static data members of a template class, which exist separately from an object.

Suppose you want to provide a template class argument to a friend function. Can you have a friend declaration like this, for example?

```
friend void report(HasFriend &);   // possible?
```

The answer is no. The reason is that there is no such thing as a `HasFriend` object. There are only particular specializations, such as `HasFriend<short>`. To provide a template class argument, then, you have to indicate a specialization. For example, you can use this:

```
template <class T>
class HasFriend
{
    friend void report(HasFriend<T> &); // bound template friend
    ...
};
```

To understand what this does, imagine the specialization produced if you declare an object of a particular type:

```
HasFriend<int> hf;
```

The compiler would replace the template parameter T with int, giving the friend declaration this form:

```
class HasFriend<int>
{
    friend void report(HasFriend<int> &); // bound template friend
    ...
};
```

That is, report() with a HasFriend<int> parameter becomes a friend to the HasFriend<int> class. Similarly, report() with a HasFriend<double> parameter would be an overloaded version of report() that is a friend to the HasFriend<double> class.

Note that report() is not itself a template function; it just has a parameter that is a template. This means that you have to define explicit specializations for the friends you plan to use:

```
void report(HasFriend<short> &) { ... };  // explicit specialization for short
void report(HasFriend<int> &) { ... };    // explicit specialization for int
```

Listing 14.22 illustrates these points. The HasFriend template has a static member ct. Note that this means that each particular specialization of the class has its own static member. The counts() method, which is a friend to all HasFriend specializations, reports the value of ct for two particular specializations: HasFriend<int> and HasFriend<double>. The program also provides two report() functions, each of which is a friend to one particular HasFriend specialization.

LISTING 14.22   frnd2tmp.cpp

```cpp
// frnd2tmp.cpp -- template class with non-template friends
#include <iostream>
using std::cout;
using std::endl;

template <typename T>
class HasFriend
{
private:
    T item;
    static int ct;
public:
    HasFriend(const T & i) : item(i) {ct++;}
```

LISTING 14.22   Continued

```
        ~HasFriend()   {ct--; }
        friend void counts();
        friend void reports(HasFriend<T> &); // template parameter
};

// each specialization has its own static data member
template <typename T>
int HasFriend<T>::ct = 0;

// non-template friend to all HasFriend<T> classes
void counts()
{
    cout << "int count: " << HasFriend<int>::ct << "; ";
    cout << "double count: " << HasFriend<double>::ct << endl;
}

// non-template friend to the HasFriend<int> class
void reports(HasFriend<int> & hf)
{
    cout <<"HasFriend<int>: " << hf.item << endl;
}

// non-template friend to the HasFriend<double> class
void reports(HasFriend<double> & hf)
{
    cout <<"HasFriend<double>: " << hf.item << endl;
}

int main()
{
    cout << "No objects declared: ";
    counts();
    HasFriend<int> hfi1(10);
    cout << "After hfi1 declared: ";
    counts();
    HasFriend<int> hfi2(20);
    cout << "After hfi2 declared: ";
    counts();
    HasFriend<double> hfdb(10.5);
    cout << "After hfdb declared: ";
    counts();
    reports(hfi1);
    reports(hfi2);
    reports(hfdb);

    return 0;
}
```

Here is the output of the program in Listing 14.22:

```
No objects declared: int count: 0; double count: 0
After hfi1 declared: int count: 1; double count: 0
After hfi2 declared: int count: 2; double count: 0
```

```
After hfdb declared: int count: 2; double count: 1
HasFriend<int>: 10
HasFriend<int>: 20
HasFriend<double>: 10.5
```

Compatibility Note

Several C++ compilers have trouble with friends to templates.

Bound Template Friend Functions to Template Classes

You can modify the preceding example by making the friend functions templates themselves. In particular, you can set things up for bound template friends, so each specialization of a class gets a matching specialization for a friend. The technique is a bit more complex than for non-template friends and involves three steps.

For the first step, you declare each template function before the class definition.

```
template <typename T> void counts();
template <typename T> void report(T &);
```

Next, you declare the templates again as friends inside the function. These statements declare specializations based on the class template parameter type:

```
template <typename TT>
class HasFriendT
{
...
    friend void counts<TT>();
    friend void report<>(HasFriendT<TT> &);
};
```

The <> in the declarations identifies these as template specializations. In the case of `report()`, the <> can be left empty because the template type argument

```
HasFriendT<TT>
```

can be deduced from the function argument. You could, however, use

```
report<HasFriendT<TT> >(HasFriendT<TT> &)
```

instead. However, the `counts()` function has no parameters, so you have to use the template argument syntax (<TT>) to indicate its specialization. Note, too, that TT is the parameter type for the `HasFriendT` class.

Again, the best way to understand these declarations is to imagine what they become when you declare an object of a particular specialization. For example, suppose you declare this object:

```
HasFriendT<int> squack;
```

Then the compiler substitutes int for TT and generates the following class definition:

```
class HasFriendT<int>
{
...
    friend void counts<int>();
    friend void report<>(HasFriendT<int> &);
};
```

One specialization is based on TT, which becomes int, and the other is based on HasFriendT<TT>, which becomes HasFriendT<int>. Thus, the template specializations counts<int>() and report<HasFriendT<int> >() are declared as friends to the HasFriendT<int> class.

The third requirement the program must meet is to provide template definitions for the friends. Listing 14.23 illustrates these three aspects. Note that Listing 14.22 has one count() function that is a friend to all HasFriend classes, whereas Listing 14.23 has two count() functions, one of which is a friend to each of the instantiated class types. Because the count() function calls have no function parameter from which the compiler can deduce the desired specialization, these calls use the count<int>() and count<double>() forms to indicate the specialization. For the calls to report(), however, the compiler can use the argument type to deduce the specialization. You could use the <> form to the same effect:

```
report<HasFriendT<int> >(hfi2);   // same as report(hfi2);
```

LISTING 14.23   tmp2tmp.cpp

```
// tmp2tmp.cpp -- template friends to a template class
#include <iostream>
using std::cout;
using std::endl;

// template prototypes
template <typename T> void counts();
template <typename T> void report(T &);

// template class
template <typename TT>
class HasFriendT
{
private:
    TT item;
    static int ct;
public:
    HasFriendT(const TT & i) : item(i) {ct++;}
    ~HasFriendT() { ct--; }
    friend void counts<TT>();
    friend void report<>(HasFriendT<TT> &);
};

template <typename T>
int HasFriendT<T>::ct = 0;
```

LISTING 14.23   Continued

```
// template friend functions definitions
template <typename T>
void counts()
{
    cout << "template size: " << sizeof(HasFriendT<T>) << "; ";
    cout << "template counts(): " << HasFriendT<T>::ct << endl;
}

template <typename T>
void report(T & hf)
{
    cout << hf.item << endl;
}

int main()
{
    counts<int>();
    HasFriendT<int> hfi1(10);
    HasFriendT<int> hfi2(20);
    HasFriendT<double> hfdb(10.5);
    report(hfi1);   // generate report(HasFriendT<int> &)
    report(hfi2);   // generate report(HasFriendT<int> &)
    report(hfdb);   // generate report(HasFriendT<double> &)
    cout << "counts<int>() output:\n";
    counts<int>();
    cout << "counts<double>() output:\n";
    counts<double>();

    return 0;
}
```

Here is the output of the program in Listing 14.23:

```
template size: 4; template counts(): 0
10
20
10.5
counts<int>() output:
template size: 4; template counts(): 2
counts<double>() output:
template size: 8; template counts(): 1
```

As you can see, `counts<double>` reports a different template size from `counts<int>`, demonstrating that each T type now gets its own `count()` friend.

Unbound Template Friend Functions to Template Classes

The bound template friend functions in the preceding section are template specializations of a template declared outside a class. An `int` class specialization gets an `int` function specialization, and so on. By declaring a template inside a class, you can create unbound friend functions for which every function specialization is a friend to every class specialization. For unbound friends, the friend template type parameters are different from the template class type parameters:

```
template <typename T>
class ManyFriend
{
...
    template <typename C, typename D> friend void show2(C &, D &);
};
```

Listing 14.24 shows an example that uses an unbound friend. In it, the function call show2(hfi1, hfi2) gets matched to the following specialization:

```
void show2<ManyFriend<int> &, ManyFriend<int> &>
        (ManyFriend<int> & c, ManyFriend<int> & d);
```

Because it is a friend to all specializations of ManyFriend, this function has access to the item members of all specializations. But it only uses access to ManyFriend<int> objects.

Similarly, show2(hfd, hfi2) gets matched to this specialization:

```
void show2<ManyFriend<double> &, ManyFriend<int> &>
        (ManyFriend<double> & c, ManyFriend<int> & d);
```

It, too, is a friend to all ManyFriend specializations, and it uses its access to the item member of a ManyFriend<int> object and to the item member of a ManyFriend<double> object.

LISTING 14.24   manyfrnd.cpp

```
// manyfrnd.cpp -- unbound template friend to a template class
#include <iostream>
using std::cout;
using std::endl;

template <typename T>
class ManyFriend
{
private:
    T item;
public:
    ManyFriend(const T & i) : item(i) {}
    template <typename C, typename D> friend void show2(C &, D &);
};

template <typename C, typename D> void show2(C & c, D & d)
{
    cout << c.item << ", " << d.item << endl;
}

int main()
{
    ManyFriend<int> hfi1(10);
    ManyFriend<int> hfi2(20);
    ManyFriend<double> hfdb(10.5);
```

LISTING 14.24 Continued

```
        cout << "hfi1, hfi2: ";
        show2(hfi1, hfi2);
        cout << "hfdb, hfi2: ";
        show2(hfdb, hfi2);

        return 0;
}
```

Here's the output of the program in Listing 14.24:

```
hfi1, hfi2: 10, 20
hfdb, hfi2: 10.5, 20
```

Compatibility Note

Several C++ compilers have trouble with friends to templates.

Summary

C++ provides several means for reusing code. Public inheritance, described in Chapter 13, "Class Inheritance," enables you to model *is-a* relationships, with derived classes being able to reuse the code of base classes. Private and protected inheritance also let you reuse base class code, this time modeling *has-a* relationships. With private inheritance, public and protected members of the base class become private members of the derived class. With protected inheritance, public and protected members of the base class become protected members of the derived class. Thus, in either case, the public interface of the base class becomes an internal interface for the derived class. This is sometimes described as inheriting the implementation but not the interface because a derived object can't explicitly use the base class interface. Thus, you can't view a derived object as a kind of base object. Because of this, a base-class pointer or reference is not allowed to refer to a derived object without an explicit type cast.

You can also reuse class code by developing a class with members that are themselves objects. This approach, called *containment*, *layering*, or *composition*, also models the *has-a* relationship. Containment is simpler to implement and use than private or protected inheritance, so it is usually preferred. However, private and protected inheritance have slightly different capabilities. For example, inheritance allows a derived class access to protected members of a base class. Also, it allows a derived class to redefine a virtual function inherited from the base class. Because containment is not a form of inheritance, neither of these capabilities are options when you reuse class code via containment. On the other hand, containment is more suitable if you need several objects of a given class. For example, a `State` class could contain an array of `County` objects.

Multiple inheritance (MI) allows you to reuse code for more than one class in a class design. Private or protected MI models the *has-a* relationship, and public MI models the *is-a* relationship. MI can create problems with multidefined names and multi-inherited bases. You can use class qualifiers to resolve name ambiguities and virtual base classes to avoid multi-inherited bases. However, using virtual base classes introduces new rules for writing initialization lists for constructors and for resolving ambiguities.

Class templates let you create a generic class design in which a type, usually a member type, is represented by a type parameter. A typical template looks like this:

```
template <class T>
class Ic
{
    T v;
    ...
public:
    Ic(const T & val) : v(val) { }
    ...
};
```

Here `T` is the type parameter, and it acts as a stand-in for a real type to be specified at a later time. (This parameter can have any valid C++ name, but `T` and `Type` are common choices.) You can also use `typename` instead of `class` in this context:

```
template <typename T>   // same as template <class T>
class Rev {...} ;
```

Class definitions (instantiations) are generated when you declare a class object and specify a particular type. For example, the declaration

```
class Ic<short> sic;    // implicit instantiation
```

causes the compiler to generate a class declaration in which every occurrence of the type parameter `T` in the template is replaced by the actual type `short` in the class declaration. In this case, the class name is `Ic<short>`, not `Ic`. `Ic<short>` is termed a *specialization* of the template. In particular, it is an implicit instantiation.

An explicit instantiation occurs when you declare a specific specialization of the class, using the keyword `template`:

```
template class IC<int>;  // explicit instantiation
```

In this situation, the compiler uses the general template to generate an `int` specialization `Ic<int>`, even though no objects have yet been requested of that class.

You can provide explicit specializations, which are specialized class declarations that override a template definition. You just define the class, starting with `template<>`, and then you use the template class name, followed by angle brackets containing the type for which you want a specialization. For example, you could provide a specialized `Ic` class for character pointers as follows:

```
template <> class Ic<char *>.
{
      char * str;
      ...
public:
      Ic(const char * s) : str(s) { }
      ...
};
```

Then a declaration of the form

```
class Ic<char *> chic;
```

would use the specialized definition for `chic` rather than using the general template.

A class template can specify more than one generic type and can also have non-type parameters:

```
template <class T, class TT, int n>
class Pals {...};
```

The declaration

```
Pals<double, string, 6> mix;
```

would generate an implicit instantiation using `double` for T, `string` for TT, and `6` for n.

A class template can also have parameters that are templates:

```
template < template <typename T> class CL, typename U, int z>
class Trophy {...};
```

Here `z` stands for an `int` value, `U` stands for the name of a type, and `CL` stands for a class template declared using `template <typename T>`.

Class templates can be partially specialized:

```
template <class T> Pals<T, T, 10> {...};
template <class T, class TT> Pals<T, TT, 100> {...};
template <class T, int n> Pals <T, T*, n> {...};
```

The first example here creates a specialization in which both types are the same and `n` has the value `6`. Similarly, the second creates a specialization for n equal to `100`, and the third creates a specialization for which the second type is a pointer to the first type.

Template classes can be members of other classes, structures, and templates.

The goal of all these methods is to allow programmers to reuse tested code without having to copy it manually. This simplifies the programming task and makes programs more reliable.

Review Questions

1. For each of the following sets of classes, indicate whether public or private derivation is more appropriate for Column B:

A	B
class Bear	class PolarBear
class Kitchen	class Home
class Person	class Programmer
class Person	class HorseAndJockey
class Person, class Automobile	class Driver

2. Suppose you have the following definitions:

```cpp
class Frabjous {
private:
    char fab[20];
public:
    Frabjous(const char * s = "C++") : fab(s) { }
    virtual void tell() { cout << fab; }
};

class Gloam {
private:
    int glip;
    Frabjous fb;
public:
    Gloam(int g = 0, const char * s = "C++");
    Gloam(int g, const Frabjous & f);
    void tell();
};
```

Given that the `Gloam` version of `tell()` should display the values of `glip` and `fb`, provide definitions for the three `Gloam` methods.

3. Suppose you have the following definitions:

```cpp
class Frabjous {
private:
    char fab[20];
public:
    Frabjous(const char * s = "C++") : fab(s) { }
    virtual void tell() { cout << fab; }
};

class Gloam : private Frabjous{
private:
    int glip;
public:
    Gloam(int g = 0, const char * s = "C++");
    Gloam(int g, const Frabjous & f);
    void tell();
};
```

Given that the `Gloam` version of `tell()` should display the values of `glip` and `fab`, provide definitions for the three `Gloam` methods.

4. Suppose you have the following definition, based on the `Stack` template of Listing 14.13 and the `Worker` class of Listing 14.10:

```
Stack<Worker *> sw;
```

Write out the class declaration that will be generated. Just do the class declaration, not the non-inline class methods.

5. Use the template definitions in this chapter to define the following:

   • An array of `string` objects

   • A stack of arrays of `double`

   • An array of stacks of pointers to `Worker` objects

   How many template class definitions are produced in Listing 14.18?

6. Describe the differences between virtual and nonvirtual base classes.

Programming Exercises

1. The `Wine` class has a `string` class object member (see Chapter 4) that holds the name of a wine and a `Pair` object (as discussed in this chapter) of `valarray<int>` objects (as discussed in this chapter). The first member of each `Pair` object holds the vintage years, and the second member holds the numbers of bottles owned for the corresponding particular vintage year. For example, the first `valarray` object of the `Pair` object might hold the years 1988, 1992, and 1996, and the second `valarray` object might hold the bottle counts 24, 48, and 144. It may be convenient for `Wine` to have an `int` member that stores the number of years. Also, some `typedefs` might be useful to simplify the coding:

```
typedef std::valarray<int> ArrayInt;
typedef Pair<ArrayInt, ArrayInt> PairArray;
```

Thus the `PairArray` type represents type `Pair<std::valarray<int>, std::valarray<int> >`. Implement the `Wine` class by using containment. The class should have a default constructor and at least the following constructors:

```
// initialize label to l, number of years to y,
// vintage years to yr[], bottles to bot[]
Wine(const char * l, int y, const int yr[], const int bot[]);
// initialize label to l, number of years to y,
// create array objects of length y
Wine(const char * l, int y);
```

The `Wine` class should have a method `GetBottles()` that, given a `Wine` object with `y` years, prompts the user to enter the corresponding number of vintage years and bottle counts. A method `Label()` should return a reference to the wine name. A method `sum()`

should return the total number of bottles in the second `valarray<int>` object in the `Pair` object.

The program should prompt the user to enter a wine name, the number of elements of the array, and the year and bottle count information for each array element. The program should use this data to construct a `Wine` object and then display the information stored in the object. For guidance, here's a sample test program:

```cpp
// pe14-1.cpp  -- using Wine class with containment
#include <iostream>
#include "winec.h"

int main ( void )
{
    using std::cin;
    using std::cout;
    using std::endl;

    cout << "Enter name of wine: ";
    char lab[50];
    cin.getline(lab, 50);
    cout << "Enter number of years: ";
    int yrs;
    cin >> yrs;

    Wine holding(lab, yrs); // store label, years, give arrays yrs elements
    holding.GetBottles();    // solicit input for year, bottle count
    holding.Show();          // display object contents

    const int YRS = 3;
    int y[YRS] = {1993, 1995, 1998};
    int b[YRS] = { 48, 60, 72};
    // create new object, initialize using data in arrays y and b
    Wine more("Gushing Grape Red",YRS, y, b);
    more.Show();
    cout << "Total bottles for " << more.Label() // use Label() method
         << ": " << more.sum() << endl;          // use sum() method
    cout << "Bye\n";
    return 0;
}
```

And here's some sample output:

```
Enter name of wine: Gully Wash
Enter number of years: 4
Enter Gully Wash data for 4 year(s):
Enter year: 1988
Enter bottles for that year: 42
Enter year: 1994
Enter bottles for that year: 58
Enter year: 1998
Enter bottles for that year: 122
Enter year: 2001
Enter bottles for that year: 144
```

```
Wine: Gully Wash
        Year    Bottles
        1988    42
        1994    58
        1998    122
        2001    144
Wine: Gushing Grape Red
        Year    Bottles
        1993    48
        1995    60
        1998    72
Total bottles for Gushing Grape Red: 180
Bye
```

2. This exercise is the same as Programming Exercise 1, except that you should use private inheritance instead of containment. Again, a few **typedefs** might prove handy. Also, you might contemplate the meaning of statements such as the following:

```
PairArray::operator=(PairArray(ArrayInt(),ArrayInt()));
cout  << (const string &)(*this);
```

The class should work with the same test program as shown in Programming Exercise 1.

3. Define a **QueueTp** template. Test it by creating a queue of pointers-to-**Worker** (as defined in Listing 14.10) and using the queue in a program similar to that in Listing 14.12.

4. A **Person** class holds the first name and the last name of a person. In addition to its constructors, it has a **Show()** method that displays both names. A **Gunslinger** class derives virtually from the **Person** class. It has a **Draw()** member that returns a type **double** value representing a gunslinger's draw time. The class also has an **int** member representing the number of notches on a gunslinger's gun. Finally, it has a **Show()** function that displays all this information.

   A **PokerPlayer** class derives virtually from the **Person** class. It has a **Draw()** member that returns a random number in the range 1 through 52, representing a card value. (Optionally, you could define a **Card** class with suit and face value members and use a **Card** return value for **Draw()**.) The **PokerPlayer** class uses the **Person show()** function. The **BadDude** class derives publicly from the **Gunslinger** and **PokerPlayer** classes. It has a **Gdraw()** member that returns a bad dude's draw time and a **Cdraw()** member that returns the next card drawn. It has an appropriate **Show()** function. Define all these classes and methods, along with any other necessary methods (such as methods for setting object values) and test them in a simple program similar to that in Listing 14.12.

5. Here are some class declarations:

```
// emp.h -- header file for abstr_emp class and children

#include <iostream>
#include <string>

class abstr_emp
{
```

```cpp
private:
    std::string fname;    // abstr_emp's first name
    std::string lname;    // abstr_emp's last name
    std::string job;
public:
    abstr_emp();
    abstr_emp(const std::string & fn, const std::string &  ln,
            const std::string &  j);
    virtual void ShowAll() const;    // labels and shows all data
    virtual void SetAll();        // prompts user for values
    friend std::ostream & operator<<(std::ostream & os, const abstr_emp & e);
    // just displays first and last name
    virtual ~abstr_emp() = 0;          // virtual base class
};

class employee : public abstr_emp
{
public:
    employee();
    employee(const std::string & fn, const std::string &  ln,
            const std::string &  j);
    virtual void ShowAll() const;
    virtual void SetAll();
};

class manager:  virtual public abstr_emp
{
private:
    int inchargeof;         // number of abstr_emps managed
protected:
    int InChargeOf() const { return inchargeof; } // output
    int & InChargeOf(){ return inchargeof; }      // input
public:
    manager();
    manager(const std::string & fn, const std::string & ln,
            const std::string & j, int ico = 0);
    manager(const abstr_emp & e, int ico);
    manager(const manager & m);
    virtual void ShowAll() const;
    virtual void SetAll();
};

class fink: virtual public abstr_emp
{
private:
    std::string reportsto;        // to whom fink reports
protected:
    const std::string ReportsTo() const { return reportsto; }
    std::string & ReportsTo(){ return reportsto; }
public:
    fink();
    fink(const std::string & fn, const std::string & ln,
        const std::string & j, const std::string & rpo);
```

```
    fink(const abstr_emp & e, const std::string & rpo);
    fink(const fink & e);
    virtual void ShowAll() const;
    virtual void SetAll();
};

class highfink: public manager, public fink // management fink
{
public:
    highfink();
    highfink(const std::string & fn, const std::string & ln,
             const std::string & j, const std::string & rpo,
             int ico);
    highfink(const abstr_emp & e, const std::string & rpo, int ico);
    highfink(const fink & f, int ico);
    highfink(const manager & m, const std::string & rpo);
    highfink(const highfink & h);
    virtual void ShowAll() const;
    virtual void SetAll();
};
```

Note that the class hierarchy uses MI with a virtual base class, so keep in mind the special rules for constructor initialization lists for that case. Also note the presence of some protected-access methods. This simplifies the code for some of the highfink methods. (Note, for example, that if highfink::ShowAll() simply calls fink::ShowAll() and manager::ShowAll(), it winds up calling abstr_emp::ShowAll() twice.) Provide the class method implementations and test the classes in a program. Here is a minimal test program:

```
// pe14-5.cpp
// useemp1.cpp -- using the abstr_emp classes

#include <iostream>
using namespace std;
#include "emp.h"

int main(void)
{
    employee em("Trip", "Harris", "Thumper");
    cout << em << endl;
    em.ShowAll();

    manager ma("Amorphia", "Spindragon", "Nuancer", 5);
    cout << ma << endl;
    ma.ShowAll();


    fink fi("Matt", "Oggs", "Oiler", "Juno Barr");
    cout << fi << endl;
    fi.ShowAll();
    highfink hf(ma, "Curly Kew");  // recruitment?
    hf.ShowAll();
    cout << "Press a key for next phase:\n";
```

```
            cin.get();
            highfink hf2;
            hf2.SetAll();

            cout << "Using an abstr_emp * pointer:\n";
            abstr_emp  * tri[4] = {&em, &fi, &hf, &hf2};
            for (int i = 0; i < 4; i++)
                tri[i]->ShowAll();

            return 0;
        }
```

Why is no assignment operator defined?

Why are ShowAll() and SetAll() virtual?

Why is abstr_emp a virtual base class?

Why does the highfink class have no data section?

Why is only one version of operator<<() needed?

What would happen if the end of the program were replaced with this code?

```
abstr_emp  tri[4] = {em, fi, hf, hf2};
for (int i = 0; i < 4; i++)
        tri[i].ShowAll();
```

CHAPTER 15

FRIENDS, EXCEPTIONS, AND MORE

> **In this chapter you'll learn about the following:**
>
> - Friend classes
> - Friend class methods
> - Nested classes
> - Throwing exceptions, `try` blocks, and `catch` blocks
> - Exception classes
> - Runtime type identification (RTTI)
> - `dynamic_cast` and `typeid`
> - `static_cast`, `const_cast`, and `reinterpret_cast`

This chapter ties up some loose ends and ventures into some of the most recent additions to the C++ language. The loose ends include friend classes, friend member functions, and nested classes, which are classes declared within other classes. The recent additions discussed here are exceptions, runtime type identification (RTTI), and improved type cast control. C++ exception handling provides a mechanism for dealing with unusual occurrences that otherwise would bring a program to a halt. RTTI is a mechanism for identifying object types. The new type cast operators improve the safety of type casts. These last three facilities are fairly new to C++, and older compilers do not support them.

Friends

Several examples in this book so far use friend functions as part of the extended interface for a class. Such functions are not the only kinds of friends a class can have. A class also can be a friend. In that case, any method of the friend class can access private and protected members of the original class. Also, you can be more restrictive and designate just particular member functions of a class to be friends to another class. A class defines which functions, member functions, or classes are friends; friendship cannot be imposed from the outside. Thus, although friends do grant outside access to a class's private portion, they don't really violate the spirit of object-oriented programming. Instead, they provide more flexibility to the public interface.

Friend Classes

When might you want to make one class a friend to another? Let's look at an example. Suppose you must program a simple simulation of a television and a remote control. You decide to define a `Tv` class representing a television and a `Remote` class representing a remote control. Clearly, there should be some sort of relationship between these classes, but what kind? A remote control is not a television and vice versa, so the *is-a* relationship of public inheritance doesn't apply. Nor is either a component of the other, so the *has-a* relationship of containment or of private or protected inheritance doesn't apply. What is true is that a remote control can modify the state of a television, and this suggests making the `Remote` class a friend to the `Tv` class.

Let's define the `Tv` class. You can represent a television with a set of state members—that is, variables that describe various aspects of the television. Here are some of the possible states:

- On/off
- Channel setting
- Volume setting
- Cable or antenna tuning mode
- TV tuner or A/V input

The tuning mode reflects the fact that, in the United States, the spacing between channels for channels 14 and up is different for cable reception than it is for UHF broadcast reception. The input selection chooses between TV, which could be either cable or broadcast TV, and a VCR. Some sets may offer more choices, such as multiple VCR/DVD inputs, but this list is enough for the purposes of this example.

Also, a television has some parameters that aren't state variables. For example, televisions vary in the number of channels they can receive, and you can include a member to track that value.

Next, you must provide the class with methods for altering the settings. Many television sets these days hide their controls behind panels, but it's still possible with most televisions to change channels, and so on, without a remote control. However, often you can go up or down one channel at a time but can't select a channel at random. Similarly, there's usually a button for increasing the volume and one for decreasing the volume.

A remote control should duplicate the controls built in to the television. Many of its methods can be implemented by using `Tv` methods. In addition, a remote control typically provides random access channel selection. That is, you can go directly from channel 2 to channel 20 without going through all the intervening channels. Also, many remotes can work in two modes—as a television controller and as a VCR controller.

These considerations suggest a definition like that shown in Listing 15.1. The definition includes several constants defined as enumerations. The following statement makes `Remote` a friend class:

```
friend class Remote;
```

A friend declaration can appear in a public, private, or protected section; the location makes no difference. Because the `Remote` class mentions the `Tv` class, the compiler has to know about the `Tv` class before it can handle the `Remote` class. The simplest way to accomplish this is to define the `Tv` class first. Alternatively, you can use a forward declaration; we'll discuss that option soon.

Compatibility Note

If your compiler doesn't support the `bool` type, you should use `int`, `0`, and `1` instead of `bool`, `false`, and `true`.

LISTING 15.1   tv.h

```cpp
// tv.h -- Tv and Remote classes
#ifndef TV_H_
#define TV_H_

class Tv
{
public:
    friend class Remote;   // Remote can access Tv private parts
    enum {Off, On};
    enum {MinVal,MaxVal = 20};
    enum {Antenna, Cable};
    enum {TV, VCR};

    Tv(int s = Off, int mc = 100) : state(s), volume(5),
        maxchannel(mc), channel(2), mode(Cable), input(TV) {}
    void onoff() {state = (state == On)? Off : On;}
    bool ison() const {return state == On;}
    bool volup();
    bool voldown();
    void chanup();
    void chandown();
    void set_mode() {mode = (mode == Antenna)? Cable : Antenna;}
    void set_input() {input = (input == TV)? VCR : TV;}
    void settings() const; // display all settings
private:
    int state;              // on or off
    int volume;             // assumed to be digitized
    int maxchannel;         // maximum number of channels
    int channel;            // current channel setting
    int mode;               // broadcast or cable
    int input;              // TV or VCR
};

class Remote
{
private:
    int mode;                   // controls TV or VCR
```

LISTING 15.1　*Continued*

```
public:
    Remote(int m = Tv::TV) : mode(m) {}
    bool volup(Tv & t) { return t.volup();}
    bool voldown(Tv & t) { return t.voldown();}
    void onoff(Tv & t) { t.onoff(); }
    void chanup(Tv & t) {t.chanup();}
    void chandown(Tv & t) {t.chandown();}
    void set_chan(Tv & t, int c) {t.channel = c;}
    void set_mode(Tv & t) {t.set_mode();}
    void set_input(Tv & t) {t.set_input();}
};
#endif
```

Most of the class methods in Listing 15.1 are defined inline. Note that each `Remote` method other than the constructor takes a reference to a `Tv` object as an argument. This reflects that a remote has to be aimed at a particular TV. Listing 15.2 shows the remaining definitions. The volume-setting functions change the volume member by one unit unless the sound has reached its minimum or maximum setting. The channel selection functions use wraparound, with the lowest channel setting, taken to be 1, immediately following the highest channel setting, `maxchannel`.

Many of the methods use the conditional operator to toggle a state between two settings:

```
void onoff() {state = (state == On)? Off : On;}
```

Provided that the two state values are 0 and 1, this can be done more compactly by using the combined bitwise exclusive OR and assignment operator (`^=`), as discussed in Appendix E, "Other Operators":

```
void onoff() {state ^= 1;}
```

In fact, you could store up to eight bivalent state settings in a single unsigned `char` variable and toggle them individually, but that's another story, one made possible by the bitwise operators discussed in Appendix E.

LISTING 15.2　`tv.cpp`

```
// tv.cpp -- methods for the Tv class (Remote methods are inline)
#include <iostream>
#include "tv.h"

bool Tv::volup()
{
    if (volume < MaxVal)
    {
        volume++;
        return true;
    }
    else
        return false;
}
```

LISTING 15.2 Continued

```
bool Tv::voldown()
{
    if (volume > MinVal)
    {
        volume--;
        return true;
    }
    else
        return false;
}

void Tv::chanup()
{
    if (channel < maxchannel)
        channel++;
    else
        channel = 1;
}

void Tv::chandown()
{
    if (channel > 1)
        channel--;
    else
        channel = maxchannel;
}

void Tv::settings() const
{
    using std::cout;
    using std::endl;
    cout << "TV is " << (state == Off? "Off" : "On") << endl;
    if (state == On)
    {
        cout << "Volume setting = " << volume << endl;
        cout << "Channel setting = " << channel << endl;
        cout << "Mode = "
            << (mode == Antenna? "antenna" : "cable") << endl;
        cout << "Input = "
            << (input == TV? "TV" : "VCR") << endl;
    }
}
```

Listing 15.3 is a short program that tests some of the features of the program so far. The same controller is used to control two separate televisions.

LISTING 15.3 use_tv.cpp

```
//use_tv.cpp -- using the Tv and Remote classes
#include <iostream>
#include "tv.h"
```

LISTING 15.3   Continued

```cpp
int main()
{
    using std::cout;
    Tv s27;
    cout << "Initial settings for 27\" TV:\n";
    s27.settings();
    s27.onoff();
    s27.chanup();
    cout << "\nAdjusted settings for 27\" TV:\n";
    s27.settings();

    Remote grey;

    grey.set_chan(s27, 10);
    grey.volup(s27);
    grey.volup(s27);
    cout << "\n27\" settings after using remote:\n";
    s27.settings();

    Tv s32(Tv::On);
    s32.set_mode();
    grey.set_chan(s32,28);
    cout << "\n32\" settings:\n";
    s32.settings();

    return 0;
}
```

Here is the output of the program in Listings 15.1, 15.2, and 15.3:

```
Initial settings for 27" TV:
TV is Off

Adjusted settings for 27" TV:
TV is On
Volume setting = 5
Channel setting = 3
Mode = cable
Input = TV

27" settings after using remote:
TV is On
Volume setting = 7
Channel setting = 10
Mode = cable
Input = TV

32" settings:
TV is On
Volume setting = 5
Channel setting = 28
Mode = antenna
Input = TV
```

The main point to this exercise is that class friendship is a natural idiom in which to express some relationships. Without some form of friendship, you would either have to make the private parts of the `Tv` class public or else construct some awkward, larger class that encompasses both a television and a remote control. And that solution wouldn't reflect the fact that a single remote control can be used with several televisions.

Friend Member Functions

Looking at the code for the last example, you may notice that most of the `Remote` methods are implemented by using the public interface for the `Tv` class. This means that those methods don't really need friend status. Indeed, the only `Remote` method that accesses a private `Tv` member directly is `Remote::set_chan()`, so that's the only method that needs to be a friend. You do have the option of making just selected class members friends to another class rather than making the entire class a friend, but that's a bit more awkward. You need to be careful about the order in which you arrange the various declarations and definitions. Let's look at why.

The way to make `Remote::set_chan()` a friend to the `Tv` class is to declare it as a friend in the `Tv` class declaration:

```
class Tv
{
    friend void Remote::set_chan(Tv & t, int c);
    ...
};
```

However, for the compiler to process this statement, it needs to have already seen the `Remote` definition. Otherwise, it won't know that `Remote` is a class and that `set_chan()` is a method of that class. This suggests putting the `Remote` definition above the `Tv` definition. But the fact that `Remote` methods mention `Tv` objects means that the `Tv` definition should appear above the `Remote` definition. Part of the way around the circular dependence is to use a *forward declaration*. To do so, you insert the statement

```
class Tv;               // forward declaration
```

above the `Remote` definition. This provides the following arrangement:

```
class Tv;  // forward declaration
class Remote { ... };
class Tv { ... };
```

Could you use the following arrangement instead?

```
class Remote;           // forward declaration
class Tv { ... };
class Remote { ... };
```

The answer is no. The reason, as mentioned earlier, is that when the compiler sees that a `Remote` method is declared as a friend in the `Tv` class declaration, the compiler needs to have already viewed the declaration of the `Remote` class in general and of the `set_chan()` method in particular.

Another difficulty remains. In Listing 15.1, the `Remote` declaration contains inline code such as the following:

```
void onoff(Tv & t) { t.onoff(); }
```

Because this calls a `Tv` method, the compiler needs to have seen the `Tv` class declaration at this point so that it knows what methods `Tv` has. But, as you've seen, that declaration necessarily follows the `Remote` declaration. The solution to this problem is to restrict `Remote` to method *declarations* and to place the actual *definitions* after the `Tv` class. This leads to the following ordering:

```
class Tv;                 // forward declaration
class Remote { ... };     // Tv-using methods as prototypes only
class Tv { ... };
// put Remote method definitions here
```

The `Remote` prototypes look like this:

```
void onoff(Tv & t);
```

All the compiler needs to know when inspecting this prototype is that `Tv` is a class, and the forward declaration supplies that information. By the time the compiler reaches the actual method definitions, it has already read the `Tv` class declaration and has the added information needed to compile those methods. By using the `inline` keyword in the method definitions, you can still make the methods inline methods. Listing 15.4 shows the revised header file.

LISTING 15.4   `tvfm.h`

```
// tvfm.h -- Tv and Remote classes using a friend member
#ifndef TVFM_H_
#define TVFM_H_

class Tv;                          // forward declaration

class Remote
{
public:
    enum State{Off, On};
    enum {MinVal,MaxVal = 20};
    enum {Antenna, Cable};
    enum {TV, VCR};
private:
    int mode;
public:
    Remote(int m = TV) : mode(m) {}
    bool volup(Tv & t);            // prototype only
    bool voldown(Tv & t);
    void onoff(Tv & t) ;
    void chanup(Tv & t) ;
    void chandown(Tv & t) ;
    void set_mode(Tv & t) ;
```

LISTING 15.4   Continued

```
    void set_input(Tv & t);
    void set_chan(Tv & t, int c);

};

class Tv
{
public:
    friend void Remote::set_chan(Tv & t, int c);
    enum State{Off, On};
    enum {MinVal,MaxVal = 20};
    enum {Antenna, Cable};
    enum {TV, VCR};

    Tv(int s = Off, int mc = 100) : state(s), volume(5),
        maxchannel(mc), channel(2), mode(Cable), input(TV) {}
    void onoff() {state = (state == On)? Off : On;}
    bool ison() const {return state == On;}
    bool volup();
    bool voldown();
    void chanup();
    void chandown();
    void set_mode() {mode = (mode == Antenna)? Cable : Antenna;}
    void set_input() {input = (input == TV)? VCR : TV;}
    void settings() const;
private:
    int state;
    int volume;
    int maxchannel;
    int channel;
    int mode;
    int input;
};

// Remote methods as inline functions
inline bool Remote::volup(Tv & t) { return t.volup();}
inline bool Remote::voldown(Tv & t) { return t.voldown();}
inline void Remote::onoff(Tv & t) { t.onoff(); }
inline void Remote::chanup(Tv & t) {t.chanup();}
inline void Remote::chandown(Tv & t) {t.chandown();}
inline void Remote::set_mode(Tv & t) {t.set_mode();}
inline void Remote::set_input(Tv & t) {t.set_input();}
inline void Remote::set_chan(Tv & t, int c) {t.channel = c;}
#endif
```

If you include `tvfm.h` instead of `tv.h` in `tv.cpp` and `use_tv.cpp`, the resulting program behaves the same as the original. The difference is that just one `Remote` method—instead of all the `Remote` methods—is a friend to the `Tv` class. Figure 15.1 illustrates this difference.

FIGURE 15.1

Class friends versus class member friends.

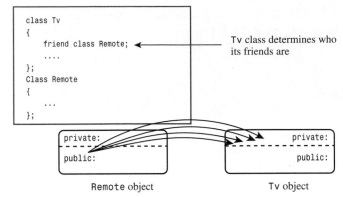

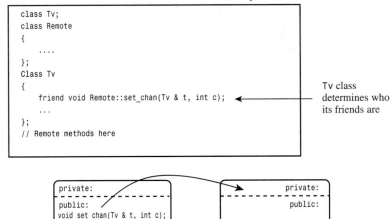

Recall that inline functions have internal linkage, which means the function definition must be in the file that uses the function. Here, the inline definitions are in the header file, so including the header file in the file that uses the definitions places the definition in the right place. You could place the definitions in the implementation file instead, provided that you remove the `inline` keyword, thus giving the functions external linkage.

By the way, making the entire `Remote` class a friend doesn't need a forward declaration because the friend statement itself identifies `Remote` as a class:

```
friend class Remote;
```

Other Friendly Relationships

Other combinations of friends and classes besides the ones discussed so far in this chapter are possible. Let's take a brief look at some of them now.

Suppose the advance of technology brings interactive remote controls. For example, an interactive remote control unit might let you enter a response to some question posed on a television program, and the television might activate a buzzer in your remote control if your response is wrong. Ignoring the possibility of television using such facilities to program the viewers, let's just look at the C++ programming aspects. The new setup would benefit from mutual friendship, with some `Remote` methods being able to affect a `Tv` object, as before, and with some `Tv` methods being able to affect a `Remote` object. This can be accomplished by making the classes friends to each other. That is, `Tv` will be a friend to `Remote` in addition to `Remote` being a friend to `Tv`. One point to keep in mind is that a `Tv` method that uses a `Remote` object can be prototyped *before* the `Remote` class declaration but must be defined *after* the declaration so that the compiler will have enough information to compile the method. The setup would look like this:

```
class Tv
{
friend class Remote;
public:
    void buzz(Remote & r);
    ...
};
class Remote
{
friend class Tv;
public:
    void Bool volup(Tv & t) { t.volup(); }
    ...
};
inline void Tv::buzz(Remote & r)
{
    ...
}
```

Because the `Remote` declaration follows the `Tv` declaration, `Remote::volup()` can be defined in the class declaration. However, the `Tv::buzz()` method has to be defined outside the `Tv` declaration so that the definition can follow the `Remote` declaration. If you don't want `buzz()` to be inline, you need to define it in a separate method definitions file.

Shared Friends

Another use for friends is when a function needs to access private data in two separate classes. Logically, such a function should be a member function of each class, but that's impossible. It could be a member of one class and a friend to the other, but sometimes it's more reasonable to make the function a friend to both. Suppose, for example, that you have a `Probe` class that represents some sort of programmable measuring device and an `Analyzer` class that represents some sort of programmable analyzing device. Each has an internal clock, and you would like to be able to synchronize the two clocks. You could use something along the following lines:

```
class Analyzer;  // forward declaration
class Probe
{
```

```
        friend void sync(Analyzer & a, const Probe & p);   // sync a to p
        friend void sync(Probe & p, const Analyzer & a);   // sync p to a
        ...
};
class Analyzer
{
        friend void sync(Analyzer & a, const Probe & p);   // sync a to p
        friend void sync(Probe & p, const Analyzer & a);   // sync p to a
        ...
};

// define the friend functions
inline void sync(Analyzer & a, const Probe & p)
{
        ...
}
inline void sync(Probe & p, const Analyzer & a)
{
        ...
}
```

The forward declaration enables the compiler to know that `Analyzer` is a type when it reaches the friend declarations in the `Probe` class declaration.

Nested Classes

In C++, you can place a class declaration inside another class. The class declared within another is called a *nested class*, and it helps avoid name clutter by giving the new type class scope. Member functions of the class containing the declaration can create and use objects of the nested class. The outside world can use the nested class only if the declaration is in the public section and if you use the scope-resolution operator. (However, older versions of C++ either don't allow nested classes or implement the concept incompletely.)

Nesting classes is not the same as containment. Recall that containment means having a class object as a member of another class. Nesting a class, on the other hand, does not create a class member. Instead, it defines a type that is known just locally to the class that contains the nested class declaration.

The usual reasons for nesting a class are to assist in the implementation of another class and to avoid name conflicts. The `Queue` class example in Listing 12.10 in Chapter 12, "Classes and Dynamic Memory Allocation," provides a disguised case of nested classes by nesting a structure definition:

```
class Queue
{
// class scope definitions
    // Node is a nested structure definition local to this class
    struct Node {Item item; struct Node * next;};
    ...
};
```

Because a structure is a class whose members are public by default, `Node` really is a nested class. However, this definition doesn't take advantage of class abilities. In particular, it lacks an explicit constructor. Let's remedy that now.

First, you need to find where `Node` objects are created in the `Queue` example. Examining the class declaration (see Listing 12.10) and the methods definitions (see Listing 12.11) reveals that the only place in which `Node` objects are created is in the `enqueue()` method:

```
bool Queue::enqueue(const Item & item)
{
    if (isfull())
        return false;
    Node * add = new Node;  // create node
    if (add == NULL)
        return false;        // quit if none available
    add->item = item;        // set node pointers
    add->next = NULL;
    ...
}
```

This code explicitly assigns values to the `Node` members after creating a `Node`. This is the sort of work that is more properly done by a constructor.

Knowing now where and how a constructor should be used, you can provide an appropriate constructor definition:

```
class Queue
{
// class scope definitions
    // Node is a nested class definition local to this class
    class Node
    {
    public:
        Item item;
        Node * next;
        Node(const Item & i) : item(i), next(0) { }
    };
    ...
};
```

This constructor initializes the node's `item` member to `i` and sets the `next` pointer to `0`, which is one way of writing the null pointer in C++. (Using `NULL` would require including a header file that defines `NULL`.) Because all nodes created by the `Queue` class have `next` initially set to the null pointer, this is the only constructor the class needs.

Next, you need to rewrite `enqueue()` by using the constructor:

```
bool Queue::enqueue(const Item & item)
{
    if (isfull())
        return false;
    Node * add = new Node(item);  // create, initialize node
    if (add == 0)
```

```
        return false;          // quit if none available
    ...
}
```

This makes the code for `enqueue()` a bit shorter and a bit safer because it automates initialization rather than requiring the programmer to correctly remember what should be done.

This example defines the constructor in the class declaration. Suppose you wanted to define it in a methods file, instead. In that case, the definition must reflect that the `Node` class is defined within the `Queue` class. This is accomplished by using the scope-resolution operator twice:

```
Queue::Node::Node(const Item & i) : item(i), next(0) { }
```

Nested Classes and Access

Two kinds of access pertain to nested classes. First, where a nested class is declared controls the scope of the nested class; that is, it establishes which parts of a program can create objects of that class. Second, as with any class, the public, protected, and private sections of a nested class provide access control to class members. Where and how a nested class can be used depends on both scope and access control. Let's examine these points further.

Scope

If a nested class is declared in a private section of a second class, it is known only to that second class. This applies, for example, to the `Node` class nested in the `Queue` declaration in the preceding example. (It may appear that `Node` was defined before the private section, but remember that private is the default access for classes.) Hence, `Queue` members can use `Node` objects and pointers to `Node` objects, but other parts of a program don't even know that the `Node` class exists. If you were to derive a class from `Queue`, `Node` would be invisible to that class, too, because a derived class can't directly access the private parts of a base class.

If the nested class is declared in a protected section of a second class, it is visible to that class but invisible to the outside world. However, in this case, a derived class would know about the nested class and could directly create objects of that type.

If a nested class is declared in a public section of a second class, it is available to the second class, to classes derived from the second class, and, because it's public, to the outside world. However, because the nested class has class scope, it has to be used with a class qualifier in the outside world. For example, suppose you have this declaration:

```
class Team
{
public:
    class Coach { ... };
    ...
};
```

Now suppose you have an unemployed coach, one who belongs to no team. To create a `Coach` object outside the `Team` class, you can use this:

```
Team::Coach forhire;  // create a Coach object outside the Team class
```

These same scope considerations apply to nested structures and enumerations, too. Indeed, many programmers use public enumerations to provide class constants that can be used by client programmers. For example, the many implementations of classes defined to support the `iostream` facility use this technique to provide various formatting options, as you've already seen (and will explore more fully in Chapter 17, "Input, Output, and Files"). Table 15.1 summarizes scope properties for nested classes, structures, and enumerations.

TABLE 15.1   Scope Properties for Nested Classes, Structures, and Enumerations

Where Declared in Nesting Class	Available to Nesting Class	Available to Classes Derived from the Nesting Class	Available to the Outside World
Private section	Yes	No	No
Protected section	Yes	Yes	No
Public section	Yes	Yes	Yes, with class qualifier

Access Control

After a class is in scope, access control comes into play. The same rules govern access to a nested class that govern access to a regular class. Declaring the `Node` class in the `Queue` class declaration does not grant the `Queue` class any special access privileges to the `Node` class, nor does it grant the `Node` class any special access privileges to the `Queue` class. Thus, a `Queue` class object can access only the public members of a `Node` object explicitly. For that reason, the `Queue` example makes all the members of the `Node` class public. This violates the usual practice of making data members private, but the `Node` class is an internal implementation feature of the `Queue` class and is not visible to the outside world. That's because the `Node` class is declared in the private section of the `Queue` class. Thus, although `Queue` methods can access `Node` members directly, a client using the `Queue` class cannot do so.

In short, the location of a class declaration determines the scope or visibility of a class. Given that a particular class is in scope, the usual access control rules (public, protected, private, friend) determine the access a program has to members of the nested class.

Nesting in a Template

You've seen that templates are a good choice for implementing container classes such as the `Queue` class. You may be wondering whether having a nested class poses any problems to converting the `Queue` class definition to a template. The answer is no. Listing 15.5 shows how this conversion can be made. As is common for class templates, the header file includes the class template, along with method function templates.

LISTING 15.5   queuetp.h

```cpp
// queuetp.h -- queue template with a nested class
#ifndef QUEUETP_H_
#define QUEUETP_H_

template <class Item>
class QueueTP
{
private:
    enum {Q_SIZE = 10};
    // Node is a nested class definition
    class Node
    {
    public:
        Item item;
        Node * next;
        Node(const Item & i):item(i), next(0){ }
    };
    Node * front;       // pointer to front of Queue
    Node * rear;        // pointer to rear of Queue
    int items;          // current number of items in Queue
    const int qsize;    // maximum number of items in Queue
    QueueTP(const QueueTP & q) : qsize(0) {}
    QueueTP & operator=(const QueueTP & q) { return *this; }
public:
    QueueTP(int qs = Q_SIZE);
    ~QueueTP();
    bool isempty() const
    {
        return items == 0;
    }
    bool isfull() const
    {
        return items == qsize;
    }
    int queuecount() const
    {
        return items;
    }
    bool enqueue(const Item &item); // add item to end
    bool dequeue(Item &item);       // remove item from front
};

// QueueTP methods
template <class Item>
QueueTP<Item>::QueueTP(int qs) : qsize(qs)
{
    front = rear = 0;
    items = 0;
}

template <class Item>
QueueTP<Item>::~QueueTP()
{
```

LISTING 15.5   *Continued*

```
    Node * temp;
    while (front != 0)          // while queue is not yet empty
    {
        temp = front;           // save address of front item
        front = front->next;//  reset pointer to next item
        delete temp;            // delete former front
    }
}

// Add item to queue
template <class Item>
bool QueueTP<Item>::enqueue(const Item & item)
{
    if (isfull())
        return false;
    Node * add = new Node(item);    // create node
    if (add == NULL)
        return false;           // quit if none available
    items++;
    if (front == 0)             // if queue is empty,
        front = add;            // place item at front
    else
        rear->next = add;       // else place at rear
    rear = add;                 // have rear point to new node
    return true;
}

// Place front item into item variable and remove from queue
template <class Item>
bool QueueTP<Item>::dequeue(Item & item)
{
    if (front == 0)
        return false;
    item = front->item;         // set item to first item in queue
    items--;
    Node * temp = front;        // save location of first item
    front = front->next;        // reset front to next item
    delete temp;                // delete former first item
    if (items == 0)
        rear = 0;
    return true;
}

#endif
```

One interesting thing about the template in Listing 15.5 is that **Node** is defined in terms of the generic type **Item**. Thus, a declaration like

```
QueueTp<double> dq;
```

leads to a **Node** defined to hold type **double** values, whereas

```
QueueTp<char> cq;
```

leads to a `Node` defined to hold type `char` values. These two `Node` classes are defined in two separate `QueueTP` classes, so there is no name conflict between the two. That is, one node is type `QueueTP<double>::Node` and the other is type `QueueTP<char>::Node`.

Listing 15.6 offers a short program for testing the new class.

LISTING 15.6   `nested.cpp`

```cpp
// nested.cpp -- using a queue that has a nested class
#include <iostream>

#include <string>
#include "queuetp.h"

int main()
{
    using std::string;
    using std::cin;
    using std::cout;

    QueueTP<string> cs(5);
    string temp;

    while(!cs.isfull())
    {
        cout << "Please enter your name. You will be "
                "served in the order of arrival.\n"
                "name: ";
        getline(cin, temp);
        cs.enqueue(temp);
    }
    cout << "The queue is full. Processing begins!\n";

    while (!cs.isempty())
    {
        cs.dequeue(temp);
        cout << "Now processing " << temp << "...\n";
    }
    return 0;
}
```

Compatibility Note

Some older compilers don't implement `getline()` correctly. In that case, you can replace

`getline(cin, temp);`

with

`cin >> temp;`

Note that this restricts each input item to a single word instead of to a single line.

Here is a sample run of the program in Listings 15.5 and 15.6:

```
Please enter your name. You will be served in the order of arrival.
name: Kinsey Millhone
Please enter your name. You will be served in the order of arrival.
name: Adam Dalgliesh
Please enter your name. You will be served in the order of arrival.
name: Andrew Dalziel
Please enter your name. You will be served in the order of arrival.
name: Kay Scarpetta
Please enter your name. You will be served in the order of arrival.
name: Richard Jury
The queue is full. Processing begins!
Now processing Kinsey Millhone...
Now processing Adam Dalgliesh...
Now processing Andrew Dalziel...
Now processing Kay Scarpetta...
Now processing Richard Jury...
```

Exceptions

Programs sometimes encounter runtime problems that prevent them from continuing normally. For example, a program may try to open an unavailable file, or it may request more memory than is available, or it may encounter values it cannot abide. Usually, programmers try to anticipate such calamities. C++ exceptions provide a powerful and flexible tool for dealing with these situations. Exceptions are a relatively recent addition to C++, so some older compilers haven't implemented them. Also, some compilers turn this feature off by default, so you may have to use the compiler options to turn it on.

Before examining exceptions, let's look at some of the more rudimentary options available to programmers. As a test case, let's look at a function that calculates the harmonic mean of two numbers. The *harmonic mean* of two numbers is defined as the inverse of the average of the inverses. This can be reduced to the following expression:

$$2.0 \times x \times y / (x + y)$$

Note that if y is the negative of x, this formula results in division by zero, a rather undesirable operation. Many newer compilers handle division by zero by generating a special floating-point value that represents infinity; cout displays this value as Inf, inf, INF, or something similar. Other compilers may produce programs that crash when division by zero occurs. It is best to write code that behaves in the same controlled fashion on all systems.

Calling abort()

One way to handle this is to have the function call the abort() function if one argument is the negative of the other. The abort() function has its prototype in the cstdlib (or stdlib.h) header file. A typical implementation, if called, sends a message such as "abnormal program termination" to the standard error stream (the same as the one used by cerr) and terminates the program. It also returns an implementation-dependent value that indicates failure to the operating system or, if the program was initiated by another program, to the parent process. Whether `abort()` flushes file buffers (that is, memory areas used to store material for transfers to and from files) depends on the implementation. If you prefer, you can use `exit()`, which does flush file buffers, but without displaying a message. Listing 15.7 shows a short program that uses `abort()`.

LISTING 15.7   error1.cpp

```
//error1.cpp -- using the abort() function
#include <iostream>
#include <cstdlib>
double hmean(double a, double b);

int main()
{
    double x, y, z;

    std::cout << "Enter two numbers: ";
    while (std::cin >> x >> y)
    {
        z = hmean(x,y);
        std::cout << "Harmonic mean of " << x << " and " << y
            << " is " << z << std::endl;
        std::cout << "Enter next set of numbers <q to quit>: ";
    }
    std::cout << "Bye!\n";
    return 0;
}

double hmean(double a, double b)
{
    if (a == -b)
    {
        std::cout << "untenable arguments to hmean()\n";
        std::abort();
    }
    return 2.0 * a * b / (a + b);
}
```

Here's a sample run of the program in Listing 15.7:

```
Enter two numbers: 3 6
Harmonic mean of 3 and 6 is 4
Enter next set of numbers <q to quit>: 10 -10
untenable arguments to hmean()
abnormal program termination
```

Note that calling the `abort()` function from `hmean()` terminates the program directly, without returning first to `main()`. (In general, different compilers issue different abort messages.)

The program could avoid aborting by checking the values of x and y before calling the hmean() function. However, it's not safe to rely on a programmer to know (or care) enough to perform such a check.

Returning an Error Code

A more flexible approach than aborting is to use a function's return value to indicate a problem. For example, the get(void) member of the ostream class ordinarily returns the ASCII code for the next input character, but it returns the special value EOF if it encounters the end-of-file. This approach doesn't work for hmean(). Any numeric value could be a valid return value, so there's no special value available to indicate a problem. In this kind of situation, you can use a pointer argument or a reference argument to get a value back to the calling program and use the function return value to indicate success or failure. The istream family of overloaded >> operators uses a variant of this technique. By informing the calling program of the success or failure, you give the program the option of taking actions other than aborting. Listing 15.8 shows an example of this approach. It redefines hmean() as a bool function whose return value indicates success or failure. It adds a third argument for obtaining the answer.

LISTING 15.8   error2.cpp

```
//error2.cpp -- returning an error code
#include <iostream>
#include <cfloat>  // (or float.h) for DBL_MAX

bool hmean(double a, double b, double * ans);

int main()
{
    double x, y, z;

    std::cout << "Enter two numbers: ";
    while (std::cin >> x >> y)
    {
        if (hmean(x,y,&z))
            std::cout << "Harmonic mean of " << x << " and " << y
                << " is " << z << std::endl;
        else
            std::cout << "One value should not be the negative "
                << "of the other - try again.\n";
        std::cout << "Enter next set of numbers <q to quit>: ";
    }
    std::cout << "Bye!\n";
    return 0;
}

bool hmean(double a, double b, double * ans)
{
    if (a == -b)
    {
```

LISTING 15.8   *Continued*

```
          *ans = DBL_MAX;
          return false;
     }
     else
     {
          *ans = 2.0 * a * b / (a + b);
          return true;
     }
}
```

Here's a sample run of the program in Listing 15.8:

```
Enter two numbers: 3 6
Harmonic mean of 3 and 6 is 4
Enter next set of numbers <q to quit>: 10 -10
One value should not be the negative of the other - try again.
Enter next set of numbers <q to quit>: 1 19
Harmonic mean of 1 and 19 is 1.9
Enter next set of numbers <q to quit>: q
Bye!
```

Program Notes

In Listing 15.8, the program design allows the user to continue, bypassing the effects of bad input. Of course, the design does rely on the user to check the function return value, something that programmers don't always do. For example, to keep the sample programs short, most of the listings in this book don't check to see if `new` returns the null pointer or if `cout` was successful in handling output.

You could use either a pointer or a reference for the third arguments. Many programmers prefer using pointers for arguments of the built-in types because that makes it obvious which argument is being used for the answer.

Another variation on the idea of storing a return condition somewhere is to use a global variable. The function with the potential problem could set the global variable to a particular value if things go wrong, and the calling program could check the variable. This is the method used by the traditional C math library, which uses the global variable `errno` for this purpose. You have to make sure, of course, that some other function doesn't try to use a global variable of the same name for some other purpose.

The Exception Mechanism

Now let's see how you can handle problems by using the exception mechanism. A C++ *exception* is a response to an exceptional circumstance that arises while a program is running, such as an attempt to divide by zero. Exceptions provide a way to transfer control from one part of a program to another. Handling an exception has three components:

- Throwing an exception

- Catching an exception with a handler

- Using a **try** block

A program throws an exception when a problem shows up. For example, you can modify **hmean()** in Listing 15.7 to throw an exception instead of call the **abort()** function. A throw statement, in essence, is a jump; that is, it tells a program to jump to statements at another location. The **throw** keyword indicates the throwing of an exception. It's followed by a value, such as a character string or an object, that indicates the nature of the exception.

A program catches an exception with an *exception handler* at the place in the program where you want to handle the problem. The **catch** keyword indicates the catching of an exception. A handler begins with the keyword **catch**, followed by a type declaration (in parentheses) that indicates the type of exception to which it responds. That, in turn, is followed by a brace-enclosed block of code that indicates the actions to take. The **catch** keyword, along with the exception type, serves as a label that identifies the point in a program to which execution should jump when an exception is thrown. An exception handler is also called a **catch** *block*.

A **try** *block* identifies a block of code for which particular exceptions will be activated. It's followed by one or more **catch** blocks. The **try** block itself is indicated by the keyword **try**, followed by a brace-enclosed block of code indicating the code for which exceptions will be noticed.

The easiest way to see how these three elements fit together is to look at a short example, such as the one in Listing 15.9.

LISTING 15.9   error3.cpp

```
// error3.cpp -- using an exception
#include <iostream>
double hmean(double a, double b);

int main()
{
    double x, y, z;

    std::cout << "Enter two numbers: ";
    while (std::cin >> x >> y)
    {
        try {                       // start of try block
            z = hmean(x,y);
        }                           // end of try block
        catch (const char * s)  // start of exception handler
        {
            std::cout << s << std::endl;
            std::cout << "Enter a new pair of numbers: ";
            continue;
        }                           // end of handler
        std::cout << "Harmonic mean of " << x << " and " << y
```

LISTING 15.9   Continued

```
                    << " is " << z << std::endl;
         std::cout << "Enter next set of numbers <q to quit>: ";
    }
    std::cout << "Bye!\n";
    return 0;
}

double hmean(double a, double b)
{
    if (a == -b)
        throw "bad hmean() arguments: a = -b not allowed";
    return 2.0 * a * b / (a + b);
}
```

Here's a sample run of the program in Listing 15.9:

```
Enter two numbers: 3 6
Harmonic mean of 3 and 6 is 4
Enter next set of numbers <q to quit>: 10 -10
bad hmean() arguments: a = -b not allowed
Enter a new pair of numbers: 1 19
Harmonic mean of 1 and 19 is 1.9
Enter next set of numbers <q to quit>: q
Bye!
```

Program Notes

The `try` block in Listing 15.9 looks like this:

```
try {                    // start of try block
    z = hmean(x,y);
}                        // end of try block
```

If any statement in this block leads to an exception being thrown, the `catch` blocks after this block will handle the exception. If the program calls `hmean()` somewhere else outside this (and any other) `try` block, it won't have the opportunity to handle an exception.

Throwing an exception looks like this:

```
if (a == -b)
    throw "bad hmean() arguments: a = -b not allowed";
```

In this case, the thrown exception is the string `"bad hmean() arguments: a = -b not allowed"`. The exception type can be a string, as in this case, or other C++ types. A class type is the usual choice, as later examples in this chapter illustrate.

Executing the `throw` is a bit like executing a return statement in that it terminates function execution. However, instead of returning control to the calling program, a `throw` causes a program to back up through the sequence of current function calls until it finds the function that contains the `try` block. In Listing 15.9, that function is the same as the calling function. Soon you'll see an example involving backing up more than one function. Meanwhile, in this case, the `throw` passes program control back to `main()`. There, the program looks for an exception handler (following the `try` block) that matches the type of exception thrown.

The handler, or `catch` block, looks like this:

```
catch (char * s)  // start of exception handler
{
    std::cout << s << std::endl;
    sdt::cout << "Enter a new pair of numbers: ";
    continue;
}                         // end of handler
```

The `catch` block looks a bit like a function definition, but it's not. The keyword `catch` identifies this as a handler, and `char * s` means that this handler matches a thrown exception that is a string. This declaration of `s` acts much like a function argument definition in that a matching thrown exception is assigned to `s`. Also, if an exception does match this handler, the program executes the code within the braces.

If a program completes executing statements in a `try` block without any exceptions being thrown, it skips the `catch` block or blocks after the `try` block and goes to the first statement following the handlers. So when the sample run of the program in Listing 15.9 processes the values 3 and 6, program execution goes directly to the output statement and reports the result.

Let's trace through the events in the sample run that occur after the values 10 and -10 are passed to the `hmean()` function. The `if` test causes `hmean()` to throw an exception. This terminates execution of `hmean()`. Searching back, the program determines that `hmean()` was called from within a `try` block in `main()`. It then looks for a `catch` block with a type that matches the exception type. The single `catch` block present has a `char *` parameter, so it does match. Detecting the match, the program assigns the string `"bad hmean() arguments: a = -b not allowed"` to the variable `s`. Next, the program executes the code in the handler. First, it prints `s`, which is the caught exception. Then it prints instructions to the user to enter new data. Finally, it executes a `continue` statement, which causes the program to skip the rest of the `while` loop and jump to its beginning again. The fact that the `continue` statement takes the program to the beginning of the loop illustrates the fact that handler statements are part of the loop and that the `catch` line acts like a label directing program flow (see Figure 15.2).

You might wonder what happens if a function throws an exception and there's no `try` block or else no matching handler. By default, the program eventually calls the `abort()` function, but you can modify that behavior. We'll return to this topic later in this chapter.

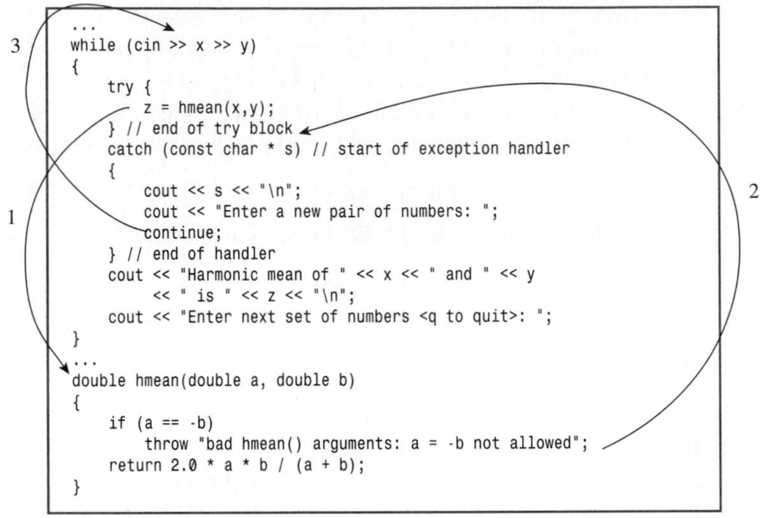

FIGURE 15.2

Program flow with exceptions.

1. The program calls `hmean()` within a try block.

2. `hmean()` throws an exception, transferring execution to the catch block, and assigning the exception string to `s`.

3. The catch block transfers execution back to the `while` loop.

Using Objects as Exceptions

Typically, functions that throw exceptions throw objects. One important advantage of this is that you can use different exception types to distinguish among different functions and situations that produce exceptions. Also, an object can carry information with it, and you can use this information to help identify the conditions that caused the exception to be thrown. Also, in principle, a `catch` block could use that information to decide which course of action to pursue. Here, for example, is one possible design for an exception to be thrown by the `hmean()` function:

```cpp
class bad_hmean
{
private:
    double v1;
    double v2;
public:
    bad_hmean(int a = 0, int b = 0) :v1(a), v2(b){}
    void mesg();
};

inline void bad_hmean::mesg()
{
    std::cout << "hmean(" << v1 << ", " << v2 <<"): "
            << "invalid arguments: a = -b\n";
}
```

A `bad_hmean` object can be initialized to the values passed to `hmean()`, and the `mesg()` method can be used to report the problem, including the values. The `hmean()` function can use code like this:

```
if (a == -b)
    throw bad_hmean(a,b);
```

This calls the `bad_hmean()` constructor, initializing the object to hold the argument values.

You can qualify a function definition with an *exception specification* to indicate which kinds of exceptions it throws. To do so, you append the exception specification, which consists of the keyword `throw` followed by a comma-separated list of exception types enclosed in parentheses:

```
double hmean(double a, double b) throw(bad_hmean);
```

This accomplishes two things. First, it tells the compiler what sort of exception or exceptions a function throws. If the function then throws some other type of exception, the program reacts to the faux pas by calling (eventually) the `abort()` function. (We'll examine this behavior and how it can be modified in more detail later in this chapter.) Second, using an exception specification alerts anyone who reads the prototype that this particular function throws an exception, reminding the reader that he or she may want to provide a `try` block and a handler. A function that throws more than one kind of exception can provide a comma-separated list of exception types; the syntax imitates that of an argument list for a function prototype. For example, the following prototype indicates a function that can throw either a `char *` exception or a `double` exception:

```
double multi_err(double z) throw(const char *, double);
```

The same information that appears in a prototype also should appear in the function definition:

```
double hmean(double a, double b) throw(bad_hmean)
{
    if (a == -b)
        throw bad_hmean(a,b);
    return 2.0 * a * b / (a + b);
}
```

Using empty parentheses in the exception specification indicates that the function does not throw exceptions:

```
double simple(double z) throw(); // DOESN'T throw an exception
```

Listings 15.10 and 15.11 add a second exception class, `bad_gmean`, and a second function, called `gmean()`, that throws a `bad_gmean` exception. The `gmean()` function calculates the geometric mean of two numbers, which is the square root of their product. This function is defined if both arguments are non-negative, so it throws an exception if it detects negative arguments. Listing 15.10 is a header file that holds the exception class definitions, and Listing 15.11 is a sample program that uses that header file. Note that the `try` block is followed by two consecutive `catch` blocks:

```
try {                    // start of try block
    ...
}// end of try block
catch (bad_hmean & bg)     // start of catch block
{
    ...
}
catch (bad_gmean & hg)
{
    ...
} // end of catch block
```

If, say, hmean() throws a **bad_hmean** exception, the first **catch** block catches it. If gmean() throws a **bad_gmean** exception, the exception falls through the first **catch** block and gets caught by the second.

LISTING 15.10   exc_mean.cpp

```cpp
// exc_mean.h  -- exception classes for hmean(), gmean()
#include <iostream>

class bad_hmean
{
private:
    double v1;
    double v2;
public:
    bad_hmean(double a = 0, double b = 0) : v1(a), v2(b){}
    void mesg();
};

inline void bad_hmean::mesg()
{
    std::cout << "hmean(" << v1 << ", " << v2 <<"): "
              << "invalid arguments: a = -b\n";
}

class bad_gmean
{
public:
    double v1;
    double v2;
    bad_gmean(double a = 0, double b = 0) : v1(a), v2(b){}
    const char * mesg();
};

inline const char * bad_gmean::mesg()
{
    return "gmean() arguments should be >= 0\n";
}
```

LISTING 15.11 error4.cpp

```cpp
//error4.cpp -- using exception classes
#include <iostream>
#include <cmath> // or math.h, unix users may need -lm flag
#include "exc_mean.h"
// function prototypes
double hmean(double a, double b) throw(bad_hmean);
double gmean(double a, double b) throw(bad_gmean);
int main()
{
    using std::cout;
    using std::cin;
    using std::endl;

    double x, y, z;

    cout << "Enter two numbers: ";
    while (cin >> x >> y)
    {
        try {                    // start of try block
            z = hmean(x,y);
            cout << "Harmonic mean of " << x << " and " << y
                << " is " << z << endl;
            cout << "Geometric mean of " << x << " and " << y
                << " is " << gmean(x,y) << endl;
            cout << "Enter next set of numbers <q to quit>: ";
        }// end of try block
        catch (bad_hmean & bg)     // start of catch block
        {
            bg.mesg();
            cout << "Try again.\n";
            continue;
        }
        catch (bad_gmean & hg)
        {
            cout << hg.mesg();
            cout << "Values used: " << hg.v1 << ", "
                << hg.v2 << endl;
            cout << "Sorry, you don't get to play any more.\n";
            break;
        } // end of catch block
    }
    cout << "Bye!\n";
    return 0;
}

double hmean(double a, double b) throw(bad_hmean)
{
    if (a == -b)
        throw bad_hmean(a,b);
    return 2.0 * a * b / (a + b);
}
```

LISTING 15.11   Continued

```
double gmean(double a, double b) throw(bad_gmean)
{
    if (a < 0 || b < 0)
        throw bad_gmean(a,b);
    return std::sqrt(a * b);
}
```

Here's a sample run of the program in Listings 15.10 and 15.11 that gets terminated by bad input for the `gmean()` function:

```
Enter two numbers: 4 12
Harmonic mean of 4 and 12 is 6
Geometric mean of 4 and 12 is 6.9282
Enter next set of numbers <q to quit>: 5 -5
hmean(5, -5): invalid arguments: a = -b
Try again.
5 -2
Harmonic mean of 5 and -2 is -6.66667
gmean() arguments should be >= 0
Values used: 5, -2
Sorry, you don't get to play any more.
Bye!
```

One point to notice is that the `bad_hmean` handler uses a `continue` statement, whereas the `bad_gmean` handler uses a `break` statement. Thus, bad input to `hmean()` leads the program to skip the rest of the loop and start the next loop cycle. But bad input for `gmean()` terminates the loop. This illustrates how a program can determine which exception is thrown (by the exception type) and tailor the response to the exception.

A second point to notice is that the `bad_gmean` design illustrates techniques that are different from what `bad_hmean` uses. In particular, `bad_gmean` uses public data and a method that returns a C-style string.

Unwinding the Stack

Suppose a `try` block doesn't contain a direct call to a function that throws an exception but that it calls a function that calls a function that throws an exception. Execution still jumps from the function in which the exception is thrown to the function that contains the `try` block and handlers. Doing so involves *unwinding the stack*, which we'll discuss now.

First, let's look at how C++ normally handles function calls and returns. C++ typically handles function calls by placing information on a stack (see Chapter 9, "Memory Models and Namespaces"). In particular, a program places the address of a calling function instruction (a *return address*) on the stack. When the called function completes, the program uses that address to determine where to continue with program execution. Also, the function call places any function arguments on the stack, where they are treated as automatic variables. If the called function creates any new automatic variables, they, too, are added to the stack. If a called function calls another function, its information is added to the stack, and so on. When a function terminates, program execution passes to the address stored when the function was called, and the top of the stack is freed. Thus a function normally returns to the function that called it, with each function liberating its automatic variables as it terminates. If an automatic variable is a class object, then the class destructor, if any, is called.

Now suppose a function terminates via a thrown exception instead of via a return call. Again, the program frees memory from the stack. But instead of stopping at the first return address on the stack, the program continues freeing the stack until it reaches a return address that resides in a **try** block (see Figure 15.3). Control then passes to the exception handlers at the end of the block rather than to the first statement following the function call. This process is called *unwinding the stack*. One very important feature of the **throw** mechanism is that, just as with function returns, the class destructors are called for any automatic class objects on the stack. However, a function return just processes objects put on the stack by that function, whereas the **throw** statement processes objects put on the stack by the entire sequence of function calls between the **try** block and the **throw**. Without the unwinding-the-stack feature, a **throw** would leave destructors uncalled for automatic class objects placed on the stack by intermediate function calls.

FIGURE 15.3

throw versus **return**.

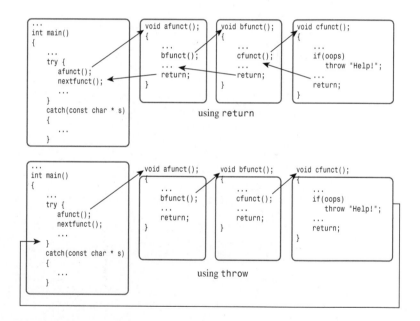

Listing 15.12 provides an example of unwinding the stack. In it, **main()** calls **means()**, which in turn calls **hmean()** and **gmean()**. The **means()** function, for the lack of anything better to do, calculates the mean of the arithmetic, harmonic, and geometric means. Both **main()** and **means()** create objects of the **demo** type (a babbling class that announces when its constructor and destructor are used) so that you can see what happens to those objects when exceptions are thrown. The **try** block in **main()** catches both **bad_hmean** and **bad_gmean** exceptions, and

the `try` block in `means()` catches just the `bad_hmean` exception. This `catch` block has the following code:

```
catch (bad_hmean & bg) // start of catch block
{
    bg.mesg();
    std::cout << "Caught in means()\n";
    throw;              // rethrows the exception
}
```

After the code responds by displaying messages, it rethrows the exception, which means, in this case, sending the exception on up to `main()`. (In general, a rethrown exception rises to the next `try-catch` combination that catches that particular type of exception. If no handler is found, the program, by default, aborts.) Listing 15.12 uses the same header file as Listing 15.11.

LISTING 15.12   error5.cpp

```
//error5.cpp -- unwinding the stack
#include <iostream>
#include <cmath> // or math.h, unix users may need -lm flag
#include <cstring>
#include "exc_mean.h"

class demo
{
private:
    char word[40];
public:
    demo (const char * str)
    {

        std::strcpy(word, str);
        std::cout << "demo " << word << " created\n";
    }
    ~demo()
    {
        std::cout << "demo " << word << " destroyed\n";
    }
    void show() const
    {
        std::cout << "demo " << word << " lives!\n";
    }
};

// function prototypes
double hmean(double a, double b) throw(bad_hmean);
double gmean(double a, double b) throw(bad_gmean);
double means(double a, double b) throw(bad_hmean, bad_gmean);

int main()
{
```

LISTING 15.12   Continued

```cpp
    using std::cout;
    using std::cin;
    using std::endl;

    double x, y, z;
    demo d1("found in main()");
    cout << "Enter two numbers: ";
    while (cin >> x >> y)
    {
        try {                      // start of try block
            z = means(x,y);
            cout << "The mean mean of " << x << " and " << y
                << " is " << z << endl;
            cout << "Enter next pair: ";
        }// end of try block
        catch (bad_hmean & bg)     // start of catch block
        {
            bg.mesg();
            cout << "Try again.\n";
            continue;
        }
        catch (bad_gmean & hg)
        {
            cout << hg.mesg();
            cout << "Values used: " << hg.v1 << ", "
                << hg.v2 << endl;
            cout << "Sorry, you don't get to play any more.\n";
            break;
        } // end of catch block
    }
    d1.show();
    cout << "Bye!\n";
    return 0;
}

double hmean(double a, double b) throw(bad_hmean)
{
    if (a == -b)
        throw bad_hmean(a,b);
    return 2.0 * a * b / (a + b);
}

double gmean(double a, double b) throw(bad_gmean)
{
    if (a < 0 || b < 0)
        throw bad_gmean(a,b);
    return std::sqrt(a * b);
}

double means(double a, double b) throw(bad_hmean, bad_gmean)
{
```

LISTING 15.12 Continued

```
    double am, hm, gm;
    demo d2("found in means()");
    am = (a + b) / 2.0;     // arithmetic mean
    try
    {
        hm = hmean(a,b);
        gm = gmean(a,b);
    }
    catch (bad_hmean & bg) // start of catch block
    {
        bg.mesg();
        std::cout << "Caught in means()\n";
        throw;               // rethrows the exception
    }
    d2.show();
    return (am + hm + gm) / 3.0;
}
```

Here's a sample run of the program in Listings 15.10 and 15.12:

```
demo found in main() created
Enter two numbers: 6 12
demo found in means() created
demo found in means() lives!
demo found in means() destroyed
The mean mean of 6 and 12 is 8.49509
6 -6
demo found in means() created
hmean(6, -6): invalid arguments: a = -b
Caught in means()
demo found in means() destroyed
hmean(6, -6): invalid arguments: a = -b
Try again.
6 -8
demo found in means() created
demo found in means() destroyed
gmean() arguments should be >= 0
Values used: 6, -8
Sorry, you don't get to play any more.
demo found in main() lives!
Bye!
demo found in main() destroyed
```

Program Notes

Let's trace through the course of the sample run shown in the preceding section. First, as the demo constructor announces, an object is created in main(). Next, means() is called, and another demo object is created. The means() function passes the values 6 and 12 on to hmean() and gmean(), and those functions return values to means(), which calculates a result and returns it. Before returning the result, means() invokes d2.show(). After returning the result, means() terminates, and the destructor for d2 is called automatically:

```
demo found in means() lives!
demo found in means() destroyed
```

The next input cycle sends the values 6 and -6 to)means(), and then means() creates a new demo object and relays the values to hmean(). The hmean() function then throws a bad_hmean exception, which is caught by the catch block in means(), as is shown by the following output:

```
hmean(6, -6): invalid arguments: a = -b
Caught in means()
```

The throw statement in this block then terminates) means() and sends the exception up to main(). The fact that d2.show() isn't called demonstrates that the execution of means() is terminated. But note that the destructor for d2 is called:

```
demo found in means() destroyed
```

This illustrates an extremely important aspect of exceptions: As the program unwinds the stack to reach where an exception is caught, it frees automatic storage class variables on the stack. If a variable happens to be a class object, then the destructor for that object is called.

Meanwhile, the rethrown exception reaches main(), where the appropriate catch block catches and handles it:

```
hmean(6, -6): invalid arguments: a = -b
Try again.
```

Now the third input cycle begins, with 6 and -8 sent on to means(). Once again, means() creates a new demo object. It passes 6 and -8 to hmean(), which processes them without a problem. Then means() passes 6 and -8 to gmean(), which throws a bad_gmean exception. Because means()) doesn't catch bad_gmean exceptions, the exception is passed on up to main(), and no further code in means() is executed. However, once again, as the program unwinds the stack, it frees local automatic variables, so the destructor for d2 is called:

```
demo found in means() destroyed
```

Finally, the bad_gmean handler in main() catches the exception and terminates the loop:

```
gmean() arguments should be >= 0
Values used: 6, -8
Sorry, you don't get to play any more.
```

Then the program terminates normally, displaying a few messages and automatically calling the constructor for d1. If the catch block used, say, exit(EXIT_FAILURE) instead of break, the program would terminate immediately, so you wouldn't see these messages:

```
demo found in main() lives!
Bye!
```

However, you would still see this message:

```
demo found in main() destroyed
```

Again, the exception mechanism would attend to freeing automatic variables on the stack.

Note the exception specification for `means()`:

```
double means(double a, double b) throw(bad_hmean, bad_gmean);
```

It indicates that)means() can throw both `bad_hmean` and `bad_gmean` exceptions. But the only exception explicitly thrown in `means()` is the `bad_hmean` that is rethrown by the `bad_hmean` handler. However, the exception specification should include not only exceptions thrown by the function itself but exceptions thrown by functions called by that function, and so on. Thus, because `means()` calls `gmean()`, it should announce that it might send along exceptions thrown by `gmean()`.

What happens if you omit `bad_gmean &` from the exception specification and `gmean()` throws that exception? This is an example of an unexpected exception, and this chapter discusses that topic a bit later, in the "When Exceptions Go Astray" section.

More Exception Features

Although the `throw-catch` mechanism is similar to function arguments and the function return mechanism, there are a few differences. One, which you've already encountered, is that a return statement in a function `fun()` transfers execution to the function that called `fun()`, but a `throw` transfers execution all the way up to the first function having a `try-catch` combination that catches the exception. For example, in Listing 15.12, when `hmean()` throws an exception, control passes up to `means()`, but when `gmean()` throws an exception, control passes up to `main()`.

Another difference is that the compiler always creates a temporary copy when throwing an exception, even if the exception specifier and `catch` blocks specify a reference. For instance, consider this code:

```
class problem {...};
...
void super() throw (problem)
{
    ...
    if (oh_no)
    {
        problem oops;   // construct object
        throw oops;     // throw it
    ...
}
...
try {
    super();
}
catch(problem & p)
{
// statements
}
```

Here, **p** would refer to a copy of **oops** rather than to **oops**. That's a good thing because **oops** no longer exists after **super()** terminates. By the way, it is simpler to combine construction with the **throw**:

```
throw problem();    // construct and throw default problem object
```

At this point you might wonder why the code uses a reference if the **throw** generates a copy. After all, the usual reason for using a reference return value is the efficiency of not having to make a copy. The answer is that references have another important property: A base-class reference can also refer to derived-class objects. Suppose you have a collection of exception types that are related by inheritance. In that case, the exception specification need only list a reference to the base type, and that would also match any derived objects thrown.

Suppose you have a class hierarchy of exceptions and you want to handle the different types separately. A base-class reference can catch all objects of a family, but a derived-class object can only catch that object and objects of classes derived from that class. A thrown object is caught by the first **catch** block that matches it. This suggests arranging the **catch** blocks in inverse order of derivation:

```
class bad_1 {...};
class bad_2 : public bad_1 {...};
class bad_3 : public bad 2 {...};
...
void duper() throw (bad_1)  // matches base- and derived-class objects
{
    ...
    if (oh_no)
        throw bad_1();
    if (rats)
        throw bad_2();
    if (drat)
        throw bad_3();

}
...
try {
    duper();
}
catch(bad_3 &be)
{ // statements }
catch(bad_2 &be)
{ // statements }
catch(bad_1 &be)
{ // statements }
```

If the **bad_1** & handler were first, it would catch the **bad_1**, **bad_2**, and **bad_3** exceptions. With the inverse order, a **bad_3** exception would be caught by the **bad_3** & handler.

Arranging `catch` blocks in the proper sequence allows you to be selective about how each type of exception is handled. But sometimes you might not know what type of exception to expect. For instance, say you write a function that calls another function, and you don't know whether that other function throws exceptions. You can still catch the exception, even if you don't know the type. The trick to catching any exception is to use an ellipsis for the exception type:

```
catch (...) { // statements }  // catches any type exception
```

If you do know some exceptions that are thrown, you can place this catchall form at the end of the `catch` block sequence, a bit like the `default` case for a `switch`:

```
try {
    duper();
}
catch(bad_3 &be)
{ // statements }
catch(bad_2 &be)
{ // statements }
catch(bad_1 &be)
{ // statements }
catch(bad_hmean & h)
{ // statements }
catch (...)            // catch whatever is left
{ // statements }
```

You can set up a handler to catch an object instead of a reference. A base-class object will catch a derived class object, but the derived aspects will be stripped off. Thus, base-class versions of virtual methods will be used.

The exception Class

The main intent for C++ exceptions is to provide language-level support for designing fault-tolerant programs. That is, exceptions make it easier to incorporate error handling into a program design so you don't have to tack on some more rigid form of error handling as an afterthought. The flexibility and relative convenience of exceptions should encourage programmers to integrate fault handling into the program design process, if appropriate. In short, exceptions are the kind of feature that, like classes, can modify your approach to programming.

Newer C++ compilers are incorporating exceptions into the language. For example, the `exception` header file (formerly `exception.h` or `except.h`) defines an `exception` class that C++ uses as a base class for other exception classes used to support the language. Your code, too, can throw an `exception` object or use the `exception` class as a base class. One virtual member function is named `what()`, and it returns a string, the nature of which is implementation dependent. However, because this method is virtual, you can redefine it in a class derived from `exception`:

```
#include <exception>
class bad_hmean : public std::exception
{
public:
    const char * what() { return "bad arguments to hmean()"; }
...
};
class bad_gmean : public std::exception
{
public:
    const char * what() { return "bad arguments to gmean()"; }
...
};
```

If you don't want to handle these derived exceptions differently from one another, you can catch them with the same base-class handler:

```
try {
...
}
catch(std::exception & e)
{
    cout << e.what() << endl;
...
}
```

Or you could catch the different types separately.

The C++ library defines many exception types based on `exception`. The `exception` header file provides `bad_exception`, which is used by the `unexpected()` function, discussed in the "When Exceptions Go Astray" section, later this chapter.

The `stdexcept` Exception Classes

The `stdexcept` header file defines several more exception classes. First, the file defines the `logic_error` and `runtime_error` classes, both of which derive publicly from `exception`:

```
class logic_error : public exception {
public:
explicit logic_error(const string& what_arg);
...
};

class domain_error : public logic_error {
public:
explicit domain_error(const string& what_arg);
...
};
```

Note that the constructors take a **string** object as an argument; this argument provides the character data returned as a C-style string by the **what()** method.

These two new classes serve, in turn, as bases for two families of derived classes. The **logic_error** family describes, as you might expect, typical logic errors. In principle, sound programming could avoid such errors, but in practice, such errors might show up. The name of each class indicates the sort of error it is intended to report:

```
domain_error

invalid_argument

length_error

out_of_bounds
```

Each class has a constructor like that of **logic_error** that allows you to provide the string to be returned by the **what()** method.

Perhaps a little amplification might be helpful. A mathematical function has a domain and a range. The domain consists of the values for which the function is defined, and the range consists of the values that a function returns. For example, the domain of the sine function is from negative infinity to positive infinity because the sine is defined for all real numbers. But the range of the sine function is from -1 to +1 because those are the extreme possible values of the sine of an angle. On the other hand, the domain of the inverse function arcsine is -1 to +1, while its range is $-\pi$ to $+\pi$. If you wrote a function that passed an argument to the **std::sin()** function, you could have your function throw a **domain_error** object if the argument were outside the -1 to +1 domain.

The **invalid_argument** exception alerts you that an unexpected value has been passed to a function. For example, if a function expects to receive a string for which each character is either a '**0**' or '**1**', it could throw the **invalid_argument** exception if some other character appeared in the string.

The **length_error** exception is used to indicate that not enough space is available for the desired action. For example, the **string** class has an **append()** method that throws a **length_error** exception if the resulting string would be larger than the maximum possible string length.

The **out_of_bounds** exception is typically used to indicate indexing errors. For example, you could define an array-like class for which **operator()[]** throws the **out_of_bounds** exception if the index used is invalid for that array.

Next, the **runtime_error** family describes errors that might show up during runtime but that could not easily be predicted and prevented. The name of each class indicates the sort of error it is intended to report:

```
range_error

overflow_error

underflow_error
```

Each class has a constructor like that of `runtime_error` that allows you to provide the string to be returned by the `what()` method.

An underflow error can occur in floating-point calculations. In general, there is a smallest nonzero magnitude that a floating-point type can represent. A calculation that would produce a smaller value would cause an underflow error. An overflow error can occur with either integer or floating-point types when the magnitude of the result of a calculation would exceed the largest representable value for that type. A computational result can lie outside the valid range of a function without being an underflow or overflow, and you can use the `range_error` exception for such situations.

In general, an exception of the `logic_error` family indicates a problem that is susceptible to a programming fix, whereas a `runtime_error` family exception is just a bit of unavoidable trouble. All these error classes have the same general characteristics. The main distinction is that the different class names allow you to handle each type of exception individually. On the other hand, the inheritance relationships allow you to lump them together, if you prefer. For example, the following code catches the `out_of_bounds` exception individually, treats the remaining `logic_error` family of exceptions as a group, and treats `exception` objects, the `runtime_error` family of objects, and any remaining exception types derived from `exception` collectively:

```
try {
...
}
catch(out_of_bounds & oe) // catch out_of_bounds error
{...}
catch(logic_error & oe)   // catch remaining logic_error family
{...}
catch(exception & oe)     // catch runtime_error, exception objects
{...}
```

If one of these library classes doesn't meet your needs, it makes sense to derive an exception class from `logic_error` or `runtime_error` so that you can fit your exceptions into the same general hierarchy.

The `bad_alloc` Exception and `new`

C++ implementations have two choices for handling memory allocation problems when using `new`. The first choice, and once the only choice, is to have `new` return the null pointer if it can't satisfy a memory request. The second choice is to have `new` throw a `bad_alloc` exception. The `new` header (formerly `new.h`) includes a declaration for the `bad_alloc` class, which is publicly derived from the `exception` class. An implementation may offer just one choice or, perhaps by using a compiler switch or some other method, let you choose the approach you prefer.

Listing 15.13 straddles the issue by trying both approaches. If the exception is caught, the program displays the implementation-dependent message returned by the inherited `what()` method and terminates early. Otherwise, it proceeds to see if the return value was the null pointer. (The purpose here is to show the two ways to check for memory allocation errors, not to suggest that a typical program would actually use both methods.)

LISTING 15.13   newexcp.cpp

```cpp
// newexcp.cpp -- the bad_alloc exception
#include <iostream>
#include <new>
#include <cstdlib>
using namespace std;

struct Big
{
    double stuff[20000];
};

int main()
{
    Big * pb;
    try {
        cout << "Trying to get a big block of memory:\n";
        pb = new Big[10000]; // 1,600,000,000 bytes
        cout << "Got past the new request:\n";
    }
    catch (bad_alloc & ba)
    {
        cout << "Caught the exception!\n";
        cout << ba.what() << endl;
        exit(EXIT_FAILURE);
    }
    if (pb != 0)
    {
        pb[0].stuff[0] = 4;
        cout << pb[0].stuff[0] << endl;
    }
    else
        cout << "pb is null pointer\n";
    delete [] pb;
    return 0;
}
```

Here's the output from a compiled version of the program in Listing 15.13 that doesn't throw an exception:

```
Trying to get a big block of memory:
Got past the new request:
pb is null pointer
```

Here's the output from a version that does throw an exception:

```
Trying to get a big block of memory:
Caught the exception!
bad allocation
```

In this case, the `what()` method returns the string `"bad allocation"`.

If the program runs without allocation problems on your system, you can try increasing the amount of memory requested.

Exceptions, Classes, and Inheritance

Exceptions, classes, and inheritance interact in a couple ways. First, you can derive one exception class from another, as the standard C++ library does. Second, you can incorporate exceptions into classes by nesting exception class declarations inside a class definition. Third, such nested declarations can be inherited and can serve as base classes themselves.

Listing 15.14 starts us on the way to exploring some of these possibilities. This header file declares a rudimentary `Sales` class that holds a year value and an array of 12 monthly sales figures. The `LabeledSales` class derives from `Sales` and adds a member to hold a label for the data.

LISTING 15.14   `sales.h`

```
// sales.h  -- exceptions and inheritance
#include <stdexcept>
#include <cstring>

class Sales
{
public:
    enum {MONTHS = 12};   // could be a static const
    class bad_index : public std::logic_error
    {
    private:
        int bi;  // bad index value
    public:
        explicit bad_index(int ix,
            const char * s = "Index error in Sales object\n");
        int bi_val() const {return bi;}
    };
    explicit Sales(int yy = 0);
    Sales(int yy, const double * gr, int n);
    virtual ~Sales() { }
    int Year() const { return year; }
    virtual double operator[](int i) const throw(std::logic_error);
    virtual double & operator[](int i) throw(std::logic_error);
private:
    double gross[MONTHS];
    int year;
};
```

LISTING 15.14   Continued

```cpp
class LabeledSales : public Sales
{
  public:
    static const int STRLEN = 50;  // could be an enum
    class nbad_index : public Sales::bad_index
    {
    private:
        char lbl[STRLEN];
    public:
        nbad_index(const char * lb, int ix,
            const char * s = "Index error in LabeledSales object\n");
        const char * label_val() {return lbl;}
    };
    explicit LabeledSales(const char * lb = "none", int yy = 0);
    LabeledSales(const char * lb, int yy, const double * gr, int n);
    virtual ~LabeledSales() { }
    const char * Label() const {return label;}
    virtual double operator[](int i) const throw(std::logic_error);
    virtual double & operator[](int i) throw(std::logic_error);
private:
    char label[STRLEN];
};
```

Let's examine a few details of Listing 15.14. First, the symbolic constant MONTHS is in the protected section of Sales; this makes the value available to derived classes, such as LabeledSales.

Next, the bad_index class is nested in the public section of Sales; this makes the class available as a type to client catch blocks. Note that the outside world requires the type to be identified as Sales::bad_index. This class derives from the standard logic_error class. The bad_index class has the ability to store and report an out-of-bounds value for an array index.

The nbad_index class is nested in the public section of LabeledSales, making it available to client code as LabeledSales::nbad_index. It derives from bad_index, adding the ability to store and report the label of a LabeledSales object. Because bad_index derives from logic_error, nbad_index also ultimately derives from logic_error.

Both classes have overloaded operator[]() methods that are designed to access the individual array elements stored in an object and to throw an exception if an index is out of bounds. Note the exception specifications:

```cpp
// Sales version
virtual double operator[](int i) const throw(std::logic_error);
// LabeledSales version
virtual double operator[](int i) const throw(std::logic_error);
```

Because of the rule that an exception specification type also matches derived classes, the std::logic_error type matches both the bad_index type and the nbad_index type.

You might recall that C++ requires that a derived-class redefinition of a base-class method have the same function signature, but the return types can differ as long as the return type for a derived-class method is derived (directly or indirectly) from the return type of the base-class method. The same rule applies for exception specifications. A derived method should have the same exception specification as the base method, or else it should be a type derived (directly or indirectly) from that used in the base-method exception specification. So, in principle, you may use `bad_index` for the exception type in `Sales::operator[]()` and `nbad_index` for the exception type in the `LabeledSales` version. However, in practice, some compilers are not yet ready to handle this option.

Listing 15.15 shows the implementation of the methods that weren't already defined inline in Listing 15.14. Note that nested classes require using the scope-resolution operator more than once. Also note that the `operator[]()` functions throw exceptions if the array index is out of bounds.

LISTING 15.15   sales.cpp

```cpp
// sales.cpp -- Sales implementation
#include "sales.h"

Sales::bad_index::bad_index(int ix, const char * s )
    : std::logic_error(s), bi(ix)
{
}

Sales::Sales(int yy)
{
    year = yy;
    for (int i = 0; i < MONTHS; ++i)
        gross[i] = 0;
}

Sales::Sales(int yy, const double * gr, int n)
{
    year = yy;
    int lim = (n < MONTHS)? n : MONTHS;
    int i;
    for (i = 0; i < lim; ++i)
        gross[i] = gr[i];
    // for i > n and i < MONTHS
    for ( ; i < MONTHS; ++i)
        gross[i] = 0;
}

double Sales::operator[](int i) const throw(std::logic_error)
{
    if(i < 0 || i >= MONTHS)
        throw bad_index(i);
    return gross[i];
}

double & Sales::operator[](int i) throw(std::logic_error)
{
```

LISTING 15.15 Continued

```
        if(i < 0 || i >= MONTHS)
            throw bad_index(i);
        return gross[i];
    }

    LabeledSales::nbad_index::nbad_index(const char * lb, int ix,
                const char * s ) : Sales::bad_index(ix, s)
    {
        std::strcpy(lbl, lb);
    }

    LabeledSales::LabeledSales(const char * lb, int yy)
            : Sales(yy)
    {
        std::strcpy(label, lb);
    }

    LabeledSales::LabeledSales(const char * lb, int yy, const double * gr, int n)
            : Sales(yy, gr, n)
    {
        std::strcpy(label, lb);
    }

    double LabeledSales::operator[](int i) const throw(std::logic_error)
    {
        if(i < 0 || i >= MONTHS)
            throw nbad_index(Label(), i);
        return Sales::operator[](i);
    }

    double & LabeledSales::operator[](int i) throw(std::logic_error)
    {
        if(i < 0 || i >= MONTHS)
            throw nbad_index(Label(), i);
        return Sales::operator[](i);
    }
```

Listing 15.16 uses the classes in a program that first tries to go beyond the end of the array in the LabeledSales object sales2, then beyond the end of the array in the Sales object sales1. These attempts are made in two separate try blocks so that you can test for each kind of exception.

LISTING 15.16 use_sales.cpp

```
// use_sales.cpp  -- nested exceptions
#include <iostream>
#include "sales.h"

int main()
{
    using std::cout;
```

LISTING 15.16 Continued

```cpp
using std::cin;
using std::endl;

double vals1[12] =
{
    1220, 1100, 1122, 2212, 1232, 2334,
    2884, 2393, 3302, 2922, 3002, 3544
};

double vals2[12] =
{
    12, 11, 22, 21, 32, 34,
    28, 29, 33, 29, 32, 35
};

Sales sales1(2004, vals1, 12);
LabeledSales sales2("Blogstar",2005, vals2, 12 );

cout << "First try block:\n";
try
{
    int i;
    cout << "Year = " << sales1.Year() << endl;
    for (i = 0; i < 12; ++i)
    {

        cout << sales1[i] << ' ';
        if (i % 6 == 5)
            cout << endl;
    }
    cout << "Year = " << sales2.Year() << endl;
    cout << "Label = " << sales2.Label() << endl;
    for (i = 0; i <= 12; ++i)
    {

        cout << sales2[i] << ' ';
        if (i % 6 == 5)
            cout << endl;
    }
    cout << "End of try block 1.\n";
}
catch(LabeledSales::nbad_index & bad)
{
    cout << bad.what();
    cout << "Company: " << bad.label_val() << endl;
    cout << "bad index: " << bad.bi_val() << endl;
}
catch(Sales::bad_index & bad)
{
    cout << bad.what();
    cout << "bad index: " << bad.bi_val() << endl;
}
```

LISTING 15.16   Continued

```
        cout << "\nNext try block:\n";
        try
         {
             sales2[2] = 37.5;
             sales1[20] = 23345;
             cout << "End of try block 2.\n";
         }
        catch(LabeledSales::nbad_index & bad)
         {
             cout << bad.what();
             cout << "Company: " << bad.label_val() << endl;
             cout << "bad index: " << bad.bi_val() << endl;
         }
        catch(Sales::bad_index & bad)
         {
             cout << bad.what();
             cout << "bad index: " << bad.bi_val() << endl;
         }
        cout << "done\n";

         return 0;
        }
```

Here is the program output of the program in Listings 15.14, 15.15, and 15.16:

```
First try block:
Year = 2004
1220 1100 1122 2212 1232 2334
2884 2393 3302 2922 3002 3544
Year = 2005
Label = Blogstar
12 11 22 21 32 34
28 29 33 29 32 35
Index error in LabeledSales object
Company: Blogstar
bad index: 12

Next try block:
Index error in Sales object
bad index: 20
done
```

When Exceptions Go Astray

After an exception is thrown, it has two opportunities to cause problems. First, if it is thrown in a function that has an exception specification, it has to match one of the types in the specification list. (Remember that in an inheritance hierarchy, a class type matches objects of that type and of types descended from it.) If the exception doesn't match the specification, the unmatched exception is branded an *unexpected exception*, and, by default, it causes the program to abort. If the exception passes this first hurdle (or avoids it because the function lacks an exception specification), it then has to be caught. If it isn't, which can happen if there is no containing `try` block or no matching `catch` block, the exception is branded an *uncaught exception*, and, by default, it causes the program to abort. However, you can alter a program's response to unexpected and uncaught exceptions. Let's see how, beginning with uncaught exceptions.

An uncaught exception doesn't initiate an immediate abort. Instead, the program first calls a function called `terminate()`. By default, `terminate()` calls the `abort()` function. You can modify the behavior of `terminate()` by *registering* a function that `terminate()` should call instead of `abort()`. To do this, you call the `set_terminate()` function. Both `set_terminate()` and `terminate()` are declared in the `exception` header file:

```
typedef void (*terminate_handler)();
terminate_handler set_terminate(terminate_handler f) throw();
void terminate();
```

Here the `typedef` makes `terminate_handler` the type name for a pointer to a function that has no arguments and no return value. The `set_terminate()` function takes, as its argument, the name of a function (that is, its address) that has no arguments and the `void` return type. It returns the address of the previously registered function. If you call the `set_terminate()` function more than once, `terminate()` calls the function set by the most recent call to `set_terminate()`.

Let's look at an example. Suppose you want an uncaught exception to cause a program to print a message to that effect and then call the `exit()` function, providing an exit status value of **5**. First, you include the `exception` header file. You can make its declarations available with a `using` directive or appropriate `using` declarations, or you can use the `std::` qualifier:

```
#include <exception>
using namespace std;
```

Next, you design a function that does the two required actions and has the proper prototype:

```
void myQuit()
{
    cout << "Terminating due to uncaught exception\n";
    exit(5);
}
```

Finally, at the start of the program, you designate this function as your chosen termination action:

```
set_terminate(myQuit);
```

Now, if an exception is thrown and not caught, the program calls `terminate()`, and `terminate()` calls `MyQuit()`.

Next, let's look at unexpected exceptions. By using exception specifications for a function, you provide the means for users of the functions to know which exceptions to catch. That is, suppose you have the following prototype:

```
double Argh(double, double) throw(out_of_bounds);
```

Then you might use the function this way:

```
try {
    x = Argh(a, b);
}
catch(out_of_bounds & ex)
{
    ...
}
```

It's good to know which exceptions to catch; recall that an uncaught exception, by default, aborts the program.

However, there's a bit more to the story. In principle, the exception specification should include exceptions thrown by functions called by the function in question. For example, if Argh() calls a Duh() function that can throw a retort object exception, then retort should appear in the Argh() exception specification as well as in the Duh() exception specification. Unless you write all the functions yourself and are careful, there's no guarantee that this will get done correctly. You might, for example, use an older commercial library whose functions don't have exception specifications. This suggests that you should look more closely at what happens if a function throws an exception that is not in its exception specification.

The behavior is much like that for uncaught exceptions. If there is an unexpected exception, the program calls the unexpected() function. (You didn't expect the unexpected() function? No one expects the unexpected() function!) This function, in turn, calls terminate(), which, by default, calls abort(). Just as there is a set_terminate() function that modifies the behavior of terminate(), there is a set_unexpected() function that modifies the behavior of unexpected(). These new functions are also declared in the exception header file:

```
typedef void (*unexpected_handler)();
unexpected_handler set_unexpected(unexpected_handler f) throw();
void unexpected();
```

However, the behavior of the function you supply for set_unexpected() is more regulated than that of a function for set_terminate(). In particular, the unexpected_handler function has the following choices:

- It can end the program by calling terminate() (the default behavior), abort(), or exit().

- It can throw an exception.

The result of throwing an exception (the second choice here) depends on the exception thrown by the replacement unexpected_handler function and the original exception specification for the function that threw the unexpected type:

- If the newly thrown exception matches the original exception specification, then the program proceeds normally from there; that is, it will look for a catch block that matches the newly thrown exception. Basically, this approach replaces an exception of an unexpected type to an exception of an expected type.

- If the newly thrown exception does not match the original exception specification and if the exception specification *does not* include the `std::bad_exception` type, the program calls `terminate()`. The bad_exception type derives from the `exception` type and is declared in the `exception` header file.

- If the newly thrown exception does not match the original exception specification and if the original exception specification *does* include the `std::bad_exception` type, the unmatched exception is replaced with an exception of the `std::bad_exception` type.

In short, if you'd like to catch all exceptions, expected or otherwise, you can do something like the following. First, you make sure the exception header file declarations are available:

```
#include <exception>
using namespace std;
```

Next, you design a replacement function that converts unexpected exceptions to the `bad_exception` type and that has the proper prototype:

```
void myUnexpected()
{
    throw std::bad_exception();  //or just throw;
}
```

Just using `throw` without an exception causes the original exception to be rethrown. However, the exception will be replaced with a `bad_exception` object if the exception specification includes that type.

Next, at the start of the program, you designate this function as your chosen unexpected exception action:

```
set_unexpected(myUnexpeced);
```

Finally, you include the `bad_exception` type in exception specifications and `catch` block sequences:

```
double Argh(double, double) throw(out_of_bounds, bad_exception);
...
try {
    x = Argh(a, b);
}
catch(out_of_bounds & ex)
{
    ...
}
catch(bad_exception & ex)
{
    ...
}
```

Exception Cautions

From the preceding discussion of using exceptions, you might gather (and gather correctly) that exception handling should be designed into a program rather than tacked on. Doing this has some disadvantages, though. For example, using exceptions adds to the size and subtracts from the speed of a program. Exception specifications don't work well with templates because template functions might throw different kinds of exceptions, depending on the particular specialization used. Exceptions and dynamic memory allocation don't always work that well together.

Let's look a little further at dynamic memory allocation and exceptions. First, consider the following function:

```
void test1(int n)
{
    string mesg("I'm trapped in an endless loop");
    ...
    if (oh_no)
        throw exception();
    ...
    return;
}
```

The `string` class uses dynamic memory allocation. Normally, the `string` destructor for `mesg` would be called when the function reached `return` and terminated. Thanks to stack unwinding, the `throw` statement, even though it terminates the function prematurely, still allows the destructor to be called. So in this case, memory is managed properly.

Now consider this function:

```
void test2(int n)
{
    double * ar = new double[n];
    ...
    if (oh_no)
        throw exception();
    ...
    delete [] ar;
    return;
}
```

Here there is a problem. Unwinding the stack removes the variable `ar` from the stack. But the premature termination of the function means that the `delete []` statement at the end of the function is skipped. The pointer is gone, but the memory block it pointed to is still intact and inaccessible. In short, there is a memory leak.

The leak can be avoided. For example, you can catch the exception in the same function that throws it, put some cleanup code into the `catch` block, and rethrow the exception:

```
void test3(int n)
{
    double * ar = new double[n];
    ...
    try {
        if (oh_no)
            throw exception();
    }
```

```
    catch(exception & ex)
    {
        delete [] ar;
        throw;
    }
    ...
    delete [] ar;
    return;
}
```

However, this clearly enhances the opportunities for oversights and other errors. Another solution is to use the `auto_ptr` template discussed in Chapter 16, "The `string` Class and the Standard Template Library."

In short, although exception handling is extremely important for some projects, it does have costs in terms of programming effort, program size, and program speed. Also, compiler exception support and user experience have not yet reached the mature level. So you might want to use this feature with moderation.

Real-World Note: Exception Handling

In modern libraries, exception handling can appear to reach new levels of complexity—much of it due to undocumented or poorly documented exception-handling routines. Anyone familiar with the use of a modern operating system has surely seen the errors and problems caused by unhandled exceptions. The programmers behind these errors often face an uphill battle, learning the complexity that lies within the libraries: what exceptions are thrown, why and when they occur, and how to handle them.

A novice programmer quickly finds that the research battle to understand exception handling in a library is as difficult as the struggle to learn the language itself; modern libraries can contain routines and paradigms as alien and difficult as any C++ syntax detail. Exposure to and understanding of the intricacies of libraries and classes is, for good software, as necessary as the time you spend learning C++ itself. The exception and error-handling details you decipher from your libraries' documentation and source code will always serve you, and your software, in good stead.

RTTI

RTTI is short for runtime type identification. It's one of the more recent additions to C++, and it isn't supported by many older implementations. Other implementations may have compiler settings for turning RTTI on and off. The intent of RTTI is to provide a standard way for a program to determine the type of object during runtime. Many class libraries have already provided ways to do so for their own class objects, but in the absence of built-in support in C++, each vendor's mechanism is typically incompatible with those of other vendors. Creating a language standard for RTTI should allow future libraries to be compatible with each other.

What Is RTTI For?

Suppose you have a hierarchy of classes descended from a common base class. You can set a base-class pointer to point to an object of any of the classes in this hierarchy. Next, you call a function that, after processing some information, selects one of these classes, creates an object of that type, and returns its address, which gets assigned to a base-class pointer. How can you tell what kind of object it points to?

Before answering this question, you need to think about why you would want to know the type. Perhaps you want to invoke the correct version of a class method. If that's the case, you don't really need to know the object type, as long as that function is a virtual function possessed by all members of the class hierarchy. But it could be that a derived object has an uninherited method. In that case, only some objects could use the method. Or maybe, for debugging purposes, you would like to keep track of which kinds of objects were generated. For these last two cases, RTTI provides an answer.

How Does RTTI Work?

C++ has three components supporting RTTI:

- The `dynamic_cast` operator generates a pointer to a derived type from a pointer to a base type, if possible. Otherwise, the operator returns **0**, the null pointer.

- The `typeid` operator returns a value identifying the exact type of an object.

- A `type_info` structure holds information about a particular type.

You can use RTTI only with a class hierarchy that has virtual functions. The reason for this is that these are the only class hierarchies for which you should be assigning the addresses of derived objects to base-class pointers.

Caution

RTTI works only for classes that have virtual functions.

Let's examine the three components of RTTI.

The `dynamic_cast` Operator

The `dynamic_cast` operator is intended to be the most heavily used RTTI component. It doesn't answer the question of what type of object a pointer points to. Instead, it answers the question of whether you can safely assign the address of an object to a pointer of a particular type. Let's look at what that means. Suppose you have the following hierarchy:

```
class Grand { // has virtual methods};
class Superb : public Grand { ... };
class Magnificent : public Superb { ... };
```

Next, suppose you have the following pointers:

```
Grand * pg = new Grand;
Grand * ps = new Superb;
Grand * pm = new Magnificent;
```

Finally, consider the following type casts:

```
Magnificent * p1 = (Magnificent *) pm;      // #1
Magnificent * p2 = (Magnificent *) pg;      // #2
Superb * p3 = (Magnificent *) pm;           // #3
```

Which of these type casts are safe? Depending on the class declarations, all of them could be safe, but the only ones guaranteed to be safe are the ones in which the pointer is the same type as the object or else a direct or indirect base type for the object. For example, Type Cast #1 is safe because it sets a type `Magnificent` pointer to point to a type `Magnificent` object. Type Cast #2 is not safe because it assigns the address of a base-class object (`Grand`) to a derived-class (`Magnificent`) pointer. Thus, the program would expect the base-class object to have derived-class properties, and that, in general, is false. A `Magnificent` object, for example, might have data members that a `Grand` object would lack. Type Cast #3, however, is safe because it assigns the address of a derived-class object to a base-class pointer. That is, public derivation promises that a `Magnificent` object also is a `Superb` object (direct base) and a `Grand` object (indirect base). Thus, it's safe to assign its address to pointers of all three types. Virtual functions ensure that using pointers of any of the three types to a `Magnificent` object will invoke `Magnificent` methods.

Note that the question of whether a type conversion is safe is both more general and more useful than the question of what kind of object is pointed to. The usual reason for wanting to know the type is so that you can know if it's safe to invoke a particular method. You don't necessarily need an exact type match to invoke a method. The type can be a base type for which a virtual version of the method is defined. The next example illustrates this point.

First, however, let's look at the `dynamic_cast` syntax. The operator is used like this, where `pg` points to an object:

```
Superb * pm = dynamic_cast<Superb *>(pg);
```

This code asks whether the pointer `pg` can be type cast safely (as described previously) to the type `Superb *`. If it can, the operator returns the address of the object. Otherwise it returns `0`, the null pointer.

Remember

In general, the expression

```
dynamic_cast<Type *>(pt)
```

converts the pointer `pt` to a pointer of type `Type *` if the pointed-to object (`*pt`) is of type `Type` or else derived directly or indirectly from type `Type`. Otherwise, the expression evaluates to `0`, the null pointer.

Listing 15.17 illustrates the process. First, it defines three classes, coincidentally named `Grand`, `Superb`, and `Magnificent`. The `Grand` class defines a virtual `Speak()` function, which each of the other classes redefines. The `Superb` class defines a virtual `Say()` function, which `Magnificent` redefines (see Figure 15.4). The program defines a `GetOne()` function that randomly creates and initializes an object of one of these three types and then returns the address as a type `Grand *` pointer. (The `GetOne()` function simulates an interactive user making decisions.) A loop assigns this pointer to a type `Grand *` variable called `pg` and then uses `pg` to invoke the `Speak()` function. Because this function is virtual, the code correctly invokes the `Speak()` version that is appropriate to the pointed-to object:

```
for (int i = 0; i < 5; i++)
{
    pg = GetOne();
    pg->Speak();
    ...
}
```

LISTING 15.17   rtti1.cpp

```cpp
// rtti1.cpp -- using the RTTI dynamic_cast operator
#include <iostream>
#include <cstdlib>
#include <ctime>

using std::cout;

class Grand
{
private:
    int hold;
public:
    Grand(int h = 0) : hold(h) {}
    virtual void Speak() const { cout << "I am a grand class!\n";}
    virtual int Value() const { return hold; }
};

class Superb : public Grand
{
public:
    Superb(int h = 0) : Grand(h) {}
    void Speak() const {cout << "I am a superb class!!\n"; }
    virtual void Say() const
        { cout << "I hold the superb value of " << Value() << "!\n";}
};

class Magnificent : public Superb
{
private:
    char ch;
public:
    Magnificent(int h = 0, char c = 'A') : Superb(h), ch(c) {}
    void Speak() const {cout << "I am a magnificent class!!!\n";}
```

LISTING 15.17   Continued

```
        void Say() const {cout << "I hold the character " << ch <<
                    " and the integer "  << Value() << "!\n"; }
};

Grand * GetOne();

int main()
{
    std::srand(std::time(0));
    Grand * pg;
    Superb * ps;
    for (int i = 0; i < 5; i++)
    {
        pg = GetOne();
        pg->Speak();
        if( ps = dynamic_cast<Superb *>(pg))
            ps->Say();
    }
    return 0;
}

Grand * GetOne()    // generate one of three kinds of objects randomly
{
    Grand * p;
    switch( std::rand() % 3)
    {
    case 0: p = new Grand(std::rand() % 100);
                    break;
        case 1: p = new Superb(std::rand() % 100);
                    break;
        case 2: p = new Magnificent(std::rand() % 100,
                            'A' + std::rand() % 26);
                    break;
    }
    return p;
}
```

However, you can't use this exact approach to invoke the Say() function; it's not defined for
the Grand class. However, you can use the dynamic_cast operator to see if pg can be type cast
to a pointer to Superb. This will be true if the object is either type Superb or Magnificent. In
either case, you can invoke the Say() function safely:

```
if (ps = dynamic_cast<Superb *>(pg))
    ps->Say();
```

Recall that the value of an assignment expression is the value of its left-hand side. Thus, the
value of the if condition is ps. If the type cast succeeds, ps is nonzero, or true. If the type cast
fails, which it will if pg points to a Grand object, ps is zero, or false. Listing 15.17 shows the
full code. (By the way, some compilers, noting that programmers usually use the == operator in
an if statement condition, may issue a warning about unintended assignment.)

FIGURE 15.4

The Grand family of classes.

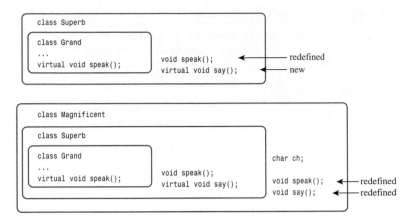

Compatibility Note

Even if your compiler supports RTTI, it might have that feature turned off by default. If the feature is inactive, the program may still compile but produce runtime errors. If you find this to be the case, you should check your documentation or explore the menu options. For example, in Microsoft Visual C++ 7.1, go to Project, select *proj* properties (where *proj* stands for the project name you're using), go the C/C++ folder, click Language, and change the Enable Run-Time Type Info setting to Yes.

The program in Listing 15.17 illustrates an important point. You should use virtual functions when possible and RTTI only when necessary. Here is some sample output:

```
I am a superb class!!
I hold the superb value of 68!
I am a magnificent class!!!
I hold the character R and the integer 68!
I am a magnificent class!!!
I hold the character D and the integer 12!
I am a magnificent class!!!
I hold the character V and the integer 59!
I am a grand class!
```

As you can see, the `Say()` methods were invoked just for the `Superb` and `Magnificent` classes. (The output will vary from run to run because the program uses `rand()` to select the object type.)

You can use `dynamic_cast` with references, too. The usage is slightly different; there is no reference value corresponding to the null-pointer type, so there's no special reference value that can be used to indicate failure. Instead, when goaded by an improper request, `dynamic_cast` throws a type `bad_cast` exception, which is derived from the `exception` class and defined in the `typeinfo` header file. Thus, the operator can be used as follows, where `rg` is a reference to a `Grand` object:

```
#include <typeinfo> // for bad_cast
...
try {
    Superb & rs = dynamic_cast<Superb &>(rg);
    ...
}
catch(bad_cast &){
    ...
};
```

The `typeid` Operator and `type_info` Class

The `typeid` operator lets you determine whether two objects are the same type. Somewhat like `sizeof`, it accepts two kinds of arguments:

- The name of a class

- An expression that evaluates to an object

The `typeid` operator returns a reference to a `type_info` object, where `type_info` is a class defined in the `typeinfo` header file (formerly `typeinfo.h`). The `type_info` class overloads the `==` and `!=` operators so that you can use these operators to compare types. For example, the expression

```
typeid(Magnificent) == typeid(*pg)
```

evaluates to the `bool` value `true` if `pg` points to a `Magnificent` object and to `false` otherwise. If `pg` happens to be a null pointer, the program throws a `bad_typeid` exception. This exception type is derived from the `exception` class and is declared in the `typeinfo` header file.

The implementation of the `type_info` class varies among vendors, but it includes a `name()` member that returns an implementation-dependent string that is typically the name of the class. For example, the statement

```
cout << "Now processing type " << typeid(*pg).name() << ".\n";
```

displays the string defined for the class of the object to which the pointer `pg` points.

Listing 15.18 modifies Listing 15.17 so that it uses the `typeid` operator and the `name()` member function. Note that they are used for situations that `dynamic_cast` and `virtual` functions don't handle. The `typeid` test is used to select an action that isn't even a class method, so it can't be invoked by a class pointer. The `name()` method statement shows how the method can be used in debugging. Note that the program includes the `typeinfo` header file.

LISTING 15.18   `rtti2.cpp`

```
// rtti2.cpp  -- using dynamic_cast, typeid, and type_info
#include <iostream>
#include <cstdlib>
#include <ctime>
#include <typeinfo>
using namespace std;
```

LISTING 15.18   Continued

```cpp
class Grand
{
private:
    int hold;
public:
    Grand(int h = 0) : hold(h) {}
    virtual void Speak() const { cout << "I am a grand class!\n";}
    virtual int Value() const { return hold; }
};

class Superb : public Grand
{
public:
    Superb(int h = 0) : Grand(h) {}
    void Speak() const {cout << "I am a superb class!!\n"; }
    virtual void Say() const
        { cout << "I hold the superb value of " << Value() << "!\n";}
};

class Magnificent : public Superb
{
private:
    char ch;
public:
    Magnificent(int h = 0, char cv = 'A') : Superb(h), ch(cv) {}
    void Speak() const {cout << "I am a magnificent class!!!\n";}
    void Say() const {cout << "I hold the character " << ch <<
                " and the integer "  << Value() << "!\n"; }
};

Grand * GetOne();
int main()
{
    srand(time(0));
    Grand * pg;
    Superb * ps;
    for (int i = 0; i < 5; i++)
    {
        pg = GetOne();
        cout << "Now processing type " << typeid(*pg).name() << ".\n";
        pg->Speak();
        if( ps = dynamic_cast<Superb *>(pg))
            ps->Say();
        if (typeid(Magnificent) == typeid(*pg))
            cout << "Yes, you're really magnificent.\n";
    }
    return 0;
}

Grand * GetOne()
{
    Grand * p;
```

LISTING 15.18   *Continued*

```
    switch( rand() % 3)
    {
        case 0: p = new Grand(rand() % 100);
                    break;
        case 1: p = new Superb(rand() % 100);
                    break;
        case 2: p = new Magnificent(rand() % 100, 'A' + rand() % 26);
                    break;
    }
    return p;
}
```

Here's a sample run of the program in Listing 15.18:

```
Now processing type Magnificent.
I am a magnificent class!!!
I hold the character P and the integer 52!
Yes, you're really magnificent.
Now processing type Superb.
I am a superb class!!
I hold the superb value of 37!
Now processing type Grand.
I am a grand class!
Now processing type Superb.
I am a superb class!!
I hold the superb value of 18!
Now processing type Grand.
I am a grand class!
```

As with the preceding example, the exact output will vary from run to run because the program uses `rand()` to select types.

Misusing RTTI

RTTI has many vocal critics within the C++ community. They view RTTI as unnecessary, a potential source of program inefficiency, and a possible contributor to bad programming practices. Without delving into the debate over RTTI, let's look at the sort of programming that you should avoid.

Consider the core of Listing 15.17:

```
Grand * pg;
Superb * ps;
for (int i = 0; i < 5; i++)
{
    pg = GetOne();
    pg->Speak();
    if( ps = dynamic_cast<Superb *>(pg))
        ps->Say();
}
```

By using `typeid` and ignoring `dynamic_cast` and virtual functions, you can rewrite this code as follows:

```
Grand * pg;
Superb * ps;
Magnificent * pm;
for (int i = 0; i < 5; i++)
{
    pg = GetOne();
    if (typeid(Magnificent) == typeid(*pg))
    {
        pm = (Magnificent *) pg;
        pm->Speak();
        pm->Say();
    }
    else if (typeid(Superb) == typeid(*pg))
    {
        ps = (Superb *) pg;
        ps->Speak();
        ps->Say();
    }
    else
        pg->Speak();
}
```

Not only is this uglier and longer than the original, it has the serious flaw of naming each class explicitly. Suppose, for example, that you find it necessary to derive an `Insufferable` class from the `Magnificent` class. The new class redefines `Speak()` and `Say()`. With the version that uses `typeid` to test explicitly for each type, you would have to modify the `for` loop code, adding a new `else if` section. The original version, however, requires no changes at all. The

```
pg->Speak();
```

statement works for all classes derived from `Grand`, and the

```
if( ps = dynamic_cast<Superb *>(pg))
    ps->Say();
```

statement works for all classes derived from `Superb`.

Tip

If you find yourself using `typeid` in an extended series of `if else` statements, you should check whether you should instead use virtual functions and `dynamic_cast`.

Type Cast Operators

The C type cast operator, in Bjarne Stroustrup's view, is too lax. For example, consider the following:

```
struct Data
{
    double data[200];
};

struct Junk
{
    int junk[100];
};
Data d = {2.5e33, 3.5e-19, 20.2e32};
char * pch = (char *) (&d);    // type cast #1 - convert to string
char ch = char (&d);           // type cast #2 - convert address to a char
Junk * pj = (Junk *) (&d);     // type cast #3 - convert to Junk pointer
```

First, which of these three type casts makes any sense? Unless you resort to the implausible, none of them make much sense. Second, which of these three type casts are allowed? In C, all of them are. Stroustrup's response to this laxity was to tighten up what is allowable for a general type cast and to add four type cast operators that provide more discipline for the casting process:

dynamic_cast

const_cast

static_cast

reinterpret_cast

Instead of using a general type cast, you can select an operator that is suited to a particular purpose. This documents the intended reason for the type cast and gives the compiler a chance to check that you did what you thought you did.

You've already seen the `dynamic_cast` operator. To summarize, suppose `High` and `Low` are two classes, that `ph` is type `High *`, and that `pl` is type `Low *`. Then the statement

```
pl = dynamic_cast<Low *> ph;
```

assigns a `Low *` pointer to `pl` only if `Low` is an accessible base class (direct or indirect) to `High`. Otherwise, the statement assigns the null pointer to `pl`. In general, the operator has this syntax:

```
dynamic_cast < type-name > (expression)
```

The purpose of this operator is to allow upcasts within a class hierarchy (such type casts being safe because of the *is-a* relationship) and to disallow other casts.

The `const_cast` operator is for making a type cast with the sole purpose of changing whether a value is `const` or `volatile`. It has the same syntax as the `dynamic_cast` operator:

```
const_cast < type-name > (expression)
```

The result of making such a type cast is an error if any other aspect of the type is altered. That is, *type_name* and *expression* must be of the same type, except that they can differ in the presence or absence of **const** or **volatile**. Again, suppose **High** and **Low** are two classes:

```
High bar;
const High * pbar = &bar;
    ...
High * pb = const_cast<High *> (pbar);     // valid
const Low * pl = const_cast<const Low *> (pbar);     // invalid
```

The first type cast makes *pb a pointer that can be used to alter the value of the **bar** object; it removes the **const** label. The second type cast is invalid because it attempts to change the type from const High * to const Low *.

The reason for this operator is that occasionally you may have a need for a value that is constant most of the time but that can be changed occasionally. In such a case, you can declare the value as **const** and use **const_cast** when you need to alter the value. This could be done using the general type cast, but the general type cast can also simultaneously change the type:

```
High bar;
const High * pbar = &bar;
...
High * pb = (High *) (pbar);        // valid
Low * pl = (Low *) (pbar);          // also valid
```

Because the simultaneous change of type and constantness may be an unintentional programming slip, using the **const_cast** operator is safer.

The **const_cast** is not all powerful. It can change the pointer access to a quantity, but the effect of attempting to change a quantity that is declared **const** is undefined. Let's clarify this statement with the short example shown in Listing 15.19.

LISTING 15.19   constcast.cpp

```
// constcast.cpp -- using const_cast<>
#include <iostream>
using std::cout;
using std::endl;

void change(const int * pt, int n);

int main()
{
    int pop1 = 38383;
    const int pop2 = 2000;

    cout << "pop1, pop2: " << pop1 << ", " << pop2 << endl;
    change(&pop1, -1);
    change(&pop2, -1);
    cout << "pop1, pop2: " << pop1 << ", " << pop2 << endl;
```

LISTING 15.19 Continued

```
        return 0;
    }

    void change(const int * pt, int n)
    {
        int * pc;
        if (n < 0)
        {
            pc = const_cast<int *>(pt);
            *pc = 100;
        }
    }
```

The `const_cast` operator can remove the `const` from `const int * pt`, thus allowing the compiler to accept the following statement in `change()`:

```
*pc = 100;
```

However, because `pop2` is declared as `const`, the compiler may protect it from any change, as is shown by the following sample output:

```
pop1, pop2: 38383, 2000
pop1, pop2: 100, 2000
```

As you can see, the calls to `change()` alter `pop1` but not `pop2`. (The particular compiler used here generates a temporary copy of `pop2` and assigns that address to `pc`, but, as mentioned, the C++ Standard says the behavior in this situation is undefined.)

The `static_cast` operator has the same syntax as the other operators:

```
static_cast < type-name > (expression)
```

It's valid only if *type_name* can be converted implicitly to the same type that *expression* has, or vice versa. Otherwise, the type cast is an error. Suppose that `High` is a base class to `Low` and that `Pond` is an unrelated class. Then conversions from `High` to `Low` and `Low` to `High` are valid, but a conversion from `Low` to `Pond` is disallowed:

```
High bar;
Low blow;
...
High * pb = static_cast<High *> (&blow);    // valid upcast
Low * pl = static_cast<Low *> (&bar);       // valid downcast
Pond * pmer = static_cast<Pond *> (&blow);  // invalid, Pond unrelated
```

The first conversion here is valid because an upcast can be done explicitly. The second conversion, from a base-class pointer to a derived-class pointer, can't be done without an explicit type conversion. But because the type cast in the other direction can be made without a type cast, it's valid to use `static_cast` for a downcast.

Similarly, because an enumeration value can be converted to an integral type without a type cast, an integral type can be converted to an enumeration value with `static_cast`. Similarly, you can use `static_cast` to convert `double` to `int`, to convert `float` to `long`, and to perform the various other numeric conversions.

The `reinterpret_cast` operator is for inherently risky type casts. It doesn't let you cast away `const`, but it does do other unsavory things. Sometimes a programmer has to do implementation-dependent, unsavory things, and using the `reinterpret_cast` operator makes it simpler to keep track of such acts. It has the same syntax as the other three operators:

```
reinterpret_cast < type-name > (expression)
```

Here is a sample use:

```
struct dat {short a; short b};
long value = 0xA224B118;
dat * pd = reinterpret_cast< dat *> (&value);
cout << pd->a;   // display first 2 bytes of value
```

Typically, such type casts would be used for low-level, implementation-dependent programming and would not be portable. For example, this code sample produces different output on an IBM-compatible machine than it does on a Macintosh because the two systems store the bytes in multibyte integer types in opposite orders.

The `reinterpret_cast` operator doesn't allow just anything, however. For example, you can cast a pointer type to an integer type that's large enough to hold the pointer representation, but you can't cast a pointer to a smaller integer type or to a floating-point type. Another restriction is that you can't cast a function pointer to a data pointer or vice versa.

The plain type cast in C++ is also restricted. Basically, it can do anything the other type casts can do, plus some combinations, such as a `static_cast` or `reinterpret_cast` followed by a `const_cast`, but it can't do anything else. Thus the type cast

```
char ch = char (&d);          // type cast #2 - convert address to a char
```

is allowed in C but, typically, not in C++ because for most C++ implementations the `char` type is too small to hold a pointer implementation.

These restrictions make sense, but if you find such enforced good judgment oppressive, you still have C available.

Summary

Friends allow you to develop a more flexible interface for classes. A class can have other functions, other classes, and member functions of other classes as friends. In some cases, you may need to use forward declarations and to exert care in the ordering of class declarations and methods in order to get friends to mesh properly.

Nested classes are classes that are declared within other classes. Nested classes facilitate the design of helper classes that implement other classes but needn't be part of a public interface.

The C++ exception mechanism provides a flexible way to deal with awkward programming events such as inappropriate values, failed I/O attempts, and the like. Throwing an exception terminates the function currently executing and transfers control to a matching `catch` block. `catch` blocks immediately follow a `try` block, and for an exception to be caught, the function call that directly or indirectly led to the exception must be in the `try` block. The program then executes the code in the `catch` block. This code may attempt to fix the problem, or it can terminate the program. A class can be designed with nested exception classes that can be thrown when problems specific to the class are detected. A function can include an exception specification that identifies the exceptions that can be thrown in that function. Uncaught exceptions (those with no matching `catch` block) by default terminate a program. So do unexpected exceptions (those not matching an exception specification.)

The RTTI features allow a program to detect the type of an object. The `dynamic_cast` operator is used to cast a derived-class pointer to a base-class pointer; its main purpose is to ensure that it's okay to invoke a virtual function call. The `typeid` operator returns a `type_info` object. Two `typeid` return values can be compared to determine whether an object is of a specific type, and the returned `type_info` object can be used to obtain information about an object.

The `dynamic_cast`, `static_cast`, `const_cast`, and `reinterpret_cast` operators provide safer, better-documented type casts than the general type cast mechanism.

Review Questions

1. What's wrong with the following attempts at establishing friends?

   a.

```
class snap {
    friend clasp;
    ...
};
class clasp { ... };
```

   b.

```
class cuff {
public:
    void snip(muff &) { ... }
    ...
};
class muff {
    friend void cuff::snip(muff &);
    ...
};
```

   c.

```
class muff {
    friend void cuff::snip(muff &);
    ...
};
class cuff {
public:
    void snip(muff &) { ... }
    ...
};
```

2. You've seen how to create mutual class friends. Can you create a more restricted form of friendship in which only some members of Class B are friends to Class A and some members of A are friends to B? Explain.

3. What problems might the following nested class declaration have?

```
class Ribs
{
private:
    class Sauce
    {
        int soy;
        int sugar;
    public:
        Sauce(int s1, int s2) : soy(s1), sugar(s2) { }
    };
    ...
};
```

4. How does `throw` differ from `return`?

5. Suppose you have a hierarchy of exception classes that are derived from a base exception class. In what order should you place `catch` blocks?

6. Consider the `Grand`, `Superb`, and `Magnificent` classes defined in this chapter. Suppose `pg` is a type `Grand *` pointer that is assigned the address of an object of one of these three classes and that `ps` is a type `Superb *` pointer. What is the difference in how the following two code samples behave?

```
if (ps = dynamic_cast<Superb *>(pg))
    ps->say();  // sample #1

if (typeid(*pg) == typeid(Superb))
    (Superb *) pg)->say();  // sample #2
```

7. How is the `static_cast` operator different from the `dynamic_cast` operator?

Programming Exercises

1. Modify the `Tv` and `Remote` classes as follows:

   a. Make them mutual friends.

   b. Add a state variable member to the `Remote` class that describes whether the remote control is in normal or interactive mode.

   c. Add a `Remote` method that displays the mode.

   d. Provide the `Tv` class with a method for toggling the new `Remote` member. This method should work only if the TV is in the on state.

   Write a short program that tests these new features.

2. Modify Listing 15.11 so that the two exception types are classes derived from the `logic_error` class provided by the `<stdexcept>` header file. Have each `what()` method report the function name and the nature of the problem. The exception objects need not hold the bad values; they should just support the `what()` method.

3. This exercise is the same as Programming Exercise 2, except that the exceptions should be derived from a base class (itself derived from `logic_error`) that stores the two argument values, the exceptions should have a method that reports these values as well as the function name, and a single `catch` block that catches the base-class exemption should be used for both exceptions, with either exception causing the loop to terminate.

4. Listing 15.16 uses two `catch` blocks after each `try` block so that the `nbad_index` exception leads to the `label_val()` method being invoked. Modify the program so that it uses a single `catch` block after each `try` block and uses RTTI to handle invoking `label_val()` only when appropriate.

CHAPTER 16

THE string CLASS AND THE STANDARD TEMPLATE LIBRARY

In this chapter you'll learn about the following:

- The standard C++ string class
- The auto_ptr template
- The Standard Template Library (STL)
- Container classes
- Iterators
- Function objects (functors)
- STL algorithms

B y now you are familiar with the C++ goal of reusable code. One of the big payoffs is when you can reuse code written by others. That's where class libraries come in. There are many commercially available C++ class libraries, and there are also libraries that come as part of the C++ package. For example, you've been using the input/output classes supported by the **ostream** header file. This chapter looks at other reusable code available for your programming pleasure.

You've already encountered the **string** class, and this chapter examines it more extensively. Then the chapter looks at **auto_ptr**, a "smart pointer" template class that makes managing dynamic memory a bit easier. Finally, it looks at the Standard Template Library (STL), a collection of useful templates for handling various kinds of container objects. The STL exemplifies a recent programming paradigm called *generic programming*.

The string Class

Many programming applications need to process strings. C provides some support with its **string.h** (**cstring** in C++) family of string functions, and many early C++ implementations provide home-grown classes to handle strings. Chapter 4, "Compound Types," introduces the ANSI/ISO C++ **string class**. Chapter 12, "Classes and Dynamic Memory Allocation," with its modest **String** class, illustrates some aspects of designing a class to represent strings.

Recall that the `string` class is supported by the `string` header file. (Note that the `string.h` and `cstring` header files support the C library string functions for C-style strings, not the `string` class.) The key to using a class is knowing its public interface, and the `string` class has an extensive set of methods, including several constructors, overloaded operators for assigning strings, concatenating strings, comparing strings, and accessing individual elements, as well as utilities for finding characters and substrings in a string, and more. In short, the `string` class has lots to offer.

Constructing a String

Let's look at the `string` constructors. After all, one of the most important things to know about a class is what your options are when creating objects of that class. Listing 16.1 uses all six of the `string` constructors (labeled `ctor`, the traditional C++ abbreviation for *constructor*). Table 16.1 briefly describes the constructors, in the order used in the program. The constructor representations are simplified in that they conceal the fact that `string` really is a `typedef` for a template specialization `basic_string<char>` and that they omit an optional argument relating to memory management. (This aspect is discussed later this chapter and in Appendix F, "The `string` Template Class.") The type `size_type` is an implementation-dependent integral type defined in the `string` header file. The class defines `string::npos` as the maximum possible length of the string. Typically, this would equal the maximum value of an `unsigned int`. Also, the table uses the common abbreviation NBTS for null-byte-terminated string—that is, the traditional C string, which is terminated with a null character.

LISTING 16.1   `str1.cpp`

```cpp
// str1.cpp -- introducing the string class
#include <iostream>
#include <string>
// using string constructors

int main()
{
    using namespace std;
    string one("Lottery Winner!");   // ctor #1
    cout << one << endl;             // overloaded <<
    string two(20, '$');             // ctor #2
    cout << two << endl;
    string three(one);               // ctor #3
    cout << three << endl;
    one += " Oops!";                 // overloaded +=
    cout << one << endl;
    two = "Sorry! That was ";
    three[0] = 'P';
    string four;                     // ctor #4
    four = two + three;              // overloaded +, =
    cout << four << endl;
    char alls[] = "All's well that ends well";
    string five(alls,20);            // ctor #5
```

LISTING 16.1   Continued

```
        cout << five << "!\n";
        string six(alls+6, alls + 10);    // ctor #6
        cout << six  << ", ";
        string seven(&five[6], &five[10]);// ctor #6 again
        cout << seven << "...\n";

        return 0;
    }
```

TABLE 16.1   string Class Constructors

Constructor	Description
string(const char * s)	Initializes a string object to the NBTS pointed to by s.
string(size_type n, char c)	Creates a string object of n elements, each initialized to the character c.
string(const string & str, string size_type n = npos)	Initializes a string object to size_type pos = 0, the object str, starting at position pos in str and going to end of str or using n characters, whichever comes first.
string()	Creates a default string object of 0 size.
string(const char * s, size_type n)	Initializes a string object to the NBTS pointed to by s and continues for n characters, even if that exceeds the size of the NBTS.
template<class Iter> string(Iter begin, Iter end)	Initializes a string object to the values in the range [begin, end), where begin and end act like pointers and specify locations; the range includes begin and is up to but not including end.

The program in Listing 16.1 also uses the overloaded += operator, which appends one string to another, the overloaded = operator for assigning one string to another, the overloaded << operator for displaying a string object, and the overloaded [] operator for accessing an individual character in a string.

Compatibility Note

Some older string implementations do not support ctor #6 in Table 16.1. (Recall that ctor is C++-speak for *constructor*.)

Here is the output of the program in Listing 16.1:

```
Lottery Winner!
$$$$$$$$$$$$$$$$$$$$
Lottery Winner!
Lottery Winner! Oops!
Sorry! That was Pottery Winner!
All's well that ends!
well, well...
```

Program Notes

The start of the program in Listing 16.1 illustrates that you can initialize a `string` object to a regular C-style string and display it by using the overloaded `<<` operator:

```
string one("Lottery Winner!");    // ctor #1
cout << one << endl;              // overloaded <<
```

The next constructor initializes the `string` object `two` to a string consisting of 20 `$` characters:

```
string two(20, '$');             // ctor #2
```

The copy constructor initializes the `string` object `three` to the `string` object `one`:

```
string three(one);               // ctor #3
```

The overloaded `+=` operator appends the string `" Oops!"` to the string `one`:

```
one += " Oops!";                 // overloaded +=
```

This particular example appends a C-style string to a `string` object. However, the `+=` operator is multiply overloaded so that you can also append `string` objects and single characters:

```
one += two;   // append a string object (not in program)
one += '!';   // append a type char value (not in program)
```

Similarly, the `=` operator is overloaded so that you can assign a `string` object to a `string` object, a C-style string to a `string` object, or a simple `char` value to a `string` object:

```
two = "Sorry! That was "; // assign a C-style string
two = one;                // assign a string object (not in program)
two = '?';                // assign a char value (not in program)
```

Overloading the `[]` operator, as the `String` example in Chapter 12 does, permits access to individual characters in a `string` object by using array notation:

```
three[0] = 'P';
```

A default constructor creates an empty string that can later be given a value:

```
string four;                     // ctor #4
four = two + three;              // overloaded +, =
```

The second line here uses the overloaded `+` operator to create a temporary `string` object, which is then assigned, using the overloaded `=` operator, to the `four` object. As you might expect, the `+` operator concatenates its two operands into a single `string` object. The operator is multiply overloaded, so the second operand can be a `string` object or a C-style string or a `char` value.

The fifth constructor takes a C-style string and an integer as arguments, with the integer indicating how many characters to copy:

```
char alls[] = "All's well that ends well";
string five(alls,20);              // ctor #5
```

Here, as the output shows, just the first 20 characters ("All's well that ends") are used to initialize the five object. As Table 16.1 notes, if the character count exceeds the length of the C-style string, the requested number of characters is still copied. So replacing 20 with 40 in the preceding example would result in 15 junk characters being copied at the end of five. (That is, the constructor would interpret the contents in memory following the string "All's well that ends well" as character codes.)

The sixth constructor has a template argument:

```
template<class Iter> string(Iter begin, Iter end);
```

The intent is that *begin* and *end* act like pointers pointing to two locations in memory. (In general, *begin* and *end* can be iterators, generalizations of pointers extensively used in the STL.) The constructor then uses the values between the locations pointed to by *begin* and *end* to initialize the string object it constructs. The notation [*begin*, *end*), borrowed from mathematics, means the range includes *begin* but doesn't include *end*. That is, *end* points to a location one past the last value to be used. Consider the following statement:

```
string six(alls+6, alls + 10);     // ctor #6
```

Because the name of an array is a pointer, both alls + 6 and alls + 10 are type char *, so the template is used with Iter replaced by type char *. The first argument points to the first w in the alls array, and the second argument points to the space following the first well. Thus, six is initialized to the string "well". Figure 16.1 shows how the constructor works.

FIGURE 16.1

A string constructor using a range.

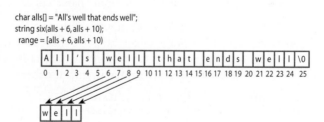

Now suppose you want to use this constructor to initialize an object to part of another string object—say, the object five. The following does not work:

```
string seven(five + 6, five + 10);
```

The reason is that the name of an object, unlike the name of an array, is not treated as the address of an object, hence five is not a pointer and five + 6 is meaningless. However, five[6] is a char value, so &five[6] is an address and can be used as an argument to the constructor:

```
string seven(&five[6], &five[10]);// ctor #6 again
```

`string` Class Input

Another useful thing to know about a class is what input options are available. For C-style strings, recall, you have three options:

```
char info[100];
cin >> info;              // read a word
cin.getline(info, 100);   // read a line, discard \n
cin.get(info, 100);       // read a line, leave \n in queue
```

For **string** objects, recall, you have two options:

```
string stuff;
cin >> stuff;             // read a word
getline(cin, stuff);      // read a line, discard \n
```

Both versions of **getline()** allow for an optional argument that specifies which character to use to delimit input:

```
cin.getline(info,100,':');    // read up to :, discard :
getline(stuff, ':');          // read up to :, discard :
```

The main operational difference is that the **string** versions automatically size the target **string** object to hold the input characters:

```
char fname[10];
string lname;
cin >> fname;       // could be a problem if input size > 9 characters
cin >> lname;       // can read a very, very long word
cin.getline(fname, 10);  // may truncate input
getline(cin, fname);     // no truncation
```

The automatic sizing feature allows the **string** version of **getline()** to dispense with the numeric parameter that limits the number of input characters to be read.

A design difference is that the C-style string input facilities are methods of the **istream** class, whereas the **string** versions are standalone functions. That's why **cin** is an invoking object for C-style string input and a function argument for **string** object input. This applies to the **>>** form, too, which is evident if the code is written in function form:

```
cin.operator>>(fname);    // ostream class method
operator>>(cin, lname);   // regular function
```

Let's examine the string input functions a bit more closely. Both, as mentioned, size the target string to fit the input. There are limits. The first limiting factor is the maximum allowable size for a string, represented by the constant **string::npos**. This, typically, is the maximum value of an **unsigned int**, so it doesn't pose a practical limit for ordinary, interactive input. It could be a factor, however, if you attempt to read the contents of an entire file into a single string. The second limiting factor is the amount of memory available to a program.

The **getline()** function for the **string** class reads characters from the input and stores them in a string until one of three things occurs:

- The end-of-file is encountered, in which case `eofbit` of the input stream is set, implying that both the `fail()` and `eof()` methods will return `true`.

- The delimiting character (`\n`, by default) is reached, in which case it is removed from the input stream but not stored.

- The maximum possible number of characters (the lesser of `string::npos` and the number of bytes in memory available for allocation) is read, in which case `failbit` of the input stream is set, implying that the `fail()` method will return `true`.

(An input stream object has an accounting system to keep track of the error state of the stream. In this system, setting `eofbit` registers detecting the end-of-file; setting `failbit` registers detecting an input error; setting `badbit` registers some unrecognized failure, such as a hardware failure; and setting `goodbit` indicates that all is well. Chapter 17 discusses this further.)

The `operator>>()` function for the `string` class behaves similarly, except that instead of reading to, and discarding, a delimiting character, it reads up to a white-space character and leaves that character in the input queue. A white-space character is a space, newline, or tab character, or, more generally, any character for which `isspace()` returns `true`.

So far in this book, you've seen several examples of console `string` input. Because the input functions for `string` objects work with streams and recognize the end-of-file, you can also use them for file input. Listing 16.2 shows a short example that reads strings from the file. It assumes that the file contains strings separated by the colon character and uses the `getline()` method of specifying a delimiter. It then numbers and displays the strings, one string to an output line.

LISTING 16.2   strfile.cpp

```cpp
// strfile.cpp -- read strings from a file
#include <iostream>
#include <fstream>
#include <string>
#include <cstdlib>
int main()
{
    using namespace std;
    ifstream fin;
    fin.open("tobuy.txt");
    if (fin.is_open() == false)
    {
        cerr << "Can't open file. Bye.\n";
        exit(EXIT_FAILURE);
    }
    string item;
    int count = 0;

    getline(fin, item, ':');
    while (fin)  // while input is good
    {
```

LISTING 16.2   Continued

```
        ++count;
        cout << count <<": " << item << endl;
        getline(fin, item,':');
    }
    cout << "Done\n";
    fin.close();
    return 0;
}
```

Here is a sample `tobuy.txt` file:

```
sardines:chocolate ice cream:pop corn:leeks:
cottage cheese:olive oil:butter:tofu:
```

Typically, for the program to find the text file, the text file should be in the same directory as the executable program, or, sometimes, in the same directory as the project file. Or you can provide the full path name. On a Windows or DOS system, keep in mind that in a C-style string the escape sequence \\ represents a single backslash:

```
fin.open("C:\\CPP\\Progs\\tobuy.txt"); // file = C:\CPP\Progs\tobuy.txt
```

Here is the output of the program in Listing 16.2:

```
1: sardines
2: chocolate ice cream
3: pop corn
4: leeks
5:
cottage cheese
6: olive oil
7: butter
8: tofu
9:

Done
```

Note that with `:` specified as the delimiting character, the newline character becomes just another regular character. Thus, the newline character at the end of the first line of the file becomes the first character of the string that continues as `"cottage cheese"`. Similarly, the newline character at the end of the second input line becomes the sole content of the ninth input string.

Working with Strings

So far, you've learned that you can create `string` objects in a variety of ways, display the contents of a `string` object, read data into a `string` object, append to a `string` object, assign to a `string` object, and concatenate two `string` objects. What else can you do?

You can compare strings. All six relational operators are overloaded for **string** objects, with one object being considered less than another if it occurs earlier in the machine collating sequence. If the machine collating sequence is the ASCII code, that implies that digits are less than uppercase characters and uppercase characters are less than lowercase characters. Each relational operator is overloaded three ways so that you can compare a **string** object with another **string** object, compare a **string** object with a C-style string, and compare a C-style string with a **string** object:

```
string snake1("cobra");
string snake2("coral");
char snake3[20] = "anaconda";
if (snake1 < snake 2)           // operator<(const string &, const string &)
    ...
if (snake1 == snake3)           // operator==(const string &, const char *)
    ...
if (snake3 != snake2)           // operator!=(const char *, const string &)
    ...
```

You can determine the size of a string. Both the **size()** and **length()** member functions return the number of characters in a string:

```
if (snake1.length() == snake2.size())
    cout << "Both strings have the same length.\n"
```

Why two functions that do the same thing? The **length()** member comes from earlier versions of the **string** class, and **size()** was added for STL compatibility.

You can search a string for a given substring or character in a variety of ways. Table 16.2 provides a short description of four variations of a **find()** method. Recall that **string::npos** is the maximum possible number of characters in a string, typically the largest **unsigned int** or **unsigned long** value.

TABLE 16.2   The Overloaded **find()** Method

Method Prototype	Description
size_type find(const string & *str*, size_type *pos* = 0) const	Finds the first occurrence of the substring *str*, starting the search at location *pos* in the invoking string. Returns the index of the first character of the substring if found, and returns string::npos otherwise.
size_type find(const char * s, size_type *pos* = 0) const	Finds the first occurrence of the substring *s*, starting the search at location *pos* in the invoking string. Returns the index of the first character of the substring if found, and returns string::npos otherwise.

TABLE 16.2   Continued

Method Prototype	Description
`size_type find(const char * s,` `size_type pos = 0, size_type n)`	Finds the first occurrence of the substring consisting of the first *n* characters in *s*, starting the search at location *pos* in the invoking string. Returns the index of the first character of the substring if found, and returns `string::npos` otherwise.
`size_type find(char ch,` `size_type pos = 0) const`	Finds the first occurrence of the character *ch*, starting the search at location *pos* in the invoking string. Returns the index of the character if found, and returns `string::npos` otherwise.

The `string` library also provides the related methods `rfind()`, `find_first_of()`, `find_last_of()`, `find_first_not_of()`, and `find_last_not_of()`, each with the same set of overloaded function signatures as the `find()` method. The `rfind()` method finds the last occurrence of a substring or character. The `find_first_of()` method finds the first occurrence in the invoking string of any of the characters in the argument. For example, the statement

```
int where = snake1.find_first_of("hark");
```

would return the location of the `r` in `"cobra"` (that is, the index 3) because that's the first occurrence of any of the letters in `"hark"` in `"cobra"`. The `find_last_of()` method works the same, except it finds the last occurrence. Thus, the statement

```
int where = snake1.last_first_of("hark");
```

would return the location of the `a` in `"cobra"`. The `find_first_not_of()` method finds the first character in the invoking string that is not a character in the argument. So

```
int where = snake1.find_first_not_of("hark");
```

would return the location of the `c` in `cobra` because `c` is not found in `hark`. (You'll learn about `find_last_not_of()` in an exercise at the end of this chapter.)

There are many more methods, but these are enough to put together a sample program that's a graphically impaired version of the word game Hangman. The game stores a list of words in an array of `string` objects, picks a word at random, and lets you guess letters in the word. Six wrong guesses, and you lose. The program uses the `find()` function to check your guesses and the `+=` operator to build a `string` object to keep track of your wrong guesses. To keep track of your good guesses, the program creates a word the same length as the mystery word but consisting of hyphens. The hyphens are then replaced by correct guesses. Listing 16.3 shows the program.

LISTING 16.3   hangman.cpp

```cpp
// hangman.cpp -- some string methods
#include <iostream>
#include <string>
#include <cstdlib>
#include <ctime>
#include <cctype>
using std::string;
const int NUM = 26;
const string wordlist[NUM] = {"apiary", "beetle", "cereal",
    "danger", "ensign", "florid", "garage", "health", "insult",
    "jackal", "keeper", "loaner", "manage", "nonce", "onset",
    "plaid", "quilt", "remote", "stolid", "train", "useful",
    "valid", "whence", "xenon", "yearn", "zippy"};

int main()
{
    using std::cout;
    using std::cin;
    using std::tolower;
    using std::endl;

    std::srand(std::time(0));
    char play;
    cout << "Will you play a word game? <y/n> ";
    cin >> play;
    play = tolower(play);
    while (play == 'y')
    {
        string target = wordlist[std::rand() % NUM];
        int length = target.length();
        string attempt(length, '-');
        string badchars;
        int guesses = 6;
        cout << "Guess my secret word. It has " << length
            << " letters, and you guess\n"
            << "one letter at a time. You get " << guesses
            << " wrong guesses.\n";
        cout << "Your word: " << attempt << endl;
        while (guesses > 0 && attempt != target)
        {
            char letter;
            cout << "Guess a letter: ";
            cin >> letter;
            if (badchars.find(letter) != string::npos
                || attempt.find(letter) != string::npos)
            {
                cout << "You already guessed that. Try again.\n";
                    continue;
            }
            int loc = target.find(letter);
            if (loc == string::npos)
            {
```

LISTING 16.3   Continued

```
                cout << "Oh, bad guess!\n";
                --guesses;
                badchars += letter; // add to string
            }
            else
            {
                cout << "Good guess!\n";
                attempt[loc]=letter;
                // check if letter appears again
                loc = target.find(letter, loc + 1);
                while (loc != string::npos)
                {
                    attempt[loc]=letter;
                    loc = target.find(letter, loc + 1);
                }
            }
            cout << "Your word: " << attempt << endl;
            if (attempt != target)
            {
                if (badchars.length() > 0)
                    cout << "Bad choices: " << badchars << endl;
                cout << guesses << " bad guesses left\n";
            }
        }
        if (guesses > 0)
            cout << "That's right!\n";
        else
            cout << "Sorry, the word is " << target << ".\n";

        cout << "Will you play another? <y/n> ";
        cin >> play;
        play = tolower(play);
    }

    cout << "Bye\n";

    return 0;
}
```

Here's a sample run of the program in Listing 16.3:

```
Will you play a word game? <y/n> y
Guess my secret word. It has 6 letters, and you guess
one letter at a time. You get 6 wrong guesses.
Your word: ------
Guess a letter: e
Oh, bad guess!
Your word: ------
Bad choices: e
5 bad guesses left
Guess a letter: a
Good guess!
Your word: a--a--
```

```
Bad choices: e
5 bad guesses left
Guess a letter: t
Oh, bad guess!
Your word: a--a--
Bad choices: et
4 bad guesses left
Guess a letter: r
Good guess!
Your word: a--ar-
Bad choices: et
4 bad guesses left
Guess a letter: y
Good guess!
Your word: a--ary
Bad choices: et
4 bad guesses left
Guess a letter: i
Good guess!
Your word: a-iary
Bad choices: et
4 bad guesses left
Guess a letter: p
Good guess!
Your word: apiary
That's right!
Will you play another? <y/n> n
Bye
```

Program Notes

In Listing 16.3, the fact that the relational operators are overloaded lets you treat strings in the same fashion you would treat numeric variables:

```
while (guesses > 0 && attempt != target)
```

This is easier to follow than, say, using `strcmp()` with C-style strings.

The program uses `find()` to check whether a character was selected earlier; if it was already selected, it will be found in either the `badchars` string (bad guesses) or in the `attempt` string (good guesses):

```
if (badchars.find(letter) != string::npos
    || attempt.find(letter) != string::npos)
```

The `npos` variable is a static member of the `string` class. Its value, recall, is the maximum allowable number of characters for a `string` object. Therefore, because indexing begins at zero, it is one greater than the largest possible index and can be used to indicate failure to find a character or a string.

The program makes use of the fact that one of the overloaded versions of the += operator lets you append individual characters to a string:

```
badchars += letter;  // append a char to a string object
```

The heart of the program begins by checking whether the chosen letter is in the mystery word:

```
int loc = target.find(letter);
```

If `loc` is a valid value, the letter can be placed in the corresponding location in the answer string:

```
attempt[loc]=letter;
```

However, a given letter might occur more than once in the mystery word, so the program has to keep checking. The program uses the optional second argument to `find()`, which specifies a starting place in the string from which to begin the search. Because the letter was found at location `loc`, the next search should begin at `loc + 1`. A `while` loop keeps the search going until no more occurrences of that character are found. Note that `find()` indicates failure if `loc` is after the end of the string:

```
// check if letter appears again
loc = target.find(letter, loc + 1);
while (loc != string::npos)
{
    attempt[loc]=letter;
    loc = target.find(letter, loc + 1);
}
```

What Else Does the `string` Class Offer?

The `string` library supplies many other facilities. There are functions for erasing part or all of a string, for replacing part or all of one string with part or all of another string, for inserting material into a string or removing material from a string, for comparing part or all of one string with part or all of another string, and for extracting a substring from a string. There's a function for copying part of one string to another string, and there's a function for swapping the contents of two strings. Most of these functions are overloaded so that they can work with C-style strings as well as with `string` objects. Appendix F describes the string library function briefly, but let's talk about a few more features here.

First, think about the automatic sizing feature. In Listing 16.3, what happens each time the program appends a letter to a string? It can't necessarily just grow the string in place because it might run into neighboring memory that is already in use. So it may have to allocate a new block and then copy the old contents to a new location. It would be inefficient to do this a lot, so many C++ implementations allocate a block of memory larger than the actual string, giving the string room to grow. Then, if the string eventually exceeds that size, the program allocates a new block twice the size, to afford more room to grow without continuous resizing. The `capacity()` method returns the size of the current block, and the `reserve()` method allows you to request a minimum size for the block. Listing 16.4 shows an example that uses these methods.

LISTING 16.4   str2.cpp

```cpp
// str2.cpp -- capacity() and reserve()
#include <iostream>
#include <string>
int main()
{
    using namespace std;
    string empty;
    string small = "bit";
    string larger = "Elephants are a girl's best friend";
    cout << "Sizes:\n";
    cout << "\tempty: " << empty.size() << endl;
    cout << "\tsmall: " << small.size() << endl;
    cout << "\tlarger: " << larger.size() << endl;
    cout << "Capacities:\n";
    cout << "\tempty: " << empty.capacity() << endl;
    cout << "\tsmall: " << small.capacity() << endl;
    cout << "\tlarger: " << larger.capacity() << endl;
    empty.reserve(50);
    cout << "Capacity after empty.reserve(50): "
         << empty.capacity() << endl;
    return 0;
}
```

Here is the output of the program in Listing 16.4 for one C++ implementation:

```
Sizes:
        empty: 0
        small: 3
        larger: 34
Capacities:
        empty: 15
        small: 15
        larger: 47
Capacity after empty.reserve(50): 63
```

Note that this implementation uses a minimum capacity of 15 characters and seems to use 1 less than multiples of 16 as standard choices for capacities. Other implementations may make different choices.

What if you have a **string** object but need a C-style string? For example, you might want to open a file whose name is in a **string** object:

```cpp
string filename;
cout << "Enter file name: ";
cin >> filename;
ofstream fout;
```

The bad news is that the **open()** method requires a C-style string argument. The good news is that the **c_str()** method returns a pointer to a C-style string that has the same contents as the invoking **string** object. So you can use this:

```cpp
fout.open(filename.c_str());
```

Real-World Note: Overloading C Functions to Use string Objects

You can use the overloaded == operator to compare `string` objects. However, the case-sensitive nature in which the == operator performs its equality comparison can be a problem in some cases. Often, two strings need to be compared for equality without respect to their case. For example, a program may compare input from a user with a constant value, and the user may not use the same case. Listing 16.3 gets around this problem by converting all input to lowercase. There may be another option. Many C libraries provide a `stricmp()` or `_stricmp()` function that does a non-case-sensitive test. (However, this function isn't listed in the C Standard, so it's not universally available.) By creating your own overloaded version of this function, you can cobble together a simple workaround:

```
#include <cstring>  // for stricmp() on many systems
#include <string>    // string object
inline bool stricmp( const std::string& strA,
                     const std::string& strB )  // overloaded function
{
   return stricmp( strA.c_str(), strB.c_str() ) == 0;    // C function
}

string strA;
cin >> strA;  // assume user enters Maplesyrup
string strB = "mapleSyrup";  // stored constant


bool bStringsAreEqual = stricmp( strA, strB );
```

Using simplified syntax, you can now compare two strings for equality without regard to case. More generally, the `c_str()` method provides a path for converting C-style string functions to `string` object functions.

This section treats the **string** class as if it were based on the **char** type. In fact, as mentioned earlier, the string library really is based on a template class:

```
template<class charT, class traits = char _traits<charT>,
      class Allocator = allocator<charT> >
basic_string {...};
```

The class includes the following two **typedef**s:

```
typedef basic_string<char> string;
typedef basic_string<wchar_t> wstring;
```

This allows you to use strings based on the wchar_t as well as the char type. You could even develop some sort of character-like class and use the **basic_string** class template with it, provided that your class met certain requirements. The **traits** class is a class that describes specific facts about the chosen character type, such as how to compare values. There are predefined specializations of the **char_traits** template for the **char** and **wchar_t** types, and these are the default values for **traits**. The **Allocator** class represents a class to manage memory allocation. There are predefined specializations of the **allocator** template for the **char** and **wchar_t** types, and these are the defaults. They use **new** and **delete** in the usual fashion, but you could reserve a chunk of memory and provide your own allocation methods.

The auto_ptr Class

The `auto_ptr` class is a template class for managing the use of dynamic memory allocation. Let's take a look at what might be needed and how it can be accomplished. Consider the following function:

```
void remodel(string & str)
{
    string * ps = new string(str);
    ...
    str = ps;
    return;
}
```

You probably see its flaw. Each time the function is called, it allocates memory from the heap but never returns it, creating a memory leak. You also know the solution—just remember to free the allocated memory by adding the following statement just before the **return** statement:

```
delete ps;
```

However, a solution involving the phrase "just remember to" is seldom the best solution. Sometimes you won't remember. Or you will remember but accidentally remove or comment out the code. And even if you do remember, there can still be problems. Consider the following variation:

```
void remodel(string & str)
{
    string * ps = new string(str);
    ...
    if (weird_thing())
        throw exception();
    str = *ps;
    delete ps;
    return;
}
```

If the exception is thrown, the **delete** statement isn't reached, and again there is a memory leak.

You can fix that oversight, as illustrated in Chapter 14, "Reusing Code in C++," but it would be nice if there were a neater solution. Let's think about what is needed. When a function such as `remodel()` terminates, either normally or by throwing an exception, local variables are removed from the stack memory—so the memory occupied by the pointer **ps** is freed. It would be nice if the memory pointed to by **ps** were also freed. That means you would want the program to take an additional action when **ps** expires. That extra service is not provided for basic types, but it can be provided for classes via the destructor mechanism. Thus, the problem with **ps** is that it is just an ordinary pointer and not a class object. If it were an object, you could have its destructor delete the pointed-to memory when the object expires. And that is the idea behind `auto_ptr`.

Using `auto_ptr`

The `auto_ptr` template defines a pointer-like object intended to be assigned an address obtained (directly or indirectly) by `new`. When an `auto_ptr` object expires, its destructor uses `delete` to free the memory. Thus, if you assign an address returned by `new` to an `auto_ptr` object, you don't have to remember to free the memory later; it will be freed automatically when the `auto_ptr` object expires. Figure 16.2 illustrates the behavioral difference between `auto_ptr` and a regular pointer.

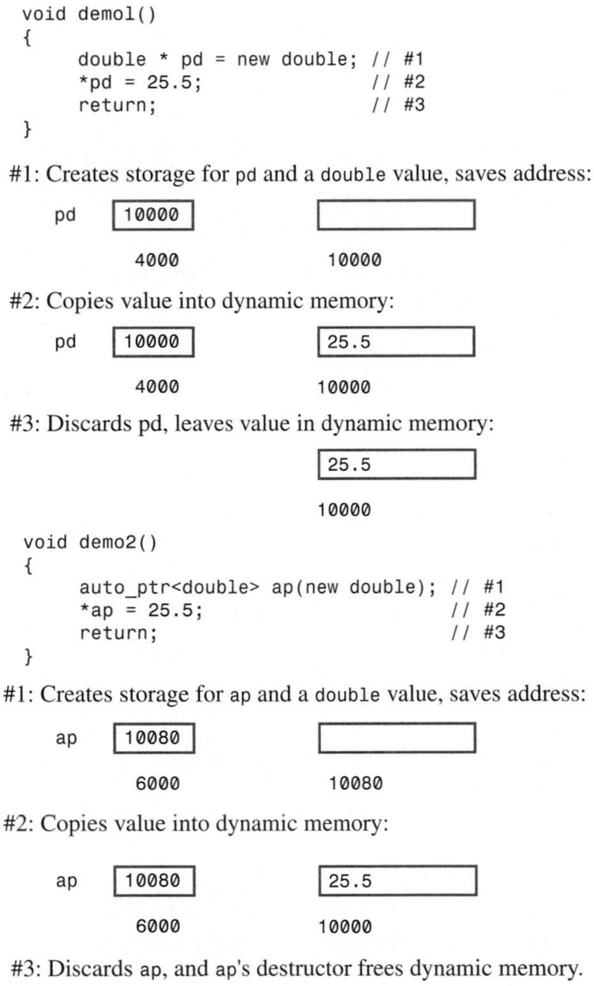

FIGURE 16.2

A regular pointer versus `auto_ptr`.

```
void demo1()
{
    double * pd = new double; // #1
    *pd = 25.5;                // #2
    return;                    // #3
}
```

#1: Creates storage for pd and a `double` value, saves address:

pd	`10000`
	4000

`        `
10000

#2: Copies value into dynamic memory:

pd	`10000`
	4000

`25.5`
10000

#3: Discards pd, leaves value in dynamic memory:

`25.5`
10000

```
void demo2()
{
    auto_ptr<double> ap(new double); // #1
    *ap = 25.5;                        // #2
    return;                            // #3
}
```

#1: Creates storage for ap and a `double` value, saves address:

ap	`10080`
	6000

`        `
10080

#2: Copies value into dynamic memory:

ap	`10080`
	6000

`25.5`
10000

#3: Discards ap, and ap's destructor frees dynamic memory.

To create an `auto_ptr` object, you include the `memory` header file, which includes the `auto_ptr` template. Then you use the usual template syntax to instantiate the kind of pointer you require. The template includes the following:

```
template<class X> class auto_ptr {
public:
    explicit auto_ptr(X* p =0) throw();
...};
```

(The `throw()` notation, recall, means this constructor doesn't throw an exception.) Thus, asking for an `auto_ptr` object of type X gives you an `auto_ptr` object that points to type X:

```
auto_ptr<double> pd(new double);  // an auto_ptr to double
                                  // (use in place of double *)
auto_ptr<string> ps(new string);  // an auto_ptr to string
                                  // (use in place of string *)
```

Here `new double` is a pointer returned by `new` to a newly allocated chunk of memory. It is the argument to the `auto_ptr<double>` constructor; that is, it is the actual argument corresponding to the formal parameter `p` in the prototype. Similarly, `new string` is also an actual argument for a constructor.

Thus, to convert the `remodel()` function, you would follow these three steps:

1. Include the `memory` header file.

2. Replace the pointer-to-`string` with an `auto_ptr` object that points to `string`.

3. Remove the `delete` statement.

Here's the function with those changes made:

```
#include <memory>
void remodel(string & str)
{
    auto_ptr<string> ps (new string(str));
    ...
    if (weird_thing())
        throw exception();
    str = *ps;
    // delete ps;  NO LONGER NEEDED
    return;
}
```

Note that the `auto_ptr` constructor is `explicit`, meaning there is no implicit type cast from a pointer to an `auto_ptr` object:

```
auto_ptr<double> pd;
double *p_reg = new double;
pd = p_reg;                     // not allowed (implicit conversion)
pd = auto_ptr<double>(p_reg); // allowed (explicit conversion
auto_ptr<double> pauto = p_reg;  // not allowed (implicit conversion)
auto_ptr<double> pauto(p_reg);   // allowed (explicit conversion
```

Note that the template allows you to initialize an `auto_ptr` object to an ordinary pointer via a constructor.

`auto_ptr` is an example of a *smart pointer*, an object that acts like a pointer but has additional features. The `auto_ptr` class is defined so that, in most respects, an `auto_ptr` object acts like a regular pointer. For example, given that `ps` is an `auto_ptr` object, you can dereference it (`*ps`), increment it (`++ps`), use it to access structure members (`ps->puffIndex`), and assign it to a regular pointer that points to the same type. You can also assign one `auto_ptr` object to another of the same type, but that raises an issue that the next section faces.

`auto_ptr` Considerations

`auto_ptr` is not a panacea. For example, consider the following code:

```
auto_ptr<int> pi(new int [200]);    // NO!
```

Remember, you must pair `delete` with `new` and `delete []` with `new []`. The `auto_ptr` template uses `delete`, not `delete []`, so it can only be used with `new`, not with `new []`. There is no `auto_ptr` equivalent for use with dynamic arrays. You could copy the `auto_ptr` template from the `memory` header file, rename it `auto_arr_ptr`, and convert the copy to use `delete []` instead of `delete`. In that case, you would want to add support for the `[]` operator.

What about the following?

```
string vacation("I wandered lonely as a cloud.");
auto_ptr<string> pvac(&vacation);  // NO!
```

This would apply the `delete` operator to non-heap memory, which is wrong.

Caution

You should use an `auto_ptr` object only for memory allocated by `new`, not for memory allocated by `new []` or by simply declaring a variable.

Now consider assignment:

```
auto_ptr<string> ps (new string("I reigned lonely as a cloud."));
auto_ptr<string> vocation;
vocation = ps;
```

What should the assignment statement accomplish? If `ps` and `vocation` were ordinary pointers, the result would be two pointers pointing to the same `string` object. That is not acceptable here because the program would wind up attempting to delete the same object twice—once when `ps` expires, and once when `vocation` expires. There are ways to avoid this problem:

- Define the assignment operator so that it makes a deep copy. This results in two pointers pointing to two distinct objects, one of which is a copy of the other.

- Institute the concept of *ownership*, with only one smart pointer allowed to own a particular object. Only if the smart pointer owns the object will its constructor delete the object. Then have assignment transfer ownership. This is the strategy used for `auto_ptr`.

- Create an even smarter pointer that keeps track of how many smart pointers refer to a particular object. This is called *reference counting*. Assignment, for example, would increase the count by one, and the expiration of a pointer would decrease the count by one. Only when the final pointer expires would `delete` be invoked.

The same strategies, of course, could also be applied to the copy constructors.

Each approach has its uses. Here's a situation, for example, that may not work properly using `auto_ptr` objects:

```
auto_ptr<string> films[5] =
{
    auto_ptr<string> (new string("Fowl Balls")),
    auto_ptr<string> (new string("Duck Walks")),
    auto_ptr<string> (new string("Chicken Runs")),
    auto_ptr<string> (new string("Turkey Errors")),
    auto_ptr<string> (new string("Goose Eggs"))
};
auto_ptr<string> pwin(films[2]);
int i;
cout << "The nominees for best avian baseball film are\n";
for (i = 0; i < 5; i++)
    cout << *films[i] << endl;
cout << "The winner is " << *pwin << "!\n";
```

The problem is that transferring ownership from `films[2]` to `pwin` may cause `films[2]` to no longer refer to the string. That is, after an `auto_ptr` object gives up ownership, it may no longer be usable. Whether it's usable or not is an implementation choice.

Smart Pointers

The C++ library `auto_ptr` object is an example of a smart pointer. A *smart pointer* is a class designed so that objects of that class have pointer-like properties. For example, a smart pointer can store the address of memory allocated by `new` and can be dereferenced. Because a smart pointer is a class object, it can modify and augment the behavior of a simple pointer. For instance, a smart pointer can institute reference counting. This allows several objects to share a single representation of a value tracked by a smart pointer. When the number of objects using the value drops to zero, the smart pointer can then delete the value. Smart pointers can allow for more efficient use of memory and help prevent memory leaks, but they do require the user to become familiar with new programming techniques.

The STL

The STL provides a collection of templates representing containers, iterators, function objects, and algorithms. A container is a unit, like an array, that can hold several values. STL containers are homogeneous; that is, they hold values all of the same kind. Algorithms are recipes for accomplishing particular tasks, such as sorting an array or finding a particular value in a list. Iterators are objects that let you move through a container much as pointers let you move through an array; they are generalizations of pointers. Function objects are objects that act like functions; they can be class objects or function pointers (including function names because a function name acts as a pointer). The STL lets you construct a variety of containers, including arrays, queues, and lists, and it lets you perform a variety of operations, including searching, sorting, and randomizing.

Alex Stepanov and Meng Lee developed STL at Hewlett-Packard Laboratories, releasing the implementation in 1994. The ISO/ANSI C++ committee voted to incorporate it as a part of the C++ Standard. The STL is not an example of object-oriented programming. Instead, it represents a different programming paradigm called *generic programming*. This makes STL interesting both in terms of what it does and in terms of its approach. There's too much information about the STL to present in a single chapter, so we'll look at some representative examples and examine the spirit of the generic programming approach. We'll begin by looking at a few specific examples. Then, when you have a hands-on appreciation for containers, iterators, and algorithms, we'll look at the underlying design philosophy and then take an overview of the whole STL. Appendix G, "The STL Methods and Functions," summarizes the various STL methods and functions.

The `vector` Template Class

In computing, the term *vector* corresponds to an array rather than to the mathematical vector discussed in Chapter 11, "Working with Classes." (Mathematically, an N-dimensional mathematical vector can be represented by a set of N components, so, in that aspect, a mathematical vector is like an N-dimensional array. However, a mathematical vector has additional properties, such as inner and outer products, that a computer vector doesn't necessarily have.) A computing-style vector holds a set of like values that can be accessed randomly. That is, you can use, say, an index to directly access the 10th element of a vector without having to access the preceding 9 elements first. So a `vector` class would provide operations similar to those of the `valarray` and `ArrayTP` classes introduced in Chapter 14. That is, you could create a `vector` object, assign one `vector` object to another, and use the `[]` operator to access `vector` elements. To make the class generic, you make it a template class. That's what the STL does, defining a `vector` template in the `vector` (formerly `vector.h`) header file.

To create a `vector` template object, you use the usual `<type>` notation to indicate the type to be used. Also, the `vector` template uses dynamic memory allocation, and you can use an initialization argument to indicate how many vector elements you want:

```
#include vector
using namespace std;
vector<int> ratings(5);      // a vector of 5 ints
int n;
cin >> n;
vector<double> scores(n);    // a vector of n doubles
```

After you create a `vector` object, operator overloading for `[]` makes it possible to use the usual array notation for accessing individual elements:

```
ratings[0] = 9;
for (int i = 0; i < n; i++)
    cout << scores[i] << endl;
```

> ## Allocators Again
>
> Like the string class, the various STL container templates take an optional template argument that specifies what allocator object to use to manage memory. For example, the vector template begins like this:
>
> ```
> template <class T, class Allocator = allocator<T> >
>     class vector {...
> ```
>
> If you omit a value for this template argument, the container template uses the allocator<T> class by default. This class uses new and delete in the standard ways.

Listing 16.5 uses this class in an undemanding application. This particular program creates two vector objects, one an int specialization and one a string specialization; each has five elements.

LISTING 16.5   vect1.cpp

```cpp
// vect1.cpp -- introducing the vector template
#include <iostream>
#include <string>
#include <vector>


const int NUM = 5;
int main()
{
    using std::vector;
    using std::string;
    using std::cin;
    using std::cout;
    using std::endl;

    vector<int> ratings(NUM);
    vector<string> titles(NUM);
    cout << "You will do exactly as told. You will enter\n"
        << NUM << " book titles and your ratings (0-10).\n";
    int i;
    for (i = 0; i < NUM; i++)
    {
        cout << "Enter title #" << i + 1 << ": ";
        getline(cin,titles[i]);
        cout << "Enter your rating (0-10): ";
        cin >> ratings[i];
        cin.get();
    }
    cout << "Thank you. You entered the following:\n"
        << "Rating\tBook\n";
    for (i = 0; i < NUM; i++)
    {
```

LISTING 16.5 Continued

```
            cout << ratings[i] << "\t" << titles[i] << endl;
    }

    return 0;
}
```

Compatibility Note

Older STL implementations use `vector.h` instead of the `vector` header file. Although the order of include files shouldn't matter, some older versions of g++ require the `string` header file to appear before STL header files. Older versions of the Microsoft Visual C++ `getline()` function have a bug that messes up synchronization of input and output.

Here's a sample run of the program in Listing 16.5:

```
You will do exactly as told. You will enter
5 book titles and your ratings (0-10).
Enter title #1: The Cat Who Knew C++
Enter your rating (0-10): 6
Enter title #2: Felonious Felines
Enter your rating (0-10): 4
Enter title #3: Warlords of Wonk
Enter your rating (0-10): 3
Enter title #4: Don't Touch That Metaphor
Enter your rating (0-10): 5
Enter title #5: Panic Oriented Programming
Enter your rating (0-10): 8
Thank you. You entered the following:
Rating  Book
6       The Cat Who Knew C++
4       Felonious Felines
3       Warlords of Wonk
5       Don't Touch That Metaphor
8       Panic Oriented Programming
```

All this program does is use the `vector` template as a convenient way to create a dynamically allocated array. The following section shows an example that uses more of the class methods.

Things to Do to Vectors

Besides allocating storage, what else can the `vector` template do for you? All the STL containers provide certain basic methods, including `size()`, which returns the number of elements in a container; `swap()`, which exchanges the contents of two containers; `begin()`, which returns an iterator that refers to the first element in a container and; `end()`, which returns an iterator that represents past-the-end for the container.

What's an iterator? It's a generalization of a pointer. In fact, it can be a pointer. Or it can be an object for which pointer-like operations such as dereferencing (for example, `operator*()`) and incrementing (for example, `operator++()`) have been defined. As you'll see later, generalizing pointers to iterators allows the STL to provide a uniform interface for a variety of container classes, including ones for which simple pointers wouldn't work. Each container class defines a suitable iterator. The type name for this iterator is a class scope typedef called iterator. For example, to declare an iterator for a type double specialization of vector, you would use this:

```
vector<double>::iterator pd;  // pd an iterator
```

Suppose scores is a vector<double> object:

```
vector<double> scores;
```

Then you can use the iterator pd use code like the following:

```
pd = scores.begin();  // have pd point to the first element
*pd = 22.3;           // dereference pd and assign value to first element
++pd;                 // make pd point to the next element
```

As you can see, an iterator behaves like a pointer.

What's *past-the-end*? It is an iterator that refers to an element one past the last element in a container. The idea is similar to the idea of the null character being one element past the last actual character in a C-style string, except that the null character is the value in the element, and past-the-end is a pointer (or iterator) to the element. The end() member function identifies the past-the-end location. If you set an iterator to the first element in a container and keep incrementing it, eventually it will reach past-the-end, and you will have traversed the entire contents of the container. Thus, if scores and pd are defined as in the preceding example, you can display the contents with this code:

```
for (pd = scores.begin(); pd != scores.end(); pd++)
    cout << *pd << endl;;
```

All containers have the methods just discussed. The vector template class also has some methods that only some STL containers have. One handy method, called push_back(), adds an element to the end of a vector. While doing so, it attends to memory management so that the vector size increases to accommodate added members. This means you can write code like the following:

```
vector<double> scores;  // create an empty vector
double temp;
while (cin >> temp && temp >= 0)
    scores.push_back(temp);
cout << "You entered " << scores.size() << " scores.\n";
```

Each loop cycle adds one more element to the scores vector. You don't have to pick the number of element when you write the program or when you run the program. As long as the program has access to sufficient memory, it will expand the size of scores as necessary.

The erase() method removes a given range of a vector. It takes two iterator arguments that define the range to be removed. It's important that you understand how the STL defines ranges using two iterators. The first iterator refers to the beginning of the range, and the second iterator is one beyond the end of the range. For example,

```
scores.erase(scores.begin(), scores.begin() + 2);
```

erases the first and second elements—that is, those referred to by `begin()` and `begin() + 1`. (Because `vector` provides random access, operations such as `begin() + 2` are defined for the `vector` class iterators.) If `it1` and `it2` are two iterators, the STL literature uses the notation [p1, p2) to indicate a range starting with `p1` and going up to, but not including, `p2`. Thus, the range [`begin()`, `end()`) encompasses the entire contents of a collection (see Figure 16.3). Also, the range [p1, p1) is an empty range. (The [) notation is not part of C++, so it doesn't appear in code; it just appears in documentation.)

Remember

A range [`it1`, `it2`) is specified by two iterators `it1` and `it2`, and it runs from `it1` up to, but not including, `it2`.

FIGURE 16.3

The STL range concept.

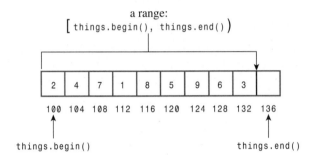

An `insert()` method complements `erase()`. It takes three iterator arguments. The first gives the position ahead of which new elements are to be inserted. The second and third iterator parameters define the range to be inserted. This range typically is part of another container object. For example, the code

```
vector<int> old;
vector<int> new;
...
old.insert(old.begin(), new.begin() + 1, new.end());
```

inserts all but the first element of the **new** vector ahead of the first element of the **old** vector. Incidentally, this is a case where having a past-the-end element is handy because it makes it simple to append something to the end of a vector. In the code

```
old.insert(old.end(), new.begin() + 1, new.end());
```

the new material is inserted ahead of `old.end()`, meaning it's placed *after* the last element in the vector.

Listing 16.6 illustrates the use of `size()`, `begin()`, `end()`, `push_back()`, `erase()`, and `insert()`. To simplify data handling, the `rating` and `title` components of Listing 16.5 are incorporated into a single `Review` structure, and `FillReview()` and `ShowReview()` functions provide input and output facilities for `Review` objects.

LISTING 16.6   vect2.cpp

```cpp
// vect2.cpp -- methods and iterators
#include <iostream>
#include <string>
#include <vector>

struct Review {
    std::string title;
    int rating;
};
bool FillReview(Review & rr);
void ShowReview(const Review & rr);
int main()
{
    using std::cout;
    using std::vector;
    vector<Review> books;
    Review temp;
    while (FillReview(temp))
        books.push_back(temp);
    int num = books.size();
    if (num > 0)
    {
        cout << "Thank you. You entered the following:\n"
            << "Rating\tBook\n";
        for (int i = 0; i < num; i++)
            ShowReview(books[i]);
        cout << "Reprising:\n"
            << "Rating\tBook\n";
        vector<Review>::iterator pr;
        for (pr = books.begin(); pr != books.end(); pr++)
            ShowReview(*pr);
        vector <Review> oldlist(books);     // copy constructor used
        if (num > 3)
        {
            // remove 2 items
            books.erase(books.begin() + 1, books.begin() + 3);
            cout << "After erasure:\n";
            for (pr = books.begin(); pr != books.end(); pr++)
                ShowReview(*pr);
            // insert 1 item
            books.insert(books.begin(), oldlist.begin() + 1,
                        oldlist.begin() + 2);
            cout << "After insertion:\n";
            for (pr = books.begin(); pr != books.end(); pr++)
                ShowReview(*pr);
        }
        books.swap(oldlist);
        cout << "Swapping oldlist with books:\n";
        for (pr = books.begin(); pr != books.end(); pr++)
            ShowReview(*pr);
    }
    else
```

LISTING 16.6   *Continued*

```
          cout << "Nothing entered, nothing gained.\n";
      return 0;
}

bool FillReview(Review & rr)
{
    std::cout << "Enter book title (quit to quit): ";
    std::getline(std::cin,rr.title);
    if (rr.title == "quit")
        return false;
    std::cout << "Enter book rating: ";
    std::cin >> rr.rating;
    if (!std::cin)
        return false;
    std::cin.get();
    return true;
}

void ShowReview(const Review & rr)
{
    std::cout << rr.rating << "\t" << rr.title << std::endl;
}
```

Compatibility Note

Older C++ implementations use `vector.h` instead of the `vector` header file. Although the order of include files shouldn't matter, some older versions of g++ require the `string` header file to appear before STL header files. Older versions of Microsoft Visual C++ 6.0 have a bug in the `getline()` implementation such that the following output doesn't appear until something is entered again. (In this example, the bug requires that the user press Enter twice after entering a title.)

Here is a sample run of the program in Listing 16.6:

```
Enter book title (quit to quit): The Cat Who Knew Vectors
Enter book rating: 5
Enter book title (quit to quit): Candid Canines
Enter book rating: 7
Enter book title (quit to quit): Warriors of Wonk
Enter book rating: 4
Enter book title (quit to quit): Quantum Manners
Enter book rating: 8
Enter book title (quit to quit): quit
Thank you. You entered the following:
Rating  Book
5       The Cat Who Knew Vectors
7       Candid Canines
4       Warriors of Wonk
8       Quantum Manners
Reprising:
Rating  Book
```

```
5          The Cat Who Knew Vectors
7          Candid Canines
4          Warriors of Wonk
8          Quantum Manners
After erasure:
5          The Cat Who Knew Vectors
8          Quantum Manners
After insertion:
7          Candid Canines
5          The Cat Who Knew Vectors
8          Quantum Manners
Swapping oldlist with books:
5          The Cat Who Knew Vectors
7          Candid Canines
4          Warriors of Wonk
8          Quantum Manners
```

More Things to Do to Vectors

There are many things programmers commonly do with arrays, such as search them, sort them, randomize the order, and so on. Does the vector template class have methods for these common operations? No! The STL takes a broader view, defining *nonmember* functions for these operations. Thus, instead of defining a separate find() member function for each container class, it defines a single find() nonmember function that can be used for all container classes. This design philosophy saves a lot of duplicate work. For example, suppose you had 8 container classes and 10 operations to support. If each class had its own member function, you'd need 8×10, or 80, separate member function definitions. But with the STL approach, you'd need just 10 separate nonmember function definitions. And if you defined a new container class, provided that you followed the proper guidelines, it, too, could use the existing 10 nonmember functions to find, sort, and so on.

Let's examine three representative STL functions: for_each(), random_shuffle(), and sort(). The for_each() function can be used with any container class. It takes three arguments. The first two are iterators that define a range in the container, and the last is a pointer to a function. (More generally, the last argument is a function object; you'll learn about function objects shortly.) The for_each() function then applies the pointed-to function to each container element in the range. The pointed-to function must not alter the value of the container elements. You can use the for_each() function instead of a for loop. For example, you can replace the code

```
vector<Review>::iterator pr;
for (pr = books.begin(); pr != books.end(); pr++)
    ShowReview(*pr);
```

with the following:

```
for_each(books.begin(), books.end(), ShowReview);
```

This enables you to avoid dirtying your hands (and code) with explicit use of iterator variables.

The `random_shuffle()` function takes two iterators that specify a range and rearranges the elements in that range in random order. For example, the statement

```
random_shuffle(books.begin(), books.end());
```

randomly rearranges the order of all the elements in the **books** vector. Unlike **for_each**, which works with any container class, this function requires that the container class allow random access, which the **vector** class does.

The **sort()** function, too, requires that the container support random access. It comes in two versions. The first version takes two iterators that define a range, and it sorts that range by using the < operator defined for the type element stored in the container. For example,

```
vector<int> coolstuff;
...
sort(coolstuff.begin(), coolstuff.end());
```

sorts the contents of **coolstuff** in ascending order, using the built-in < operator to compare values.

If the container elements are user-defined objects, then there has to be an **operator<()** function defined that works with that type of object in order to use **sort()**. For example, you could sort a vector containing **Review** objects if you provided either a **Review** member function or a nonmember function for **operator<()**. Because **Review** is a structure, its members are public, and a nonmember function like this would serve:

```
bool operator<(const Review & r1, const Review & r2)
{
    if (r1.title < r2.title)
        return true;
    else if (r1.title == r2.title && r1.rating < r2.rating)
        return true;
    else
        return false;
}
```

With a function like this in place, you could then sort a vector of **Review** objects (such as **books**):

```
sort(books.begin(), books.end());
```

This version of the **operator<()** function sorts in lexicographic order of the title members. If two objects have the same title members, they are then sorted in ratings order. But suppose you want to sort in decreasing order or in order of ratings instead of titles. In such a case, you can use the second form of **sort()**. It takes three arguments. The first two, again, are iterators that indicate the range. The final argument is a pointer to a function (more generally, a function object) to be used instead of **operator<()** for making the comparison. The return value should be convertible to **bool**, with **false** meaning the two arguments are in the wrong order. Here's an example of such a function:

```
bool WorseThan(const Review & r1, const Review & r2)
{
    if (r1.rating < r2.rating)
```

```
        return true;
    else
        return false;
}
```

With this function in place, you can use the following statement to sort the books vector of Review objects in order of increasing rating values:

```
sort(books.begin(), books.end(), WorseThan);
```

Note that the WorseThan() function does a less complete job than operator<() of ordering Review objects. If two objects have the same title member, the operator<() function sorts by using the rating member. But if two objects have the same rating member, WorseThan() treats them as equivalent. The first kind of ordering is called *total ordering*, and the second kind is called *strict weak ordering*. With total ordering, if both *a* < *b* and *b* < *a* are false, then *a* and *b* must be identical. With strict weak ordering, that's not so. They might be identical, or they might just have one aspect that is the same, such as the rating member in the WorseThan() example. So instead of saying the two objects are identical, the best you can say for strict weak ordering is that they are *equivalent*.

Listing 16.7 illustrates the use of these STL functions.

LISTING 16.7   vect3.cpp

```cpp
// vect3.cpp -- using STL functions
#include <iostream>
#include <string>
#include <vector>
#include <algorithm>

struct Review {
    std::string title;
    int rating;
};

bool operator<(const Review & r1, const Review & r2);
bool worseThan(const Review & r1, const Review & r2);
bool FillReview(Review & rr);
void ShowReview(const Review & rr);
int main()
{
    using namespace std;

    vector<Review> books;
    Review temp;
    while (FillReview(temp))
        books.push_back(temp);
    cout << "Thank you. You entered the following "
         << books.size() << " ratings:\n"
          << "Rating\tBook\n";
    for_each(books.begin(), books.end(), ShowReview);
```

LISTING 16.7   *Continued*

```cpp
    sort(books.begin(), books.end());
    cout << "Sorted by title:\nRating\tBook\n";
    for_each(books.begin(), books.end(), ShowReview);

    sort(books.begin(), books.end(), worseThan);
    cout << "Sorted by rating:\nRating\tBook\n";
    for_each(books.begin(), books.end(), ShowReview);

    random_shuffle(books.begin(), books.end());
    cout << "After shuffling:\nRating\tBook\n";
    for_each(books.begin(), books.end(), ShowReview);
    cout << "Bye.\n";
    return 0;
}

bool operator<(const Review & r1, const Review & r2)
{
    if (r1.title < r2.title)
        return true;
    else if (r1.title == r2.title && r1.rating < r2.rating)
        return true;
    else
        return false;
}

bool worseThan(const Review & r1, const Review & r2)
{
    if (r1.rating < r2.rating)
        return true;
    else
        return false;
}

bool FillReview(Review & rr)
{
    std::cout << "Enter book title (quit to quit): ";
    std::getline(std::cin,rr.title);
    if (rr.title == "quit")
        return false;
    std::cout << "Enter book rating: ";
    std::cin >> rr.rating;
    if (!std::cin)
        return false;
    std::cin.get();
    return true;
}

void ShowReview(const Review & rr)
{
    std::cout << rr.rating << "\t" << rr.title << std::endl;
}
```

Compatibility Note

Older C++ implementations use `vector.h` instead of the `vector` header file and `algo.h` instead of the `algorithm` header file. Although the order of include files shouldn't matter, g++ 2.7.1 requires the `string` header file to appear before STL header files. This is not an issue with the current version. Older versions of the Microsoft Visual C++ `getline()` have a bug that delays the next output line appearing until after the next input. Also, older versions of Microsoft Visual C++ require you to define `operator==()` in addition to `operator<()`. Borland C++BuilderX requires that the statement

```
using std::rand;
```

be added to the global namespace.

Here's a sample run of the program in Listing 16.7:

```
Enter book title (quit to quit): The Cat Who Can Teach You Weight Loss
Enter book rating: 8
Enter book title (quit to quit): The Dogs of Dharma
Enter book rating: 6
Enter book title (quit to quit): The Wimps of Wonk
Enter book rating: 3
Enter book title (quit to quit): Farewell and Delete
Enter book rating: 7
Enter book title (quit to quit): quit
Thank you. You entered the following 4 ratings:
Rating  Book
8       The Cat Who Can Teach You Weight Loss
6       The Dogs of Dharma
3       The Wimps of Wonk
7       Farewell and Delete
Sorted by title:
Rating  Book
7       Farewell and Delete
8       The Cat Who Can Teach You Weight Loss
6       The Dogs of Dharma
3       The Wimps of Wonk
Sorted by rating:
Rating  Book
3       The Wimps of Wonk
6       The Dogs of Dharma
7       Farewell and Delete
8       The Cat Who Can Teach You Weight Loss
After shuffling:
Rating  Book
7       Farewell and Delete
3       The Wimps of Wonk
6       The Dogs of Dharma
8       The Cat Who Can Teach You Weight Loss
Bye.
```

Generic Programming

Now that you have some experience using the STL, let's look at the underlying philosophy. The STL is an example of *generic programming*. Object-oriented programming concentrates on the data aspect of programming, whereas generic programming concentrates on algorithms. The main things the two approaches have in common are abstraction and the creation of reusable code, but the philosophies are quite different.

A goal of generic programming is to write code that is independent of data types. Templates are the C++ tools for creating generic programs. Templates, of course, let you define a function or class in terms of a generic type. The STL goes further by providing a generic representation of algorithms. Templates make this possible, but not without the added element of careful and conscious design. To see how this mixture of templates and design works, let's look at why iterators are needed.

Why Iterators?

Understanding iterators is perhaps the key to understanding the STL. Just as templates make algorithms independent of the type of data stored, iterators make the algorithms independent of the type of container used. Thus, they are an essential component of the STL's generic approach.

To see why iterators are needed, let's look at how you might implement a `find` function for two different data representations and then see how you could generalize the approach. First, let's consider a function that searches an ordinary array of `double` for a particular value. You could write the function like this:

```
double * find_ar(double * ar, int n, const double & val)
{
    for (int i = 0; i < n; i++)
        if (ar[i] == val)
            return &ar[i];
    return 0;
}
```

If the function finds the value in the array, it returns the address in the array where the value is found; otherwise, it returns the null pointer. It uses subscript notation to move through the array. You could use a template to generalize to arrays of any type having an `==` operator. Nonetheless, this algorithm is still tied to one particular data structure—the array.

So let's look at searching another kind of data structure, the linked list. (Chapter 12 uses a linked list to implement a `Queue` class.) The list consists of linked `Node` structures:

```
struct Node
{
    double item;
    Node * p_next;
};
```

Suppose you have a pointer that points to the first node in the list. The p_next pointer in each node points to the next node, and the p_next pointer for the last node in the list is set to 0. You could write a find_ll() function this way:

```
Node* find_ll(Node * head, const double & val)
{
    Node * start;
    for (start = head; start!= 0; start = start->p_next)
        if (start->item == val)
            return start;
    return 0;
}
```

Again, you could use a template to generalize this to lists of any data type supporting the == operator. Nonetheless, this algorithm is still tied to one particular data structure—the linked list.

If you consider details of implementation, the two find functions use different algorithms: One uses array indexing to move through a list of items, and the other resets start to start->p_next. But broadly, the two algorithms are the same: Compare the value with each value in the container in sequence until you find a match.

The goal of generic programming in this case would be to have a single find function that would work with arrays or linked lists or any other container type. That is, not only should the function be independent of the data type stored in the container, it should be independent of the data structure of the container itself. Templates provide a generic representation for the data type stored in a container. What's needed is a generic representation of the process of moving through the values in a container. The iterator is that generalized representation.

What properties should an iterator have in order to implement a find function? Here's a short list:

- You should be able to dereference an iterator in order to access the value to which it refers. That is, if p is an iterator, *p should be defined.

- You should be able to assign one iterator to another. That is, if p and q are iterators, the expression p = q should be defined.

- You should be able to compare one iterator to another for equality. That is, if p and q are iterators, the expressions p == q and p != q should be defined.

- You should be able to move an iterator through all the elements of a container. This can be satisfied by defining ++p and p++ for an iterator p.

There are more things an iterator could do, but nothing more it need do—at least, not for the purposes of a find function. Actually, the STL defines several levels of iterators of increasing capabilities, and we'll return to that matter later. Note, by the way, that an ordinary pointer meets the requirements of an iterator. Hence, you can rewrite the find_arr() function like this:

```
typedef double * iterator;
iterator find_ar(iterator ar, int n, const double & val)
{
    for (int i = 0; i < n; i++, ar++)
        if (*ar == val)
            return ar;
    return 0;
}
```

Then you can alter the function parameter list so that it takes a pointer to the beginning of the array and a pointer to one past-the-end of the array as arguments to indicate a range. (Listing 7.8 in Chapter 7, "Functions: C++'s Programming Modules," does something similar.) And the function can return the end pointer as a sign the value was not found. The following version of find_ar() makes these changes:

```
typedef double * iterator;
iterator find_ar(iterator begin, iterator end, const double & val)
{
    iterator ar;
    for (ar = begin; ar != end;  ar++)
        if (*ar == val)
            return ar;
    return end;   // indicates val not found
}
```

For the find_ll() function, you can define an iterator class that defines the * and ++ operators:

```
struct Node
{
    double item;
    Node * p_next;
};

class iterator
{
    Node * pt;
public:
    iterator() : pt(0) {}
    iterator (Node * pn) : pt(pn) {}
    double operator*() { return pt->item;}
    iterator& operator++()     // for ++it
    {
        pt = pt->p_next;
        return *this;
    }
    iterator operator++(int)  // for it++
    {
        iterator tmp = *this;
        pt = pt->p_next;
        return tmp;
    }
// ... operator==(), operator!=(), etc.
};
```

(To distinguish between the prefix and postfix versions of the ++ operator, C++ adopted the convention of letting `operator++()` be the prefix version and `operator++(int)` be the suffix version; the argument is never used and hence needn't be given a name.)

The main point here is not how, in detail, to define the `iterator` class, but that with such a class, the second `find` function can be written like this:

```
iterator find_ll(iterator head, const double & val)
{
    iterator start;
    for (start = head; start!= 0; ++start)
        if (*start == val)
            return start;
    return 0;
}
```

This is very nearly the same as `find_ar()`. The point of difference is in how the two functions determine whether they've reached the end of the values being searched. The `find_ar()` function uses an iterator to one-past-the-end, whereas `find_ll()` uses a null value stored in the final node. Remove that difference, and you can make the two functions identical. For example, you could require that the linked list have one additional element after the last official element. That is, you could have both the array and the linked list have a past-the-end element, and you could end the search when the iterator reaches the past-the-end position. Then `find_ar()` and `find_ll()` would have the same way of detecting the end of data and become identical algorithms. Note that requiring a past-the-end element moves from making requirements on iterators to making requirements on the container class.

The STL follows the approach just outlined. First, each container class (`vector`, `list`, `deque`, and so on) defines an iterator type appropriate to the class. For one class, the iterator might be a pointer; for another, it might be an object. Whatever the implementation, the iterator will provide the needed operations, such as * and ++. (Some classes may need more operations than others.) Next, each container class will have a past-the-end marker, which is the value assigned to an iterator when it has been incremented one past the last value in the container. Each container class will have `begin()` and `end()` methods that return iterators to the first element in a container and to the past-the-end position. And each container class will have the ++ operation take an iterator from the first element to past-the-end, visiting every container element en route.

To use a container class, you don't need to know how its iterators are implemented nor how past-the-end is implemented. It's enough to know that it does have iterators, that `begin()` returns an iterator to the first element, and that `end()` returns an iterator to past-the-end. For example, suppose you want to print the values in a `vector<double>` object. In that case, you can use this:

```
vector<double>::iterator pr;
for (pr = scores.begin(); pr != scores.end(); pr++)
    cout << *pr << endl;
```

Here the line

```
vector<double>::iterator pr;
```

identifies `pr` as the iterator type defined for the `vector<double>` class. If you used the `list<double>` class template instead to store scores, you could use this code:

```
list<double>::iterator pr;
for (pr = scores.begin(); pr != scores.end(); pr++)
    cout << *pr << endl;
```

The only change is in the type declared for `pr`. Thus, by having each class define appropriate iterators and designing the classes in a uniform fashion, the STL lets you write the same code for containers that have quite dissimilar internal representations.

Actually, as a matter of style, it's better to avoid using the iterators directly; instead, if possible, you should use an STL function, such as `for_each()`, that takes care of the details for you.

So, to summarize the STL approach, you start with an algorithm for processing a container. You express it in as general terms as possible, making it independent of data type and container type. To make the general algorithm work with specific cases, you define iterators that meet the needs of the algorithm and place requirements on the container design. That is, basic iterator properties and container properties stem from requirements placed on the algorithm.

Kinds of Iterators

Different algorithms have different requirements for iterators. For example, a find algorithm needs the `++` operator to be defined so the iterator can step through the entire container. It needs read access to data but not write access. (It just looks at data and doesn't change it.) The usual sort algorithm, on the other hand, requires random access so that it can swap the two non-adjacent elements. If `iter` is an iterator, you can get random access by defining the `+` operator so that you can use expressions such as `iter + 10`. Also, a sort algorithm needs to be able to both read and write data.

The STL defines five kinds of iterators and describes its algorithms in terms of which kinds of iterators it needs. The five kinds are the input iterator, output iterator, forward iterator, bidirectional iterator, and random access iterator. For example, the `find()` prototype looks like this:

```
template<class InputIterator, class T>
InputIterator find(InputIterator first, InputIterator last, const T& value);
```

This tells you that this algorithm requires an input iterator. Similarly, the prototype

```
template<class RandomAccessIterator>
void sort(RandomAccessIterator first, RandomAccessIterator last);
```

tells you that the sort algorithm requires a random access iterator.

All five kinds of iterators can be dereferenced (that is, the `*` operator is defined for them) and can be compared for equality (using the `==` operator, possibly overloaded) and inequality (using the != operator, possibly overloaded). If two iterators test as equal, then dereferencing one should produce the same value as dereferencing the second. That is, if

```
iter1 == iter2
```

is true, then the following is also true:

```
*iter1 == *iter2
```

Of course, these properties hold true for built-in operators and pointers, so these requirements are guides for what you must do when overloading these operators for an iterator class. Now let's look at other iterator properties.

Input Iterators

The term *input* is used from the viewpoint of a program. That is, information going from the container to the program is considered input, just as information from a keyboard to the program is considered input. So an *input iterator* is one that a program can use to read values from a container. In particular, dereferencing an input iterator must allow a program to read a value from a container, but it needn't allow a program to alter that value. So algorithms that require an input iterator are algorithms that don't change values held in a container.

An input iterator has to allow you to access all the values in a container. It does so by supporting the ++ operator, both in prefix and suffix form. If you set an input operator to the first element in a container and increment it until it reaches past-the-end, it will point to every container item once en route. Incidentally, there is no guarantee that traversing a container a second time with an input iterator will move through the values in the same order. Also, after an input iterator has been incremented, there is no guarantee that its prior value can still be dereferenced. Any algorithm based on an input iterator, then, should be a single-pass algorithm that doesn't rely on iterator values from a previous pass or on earlier iterator values from the same pass.

Note that an input iterator is a one-way iterator; it can increment, but it can't back up.

Output Iterators

In STL usage, the term *output* indicates that the iterator is used for transferring information from a program to a container. (Thus the output for the program is input for the container.) An output iterator is similar to an input iterator, except that dereferencing is guaranteed to allow a program to alter a container value but not to read it. If the ability to write without reading seems strange, keep in mind that this property also applies to output sent to your display; cout can modify the stream of characters sent to the display, but it can't read what's onscreen. The STL is general enough that its containers can represent output devices, so you can run into the same situation with containers. Also, if an algorithm modifies the contents of a container (for example, by generating new values to be stored) without reading the contents, there's no reason to require that it use an iterator that can read the contents.

In short, you can use an input iterator for single-pass, read-only algorithms and an output operator for single-pass, write-only algorithms.

Forward Iterators

Like input and output iterators, forward iterators use only the ++ operators for navigating through a container. So a forward iterator can only go forward through a container one element at a time. However, unlike input and output iterators, it necessarily goes through a sequence of values in the same order each time you use it. Also, after you increment a forward iterator, you can still dereference the prior iterator value, if you've saved it, and get the same value. These properties make multiple-pass algorithms possible.

A forward iterator can allow you to both read and modify data, or it can allow you just to read it:

```
int * pirw;       // read-write iterator
const int * pir;  // read-only iterator
```

Bidirectional Iterators

Suppose you have an algorithm that needs to be able to traverse a container in both directions. For example, a reverse function could swap the first and last elements, increment the pointer to the first element, decrement the pointer to a second element, and repeat the process. A bidirectional iterator has all the features of a forward iterator and adds support for the two decrement operators (prefix and postfix).

Random Access Iterators

Some algorithms, such as standard sort and binary search, require the ability to jump directly to an arbitrary element of a container. This is termed *random access*, and it requires a random access iterator. This type of iterator has all the features of a bidirectional iterator, plus it adds operations (such as pointer addition) that support random access and relational operators for ordering the elements. Table 16.3 lists the operations a random access iterator has beyond those of a bidirectional iterator. In this table, X represents a random iterator type, T represents the type pointed to, a and b are iterator values, n is an integer, and r is a random iterator variable or reference.

TABLE 16.3   Random Access Iterator Operations

Expression	Description
a + n	Points to the nth element after the one a points to
n + a	Same as a + n
a - n	Points to the nth element before the one a points to
r += n	Equivalent to r = r + n
r -= n	Equivalent to r = r - n
a[n]	Equivalent to *(a + n)

TABLE 16.3   Continued

Expression	Description
b - a	The value of n such that b = a + n
a < b	True if b - a > 0
a > b	True if b < a
a >= b	True if !(a < b)
a <= b	True if !(a > b)

Expressions such as a + n are valid only if both a and a + n lie within the range of the container (including past-the-end).

Iterator Hierarchy

You have probably noticed that the iterator kinds form a hierarchy. A forward iterator has all the capabilities of an input iterator and of an output iterator, plus its own capabilities. A bidirectional iterator has all the capabilities of a forward iterator, plus its own capabilities. And a random access iterator has all the capabilities of a forward iterator, plus its own capabilities. Table 16.4 summarizes the main iterator capabilities. In it, i is an iterator, and n is an integer.

TABLE 16.4   Iterator Capabilities

Iterator Capability	Input	Output	Forward	Bidirectional	Random Access
Dereferencing read	Yes	No	Yes	Yes	Yes
Dereferencing write	No	Yes	Yes	Yes	Yes
Fixed and repeatable order	No	No	Yes	Yes	Yes
++i i++	Yes	Yes	Yes	Yes	Yes
--i i--	No	No	No	Yes	Yes
i[n]	No	No	No	No	Yes
i + n	No	No	No	No	Yes

TABLE 16.4   Continued

Iterator Capability	Input	Output	Forward	Bidirectional	Random Access
i - n	No	No	No	No	Yes
i += n	No	No	No	No	Yes
i -=n	No	No	No	No	Yes

An algorithm written in terms of a particular kind of iterator can use that kind of iterator or any other iterator that has the required capabilities. So a container with, say, a random access iterator can use an algorithm written for an input iterator.

Why all these different kinds of iterators? The idea is to write an algorithm using the iterator with the fewest requirements possible, allowing it to be used with the largest range of containers. Thus, the `find()` function, by using a lowly input iterator, can be used with any container that contains readable values. The `sort()` function, however, by requiring a random access iterator, can be used just with containers that support that kind of iterator.

Note that the various iterator kinds are not defined types; rather, they are conceptual characterizations. As mentioned earlier, each container class defines a class scope `typedef` name called `iterator`. So the `vector<int>` class has iterators of type `vector<int>::iterator`. But the documentation for this class would tell you that vector iterators are random access iterators. That, in turn, allows you to use algorithms based on any iterator type because a random access iterator has all the iterator capabilities. Similarly, a `list<int>` class has iterators of type `list<int>::iterator`. The STL implements a doubly linked list, so it uses a bidirectional iterator. Thus, it can't use algorithms based on random access iterators, but it can use algorithms based on less demanding iterators.

Concepts, Refinements, and Models

The STL has several features, such as kinds of iterators, that aren't expressible in the C++ language. That is, although you can design, say, a class that has the properties of a forward iterator, you can't have the compiler restrict an algorithm to using only that class. The reason is that the forward iterator is a set of requirements, not a type. The requirements could be satisfied by an iterator class you've designed, but they could also be satisfied by an ordinary pointer. An STL algorithm works with any iterator implementation that meets its requirements. STL literature uses the word *concept* to describe a set of requirements. Thus, there is an input iterator concept, a forward iterator concept, and so on. By the way, if you do need iterators for, say, a container class you're designing, you can look to the STL, which include iterator templates for the standard varieties.

Concepts can have an inheritance-like relationship. For example, a bidirectional iterator inherits the capabilities of a forward iterator. However, you can't apply the C++ inheritance mechanism to iterators. For example, you might implement a forward iterator as a class and a bidirectional iterator as a regular pointer. So, in terms of the C++ language, this particular bidirectional iterator, being a built-in type, couldn't be derived from a class. Conceptually, however, it does inherit. Some STL literature uses the term *refinement* to indicate this conceptual inheritance. Thus, a bidirectional iterator is a refinement of the forward iterator concept.

A particular implementation of a concept is termed a *model*. Thus, an ordinary pointer-to-int is a model of the concept random access iterator. It's also a model of a forward iterator, for it satisfies all the requirements of that concept.

The Pointer as Iterator

Iterators are generalizations of pointers, and a pointer satisfies all the iterator requirements. Iterators form the interface for STL algorithms, and pointers are iterators, so STL algorithms can use pointers to operate on non-STL containers that are based on pointers. For example, you can use STL algorithms with arrays. Suppose `Receipts` is an array of `double` values, and you would like to sort in ascending order:

```
const int SIZE = 100;
double Receipts[SIZE];
```

The STL `sort()` function, recall, takes as arguments an iterator pointing to the first element in a container and an iterator pointing to past-the-end. Well, `&Receipts[0]` (or just `Receipts`) is the address of the first element, and `&Receipts[SIZE]` (or just `Receipts + SIZE`) is the address of the element following the last element in the array. Thus, the function call

```
sort(Receipts, Receipts + SIZE);
```

sorts the array. C++ guarantees that the expression `Receipts + n` is defined as long as the result lies in the array or one past-the-end. Thus, C++ supports the "one-past-the-end" concept for pointers into an array, and this makes it possible to apply STL algorithms to ordinary arrays. Thus, the fact that pointers are iterators and that algorithms are iterator based makes it possible to apply STL algorithms to ordinary arrays. Similarly, you can apply STL algorithms to data forms of your own design, provided that you supply suitable iterators (which may be pointers or objects) and past-the-end indicators.

copy(), ostream_iterator, and istream_iterator

The STL provides some predefined iterators. To see why, let's establish some background. There is an algorithm called `copy()` for copying data from one container to another. This algorithm is expressed in terms of iterators, so it can copy from one kind of container to another or even from or to an array, because you can use pointers into an array as iterators. For example, the following copies an array into a vector:

```
int casts[10] = {6, 7, 2, 9 ,4 , 11, 8, 7, 10, 5};
vector<int> dice[10];
copy(casts, casts + 10, dice.begin());   // copy array to vector
```

The first two iterator arguments to `copy()` represent a range to be copied, and the final iterator argument represents the location to which the first item is copied. The first two arguments must be input iterators (or better), and the final argument must be an output iterator (or better). The `copy()` function overwrites existing data in the destination container, and the container has to be large enough to hold the copied elements. So you can't use `copy()` to place data in an empty vector—at least not without resorting to a trick that is revealed later in this chapter.

Now suppose you want to copy information to the display. You could use `copy()` if there was an iterator representing the output stream. The STL provides such an iterator with the `ostream_iterator` template. Using STL terminology, this template is a *model* of the output iterator concept. It is also an example of an *adapter*—a class or function that converts some other interface to an interface used by the STL. You could create an iterator of this kind by including the `iterator` (formerly `iterator.h`) header file and making a declaration:

```
#include <iterator>
...
ostream_iterator<int, char> out_iter(cout, " ");
```

The `out_iter` iterator now becomes an interface that allows you to use `cout` to display information. The first template argument (`int`, in this case) indicates the data type being sent to the output stream. The second template argument (`char`, in this case) indicates the character type used by the output stream. (Another possible value would be `wchar_t`.) The first constructor argument (`cout`, in this case) identifies the output stream being used. It could also be a stream used for file output. The final character string argument is a separator to be displayed after each item sent to the output stream.

Caution

Older C++ implementations use just the first template argument for the `ostream_iterator`:

```
ostream_iterator<int> out_iter(cout, " "); // older implementation
```

You could use the iterator like this:

```
*out_iter++ = 15;   // works like cout << 15 << " ";
```

For a regular pointer, this would mean assigning the value **15** to the pointed-to location and then incrementing the pointer. For this `ostream_iterator`, however, the statement means send **15** and then a string consisting of a space to the output stream managed by `cout`. Then it should get ready for the next output operation. You could use the iterator with `copy()` as - follows:

```
copy(dice.begin(), dice.end(), out_iter);   // copy vector to output stream
```

This would mean to copy the entire range of the `dice` container to the output stream—that is, to display the contents of the container.

Or, you could skip creating a named iterator and construct an anonymous iterator instead. That is, you could use the adapter like this:

```
copy(dice.begin(), dice.end(), ostream_iterator<int, char>(cout, " ") );
```

Similarly, the `iterator` header file defines an `istream_iterator` template for adapting `istream` input to the iterator interface. It is a model of the input iterator concept. You could use two `istream_iterator` objects to define an input range for `copy()`:

```
copy(istream_iterator<int, char>(cin),
    istream_iterator<int, char>(), dice.begin());
```

Like `ostream_iterator`, `istream_iterator` uses two template arguments. The first indicates the data type to be read, and the second indicates the character type used by the input stream. Using a constructor argument of `cin` means to use the input stream managed by `cin`. Omitting the constructor argument indicates input failure, so the previous code means to read from the input stream until end-of-file, type mismatch, or some other input failure.

Other Useful Iterators

The iterator header file provides some other special-purpose predefined iterator types in addition to `ostream_iterator` and `istream_iterator`. They are `reverse_iterator`, `back_insert_iterator`, `front_insert_iterator`, and `insert_iterator`.

Let's start with seeing what a reverse iterator does. In essence, incrementing a reverse iterator causes it to decrement. Why not just decrement a regular iterator? The main reason is to simplify using existing functions. Suppose you want to display the contents of the `dice` container. As you just saw, you can use `copy()` and `ostream_iterator` to copy the contents to the output stream:

```
ostream_iterator<int, char> out_iter(cout, " ");
copy(dice.begin(), dice.end(), out_iter);  // display in forward order
```

Now suppose you want to print the contents in reverse order. (Perhaps you are performing time-reversal studies.) There are several approaches that don't work, but rather than wallow in them, let's go to one that does. The `vector` class has a member function called `rbegin()` that returns a reverse iterator pointing to past-the-end and a member `rend()` that returns a reverse iterator pointing to the first element. Because incrementing a reverse iterator makes it decrement, you can use the statement

```
copy(dice.rbegin(), dice.rend(), out_iter); // display in reverse order
```

to display the contents backward. You don't even have to declare a reverse iterator.

Remember

Both `rbegin()` and `end()` return the same value (past-the-end), but as a different type (`reverse_iterator` versus `iterator`). Similarly, both `rend()` and `begin()` return the same value (an iterator to the first element), but as a different type.

Reverse pointers have to make a special compensation. Suppose `rp` is a reverse pointer initialized to `dice.rbegin()`. What should `*rp` be? Because `rbegin()` returns past-the-end, you shouldn't try to dereference that address. Similarly, if `rend()` is really the location of the first element, `copy()` stops one location earlier because the end of the range is not in a range.

Reverse pointers solve both problems by decrementing first and then dereferencing. That is, *rp dereferences the iterator value immediately preceding the current value of *rp. If rp points to position six, *rp is the value of position five, and so on. Listing 16.8 illustrates using copy(), an istream iterator, and a reverse iterator.

LISTING 16.8   copyit.cpp

```
// copyit.cpp -- copy() and iterators
#include <iostream>
#include <iterator>
#include <vector>

int main()
{
    using namespace std;

    int casts[10] = {6, 7, 2, 9 ,4 , 11, 8, 7, 10, 5};
    vector<int> dice(10);
    // copy from array to vector
    copy(casts, casts + 10, dice.begin());
    cout << "Let the dice be cast!\n";
    // create an ostream iterator
    ostream_iterator<int, char> out_iter(cout, " ");
    // copy from vector to output
    copy(dice.begin(), dice.end(), out_iter);
    cout << endl;
    cout <<"Implicit use of reverse iterator.\n";
    copy(dice.rbegin(), dice.rend(), out_iter);
    cout << endl;
    cout <<"Explicit use of reverse iterator.\n";
    vector<int>::reverse_iterator ri;
    for (ri = dice.rbegin(); ri != dice.rend(); ++ri)
        cout << *ri << ' ';
    cout << endl;

    return 0;
}
```

Compatibility Notes

Older C++ implementations may use the iterator.h and vector.h header files instead of iterator and vector. Also, some implementations use ostream_iterator<int> instead of ostream_iterator<int, char>.

Here is the output of the program in Listing 16.8:

```
Let the dice be cast!
6 7 2 9 4 11 8 7 10 5
Implicit use of reverse iterator.
5 10 7 8 11 4 9 2 7 6
Explicit use of reverse iterator.
5 10 7 8 11 4 9 2 7 6
```

If you have the choice of explicitly declaring iterators or using STL functions to handle the matter internally, for example, by passing an `rbegin()` return value to a function, you should take the latter course. It's one less thing to do and one less opportunity to experience human fallibility.

The other three iterators (`back_insert_iterator`, `front_insert_iterator`, and `insert_iterator`) also increase the generality of the STL algorithms. Many STL functions are like `copy()` in that they send their results to a location indicated by an output iterator. Recall that

```
copy(casts, casts + 10, dice.begin());
```

copies values to the location beginning at `dice.begin()`. These values overwrite the prior contents in `dice`, and the function assumes that `dice` has enough room to hold the values. That is, `copy()` does not automatically adjust the size of the destination to fit the information sent to it. Listing 16.8 takes care of that situation by declaring `dice` to have 10 elements, but suppose you don't know in advance how big `dice` should be. Or suppose you want to add elements to `dice` rather than overwrite existing ones.

The three insert iterators solve these problems by converting the copying process to an insertion process. Insertion adds new elements without overwriting existing data, and it uses automatic memory allocation to ensure that the new information fits. A `back_insert_iterator` inserts items at the end of the container, and a `front_insert_iterator` inserts items at the front. Finally, the `insert_iterator` inserts items in front of the location specified as an argument to the `insert_iterator` constructor. All three of these iterators are models of the output container concept.

There are restrictions. A `back_insert_iterator` can be used only with container types that allow rapid insertion at the end. (*Rapid* refers to a constant time algorithm; the section "Container Concepts," later in this chapter, discusses the constant time concept further.) The `vector` class qualifies. A `front_insert_iterator` can be used only with container types that allow constant time insertion at the beginning. Here the `vector` class doesn't qualify, but the `queue` class does. The `insert_iterator` doesn't have these restrictions. Thus, you can use it to insert material at the front of a vector. However, a `front_insert_iterator` does so faster for the container types that support it.

Tip

You can use an `insert_iterator` to convert an algorithm that copies data into one that inserts data.

These iterators take the container type as a template argument and the actual container identifier as a constructor argument. That is, to create a `back_insert_iterator` for a `vector<int>` container called `dice`, you use this:

```
back_insert_iterator<vector<int> > back_iter(dice);
```

The reason you have to declare the container type is that the iterator has to make use of the appropriate container method. The code for the `back_insert_iterator` constructor will assume that a `push_back()` method exists for the type passed to it. The `copy()` function, being a standalone function, doesn't have the access rights to resize a container. But the declaration just shown allows `back_iter` to use the `vector<int>::push_back()` method, which does have access rights.

Declaring a `front_insert_iterator` has the same form. An `insert_iterator` declaration has an additional constructor argument to identify the insertion location:

```
insert_iterator<vector<int> > insert_iter(dice, dice.begin() );
```

Listing 16.9 illustrates using two of these iterators.

LISTING 16.9   inserts.cpp

```cpp
// inserts.cpp -- copy() and insert iterators
#include <iostream>
#include <string>
#include <iterator>
#include <vector>

int main()
{
    using namespace std;
    string s1[4] = {"fine", "fish", "fashion", "fate"};
    string s2[2] = {"busy", "bats"};
    string s3[2] = {"silly", "singers"};
    vector<string> words(4);
    copy(s1, s1 + 4, words.begin());
    ostream_iterator<string, char> out(cout, " ");
    copy (words.begin(), words.end(), out);
    cout << endl;

// construct anonymous back_insert_iterator object
    copy(s2, s2 + 2, back_insert_iterator<vector<string> >(words));
    copy (words.begin(), words.end(), out);
    cout << endl;

// construct anonymous insert_iterator object
    copy(s3, s3 + 2, insert_iterator<vector<string> >(words, words.begin()));
    copy (words.begin(), words.end(), out);
    cout << endl;

    return 0;
}
```

Compatibility Note

Older compilers may use `list.h` and `iterator.h`. Also, some compilers may use `ostream_iterator<int>` instead of `ostream_iterator<int,char>`.

Here is the output of the program in Listing 16.9:

```
fine fish fashion fate
fine fish fashion fate busy bats
silly singers fine fish fashion fate busy bats
```

The first `copy()` copies the four strings from `s1` into `words`. This works in part because `words` is declared to hold four strings, which equals the number of strings being copied. Then the `back_insert_iterator` inserts the strings from `s2` just in front of the end of the `words` array, expanding the size of `words` to six elements. Finally, the `insert_iterator` inserts the two strings from `s3` just in front of the first element of `words`, expanding the size of `words` to eight elements. If the program attempted to copy `s2` and `s3` into `words` by using `words.end()` and `words.begin()` as iterators, there would be no room in `words` for the new data, and the program would probably abort because of memory violations.

If you're feeling overwhelmed by all the iterator varieties, keep in mind that using them will make them familiar. Also keep in mind that these predefined iterators expand the generality of the STL algorithms. Thus, not only can `copy()` copy information from one container to another, it can copy information from a container to the output stream and from the input stream to a container. And you can also use `copy()` to insert material into another container. So you wind up with a single function doing the work of many. And because `copy()` is just one of several STL functions that use an output iterator, these predefined iterators multiply the capabilities of those functions, too.

Kinds of Containers

The STL has both container concepts and container types. The concepts are general categories with names such as container, sequence container, and associative container. The container types are templates you can use to create specific container objects. The 11 container types are `deque`, `list`, `queue`, `priority_queue`, `stack`, `vector`, `map`, `multimap`, `set`, `multiset`, and `bitset`. (This chapter doesn't discuss `bitset`, which is a container for dealing with data at the bit level.) Because the concepts categorize the types, let's start with them.

Container Concepts

No type corresponds to the basic container concept, but the concept describes elements common to all the container classes. It's sort of a conceptual abstract base class—conceptual because the container classes don't actually use the inheritance mechanism. Or to put it another way, the container concept lays down a set of requirements that all STL container classes must satisfy.

A *container* is an object that stores other objects, which are all of a single type. The stored objects may be objects in the OOP sense, or they may be values of built-in types. Data stored in a container is *owned* by the container. That means when a container expires, so do the data stored in the container. (However, if the data is pointers, the pointed-to data does not necessarily expire.)

You can't store just any kind of object in a container. In particular, the type has to be *copy constructable* and *assignable*. Basic types satisfy these requirements, as do class types—unless the class definition makes one or both of the copy constructor and the assignment operator private or protected.

The basic container doesn't guarantee that its elements are stored in any particular order or that the order doesn't change, but refinements to the concept may add such guarantees. All containers provide certain features and operations. Table 16.5 summarizes several of these common features. In the table, X represents a container type, such as vector, T represents the type of object stored in the container, a and b represent values of type X, and u represents an identifier of type X.

TABLE 16.5 Some Basic Container Properties

Expression	Return Type	Description	Complexity
X::iterator	Iterator type pointing to T	Any iterator category except output iterator	Compile time
X::value_type	T	The type for T	Compile time
X u;		Creates 0-size container called u	Constant
X();		Creates 0-size anonymous container	Constant
X u(a);		Copy constructor	Linear
X u = a;		Same effect as X u(a);	
(&a)->~X();	void	Applies destructor to every element of a container	Linear
a.begin()	iterator	Returns an iterator referring to the first element of the container	Constant
a.end()	iterator	Returns an iterator that is a past-the-end value	Constant
a.size()	unsigned integral type	Returns number of elements equal to a.end() - a.begin()	Constant
a.swap(b)	void	Swaps contents of a and b	Constant
a == b	convertible to bool	Returns true if a and b have the same size and each element in a is equivalent to (== is true) the corresponding element in b	Linear
a != b	convertible to bool	Returns !(a == b)	Linear

The Complexity column in Table 16.5 describes the time needed to perform an operation. This table lists three possibilities, which, from fastest to slowest, are as follows:

- Compile time
- Constant time
- Linear time

If the complexity is compile time, the action is performed during compilation and uses no execution time. A constant complexity means the operation takes place during runtime but doesn't depend on the number of elements in an object. A linear complexity means the time is proportional to the number of elements. Thus, if **a** and **b** are containers, **a == b** has linear complexity because the **==** operation may have to be applied to each element of the container. Actually, that is a worst-case scenario. If two containers have different sizes, no individual comparisons need to be made.

Constant-Time and Linear-Time Complexity
Imagine a long, narrow box filled with large packages arranged in a line, and suppose the box is open at just one end. Suppose your task is to unload the package at the open end. This is a constant time task. Whether there are 10 packages or 1,000 packages behind the one at the end makes no difference.
Now suppose your task is to fetch the package at the closed end of the box. This is a linear time task. If there are 10 packages altogether, you have to unload 10 packages to get the one at the closed end. If there are 100 packages, you have to unload 100 packages at the end. Assuming that you are a tireless worker who can move only 1 package at a time, this task will take 10 times longer than the first one.
Now suppose your task is to fetch an arbitrary package. It might happen that the package you are supposed to get is the first one at hand. However, on the average, the number of packages you have to move is still proportional to the number of packages in the container, so the task still has linear-time complexity.
Replacing the long, narrow box with a similar box having open sides would change the task to constant-time complexity because then you could move directly to the desired package and remove it without moving the others.
The idea of time complexity describes the effect of container size on execution time but ignores other factors. If a superhero can unload packages from a box with one open end 1,000 times faster than you can, the task as executed by her still has linear-time complexity. In this case, the super hero's linear time performance with a closed box (open end) would be faster than your constant time performance with an open box, as long as the boxes didn't have too many packages.

Complexity requirements are characteristic of the STL. Although the details of an implementation may be hidden, the performance specifications should be public so that you know the computing cost of doing a particular operation.

Sequences

You can refine the basic container concept by adding requirements. The *sequence* is an important refinement because six of the STL container types (**deque**, **list**, **queue**, **priority_queue**, stack, and vector) are sequences. (Recall that a queue allows elements to be added at the rear end and removed from the front. A double-ended queue, represented by deque, allows addition and removal at both ends.) The sequence concept adds the requirement that the iterator be at least a forward iterator. This, in turn, guarantees that the elements are arranged in a definite order that doesn't change from one cycle of iteration to the next.

The sequence also requires that its elements be arranged in strict linear order. That is, there is a first element, there is a last element, and each element but the first and last has exactly one element immediately ahead of it and one element immediately after it. An array and a linked list are examples of sequences, whereas a branching structure (in which each node points to two daughter nodes) is not.

Because elements in sequence have a definite order, operations such as inserting values at a particular location and erasing a particular range become possible. Table 16.6 lists these and other operations required of a sequence. The table uses the same notation as Table 16.5, with the addition of t representing a value of type T—that is, the type of value stored in the container, of n, an integer, and of p, q, i, and j, representing iterators.

TABLE 16.6   Sequence Requirements

Expression	Return Type	Description
X a(n,t);		Declares a sequence a of n copies of value t
X(n, t)		Creates an anonymous sequence of n copies of value t
X a(i, j)		Declares a sequence a initialized to the contents of range [i, j)
X(i, j)		Creates an anonymous sequence initialized to the contents of range [i, j)
a.insert(p,t)	iterator	Inserts a copy of t before p
a.insert(p,n,t)	void	Inserts n copies of t before p
a.insert(p,i,j)	void	Insert copies of elements in the range [i, j) before p
a.erase(p)	iterator	Erases the element pointed to by p
a.erase(p,q)	iterator	Erases the elements in the range [p, q)
a.clear()	void	Is the same as erase(begin(), end())

Because the deque, list, queue, priority_queue, stack, and vector template classes are all models of the sequence concept, they all support the operators in Table 16.6. In addition, there are operations that are available to some of these six models. When allowed, they have constant-time complexity. Table 16.7 lists these additional operations.

TABLE 16.7   Optional Sequence Requirements

Expression	Return Type	Meaning	Container
`a.front()`	T&	`*a.begin()`	vector, list, deque
`a.back()`	T&	`*--a.end()`	vector, list, deque
`a.push_front(t)`	void	`a.insert(a.begin(), t)`	list, deque
`a.push_back(t)`	void	`a.insert(a.end(), t)`	vector, list, deque
`a.pop_front(t)`	void	`a.erase(a.begin())`	list, deque
`a.pop_back(t)`	void	`a.erase(--a.end())`	vector, list, deque
`a[n]`	T&	`*(a.begin() + n)`	vector, deque
`a.at(n)`	T&	`*(a.begin() + n)`	vector, deque

Table 16.7 merits a comment or two. First, notice that `a[n]` and `a.at(n)` both return a reference to the nth element (numbering from 0) in a container. The difference between the two is that `a.at(n)` does bounds checking and throws an `out_of_range` exception if n is outside the valid range for the container. Next, you might wonder why, say, `push_front()` is defined for **list** and **deque** and not for **vector**. Suppose you want to insert a new value at the front of a vector of 100 elements. To make room, you have to move element 99 to position 100, and then you have to move element 98 to position 99, and so on. This is an operation with linear-time complexity because moving 100 elements would take 100 times as long as moving a single element. But the operations in Table 16.7 are supposed to be implemented only if they can be performed with constant-time complexity. The design for lists and double-ended queues, however, allows an element to be added to the front without moving the other elements to new locations, so they can implement `push_front()` with constant-time complexity. Figure 16.4 illustrates `push_front()` and `push_back()`.

FIGURE 16.4
push_front() and
push_back().

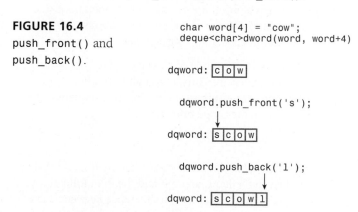

Let's take a closer look at the six sequence container types.

vector

You've already seen several examples using the `vector` template, which is declared in the `vector` header file. In brief, `vector` is a class representation of an array. The class provides automatic memory management that allows the size of a `vector` object to vary dynamically, growing and shrinking as elements are added or removed. It provides random access to elements. Elements can be added to or removed from the end in constant time, but insertion and removal from the beginning and the middle are linear-time operations.

In addition to being a sequence, a `vector` container is also a model of the *reversible container* concept. This adds two more class methods: `rbegin()` returns an iterator to the first element of the reversed sequence, and `rend()` returns a past-the-end iterator for the reversed sequence. So if `dice` is a `vector<int>` container and `Show(int)` is a function that displays an integer, the following code displays the contents of `dice` first in forward order and then in reverse order:

```
for_each(dice.begin(), dice.end(), Show);    // display in order
cout << endl;
for_each(dice.rbegin(), dice.rend(), Show);  // display in reversed order
cout << endl;
```

The iterator returned by the two methods is of a class scope type `reverse_iterator`. Recall that incrementing such an iterator causes it to move through a reversible container in reverse order.

The `vector` template class is the simplest of the sequence types and is considered the type that should be used by default unless the program requirements are better satisfied by the particular virtues of the other types.

deque

The `deque` template class (declared in the `deque` header file) represents a double-ended queue, a type often called a *deque* (pronounced "deck"), for short. As implemented in the STL, it's a lot like a `vector` container, supporting random access. The main difference is that inserting and removing items from the beginning of a `deque` object are constant-time operations instead of being linear-time operations the way they are for `vector`. So if most operations take place at the beginning and ends of a sequence, you should consider using a `deque` data structure.

The goal of constant-time insertion and removal at both ends of a `deque` makes the design of a `deque` object more complex than that of a `vector` object. Thus, although both offer random access to elements and linear-time insertion and removal from the middle of a sequence, the `vector` container should allow faster execution of these operations.

list

The `list` template class (declared in the `list` header file) represents a doubly linked list. Each element, other than the first and last, is linked to the item before it and the item following it, implying that a list can be traversed in both directions. The crucial difference between `list` and `vector` is that `list` provides for constant-time insertion and removal of elements at any location in the list. (Recall that the `vector` template provides linear-time insertion and removal except at the end, where it provides constant-time insertion and removal.) Thus, vector emphasizes rapid access via random access, whereas list emphasizes rapid insertion and removal of elements.

Like vector, list is a reversible container. Unlike vector, list does not support array notation and random access. Unlike a vector iterator, a list iterator remains pointing to the same element even after items are inserted into or removed from a container. For example, suppose you have an iterator pointing to the fifth element of a vector container. Then suppose you insert an element at the beginning of the container. All the other elements have to be moved to make room, so after the insertion, the fifth element now contains the value that used to be in the fourth element. Thus, the iterator points to the same location but to different data. Inserting a new element into a list, however, doesn't move the existing elements; it just alters the link information. An iterator pointing to a certain item still points to the same item, but it may be linked to different items than before.

The list template class has some list-oriented member functions in addition to those that come with sequences and reversible containers. Table 16.8 lists many of them. (For a complete list of STL methods and functions, see Appendix G.) The Alloc template parameter is one you normally don't have to worry about because it has a default value.

TABLE 16.8   Some list Member Functions

Function	Description
void merge(list<T, Alloc>& x)	Merges list x with the invoking list. Both lists must be sorted. The resulting sorted list is in the invoking list, and x is left empty. This function has linear-time complexity.
void remove(const T & val)	Removes all instances of val from the list. This function has linear-time complexity.
void sort()	Sorts the list by using the < operator; the complexity is N log N for N elements.
void splice(iterator pos, list<T, Alloc> x)	Inserts the contents of list x in front of position pos, and x is left empty. This function has constant-time complexity.
void unique()	Collapses each consecutive group of equal elements to a single element. This function has linear-time complexity.

Listing 16.10 illustrates these methods, along with the insert() method, which comes with all STL classes that model sequences.

LISTING 16.10   `list.cpp`

```cpp
// list.cpp -- using a list
#include <iostream>
#include <list>
#include <iterator>

int main()
{
    using namespace std;
    list<int> one(5, 2); // list of 5 2s
    int stuff[5] = {1,2,4,8, 6};
    list<int> two;
    two.insert(two.begin(),stuff, stuff + 5 );
    int more[6] = {6, 4, 2, 4, 6, 5};
    list<int> three(two);
    three.insert(three.end(), more, more + 6);

    cout << "List one: ";
    ostream_iterator<int,char> out(cout, " ");
    copy(one.begin(), one.end(), out);
    cout << endl << "List two: ";
    copy(two.begin(), two.end(), out);
    cout << endl << "List three: ";
    copy(three.begin(), three.end(), out);
    three.remove(2);
    cout << endl << "List three minus 2s: ";
    copy(three.begin(), three.end(), out);
    three.splice(three.begin(), one);
    cout << endl << "List three after splice: ";
    copy(three.begin(), three.end(), out);
    cout << endl << "List one: ";
    copy(one.begin(), one.end(), out);
    three.unique();
    cout << endl << "List three after unique: ";
    copy(three.begin(), three.end(), out);
    three.sort();
    three.unique();
    cout << endl << "List three after sort & unique: ";
    copy(three.begin(), three.end(), out);
    two.sort();
    three.merge(two);
    cout << endl << "Sorted two merged into three: ";
    copy(three.begin(), three.end(), out);
    cout << endl;

    return 0;
}
```

Compatibility Note

Older versions of the STL may use `list.h` and `iterator.h`. Also, older versions may use `ostream_iterator<int>` instead of `ostream_iterator<int,char>`.

Here is the output of the program in Listing 16.10:

```
List one: 2 2 2 2
List two: 1 2 4 8 6
List three: 1 2 4 8 6 6 4 2 4 6 5
List three minus 2s: 1 4 8 6 6 4 4 6 5
List three after splice: 2 2 2 2 1 4 8 6 6 4 4 6 5
List one:
List three after unique: 2 1 4 8 6 4 6 5
List three after sort & unique: 1 2 4 5 6 8
Sorted two merged into three: 1 1 2 2 4 4 5 6 6 8 8
```

Program Notes

The program in Listing 16.10 uses the technique discussed earlier for using the general STL `copy()` function and an `ostream_iterator` object to display the contents of a container.

The main difference between `insert()` and `splice()` is that `insert()` inserts a copy of the original range into the destination, whereas `splice()` moves the original range into the destination. Thus, after the contents of `one` are spliced to `three`, `one` is left empty. (The `splice()` method has additional prototypes for moving single elements and a range of elements.) The `splice()` method leaves iterators valid. That is, if you set a particular iterator to point to an element in `one`, that iterator still points to the same element after `splice()` relocates it in `three`.

Notice that `unique()` only reduces adjacent equal values to a single value. After the program executes `three.unique()`, `three` still contains two fours and two sixes that weren't adjacent. But applying `sort()` and then `unique()` does limit each value to a single appearance.

There is a nonmember `sort()` function (Listing 16.7), but it requires random access iterators. Because the trade-off for rapid insertion is to give up random access, you can't use the nonmember `sort()` function with a list. Therefore, the class includes a member version that works within the restrictions of the class.

The list Toolbox

The `list` methods form a handy toolbox. Suppose, for example, that you have two mailing lists to organize. You could sort each list, merge them, and then use `unique()` to remove multiple entries.

The `sort()`, `merge()`, and `unique()` methods also each have a version that accepts an additional argument to specify an alternative function to be used for comparing elements. Similarly, the `remove()` method has a version with an additional argument that specifies a function used to determine whether an element is removed. These arguments are examples of predicate functions, a topic to which we'll return later.

queue

The `queue` template class (declared in the `queue`—formerly `queue.h`—header file) is an adapter class. Recall that the `ostream_iterator` template is an adapter that allows an output stream to use the iterator interface. Similarly, the `queue` template allows an underlying class (`deque`, by default) to exhibit the typical queue interface.

The `queue` template is more restrictive than `deque`. Not only does it not permit random access to elements of a queue, the `queue` class doesn't even allow you to iterate through a queue. Instead, it limits you to the basic operations that define a queue. You can add an element to the rear of a queue, remove an element from the front of a queue, view the values of the front and rear elements, check the number of elements, and test to see if a queue is empty. Table 16.9 lists these operations.

TABLE 16.9   `queue` Operations

Method	Description
`bool empty() const`	Returns `true` if the queue is empty and `false` otherwise.
`size_type size() const`	Returns the number of elements in the queue.
`T& front()`	Returns a reference to the element at the front of the queue.
`T& back()`	Returns a reference to the element at the back of the queue.
`void push(const T& x)`	Inserts `x` at the back of the queue.
`void pop()`	Removes the element at the front of the queue.

Note that `pop()` is a data removal method, not a data retrieval method. If you want to use a value from a queue, you first use `front()` to retrieve the value and then use `pop()` to remove it from the queue.

priority_queue

The `priority_queue` template class (declared in the `queue` header file) is another adapter class. It supports the same operations as `queue`. The main difference between the two is that with `priority_queue`, the largest item gets moved to the front of the queue. (Life is not always fair, and neither are queues.) An internal difference is that the default underlying class is `vector`. You can alter the comparison used to determine what gets to the head of the queue by providing an optional constructor argument:

```
priority_queue<int> pq1;               // default version
priority_queue<int> pq2(greater<int>); // use greater<int> to order
```

The `greater<>()` function is a predefined function object, and it is discussed later in this chapter.

stack

Like `queue`, `stack` (declared in the `stack`—formerly `stack.h`—header file) is an adapter class. It gives an underlying class (`vector`, by default) the typical stack interface.

The `stack` template is more restrictive than `vector`. Not only does it not permit random access to elements of a stack, the `stack` class doesn't even allow you to iterate through a stack. Instead, it limits you to the basic operations that define a stack. You can push a value onto the top of a stack, pop an element from the top of a stack, view the value at the top of a stack, check the number of elements, and test whether the stack is empty. Table 16.10 lists these operations.

TABLE 16.10 `stack` Operations

Method	Description
`bool empty() const`	Returns `true` if the stack is empty and `false` otherwise.
`size_type size() const`	Returns the number of elements in the stack.
`T& top()`	Returns a reference to the element at the top of the stack.
`void push(const T& x)`	Inserts `x` at the top of the stack.
`void pop()`	Removes the element at the top of the stack.

Much as with `queue`, if you want to use a value from a stack, you first use `top()` to retrieve the value, and then you use `pop()` to remove it from the stack.

Associative Containers

An *associative container* is another refinement of the container concept. An associative container associates a value with a key and uses the key to find the value. For example, the values could be structures representing employee information, such as name, address, office number, home and work phones, health plan, and so on, and the key could be a unique employee number. To fetch the employee information, a program would use the key to locate the employee structure. Recall that for a container X, in general, the expression `X::value_type` indicates the type of value stored in the container. For an associative container, the expression `X::key_type` indicates the type used for the key.

The strength of an associative container is that it provides rapid access to its elements. Like a sequence, an associative container allows you to insert new elements; however, you can't specify a particular location for the inserted elements. The reason is that an associative container usually has a particular algorithm for determining where to place data so that it can retrieve information quickly.

The STL provides four associative containers: `set`, `multiset`, `map`, and `multimap`. The first two types are defined in the `set` header file (formerly separately in `set.h` and `multiset.h`), and the second two types are defined in the `map` header file (formerly separately in `map.h` and `multimap.h`).

The simplest of the bunch is `set`; the value type is the same as the key type, and the keys are unique, meaning there is no more than one instance of a key in a set. Indeed, for `set`, the value is the key. The `multiset` type is like the `set` type except that it can have more than one value with the same key. For example, if the key and value type are `int`, a `multiset` object could hold, say 1, 2, 2, 2, 3, 5, 7, and 7.

For the `map` type, the value type is different from the key type, and the keys are unique, with only one value per key. The `multimap` type is similar to `map`, except one key can be associated with multiple values.

There's too much information about these types to cover in this chapter (but Appendix G does list the methods), so let's just look at a simple example that uses `set` and a simple example that uses `multimap`.

A set Example

The STL `set` models several concepts. It is an associative set, it is reversible, it is sorted, and the keys are unique, so it can hold no more than one of any given value. Like `vector` and `list`, `set` uses a template parameter to provide the type stored:

```
set<string> A;  // a set of string objects
```

An optional second template argument can be used to indicate a comparison function or object to be used to order the key. By default, the `less<>` template (discussed later) is used. Older C++ implementations may not provide a default value and thus require an explicit template parameter:

```
set<string, less<string> > A;  // older implementation
```

Consider the following code:

```
const int N = 6;
string s1[N] = {"buffoon", "thinkers", "for", "heavy", "can", "for"};
set<string> A(s1, s1 + N);        // initialize set A using a range from array
ostream_iterator<string, char> out(cout, " ");
copy(A.begin(), A.end(), out);
```

Like other containers, `set` has a constructor (refer to Table 16.6) that takes a range of iterators as arguments. This provides a simple way to initialize a set to the contents of an array. Remember that the last element of a range is one past-the-end, and `s1 + N` points to one position past-the-end of array `s1`. The output for this code fragment illustrates that keys are unique (the string `"for"` appears twice in the array but once in the set) and that the set is sorted:

```
buffoon can for heavy thinkers
```

Mathematics defines some standard operations for sets. For example, the union of two sets is a set that combines the contents of the two sets. If a particular value is common to both sets, it appears just once in the union because of the unique key feature. The intersection of two sets is a set that consists of the elements that are common to both sets. The difference between two sets is the first set minus the elements common to both sets.

The STL provides algorithms that support these operations. They are general functions rather than methods, so they aren't restricted to **set** objects. However, all **set** objects automatically satisfy the precondition for using these algorithms—namely, that the container be sorted. The **set_union()** function takes five iterators as arguments. The first two define a range in one set, the second two define a range in a second set, and the final iterator is an output iterator that identifies a location to which to copy the resultant set. For example, to display the union of sets **A** and **B**, you can use this:

```
set_union(A.begin(), A.end(), B.begin(), B.end(),
          ostream_iterator<string, char> out(cout, " "));
```

Suppose you want to place the result into a set **C** instead of displaying it. In this case, you would want the last argument to be an iterator into **C**. The obvious choice is **C.begin()**, but that doesn't work for two reasons. The first reason is that associative sets treat keys as constant values, so the iterator returned by **C.begin()** is a constant iterator and can't be used as an output iterator. The second reason not to use **C.begin()** directly is that **set_union()**, like **copy()**, overwrites existing data in a container and requires the container to have sufficient space to hold the new information. **C**, being empty, does not satisfy that requirement. But the **insert_iterator** template discussed earlier solves both problems. Earlier you saw that it converts copying to insertion. Also, it models the output iterator concept, so you can use it to write to a container. So you can construct an anonymous **insert_iterator** to copy information to **C**. The constructor, recall, takes the name of the container and an iterator as arguments:

```
set_union(A.begin(), A.end(), B.begin(), B.end(),
          insert_iterator<set<string> >(C, C.begin()));
```

The **set_intersection()** and **set_difference()** functions find the set intersection and set difference of two sets, and they have the same interface as **set_union()**.

Two useful **set** methods are **lower_bound()** and **upper_bound()**. The **lower_bound()** method takes a key-type value as its argument and returns an iterator that points to the first member of the set that is not less than the key argument. Similarly, the **upper_bound()** method takes a key as its argument and returns an iterator that points to the first member of the set that is greater than the key argument. For example, if you had a set of strings, you could use these methods to identify a range encompassing all strings from **"b"** up to **"f"** in the set.

Because sorting determines where additions to a set go, the class has insertion methods that just specify the material to be inserted, without specifying a position. If **A** and **B** are sets of strings, for example, you can use this:

```
string s("tennis");
A.insert(s);                     // insert a value
B.insert(A.begin(), A.end());    // insert a range
```

Listing 16.11 illustrates these uses of sets.

LISTING 16.11   setops.cpp

```
// setops.cpp -- some set operations
#include <iostream>
#include <string>
```

LISTING 16.11   Continued

```cpp
#include <set>
#include <algorithm>
#include <iterator>

int main()
{
    using namespace std;
    const int N = 6;
    string s1[N] = {"buffoon", "thinkers", "for", "heavy", "can", "for"};
    string s2[N] = {"metal", "any", "food", "elegant", "deliver","for"};

    set<string> A(s1, s1 + N);
    set<string> B(s2, s2 + N);

    ostream_iterator<string, char> out(cout, " ");
    cout << "Set A: ";
    copy(A.begin(), A.end(), out);
    cout << endl;
    cout << "Set B: ";
    copy(B.begin(), B.end(), out);
    cout << endl;

    cout << "Union of A and B:\n";
    set_union(A.begin(), A.end(), B.begin(), B.end(), out);
    cout << endl;

    cout << "Intersection of A and B:\n";
    set_intersection(A.begin(), A.end(), B.begin(), B.end(), out);
    cout << endl;

    cout << "Difference of A and B:\n";
    set_difference(A.begin(), A.end(), B.begin(), B.end(), out);
    cout << endl;

    set<string> C;
    cout << "Set C:\n";
    set_union(A.begin(), A.end(), B.begin(), B.end(),
        insert_iterator<set<string> >(C, C.begin()));
    copy(C.begin(), C.end(), out);
    cout << endl;

    string s3("grungy");
    C.insert(s3);
    cout << "Set C after insertion:\n";
    copy(C.begin(), C.end(),out);
    cout << endl;

    cout << "Showing a range:\n";
    copy(C.lower_bound("ghost"),C.upper_bound("spook"), out);
    cout << endl;

    return 0;
}
```

Here is the output of the program in Listing 16.11:

```
Set A: buffoon can for heavy thinkers
Set B: any deliver elegant food for metal
Union of A and B:
any buffoon can deliver elegant food for heavy metal thinkers
Intersection of A and B:
for
Difference of A and B:
buffoon can heavy thinkers
Set C:
any buffoon can deliver elegant food for heavy metal thinkers
Set C after insertion:
any buffoon can deliver elegant food for grungy heavy metal thinkers
Showing a range:
grungy heavy metal
```

Like most of the examples in this chapter, the code in Listing 16.11 takes the lazy route for handling the `std` namespace:

```
using namespace std;
```

It does so in order to simplify the presentation. The examples use so many elements of the `std` namespace that using directives or the scope-resolution operators would tend to make the code look a bit fussy:

```
std::set<std::string> B(s2, s2 + N);
std::ostream_iterator<std::string, char> out(std::cout, " ");
std::cout << "Set A: ";
std::copy(A.begin(), A.end(), out);
```

A multimap Example

Like `set`, `multimap` is a reversible, sorted, associative container. However, with `multimap`, the key type is different from the value type, and a `multimap` object can have more than one value associated with a particular key.

The basic `multimap` declaration specifies the key type and the type of value, stored as template arguments. For example, the following declaration creates a `multimap` object that uses `int` as the key type and `string` as the type of value stored:

```
multimap<int,string> codes;
```

An optional third template argument can be used to indicate a comparison function or an object to be used to order the key. By default, the `less<>` template (discussed later) is used with the key type as its parameter. Older C++ implementations may require this template parameter explicitly.

To keep information together, the actual value type combines the key type and the data type into a single pair. To do this, the STL uses a `pair<class T, class U>` template class for storing two kinds of values in a single object. If `keytype` is the key type and `datatype` is the type of the stored data, the value type is `pair<const keytype, datatype>`. For example, the value type for the `codes` object declared earlier is `pair<const int, string>`.

Suppose, for example, that you want to store city names, using the area code as a key. This happens to fit the `codes` declaration, which uses an `int` for a key and a `string` as a data type. One approach is to create a pair and then insert it:

```
pair<const int, string> item(213, "Los Angeles");
codes.insert(item);
```

Or you can create an anonymous `pair` object and insert it in a single statement:

```
codes.insert(pair<const int, string> (213, "Los Angeles"));
```

Because items are sorted by key, there's no need to identify an insertion location.

Given a `pair` object, you can access the two components by using the `first` and `second` members:

```
pair<const int, string> item(213, "Los Angeles");
cout << item.first << ' ' << item.second << endl;
```

What about getting information about a `multimap` object? The `count()` member function takes a key as its argument and returns the number of items that have that key. The `lower_bound()` and `upper_bound()` member functions take a key and work as they do for `set`. Also, the `equal_range()` member function takes a key as its argument and returns iterators representing the range matching that key. In order to return two values, the method packages them into a `pair` object, this time with both template arguments being the iterator type. For example, the following would print a list of cities in the `codes` object with area code 718:

```
pair<multimap<KeyType, string>::iterator,
    multimap<KeyType, string>::iterator> range
                      = codes.equal_range(718);
cout << "Cities with area code 718:\n";
for (it = range.first; it != range.second; ++it)
    cout <<  (*it).second    << endl;
```

Listing 16.12 demonstrates most of these techniques. It also uses `typedef` to simplify some of the code writing.

LISTING 16.12   multmap.cpp

```
// multmap.cpp -- use a multimap
#include <iostream>
#include <string>
#include <map>
#include <algorithm>
```

LISTING 16.12   Continued

```
typedef int KeyType;
typedef std::pair<const KeyType, std::string> Pair;
typedef std::multimap<KeyType, std::string> MapCode;

int main()
{
    using namespace std;
    MapCode codes;

    codes.insert(Pair(415, "San Francisco"));
    codes.insert(Pair(510, "Oakland"));
    codes.insert(Pair(718, "Brooklyn"));
    codes.insert(Pair(718, "Staten Island"));
    codes.insert(Pair(415, "San Rafael"));
    codes.insert(Pair(510, "Berkeley"));

    cout << "Number of cities with area code 415: "
        << codes.count(415) << endl;
    cout << "Number of cities with area code 718: "
        << codes.count(718) << endl;
    cout << "Number of cities with area code 510: "
        << codes.count(510) << endl;
    cout << "Area Code   City\n";
    MapCode::iterator it;
    for (it = codes.begin(); it != codes.end(); ++it)
        cout << "    " << (*it).first << "    "
            << (*it).second    << endl;

    pair<MapCode::iterator, MapCode::iterator> range
        = codes.equal_range(718);
    cout << "Cities with area code 718:\n";
    for (it = range.first; it != range.second; ++it)
        cout << (*it).second    << endl;

    return 0;
}
```

Compatibility Note

Older STL implementations may use `multimap.h` and `algo.h`. Older implementations may require `less<Pair>` as a third template argument for `multimap`. Also, older versions may use `ostream_iterator<string>` instead of `ostream_iterator<string,char>`. Borland's C++Builder 1.0 wants the `const` omitted from the `Pair` typedef.

Here is the output of the program in Listing 16.12:

```
Number of cities with area code 415: 2
Number of cities with area code 718: 2
Number of cities with area code 510: 2
```

```
Area Code   City
    415     San Francisco
    415     San Rafael
    510     Oakland
    510     Berkeley
    718     Brooklyn
    718     Staten Island
Cities with area code 718:
Brooklyn
Staten Island
```

Function Objects (aka Functors)

Many STL algorithms use *function objects*, also known as *functors*. A *functor* is any object that can be used with () in the manner of a function. This includes normal function names, pointers to functions, and class objects for which the () operator is overloaded—that is, classes for which the peculiar-looking function `operator()()` is defined. For example, you could define a class like this:

```cpp
class Linear
{
private:
    double slope;
    double y0;
public:
    Linear(double _sl = 1, double _y = 0)
        : slope(_sl), y0(_y) {}
    double operator()(double x) {return y0 + slope * x; }
};
```

The overloaded () operator then allows you to use `Linear` objects like functions:

```cpp
Linear f1;
Linear f2(2.5, 10.0);
double y1 = f1(12.5);     // right-hand side is f1.operator()(12.5)
double y2 = f2(0.4);
```

Here `y1` is calculated using the expression $0 + 1 * 12.5$, and `y2` is calculated using the expression $10.0 + 2.5 * 0.4$. In the expression `y0 + slope * x`, the values for `y0` and `slope` come from the constructor for the object, and the value of `x` comes from the argument to `operator()()`.

Remember the `for_each` function? It applied a specified function to each member of a range:

```cpp
for_each(books.begin(), books.end(), ShowReview);
```

In general, the third argument could be a functor, not just a regular function. Actually, this raises a question: How do you declare the third argument? You can't declare it as a function pointer because a function pointer specifies the argument type. Because a container can contain just about any type, you don't know in advance what particular argument type should be used. The STL solves that problem by using templates. The `for_each` prototype looks like this:

```
template<class InputIterator, class Function>
Function for_each(InputIterator first, InputIterator last, Function f);
```

The `ShowReview()` prototype is this:

```
void ShowReview(const Review &);
```

This makes the identifier `ShowReview` have the type `void (*)(const Review &)`, so that is the type assigned to the template argument `Function`. With a different function call, the `Function` argument could represent a class type that has an overloaded `()` operator. Ultimately, the `for_each()` code will have an expression using `f(...)`. In the `ShowReview()` example, `f` is a pointer to a function, and `f(...)` invokes the function. If the final `for_each()` argument is an object, then `f(...)` becomes the object that invokes its overloaded `()` operator.

Functor Concepts

Just as the STL defines concepts for containers and iterators, it defines functor concepts:

- A *generator* is a functor that can be called with no arguments.

- A *unary function* is a functor that can be called with one argument.

- A *binary function* is a functor that can be called with two arguments.

For example, the functor supplied to `for_each()` should be a unary function because it is applied to one container element at a time.

Of course, these concepts come with refinements:

- A unary function that returns a `bool` value is a *predicate*.

- A binary function that returns a `bool` value is a *binary predicate*.

Several STL functions require predicate or binary predicate arguments. For example, Listing 16.7 uses a version of `sort()` that takes a binary predicate as its third argument:

```
bool WorseThan(const Review & r1, const Review & r2);
...
sort(books.begin(), books.end(), WorseThan);
```

The `list` template has a `remove_if()` member that takes a predicate as an argument. It applies the predicate to each member in the indicated range, removing those elements for which the predicate returns `true`. For example, the following code would remove all elements greater than 100 from the list `three`:

```
bool tooBig(int n){ return n > 100; }
list<int> scores;
...
scores.remove_if(tooBig);
```

Incidentally, this last example shows where a class functor might be useful. Suppose you want to remove every value greater than 200 from a second list. It would be nice if you could pass the cut-off value to `tooBig()` as a second argument so you could use the function with different values, but a predicate can have but one argument. If, however, you design a `TooBig` class, you can use class members instead of function arguments to convey additional information:

```cpp
template<class T>
class TooBig
{
private:
    T cutoff;
public:
    TooBig(const T & t) : cutoff(t) {}
    bool operator()(const T & v) { return v > cutoff; }
};
```

Here one value (v) is passed as a function argument, and the second argument (`cutoff`) is set by the class constructor. Given this definition, you can initialize different `TooBig` objects to different cut-off values to be used in calls to `remove_if()`. Listing 16.13 illustrates the technique.

LISTING 16.13 `functor.cpp`

```cpp
// functor.cpp -- using a functor
#include <iostream>
#include <list>
#include <iterator>

template<class T>  // functor class defines operator()()
class TooBig
{
private:
    T cutoff;
public:
    TooBig(const T & t) : cutoff(t) {}
    bool operator()(const T & v) { return v > cutoff; }
};

int main()
{
    using std::list;
    using std::cout;
    using std::endl;

    TooBig<int> f100(100); // limit = 100
    list<int> yadayada;
    list<int> etcetera;
    int vals[10] = {50, 100, 90, 180, 60, 210, 415, 88, 188, 201};

    yadayada.insert(yadayada.begin(), vals, vals + 10);
    etcetera.insert(etcetera.begin(), vals, vals + 10);
    std::ostream_iterator<int, char> out(cout, " ");
    cout << "Original lists:\n";
    copy(yadayada.begin(), yadayada.end(), out);
    cout << endl;
```

LISTING 16.13   *Continued*

```
        copy(etcetera.begin(), etcetera.end(), out);
        cout << endl;
        yadayada.remove_if(f100);                  // use a named function object
        etcetera.remove_if(TooBig<int>(200));   // construct a function object
        cout <<"Trimmed lists:\n";
        copy(yadayada.begin(), yadayada.end(), out);
        cout << endl;
        copy(etcetera.begin(), etcetera.end(), out);
        cout << endl;

        return 0;
}
```

One functor (`f100`) is a declared object, and the second (`TooBig<int>(200)`) is an anonymous object created by a constructor call. Here's the output of the program in Listing 16.13:

```
Original lists:
50 100 90 180 60 210 415 88 188 201
50 100 90 180 60 210 415 88 188 201
Trimmed lists:
50 100 90 60 88
50 100 90 180 60 88 188
```

Compatibility Note

The `remove_if()` method is a template method of a template class. Template methods are a recent extension to C++ template facilities, so older compilers may not support this method. However, there is also a nonmember `remove_if()` function that takes a range (two iterators) and a predicate as arguments.

Suppose that you already have a template function with two arguments:

```
template <class T>
bool tooBig(const T & val, const T & lim)
{
    return val > lim;
}
```

You can use a class to convert it to a one-argument function object:

```
template<class T>
class TooBig2
{
private:
    T cutoff;
public:
    TooBig2(const T & t) : cutoff(t) {}
    bool operator()(const T & v) { return tooBig<T>(v, cutoff); }
};
```

That is, you can use the following:

```
TooBig2<int> tB100(100);
int x;
cin >> x;
if (tB100(x))    // same as if (tooBig(x,100))
    ...
```

So the call `tB100(x)` is the same as `tooBig(x,100)`, but the two-argument function is converted to a one-argument function object, with the second argument being used to construct the function object. In short, the class functor `TooBig2` is a function adapter that adapts a function to meet a different interface.

Predefined Functors

The STL defines several elementary functors. They perform actions such as adding two values and comparing two values for equality. They are provided to help support STL functions that take functions as arguments. For example, consider the `transform()` function. It has two versions. The first version takes four arguments. The first two arguments are iterators that specify a range in a container. (By now you must be familiar with that approach.) The third is an iterator that specifies where to copy the result. The final is a functor that is applied to each element in the range to produce each new element in the result. For example, consider the following:

```
const int LIM = 5;
double arr1[LIM] = {36, 39, 42, 45, 48};
vector<double> gr8(arr1, arr1 + LIM);
ostream_iterator<double, char> out(cout, " ");
transform(gr8.begin(), gr8.end(), out, sqrt);
```

This code calculates the square root of each element and sends the resulting values to the output stream. The destination iterator can be in the original range. For example, replacing `out` in this example with `gr8.begin()` would copy the new values over the old values. Clearly, the functor used must be one that works with a single argument.

The second version uses a function that takes two arguments, applying the function to one element from each of two ranges. It takes an additional argument, which comes third in order, identifying the start of the second range. For example, if `m8` were a second `vector<double>` object and if `mean(double, double)` returned the mean of two values, the following would output the average of each pair of values from `gr8` and `m8`:

```
transform(gr8.begin(), gr8.end(), m8.begin(), out, mean);
```

Now suppose you want to add the two arrays. You can't use + as an argument because, for type `double`, + is a built-in operator, not a function. You could define a function to add two numbers and use it:

```
double add(double x, double y) { return x + y; }
...
transform(gr8.begin(), gr8.end(), m8.begin(), out, add);
```

But then you'd have to define a separate function for each type. It would be better to define a template, except that you don't have to because the STL already has. The functional (formerly function.h) header defines several template class function objects, including one called plus<>().

Using the plus<> class for ordinary addition is possible, if awkward:

```
#include <functional>
...
plus<double> add;  // create a plus<double> object
double y = add(2.2, 3.4); // using plus<double>::operator()()
```

But it makes it easy to provide a function object as an argument:

```
transform(gr8.begin(), gr8.end(), m8.begin(), out, plus<double>() );
```

Here, rather than create a named object, the code uses the plus<double> constructor to construct a functor to do the adding. (The parentheses indicate calling the default constructor; what's passed to transform() is the constructed function object.)

The STL provides functor equivalents for all the built-in arithmetic, relational, and logical operators. Table 16.11 shows the names for these functor equivalents. They can be used with the C++ built-in types or with any user-defined type that overloads the corresponding operator.

Caution

Older C++ implementations use the functor name times instead of multiplies.

TABLE 16.11 Operators and Functor Equivalents

Operator	Functor Equivalent
+	plus
-	minus
*	multiplies
/	divides
%	modulus
-	negate
==	equal_to
!=	not_equal_to
>	greater

TABLE 16.11   Continued

Operator	Functor Equivalent
<	less
>=	greater_equal
<=	less_equal
&&	logical_and
||	logical_or
!	logical_not

Adaptable Functors and Function Adapters

The predefined functors in Table 16.11 are all *adaptable*. Actually, the STL has five related concepts: adaptable generators, adaptable unary functions, adaptable binary functions, adaptable predicates, and adaptable binary predicates.

What makes a functor adaptable is that it carries `typedef` members identifying its argument types and return type. The members are called `result_type`, `first_argument_type`, and `second_argument_type`, and they represent what they sound like. For example, the return type of a `plus<int>` object is identified as `plus<int>::result_type`, and this would be a `typedef` for `int`.

The significance of a functor being adaptable is that it can then be used by function adapter objects, which assume the existence of these `typedef` members. For example, a function with an argument that is an adaptable functor can use the `result_type` member to declare a variable that matches the function's return type.

Indeed, the STL provides function adapter classes that use these facilities. For example, suppose you want to multiply each element of the vector `gr8` by 2.5. That calls for using the `transform()` version with a unary function argument, like the

```
transform(gr8.begin(), gr8.end(), out, sqrt);
```

example shown earlier. The `multiplies()` functor can do the multiplication, but it's a binary function. So you need a function adapter that converts a functor that has two arguments to one that has one argument. The earlier `TooBig2` example shows one way, but the STL has automated the process with the `binder1st` and `binder2nd` classes, which convert adaptable binary functions to adaptable unary functions.

Let's look at `binder1st`. Suppose you have an adaptable binary function object `f2()`. You can create a `binder1st` object that binds a particular value, called `val`, to be used as the first argument to `f2()`:

```
binder1st(f2, val) f1;
```

Then, invoking f1(x) with its single argument returns the same value as invoking f2() with val as its first argument and f1()'s argument as its second argument. That is, f1(x) is equivalent to f2(val, x), except that it is a unary function instead of a binary function. The f2() function has been adapted. Again, this is possible only if f2() is an adaptable function.

This might seem a bit awkward. However, the STL provides the bind1st() function to simplify using the binder1st class. You give it the function name and value used to construct a binder1st object, and it returns an object of that type. For example, you can convert the binary function multiplies() to a unary function that multiplies its argument by 2.5. Just do this:

```
bind1st(multiplies<double>(), 2.5)
```

Thus, the solution to multiplying every element in gr8 by 2.5 and displaying the results is this:

```
transform(gr8.begin(), gr8.end(), out,
        bind1st(multiplies<double>(), 2.5));
```

The binder2nd class is similar, except that it assigns the constant to the second argument instead of to the first. It has a helper function called bind2nd that works analogously to bind1st.

> **Tip**
>
> If an STL function calls for a unary function and you have an adaptable binary function that does the right thing, you can use bind1st() or bind2nd() to adapt the binary function to a unary interface.

Listing 16.14 incorporates some of the recent examples into a short program.

LISTING 16.14   funadap.cpp

```cpp
// funadap.cpp -- using function adapters
#include <iostream>
#include <vector>
#include <iterator>
#include <algorithm>
#include <functional>

void Show(double);
const int LIM = 5;
int main()
{
    using namespace std;
    double arr1[LIM] = {36, 39, 42, 45, 48};
    double arr2[LIM] = {25, 27, 29, 31, 33};
    vector<double> gr8(arr1, arr1 + LIM);
    vector<double> m8(arr2, arr2 + LIM);
    cout.setf(ios_base::fixed);
    cout.precision(1);
    cout << "gr8:\t";
```

LISTING 16.14 Continued

```
    for_each(gr8.begin(), gr8.end(), Show);
    cout << endl;
    cout << "m8: \t";
    for_each(m8.begin(), m8.end(), Show);
    cout << endl;

    vector<double> sum(LIM);
    transform(gr8.begin(), gr8.end(), m8.begin(), sum.begin(),
            plus<double>());
    cout << "sum:\t";
    for_each(sum.begin(), sum.end(), Show);
    cout << endl;

    vector<double> prod(LIM);
    transform(gr8.begin(), gr8.end(), prod.begin(),
            bind1st(multiplies<double>(), 2.5));
    cout << "prod:\t";
    for_each(prod.begin(), prod.end(), Show);
    cout << endl;

    return 0;
}

void Show(double v)
{
    std::cout.width(6);
    std::cout << v << ' ';
}
```

Compatibility Note

Older STL implementations may use `vector.h`, `iterator.h`, `algo.h`, and `function.h`. Also, older implementations may use `times` instead of `multiplies`.

Here is the output of the program in Listing 16.14:

```
gr8:    36.0   39.0   42.0    45.0    48.0
m8:     25.0   27.0   29.0    31.0    33.0
sum:    61.0   66.0   71.0    76.0    81.0
prod:   90.0   97.5  105.0   112.5   120.0
```

Algorithms

The STL contains many nonmember functions for working with containers. You've seen a few of them already: `sort()`, `copy()`, `find()`, `for_each()`, `random_shuffle()`, `set_union()`, `set_intersection()`, `set_difference()`, and `transform()`. You've probably noticed that they feature the same overall design, using iterators to identify data ranges to be processed and to identify where results are to go. Some also take a function object argument to be used as part of the data processing.

There are two main generic components to the algorithm function designs. First, they use templates to provide generic types. Second, they use iterators to provide a generic representation for accessing data in a container. Thus, the `copy()` function can work with a container that holds type `double` values in an array, with a container that holds `string` values in a linked list, or with a container that stores user-defined objects in a tree structure, such as is used by `set`. Because pointers are a special case of iterators, STL functions such as `copy()` can be used with ordinary arrays.

The uniform container design allows meaningful relationships between containers of different kinds. For example, you can use `copy()` to copy values from an ordinary array to a `vector` object, from a `vector` object to a `list` object, and from a `list` object to a `set` object. You can use `==` to compare different kinds of containers—for example, `deque` and `vector`. This is possible because the overloaded `==` operator for containers uses iterators to compare contents, so a `deque` object and a `vector` object test as equal if they have the same content in the same order.

Algorithm Groups

The STL divides the algorithm library into four groups:

- Nonmodifying sequence operations
- Mutating sequence operations
- Sorting and related operations
- Generalized numeric operations

The first three groups are described in the `algorithm` (formerly `algo.h`) header file, and the fourth group, being specifically oriented toward numeric data, gets its own header file, called `numeric`. (Formerly, they, too, were in `algo.h`.)

Nonmodifying sequence operations operate on each element in a range. These operations leave a container unchanged. For example, `find()` and `for_each()` belong to this category.

Mutating sequence operations also operate on each element in a range. As the name suggests, however, they can change the contents of a container. The change could be in values or in the order in which the values are stored. For example, `transform()`, `random_shuffle()`, and `copy()` fall into this category.

Sorting and related operations include several sorting functions (including `sort()`) and a variety of other functions, including the set operations.

The numeric operations include functions to sum the contents of a range, calculate the inner product of two containers, calculate partial sums, and calculate adjacent differences. Typically, these are operations that are characteristic of arrays, so `vector` is the container most likely to be used with them.

Appendix G provides a complete summary of these functions.

General Properties of Algorithms

As you've seen again and again in this chapter, STL functions work with iterators and iterator ranges. The function prototype indicates the assumptions made about the iterators. For example, the `copy()` function has this prototype:

```
template<class InputIterator, class OutputIterator>
OutputIterator copy(InputIterator first, InputIterator last,
                    OutputIterator result);
```

Because the identifiers `InputIterator` and `OutputIterator` are template parameters, they just as easily could have been `T` and `U`. However, the STL documentation uses the template parameter names to indicate the concept that the parameter models. So this declaration tells you that the range parameters must be input iterators or better and that the iterator indicating where the result goes must be an output parameter or better.

One way of classifying algorithms is on the basis of where the result of the algorithm is placed. Some algorithms do their work in place, and others create copies. For example, when the `sort()` function is finished, the result occupies the same location that the original data did. So `sort()` is an *in-place algorithm*. The `copy()` function, however, sends the result of its work to another location, so it is a *copying algorithm*. The `transform()` function can do both. Like `copy()`, it uses an output iterator to indicate where the results go. Unlike `copy()`, `transform()` allows the output iterator to point to a location in the input range, so it can copy the transformed values over the original values.

Some algorithms come in two versions: an in-place version and a copying version. The STL convention is to append `_copy` to the name of the copying version. The latter version takes an additional output iterator parameter to specify the location to which to copy the outcome. For example, there is a `replace()` function that has this prototype:

```
template<class ForwardIterator, class T>
void replace(ForwardIterator first, ForwardIterator last,
             const T& old_value, const T& new_value);
```

It replaces each instance of `old_value` with `new_value`. This occurs in place. Because this algorithm both reads from and writes to container elements, the iterator type has to be `ForwardIterator` or better. The copying version has this prototype:

```
template<class InputIterator, class OutputIterator, class T>
OutputIterator replace_copy(InputIterator first, InputIterator last,
             OutputIterator result,
             const T& old_value, const T& new_value);
```

This time the resulting data is copied to a new location, given by `result`, so the read-only input iterator is sufficient for specifying the range.

Note that `replace_copy()` has an `OutputIterator` return type. The convention for copying algorithms is that they return an iterator pointing to the location one past the last value copied.

Another common variation is that some functions have a version that performs an action conditionally, depending on the result of applying a function to a container element. These versions typically append `_if` to the function name. For example, `replace_if()` replaces an old value with a new value if applying a function to the old value returns the value `true`. Here's the prototype:

```
template<class ForwardIterator, class Predicate class T>
void replace_if(ForwardIterator first, ForwardIterator last,
             Predicate pred, const T& new_value);
```

(Recall that a predicate is a unary function that returns a `bool` value.) There's also a version called `replace_copy_if()`. You can probably figure out what it does and what its prototype is like.

As with `InputIterator`, `Predicate` is a template parameter name and could just as easily be called `T` or `U`. However, the STL chooses to use `Predicate` to remind the user that the actual argument should be a model of the `Predicate` concept. Similarly, the STL uses terms such as `Generator` and `BinaryPredicate` to identify arguments that should model other function object concepts.

The STL and the `string` Class

The `string` class, although not part of the STL, is designed with the STL in mind. For example, it has `begin()`, `end()`, `rbegin()`, and `rend()` members. Thus, it can use the STL interface. Listing 16.15 uses the STL to show all the permutations you can form from the letters in a word. A *permutation* is a rearrangement of the order of the elements in a container. The `next_permutation()` algorithm transforms the contents of a range to the next permutation; in the case of a string, the permutations are arranged in increasing alphabetical order. The algorithm returns `true` if it succeeds and `false` if the range already is in the final sequence. To get all the permutations of a range, you should start with the elements in the earliest possible order, and the program uses the STL `sort()` algorithm for that purpose.

LISTING 16.15   `strgstl.cpp`

```cpp
// strgstl.cpp -- applying the STL to a string
#include <iostream>
#include <string>
#include <algorithm>

int main()
{
    using namespace std;
    string letters;

    cout << "Enter the letter grouping (quit to quit): ";
    while (cin >> letters && letters != "quit")
    {
        cout << "Permutations of " << letters << endl;
        sort(letters.begin(), letters.end());
        cout << letters << endl;
        while (next_permutation(letters.begin(), letters.end()))
```

LISTING 16.15 *Continued*

```
            cout << letters << endl;
        cout << "Enter next sequence (quit to quit): ";
    }
    cout << "Done.\n";

    return 0;
}
```

Here's a sample run of the program in Listing 16.15:

```
Enter the letter grouping (quit to quit): wed
Permutations of wed
dew
dwe
edw
ewd
wde
wed
Enter next sequence (quit to quit): wee
Permutations of wee
eew
ewe
wee
Enter next sequence (quit to quit): quit
Done.
```

Note that the `next_permutation()` algorithm automatically provides only unique permutations, which is why the output shows more permutations for the word *wed* than for the word *wee*, which has duplicate letters.

Functions Versus Container Methods

Sometimes you have a choice between using an STL method and an STL function. Usually, the method is the better choice. First, it should be better optimized for a particular container. Second, being a member function, it can use a template class's memory management facilities and resize a container when needed.

Suppose, for example, that you have a list of numbers and you want to remove all instances of a certain value, say **4**, from the list. If `la` is a `list<int>` object, you can use the list `remove()` method:

```
la.remove(4);  // remove all 4s from the list
```

After this method call, all elements with the value **4** are removed from the list, and the list is automatically resized.

There is also an STL algorithm called `remove()` (see Appendix G). Instead of being invoked by an object, it takes range arguments. So, if `lb` is a `list<int>` object, a call to the function could look like this:

```
remove(lb.begin(), lb.end(), 4);
```

However, because this `remove()` is not a member, it can't adjust the size of the list. Instead, it makes sure all the non-removed items are at the beginning of the list, and it returns an iterator to the new past-the-end value. You can then use this iterator to fix the list size. For example, you can use the list `erase()` method to remove a range that describes the part of the list that is no longer needed. Listing 16.16 shows how this process works.

LISTING 16.16   `listrmv.cpp`

```cpp
// listrmv.cpp -- applying the STL to a string
#include <iostream>
#include <list>
#include <algorithm>

void Show(int);
const int LIM = 10;
int main()
{
    using namespace std;
    int ar[LIM] = {4, 5, 4, 2, 2, 3, 4, 8, 1, 4};
    list<int> la(ar, ar + LIM);
    list<int> lb(la);

    cout << "Original list contents:\n\t";
    for_each(la.begin(), la.end(), Show);
    cout << endl;
    la.remove(4);
    cout << "After using the remove() method:\n";
    cout << "la:\t";
    for_each(la.begin(), la.end(), Show);
    cout << endl;
    list<int>::iterator last;
    last = remove(lb.begin(), lb.end(), 4);
    cout << "After using the remove() function:\n";
    cout << "lb:\t";
    for_each(lb.begin(), lb.end(), Show);
    cout << endl;
    lb.erase(last, lb.end());
    cout << "After using the erase() method:\n";
    cout << "lb:\t";
    for_each(lb.begin(), lb.end(), Show);
    cout << endl;

    return 0;
}

void Show(int v)
{
    std::cout << v << ' ';
}
```

Here's the output of the program in Listing 16.16:

```
Original list contents:
    4 5 4 2 2 3 4 8 1 4
After using the remove() method:
la: 5 2 2 3 8 1
After using the remove() function:
lb: 5 2 2 3 8 1 4 8 1 4
After using the erase() method:
lb: 5 2 2 3 8 1
```

As you can see, the `remove()` method reduces the list `la` from 10 elements to 6 elements. However, list `lb` still contains 10 elements after the `remove()` function is applied to it. The last 4 elements are disposable, because each is either the value `4` or a duplicate of a value moved farther to the front of the list.

Although the methods are usually better suited, the nonmethod functions are more general. As you've seen, you can use them on arrays and `string` objects as well as STL containers, and you can use them with mixed container types—for example, to save data from a vector container in a list or a set.

Using the STL

The STL is a library whose parts are designed to work together. The STL components are tools, but they are also building blocks to create other tools. Let's illustrate this with an example. Suppose you want to write a program that lets the user enter words. At the end, you'd like a record of the words as they were entered, an alphabetical list of the words used (capitalization differences ignored), and a record of how many times each word was entered. To keep things simple, let's assume that the input contains no numbers or punctuation.

Entering and saving the list of words is simple enough. Following the example of Listings 16.5 and 16.6, you can create a `vector<string>` object and use `push_back()` to add input words to the vector:

```
vector<string> words;
string input;
while (cin >> input && input != "quit")
    words.push_back(input);
```

What about getting the alphabetic word list? You can use `sort()` followed by `unique()`, but that approach overwrites the original data because `sort()` is an in-place algorithm. There is an easier way that avoids this problem. You can create a `set<string>` object and copy (using an insert iterator) the words from the vector to the set. A set automatically sorts its contents, which means you don't have to call `sort()`, and a set allows only one copy of a key, so that takes the place of calling `unique()`. Wait! The specification called for ignoring the case differences. One way to handle that is to use `transform()` instead of `copy()` to copy data from the vector to the set. For the transformation function, you can use one that converts a string to lowercase:

```
set<string> wordset;
transform(words.begin(), words.end(),
    insert_iterator<set<string> > (wordset, wordset.begin()), ToLower);
```

The ToLower() function is easy to write. You just use transform() to apply the tolower() function to each element in the string, using the string both as source and destination. Remember, string objects, too, can use the STL functions. Passing and returning the string as a reference means the algorithm works on the original string without having to make copies. Here's the code for ToLower():

```
string & ToLower(string & st)
{
    transform(st.begin(), st.end(), st.begin(), tolower);
    return st;
}
```

One possible problem is that the tolower() function is defined as int tolower(int), and some compilers want the function to match the element type, which is char. One solution is to replace tolower with toLower and to provide the following definition:

```
char toLower(char ch) { return tolower(ch); }
```

To get the number of times each word appears in the input, you can use the count() function. It takes a range and a value as arguments, and it returns the number of times the value appears in the range. You can use the vector object to provide the range and the set object to provide the list of words to count. That is, for each word in the set, you can count how many times it appears in the vector. To keep the resulting count associated with the correct word, you can store the word and the count as a pair<const string, int> object in a map object. The word will be the key (just one copy), and the count will be the value. This can be done in a single loop:

```
map<string, int> wordmap;
set<string>::iterator  si;
for (si = wordset.begin(); si != wordset.end(); si++)
    wordmap.insert(pair<string, int>(*si, count(words.begin(),
    words.end(), *si)));
```

Caution

Older STL implementations declare count() as type void. Instead of using a return value, you provide a fourth argument passed as a reference, and the number of items is added to that argument:

```
int ct = 0;
count(words.begin(), words.end(), *si), ct));     count added to ct
```

The map class has an interesting feature: You can use array notation with keys that serve as indexes to access the stored values. For example, wordmap["the"] would represent the value associated with the key "the", which in this case is the number of occurrences of the string "the". Because the wordset container holds all the keys used by wordmap, you can use the following code as an alternative and more attractive way of storing results:

```
for (si = wordset.begin(); si != wordset.end(); si++)
    wordmap[*si] = count(words.begin(), words.end(), *si);
```

Because `si` points to a string in the `wordset` container, `*si` is a string and can serve as a key for `wordmap`. This code places both keys and values into the `wordmap` map.

Similarly, you can use the array notation to report results:

```
for (si = wordset.begin(); si != wordset.end(); si++)
    cout << *si << ": " << wordmap[*si] << endl;
```

If a key is invalid, the corresponding value is **0**.

Listing 16.17 puts these ideas together and includes code to display the contents of the three containers (a vector with the input, a set with a word list, and a map with a word count).

LISTING 16.17   `usealgo.cpp`

```
//usealgo.cpp -- using several STL elements
#include <iostream>
#include <string>
#include <vector>
#include <set>
#include <map>
#include <iterator>
#include <algorithm>
#include <cctype>
using namespace std;

char toLower(char ch) { return tolower(ch); }
string & ToLower(string & st);
void display(const string & s);

int main()
{
    vector<string> words;
    cout << "Enter words (enter quit to quit):\n";
    string input;
    while (cin >> input && input != "quit")
        words.push_back(input);

    cout << "You entered the following words:\n";
    for_each(words.begin(), words.end(), display);
    cout << endl;

    // place words in set, converting to lowercase
    set<string> wordset;
    transform(words.begin(), words.end(),
        insert_iterator<set<string> > (wordset, wordset.begin()),
        ToLower);
    cout << "\nAlphabetic list of words:\n";
    for_each(wordset.begin(), wordset.end(), display);
    cout << endl;

    // place word and frequency in map
    map<string, int> wordmap;
```

LISTING 16.17   *Continued*

```
    set<string>::iterator si;
    for (si = wordset.begin(); si != wordset.end(); si++)
        wordmap[*si] = count(words.begin(), words.end(), *si);

    // display map contents
    cout << "\nWord frequency:\n";
    for (si = wordset.begin(); si != wordset.end(); si++)
        cout << *si << ": " << wordmap[*si] << endl;

    return 0;
}

string & ToLower(string & st)
{
    transform(st.begin(), st.end(), st.begin(), toLower);
    return st;
}

void display(const string & s)
{
    cout << s << " ";
}
```

Compatibility Note

Older C++ implementations may use `vector.h`, `set.h`, `map.h`, `iterator.h`, `algo.h`, and `ctype.h`. Also, older implementations may require the `set` and `map` templates to use an additional `less<string>` template parameter. Older versions use the type `void count()` function mentioned earlier.

Here is a sample run of the program in Listing 16.17:

```
Enter words (enter quit to quit):
The dog saw the cat and thought the cat fat
The cat thought the cat perfect
quit
You entered the following words:
The dog saw the cat and thought the cat fat The cat thought the cat perfect

Alphabetic list of words:
and cat dog fat perfect saw the thought

Word frequency:
and: 1
cat: 4
dog: 1
fat: 1
perfect: 1
saw: 1
the: 5
thought: 2
```

The moral here is that your attitude when using the STL should be to avoid writing as much code as possible. STL's generic and flexible design should save you lots of work. Also, the STL designers are algorithm people who are very much concerned with efficiency. So the algorithms are well chosen and inline.

Other Libraries

C++ provides some other class libraries that are more specialized than the examples covered so far in this chapter. The `complex` header file provides a `complex` class template for complex numbers, with specializations for `float`, `long`, and `long double`. The class provides standard complex number operations, along with standard functions that can be used with complex numbers.

Chapter 14 introduces the `valarray` template class, supported by the `valarray` header file. This class template is designed to represent numeric arrays and provides support for a variety of numeric array operations, such as adding the contents of one array to another, applying math functions to each element of an array, and applying linear algebra operations to arrays.

vector **and** valarray

Perhaps you are wondering why C++ has two array templates: `vector` and `valarray`. These classes were developed by different groups for different purposes. The `vector` template class is part of a system of container classes and algorithms. The `vector` class supports container-oriented activities, such as sorting, insertion, rearrangement, searching, transferring data to other containers, and other manipulations. The `valarray` class template, on the other hand, is oriented toward numeric computation, and it is not part of the STL. It doesn't have `push_back()` and `insert()` methods, for example, but it does provide a simple, intuitive interface for many mathematical operations.

Suppose, for example, that you have these declarations:

```
vector<double> ved1(10), ved2(10), ved3(10);
valarray<double> vad1(10), vad2(10), vad3(10);
```

Furthermore, assume that `ved1`, `ved2`, `vad1`, and `vad2` all acquire suitable values. Suppose you want to assign the sum of the first elements of two arrays to the first element of a third array, and so on. With the `vector` class, you would do this:

```
transform(ved1.begin(), ved1.end(), ved2.begin(), ved3.begin(),
        plus<double>());
```

However, the `valarray` class overloads all the arithmetic operators to work with `valarray` objects, so you would use this:

```
vad3 = vad1 + vad2;    // + overloaded
```

Similarly,

```
vad3 = vad1 * vad2;    // * overloaded
```

would result in each element of vad3 being the product of the corresponding elements in vad1 and vad2.

Suppose you want to replace every value in an array with that value multiplied by 2.5. The STL approach is this:

```
transform(ved3.begin(), ved3.end(), ved3.begin(),
        bind1st(multiplies<double>(), 2.5));
```

The valarray class overloads multiplying a valarray object by a single value, and it also overloads the various computed assignment operators, so you could use either of the following:

```
vad3 = 2.5 * vad3;      // * overloaded
vad3 *= 2.5;            // *= overloaded
```

Suppose you want to take the natural logarithm of every element of one array and store the result in the corresponding element of a second array. The STL approach is this:

```
transform(ved1.begin(), ved1.end(), ved3.begin(),
        log);
```

The valarray class overloads the usual math function to take a valarray argument and to return a valarray object, so you can use this:

```
vad3 = log(vad1);       // log() overloaded
```

Or you could use the apply() method, which also works for non-overloaded functions:

```
vad3 = vad1.apply(log);
```

The apply() method doesn't alter the invoking object; instead, it returns a new object that contains the resulting values.

The simplicity of the valarray interface is even more apparent when you do a multistep calculation:

```
vad3 = 10.0* ((vad1 + vad2) / 2.0 + vad1 * cos(vad2));
```

The vector-STL version is left as an exercise for the motivated reader.

The valarray class also provides a sum() method that sums the contents of a valarray object, a size() method that returns the number of elements, a max() method that returns the largest value in an object, and a min() method that returns the smallest value.

As you can see, valarray has a clear notational advantage over vector for mathematical operations, but it is also much less versatile. The valarray class does have a resize() method, but there's no automatic resizing of the sort you get when you use the vector push_back() method. There are no methods for inserting values, searching, sorting, and the like. In short, the valarray class is more limited than the vector class, but its narrower focus allows a much simpler interface.

Does the simpler interface that valarray provides translate to better performance? In most cases, no. The simple notation is typically implemented with the same sort of loops you would use with ordinary arrays. However, some hardware designs allow vector operations in which the values in an array are loaded simultaneous into an array of registers and then processed simultaneously. In principle, `valarray` operations could be implemented to take advantage of such designs.

Can you use the STL with `valarray` objects? Answering this question provides a quick review of some STL principles. Suppose you have a `valarray<double>` object that has 10 elements:

```
valarray<double> vad(10);
```

After the array has been filled with numbers, can you, say, use the STL sort function on it? The `valarray` class doesn't have `begin()` and `end()` methods, so you can't use them as the range arguments:

```
sort(vad.begin(), vad.end());  // NO, no begin(), end()
```

You can't imitate ordinary array usage and provide `vad` and `vad + 10` as range arguments because `vad` is not the name of an array; it is the name of an object, and hence it is not an address. So the following doesn't work:

```
sort(vad, vad + 10);  // NO, vad an object, not an address
```

Perhaps you can use the address operator:

```
sort(&vad[0], &vad[10]);  // maybe?
```

This looks promising; `vad` is type `valarray<double>`, `vad[0]` is type `double`, and `&vad[0]` is type `double *`, so its value can be assigned to a type `double *` pointer, which can act as an iterator. Next, let's see if this pointer (let's call it `pt`) satisfies the STL requirements for random access iterators. First, it can be dereferenced: `*pt` is `vad[0]`, the value of the first element in the array. What about `pt++`? Certainly a pointer can be incremented, but will it then point to the second element of the array? The class description says that `&a[i+j]` and `&a[i] + j` are equivalent. In particular, `&a[i] + 1` is `&a[i+1]`; that is, adding one to an address provides the address of the next element, so incrementing `pt` does, indeed, make it point to the next element. The general equivalence rule also means that random access works. So far, so good.

But then you come to `&vad[10]`. Here there are two problems. The rule about `&a[i+j]` being the same as `&a[i] + j` has the restriction that `i + j` is less than the size of the array. Thus, for our example, it only extends to `&vad[9]`. Furthermore, the effect of using a subscript equal to or larger than the array size is described as leading to undefined behavior. Hence the behavior resulting from using `vad[10]` is undefined. This doesn't mean that using `sort()` does not work. (In fact, it did work for all six compilers used to test this code.) But it does mean that it might not work. For the code to fail, you probably would need a very unlikely circumstance, such as the array being butted against the end of the block of memory set aside for the heap. But, if a $350 million mission depended on your code, you might not want to risk that failure.

You could get around the one-past-the-end problem by making a `valarray` object one element larger than needed, but that would create problems with the `sum()`, `max()`, `min()`, and `size()` methods.

Listing 16.18 illustrates some of the relative strengths of the `vector` and `valarray` classes. It uses `push_back()` and the automatic sizing feature of `vector` to collect data. Then after sorting the numbers, the program copies them from the vector object to a valarray object of the same size and does a few math operations.

LISTING 16.18 valvect.cpp

```cpp
// valvect.cpp -- comparing vector and valarray
#include <iostream>
#include <valarray>
#include <vector>
#include <algorithm>
int main()
{
    using namespace std;
    vector<double> data;
    double temp;

    cout << "Enter numbers (<=0 to quit):\n";
    while (cin >> temp && temp > 0)
        data.push_back(temp);
    sort(data.begin(), data.end());
    int size = data.size();
    valarray<double> numbers(size);
    int i;
    for (i = 0; i < size; i++)
        numbers[i] = data[i];
    valarray<double> sq_rts(size);
    sq_rts = sqrt(numbers);
    valarray<double> results(size);
    results = numbers + 2.0 * sq_rts;
    cout.setf(ios_base::fixed);
    cout.precision(4);
    for (i = 0; i < size; i++)
    {
        cout.width(8);
        cout << numbers[i] << ": ";
        cout.width(8);
        cout << results[i] << endl;
    }
    cout << "done\n";
    return 0;
}
```

Here is a sample run of the program in Listing 16.18:

```
Enter numbers (<=0 to quit):
5 21.2 6 8 2 10 14.4 0
  2.0000:   4.8284
  5.0000:   9.4721
  6.0000:  10.8990
  8.0000:  13.6569
 10.0000:  16.3246
 14.4000:  21.9895
 21.2000:  30.4087
```

Compatibility Note

At the time this book was prepared, the default library used with Borland C++BuilderX had a bug in implementing the `valarray` math functions. One workaround is to have the compiler use an older version of the STL by using the following option on the command line:

`-D_USE_OLD_RW_STL`

Or, in IDE mode, you can specify the _USE_OLD_RW_STL option by selecting Project, Build Options Explorer, clicking bcc32, and then adding the option to the Conditional Defines text box.

The `valarray` class has many features besides the ones discussed so far. For example, if `numbers` is a `valarray<double>` object, the statement

`valarray<bool> vbool = numbers > 9;`

creates an array of `bool` values, with `vbool[i]` set to the value of `numbers[i]` > `9`—that is, to `true` or `false`.

There are extended versions of subscripting. Let's look at one—the `slice` class. A `slice` class object can be used as an array index, in which case it represents, in general, not just one value but a subset of values. A `slice` object is initialized to three integer values: the start, the number, and the stride. The *start* indicates the index of the first element to be selected, the *number* indicates the number of elements to be selected, and the *stride* represents the spacing between elements. For example, the object constructed by `slice(1,4,3)` means select the four elements whose indexes are 1, 4, 7, and 10. That is, start with the start element, add the stride to get the next element, and so on until four elements are selected. If, say, `varint` is a `vararray<int>` object, then the following statement would set elements 1, 4, 7, and 10 to the value `10`:

`varint[slice(1,4,3)] = 10;   // set selected elements to 10`

This special subscripting facility allows you to use a one-dimensional `valarray` object to represent two-dimensional data. For example, suppose you want to represent an array with 4 rows and 3 columns. You can store the information in a 12-element `valarray` object. Then a `slice(0,3,1)` object used as a subscript would represent elements 0, 1, and 2—that is, the first row. Similarly, a `slice(0,4,3)` subscript would represent elements 0, 3, 6, and 9—that is, the first column. Listing 16.19 illustrates some features of `slice`.

LISTING 16.19   vslice.cpp

```
// vslice.cpp -- using valarray slices
#include <iostream>
#include <valarray>
#include <cstdlib>

const int SIZE = 12;
typedef std::valarray<int> vint;    // simplify declarations
void show(const vint & v, int cols);
```

LISTING 16.19   Continued

```
int main()
{
    using std::slice;                    // from <valarray>
    using std::cout;
    vint valint(SIZE);                   // think of as 4 rows of 3

    int i;
    for (i = 0; i < SIZE; ++i)
        valint[i] = std::rand() % 10;
    cout << "Original array:\n";
    show(valint, 3);                     // show in 3 columns
    vint vcol(valint[slice(1,4,3)]); // extract 2nd column
    cout << "Second column:\n";
    show(vcol, 1);                       // show in 1 column
    vint vrow(valint[slice(3,3,1)]); // extract 2nd row
    cout << "Second row:\n";
    show(vrow, 3);
    valint[slice(2,4,3)]  = 10;      // assign to 2nd column
    cout << "Set last column to 10:\n";
    show(valint, 3);
    cout << "Set first column to sum of next two:\n";
    // + not defined for slices, so convert to valarray<int>
    valint[slice(0,4,3)]  = vint(valint[slice(1,4,3)])
                                + vint(valint[slice(2,4,3)]);
    show(valint, 3);
    return 0;
}

void show(const vint & v, int cols)
{
    using std::cout;
    using std::endl;

    int lim = v.size();
    for (int i = 0; i < lim; ++i)
    {
        cout.width(3);
        cout << v[i];
        if (i % cols == cols - 1)
            cout << endl;
        else
            cout << ' ';
    }
    if (lim % cols != 0)
        cout << endl;
}
```

The + operator is defined for **valarray** objects, such as **valint**, and it's defined for a single **int** element, such as **valint[1]**. But, as the code in Listing 16.19 notes, the + operator isn't defined for `slice`-subscripted `valarray` units, such as `valint[slice(1,4,3)]`. Therefore, the program constructs full objects from the slices to enable addition:

```
vint(valint[slice(1,4,3)])    // calls a slice-based constructor
```

The `valarray` class provides constructors just for this purpose.

Here is a sample run of the program in Listing 16.19:

```
Original array:
  1   7   4
  0   9   4
  8   8   2
  4   5   5
Second column:
  7
  9
  8
  5
Second row:
  0   9   4
Set last column to 10:
  1   7  10
  0   9  10
  8   8  10
  4   5  10
Set first column to sum of next two:
 17   7  10
 19   9  10
 18   8  10
 15   5  10
```

Because values are set using `rand()`, different implementations of `rand()` will result in different values.

There's more, including the `gslice` class to represent multidimensional slices, but this should be enough to give you a sense of what `valarray` is about.

Summary

C++ includes a powerful set of libraries that provide solutions to many common programming problems and the tools to simplify many more problems. The `string` class provides a convenient means to handle strings as objects. The `string` class provides automatic memory management and a host of methods and functions for working with strings. For example, these methods and functions allow you to concatenate strings, insert one string into another, reverse a string, search a string for characters or substrings, and perform input and output operations.

The `auto_ptr` template makes it easier to manage memory allocated by `new`. If you use an `auto_ptr` object instead of a regular pointer to hold the address returned by `new`, you don't have to remember to use the `delete` operator later. When the `auto_ptr` object expires, its destructor calls the `delete` operator automatically.

The STL is a collection of container class templates, iterator class templates, function object templates, and algorithm function templates that feature a unified design based on generic programming principles. The algorithms use templates to make them generic in terms of type of stored object and an iterator interface to make them generic in terms of the type of container. Iterators are generalizations of pointers.

The STL uses the term *concept* to denote a set of requirements. For example, the concept of forward iterators includes the requirements that a forward iterator object can be dereferenced for reading and writing and that it can be incremented. Actual implementations of the concept are said to *model* the concept. For example, the forward iterator concept could be modeled by an ordinary pointer or by an object designed to navigate a linked list. Concepts based on other concepts are termed *refinements*. For example, the bidirectional iterator is a refinement of the forward iterator concept.

Container classes, such as `vector` and `set`, are models of container concepts, such as containers, sequences, and associative containers. The STL defines several container class templates: `vector`, `deque`, `list`, `set`, `multiset`, `map`, `multimap`, and `bitset`. It also defines the adapter class templates `queue`, `priority_queue`, and `stack`; these classes adapt an underlying container class to give it the characteristic interface suggested by the adapter class template name. Thus, `stack`, although based, by default, on `vector`, allows insertion and removal only at the top of the stack.

Some algorithms are expressed as container class methods, but the bulk are expressed as general, nonmember functions. This is made possible by using iterators as the interface between containers and algorithms. One advantage to this approach is that there needs to be just one `for_each()` or `copy()` function, and so on, instead of a separate version for each container. A second advantage is that STL algorithms can be used with non-STL containers, such as ordinary arrays, `string` objects, and any classes you design consistent with the STL iterator and container idiom.

Both containers and algorithms are characterized by the type of iterator they provide or need. You should check that a container features an iterator concept that supports the algorithm's needs. For example, the `for_each()` algorithm uses an input iterator, whose minimal requirements are met by all the STL container class types. But `sort()` requires random access iterators, which not all container classes support. A container class may offer a specialized method as an option if it doesn't meet the requirements for a particular algorithm. For example, the `list` class has a `sort()` method that is based on bidirectional iterators, so it can use that method instead of the general function.

The STL also provides function objects, or functors, that are classes for which the `()` operator is overloaded—that is, for which the `operator()()` method is defined. Objects of such classes can be invoked by using function notation but can carry additional information. Adaptable functors, for example, have `typedef` statements that identify the argument types and the return value type for the functor. This information can be used by other components, such as function adapters.

By representing common container types and providing a variety of common operations implemented with efficient algorithms, all done in a generic manner, the STL provides an excellent source of reusable code. You may be able to solve a programming problem directly with the STL tools, or you may be able to use them as building blocks to construct the solution you need.

The `complex` and `valarray` template classes support numeric operations for complex numbers and arrays.

Review Questions

1. Consider the following class declaration:

```
class RQ1
{
private:
    char * st;          // points to C-style string
public:
    RQ1() { st = new char [1]; strcpy(st,""); }
    RQ1(const char * s)
    {st = new char [strlen(s) + 1]; strcpy(st, s); }
    RQ1(const RQ1 & rq)
    {st = new char [strlen(rq.st) + 1]; strcpy(st, rq.st); }
    ~RQ1() {delete [] st};
    RQ & operator=(const RQ & rq);
    // more stuff
};
```

Convert this to a declaration that uses a `string` object instead. What methods no longer need explicit definitions?

2. Name at least two advantages `string` objects have over C-style strings in terms of ease-of-use.

3. Write a function that takes a reference to a `string` object as an argument and that converts the `string` object to all uppercase.

4. Which of the following are not examples of correct usage (conceptually or syntactically) of `auto_ptr`? (Assume that the needed header files have been included.)

```
auto_ptr<int> pia(new int[20]);
auto_ptr<string> (new string);
int rigue = 7;
auto_ptr<int>pr(&rigue);
auto_ptr dbl (new double);
```

5. If you could make the mechanical equivalent of a stack that held golf clubs instead of numbers, why would it (conceptually) be a bad golf bag?

6. Why would a `set` container be a poor choice for storing a hole-by-hole record of your golf scores?

7. Because a pointer is an iterator, why didn't the STL designers simply use pointers instead of iterators?

8. Why didn't the STL designers simply define a base iterator class, use inheritance to derive classes for the other iterator types, and express the algorithms in terms of those iterator classes?

9. Give at least three examples of convenience advantages that a vector object has over an ordinary array.

10. If Listing 16.7 were implemented with list instead of vector, what parts of the program would become invalid? Could the invalid part be fixed easily? If so, how?

Programming Exercises

1. A *palindrome* is a string that is the same backward as it is forward. For example, "tot" and "otto" are rather short palindromes. Write a program that lets a user enter a string and that passes to a bool function a reference to the string. The function should return true if the string is a palindrome and false otherwise. At this point, don't worry about complications such as capitalization, spaces, and punctuation. That is, this simple version should reject "Otto" and "Madam, I'm Adam." Feel free to scan the list of string methods in Appendix F for methods to simplify the task.

2. Do the same problem as given in Programming Exercise 1, but do worry about complications such as capitalization, spaces, and punctuation. That is, "Madam, I'm Adam" should test as a palindrome. For example, the testing function could reduce the string to "madamimadam" and then test whether the reverse is the same. Don't forget the useful cctype library. You might find an STL function or two useful although not necessary.

3. Redo Listing 16.3 so that it gets it words from a file. One approach is to use a vector<string> object instead of an array of string. Then you can use push_back() to copy how ever many words are in your data file into the vector<string> object and use the size() member to determine the length of the word list. Because the program should read one word at a time from the file, you should use the >> operator rather than getline(). The file itself should contain words separated by spaces, tabs, or new lines.

4. Write a function with an old-style interface that has this prototype:

```
int reduce(long ar[], int n);
```

The actual arguments should be the name of an array and the number of elements in the array. The function should sort an array, remove duplicate values, and return a value equal to the number of elements in the reduced array. Write the function using STL functions. (If you decide to use the general unique() function, note that it returns the end of the resulting range.) Test the function in a short program.

5. Do the same problem as described in Programming Exercise 4, except make it a template function:

```
template <class T>
int reduce(T ar[], int n);
```

Test the function in a short program, using both a `long` instantiation and a `string` instantiation.

6. Redo the example shown in Listing 12.15, using the STL `queue` template class instead of the `Queue` class described in Chapter 12.

7. A common game is the lottery card. The card has numbered spots of which a certain number are selected at random. Write a `Lotto()` function that takes two arguments. The first should be the number of spots on a lottery card, and the second should be the number of spots selected at random. The function should return a `vector<int>` object that contains, in sorted order, the numbers selected at random. For example, you could use the function as follows:

```
vector<int> winners;
winners = Lotto(51,6);
```

This would assign to `winners` a vector that contains six numbers selected randomly from the range 1 through 51. Note that simply using `rand()` doesn't quite do the job because it may produce duplicate values. Suggestion: Have the function create a vector that contains all the possible values, use `random_shuffle()`, and then use the beginning of the shuffled vector to obtain the values. Also write a short program that lets you test the function.

8. Mat and Pat want to invite their friends to a party. They ask you to write a program that does the following:

- Allows Mat to enter a list of his friends' names. The names are stored in a container and then displayed in sorted order.

- Allows Pat to enter a list of her friends' names. The names are stored in a second container and then displayed in sorted order.

- Creates a third container that merges the two lists, eliminates duplicates, and displays the contents of this container.

CHAPTER 17

INPUT, OUTPUT, AND FILES

In this chapter you'll learn about the following:

- The C++ view of input and output
- The `iostream` family of classes
- Redirection
- `ostream` class methods
- Formatting output
- `istream` class methods
- Stream states
- File I/O
- Using the `ifstream` class for input from files

- Using the `ofstream` class for output to files
- Using the `fstream` class file input and output
- Command-line processing
- Binary files
- Random file access
- Incore formatting

iscussing C++ input and output (I/O) poses a problem. On the one hand, practically every program uses input and output, and learning how to use them is one of the first tasks facing someone learning a computer language. On the other hand, C++ uses many of its more advanced language features to implement input and output, including classes, derived classes, function overloading, virtual functions, templates, and multiple inheritance. Thus, to really understand C++ I/O, you must know a lot of C++. To get you started, the early chapters of this book outline the basic ways for using the `istream` class object `cin` and the `ostream` class object `cout` for input and output, and, to a lesser degree, using `ifstream` and `ofstream` objects for file input and output. This chapter takes a longer look at C++'s input and output classes, showing how they are designed and explaining how to control the output format. (If you've skipped a few chapters just to learn advanced formatting, you can read the sections on formatting, noting the techniques and ignoring the explanations.)

The C++ facilities for file input and output are based on the same basic class definitions that `cin` and `cout` are based on, so this chapter uses the discussion of console I/O (keyboard and screen) as a springboard to investigating file I/O.

The ANSI/ISO C++ standards committee has worked to make C++ I/O more compatible with existing C I/O, and this has produced some changes from traditional C++ practices.

An Overview of C++ Input and Output

Most computer languages build input and output into the language itself. For example, if you look through the lists of keywords for languages such as BASIC and Pascal, you see that PRINT statements, writeln statements, and the like are part of the language vocabulary. But neither C nor C++ has built input and output into the language. If you look through the keywords for these languages, you find for and if but nothing relating to I/O. C originally left I/O to compiler implementers. One reason for this was to give implementers the freedom to design I/O functions that best fit the hardware requirements of the target computer. In practice, most implementers based I/O on a set of library functions originally developed for the Unix environment. ANSI C formalized recognition of this I/O package, called the Standard Input/Output package, by making it a mandatory component of the standard C library. C++ also recognizes this package, so if you're familiar with the family of C functions declared in the stdio.h file, you can use them in C++ programs. (Newer implementations use the cstdio header file to support these functions.)

However, C++ relies on a C++ solution rather than a C solution to I/O, and that solution is a set of classes defined in the iostream (formerly iostream.h) and fstream (formerly fstream.h) header files. This class library is not part of the formal language definition (cin and istream are not keywords); after all, a computer language defines rules for how to do things, such as create classes, and doesn't define what you should create by following those rules. But, just as C implementations come with a standard library of functions, C++ comes with a standard library of classes. At first, that standard class library was an informal standard consisting solely of the classes defined in the iostream and fstream header files. The ANSI/ISO C++ committee decided to formalize this library as a standard class library and to add a few more standard classes, such as those discussed in Chapter 16, "The string Class and the Standard Template Library." This chapter discusses standard C++ I/O. But first, let's examine the conceptual framework for C++ I/O.

Streams and Buffers

A C++ program views input or output as a stream of bytes. On input, a program extracts bytes from an input stream, and on output, a program inserts bytes into the output stream. For a text-oriented program, each byte can represent a character. More generally, the bytes can form a binary representation of character or numeric data. The bytes in an input stream can come from the keyboard, but they can also come from a storage device, such as a hard disk, or from another program. Similarly, the bytes in an output stream can flow to the display, to a printer, to a storage device, or to another program. A stream acts as an intermediary between the program and the stream's source or destination. This approach enables a C++ program to treat input from a keyboard in the same manner it treats input from a file; the C++ program merely examines the stream of bytes, without needing to know where the bytes come from. Similarly, by using streams, a C++ program can process output in a manner independent of where the bytes are going. Managing input, then, involves two stages:

- Associating a stream with an input to a program

- Connecting the stream to a file

In other words, an input stream needs two connections, one at each end. The file-end connection provides a source for the stream, and the program-end connection dumps the stream outflow into the program. (The file-end connection can be a file, but it can also be a device, such as a keyboard.) Similarly, managing output involves connecting an output stream to the program and associating some output destination with the stream. It's like plumbing with bytes instead of water (see Figure 17.1).

FIGURE 17.1

C++ input and output.

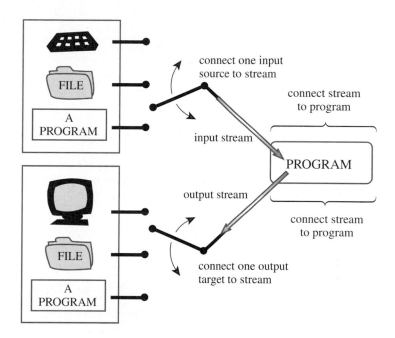

Usually, input and output can be handled more efficiently by using a buffer. A *buffer* is a block of memory used as an intermediate, temporary storage facility for the transfer of information from a device to a program or from a program to a device. Typically, devices such as disk drives transfer information in blocks of 512 bytes or more, whereas programs often process information 1 byte at a time. The buffer helps match these two disparate rates of information transfer. For example, assume that a program is supposed to count the number of dollar signs in a hard-disk file. The program could read one character from the file, process it, read the next character from the file, and so on. Reading a file a character at a time from a disk requires a lot of hardware activity and is slow. The buffered approach is to read a large chunk from the disk, store the chunk in the buffer, and read the buffer one character at a time. Because it is much quicker to read individual bytes of data from memory than from a hard disk, this approach is much faster as well as easier on the hardware. Of course, after the program reaches the end of the buffer, the program should then read another chunk of data from the disk. The principle is similar to that of a water reservoir that collects megagallons of runoff water during a big storm and then feeds water to your home at a more civilized rate of flow (see Figure 17.2). Similarly, on output, a program can first fill the buffer and then transfer the entire block of data to a hard disk, clearing the buffer for the next batch of output. This is called *flushing the buffer*. Perhaps you can come up with your own plumbing-based analogy for that process.

FIGURE 17.2
A stream with a buffer.

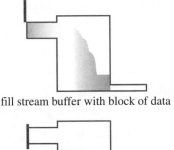

fill stream buffer with block of data

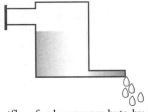

stream outflow feeds program byte-by-byte

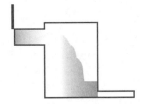

refill stream buffer with next block of data

Keyboard input provides one character at a time, so in that case, a program doesn't need a buffer to help match different data transfer rates. However, buffered keyboard input allows the user to back up and correct input before transmitting it to a program. A C++ program normally flushes the input buffer when you press Enter. That's why the examples in this book don't begin processing input until you press Enter. For output to the display, a C++ program normally flushes the output buffer when you transmit a newline character. Depending on the implementation, a program may flush input on other occasions, too, such as at impending input. That is, when a program reaches an input statement, it flushes any output currently in the output buffer. C++ implementations that are consistent with ANSI C should behave in that manner.

Streams, Buffers, and the `iostream` File

The business of managing streams and buffers can get a bit complicated, but including the `iostream` (formerly `iostream.h`) file brings in several classes designed to implement and manage streams and buffers for you. The newest version of C++ I/O actually defines class templates in order to support both `char` and `wchar_t` data. By using the `typedef` facility, C++ makes the `char` specializations of these templates mimic the traditional non-template I/O implementation. Here are some of those classes (see Figure 17.3):

- The `streambuf` class provides memory for a buffer, along with class methods for filling the buffer, accessing buffer contents, flushing the buffer, and managing the buffer memory.

- The `ios_base` class represents general properties of a stream, such as whether it's open for reading and whether it's a binary or a text stream.

- The `ios` class is based on `ios_base`, and it includes a pointer member to a `streambuf` object.

- The `ostream` class derives from the `ios` class and provides output methods.

- The `istream` class derives from the `ios` class and provides input methods.

- The `iostream` class is based on the `istream` and `ostream` classes and thus inherits both input and output methods.

FIGURE 17.3

Some I/O classes.

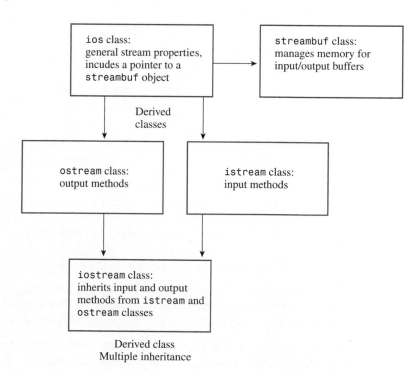

To use these facilities, you use objects of the appropriate classes. For example, you use an `ostream` object such as `cout` to handle output. Creating such an object opens a stream, automatically creates a buffer, and associates it with the stream. It also makes the class member functions available to you.

Redefining I/O

The ISO/ANSI C++ Standard has revised I/O a couple ways. First, there's the change from `ostream.h` to `ostream`, with `ostream` placing the classes in the `std` namespace. Second, the I/O classes have been rewritten. To be an international language, C++ has to be able to handle international character sets that require a 16-bit or wider character type. So the language added the `wchar_t` (or "wide") character type to the traditional 8-bit `char` (or "narrow") type. Each type needs its own I/O facilities. Rather than develop two separate sets of classes, the standards committee developed a template set of I/O classes, including `basic_istream<charT, traits<charT> >` and `basic_ostream<charT, traits<charT> >`. The `traits<charT>` template, in turn, is a template class that defines particular traits for a character type, such as how to compare for equality and its EOF value. The C++ Standard provides `char` and `wchar_t` specializations of the I/O classes. For example, `istream` and `ostream` are `typedef`s for `char` specializations. Similarly, `wistream` and `wostream` are `wchar_t` specializations. For example, there is a `wcout` object for outputting wide character streams. The `ostream` header file contains these definitions.

Certain type-independent information that used to be kept in the `ios` base class has been moved to the new `ios_base` class. This includes the various formatting constants such as `ios::fixed`, which is now `ios_base::fixed`. Also, `ios_base` contains some options that aren't available in the old `ios`.

The C++ `iostream` class library takes care of many details for you. For example, including the `iostream` file in a program creates eight stream objects (four for narrow character streams and four for wide character streams) automatically:

- The `cin` object corresponds to the standard input stream. By default, this stream is associated with the standard input device, typically a keyboard. The `wcin` object is similar but works with the `wchar_t` type.

- The `cout` object corresponds to the standard output stream. By default, this stream is associated with the standard output device, typically a monitor. The `wcout` object is similar but works with the `wchar_t` type.

- The `cerr` object corresponds to the standard error stream, which you can use for displaying error messages. By default, this stream is associated with the standard output device, typically a monitor, and the stream is unbuffered. This means that information is sent directly to the screen, without waiting for a buffer to fill or for a newline character. The `wcerr` object is similar but works with the `wchar_t` type.

- The `clog` object also corresponds to the standard error stream. By default, this stream is associated with the standard output device, typically a monitor, and the stream is buffered. The `wclog` object is similar but works with the `wchar_t` type.

What does it mean to say that an object represents a stream? Well, for example, when the `iostream` file declares a `cout` object for a program, that object has data members holding information relating to output, such as the field widths to be used in displaying data, the number of places after the decimal to use, what number base to use for displaying integers, and the address of a `streambuf` object that describes the buffer used to handle the output flow. A statement such as

```
cout << "Bjarne free";
```

places the characters from the string `"Bjarne free"` into the buffer managed by `cout` via the pointed-to `streambuf` object. The `ostream` class defines the `operator<<()` function used in this statement, and the `ostream` class also supports the `cout` data members with a variety of other class methods, such as the ones this chapter discusses later. Furthermore, C++ sees to it that the output from the buffer is directed to the standard output, usually a monitor, provided by the operating system. In short, one end of a stream is connected to the program, the other end is connected to the standard output, and the `cout` object, with the help of a type `streambuf` object, manages the flow of bytes through the stream.

Redirection

The standard input and output streams normally connect to the keyboard and the screen. But many operating systems, including Unix, Linux, and MS-DOS, support redirection, a facility that lets you change the associations for the standard input and the standard output. Suppose, for example, that you have an executable DOS C++ program called `counter.exe` that counts the number of characters in its input and reports the result. (From most versions of Windows you can select Start, Programs and then click the MS-DOS Command Prompt icon or Command Prompt icon to open an MD-DOS window.) A sample run might look like this:

```
C>counter
Hello
and goodbye!
Control-Z            <- simulated end-of-file
Input contained 19 characters.
C>
```

In this case, input came from the keyboard, and output went to the screen.

With input redirection (`<`) and output redirection (`>`), you can use the same program to count the number of characters in the `oklahoma` file and to place the results in the `cow_cnt` file:

```
C>counter <oklahoma >cow_cnt
C>
```

The `<oklahoma` part of the command line associates the standard input with the `oklahoma` file, causing `cin` to read input from that file instead of the keyboard. In other words, the operating system changes the connection at the inflow end of the input stream, while the outflow end remains connected to the program. The `>cow_cnt` part of the command line associates the standard output with the `cow_cnt` file, causing `cout` to send output to that file instead of to the screen. That is, the operating system changes the outflow end connection of the output stream, leaving its inflow end still connected to the program. DOS (2.0 and later), Linux, and Unix automatically recognize this redirection syntax. (Unix, Linux, and DOS 3.0 and later also permit optional space characters between the redirection operators and the filenames.)

The standard output stream, represented by `cout`, is the normal channel for program output. The standard error streams (represented by `cerr` and `clog`) are intended for a program's error messages. By default, all three of these objects are typically sent to the monitor. But redirecting the standard output doesn't affect `cerr` or `clog`; thus, if you use one of these objects to print an error message, a program will display the error message on the screen even if the regular `cout` output is redirected elsewhere. For example, consider this code fragment:

```cpp
if (success)
    std::cout << "Here come the goodies!\n";
else
{
    std::cerr << "Something horrible has happened.\n";
    exit(1);
}
```

If redirection is not in effect, whichever message is selected is displayed onscreen. If, however, the program output has been redirected to a file, the first message, if selected, would go to the file but the second message, if selected, would go to the screen. By the way, some operating systems permit redirecting the standard error, too. In Unix and Linux, for example, the `2>` operator redirects the standard error.

Output with `cout`

As mentioned previously, C++ considers output to be a stream of bytes. (Depending on the implementation and platform, these may be 16-bit or 32-bit bytes, but they're bytes nonetheless.) But many kinds of data in a program are organized into larger units than a single byte. An `int` type, for example, may be represented by a 16-bit or 32-bit binary value. And a `double` value may be represented by 64 bits of binary data. But when you send a stream of bytes to a screen, you want each byte to represent a character value. That is, to display the number -2.34 onscreen, you should send the five characters -, 2, ., 3, and 4 to the screen, and not the internal 64-bit floating-point representation of that value. Therefore, one of the most important tasks facing the `ostream` class is converting numeric types, such as `int` or `float`, into a stream of characters that represents the values in text form. That is, the `ostream` class translates the internal representation of data as binary bit patterns to an output stream of character bytes. (Some day we may have bionic implants to enable us to interpret binary data directly. I leave that development as another exercise for the reader.) To perform these translation tasks, the `ostream` class provides several class methods. We'll look at them now, summarizing methods used throughout the book and describing additional methods that provide finer control over the appearance of the output.

The Overloaded << Operator

Most often, this book has used `cout` with the `<<` operator, also called the *insertion* operator:

```cpp
int clients = 22;
cout << clients;
```

In C++, as in C, by default the << operator is used as the bitwise left-shift operator (see Appendix E, "Other Operators"). An expression such as x<<3 means to take the binary representation of x and shift all the bits three units to the left. Obviously, this doesn't have a lot to do with output. But the ostream class redefines the << operator through overloading to output for the ostream class. In this guise, the << operator is called the insertion operator instead of the left-shift operator. (The left-shift operator earned this new role through its visual aspect, which suggests a flow of information to the left.) The insertion operator is overloaded to recognize all the basic C++ types:

- unsigned char

- signed char

- char

- short

- unsigned short

- int

- unsigned int

- long

- unsigned long

- float

- double

- long double

The ostream class provides a definition for the operator<<() function for each of these data types. (Functions that have *operator* in their names are used to overload operators, as discussed in Chapter 11, "Working with Classes.") Thus, if you use a statement of the form

```
cout << value;
```

and if *value* is one of the preceding types, a C++ program can match it to an operator function with the corresponding signature. For example, the expression cout << 88 matches the following method prototype:

```
ostream & operator<<(int);
```

Recall that this prototype indicates that the operator<<() function takes one type int argument. That's the part that matches the 88 in the previous statement. The prototype also indicates that the function returns a reference to an ostream object. That property makes it possible to concatenate output, as in the following old rock hit:

```
cout << "I'm feeling sedimental over " << boundary << "\n";
```

If you're a C programmer who has suffered through C's multitudinous % type specifiers and the problems that arise when you mismatch a specifier type to a value, using cout is almost sinfully easy. (And C++ input, of course, *is* cinfully easy.)

Output and Pointers

The `ostream` class defines insertion operator functions for the following pointer types:

- `const signed char *`
- `const unsigned char *`
- `const char *`
- `void *`

C++ represents a string, don't forget, by using a pointer to the location of the string. The pointer can take the form of the name of an array of `char` or of an explicit `pointer-to-char` or of a quoted string. Thus, all the following `cout` statements display strings:

```
char name[20] = "Dudly Diddlemore";
char * pn = "Violet D'Amore";
cout << "Hello!";
cout << name;
cout << pn;
```

The methods use the terminating null character in the string to determine when to stop displaying characters.

C++ matches a pointer of any other type with type `void *` and prints a numeric representation of the address. If you want the address of the string, you have to type cast it to another type, as shown in the following code fragment:

```
int eggs = 12;
char * amount = "dozen";
cout << &eggs;              // prints address of eggs variable
cout << amount;            // prints the string "dozen"
cout << (void *) amount;   // prints the address of the "dozen" string
```

Note

Some older implementations of C++ lack a prototype with the `void *` argument. In that case, you have to type cast a pointer to `unsigned` or, perhaps, `unsigned long`, if you want to print the value of the address.

Output Concatenation

All the incarnations of the insertion operator are defined to return type `ostream &`. That is, the prototypes have this form:

```
ostream & operator<<(type);
```

(Here, *type* is the type to be displayed.) The `ostream &` return type means that using this operator returns a reference to an `ostream` object. Which object? The function definitions say that the reference is to the object used to evoke the operator. In other words, an operator function's return value is the same object that evokes the operator. For example, `cout <<` `"potluck"` returns the `cout` object. That's the feature that lets you concatenate output by using insertion. For example, consider the following statement:

```
cout << "We have " << count << " unhatched chickens.\n";
```

The expression `cout << "We have "` displays the string and returns the `cout` object, reducing the statement to the following:

```
cout << count << " unhatched chickens.\n";
```

Then the expression `cout << count` displays the value of the `count` variable and returns `cout`, which can then handle the final argument in the statement (see Figure 17.4). This design technique really is a nice feature, which is why the examples of overloading the `<<` operator in the previous chapters shamelessly imitate it.

FIGURE 17.4

Output concatenation.

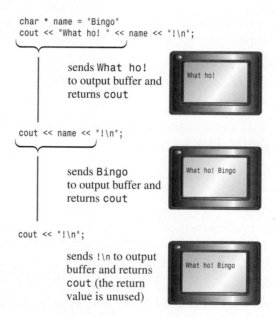

The Other `ostream` Methods

Besides the various `operator<<()` functions, the `ostream` class provides the `put()` method for displaying characters and the `write()` method for displaying strings.

Originally, the `put()` method had the following prototype:

```
ostream & put(char);
```

The current standard is equivalent, except it's templated to allow for `wchar_t`. You invoke it by using the usual class method notation:

```
cout.put('W');        // display the W character
```

Here `cout` is the invoking object and `put()` is the class member function. Like the `<<` operator functions, this function returns a reference to the invoking object, so you can concatenate output with it:

```
cout.put('I').put('t'); // displaying It with two put() calls
```

The function call `cout.put('I')` returns `cout`, which then acts as the invoking object for the `put('t')` call.

Given the proper prototype, you can use `put()` with arguments of numeric types other than `char`, such as `int`, and let function prototyping automatically convert the argument to the correct type `char` value. For example, you could use the following:

```
cout.put(65);       // display the A character
cout.put(66.3);     // display the B character
```

The first statement converts the `int` value 65 to a `char` value and then displays the character having 65 as its ASCII code. Similarly, the second statement converts the type `double` value 66.3 to a type `char` value 66 and displays the corresponding character.

This behavior comes in handy with versions prior to Release 2.0 C++; in those versions, the language represents character constants with type `int` values. Thus, a statement such as

```
cout << 'W';
```

would interpret `'W'` as an `int` value, and hence displays it as the integer 87, the ASCII value for the character. But the statement

```
cout.put('W');
```

works fine. Because current C++ represents `char` constants as type `char`, you can now use either method.

Some older compilers erroneously overload `put()` for three argument types: `char`, `unsigned char`, and `signed char`. This makes using `put()` with an `int` argument ambiguous because an `int` can be converted to any one of those three types.

The `write()` method writes an entire string and has the following template prototype:

```
basic_ostream<charT,traits>& write(const char_type* s, streamsize n);
```

The first argument to `write()` provides the address of the string to be displayed, and the second argument indicates how many characters to display. Using `cout` to invoke `write()` invokes the `char` specialization, so the return type is `ostream &`. Listing 17.1 shows how the `write()` method works.

LISTING 17.1 `write.cpp`

```
// write.cpp -- using cout.write()
#include <iostream>
#include <cstring>  // or else string.h

int main()
{
```

LISTING 17.1   Continued

```
        using std::cout;
        using std::endl;
        const char * state1 = "Florida";
        const char * state2 = "Kansas";
        const char * state3 = "Euphoria";
        int len = std::strlen(state2);
        cout << "Increasing loop index:\n";
        int i;
        for (i = 1; i <= len; i++)
        {
            cout.write(state2,i);
            cout << endl;
        }

// concatenate output
        cout << "Decreasing loop index:\n";
        for (i = len; i > 0; i--)
            cout.write(state2,i) << endl;

// exceed string length
        cout << "Exceeding string length:\n";
        cout.write(state2, len + 5) << endl;

        return 0;
}
```

Some compilers may observe that the program defines but doesn't use the arrays **state1** and **state3**. That's okay because those two arrays are there just to provide data before and after the **state2** array so that you can see what happens when the program miscodes access to **state2**. Here is the output of the program in Listing 17.1:

```
Increasing loop index:
K
Ka
Kan
Kans
Kansa
Kansas
Decreasing loop index:
Kansas
Kansa
Kans
Kan
Ka
K
Exceeding string length:
Kansas Euph
```

Note that the **cout.write()** call returns the **cout** object. This is because the **write()** method returns a reference to the object that invokes it, and in this case, the **cout** object invokes it.

This makes it possible to concatenate output because `cout.write()` is replaced by its return value, `cout`:

```
cout.write(state2,i) << endl;
```

Also, note that the `write()` method doesn't stop printing characters automatically when it reaches the null character. It simply prints how many characters you tell it to, even if that goes beyond the bounds of a particular string! In this case, the program brackets the string `"Kansas"` with two other strings so that adjacent memory locations would contain data. Compilers differ in the order in which they store data in memory and in how they align memory. For example, `"Kansas"` occupies 6 bytes, but this particular compiler appears to align strings by using multiples of 4 bytes, so `"Kansas"` is padded out to 8 bytes. Some compilers store `"Florida"` after `"Kansas"`. So, because of compiler differences, you may get a different result for the final line of output.

The `write()` method can also be used with numeric data. You would pass it the address of a number, type cast to `char *`:

```
long val = 560031841;
cout.write( (char *) &val, sizeof (long));
```

This doesn't translate a number to the correct characters; instead, it transmits the bit representation as stored in memory. For example, a 4-byte `long` value such as `560031841` would be transmitted as 4 separate bytes. An output device such as a monitor would then try to interpret each byte as if it were ASCII (or whatever) code. So `560031841` would appear onscreen as some 4-character combination, most likely gibberish. (But maybe not; try it and see.) However, `write()` does provide a compact, accurate way to store numeric data in a file. We'll return to this possibility later in this chapter.

Flushing the Output Buffer

Consider what happens as a program uses `cout` to send bytes on to the standard output. Because the `ostream` class buffers output handled by the `cout` object, output isn't sent to its destination immediately. Instead, it accumulates in the buffer until the buffer is full. Then the program *flushes* the buffer, sending the contents on and clearing the buffer for new data. Typically, a buffer is 512 bytes or an integral multiple thereof. Buffering is a great time-saver when the standard output is connected to a file on a hard disk. After all, you don't want a program to access the hard disk 512 times to send 512 bytes. It's much more effective to collect 512 bytes in a buffer and write them to a hard disk in a single disk operation.

For screen output, however, filling the buffer first is less critical. Indeed, it would be inconvenient if you had to reword the message "Press any key to continue" so that it consumed the prerequisite 512 bytes to fill a buffer. Fortunately, in the case of screen output, the program doesn't necessarily wait until the buffer is full. Sending a newline character to the buffer, for example, normally flushes the buffer. Also, as mentioned before, most C++ implementations flush the buffer when input is pending. That is, suppose you have the following code:

```
cout << "Enter a number: ";
float num;
cin >> num;
```

The fact that the program expects input causes it to display the **cout** message (that is, flush the "Enter a number: " message) immediately, even though the output string lacks a newline character. Without this feature, the program would wait for input without prompting the user with the **cout** message.

If your implementation doesn't flush output when you want it to, you can force flushing by using one of two manipulators. The **flush** manipulator flushes the buffer, and the **endl** manipulator flushes the buffer and inserts a newline character. You use these manipulators the way you would use a variable name:

```
cout << "Hello, good-looking! " << flush;
cout << "Wait just a moment, please." << endl;
```

Manipulators are, in fact, functions. For example, you can flush the **cout** buffer by calling the **flush()** function directly:

```
flush(cout);
```

However, the **ostream** class overloads the **<<** insertion operator in such a way that the expression

```
cout << flush
```

gets replaced with the **flush(cout)** function call. Thus, you can use the more convenient insertion notation to flush with success.

Formatting with cout

The **ostream** insertion operators convert values to text form. By default, they format values as follows:

- A type **char** value, if it represents a printable character, is displayed as a character in a field one character wide.

- Numeric integer types are displayed as decimal integers in a field just wide enough to hold the number and, if present, a minus sign.

- Strings are displayed in a field equal in width to the length of the string.

The default behavior for floating-point types has changed. The following are the differences between older and newer C++ implementations:

- **New style**—Floating-point types are displayed with a total of six digits, except that trailing zeros aren't displayed. (Note that the number of digits displayed has no connection with the precision to which the number is stored.) The number is displayed in fixed-point notation or else in E notation (see Chapter 3, "Dealing with Data"), depending on the value of the number. In particular, E notation is used if the exponent is 6 or larger or -5 or smaller. Again, the field is just wide enough to hold the number and, if present, a minus sign. The default behavior corresponds to using the standard C library function **fprintf()** with a **%g** specifier.

- **Old style**—Floating-point types are displayed with six places to the right of the decimal, except that trailing zeros aren't displayed. (Note that the number of digits displayed has no connection with the precision to which the number is stored.) The number is displayed in fixed-point notation or else in E notation (see Chapter 3), depending on the value of the number. Again, the field is just wide enough to hold the number and, if present, a minus sign.

Because each value is displayed in a width equal to its size, you have to provide spaces between values explicitly; otherwise, consecutive values would run together.

There are several small differences between early C++ formatting and formatting in the current C++ Standard; they are summarized in Table 17.3, later in this chapter.

Listing 17.2 illustrates the output defaults. It displays a colon (:) after each value so you can see the width of the field used in each case. The program uses the expression `1.0 / 9.0` to generate a nonterminating fraction so you can see how many places get printed.

Compatibility Note

Not all compilers generate output formatted in accordance with the current C++ Standard. Also, the current standard allows for regional variations. For example, a European implementation can follow the continental fashion of using a comma instead of a period for displaying decimal fractions. That is, it may write `2,54` instead of `2.54`. The locale library (header file `locale`) provides a mechanism for *imbuing* an input or output stream with a particular style, so a single compiler can offer more than one locale choice. This chapter uses the U.S. locale.

LISTING 17.2   defaults.cpp

```cpp
// defaults.cpp -- cout default formats
#include <iostream>

int main()
{
    using std::cout;
    cout << "12345678901234567890\n";
    char ch = 'K';
    int t = 273;
    cout << ch << ":\n";
    cout << t << ":\n";
    cout << -t <<":\n";

    double f1 = 1.200;
    cout << f1 << ":\n";
    cout << (f1 + 1.0 / 9.0) << ":\n";

    double f2 = 1.67E2;
    cout << f2 << ":\n";
    f2 += 1.0 / 9.0;
```

LISTING 17.2   Continued

```
    cout << f2 << ":\n";
    cout << (f2 * 1.0e4) << ":\n";


    double f3 = 2.3e-4;
    cout << f3 << ":\n";
    cout << f3 / 10 << ":\n";

    return 0;
}
```

Here is the output of the program in Listing 17.2:

```
12345678901234567890
K:
273:
-273:
1.2:
1.31111:
167:
167.111:
1.67111e+006:
0.00023:
2.3e-005:
```

Each value fills its field. Note that the trailing zeros of 1.200 are not displayed but that float-ing-point values without terminating zeros have six places to the right of the decimal dis-played. Also, this particular implementation displays three digits in the exponent; others might use two.

Changing the Number Base Used for Display

The `ostream` class inherits from the `ios` class, which inherits from the `ios_base` class. The `ios_base` class stores information that describes the format state. For example, certain bits in one class member determine the number base used, whereas another member determines the field width. By using *manipulators*, you can control the number base used to display integers. By using `ios_base` member functions, you can control the field width and the number of places displayed to the right of the decimal. Because the `ios_base` class is an indirect base class for `ostream`, you can use its methods with `ostream` objects (or descendants), such as `cout`.

Note

The members and methods found in the `ios_base` class were formerly found in the `ios` class. Now `ios_base` is a base class to `ios`. In the new system, `ios` is a template class with `char` and `wchar_t` specializations, and `ios_base` contains the non-template features.

Let's look at how to set the number base to be used in displaying integers. To control whether integers are displayed in base 10, base 16, or base 8, you can use the dec, hex, and oct manipulators. For example, the function call

```
hex(cout);
```

sets the number base format state for the cout object to hexadecimal. After you do this, a program will print integer values in hexadecimal form until you set the format state to another choice. Note that the manipulators are not member functions, hence they don't have to be invoked by an object.

Although the manipulators really are functions, you normally see them used this way:

```
cout << hex;
```

The ostream class overloads the << operator to make this usage equivalent to the function call hex(cout). The manipulators are in the std namespace. Listing 17.3 illustrates using these manipulators. It shows the value of an integer and its square in three different number bases. Note that you can use a manipulator separately or as part of a series of insertions.

LISTING 17.3 manip.cpp

```
// manip.cpp -- using format manipulators
#include <iostream>
int main()
{
    using namespace std;
    cout << "Enter an integer: ";
    int n;
    cin >> n;

    cout << "n      n*n\n";
    cout << n << "        " << n * n << " (decimal)\n";
// set to hex mode
    cout << hex;
    cout << n << "        ";
    cout << n * n << " (hexadecimal)\n";

// set to octal mode
    cout << oct << n << "        " << n * n << " (octal)\n";

// alternative way to call a manipulator
    dec(cout);
    cout << n << "        " << n * n << " (decimal)\n";

    return 0;
}
```

Here is some sample output from the program in Listing 17.3:

```
Enter an integer: 13
n      n*n
13     169 (decimal)
```

```
d       a9 (hexadecimal)
15      251 (octal)
13      169 (decimal)
```

Adjusting Field Widths

You probably noticed that the columns in output from Listing 17.3 don't line up; that's because the numbers have different field widths. You can use the `width` member function to place differently sized numbers in fields that have equal widths. The method has these prototypes:

```
int width();
int width(int i);
```

The first form returns the current setting for field width. The second sets the field width to `i` spaces and returns the previous field width value. This allows you to save the previous value in case you want to restore the width to that value later.

The `width()` method affects only the next item displayed, and the field width reverts to the default value afterward. For example, consider the following statements:

```
cout << '#';
cout.width(12);
cout << 12 << "#" <<  24 << "#\n";
```

Because `width()` is a member function, you have to use an object (`cout`, in this case) to invoke it. The output statement produces the following display:

```
#          12#24#
```

The `12` is placed in a field 12 characters wide at the right end of the field. This is called right-justification. After that, the field width reverts to the default, and the two `#` characters and the `24` are printed in fields equal to their own size.

Remember
The `width()` method affects only the next item displayed, and the field width reverts to the default value afterward.

C++ never truncates data, so if you attempt to print a seven-digit value in a field with a width of two, C++ expands the field to fit the data. (Some languages just fill the field with asterisks if the data doesn't fit. The C/C++ philosophy is that showing all the data is more important than keeping the columns neat; C++ puts substance before form.) Listing 17.4 shows how the `width()` member function works.

LISTING 17.4 width.cpp

```
// width.cpp -- using the width method
#include <iostream>
```

LISTING 17.4 Continued

```cpp
int main()
{
    using std::cout;
    int w = cout.width(30);
    cout << "default field width = " << w << ":\n";

    cout.width(5);
    cout << "N" <<':';
    cout.width(8);
    cout << "N * N" << ":\n";

    for (long i = 1; i <= 100; i *= 10)
    {
        cout.width(5);
        cout << i <<':';
        cout.width(8);
        cout << i * i << ":\n";
    }

    return 0;
}
```

Here is the output of the program in Listing 17.4:

```
       default field width = 0:
   N:    N * N:
   1:        1:
  10:      100:
 100:    10000:
```

The output displays values right-justified in their fields. The output is padded with spaces. That is, **cout** achieves the full field width by adding spaces. With right-justification, the spaces are inserted to the left of the values. The character used for padding is termed the *fill character*. Right-justification is the default.

Note that the program in Listing 17.4 applies the field width of 30 to the string displayed by the first **cout** statement but not to the value of w. This is because the **width()** method affects only the next single item displayed. Also, note that w has the value **0**. This is because **cout.width(30)** returns the previous field width, not the width to which it was just set. The fact that w is **0** means that zero is the default field width. Because C++ always expands a field to fit the data, this one size fits all. Finally, the program uses **width()** to align column headings and data by using a width of five characters for the first column and a width of eight characters for the second column.

Fill Characters

By default, **cout** fills unused parts of a field with spaces. You can use the **fill()** member function to change that. For example, the call

```cpp
cout.fill('*');
```

changes the fill character to an asterisk. That can be handy for, say, printing checks so that recipients can't easily add a digit or two. Listing 17.5 illustrates using this member function.

LISTING 17.5   fill.cpp

```cpp
// fill.cpp -- changing fill character for fields
#include <iostream>

int main()
{
    using std::cout;
    cout.fill('*');
    const char * staff[2] = { "Waldo Whipsnade", "Wilmarie Wooper"};
    long bonus[2] = {900, 1350};

    for (int i = 0; i < 2; i++)
    {
        cout << staff[i] << ": $";
        cout.width(7);
        cout << bonus[i] << "\n";
    }

    return 0;
}
```

Here's the output of the program in Listing 17.5:

```
Waldo Whipsnade: $****900
Wilmarie Wooper: $***1350
```

Note that, unlike the field width, the new fill character stays in effect until you change it.

Setting Floating-Point Display Precision

The meaning of floating-point *precision* depends on the output mode. In the default mode, it means the total number of digits displayed. In the fixed and scientific modes, to be discussed soon, *precision* means the number of digits displayed to the right of the decimal place. The precision default for C++, as you've seen, is **6**. (Recall, however, that trailing zeros are dropped.) The `precision()` member function lets you select other values. For example, the statement

```cpp
cout.precision(2);
```

causes `cout` to set the precision to **2**. Unlike the case with `width()`, but like the case for `fill()`, a new precision setting stays in effect until it is reset. Listing 17.6 demonstrates precisely this point.

LISTING 17.6   precise.cpp

```cpp
// precise.cpp -- setting the precision
#include <iostream>
```

LISTING 17.6   Continued

```
int main()
{
    using std::cout;
    float price1 = 20.40;
    float price2 = 1.9 + 8.0 / 9.0;

    cout << "\"Furry Friends\" is $" << price1 << "!\n";
    cout << "\"Fiery Fiends\" is $" << price2 << "!\n";

    cout.precision(2);
    cout << "\"Furry Friends\" is $" << price1 << "!\n";
    cout << "\"Fiery Fiends\" is $" << price2 << "!\n";

    return 0;
}
```

Compatibility Note

Older versions of C++ interpret the precision for the default mode as the number of digits to the right of the decimal instead of as the total number of digits.

Here is the output of the program in Listing 17.6:

```
"Furry Friends" is $20.4!
"Fiery Fiends" is $2.78889!
"Furry Friends" is $20!
"Fiery Fiends" is $2.8!
```

Note that the third line of this output doesn't include a trailing decimal point. Also, the fourth line displays a total of two digits.

Printing Trailing Zeros and Decimal Points

Certain forms of output, such as prices or numbers in columns, look better if trailing zeros are retained. For example, the output to Listing 17.6 would look better as $20.40 than as $20.4. The `iostream` family of classes doesn't provide a function whose sole purpose is to accomplish that. However, the `ios_base` class provides a `setf()` (for *set flag*) function that controls several formatting features. The class also defines several constants that can be used as arguments to this function. For example, the function call

```
cout.setf(ios_base::showpoint);
```

causes `cout` to display trailing decimal points. In the default floating-point format, it also causes trailing zeros to be displayed. That is, instead of displaying **2.00** as 2, `cout` will display it as **2.00000** if the default precision of 6 is in effect. Listing 17.7 adds this statement to Listing 17.6.

> **Caution**
>
> If your compiler uses the `iostream.h` header file instead of `iostream`, you most likely will have to use `ios` instead of `ios_base` in `setf()` arguments.

In case you're wondering about the notation `ios_base::showpoint`, `showpoint` is a class-scope static constant that is defined in the `ios_base` class declaration. Class scope means that you have to use the scope-resolution operator (`::`) with the constant name if you use the name outside a member function definition. So `ios_base::showpoint` names a constant defined in the `ios_base` class.

LISTING 17.7   showpt.cpp

```cpp
// showpt.cpp -- setting the precision, showing trailing point
#include <iostream>

int main()
{
    using std::cout;
    using std::ios_base;

    float price1 = 20.40;
    float price2 = 1.9 + 8.0 / 9.0;

    cout.setf(ios_base::showpoint);
    cout << "\"Furry Friends\" is $" << price1 << "!\n";
    cout << "\"Fiery Fiends\" is $" << price2 << "!\n";

    cout.precision(2);
    cout << "\"Furry Friends\" is $" << price1 << "!\n";
    cout << "\"Fiery Fiends\" is $" << price2 << "!\n";

    return 0;
}
```

Here is the output of the program in Listing 17.7, using the current C++ formatting:

```
"Furry Friends" is $20.4000!
"Fiery Fiends" is $2.78889!
"Furry Friends" is $20.!
"Fiery Fiends" is $2.8!
```

Note that in this output, trailing zeros are not shown, but the trailing decimal point for the third line is shown.

More About `setf()`

The `setf()` method controls several other formatting choices besides when the decimal point is displayed, so let's take a closer look at it. The `ios_base` class has a protected data member in which individual bits (called *flags* in this context) control different formatting aspects, such as the number base and whether trailing zeros are displayed. Turning a flag on is called *setting the flag* (or bit) and means setting the bit to 1. (Bit flags are the programming equivalent to setting DIP switches to configure computer hardware.) The `hex`, `dec`, and `oct` manipulators, for example, adjust the three flag bits that control the number base. The `setf()` function provides another means of adjusting flag bits.

The `setf()` function has two prototypes. The first is this:

```
fmtflags setf(fmtflags);
```

Here `fmtflags` is a `typedef` name for a *bitmask* type (see the following Note) used to hold the format flags. The name is defined in the `ios_base` class. This version of `setf()` is used for setting format information controlled by a single bit. The argument is a `fmtflags` value that indicates which bit to set. The return value is a type `fmtflags` number that indicates the former settings of all the flags. You can then save that value if you later want to restore the original settings. What value do you pass to `setf()`? If you want to set bit number 11 to 1, you pass a number that has its number 11 bit set to 1. The return value would have its number 11 bit assigned the prior value for that bit. Keeping track of bits sounds (and is) tedious. However, you don't have to do that job; the `ios_base` class defines constants that represent the bit values. Table 17.1 shows some of these definitions.

Note

A *bitmask type* is a type that is used to store individual bit values. It could be an integer type, an `enum`, or an STL `bitset` container. The main idea is that each bit is individually accessible and has its own meaning. The `iostream` package uses bitmask types to store state information.

TABLE 17.1   Formatting Constants

Constant	Meaning
`ios_base::boolalpha`	Input and output `bool` values as `true` and `false`
`ios_base::showbase`	Use C++ base prefixes (0,0x) on output
`ios_base::showpoint`	Show trailing decimal point
`ios_base::uppercase`	Use uppercase letters for hex output, E notation
`ios_base::showpos`	Use + before positive numbers

Because these formatting constants are defined within the `ios_base` class, you must use the scope-resolution operator with them. That is, you must use `ios_base::uppercase`, not just `uppercase`. If you don't use a `using` directive or `using` declaration, you can use the scope-resolution operator to indicate that these names are in the `std` namespace. That is, you can use `std::ios_base::showpos`, and so on. Changes remain in effect until they are overridden. Listing 17.8 illustrates using some of these constants.

LISTING 17.8   `setf.cpp`

```cpp
// setf.cpp -- using setf() to control formatting
#include <iostream>

int main()
{
    using std::cout;
    using std::endl;
    using std::ios_base;

    int temperature = 63;

    cout << "Today's water temperature: ";
    cout.setf(ios_base::showpos);    // show plus sign
    cout << temperature << endl;

    cout << "For our programming friends, that's\n";
    cout << std::hex << temperature << endl; // use hex
    cout.setf(ios_base::uppercase);     // use uppercase in hex
    cout.setf(ios_base::showbase);     // use 0X prefix for hex
    cout << "or\n";
    cout << temperature << endl;
    cout << "How " << true << "!  oops -- How ";
    cout.setf(ios_base::boolalpha);
    cout << true << "!\n";

    return 0;
}
```

Compatibility Note

Some C++ implementations may use `ios` instead of `ios_base`, and they may fail to provide a `boolalpha` choice.

Here is the output of the program in Listing 17.8:

```
Today's water temperature: +63
For our programming friends, that's
3f
or
0X3F
How 0X1!  oops -- How true!
```

Note that the plus sign is used only with the base 10 version. C++ treats hexadecimal and octal values as unsigned; therefore no sign is needed for them. (However, some C++ implementations may still display a plus sign.)

The second `setf()` prototype takes two arguments and returns the prior setting:

```cpp
fmtflags setf(fmtflags , fmtflags );
```

This overloaded form of the function is used for format choices controlled by more than 1 bit. The first argument, as before, is a `fmtflags` value that contains the desired setting. The second argument is a value that first clears the appropriate bits. For example, suppose setting bit 3 to 1 means base 10, setting bit 4 to 1 means base 8, and setting bit 5 to 1 means base 16. Suppose output is in base 10, and you want to set it to base 16. Not only do you have to set bit 5 to 1, you also have to set bit 3 to 0; this is called *clearing the bit*. The clever `hex` manipulator does both tasks automatically. Using the `setf()` function requires a bit more work because you use the second argument to indicate which bits to clear and then use the first argument to indicate which bit to set. This is not as complicated as it sounds because the `ios_base` class defines constants (shown in Table 17.2) for this purpose. In particular, you should use the constant `ios_base::basefield` as the second argument and `ios_base::hex` as the first argument if you're changing bases. That is, the function call

```
cout.setf(ios_base::hex, ios_base::basefield);
```

has the same effect as using the `hex` manipulator.

TABLE 17.2 Arguments for `setf(long, long)`

Second Argument	First Argument	Meaning
ios_base::basefield	ios_base::dec	Use base 10
	ios_base::oct	Use base 8
	ios_base::hex	Use base 16
ios_base::floatfield	ios_base::fixed	Use fixed-point notation
	ios_base::scientific	Use scientific notation
ios_base::adjustfield	ios_base::left	Use left-justification
	ios_base::right	Use right-justification
	ios_base::internal	Left-justify sign or base prefix, right-justify value

The `ios_base` class defines three sets of formatting flags that can be handled this way. Each set consists of one constant to be used as the second argument and two to three constants to be used as a first argument. The second argument clears a batch of related bits; then the first argument sets one of those bits to 1. Table 17.2 shows the names of the constants used for the second `setf()` argument, the associated choice of constants for the first argument, and their meanings. For example, to select left-justification, you use `ios_base::adjustfield` for the second argument and `ios_base::left` as the first argument. Left-justification means starting a value at the left end of the field, and right-justification means ending a value at the right end of the field. Internal justification means placing any signs or base prefixes at the left of the field and the rest of the number at the right of the field. (Unfortunately, C++ does not provide a self-justification mode.)

Fixed-point notation means using the 123.4 style for floating-point values, regardless of the size of the number, and scientific notation means using the 1.23e04 style, regardless of the size of the number. If you are familiar with C's `printf()` specifiers, it may help you to know that the default C++ mode corresponds to the `%g` specifier, `fixed` corresponds to the `%f` specifier, and `scientific` corresponds to the `%e` specifier.

Under the C++ Standard, both fixed and scientific notation have the following two properties:

- *Precision* means the number of digits to the right of the decimal rather than the total number of digits.

- Trailing zeros are displayed.

Under the older usage, trailing zeros are not shown unless `ios::showpoint` is set. Also, under older usage, precision always meant the number of digits to the right of the decimal, even in the default mode.

The `setf()` function is a member function of the `ios_base` class. Because that's a base class for the `ostream` class, you can invoke the function by using the `cout` object. For example, to request left-justification, you use this call:

```
ios_base::fmtflags old = cout.setf(ios::left, ios::adjustfield);
```

To restore the previous setting, you use this:

```
cout.setf(old, ios::adjustfield);
```

Listing 17.9 illustrates further examples of using `setf()` with two arguments.

Compatibility Note

The program in Listing 17.9 uses a math function, and some C++ systems don't automatically search the math library. For example, some Unix systems require that you use the following:

```
$ CC setf2.C -lm
```

The `-lm` option instructs the linker to search the math library. Similarly, some Linux systems using g++ require the same flag.

LISTING 17.9   `setf2.cpp`

```cpp
// setf2.cpp -- using setf() with 2 arguments to control formatting
#include <iostream>
#include <cmath>

int main()
{
    using namespace std;
  // use left justification, show the plus sign, show trailing
  // zeros, with a precision of 3
    cout.setf(ios_base::left, ios_base::adjustfield);
    cout.setf(ios_base::showpos);
```

LISTING 17.9   Continued

```
        cout.setf(ios_base::showpoint);
        cout.precision(3);
        // use e-notation and save old format setting
        ios_base::fmtflags old = cout.setf(ios_base::scientific,
            ios_base::floatfield);
        cout << "Left Justification:\n";
        long n;
        for (n = 1; n <= 41; n+= 10)
        {
            cout.width(4);
            cout << n << "|";
            cout.width(12);
            cout << sqrt(double(n)) << "|\n";
        }

        // change to internal justification
        cout.setf(ios_base::internal, ios_base::adjustfield);
        // restore default floating-point display style
        cout.setf(old, ios_base::floatfield);

        cout << "Internal Justification:\n";
        for (n = 1; n <= 41; n+= 10)
        {
            cout.width(4);
            cout << n << "|";
            cout.width(12);
            cout << sqrt(double(n)) << "|\n";
        }

        // use right justification, fixed notation
        cout.setf(ios_base::right, ios_base::adjustfield);
        cout.setf(ios_base::fixed, ios_base::floatfield);
        cout << "Right Justification:\n";
        for (n = 1; n <= 41; n+= 10)
        {
            cout.width(4);
            cout << n << "|";
            cout.width(12);
            cout << sqrt(double(n)) << "|\n";
        }

        return 0;
    }
```

Here is the output of the program in Listing 17.9:

```
Left Justification:
+1  |+1.000e+00  |
+11 |+3.317e+00  |
+21 |+4.583e+00  |
+31 |+5.568e+00  |
+41 |+6.403e+00  |
```

```
Internal Justification:
+  1|+        1.00|
+ 11|+        3.32|
+ 21|+        4.58|
+ 31|+        5.57|
+ 41|+        6.40|
Right Justification:
  +1|        +1.000|
 +11|        +3.317|
 +21|        +4.583|
 +31|        +5.568|
 +41|        +6.403|
```

Note how a precision of 3 causes the default floating-point display (used for internal justification in this program) to display a total of three digits, while the fixed and scientific modes display three digits to the right of the decimal. (The number of digits displayed in the exponent for e-notation depends on the implementation.)

The effects of calling `setf()` can be undone with `unsetf()`, which has the following prototype:

```
void unsetf(fmtflags mask);
```

Here `mask` is a bit pattern. All bits set to `1` in `mask` cause the corresponding bits to be unset. That is, `setf()` sets bits to `1`, and `unsetf()` sets bits back to `0`. Here's an example:

```
cout.setf(ios_base::showpoint);    // show trailing decimal point
cout.unsetf(ios_base::boolalpha);  // don't show trailing decimal point
cout.setf(ios_base::boolalpha);    // display true, false
cout.unsetf(ios_base::boolalpha);  // display 1, 0
```

You may have noticed that there is no special flag to indicate the default mode for displaying floating-point numbers. Here's how the system works. Fixed notation is used if the fixed bit and only the fixed bit is set. Scientific notation is used if the scientific bit and only the scientific bit is set. Any other combination, such as no bits set or both bits set, results in the default mode being used. So one way to invoke the default mode is this:

```
cout.setf(0, ios_base::floatfield);  // go to default mode
```

The second argument turns both bits off, and the first argument doesn't set any bits. A shorter way to accomplish the same end is to use `unsetf()` with `ios_base::floatfield`:

```
cout.unsetf(ios_base::floatfield);  // go to default mode
```

If you knew for certain that `cout` were in the fixed state, you could use `ios_base::fixed` as an argument to `unsetf()`, but using `ios_base::floatfield` works, regardless of the current state of `cout`, so it's a better choice.

Standard Manipulators

Using `setf()` is not the most user-friendly approach to formatting, so C++ offers several manipulators to invoke `setf()` for you, automatically supplying the right arguments. You've already seen `dec`, `hex`, and `oct`. These manipulators, most of which are not available to older C++ implementations, work like `hex`. For example, the statement

```
cout << left << fixed;
```

turns on left-justification and the fixed decimal point option. Table 17.3 lists these along with several other manipulators.

Tip

If your system supports these manipulators, take advantage of them; if it doesn't, you still have the option of using `setf()`.

TABLE 17.3 Some Standard Manipulators

Manipulator	Calls
boolalpha	setf(ios_base::boolalpha)
noboolalpha	unset(ios_base::noboolalpha)
showbase	setf(ios_base::showbase)
noshowbase	unsetf(ios_base::showbase)
showpoint	setf(ios_base::showpoint)
noshowpoint	unsetf(ios_base::showpoint)
showpos	setf(ios_base::showpos)
noshowpos	unsetf(ios_base::showpos)
uppercase	setf(ios_base::uppercase)
nouppercase	unsetf(ios_base::uppercase)
internal	setf(ios_base::internal, ios_base::adjustfield)
left	setf(ios_base::left, ios_base::adjustfield)
right	setf(ios_base::right, ios_base::adjustfield)
dec	setf(ios_base::dec, ios_base::basefield)
hex	setf(ios_base::hex, ios_base::basefield)
oct	setf(ios_base::oct, ios_base::basefield)
fixed	setf(ios_base::fixed, ios_base::floatfield)
scientific	setf(ios_base::scientific, ios_base::floatfield)

The `iomanip` Header File

Setting some format values, such as the field width, can be awkward using the `iostream` tools. To make life easier, C++ supplies additional manipulators in the `iomanip` header file. They provide the same services already discussed, but in a notationally more convenient manner. The three most commonly used are `setprecision()` for setting the precision, `setfill()` for setting the fill character, and `setw()` for setting the field width. Unlike the manipulators discussed previously, these take arguments. The `setprecision()` manipulator takes an integer argument that specifies the precision, the `setfill()` manipulator takes a `char` argument that indicates the fill character, and the `setw()` manipulator takes an integer argument that specifies the field width. Because they are manipulators, they can be concatenated in a `cout` statement. This makes the `setw()` manipulator particularly convenient when you're displaying several columns of values. Listing 17.10 illustrates this by changing the field width and fill character several times for one output line. It also uses some of the newer standard manipulators.

Compatibility Note

The program in Listing 17.10 uses a math function, and some C++ systems don't automatically search the math library. For example, some Unix systems require that you use the following:

```
$ CC iomanip.C -lm
```

The `-lm` option instructs the linker to search the math library. Some Linux systems using g++ use the same option. Also, older compilers may not recognize the new standard manipulators, such as `show-point`. In that case, you can use the `setf()` equivalents.

LISTING 17.10   `iomanip.cpp`

```cpp
// iomanip.cpp -- using manipulators from iomanip
// some systems require explicitly linking the math library
#include <iostream>
#include <iomanip>
#include <cmath>

int main()
{
    using namespace std;
    // use new standard manipulators
    cout << showpoint << fixed << right;

    // use iomanip manipulators
    cout << setw(6) << "N" << setw(14) << "square root"
         << setw(15) << "fourth root\n";

    double root;
    for (int n = 10; n <=100; n += 10)
    {
        root = sqrt(double(n));
```

LISTING 17.10 Continued

```
        cout << setw(6) << setfill('.') << n << setfill(' ')
             << setw(12) << setprecision(3) << root
             << setw(14) << setprecision(4) << sqrt(root)
             << endl;
    }

    return 0;
}
```

Here is the output of the program in Listing 17.10:

```
    N   square root    fourth root
....10        3.162        1.7783
....20        4.472        2.1147
....30        5.477        2.3403
....40        6.325        2.5149
....50        7.071        2.6591
....60        7.746        2.7832
....70        8.367        2.8925
....80        8.944        2.9907
....90        9.487        3.0801
...100       10.000        3.1623
```

Now you can produce neatly aligned columns. Note that this program produces the same formatting with either the older or current implementations. Using the `showpoint` manipulator causes trailing zeros to be displayed in older implementations, and using the `fixed` manipulator causes trailing zeros to be displayed in current implementations. Using `fixed` makes the display fixed-point in either system, and in current systems it makes precision refer to the number of digits to the right of the decimal. In older systems, precision always has that meaning, regardless of the floating-point display mode.

Table 17.4 summarizes some of the differences between older C++ formatting and the current state. One moral of this table is that you shouldn't feel baffled if you run a sample program you've seen somewhere and the output format doesn't match what is shown for the example.

TABLE 17.4 Formatting Changes

Feature	Older C++ Meaning	Current C++ Meaning
`precision(n)`	Display n digits to the right of the decimal point	Display a total of n digits in the default mode, and display n digits to the right of the decimal point in fixed and scientific modes
`ios::showpoint`	Display trailing decimal point and trailing zeros	Display trailing decimal point
`ios::fixed`, `ios::scientific`		Show trailing zeros (also see comments under `precision(n)`)

Input with `cin`

Now it's time to turn to input and getting data into a program. The `cin` object represents the standard input as a stream of bytes. Normally, you generate that stream of characters at the keyboard. If you type the character sequence **2005**, the `cin` object extracts those characters from the input stream. You may intend that input to be part of a string, to be an `int` value, to be a `float` value, or to be some other type. Thus, extraction also involves type conversion. The `cin` object, guided by the type of variable designated to receive the value, must use its methods to convert that character sequence into the intended type of value.

Typically, you use `cin` as follows:

```
cin >> value_holder;
```

Here *value_holder* identifies the memory location in which to store the input. It can be the name of a variable, a reference, a dereferenced pointer, or a member of a structure or of a class. How `cin` interprets the input depends on the data type for *value_holder*. The `istream` class, defined in the `iostream` header file, overloads the `>>` extraction operator to recognize the following basic types:

- `signed char &`
- `unsigned char &`
- `char &`
- `short &`
- `unsigned short &`
- `int &`
- `unsigned int &`
- `long &`
- `unsigned long &`
- `float &`
- `double &`
- `long double &`

These are referred to as *formatted input functions* because they convert the input data to the format indicated by the target.

A typical operator function has a prototype like the following:

```
istream & operator>>(int &);
```

Both the argument and the return value are references. With a reference argument (see Chapter 8, "Adventures in Functions"), a statement such as

```
cin >> staff_size;
```

causes the `operator>>()` function to work with the variable `staff_size` itself rather than with a copy, as would be the case with a regular argument. Because the argument type is a reference, `cin` is able to directly modify the value of a variable used as an argument. The preceding statement, for example, directly modifies the value of the `staff_size` variable. We'll get to the significance of a reference return value in a moment. First, let's examine the type conversion aspect of the extraction operator. For arguments of each type in the preceding list of types, the extraction operator converts the character input to the indicated type of value. For example, suppose `staff_size` is type `int`. In this case, the compiler matches

```
cin >> staff_size;
```

to the following prototype:

```
istream & operator>>(int &);
```

The function corresponding to that prototype then reads the stream of characters being sent to the program—say, the characters 2, 3, 1, 8, and 4. For a system using a 2-byte `int`, the function then converts these characters to the 2-byte binary representation of the integer 23184. If, on the other hand, `staff_size` were type `double`, `cin` would use `operator>>(double &)` to convert the same input into the 8-byte floating-point representation of the value 23184.0.

Incidentally, you can use the `hex`, `oct`, and `dec` manipulators with `cin` to specify that integer input is to be interpreted as hexadecimal, octal, or decimal format. For example, the statement

```
cin >> hex;
```

causes an input of 12 or 0x12 to be read as hexadecimal 12, or decimal 18, and it causes ff or FF to be read as decimal 255.

The `istream` class also overloads the `>>` extraction operator for character pointer types:

- `signed char *`
- `char *`
- `unsigned char *`

For this type of argument, the extraction operator reads the next word from input and places it at the indicated address, adding a null character to make a string. For example, suppose you have this code:

```
cout << "Enter your first name:\n";
char name[20];
cin >> name;
```

If you respond to the request by typing **Liz**, the extraction operator places the characters `Liz\0` in the `name` array. (As usual, `\0` represents the terminating null character.) The `name` identifier, being the name of a `char` array, acts as the address of the array's first element, making `name` type `char *` (pointer-to-`char`).

The fact that each extraction operator returns a reference to the invoking object lets you concatenate input, just as you can concatenate output:

```
char name[20];
float fee;
int group;
cin >> name >> fee >> group;
```

Here, for example, the `cin` object returned by `cin >> name` becomes the object that handles `fee`.

How `cin >>` Views Input

The various versions of the extraction operator share a common way of looking at the input stream. They skip over white space (blanks, newlines, and tabs) until they encounter a non-white-space character. This is true even for the single-character modes (those in which the argument is type `char`, `unsigned char`, or `signed char`), which is not true of C's character input functions (see Figure 17.5). In the single-character modes, the `>>` operator reads that character and assigns it to the indicated location. In the other modes, the operator reads in one unit of the indicated type. That is, it reads everything from the initial non-white-space character up to the first character that doesn't match the destination type.

FIGURE 17.5

`cin >>` skips over white space.

```
char philosophy[20];
int distance;
char initial;

cin >> philosophy >> distance >> initial;
```

skips over spaces, newlines, and tabs

stoic 100 Blaise

philosophy	distance	initial
stoic	100	B

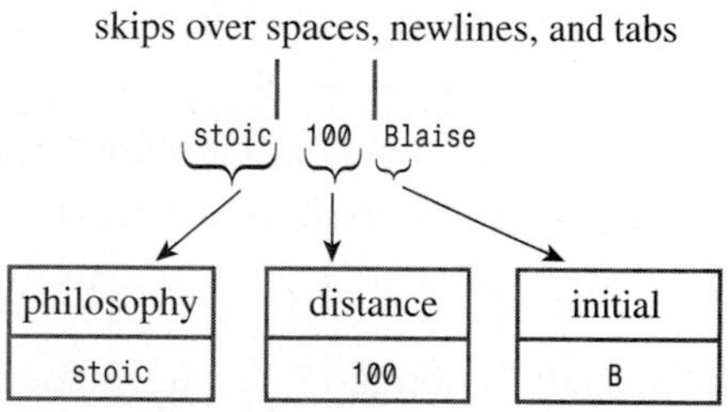

For example, consider the following code:

```
int elevation;
cin >> elevation;
```

Suppose you type the following characters:

`-123Z`

The operator will read the `-`, `1`, `2`, and `3` characters, because they are all valid parts of an integer. But the `Z` character isn't valid, so the last character accepted for input is the `3`. The `Z` remains in the input stream, and the next `cin` statement will start reading at that point. Meanwhile, the operator converts the character sequence `-123` to an integer value and assigns it to `elevation`.

It can happen that input fails to meet a program's expectation. For example, suppose you enter Zcar instead of -123Z. In that case, the extraction operator leaves the value of elevation unchanged and returns the value 0. (More technically, an if or while statement evaluates an istream object as false if it's had an error state set; we'll discuss this in more depth later in this chapter.) The false return value allows a program to check whether input meets the program requirements, as Listing 17.11 shows.

LISTING 17.11   check_it.cpp

```cpp
// check_it.cpp -- checking for valid input
#include <iostream>

int main()
{
    using namespace std;
    cout << "Enter numbers: ";

    int sum = 0;
    int input;
    while (cin >> input)
    {
        sum += input;
    }

    cout << "Last value entered = " << input << endl;
    cout << "Sum = " << sum << endl;
    return 0;
```

Compatibility Note

If your compiler doesn't support the showpoint and fixed manipulators, you can use the setf() equivalents.

Here's the output of the program in Listing 17.11 when some inappropriate input (-123Z) sneaks into the input stream:

```
Enter numbers: 200
10 -50 -123Z 60
Last value entered = -123
Sum = 37
```

Because input is buffered, the second line of keyboard input values didn't get sent to the program until you pressed Enter at the end of the line. But the loop quit processing input at the Z character because it didn't match any of the floating-point formats. The failure of input to match the expected format, in turn, caused the expression cin>> input to evaluate to false, thus terminating the while loop.

Stream States

Let's take a closer look at what happens for inappropriate input. A `cin` or `cout` object contains a data member (inherited from the `ios_base` class) that describes the *stream state*. A stream state (defined as type `iostate`, which, in turn, is a bitmask type, such as described earlier) consists of the three `ios_base` elements: `eofbit`, `badbit`, and `failbit`. Each element is a single bit that can be 1 (set) or 0 (cleared). When a `cin` operation reaches the end of a file, it sets `eofbit`. When a `cin` operation fails to read the expected characters, as in the earlier example, it sets `failbit`. I/O failures, such as trying to read a non-accessible file or trying to write to a write-protected disk, also can set `failbit` to 1. The `badbit` element is set when some undiagnosed failure may have corrupted the stream. (Implementations don't necessarily agree about which events set `failbit` and which set `badbit`.) When all three of these state bits are set to 0, everything is fine. Programs can check the stream state and use that information to decide what to do next. Table 17.5 lists these bits, along with some `ios_base` methods that report or alter the stream state. (Older compilers don't provide the two `exceptions()` methods.)

TABLE 17.5 Stream States

Member	Description
`eofbit`	Is set to 1 if end-of-file reached.
`badbit`	Is set to 1 if the stream may be corrupted; for example, there could have been a file read error.
`failbit`	Is set to 1 if an input operation failed to read the expected characters or an output operation failed to write the expected characters.
`goodbit`	Just another way of saying 0.
`good()`	Returns `true` if the stream can be used (all bits are cleared).
`eof()`	Returns `true` if `eofbit` is set.
`bad()`	Returns `true` if `badbit` is set.
`fail()`	Returns `true` if `badbit` or `failbit` is set.
`rdstate()`	Returns the stream state.
`exceptions()`	Returns a bit mask that identifies which flags cause an exception to be thrown.
`exceptions(iostate ex)`	Sets which states will cause `clear()` to throw an exception; for example, if `ex` is `eofbit`, then `clear()` will throw an exception if `eofbit` is set.
`clear(iostate s)`	Sets the stream state to s; the default for s is 0 (goodbit); throws a `basic_ios::failure` exception if `rdstate() & exceptions()) != 0`.
`setstate(iostate s)`	Calls `clear(rdstate()	s)`. This sets stream state bits corresponding to those bits set in s; other stream state bits are left unchanged.

Setting States

Two of the methods in Table 17.5, `clear()` and `setstate()`, are similar. Both reset the state, but they do so in a different fashion. The `clear()` method sets the state to its argument. Thus, the call

```
clear();
```

uses the default argument of `0`, which clears all three state bits (`eofbit`, `badbit`, and `failbit`). Similarly, the call

```
clear(eofbit);
```

makes the state equal to `eofbit`; that is, `eofbit` is set, and the other two state bits are cleared.

The `setstate()` method, however, affects only those bits that are set in its argument. Thus, the call

```
setstate(eofbit);
```

sets `eofbit` without affecting the other bits. So if `failbit` was already set, it stays set.

Why would you reset the stream state? For a program writer, the most common reason is to use `clear()` with no argument to reopen input after encountering mismatched input or end-of-file; whether doing so makes sense depends on what the program is trying to accomplish. You'll see some examples shortly. The main purpose for `setstate()` is to provide a means for input and output functions to change the state. For example, if `num` is an `int`, the call

```
cin >> num;   // read an int
```

can result in `operator>>(int &)` using `setstate()` to set `failbit` or `eofbit`.

I/O and Exceptions

Suppose that an input function sets `eofbit`. Does this cause an exception to be thrown? By default, the answer is no. However, you can use the `exceptions()` method to control how exceptions are handled.

First, here's some background. The `exceptions()` method returns a bitfield with three bits corresponding to `eofbit`, `failbit`, and `badbit`. Changing the stream state involves either `clear()` or `setstate()`, which uses `clear()`. After changing the stream state, the `clear()` method compares the current stream state to the value returned by `exceptions()`. If a bit is set in the return value and the corresponding bit is set in the current state, `clear()` throws an `ios_base::failure` exception. This would happen, for example, if both values had `badbit` set. It follows that if `exceptions()` returns `goodbit`, no exceptions are thrown. The `ios_base::failure` exception class derives from the `std::exception` class and thus has a `what()` method.

The default setting for `exceptions()` is `goodbit`—that is, no exceptions thrown. However, the overloaded `exceptions(iostate)` function gives you control over the behavior:

```
cin.exceptions(badbit);   // setting badbit causes exception to be thrown
```

The bitwise OR operator (|), as discussed in Appendix E, allows you to specify more than one bit. For example, the statement

```
cin.exceptions(badbit | eofbit);
```

results in an exception being thrown if either **badbit** or **eofbit** is subsequently set.

Listing 17.12 modifies Listing 17.11 so that the program throws and catches an exception if **failbit** is set.

LISTING 17.12   cinexcp.cpp

```cpp
// cinexcp.cpp -- having cin throw an exception
#include <iostream>
#include <exception>

int main()
{
    using namespace std;
    // have failbit cause an exception to be thrown
    cin.exceptions(ios_base::failbit);
    cout << "Enter numbers: ";
    int sum = 0;
    int input;
    try {
        while (cin >> input)
        {
            sum += input;
        }
    } catch(ios_base::failure & bf)
    {
        cout << bf.what() << endl;
        cout << "O! the horror!\n";
    }

    cout << "Last value entered = " << input << endl;
    cout << "Sum = " << sum << endl;
    return 0;
}
```

Here is a sample run of the program in Listing 17.12; the **what()** message depends on the implementation:

```
Enter numbers: 20 30 40 pi 6
ios_base failure in clear
O! the horror!
Last value entered = 40.00
Sum = 90.00
```

So that's how you can use exceptions for input. But should you use them? It depends on the context. For this example, the answer is no. An exception should catch an unusual, unexpected occurrence, but this particular program uses a type mismatch as the intended way to exit the loop. It might make sense, however, for this program to throw an exception for `badbit` because that circumstance would be unexpected. Or if the program were designed to read numbers from a data file up to end-of-file, it might make sense to throw an exception for `failbit` because that would represent a problem with the data file.

Stream State Effects

An `if` or `while` test such as

```
while (cin >> input)
```

tests as `true` only if the stream state is good (all bits cleared). If a test fails, you can use the member functions in Table 17.5 to discriminate among possible causes. For example, you could modify the central part of Listing 17.11 to look like this:

```
while (cin >> input)
{
    sum += input;
}
if (cin.eof())
    cout << "Loop terminated because EOF encountered\n";
```

Setting a stream state bit has a very important consequence: The stream is closed for further input or output until the bit is cleared. For example, the following code won't work:

```
while (cin >> input)
{
    sum += input;
}
cout << "Last value entered = " << input << endl;
cout << "Sum = " << sum << endl;
cout << "Now enter a new number: ";
cin >> input;    // won't work
```

If you want a program to read further input after a stream state bit has been set, you have to reset the stream state to good. This can be done by calling the `clear()` method:

```
while (cin >> input)
{
    sum += input;
}
cout << "Last value entered = " << input << endl;
cout << "Sum = " << sum << endl;
cout << "Now enter a new number: ";
cin.clear();          // reset stream state
while (!isspace(cin.get()))
    continue;         // get rid of bad input
cin >> input;         // will work now
```

Note that it is not enough to reset the stream state. The mismatched input that terminated the input loop is still in the input queue, and the program has to get past it. One way is to keep reading characters until reaching white space. The `isspace()` function (see Chapter 6,

"Branching Statements and Logical Operators") is a `cctype` function that returns `true` if its argument is a white-space character. Or you can discard the rest of the line instead of just the next word:

```
while (cin.get() != '\n')
    continue;  // get rid rest of line
```

This example assumes that the loop terminated because of inappropriate input. Suppose, instead, that the loop terminated because of end-of-file or because of a hardware failure. Then the new code disposing of bad input makes no sense. You can fix matters by using the `fail()` method to test whether the assumption was correct. Because, for historical reasons, `fail()` returns `true` if either `failbit` or `eofbit` is set, the code has to exclude the latter case. The following code shows an example of such exclusion:

```
while (cin >> input)
{
    sum += input;
}
cout << "Last value entered = " << input << endl;
cout << "Sum = " << sum << endl;
if (cin.fail() && !cin.eof() ) // failed because of mismatched input
{

    cin.clear();       // reset stream state
    while (!isspace(cin.get()))
        continue;      // get rid of bad input
}
else // else bail out
{
    cout << "I cannot go on!\n";
    exit(1);
}
cout << "Now enter a new number: ";
cin >> input;  // will work now
```

Other `istream` Class Methods

Chapters 3, 4, "Compound Types," and 5, "Loops and Relational Expressions," discuss the `get()` and `getline()` methods. As you may recall, they provide the following additional input capabilities:

- The `get(char &)` and `get(void)` methods provide single-character input that doesn't skip over white space.

- The `get(char *, int, char)` and `getline(char *, int, char)` functions by default read entire lines rather than single words.

These are termed *unformatted input functions* because they simply read character input as it is, without skipping over white space and without performing data conversions.

Let's look at these two groups of `istream` class member functions.

Single-Character Input

When used with a `char` argument or no argument at all, the `get()` methods fetch the next input character, even if it is a space, tab, or newline character. The `get(char & ch)` version assigns the input character to its argument, and the `get(void)` version uses the input character, converted to an integer type (typically `int`), as its return value.

Let's try `get(char &)` first. Suppose you have the following loop in a program:

```
int ct = 0;
char ch;
cin.get(ch);
while (ch != '\n')
{
    cout << ch;
    ct++;
    cin.get(ch);
}
cout << ct << endl;
```

Next, suppose you type the following optimistic input:

I C++ clearly.<Enter>

Pressing the Enter key sends this input line to the program. The program fragment reads the **I** character, displays it with `cout`, and increments `ct` to **1**. Next, it reads the space character following the **I**, displays it, and increments `ct` to **2**. This continues until the program processes the Enter key as a newline character and terminates the loop. The main point here is that, by using `get(ch)`, the code reads, displays, and counts the spaces as well as the printing characters.

Suppose, instead, that the program tried to use >>:

```
int ct = 0;
char ch;
cin >> ch;
while (ch != '\n')     // FAILS
{
    cout << ch;
    ct++;
    cin >> ch;
}
cout << ct << endl;
```

First, the code would skip the spaces, thus not counting them and compressing the corresponding output to this:

```
IC++clearly.
```

Worse, the loop would never terminate! Because the extraction operator skips newlines, the code would never assign the newline character to `ch`, so the `while` loop test would never terminate the loop.

The `get(char &)` member function returns a reference to the `istream` object used to invoke it. This means you can concatenate other extractions following `get(char &)`:

```
char c1, c2, c3;
cin.get(c1).get(c2) >> c3;
```

First, `cin.get(c1)` assigns the first input character to `c1` and returns the invoking object, which is `cin`. This reduces the code to `cin.get(c2) >> c3`, which assigns the second input character to `c2`. The function call returns `cin`, reducing the code to `cin >> c3`. This, in turn, assigns the next non-white-space character to `c3`. Note that `c1` and `c2` could wind up being assigned white space, but `c3` couldn't.

If `cin.get(char &)` encounters the end of a file, either real or simulated from the keyboard (Ctrl+Z for DOS, Ctrl+D at the beginning of a line for Unix), it does not assign a value to its argument. This is quite right because if the program has reached the end of the file, there is no value to be assigned. Furthermore, the method calls `setstate(failbit)`, which causes `cin` to test as `false`:

```
char ch;
while (cin.get(ch))
{
    // process input
}
```

As long as there's valid input, the return value for `cin.get(ch)` is `cin`, which evaluates as `true`, so the loop continues. Upon reaching end-of-file, the return value evaluates as `false`, terminating the loop.

The `get(void)` member function also reads white space, but it uses its return value to communicate input to a program. So you would use it this way:

```
int ct = 0;
char ch;
ch = cin.get();        // use return value
while (ch != '\n')
{
    cout << ch;
    ct++;
    ch = cin.get();
}
cout << ct << endl;
```

Some older C++ implementation functions don't provide this member function.

The `get(void)` member function returns type `int` (or some larger integer type, depending on the character set and locale). This makes the following invalid:

```
char c1, c2, c3;
cin.get().get() >> c3;  // not valid
```

Here `cin.get()` returns a type `int` value. Because that return value is not a class object, you can't apply the membership operator to it. Thus, you get a syntax error. However, you can use `get()` at the end of an extraction sequence:

```
char c1;
cin.get(c1).get();   // valid
```

The fact that `get(void)` returns type `int` means you can't follow it with an extraction operator. But because `cin.get(c1)` returns `cin`, it makes it a suitable prefix to `get()`. This particular code would read the first input character, assign it to `c1`, and then read the second input character and discard it.

Upon reaching the end-of-file, real or simulated, `cin.get(void)` returns the value `EOF`, which is a symbolic constant provided by the `iostream` header file. This design feature allows the following construction for reading input:

```
int ch;
while ((ch = cin.get()) != EOF)
{
    // process input
}
```

You should use type `int` for `ch` instead of type `char` here because the value `EOF` may not be expressed as a `char` type.

Chapter 5 describes these functions in a bit more detail, and Table 17.6 summarizes the features of the single-character input functions.

TABLE 17.6   `cin.get(ch)` Versus `cin.get()`

Property	`cin.get(ch)`	`ch = cin.get()`
Method for conveying input character	Assign to argument `ch`	Use function return value to assign to `ch`
Function return value for character input	Reference to a class `istream` object	Code for character as type `int` value
Function return value at end-of-file	Converts to `false`	`EOF`

Which Form of Single-Character Input to Use?

Given the choice of `>>`, `get(char &)`, and `get(void)`, which should you use? First, you need to decide whether you want input to skip over white space. If skipping white space is convenient, you should use the extraction operator, `>>`. For example, skipping white space is convenient for offering menu choices:

```
cout  << "a. annoy client       b. bill client\n"
      << "c. calm client        d. deceive client\n"
      << "q.\n";
cout  << "Enter a, b, c, d, or q: ";
char ch;
cin >> ch;
```

```
while (ch != 'q')
{
    switch(ch)
    {
        ...
    }
    cout << "Enter a, b, c, d, or q: ";
    cin >> ch;
}
```

To enter, say, a **b** response, you type **b** and press Enter, generating the two-character response `b\n`. If you used either form of `get()`, you would have to add code to process that `\n` character on each loop cycle, but the extraction operator conveniently skips it. (If you've programmed in C, you've probably encountered a situation in which the newline appears to the program as an invalid response. It's an easy problem to fix, but it is a nuisance.)

If you want a program to examine every character, you should use one of the `get()` methods. For example, a word-counting program could use white space to determine when a word came to an end. Of the two `get()` methods, the `get(char &)` method has the classier interface. The main advantage of the `get(void)` method is that it closely resembles the standard C `getchar()` function, which means you can convert a C program to a C++ program by including `iostream` instead of `stdio.h`, globally replacing `getchar()` with `cin.get()`, and globally replacing C's `putchar(ch)` with `cout.put(ch)`.

String Input: `getline()`, `get()`, and `ignore()`

Next, let's review the string input member functions introduced in Chapter 4. The `getline()` member function and the string-reading version of `get()` both read strings, and both have the same function signatures (here simplified from the more general template declaration):

```
istream & get(char *, int, char);
istream & get(char *, int);
istream & getline(char *, int, char);
istream & getline(char *, int);
```

The first argument, recall, is the address of the location to place the input string. The second argument is one greater than the maximum number of characters to be read. (The additional character leaves space for the terminating null character used in storing the input as a string.) The third argument specifies a character to act as a delimiter to input. The versions with just two arguments use the newline character as a delimiter. Each function reads up to the maximum characters or until it encounters the delimiter character, whichever comes first.

For example, the code

```
char line[50];
cin.get(line, 50);
```

reads character input into the character array `line`. The `cin.get()` function quits reading input into the array after encountering 49 characters or, by default, after encountering a newline character, whichever comes first. The chief difference between `get()` and `getline()` is that `get()` leaves the newline character in the input stream, making it the first character seen by the next input operation, whereas `getline()` extracts and discards the newline character from the input stream.

Chapter 4 illustrated using the two-argument form for these two member functions. Now let's look at the three-argument versions. The third argument is the delimiter character. Encountering the delimiter character causes input to cease, even if the maximum number of characters hasn't been reached. So, by default, both methods quit reading input if they reach the end of a line before reading the allotted number of characters. Just as in the default case, `get()` leaves the delimiter character in the input queue, and `getline()` does not.

Listing 17.13 demonstrates how `getline()` and `get()` work. It also introduces the `ignore()` member function. `ignore()` takes two arguments: a number specifying a maximum number of characters to read and a character that acts as a delimiter character for input. For example, the function call

```
cin.ignore(255, '\n');
```

reads and discards the next 255 characters or up through the first newline character, whichever comes first. The prototype provides defaults of `1` and `EOF` for the two arguments, and the function return type is `istream &`:

```
istream & ignore(int = 1, int = EOF);
```

(The `EOF` default value causes `ignore()` to read up to the specified number of characters or until end-of-file, whichever comes first.)

The function returns the invoking object. This lets you concatenate function calls, as in the following:

```
cin.ignore(255, '\n').ignore(8255, '\n');
```

Here the first `ignore()` method reads and discards one line, and the second call reads and discards the second line. Together the two functions read through two lines.

Now check out Listing 17.13.

LISTING 17.13   get_fun.cpp

```
// get_fun.cpp -- using get() and getline()
#include <iostream>
const int Limit = 255;

int main()
{
    using std::cout;
    using std::cin;
    using std::endl;

    char input[Limit];

    cout << "Enter a string for getline() processing:\n";
    cin.getline(input, Limit, '#');
```

LISTING 17.13   Continued

```
    cout << "Here is your input:\n";
    cout << input << "\nDone with phase 1\n";

    char ch;
    cin.get(ch);
    cout << "The next input character is " << ch << endl;

    if (ch != '\n')
        cin.ignore(Limit, '\n');    // discard rest of line

    cout << "Enter a string for get() processing:\n";
    cin.get(input, Limit, '#');
    cout << "Here is your input:\n";
    cout << input << "\nDone with phase 2\n";

    cin.get(ch);
    cout << "The next input character is " << ch << endl;

    return 0;
}
```

Compatibility Note

Some older C++ implementations of `getline()` have a bug that causes the display of the next output line to be delayed until after you enter the data requested by the undisplayed line.

Here is a sample run of the program in Listing 17.13:

```
Enter a string for getline() processing:
Please pass
me a #3 melon!
Here is your input:
Please pass
me a
Done with phase 1
The next input character is 3
Enter a string for get() processing:
I still
want my #3 melon!
Here is your input:
I still
want my
Done with phase 2
The next input character is #
```

Note that the `getline()` function discards the # termination character in the input, and the `get()` function does not.

Unexpected String Input

Some forms of input for `get(char *, int)` and `getline()` affect the stream state. As with the other input functions, encountering end-of-file sets `eofbit`, and anything that corrupts the stream, such as device failure, sets `badbit`. Two other special cases are no input and input that meets or exceeds the maximum number of characters specified by the function call. Let's look at those cases now.

If either method fails to extract any characters, the method places a null character into the input string and uses `setstate()` to set `failbit`. (Older C++ implementations don't set `failbit` if no characters are read.) When would a method fail to extract any characters? One possibility is if an input method immediately encounters end-of-file. For `get(char *, int)`, another possibility is if you enter an empty line:

```
char temp[80];
while (cin.get(temp,80))  // terminates on empty line
    ...
```

Interestingly, an empty line does not cause `getline()` to set `failbit`. That's because `getline()` still extracts the newline character, even if it doesn't store it. If you want a `getline()` loop to terminate on an empty line, you can write it this way:

```
char temp[80];
while (cin.getline(temp,80) && temp[0] != '\0') // terminates on empty line
```

Now suppose the number of characters in the input queue meets or exceeds the maximum specified by the input method. First, consider `getline()` and the following code:

```
char temp[30];
while (cin.getline(temp,30))
```

The `getline()` method will read consecutive characters from the input queue, placing them in successive elements of the `temp` array, until (in order of testing) end-of-file is encountered, until the next character to be read is the newline character, or until 29 characters have been stored. If end-of-file is encountered, `eofbit` is set. If the next character to be read is a newline character, that character is read and discarded. And if 29 characters were read, `failbit` is set, unless the next character is a newline. Thus, an input line of 30 characters or more will terminate input.

Now consider the `get(char *, int)` method. It tests the number of characters first, end-of-file second, and for the next character being a newline third. It does not set the `failbit` flag if it reads the maximum number of characters. Nonetheless, you can tell if too many input characters caused the method to quit reading. You can use `peek()` (see the next section) to examine the next input character. If it's a newline, then `get()` must have read the entire line. If it's not a newline, then `get()` must have stopped before reaching the end. This technique doesn't necessarily work with `getline()` because `getline()` reads and discards the newline, so looking at the next character doesn't tell you anything. But if you use `get()`, you have the option of doing something if less than an entire line is read. The next section includes an example of this approach. Meanwhile, Table 17.7 summarizes some of the differences between older C++ input methods and the current standard.

TABLE 17.7 Changes in Input Behavior

Method	Older C++	Current C++
getline()	Doesn't set failbit if no characters are read.	Sets failbit if no characters are read (but newline counts as a character read).
	Doesn't set failbit if the maximum number of characters are read.	Sets failbit if the maximum number of characters are read and more are stil left in the line.
get(char *, int)	Doesn't set failbit if no characters are read.	Sets failbit if no characters are read.

Other istream Methods

Other istream methods besides the ones discussed so far include read(), peek(), gcount(), and putback(). The read() function reads a given number of bytes and stores them in the specified location. For example, the statement

```
char gross[144];
cin.read(gross, 144);
```

reads 144 characters from the standard input and places them in the gross array. Unlike getline() and get(), read() does not append a null character to input, so it doesn't convert input to string form. The read() method is not intended for keyboard input. Instead, it is most often used in conjunction with the ostream write() function for file input and output. The method's return type is istream &, so it can be concatenated as follows:

```
char gross[144];
char score[20];
cin.read(gross, 144).read(score, 20);
```

The peek() function returns the next character from input without extracting from the input stream. That is, it lets you peek at the next character. Suppose you want to read input up to the first newline or period, whichever comes first. You can use peek() to peek at the next character in the input stream in order to judge whether to continue:

```
char great_input[80];
char ch;
int i = 0;
while ((ch = cin.peek()) != '.' && ch != '\n')
    cin.get(great_input[i++]);
great_input [i] = '\0';
```

The call to cin.peek() peeks at the next input character and assigns its value to ch. Then the while loop test condition checks that ch is neither a period nor a newline. If this is the case, the loop reads the character into the array and updates the array index. When the loop terminates, the period or newline character remains in the input stream, positioned to be the first character read by the next input operation. Then the code appends a null character to the array, making it a string.

The gcount() method returns the number of characters read by the last unformatted extraction method. That means characters read by a get(), getline(), ignore(), or read() method but not by the extraction operator (>>), which formats input to fit particular data types. For example, suppose you've just used cin.get(myarray, 80) to read a line into the myarray array and you want to know how many characters were read. You could use the strlen() function to count the characters in the array, but it would be quicker to use cin.gcount() to report how many characters were just read from the input stream.

The putback() function inserts a character back in the input string. The inserted character then becomes the first character read by the next input statement. The putback() method takes one char argument, which is the character to be inserted, and it returns type istream &, which allows the call to be concatenated with other istream methods. Using peek() is like using get() to read a character and then using putback() to place the character back in the input stream. However, putback() gives you the option of putting back a character that is different from the one just read.

Listing 17.14 uses two approaches to read and echo input up to, but not including, a # character. The first approach reads through the # character and then uses putback() to insert the character back into the input. The second approach uses peek() to look ahead before reading input.

LISTING 17.14 peeker.cpp

```cpp
// peeker.cpp -- some istream methods
#include <iostream>

int main()
{
    using std::cout;
    using std::cin;
    using std::endl;

//  read and echo input up to a # character
    char ch;

    while(cin.get(ch))            // terminates on EOF
    {
        if (ch != '#')
            cout << ch;
        else
        {
            cin.putback(ch);      // reinsert character
            break;
        }
    }
```

LISTING 17.14   Continued

```
        if (!cin.eof())
        {
            cin.get(ch);
            cout << endl << ch << " is next input character.\n";
        }
        else
        {
            cout << "End of file reached.\n";
            std::exit(0);
        }

        while(cin.peek() != '#')     // look ahead
        {
            cin.get(ch);
            cout << ch;
        }
        if (!cin.eof())
        {
            cin.get(ch);
            cout << endl << ch << " is next input character.\n";
        }
        else
            cout << "End of file reached.\n";

        return 0;
    }
```

Here is a sample run of the program in Listing 17.14:

I used a #3 pencil when I should have used a #2.
```
I used a
# is next input character.
3 pencil when I should have used a
# is next input character.
```

Program Notes

Let's look more closely at some of the code in Listing 17.14. The first approach uses a `while` loop to read input:

```
while(cin.get(ch))              // terminates on EOF
{
    if (ch != '#')
        cout << ch;
    else
    {
        cin.putback(ch);  // reinsert character
        break;
    }
}
```

The expression `cin.get(ch)` returns `false` on reaching the end-of-file condition, so simulating end-of-file from the keyboard terminates the loop. If the # character shows up first, the program puts the character back in the input stream and uses a break statement to terminate the loop.

The second approach is simpler in appearance:

```
while(cin.peek() != '#')       // look ahead
{
    cin.get(ch);
    cout << ch;
}
```

The program peeks at the next character. If it is not the # character, the program reads the next character, echoes it, and peeks at the next character. This continues until the terminating character shows up.

Now let's look, as promised, at an example that uses `peek()` to determine whether an entire line has been read (see Listing 17.15). If only part of a line fits in the input array, the program discards the rest of the line.

LISTING 17.15 `truncate.cpp`

```
// truncate.cpp -- using get() to truncate input line, if necessary
#include <iostream>
const int SLEN = 10;
inline void eatline() { while (std::cin.get() != '\n') continue; }
int main()
{
    using std::cin;
    using std::cout;
    using std::endl;

    char name[SLEN];
    char title[SLEN];
    cout << "Enter your name: ";
    cin.get(name,SLEN);
    if (cin.peek() != '\n')
        cout << "Sorry, we only have enough room for "
                << name << endl;
    eatline();
    cout << "Dear " << name << ", enter your title: \n";
    cin.get(title,SLEN);
    if (cin.peek() != '\n')
        cout << "We were forced to truncate your title.\n";
    eatline();
    cout << " Name: " << name
        << "\nTitle: " << title << endl;

    return 0;
}
```

Here is a sample run of the program in Listing 17.15:

```
Enter your name: Ella Fishsniffer
Sorry, we only have enough room for Ella Fish
Dear Ella Fish, enter your title:
Executive Adjunct
We were forced to truncate your title.
 Name: Ella Fish
Title: Executive
```

Note that the following code makes sense whether or not the first input statement reads the entire line:

```
while (cin.get() != '\n') continue;
```

If `get()` reads the whole line, it still leaves the newline in place, and this code reads and discards the newline character. If `get()` reads just part of the line, this code reads and discards the rest of the line. If you didn't dispose of the rest of line, the next input statement would begin reading at the beginning of the remaining input on the first input line. With this example, that would result in the program reading the string `arpride` into the `title` array.

File Input and Output

Most computer programs work with files. Word processors create document files. Database programs create and search files of information. Compilers read source code files and generate executable files. A file itself is a bunch of bytes stored on some device, perhaps magnetic tape, perhaps an optical disk, a floppy disk, or a hard disk. Typically, the operating system manages files, keeping track of their locations, their sizes, when they were created, and so on. Unless you're programming on the operating system level, you normally don't have to worry about those things. What you do need is a way to connect a program to a file, a way to have a program read the contents of a file, and a way to have a program create and write to files. Redirection (as discussed earlier in this chapter) can provide some file support, but it is more limited than explicit file I/O from within a program. Also, redirection comes from the operating system, not from C++, so it isn't available on all systems. This book has already touched on file I/O, and this chapter explores the topic more thoroughly.

The C++ I/O class package handles file input and output much as it handles standard input and output. To write to a file, you create an `ofstream` object and use the `ostream` methods, such as the `<<` insertion operator or `write()`. To read a file, you create an `ifstream` object and use the `istream` methods, such as the `>>` extraction operator or `get()`. Files require more management than the standard input and output, however. For example, you have to associate a newly opened file with a stream. You can open a file in read-only mode, write-only mode, or read-and-write mode. If you write to a file, you might want to create a new file, replace an old file, or add to an old file. Or you might want to move back and forth through a file. To help handle these tasks, C++ defines several new classes in the `fstream` (formerly `fstream.h`) header file, including the `ifstream` class for file input and the `ofstream` class for file output. C++ also defines the `fstream` class for simultaneous file I/O. These classes are derived from the classes in the `iostream` header file, so objects of these new classes are able to use the methods you've already learned.

Simple File I/O

Suppose you want a program to write to a file. You must do the following:

1. Create an `ofstream` object to manage the output stream.

2. Associate that object with a particular file.

3. Use the object the same way you would use `cout`; the only difference is that output goes to the file instead of to the screen.

To accomplish this, you begin by including the `fstream` header file. Including this file automatically includes the `iostream` file for most, but not all, implementations, so you may not have to include `iostream` explicitly. Then you declare an `ofstream` object:

```
ofstream fout;      // create an ofstream object named fout
```

The object's name can be any valid C++ name, such as `fout`, `outFile`, `cgate`, or `didi`.

Next, you must associate this object with a particular file. You can do so by using the `open()` method. Suppose, for example, that you want to open the `jar` file for output. You would do the following:

```
fout.open("jar.txt");  // associate fout with jar.txt
```

You can combine these two steps (creating the object and associating a file) into a single statement by using a different constructor:

```
ofstream fout("jar.txt");  // create fout object, associate it with jar.txt
```

When you've gotten this far, you use `fout` (or whatever name you choose) in the same manner as `cout`. For example, if you want to put the words `Dull Data` into the file, you can do the following:

```
fout << "Dull Data";
```

Indeed, because `ostream` is a base class for the `ofstream` class, you can use all the `ostream` methods, including the various insertion operator definitions and the formatting methods and manipulators. The `ofstream` class uses buffered output, so the program allocates space for an output buffer when it creates an `ofstream` object such as `fout`. If you create two `ofstream` objects, the program creates two buffers, one for each object. An `ofstream` object such as `fout` collects output byte-by-byte from the program; then, when the buffer is filled, it transfers the buffer contents en masse to the destination file. Because disk drives are designed to transfer data in larger chunks, not byte-by-byte, the buffered approach greatly speeds up the transfer rate of data from a program to a file.

Opening a file for output this way creates a new file if there is no file of that name. If a file by that name exists prior to opening it for output, the act of opening it truncates it so that output starts with a clean file. Later in this chapter you'll see how to open an existing file and retain its contents.

> **Caution**
>
> Opening a file for output in the default mode automatically truncates the file to zero size, in effect disposing of the prior contents.

The requirements for reading a file are much like those for writing to a file:

1. Create an `ifstream` object to manage the input stream.

2. Associate that object with a particular file.

3. Use the object the same way you would use `cin`.

The steps for reading a file are similar to those for writing to a file. First, of course, you include the `fstream` header file. Then you declare an `ifstream` object and associate it with the filename. You can do so in two statements or one:

```
// two statements
ifstream fin;              // create ifstream object called fin
fin.open("jellyjar.dat");  // open jellyjar.dat for reading
// one statement
ifstream fis("jamjar.dat"); // create fis and associate with jamjar.dat
```

You can then use `fin` or `fis` much as you would use `cin`. For example, you can use the following:

```
char ch;
fin >> ch;                 // read a character from the jellyjar.dat file
char buf[80];
fin >> buf;                // read a word from the file
fin.getline(buf, 80);      // read a line from the file
string line;
getline(fin, line);        // read from a file to a string object
```

Input, like output, is buffered, so creating an `ifstream` object such as `fin` creates an input buffer, which the `fin` object manages. As with output, buffering moves data much faster than byte-by-byte transfer.

The connections with a file are closed automatically when the input and output stream objects expire—for example, when the program terminates. Also, you can close a connection with a file explicitly by using the `close()` method:

```
fout.close();    // close output connection to file
fin.close();     // close input connection to file
```

Closing such a connection does not eliminate the stream; it just disconnects it from the file. However, the stream management apparatus remains in place. For example, the `fin` object still exists, along with the input buffer it manages. As you'll see later, you can reconnect the stream to the same file or to another file.

Let's look at a short example. The program in Listing 17.16 asks for a filename. It creates a file that has that name, writes some information to it, and closes the file. Closing the file flushes the buffer, guaranteeing that the file is updated. Then the program opens the same file for reading and displays its contents. Note that the program uses `fin` and `fout` in the same manner as you'd use `cin` and `cout`. Also, the program reads the filename into a `string` object and then uses the `c_str()` method to provide C-style string arguments for the `ofstream` and `ifstream` constructors.

LISTING 17.16   `fileio.cpp`

```
// fileio.cpp -- saving to a file
#include <iostream> // not needed for many systems
#include <fstream>
#include <string>

int main()
{
    using namespace std;
    string filename;

    cout << "Enter name for new file: ";
    cin >> filename;

// create output stream object for new file and call it fout
    ofstream fout(filename.c_str());

    fout << "For your eyes only!\n";        // write to file
    cout << "Enter your secret number: ";   // write to screen
    float secret;
    cin >> secret;
    fout << "Your secret number is " << secret << endl;
    fout.close();            // close file

// create input stream object for new file and call it fin
    ifstream fin(filename.c_str());
    cout << "Here are the contents of " << filename << ":\n";
    char ch;
    while (fin.get(ch))      // read character from file and
        cout << ch;          // write it to screen
    cout << "Done\n";
    fin.close();

    return 0;
}
```

Here is a sample run of the program in Listing 17.16:

```
Enter name for new file: pythag
Enter your secret number: 3.14159
Here are the contents of pythag:
For your eyes only!
Your secret number is 3.14159
Done
```

If you check the directory that contains the program, you should find a file named `pythag`, and any text editor should show the same contents that the program output displays. (So much for secrecy.)

Stream Checking and `is_open()`

The C++ file stream classes inherit a stream-state member from the `ios_base` class. This member, as discussed earlier, stores information that reflects the stream status: All is well, end-of-file has been reached, I/O operation failed, and so on. If all is well, the stream state is zero (no news is good news). The various other states are recorded by setting particular bits to `1`. The file stream classes also inherit the `ios_base` methods that report about the stream state and that are summarized in Table 17.5. You can check the stream state to find whether the most recent stream operation succeeded or failed. For file streams, this includes checking the success of an attempt to open a file. For example, attempting to open a non-existent file for input sets `failbit`. So you could check this way:

```
fin.open(argv[file]);
if (fin.fail())  // open attempt failed
{
    ...
}
```

Or, because an `ifstream` object, like an `istream` object, is converted to a `bool` type where a `bool` type is expected, you could use this:

```
fin.open(argv[file]);
if (!fin)  // open attempt failed
{
    ...
}
```

However, newer C++ implementations have a better way to check whether a file has been opened—the `is_open()` method:

```
if (!fin.is_open())  // open attempt failed
{
    ...
}
```

The reason this is better is that it tests for some subtle problems that the other forms miss, as discussed in the following Caution.

Caution

In the past, the usual tests for successful opening of a file were the following:

```
if(fin.fail()) ...   // failed to open
if(!fin.good()) ...  // failed to open
if (!fin) ...        // failed to open
```

The `fin` object, when used in a test condition, is converted to `false` if `fin.good()` is false and to `true` otherwise, so the two forms are equivalent. However, these tests fail to detect one circumstance, which is attempting to open a file by using an inappropriate file mode (see the "File Modes" section, later in this chapter). The `is_open()` method catches this form of error, along with those caught by the `good()` method. However, older C++ implementations do not have `is_open()`.

Opening Multiple Files

You might require that a program open more than one file. The strategy for opening multiple files depends on how they will be used. If you need two files open simultaneously, you must create a separate stream for each file. For example, a program that collates two sorted files into a third file would create two `ifstream` objects for the two input files and an `ofstream` object for the output file. The number of files you can open simultaneously depends on the operating system, but it typically is on the order of 20.

However, you may plan to process a group of files sequentially. For example, you might want to count how many times a name appears in a set of 10 files. In this case, you can open a single stream and associate it with each file in turn. This conserves computer resources more effectively than opening a separate stream for each file. To use this approach, you declare an `ifstream` object without initializing it and then use the `open()` method to associate the stream with a file. For example, this is how you could handle reading two files in succession:

```
ifstream fin;            // create stream using default constructor
fin.open("fat.dat");     // associate stream with fat.dat file
...                      // do stuff
fin.close();             // terminate association with fat.dat
fin.clear();             // reset fin (may not be needed)
fin.open("rat.dat");     // associate stream with rat.dat file
...
fin.close();
```

We'll look at an example shortly, but first, let's examine a technique for feeding a list of files to a program in a manner that allows the program to use a loop to process them.

Command-Line Processing

File-processing programs often use command-line arguments to identify files. *Command-line arguments* are arguments that appear on the command line when you type a command. For example, to count the number of words in some files on a Unix or Linux system, you would type this command at the command-line prompt:

```
wc report1 report2 report3
```

Here `wc` is the program name, and `report1`, `report2`, and `report3` are filenames passed to the program as command-line arguments.

C++ has a mechanism for letting a program running in a command-line environment access the command-line arguments. You can use the following alternative function heading for `main()`:

```
int main(int argc, char *argv[])
```

The `argc` argument represents the number of arguments on the command line. The count includes the command name itself. The `argv` variable is a pointer to a pointer to a `char`. This sounds a bit abstract, but you can treat `argv` as if it were an array of pointers to the command-line arguments, with `argv[0]` being a pointer to the first character of a string holding the command name, `argv[1]` being a pointer to the first character of a string holding the first command-line argument, and so on. That is, `argv[0]` is the first string from the command line, and so on. For example, suppose you have the following command line:

```
wc report1 report2 report3
```

In this case, `argc` would be `4`, `argv[0]` would be `wc`, `argv[1]` would be `report1`, and so on. The following loop would print each command-line argument on a separate line:

```
for (int i = 1; i < argc; i++)
    cout << argv[i] << endl;
```

Starting with `i = 1` just prints the command-line arguments; starting with `i = 0` would print the command name as well.

Command-line arguments, of course, go hand-in-hand with command-line operating systems such as DOS, Unix, and Linux. Other setups may still allow you to use command-line arguments:

- Many DOS and Windows IDEs (Integrated Development Environments) have an option for providing command-line arguments. Typically, you have to navigate through a series of menu choices that lead to a box into which you can type the command-line arguments. The exact set of steps varies from vendor to vendor and from upgrade to upgrade, so check your documentation.

- DOS IDEs and many Windows IDEs can produce executable files that run under DOS or in a DOS window in the usual DOS command-line mode.

- Under Metrowerks CodeWarrior for the Macintosh, you can simulate command-line arguments by placing the following code in a program:

    ```
    ...
    #include <console.h> // for emulating command-line arguments
    int main(int argc, char * argv[])
    {
        argc = ccommand(&argv); // yes, ccommand, not command
        ...
    ```

    When you run the program, the `ccommand()` function places a dialog box onscreen, with a box in which you can type the command-line arguments. It also lets you simulate redirection.

Listing 17.17 combines the command-line technique with file stream techniques to count characters in files listed on the command line.

LISTING 17.17 `count.cpp`

```cpp
// count.cpp -- counting characters in a list of files
#include <iostream>
#include <fstream>
#include <cstdlib>           // or stdlib.h
// #include <console.h>      // for Macintosh
int main(int argc, char * argv[])
{
    using namespace std;
    // argc = ccommand(&argv);      // for Macintosh
    if (argc == 1)              // quit if no arguments
    {
        cerr << "Usage: " << argv[0] << " filename[s]\n";
        exit(EXIT_FAILURE);
    }

    ifstream fin;              // open stream
    long count;
    long total = 0;
    char ch;

    for (int file = 1; file < argc; file++)
    {
        fin.open(argv[file]);  // connect stream to argv[file]
        if (!fin.is_open())
        {
            cerr << "Could not open " << argv[file] << endl;
            fin.clear();
            continue;
        }
        count = 0;
        while (fin.get(ch))
            count++;
        cout << count << " characters in " << argv[file] << endl;
        total += count;
        fin.clear();           // needed for some implementations
        fin.close();           // disconnect file
    }
    cout << total << " characters in all files\n";

    return 0;
}
```

Compatibility Note

Some C++ implementations require using `fin.clear()` at the end of the program and others do not. It depends on whether associating a new file with the `ifstream` object automatically resets the stream state. In does no harm to use `fin.clear()` even if it isn't needed.

On a DOS system, for example, you could compile Listing 17.17 to an executable file called `count.exe`. Then sample runs could look like this:

```
C>count
Usage: c:\count.exe filename[s]
C>count paris rome
3580 characters in paris
4886 characters in rome
8466 characters in all files
C>
```

Note that the program uses `cerr` for the error message. A minor point is that the message uses `argv[0]` instead of `count.exe`:

```
cerr << "Usage: " << argv[0] << " filename[s]\n";
```

This way, if you change the name of the executable file, the program will automatically use the new name.

The program uses the `is_open()` method to verify that it was able to open the requested file. Let's examine that matter further.

File Modes

The file mode describes how a file is to be used: read it, write to it, append it, and so on. When you associate a stream with a file, either by initializing a file stream object with a filename or by using the `open()` method, you can provide a second argument that specifies the file mode:

```
ifstream fin("banjo", mode1);   // constructor with mode argument
ofstream fout();
fout.open("harp", mode2);        // open() with mode arguments
```

The `ios_base` class defines an `openmode` type to represent the mode; like the `fmtflags` and `iostate` types, it is a `bitmask` type. (In the old days, it was type `int`.) You can choose from several constants defined in the `ios_base` class to specify the mode. Table 17.8 lists the constants and their meanings. C++ file I/O has undergone several changes to make it compatible with ANSI C file I/O.

TABLE 17.8 File Mode Constants

Constant	Meaning
ios_base::in	Open file for reading.
ios_base::out	Open file for writing.
ios_base::ate	Seek to end-of-file upon opening file.
ios_base::app	Append to end-of-file.
ios_base::trunc	Truncate file if it exists.
ios_base::binary	Binary file.

If the `ifstream` and `ofstream` constructors and the `open()` methods each take two arguments, how have we gotten by using just one in the previous examples? As you have probably guessed, the prototypes for these class member functions provide default values for the second argument (the file mode argument). For example, the `ifstream open()` method and constructor use `ios_base::in` (open for reading) as the default value for the mode argument, and the `ofstream open()` method and constructor use `ios_base::out | ios_base::trunc` (open for writing and truncate the file) as the default. The bitwise OR operator (`|`) is used to combine two bit values into a single value that can be used to set both bits. The `fstream` class doesn't provide a mode default, so you have to provide a mode explicitly when creating an object of that class.

Note that the `ios_base::trunc` flag means an existing file is truncated when opened to receive program output; that is, its previous contents are discarded. Although this behavior commendably minimizes the danger of running out of disk space, you can probably imagine situations in which you don't want to wipe out a file when you open it. Of course, C++ provides other choices. If, for example, you want to preserve the file contents and add (append) new material to the end of the file, you can use the `ios_base::app` mode:

```
ofstream fout("bagels", ios_base::out | ios_base::app);
```

Again, the code uses the `|` operator to combine modes. So `ios_base::out | ios_base::app` means to invoke both the `out` mode and the `app` mode (see Figure 17.6).

FIGURE 17.6

Some file-opening modes.

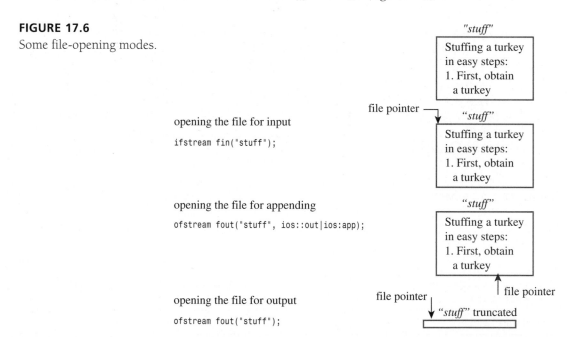

You can expect to find some differences among older C++ implementations. For example, some allow you to omit the `ios_base::out` in the previous example, and some don't. If you aren't using the default mode, the safest approach is to provide all the mode elements explicitly. Some compilers don't support all the choices in Table 17.7, and some may offer choices beyond those in the table. One consequence of these differences is that you may have to make some alterations in the following examples to use them on your system. The good news is that the development of the C++ Standard is providing greater uniformity.

Standard C++ defines parts of file I/O in terms of ANSI C standard I/O equivalents. A C++ statement like

```
ifstream fin(filename, c++mode);
```

is implemented as if it uses the C `fopen()` function:

```
fopen(filename, cmode);
```

Here *c++mode* is a type `openmode` value, such as `ios_base::in`, and *cmode* is the corresponding C-mode string, such as `"r"`. Table 17.9 shows the correspondence between C++ modes and C modes. Note that `ios_base::out` by itself causes truncation but that it doesn't cause truncation when combined with `ios_base::in`. Unlisted combinations, such as `ios_base::in` [vn] `ios_base::trunc`, prevent the file from being opened. The `is_open()` method detects this failure.

TABLE 17.9   C++ and C File-Opening Modes

C++ mode	C mode	Meaning
ios_base::in	"r"	Open for reading.
ios_base::out	"w"	(Same as ios_base::out | ios_base::trunc.)
ios_base::out | ios_base::trunc	"w"	Open for writing, truncating file if it already exists.
ios_base::out | ios_base::app	"a"	Open for writing, append only.
ios_base::in | ios_base::out	"r+"	Open for reading and writing, with writing permitted anywhere in the file.
ios_base::in | ios_base ::out | ios_base::trunc	"w+"	Open for reading and writing, first truncating file if it already exists.
c++mode | ios_base::binary	"cmodeb"	Open in *c++mode* or corresponding *cmode* and in binary mode; for example, ios_base::in | ios_base::binary becomes "rb".
c++mode | ios_base::ate	"cmode"	Open in indicated mode and go to end of file. C uses a separate function call instead of a mode code. For example, ios_base::in | ios_base::ate translates to the "r" mode and the C function call fseek(file, 0, SEEK_END).

Note that both `ios_base::ate` and `ios_base::app` place you (or, more precisely, a file pointer) at the end of the file just opened. The difference between the two is that the `ios_base::app` mode allows you to add data to the end of the file only, while the `ios_base::ate` mode merely positions the pointer at the end of the file.

Clearly, there are many possible combinations of modes. We'll look at a few representative ones.

Appending to a File

Let's look at a program that appends data to the end of a file. The program maintains a file that contains a guest list. When the program begins, it displays the current contents of the file, if it exists. It can use the `is_open()` method after attempting to open the file to check whether the file exists. Next, the program opens the file for output, using the `ios_base::app` mode. Then it solicits input from the keyboard to add to the file. Finally, the program displays the revised file contents. Listing 17.18 illustrates how to accomplish these goals. Note how the program uses the `is_open()` method to test whether the file has been opened successfully.

Compatibility Note

File I/O was perhaps the least standardized aspect of C++ in its earlier days, and many older compilers don't quite conform to the current standard. Some, for example, used modes such as `nocreate` that are not part of the current standard. Also, only some compilers require the `fin.clear()` call before opening the same file a second time for reading.

LISTING 17.18   `append.cpp`

```cpp
// append.cpp -- appending information to a file
#include <iostream>
#include <fstream>
#include <string>
#include <cstdlib>        // (or stdlib.h) for exit()

const char * file = "guests.txt";
int main()
{
    using namespace std;
    char ch;

// show initial contents
    ifstream fin;
    fin.open(file);

    if (fin.is_open())
    {
        cout << "Here are the current contents of the "
            << file << " file:\n";
        while (fin.get(ch))
            cout << ch;
```

LISTING 17.18 Continued

```cpp
        fin.close();
    }

// add new names
    ofstream fout(file, ios::out | ios::app);
    if (!fout.is_open())
    {
        cerr << "Can't open " << file << " file for output.\n";
        exit(EXIT_FAILURE);
    }

    cout << "Enter guest names (enter a blank line to quit):\n";
    string name;
    while (getline(cin,name) && name.size() > 0)
    {
        fout << name << endl;
    }
    fout.close();

// show revised file
    fin.clear();      // not necessary for some compilers
    fin.open(file);
    if (fin.is_open())
    {
        cout << "Here are the new contents of the "
            << file << " file:\n";
        while (fin.get(ch))
            cout << ch;
        fin.close();
    }
    cout << "Done.\n";
    return 0;
}
```

Here's a sample first run of the program in Listing 17.18:

```
Enter guest names (enter a blank line to quit):
Sylvester Ballone
Phil Kates
Bill Ghan

Here are the new contents of the guests.txt file:
Sylvester Ballone
Phil Kates
Bill Ghan
Done.
```

At this point the `guests.txt` file hasn't been created, so the program doesn't preview the file.

Next time the program is run, however, the `guests.txt` file does exist, so the program does preview the file. Also, note that the new data are appended to the old file contents rather than replacing them:

```
Here are the current contents of the guests.txt file:
Sylvester Ballone
Phil Kates
Bill Ghan
Enter guest names (enter a blank line to quit):
Greta Greppo
LaDonna Mobile
Fannie Mae

Here are the new contents of the guests.txt file:
Sylvester Ballone
Phil Kates
Bill Ghan
Greta Greppo
LaDonna Mobile
Fannie Mae
Done.
```

You should be able to read the contents of `guest.txt` with any text editor, including the editor you use to write your source code.

Binary Files

When you store data in a file, you can store the data in text form or in binary format. Text form means you store everything as text, even numbers. For example, storing the value -2.324216e+07 in text form means storing the 13 characters used to write this number. That requires converting the computer's internal representation of a floating-point number to character form, and that's exactly what the `<<` insertion operator does. Binary format, on the other hand, means storing the computer's internal representation of a value. That is, instead of storing characters, the computer stores the (typically) 64-bit `double` representation of the value. For a character, the binary representation is the same as the text representation—the binary representation of the character's ASCII code (or equivalent). For numbers, however, the binary representation is much different from the text representation (see Figure 17.7).

FIGURE 17.7
Binary and text representations of a floating-point number.

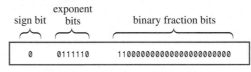

Binary representation of 0.375

sign bit   exponent bits   binary fraction bits

| 0 | 0111110 | 11000000000000000000000 |

Text representation of 0.375

00110000	00101110	00110011	00110111	00110111
code for the 0 character	code for the . character	code for the 3 character	code for the 7 character	code for the 5 character

Each format has advantages. The text format is easy to read. With it, you can use an ordinary editor or word processor to read and edit a text file. You can easily transfer a text file from one computer system to another. The binary format is more accurate for numbers because it stores the exact internal representation of a value. There are no conversion errors or round-off errors. Saving data in binary format can be faster because there is no conversion and because you may be able to save data in larger chunks. And the binary format usually takes less space, depending on the nature of the data. Transferring to another system can be a problem, however, if the new system uses a different internal representation for values. Even different compilers on the same system may use different internal representations for structure layouts. In these cases, you (or someone) may have to write a program to translate one data format to another.

Let's look at a more concrete example. Consider the following structure definition and declaration:

```
const int LIM = 20;
struct planet
{
    char name[LIM];        // name of planet
    double population;     // its population
    double g;              // its acceleration of gravity
};
planet pl;
```

To save the contents of the structure `pl` in text form, you can use this:

```
ofstream fout("planets.dat", ios_base:: out | ios_base::app);
fout << pl.name << " " << pl.population << " " << pl.g << "\n";
```

Note that you have to provide each structure member explicitly by using the membership operator, and you have to separate adjacent data for legibility. If the structure contained, say, 30 members, this could get tedious.

To save the same information in binary format, you can use this:

```
ofstream fout("planets.dat",
              ios_base:: out | ios_base::app | ios_base::binary);
fout.write( (char *) &pl, sizeof pl);
```

This code saves the entire structure as a single unit, using the computer's internal representation of data. You won't be able to read the file as text, but the information will be stored more compactly and precisely than as text. And it is certainly easier to type the code. This approach makes two changes:

- It uses a binary file mode.
- It uses the `write()` member function.

Let's examine these changes more closely.

Some systems, such as DOS, support two file formats: text and binary. If you want to save data in binary form, you should use the binary file format. In C++ you do so by using the `ios_base::binary` constant in the file mode. If you want to know why you should do this on a DOS system, check the discussion in the following sidebar, "Binary Files and Text Files."

Binary Files and Text Files

Using a binary file mode causes a program to transfer data from memory to a file, or vice versa, without any hidden translation taking place. Such is not necessarily the case for the default text mode. For example, consider DOS text files. They represent a newline with a two-character combination: carriage return, linefeed. Macintosh text files represent a newline with a carriage return. Unix and Linux files represent a newline with a linefeed. C++, which grew up on Unix, also represents a newline with a linefeed. For portability, a DOS C++ program automatically translates the C++ newline to a carriage return and linefeed when writing to a text mode file; and a Macintosh C++ program translates the newline to a carriage return when writing to a file. When reading a text file, these programs convert the local newline back to the C++ form. The text format can cause problems with binary data because a byte in the middle of a `double` value could have the same bit pattern as the ASCII code for the newline character. Also, there are differences in how end-of-file is detected. So you should use the binary file mode when saving data in binary format. (Unix systems have just one file mode, so on them the binary mode is the same as the text mode.)

To save data in binary form instead of text form, you can use the `write()` member function. This method, recall, copies a specified number of bytes from memory to a file. You used it earlier in this chapter to copy text, but it will copy any type of data byte-by-byte with no conversion. For example, if you pass to it the address of a `long` variable and tell it to copy 4 bytes, it will copy the 4 bytes constituting the `long` value verbatim to a file and not convert it to text. The only awkwardness is that you have to type cast the address to type pointer-to-`char`. You can use the same approach to copy an entire `planet` structure. To get the number of bytes, you use the `sizeof` operator:

```
fout.write( (char *) &pl, sizeof pl);
```

This statement goes to the address of the `pl` structure and copies the 36 bytes (the value of the `sizeof pl` expression) beginning at this address to the file connected to `fout`.

To recover the information from a file, you use the corresponding `read()` method with an `ifstream` object:

```
ifstream fin("planets.dat", ios_base::in | ios_base::binary);
fin.read((char *) &pl, sizeof pl);
```

This copies `sizeof pl` bytes from the file to the `pl` structure. This same approach can be used with classes that don't use virtual functions. In that case, just the data members are saved, not the methods. If the class does have virtual methods, then a hidden pointer to a table of pointers to virtual functions is also copied. Because the next time you run the program it might locate the virtual function table at a different location, copying old pointer information into objects from a file can create havoc. (Also, see the Note in Programming Exercise 6.)

Tip

The `read()` and `write()` member functions complement each other. You use `read()` to recover data that has been written to a file with `write()`.

Listing 17.19 uses these methods to create and read a binary file. In form, the program is similar to Listing 17.18, but it uses `write()` and `read()` instead of the insertion operator and the `get()` method. It also uses manipulators to format the screen output.

Compatibility Note

Although the binary file concept is part of ANSI C, some C and C++ implementations do not provide support for the binary file mode. The reason for this oversight is that some systems have only one file type in the first place, so you can use binary operations such as `read()` and `write()` with the standard file format. Therefore, if your implementation rejects `ios_base::binary` as a valid constant, you can just omit it from your program. If your implementation doesn't support the `fixed` and `right` manipulators, you can use `cout.setf(ios_base::fixed, ios_base::floatfield)` and `cout.setf(ios_base::right, ios_base::adjustfield)`. Also, you may have to substitute `ios` for `ios_base`. Other compilers, particularly older ones, may have other idiosyncrasies.

LISTING 17.19   `binary.cpp`

```cpp
// binary.cpp -- binary file I/O
#include <iostream> // not required by most systems
#include <fstream>
#include <iomanip>
#include <cstdlib>  // (or stdlib.h) for exit()

inline void eatline() { while (std::cin.get() != '\n') continue; }
struct planet
{
    char name[20];      // name of planet
    double population;  // its population
    double g;           // its acceleration of gravity
};

const char * file = "planets.dat";

int main()
{
    using namespace std;
    planet pl;
    cout << fixed << right;

// show initial contents
    ifstream fin;
    fin.open(file, ios_base::in |ios_base::binary);  // binary file
    //NOTE: some systems don't accept the ios_base::binary mode
    if (fin.is_open())
    {
    cout << "Here are the current contents of the "
        << file << " file:\n";
    while (fin.read((char *) &pl, sizeof pl))
    {
```

LISTING 17.19 *Continued*

```
        cout << setw(20) << pl.name << ": "
             << setprecision(0) << setw(12) << pl.population
             << setprecision(2) << setw(6) << pl.g << endl;
    }
    fin.close();
    }

// add new data
    ofstream fout(file,
            ios_base::out | ios_base::app | ios_base::binary);
    //NOTE: some systems don't accept the ios::binary mode
    if (!fout.is_open())
    {
        cerr << "Can't open " << file << " file for output:\n";
        exit(EXIT_FAILURE);
    }

    cout << "Enter planet name (enter a blank line to quit):\n";
    cin.get(pl.name, 20);
    while (pl.name[0] != '\0')
    {
        eatline();
        cout << "Enter planetary population: ";
        cin >> pl.population;
        cout << "Enter planet's acceleration of gravity: ";
        cin >> pl.g;
        eatline();
        fout.write((char *) &pl, sizeof pl);
        cout << "Enter planet name (enter a blank line "
                "to quit):\n";
        cin.get(pl.name, 20);
    }
    fout.close();

// show revised file
    fin.clear();    // not required for some implementations, but won't hurt
    fin.open(file, ios_base::in | ios_base::binary);
    if (fin.is_open())
    {
        cout << "Here are the new contents of the "
             << file << " file:\n";
        while (fin.read((char *) &pl, sizeof pl))
        {
            cout << setw(20) << pl.name << ": "
                 << setprecision(0) << setw(12) << pl.population
                 << setprecision(2) << setw(6) << pl.g << endl;
        }
        fin.close();
    }
    cout << "Done.\n";
    return 0;
}
```

Here is a sample initial run of the program in Listing 17.19:

```
Enter planet name (enter a blank line to quit):
Earth
Enter planetary population: 5962000000
Enter planet's acceleration of gravity: 9.81
Enter planet name (enter a blank line to quit):

Here are the new contents of the planets.dat file:
          Earth:   5932000000  9.81
Done.
```

And here is a sample follow-up run:

```
Here are the current contents of the planets.dat file:
          Earth:   5932000000  9.81
Enter planet name (enter a blank line to quit):
Bill's Planet
Enter planetary population: 23020020
Enter planet's acceleration of gravity: 8.82
Enter planet name (enter a blank line to quit):

Here are the new contents of the planets.dat file:
          Earth:   5932000000    9.81
    Bill's Planet:   23020020    8.82
Done.
```

You've already seen the major features of the program, but let's reexamine an old point. The program uses this code (in the form of the inline `eatline()` function) after reading the planet's g value:

```
while (std::cin.get() != '\n') continue;
```

This reads and discards input up through the newline character. Consider the next input statement in the loop:

```
cin.get(pl.name, 20);
```

If the newline were left in place, this statement would read the newline as an empty line, terminating the loop.

You might wonder if this program could use a `string` object instead of a character array for the `name` member of the `planet` structure. The answer is no—at least not without major changes in design. The problem is that a `string` object doesn't actually contain the string within itself; instead, it contains a pointer to the memory location where the string is stored. So if you copy the structure to a file, you don't copy the string data, you just copy the address of where the string was stored. When you run the program again, that address is meaningless.

Random Access

For our last example, let's look at random access. *Random access* means moving directly to any location in the file instead of moving through it sequentially. The random access approach is often used with database files. A program will maintain a separate index file, giving the location of data in the main data file. Then it can jump directly to that location, read the data there, and perhaps modify it. This approach is done most simply if the file consists of a collection of equal-sized records. Each record represents a related collection of data. For example, in the example in Listing 17.19, each file record would represent all the data about a particular planet. A file record corresponds rather naturally to a program structure or class.

This example is based on the binary file program in Listing 17.19, to take advantage of the fact that the `planet` structure provides a pattern for a file record. To add to the creative tension of programming, the example opens the file in a read-and-write mode so that it can both read and modify a record. You can do this by creating an `fstream` object. The `fstream` class derives from the `iostream` class, which, in turn, is based on both the `istream` and `ostream` classes, so it inherits the methods of both. It also inherits two buffers, one for input and one for output, and synchronizes the handling of the two buffers. That is, as the program reads the file or writes to it, it moves both an input pointer in the input buffer and an output pointer in the output buffer in tandem.

The example does the following:

1. Displays the current contents of the `planets.dat` file.

2. Asks which record you want to modify.

3. Modifies that record.

4. Shows the revised file.

A more ambitious program would use a menu and a loop to let you select from the list of actions indefinitely, but this version performs each action just once. This simplified approach allows you to examine several aspects of read/write files without getting bogged down in matters of program design.

Caution

This program assumes that the `planets.dat` file already exists and was created by the `binary.cpp` program in Listing 17.19.

The first question to answer is what file mode to use. In order to read the file, you need the `ios_base::in` mode. For binary I/O, you need the `ios_base::binary` mode. (Again, on some nonstandard systems you can omit—indeed, you may have to omit—this mode.) In order to write to the file, you need the `ios_base::out` or the `ios_base::app` mode. However, the append mode allows a program to add data to the end of the file only. The rest of the file is read-only; that is, you can read the original data but not modify it—so you have to use `ios_base::out`. As Table 17.9 indicates, using the in and out modes simultaneously provides a read/write mode, so you just have to add the binary element. As mentioned earlier, you use the | operator to combine modes. Thus, you need the following statement to set up business:

```
finout.open(file,ios_base::in | ios_base::out | ios_base::binary);
```

Next, you need a way to move through a file. The `fstream` class inherits two methods for this: `seekg()` moves the input pointer to a given file location, and `seekp()` moves the output pointer to a given file location. (Actually, because the `fstream` class uses buffers for intermediate storage of data, the pointers point to locations in the buffers, not in the actual file.) You can also use `seekg()` with an `ifstream` object and `seekp()` with an `ofstream` object. Here are the `seekg()` prototypes:

```
basic_istream<charT,traits>& seekg(off_type, ios_base::seekdir);
basic_istream<charT,traits>& seekg(pos_type);
```

As you can see, they are templates. This chapter uses a template specialization for the `char` type. For the `char` specialization, the two prototypes are equivalent to the following:

```
istream & seekg(streamoff, ios_base::seekdir);
istream & seekg(streampos);
```

The first prototype represents locating a file position measured, in bytes, as an offset from a file location specified by the second argument. The second prototype represents locating a file position measured, in bytes, from the beginning of a file.

Type Escalation

When C++ was young, life was simpler for the `seekg()` methods. The `streamoff` and `streampos` types were `typedef`s for some standard integer type, such as `long`. However, the quest for creating a portable standard had to deal with the realization that an integer argument might not provide enough information for some file systems, so `streamoff` and `streampos` were allowed to be structure or class types, as long as they allowed some basic operations, such as using an integer value as an initialization value. Next, the old `istream` class was replaced with the `basic_istream` template, and `streampos` and `streamoff` were replaced with the template-based types `pos_type` and `off_type`. However, `streampos` and `streamoff` continue to exist as `char` specializations of `pos_type` and `off_type`. Similarly, you can use the `wstreampos` and `wstreamoff` types if you use `seekg()` with a `wistream` object.

Let's take a look at the arguments to the first prototype of `seekg()`. Values of the `streamoff` type are used to measure offsets, in bytes, from a particular location in a file. The `streamoff` argument represents the file position, in bytes, measured as an offset from one of three locations. (The type may be defined as an integral type or as a class.) The `seek_dir` argument is another integer type that is defined, along with three possible values, in the `ios_base` class. The constant `ios_base::beg` means measure the offset from the beginning of the file. The constant `ios_base::cur` means measure the offset from the current position. The constant `ios_base::end` means measure the offset from the end of the file. Here are some sample calls, assuming that `fin` is an `ifstream` object:

```
fin.seekg(30, ios_base::beg);    // 30 bytes beyond the beginning
fin.seekg(-1, ios_base::cur);    // back up one byte
fin.seekg(0, ios_base::end);     // go to the end of the file
```

Now let's look at the second prototype. Values of the `streampos` type locate a position in a file. It can be a class, but, if so, the class includes a constructor with a `streamoff` argument and a constructor with an integer argument, providing a path to convert both types to `streampos` values. A `streampos` value represents an absolute location in a file, measured from the beginning of the file. You can treat a `streampos` position as if it measures a file location in bytes from the beginning of a file, with the first byte being byte 0. So the statement

```
fin.seekg(112);
```

locates the file pointer at byte 112, which would be the 113th byte in the file. If you want to check the current position of a file pointer, you can use the `tellg()` method for input streams and the `tellp()` methods for output streams. Each returns a `streampos` value representing the current position, in bytes, measured from the beginning of the file. When you create an `fstream` object, the input and output pointers move in tandem, so `tellg()` and `tellp()` return the same value. But if you use an `istream` object to manage the input stream and an `ostream` object to manage the output stream to the same file, the input and output pointers move independently of one another, and `tellg()` and `tellp()` can return different values.

You can then use `seekg()` to go to the file beginning. Here is a section of code that opens a file, goes to the beginning, and displays the file contents:

```
fstream finout;     // read and write streams
finout.open(file,ios::in | ios::out |ios::binary);
//NOTE: Some Unix systems require omitting | ios::binary
int ct = 0;
if (finout.is_open())
{
    finout.seekg(0);    // go to beginning
    cout << "Here are the current contents of the "
         << file << " file:\n";
    while (finout.read((char *) &pl, sizeof pl))
    {
        cout << ct++ << ": " << setw(LIM) << pl.name << ": "
        << setprecision(0) << setw(12) << pl.population
        << setprecision(2) << setw(6) << pl.g << endl;
    }
    if (finout.eof())
        finout.clear(); // clear eof flag
    else
    {
        cerr << "Error in reading " << file << ".\n";
        exit(EXIT_FAILURE);
    }
}
else
{
    cerr << file << " could not be opened -- bye.\n";
    exit(EXIT_FAILURE);
}
```

This is similar to the start of Listing 17.19, but there are some changes and additions. First, as just described, the program uses an `fstream` object with a read/write mode, and it uses `seekg()` to position the file pointer at the start of the file. (This isn't really needed for this example, but it shows how `seekg()` is used.) Next, the program makes the minor change of numbering the records as they are displayed. Then it makes the following important addition:

```
if (finout.eof())
    finout.clear(); // clear eof flag
else
{
    cerr << "Error in reading " << file << ".\n";
    exit(EXIT_FAILURE);
}
```

The problem is that when the program reads and displays the entire file, it sets the `eofbit` element. This convinces the program that it's finished with the file and disables any further reading of or writing to the file. Using the `clear()` method resets the stream state, turning off `eofbit`. Now the program can once again access the file. The `else` part handles the possibility that the program quit reading the file for some reason other than reaching the end-of-file, such as a hardware failure.

The next step is to identify the record to be changed and then change it. To do this, the program asks the user to enter a record number. Multiplying the number by the number of bytes in a record yields the byte number for the beginning of the record. If `record` is the record number, the desired byte number is `record * sizeof pl`:

```
cout << "Enter the record number you wish to change: ";
long rec;
cin >> rec;
eatline();                  // get rid of newline
if (rec < 0 || rec >= ct)
{
    cerr << "Invalid record number -- bye\n";
    exit(EXIT_FAILURE);
}
streampos place = rec * sizeof pl;  // convert to streampos type
finout.seekg(place);        // random access
```

The variable `ct` represents the number of records; the program exits if you try to go beyond the limits of the file.

Next, the program displays the current record:

```
finout.read((char *) &pl, sizeof pl);
cout << "Your selection:\n";
cout << rec << ": " << setw(LIM) << pl.name << ": "
<< setprecision(0) << setw(12) << pl.population
<< setprecision(2) << setw(6) << pl.g << endl;
if (finout.eof())
    finout.clear();        // clear eof flag
```

After displaying the record, the program lets you change the record:

```
cout << "Enter planet name: ";
cin.get(pl.name, LIM);
eatline();
cout << "Enter planetary population: ";
cin >> pl.population;
cout << "Enter planet's acceleration of gravity: ";
cin >> pl.g;
```

```
finout.seekp(place);     // go back
finout.write((char *) &pl, sizeof pl) << flush;

if (finout.fail())
{
    cerr << "Error on attempted write\n";
    exit(EXIT_FAILURE);
}
```

The program flushes the output to guarantee that the file is updated before proceeding to the next stage.

Finally, to display the revised file, the program uses `seekg()` to reset the file pointer to the beginning. Listing 17.20 shows the complete program. Don't forget that it assumes that a `planets.dat` file created using the `binary.cpp` program is available.

Compatibility Note

The older the implementation, the more likely it is to run afoul of the C++ Standard. Some systems don't recognize the binary flag, the `fixed` and `right` manipulators, and `ios_base`.

LISTING 17.20   random.cpp

```
// random.cpp -- random access to a binary file
#include <iostream>      // not required by most systems
#include <fstream>
#include <iomanip>
#include <cstdlib>       // (or stdlib.h) for exit()
const int LIM = 20;
struct planet
{
    char name[LIM];      // name of planet
    double population;   // its population
    double g;            // its acceleration of gravity
};

const char * file = "planets.dat";  // ASSUMED TO EXIST (binary.cpp example)
inline void eatline() { while (std::cin.get() != '\n') continue; }

int main()
{
    using namespace std;
    planet pl;
    cout << fixed;

// show initial contents
    fstream finout;      // read and write streams
    finout.open(file,
            ios_base::in | ios_base::out | ios_base::binary);
    //NOTE: Some Unix systems require omitting | ios::binary
```

LISTING 17.20 *Continued*

```
        int ct = 0;
        if (finout.is_open())
        {
            finout.seekg(0);     // go to beginning
            cout << "Here are the current contents of the "
                << file << " file:\n";
            while (finout.read((char *) &pl, sizeof pl))
            {
                cout << ct++ << ": " << setw(LIM) << pl.name << ": "
                    << setprecision(0) << setw(12) << pl.population
                    << setprecision(2) << setw(6) << pl.g << endl;
            }
            if (finout.eof())
                finout.clear(); // clear eof flag
            else
            {
                cerr << "Error in reading " << file << ".\n";
                exit(EXIT_FAILURE);
            }
        }
        else
        {
            cerr << file << " could not be opened -- bye.\n";
            exit(EXIT_FAILURE);
        }

    // change a record
        cout << "Enter the record number you wish to change: ";
        long rec;
        cin >> rec;
        eatline();              // get rid of newline
        if (rec < 0 || rec >= ct)
        {
            cerr << "Invalid record number -- bye\n";
            exit(EXIT_FAILURE);
        }
        streampos place = rec * sizeof pl;  // convert to streampos type
        finout.seekg(place);    // random access
        if (finout.fail())
        {
            cerr << "Error on attempted seek\n";
            exit(EXIT_FAILURE);
        }

        finout.read((char *) &pl, sizeof pl);
        cout << "Your selection:\n";
        cout << rec << ": " << setw(LIM) << pl.name << ": "
            << setprecision(0) << setw(12) << pl.population
            << setprecision(2) << setw(6) << pl.g << endl;
        if (finout.eof())
            finout.clear();      // clear eof flag
```

LISTING 17.20 *Continued*

```
    cout << "Enter planet name: ";
    cin.get(pl.name, LIM);
    eatline();
    cout << "Enter planetary population: ";
    cin >> pl.population;
    cout << "Enter planet's acceleration of gravity: ";
    cin >> pl.g;
    finout.seekp(place);      // go back
    finout.write((char *) &pl, sizeof pl) << flush;
    if (finout.fail())
    {
        cerr << "Error on attempted write\n";
        exit(EXIT_FAILURE);
    }

// show revised file
    ct = 0;
    finout.seekg(0);                // go to beginning of file
    cout << "Here are the new contents of the " << file
         << " file:\n";
    while (finout.read((char *) &pl, sizeof pl))
    {
        cout << ct++ << ": " << setw(LIM) << pl.name << ": "
             << setprecision(0) << setw(12) << pl.population
             << setprecision(2) << setw(6) << pl.g << endl;
    }
    finout.close();
    cout << "Done.\n";
    return 0;
}
```

Here's a sample run of the program in Listing 17.20, based on a `planets.dat` file that has had a few more entries added since you last saw it:

```
Here are the current contents of the planets.dat File:
0:      Earth:         5333000000        9.81
1:      Bill's Planet: 23020020          8.82
2:      Trantor:       58000000000       15.03
3:      Trellan:       4256000           9.62
4:      Freestone:     3845120000        8.68
5:      Taanagoot:     350000002         10.23
6:      Marin:         232000            9.79
Enter the record number you wish to change: 2
Your selection:
2:      Trantor:       58000000000       15.03
Enter planet name: Trantor
Enter planetary population: 59500000000
Enter planet's acceleration of gravity:  10.53
Here are the new contents of the planets.dat file:
0:      Earth:         5333000000        9.81
1:      Bill's Planet: 23020020          8.82
2:      Trantor:       59500000000       10.53
```

```
3:      Trellan:        4256000         9.62
4:      Freestone:      3845120000      8.68
5:      Taanagoot:      350000002       10.23
6:      Marin:          232000          9.79
Done.
```

By using the techniques in this program, you can extend it so that it allows you to add new material and delete records. If you were to expand the program, it would be a good idea to reorganize it by using classes and functions. For example, you could convert the `planet` structure to a class definition; then you could overload the `<<` insertion operator so that `cout <<` `pl` displays the class data members formatted as in the example. Also, the example doesn't bother to verify input, so you could add code to check for numeric input where appropriate.

Real-World Note: Working with Temporary Files

Developing applications often requires the use of temporary files whose lifetimes are transient and must be controlled by the program. Have you ever thought about how to go about this in C++? It's really quite easy to create a temporary file, copy the contents of another file, and delete the file. First of all, you need to come up with a naming scheme for your temporary file(s). But wait…how can you ensure that each file is assigned a unique name? The `tmpnam()` standard function declared in `cstdio` has you covered:

```
char* tmpnam( char* pszName );
```

The `tmpnam()` function creates a temporary name and places it in the C-style string that is pointed to by `pszName`. The constants `L_tmpnam` and `TMP_MAX`, both defined in `cstdio`, limit the number of characters in the filename and the maximum number of times `tmpnam()` can be called without generating a duplicate filename in the current directory. The following example generates 10 temporary names:

```cpp
#include <cstdio>
#include <iostream>

int main()
{
    using namespace std;
    cout << "This system can generate up to " << TMP_MAX
        << " temporary names of up to " << L_tmpnam
        << " characters.\n";
    char pszName[ L_tmpnam ] = {'\0'};
    cout << "Here are ten names:\n";
    for( int i=0; 10 > i; i++ )
    {
        tmpnam( pszName );
        cout << pszName << endl;
    }
    return 0;
}
```

More generally, by using `tmpnam()`, you can now generate `TMP_NAM` unique filenames with up to `L_tmpnam` characters per name. The names themselves depend on the compiler. You can run this program to see what names your compiler comes up with.

Incore Formatting

The `iostream` family supports I/O between a program and a terminal. The `fstream` family uses the same interface to provide I/O between a program and a file. The C++ library also provides an `sstream` family, which uses the same interface to provide I/O between a program and a `string` object. That is, you can use the same `ostream` methods you've used with `cout` to write formatted information into a `string` object, and you can use `istream` methods such as `getline()` to read information from a `string` object. The process of reading formatted information from a `string` object or of writing formatted information to a `string` object is termed *incore* formatting. Let's take a brief look at these facilities. (The `sstream` family of `string` support supersedes the `strstream.h` family of `char`-array support.)

The `sstream` header file defines an `ostringstream` class that is derived from the `ostream` class. (There is also a `wostringstream` class based on `wostream`, for wide character sets.) If you create an `ostringstream` object, you can write information to it, which it stores. You can use the same methods with an `ostringstream` object that you can with `cout`. That is, you can do something like the following:

```
ostringstream outstr;
double price = 281.00;
char * ps = " for a copy of the ISO/EIC C++ standard!";
outstr.precision(2);
outstr << fixed;
outstr << "Pay only $" << price << ps << end;
```

The formatted text goes into a buffer, and the object uses dynamic memory allocation to expand the buffer size as needed. The `ostringstream` class has a member function, called `str()`, that returns a string object initialized to the buffer's contents:

```
string mesg = outstr.str();    // returns string with formatted information
```

Using the `str()` method "freezes" the object, and you can no longer write to it.

Listing 17.21 provides a short example of incore formatting.

LISTING 17.21 `strout.cpp`

```
// strout.cpp -- incore formatting (output)
#include <iostream>
#include <sstream>
#include <string>
int main()
{
    using namespace std;
    ostringstream outstr;   // manages a string stream

    string hdisk;
    cout << "What's the name of your hard disk? ";
    getline(cin, hdisk);
    int cap;
    cout << "What's its capacity in GB? ";
```

LISTING 17.21   Continued

```
    cin >> cap;
    // write formatted information to string stream
    outstr << "The hard disk " << hdisk << " has a capacity of "
           << cap << " gigabytes.\n";
    string result = outstr.str();    // save result
    cout << result;                  // show contents

    return 0;
}
```

Here's a sample run of the program in Listing 17.21:

```
What's the name of your hard disk? Datarapture
What's its capacity in GB? 250
The hard disk Datarapture has a capacity of 250 gigabytes.
```

The `istringstream` class lets you use the `istream` family of methods to read data from an `istringstream` object, which can be initialized from a `string` object. Suppose `facts` is a `string` object. To create an `istringstream` object associated with this string, you can use the following:

```
istringstream instr(facts);    // use facts to initialize stream
```

Then you use `istream` methods to read data from `instr`. For example, if `instr` contained a bunch of integers in character format, you could read them as follows:

```
int n;
int sum = 0;
while (instr << n)
    sum += num;
```

Listing 17.22 uses the overloaded `>>` operator to read the contents of a string one word at a time.

LISTING 17.22   strin.cpp

```
// strin.cpp -- formatted reading from a char array
#include <iostream>
#include <sstream>
#include <string>
int main()
{
    using namespace std;
    string lit = "It was a dark and stormy day, and "
                 " the full moon glowed brilliantly. ";
    istringstream instr(lit);    // use buf for input
    string word;;
    while (instr >> word)        // read a word a time
        cout << word << endl;
    return 0;
}
```

Here is the output of the program in Listing 17.22:

```
It
was
a
dark
and
stormy
day,
and
the
full
moon
glowed
brilliantly.
```

In short, the `istringstream` and `ostringstream` classes give you the power of the `istream` and `ostream` class methods to manage character data stored in strings.

What Now?

If you have worked your way through this book, you should have a good grasp of the rules of C++. However, that's just the beginning in learning this language. The second stage is learning to use the language effectively, and that is the longer journey. The best situation to be in is a work or learning environment that brings you into contact with good C++ code and programmers. Also, now that you know C++, you can read books that concentrate on more advanced topics and on object-oriented programming. Appendix H, "Selected Readings and Internet Resources," lists some of these resources.

One promise of OOP is to facilitate the development and enhance the reliability of large projects. One of the essential activities of the OOP approach is to invent the classes that represent the situation (called the *problem domain*) that you are modeling. Because real problems are often complex, finding a suitable set of classes can be challenging. Creating a complex system from scratch usually doesn't work; instead, it's best to take an iterative, evolutionary approach. Toward this end, practitioners in the field have developed several techniques and strategies. In particular, it's important to do as much of the iteration and evolution in the analysis and design stages as possible instead of writing and rewriting actual code.

Two common techniques are *use-case analysis* and *CRC cards*. In use-case analysis, the development team lists the common ways, or scenarios, in which it expects the final system to be used, identifying elements, actions, and responsibilities that suggest possible classes and class features. Using CRC (short for Class/Responsibilities/Collaborators) cards is a simple way to analyze such scenarios. The development team creates an index card for each class. On the card are the class name; class responsibilities, such as data represented and actions performed; and class collaborators, such as other classes with which the class must interact. Then the team can walk through a scenario, using the interface provided by the CRC cards. This can lead to suggestions for new classes, shifts of responsibility, and so on.

On a larger scale are the systematic methods for working on entire projects. The most recent of these is the Unified Modeling Language (UML). UML is not a programming language; rather, it is a language for representing the analysis and design of a programming project. It was developed by Grady Booch, Jim Rumbaugh, and Ivar Jacobson, who had been the primary developers of three earlier modeling languages: the Booch Method, OMT (Object Modeling Technique), and OOSE (Object-Oriented Software Engineering), respectively. UML is the evolutionary successor of these three.

In addition to increasing your understanding of C++ in general, you might want to learn about specific class libraries. Microsoft, Borland, and Metrowerks, for example, offer extensive class libraries to facilitate programming for the Windows environment, and Metrowerks offers similar facilities for Macintosh programming.

Summary

A stream is a flow of bytes into or out of a program. A buffer is a temporary holding area in memory that acts as an intermediary between a program and a file or other I/O devices. Information can be transferred between a buffer and a file, using large chunks of data of the size most efficiently handled by devices such as disk drives. And information can be transferred between a buffer and a program in a byte-by-byte flow that often is more convenient for the processing done in a program. C++ handles input by connecting a buffered stream to a program and to its source of input. Similarly, C++ handles output by connecting a buffered stream to a program and to its output target. The `iostream` and `fstream` files constitute an I/O class library that defines a rich set of classes for managing streams. C++ programs that include the `iostream` file automatically open eight streams, managing them with eight objects. The `cin` object manages the standard input stream, which, by default, connects to the standard input device, typically a keyboard. The `cout` object manages the standard output stream, which, by default, connects to the standard output device, typically a monitor. The `cerr` and `clog` objects manage unbuffered and buffered streams connected to the standard error device, typically a monitor. These four objects have four wide character counterparts, named `wcin`, `wcout`, `wcerr`, and `wclog`.

The I/O class library provides a variety of useful methods. The `istream` class defines versions of the extraction operator (`>>`) that recognize all the basic C++ types and that convert character input to those types. The `get()` family of methods and the `getline()` method provide further support for single-character input and for string input. Similarly, the `ostream` class defines versions of the insertion operator (`<<`) that recognize all the basic C++ types and that convert them to suitable character output. The `put()` method provides further support for single-character output. The `wistream` and `wostream` classes provide similar support for wide characters.

You can control how a program formats output by using `ios_base` class methods and by using manipulators (functions that can be concatenated with insertion) defined in the `iostream` and `iomanip` files. These methods and manipulators let you control the number base, the field width, the number of decimal places displayed, the system used to display floating-point values, and other elements.

The `fstream` file provides class definitions that extend the `iostream` methods to file I/O. The `ifstream` class derives from the `istream` class. By associating an `ifstream` object with a file, you can use all the `istream` methods for reading the file. Similarly, associating an `ofstream` object with a file lets you use the `ostream` methods to write to a file. And associating an `fstream` object with a file lets you employ both input and output methods with the file.

To associate a file with a stream, you can provide the filename when initializing a file stream object or you can first create a file stream object and then use the `open()` method to associate the stream with a file. The `close()` method terminates the connection between a stream and a file. The class constructors and the `open()` method take an optional second argument that provides the file mode. The file mode determines such things as whether the file is to be read and/or written to, whether opening a file for writing truncates it, whether attempting to open a non-existent file is an error, and whether to use the binary or text mode.

A text file stores all information in character form. For example, numeric values are converted to character representations. The usual insertion and extraction operators, along with `get()` and `getline()`, support this mode. A binary file stores all information by using the same binary representation the computer uses internally. Binary files store data, particularly floating-point values, more accurately and compactly than text files, but they are less portable. The `read()` and `write()` methods support binary input and output.

The `seekg()` and `seekp()` functions provide C++ random access for files. These class methods let you position a file pointer relative to the beginning of a file, relative to the end, or relative to the current position. The `tellg()` and `tellp()` methods report the current file position.

The `sstream` header file defines `istringstream` and `ostringstream` classes that let you use `istream` and `ostream` methods to extract information from a string and to format information placed into a string.

Review Questions

1. What role does the `iostream` file play in C++ I/O?

2. Why does typing a number such as 121 as input require a program to make a conversion?

3. What's the difference between the standard output and the standard error?

4. Why is `cout` able to display various C++ types without being provided explicit instructions for each type?

5. What feature of the output method definitions allows you to concatenate output?

6. Write a program that requests an integer and then displays it in decimal, octal, and hexadecimal forms. Display each form on the same line, in fields that are 15 characters wide, and use the C++ number base prefixes.

7. Write a program that requests the following information and that formats it as shown:

```
Enter your name: Billy Gruff
Enter your hourly wages: 12
Enter number of hours worked: 7.5
First format:
                    Billy Gruff: $      12.00:  7.5
Second format:
Billy Gruff                     : $12.00      :7.5
```

8. Consider the following program:

```
//rq17-8.cpp
#include <iostream>

int main()
{
    using namespace std;
    char ch;
    int ct1 = 0;

    cin >> ch;
    while (ch != 'q')
    {
        ct1++;
        cin >> ch;
    }

    int ct2 = 0;
    cin.get(ch);
    while (ch != 'q')
    {
        ct2++;
        cin.get(ch);
    }
    cout << "ct1 = " << ct1 << "; ct2 = " << ct2 << "\n";

    return 0;
}
```

What does it print, given the following input:

```
I see a q<Enter>
I see a q<Enter>
```

Here <Enter> signifies pressing the Enter key.

9. Both of the following statements read and discard characters up to and including the end of a line. In what way does the behavior of one differ from that of the other?

```
while (cin.get() != '\n')
    continue;
cin.ignore(80, '\n');
```

Programming Exercises

1. Write a program that counts the number of characters up to the first $ in input and that leaves the $ in the input stream.

2. Write a program that copies your keyboard input (up to the simulated end-of-file) to a file named on the command line.

3. Write a program that copies one file to another. Have the program take the filenames from the command line. Have the program report if it cannot open a file.

4. Write a program that opens two text files for input and one for output. The program should concatenate the corresponding lines of the input files, use a space as a separator, and write the results to the output file. If one file is shorter than the other, the remaining lines in the longer file should also be copied to the output file. For example, suppose the first input file has these contents:

```
eggs kites donuts
balloons hammers
stones
```

And suppose the second input file has these contents:

```
zero lassitude
finance drama
```

The resulting file would have these contents:

```
eggs kites donuts zero lassitude
balloons hammers finance drama
stones
```

5. Mat and Pat want to invite their friends to a party, much as they did in Programming Exercise 8 in Chapter 16, except now they want a program that uses files. They have asked you to write a program that does the following:

   - Reads a list of Mat's friends' names from a text file called `mat.dat`, which lists one friend per line. The names are stored in a container and then displayed in sorted order.

   - Reads a list of Pat's friends' names from a text file called `pat.dat`, which lists one friend per line. The names are stored in a container and then displayed in sorted order.

   - Merges the two lists, eliminating duplicates, and stores the result in the file `matnpat.dat`, one friend per line.

6. Consider the class definitions of Programming Exercise 5 in Chapter 14. If you haven't yet done that exercise, do so now. Then do the following:

   Write a program that uses standard C++ I/O and file I/O in conjunction with data of types `employee`, `manager`, `fink`, and `highfink`, as defined in Programming Exercise 5 in Chapter 14. The program should be along the general lines of Listing 17.17 in that it should let you add new data to a file. The first time through, the program should solicit data from the user, show all the entries, and save the information in a file. On subsequent uses, the program should first read and display the file data, let the user add data, and show all the data. One difference is that data should be handled by an array of pointers to type `employee`. That way, a pointer can point to an `employee` object or to objects of any of the three derived types. Keep the array small to facilitate checking the program; for example, you might limit the array to 10 elements:

```
const int MAX = 10;     // no more than 10 objects
...
employee * pc[MAX];
```

For keyboard entry, the program should use a menu to offer the user the choice of which type of object to create. The menu should use a switch to use `new` to create an object of the desired type and to assign the object's address to a pointer in the `pc` array. Then that object can use the virtual `setall()` function to elicit the appropriate data from the user:

```
pc[i]->setall();  // invokes function corresponding to type of object
```

To save the data to a file, devise a virtual `writeall()` function for that purpose:

```
for (i = 0; i < index; i++)
    pc[i]->writeall(fout);// fout ofstream connected to output file
```

Note

Use text I/O, not binary I/O, for Programming Exercise 6. (Unfortunately, virtual objects include pointers to tables of pointers to virtual functions, and `write()` copies this information to a file. An object filled by using `read()` from the file gets weird values for the function pointers, which really messes up the behavior of virtual functions.) Use a newline character to separate each data field from the next; this makes it easier to identify fields on input. Or you could still use binary I/O, but not write objects as a whole. Instead, you could provide class methods that apply the `write()` and `read()` functions to each class member individually rather than to the object as a whole. That way, the program could save just the intended data to a file.

The tricky part is recovering the data from the file. The problem is, how can the program know whether the next item to be recovered is an `employee` object, a `manager` object, a `fink` type, or a `highfink` type? One approach is, when writing the data for an object to a file, precede the data with an integer that indicates the type of object to follow. Then, on file input, the program can read the integer and then use `switch` to create the appropriate object to receive the data:

```
enum classkind{Employee, Manager, Fink, Highfink}; // in class header
...
int classtype;
while((fin >> classtype).get(ch)){ // newline separates int from data
    switch(classtype) {
        case Employee  : pc[i] = new employee;
                    : break;
```

Then you can use the pointer to invoke a virtual `getall()` function to read the information:

```
pc[i++]->getall();
```

7. Here is part of a program that reads keyboard input into a vector of **string** objects, stores the string contents (not the objects) in a file, and then copies the file contents back into a vector of **string** objects:

```cpp
int main()
{
    using namespace std;
    vector<string> vostr;
    string temp;

// acquire strings
    cout << "Enter strings (empty line to quit):\n";
    while (getline(cin,temp) && temp[0] != '\0')
        vostr.push_back(temp);
    cout << "Here is your input.\n";
    for_each(vostr.begin(), vostr.end(), ShowStr);

// store in a file
    ofstream fout("strings.dat", ios_base::out | ios_base::binary);
    for_each(vostr.begin(), vostr.end(), Store(fout));
    fout.close();

// recover file contents
    vector<string> vistr;
    ifstream fin("strings.dat", ios_base::in | ios_base::binary);
    if (!fin.is_open())
    {
        cerr << "Could not open file for input.\n";
        exit(EXIT_FAILURE);
    }
    GetStrs(fin, vistr);
    cout << "\nHere are the strings read from the file:\n";
    for_each(vistr.begin(), vistr.end(), ShowStr);

    return 0;
}
```

Note that the file is opened in binary format and that the intention is that I/O be accomplished with `read()` and `write()`. Quite a bit remains to be done:

- Write a `void ShowStr(const string &)` function that displays a **string** object followed by a newline character.

- Write a `Store` functor that writes string information to a file. The `Store` constructor should specify an **ifstream** object, and the overloaded `operator()(const string &)` should indicate the string to write. A workable plan is to first write the string's size to the file and then write the string contents. For example, if `len` holds the string size, you could use this:

```
os.write((char *)&len, sizeof(std::size_t));  // store length
os.write(s.data(), len);                       // store characters
```

The `data()` member returns a pointer to an array that holds the characters in the string. It's similar to the `c_str()` member except that the latter appends a null character.

- Write a `GetStrs()` function that recovers information from the file. It can use `read()` to obtain the size of a string and then use a loop to read that many characters from the file, appending them to an initially empty temporary string. Because a string's data is private, you have to use a class method to get data into the string rather than read directly into it.

NUMBER BASES

Civilizations have used many systems to represent numbers. Some systems, such as Roman numerals, are ill suited for doing arithmetic. On the other hand, the Hindi number system, modified and transmitted to Europe as the Arabic number system, facilitated calculations for mathematicians, scientists, and merchants. Modern computer number systems are based on the placeholder concept and use of zero that first appeared with the Hindi number system. However, they generalize the principles to other number bases. So, although our everyday notation is based on the number 10, as described in the next section, the computing world often uses numbers based on 8 (octal), 16 (hexadecimal), and 2 (binary).

Decimal Numbers (Base 10)

The method we use for writing numbers is based on powers of 10. For example, consider the number 2,468. The 2 represents 2 thousands, the 4 represents 4 hundreds, the 6 represents 6 tens, and the 8 represents 8 ones:

$$2,468 = 2 \times 1,000 + 4 \times 100 + 6 \times 10 + 8 \times 1$$

One thousand is $10 \times 10 \times 10$, or 10 to the third power, which can be written as 10^3. Using this notation, you can write the preceding relationship this way:

$$2,468 = 2 \times 10^3 + 4 \times 10^2 + 6 \times 10^1 + 8 \times 10^0$$

Because this number notation is based on powers of 10, we refer to it as base 10, or decimal, notation. You can also use another number as a base. For example, C++ lets you use base 8 (octal) and base 16 (hexadecimal or hex) notation for writing integer numbers. (Note: 10^0 is 1, as is any nonzero number to the zero power.)

Octal Integers (Base 8)

Octal numbers are based on powers of 8, so base 8 notation uses the digits 0–7 in writing numbers. C++ uses a 0 prefix to indicate octal notation. Thus, 0177 is an octal value. You can use powers of 8 to find the equivalent base 10 value:

Octal	Decimal
0177	$= 1 \times 8^2 + 7 \times 8^1 + 7 \times 8^0$
	$= 1 \times 64 + 7 \times 8 + 7 \times 1$
	$= 127$

Because the Unix operating system often uses octal representation of values, C++ and C provide octal notation.

Hexadecimal Numbers (Base 16)

Hexadecimal numbers are based on powers of 16. This means that 10 in hexadecimal represents the value $16 + 0$, or 16. To represent the values between 9 and hexadecimal 16, you need a few more digits. Standard hexadecimal notation uses the letters a–f for that purpose. C++ accepts either lowercase or uppercase versions of these characters, as shown in Table A.1.

TABLE A.1 Hexadecimal Digits

Hexadecimal Digit	Decimal Value
a or A	10
b or B	11
c or C	12
d or D	13
e or E	14
f or F	15

C++ uses 0x or 0X notation to indicate hexadecimal notation. Thus, 0x2B3 is a hexadecimal value. To find the decimal equivalent of 0x2B3, you can evaluate the powers of 16:

Hexadecimal	Decimal
0x2B3	$= 2 \times 16^2 + 11 \times 16^1 + 3 \times 16^0$
	$= 2 \times 256 + 11 \times 16 + 3 \times 1$
	$= 691$

Hardware documentation often uses hexadecimal notation to represent values such as memory locations and port numbers.

Binary Numbers (Base 2)

Whether you use decimal, octal, or hexadecimal notation for writing an integer, the computer stores it as a binary, or base 2, value. Binary notation uses just two digits, 0 and 1. For example, 10011011 is a binary number. Note, however, that C++ doesn't provide for writing a number in binary notation. Binary numbers are based on powers of 2:

Binary	Decimal
100110111	$= 1{\times}2^7 + 0{\times}2^6 + 0{\times}2^5 + 1{\times}2^4$
	$+ \ 1{\times}2^3 + 0{\times}2^2 + 1{\times}2^1 + 1{\times}2^0$
	$= 128 + 0 + 0 + 16 + 8 + 0 + 2 + 1$
	$= 155$

Binary notation makes a nice match to computer memory, in which each individual unit, called a *bit*, can be set to off or on. You just identify the off setting with 0 and the on setting with 1. Memory is commonly organized in units called *bytes*, with each byte being 8 bits. The bits in a byte are numbered corresponding to the associated power of 2. Thus, the rightmost bit is bit number 0, the next bit is bit 1, and so on. For example, Figure A.1 represents a 2-byte integer.

FIGURE A.1

A 2-byte integer value.

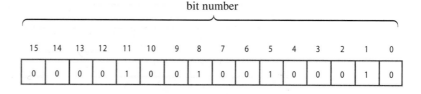

$$\text{value} = 1 \times 2^{11} + 1 \times 2^8 + 1 \times 2^5 + 1 \times 2^1$$
$$= 2048 + 256 + 32 + 2$$
$$= 2338$$

Binary and Hex

Hex notation is often used to provide a more convenient view of binary data, such as memory addresses or integers holding bit-flag settings. The reason for this is that each hexadecimal digit corresponds to a 4-bit unit. Table A.2 shows this correspondence.

TABLE A.2 Hexadecimal Digits and Binary Equivalents

Hexadecimal Digit	Binary Equivalent
0	0000
1	0001
2	0010
3	0011
4	0100
5	0101
6	0110
7	0111
8	1000
9	1001
A	1010
B	1011
C	1100
D	1101
E	1110
F	1111

To convert a hex value to binary, you just replace each hex digit with the corresponding binary equivalent. For example, the hex number 0xA4 corresponds to binary 1010 0100. Similarly, you can easily convert binary values to hex notation by converting each 4-bit unit into the equivalent hex digit. For example, the binary value 1001 0101 becomes 0x95.

Real-World Note: Big Endian and Little Endian

Oddly, two computing platforms that both use binary representation of integers might not represent the same number identically. Intel machines, for example, store bytes using the Little Endian architecture, whereas Motorola, RISC-based MIPS computers and DEC Alpha computers employ the Big Endian scheme. (However, the last two systems can be configured to use either scheme.)

The terms *Big Endian* and *Little Endian* can be thought of as meaning "Big End In" and "Little End In"—a reference to the order of bytes in a word (typically a 2-byte unit) of memory. On an Intel computer (Little Endian), the low-order byte is stored first. This means a hex value such as 0xABCD would be stored in memory as 0xCD 0xAB. A Motorola (Big Endian) machine would store the same value in reverse, so 0xABCD would be stored in memory as 0xAB 0xCD.

Jonathan Swift's book *Gulliver's Travels* is the ultimate source for these terms. Swift satirized the irrationality of many political disputes by inventing two contentious political factions in Lilliput: the Big Endians, who maintained that the proper end to break an egg is the large end, and the Little Endians, who championed breaking the small end of the egg.

You, as a software engineer, should understand the word order of the platform you are targeting. Among other things, it affects the interpretation of data transmitted over a network and how data is stored in binary files. In the preceding example, the 2-byte memory pattern `0xABCD` would represent the decimal value 52,651 on a Little Endian machine and the decimal value 43,981 on a Big Endian machine.

APPENDIX B

C++ RESERVED WORDS

C++ reserves some words for its own use and for use in C++ libraries. You shouldn't use a reserved word as an identifier in a declaration. Reserved words come in three categories: keywords, alternative tokens, and C++ library reserved names.

C++ Keywords

Keywords are identifiers that form the vocabulary of a programming language. They may not be used for other purposes, such as serving as variable names. The following list shows C++'s keywords. Keywords shown in boldface are also keywords in ANSI C99. Table B.1 lists the keywords.

TABLE B.1 C++ Keywords

asm	**auto**	bool	**break**	**case**
catch	**char**	class	**const**	const_cast
continue	**default**	delete	**do**	**double**
dynamic_cast	**else**	**enum**	explicit	export
extern	false	**float**	**for**	friend
goto	**if**	inline	**int**	**long**
mutable	namespace	new	operator	private
protected	public	**register**	reinterpret_cast	**return**
short	**signed**	**sizeof**	**static**	static_cast
struct	**switch**	template	this	throw
true	try	**typedef**	typeid	typename
union	**unsigned**	using	virtual	**void**
volatile	wchar_t	**while**		

Alternative Tokens

In addition to keywords, C++ has some alphabetic alternative representations of operators, termed *alternative tokens*. These, too, are reserved. Table B.2 lists the alphabetic alternative tokens and the operators they represent.

TABLE B.2 C++ Reserved Alternative Tokens and Their Meanings

Token	Meaning
and	&&
and_eq	&=
bitand	&
bitor	|
compl	~
not	!
not_e	!=
or	||
or_eq	|=
xor	^
xor_eq	^=

C++ Library Reserved Names

The compiler won't let you use keywords and alternative tokens as names. There's another class of forbidden names for which the protection is not as absolute—*reserved names*, which are names reserved for use by the C++ library. If you use one of these as an identifier, the effect is undefined. That is, it might generate a compiler error, it might generate a warning, it might cause a program to run incorrectly, or it might cause no problems at all.

The C++ language reserves macro names used in a library header file. If a program includes a particular header file, then you shouldn't use the names of macros defined in that header (or in headers included by that header file, and so on) for other purposes. For example, if you include the header file `<climits>` directly or indirectly, you shouldn't use `CHAR_BIT` as an identifier because that name is already used as a macro in that header file.

The C++ language reserves names beginning with two underscores or a single underscore followed by an uppercase letter for any use, and it reserves names beginning with a single underscore for use as a global variable. So don't create names such as `__gink` or `__Lynx` in any case and names such as `_lynx` in the global namespace.

The C++ language reserves names declared with external linkage in library header files. For functions, this includes the function signature (name and parameter list). For example, suppose you have this code:

```
#include <cmath>
using namespace std;
```

In this case, the function signature `tan(double)` is reserved. That means your program should not declare a function that has this prototype:

```
int tan(double);  // don't do it
```

This doesn't match the library `tan()` prototype, which returns type `double`, but it does match the signature portion. However, it would be okay to have the following prototype:

```
char * tan(char *);  // ok
```

That's because even though it matches the `tan()` identifier, it doesn't match the signature.

APPENDIX C

THE ASCII CHARACTER SET

*C*omputers store characters by using numeric codes. The ASCII (American Standard Code for Information Interchange) code is the most commonly used code in the United States. It's also a subset (a very small subset) of Unicode. C++ lets you represent most single characters directly, by including the character in single quotation marks, as in 'A' for the A character. You can also represent a single character by using the octal or hex code preceded by a backslash; for example, '\012' and '\0xa' both represent the linefeed (LF) character. Such escape sequences can also be part of a string, as in "Hello,\012my dear".

Table C.1 shows the ASCII character set in various representations. When used as a prefix in the table, the ^ character denotes using the Ctrl key.

TABLE C.1   The ASCII Character Set

Decimal	Octal	Hex	Binary	Character	ASCII Name
0	0	0	00000000	^@	NUL
1	01	0x1	00000001	^A	SOH
2	02	0x2	00000010	^B	STX
3	03	0x3	00000011	^C	ETX
4	04	0x4	00000100	^D	EOT
5	05	0x5	00000101	^E	ENQ
6	06	0x6	00000110	^F	ACK
7	07	0x7	00000111	^G	BEL
8	010	0x8	00001000	^H	BS
9	011	0x9	00001001	^I, Tab	HT
10	012	0xa	00001010	^J	LF
11	013	0xb	00001011	^K	VT
12	014	0xc	00001100	^L	FF

TABLE C.1 Continued

Decimal	Octal	Hex	Binary	Character	ASCII Name
13	015	0xd	00001101	^M	CR
14	016	0xe	00001110	^N	SO
15	017	0xf	00001111	^O	SI
16	020	0x10	00010000	^P	DLE
17	021	0x11	00010001	^Q	DC1
18	022	0x12	00010010	^R	DC2
19	023	0x13	00010011	^S	DC3
20	024	0x14	00010100	^T	DC4
21	025	0x15	00010101	^U	NAK
22	026	0x16	00010110	^V	SYN
23	027	0x17	00010111	^W	ETB
24	030	0x18	00011000	^X	CAN
25	031	0x19	00011001	^Y	EM
26	032	0x1a	00011010	^Z	SUB
27	033	0x1b	00011011	^[, Esc	ESC
28	034	0x1c	00011100	^\	FS
29	035	0x1d	00011101	^]	GS
30	036	0x1e	00011110	^^	RS
31	037	0x1f	00011111	^_	US
32	040	0x20	00100000	Spacebar	SP
33	041	0x21	00100001	!	
34	042	0x22	00100010	"	
35	043	0x23	00100011	#	
36	044	0x24	00100100	$	
37	045	0x25	00100101	%	
38	046	0x26	00100110	&	
39	047	0x27	00100111	'	
40	050	0x28	00101000	(	

Decimal	Octal	Hex	Binary	Character	ASCII Name
41	051	0x29	00101001	)	
42	052	0x2a	00101010	*	
43	053	0x2b	00101011	+	
44	054	0x2c	00101100	,	
45	055	0x2d	00101101	-	
46	056	0x2e	00101110	.	
47	057	0x2f	00101111	/	
48	060	0x30	00110000	0	
49	061	0x31	00110001	1	
50	062	0x32	00110010	2	
51	063	0x33	00110011	3	
52	064	0x34	00110100	4	
53	065	0x35	00110101	5	
54	066	0x36	00110110	6	
55	067	0x37	00110111	7	
56	070	0x38	00111000	8	
57	071	0x39	00111001	9	
58	072	0x3a	00111010	:	
59	073	0x3b	00111011	;	
60	074	0x3c	00111100	<	
61	075	0x3d	00111101	=	
62	076	0x3e	00111110	>	
63	077	0x3f	00111111	?	
64	0100	0x40	01000000	@	
65	0101	0x41	01000001	A	
66	0102	0x42	01000010	B	
67	0103	0x43	01000011	C	
68	0104	0x44	01000100	D	

TABLE C.1 Continued

Decimal	Octal	Hex	Binary	Character	ASCII Name
69	0105	0x45	01000101	E	
70	0106	0x46	01000110	F	
71	0107	0x47	01000111	G	
72	0110	0x48	01001000	H	
73	0111	0x49	01001001	I	
74	0112	0x4a	01001010	J	
75	0113	0x4b	01001011	K	
76	0114	0x4c	01001100	L	
77	0115	0x4d	01001101	M	
78	0116	0x4e	01001110	N	
79	0117	0x4f	01001111	O	
80	0120	0x50	01010000	P	
81	0121	0x51	01010001	Q	
82	0122	0x52	01010010	R	
83	0123	0x53	01010011	S	
84	0124	0x54	01010100	T	
85	0125	0x55	01010101	U	
86	0126	0x56	01010110	V	
87	0127	0x57	01010111	W	
88	0130	0x58	01011000	X	
89	0131	0x59	01011001	Y	
90	0132	0x5a	01011010	Z	
91	0133	0x5b	01011011	[	
92	0134	0x5c	01011100	\	
93	0135	0x5d	01011101	]	
94	0136	0x5e	01011110	^	
95	0137	0x5f	01011111	_	
96	0140	0x60	01100000	'	

Decimal	Octal	Hex	Binary	Character	ASCII Name
97	0141	0x61	01100001	a	
98	0142	0x62	01100010	b	
99	0143	0x63	01100011	c	
100	0144	0x64	01100100	d	
101	0145	0x65	01100101	e	
102	0146	0x66	01100110	f	
103	0147	0x67	01100111	g	
104	0150	0x68	01101000	h	
105	0151	0x69	01101001	i	
106	0152	0x6a	01101010	j	
107	0153	0x6b	01101011	k	
108	0154	0x6c	01101100	l	
109	0155	0x6d	01101101	m	
110	0156	0x6e	01101110	n	
111	0157	0x6f	01101111	o	
112	0160	0x70	01110000	p	
113	0161	0x71	01110001	q	
114	0162	0x72	01110010	r	
115	0163	0x73	01110011	s	
116	0164	0x74	01110100	t	
117	0165	0x75	01110101	u	
118	0166	0x76	01110110	v	
119	0167	0x77	01110111	w	
120	0170	0x78	01111000	x	
121	0171	0x79	01111001	y	
122	0172	0x7a	01111010	z	
123	0173	0x7b	01111011	{	
124	0174	0x7c	01111100			

TABLE C.1   Continued

Decimal	Octal	Hex	Binary	Character	ASCII Name
125	0175	0x7d	01111101	}	
126	0176	0x7e	01111110	~	
127	0177	0x7f	01111111	Del	

APPENDIX D

OPERATOR PRECEDENCE

Operator precedence determines the order in which operators are applied to a value. C++ operators come in 18 precedence groups, which are presented in Table D.1. Those in Group 1 have the highest precedence, those in Group 2 have the next-highest precedence, and so on. If two operators apply to the same operand (something on which an operator operates), the operator with the higher precedence applies first. If the two operators have the same precedence, C++ uses associativity rules to determine which operator binds more tightly. All operators in the same group have the same precedence and the same associativity, which is either left to right (L–R in the table) or right to left (R–L in the table). Left-to-right associativity means to apply the leftmost operator first, while right-to-left associativity means to apply the rightmost operator first.

Some symbols, such as * and &, are used for more than one operator. In such cases, one form is *unary* (one operand) and the other form is *binary* (two operands), and the compiler uses the context to determine which is meant. Table D.1 labels operator groups unary or binary for those cases in which the same symbol is used two ways.

The following are some examples of precedence and associativity.

Here's an example in which the compiler has to decide whether to add 5 to 3 or multiply 5 by 6:

```
3 + 5 * 6
```

The * operator has higher precedence than the + operator, so it is applied to the **5** first, making the expression **3 + 30**, or **33**.

Here's an example in which the compiler has to decide whether to divide 6 into 120 or multiply 6 by 5:

```
120 / 6 * 5
```

Both / and * have the same precedence, but these operators associate from left to right. That means the operator to the left of the shared operand (**6**) is applied first, so the expression becomes **20 * 5**, or **100**.

Here's an example in which the compiler has to decide whether to begin by incrementing str or by dereferencing str:

```
char * str = "Whoa";
char ch = *str++;
```

The postfix ++ operator has higher precedence than the unary * operator. This means the increment operator operates on str and not *str. That is, the operation increments the pointer, making it point to the next character, rather than altering the character pointed to. However, because ++ is the postfix form, the pointer is incremented after the original value of *str is assigned to ch. Therefore, this expression assigns the character W to ch and then moves str to point to the h character.

Here's a similar example:

```cpp
char * str = "Whoa";
char ch = *++str;
```

The prefix ++ operator and the unary * operator have the same precedence, but they associate right-to-left. So, again, str and not *str is incremented. Because the ++ operator is in prefix form, first str is incremented and then the resulting pointer is dereferenced. Thus, str moves to point to the h character, and the h character is assigned to ch.

Note that Table D.1 uses *binary* or *unary* in the "Precedence" column to distinguish between two operators that use the same symbol, such as the unary address operator and the binary bitwise AND operator.

TABLE D.1 C++ Operator Precedence and Associativity

Operator	Assoc.	Meaning
		Precedence Group 1
::		Scope resolution operator
		Precedence Group 2
(*expression*)		Grouping
()	L–R	Function call
()		Value construction—that is, *type* (*expr*)
[]		Array subscript
->		Indirect membership operator
.		Direct membership operator
const_cast		Specialized type cast
dynamic_cast		Specialized type cast
reinterpret_cast		Specialized type cast
static_cast		Specialized type cast
typeid		Type identification

Operator	Assoc.	Meaning
Precedence Group 2		
++		Increment operator, postfix
--		Decrement operator, postfix
Precedence Group 3 (All Unary)		
!	R–L	Logical negation
~		Bitwise negation
+		Unary plus (positive sign)
-		Unary minus (negative sign)
++		Increment operator, prefix
--		Decrement operator, prefix
&		Address
*		Dereference (indirect value)
()		Type cast—that is, *(type) expr*
sizeof		Size in bytes
new		Dynamically allocate storage
new []		Dynamically allocate array
delete		Dynamically free storage
delete []		Dynamically free array
Precedence Group 4		
.*	L–R	Member dereference
->*		Indirect member dereference
Precedence Group 5 (All Binary)		
*	L–R	Multiply
/		Divide
%		Modulus (remainder)
Precedence Group 6 (All Binary)		
+	L–R	Addition
-		Subtraction

TABLE D.1 Continued

Operator	Assoc.	Meaning
		Precedence Group 7
<<	L–R	Left shift
>>		Right shift
		Precedence Group 8
<	L–R	Less than
<=		Less than or equal to
>=		Greater than or equal to
>		Greater than
		Precedence Group 9
==	L–R	Equal to
!=		Not equal to
		Precedence Group 10 (Binary)
&	L–R	Bitwise AND
		Precedence Group 11
^	L–R	Bitwise XOR (exclusive OR)
		Precedence Group 12
|	L–R	Bitwise OR
		Precedence Group 13
&&	L–R	Logical AND
		Precedence Group 14
||	L–R	Logical OR
		Precedence Group 15
:?	R–L	Conditional
		Precedence Group 16
=	R–L	Simple assignment
*=		Multiply and assign

Operator	Assoc.	Meaning
		Precedence Group 16
/=		Divide and assign
%=		Take remainder and assign
+=		Add and assign
-=		Subtract and assign
&=		Bitwise AND and assign
^=		Bitwise XOR and assign
|=		Bitwise OR and assign
<<=		Left shift and assign
>>=		Right shift and assign
		Precedence Group 17
throw	L–R	Throw exception
		Precedence Group 18
,	L–R	Combine two expressions into one

OTHER OPERATORS

*I*n order to avoid terminal obesity, the main text of this book doesn't cover two groups of operators. The first group consists of the bitwise operators, which let you manipulate individual bits in a value; these operators were inherited from C. The second group consists of two-member dereferencing operators; they are C++ additions. This appendix briefly summarizes these operators.

Bitwise Operators

The bitwise operators operate on the bits of integer values. For example, the left-shift operator moves bits to the left, and the bitwise negation operator turns each 1 to a 0, and each 0 to a 1. Altogether, C++ has six such operators: <<, >>, ~, &, |, and ^.

The Shift Operators

The left-shift operator has the following syntax:

```
value << shift
```

Here *value* is the integer value to be shifted, and *shift* is the number of bits to shift. For example,

```
13 << 3
```

means shift all the bits in the value 13 three places to the left. The vacated places are filled with zeros, and bits shifted past the end are discarded (see Figure E.1).

Because each bit position represents a value twice that of the bit to the right (see Appendix A, "Number Bases"), shifting one bit position is equivalent to multiplying the value by 2. Similarly, shifting two bit positions is equivalent to multiplying by 2^2, and shifting n positions is equivalent to multiplying by 2^n. Thus, the value of 13 << 3 is 13×2^3, or 104.

The left-shift operator provides a capability often found in assembly languages. However, an assembly language left-shift operator directly alters the contents of a register, whereas the C++ left-shift operator produces a new value without altering existing values. For example, consider the following:

```
int x = 20;
int y = x << 3;
```

FIGURE E.1

The left-shift operator.

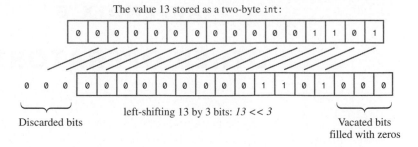

The value 13 stored as a two-byte int:

left-shifting 13 by 3 bits: *13 << 3*

Discarded bits

Vacated bits
filled with zeros

This code doesn't change the value of **x**. The expression **x << 3** uses the value of **x** to produce a new value, much as **x + 3** produces a new value without altering **x**.

If you want to use the left-shift operator to change the value of a variable, you must also use assignment. You can use regular assignment or the <<= operator, which combines shifting with assignment:

```
x = x << 4;        // regular assignment
y <<= 2;           // shift and assign
```

The right-shift operator (>>), as you might expect, shifts bits to the right. It has the following syntax:

value >> shift

Here *value* is the integer value to be shifted, and *shift* is the number of bits to shift. For example,

```
17 >> 2
```

means shift all the bits in the value **17** two places to the right. For unsigned integers, the vacated places are filled with zeros, and bits shifted past the end are discarded. For signed integers, vacated places may be filled with zeros or else with the value of the original leftmost bit. The choice depends on the C++ implementation. (Figure E.2 shows an example that illustrates filling with zeros.)

FIGURE E.2

The right-shift operator.

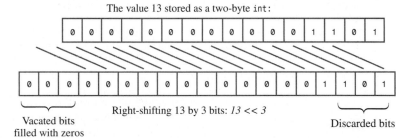

The value 13 stored as a two-byte int:

Right-shifting 13 by 3 bits: *13 << 3*

Vacated bits
filled with zeros

Discarded bits

Shifting one place to the right is equivalent to integer division by 2. In general, shifting n places to the right is equivalent to integer division by 2[n].

C++ also defines a right-shift-and-assign operator that you can use to replace the value of a variable by the shifted value:

```
int q = 43;
q >>= 2;                // replace 43 by 43 >> 2, or 10
```

On some systems, using left- and right-shift operators may produce faster integer multiplication and division by 2 than using the division operator, but as compilers get better at optimizing code, such differences are fading.

The Logical Bitwise Operators

The logical bitwise operators are analogous to the regular logical operators, except they apply to a value on a bit-by-bit basis rather than to the whole. For example, consider the regular negation operator (!) and the bitwise negation (or complement) operator (~). The ! operator converts a `true` (or nonzero) value to `false` and a `false` value to `true`. The ~ operator converts each individual bit to its opposite (1 to 0 and 0 to 1). For example, consider the `unsigned char` value of 3:

```
unsigned char x = 3;
```

The expression !x has the value 0. To see the value of ~x, you write it in binary form: 00000011. Then you convert each 0 to 1 and each 1 to 0. This produces the value 11111100, which in base 10 is the value 252. (Figure E.3 shows a 16-bit example.) The new value is termed the *complement* of the original value.

FIGURE E.3

The bitwise negation operator.

The value 13 stored as a two-byte int:

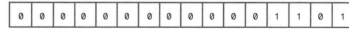

The value ~13— each 1 becomes a 0, and each 0 becomes a 1

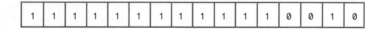

The bitwise OR operator (|) combines two integer values to produce a new integer value. Each bit in the new value is set to 1 if one or the other, or both, of the corresponding bits in the original values is set to 1. If both corresponding bits are 0, then the final bit is set to 0 (see Figure E.4).

Table E.1 summarizes how the | operator combines bits.

FIGURE E.4
The bitwise OR operator.

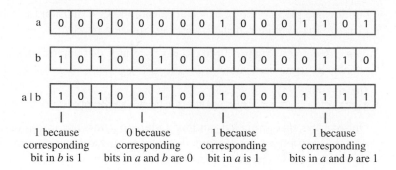

1 because corresponding bit in *b* is 1

0 because corresponding bits in *a* and *b* are 0

1 because corresponding bit in *a* is 1

1 because corresponding bits in *a* and *b* are 1

TABLE E.1   The Value of b1 | b2

Bit Values	b1 = 0	b1 = 1
b2 = 0	0	1
b2 = 1	1	1

The |= operator combines the bitwise OR operator with assignment:

```
a |= b;  // set a to a | b
```

The bitwise XOR operator (^) combines two integer values to produce a new integer value. Each bit in the new value is set to 1 if one or the other, but not both, of the corresponding bits in the original values is set to 1. If both corresponding bits are 0 or both are 1, the final bit is set to 0 (see Figure E.5).

FIGURE E.5
The bitwise XOR operator.

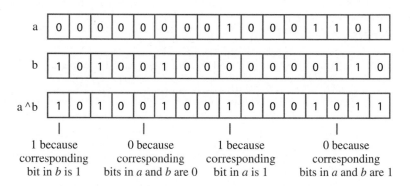

1 because corresponding bit in *b* is 1

0 because corresponding bits in *a* and *b* are 0

1 because corresponding bit in *a* is 1

0 because corresponding bits in *a* and *b* are 1

Table E.2 summarizes how the ^ operator combines bits.

TABLE E.2 The Value of b1 ^ b2

Bit Values	b1 = 0	b1 = 1
b2 = 0	0	1
b2 = 1	1	0

The ^= operator combines the bitwise XOR operator with assignment:

```
a ^= b;  // set a to a ^ b
```

The bitwise AND operator (&) combines two integer values to produce a new integer value. Each bit in the new value is set to 1 only if both of the corresponding bits in the original values are set to 1. If either or both corresponding bits are 0, the final bit is set to 0 (see Figure E.6).

FIGURE E.6
The bitwise AND operator.

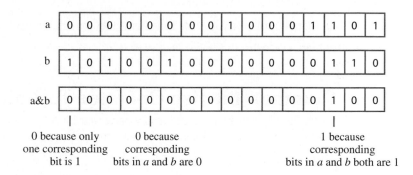

Table E.3 summarizes how the & operator combines bits.

TABLE E.3 The Value of b1 & b2

Bit Values	b1 = 0	b1 = 1
b2 = 0	0	0
b2 = 1	0	1

The &= operator combines the bitwise AND operator with assignment:

```
a &= b;  // set a to a & b
```

Alternative Representations of Bitwise Operators

C++ provides alternative representations of several bitwise operators, as shown in Table E.4. They are provided for locales that do not have the traditional bitwise operators as part of their character sets.

TABLE E.4   Bitwise Operator Representations

Standard Representation	Alternative Representation
&	bitand
&=	and_eq
|	bitor
|=	or_eq
~	compl
^	xor
^=	xor_eq

These alternative forms let you write statements like the following:

```
b = compl a bitand b;   // same as b = ~a & b;
c = a xor b;            // same as c = a ^ c;
```

A Few Common Bitwise Operator Techniques

Often, controlling hardware involves turning particular bits on or off or checking their status. The bitwise operators provide the means to perform such actions. We'll go through the methods quickly.

In the following examples, `lottabits` represents a general value, and `bit` represents the value corresponding to a particular bit. Bits are numbered from right to left, beginning with bit 0, so the value corresponding to bit position n is 2[n]. For example, an integer with only bit number 3 set to 1 has the value 2[3] or **8**. In general, each individual bit corresponds to a power of 2, as described for binary numbers in Appendix A. So we'll use the term *bit* to represent a power of 2; this corresponds to a particular bit being set to 1 and all other bits being set to **0**.

Turning a Bit On

The following two operations each turn on the bit in `lottabits` that corresponds to the bit represented by `bit`:

```
lottabits = lottabits | bit;
lottabits |= bit;
```

Each sets the corresponding bit to 1, regardless of the former value of the bit. That's because ORing 1 with either **0** or 1 produces 1. All other bits in `lottabits` remain unaltered. That's because ORing **0** with **0** produces **0**, and ORing **0** with 1 produces 1.

Toggling a Bit

The following two operations each toggle the bit in `lottabits` that corresponds to the bit represented by `bit`. That is, they turn the bit on if it is off, and they turn it off if it is on:

```
lottabits = lottabits ^ bit;
lottabits ^= bit;
```

XORing 1 with 0 produces 1, turning an off bit on, and XORing 1 with 1 produces 0, turning an on bit off. All other bits in `lottabits` remain unaltered. That's because XORing 0 with 0 produces 0, and XORing 0 with 1 produces 1.

Turning a Bit Off

The following operation turns off the bit in `lottabits` that corresponds to the bit represented by `bit`:

```
lottabits = lottabits & ~bit;
```

These statements turn the bit off, regardless of its prior state. First, the operator `~bit` produces an integer with all its bits set to 1 *except* the bit that originally was set to 1; that bit becomes 0. ANDing a 0 with any bit results in 0, thus turning that bit off. All other bits in `lottabits` are unchanged. That's because ANDing a 1 with any bit produces the value that bit had before.

Here's a briefer way of doing the same thing:

```
lottabits &= ~bit;
```

Testing a Bit Value

Suppose you want to determine whether the bit corresponding to `bit` is set to 1 in `lottabits`. The following test does not necessarily work:

```
if (lottabits == bit)          // no good
```

That's because even if the corresponding bit in `lottabits` is set to 1, other bits might also be set to 1. The equality above is true *only* when the corresponding bit is 1. The fix is to first AND `lottabits` with `bit`. This produces a value that is 0 in all the other bit positions because 0 AND any value is 0. Only the bit corresponding to the bit value is left unchanged because 1 AND any value is that value. Thus the proper test is this:

```
if (lottabits & bit == bit)    // testing a bit
```

Real-world programmers often simplify this test to the following:

```
if (lottabits & bit)         // testing a bit
```

Because `bit` consists of one bit set to 1 and the rest set to 0, the value of `lottabits & bit` is either 0 (which tests as `false`) or `bit`, which, being nonzero, tests as `true`.

Member Dereferencing Operators

C++ lets you define pointers to members of a class. These pointers involve special notations to declare them and to dereference them. To see what's involved, let's start with a sample class:

```
class Example
{
private:
    int feet;
    int inches;
public:
    Example();
    Example(int ft);
    ~Example();
    void show_in() const;
    void show_ft() const;
    void use_ptr() const;
};
```

Consider the `inches` member. Without a specific object, `inches` is a label. That is, the class defines `inches` as a member identifier, but you need an object before you actually have memory allocated:

```
Example ob;   // now ob.inches exists
```

Thus, you specify an actual memory location by using the identifier `inches` in conjunction with a specific object. (In a member function, you can omit the name of the object, but then the object is understood to be the one pointed to by the pointer.)

C++ lets you define a member pointer to the identifier `inches` like this:

```
int Example::*pt = &Example::inches;
```

This pointer is a bit different from a regular pointer. A regular pointer points to a specific memory location. But the `pt` pointer doesn't point to a specific memory location because the declaration doesn't identify a specific object. Instead, the pointer `pt` identifies the location of `inches` member within any `Example` object. Like the identifier `inches`, `pt` is designed to be used in conjunction with an object identifier. In essence, the expression `*pt` assumes the role of the identifier `inches`. Therefore, you can use an object identifier to specify which object to access and the `pt` pointer to specify the `inches` member of that object. For example, a class method could use this code:

```
int Example::*pt = &Example::inches;
Example ob1;
Example ob2;
Example *pq = new Example;
cout << ob1.*pt << endl; // display inches member of ob1
cout << ob2.*pt << endl; // display inches member of ob2
cout << po->pt << endl;  // display inches member of *po
```

Here `.*` and `->*` are *member dereferencing operators*. When you have a particular object, such as `ob1`, then `ob1.*pi` identifies the `inches` member of the `ob1` object. Similarly, `pq->*pt` identifies the `inches` member of an object pointed to by `pq`.

Changing the object in the preceding example changes which `inches` member is used. But you can also change the `pt` pointer itself. Because `feet` is of the same type as `inches`, you can reset `pt` to point to the `feet` member instead of the `inches` member; then `ob1.*pt` will refer to the feet member of `ob1`:

```
pt = &Example::feet;        // reset pt
cout << ob1.*pt << endl;   // display feet member of ob1
```

In essence, the combination `*pt` takes the place of a member name and can be used to identify different member names (of the same type).

You can also use member pointers to identify member functions. The syntax for this is relatively involved. Recall that declaring a pointer to an ordinary type `void` function with no arguments looks like this:

```
void (*pf)();  // pf points to a function
```

Declaring a pointer to a member function has to indicate that the function belongs to a particular class. Here, for instance, is how to declare a pointer to an `Example` class method:

```
void (Example::*pf)() const;  // pf points to an Example member function
```

This indicates that `pf` can be used the same places that `Example` method can be used. Note that the term `Example::*pf` has to be in parentheses. You can assign the address of a particular member function to this pointer:

```
pf = &Example::show_inches;
```

Note that, unlike in the case of ordinary function pointer assignment, here you can and must use the address operator. Having made this assignment, you can then use an object to invoke the member function:

```
Example ob3(20);
(ob3.*pf)();      // invoke show_inches() using the ob3 object
```

You need to enclose the entire `ob3.*pf` construction in parentheses in order to clearly identify the expression as representing a function name.

Because `show_feet()` has the same prototype form as `show_inches()`, you can use `pf` to access the `show_feet()` method, too:

```
pf = &Example::show_feet;
(ob3.*pf)();      // apply show_feet() to the ob3 object
```

The class definition presented in Listing E.1 has a `use_ptr()` method that uses member pointers to access both data members and function members of the `Example` class.

LISTING E.1   `memb_pt.cpp`

```
// memb_pt.cpp -- dereferencing pointers to class members
#include <iostream>
using namespace std;

class Example
{
```

LISTING E.1   Continued

```cpp
private:
    int feet;
    int inches;
public:
    Example();
    Example(int ft);
    ~Example();
    void show_in() const;
    void show_ft() const;
    void use_ptr() const;
};

Example::Example()
{
    feet = 0;
    inches = 0;
}

Example::Example(int ft)
{
    feet = ft;
    inches = 12 * feet;
}

Example::~Example()
{
}

void Example::show_in() const
{
    cout << inches << " inches\n";
}

void Example::show_ft() const
{
    cout << feet << " feet\n";
}

void Example::use_ptr() const
{
    Example yard(3);
    int Example::*pt;
    pt = &Example::inches;
    cout << "Set pt to &Example::inches:\n";
    cout << "this->pt: " << this->*pt << endl;
    cout << "yard.*pt: " << yard.*pt << endl;
    pt = &Example::feet;
    cout << "Set pt to &Example::feet:\n";
    cout << "this->pt: " << this->*pt << endl;
    cout << "yard.*pt: " << yard.*pt << endl;
    void (Example::*pf)() const;
    pf = &Example::show_in;
```

```
        cout << "Set pf to &Example::show_in:\n";
        cout << "Using (this->*pf)(): ";
        (this->*pf)();
        cout << "Using (yard.*pf)(): ";
        (yard.*pf)();
}

int main()
{
        Example car(15);
        Example van(20);
        Example garage;

        cout << "car.use_ptr() output:\n";
        car.use_ptr();
        cout << "\nvan.use_ptr() output:\n";
        van.use_ptr();

        return 0;
}
```

Here is a sample run of the program in Listing E.1:

```
car.use_ptr() output:
Set pt to &Example::inches:
this->pt: 180
yard.*pt: 36
Set pt to &Example::feet:
this->pt: 15
yard.*pt: 3
Set pf to &Example::show_in:
Using (this->*pf)(): 180 inches
Using (yard.*pf)(): 36 inches

van.use_ptr() output:
Set pt to &Example::inches:
this->pt: 240
yard.*pt: 36
Set pt to &Example::feet:
this->pt: 20
yard.*pt: 3
Set pf to &Example::show_in:
Using (this->*pf)(): 240 inches
Using (yard.*pf)(): 36 inches
```

This example assigned pointer values at compile time. In a more sophisticated class, you can use member pointers to data members and methods for which the exact member associated with the pointer is determined at runtime.

THE `string` TEMPLATE CLASS

M uch of this appendix is a bit technical. However, if you just want to know the capabilities of the `string` template class, you can concentrate on the descriptions of the various `string` methods.

The `string` class is based on a template definition:

```
template<class charT, class traits = char_traits<charT>,
            class Allocator = allocator<charT> >
class basic_string {...};
```

Here `charT` represents the type stored in the string. The **traits** parameter represents a class that defines necessary properties that a type must possess to be represented as a string. For example, it should have a `length()` method that returns the length of a string, represented as an array of type `charT`. The end of such an array is indicated by the value `charT(0)`, the generalization of the null character. (The expression `charT(0)` is a type cast of `0` to type `charT`. It could be just `0`, as it is for type `char`, or, more generally, it could be an object created by a `charT` constructor.) The class also includes methods for comparing values, and so on. The `Allocator` parameter represents a class to handle memory allocation for the string. The default `allocator<charT>` template uses `new` and `delete` in the standard ways.

There are two predefined specializations:

```
typedef basic_string<char> string;
typedef basic_string<wchar_t> wstring;
```

These specializations, in turn, use the following specializations:

```
char_traits<char>
allocator<char>
char_traits<wchar_t>
allocator<wchar_t>
```

You can create a `string` class for some type other than `char` or `wchar_t` by defining a `traits` class and using the `basic_string` template.

Thirteen Types and a Constant

The `basic_string` template defines several types that are used later in defining the methods:

```
typedef traits                                    traits_type;
typedef typename traits::char_type                value_type;
typedef Allocator                                 allocator_type;
typedef typename Allocator::size_type             size_type;
typedef typename Allocator::difference_type       difference_type;
typedef typename Allocator::reference             reference;
typedef typename Allocator::const_reference       const_reference;
typedef typename Allocator::pointer               pointer;
typedef typename Allocator::const_pointer         const_pointer;
```

Note that `traits` is a template parameter that corresponds to some specific type, such as `char_traits<char>`; `traits_type` becomes a `typedef` for that specific type. The notation

```
typedef typename traits::char_type                value_type;
```

means that `char_type` is a type name defined in the class represented by `traits`. The keyword `typename` is used to tell the compiler that the expression `traits::char_type` is a type. For the `string` specialization, for example, `value_type` is `char`.

`size_type` is used like `size_of`, except that it returns the size of a string in terms of the stored type. For the `string` specialization, that would be in terms of `char`, in which case `size_type` is the same as `size_of`. It is an unsigned type.

`difference_type` is used to measure the distance between two elements of a string, again in units corresponding to the size of a single element. Typically, it would be a signed version of the type underlying `size_type`.

For the `char` specialization, `pointer` is type `char *`, and `reference` is type `char &`. However, if you create a specialization for a type of your own design, these types (`pointer` and `reference`) could refer to classes that have the same properties as the more basic pointers and references.

To allow Standard Template Library (STL) algorithms to be used with strings, the template defines some iterator types:

```
typedef (models random access iterator)           iterator;
typedef (models random access iterator)           const_iterator;
typedef std::reverse_iterator<iterator>           reverse_iterator;
typedef std::reverse_iterator<const_iterator>     const_reverse_iterator;
```

The template defines a static constant:

```
static const size_type npos = -1;
```

Because `size_type` is unsigned, assigning the value `-1` actually amounts to assigning the largest possible unsigned value to `npos`. This value corresponds to one greater than the largest possible array index.

Data Information, Constructors, and Odds and Ends

Constructors can be described in terms of the effects they have. Because the private portions of a class can be implementation dependent, these effects should be described in terms of information available as part of the public interface. Table F.1 lists several methods whose return values can be used to describe the effects of constructors and of other methods. Note that much of the terminology is from the STL.

TABLE F.1 Some `string` Data Methods

Method	Returns
`begin()`	An iterator to the first character in a string (also available in a `const` version, which returns a `const` iterator).
`end()`	An iterator that is the past-the-end value (also available in a `const` version).
`rbegin()`	A reverse iterator that is the past-the-end value (also available in a `const` version).
`rend()`	A reverse iterator that refers to the first character (also available in a `const` version).
`size()`	The number of elements in a string, equal to the distance from `begin()` to `end()`.
`length()`	The same as `size()`.
`capacity()`	The allocated number of elements in a string. This can be greater than the actual number of characters. The value of `capacity() - size()` represents the number of characters that can be appended to a string before more memory needs be allocated.
`max_size()`	The maximum allowable size of a string.
`data()`	A pointer of type `const charT*` that points to the first element of an array whose first `size()` elements equal the corresponding elements in the string controlled by `*this`. The pointer should not be assumed to be valid after the `string` object itself has been modified.
`c_str()`	A pointer of type `const charT*` that points to the first element of an array whose first `size()` elements equal the corresponding elements in the string controlled by `*this` and whose next element is the `charT(0)` character (end-of-string marker) for the `charT` type. The pointer should not be assumed to be valid after the string object itself has been modified.
`get_allocator()`	A copy of the `allocator` object that is used to allocate memory for the `string` object.

Be careful of the differences among `begin()`, `rend()`, `data()`, and `c_str()`. All relate to the first character in a string, but in different ways. The `begin()` and `rend()` methods return iterators, which are generalizations of pointers, as described in Chapter 16, "The `string` Class and the Standard Template Library," discussion of the STL. In particular, `begin()` returns a model of a forward iterator, and `rend()` returns a copy of a reverse iterator. Both refer to the actual string managed by the `string` object. (Because the `string` class uses dynamic memory allocation, the actual string contents need not be inside the object, so we use the term *manage* to describe the relationship between object and string.) You can use the methods that return iterators with the iterator-based algorithms of the STL. For example, you can use the STL `reverse()` function to reverse the contents of a string:

```
string word;
cin >> word;
reverse(word.begin(), word.end());
```

The `data()` and `c_str()` methods, on the other hand, do return ordinary pointers. Furthermore, the returned pointers point to the first element of an *array* that holds the string characters. This array can, but need not, be a copy of the original string managed by the `string` object. (The internal representation used by the `string` object can be an array, but it doesn't have to be.) Because it is possible that the returned pointers point to the original data, they are `const`, so they can't be used to alter the data. Also, the pointers are not guaranteed to be valid after the string is modified; this reflects that they may point to the original data. The difference between `data()` and `c_str()` is that the array `c_str()` points to is terminated with a null character (or equivalent), whereas `data()` just guarantees that the actual string characters are present. Thus, the `c_str()` method can be used, for example, as an argument to a function that expects to receive a C-style string:

```
string file("tofu.man");
ofstream outFile(file.c_str());
```

Similarly, `data()` and `size()` could be used with a function that expects to receive a pointer to an array element and a value that represents the number of elements to process:

```
string vampire("Do not stake me, oh my darling!");
int vlad = byte_check(vampire.data(), vampire.size());
```

A C++ implementation could choose to represent a `string` object's string as a dynamically allocated C-style string and to implement the forward iterator as a `char *` pointer. In that case, the implementation could choose to have `begin()`, `data()`, and `c_str()` all return the same pointer. But it could just as legitimately (if not as easily) return references to three different data objects.

Here are the six constructors and one destructor for the `basic_string` template class:

```
explicit basic_string(const Allocator& a = Allocator());

basic_string(const charT* s, const Allocator& a = Allocator());

basic_string(const basic_string& str, size_type pos = 0,
    size_type n = npos, const Allocator& a = Allocator());
```

```
basic_string(const charT* s, size_type n,
    const Allocator& a = Allocator());

basic_string(size_type n, charT c, const Allocator& a = Allocator());

template<class InputIterator>
basic_string(InputIterator begin, InputIterator end,
    const Allocator& a = Allocator());

~basic_string();
```

Note that each of the six constructors has an argument of the following form:

```
const Allocator& a = Allocator()
```

Recall that the term **Allocator** is the template parameter name for an **allocator** class to manage memory. The term **Allocator()** is the default constructor for that class. Thus, the constructors, by default, use the default version of the **allocator** object, but they give you the option of using some other version of the **allocator** object. The following sections examine the constructors individually.

Default Constructors

This is the prototype for the default constructor:

```
explicit basic_string(const Allocator& a = Allocator());
```

Typically, you would accept the default argument for the **allocator** class and would use the constructor to create empty strings:

```
string bean;
wstring theory;
```

The following relationships hold after the constructor is called:

- The **data()** method returns a non-null pointer to which **0** can be added.
- The **size()** method returns **0**.
- The return value for **capacity()** is not specified.

Suppose you assign the value returned by **data()** to the pointer **str**. In this case, the first condition means **str + 0** is valid.

Constructors That Use Arrays

Constructors that use arrays let you initialize a **string** object from a C-style string; more generally, they let you initialize a **charT** specialization from an array of **charT** values:

```
basic_string(const charT* s, const Allocator& a = Allocator());
```

To determine how many characters to copy, the constructor applies the **traits::length()** method to the array pointed to by **s**. (The pointer **s** should not be a null pointer.) For example, the statement

```
string toast("Here's looking at you, kid.");
```

initializes the `toast` object, using the indicated character string. The `traits::length()` method for type `char` uses the null character to determine how many characters to copy.

The following relationships hold after the constructor is called:

- The `data()` method returns a pointer to the first element of a copy of the array `s`.

- The `size()` method returns a value equal to `traits::length()`.

- The `capacity()` method returns a value at least as large as `size()`.

Constructors That Use Part of an Array

Constructors that use part of an array let you initialize a `string` object from part of a C-style string; more generally, they let you initialize a `charT` specialization from part of an array of `charT` values:

```
basic_string(const charT* s, size_type n, const Allocator& a = Allocator());
```

This constructor copies to the constructed object a total of `n` characters from the array pointed to by `s`. Note that it doesn't stop copying if `s` has fewer characters than `n`. If `n` exceeds the length of `s`, the constructor interprets the contents of memory following the string as if they held data of type `charT`.

This constructor requires that `s` is not a null pointer and that `n < npos`. (Recall that `npos` is a static class constant equal to the maximum possible number of elements in a string.) If `n` equals `npos`, the constructor throws an `out_of_range` exception. (Because `n` is of type `size_type` and `npos` is the maximum `size_type` value, `n` cannot be greater than `npos`.) Otherwise, the following relationships hold after the constructor is called:

- The `data()` method returns a pointer to the first element of a copy of the array `s`.

- The `size()` method returns `n`.

- The `capacity()` method returns a value at least as large as `size()`.

Copy Constructors

A copy constructor provides several arguments with default values:

```
basic_string(const basic_string& str, size_type pos = 0, size_type n = npos,
    const Allocator& a = Allocator());
```

Calling a copy constructor with only a `basic_string` argument initializes the new object to the `string` argument:

```
string mel("I'm ok!");
string ida(mel);
```

Here `ida` would get a copy of the string managed by `mel`.

The optional second argument `pos` specifies a location in the source string from which to begin the copying:

```
string att("Telephone home.");
string et(att, 4);
```

Position numbers begin with `0`, so position `4` is the `p` character. Thus, `et` is initialized to `"Telephone home."`.

The optional third argument `n` specifies the maximum number of characters to copy. Thus,

```
string att("Telephone home.");
string pt(att, 4, 5);
```

initializes `pt` to the string `"Telephone"`. However, this constructor does not go past the end of the source string; for example,

```
string pt(att, 4, 200)
```

stops after copying the period. Thus, the constructor actually copies a number of characters equal to the lesser of `n` and `str.size() - pos`.

This constructor requires that `pos <= str.size()`—that is, that the initial position copied to is inside the source string; if this is not the case, the constructor throws an `out_of_range` exception. Otherwise, if `copy_len` represents the lesser of `n` and `str.size() - pos`, the following relationships hold after the constructor is called:

- The `data()` method returns a pointer to a copy of `copy_len` elements copied from the string `str`, starting with position `pos` in `str`.
- The `size()` method returns `copy_len`.
- The `capacity()` method returns a value at least as large as `size()`.

Constructors That Use n Copies of a Character

A constructor that uses `n` copies of a character creates a `string` object that consists of `n` consecutive characters, all having the value `c`:

```
basic_string(size_type n, charT c, const Allocator& a = Allocator());
```

This constructor requires that `n < npos`. If `n` equals `npos`, the constructor throws an `out_of_range` exception. Otherwise, the following relationships hold after the constructor is called:

- The `data()` method returns a pointer to the first element of a string of `n` elements, each set to `c`.
- The `size()` method returns `n`.
- The `capacity()` method returns a value at least as large as `size()`.

Constructors That Use a Range

A constructor that uses a range uses an iterator-defined range in the style of the STL:

```
template<class InputIterator>
basic_string(InputIterator begin, InputIterator end,
             const Allocator& a = Allocator());
```

The `begin` iterator points to the element in the source at which copying begins, and `end` points to one past the last location to be copied.

You can use this form with arrays, strings, or STL containers:

```
char cole[40] = "Old King Cole was a merry old soul.";
string title(cole + 4, cole + 8);
vector<char> input;
char ch;
while (cin.get(ch) && ch != '\n')
    input.push_back(ch);
string str_input(input.begin(), input.end());
```

In the first use, `InputIterator` is evaluated to type `const char *`. In the second use, `InputIterator` is evaluated to type `vector<char>::iterator`.

The following relationships hold after the constructor is called:

- The `data()` method returns a pointer to the first element of a string formed by copying elements from the range [begin, end).

- The `size()` method returns the distance between `begin` and `end`. (The distance is measured in units equal to the size of data type obtained when the iterator is dereferenced.)

- The `capacity()` method returns a value at least as large as `size()`.

Memory Miscellany

Several methods deal with memory—for example, clearing memory contents, resizing a string, adjusting the capacity of a string. Table F.2 lists some memory-related methods.

TABLE F.2   Some Memory-Related Methods

Method	Effect
`void resize(size_type n)`	Throws an `out_of_range` exception if n > npos. Otherwise, changes the size of a string to n, truncating the end of the string if n < `size()` and padding the string with `charT(0)` characters if n > `size()`.
`void resize(size_type n, charT c)`	Throws an `out_of_range` exception if n > npos. Otherwise, changes the size of a string to n, truncating the end of the string if n < `size()` and padding the string with the character c if n > `size()`.

Method	Effect
void reserve(size_type res_arg = 0)	Sets capacity() to greater than or equal to res_arg. Because this reallocates the string, it voids previous references, iterators, and pointers into the string.
void clear()	Removes all characters from a string.
bool empty() const	Returns true if size() == 0.

String Access

There are four methods for accessing individual characters, two of which use the [] operator, and two of which use the at() method:

```
reference operator[](size_type pos);

const_reference operator[](size_type pos) const;

reference at(size_type n);

const_reference at(size_type n) const;
```

The first operator[]() method allows you to access an individual element of a string by using array notation; it can be used to retrieve or alter the value. The second operator[]() method can be used with const objects, and it can be used only to retrieve the value:

```
string word("tack");
cout << word[0];     // display the t
word[3] = 't';       // overwrite the k with a t
const ward("garlic");
cout << ward[2];     // display the r
```

The at() methods provide similar access, except that the index is provided in function argument notation:

```
string word("tack");
cout << word.at(0);     // display the t
```

The difference (besides the syntax difference) is that the at() methods provide bounds checking and throw an out_of_range exception if pos >= size(). Note that pos is type size_type, which is unsigned; therefore, a negative value is impossible for pos. The operator[]() methods don't do bounds checking, so the behavior is undefined if pos >= size(), except that the const version returns the null character equivalent if pos == size().

Thus, you get a choice between safety (using at() and testing for exceptions) and execution speed (using array notation).

There is also a function that returns a new string that is a substring of the original:

```
basic_string substr(size_type pos = 0, size_type n = npos) const;
```

It returns a string that's a copy of the string starting at position **pos** and going for **n** characters or to the end of the string, whichever comes first. For example, the following initializes **pet** to "donkey":

```
string message("Maybe the donkey will learn to sing.");
string pet(message.substr(10, 6));
```

Basic Assignment

There are three overloaded assignment methods:

```
basic_string& operator=(const basic_string& str);

basic_string& operator=(const charT* s);

basic_string& operator=(charT c);
```

The first assigns one **string** object to another, the second assigns a C-style string to a **string** object, and the third assigns a single character to a **string** object. Thus, all the following operations are possible:

```
string name("George Wash");
string pres, veep, source;
pres = name;
veep = "Road Runner";
source = 'X';
```

String Searching

The **string** class provides six search functions, each with four prototypes. The following sections describe them briefly.

The find() Family

Here are the **find()** prototypes:

```
size_type find (const basic_string& str, size_type pos = 0) const;

size_type find (const charT* s, size_type pos = 0) const;

size_type find (const charT* s, size_type pos, size_type n) const;

size_type find (charT c, size_type pos = 0) const;
```

The first member returns the beginning position of the **str** substring's first occurrence in the invoking object, with the search beginning at position **pos**. If the substring is not found, the method returns **npos**.

Here's code for finding the location of the substring "hat" in a longer string:

```
string longer("That is a funny hat.");
string shorter("hat");
size_type loc1 = longer.find(shorter);          // sets loc1 to 1
size_type loc2 = longer.find(shorter, loc1 + 1); // sets loc2 to 16
```

Because the second search begins at position 2 (the a in That), the first occurrence of hat it finds is near the end of the string. To test for failure, you use the string::npos value:

```
if (loc1 == string::npos)
    cout << "Not found\n";
```

The second method does the same thing, except that it uses an array of characters instead of a string object as the substring:

```
size_type loc3 = longer.find("is");             //sets loc3 to 5
```

The third method does the same as the second, except that it uses only the first n characters of the string s. The effect is the same as using the basic_string(const charT* s, size_type n) constructor and using the resulting object as the string argument to the first form of find(). For example, the following searches for the substring "fun":

```
size_type loc4 = longer.find("funds", 3);       //sets loc4 to 10
```

The fourth method does the same thing as the first, except that it uses a single character instead of a string object as the substring:

```
size_type loc5 = longer.find('a');              //sets loc5 to 2
```

The rfind() Family

The rfind() methods have these prototypes:

```
size_type rfind(const basic_string& str, size_type pos = npos) const;

size_type rfind(const charT* s, size_type pos = npos) const;

size_type rfind(const charT* s, size_type pos, size_type n) const;

size_type rfind(charT c, size_type pos = npos) const;
```

These methods work like the analogous find() methods, except that they find the last occurrence of a string or character that starts at or before position pos. If the substring is not found, the method returns npos.

Here's code for finding the location of the substring "hat" in a longer string, starting at the end of the longer string:

```
string longer("That is a funny hat.");
string shorter("hat");
size_type loc1 = longer.rfind(shorter);          // sets loc1 to 16
size_type loc2 = longer.rfind(shorter, loc1 - 1); // sets loc2 to 1
```

The `find_first_of()` Family

The `find_first_of()` methods have these prototypes:

```
size_type find_first_of(const basic_string& str, size_type pos = 0) const;

size_type find_first_of(const charT* s, size_type pos, size_type n) const;

size_type find_first_of(const charT* s, size_type pos = 0) const;
size_type find_first_of(charT c, size_type pos = 0) const;
```

These methods work like the corresponding `find()` methods, except that instead of looking for a match of the entire substring, they look for the first match for any single character in the substring.

```
string longer("That is a funny hat.");
string shorter("fluke");
size_type loc1 = longer.find_first_of(shorter);  // sets loc1 to 10
size_type loc2 = longer.find_first_of("fat");    // sets loc2 to 2
```

The first occurrence of any of the five characters of `fluke` in `longer` is the `f` in `funny`. The first occurrence of any of three characters of `fat` in `longer` is the `a` in `That`.

The `find_last_of()` Family

The `find_last_of()` methods have these prototypes:

```
size_type find_last_of (const basic_string& str,
                        size_type pos = npos) const;

size_type find_last_of (const charT* s, size_type pos, size_type n) const;

size_type find_last_of (const charT* s, size_type pos = npos) const;

size_type find_last_of (charT c, size_type pos = npos) const;
```

These methods work like the corresponding `rfind()` methods, except that instead of looking for a match of the entire substring, they look for the last match for any single character in the substring.

Here's code for finding the location of the last and next to last occurrences of any of the letters in `"fluke"` in a longer string:

```
string longer("That is a funny hat.");
string shorter("hat");
size_type loc1 = longer.find_last_of(shorter);  // sets loc1 to 18
size_type loc2 = longer.find_last_of("any");    // sets loc2 to 17
```

The last occurrence of any of the three letters of `hat` in `longer` is the `t` in `hat`. The last occurrence of any of the three characters of `any` in `longer` is the `a` in `hat`.

The `find_first_not_of()` Family

The `find_first_not_of()` methods have these prototypes:

```
size_type find_first_not_of(const basic_string& str,
                            size_type pos = 0) const;

size_type find_first_not_of(const charT* s, size_type pos,
                            size_type n) const;

size_type find_first_not_of(const charT* s, size_type pos = 0) const;

size_type find_first_not_of(charT c, size_type pos = 0) const;
```

These methods work like the corresponding `find_first_of()` methods, except that they search for the first occurrence of any character not in the substring.

Here's code for finding the location of the first two occurrences of any of the letters not in `"This"` in a longer string:

```
string longer("That is a funny hat.");
string shorter("This");
size_type loc1 = longer.find_first_not_of(shorter);    // sets loc1 to 2
size_type loc2 = longer.find_first_not_of("Thatch"); // sets loc2 to 4
```

The `a` in `That` is the first character in `longer` that does not appear in `This`. The first space in the `longer` string is the first character not present in `Thatch`.

The `find_last_not_of()` Family

The `find_last_not_of()` methods have these prototypes:

```
size_type find_last_not_of (const basic_string& str,
                            size_type pos = npos) const;

size_type find_last_not_of (const charT* s, size_type pos,
                            size_type n) const;

size_type find_last_not_of (const charT* s, size_type pos = npos) const;

size_type find_last_not_of (charT c, size_type pos = npos) const;
```

These methods work like the corresponding `find_last_of()` methods, except that they search for the last occurrence of any character not in the substring.

Here's code for finding the location of the last two occurrences of any of the letters not in `"This"` in a longer string:

```
string longer("That is a funny hat.");
string shorter("That.");
size_type loc1 = longer.find_last_not_of(shorter);    // sets loc1 to 15
size_type loc2 = longer.find_last_not_of(shorter, 10); // sets loc2 to 10
```

The last space in `longer` is the last character in `longer` that does not appear in `shorter`. The `f` in the `longer` string is the last character not present in `shorter` found up through position 10.

Comparison Methods and Functions

The `string` class offers methods and functions for comparing two strings. First, here are the method prototypes:

```
int compare(const basic_string& str) const;

int compare(size_type pos1, size_type n1,
         const basic_string& str) const;

int compare(size_type pos1, size_type n1,
         const basic_string& str,
         size_type pos2, size_type n2) const;

int compare(const charT* s) const;

int compare(size_type pos1, size_type n1,
         const charT* s, size_type n2 = npos) const;
```

These methods use a `traits::compare()` method that is defined for the particular character type used for the string. The first method returns a value less than 0 if the first string precedes the second string according to the ordering supplied by `traits::compare()`. It returns **0** if the two strings are the same, and it returns a value greater than 0 if the first string follows the second. If two string are identical to the end of the shorter of the two strings, the shorter string precedes the longer string.

The following examples compare strings **s3** with **s3** and **s1** with **s2**:

```
string s1("bellflower");
string s2("bell");
string s3("cat");
int a13 = s1.compare(s3); // a13 is < 0
int a12 = s1.compare(s2); // a12 is> 0
```

The second method is like the first, except that it just uses **n1** characters, starting from position **pos1** in the first string, for the comparison.

The following example compares the first four characters in **s1** with **s2**:

```
string s1("bellflower");
string s2("bell");
int a2 = s1.compare(0, 4, s2); // a2 is 0
```

The third method is like the first, except that it just uses **n1** characters, starting from position **pos1** in the first string, and **n2** characters, starting from position **pos2** in the second string, for the comparison. For example, the following compares the **out** in **stout** to the **out** in **about**:

```
string st1("stout boar");
string st2("mad about ewe");
int a3 = st1.compare(2, 3, st2, 6, 3);  // a3 is 0
```

The fourth method is like the first, except that it uses a character array instead of a `string` object for the second string.

The fifth method is like the third, except that it uses a character array instead of a `string` object for the second string.

The non-member comparison functions are overloaded relational operators:

```
operator==()
operator<()
operator<=()
operator>()
operator>=()
operator!=()
```

Each operator is overloaded so that it can compare a `string` object to a `string` object, a `string` object to a string array, and a string array to a `string` object. These operators are defined in terms of the `compare()` method, so they provide a notationally more convenient way of making comparisons.

String Modifiers

The `string` class provides several methods for modifying strings. Most come with an abundance of overloaded versions so that they can be used with `string` objects, string arrays, individual characters, and iterator ranges.

Methods for Appending and Adding

You can append one string to another by using the overloaded `+=` operator or by using an `append()` method. All throw a `length_error` exception if the result would be longer than the maximum string size. The `+=` operators let you append a `string` object, a string array, or an individual character to another string:

```
basic_string& operator+=(const basic_string& str);

basic_string& operator+=(const charT* s);

basic_string& operator+=(charT c);
```

The `append()` methods also let you append a `string` object, a string array, or an individual character to another string. In addition, they let you append part of a `string` object by specifying an initial position and a number of characters to append or else by specifying a range. You can append part of a string by specifying how many characters of the string to use. The version for appending a character lets you specify how many instances of that character to copy. Here are the prototypes for the various `append()` methods:

```
basic_string& append(const basic_string& str);

basic_string& append(const basic_string& str, size_type pos,
                     size_type n);
```

```
template<class InputIterator>
  basic_string& append(InputIterator first, InputIterator last);

basic_string& append(const charT* s);

basic_string& append(const charT* s, size_type n);

basic_string& append(size_type n, charT c);   // append n copies of c
```

Here are a couple examples:

```
string test("The");
test.append("ory");   // test is "Theory"
test.append(3,'!');   // test is "Theory!!!"
```

The `operator+()` function is overloaded to enable string concatenation. The overloaded functions don't modify a string; instead, they create a new string that consists of one string appended to a second. The addition functions are not member functions, and they allow you to add a **string** object to a **string** object, a string array to a **string** object, a **string** object to a string array, a character to a **string** object, and a **string** object to a character. Here are some examples:

```
string st1("red");
string st2("rain");
string st3 = st1 + "uce"; // st3 is "reduce"
string st4 = 't' + st2;    // st4 is "train"
string st5 = st1 + st2;    // st5 is "redrain"
```

More Assignment Methods

In addition to the basic assignment operator, the **string** class provides **assign()** methods, which allow you to assign a whole string or a part of a string or a sequence of identical characters to a **string** object. Here are the prototypes for the various **assign()** methods:

```
basic_string& assign(const basic_string&);

basic_string& assign(const basic_string& str, size_type pos,
                     size_type n);

basic_string& assign(const charT* s, size_type n);

basic_string& assign(const charT* s);

basic_string& assign(size_type n, charT c); // assign n copies of c

template<class InputIterator>
  basic_string& assign(InputIterator first, InputIterator last);
```

Here are a couple examples:

```
string test;
string stuff("set tubs clones ducks");
test.assign(stuff, 1, 5);   // test is "et tu"
test.assign(6, '#');        // test is "######"
```

Insertion Methods

The insert() methods let you insert a **string** object, a string array, a character, or several characters into a **string** object. The methods are similar to the **append()** methods, except that they take an additional argument, indicating where to insert the new material. This argument may be a position or an iterator. The material is inserted before the insertion point. Several of the methods return a reference to the resulting string. If **pos1** is beyond the end of the target string or if **pos2** is beyond the end of the string to be inserted, a method throws an **out_of_range** exception. If the resulting string will be larger than the maximum size, a method throws a **length_error** exception. Here are the prototypes for the various **insert()** methods:

```
basic_string& insert(size_type pos1, const basic_string& str);

basic_string& insert(size_type pos1, const basic_string& str,
                     size_type pos2, size_type n);

basic_string& insert(size_type pos, const charT* s, size_type n);

basic_string& insert(size_type pos, const charT* s);

basic_string& insert(size_type pos, size_type n, charT c);

iterator insert(iterator p, charT c = charT());

void insert(iterator p, size_type n, charT c);

template<class InputIterator>
  void insert(iterator p, InputIterator first, InputIterator last);
```

For example, the following code inserts the string `"former "` before the **b** in `"The banker."`:

```
string st3("The banker.");
st3.insert(4, "former ");
```

Then the following code inserts the string `" waltzed"` (not including the !, which would be the ninth character) just before the period at the end of `"The former banker."`:

```
st3.insert(st3.size() - 1, " waltzed!", 8);
```

Erase Methods

The erase() methods remove characters from a string. Here are their prototypes:

```
basic_string& erase(size_type pos = 0, size_type n = npos);

iterator erase(iterator position);

iterator erase(iterator first, iterator last);
```

The first form removes the character from position **pos** to n characters later, or the end of the string, whichever comes first. The second removes the single character referenced by the iterator position and returns an iterator to the next element, or, if there are no more elements, returns `end()`. The third removes the characters in the range [`first`, `last`); that is, including `first` and up to but not including `last`. The method returns an iterator to the element following the last element erased.

Replacement Methods

The various `replace()` methods identify part of a string to be replaced and identify the replacement. The part to be replaced can be identified by an initial position and a character count or by an iterator range. The replacement can be a `string` object, a string array, or a particular character duplicated several times. Replacement `string` objects and arrays can further be modified by indicating a particular portion, using a position and a count, just a count, or an iterator range. Here are the prototypes for the various `replace()` methods:

```
basic_string& replace(size_type pos1, size_type n1, const basic_string& str);

basic_string& replace(size_type pos1, size_type n1, const basic_string& str,
                      size_type pos2, size_type n2);

basic_string& replace(size_type pos, size_type n1, const charT* s,
                      size_type n2);

basic_string& replace(size_type pos, size_type n1, const charT* s);

basic_string& replace(size_type pos, size_type n1, size_type n2, charT c);

basic_string& replace(iterator i1, iterator i2, const basic_string& str);

basic_string& replace(iterator i1, iterator i2, const charT* s, size_type n);

basic_string& replace(iterator i1, iterator i2, const charT* s);

basic_string& replace(iterator i1, iterator i2,
                      size_type n, charT c);

template<class InputIterator>
  basic_string& replace(iterator i1, iterator i2,
                        InputIterator j1, InputIterator j2);
```

Here is an example:

```
string test("Take a right turn at Main Street.");
test.replace(7,5,"left"); // replace right with left
```

Note that you can use `find()` to find the positions used in `replace`:

```
string s1 = "old";
string s2 = "mature";
string s3 = "The old man and the sea";
string::size_type pos = s3.find(s1);
if (pos != string::npos)
    s3.replace(pos, s1.size(), s2);
```

This example would replace `old` with `mature`.

Other Modifying Methods: copy() and swap()

The copy() method copies a string object, or part thereof, to a designated character array:

```
size_type copy(charT* s, size_type n, size_type pos = 0) const;
```

In this case, s points to the destination array, n indicates the number of characters to copy, and pos indicates the position in the string object from which copying begins. Copying proceeds for n characters or until the last character in the string object, whichever comes first. The function returns the number of characters copied. The method does not append a null character, and it is up to the programmer to see that the array is large enough to hold the copy.

Caution

The copy() method does not append a null character, nor does it check whether the destination array is large enough.

The swap() method swaps the contents of two string objects by using a constant time algorithm:

```
void swap(basic_string<charT,traits,Allocator>&);
```

Output and Input

The string class overloads the << operator to display string objects. It returns a reference to the istream object so that output can be concatenated:

```
string claim("The string class has many features.");
cout << claim << endl;
```

The string class overloads the >> operator so that you can read input into a string:

```
string who;
cin >> who;
```

Input terminates on the end-of-file, on reading the maximum number of characters allowed in a string, or on reaching a white-space character. (The definition of white space depends on the character set and on the type that charT represents.)

There are two getline() functions. The first has this prototype:

```
template<class charT, class traits, class Allocator>
  basic_istream<charT,traits>& getline(basic_istream<charT,traits>& is,
            basic_string<charT,traits,Allocator>& str, charT delim);
```

It reads characters from the input stream is into the string str until it encounters the delim delimiter character, reaches the maximum size of the string, or encounters the end-of-file. The delim character is read (that is, removed from the input stream) but not stored. The second version lacks the third argument and uses the newline character (or its generalization) instead of `delim`:

```
string str1, str2;
getline(cin, str1);        // read to end-of-line
getline(cin, str2, '.');  // read to period
```

THE STL METHODS AND FUNCTIONS

The Standard Template Library (STL) aims to provide efficient implementations of common algorithms. It expresses these algorithms in general functions that can be used with any container that satisfies the requirements for the particular algorithm and in methods that can be used with instantiations of particular container classes. This appendix assumes that you have some familiarity with the STL, such as might be gained from reading Chapter 16, "The `string` Class and the Standard Template Library." For example, this chapter assumes that you know about iterators and constructors.

Members Common to All Containers

All containers define the types in Table G.1. In this table, X is a container type, such as `vector<int>`, and T is the type stored in the container, such as `int`. The examples following the table clarify the meanings.

TABLE G.1 Types Defined for All Containers

Type	Value
X::value_type	T, the element type
X::reference	T &
X::const_reference	const T &
X::iterator	Iterator type pointing to T, behaves like type T *
X::const_iterator	Iterator type pointing to const T, behaves like type const T *
X::difference_type	Signed integral type used to represent the distance from one iterator to another (for example, the difference between two pointers)
X::size_type	Unsigned integral type size_type can represent size of data objects, number of elements, and subscripts

The class definition uses a **typedef** to define these members. You can use these types to declare suitable variables. For example, the following code uses a roundabout way to replace the first occurrence of `"bonus"` in a vector of **string** objects with `"bogus"` in order to show how you can use member types to declare variables:

```
vector<string> input;
string temp;
while (cin >> temp && temp != "quit")
    input.push_back(temp);
vector<string>::iterator want=
    find(input.begin(), input.end(), string("bonus"));
if (want != input.end())
{
    vector<string>::reference r = *want;
    r = "bogus";
}
```

This code makes `r` a reference to the element in **input** to which `want` points. Similarly, continuing with the preceding example, you can write code like the following:

```
vector<string>::value_type s1 = input[0];   // s1 is type string
vector<string>::reference s2 = input[1];    // s2 is type string &
```

This results in `s1` being a new **string** object that's a copy of `input[0]` and in `s2` being a reference to `input[1]`. In this example, given that you already know that the template is based on the **string** type, it would be simpler to write the following code, which is equivalent in its effect:

```
string s1 = input[0];      // s1 is type string
string & s2 = input[1];    // s2 is type string &
```

However, the more elaborate types from Table G.1 can also be used in more general code in which the type of container and element are generic. For example, suppose you want a **min()** function that takes as its argument a reference to a container and returns the smallest item in the container. This assumes that the < operator is defined for the value type used to instantiate the template and that you don't want to use the STL **min_element()** algorithm, which uses an iterator interface. Because the argument could be **vector<int>** or **list<string>** or **deque<double>**, you use a template with a template parameter, such as **Bag**, to represent the container. (That is, **Bag** is a template type that might be instantiated as **vector<int>**, **list<string>**, or some other container type.) So the argument type for the function is **const Bag & b**. What about the return type? It should be the value type for the container—that is, **Bag::value_type**. However, at this point, **Bag** is just a template parameter, and the compiler has no way of knowing that the **value_type** member is actually a type. But you can use the **typename** keyword to clarify that a class member is a **typedef**:

```
vector<string>::value_type st;   // vector<string> a defined class
typename Bag::value_type m;       // Bag an as yet undefined type
```

For the first definition here, the compiler has access to the **vector** template definition, which states that **value_type** is a **typedef**. For the second definition, the **typename** keyword promises that, whatever **Bag** may turn out to be, the combination **Bag::value_type** is the name of a type. These considerations lead to the following definition:

```
template<typename Bag>
typename Bag::value_type min(const Bag & b)
{
    typename Bag::const_iterator it;
    typename Bag::value_type m = *b.begin();
    for (it = b.begin(); it != b.end(); ++it)
        if (*it < m)
            m = *it;
    return m;
}
```

You then could use this template function as follows:

```
vector<int> temperatures;
// input temperature values into the vector
int coldest = min(temperatures);
```

The `temperatures` parameter would cause `Bag` to be evaluated as `vector<int>` and `typename Bag::value_type` to be evaluated as `vector<int>::value_type`, which, in turn, is `int`.

All containers also contain the member functions or operations listed in Table G.2. Again, `X` is a container type, such as `vector<int>`, and `T` is the type stored in the container, such as `int`. Also, `a` and `b` are values of type `X`.

TABLE G.2   Methods Defined for All Containers

Method/Operation	Description
begin()	Returns an iterator to the first element
end()	Returns an iterator to past the end
rbegin()	Returns a reverse iterator to past the end
rend()	Returns a reverse iterator to the first element
size()	Returns the number of elements
maxsize()	Returns the size of the largest possible container
empty()	Returns true if the container is empty
swap()	Swaps the contents of two containers
==	Returns true if two containers are the same size and have the same elements in the same order
!=	a != b returns !(a == b)
<	a < b returns true if a lexicographically precedes b
>	a > b returns b < a
<=	a <= b returns !(a > b)
>=	a >= b returns !(a < b)

The > operator for a container assumes that the > operator is defined for the value type. A lexicographic comparison is a generalization of alphabetical sorting. It compares two containers, element-by-element, until it encounters an element in one container that doesn't equal the corresponding element in the other container. In that case, the containers are considered to be in the same order as the noncorresponding pair of elements. For example, if two containers are identical through the first 10 elements, but the 11th element in the first container is less than the 11th element in the second container, the first container precedes the second. If two containers compare equally until one runs out of elements, the shorter container precedes the longer.

Additional Members for Vectors, Lists, and Deques

Vectors, lists, and deques are all sequences, and they all have the methods listed in Table G.3. Again, X is a container type, such as `vector<int>`, and T is the type stored in the container, such as `int`, a is a value of type X, t is a value of `type X::value_type`, i and j are input iterators, q2 and p are iterators, q and q1 are dereferenceable iterators (that is, you can apply the * operator to them), and n is an integer of `X::size_type`.

TABLE G.3   Methods Defined for Vectors, Lists, and Deques

Method	Description
`a.insert(p,t)`	Inserts a copy of t before p; returns an iterator pointing to the inserted copy of t. The default value for t is `T()`—that is, the value used for type T in the absence of explicit initialization.
`a.insert(p,n,t)`	Inserts n copies of t before p; no return value.
`a.insert(p,i,j)`	Inserts copies of the elements in the range [i, j) before p; no return value.
`a.resize(n,t)`	If n > a.size(), inserts n - a.size() copies of t before a.end(); t has a default value of `T()`—that is, the value used for type T in the absence of explicit initialization. If n < a.size(), the elements following the nth element are erased.
`a.assign(i,j)`	Replaces the current contents of a with copies of the elements in the range [i, j).
`a.assign(n,t)`	Replaces the current contents of a with n copies of t. The default value for t is `T()`,the value used for type T in the absence of explicit initialization.
`a.erase(q)`	Erases the element pointed to by q; returns an iterator to the element that had followed q.
`a.erase(q1,q2)`	Erases the elements in the range [q1, q2); returns an iterator pointing to the element that q2 originally pointed to.

TABLE G.3 Continued

Method	Description
`a.clear()`	Does the same thing as `erase(a.begin(), a.end())`.
`a.front()`	Returns `*a.begin()` (the first element).
`a.back()`	Returns `*--a.end()` (the last element).
`a.push_back(t)`	Inserts `t` before `a.end()`.
`a.pop_back()`	Erases the last element.

Table G.4 lists methods common to two of the three sequence classes (`vector`, `list`, and `deque`).

TABLE G.4 Methods Defined for Some Sequences

Method	Description	Container
`a.push_front(t)`	Inserts a copy of `t` before the first element.	`list`, `deque`
`a.pop_front()`	Erases the first element.	`list`, `deque`
`a[n]`	Returns `*(a.begin() + n)`.	`vector`, `deque`
`a.at(n)`	Returns `*(a.begin() + n)`; throws `out_of_range` exception if `n > a.size()`.	`vector`, `deque`

The `vector` template additionally has the methods in Table G.5. Here, `a` is a `vector` container and `n` is an integer of `X::size_type`.

TABLE G.5 Additional Methods for Vectors

Method	Description
`a.capacity()`	Returns the total number of elements the vector can hold without requiring reallocation.
`a.reserve(n)`	Alerts object `a` that memory for at least `n` elements is needed. After the method call, the capacity will be at least `n` elements. Reallocation occurs if `n` is greater than the current capacity. If `n` is greater than `a.max_size()`, the method throws a `length_error` exception.

The `list` template additionally has the methods in Table G.6. Here, `a` and `b` are `list` containers, and `T` is the type stored in the list, such as `int`, `t` is a value of type `T`, `i` and `j` are input iterators, `q2` and `p` are iterators, `q` and `q1` are dereferenceable iterators, and `n` is an integer of `X::size_type`. The table uses the standard STL notation `[i, j)`, meaning the range from `i` up to, but not including, `j`.

TABLE G.6   Additional Methods for Lists

Method	Description
`a.splice(p,b)`	Moves the contents of list `b` to list `a`, inserting them before `p`.
`a.splice(p,b,i)`	Moves the element in list `b` pointed to by `i` to before position `p` in list `a`.
`a.splice(p,b,i,j)`	Moves the elements in the range `[i, j)` of list `b` to before position `p` in list `a`.
`a.remove(const T& t)`	Erases all elements in list `a` that have the value `t`.
`a.remove_if(Predicate pred)`	Given that `i` is an iterator into list `a`, erases all values for which `pred(*i)` is `true`. (`Predicate` is a Boolean function or function object, as discussed in Chapter 15, "Friends, Exceptions, and More.")
`a.unique()`	Erases all but the first element from each group of consecutive equal elements.
`a.unique(BinaryPredicate bin_pred)`	Erases all but the first element from each group of consecutive elements for which `bin_pred(*i, *(i - 1))` is `true`. (`BinaryPredicate` is a Boolean function or function object, as discussed in Chapter 15.)
`a.merge(b)`	Merges the contents of list `b` with list `a`, using the `<` operator defined for the value type. If an element in `a` is equivalent to an element in `b`, the element from `a` is placed first. List `b` is empty after the merge.
`a.merge(b, Compare comp)`	Merges the contents of list `b` with list `a`, using the `comp` function or function object. If an element in `a` is equivalent to an element in `b`, the element from `a` is placed first. List `b` is empty after the merge.
`a.sort()`	Sorts list `a`, using the `<` operator.
`a.sort(Compare comp)`	Sorts list `a`, using the `comp` function or function object.
`a.reverse()`	Reverses the order of the elements in list `a`.

Additional Members for Sets and Maps

Associative containers, of which sets and maps are models, have a `Key` template parameter and a `Compare` template parameter, which indicate, respectively, the type of the `key` used to order the contents and the function object, termed a *comparison object*, used to compare key values. For the `set` and `multiset` containers, the stored keys are the stored values, so the key type is the same as the value type. For the `map` and `multimap` containers, the stored values of one type (template parameter `T`) are associated with a key type (template parameter `Key`), and the value type is `pair<const Key, T>`. Associative containers have additional members to describe these features, as listed in Table G.7.

TABLE G.7 Types Defined for Associative Containers

Type	Value
X::key_type	Key, the key type
X::key_compare	Compare, which has a default value of less<key_type>
X::value_compare	A binary predicate type that is the same as key_compare for set and multiset and that supplies ordering for the pair<const Key, T> values in a map or multimap container
X::mapped_type	T, the type of the associated data (map and multimap only)

Associative containers provide the methods listed in Table G.8. In general, the comparison object need not require that values with the same key be identical; the term *equivalent keys* means that two values, which may or may not be equal, have the same key. In the table, `X` is a container class, and `a` is an object of type `X`. If `X` uses unique keys (that is, is `set` or `map`), `a_uniq` is an object of type `X`. If `X` uses multiple keys (that is, is `multiset` or `multimap`), `a_eq` is an object of type `X`. As before, `i` and `j` are input iterators referring to elements of `value_type`, `[i, j)` is a valid range, `p` and `q2` are iterators to `a`, `q` and `q1` are dereferenceable iterators to `a`, `[q1, q2)` is a valid range, `t` is a value of `X::value_type` (which may be a pair), and `k` is a value of `X::key_type`.

TABLE G.8 Methods Defined for Sets, Multisets, Maps, and Multimaps

Method	Description
a.key_comp()	Returns the comparison object used in constructing a.
a.value_comp()	Returns an object of the value_compare type.

TABLE G.8 Continued

Method	Description
a_uniq.insert(t)	Inserts the value t into the container a if and only if a does not yet contain a value with an equivalent key. The method returns a value of type pair<iterator,bool>. The bool component is true if insertion occurred and false otherwise. The iterator component points to the element whose key is equivalent to the key of t.
a_eq.insert(t)	Inserts t and returns an iterator that points to its location.
a.insert(p,t)	Inserts t, using p as a hint to where insert() should begin its search. If a is a container with unique keys, insertion takes place if and only if a doesn't contain an element with an equivalent key; otherwise, insertion takes place. Whether or not insertion takes place, the method returns an iterator that points to the location with an equivalent key.
a.insert(i,j)	Inserts elements from the range [i, j) into a.
a.erase(k)	Erases all elements in a whose keys are equivalent to k and returns the number of elements erased.
a.erase(q)	Erases the element pointed to by q.
a.erase(q1,q2)	Erases the elements in the range [q1, q2).
a.clear()	Does the same thing as erase(a.begin(), a.end()).
a.find(k)	Returns an iterator that points to an element whose key is equivalent to k; returns a.end() if no such element is found.
a.count(k)	Returns the number of elements that have keys equivalent to k.
a.lower_bound(k)	Returns an iterator to the first element that have a key not less than k.
a.upper_bound(k)	Returns an iterator to the first element that have a key greater than k.
a.equal_range(k)	Returns a pair whose first member is a.lower_bound(k) and whose second member is a.upper_bound(k).
a.operator[](k)	Returns a reference to the value associated with the key k (map containers only).

STL Functions

The STL algorithm library, supported by the algorithm and numeric header files, provides a large number of nonmember, iterator-based template functions. As discussed in Chapter 16, the template parameter names are chosen to indicate what concept particular parameters should model. For example, ForwardIterator is used to indicate that a parameter should, at the minimum, model the requirements of a forward iterator, and `Predicate` is used to indicate a parameter that should be a function object with one argument and a `bool` return value. The C++ Standard divides the algorithms into four groups: nonmodifying sequence operations, mutating sequence operations, sorting and related operators, and numeric operations. The term *sequence operation* indicates that the function takes a pair of iterators as arguments to define a range, or sequence, to be operated on. The term *mutating* means the function is allowed to alter the container.

Nonmodifying Sequence Operations

Table G.9 summarizes the nonmodifying sequence operations. Arguments are not shown, and overloaded functions are listed just once. A fuller description, including the prototypes, follows the table. Thus, you can scan the table to get an idea of what a function does and then look up the details if you find the function appealing.

TABLE G.9 Nonmodifying Sequence Operations

Function	Description
`for_each()`	Applies a nonmodifying function object to each element in a range.
`find()`	Finds the first occurrence of a value in a range.
`find_if()`	Finds the first value that satisfies a predicate test criterion in a range.
`find_end()`	Finds the last occurrence of a subsequence whose values match the values of a second sequence. Matching may be by equality or by applying a binary predicate.
`find_first_of()`	Finds the first occurrence of any element of a second sequence that matches a value in the first sequence. Matching may be by equality or may be evaluated with a binary predicate.
`adjacent_find()`	Finds the first element that matches the element immediately following it. Matching may be by equality or may be evaluated with a binary predicate.
`count()`	Returns the number of times a given value occurs in a range.
`count_if()`	Returns the number of times a given value matches values in a range, with a match determined by using a binary predicate.
`mismatch()`	Finds the first element in one range that does not match the corresponding element in a second range and returns iterators to both. Matching may be by equality or may be evaluated with a binary predicate.
`equal()`	Returns `true` if each element in one range matches the corresponding element in a second range. Matching may be by equality or may be evaluated with a binary predicate.

TABLE G.9 Continued

Function	Description
search()	Finds the first occurrence of a subsequence whose values match the values of a second sequence. Matching may be by equality or by applying a binary predicate.
search_n()	Finds the first subsequence of n elements that each match a given value. Matching may be by equality or by applying a binary predicate.

Now let's take a more detailed look at these nonmodifying sequence operations. For each function, the discussion shows the prototype(s), followed by a brief explanation. Pairs of iterators indicate ranges, with the chosen template parameter name indicating the type of iterator. As usual a range in the form [first, last) goes from first up to, but not including, last. Some functions take two ranges, which need not be in the same kind of container. For example, you can use equal() to compare a list to a vector. Functions passed as arguments are function objects, which can be pointers (of which function names are an example) or objects for which the () operation is defined. As in Chapter 16, a predicate is a Boolean function with one argument, and a binary predicate is a Boolean function with two arguments. (The functions need not be type bool, as long as they return 0 for false and a nonzero value for true.)

for_each()

```
template<class InputIterator, class Function>
Function for_each(InputIterator first, InputIterator last, Function f);
```

The for_each() function applies function object f to each element in the range [first, last). It also returns f.

find()

```
template<class InputIterator, class T>
InputIterator find(InputIterator first, InputIterator last, const T& value);
```

The find() function returns an iterator to the first element in the range [first, last) that has the value value; it returns last if the item is not found.

find_if()

```
template<class InputIterator, class Predicate>
InputIterator find_if(InputIterator first, InputIterator last,
                      Predicate pred);
```

The find_if() function returns an iterator it to the first element in the range [first, last) for which the function object call pred(*i) is true; it returns last if the item is not found.

find_end()

```
template<class ForwardIterator1, class ForwardIterator2>
ForwardIterator1 find_end(ForwardIterator1 first1, ForwardIterator1 last1,
                          ForwardIterator2 first2, ForwardIterator2 last2);
```

```
template<class ForwardIterator1, class ForwardIterator2,
    class BinaryPredicate>
ForwardIterator1 find_end(ForwardIterator1 first1, ForwardIterator1 last1,
                    ForwardIterator2 first2, ForwardIterator2 last2,
                    BinaryPredicate pred);
```

The `find_end()` function returns an iterator `it` to the last element in the range [`first1`, `last1`) that marks the beginning of a subsequence that matches the contents of the range [`first2`, `last2`). The first version uses the == operator for the value type to compare elements. The second version uses the binary predicate function object `pred` to compare elements. That is, elements pointed to by `it1` and `it2` match if `pred(*it1, *it2)` is `true`. Both return `last1` if the item is not found.

find_first_of()

```
template<class ForwardIterator1, class ForwardIterator2>
ForwardIterator1 find_first_of(
                    ForwardIterator1 first1, ForwardIterator1 last1,
                    ForwardIterator2 first2, ForwardIterator2 last2);

template<class ForwardIterator1, class ForwardIterator2,
        class BinaryPredicate>
ForwardIterator1 find_first_of(
                    ForwardIterator1 first1, ForwardIterator1 last1,
                    ForwardIterator2 first2, ForwardIterator2 last2,
                    BinaryPredicate pred);
```

The `find_first_of()` function returns an iterator `it` to the first element in the range [`first1`, `last1`) that matches any element of the range [`first2`, `last2`). The first version uses the == operator for the value type to compare elements. The second version uses the binary predicate function object `pred` to compare elements. That is, elements pointed to by `it1` and `it2` match if `pred(*it1, *it2)` is `true`. Both return `last1` if the item is not found.

adjacent_find()

```
template<class ForwardIterator>
ForwardIterator adjacent_find(ForwardIterator first, ForwardIterator last);

template<class ForwardIterator, class BinaryPredicate>
ForwardIterator adjacent_find(ForwardIterator first, ForwardIterator last,
                        BinaryPredicate pred);
```

The `adjacent_find()` function returns an iterator `it` to the first element in the range [`first1`, `last1`) such that the element matches the following element. The function returns `last` if no such pair is found. The first version uses the == operator for the value type to compare elements. The second version uses the binary predicate function object `pred` to compare elements. That is, elements pointed to by `it1` and `it2` match if `pred(*it1, *it2)` is `true`.

count()

```
template<class InputIterator, class T>
iterator_traits<InputIterator>::difference_type count(
                InputIterator first, InputIterator last, const T& value);
```

The count() function returns the number of elements in the range [first, last) that match the value value. The == operator for the value type is used to compare values. The return type is an integer type that is large enough to contain the maximum number of items the container can hold.

count_if()

```
template<class InputIterator, class Predicate>
iterator_traits<InputIterator>::difference_type count_if(
            InputIterator first, InputIterator last, Predicate pred);
```

The count if() function returns the number of elements in the range [first, last) for which the function object pred returns a true value when passed the element as an argument.

mismatch()

```
template<class InputIterator1, class InputIterator2>
pair<InputIterator1, InputIterator2> mismatch(InputIterator1 first1,
                InputIterator1 last1, InputIterator2 first2);

template<class InputIterator1, class InputIterator2, class BinaryPredicate>
pair<InputIterator1, InputIterator2> mismatch(InputIterator1 first1,
                InputIterator1 last1, InputIterator2 first2,
                BinaryPredicate pred);
```

Each of the mismatch() functions finds the first element in the range [first1, last1) that doesn't match the corresponding element in the range beginning at first2 and returns a pair holding iterators to the two mismatching elements. If no mismatch is found, the return value is pair<last1, first2 + (last1 - first1)>. The first version uses the == operator to test matching. The second version uses the binary predicate function object pred to compare elements. That is, elements pointed to by it1 and it2 don't match if pred(*it1, *it2) is false.

equal()

```
template<class InputIterator1, class InputIterator2>
bool equal(InputIterator1 first1, InputIterator1 last1,
        InputIterator2 first2);

template<class InputIterator1, class InputIterator2, class BinaryPredicate>
bool equal(InputIterator1 first1, InputIterator1 last1,
        InputIterator2 first2, BinaryPredicate pred);
```

The equal() function returns true if each element in the range [first1, last1) matches the corresponding element in the sequence beginning at first2 and false otherwise. The first version uses the == operator for the value type to compare elements. The second version uses the binary predicate function object pred to compare elements. That is, elements pointed to by it1 and it2 match if pred(*it1, *it2) is true.

search()

```
template<class ForwardIterator1, class ForwardIterator2>
ForwardIterator1 search(ForwardIterator1 first1, ForwardIterator1 last1,
                    ForwardIterator2 first2, ForwardIterator2 last2);

template<class ForwardIterator1, class ForwardIterator2,
        class BinaryPredicate>
ForwardIterator1 search(ForwardIterator1 first1, ForwardIterator1 last1,
                    ForwardIterator2 first2, ForwardIterator2 last2,
                    BinaryPredicate pred);
```

The search() function finds the first occurrence in the range [first1, last1) that matches the corresponding sequence found in the range [first2, last2). It returns last1 if no such sequence is found. The first version uses the == operator for the value type to compare elements. The second version uses the binary predicate function object pred to compare elements. That is, elements pointed to by it1 and it2 match if pred(*it1, *it2) is true.

search_n()

```
template<class ForwardIterator, class Size, class T>
ForwardIterator  search_n(ForwardIterator first, ForwardIterator last,
                    Size count, const T& value);

template<class ForwardIterator, class Size, class T, class BinaryPredicate>
ForwardIterator search_n(ForwardIterator first, ForwardIterator last,
                    Size count, const T& value, BinaryPredicate pred);
```

The search_n() function finds the first occurrence in the range [first1, last1) that matches the sequence consisting of count consecutive occurrences of value. It returns last1 if no such sequence is found. The first version uses the == operator for the value type to compare elements. The second version uses the binary predicate function object pred to compare elements. That is, elements pointed to by it1 and it2 match if pred(*it1, *it2) is true.

Mutating Sequence Operations

Table G.10 summarizes the mutating sequence operations. Arguments are not shown, and overloaded functions are listed just once. A fuller description, including the prototypes, follows the table. Thus, you can scan the table to get an idea of what a function does and then look up the details if you find the function appealing.

TABLE G.10 Mutating Sequence Operations

Function	Description
copy()	Copies elements from a range to a location identified by an iterator.
copy_backward()	Copies elements from a range to a location identified by an iterator. Copying begins at the end of the range and proceeds backward.
swap()	Exchanges two values stored at locations specified by references.

TABLE G.10   Continued

Function	Description
swap_ranges()	Exchanges corresponding values in two ranges.
iter_swap()	Exchanges two values stored at locations specified by iterators.
transform()	Applies a function object to each element in a range (or to each pair of elements in a pair of ranges) and copies the return value to the corresponding location of another range.
replace()	Replaces each occurrence of a value in a range with another value.
replace_if()	Replaces each occurrence of a value in a range with another value if a predicate function object applied to the original value returns true.
replace_copy()	Copies one range to another and replaces each occurrence of a specified value with another value.
replace_copy_if()	Copies one range to another and replaces each value for which a predicate function object is true with an indicated value.
fill()	Sets each value in a range to an indicated value.
fill_n()	Sets n consecutive elements to a value.
generate()	Sets each value in a range to the return value of a generator, which is a function object that takes no arguments.
generate_n()	Sets the first n values in a range to the return value of a generator, which is a function object that takes no arguments.
remove()	Removes all occurrences of an indicated value from a range and returns a past-the-end iterator for the resulting range.
remove_if()	Removes all occurrences of values for which a predicate object returns true from a range and returns a past-the-end iterator for the resulting range.
remove_copy()	Copies elements from one range to another, omitting elements that equal a specified value.
remove_copy_if()	Copies elements from one range to another, omitting elements for which a predicate function object returns true.
unique()	Reduces each sequence of two or more equivalent elements in a range to a single element.
unique_copy()	Copies elements from one range to another, reducing each sequence of two or more equivalent elements to one.
reverse()	Reverses the elements in a range.
reverse_copy()	Copies a range in reverse order to a second range.

Function	Description
rotate()	Treats a range as a circular ordering and rotates the elements left.
rotate_copy()	Copies one range to another in a rotated order.
random_shuffle()	Randomly rearranges the elements in a range.
partition()	Places all the elements that satisfy a predicate function object before all elements that don't.
stable_partition()	Places all the elements that satisfy a predicate function object before all elements that don't. The relative order of elements in each group is preserved.

Now let's take a more detailed look at these mutating sequence operations. For each function, the discussion shows the prototype(s), followed by a brief explanation. As you saw earlier, pairs of iterators indicate ranges, with the chosen template parameter name indicating the type of iterator. As usual, a range in the form [first, last) goes from first up to, but not including, last. Functions passed as arguments are function objects, which can be function pointers or objects for which the () operation is defined. As in Chapter 16, a predicate is a Boolean function with one argument, and a binary predicate is a Boolean function with two arguments. (The functions need not be type bool, as long as they return 0 for false and a nonzero value for true.) Also, as in Chapter 16, a unary function object is one that takes a single argument, and a binary function object is one that takes two arguments.

copy()

```
template<class InputIterator, class OutputIterator>
OutputIterator copy(InputIterator first, InputIterator last,
                    OutputIterator result);
```

The copy() function copies the elements in the range [first, last) into the range [result, result + (last - first)). It returns result + (last - first)— that is, an iterator pointing one past the last copied-to location. The function requires that result not be in the range [first, last)— that is, the target can't overlap the source.

copy_backward()

```
template<class BidirectionalIterator1, class BidirectionalIterator2>
BidirectionalIterator2 copy_backward(BidirectionalIterator1 first,
        BidirectionalIterator1 last, BidirectionalIterator2 result);
```

The copy_backward() function copies the elements in the range [first, last) into the range [result -(last - first), result). Copying begins with the element at last -1 being copied to location result - 1 and proceeds backward from there to first. It returns result - (last - first)—that is, an iterator pointing one past the last copied-to location. The function requires that result not be in the range [first, last). However, because copying is done backward, it is possible for the target and source to overlap.

swap()

```
template<class T> void swap(T& a, T& b);
```

The `swap()` function exchanges values stored at two locations specified by references.

swap_ranges()

```
template<class ForwardIterator1, class ForwardIterator2>
ForwardIterator2 swap_ranges(
                    ForwardIterator1 first1, ForwardIterator1 last1,
                    ForwardIterator2 first2);
```

The `swap_ranges()` function exchanges values in the range [`first1`, `last1`) with the corresponding values in the range beginning at `first2`. The two ranges should not overlap.

```
template<class ForwardIterator1, class ForwardIterator2>
void iter_swap(ForwardIterator1 a, ForwardIterator2 b);
```

The `iter_swap()` function exchanges values stored at two locations specified by iterators.

transform()

```
template<class InputIterator, class OutputIterator, class UnaryOperation>
OutputIterator transform(InputIterator first, InputIterator last,
OutputIterator result, UnaryOperation op);
```

```
template<class InputIterator1, class InputIterator2, class OutputIterator,
        class BinaryOperation>
OutputIterator transform(InputIterator1 first1, InputIterator1 last1,
                    InputIterator2 first2, OutputIterator result,
                    BinaryOperation binary_op);
```

The first version of `transform()` applies the unary function object `op` to each element in the range [`first`, `last`) and assigns the return value to the corresponding element in the range beginning at `result`. So `*result` is set to `op(*first)`, and so on. It returns `result + (last - first)`—that is, the past-the-end value for the target range.

The second version of `transform()` applies the binary function object `op` to each element in the range [`first1`, `last1`) and to each element in the range [`first2`, `last2`) and assigns the return value to the corresponding element in the range beginning at `result`. So `*result` is set to `op(*first1, *first2)`, and so on. It returns `result + (last - first)`, the past-the-end value for the target range.

replace()

```
template<class ForwardIterator, class T>
void replace(ForwardIterator first, ForwardIterator last,
            const T& old_value, const T& new_value);
```

The `replace()` function replaces each occurrence of the value `old_value` in the range [`first`, `last`) with the value `new_value`.

replace_if()

```
template<class ForwardIterator, class Predicate, class T>
void replace_if(ForwardIterator first, ForwardIterator last,
                Predicate pred, const T& new_value);
```

The replace()_if function replaces each value old in the range [first, last) for which pred(old) is true with the value new_value.

replace_copy()

```
template<class InputIterator, class OutputIterator, class T>
OutputIterator replace_copy(InputIterator first, InputIterator last,
    OutputIterator result,const T& old_ value, const T& new_ value);
```

The replace_copy() function copies the elements in the range [first, last) to a range beginning at result but substituting new_value for each occurrence of old_value. It returns result + (last - first), the past-the-end value for the target range.

replace_copy_if()

```
template<class Iterator, class OutputIterator, class Predicate, class T>
OutputIterator replace_copy_if(Iterator first, Iterator last,
    OutputIterator result, Predicate pred, const T& new_ value);
```

The replace_copy_if() function copies the elements in the range [first, last) to a range beginning at result but substituting new_value for each value old for which pred(old) is true. It returns result + (last - first), the past-the-end value for the target range.

fill()

```
template<class ForwardIterator, class T>
void fill(ForwardIterator first, ForwardIterator last, const T& value);
```

The fill() function sets each element in the range [first, last) to value.

fill_n()

```
template<class OutputIterator, class Size, class T>
void fill_n(OutputIterator first, Size n, const T& value);
```

The fill_n() function sets each of the first n elements beginning at location first to value.

generate()

```
template<class ForwardIterator, class Generator>
void generate(ForwardIterator first, ForwardIterator last, Generator gen);
```

The generate() function sets each element in the range [first, last) to gen(), where gen is a generator function object—that is, one that takes no arguments. For example, gen can be a pointer to rand().

generate_n()

```
template<class OutputIterator, class Size, class Generator>
void generate_n(OutputIterator first, Size n, Generator gen);
```

The `generate_n()` function sets each of the first n elements in the range beginning at `first` to `gen()`, where `gen` is a generator function object—that is, one that takes no arguments. For example, `gen` can be a pointer to `rand()`.

remove()

```
template<class ForwardIterator, class T>
ForwardIterator remove(ForwardIterator first, ForwardIterator last,
                       const T& value);
```

The `remove()` function removes all occurrences of `value` from the range [`first`, `last`) and returns a past-the-end iterator for the resulting range. The function is stable, meaning that the order of the unremoved elements is unaltered.

Note

Because the various `remove()` and `unique()` functions are not member functions, and also because they aren't restricted to STL containers, they can't reset the size of a container. Instead, they return an iterator that indicates the new past-the-end location. Typically, the removed items are simply shifted to the end of the container. However, for STL containers, you can use the returned iterator and one of the `erase()` methods to reset `end()`.

remove_if()

```
template<class ForwardIterator, class Predicate>
ForwardIterator remove_if(ForwardIterator first, ForwardIterator last,
                          Predicate pred);
```

The `remove_if()` function removes all occurrences of values `val` for which `pred(val)` is `true` from the range [`first`, `last`) and returns a past-the-end iterator for the resulting range. The function is stable, meaning that the order of the unremoved elements is unaltered.

remove_copy()

```
template<class InputIterator, class OutputIterator, class T>
OutputIterator remove_copy(InputIterator first, InputIterator last,
                           OutputIterator result, const T& value);
```

The `remove_copy()` function copies values from the range [`first`, `last`) to the range beginning at `result`, skipping instances of `value` as it copies. It returns a past-the-end iterator for the resulting range. The function is stable, meaning that the order of the unremoved elements is unaltered.

remove_copy_if()

```
template<class InputIterator, class OutputIterator, class Predicate>
OutputIterator remove_copy_if(InputIterator first, InputIterator last,
                              OutputIterator result, Predicate pred);
```

The `remove_copy_if()` function copies values from the range [`first`, `last`) to the range beginning at `result`, skipping instances of `val` for which `pred(val)` is `true` as it copies. It returns a past-the-end iterator for the resulting range. The function is stable, meaning that the order of the unremoved elements is unaltered.

unique()

```
template<class ForwardIterator>
ForwardIterator unique(ForwardIterator first, ForwardIterator last);

template<class ForwardIterator, class BinaryPredicate>
ForwardIterator unique(ForwardIterator first, ForwardIterator last,
                       BinaryPredicate pred);
```

The unique() function reduces each sequence of two or more equivalent elements in the range [first, last) to a single element and returns a past-the-end iterator for the new range. The first version uses the == operator for the value type to compare elements. The second version uses the binary predicate function object pred to compare elements. That is, elements pointed to by it1 and it2 match if pred(*it1, *it2) is true.

unique_copy()

```
template<class InputIterator, class OutputIterator>
OutputIterator unique_copy(InputIterator first, InputIterator last,
                           OutputIterator result);

template<class InputIterator, class OutputIterator, class BinaryPredicate>
OutputIterator unique_copy(InputIterator first, InputIterator last,
                           OutputIterator result, BinaryPredicate pred);
```

The unique_copy() function copies elements from the range [first, last) to the range beginning at result, reducing each sequence of two or more identical elements to a single element. It returns a past-the-end iterator for the new range. The first version uses the == operator for the value type to compare elements. The second version uses the binary predicate function object pred to compare elements. That is, elements pointed to by it1 and it2 match if pred(*it1, *it2) is true.

```
template<class BidirectionalIterator>
void reverse(BidirectionalIterator first, BidirectionalIterator last);
```

The reverse() function reverses the elements in the range [first, last) by invoking swap(first, last - 1), and so on.

reverse_copy()

```
template<class BidirectionalIterator, class OutputIterator>
OutputIterator reverse_copy(BidirectionalIterator first,
                            BidirectionalIterator last,
                            OutputIterator result);
```

The reverse copy() function copies the elements in the range [first, last) to the range beginning at result in reverse order. The two ranges should not overlap.

rotate()

```
template<class ForwardIterator>
void rotate(ForwardIterator first, ForwardIterator middle,
            ForwardIterator last);
```

The `rotate()`function performs a left rotation on the elements in the range [`first`, `last`). The element at `middle` is moved to `first`, the element at `middle + 1` is moved to `first + 1`, and so on. The elements preceding `middle` are wrapped around to the end of the container so that the element at `first` follows the element formerly at `last - 1`.

rotate_copy()

```
template<class ForwardIterator, class OutputIterator>
OutputIterator rotate_copy(ForwardIterator first, ForwardIterator middle,
                           ForwardIterator last, OutputIterator result);
```

The `rotate_copy()` function copies the elements in the range [`first`, `last`) to the range beginning at `result`, using the rotated sequence described for `rotate()`.

replace()

```
template<class RandomAccessIterator>
void random_shuffle(RandomAccessIterator first, RandomAccessIterator last);
```

This version of the `random_shuffle()` function shuffles the elements in the range [`first`, `last`). The distribution is uniform; that is, each possible permutation of the original order is equally likely.

random_shuffle()

```
template<class RandomAccessIterator, class RandomNumberGenerator>
void random_shuffle(RandomAccessIterator first, RandomAccessIterator last,
                    RandomNumberGenerator& random);
```

This version of the `random_shuffle()` function shuffles the elements in the range [`first`, `last`). The function object `random` determines the distribution. Given n elements, the expression `random(n)` should return a value in the range [`0`,n).

partition()

```
template<class BidirectionalIterator, class Predicate>
BidirectionalIterator partition(BidirectionalIterator first,
                                BidirectionalIterator last,
                                Predicate pred);
```

The `partition()` function places each element whose value `val` is such that `pred(val)` is `true` before all elements that don't meet that test. It returns an iterator to the position following that last position, holding a value for which the predicate object function was `true`.

stable_partition()

```
template<class BidirectionalIterator, class Predicate>
BidirectionalIterator stable_partition(BidirectionalIterator first,
```

```
BidirectionalIterator last,
Predicate pred);
```

The `stable_partition()` function places each element whose value `val` is such that `pred(val)` is `true` before all elements that don't meet that test. This function preserves the relative ordering within each of the two groups. It returns an iterator to the position following that last position, holding a value for which the predicate object function was `true`.

Sorting and Related Operations

Table G.11 summarizes the sorting and related operations. Arguments are not shown, and overloaded functions are listed just once. Each function has a version that uses < for ordering elements and a version that uses a comparison function object for ordering elements. A fuller description, including the prototypes, follows the table. Thus, you can scan the table to get an idea of what a function does and then look up the details if you find the function appealing.

TABLE G.11   Sorting and Related Operations

Function	Description
sort()	Sorts a range.
stable_sort()	Sorts a range, preserving the relative order of equivalent elements.
partial_sort()	Partially sorts a range, providing the first n elements of a full sort.
partial_sort_copy()	Copies a partially sorted range to another range.
nth_element()	Given an iterator into a range, finds the element that would be there if the range were sorted and places that element there.
lower_bound()	Given a value, finds the first position in a sorted range before which the value can be inserted while maintaining the ordering.
upper_bound()	Given a value, finds the last position in a sorted range before which the value can be inserted while maintaining the ordering.
equal_range()	Given a value, finds the largest subrange of a sorted range such that the value can be inserted before any element in the subrange without violating the ordering.
binary_search()	Returns `true` if a sorted range contains a value that is equivalent to a given value; returns `false` otherwise.
merge()	Merges two sorted ranges into a third range.
inplace_merge()	Merges two consecutive sorted ranges in place.
includes()	Returns `true` if every element in one set is also found in another set.

TABLE G.11   Continued

Function	Description
`set_union()`	Constructs the union of two sets—that is, a set that contains all elements present in each set.
`set_intersection()`	Constructs the intersection of two sets—that is, a set that contains only those elements found in both sets.
`set_difference()`	Constructs the difference of two sets—that is, a set that contains only those elements found in the first set but not the second.
`set_symmetric_difference()`	Constructs a set that contains elements found in one set or the other, but not both.
`make_heap`	Converts a range to a heap.
`push_heap()`	Adds an element to a heap.
`pop_heap()`	Removes the largest element from a heap.
`sort_heap()`	Sorts a heap.
`min()`	Returns the lesser of two values.
`max()`	Returns the greater of two values.
`min_element()`	Finds the first occurrence of the smallest value in a range.
`max_element()`	Finds the first occurrence of the largest value in a range.
`lexicographic_compare()`	Compares two sequences lexicographically, returning `true` if the first sequence is lexicographically less than the second and `false` otherwise.
`next_permutation()`	Generates the next permutation in a sequence.
`previous_permutation()`	Generates the preceding permutation in a sequence.

The functions in this section determine the order of two elements by using the `<` operator defined for the elements or by using a comparison object designated by the template type `Compare`. If `comp` is an object of type `Compare`, then `comp(a,b)` is a generalization of `a < b` and returns `true` if `a` precedes `b` in the ordering scheme. If `a < b` is `false` and `b < a` is also `false`, `a` and `b` are equivalent. A comparison object must provide at least *strict weak ordering*. This means the following:

- The expression `comp(a,a)` must be `false`, a generalization of the fact that a value can't be less than itself. (This is the strict part.)

- If `comp(a,b)` is `true` and `comp(b,c)` is `true`, then `comp(a,c)` is `true` (that is, comparison is a transitive relationship).

- If `a` is equivalent to `b` and `b` is equivalent to `c`, then `a` is equivalent to `c` (that is, equivalency is a transitive relationship).

If you think of applying < to integers, then equivalency implies equality, but this doesn't have to hold for more general cases. For example, you could define a structure with several members describing a mailing address and define a `comp` comparison object that orders the structures according to zip code. Then any two addresses with the same zip code would be equivalent but not equal.

Now let's take a more detailed look at these sorting and related operations. For each function, the discussion shows the prototype(s), followed by a brief explanation. This section is divided into several subsections. As you saw earlier, pairs of iterators indicate ranges, with the chosen template parameter name indicating the type of iterator. As usual, a range in the form [`first`, `last`) goes from `first` up to, but not including, `last`. Functions passed as arguments are function objects, which can be pointers or objects for which the `()` operation is defined. As you learned in Chapter 16, a predicate is a Boolean function with one argument, and a binary predicate is a Boolean function with two arguments. (The functions need not be type `bool`, as long as they return `0` for `false` and a nonzero value for `true`.) Also, as in Chapter 16, a unary function object is one that takes a single argument, and a binary function object is one that takes two arguments.

Sorting

First, let's examine the sorting algorithms.

sort()

```
template<class RandomAccessIterator>
void sort(RandomAccessIterator first, RandomAccessIterator last);

template<class RandomAccessIterator, class Compare>
void sort(RandomAccessIterator first, RandomAccessIterator last,
          Compare comp);
```

The `sort()` function sorts the range [`first`, `last`) in increasing order, using the value type < operator for comparison. The first version uses <, and the second version uses the comparison object `comp` to determine the order.

stable_sort()

```
template<class RandomAccessIterator>
void stable_sort(RandomAccessIterator first, RandomAccessIterator last);

template<class RandomAccessIterator, class Compare>
void stable_sort(RandomAccessIterator first, RandomAccessIterator last,
                 Compare comp);
```

The `stable_sort()` function sorts the range [`first`, `last`), preserving the relative order of equivalent elements. The first version uses <, and the second version uses the comparison object `comp` to determine the order.

partial_sort()

```
template<class RandomAccessIterator>
void partial_sort(RandomAccessIterator first, RandomAccessIterator middle,
              RandomAccessIterator last);

template<class RandomAccessIterator, class Compare>
void partial_sort(RandomAccessIterator first, RandomAccessIterator middle,
RandomAccessIterator last, Compare comp);
```

The partial_sort() function partially sorts the range [first, last). The first middle - first elements of the sorted range are placed in the range [first, middle), and the remaining elements are unsorted. The first version uses <, and the second version uses the comparison object comp to determine the order.

partial_sort_copy()

```
template<class InputIterator, class RandomAccessIterator>
RandomAccessIterator partial_sort_copy(InputIterator first,
                   InputIterator last,
                   RandomAccessIterator result_first,
                   RandomAccessIterator result_last);

template<class InputIterator, class RandomAccessIterator, class Compare>
RandomAccessIterator
partial_sort_copy(InputIterator first, InputIterator last,
              RandomAccessIterator result_first,
              RandomAccessIterator result_last,
              Compare comp);
```

The partial_sort_copy() function copies the first *n* elements of the sorted range [first, last) to the range [result_first, result_first + n). The value of n is the lesser of last - first and result_last - result_first. The function returns result_first + n. The first version uses <, and the second version uses the comparison object comp to determine the order.

nth_element()

```
template<class RandomAccessIterator>
void nth_element(RandomAccessIterator first, RandomAccessIterator nth,
              RandomAccessIterator last);

template<class RandomAccessIterator, class Compare>
void nth_element(RandomAccessIterator first, RandomAccessIterator nth,
RandomAccessIterator last, Compare comp);
```

The nth_element() function finds the element in the range [first, last) that would be at position nth were the range sorted, and it places that element at position nth. The first version uses <, and the second version uses the comparison object comp to determine the order.

Binary Searching

The algorithms in the binary searching group assume that the range is sorted. They only require a forward iterator but are most efficient for random iterators.

lower_bound()

```
template<class ForwardIterator, class T>
ForwardIterator lower_bound(ForwardIterator first, ForwardIterator last,
                            const T& value);

template<class ForwardIterator, class T, class Compare>
ForwardIterator lower_bound(ForwardIterator first, ForwardIterator last,
                            const T& value, Compare comp);
```

The lower_bound() function finds the first position the a sorted range [first, last) in front of which value can be inserted without violating the order. It returns an iterator that points to this position. The first version uses <, and the second version uses the comparison object comp to determine the order.

upper_bound()

```
template<class ForwardIterator, class T>
ForwardIterator upper_bound(ForwardIterator first, ForwardIterator last,
                            const T& value);

template<class ForwardIterator, class T, class Compare>
ForwardIterator upper_bound(ForwardIterator first, ForwardIterator last,
const T& value, Compare comp);
```

The upper_bound() function finds the last position in the sorted range [first, last) in front of which value can be inserted without violating the order. It returns an iterator that points to this position. The first version uses <, and the second version uses the comparison object comp to determine the order.

equal_range()

```
template<class ForwardIterator, class T>
pair<ForwardIterator, ForwardIterator> equal_range(
    ForwardIterator first, ForwardIterator last, const T& value);

template<class ForwardIterator, class T, class Compare>
pair<ForwardIterator, ForwardIterator> equal_range(
    ForwardIterator first, ForwardIterator last, const T& value,
    Compare comp);
```

The equal_range() function finds the largest subrange [it1, it2) in the sorted range [first, last) such that value can be inserted in front of any iterator in this range without violating the order. The function returns a pair formed of it1 and it2. The first version uses <, and the second version uses the comparison object comp to determine the order.

binary_search()

```
template<class ForwardIterator, class T>
bool binary_search(ForwardIterator first, ForwardIterator last,
                   const T& value);

template<class ForwardIterator, class T, class Compare>
bool binary_search(ForwardIterator first, ForwardIterator last,
                   const T& value, Compare comp);
```

The `binary_search()` function returns `true` if the equivalent of `value` is found in the sorted range [`first`, `last`); it returns `false` otherwise. The first version uses <, and the second version uses the comparison object `comp` to determine the order.

> **Note**
>
> Recall that if < is used for ordering, the values a and b are equivalent if both a < b and b < a are false. For ordinary numbers, equivalency implies equality, but this is not the case for structures sorted on the basis of just one member. Thus, there may be more than one location where a new value can be inserted and still keep the data ordered. Similarly, if the comparison object `comp` is used for ordering, equivalency means both `comp(a,b)` and `comp(b,a)` are `false`. (This is a generalization of the statement that a and b are equivalent if a is not less than b and b is not less than a.)

Merging

The merging functions assume that ranges are sorted.

merge()

```
template<class InputIterator1, class InputIterator2, class OutputIterator>
OutputIterator merge(InputIterator1 first1, InputIterator1 last1,
                     InputIterator2 first2, InputIterator2 last2,
                     OutputIterator result);

template<class InputIterator1, class InputIterator2, class OutputIterator,
class Compare>
OutputIterator merge(InputIterator1 first1, InputIterator1 last1,
                     InputIterator2 first2, InputIterator2 last2,
                     OutputIterator result, Compare comp);
```

The `merge()` function merges elements from the sorted range [`first1`, `last1`) and from the sorted range [`first2`, `last2`), placing the result in a range starting at `result`. The target range should not overlap either of the merged ranges. When equivalent elements are found in both ranges, elements from the first range precede elements of the second. The return value is the past-the-end iterator for the resulting merge. The first version uses <, and the second version uses the comparison object `comp` to determine the order.

inplace_merge()

```
template<class BidirectionalIterator>
void inplace_merge(BidirectionalIterator first,
            BidirectionalIterator middle, BidirectionalIterator last);

template<class BidirectionalIterator, class Compare>
void inplace_merge(BidirectionalIterator first,
            BidirectionalIterator middle, BidirectionalIterator last,
            Compare comp);
```

The `inplace_merge()` function merges two consecutive sorted ranges—[`first`, `middle`) and [`middle`, `last`)—into a single sorted sequence stored in the range [`first`, `last`). Elements from the first range precede equivalent elements from the second range. The first version uses <, and the second version uses the comparison object `comp` to determine the order.

Working with Sets

Set operations work with all sorted sequences, including `set` and `multiset`. For containers that hold more than one instance of a value, such as `multiset`, definitions are generalized. A union of two multisets contains the larger number of occurrences of each element, and an intersection contains the lesser number of occurrences of each element. For example, suppose Multiset `A` contains the string `"apple"` seven times and Multiset `B` contains the same string four times. Then the union of `A` and `B` will contain seven instances of `"apple"`, and the intersection will contain four instances.

includes()

```
template<class InputIterator1, class InputIterator2>
bool includes(InputIterator1 first1, InputIterator1 last1,
            InputIterator2 first2, InputIterator2 last2);

template<class InputIterator1, class InputIterator2, class Compare>
bool includes(InputIterator1 first1, InputIterator1 last1,
            InputIterator2 first2, InputIterator2 last2, Compare comp);
```

The `includes()` function returns `true` if every element in the range [`first2`, `last2`) is also found in the range [`first1`, `last1`); it returns `false` otherwise. The first version uses <, and the second version uses the comparison object `comp` to determine the order.

set_union()

```
template<class InputIterator1, class InputIterator2, class OutputIterator>
OutputIterator set_union(InputIterator1 first1, InputIterator1 last1,
                    InputIterator2 first2, InputIterator2 last2,
                    OutputIterator result);

template<class InputIterator1, class InputIterator2, class OutputIterator,
        class Compare>
OutputIterator set_union(InputIterator1 first1, InputIterator1 last1,
                    InputIterator2 first2, InputIterator2 last2,
                    OutputIterator result, Compare comp);
```

The `set_union()` function constructs the set that is the union of the ranges [`first1`, `last1`) and [`first2`, `last2`) and copies the result to the location pointed to by `result`. The resulting range should not overlap either of the original ranges. The function returns a past-the-end iterator for the constructed range. The union is the set that contains all elements found in either or both sets. The first version uses <, and the second version uses the comparison object `comp` to determine the order.

set_intersection()

```
template<class InputIterator1, class InputIterator2, class OutputIterator>
OutputIterator set_intersection(InputIterator1 first1, InputIterator1 last1,
```

```
                        InputIterator2 first2, InputIterator2 last2,
                        OutputIterator result);

template<class InputIterator1, class InputIterator2, class OutputIterator,
        class Compare>
OutputIterator set_intersection(InputIterator1 first1, InputIterator1 last1,
                        InputIterator2 first2, InputIterator2 last2,
                        OutputIterator result, Compare comp);
```

The `set_intersection()` function constructs the set that is the intersection of the ranges [`first1`, `last1`) and [`first2`, `last2`) and copies the result to the location pointed to by `result`. The resulting range should not overlap either of the original ranges. The function returns a past-the-end iterator for the constructed range. The intersection is the set that contains the elements that are common to both sets. The first version uses <, and the second version uses the comparison object `comp` to determine the order.

set_difference()

```
template<class InputIterator1, class InputIterator2, class OutputIterator>
OutputIterator set_difference(InputIterator1 first1, InputIterator1 last1,
                        InputIterator2 first2, InputIterator2 last2,
                        OutputIterator result);

template<class InputIterator1, class InputIterator2, class OutputIterator,
        class Compare>
OutputIterator set_difference(InputIterator1 first1, InputIterator1 last1,
                        InputIterator2 first2, InputIterator2 last2,
                        OutputIterator result, Compare comp);
```

The `set_difference()` function constructs the set that is the difference between the ranges [`first1`, `last1`) and [`first2`, `last2`) and copies the result to the location pointed to by `result`. The resulting range should not overlap either of the original ranges. The function returns a past-the-end iterator for the constructed range. The difference is the set that contains the elements found in the first set but not in the second. The first version uses <, and the second version uses the comparison object `comp` to determine the order.

```
template<class InputIterator1, class InputIterator2, class OutputIterator>
OutputIterator set_symmetric_difference(
                        InputIterator1 first1, InputIterator1 last1,
                        InputIterator2 first2, InputIterator2 last2,
                        OutputIterator result);

template<class InputIterator1, class InputIterator2, class OutputIterator,
        class Compare>
OutputIterator set_symmetric_difference(
                        InputIterator1 first1, InputIterator1 last1,
                        InputIterator2 first2, InputIterator2 last2,
                        OutputIterator result, Compare comp);
```

The `set_symmetric_difference()` function constructs the set that is the symmetric difference between the ranges [`first1`, `last1`) and [`first2`, `last2`) and copies the result to the location pointed to by `result`. The resulting range should not overlap either of the original ranges. The function returns a past-the-end iterator for the constructed range. The symmetric difference is the set that contains the elements found in the first set but not in the second and the elements found in the second set but not the first. It's the same as the difference between the union and the intersection. The first version uses <, and the second version uses the comparison object `comp` to determine the order.

Working with Heaps

A *heap* is a common data form with the property that the first element in a heap is the largest. Whenever the first element is removed or any element is added, the heap may have to be rearranged to maintain that property. A heap is designed so that these two operations are done efficiently.

make_heap()

```
template<class RandomAccessIterator>
void make_heap(RandomAccessIterator first, RandomAccessIterator last);

template<class RandomAccessIterator, class Compare>
void make_heap(RandomAccessIterator first, RandomAccessIterator last,
               Compare comp);
```

The `make_heap()` function makes a heap of the range [`first`, `last`). The first version uses < to determine the ordering, and the second version uses the `comp` comparison object.

push_heap()

```
template<class RandomAccessIterator>
void push_heap(RandomAccessIterator first, RandomAccessIterator last);

template<class RandomAccessIterator, class Compare>
void push_heap(RandomAccessIterator first, RandomAccessIterator last,
               Compare comp);
```

The `push_heap()` function assumes that the range [`first`, `last` - 1) is a valid heap, and it adds the value at location `last` - 1 (that is, one past the end of the heap that is assumed to be valid) into the heap, making [`first`, `last`) a valid heap. The first version uses < to determine the ordering, and the second version uses the `comp` comparison object.

pop_heap()

```
template<class RandomAccessIterator>
void pop_heap(RandomAccessIterator first, RandomAccessIterator last);

template<class RandomAccessIterator, class Compare>
void pop_heap(RandomAccessIterator first, RandomAccessIterator last,
              Compare comp);
```

The `pop_heap()` function assumes that the range [`first`, `last`) is a valid heap. It swaps the value at location `last` - 1 with the value at `first` and makes the range [`first`, `last` - 1) a valid heap. The first version uses < to determine the ordering, and the second version uses the `comp` comparison object.

sort_heap()

```
template<class RandomAccessIterator>
void sort_heap(RandomAccessIterator first, RandomAccessIterator last);

template<class RandomAccessIterator, class Compare>
void sort_heap(RandomAccessIterator first, RandomAccessIterator last,
               Compare comp);
```

The `sort_heap()` function assumes that the range [`first`, `last`) is a heap and sorts it. The first version uses < to determine the ordering, and the second version uses the `comp` comparison object.

Finding Minimum and Maximum Values

The minimum and maximum functions return the minimum and maximum values of pairs of values and of sequences of values.

min()

```
template<class T> const T& min(const T& a, const T& b);

template<class T, class Compare>
const T& min(const T& a, const T& b, Compare comp);
```

The `min()` function returns the lesser of two values. If the two values are equivalent, it returns the first value. The first version uses < to determine the ordering, and the second version uses the `comp` comparison object.

max()

```
template<class T> const T& max(const T& a, const T& b);

template<class T, class Compare>
const T& max(const T& a, const T& b, Compare comp);
```

The `max()` function returns the greater of two values. If the two values are equivalent, it returns the first value. The first version uses < to determine the ordering, and the second version uses the `comp` comparison object.

min_element()

```
template<class ForwardIterator>
ForwardIterator min_element(ForwardIterator first, ForwardIterator last);

template<class ForwardIterator, class Compare>
ForwardIterator min_element(ForwardIterator first, ForwardIterator last,
Compare comp);
```

The `min_element()` function returns the first iterator `it` in the range [`first`, `last`) such that no element in the range is less than `*it`. The first version uses < to determine the ordering, and the second version uses the `comp` comparison object.

max_element()

```
template<class ForwardIterator>
ForwardIterator max_element(ForwardIterator first, ForwardIterator last);

template<class ForwardIterator, class Compare>
ForwardIterator max_element(ForwardIterator first, ForwardIterator last,
Compare comp);
```

The max_element() function returns the first iterator it in the range [first, last) such that there is no element that *it is less than. The first version uses < to determine the ordering, and the second version uses the comp comparison object.

lexicographical_compare()

```
template<class InputIterator1, class InputIterator2>
bool lexicographical_compare(InputIterator1 first1, InputIterator1 last1,
                             InputIterator2 first2, InputIterator2 last2);

template<class InputIterator1, class InputIterator2, class Compare>
bool lexicographical_compare(InputIterator1 first1, InputIterator1 last1,
                             InputIterator2 first2, InputIterator2 last2,
                             Compare comp);
```

The lexicographical_compare() function returns true if the sequence of elements in the range [first1, last1) is lexicographically less than the sequence of elements in the range [first2, last2); it returns false otherwise. A lexicographic comparison compares the first element of one sequence to the first of the second—that is, it compares *first1 to *first2. If *first1 is less than *first2, the function returns true. If *first2 is less than *first1, the function returns false. If the two are equivalent, comparison proceeds to the next element in each sequence. This process continues until two corresponding elements are not equivalent or until the end of a sequence is reached. If two sequences are equivalent until the end of one is reached, the shorter sequence is less. If the two sequences are equivalent and of the same length, neither is less, so the function returns false. The first version of the function uses < to compare elements, and the second version uses the comp comparison object. The lexicographic comparison is a generalization of an alphabetic comparison.

Working with Permutations

A *permutation* of a sequence is a reordering of the elements. For example, a sequence of three elements has six possible orderings because you have a choice of three elements for the first element. Choosing a particular element for the first position leaves a choice of two for the second, and one for the third. For example, the six permutations of the digits 1, 2, 3 are as follows:

123 132 213 232 312 321

In general, a sequence of n elements has $n \times (n-1) \times \ldots \times 1$, or $n!$ possible permutations.

The permutation functions assume that the set of all possible permutations can be arranged in lexicographic order, as in the previous example of six permutations. That means, in general, that there is a specific permutation that precedes and follows each permutation. For example, 213 immediately precedes 232, and 312 immediately follows it. However, the first permutation (123 in the example) has no predecessor, and the last permutation (321 in the example) has no follower.

next_permutation()

```
template<class BidirectionalIterator>
bool next_permutation(BidirectionalIterator first,
                      BidirectionalIterator last);

template<class BidirectionalIterator, class Compare>
bool next_permutation(BidirectionalIterator first,
                      BidirectionalIterator last, Compare comp);
```

The `next_permutation()` function transforms the sequence in the range [`first`, `last`) to the next permutation in lexicographic order. If the next permutation exists, the function returns `true`. If it doesn't exist (that is, the range contains the last permutation in lexicographic order), the function returns `false` and transforms the range to the first permutation in lexicographic order. The first version uses < to determine the ordering, and the second version uses the `comp` comparison object.

prev_permutation()

```
template<class BidirectionalIterator>
bool prev_permutation(BidirectionalIterator first,
                      BidirectionalIterator last);

template<class BidirectionalIterator, class Compare>
bool prev_permutation(BidirectionalIterator first,
                      BidirectionalIterator last, Compare comp);
```

The `previous_permutation()` function transforms the sequence in the range [`first`, `last`) to the previous permutation in lexicographic order. If the previous permutation exists, the function returns `true`. If it doesn't exist (that is, the range contains the first permutation in lexicographic order), the function returns `false` and transforms the range to the last permutation in lexicographic order. The first version uses < to determine the ordering, and the second version uses the `comp` comparison object.

Numeric Operations

Table G.12 summarizes the numeric operations, which are described by the `numeric` header file. Arguments are not shown, and overloaded functions are listed just once. Each function has a version that uses < for ordering elements and a version that uses a comparison function object for ordering elements. A fuller description, including the prototypes, follows the table. Thus, you can scan the table to get an idea of what a function does and then look up the details if you find the function appealing.

TABLE G.12 Sorting and Related Operations

Function	Description
accumulate()	Calculates a cumulative total for values in a range.
inner_product()	Calculates the inner product of two ranges.
partial_sum()	Copies partial sums calculated from one range into a second range.
adjacent_difference()	Copies adjacent differences calculated from elements in one range to a second range.

Now let's take a more detailed look at these numeric operations. For each function, the discussion shows the prototype(s), followed by a brief explanation.

accumulate()

```
template <class InputIterator, class T>
T accumulate(InputIterator first, InputIterator last, T init);

template <class InputIterator, class T, class BinaryOperation>
T accumulate(InputIterator first, InputIterator last, T init,
             BinaryOperation binary_op);
```

The accumulate() function initializes a value acc to init; then it performs the operation acc = acc + *i (first version) or acc = binary_op(acc, *i) (second version) for each iterator i in the range [first, last), in order. It then returns the resulting value of acc.

inner_product()

```
template <class InputIterator1, class InputIterator2, class T>
T inner_product(InputIterator1 first1, InputIterator1 last1,
                InputIterator2 first2, T init);

template <class InputIterator1, class InputIterator2, class T,
class BinaryOperation1, class BinaryOperation2>
T inner_product(InputIterator1 first1, InputIterator1 last1,
                InputIterator2 first2, T init,
                BinaryOperation1 binary_op1, BinaryOperation2 binary_op2);
```

The inner_product() function initializes a value acc to init; then it performs the operation acc = *i * *j (first version) or acc = binary_op(*i, *j) (second version) for each iterator i in the range [first1, last1), in order, and each corresponding iterator j in the range [first2, first2 + (last1 - first1)). That is, it calculates a value from the first elements from each sequence, then from the second elements of each sequence, and so on, until it reaches the end of the first sequence. (Hence the second sequence should be at least as long as the first.) The function then returns the resulting value of acc.

partial_sum()

```
template <class InputIterator, class OutputIterator>
OutputIterator partial_sum(InputIterator first, InputIterator last,
                           OutputIterator result);

template <class InputIterator, class OutputIterator, class BinaryOperation>
OutputIterator partial_sum(InputIterator first, InputIterator last,
                           OutputIterator result,
                           BinaryOperation binary_op);
```

The partial_sum() function assigns *first to *result or *first + *(first + 1) to *(result + 1) (first version) or it assigns binary_op(*first, *(first + 1)) to *(result + 1) (second version), and so on. That is, the nth element of the sequence beginning at result contains the sum (or binary_op equivalent) of the first n elements of the sequence beginning at first. The function returns the past-the-end iterator for the result. The algorithm allows result to be first—that is, it allows the result to be copied over the original sequence, if desired.

adjacent_difference()

```
template <class InputIterator, class OutputIterator>
OutputIterator adjacent_difference(InputIterator first, InputIterator last,
                                   OutputIterator result);

template <class InputIterator, class OutputIterator, class BinaryOperation>
OutputIterator adjacent_difference(InputIterator first, InputIterator last,
                                   OutputIterator result,
                                   BinaryOperation binary_op);
```

The adjacent_difference() function assigns *first to the location result (*result = *first). Subsequent locations in the target range are assigned the differences (or binary_op equivalent) of adjacent locations in the source range. That is, the next location in the target range (result + 1) is assigned *(first + 1) - *first (first version) or binary_op(*(first + 1), *first) (second version), and so on. The function returns the past-the-end iterator for the result. The algorithm allows result to be first—that is, it allows the result to be copied over the original sequence, if desired.

APPENDIX H

SELECTED READINGS AND INTERNET RESOURCES

*T*here are many good books and Internet resources about C++ and programming. The following list is intended to be representative rather than comprehensive. Thus, there are many fine books and sites not listed here. However, the list does cover a broad range of presentations.

Selected Readings

- Booch, Grady. *Object-Oriented Analysis and Design*, Second Edition. Reading, MA: Addison-Wesley, 1993.

  This book presents the concepts behind object-oriented programming (OOP), discusses OOP methods, and presents sample applications. The examples are in C++.

- Booch, Grady, Jim Rumbaugh, and Ivar Jacobson. *Unified Modeling Language User Guide*. Reading, MA: Addison-Wesley, 1998.

  This book by the creators of the Unified Modeling Language (UML) presents the core of UML along with many examples of its use.

- Cline, Marshall, Greg Lomow, and Mike Girou. *C++ FAQs,* Second Edition. Reading, MA: Addison-Wesley, 1999.

  This book addresses a great number of frequently asked questions about the C++ language.

- Jacobson, Ivar. *Object-Oriented Software Engineering: A Use Case Driven Approach*. Reading, MA: Addison-Wesley, 1994.

  This book describes successful guidelines and methods (Object-Oriented Software Engineering [OOSE]) for developing large-scale software systems.

- Josuttis, Nicolai M. *The C++ Standard Library: A Tutorial and Reference*. Reading, MA: Addison-Wesley, 1999.

  This book describes the Standard Template Library (STL) as well as other C++ library features, such as complex number support, locales, and input/output streams.

- Lee, Richard C and William M. Tepfenhart. *UML and C++*, Second Edition. Upper Saddle River, New Jersey: Prentice Hall, 2001.

  This book is a self-teaching guide to UML, and it includes a review of C++ fundamentals.

- Meyers, Scott. *Effective C++: 50 Specific Ways to Improve Your Programs and Designs*, Second Edition. Reading, MA: Addison-Wesley, 1998.

  This book is aimed at programmers who already know C++, and it provides 50 rules and guidelines. Some are technical, such as explaining when you should define copy constructors and assignment operators. Others are more general, such as discussing *is-a* and *has-a* relationships.

- Meyers, Scott. *Effective STL: 50 Specific Ways to Improve Your Use of the Standard Template Library*. Reading, MA: Addison-Wesley, 2001.

  This book provides guidance in choosing containers and algorithms and in other facets of using the STL.

- Meyers, Scott. *More Effective C++: 35 New Ways to Improve Your Programs and Designs*. Reading, MA: Addison-Wesley, 1996.

  This book continues in the tradition of *Effective C++*, clarifying some of the more obscure aspects of the language and showing how to accomplish various goals, such as designing smart pointers. It reflects the additional experience C++ programmers have gained in the past few years.

- Rumbaugh, James, Michael Blaha, William Premerlani, Frederick Eddy, Bill Lorensen, and William Lorenson. *Object-Oriented Modeling and Design*. Englewood Cliffs, NJ: Prentice Hall, 1991.

  This book presents and explores the Object Modeling Technique (OMT), a method for breaking problems into suitable objects.

- Rumbaugh, James, Ivar Jacobson, and Grady Booch. *Unified Modeling Reference Manual*. Reading, MA: Addison-Wesley, 1998.

  This book by the creators of UML presents the complete description, in reference manual format, of the UML.

- Stroustrup, Bjarne. *The C++ Programming Language*, Third Edition. Reading, MA: Addison-Wesley, 1997.

  Stroustrup created C++, so this is the definitive text. However, it is most easily digested if you already have some knowledge of C++. It not only describes the language, it also provides many examples of how to use it, as well as discussions of OOP methodology. Successive editions of this book have grown with the language, and this edition includes a discussion of standard library elements such as the STL and strings.

- Stroustrup, Bjarne. *The Design and Evolution of C++*. Reading, MA: Addison-Wesley, 1994.

  If you're interested in learning how C++ evolved and why it is the way it is, read this book.

- Vandevoorde, David and Nocolai M. Jpsittos. *C++ Templates: The Complete Guide*. Reading, MA: Addison-Wesley, 2003.

  A lot can be said about templates, as this detailed reference demonstrates.

Internet Resources

- The ISO/ANSI C++ Standard (ISO/IEC 14882:2003) is a technical revision of the 1998 version of the Standard (14882:1998), and it is available from both the American National Standards Institute (ANSI) and the International Organization for Standardization (ISO).

  ANSI has a printed version available for $281 and a downloadable electronic version (PDF format, single-user restrictions) available for $18. Either can be ordered from the following website:

  http://webstore.ansi.org

  The ISO offers the document as a downloadable PDF file for CHF 352 or on a CD-ROM, also for CHF 352 (Swiss Francs), at the following site:

  www.iso.org

- The C++ FAQ Lite site for frequently asked questions (in English, Chinese, French, Russian, and Portuguese) is a slimmed-down version of the book by Cline, et al. Currently it has the following URL:

  www.parashift.com/c++-faq-lite

- You can find a moderated discussion of C++ questions in the following newsgroup:

  comp.lang.c++.moderated

- *C/C++ Users Journal*

  This monthly magazine primarily targets professional programmers. Its website (www.cuj.com) provides several useful resources.

APPENDIX I

CONVERTING TO ANSI/ISO STANDARD C++

You might have programs (or programming habits) that you developed in C or in older versions of C++ and you want to convert to standard C++. This appendix provides some guidelines. Some pertain to moving from C to C++ and others pertain to moving from older C++ to standard C++.

Use Alternatives for Some Preprocessor Directives

The C/C++ preprocessor provides an array of directives. In general, C++ practice is to use those directives that are designed to manage the compilation process and to avoid using directives as a substitute for code. For example, the `#include` directive is an essential component for managing program files. Other directives, such as `#ifndef` and `#endif`, let you control whether particular blocks of code get compiled. The `#pragma` directive lets you control compiler-specific compilation options. These are all useful, sometimes necessary, tools. You should exert caution, however, when it comes to the `#define` directive.

Use `const` Instead of `#define` to Define Constants

Symbolic constants make code more readable and maintainable. The constant's name indicates its meaning, and if you need to change the value, you just have to change the value once, in the definition, and then recompile. C uses the preprocessor to create symbolic names for a constant:

```
#define MAX_LENGTH 100
```

The preprocessor then does a text substitution in your source code, replacing occurrences of `MAX_LENGTH` with `100` prior to compilation.

The C++ approach is to apply the `const` modifier to a variable declaration:

```
const int MAX_LENGTH = 100;
```

This treats `MAX_LENGTH` as a read-only `int`.

There are several advantages to using the `const` approach. First, the declaration explicitly names the type. With `#define`, you must use various suffixes to a number to indicate types other than `char`, `int`, or `double`; for example, you use `100L` to indicate a `long` type and `3.14F` to indicate a `float` type. More importantly, the `const` approach can just as easily be used with compound types, as in this example:

```
const int base_vals[5] = {1000, 2000, 3500, 6000, 10000};
const string ans[3] = {"yes", "no", "maybe"};
```

Finally, `const` identifiers obey the same scope rules as variables. Thus, you can create constants with global scope, named namespace scope, and block scope. If, say, you define a constant in a particular function, you don't have to worry about the definition conflicting with a global constant used elsewhere in a program. For example, consider the following:

```
#define n 5
const int dz = 12;
...
void fizzle()
{
    int n;
    int dz;
    ...
}
```

The preprocessor will replace

```
int n;
```

with

```
int 5;
```

and induce a compilation error. The `dz` defined in `fizzle()`, however, will be a local variable. Also, if necessary, `fizzle()`can use the scope-resolution operator (`::`) and access the constant as `::dz`.

C++ has borrowed the `const` keyword from C, but the C++ version is more useful. For example, the C++ version has internal linkage for external `const` values rather than the default external linkage used by variables and by the C `const`. This means that each file in a program using a `const` needs that `const` defined in that particular file. This might sound like extra work, but, in fact, it makes life easier. With internal linkage, you can place `const` definitions in a header file used by various files in a project. That is a compiler error for external linkage but not for internal linkage. Also, because a `const` must be defined in the file that uses it (being in a header file used by that file satisfies the requirement), you can use `const` values as array size arguments:

```
const int MAX_LENGTH = 100;
...
double loads[MAX_LENGTH];
for (int i = 0; i < MAX_LENGTH; i++)
    loads[i] = 50;
```

This won't work in C because the defining declaration for `MAX_LENGTH` could be in a separate file and not be available when this particular file is compiled. In fairness, it should be added that, in C, you could use the `static` modifier to create constants with internal linkage. It's just that C++, by making `static` the default, requires one fewer thing for you to remember.

Incidentally, the revised C Standard (C99) allows you to use a const as an array size specification, but the array is treated as a new form of array, called a *variable array*, that is not part of the C++ Standard.

One role for the #define directive is still quite useful—the standard idiom for controlling when a header file is compiled:

```
// blooper.h
#ifndef _BLOOPER_H_
#define _BLOOPER_H_
// code goes here
#endif
```

For typical symbolic constants, however, you should get into the habit of using const instead of #define. Another good alternative, particularly when you have a set of related integer constants, is to use enum:

```
enum {LEVEL1 = 1, LEVEL2 = 2, LEVEL3 = 4, LEVEL4 = 8};
```

Use inline Instead of #define to Define Short Functions

The traditional C way to create the near-equivalent of an inline function is to use a #define macro definition:

```
#define Cube(X) X*X*X
```

This leads the preprocessor to do text substitution, with X being replaced by the corresponding argument to Cube():

```
y = Cube(x);       // replaced with y = x*x*x;
y = Cube(x + z++); // replaced with x + z++*x + z++*x + z++;
```

Because the preprocessor uses text substitution instead of true passing of arguments, using such macros can lead to unexpected and incorrect results. Such errors can be reduced by using lots of parentheses in the macro to ensure the correct order of operations:

```
#define Cube(X) ((X)*(X)*(X))
```

Even this, however, doesn't deal with cases such as using values like z++.

The C++ approach of using the keyword inline to identify inline functions is much more dependable because it uses true argument passing. Furthermore, C++ inline functions can be regular functions or class methods:

```
class dormant
{
private:
    int period;
    ...
public:
    int Period() const { return period; } // automatically inline
    ...
};
```

One positive feature of the #define macro is that it is typeless, so it can be used with any type for which the operation makes sense. In C++ you can create inline templates to achieve type-independent functions while retaining argument passing.

In short, you should use C++ inlining instead of C #define macros.

Use Function Prototypes

Actually, you don't have a choice: Although prototyping is optional in C, it is mandatory in C++. Note that a function that is defined before its first use, such as an inline function, serves as its own prototype.

You should use const in function prototypes and headers when appropriate. In particular, you should use const with pointer parameters and reference parameters representing data that is not to be altered. Not only does this allow the compiler to catch errors that change data, it also makes a function more general. That is, a function with a const pointer or reference can process both const and non-const data, whereas a function that fails to use const with a pointer or reference can process only non-const.

Use Type Casts

One of Stroustrup's pet peeves about C is its undisciplined type cast operator. True, type casts are often necessary, but the standard type cast is too unrestrictive. For example, consider the following code:

```
struct Doof
{
    double feeb;
    double steeb;
    char sgif[10];
};
Doof leam;
short * ps = (short *) & leam;   // old syntax
int * pi = int * (&leam);        // new syntax
```

Nothing in the C language prevents you from casting a pointer of one type to a pointer to a totally unrelated type.

In a way, the situation is similar to that of the goto statement. The problem with the goto statement was that it was too flexible, leading to twisted code. The solution was to provide more limited, structured versions of goto to handle the most common tasks for which goto was needed. This was the genesis of language elements such as for and while loops and if else statements. Standard C++ provides a similar solution for the problem of the undisciplined type cast—namely, restricted type casts to handle the most common situations requiring type casts. The following are the type cast operators discussed in Chapter 15, "Friends, Exceptions, and More":

```
dynamic_cast
static_cast
const_cast
reinterpret_cast
```

So, if you are doing a type cast involving pointers, you should use one of these operators if possible. Doing so both documents the intent of the type cast and provides checking that the type cast is being used as intended.

Become Familiar with C++ Features

If you've been using `malloc()` and `free()`, you should switch to using `new` and `delete` instead. If you've been using `setjmp()` and `longjmp()` for error handling, you should use `try`, `throw`, and `catch` instead. You should try using the `bool` type for values representing `true` and `false`.

Use the New Header Organization

The C++ Standard specifies new names for the header files, as described in Chapter 2, "Setting Out to C++." If you've been using the old-style header files, you should change over to using the new-style names. This is not just a cosmetic change because the new versions sometimes add new features. For example, the `ostream` header file provides support for wide-character input and output. It also provides new manipulators such as `boolalpha` and `fixed` (as described in Chapter 17, "Input, Output, and Files"). These offer a simpler interface than using `setf()` or the `iomanip` functions for setting many formatting options. If you do use `setf()`, you should use `ios_base` instead of `ios` when specifying constants; that is, you should use `ios_base::fixed` instead of `ios::fixed`. Also, the new header files incorporate namespaces.

Use Namespaces

Namespaces help organize identifiers used in a program in order to avoid name conflicts. Because the standard library, as implemented with the new header file organization, places names in the `std` namespace, using these header files requires that you deal with namespaces.

The examples in this book, for simplicity, typically utilize a `using` directive to make all the names from the `std` namespace available:

```
#include <iostream>
#include <string>
#include <vector>
using namespace std;            // a using-directive
```

However, the wholesale exporting of all the names in a namespace, whether needed or not, runs counter to the goals of namespaces.

Somewhat better is placing a `using` directive inside a function; this makes the names available just inside that function.

Even better, and the recommended approach, is to use either `using` declarations or the scope-resolution operator (`::`) to make available just those names a program needs. For example,

```
#include <iostream>
using std::cin;                         // a using-declaration
using std::cout;
using std::endl;
```

makes `cin`, `cout`, and `endl` available for the rest of the file. Using the scope-resolution operator, however, makes a name available just in the expression that uses the operator:

```
cout << std::fixed << x << endl;     //using the scope resolution operator
```

This could get wearisome, but you could collect your common `using` declarations in a header file:

```
// mynames -- a header file
using std::cin;                         // a using-declaration
using std::cout;
using std::endl;
```

Going a step further, you could collect `using` declarations in namespaces:

```
// mynames -- a header file
#include <iostream>

namespace io
{
    using std::cin;
    using std::cout;
    using std::endl;
}

namespace formats
{
    using std::fixed;
....using std::scientific;
    using std:boolalpha;
}
```

Then a program could include this file and use the namespaces it needs:

```
#include "mynames"
using namespace io;
```

Use the `autoptr` Template

Each use of `new` should be paired with a use of `delete`. This can lead to problems if a function in which `new` is used terminates early via an exception being thrown. As discussed in

Chapter 15, using an `autoptr` object to keep track of an object created by `new` automates the activation of `delete`.

Use the `string` Class

The traditional C-style string suffers from not being a real type. You can store a string in a character array, and you can initialize a character array to a string. But you can't use the assignment operator to assign a string to a character array; instead, you must remember to use `strcpy()` or `strncpy()`. You can't use the relational operators to compare C-style strings; instead, you must remember to use `strcmp()`. (And if you forget and use, say, the > operator, you don't get a syntax error; instead, the program compares string addresses instead of string contents.)

The `string` class (see Chapter 16, "The `string` Class and the Standard Template Library," and Appendix F, "The `string` Template Class"), on the other hand, lets you use objects to represent strings. Assignment operators, relational operators, and the addition operator (for concatenation) are all defined. Furthermore, the `string` class provides automatic memory management so that you normally don't have to worry about someone entering a string that either overruns an array or gets truncated before being stored.

The `string` class provides many convenience methods. For example, you can append one `string` object to another, but you can also append a C-style string or even a `char` value to a `string` object. For functions that require a C-style string argument, you can use the `c_str()` method to return a suitable pointer-to-`char`.

Not only does the `string` class provide a well-designed set of methods for handling string-related tasks, such as finding substrings, but it also features a design that is compatible with the Standard Template Library (STL) so that you can use STL algorithms with `string` objects.

Use the STL

The STL (see Chapter 16 and Appendix G, "The STL Templates and Functions") provides ready-made solutions to many programming needs, so you should use it. For example, instead of declaring an array of `double` or of `string` objects, you can create a `vector<double>` object or a `vector<string>` object. The advantages are similar to those of using `string` objects instead of C-style strings. Assignment is defined, so you can use the assignment operator to assign one `vector` object to another. You can pass a `vector` object by reference, and a function receiving such an object can use the `size()` method to determine the number of elements in the `vector` object. Built-in memory management allows for automatic resizing when you use the `pushback()` method to add elements to a `vector` object. And, of course, several useful class methods and general algorithms are at your service.

If you need a list, a double-ended queue (or deque), a stack, a regular queue, a set, or a map, you should use the STL, which provides useful container templates. The algorithm library is designed so that you can easily copy the contents of a vector to a list or compare the contents of a set to a vector. This design makes the STL a toolkit that provides basic units that you can assemble as needed.

The extensive algorithm library was designed with efficiency as one of the main design goals, so you can get top-flight results with relatively little programming effort on your part. And the iterator concept used to implement the algorithms means that the algorithms aren't limited to being used with STL containers. In particular, they can be applied to traditional arrays, too.

ANSWERS TO THE REVIEW QUESTIONS

Answers to Review Questions for Chapter 2

1. They are called functions.

2. It causes the contents of the `iostream` file to be substituted for this directive before final compilation.

3. It makes definitions made in the `std` namespace available to a program.

4. ```cpp
   cout << "Hello, world\n";
   ```

   or

   ```cpp
   cout << "Hello, world" << endl;
   ```

5. ```cpp
   int cheeses;
   ```

6. ```cpp
   cheeses = 32;
   ```

7. ```cpp
   cin >> cheeses;
   ```

8. ```cpp
   cout << "We have " << cheeses << " varieties of cheese\n";
   ```

9. The function `froop()` expects to be called with one argument, which will be type `double`, and that the function will return a type `int` value. For instance, it could be used as follows:

   ```cpp
   int gval = froop(3.14159);
   ```

   The function `rattle()` has no return value and expects an `int` argument. For instance, it could be used as follows:

   ```cpp
   rattle(37);
   ```

   The function `prune()` returns an `int` and expects to be used without an argument. For instance, it could be used as follows:

   ```cpp
   int residue = prune();
   ```

10. You don't have to use `return` in a function when the function has the return type `void`. However, you can use it if you don't give a return value:

    ```cpp
    return;
    ```
    ```

Answers to Review Questions for Chapter 3

1. Having more than one integer type lets you choose the type that is best suited to a particular need. For example, you could use **short** to conserve space or **long** to guarantee storage capacity or to find that a particular type speeds up a particular calculation.

2.

```
short rbis = 80;              // or short int rbis = 80;
unsigned int q = 42110;       // or unsigned q = 42110;
unsigned long ants = 3000000000;
```

   Note: Don't count on **int** being large enough to hold 3,000,000,000.

3. C++ provides no automatic safeguards to keep you from exceeding integer limits; you can use the **climits** header file to determine what the limits are.

4. The constant **33L** is type **long**, whereas the constant **33** is type **int**.

5. The two statements are not really equivalent, although they have the same effect on some systems. Most importantly, the first statement assigns the letter A to **grade** only on a system using the ASCII code, while the second statement also works for other codes. Second, 65 is a type **int** constant, whereas **'A'** is a type **char** constant.

6. Here are four ways:

```
char c = 88;
cout << c << endl;         // char type prints as character

cout.put(char(88));        // put() prints char as character

cout << char(88) << endl;  // new-style type cast value to char

cout << (char)88 << endl;  // old-style type cast value to char
```

7. The answer depends on how large the two types are. If **long** is 4 bytes, there is no loss. That's because the largest **long** value would be about 2 billion, which is 10 digits. Because **double** provides at least 13 significant figures, no rounding would be needed.

8. a. 8 * 9 + 2 is 72 + 2 is 74

    b. 6 * 3 / 4 is 18 / 4 is 4

    c. 3 / 4 * 6 is 0 * 6 is 0

    d. 6.0 * 3 / 4 is 18.0 / 4 is 4.5

    e. 15 % 4 is 3

9. Either of the following would work:

```
int pos = (int) x1 + (int) x2;

int pos = int(x1) + int(x2);
```

Answers to Review Questions for Chapter 4

1.
   a. `char actors[30];`

   b. `short betsie[100];`

   c. `float chuck[13];`

   d. `long double dipsea[64];`

2. `int oddly[5] = {1, 3, 5, 7, 9};`

3. `int even = oddly[0] + oddly[4];`

4. `cout << ideas[1] << "\n";  // or << endl;`

5. `char lunch[13] = "cheeseburger"; // number of characters + 1`

   or

   `char lunch[] = "cheeseburger";  // let the compiler count elements`

6.
```
struct fish {
    char kind[20];
    int weight;
    float length;
};
```

7.
```
fish petes =
{
    "trout",
    13,
    12.25
};
```

8. `enum Response {No, Yes, Maybe};`

9.
```
double * pd = &ted;
cout << *pd << "\n";
```

10.
```
float * pf = treacle;    // or = &treacle[0]
cout << pf[0] << " " << pf[9] << "\n";
            // or use *pf and *(pf + 9)
```

11.
```
unsigned int size;
cout << "Enter a positive integer: ";
cin >> size;
int * dyn = new int [size];
```

12. Yes, it is valid. The expression `"Home of the jolly bytes"` is a string constant; hence it evaluates as the address of the beginning of the string. The `cout` object interprets the address of a `char` as an invitation to print a string, but the type cast `(int *)` converts the address to type pointer-to-`int`, which is then printed as an address. In short, the statement prints the address of the string.

13.

```
struct fish
{
    char kind[20];
    int weight;
    float length;
};

fish * pole = new fish;
cout << "Enter kind of fish: ";
cin >> pole->kind;
```

14. Using `cin >> address` causes a program to skip over whitespace until it finds non-whitespace. It then reads characters until it encounters whitespace again. Thus, it will skip over the newline following the numeric input, avoiding that problem. On the other hand, it will read just a single word, not an entire line.

Answers to Review Questions for Chapter 5

1. An entry-condition loop evaluates a test expression before entering the body of the loop. If the condition is initially `false`, the loop never executes its body. An exit-condition loop evaluates a test expression after processing the body of the loop. Thus, the loop body is executed once, even if the test expression is initially `false`. The `for` and `while` loops are entry-condition loops, and the `do while` loop is an exit-condition loop.

2. It would print the following:

   ```
   01234
   ```

   Note that `cout << endl;` is not part of the loop body (because there are no braces).

3. It would print the following:

   ```
   0369
   12
   ```

4. It would print the following:

   ```
   6
   8
   ```

5. It would print the following:

   ```
   k = 8
   ```

6. It's simplest to use the `*=` operator:

```
for (int num = 1; num <= 64; num *= 2)
    cout << num << " ";
```

7. You enclose the statements within paired braces to form a single compound statement, or block.

8. Yes, the first statement is valid. The expression 1,024 consists of two expressions—1 and 024—joined by a comma operator. The value is the value of the right-hand expression. This is 024, which is octal for 20, so the declaration assigns the value **20** to **x**. The second statement is also valid. However, operator precedence causes it to be evaluated as follows:

```
(y = 1), 024;
```

That is, the left expression sets **y** to **1**, and the value of the entire expression, which isn't used, is **024**, or **20**.

9. The `cin >> ch` form skips over spaces, newlines, and tabs when it encounters them. The other two forms read those characters.

Answers to Review Questions for Chapter 6

1. Both versions give the same answers, but the `if else` version is more efficient. Consider what happens, for example, when `ch` is a space. Version 1, after incrementing spaces, tests whether the character is a newline. This wastes time because the program has already established that `ch` is a space and hence could not be a newline. Version 2, in the same situation, skips the newline test.

2. Both `++ch` and `ch + 1` have the same numerical value. But `++ch` is type `char` and prints as a character, while `ch + 1`, because it adds a `char` to an `int`, is type `int` and prints as a number.

3. Because the program uses `ch = '$'` instead of `ch == '$'`, the combined input and output looks like this:

```
Hi!
H$i$!$
$Send $10 or $20 now!
S$e$n$d$ $ct1 = 9, ct2 = 9
```

Each character is converted to the `$` character before being printed the second time. Also, the value of the expression `ch = $` is the code for the `$` character, hence nonzero, hence `true`; so `ct2` is incremented each time.

4.   a. `weight >= 115 && weight < 125`

     b. `ch == 'q' || ch == 'Q'`

     c. `x % 2 == 0 && x != 26`

     d. `x % 2 == 0 && !(x % 26 == 0)`

     e. `donation >= 1000 && donation <= 2000 || guest == 1`

     f. `(ch >= 'a' && ch <= 'z') ||(ch >= 'A' && ch <= 'Z')`

5. Not necessarily. For example, if `x` is `10`, then `!x` is `0` and `!!x` is `1`. However, if `x` is a `bool` variable, then `!!x` is `x`.

6. `(x < 0)? -x : x`

   or

   `(x >= 0)? x : -x;`

7.

```
switch (ch)
{
    case 'A': a_grade++;
            break;
    case 'B': b_grade++;
            break;
    case 'C': c_grade++;
            break;
    case 'D': d_grade++;
            break;
    default:  f_grade++;
            break;
}
```

8. If you use integer labels and the user types a noninteger such as **q**, the program hangs because integer input can't process a character. But if you use character labels and the user types an integer such as **5**, character input will process 5 as a character. Then the default part of the switch can suggest entering another character.

9. Here is one version:

```
int line = 0;
char ch;
while (cin.get(ch) && ch != 'Q')
{
    if (ch == '\n')
        line++;
}
```

Answers to Review Questions for Chapter 7

1. The three steps are defining the function, providing a prototype, and calling the function.

2. a. `void igor(void);   // or void igor()`

    b. `float tofu(int n);   // or  float tofu(int);`

    c. `double mpg(double miles, double gallons);`

    d. `long summation(long harray[], int size);`

    e. `double doctor(const char * str);`

    f. `void ofcourse(boss dude);`

    g. `char * plot(map *pmap);`

3.
```
void set_array(int arr[], int size, int value)
{
    for (int i = 0; i < size; i++)
        arr[i] = value;
}
```

4.
```
void set_array(int * begin, int * end, int value)
{
    for (int * pt = begin; pt != end; pt++)
        pt* = value;
}
```

5.
```
double biggest (const double foot[], int size)
{
    double max;
    if (size < 1)
    {
        cout << "Invalid array size of " << size << endl;
        cout << "Returning a value of 0\n";
        return 0;
    }
    else    // not necessary because return terminates program
    {
        max = foot[0];
        for (int i = 1; i < size; i++)
            if (foot[i] > max)
                max = foot[i];
        return max;
    }
}
```

6. You use the `const` qualifier with pointers to protect the original pointed-to data from being altered. When a program passes a fundamental type such as an `int` or a `double`, it passes it by value so that the function works with a copy. Thus, the original data is already protected.

7. A string can be stored in a `char` array, it can be represented by a string constant in double quotation marks, and it can be represented by a pointer pointing to the first character of a string.

8.

```
int replace(char * str, char c1, char c2)
{
    int count = 0;
    while (*str)        // while not at end of string
    {
        if (*str == c1)
        {
            *str = c2;
            count++;
        }
        str++;          // advance to next character
    }
    return count;
}
```

9. Because C++ interprets `"pizza"` as the address of its first element, applying the `*` operator yields the value of that first element, which is the character `p`. Because C++ interprets `"taco"` as the address of its first element, it interprets `"taco"[2]` as the value of the element two positions down the line—that is, as the character `c`. In other words, the string constant acts the same as an array name.

10. To pass it by value, you just pass the structure name `glitz`. To pass its address, you use the address operator `&glitz`. Passing by value automatically protects the original data, but it takes time and memory. Passing by address saves time and memory but doesn't protect the original data unless you use the `const` modifier for the function parameter. Also, passing by value means you can use ordinary structure member notation, but passing a pointer means you have to remember to use the indirect membership operator.

11. `int judge (int (*pf)(const char *));`

Answers to Review Questions for Chapter 8

1. Short, nonrecursive functions that can fit in one line of code are good candidates for inline status.

2.   a. `void song(char * name, int times = 1);`

   b. None. Only prototypes contain the default value information.

   c. Yes, provided that you retain the default value for `times`:

   `void song(char * name = "O, My Papa", int times = 1);`

3. You can use either the string `"\""` or the character `'"'` to print a quotation mark. The following functions show both methods:

```cpp
#include <iostream.h>
void iquote(int n)
{
    cout << "\"" << n << "\"";
}

void iquote(double x)
{
    cout << '"' << x << '"';
}

void iquote(const char * str)
{
    cout << "\"" << str << "\"";
}
```

4. a. This function shouldn't alter the structure members, so use the **const** qualifier:

```cpp
void show_box(const box & container)
{
    cout << "Made by " << container. maker << endl;
    cout << "Height = " << container.height << endl;
    cout << "Width = " << container.width << endl;
    cout << "Length = " << container.length << endl;
    cout << "Volume = " << container.volume << endl;
}
```

   b.

```cpp
void set_volume(box & crate)
{
    crate.volume = crate.height * crate.width * crate.length;
}
```

5. a. This can be done by using a default value for the second argument:

```cpp
double mass(double d, double v = 1.0);
```

It can also be done by using function overloading:

```cpp
double mass(double d, double v);
double mass(double d);
```

   b. You can't use a default for the repeat value because you have to provide default values from right to left. You can use overloading:

```cpp
void repeat(int times, const char * str);
void repeat(const char * str);
```

   c. You can use function overloading:

```cpp
int average(int a, int b);
double average(double x, double y);
```

   d. You can't do this because both versions would have the same signature.

6.

```
template<class T>
T max(T t1, T t2)  // or T max(const T & t1, const T & t2)
{
    return t1 > t2? t1 : t2;
}
```

7.

```
template<> box max(box b1, box b2)
{
    return b1.volume > b2.volume? b1 : b2;
}
```

Answers to Review Questions for Chapter 9

1.   a. `homer` is automatically an automatic variable.

   b. `secret` should be defined as an external variable in one file and declared using `extern` in the second file.

   c. `topsecret` could be defined as a static variable with internal linkage by prefacing the external definition with the keyword `static`. Or it could be defined in an unnamed namespace.

   d. `beencalled` should be defined as a local static variable by prefacing a declaration in the function with the keyword `static`.

2. A `using` declaration makes available a single name from a namespace, and it has the scope corresponding to the declarative region in which the `using` declaration occurs. A `using` directive makes available all the names in a namespace. When you use a `using` directive, it is as if you have declared the names in the smallest declarative region containing both the `using` declaration and the namespace itself.

3.

```
#include <iostream>
int main()
{
    double x;
    std::cout << "Enter value: ";
    while (! (std::cin >> x) )
    {
        std::cout << "Bad input. Please enter a number: ";
        std::cin.clear();
        while (std::cin.get() != '\n')
            continue;
    }
    std::cout << "Value = " << x << std::endl;
    return 0;
}
```

4. Here is the revised code:

```cpp
#include <iostream>
int main()
{
    using std::cin;
    using std::cout;
    using std::endl;
    double x;
    cout << "Enter value: ";
    while (! (cin >> x) )
    {
        cout << "Bad input. Please enter a number: ";
        cin.clear();
        while (cin.get() != '\n')
            continue;
    }
    cout << "Value = " << x << endl;
    return 0;
}
```

5. You could have separate static function definitions in each file. Or each file could define the appropriate `average()` function in an unnamed namespace.

6.

```
10
4
0
Other: 10, 1
another(): 10, -4
```

7.

```
1
4, 1, 2
2
2
4, 1, 2
2
```

Answers to Review Questions for Chapter 10

1. A class is a definition of a user-defined type. A class declaration specifies how data is to be stored, and it specifies the methods (class member functions) that can be used to access and manipulate that data.

2. A class represents the operations you can perform on a class object with a public interface of class methods; this is abstraction. The class can use private visibility (the default) for data members, meaning that the data can be accessed only through the member functions; this is data hiding. Details of the implementation, such as data representation and method code, are hidden; this is encapsulation.

3. A class defines a type, including how it can be used. An object is a variable or another data object, such as that produced by `new`, which is created and used according to the class definition. The relationship between a class and an object is the same as that between a standard type and a variable of that type.

4. If you create several objects of a given class, each object comes with storage for its own set of data. But all the objects use the one set of member functions. (Typically, methods are public and data members are private, but that's a matter of policy, not of class requirements.) Note: The program uses `cin.get(char *, int)` instead of `cin >>` to read names because `cin.get()` reads a whole line instead of just one word (see Chapter 4).

5. This example use `char` arrays to hold the character data, but you could use `string` class objects instead.

```
// #include <cstring>

// class definition
class BankAccount
{
private:
    char name[40];      // or std::string name;
    char acctnum[25];   // or std::string acctnum;
    double balance;
public:
    BankAccount(const char * client, const char * num, double bal = 0.0);
//or BankAccount(const std::string & client,
//                 const std::string & num, double bal = 0.0);

    void show(void) const;
    void deposit(double cash);
    void withdraw(double cash);
};
```

6. A class constructor is called when you create an object of that class or when you explicitly call the constructor. A class destructor is called when the object expires.

7. These are two possible solutions (note that you must include `cstring` or `string.h` in order to use `strncpy()` or else you must include `string` to use the `string` class):

```
BankAccount::BankAccount(const char * client, const char * num, double bal)
{
    strncpy(name, client, 39);
    name[39] = '\0';
    strncpy(acctnum, num, 24);
    acctnum[24] = '\0';
    balance = bal;
}
```

or

```
BankAccount::BankAccount(const std::string & client,
                        const std::string & num, double bal)
{
    name = client;
    acctnum = num;
    balance = bal;
}
```

Keep in mind that default arguments go in the prototype, not in the function definition.

8. A default constructor either has no arguments or has defaults for all the arguments. Having a default constructor enables you to declare objects without initializing them, even if you've already defined an initializing constructor. It also allows you to declare arrays.

9.

```
// stock3.h
#ifndef STOCK3_H_
#define STOCK3_H_

class Stock
{
private:
    std::string company;
    int shares;
    double share_val;
    double total_val;
    void set_tot() { total_val = shares * share_val; }
public:
    Stock();                // default constructor
    Stock(const std::string & co, int n, double pr);
    ~Stock() {}             // do-nothing destructor
    void buy(int num, double price);
    void sell(int num, double price);
    void update(double price);
    void show() const;
    const Stock & topval(const Stock & s) const;
    int numshares() const { return shares; }
    double shareval() const { return share_val; }
    double totalval() const { return total_val; }
    string co_name() const { return company; }
};
```

10. The **this** pointer is a pointer that is available to class methods. It points to the object used to invoke the method. Thus, **this** is the address of the object, and ***this** represents the object itself.

Answers to Review Questions for Chapter 11

1. Here's a prototype for the class definition file and a function definition for the methods file:

```
// prototype
Stonewt operator*(double mult);

// definition -- let constructor do the work
Stonewt Stonewt::operator*(double mult)
{
    return Stonewt(mult * pounds);
}
```

2. A member function is part of a class definition and is invoked by a particular object. The member function can access members of the invoking object implicitly, without using the membership operator. A friend function is not part of a class, so it's called as a straight function call. It can't access class members implicitly, so it must use the membership operator applied to an object passed as an argument. Compare, for instance, the answer to Review Question 1 with the answer to Review Question 4.

3. It must be a friend to access private members, but it doesn't have to be a friend to access public members.

4. Here's a prototype for the class definition file and a function definition for the methods file:

```
// prototype
friend Stonewt operator*(double mult, const Stonewt & s);

// definition -- let constructor do the work
Stonewt operator*(double mult, const Stonewt & s)
{
    return Stonewt(mult * s.pounds);
}
```

5. The following five operators cannot be overloaded:

```
sizeof
.
.*
::
? :
```

6. These operators must be defined by using a member function.

7. Here are a possible prototype and definition:

```
// prototype and inline definition
operator double () {return mag;}
```

Note, however, that it makes better sense to use the `magval()` method than to define this conversion function.

Answers to Review Questions for Chapter 12

1. a. The syntax is fine, but this constructor leaves the `str` pointer uninitialized. The constructor should either set the pointer to `NULL` or use `new []` to initialize the pointer.

    b. This constructor does not create a new string; it merely copies the address of the old string. It should use `new []` and `strcpy()`.

    c. It copies the string without allocating the space to store it. It should use `new char[len + 1]` to allocate the proper amount of memory.

2. First, when an object of that type expires, the data pointed to by the object's member pointer remains in memory, using space and remaining inaccessible because the pointer has been lost. That can be fixed by having the class destructor delete memory allocated by `new` in the constructor functions. Second, after the destructor deletes such memory, it might end up trying to delete it twice if a program initializes one such object to another. That's because the default initialization of one object to another copies pointer values but does not copy the pointed-to data, and this produces two pointers to the same data. The solution is to define a class copy constructor that causes initialization to copy the pointed-to data. Third, assigning one object to another can produce the same situation of two pointers pointing to the same data. The solution is to overload the assignment operator so that it copies the data, not the pointers.

3. C++ automatically provides the following member functions:

    - A default constructor if you define no constructors

    - A copy constructor if you don't define one

    - An assignment operator if you don't define one

    - A default destructor if you don't define one

    - An address operator if you don't define one

    The default constructor does nothing, but it allows you to declare arrays and uninitialized objects. The default copy constructor and the default assignment operator use memberwise assignment. The default destructor does nothing. The implicit address operator returns the address of the invoking object (that is, the value of the `this` pointer).

4. The `personality` member should be declared either as a character array or as a pointer-to-`char`. Or you could make it a `String` object or a `string` object. The declaration fails to make the methods public. Then there are several small errors. Here is a possible solution, with changes (other than deletions) in boldface:

```
#include <iostream>
#include <cstring>
using namespace std;
class nifty
{
```

```
private: // optional
    char personality[40];    // provide array size
    int talents;
public: // needed
// methods
    nifty();
    nifty(const char * s);
    friend ostream & operator<<(ostream & os, const nifty & n);
};    // note closing semicolon

nifty::nifty()
{
    personality[0] = '\0';
    talents = 0;
}

nifty::nifty(const char * s)
{
    strcpy(personality, s);
    talents = 0;
}

ostream & operator<<(ostream & os, const nifty & n)
{
    os << n.personality << '\n';
    os << n.talent << '\n';
    return os;
}
```

Here is another possible solution:

```
#include <iostream>
#include <cstring>
using namespace std;
class nifty
{
private: // optional
    char * personality;    // create a pointer
    int talents;
public: // needed
// methods
    nifty();
    nifty(const char * s);
    nifty(const nifty & n);
    ~nifty() { delete [] personality; }
    nifty & operator=(const nifty & n) const;
    friend ostream & operator<<(ostream & os, const nifty & n);
};    // note closing semicolon

nifty::nifty()
{
    personality = NULL;
    talents = 0;
}
```

```
nifty::nifty(const char * s)
{
    personality = new char [strlen(s) + 1];
    strcpy(personality, s);
    talents = 0;
}

ostream & operator<<(ostream & os, const nifty & n)
{
    os << n.personality << '\n';
    os << n.talent << '\n';
    return os;
}
```

5.   a.
```
Golfer nancy; // default constructor
Golfer lulu("Little Lulu"); // Golfer(const char * name, int g)
Golfer roy("Roy Hobbs", 12); // Golfer(const char * name, int g)
Golfer * par = new Golfer; // default constructor
Golfer next = lulu; // Golfer(const Golfer &g)
Golfer hazard = "Weed Thwacker"; // Golfer(const char * name, int g)
*par = nancy; // default assignment operator
nancy = "Nancy Putter";// Golfer(const char * name, int g), then
                       // the default assignment operator
```

Note that some compilers additionally call the default assignment operator for Statements 5 and 6.

   b.   The class should define an assignment operator that copies data rather than addresses.

Answers to Review Questions for Chapter 13

1. The public members of the base class become public members of the derived class. The protected members of the base class become protected members of the derived class. The private members of the base class are inherited but cannot be accessed directly. The answer to Review Question 2 provides the exceptions to these general rules.

2. The constructor methods are not inherited, the destructor is not inherited, the assignment operator is not inherited, and friends are not inherited.

3. If the return type were void, you would still be able to use single assignment but not chain assignment:

```
baseDMA magazine("Pandering to Glitz", 1);
baseDMA gift1, gift2, gift3;
gift1 = magazine;        // ok
gift 2 = gift3 = gift1;  // no longer valid
```

If the method returned an object instead of a reference, the method execution would be slowed a bit because the return statement would involve copying the object.

4. Constructors are called in the order of derivation, with the most ancestral constructor called first. Destructors are called in the opposite order.

5. Yes, every class requires its own constructors. If the derived class adds no new members, the constructor can have an empty body, but it must exist.

6. Only the derived-class method is called. It supersedes the base-class definition. A base-class method is called only if the derived class does not redefine the method or if you use the scope-resolution operator. However, you really should declare as virtual any functions that will be redefined.

7. The derived class should define an assignment operator if the derived-class constructors use the `new` or `new []` operator to initialize pointers that are members of that class. More generally, the derived class should define an assignment operator if the default assignment is incorrect for derived-class members.

8. Yes, you can assign the address of an object of a derived class to a pointer to the base class. You can assign the address of a base-class object to a pointer to a derived class (downcasting) only by making an explicit type cast, and it is not necessarily safe to use such a pointer.

9. Yes, you can assign an object of a derived class to an object of the base class. Any data members that are new to the derived type are not passed to the base type, however. The program uses the base-class assignment operator. Assignment in the opposite direction (base to derived) is possible only if the derived class defines a conversion operator, which is a constructor that has a reference to the base type as its sole argument, or else defines an assignment operator with a base-class parameter.

10. It can do so because C++ allows a reference to a base type to refer to any type derived from that base.

11. Passing an object by value invokes the copy constructor. Because the formal argument is a base-class object, the base-class copy constructor is invoked. The copy constructor has as its argument a reference to the base class, and this reference can refer to the derived object passed as an argument. The net result is that a new base-class object whose members correspond to the base class portion of the derived object is produced.

12. Passing an object by reference instead of by value enables the function to avail itself of virtual functions. Also, passing an object by reference instead of by value may use less memory and time, particularly for large objects. The main advantage of passing by value is that it protects the original data, but you can accomplish the same end by passing the reference as a `const` type.

13. If `head()` is a regular method, then `ph->head()` invokes `Corporation::head()`. If `head()` is a virtual function, then `ph->head()` invokes `PublicCorporation::head()`.

14. First, the situation does not fit the *is-a* model, so public inheritance is not appropriate. Second, the definition of `area()` in `House` hides the `Kitchen` version of `area()` because the two methods have different signatures.

Answers to Review Questions for Chapter 14

1.

class Bear	class PolarBear	Public; a polar bear is a kind of bear
class Kitchen	class Home	Private; a home has a kitchen
class Person	class Programmer	Public; a programmer is a kind of person
class Person	class HorseAndJockey	Private; a horse and jockey team contains a person
class Person, class Automobile	class Driver	Person public because a driver is a person; Automobile private because a driver has an automobile

2.

```
Gloam::Gloam(int g, const char * s) : glip(g), fb(s) { }
Gloam::Gloam(int g, const Frabjous & fr) : glip(g), fb(fr) { }
// note: the above uses the default Frabjous copy constructor
void Gloam::tell()
{
    fb.tell();
    cout << glip << endl;
}
```

3.

```
Gloam::Gloam(int g, const char * s)
            : glip(g), Frabjous(s) { }
Gloam::Gloam(int g, const Frabjous & fr)
            : glip(g), Frabjous(fr) { }
// note: the above uses the default Frabjous copy constructor
void Gloam::tell()
{
    Frabjous::tell();
    cout << glip << endl;
}
```

4.

```
class Stack<Worker *>
{
private:
    enum {MAX = 10};        // constant specific to class
    Worker * items[MAX];    // holds stack items
    int top;                // index for top stack item
public:
    Stack();
    Boolean isempty();
```

```
         Boolean isfull();
         Boolean push(const Worker * & item); // add item to stack
         Boolean pop(Worker * & item);        // pop top into item
     };
```

5.

```
     ArrayTP<string> sa;
     StackTP< ArrayTP<double> > stck_arr_db;
     ArrayTP< StackTP<Worker *> > arr_stk_wpr;
```

Listing 14.18 generates four templates: `ArrayTP<int, 10>`, `ArrayTP<double, 10>`, `ArrayTP<int,5>`, and `Array< ArrayTP<int,5>, 10>`.

6. If two lines of inheritance for a class share a common ancestor, the class winds up having two copies of the ancestor's members. Making the ancestor class a virtual base class to its immediate descendants solves that problem.

Answers to Review Questions for Chapter 15

1.   a. The friend declaration should be as follows:

```
     friend class clasp;
```

   b. This needs a forward declaration so that the compiler can interpret `void snip(muff &)`:

```
     class muff;    // forward declaration
     class cuff {
     public:
         void snip(muff &) { ... }
         ...
     };
     class muff {
         friend void cuff::snip(muff &);
         ...
     };
```

   c. First, the `cuff` class declaration should precede the `muff` class so that the compiler can understand the term `cuff::snip()`. Second, the compiler needs a forward declaration of `muff` so that it can understand `snip(muff &)`:

```
     class muff;    // forward declaration
     class cuff {
     public:
         void snip(muff &) { ... }
         ...
     };
     class muff {
         friend void cuff::snip(muff &);
         ...
     };
```

2. No. For Class **A** to have a friend that's a member function of Class **B**, the **B** declaration must precede the **A** declaration. A forward declaration is not enough because it would tell **A** that **B** is a class, but it wouldn't reveal the names of the class members. Similarly, if **B** has a friend that's a member function of **A**, the complete **A** declaration must precede the **B** declaration. These two requirements are mutually exclusive.

3. The only access to a class is through its public interface, which means the only thing you can do with a **Sauce** object is call the constructor to create one. The other members (**soy** and **sugar**) are private by default.

4. Suppose the function **f1()** calls the function **f2()**. A return statement in **f2()** causes program execution to resume at the next statement following the **f2()** function call in function **f1()**. A **throw** statement causes the program to back up through the current sequence of function calls until it finds a **try** block that directly or indirectly contains the call to **f2()**. This might be in **f1()** or in a function that called **f1()**, and so on. Once there, execution goes to the next matching **catch** block, not to the first statement after the function call.

5. You should arrange the **catch** blocks in order, from most derived class to least derived.

6. For Sample #1, the **if** condition is **true** if pg points to a **Superb** object or to an object of any class descended from **Superb**. In particular, it is also **true** if pg points to a **Magnificent** object. In Sample #2, the **if** condition is **true** only for a **Superb** object, not for objects derived from **Superb**.

7. The **dynamic_cast** operator only allows upcasting in a class hierarchy, whereas a **static_cast** operator allows both upcasting and downcasting. The **static_cast** operator also allows conversions from enumeration types to integer types, and vice versa, and between various numeric types.

Answers to Review Questions for Chapter 16

1.

```
#include <string>
using namespace std;
class RQ1
{
private:
    string st;        // a string object
public:
    RQ1() : st("") {}
    RQ1(const char * s) : st(s) {}
    ~RQ1() {};
// more stuff
};
```

The explicit copy constructor, destructor, and assignment operator are no longer needed because the **string** object provides its own memory management.

2. You can assign one **string** object to another. A **string** object provides its own memory management so that you normally don't have to worry about a string exceeding the capacity of its holder.

3.

```
#include <string>
#include <cctype>
using namespace std;
void ToUpper(string & str)
{
    for (int i = 0; i < str.size(); i++)
        str[i] = toupper(str[i]);
}
```

4.

```
auto_ptr<int> pia= new int[20];   // wrong, use with new, not new[]
auto_ptr<string>(new string);     // wrong, no name for pointer
int rigue = 7;
auto_ptr<int>(&rigue);            // wrong, memory not allocated by new
auto_ptr dbl (new double);        // wrong, omits <double>
```

5. The LIFO aspect of a stack means you might have to remove a lot of clubs before reaching the one you need.

6. The set will store just one copy of each value, so, say, five scores of **5** would be stored as a single **5**.

7. Using iterators allows you to use objects with a pointer-like interface to move through data that is organized in some fashion other than an array (for example, data in a doubly linked list).

8. The STL approach allows STL functions to be used with ordinary pointers to ordinary arrays as well as with iterators to STL container classes, thus increasing generality.

9. You can assign one **vector** object to another. A **vector** manages its own memory, so you can insert items into a vector and have it resize itself automatically. By using the **at()** method, you can get automatic bounds checking.

10. The two **sort()** functions and the **random_shuffle()** function require a random access iterator, whereas a **list** object just has a bidirectional iterator. You can use the list template class **sort()** member functions (see Appendix G) instead of the general-purpose functions to do the sorting, but there is no member function equivalent to **random_shuffle()**. However, you could copy the list to a vector, shuffle the vector, and copy the results back to the list.

Answers to Review Questions for Chapter 17

1. The **iostream** file defines the classes, constants, and manipulators used to manage input and output. These objects manage the streams and buffers used to handle I/O. The file

also creates standard objects (`cin`, `cout`, `cerr`, and `clog` and their wide-character equivalents) used to handle the standard input and output streams connected to every program.

2. Keyboard entry generates a series of characters. Typing **121** generates three characters, each represented by a 1-byte binary code. If the value is to be stored as type `int`, these three characters have to be converted to a single binary representation of the value 121.

3. By default, both the standard output and the standard error send output to the standard output device, typically a monitor. If you have the operating system redirect output to a file, however, the standard output connects to the file instead of to the screen, but the standard error continues to be connected to the screen.

4. The `ostream` class defines a version of the `operator<<()` function for each basic C++ type. The compiler interprets an expression like

```
cout << spot
```

as the following:

```
cout.operator<<(spot)
```

It can then match this method call to the function prototype that has the same argument type.

5. You can concatenate output methods that return type `ostream &`. This causes the invoking of a method with an object to return that object. The returned object can then invoke the next method in a sequence.

6.
```
//rq17-6.cpp
#include <iostream>
#include <iomanip>

int main()
{
    using namespace std;
    cout << "Enter an integer: ";
    int n;
    cin >> n;
    cout << setw(15) << "base ten" << setw(15)
         << "base sixteen" << setw(15) << "base eight" << "\n";
    cout.setf(ios::showbase);    // or cout << showbase;
    cout << setw(15) << n << hex << setw(15) << n
         << oct << setw(15) << n << "\n";

    return 0;
}
```

7.

```
//rq17-7.cpp
#include <iostream>
#include <iomanip>

int main()
{
    using namespace std;
    char name[20];
    float hourly;
    float hours;

    cout << "Enter your name: ";
    cin.get(name, 20).get();
    cout << "Enter your hourly wages: ";
    cin >> hourly;
    cout << "Enter number of hours worked: ";
    cin >> hours;

    cout.setf(ios::showpoint);
    cout.setf(ios::fixed, ios::floatfield);
    cout.setf(ios::right, ios::adjustfield);
// or cout << showpoint << fixed << right;
    cout << "First format:\n";
    cout << setw(30) << name << ": $" << setprecision(2)
        << setw(10) << hourly << ":" << setprecision(1)
        << setw(5) << hours << "\n";
    cout << "Second format:\n";
    cout.setf(ios::left, ios::adjustfield);
    cout << setw(30) << name << ": $" << setprecision(2)
        << setw(10) << hourly << ":" << setprecision(1)
        << setw(5) << hours << "\n";

    return 0;
}
```

8. Here is the output:

```
ct1 = 5; ct2 = 9
```

The first part of the program ignores spaces and newline characters; the second part doesn't. Note that the second part of the program begins reading at the newline character following the first **q**, and it counts that newline character as part of its total.

9. The `ignore()` form falters if the input line exceeds 80 characters. In that case, it skips only the first 80 characters.

INDEX

Symbols

+ (addition operator), 506-510
= (assignment operator), 45, 577, 687, 691-693
    compared to equality operator, 199-201
    custom definitions, 578-579
    enumerator values, setting, 142-143
    overloading, 584-590
        sayings1.cpp, 588-589
        string1.cpp, 586-588
        string1.h, 585
    potential problems, 578
    strings, 126-127
    structures, 136-137
    when to use, 577
*= (assignment operator), 193
+= (assignment operator), 193
/= (assignment operator), 193
-= (assignment operator), 193
%= (assignment operator), 193
& (bitwise AND operator), 1067
~ (bitwise negation operator), 1065
| (bitwise OR operator), 1065-1066
^ (bitwise XOR operator), 1066
{} (braces), 235
[] (brackets), 582-583
, (comma operator), 195-198
/*...*/ comment notation, 35
// comment notation, 29, 34-35
+ (concatenation operator), 126-127
?: (conditional operator), 250-251
— (decrement operator), 189-192
* (dereferencing operator), 145-149, 160
/ (division operator), 97-98
== (equality operator), 198-201
>= (greater than or equal to operator), 198
> (greater than operator), 198
++ (increment operator), 178, 189-192
!= (inequality operator), 198
<< (insertion operator)
    concatenation, 960-961
    data types recognized, 958-959
    pointers, 960

<<= (left shift and assign operator), 1064
<< (left shift operator), 518-524, 606, 1063-1064
< (less than operator), 198
<= (less than or equal to operator), 198
&& (logical AND operator), 239
    alternative representations, 247
    example, 240-242
    precedence, 246-247
    ranges, 242-244
! (logical NOT operator), 244-245
    alternative representations, 247
    precedence, 246
|| (logical OR operator), 238-239, 246-247
->* (member dereferencing operator), 1070-1073
.* (member dereferencing operator), 1070-1073
% (modulus operator), 99-100
* (multiplication operator), 512-515
. (period), 232
(pound sign), 214
" (quotation marks), 38
& (reference operator), 341-344
>>= (right shift and assign operator), 1065
>> (right shift operator), 1064-1065
:: (scope resolution operator), 409, 453, 1138
; (semicolon), 32
- (subtraction operator), 512-515
~ (tilde), 468
_ (underscore), 1049

A

ABCs (abstract base classes), 670-672
    ABC philosophy, 677
    AcctABC example, 672-676
    enforcing interface rules with, 677
abort() function, 805-807, 835-836
abstract base classes. *See* ABCs
abstract data types (ADTs), 489-494
abstraction, 447
access control (classes), 451-453, 801
AcctABC class, 672-676

arrays
- array notation, 161
- arrays of objects
  - declaring, 483
  - example, 484-486
  - initializing, 483
- const keyword, 299-300
- declaring, 110-113
- defined, 110
- design decisions, 297-298
- displaying contents of, 299-300
- dynamic arrays, 161
  - creating, 153-155
  - sample program, 155-156
- examples, 300-303
- external arrays, 243
- filling, 298-299
- as function arguments, 293-297
- indexes, 110-111
- initializing, 111-114
- modifying, 300
- naming, 160
- one-dimensional arrays, 223
- pointer arithmetic, 156-161
- pointers, 294-295
- ranges, 303-304
- static binding, 161
- strings, 114-117
- structures, 137-139
- subscripts, 111
- templates, 756-758
- two-dimensional arrays, 223-227, 308-309
  - declaring, 224-225
  - initializing, 225-227
- variable arrays, 1135

arraytp.h, 756-757
arrfun1.cpp, 293
arrfun2.cpp, 296
arrfun3.cpp, 300
arrfun4.cpp, 303
arrstruc.cpp, 138
ASCII character set, 1051-1056
assgn_st.cpp, 136
assign() function, 1090, 1098
assign.cpp, 101
assignable objects, 905

assignment
- assignable objects, 905
- assignment functions, 1084
- assignment operator (=), 45, 577, 687, 691-693
  - combination assignment operators, 192-193
  - compared to equality operator, 199-201
  - custom definitions, 578-579
  - enumerator values, setting, 142-143
  - overloading, 584-590

- potential problems, 578
- strings, 126-127
- structures, 136-137
- when to use, 577
- assignment statements, 45
- pointers, 160
- strings, 126, 1090
- type conversions, 100-102
- variable values, 45

assignment operator (=), 45, 577, 687, 691-693
- combination assignment operators, 192-193
- compared to equality operator, 199, 201
- custom definitions, 578-579
- enumerator values, setting, 142-143
- overloading, 584-590
  - sayings1.cpp, 588-589
  - string1.cpp, 586-588
  - string1.h, 585
- potential problems, 578
- strings, 126-127
- structures, 136-137
- when to use, 577

assignment statements, 45
associative containers, 915
- functions, 1101-1102
- multimap, 919-922
- set, 916-919

associativity of operators
- arithmetic operators, 96-97
- examples, 1057-1058
- table of, 1058-1061

asterisk (*), 145, 149, 160
at() function, 1083, 1099
atan() function, 318
atan2() function, 318
ATM queue simulation, 607-608
- bank.cpp simulation, 621-626
- Customer class, 618-621
- Queue class
  - class declaration, 618-621
  - design, 608-609
  - implementation, 609-612
  - functions, 612-618
  - public interface, 609

auto keyword, 416
auto_ptr class, 873-877
auto.cpp, 401-402
automatic memory storage, 170-171
automatic sizing (strings), 870-872
automatic teller machine simulation. *See* ATM queue simulation
automatic type conversion. *See* type conversion
automatic variables, 170-171, 287, 399-403
- example, 401-402
- initializing, 403
- register keyword, 405
- stacks, 403-404

user-defined functions
    example, 55-56
    function form, 56
    function headers, 56-58
    return values, 58-60
    using directive, 60-61
virtual functions, 671
void, 281
functor.cpp, 924-925
functors, 922-923
    adaptable, 928
    concepts, 923-926
    predefined, 926-928
funtemp.cpp, 372-373

G

g++ compiler, 23-24
gcount() function, 999-1003
generate() function, 1108, 1111
generate_n() function, 1108, 1111
generators, 923
get() function, 121-123, 215-217, 220-223, 735, 992-999
get_allocator() function, 1077
get_fun.cpp, 996
getinfo.cpp, 47
getline() function, 120-121, 449, 728, 862-864, 995-999, 1093
getname() function, 168-170
global namespaces, 426
global objects, 555
global scope, 399
global variables, 410
good() function, 270, 987-991
goodbit stream state, 987-991
gpp compiler, 24
greater than operator (>), 198
greater than or equal to operator (>=), 198

H

handling exceptions. *See* exception handling
hangman.cpp, 867-869
harmonic mean, 805
harpo() function, 363
has-a relationships, 645, 703-705
header files, 394-395
    climits, 71-72
    cmath, 319, 322
    converting to standard C++, 1137
    creating, 469
    cstring, 116-117

ctime, 209
filenames, 36-37
iomanip, 981-982
iostream, 265
managing, 396
headers (function), 32-34, 56-58
heaps (memory), 170
    creating, 1123
    defined, 1123
    heap operations
        make_heap() function, 1116, 1123
        pop_heap() function, 1116, 1123
        push_heap() function, 1116, 1123
        sort_heap() function, 1116, 1124
    popping values off, 1123
    pushing values onto, 1123
    sorting, 1124
hex manipulator, 968-969, 980
hexadecimal numbers, 1042-1044
hexoct1.cpp, 77
hexoct2.cpp, 78
high-level languages, 13
history of C++, 12-17
    C language, 13-14
    generic programming, 15-16
    OOP, 14-15
hmean() function, 807-814

I

I/O, 952
    buffers, 953-957
    cin object, 47-48, 956, 983-985
        get() function, 122-123, 215-217, 220-223, 290, 993-994
        getline() function, 120-121
        loops, 214-215
        operator overloading, 985-986
        stream states, 987-991
    cout object, 39, 956-958
        buffers, flushing, 964-965
        concatenation, 48, 960-961
        endl manipulator, 40
        field width display, 969-970
        fill characters, 970-971
        floating-point display precision, 971-972
        formatting data types, 965-967
        integer values, displaying, 46
        functions, 81-82, 961-964
        \n newline character, 40-41
        number base display, 967, 969
        overloaded << operator, 958-959
        printing trailing zeros/decimal points, 972-979

S

How can we make this index more useful? Email us at indexes@samspublishing.com

T

U

V

W

X-Z